The New York
Botanical Garden
Illustrated Encyclopedia
of Horticulture

The New York Botanical Garden Illustrated Encyclopedia of Horticulture

Thomas H. Everett

Volume 8
Par-Py

Garland Publishing, Inc.
New York & London

15 14 13 12 11 10 9 8 7 6 5 4 3 2 1

Library of Congress Cataloging in Publication Data

Everett, Thomas H
    The New York Botanical Garden illustrated encyclopedia of horticulture.

    1. Horticulture—Dictionaries. 2. Gardening—Dictionaries. 3. Plants, Ornamental—Dictionaries. 4. Plants, Cultivated—Dictionaries. I. New York (City). Botanical Garden. II. Title.
SB317.58.E94   635.9′03′21   80-65941
ISBN 0-8240-7238-3

PHOTO CREDITS

Black and White

American Association of Nurserymen: A shade tree and a flowering tree set in a well-kept lawn, p. 2674. George J. Ball, Inc.: Single varieties of *Petunia hybrida* (both pictures), p. 2575. Ferry-Morse Seed Company: A border of mixed annuals and hardy perennials, p. 2677. Netherlands Flower Institute: *Puschkinia scilloides*, p. 2852; *Puschkinia scilloides libanotica* in a rock garden, p. 2852. The New York Botanical Garden: *Parkinsonia aculeata*, p. 2494; *Parnassia glauca*, p. 2495; Properly thinned peaches develop without crowding, p. 2517; *Pedilanthus tithymaloides* with foliage, p. 2526; *Penstemon nitidus*, p. 2545; *Penstemon wilcoxii*, p. 2547; *Penstemon hirsutus pygmaeus*, p. 2547; *Pereskia*, undetermined species in Cuba, p. 2561; *Phacelia purshii*, p. 2579; *Phalaenopsis schillerana*, p. 2582; *Philadelphus coronarius*, p. 2588; Phoenix palms are elegant as indoor decoratives, p. 2608; *Pilea involucrata*, p. 2637; *Platanus occidentalis* (fruits—seed balls), p. 2712; *Platanus acerifolia* at The New York Botanical Garden, p. 2713; *Podophyllum peltatum* in a woodland, p. 2735; *Podophyllum peltatum* (flowers), p. 2735; *Podophyllum peltatum* (fruits), p. 2735; *Pogonia ophioglossoides*, p. 2736; A Christmas display of poinsettias, p. 2737; A white-bracted poinsettia showing the true flowers clustered at the centers of the inflorescences, p. 2737; Propagating poinsettias (parts a, b, c, d, e & f), p. 2738; *Polygonatum commutatum*, p. 2746; *Polygonatum commutatum* (fruits), p. 2746; *Pontederia cordata*, a native stand, p. 2759; *Populus alba* (part b), p. 2763; *Populus grandidentata*, p. 2764; A group of plants assembled for repotting, p. 2776; To repot a well-rooted leafy plant (parts a, b, c, d, e & f), p. 2780; To repot a well-rooted leafy plant (part g), p. 2781; *Prunus serrulata* variety, p. 2824; *Prunus serotina*, p. 2826; *Prunus serotina* (flowers), p. 2826; *Prunus serotina* (fruits), p. 2826; *Pseudosasa japonica* as a pot plant, p. 2836. Department of Horticulture, Ohio State University: Symmetrical balance is achieved by the use of a specimen boxwood and a vine on each side of this door, p. 2675. United States National Arboretum: *Phillyrea decora*, p. 2591; A young specimen of *Pinus wallichiana*, p. 2654. Roy F. Wilcox & Company: *Philodendron erubescens*, p. 2593. Other photographs by Thomas H. Everett.

Color

Harold Frisch: *Podophyllum hexandrum*, *Primula malacoides*. The New York Botanical Garden: *Parnassia grandifolia*, *Phacelia*, undetermined species (both pictures), *Phalaenopsis lueddemanniana*, *Phlox procumbens*, *Phyllodoce empetriformis*, *Pittosporum tobira*, *Podophyllum peltatum* as a groundcover, *Pogonia ophioglossoides*, *Polygala californica*. Other photographs by Thomas H. Everett.

Published by Garland Publishing, Inc.
136 Madison Avenue, New York, New York 10016

Printed in the United States of America

This work is dedicated to the honored memory of the distinguished horticulturists and botanists who most profoundly influenced my professional career: Allan Falconer of Cheadle Royal Gardens, Cheshire, England; William Jackson Bean, William Dallimore, and John Coutts of the Royal Botanic Gardens, Kew, England; and Dr. Elmer D. Merrill and Dr. Henry A. Gleason of The New York Botanical Garden.

Foreword

According to Webster, an encyclopedia is a book or set of books giving information on all or many branches of knowledge generally in articles alphabetically arranged. To the horticulturist or grower of plants, such a work is indispensable and one to be kept close at hand for frequent reference.

The appearance of *The New York Botanical Garden Illustrated Encyclopedia of Horticulture* by Thomas H. Everett is therefore welcomed as an important addition to the library of horticultural literature. Since horticulture is a living, growing subject, these volumes contain an immense amount of information not heretofore readily available. In addition to detailed descriptions of many thousands of plants given under their generic names and brief description of the characteristics of the more important plant families, together with lists of their genera known to be in cultivation, this Encyclopedia is replete with well-founded advice on how to use plants effectively in gardens and, where appropriate, indoors. Thoroughly practical directions and suggestions for growing plants are given in considerable detail and in easily understood language. Recommendations about what to do in the garden for all months of the year and in different geographical regions will be helpful to beginners and will serve as reminders to others.

The useful category of special subject entries (as distinct from the taxonomic presentations) consists of a wide variety of topics. It is safe to predict that one of the most popular will be Rock and Alpine Gardens. In this entry the author deals helpfully and adequately with a phase of horticulture that appeals to a growing group of devotees, and in doing so presents a distinctly fresh point of view. Many other examples could be cited.

The author's many years as a horticulturist and teacher well qualify him for the task of preparing this Encyclopedia. Because he has, over a period of more than a dozen years, written the entire text (submitting certain critical sections to specialists for review and suggestions) instead of farming out sections to a score or more specialists to write, the result is remarkably homogeneous and cohesive. The Encyclopedia is fully cross referenced so that one may locate a plant by either its scientific or common name.

If, as has been said, an encyclopedia should be all things to all people, then the present volumes richly deserve that accolade. Among the many who call it "friend" will be not only horticulturists ("gardeners," as our author likes to refer to them), but growers, breeders, writers, lecturers, arborists, ecologists, and professional botanists who are frequently called upon to answer questions to which only such a work can provide answers. It seems safe to predict that it will be many years before lovers and growers of plants will have at their command another reference work as authoritative and comprehensive as T. H. Everett's Encyclopedia.

John M. Fogg, Jr.
Director Emeritus, Arboretum of the Barnes Foundation
Emeritus Professor of Botany, University of Pennsylvania

Preface

The primary objective of *The New York Botanical Garden Illustrated Encyclopedia of Horticulture* is a comprehensive description and evaluation of horticulture as it is known and practiced in the United States and Canada by amateurs and by professionals, including those responsible for botanical gardens, public parks, and industrial landscapes. Although large-scale commercial methods of cultivating plants are not stressed, much of the content of the Encyclopedia is as basic to such operations as it is to other horticultural enterprises. Similarly, although landscape design is not treated on a professional level, landscape architects will find in the Encyclopedia a great deal of importance and interest to them. Emphasis throughout is placed on the appropriate employment of plants both outdoors and indoors, and particular attention is given to explaining in considerable detail the how-and when-to-do-it aspects of plant growing.

It may be useful to assess the meanings of two words I have used. Horticulture is simply gardening. It derives from the Latin *hortus*, garden, and *cultura*, culture, and alludes to the intensive cultivation in gardens and nurseries of flowers, fruits, vegetables, shrubs, trees, and other plants. The term is not applicable to the extensive field practices that characterize agriculture and forestry. Amateur, as employed by me, retains its classic meaning of a lover from the Latin *amator*; it refers to those who garden for pleasure rather than for financial gain or professional status. It carries no implication of lack of knowledge or skills and is not to be equated with novice, tyro, or dabbler. In truth, amateurs provide the solid basis upon which American horticulture rests; without them the importance of professionals would diminish. Numbered in millions, amateur gardeners are devotees of the most widespread avocation in the United States. This avocation is serviced by a great complex of nurseries, garden centers, and other suppliers; by landscape architects and landscape contractors; and by garden writers, garden lecturers, Cooperative Extension Agents, librarians, and others who dispense horticultural information. Numerous horticultural societies, garden clubs, and botanical gardens inspire and promote interest in America's greatest hobby and stand ready to help its enthusiasts.

Horticulture as a vocation presents a wide range of opportunities which appeal equally to women and men. It is a field in which excellent prospects still exist for capable entrepreneurs. Opportunities at professional levels occur too in nurseries and greenhouses, in the management of landscaped grounds of many types, and in teaching horticulture.

Some people confuse horticulture with botany. They are not the same. The distinction becomes more apparent if the word gardening is substituted for horticulture. Botany is the science that encompasses all systematized factual knowledge about plants, both wild and cultivated. It is only one of the several disciplines upon which horticulture is based. To become a capable gardener or a knowledgeable plantsman or plantswoman (I like these designations for gardeners who have a wide, intimate, and discerning knowledge of plants in addition to skill in growing them) it is not necessary to study botany formally, although such study is likely to add greatly to one's pleasure. In the practice of gardening many botanical truths are learned from experience. I have known highly competent gardeners without formal training in botany and able and indeed distinguished botanists possessed of minimal horticultural knowledge and skills.

Horticulture is primarily an art and a craft, based upon science, and at some levels perhaps justly regarded as a science in its own right. As an art it calls for an appreciation of beauty and form as expressed in three-dimensional spatial relationships and an ability to translate aesthetic concepts into reality. The chief materials used to create gardens are living plants, most of which change in size and form with the passing of time and often show differences in color and texture and in other ways from season to season. Thus it is important that designers of gardens have a wide familiarity with the sorts of plants that lend themselves to their purposes and with plants' adaptability to the regions and to the sites where it is proposed to plant them.

As a craft, horticulture involves special skills often derived from ancient practices passed from generation to generation by word of mouth and apprenticeship-like contacts. As a technology it relies on this backlog of empirical knowledge supplemented by that acquired by scientific experiment and investigation, the results of which often serve to explain rather than supplant old beliefs and practices but sometimes point the way to more expeditious methods of attaining similar results. And from time to time new techniques are developed that add dimensions to horticultural practice; among such of fairly recent years that come to mind are the manipulation of blooming season by artificial daylength, the propagation of orchids and some other plants by meristem tissue culture, and the development of soilless growing mixes as substitutes for soil.

One of the most significant developments in American horticulture in recent decades is the tremendous increase in the number of different kinds of plants that are cultivated by many more people than formerly. This is particularly true of indoor plants or houseplants, the sorts grown in homes, offices, and other interiors, but is by no means confined to that group. The relative affluence of our society and the freedom and frequency of travel both at home and abroad has contributed to this expansion, a phenomenon that will surely continue as avid collectors of the unusual bring into cultivation new plants from the wild and promote wider interest in sorts presently rare. Our garden flora is also constantly and beneficially expanded as a result of the work of both amateur and professional plant breeders.

It is impracticable in even the most comprehensive encyclopedia to describe or even list all plants that somewhere within a territory as large as the United States and Canada are grown in gardens. In this Encyclopedia the majority of genera known to be in cultivation are described, and descriptions and often other pertinent information about a complete or substantial number of their species and lesser categories are given. Sorts likely to be found only in collections of botanical gardens or in those of specialists may be omitted.

The vexing matter of plant nomenclature inevitably presents itself when an encyclopedia of horticulture is contemplated. Conflicts arise chiefly between the very understandable desire of gardeners and others who deal with cultivated plants to retain longfamiliar names and the need to reflect up-to-date botanical interpretations. These points of view are basically irreconcilable and so accommodations must be reached.

As has been well demonstrated in the past, it is unrealistic to attempt to standardize the horticultural usage of plant names by decree or edict. To do so would negate scientific progress. But it is just as impracticable to expect gardeners, nurserymen, arborists, seedsmen, dealers in bulbs, and other amateur and professional horticulturists to keep current with the interpretations and recommendations of plant taxonomists; particularly as these sometimes fail to gain the acceptance even of other botanists and it is not unusual for scientists of equal stature and competence to prefer different names for the same plant.

In practice time is the great leveler. Newly proposed plant names accepted in botanical literature are likely to filter gradually into horticultural usage and eventually gain currency value, but this sometimes takes several years. The complete up-to-dateness and niceties of botanical naming are less likely to bedevil horticulturists than uncertainties concerned with correct plant identification. This is of prime importance. Whether a tree is labeled *Pseudotsuga douglasii, P. taxifolia,* or *P. menziesii* is of less concern than that the specimen so identified is indeed a Douglas-fir and not some other conifer.

After reflection I decided that the most sensible course to follow in *The New York Botanical Garden Illustrated Encyclopedia of Horticulture* was to accept almost in its entirety the nomenclature adopted in *Hortus Third* published in 1976. By doing so, much of the confusion that would result from two major comprehensive horticultural works of the late twentieth century using different names for the same plant is avoided, and it is hoped that for a period of years a degree of stability will be attained. Always those deeply concerned with critical groups of plants can adopt the recommendations of the latest monographers. Exceptions to the parallelism in nomenclature in this Encyclopedia and *Hortus Third* are to be found in the CACTACEAE for which, with certain reservations but for practical purposes, as explained in the Encyclopedia entry Cactuses, the nomenclature of Curt Backeburg's *Die Cactaceae,* published in 1958–62, is followed; and the ferns, where I mostly accepted the guidance of Dr. John T. Mickel of The New York Botanical Garden. The common or colloquial names employed are those deemed to have general acceptance. Cross references and synonymy are freely provided.

The convention of indicating typographically whether or not plants of status lesser than species represent entities that propagate and persist in the wild or are sorts that persist only in cultivation is not followed. Instead, as explained in the Encyclopedia entry Plant Names, the word variety is employed for all entities below specific rank and if in Latin form the name is written in italic, if in English or other modern language, in Roman type, with initial capital letter, and enclosed in single quotation marks.

Thomas H. Everett
Senior Horticulture Specialist
The New York Botanical Garden

Acknowledgments

I am indebted to many people for help and support generously given over the period of more than twelve years it has taken to bring this Encyclopedia to fruition. Chief credit belongs to four ladies. They are Lillian M. Weber and Nancy Callaghan, who besides accepting responsibility for the formidable task of filing and retrieving information, typing manuscript, proofreading, and the management of a vast collection of photographs, provided much wise council; Elizabeth C. Hall, librarian extraordinary, whose superb knowledge of horticultural and botanical literature was freely at my disposal; and Ellen, my wife, who displayed a deep understanding of the demands on time called for by an undertaking of this magnitude, and with rare patience accepted inevitable inconvenience. I am also obliged to my sister, Hette Everett, for the valuable help she freely gave on many occasions.

Of the botanists I repeatedly called upon for opinions and advice and from whom I sought elucidation of many details of their science abstruse to me, the most heavily burdened have been my friends and colleagues at The New York Botanical Garden, Dr. Rupert C. Barneby, Dr. Arthur Cronquist, and Dr John T. Mickel. Other botanists and horticulturists with whom I held discussions or corresponded about matters pertinent to my text include Dr. Theodore M. Barkley, Dr. Lyman Benson, Dr. Ben Blackburn, Professor Harold Davidson, Dr. Otto Degener, Harold Epstein, Dr. John M. Fogg, Jr., Dr. Alwyn H. Gentry, Dr. Alfred B. Graf, Brian Halliwell, Dr. David R. Hunt, Dr. John P. Jessop, Dr. Tetsuo Koyama, Dr. Bassett Maguire, Dr. Roy A. Mecklenberg, Everitt L. Miller, Dr. Harold N. Moldenke, Dr. Dan H. Nicolson, Dr. Pascal P. Pirone, Dr. Ghillean Prance, Don Richardson, Stanley J. Smith, Ralph L. Snodsmith, Marco Polo Stufano, Dr. Bernard Verdcourt, Dr. Edgar T. Wherry, Dr. Trevor Whiffin, Dr. Richard P. Wunderlin, Dr. John J. Wurdack, Yuji Yoshimura, and Rudolf Ziesenhenne.

Without either exception or stint these conferees and correspondents shared with me their knowledge, thoughts, and judgments. Much of the bounty so gleaned is reflected in the text of the Encyclopedia but none other than I am responsible for interpretations and opinions that appear there. To all who have helped, my special thanks are due and are gratefully proferred.

I acknowledge with much pleasure the excellent cooperation I have received from the Garland Publishing Company and most particularly from its President, Gavin Borden. To Ruth Adams, Geoffrey Braine, Nancy Isaac, Carol Miller, Melinda Wirkus, I say thank you for working so understandingly and effectively with me and for shepherding my raw typescript through the necessary stages.

How to Use This Encyclopedia

A vast amount of information about how to use, propagate, and care for plants both indoors and outdoors is contained in the thousands of entries that compose *The New York Botanical Garden Illustrated Encyclopedia of Horticulture* Some understanding of the Encyclopedia's organization is necessary in order to find what you want to know.

Arrangement of the Entries

Genera

The entries are arranged in alphabetical order. Most numerous are those that deal with taxonomic groups of plants. Here belong approximately 3,500 items entered under the genus name, such as ABIES, DIEFFENBACHIA, and JUGLANS. If instead of referring to these names you consult their common name equivalents of FIR, DUMB CANE, and WALNUT, you will find cross references to the genus names.

Bigeneric Hybrids & Chimeras

Hybrids between genera that have names equivalent to genus names—most of these belonging in the orchid family—are accorded separate entries. The same is true for the few chimeras or graft hybrids with names of similar status. Because bigeneric hybrids frequently have characteristics similar to those of their parents and require similar care, the entries for them are often briefer than the regular genus entries.

Families

Plant families are described under their botanical names, with their common name equivalents also given. Each description is followed by a list of the genera accorded separate entries in this Encyclopedia.

Vegetables, Fruits, Herbs, & Ornamentals

Vegetables and fruits that are commonly cultivated, such as broccoli, cabbage, potato, tomato, apple, peach, and raspberry; most culinary herbs, including basil, chives, parsley, sage, and tarragon; and a few popular ornamentals, such as azaleas, carnations, pansies, and poinsettias, are treated under their familiar names, with cross references to their genera. Discussions of a few herbs and some lesser known vegetables and fruits are given under their Latin scientific names with cross references to the common names.

Other Entries

The remaining entries in the Encyclopedia are cross references, definitions, and more substantial discussions of many subjects of interest to gardeners and others concerned with plants. For example, a calendar of gardening activity, by geographical area, is given under the names of the months and a glossary of frequently applied species names (technically, specific epithets) is provided in the entry Plant Names. A list of these general topics, which may provide additional information about a particular plant, is provided at the beginning of each volume of the Encyclopedia.

Cross References & Definitions

The cross references are of two chief types: those that give specific information, which may be all you wish to know at the moment:
Boojam Tree is *Idria columnaris*
Cobra plant is *Darlingtonia californica*.
and those that refer to entries where fuller explanations are to be found:
Adhatoda. See Justicia.
Clubmoss. See Lycopodium and Selaginella.

Additional information about entries of the former type can, of course, be found by looking up the genus to which the plant belongs—*Idria* in the case of the boojam tree and *Darlingtonia* for the cobra plant.

ORGANIZATION OF THE GENUS ENTRIES

Pronunciation

Each genus name is followed by its pronunciation in parentheses. The stressed syllable is indicated by the diacritical mark ´ if the vowel sound is short as in man, pet, pink, hot, and up; or by if the vowel sound is long as in mane, pete, pine, home, and fluke.

Genus Common Names
Family Common Names
General Characteristics

Following the pronunciation, there may be one or more common names applicable to the genus as a whole or to certain of its kinds. Other names may be introduced later with the descriptions of the species or kinds. Early in the entry you will find the common and botanical names of the plant family to which the genus belongs, the number of species the genus contains, its natural geographical distribution, and the derivation of its name. A description that stresses the general characteristics of the genus follows, and this may be supplemented by historical data, uses of some or all of its members, and other pertinent information.

Identification of Plants

Descriptions of species, hybrids, and varieties appear next. The identification of unrecognized plants is a fairly common objective of gardeners; accordingly, in this Encyclopedia various species have been grouped within entries in ways that make their identification easier. The groupings may bring into proximity sorts that can be adapted for similar landscape uses or that require the same cultural care, or they may emphasize geographical origins of species or such categories as evergreen and deciduous or tall and low members of the same genus. Where the description of a species occurs, its name is designated in ***bold italic***. Under this plan, the description of a particular species can be found by referring to the group to which it belongs, scanning the entry for the species name in bold italic, or referring to the opening sentences of paragraphs which have been designed to serve as lead-ins to descriptive groupings.

Gardening & Landscape Uses
Cultivation
Pests & Diseases

At the end of genus entries, subentries giving information on garden and landscape uses, cultivation, and pests or diseases or both are included, or else reference is made to other genera or groupings for which these are similar.

xvi

General Subject Listings

The lists below organize some of the Encyclopedia entries into topics which may be of particular interest to the reader. They are also an aid in finding information other than Latin or common names of plants.

PLANT ANATOMY AND TERMS USED IN PLANT DESCRIPTIONS

All-America Selections
Alternate
Annual Rings
Anther
Apex
Ascending
Awl-Shaped
Axil, Axillary
Berry
Bloom
Bracts
Bud
Bulb
Bulbils
Bulblet
Bur
Burl
Calyx
Cambium Layer
Capsule
Carpel
Catkin
Centrals
Ciliate
Climber
Corm
Cormel
Cotyledon
Crown
Deciduous
Disk or Disc
Double Flowers
Drupe
Florets
Flower
Follicle
Frond
Fruit
Glaucous
Gymnosperms
Head
Hips
Hose-in-Hose

Inflorescence
Lanceolate
Leader
Leaf
Leggy
Linear
Lobe
Midrib
Mycelium
Node
Nut and Nutlet
Oblanceolate
Oblong
Obovate
Offset
Ovate
Palmate
Panicle
Pedate
Peltate
Perianth
Petal
Pinnate
Pip
Pistil
Pit
Pod
Pollen
Pompon
Pseudobulb
Radials
Ray Floret
Rhizome
Runners
Samara
Scion or Cion
Seeds
Sepal
Set
Shoot
Spore
Sprigs
Spur
Stamen
Stigma
Stipule

Stolon
Stool
Style
Subshrub
Taproot
Tepal
Terminal
Whorl

GARDENING TERMS AND INFORMATION

Acid and Alkaline Soils
Adobe
Aeration of the Soil
Air and Air Pollution
Air Drainage
Air Layering
Alpine Greenhouse or Alpine House
Amateur Gardener
April, Gardening Reminders For
Aquarium
Arbor
Arboretum
Arch
Asexual or Vegetative Propagation
Atmosphere
August, Gardening Reminders For
Balled and Burlapped
Banks and Steep Slopes
Bare-Root
Bark Ringing
Baskets, Hanging
Bed
Bedding and Bedding Plants
Bell Jar
Bench, Greenhouse
Blanching
Bleeding
Bog
Bolting
Border
Bottom Heat
Break, Breaking
Broadcast
Budding
Bulbs or Bulb Plants

Gardening Terms and Information (Continued)

State Agricultural Experimental Stations
Stock or Understock
Straightedge
Strawberry Jars
Strike
Stunt
Succession Cropping
Sundials
Syringing
Thinning or Thinning Out
Tillage
Tilth
Tools
Top-Dressing
Topiary Work
Training Plants
Tree Surgery
Tree Wrapping
Trenching
Trowels
Tubs
Watering
Weeds and Their Control
Window Boxes

FERTILIZERS AND OTHER SUBSTANCES RELATED TO GARDENING

Algicide
Aluminum Sulfate
Ammonium Nitrate
Ammonium Sulfate
Antibiotics
Ashes
Auxins
Basic Slag
Blood Meal
Bonemeal
Bordeaux Mixture
Calcium Carbonate
Calcium Chloride
Calcium Metaphosphate
Calcium Nitrate
Calcium Sulfate
Carbon Disulfide
Chalk
Charcoal
Coal Cinders
Cork Bark
Complete Fertilizer
Compost and Composting
Cottonseed Meal
Creosote
DDT
Dormant Sprays
Dried Blood
Fermate or Ferbam
Fertilizers
Fishmeal
Formaldehyde
Fungicides
Gibberellic Acid
Green Manuring
Growth Retardants
Guano
Herbicides or Weed-Killers
Hoof and Horn Meal

Hormones
Humus
Insecticide
John Innes Composts
Lime and Liming
Liquid Fertilizer
Liquid Manure
Manures
Mulching and Mulches
Muriate of Potash
Nitrate of Ammonia
Nitrate of Lime
Nitrate of Potash
Nitrate of Soda
Nitrogen
Orchid Peat
Organic Matter
Osmunda Fiber or Osmundine
Oyster Shells
Peat
Peat Moss
Permanganate of Potash
Potassium
Potassium Chloride
Potassium-Magnesium Sulfate
Potassium Nitrate
Potassium Permanganate
Potassium Sulfate
Pyrethrum
Rock Phosphate
Rotenone
Salt Hay or Salt Marsh Hay
Sand
Sawdust
Sodium Chloride
Sprays and Spraying
Sulfate
Superphosphate
Trace Elements
Urea
Urea-Form Fertilizers
Vermiculite
Wood Ashes

TECHNICAL TERMS

Acre
Alternate Host
Annuals
Antidessicant or Antitranspirant
Biennals
Binomial
Botany
Chromosome
Climate
Clone
Composite
Conservation
Cross or Crossbred
Cross Fertilization
Cross Pollination
Cultivar
Decumbent
Dicotyledon
Division
Dormant
Endemic
Environment
Family

Fasciation
Fertility
Fertilization
Flocculate
Floriculture
Genus
Germinate
Habitat
Half-Hardy
Half-Ripe
Hardy Annual
Hardy Perennial
Heredity
Hybrid
Indigenous
Juvenile Forms
Juvenility
Legume
Monocotyledon
Monoecious
Mutant or Sport
Mycorrhiza or Mycorhiza
Nitrification
Perennials
pH
Plant Families
Photoperiodism
Photosynthesis
Pollination
Pubescent
Saprophyte
Self-Fertile
Self-Sterile
Species
Standard
Sterile
Strain
Terrestrial
Tetraploid
Transpiration
Variety

TYPES OF GARDENS AND GARDENING

Alpine Garden
Artificial Light Gardening
Backyard Gardens
Biodynamic Gardening
Bog Gardens
Botanic Gardens and Arboretums
Bottle Garden
City Gardening
Colonial Gardens
Conservatory
Container Gardening
Cutting Garden
Desert Gardens
Dish Gardens
Flower Garden
Fluorescent Light Gardening
Formal and Semiformal Gardens
Greenhouses and Conservatories
Heath or Heather Garden
Herb Gardens
Hydroponics or Nutriculture
Indoor Lighting Gardening
Japanese Gardens
Kitchen Garden
Knot Gardens

The New York
Botanical Garden
Illustrated Encyclopedia
of Horticulture

PARAPHALAENOPSIS (Paraphalaen-ópsis). Three species of the orchid family ORCHIDACEAE, formerly included in *Phalaenopsis*, constitute *Paraphalaenopsis*. All are natives of Borneo. The name comes from the Greek *para*, near, and *Phalaenopsis*.

These differ from *Phalaenopsis* in having cylindrical leaves and in sometimes developing more than one flower group from the same point on the stem. They look more like *Vanda* than *Phalaenopsis* and have been hybridized with that genus to produce *Paravanda*. They have also been hybridized with *Arachnis* and *Renanthera*, but not successfully with *Phalaenopsis*. There are hybrids between the species of *Paraphalaenopsis*.

Paraphalaenopsises grow as epiphytes (tree-perchers that take no nourishment from their hosts) or on mossy rocks. They have short stems and long, slender, drooping, cylindrical leaves, grooved along their upper sides. In clusters, the fragrant flowers have spreading or slightly backward-bending, more or less wavy or twisted, similar sepals and petals, three of the former, two of the latter, and a three-lobed lip.

The first species, discovered in 1925, *P. denevei* (syn. *Phalaenopsis denevei*) has a short stem and three to six dark bluish-green leaves up to 2½ feet long. From below the leaves in clusters up to 6 inches long, the fifteen or fewer blooms of each cluster come from approximately the same point on the stem. The flowers, long-lasting and about 2 inches wide, have usually very wavy sepals and petals, often bent backward, greenish-yellow to deep yellow-brown, with paler borders. The three-lobed lip is white, striped and blotched with red or violet, with a red-lined, yellow to orange callus. The leaves of *P. laycockii* (syn. *Phalaenopsis laycockii*) are more deeply channeled than those of *P. denevei*. Its somewhat larger, lemon-fragrant blooms are whitish to light mauve or rose suffused with mauve, the lip shading to reddish-brown and blotched, with a red-striped, yellow callus. The flowers of *P. serpentilingua* (syn. *Phalaenopsis serpentilingua*), a little smaller than those of *P. denevei*, are in larger racemes. Fragrant, they have white sepals and petals and white to lemon-yellow lips, their middle lobes deeply forked at their apexes, with red markings and a red-dotted callus.

Garden Uses and Cultivation. These choice collectors' orchids require the same conditions and care as *Phalaenopsis*. For further details see Phalaenopsis, and Orchids.

PARASITE. A plant or creature that lives on or in the tissues of another living plant or creature and derives nourishment from it to the latter's detriment is called a parasite. The supplier of the nourishment is known as the host. From parasites sapro-phytes differ in that they obtain their nutrients from dead plant tissues, epiphytes in that they perch on trees or other plants without taking nourishment from them. Organisms that live with other organisms in symbiotic relationship (one from which they mutually benefit) are not ordinarily defined as parasites.

The funguses, bacteria, and other non-animal organisms that cause plant diseases are mostly parasites. Some are primarily saprophytes that, under some circumstances, become more or less parasitic. A common example of a higher plant that is parasitic is dodder, a member of the morning glory family CONVOLVULACEAE, that lives on a wide variety of other plants.

Plants like dodder, which are complete parasites, are without chlorophyll and depend entirely upon their hosts for nourishment. Others, of which the best-known example is mistletoe, which are partial parasites, contain chlorophyll and so photosynthesize some of the food they need, but satisfy part of their requirements from their hosts.

Animal parasites that live on plants include a wide variety of insects, mites, nematodes, and other small creatures.

PARASOL TREE, CHINESE. This is *Firmiana simplex*.

PARASYRINGA SEMPERVIRENS is *Ligustrum sempervirens*.

PARAVANDA. This is the name of hybrids between the orchid genera *Paraphalaenopsis* and *Vanda*.

PARDANTHOPSIS DICHOTOMUS is *Iris dichotoma*.

PARIETARIA (Pariet-ària)—Pellitory. Nettle relatives, without stinging hairs, the thirty species of *Parietaria*, of the nettle family URTICACEAE, are of little horticultural importance. The genus, widely distributed in temperate and tropical regions of the Old World and the New World has a name derived from the Latin *paries*, a wall, in allusion to favored habitats of *P. officinalis* and some other species.

Dioscorides knew the pellitory and recommended it for producing cooling relief for patients suffering from "Erysipelata, Condylomata, adustions, ye Pani beginning and all manner of inflammation, ye Oedemata" as well as for "ye Herpetas and feet gouts" and for "enflamed Tonsillae" and "ear pains." Many centuries later Ben Jonson reported with satisfaction "A good old woman . . . did cure me with sodden ale and pellitorie of the wall."

Annual and perennial herbaceous plants, sometimes becoming woody at their bases, parietarias have opposite, undivided, fleshy leaves, and spherical clusters of tiny green flowers and bracts, in the leaf axils. The blooms are bisexual or unisexual, the sexes on the same or separate plants. Bisexual and male flowers have four-parted perianths and four stamens; females have a solitary style and four-toothed, persistent perianths that enclose loosely the fruits (technically achenes). As in *Pilea*, of the same family, the pollen is discharged explosively.

Native to central and southern, but not western, Europe, *P. officinalis* is erect and 1 foot to 3 feet tall, with densely-hairy stems little or not branched. Its stalked, long-pointed, ovate-lanceolate to elliptic leaves are 1½ to 4½ inches long. Its fruits (often called seeds) are black. A lower, much-branched species with procumbent or erect stems, and leaves up to 2 inches long that differs from the last in having the bracts of its flower clusters joined instead of free at their bases, is often mistakenly referred to as *P. officinalis*. It is *P. diffusa*, of central and southwestern Europe.

Garden Uses and Cultivation. Apart from its interest as a plant once employed medicinally and thus a candidate for inclusion in gardens devoted to species of historic medical importance, the pellitory has no merit. Hardy and growing without difficulty in ordinary porous garden soil, it is easily raised from seed and cuttings.

PARIS (Par-is)—Herb Paris. This genus of twenty species is little known to American gardeners. It is very like *Trillium*, but whereas *Trillium* is indigenous to North America but not Europe, the reverse is true of *Paris*. Both occur in Japan and some other temperate parts of Asia. The chief difference between *Trillium* and *Paris* is that in the former the leaves and floral parts are in threes, in the latter in fours or higher numbers. In the lily family LILIACEAE, to which both genera belong, the floral parts are typically in threes or sixes, a quadruple arrangement is very unusual, but not unique to *Paris*; it occurs also in *Aspidistra*. As a member of the lily family, *Paris* is also unusual, but not unique, in that its leaves do not have parallel veins but are net-veined. The origin of the name *Paris* is uncertain. It may come from the Latin *par*, equal, and allude to the plants commonly having the same number of leaves as floral parts. Herb paris was once held in repute as a medicine and aphrodisiac. It is poisonous and overdoses have resulted in the deaths of children. The berries have also proved fatal to poultry.

The genus *Paris* consists of deciduous herbaceous plants with creeping rhizomes and erect, branchless stems that, except for some scales near their bases, have their leaves in a collar or ruff (whorl) at the top of the stem and beneath the bloom. The leaves are lanceolate to ovate and have three main veins. The perianth segments are in two series of four to ten according to kind. There are as many styles and twice as many stamens as petals. The fruits are capsules.

Herb paris (*P. quadrifolia*) is up to 1 foot tall. The yellowish-green flower is held 1 inch to 2 inches above the spreading leaves and is 2 to 3 inches in diameter. The four or very rarely five outer perianth segments are greener, broader, and longer than the inner ones. The leaves are obovate, 1¼ to 2½ inches long, and normally number four, rarely five. The fruits are spherical, black, and berry-like. This inhabits moist woodlands throughout most of Europe and adjacent Asia north to the Arctic Circle. Himalayan *P. polyphylla*, up to 3 feet tall, has four to nine linear to oblong-lanceolate leaves up to 6 inches long. Sometimes exceeding 4 inches across, the flower has four to six green outer perianth segments and as many yellow inner ones. The fruits, up to 2½ inches in diameter, contain red seeds.

Garden Uses and Cultivation. These plants, less showy than the better trilliums, are scarcely worth planting for display. As a variant from more typical members of the lily family they interest students of botany, and as an old-time source of medicine herb paris appeals to people interested in plants thought to possess healing virtues. Environmental needs and cultivation are as for *Trillium*.

PARIS-DAISY. See Marguerite or Paris-Daisy.

PARKERIACEAE — Water-Fern Family. The characteristics of this family of ferns are those of its only genus, *Ceratopteris*.

PARKIA (Pàrk-ia). The famous African explorer Mungo Park, who died about 1806, is commemorated by *Parkia*, a genus of forty species of the pea family LEGUMINOSAE. It is a native of the tropics of both the Old World and the New World.

Parkias are tall, thornless trees. Their twice-pinnate leaves have numerous small leaflets. Their flowers are in large, compact, ovoid, pear- or club-shaped, long-stalked heads that suggest giant ones of acacias, but are generally less lovely. The heads are solitary from the leaf axils or grouped at the branch ends. The upper flowers of each head are fertile and yellow to red, those below are white or red and sterile. Each tiny bloom has a shortly-five-toothed, tubular calyx, a tubular corolla of five petals united or not in their lower parts, ten stamens separate or joined below, and a slender style. The fruits are flat, strap-shaped, black pods. Those of *P. filicoidea* contain sweetish edible pulp and seeds used like coffee. The pods of *P. javanica* and *P. speciosa* are edible and used for flavoring.

Cultivated in Florida, *P. javanica*, 60 feet tall or taller, has ferny leaves up to 3 feet long. Its heads of whitish flowers are rounded or club-shaped. The seed pods are up to 1 foot long and 1½ inches wide. From the Philippine Islands and Timor, *P. timorana* exceeds 100 feet in height and has a broad, vase-shaped crown. Its little white-and-yellow flowers are in pear-shaped heads. The pendulous seed pods are about 1½ feet long.

Garden and Landscape Uses and Cultivation. In tropical and near tropical climates parkias are satisfactory ornamental trees that grow in ordinary soils and locations. They are propagated by seed.

PARKINSONIA (Parkin-sònia)—Palo Verde or Jerusalem-Thorn or Ratama or Horse-Bean. The common name of these plants is also applied to the related genus *Cercidium*. There are two species of *Parkinsonia*, one American, one South African. Other species previously included here have been transferred to *Cercidium*. Parkinsonias belong in the pea family LEGUMINOSAE and bear a name that commemorates the great English herbalist and author John Parkinson, who died in 1650.

Parkinsonias are low trees with conspicuously green branches and branchlets, a circumstance recognized by the common name palo verde (green tree). At each node on the stems are two spines and one at the end of the extremely short main midrib of each leaf. The leaves are twice-pinnate. They have one to three pairs of primary divisions with long, flattened, winged midribs crowded with tiny leaflets that soon fall. The flowers, which are not pea-like, but are structured like those of senna (*Cassia*), are in long racemes. They have five-parted calyxes and five spreading petals much narrowed at their bases. The upper petal is inside the others and is broader than them. The ten separate stamens have stalks hairy at their bases. The fruits are pods, strongly constricted between the seeds.

The palo verde, Jerusalem-thorn, ratama, or horse-bean (*P. aculeata*) is a graceful, feathery-looking shrub or tree up to 30 feet tall. It has slender, pendulous branches and leaves with primary divisions up to 8 inches long and necklaced with leaflets not over 8 inch long, but usually smaller. The flowers, yellow dotted with red, have petals 8 to ½ inch long. They are in racemes 4 to 6 inches long. The seed pods are 2 to 4 inches long. This species is native from Arizona to Florida, the West Indies, Mexico, and South America.

Garden and Landscape Uses and Cultivation. Parkinsonias provide elegant furnishing for gardens and other landscapes in areas with warm, moist or arid climates. They are popular from South Carolina to Florida and along the Gulf Coast and in California. They are pleasing as single specimens or grouped, and form good screens and hedges. Because they are light and airy sufficient light reaches the ground for lawn grass to grow beneath them. Exposure to full sun and dryish, well-drained soil provide suitable growing conditions. Although none is needed, except to restrict them to size or shape, they stand pruning and shearing well. Immediately after flowering is an appropriate time to do this. Propagation is by seed.

PARMENTIERA (Parmen-tièra) — Candle Tree. The name *Parmentiera* commemorates Antoine Parmentier, a French apothecary interested in food plants, who died in 1813. The genus it identifies belongs in the bignonia family BIGNONIACEAE and comprises three or four species of trees indigenous to Mexico and Central America.

Parmentieras have alternate to nearly opposite leaves, usually with three, or sometimes five leaflets and winged stalks. Their large, stalked, slightly two-lipped, bell- to funnel-shaped flowers, solitary or clustered, mostly grow on the trunk and older branches. They have calyxes split so that they look like spathes and five-lobed, nearly symmetrical corollas from which the four stamens scarcely protrude.

The candle tree (*P. cereifera*), of Panama, is so named because its pendant

Parkinsonia aculeata

Parkinsonia aculeata (flowers)

fruits look like great wax candles. Yellowish, cylindrical, and 1 foot to 4 feet long by up to 1 inch wide, they have an apple-like odor and are relished by cattle. The tree that bears these curious fruits is 20 to 25 feet tall and well-branched from its base. Its thinnish leaves have ovate-elliptic to obovate, short-stalked leaflets up to 2 inches long that are usually toothed on young trees, but not on mature ones. The wavy-edged, whitish, sometimes pink-tinged flowers are up to 3 inches long by 2 inches wide or somewhat wider.

The guajilote or cuachilote (*P. edulis*) is much like the candle tree, but has yellowish-green, fleshy, pointed fruits, ridged, and 4 to 8 inches long by ¾ inch to 2 inches wide. They are sweet, but of poor eating quality. In Mexico they are eaten raw, cooked, and pickled and are fed to cattle. Also, at the bases of the leafstalks of this species are short spines. Its flowers are pale green tinged with purple. The guajilote tree, sometimes 40 feet tall, is indigenous to Mexico and Guatemala.

Parmentiera edulis

A tree of curious aspect 15 to 45 feet high, *P. alata* (syn. *Crescentia alata*) is native from Mexico to Guatemala and San Salvador. It has erect, whiplike branches and leaves with broadly-winged stalks and three oblanceolate to spatula-shaped leaflets, the longest, the center one, up to 3 inches long. The subspherical fruits 2½ to 4½ inches in diameter, and like the ill-scented flowers borne on main branches and trunk, are used as gourds for making drinking cups and small flasks, and their pulp is employed in domestic medicines.

Garden and Landscape Uses and Cultivation. Parmentieras are cultivated in warm-climate regions for ornament and for the interest of their unusual fruits. They are bushy, evergreen trees that provide good screening and are suitable for grouping, boundary plantings, and display as single specimens. They thrive in ordinary soils, but are most responsive to those that are both fertile and moist. Seed and cuttings afford ready means of increase.

PARNASSIA (Parnás-sia) — Grass-of-Parnassus. By some botanists *Parnassia* is considered sufficiently distinct from the saxifrage family SAXIFRAGACEAE, to which it is generally allotted, to warrant segregating it as the only genus of the grass-of-Parnassus family PARNASSIACEAE. Its fifty members are hairless herbaceous perennials, about as unlike grasses as plants can be, of temperate and arctic regions in North America, Europe, and Asia. The name is derived from that of Mount Parnassus, in Greece, which is dedicated to Apollo and the Muses.

Inhabiting damp and wet soils, parnassias have basal rosettes of thickish, usually evergreen, more or less shiny, undivided, long-stalked leaves and slender, erect flower stems, each with usually a single stalkless leaf. The solitary, white to pale yellowish blooms, generally veined with green or yellow, are somewhat buttercup-like. They have five sepals joined somewhat at their bases, five spreading petals, five stamens, and at the base of each petal a cluster of three or more sterile stamens (staminodes) in which the anthers are usually represented by glossy, knoblike glands. These often add to the attractiveness of the blooms. There are three or four nearly stalkless stigmas. The fruits are many-seeded capsules.

Large-flowered *P. grandifolia*, sometimes 1½ feet tall, has blooms up to 2 inches in diameter. They have petals with seven to nine veins and staminodes, joined for one-tenth or more of their lengths from their bases, much longer than the stamens. The basal leaves have broad, ovate to nearly round blades, 2 to 3½ inches long, and a leaf below the middle of the stem, smaller than the basal ones. This grows in wet, calcareous soils in the mountains from Virginia and West Virginia to Georgia, and in Missouri.

Native to North America, Europe, and Asia, *P. palustris* grows in wet, calcareous soils along shores and in meadows. From 6 inches to over 1 foot tall, it has broadly-ovate to nearly round basal leaves, ½ inch to 1½ inches across, and stem leaves as large or smaller than the basal ones, with clasping bases. The blooms have three- to thirteen-veined petals. The staminodes are conspicuously longer than the stamens. Each is divided into from nine to more than twenty slender filaments. The flowers are ½ to 1 inch across and have petals at least one-half as long as the sepals. This occurs from Labrador to Alaska, New York, Minnesota, and Oregon. In *P. p. californica*, the stem leaf (sometimes wanting) does not clasp the stem.

Two North American species in which the staminodes of the flowers are somewhat shorter than the stamens are *P. glauca* (formerly called *P. caroliniana*) and *P. asarifolia*. The former favors calcareous bogs, meadows, and shores from Canada

Parnassia glauca

to Virginia and South Dakota, the latter, stream banks and bogs in the mountains from Virginia to Georgia, and in Arkansas. Both are from 8 inches to over 1 foot in height. The basal leaves of *P. glauca* are ovate to round-ovate, up to 2 inches in length, and longer than broad; those of *P. asarifolia* are kidney-shaped and broader than their 1- to 2-inch lengths. The flowers of the former are ¾ inch to 1½ inches wide; those of the latter up to 2 inches wide.

Wild from the Rocky Mountains and mountains of California to Alaska, and growing in wet meadows, *P. fimbriata* is distinct by reason of its flowers having petals fringed along their sides toward the bases. The plant is 8 inches to a little over 1 foot tall. Its elliptic to broad-elliptic basal leaves have kidney- to heart-shaped blades 1 inch to 1¾ inches across. The stem leaf is small, heart-shaped, and bractlike. The 1-inch-wide blooms have their staminodes joined as fleshy, short-lobed scales.

Garden Uses and Cultivation. Parnassias are dainty plants for cool bog gardens and wet places in native plant gardens and rock gardens. They appreciate an abundance of peat or other humus in the soil and, many kinds, plenty of crushed limestone mixed in. Spring is the best planting season. The plants may be spaced 4 to 6 inches apart. Once established they may be left undisturbed, except if they are to be divided as a means of increase. This is done by digging the plants up and pulling them apart in spring. Seeds, sown as soon as they are ripe in pans (shallow pots) of sandy peaty soil, with the pans kept standing in saucers of water so that the soil never dries, and shaded from direct sun, afford another simple means of propagation.

PAROCHETUS (Paróch-etus) — Shamrock-Pea. The shamrock-pea (*Parochetus communis*) is the only species of this genus of the pea family LEGUMINOSAE. Indigenous to temperate parts of the Himalayas and

East Africa, it is moderately hardy, but not sufficiently so to winter outdoors at New York City. Its name, from the Greek *para,* beside, and *ochetos,* a ditch or brook, alludes to its liking for moist soils.

A prostrate herbaceous perennial 2 to 3 inches tall, **P. communis** has slender, almost threadlike, freely-branching, rooting stems that spread widely and clover-like leaves, with 2-inch-long stalks, and three obovate, toothed leaflets. Its bright azure-blue, pea-like flowers, ½ to ¾ inch across and lightly tinged with yellow, are borne singly or in clusters of two or three from the leaf axils. The fruits are hairless, straight, linear pods ¾ to 1 inch long.

Garden Uses and Cultivation. Rock gardens and suchlike intimate plantings are the best sites for this pretty, interesting creeper. It thrives with abandon in well-drained, not excessively dry soil in full sun, and one plant will clothe several square feet. Propagation is by division and by seed. In regions where it is not winter-hardy, it is easy to keep by removing pieces in late summer, potting them, and overwintering them in a well-protected cold frame or cool greenhouse. The shamrock-pea is also susceptible to cultivation in pots and hanging baskets in cool greenhouses. When so cultivated its soil should be fertile and always moist. Winter night temperatures of 45 to 50°F are satisfactory, with a few degrees increase by day.

PARODIA (Par-òdia). Its name honoring the Argentinian botanist Lorenzo Raimundo Parodi, who died in 1966, *Parodia* accommodates thirty-five charming South American species of the cactus family CACTACEAE.

Parodia, undetermined species

Parodias are small plants with spherical to cylindrical, solitary or clustered, very spiny stems or plant bodies with low, notched, straight or spiraled ribs and usually abundant white wool at the bases of the spine clusters especially near the tops of the plants. Their bristly to awl-shaped spines, often beautifully colored, are all

straight or one of the centrals may be hooked. The funnel-shaped flowers originate from the tops of the plants. They are expanded by day and have their perianth tubes and ovaries clothed, like the fruits, with woolly hairs and bristles. The fruits are berry-like.

Species cultivated include these: **P. alacriportana,** a Brazilian, has spherical to short-cylindrical stems 3 to 3½ inches in diameter with about twenty-three ribs and clusters of up to twenty yellowish, ¼-inch-long radial spines and up to seven ⅝-inch-long centrals, one hooked. Its flowers are yellow. **P. aureicentra,** of Argentina, forms clusters of flattened-spherical plant bodies some 6 inches across with about fifteen slightly notched ribs. The spine clusters are of about forty bristly, ½-inch-long, white radials and one to four yellow to brownish, needle-like centrals, approximately ¾ inch long. The blood-red flowers are 1½ inches across. **P. aureispina,** of Argentina, has bluish-green, spherical plant

Parodia aureispina

bodies up to 3 inches in diameter with slightly spiraled ribs. The bristle-like radial spines of each cluster number thirty to forty. There are six or seven bright yellow, ½-inch-long centrals, one hooked. Golden-yellow, the blooms are about 1¼ inches in diameter. **P. chrysacanthion,** of Argentina, has globose to slightly cylindrical plant bodies 3 inches tall with about twenty ribs, densely-white-woolly at their apexes, and thickly covered with bristly spines ¼ to ¾ inch long. The outer spines of each cluster of twenty-five to forty are white, the others stouter and yellow. None is hooked. The blooms are rich yellow, ½ to 1 inch in diameter. **P. erythrantha,** an Argentinian, has spherical, 2-inch-tall plant bodies with spiraled ribs. Its spine clusters are of twenty radials about ¼ inch long and four white-based, reddish-brown centrals, one hooked. The flowers, 1 inch in diameter, are brick-red to dark red. **P. maassii,** remarkable in its genus for its unusually large size, is a native of Bolivia and Argentina. This has spherical to cylindrical plant

Parodia chrysacanthion

bodies, sometimes 10 inches in diameter, with thirteen to twenty-one high, spiraled ribs. The spine clusters are of eight to fifteen needle-like, twisted, honey-yellow to white radials up to ⅓ inch long or sometimes longer, and four twisted, light brown centrals, 1¼ to 2½ inches long, at least one strongly hooked. The coppery-orange-red blooms are ½ to 1 inch in diameter. All the spines of *P. m. rectispina* are straight. **P. mairanana,** of Bolivia, has plant bodies about 2 inches wide with thirteen or fourteen ribs. The spine clusters are of nine to fourteen radials up to ½ inch long and one to three centrals up to ¾ inch long, one hooked. All are whitish to yellowish. The 1-inch-wide blooms are orange-yellow. **P. microsperma,** of Argentina, is a variable sort with spherical to short-cylindrical plant bodies, usually in clusters. They are up to 8 inches tall by 2 to 4 inches wide and have irregularly disposed tubercles. The spine clusters are of ten to twenty-five, ¼-inch-long, glassy-white, bristly radials and three or four ½- to ¾-inch-long reddish or brown centrals, one hooked. The orange-yellow flowers with reddish outer petals are 1 inch to 2 inches across. **P. mutabilis,** a variable native of Argentina, has spherical plant bodies 3 to 3½ inches wide with irregularly arranged tubercles and clusters of about fifty bristly, white radial spines and usually four dark-tipped white to orange-yellow centrals, one hooked. The brilliant orange-yellow to golden-yellow flowers, frequently with red throats, are 1½ to 2 inches wide. There are varieties with pink, rusty-red, or nearly black central spines. **P. nivosa,** an Argentinian, resembles *P. microsperma,* but has spine clusters without any of the ¾-inch-long centrals hooked. Its fiery-red flowers are 1½ to 2 inches in diameter. **P. sanguiniflora,** of Argentina, is a delightful sort with solitary, flattened to spherical plant bodies with spiraled ribs. Its spine clusters are of about fifteen bristly, ¼-inch-long, white radials and four longer reddish-brown centrals up to ¾ inch long or longer, one hooked. The glowing blood-red blooms are 1½ to 1¾ inches in diameter. Variety *P. s. violacea* has reddish-violet blooms. *P. schwebsiana*, a variable Bolivian, resembles *P. maassii*, but is smaller. It has 2-inch-wide, flattened-spherical plant bodies with twelve to twenty ribs and spine clusters of about ten nearly ½-inch-long, grayish or yellowish radials and one to four down-curved, yellowish-brown centrals ½ to ¾ inch long. The carmine-red blooms are ¾ to 1 inch wide. *P. setifera,* of Bolivia, has solitary, flattened-spherical plant bodies about 2 inches wide with seventeen or eighteen ribs and clusters of about twenty white radials and three or four pale pink to blackish central spines. The former are about ⅓ inch long, the others, one hooked, a little over ½ inch long. The light yellow flowers are 1½ inches across. *P. s. longihamata* is bigger, with central spines about 2 inches long. *P. stuemeri,* of Argentina, has very spiny, spherical plant bodies about 4 inches in diameter and with about twenty ribs. Its spine clusters are of about twenty-five twisted, ½-inch-long, white radials and four stout, blackish-brown, 1-inch-long centrals. The orange-yellow to light red flowers are 1 inch or somewhat more in diameter. *P. tilcarensis* (syn. *P. stuemeri tilcarensis*), of Argentina, much resembles *P. stuemeri,* but differs in having fewer spines and rather smaller, orange-red flowers.

Garden Uses and Cultivation. Parodias are among the very best cactuses for beginners' collections as well as for inclusion in those of advanced cactus fanciers. In warm regions, with semidesert climates, they can be grown in rock gardens and similar places outdoors. They are well suited for greenhouses and window gardens, responding well to conditions and care that suit the majority of small desert cactuses, such as mammillarias. For more information see Cactuses.

PARONYCHIA (Paro-nýchia) — Whitlow-Wort, Nailwort. The lowly *Dianthus* relatives that compose *Paronychia* number about fifty species scattered through most temperate regions of the world. They are annual and perennial herbaceous plants of the pink family CARYOPHYLLACEAE. The name, like their common one whitlow-wort, alludes to their supposed virtues for curing an inflammatory condition of the fingers and toes called whitlow. It derives from the Greek *para,* by, and *onyx,* a finger-nail.

Paronychias have slender, usually much-branched stems and opposite or sometimes apparently alternate, elliptic to linear, toothless leaves with conspicuous papery stipules (basal appendages). The flowers, in dense or loose, axillary or more rarely terminal clusters, generally have deeply-five-lobed calyxes. They are without petals or have very minute ones.

There are five stamens and two styles, which may be joined in their lower parts, sometimes up to the stigma, which then is two-lobed. The flowers are frequently more or less concealed among conspicuous, silvery, papery bracts. The fruits are dry achenes.

Paronychia, undetermined species

A few European perennial paronychias are sufficiently attractive to be admitted to gardens, among them *P. kapela.* This has stems up to 6 inches long. Its leaves, often hairy, have stipules shorter than or equaling the blades in length. The flower clusters, conspicuous by reason of their silvery-white bracts, are up to ¾ inch or slightly more in diameter. Variety *P. k. serpyliifolia* (syn. *P. serpyllifolia*) differs from the typical species in forming definite mats

Paronychia kapela serpyllifolia

or sods of stems and foliage up to 6 inches tall. These are chiefly plants of southern Europe. Another attractive southern European, *P. capitata* (syn. *P. nivea*) may be distinguished from *P. kapela* and its variety by its calyx lobes being of very uneven rather than of nearly equal sizes. It has freely-branching stems up to 6 inches long, with grayish-green, up to ¼-inch-long, linear-lanceolate leaves. The flowers are nearly concealed by bracts of pleasing

Paronychia kapela serpyllifolia (flowers)

appearance. Usually procumbent, *P. argentea* has much-branched matted stems up to 1 foot long and ovate to lanceolate leaves up to 8 inch long. The flowers, hidden by silvery bracts, are in clusters mostly over 8 inch across. The calyx lobes are of even size. This is a native of Europe.

One of the best American species, *P. argyrocoma* occurs chiefly at high altitudes in mountains from Virginia to North Carolina, Georgia, and Tennessee. A taprooted, erect or semiprostrate, mat-forming perennial, it has stems up to 1 foot long and silky-hairy, linear to linear-lanceolate leaves up to a little over 1 inch long. The flowers, nearly hidden by silvery bracts, are in dense clusters.

Paronychia argentea

Garden Uses and Cultivation. Sunny rock gardens afford the most suitable sites for paronychias. They are simple to manage in porous, well-drained soil and are easily multiplied by seed and by division. Too rich soil is likely to encourage gross growth and diminish the silvery appearance of these little plants.

PARROT and PARROT'S. As part of the common names of plants parrot or parrot's appears in these: parrot beak or parrot's bill (*Clianthus*), and parrot's feather (*Myriophyllum brasiliense*).

PARROTIA (Parròt-ia) — Iron Tree. One handsome, deciduous tree or large shrub, a native from Iran to the Caucasus, is the only member of *Parrotia*, of the witch-hazel family HAMAMELIDACEAE. Another species previously known as *P. jacquemontia* is now *Parrotiopsis involucrata*. The genus name commemorates F. W. Parrot, a German naturalist, traveler, and professor of medicine, who died in 1841. He was the first to climb Mt. Ararat, in 1829.

In the British Isles known as the iron tree because of its exceedingly hard wood, **P. persica** is a broad specimen that may attain a height of 40 feet, but often is lower. It usually branches low. The bark flakes from the trunk and older branches to produce an attractive mottled effect. Its broad-ovate to nearly round, witch-hazel-like leaves, with stalks up to ½ inch long, are 2 to 3½ inches long and have a few sharp teeth at their margins. They have strongly marked parallel veins. The flowers, which appear in earliest spring, have burgundy-red anthers at first displayed in tight clusters. As the blooms mature the filaments (stalks) of the stamens lengthen considerably and the anthers then hang in loose brushes. The filaments are white. Each cluster of stamens is surrounded by an involucre (collar) of bracts much as are the true flowers of the flowering dogwood and the poinsettia. In *Parrotia* the entire flower head, including the bracts, does not exceed ¾ inch in diameter. The bracts are pale green inside and brown on their outsides. Associated with the flower heads are brown, hairy bracts up to ¼ inch long. The foliage assumes brilliant autumnal shades of yellow, orange, and scarlet and persists until early winter.

Garden and Landscape Uses. Hardy at least as far north as Massachusetts, *P. persica* is excellent for landscape planting and well suited for small properties. Although pleasing in flower, especially in sunshine, it makes no extravagant display. For this it compensates by its glorious show of fall color. Its mottled bark is attractive, especially in winter. At all seasons this is a tidy tree that fits pleasingly into the landscape. As a lawn specimen or associated with other trees and shrubbery *P. persica* can be very effective. It prefers deep, well-drained, fertile soil and is not subject to serious attacks of pests or diseases.

Cultivation. Early spring and early fall are appropriate times to plant. No special aftercare is required, but judicious pruning in the early years is helpful in persuading it to develop as a tree rather than a shrub. Propagation is by seed, summer cuttings under mist, and layering.

PARROTIOPSIS (Parroti-ópsis). Formerly included in the allied genus *Parrotia*, the only species of *Parrotiopsis* is a native of the Himalayas. It belongs in the witch-hazel family HAMAMELIDACEAE. Its name is formed of that of the related genus and the Greek *opsis*, resembling.

Little known in cultivation, *Parrotiopsis* is a deciduous tree up to 20 feet in height that differs technically from *Parrotia* in having ten to twenty-four stamens with upright filaments (stalks), and more obviously in having its flower heads surrounded by large, white bracts in the fashion of the flowering dogwood.

Hardy in sheltered places in southern New England, **P. jacquemontia** (syn. *Parrotia jacquemontia*) has smooth gray bark.

Its leaves are much like those of the black alder (*Alnus glutinosa*). Alternate and nearly round, they have short, sharp teeth and are 2 to 3 inches long. Their stalks are short. In fall they change to pale yellow before they drop. The small, bisexual flowers, without petals but with many densely-packed yellow stamens, are many together in heads surrounded by four to six spreading, white, round-ovate, petal-like bracts, their outsides spotted with brown, scurfy hairs. The flower head, including the bracts, is 1½ to 2 inches across. The fruits are capsules with spreading beaks. In Kashmir and other Himalayan countries, the tough twigs of this species are used for constructing rope bridges. The hard wood is employed locally for various purposes.

Garden and Landscape Uses and Cultivation. Although not a very showy tree, certainly much less so than the flowering dogwoods, *Parrotiopsis* belongs to a particularly interesting family that includes the American genus *Fothergilla*, to which *Parrotiopsis* is quite closely related, the witch-hazels (*Hamamelis*), *Corylopsis*, and the sweet gum (*Liquidambar*), as well as, of course, *Parrotia*. It is chiefly a plant for collectors and those interested in the unusual. It may be used to best advantage as a lawn specimen or planted with, but not crowded against, other trees and shrubs. The cultural requirements are the same as for *Parrotia*.

PARRYA. See Phoenicaulis.

PARSLEY. This word is used as well as for the name of the herb treated in the next entry as part of the common names of these plants: desert-parsley (*Lomatium*), horse-parsley (*Smyrnium olusatrum*), mountain-parsley (*Pseudocymopteris montanus*), and parsley fern (*Cryptogramma crispa*).

PARSLEY. Of all vegetable garden products this is the most useful for garnishing. It serves also as a herb for flavoring soups, fish dishes, boiled potatoes, and other foods. A hardy biennial, parsley is *Petroselinum crispum*, under which name it is described in this Encyclopedia. Because of its attractive appearance this crop, especially curled-leaved varieties, makes an elegant edging to paths. It may even be grown in boxes on window sills, porches, roofs, and other places, and of course in garden beds. As few as a dozen plants may supply the needs of an ordinary family. For good results deep, fertile soil that contains appreciable amounts of organic matter and that is not acid is needed. Acid soils should be limed to bring them at least to a neutral (pH 7) or near neutral condition. Poor, dry earths give skimpy, unproductive plants that tend to run to seed prematurely. Sunny locations are generally satisfactory, but if the soil is very sandy a

Parrotia persica (flowers)

Parsley as a path edging

little part-day shade is likely to be beneficial.

Sow in early spring, and for a follow-up crop about midsummer, in shallow drills spaced, if more than one row is involved, 1 foot to 1¼ feet apart. Cover the seeds with soil to a depth of rather less than ½ inch. The seeds germinate slowly; therefore it is a good plan to sow a few radish seeds along with the parsley in such proportions that three or four seeds of radish are dropped along each foot of drill. The radishes sprout long before the parsley and serve to mark the rows. Later they are harvested for eating. It is a great mistake to crowd parsley. Thin the young plants in two or three stages to a final spacing in the row of 6 to 8 inches between individuals. The later thinnings can be used in the kitchen. In dry weather deep watering at intervals stimulates growth. A mulch of compost, peat moss, or other organic material is helpful.

Harvest parsley by picking a few leaves at a time rather than by denuding the plants of foliage. By leaving a fair number of leaves the growth of additional young ones is encouraged. In mild climates parsley continues to grow through the winter, but not in harsher ones even though the plants live over. In climates too severe for

Picking parsley

winter production the picking season can be prolonged by covering the plants with a cold frame, insulated on cold nights by thick mats. Alternatively, plants from summer sowings can be dug carefully in early fall, planted in pots or boxes and placed in a cool greenhouse or even in a sunny window in a cool room. Water such plants well immediately after transplanting and keep them shaded and out of drafts for the first two or three weeks. A simpler way of ensuring a supply of "fresh" parsley for winter use is to harvest the leaves in summer, place them in plastic bags, and freeze them. Parsley can also be dried in a slow oven, crumpled by rubbing between the palms of the hands, and stored in tightly stoppered containers.

To have fresh parsley in winter: (a) Pot plants dug from the garden in early fall

(b) Harvest the leaves

Varieties of parsley are not many. They fall into two classes, those with flat leaves and those with leaves much curled and crisped. The first is offered as plain or single parsley. Good varieties of the other are 'Extra Curled Dwarf' and 'Paramount'. For parsnip-rooted or Hamburg parsley see Hamburg Parsley.

PARSNIP. Besides its use as the name of the vegetable treated in the next entry, the word parsnip appears as parts of the common names of these plants: cow-parsnip (*Heracleum*) and water-parsnip (*Sium suave*).

PARSNIP. Less popular in America than northern Europe, parsnips are a very worthwhile garden vegetable. They are grown for their pale yellow, carrot-like roots, which are eaten boiled and in soups. The botanical name of parsnip is *Pastinaca sativa hortensis*. It belongs to the carrot family UMBELLIFERAE. The wild species is a native of Europe.

Parsnips require a long growing season. They occupy the ground from spring to fall. For their satisfactory development they must have deep, mellow, fertile, stone-free, clod-free soil. In shallow, stony, lumpy, and excessively clayey earths the roots become crooked and forked. To prepare the soil, work it to a depth of 10 inches or more with spade, rotary tiller, or plow, mixing in liberal amounts of decayed compost or, well before seed sowing time, a green manure crop. Do not use animal manure, but land that has been well manured for a previous crop, such as cabbage, beans, peas, or onions, is excellent for parsnips. In addition to organic additives, mix in a dressing of fertilizer that has a comparatively high content of phosphorus and potash.

Sow the seeds at the first opportunity spring affords in drills ½ to 1 inch deep, 1¼ to 1½ feet apart. Often not all seeds germinate, therefore it is advisable to sow fairly thickly. An alternative plan that calls for less seeds is to drop three or four at 6- to 8-inch intervals along the drills. Because parsnip seeds are slow to germinate, it is good practice to scatter radish seeds very thinly with them along the drills. These sprout quickly (mark the drills so you can cultivate between them to destroy weeds and admit air even before the parsnips come up) and aid in breaking any surface crust that may develop to hinder the seedling parsnips from breaking through. The radishes also provide an extra dividend in edibles. Pull them when ready for eating. Recommended varieties of parsnips are 'Guernsey', 'Hollow Crown', 'Model', and 'Student'.

Parsnips growing vigorously in a home garden

Care after sowing is not onerous. Before the seedlings crowd, any surplus must be thinned by hand pulling. By doing this in two operations rather than at one time it is easier to choose for retention the most vigorous and most suitably located seedlings. A final spacing of 6 to 8 inches between individuals is satisfactory. Keep weeds down by frequent shallow cultivation between, and by hand pulling along, the rows. In dry weather deep watering at approximately weekly intervals promotes growth.

Harvesting may be done in fall and the roots stored, or the crop, which is perfectly hardy, indeed its flavor improves after exposure to frost or even freezing, may be left in the ground until spring and dug as needed. In severe climates the last procedure has the disadvantage that it may be difficult or impossible to dig the roots when the ground is frozen deeply. If left in the ground in cold climates it is advisable, after the foliage has died in fall and the soil has frozen to a depth of an inch or two, to place over the rows a thick layer of dry straw or leaves covered with a strip of polyethylene plastic film weighted down along its edges with stones or loose earth. When digging the crop take particular care. Insert the fork nearly vertically some little distance from the crowns and dig deeply so that the tines are raised from well below the roots and do not pierce them. Damaged and broken roots will not store well. Storage may be in pits dug in a well-drained location and covered to keep out rain, or between layers of slightly damp soil, sand, or peat moss in a cool garage or other building.

PARSONSIA (Par-sònsia). Trees, shrubs, and vines of the dogbane family APOCYNACEAE constitute *Parsonsia*, a genus of some 100 species that inhabits Australia, New Zealand, islands of the Pacific, and tropical Asia. The name commemorates Dr. John Parsons, a Scots physician and naturalist, who died in 1770.

Parsonsias have twining stems and opposite, undivided leaves. Their small, clustered flowers have five-parted calyxes, tubular corollas with five spreading lobes (petals), five stamens with twisted stalks, and one style. The fruits are paired follicles (pods) at first joined, but eventually separating, containing seeds with a tuft of hair at the apex.

The name *P. heterophylla* (the specific epithet derives from the Greek *heteros*, different, and *phyllon*, leaf) directs attention to the variously shaped leaves that are not only found on plants of different ages, but often on the same plant. Native to New Zealand, this species is a slender, but robust vine with stems often twining about each other. It has glossy, leathery leaves, those of adult type from 1½ to 3 or some-times 4 inches long, up to 1½ inches broad, and linear to broadly-ovate. Juvenile-type leaves are often wavy-edged or may be lobed at their bases. The approximately ¼-inch-long, white to yellow, fragrant blooms are in terminal and axillary panicled clusters up to 4 inches long. Their anthers do not protrude. From the last, *P. capsularis,* a more slender-stemmed vine, differs in its smaller flowers, in fewer-flowered clusters, having protruding anthers. In variety *P. c. rosea* the blooms are rose-pink to dark red. The flowers of *P. c. ochracea* are yellow.

Garden and Landscape Uses and Cultivation. Reports about these robust vines in cultivation in North America are scant and incomplete. It is to be expected that they will adapt to ordinary soils in lightly shaded places in regions of little frost. They may be used to clothe pergolas and other supports. Propagation is by seed, and probably by cuttings.

PARTHENIUM (Parthèn-ium) — Guayule. The shrubs, herbaceous perennials, and in some cases perhaps annuals, that constitute *Parthenium* belong in the daisy family COMPOSITAE. The genus ranges as a native from North America to the West Indies and northern South America. It comprises fifteen species. One, the guayule, has been exploited commercially as a source of rubber. The genus name is an ancient classical one.

Partheniums have alternate leaves and clusters or panicles of small, white or yellow flower heads, each with disk and ray florets. The corollas of the florets are five-toothed, the styles are undivided. The seedlike fruits are achenes.

Guayule (*P. argenteum*), a native of limestone soils in semiarid parts of Texas and Mexico, is a densely-gray-hairy, much-branched, aromatic shrub up to about 3 feet in height. It has lanceolate, lobed or lobeless leaves ½ inch to 2 inches long and long-stalked clusters of ¼-inch-wide flower heads with white rays.

Garden Uses and Cultivation. Except for its interest as a rubber-producing plant, guayule is without horticultural significance. It is occasionally cultivated in collections of plants useful to man. Outdoors it needs a climate similar to those in which it grows in the wild, porous, preferably alkaline soil and full sun. In greenhouses it prospers under conditions that suit cactuses and other succulents. It is propagated by seed.

PARTHENOCISSUS (Partheno-císsus) — Boston-Ivy, Virginia Creeper. The plants belonging here called Boston-ivy and Virginia creeper are by far the best known of this genus of fifteen North American and Asian species of the grape family VITACEAE. Consisting of woody vines and trailers, *Parthenocissus* differs from *Vitis* in its flowers being without a conspicuous disk surrounding the ovary and in the petals falling separately instead of cohering and dropping together as one, and from *Cissus* in the flower parts usually being in fours and its leaves not being fleshy. The name *Parthenocissus*, from the Greek *parthenos*, virgin, and *kissos*, ivy, is a translation of its French name.

Parthenocissuses climb by tendrils, those of some species twining, but more commonly having disklike ends that attach themselves to tree trunks, walls, and other supports. The leaves are alternate, long-stalked, and palmately- (in hand-fashion) lobed or of separate leaflets radiating from the top of the leafstalk. Not showy, the small, greenish flowers are in branched clusters. They have minute calyxes and five, or rarely four, each petals and stamens. There is one short, thick style. The fruits are little berries containing one to four seeds.

Boston-ivy (*P. tricuspidata*), or Japanese-ivy as it is less commonly called, is

Parthenocissus tricuspidata

not, as the first of these vernacular names suggests, a native of North America, but of China and Japan. An exceedingly vigorous clinging vine, it is hardy throughout most of New England. Unrestrained, it attains tremendous heights, not infrequently climbing to the tops of five-story buildings, and hides its supports with curtains of lustrous foliage that before it drops in fall becomes rich scarlet or crimson. Its leaves exhibit variation in shape and size, the differences related in large measure to the age and vigor of the vines, and of the shoots. Well-established, lush-growing specimens have leaves up to 8 inches in diameter and three-lobed, or divided into three stalkless leaflets, or they may be three-lobed and not over 2 to 4 inches across. Even smaller foliage, of heart-shaped, merely toothed leaves, is often displayed by young plants and weak shoots. The leaves of *P. t. purpurea* are deep purple, those of *P. t. veitchii* are smaller than those of the typical species and when young are purple or bronzy-purple. With the smallest foliage of all varieties, *P. t. lowii* has apple-green leaves, purplish when young, and often broader than long.

Virginia creeper (*P. quinquefolia* syn. *Ampelopsis quinquefolia*) is hardy as far north as southern Canada. A deciduous, high climber with much-branched, disk-tipped tendrils, or when growing where supports are not handy, a long, trailing vine, this makes less dense curtains of foliage than Boston-ivy. Its leaves are of five, or occasionally six, coarsely-toothed, elliptic to obovate-oblong, pointed leaflets.

Parthenocissus quinquefolia climbing a tree; the groundcover is *Vinca minor*

Their upper sides are dull green. In early fall they become brilliant scarlet and crimson. The flower clusters are in terminal, umbel-like clusters with a definite central axis. The almost black berries are about ¼ inch in diameter. Very similar to *P. quinquefolia*, and also often known as Virginia creeper, *P. inserta* (syn. *P. vitacea*) differs chiefly in its fewer-branched tendrils rarely ending in adhering disks, and in its foliage being glossy instead of dull. Also, the broad, rounded, repeatedly two-forked flower clusters are without a well-marked central axis. This species inhabits moist soils from Quebec and northern New England to Manitoba and Texas. Endemic to Texas, *P. heptaphylla* has leaves of seven coarsely-toothed leaflets 1¼ to 2 inches long, and decidedly more fleshy than those of *P. quinquefolia*. Their upper surfaces are glossy. This is not hardy in the north. These native American species are sometimes called woodbine.

Strikingly variegated foliage characterizes *P. henryana* (syn. *Ampelopsis henryana*), a high-climbing, quite fast-growing, deciduous vine of China, which, sadly, is not hardy in the north. In milder climes it is quite stunning. It has five- to seven-branched tendrils and leaves with five-stalked, elliptic-ovate to obovate leaflets 1½ to 2½ inches long, coarsely-toothed above their middles. Above, they are a

Parthenocissus henryana in a conservatory at the botanic gardens, Brussels, Belgium

Parthenocissus henryana (foliage)

somber velvety green tinted with red, with the veins picked out in white. The contrast is most pronounced in young foliage and when the vine is grown in partial shade. In the sun the variegation sometimes disappears. The undersides of the leaves, hairless except sometimes along the midrib, are purplish. Before they fall the leaves assume brilliant autumn colors. The blue-black fruits make no appreciable display, but are esteemed by birds.

Asian species less commonly cultivated include *P. himalayana* (syn. *Ampelopsis himalayana*), a nonhardy, vigorous climber from the Himalayan region and China. It has tendrils with adhering disks, and toothed leaves with three stalked leaflets 3 to 5 inches long, the center one ovate, the others very asymmetrically so. In fall the foliage turns brilliant red. Variety *P. h. rubrifolia* has leaves that when young are purplish. Also a native of China and the Himalayas, *P. thomsonii* is a slender-stemmed vine with toothed leaves of five broad-elliptic to obovate leaflets, 1½ to 4½ inches in length, lustrous on their upper surfaces and downy on the midrib beneath. The shoots are claret-purple when young, duller and red-purple later.

Parthenocissus himalayana

Garden and Landscape Uses and Cultivation. These vines are esteemed for their attractive foliage and splendid fall colors as well as for their self-clinging propensities, which enable them to cover vast surfaces of masonry and tall tree trunks without special aid. The small-foliaged varieties of Boston-ivy and Virginia creeper provide more refined patterns of foliage than larger leaved types and are less vigorous.

Boston-ivy (*Parthenocissus tricuspidata*) clothing the pillars of an entranceway

Because of this they are better adapted for use where space is limited. Of the kinds discussed, Boston-ivy and Virginia creeper are especially well suited for city gardens and succeed in sun or part-shade. Virginia creeper is excellent near the sea. It does well even exposed to salt spray. To give of its best, *P. henryana* needs light shade. These vines succeed in any ordinary soil. Once established they need practically no attention other than any cutting back necessary to keep them from choking gutters, covering windows, or other such extravagancies of growth. They are easily increased by cuttings, by layering, and by seed. Before sowing, the seeds should be freed from their surrounding pulp and placed, mixed with slightly damp sand or vermiculite, in polyethylene plastic and stored at 40°F for three months.

Pests and Diseases. Japanese beetles and certain caterpillars are very fond of the foliage of Boston-ivy, Virginia creeper, and probably other kinds. Leaf spot and mildew diseases sometimes mar the foliage.

PARTRIDGE-BERRY is *Mitchella repens*.

PARTRIDGE WOOD is *Andira inermis*.

PASITHEA (Pasith-èa). A native of Peru and Chile related to and rather resembling *Anthericum*, the only species of *Pasithea* belongs to the lily family LILIACEAE. Its name is that of a mythological nymph.

Rhizomatous *P. caerulea* forms clumps of hairless, grasslike leaves 1 foot to 1½ feet tall, with loosely-branched panicles taller than the foliage of the starry, 1-inch-wide, blue or purple-blue flowers in spring and early summer. The blooms have each six petals, or more correctly, tepals, six stamens, one style, and a three-branched stigma. The fruits are capsules.

Pasithea caerulea

Garden Uses. Hardy only where little or no frost is experienced, this species, little tried in North America, survives outdoors in southern England. It is well adapted for flower borders and for growing in cool, sunny greenhouses.

Cultivation. Peaty, well-drained soil kept moderately moist and exposure to full sun suit this plant, which may be propagated by division in spring and by seeds sown in sandy peaty soil.

PASPALUM (Pás-palum). The majority of the more than 250 species of this genus, of the grass family GRAMINEAE, are indigenous to the Americas, a few are of the Old World. They are annuals and perennials of diverse appearance. Their name is from *paspalos*, the ancient Greek one for a kind of millet. Several species, including *Paspalum dilatatum*, are good forage grasses and the Bahia grasses are used as lawn grasses in the south.

Paspalums have flat, folded, or rolled, narrowly-linear, lanceolate, or ovate leaf blades. Their spikelets of flowers, in one-sided spikelike racemes, are without awns (bristles). Each contains one sterile and one bisexual flower. The racemes are solitary, paired, or clustered.

Bahia grass (*P. notatum*), of Mexico, South America, and the West Indies, is a rhizomatous perennial with stems up to 1½ feet tall and flat or folded leaf blades. Mostly in pairs, the racemes of flowers, up to 2¾ inches long, are of glossy, ovate to obovate spikelets about ⅛ inch long. Pensacola Bahia grass, Paraguay Bahia grass, or Wilmington Bahia grass (*P. n. saurae*), taller than the typical species and a native of Argentina and Paraguay, has leaf blades up to 1 foot long. These are among the easiest-to-care-for grasses for southern lawns.

A summer-flowering perennial, native of subtropical and warm-temperate parts of South America and naturalized in the United States, Dallis grass (*P. dilatatum*) is up to 6 feet tall and has pointed-linear leaf blades 1 foot to 1½ feet long, up to ½ inch wide, and hairy at their bases. Its very slender, green or purplish, erect or nodding racemes of flowers are in clusters of usually three to five, sometimes only two or as many as twelve. Up to 4 inches long, they have solitary or paired spikelets, fringed with white hairs, about ⅛ inch long.

An annual of tropical South America, *P. racemosum* is up to 3 feet tall. It has slender, spreading, branched stems, and hairless, lanceolate to ovate, pointed leaf blades up to 6 inches long by 1 inch wide, but often smaller. The brownish or purplish, erect or spreading racemes of spikelets are in crowded clusters 3 to 8 inches long by up to 1½ inches wide. There are twenty to eighty racemes in each cluster. This species blooms in late summer and fall.

Paspalum racemosum

Garden and Landscape Uses and Cultivation. Except for the Bahia grasses, which are used for lawns, the paspalums discussed above are raised to decorate flower beds and borders and for fresh and dried bouquets. The exact hardiness of *P. dilatatum* is not known, but it withstands some freezing. Paspalums respond to fertile soil and sunny locations. Division and seeds afford means of increasing the perennials. The annuals are raised from seeds sown outdoors in spring, or earlier in a greenhouse and the young plants set in the garden after the last frost.

PASQUE FLOWER. See Anemone.

PASSIFLORA (Passi-flòra)—Passion Flower, Maypop, Granadilla. This intriguing, and from the point of view of identification, often confusing genus is the only one important horticulturally of the dozen that constitute the passion flower family PASSIFLORACEAE. Its name is derived from the Latin, *passio*, passion, and *flos*, a flower, and alludes to the supposed representation by parts of the flowers and other organs of the instruments of Christ's crucifixion.

There are about 400 species of *Passiflora*, of which 350 are natives of the New World. The others mostly occur in southeast Asia and Australia; one is native of Malagasy (Madagascar). Passion flowers are chiefly tropical, the vast majority vines. The northernmost representatives of the group are seven species native in the United States. Of these the maypop ventures farthest north. Comparatively few, probably thirty species or less, are known to be cultivated. These include the tropical fruits called granadillas, which are esteemed for making cooling beverages and sherbets.

The association of these plants with Christ's passion stems from early Spanish colonial days in South America. Spanish and Italian travelers professed to see in the curious and wonderful blooms and other parts of these plants symbols of the crucifixion, which they accepted as Divine assurance of success for their enthusiastic, but unfortunately often fatal efforts to convert the heathen Indians. The five petals and five sepals were thought to represent the ten apostles present at Christ's death, Peter and Judas being absent. The conspicuous fringed corona was considered emblematic of the crown of thorns or of the halo, and the five stamens of the five wounds or of the hammers employed to drive the nails. The latter, three in number, were symbolized for these devout Christians by the stigmas. Recalling the scourges or the cords were the tendrils of the passion flower and the fingered leaves of some kinds suggested the persecutor's hands or the head of the lance that pierced the Savior's side. Beginning early in the seventeenth century, stylized drawings of passion flowers, showing the parts with varying degrees of realism, were published.

Passion flowers have round, sometimes grooved, or sharp-angled or winged stems, and alternate, often lobed leaves with stalks that in most kinds bear easy-to-see glands. Branchless, coiled tendrils arise from the leaf axils. The often large and showy flowers, solitary or in pairs or racemes, are mostly axillary. They have five sepals and usually five petals (the latter in some kinds absent), five stamens united to form a tube around the stalk that supports the ovary, and three styles. One of the most striking features of the blooms is the corona or crown of one or more rows of filaments, which may be separate to their bases or joined in their lower parts to form a circle or tube. To the casual observer these may be mistaken for staminodes (abortive stamens), but actually they are outgrowths of the enlarged end of the stem, called the receptacle, on which the parts of the flower are borne. Usually there are three to five leafy or threadlike green bracts on the flower stalks, close to the blooms or distinctly separate from them. When close to the flower they appear to form a second calyx. The many-seeded fruits, technically berries, are often comparatively large.

Granadillas, cultivated for their edible fruits, belong with the large-flowered passion flowers and are decidedly ornamental in foliage and bloom. In addition to those listed here the fruits of several others are eaten locally in the tropics. All now to be described except the first have round stems. The giant granadilla (*P. quadrangularis*) has stems markedly four-angled and winged. A native of tropical America,

this very vigorous, hairless vine has lobeless, ovate to round-ovate leaves 6 to 8 inches long with six glands on their stalks. The fragrant flowers, 3 to 5 inches in diameter, have white or pinkish sepals with green backs, pink petals, and a large corona banded blue-purple and white. The floral bracts are distant from the blooms. The oblong fruits, 5 to 9 inches long, are yellowish-green. The sweet granadilla (*P. ligularis*) and the yellow granadilla water-lemon, or Jamaica-honeysuckle (*P. laurifolia*), both natives of tropical America, have lobeless leaves, those of the former with four to six glands on their stalks, those of the latter with two. Another difference is that the floral bracts of the sweet granadilla are united to about their middles, whereas those of the other are separate to their bases. The sweet granadilla is a hairless, vigorous climber with broad-ovate leaves 5 to 6 inches long. Its blooms about 3 to 4 inches in diameter have greenish-white sepals, white petals tinged with pink, and white and reddish-purple coronas. The 2- to 3-inch-long, hard-shelled, orange-brown or purplish fruits have white pulp. The yellow granadilla, a vigorous, hairless vine with ovate-oblong to oblong leaves 3 to 5 inches long, has blooms up to 4 inches across. They are purplish-red or white with red markings and have coronas zoned with blue, purple, and pink or white. Its hard-shelled, egg-shaped, yellow fruits about 3 inches long, have whitish flesh. The purple granadilla (*P. edulis*) has grooved stems and is easily distinguished from other sorts by its deeply-three-lobed and toothed, 3- to 5-inch-long, glossy leaves with two small glands on their stalks. A vigorous, hairless climber of tropical America, this has blooms 2 to 3 inches across with white sepals with green outsides, white petals, and a corona of filaments purple at their bases and white above. The ovate fruits, deep purple-yellow at maturity and with hard rinds, are 2 to 3 inches long.

Other large-flowered passion flowers, kinds with blooms normally over 2 inches in diameter, are cultivated for ornament. The most common, a hybrid between *P. alata* and *P. caerulea*, is **P. alato-caerulea.**

Passiflora alato-caerulea

Passiflora alato-caerulea (flower)

From the first-named parent this is distinct in having lobed leaves and from the second in the lobes numbering three instead of five or sometimes more. This kind is sometimes labeled with the completely untenable name *P. pfordtii*. It has four-angled stems, leaves 4 to 5 inches long with two to four glands on their stems, and fragrant blooms about 4 inches wide with white sepals and petals pink on their insides and greenish on their outsides. The corona, much shorter than the petals, is of filaments with dark purple bases, white tips, and bluish between. Native from Brazil to Argentina, *P. caerulea* is the parent of several fine horticultural hybrids. Vigorous, hairless and of somewhat varied aspect, it typically has rather glaucous, palmately-cleft leaves with three to nine, but most commonly five toothless lobes extending at least two-thirds way to the base of the blade. The flowers, 3 to 4 inches across, have white or pinkish petals and corona filaments with blue apexes, white middles, and purple bases. The yellow or orange, ovoid fruits are 2 inches long or a

Passiflora quadrangularis

Passiflora edulis

Passiflora caerulea

Passiflora racemosa in a large conservatory

Passiflora antioquiensis

little longer. This species is sometimes confused with the purple granadilla, but is easily distinguished by its stipules (appendages at the base of the leafstalk) being linear to bristle-like, whereas those of *P. edulis* are leaflike. The passion flower 'Constance Elliott' is a variety or perhaps a hybrid of *P. caerulea*. It has beautiful ivory-white flowers. Another, also possibly a hybrid, with blooms 4½ to 8 inches in diameter, is *P. c. grandiflora*.

Passiflora 'Constance Elliott'

Kinds with large brilliant red flowers that have sepals and petals of similar coloring are especially showy. The most familiar of these is *P. racemosa* (syn. *P. princeps*). A native of Brazil, this elegant, tall-growing, hairless vine has round, grooved stems and usually deeply-three-lobed leaves 3 to 5 inches long with two small glands on their stalks. Its flowers are in leafless racemes two of which usually develop from each upper leaf axil. They are 3 to 4 inches in diameter with the petals shorter than the sepals and the coronas with white and purple outer filaments and red inner ones. Quite different is the brilliant red-flowered *P. coccinea*, native from Venezuela to Bolivia, which has ovate, lobeless, coarsely-toothed leaves up to 6 inches long and solitary flowers some 3 inches wide.

Passiflora coccinea

Sorts previously called *Tacsonia* and once regarded as a separate genus are now included in *Passiflora*. They are especially spectacular in bloom, but unfortunately are rare in gardens. From other passion flowers these are distinguished by their hypanthium (part of the bloom behind the spreading segments that looks like a calyx tube, but actually is the result of a fusion of the lower parts of the sepals and petals). In kinds that were previously tacsonias the hypanthium is long and cylindrical and often exceeds the sepals in length. In other passion flowers it is conspicuously shorter than the sepals and typically is bell- or urn-shaped. The species with a long tube most likely to be cultivated is *P. antioquiensis* (syn. *Tacsonia van-volxemii*), of Colombia. This has slender stems covered with fine down. Its leaves, 4 to 5 inches long, are of two shapes, lanceolate and lobeless or with three deep lanceolate lobes. Toothed and downy on the veins on their undersides, they have many glands on their stalks. The blooms are pendulous, 4 to 5 inches or more in diameter and with tubes 1 inch to 2 inches long, but shorter than the sepals. Beautiful rose-red and with small violet coronas that are scarcely more than rims, they are on slender stalks 10 inches to 1½ feet long. Indigenous to the Andes, *P. mollissima* (syn. *Tacsonia*

mollissima) is a softly-pubescent vine with round or slightly-angled stems and leaves 2½ to 4½ inches long, deeply divided into three ovate-lanceolate, toothed lobes. Its leafstalks have eight to twelve glands. The brilliant scarlet blooms, about 3 inches in diameter, have tubes 4 to 5 inches long. They are rose-pink and have the corona represented by a short, warty rim. The egg-shaped, pubescent fruits, about 2¼ inches long, are yellow. A very fine hybrid, *P. exoniensis* (syn. *Tacsonia exoniensis*) has *P. antioquiensis* and *P. mollissima* as parents. Its stems and leaves, the latter deeply-three-lobed and with 1-inch-long stalks bearing two glands, are downy. The rose-pink blooms, brick-red on their outsides and with small whitish coronas, have cylindrical tubes 2½ inches in length. They are 4 to 5 inches in diameter. From northern South America comes *P. manicata* (syn. *Tacsonia manicata*). Its leaves, deeply divided into three coarsely-toothed

Passiflora manicata (flower)

lobes and pubescent beneath, have stalks with four to ten glands. The brilliant scarlet flowers have tubes about 1½ inches long by 4 inches across. The outer parts of their coronas consist of blue filaments, the inner of a membrane. The glossy, yellowish-green, more or less egg-shaped fruits are 1½ to 2 inches long. Handsome *P. vitifolia* (syn. *Tacsonia sanguinea*), of Central and South America, has shallowly-toothed leaves, often variable on the same plant, up to 6 inches long or sometimes longer and sometimes as broad as long, and three-lobed to their middles or below. The flowers, 5 to 6 inches in diameter, have a cylindrical calyx tube and orange-scarlet to blood-red sepals and petals. The corona is bright red with some of its inner filaments paler. The protruding column of stamens is about 2 inches long. The ovoid fruits are about 2½ inches long.

Sorts native in the United States mostly have flowers under 2 inches in diameter. The wild yellow passion flower (**P. lutea**), a trailing or climbing plant with stems 3 feet long, toothless, shallowly-three-lobed leaves with nonglandular stalks, greenish-yellow to yellow blooms about 1 inch wide, and purple fruits under ½ inch in diameter is wild from Pennsylvania to Oklahoma, Florida, and Texas. The maypop (**P. incarnata**), native from Virginia to Ohio, Oklahoma, Florida, and Texas, has larger, rather showier flowers than the last and stems up to 25 feet long. Its deeply-three-lobed, finely-toothed leaves have glands on their stalks. The flowers, 1½ to 2¼ inches wide, have white or pale lavender petals and sepals and pink or purple coronas. The fruits, yellow and about 3 inches long, are edible.

Other passion flowers in cultivation include these: **P. alata**, a variable native of tropical America, has four-angled stems and roundish to ovate, toothless, hairless leaves with usually four, sometimes two glands on their stalks. Its fragrant flowers, 3 to 5 inches across and red or white with red centers, have the corona banded with red, purple, and white. The fruits are edible, yellow, and about 5 inches long. **P. banksii**, of Australia, has three-lobed, toothless leaves and 3-inch-wide blooms, pale when they first open gradually deepening to orange- or brick-red. They have petals about one-half as long as the sepals. The corona is red. **P. biflora**, native from Mexico to Venezuela and the Bahamas, has five-angled stems and two- or rarely three-lobed, kidney- to sickle-shaped leaves up to 4 inches long and wide, but often smaller. The flowers, in pairs and 1 inch to 1½ inches in diameter, are white with green coronas. The fruits, spherical to subspherical, are up to ¾ inch in diameter. **P. bryonioides**, of Arizona and Mexico, slender-stemmed, has leaves 1½ to 3½ inches in length, broader than long, and deeply cleft into three-toothed lobes, the side ones often again lobed. From ¾ inch to 1¼ inches wide, the flowers are white with the rays of the corona violet-purple at their bases. The fruits are ovoid, 1 inch or slightly more in length. *P. caerulea-racemosa* is a robust hybrid, its parents *P. caerulea* and *P. racemosa*. This has

Passiflora caerulea-racemosa

Passiflora colvillei

lustrous leaves very deeply cleft into three to five lobes and rosy-purple, 3-inch-wide blooms with white-tipped, purple coronas. The stamens are pale green, the stigmas pink. *P. capsularis*, of tropical America, has slender, angled stems and

Passiflora capsularis

leaves 1½ to 4 inches long and broad, more or less hairy on both surfaces, with two deep or shallow divergent lobes. The greenish-white to yellow-green flowers sometimes flushed with pink are 1 inch to 2 inches in diameter. The fruits are red. *P. cinnabarina*, of Australia, has mostly three-lobed, toothless leaves up to 2 inches in diameter. Its solitary scarlet flowers, 2½ inches across, have petals about one-half as long as the sepals and a short, yellowish corona. *P. colvillei* is a hybrid between *P. incarnata* and *P. caerulea*. Its leaves are cleft less than halfway to their bases into usually five to seven lobes. The 3½-inch wide, white, spotted-with-reddish-brown flowers have purple, white, and blue coronas. *P. coriacea*, native from Mexico to Peru, has angular stems and

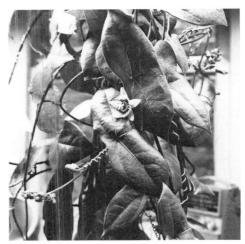
Passiflora coriacea

lobeless, toothless leaves up to 10 inches wide, much shorter than wide, and pointed at each lateral extremity. The leafstalk, joined to the blade well in from the margin, has two or rarely four glands. From 1 inch to 1½ inches across, the yellowish-green flowers are unusual, but not unique in the genus in being without petals. The spherical fruits are up to ¾ inch in diameter. *P. foetida* is a very variable native of the American tropics. A herbaceous, ill-scented vine, it has broadly-shallowly-ovate, three- to five-lobed, hairy or hairless leaves with heart-shaped bases. The flowers are ¾ inch to 2 inches across and white, pink, lilac, or purplish. The bracts below them are finely dissected in fernlike fashion. The spherical to subspherical fruits are 1 inch to 1½ inches in diameter. *P. organensis* (syns. *P. maculosa*, *P. maculifolia*), of Brazil, has leaves somewhat variable in shape, but usually broadly-wedge-shaped, and with two or less commonly three very shallow to quite deep lobes at their broad apexes. Their upper surfaces are prettily irregularly marbled and spotted with yellow. Their undersides are often purple, sometimes glandular-hairy. Up to 2 inches wide, the flowers are cream-colored to dull purple. The spherical fruits are up to ¾ inch in diameter. *P. subpeltata,* sometimes misnamed *P. alba,* is native from Mexico to Venezuela. Essentially hairless, it has toothless, three-lobed leaves 2 to 6 inches wide by up to 4 inches long. The flowers, up to 2 inches across, are white with the outsides of the sepals green. The corona is white. The yellowish, egg-shaped fruits are 1 inch to 1½ inches long. *P. trifasciata,* Brazilian, has fragrant, yellowish flowers up to 1½ inches wide and coronas under ½ inch long. Its three-lobed, dark dull green leaves are attractively mottled with yellowish or pale greenish markings.

Passiflora trifasciata

Their stalks are without glands. *P. violacea,* of Brazil, essentially hairless, has toothless or nearly toothless, three-lobed leaves, the lobes occasionally lobed again, slightly glaucous on their undersides, 2½ to 6 inches long and rather broader than long. The side lobes diverge at nearly right angles to the center one. The long-stalked flowers, up to 4 inches wide, have pinkish-lilac sepals, violet petals, and the corona violet with white bases to its filaments.

Garden and Landscape Uses. The cultivated passion flowers include some of the most attractive and satisfactory evergreen vines for tropical and subtropical climates where frost is rarely or never experienced and for ornamenting greenhouses. A few, such as *P. alato-caerulea,* can be cultivated as houseplants where especially favorable conditions can be provided, such as perhaps exist in connection with a large picture window. Always they are good "conversation pieces." Their curious and beautiful blooms never fail to attract attention and spark interest whether on the vine or displayed floating in an inch or so of water in shallow containers as floral decorations. The native kinds of the United States, including the maypop (*P. incarnata*) and the wild yellow passion flower (*P. lutea*), are rather weedy plants of no great interest as garden subjects, but legitimate for including in wild gardens and native plant collections.

Cultivation. No trouble is likely to be encountered in raising passion flowers from seeds or in rooting cuttings. They can also be increased by layering. Whichever method is chosen they are responsive to warm, humid conditions. A minimum propagating temperature of 60 to 65°F favors good results. Late winter and early spring is a good time to undertake their multiplication. They appreciate deep, fertile, well-drained soil not subject to drought and require good light, although a little broken shade from strong summer sun is beneficial. When grown in greenhouses, a minimum winter night temperature of 55 to 60°F is appropriate. During the day this may be increased by five to ten degrees and at other seasons both night and day temperatures should be higher by about ten degrees than those maintained in winter. Fairly moist atmospheric conditions favor good growth, but the air should not be stagnant nor oppressively humid. Young plants need pinching once or twice to induce branching, and wires or other supports must be suitably placed for the plants to attach themselves to. So far as they can be carried out, the same suggestions apply to specimens grown as houseplants. In greenhouses and conservatories these plants may be grown in large pots or other receptacles, but the best results are obtained when they are set out in well-drained ground beds. Planted-out specimens benefit from having the soil refurbished each spring by removing the surface inch or two and replacing it with new soil enriched by the addition of a complete fertilizer. Plants established in containers benefit from repotting or top dressing with a mixture of soil and fertilizer at that same time. Pruning is done in late winter or spring and consists of cutting out old, worn-out branches and shoots, as well as very weak and crowded ones, and shortening others; the blooms are produced from current season's shoots. Specimens well established in pots or other containers benefit immensely from regular applications of dilute liquid fertilizer from spring to fall and during that same period they need quite copious supplies of water. In winter the soil is kept drier and fertilizer is withheld.

PASSIFLORACEAE — Passion Flower Family. A dozen genera totaling 600 species, mostly natives of the tropics, subtropics, and warm-temperate regions, compose this family of herbaceous and woody dicotyledons, mostly climbing by tendrils. They have alternate, often lobed leaves. The flowers, bisexual or unisexual and solitary or clustered, have three or five often petal-like sepals, as many petals as sepals or none, three or five or rarely ten stamens, and either a branchless or branched style or three to five separate styles. The fruits are berries, sometimes large, or capsules. Cultivated genera are *Adenia, Passiflora,* and *Tetrapathaea.*

PASSION FLOWER. See Passiflora. The New-Zealand-passion-flower is *Tetrapathaea tetrandra.*

PASSION VINE. This name is sometimes applied to *Passiflora.* The name purple passion vine is used for *Gynura aurantiaca* Purple Passion'.

PASTINACA (Pastin-àca)—Parsnip. Of this genus of the carrot family UMBELLIFERAE, only the cultivated parsnip (*Pastinaca sativa hortensis*) has garden importance. Its wild progenitor, *P. sativa,* a native of Europe and Asia, is widely naturalized in waste places, fields, and roadsides in North America. The genus, consisting of fifteen European and Asian species of mostly thick-rooted biennials, bears a Latin name originally used for the carrot. Its members have usually pinnate leaves with the leaflets sometimes lobed. The tiny, five-petaled, yellow flowers, many together in large umbels composed of smaller umbels, are without sepals. The elliptic to obovate fruits are flattened and winged. The wild parsnip, up to 4½ feet tall, has leaves, of five to fifteen leaflets, variously lobed and toothed. For information about cultivated parsnips see Parsnip.

Pastinaca sativa

PATCHOULI is *Pogostemon patchouly.*

PATERSONIA (Pater-sònia). Except for three species of New Guinea, Borneo, and the Philippines, all twenty that constitute *Patersonia,* of the iris family IRIDACEAE, are endemic to Australia. The name commemorates William Paterson, Scottish botanical collector in Australia, who became Lieutenant-Governor of New South Wales, and died in 1810.

Patersonias are herbaceous perennials with short rhizomes and basal clusters of fans of often rigid leaves. The short-lived blooms, in terminal cluster-like spikes from between two stiff bracts, open in succession and are usually blue, less commonly yellow or white. They have slender corolla tubes, three broad, spreading perianth lobes (usually called petals), and three much smaller, erect inner ones. There are three stamens with their stalks united into a tube and a style with three obovate branches. The fruits are capsules.

Native to eastern and southern Australia and Tasmania, *P. glauca* has sharp-pointed, narrowly-linear, hairless leaves about 1½ feet in length, and normally spikes of two to four blooms topping stems shorter than the leaves. The flowers are blue and about 1 inch in diameter. Closely related *P. longiscapa* is very similar, but has flower stems longer, usually much longer, than the leaves. This also is a native of southern and eastern Australia and Tasmania. Its linear leaves more rigid than those of *P. glauca* and up to 2 feet in length, western Australian *P. umbrosa* has also blue flowers about 1 inch in width.

Garden and Landscape Uses and Cultivation. Patersonias are hardy only in regions of mild winters. They are appropriate for beds, informal plantings, and large rock gardens. They prosper in sunny locations in well-drained soils and are propagated by division and by seed.

PATETE is *Schefflera digitata.*

PATHS, GARDEN. As convenient means for getting from here to there paths are necessary in all gardens except the most miniscule, such as, for example, "viewing gardens" occupying enclosures or other small spaces designed in Japanese fashion to be admired from a window rather than walked in. Besides serving usefully, paths, if well planned and of appropriate materials, create charm. They should form an integral part of the garden design, their lines, proportions, and surfacings contributing to satisfactory over-all effects. It is all too easy to find examples that fail in this, that are incongruous, harsh, and ungarden-like. For more about this see Planning Gardens and Home Grounds; here we are chiefly concerned with types of materials to use and construction.

Broadly speaking, garden paths are of two sorts, solid-surfaced and soft- or loose-surfaced. The first, the more formal and insistent in the landscape, are usually reserved for the most traversed routes such as from street to front and back doors and for strictly formal gardens. They are commonly costlier to install than types satisfactory and appropriate for less frequented routes and for informal landscapes. Maintenance of well-made solid-surfaced paths is usually less than for others chiefly because most sorts give weeds little opportunity and if properly made are

not heaved or otherwise disturbed by freezing. Among the simplest and, in many situations, the loveliest paths are strips of lawn kept neatly mown and edged, but these are satisfactory only in sunny areas and where traffic is minimal.

Good subsurface drainage is a prime requirement for all paths. In gravelly and sandy areas it may be assured by the character of the soil and underlying strata, but where clayey earth, hardpan, or other impervious under layers exist, provision must be made for rapid drainage of excess water before the path is laid.

Grass paths are useful only where traffic is minimal

Patersonia longiscapa

Set flagstones, where subsurface drainage is satisfactory, on a soil base with lawn grass: (a) Rectangular flagstones

(b) Irregularly shaped flagstones

(c) Plant low rock garden plants between the joints

A foundation 4 to 8 inches thick of gravel, broken stone, or coarse cinders may be all that is needed to assure this if the substratum is moderately porous, otherwise it may be necessary to install a line of agricultural tile drain below the center of the path to conduct the water to a suitable outlet. Even in comparatively poorly drained ground, such treatment is usually only imperative with paths of concrete or of bricks, flagstones, or other surfacings laid in concrete, and with black top paths. Heaving by freezing breaks paths of these materials beyond easy repair.

Flagstone 1½ to 2 inches thick and flagstone substitutes 3 to 4 inches thick, the latter fashioned of concrete and often colored to simulate natural stone, are attractive and assure dry footing. The pieces may be rectangular and of the same or different sizes or be irregularly shaped and of various sizes. Surfacings of the latter, called random or crazy paving, are less formal than those made of rectangular components. In any case avoid using too many small pieces and establish a pattern in sensible scale with the surroundings.

In preparation for laying the path, excavate to a depth of about 8 inches. Re-move any large stones, rake the bottom to an even grade, and if loose firm it by treading or rolling. Then fill to within about 3 inches of the final grade with ½- or ¾-inch crushed stone topped off with finer stone, or gravel or use only coarse gravel, coarse cinders, or other suitable drainage material. Tamp this firm.

Next spread an inch or more of sand or fine coal cinders upon which to set the flagstones or precast substitutes. Begin by positioning the pieces for a section of the path on the surface without setting or "bedding" them. This allows the opportunity to arrange them most effectively and with least wastage and to view the pattern created. After you are satisfied with the layout, settle each piece so that its surface is at the proper level and it rests quite firmly without any tendency to tip when stepped upon. In laying random paving begin by establishing the edges of the path by placing pieces with one straight side so the straight side faces out, then fill between with pieces chosen for their suitability of shape and size. Inevitably, a certain amount of cutting will be needed, but this can be kept to a minimum by careful selection and laying out.

Instead of precasting substitute flagstones and laying them as just described, they may be formed in place. Made in this way, the pieces conform to the configuration of the top of the underlying drainage layer so there is no likelihood of tipping or rocking.

To cast "flagstones" in place, after installing the underdrainage set shallow wooden forms to define the edges of the path and between them strips of lath painted with heavy oil to serve as dividers to mark where the joints between the pieces are to be. Then fill in the concrete mix and finish to a smooth or rougher surface as desired. When the concrete has partly set, cover it with straw, hay, burlap or similar material kept moist so that the concrete dries slowly. After it has dried, pull out the divider strips and fill the crevices between the artificial flagstones with sand.

Brick and tile paths blend well with all kinds of vegetation and many types of architecture and are of pleasing colors and textures and agreeable to walk upon. They have a charm and old worldliness well suited for rose gardens, herb gardens, and other intricately patterned areas. But be-

These attractive paths are of flagstones butted closely together and laid on a 3-inch layer of sand spread over 5 to 6 inches of crushed stone or other coarse drainage; the joints are not grouted

Bed flagstones in 3 to 4 inches of concrete and grout the joints with cement to create good-looking, maintenance-free paths: (a) Irregularly shaped flagstones

(b) Rectangular flagstones

Square tiles form an attractive surface for this path

cause bricks and tiles do not lend themselves well to laying in other than straight lines they are not readily adapted to curved paths. Be sure to use only hard-burned bricks suitable for outdoor use. Soft ones made for interior walls disintegrate rapidly if exposed to freezing temperatures. Many charming patterns, including those that give herringbone and basket-weave effects, can be worked out with bricks.

Laying a brick path on a bed of cinders and sand

Brick paths, pleasing complements to garden greenery, can be laid in many different patterns

Concrete and blacktop (asphalt) paths if properly installed are exceedingly durable, but unless carefully made and finished, they are of too harsh appearance for the best garden effects. Concrete can, of course, be surfaced with flagstones, brick, or by having pebbles or small stones of attractive color pressed into its surfaces while still moist and then can be very acceptable; it is even possible to relieve the poor appearance of blacktop to a degree by rolling chips of stone into its surface. The device of scratching into the moist surface of newly laid concrete grooves that simulate the crevices of flagstone pavement is frequently attempted, although rarely convincing, and generally is best avoided. All in all, concrete is not highly agreeable as a surface for garden paths, although, as indicated under the discussion of the use of flagstones, it can be made into very acceptable artificial "flagstones." If employed without any special finishing, tinting it gray or brown helps to remove the harsh objectionable effect of uncolored concrete. Paths of concrete must have perfect underdrainage and be of sufficient thickness to preclude the possibility of damage from heaving as a result of freezing (the danger of which varies according to geographical location). Leave cross joints as is done with concrete highways at intervals of 5 to 10 feet to allow for expansion without buckling in hot weather.

Stepping-stone paths are casual and when appropriately located charming. Simple to install, they can be of natural stone or precast concrete, their elements rectangular or of other formal shapes or irregular. Stepping-stones may be used to good purpose across lawns and to give delightful effects appropriately spaced in loose-surfaced paths of gravel or crushed stone. Spacing is important. The distance from stone to stone should just accommodate an easy stride.

Stepping-stones may be set in turf, low enough for a lawn mower to pass over easily, without special underdrainage.

Stepping-stone paths are charming:
(a) Across lawns

(b) In informal settings

They do then present the maintenance chore of keeping the grass neatly clipped around each stone so that it does not grow over them to give a frowsy appearance.

Gravel and crushed stone are very commonly employed as loose surfacings for garden paths and are generally satisfactory. Those of brown and other earthy colors are decidedly preferable to glistening white or even dark gray, but usually the gardener must be satisfied with the sort or sorts available locally. These materials may be laid on firmly packed bases a few inches deep of gravel, cinders, or po-

Paths surfaced with loose crushed stone or gravel: (a) Are inexpensive

(b) Require frequent raking

(c) Necessitate weed control; here a granular weedicide is distributed from a can with a perforated bottom

rous soil, with good drainage assured. A mistake sometimes made is to have too thick a loose layer on top of the firmly tamped base. This makes for unpleasant walking and makes more difficult keeping the surface even by raking.

Excellent results are had by treating the finished surface of gravel and crushed stone paths with epoxy cements sold especially for the purpose. These glue firmly together the small pieces of stone, preventing them being moved by walking upon or by rains, yet preserving the pleasing appearance of the natural material. Such "glued" paths are not strictly loose-surfaced, but they look as though they were and water seeps through them as it does with truly loose-surfaced paths.

Other loose surfacings that, laid over firm, porous bases, make satisfactory garden paths for particular locations include coal cinders, tan bark, wood chips, and sawdust. The first, if readily available is inexpensive, makes a good path, but is too ordinary and work-a-day in appearance for use other than in such utilitarian areas as vegetable gardens and in informal landscapes.

Tan bark, wood chips, and sawdust are all best adapted for woodland paths. They are springy, pleasant to walk upon, and easy to maintain. The first, which lasts longest, is rich brown. The others have a somewhat raw appearance when first installed, but soon weather to a more acceptable hue. They have shorter lives than tan bark and may need a little resurfacing every two or three years, but that is easy to do.

PATIENCE PLANT is *Impatiens wallerana.* Herb-patience is *Rumex patientia.*

PATIO AND TERRACE PLANTINGS. For a variety of reasons including the decrease in indoor living space in most contemporary homes, as compared with those of yesteryear and the notable upsurge of population in warmer and drier parts of the United States, patios and terraces have become increasingly popular. Not the least reason for this stems from changed life styles. Everywhere greater emphasis is placed on eating, playing, entertaining, and in other ways spending leisure time outdoors. Patios and terraces afford additional living space, informal, charming, and different from that indoors.

Patios differ from terraces in being bounded on one or more sides by the walls of a dwelling and on their others,

An informal path surfaced with tan bark

except possibly for one opening on a garden or other pleasant view, by walls or fences high enough to afford considerable seclusion. They serve more obviously than terraces as rooms. The latter, other than sometimes for low, see-over boundaries, are open on all sides except against the house. But no sharp lines of distinction exist, what one calls a patio another may call a terrace.

Modern patios, like their name, derive from those of Spain, but their more remote origin is traceable to the Orient. In both regions women were secluded from the outside world and houses were designed to enclose a garden-like area where the ladies could enjoy fresh air, sunshine, and other advantages of the outdoors without being exposed to public view.

The floors of patios and terraces that are to be much used are usually of flagstones, slate, brick, or other attractive material

that affords a clean, quick-drying surface. Terraces intended more as architectural decorative complements to the house than for hard use are sometimes of grass turf.

Often terraces are raised from a little to considerably above the adjacent ground, sometimes to the extent that steps are necessary. Such differences of grade call for boundaries that will be effective in preventing people from stumbling or falling. Low shrubs or hedges may suffice if the drop is small, or long planters stood along the edge of the terrace may be a good choice. Where more severe drops are involved low walls or railings are safest.

Satisfactory planting for patios and terraces adds much to their appeal and amenities. Trees suitably located just outside or within the paved part can afford welcome shade. To be most effective they must shadow the area during the hottest parts of summer days.

Terraces give opportunity for outdoor living and entertaining

Three views of a well-planted patio in New Orleans, Louisiana

Boundary walls and fences provide a splendid opportunity to exercise skill and imagination in training vines and espaliered shrubs and trees against them, not to hide their entire surfaces but to decorate and complement them. Narrow borders at the bases of such boundaries may be planted with a variety of choice evergreen and deciduous shrubs with spaces between perhaps for spring bulbs, hardy perennials of quality, and whichever annuals and other summer bedding plants appeal, and in crevices between flagstone or brick it may be practicable to have a few plants

such as creeping thymes and other low carpeters. Plants in tubs or other containers are frequently very well suited for use on patios and terraces, as are, sometimes, hanging baskets filled with plants.

Furnish patios and terraces with container-grown specimens:
(a) Agapanthuses

(b) Hydrangeas

(c) Oranges

Restraint should be the keynote of the plantings. Locate specimens as carefully as you would furniture in a room. Make sure each serves a visual purpose and contributes to a harmonious whole. As with rooms, the center area should be uncluttered to permit easy movement. It may ac-

commodate appropriate garden furniture but the plants for the most part should be placed at or near the perimeter.

Of first importance is that the plants be of choice sorts that present a good appearance throughout the year and will not become too large for their places or can be pruned without detracting from their appearance. Where climate permits use evergreens generously, but do not entirely neglect deciduous sorts, many of which are attractive in bloom. Among those that commend themselves are boxwoods, ceanothuses, cotoneasters, hollies, osmanthuses, and certain viburnums. There are numerous others, not all suited for all climates.

If you regard the evergreens and importantly featured deciduous trees, such as a flowering dogwood or a mimosa (*Albizia julibrissin*), and shrubs as the major furnishings, you may think of spring bulbs, summer- and fall-flowering perennials, and temporary bedding plants as pictures that provide seasonal color and beauty. Do not use too many of these, just enough to give contrast and relief. A terrace or patio planting should not be riotous, but calm and peaceful. Most of the plants will, of necessity, be in narrow borders or in planters or other containers. Often the best effects are had if these last are grouped rather than scattered. See also Container Gardening.

Geraniums in containers on a terrace

PATRINIA (Pat-rínia). Ranging in the wild from central to eastern Asia, *Patrinia*, of the valerian family VALERIANACEAE, consists of twenty species. Its name commemorates the French explorer and traveler Eugène Louis Melchior Patrin, who died in 1815.

Patrinias are hardy herbaceous perennials with opposite leaves that, except for the basal ones, which are sometimes cleftless, are once- or twice-lobed or -divided. The small white or yellow blooms, in more or less panicle-like clusters, have short, slightly-toothed calyxes and short-tubed corollas with five spreading lobes (petals).

The stamens usually number four, and there is one style. The fruits are achenes.

Japanese *P. triloba* (syn. *P. palmata*) is a variable, attractive, bright yellow-flowered species up to 2 feet tall, but often lower.

Patrinia triloba

Mostly basal, its foliage is palmately- (in hand-fashion) lobed or cleft into five, or less often three, coarsely-toothed segments. The flowers, in loose, three-branched clusters 3 to 4 inches wide, are carried well above the foliage. They are ¼ inch wide or a little wider. Those of *P. t. palmata* (syn. *P. palmata*) have brief spurs. White-flowered *P. villosa* is a coarser, finely-downy, leafy-stemmed native of Japan, Korea, and China. From 2 to 3 feet tall, it has pinnately-cleft leaves, the basal ones stalked, the stem leaves stalkless. The flowers are about ⅕ inch wide.

Other species that may be cultivated are *P. intermedia,* a Siberian native about 1½ feet tall, with pinnately-lobed leaves each with a large terminal lobe and yellow flowers; *P. sibirica,* as its name suggests, also Siberian, but occurring as well in Japan, which grows 6 inches to 1 foot tall, and has bluntly-toothed or toothless, long spatula-shaped basal leaves and pinnately-lobed upper ones, and fragrant, yellow, ¼-inch-wide blooms; and *P. scabiosae-folia,* of Japan, Taiwan, China, Korea, and Siberia, which is 2 to 3 feet in height and has toothed, ovate-oblong to fiddle-shaped basal leaves, the upper leaves pinnately-cleft into narrow, toothed lobes, and yellow flowers under ¼ inch wide, in flattish-topped clusters.

Garden and Landscape Uses and Cultivation. Patrinias are useful furnishings for the fronts of flower beds and rock gardens and for informal planting in naturalistic settings. They are easy to grow in fertile, well-drained, not excessively dry soil, in sun or part-day shade. Increase is by division in early fall or spring and by seed.

PATTONIHEADIA. This is the name of orchid hybrids the parents of which are *Bromheadia* and *Pattonia.*

PAULLINIA (Paul-línia). One species of this genus of 180 tropical American woody vines, of the soapberry family SAPINDA-CEAE, is rarely included in collections of tropical foliage plants. The name of the genus it is believed honors Simon Paulli, a professor of botany and surgery at Copenhagen, Denmark, who died in 1680.

Evergreen *Paullinia thalictrifolia* has slender stems and alternate, maidenhair fernlike leaves, up to 10 inches long, and finely-three-times-pinnately-divided into many small leaflets. When they first expand the leaves are a beautiful bronzy hue, later they become bright green. This plant climbs by tendrils. Of no display value, the small, pinkish flowers are in racemes from the leaf axils. They are tubular and have five spreading corolla lobes. The fruits are fleshy, winged capsules, about 1 inch long. This is a native of Brazil.

Garden Uses and Cultivation. Essentially, this is a plant for outdoor planting in the humid tropics and pot culture in humid, tropical greenhouses where a minimum winter night temperature of 60°F is maintained. By day and at other seasons temperatures may, with benefit, be considerably higher. Attractive specimens can be had in pots 4 or 5 inches in diameter and in hanging baskets. They prosper in rich, well-drained soil and stand considerable sun, but light shade in summer is advisable. Needed pruning to size and shape, and repotting is done in spring. Propagation is by cuttings taken in spring and inserted in a propagating bench with bottom heat. The tips of the shoots of young plants should be pinched out once or twice to encourage branching. Unless grown in hanging baskets light stakes for support are needed.

PAULOWNIA (Paul-òwnia). A most lovely species is a familiar example of this eastern Asian genus, of the bignonia family BIG-NONIACEAE. This genus of about six species of deciduous trees shows many similarities to the figwort family, *Scrophulariaceae,* and by some botanists is included there. A princess of the Netherlands, Anna Paulowna, who died in 1865, is honored by the name *Paulownia.*

Paulownias have large, opposite, undivided, sometimes lobed leaves and terminal panicles of blooms with deeply-five-cleft calyxes and long, tubular corollas with five lobes (petals) that spread obliquely and are slightly unequal in size. There are four stamens, and a long style with a slightly two-lobed stigma. The fruits are large capsules enclosing many winged seeds.

The empress tree (*P. tomentosa* syn. *P. imperialis*) has never certainly been located in the wild. In the United States, it has escaped from cultivation and become naturalized from southern New York, where it is a common inhabitant of the Palisades

Paulownia tomentosa, a twin-trunked specimen: (a) In summer

(b) In winter

along the Hudson River, to Georgia. Undoubtedly it originated in China, where it has been cultivated for many hundreds of years. A Chinese manuscript of the third century B.C mentions it, and another dated 1049 is devoted entirely to a discussion of this species The Chinese used the

Paulownia tomentosa, a shapely specimen in full bloom

Paulownia tomentosa (bark)

empress tree medicinally and for other purposes, such as washing the hair and skin. Its unusually light lumber is employed for a variety of purposes. Broadly-round-topped and up to about 50 feet tall, the empress tree looks much like a catalpa. Its young shoots are densely-downy, so are the undersides of its leaves. The smaller leaves are ovate. Larger ones, up to 10 inches in length, are shallowly-three- to five-lobed. Their bases are heart-shaped. The flower buds develop in fall and open the following spring just before or with the new foliage. The blooms are in

Paulownia tomentosa (flowers)

panicles about 1 foot in length. Each is 1½ to 2 inches long, slightly fragrant, hairy on the outside, and of a lovely blue-purple hue, with darker spots and yellow lines inside. The podlike seed capsules, 1½ to 2 inches long, are retained for a long time, becoming somewhat untidy. In *P. t. pallida* the blooms are whitish-lavender. Variety *P. t. lanata* has denser, yellowish hair on the undersides of the leaves.

Hardy only in the south and elsewhere where climates are mild, **P. fargesii**, of western China, is up to 60 feet in height.

At first hairy, its young branches soon lose their down. Its leaves are much less densely-hairy beneath than those of the empress tree and are only slightly hairy above. They are also smaller than those of the more familiar species and may or may not have a few teeth. The whitish or lavender blooms, a little over 2 inches long and slightly hairy on their outsides, are in panicles smaller than those of *P. tomentosa*.

Paulownia tomentosa (fruits)

Other paulownias for mild climates are Chinese *P. fortunei* and *P. kawakamii*, the latter native of Taiwan and southern China. Up to about 20 feet tall, **P. fortunei** in form resembles the empress tree. It has leaves up to 1 foot long and almost as broad and densely-hairy on their undersides. The 3- to 4-inch-long, fragrant, creamy-white flowers are tinged with lilac on their outsides and heavily marked on their insides with dark purple. From 30 to 35 feet tall, **P. kawakamii** has three- or five-lobed, ovate leaves with heart-shaped bases. From 9 inches to 1 foot long they are glandular-hairy on both surfaces. The flowers, 1 inch to 1¾ inches long, are white or purplish-white with purple lines in their throats.

Garden and Landscape Uses. Paulownias are handsome as single specimens and for avenues. In parts of Europe they are much used as street trees. The hardiest, the empress tree, cannot be relied to bloom regularly north of Philadelphia. At New York City the flower buds are killed in severe winters even though the tree itself is quite hardy. In colder climates, even as severe as that of Montreal, Canada, the roots survive even though the tops are killed to the ground each year. Under such conditions it is perhaps worthwhile, as is sometimes done in England, to cultivate the empress tree for its foliage alone. This is done by planting several young trees 3 or 4 feet apart in a large bed of deep, fertile soil. In early spring the stems are cut back almost to the ground or to within an inch or two of older wood. Of the new shoots that develop all except two are

eliminated as soon as possible and as soon as their establishment is assured, the weaker of the two is cut out. Generous fertilizing and watering in dry weather encourages the production of leaves of astonishing size, fully 2 to 3 feet across, on stems up to 12 feet tall. In cold climates it is well to protect the bases of the stems of specimens grown in this way by applying a thick mulch in fall.

Part of an avenue of *Paulownia tomentosa* at Longwood Gardens, Kennett Square, Pennsylvania

Cultivation. Paulownias thrive in ordinary, well-drained soils in sunny locations and are fast growers. They need no special care. Except perhaps to shape them when young, or to remove or shorten an unwanted branch, pruning is not needed. Seeds afford the most satisfactory means of multiplication. Root cuttings may also be used.

PAUPER'S-TEA is *Sageretia thea*.

PAUROTIS. The palm previously known by this name is *Acoelorrhaphe*.

PAVETTA (Pav-étta). Little known to American gardeners, *Pavetta*, of the madder family RUBIACEAE, comprises perhaps 400 species of shrubs and small trees. Natives of the tropics and subtropics of the Old and the New World, these close relatives of *Ixora* are less showy than the more brilliant members of that clan, but some are well worth having as garden ornamentals. They have a name derived from one applied to one species in Malabar. An interesting feature of these plants is that tiny spots on their leaves contain bacteria that fix free nitrogen from the air and so help to nourish their hosts.

Pavettas have leaves opposite or in whorls (circles) of three. They are undivided. The flowers are predominantly in clusters at the branch ends. They have top- to bell-shaped, usually four- or five-lobed calyxes. The corollas have cylindrical or funnel-shaped tubes and usually five, more rarely four, lobes (petals) that spread like the spokes of a wheel. There are four or five stamens and a long-protruding style. The fruits are two-stoned berries.

As its name indicates, a native of India, but indigenous also from China to Australia, *P. indica* is a shrub 6 to 10 feet tall or sometimes taller. Its dark green, narrowly- to broadly-elliptic, stalked leaves are 2 to 9 inches long and downy or hairless. The fragrant white flowers are many together in branched, up-facing clusters up to 5 inches across.

Pavetta indica

Two South African species are cultivated, *P. caffra* and *P. natalensis*. An evergreen, sprawling shrub 3 to 6 feet tall, *P. caffra* has obovate to spatula-shaped leaves, 1 inch to 2 inches long, and terminating short shoots, dense clusters 1 inch to 1½ inches wide of fragrant white flowers with corolla tubes ½ inch long. Except in variety *P. c. pubescens* the leaves are hairless. Bigger, looser clusters of larger white flowers are carried by *P. natalensis*, a hairless shrub with lustrous, pointed-lanceolate leaves 3 to 4 inches long.

Garden and Landscape Uses and Cultivation. For gardens in the tropics and subtropics that are unaffected by frost, pavettas are useful for locations in sun or part-day shade. They are also excellent for greenhouses. They succeed in reasonably fertile, well-drained soil with fair supplies of moisture and are easily increased by seeds and cuttings. In greenhouses a minimum winter night temperature of 55 to 60°F with increases of five to fifteen degrees by day permitted and higher temperatures at other seasons, are appropriate. In general the treatment satisfactory for ixoras suits pavettas.

PAVONIA (Pav-ònia). The genus *Pavonia*, which occurs natively in warm parts of the Americas, Africa, Asia, and islands of the Pacific, belongs to the mallow family MALVACEAE. Its name commemorates José Antonio Pavon, a distinguished botanical au-

thor, who died in 1844. There are approximately 200 species. The plant previously known as *P. multiflora* is *Triplochlamys multiflora*.

Pavonias are herbaceous plants and shrubs of diverse forms. They have more or less hairy stems and foliage. Their leaves are alternate and often lobed or angled. Solitary or in clusters from the leaf axils, the yellow, pink, or purple flowers have in addition to a calyx with five lobes or teeth, an involucre (collar) below it of five or more linear bracts. There are five spreading or upright petals, a prominent column formed of many united stamens, and a style with ten branches. The dry fruits are of five sections or carpels that eventually part.

A tropical American shrub up to 20 feet in height, *P. spinifex* has a few wandlike branches, and ovate to heart-shaped, sometimes angled, thinly-pubescent, short-stalked leaves 2 to 4 inches long. They have round- or double-toothed margins. The 1-inch-wide, long-stalked, yellow blooms, solitary from the leaf axils, have obovate petals about as long as the column of stamens. The seed capsules are furnished with three spines. Similar to *P. spinifex* and sometimes misidentified as that species, South American *P. sepium* has narrower leaves and smaller flowers. South African *P. praemorsa* differs from *P. spinifex* in having dark-centered flowers and in its capsules being downy but not spiny. The flowers of this sort do not open widely.

Naturalized in the southern United States, and sometimes recommended for cultivation, *P. hastata* is rather too weedy in appearance to make wide appeal despite its flowers being quite pretty. It is a 6-foot-tall shrub, of South America, that has solitary, 1-inch-long blooms, light red with a dark spot at the base.

Garden and Landscape Uses and Cultivation. As outdoor plants, pavonias can be grown in the United States only in the warmer parts. Most are chiefly appropriate for informal areas. They succeed in ordinary soils and sunny locations and are easily propagated by seed sown in well-drained soil and by cuttings.

PAWPAW. This is a common name for *Asimina triloba* and *Carica papaya*.

PAXISTIMA (Pax-ístima)—Ratstripper, Oregon-Boxwood. After being variously *Pachystigma*, *Pachystima*, and *Pachistima*, the name of this genus, of the staff tree family CELASTRACEAE, is now, for a while at least, *Paxistima*. The group is entirely North American and is usually conceded as comprising two species, although some botanists admit more. The name derives from the Greek *pachys*, thick, and *stima*, a stigma, in allusion to the slightly thickened stigma.

Paxistimas are low evergreen shrubs with warted, four-angled branches and opposite, undivided, short-stalked leaves. The little, insignificant greenish or reddish flowers are few together in axillary clusters. They have four each sepals, petals, and short stamens and a short style topped with a slightly two-lobed stigma. The fruits are small leathery capsules containing one or two seeds.

Known locally as ratstripper, *P. canbyi* inhabits the mountains of Virginia and West Virginia. A trailer, it has rooting stems, and linear to narrowly-oblong leaves, ¼ to 1 inch long, with turned under margins usually toothed above their middles. The flowers are about ⅙ inch in diameter. This species is hardy in New England.

Paxistima canbyi

Less hardy, scarcely persisting outside in the vicinity of New York City, except in very sheltered locations, the Oregon-boxwood (*P. myrsinites*) ranges as a native from California and New Mexico to British Columbia. It is a variable, spreading, stiff-branched shrub, not exceeding 2 feet in height, with broad-elliptic to slightly obovate leaves from ½ inch to slightly over 1 inch long. The leaf margins, toothed or not, are slightly turned under. The flowers are ⅛ inch in diameter and green or purplish.

Garden and Landscape Uses and Cultivation. Paxistimas are excellent low evergreen shrubs. As a superior groundcover *P. canbyi* is unsurpassed. It is at its best and most compact in sun, but flourishes in part-shade, although then a little looser in growth. It is very worthy of planting at the fringes of shrub beds, on banks, and in rock gardens. Preferring light shade, *P. myrsinites* is suitable for planting wherever that is available and a low evergreen is appropriate. It makes good undercover in open woodlands. Both species are adaptable to a variety of soils provided drainage is good. They prefer those that contain a reasonable amount of organic matter, such as leaf mold or peat moss, and sand, and that do not dry excessively. Cuttings taken in summer and planted under mist in a shaded cold frame, or in a cool greenhouse propagating bench, root with facility. Layering affords a ready means of securing increase. Division is satisfactory with *P. canbyi*. Seeds sown in sandy, peaty soil also produce good results.

PE-TSAI. See Chinese Cabbage.

PEA. The word pea occurs in the common names of these plants: asparagus-pea (*Psophocarpus tetragonolobus* and *Lotus tetragonolobus*), Australian-pea (*Dolichos lignosus*), beach-pea (*Lathyrus maritimus*), black-eyed-pea, cow-pea, or Southern table-pea (*Vigna unguiculata*), bush-flame-pea (*Chorizema*), butterfly-pea (*Centrosema virginianum* and *Ciitoria*), chapparal-pea (*Pickeringia montana*), chick-pea (*Cicer arietinum*), Darling-River-pea (*Swainsona greyana*), everlasting-pea or perennial-pea (*Lathyrus latifolius*), glory-pea or Sturt's desert-pea (*Clianthus formosus*), grass-pea (*Lathyrus sativus*), Lord Anson's blue-pea (*Lathyrus magelianicus*), marsh-pea (*Lathyrus palustris*), pea-bush (*Pultenaea*), pea-shrub and pea-tree (*Caragana*), pigeon-pea (*Cajanus cajan*), rosary-pea (*Abrus precatorius*), scarlet coral-pea (*Kennedia prostrata*), scurfy-pea (*Psoralea*), shamrock-pea (*Parochetus communis*), Swan-River-pea (*Brachysema lanceolatum*), sweet-pea (*Lathyrus odoratus*), Tangier-pea (*Lathyrus tingitanus*), two-flowered-pea (*Lathyrus grandiflorus*), wedge-pea (*Gompholobium*), wild-pea (*Lathyrus*), and winged-pea (*Lotus tetragonolobus*.)

PEA STICKS or PEA BRUSH. These are names used for twiggy, leafless branches of trees sharpened at their bases and stuck into the ground as supports for peas and other vining plants such as sweet-peas and morning glories.

PEACH. For flowering peaches grown as landscape ornamentals rather than for their fruits see Prunus. Here we are concerned with pomological or orchard kinds. More sensitive to cold than other temperate-region fruits, peaches, varieties of *Prunus persica*, of the rose family ROSACEAE, are nevertheless grown successfully as far north as western New York, the Great Lakes region, northern Ohio, the Rocky Mountain states, and Ontario, Canada. Despite their sensitivity to very low temperatures, peach trees need a period of definite chilling. Very few varieties succeed in regions of extremely mild winters.

Derived through long centuries of breeding and selection from a species probably originally native of China, modern varieties are among the most esteemed of fruits for eating out of hand, cooking, canning, and freezing. Because of the comparatively small sizes of the trees, their adaptability to varied environments, and their ease of management peaches are well suited for home orchards.

Planting sites should be open and sunny with good air drainage assured. Low sites into which cold air drains and collects on still nights in winter and spring are to be avoided. Proximity to large bodies of water is favorable because such features tend to check sudden drops in temperature and in late winter and spring to delay premature blooming that may subject the flowers to injury by late frosts.

Soils lighter than those best for apples, pears, plums, and most other tree fruits suit peaches. Best are deep, fertile, sandy loams that encourage root penetration. Those underlain with hardpan or plagued with poor subsurface drainage will not do. Trees planted on them are unproductive and soon deteriorate and die. Do not, until after an interval of several years, plant peaches on land from which old peach

trees have been removed. Experience indicates that if this is done the newly set trees behave poorly.

Planting may be done in fall in mild climates, but is better deferred until early spring where winters are severe. Spacing may be 20 feet apart each way, or in home orchards a little closer and the trees kept to smaller size by pruning. For very vigorous varieties, 25 feet between individuals is not too much. The planting procedure is as for apples and other fruit trees. During the first two or three years following planting, vegetables or flowers may be grown in rows between the peaches, but not close enough to them to interfere with the growth of the trees.

Young peach trees with vegetables planted between them

Training and pruning need attention. Peaches carry heavy crops, and if narrow-angled, weak crotches are allowed to develop at branching points, breakage is likely to result from the weight of the crop as well as from storms. Nursery-grown trees at planting time will usually be 3 to 7 feet tall and somewhat branched. Prune them to a height of 3 feet, the weak branches back to about 1 inch from their bases. Some orchardists cut lower, but more height allows for better spacing of

Pea sticks: (a) Sharpening their bases

(b) The sharpened stakes tied in bundles

An established peach orchard

the scaffold branches-to-be. Select these last from among the new shoots that develop in response to the pruning. Do this when they are a few inches long by retaining three that diverge from the trunk at wide angles and are most advantageously placed and spaced to form a shapely head.

The next spring prune the branches selected as scaffolds lightly and cut out all weak and crowded lateral shoots that have developed. Repeat this procedure at the third and fourth spring prunings. After that the trees will come into full cropping and more severe pruning is in order.

Peaches are occasionally trained as fan-form espaliers. With such specimens, after the main framework of branches is established, routine pruning is done to replace shoots that have borne fruits with new ones that sprout from the bases of the old ones and that will bear fruits the following year. Retain only enough new shoots, ordinarily one replacement shoot for each older one that is to be cut out, to furnish the available space without crowding, and tie them into place alongside the older shoots, which, as soon as the fruits are harvested, should be cut down completely to the replacement shoot. Other pruning consists of shortening the terminal growths that grow from shoots of the previous year's growth by cutting them back just above the fourth or fifth leaf as soon as they have developed eight or nine leaves.

A peach tree espaliered against a wall

Pruning older, established trees is done annually to stimulate satisfactory growth and the production of new fruiting shoots of sufficient, but not excessive vigor. If the terminal shoots grow to a length of more than 1 foot to 1¼ feet in a season it is indicative of excessive vigor likely to result in poorly colored fruits and possible winter injury to the trees. Both pruning and fertilizing practices should be done in such ways as to avoid these happening.

The chief pruning of trees making adequate growth consists of thinning out the weaker shoots. Older specimens growing less robustly may be treated in the same manner and additionally by heading back two- and three-year-old branches to advantageously located laterals. Do the work in such a way that the head is pruned uniformly throughout, not just its top.

Routine management involves the maintenance of favorable conditions at the soil surface. Unlike apples, peaches do not thrive in heavy permanent sod. Often clean cultivation in which grass, weeds, and cover crops play no part is practiced, but this involves frequent use of a cultivator or hoe and is less satisfactory than an intermediate routine called trashy cultivation.

This last is achieved by using a disk harrow to break the sod between the trees without turning it under, leaving it as a mulch of sorts to check erosion and absorb rains. In home gardens a mulch of coarse compost or other organic material may be substituted.

Fertilizing in spring is needed by young trees, the terminal shoots of which make under 1½ feet of growth each season and by older ones making not over 1 foot. For trees one to three years old nitrate of soda may be applied at the rate of ½ pound for each tree; for four- and five-year-old trees up to 2 pounds; and for older ones up to twice that amount. Other fertilizers in amounts supplying equivalent nitrogen may be substituted for nitrate of soda.

Thinning the fruits so the shoots carry to maturity no more than one for every thirty to fifty leaves is important to the production of large-sized, high quality fruits. This is sometimes done in commercial orchards by chemical sprays, but for home production hand thinning is preferred. Should you contemplate spraying consult a Cooperative Extension Agent or State Agricultural Experiment Station for advice about procedures. Hand thinning may be achieved by removing blooms or young fruits. The latter is preferable. Excessive young fruits should be taken off immediately following the 'June drop" at which time the trees naturally shed some of their small fruits. When thinning, leave proportionately more fruits on vigorous shoots at the top of the tree than on weaker shoots toward the interior.

Harvesting should not be done until the ground color of the fruit changes from green to yellow or whitish, according to whether the variety is yellow- or white-fleshed. Two or three pickings are usually desirable to assure collecting the fruit in optimum condition. Too often fruit for market is harvested before it is sufficiently ripe, a deplorable practice that results in a lighter crop and impaired flavor. Peaches, unlike some other fruits, do not improve in flavor after being taken from the tree.

Varieties are very numerous and it is well to check locally for those that do best

Peach fruits are thinned when about this size

Neglect of thinning results in crowded, inferior fruits

Properly thinned peaches develop without crowding

in particular areas. Cooperative Extension Agents and State Agricultural Experiment Stations can be very helpful in offering recommendations. When making selections consider whether the fruits are chiefly to be used for eating out of hand, canning, freezing, or drying. Consider also the hardiness of the variety and whether it ripens early, midseason, or late. Peaches come with yellow or white flesh, and as clingstones and freestones. In most regions yellow-fleshed freestones are preferred, but there may be reasons for planting other types.

Dwarf peach trees often have special appeal for home gardeners, especially those with limited space at their disposal. Unlike many other sorts of dwarf fruits, apples and pears, for example, these miniature peach trees are not produced by grafting onto dwarfing understocks; they are natural genetic dwarfs. One of the most popular, 'Bonanza', eventually reaches 6 feet and begins bearing when about 2 feet tall. It is a yellow-fleshed freestone of good quality. 'Golden Glory' is a yellow-fleshed freestone 8 to 9 feet tall. A white-fleshed freestone, 'Flory', slightly smaller than 'Bonanza', has fruits of bland flavor.

Propagation is done by shield or T budding, in June in the south, in July or August in the north, onto seedling understocks, those of the variety Lovell', the fruit of which is used in California for drying, being often used by commercial nurserymen simply because seeds are available in the large quantities they need. Seedlings of other varieties are also suitable. Where soil nematodes are troublesome, the resistant understocks 'Bokhara' and 'Shalil' are preferred. Seedling plums and apricots are also sometimes used as understocks, but are generally considered less satisfactory than seedling peaches.

Understocks are raised by sowing the seeds in spring in outdoor nursery rows after they have been stratified over winter mixed with damp peat moss and kept at 35 to 40°F. The seedlings are budded in the summer of their first year. The following spring when the buds begin to grow, the tops of the understocks are cut off and the young trees can be planted in fall or spring in their permanent locations.

Pests and Diseases. The chief pests of peaches, serious unless adequately controlled, include borers, of which there are two sorts, one of which invades the trunk and branches, another that does its damaging work at about soil level. Root nematodes are troublesome in some regions. Among more common diseases are leaf curl, scab, and brown rot. There are many others. Seek the advice of a Cooperative Extension Agent or State Agricultural Experiment Station about these and other troubles that may come and follow their recommendations to the letter.

PEACOCK. This word appears as part of the common names of these plants: peacock flower (*Caesalpinia pulcherrima* and *Moraea villosa*), peacock flower fence (*Adenanthera pavonina*), peacock-iris (*Moraea villosa*), and peacock plant (*Calathea* and *Kaempferia roscoeana*).

PEANUT. The peanut, goober, or groundnut, only occasionally grown in gardens, is an important field crop in the south and warm countries abroad. In this Encyclopedia its description and information about its uses are given under its botanical name *Arachis*. Here we deal only with the cultivation of peanuts in gardens and in greenhouses for educational purposes. Outdoors they are unlikely to produce substantial crops north of Washington, D.C., but it is possible to have some success with them even in central New York.

Peanuts are raised as annuals. Before sowing, the seeds of thick-shelled varieties are removed from the shells, but thin-shelled "nuts" may be planted intact. This is done as soon in spring as the ground has warmed and the weather is settled, at the time the first corn is planted. Peanuts thrive in well-drained, fertile, sandy soil. If it is at all acid, liming is highly beneficial. They need full sun. There are both vining and compact varieties, the latter being preferred for gardens because they need less room. They may be set in rows 2½ to 3 feet apart with 6 to 9 inches between the plants in the row. Summer care consists principally of keeping down weeds and watering in dry weather. After the vines are touched with frost the entire plants are dug, freed of soil, and cured by stacking them in the open around stakes fitted with cross cleats in such a way that the roots point inward, but do not touch the ground, and the tops provide the roots and attached "nuts" protection from the weather. Alternatively, after digging and freeing of soil the plants can be spread on a dry surface in a shed, garage, attic, or similar place to cure.

Peanuts: (a) A growing plant

(b) A dug-up plant showing the "nuts"

In greenhouses peanuts are better grown in broad pans (shallow pots) or boxes than in regular flower pots. They flourish in rich earth kept moderately moist and in a sunny location. They need no special care. As soon as their containers are well filled with roots a program of weekly or semiweekly applications of dilute liquid fertilizer should be instituted. The seeds are sown in spring and the plants grown in a minimum temperature of 60°F.

PEAR. Members of the genus *Pyrus*, called pears, are discussed in this Encyclopedia under the entries Pears and Pyrus. Other plants with common names including the word pear are alligator-pear or avocado-pear (*Persea americana*), balsam-pear (*Momordica charantia*), Bollwyller-pear (*Sorbopyrus auricularis*), and prickly-pear (*Opuntia*).

PEAR-MELON is *Solanum muricatum*.

PEARL. The words pearl or pearly form part of these common names: pearl bush (*Exochorda*), pearl fruit (*Margyricarpus setosus*), pearl-millet (*Pennisetum americanum*), and pearly everlasting (*Anaphalis*).

PEARLBERRY, CREEPING is *Gaultheria hispidula*.

PEARLWORT. See Sagina.

PEARS. These familiar fruits, members of the genus *Pyrus*, of the rose family ROSACEAE, are greatly esteemed for eating out of hand, for canning, and some sorts for cooking. Less hardy to cold than apples, but more resistant than peaches, they are adaptable for cultivation in temperate regions where temperatures below −20 to −25°F are not experienced. Except for hybrids of the sand pear, which are inferior to varieties of the European pear, but more blight resistant, pears are ill-suited to such regions as the southern United States where high temperatures and humidities prevail in summer.

Parnassia grandifolia

Passiflora alato-caerulea

Pelargonium zonale (geranium) variety in a decorative container

Parthenocissus tricuspidata in fall

Peaches

Pelargonium zonale (geranium), a semidouble-flowered variety

Paulownia tomentosa

Pelargonium zonale 'Mrs. Henry Cox'

Pelargonium tomentosum

Lady Washington pelargonium
(*Pelargonium domesticum* variety)

Espaliered pear trees: (a) In bloom   (b) In leaf

Compared with apples, pears generally take longer to come into bearing. Because they bloom earlier even more care must be taken than with apples when choosing sites for them to avoid low-lying places that on cold, still nights become frost pockets as a result of cold air draining into them from surrounding land. Like apples, pears lend themselves well to training as espaliers.

Soils for pears must be well drained, but not excessively dry. Those of a somewhat clayey nature overlying porous subsoil are most satisfactory, but for home gardens more latitude in respect to choice of soils is permissible than for commercial orchards. Land of moderate to rather low fertility that will not stimulate lush growth likely to fall victim to fire blight disease is to be preferred to excessively nourishing or too-moist ground. Preparation for planting and after-management is as for apples, with more care taken not to fertilize too heavily with nitrogen. The objective should be to promote sturdy, firm, moderate growth least likely to suffer from fire blight.

In selecting varieties remember that, unlike apples, for practical purposes nearly all pears are self-sterile and to assure cropping it is necessary to have two or more compatible (mutually interfertile) varieties growing near enough together for bees to transfer pollen from one to the other. The varieties 'Bartlett' and 'Seckel' are not compatible, that is, they do not fertilize each other.

Plant in fall in regions of fairly mild winters or in early spring. Distances between trees may be 20 to 25 feet depending upon the vigor of the variety or for pears dwarfed by grafting onto quince understocks 12 to 15 feet. Planting procedures and immediate aftercare are as for apples.

Pruning pears follows closely the style recommended for apples, except that excessive cutting is to be avoided as likely to stimulate lush, sappy shoots especially subject to fire blight. Free-standing, as op-posed to espaliered trees, are usually trained according to the modified leader plan. This calls for pruning back to a height of 3½ to 4 feet one-year-old trees at planting time and at the end of another year selecting for retention four to six shoots to form the main framework, the scaffold branches, of the head of the tree. Should insufficient suitable shoots for scaffolds be developed by the end of the first season after planting, additional ones may be selected the following year. In succeeding years prune correctively, but lightly to develop a well-shaped head without crossed branches, capable of carrying heavy crops and without bad crotches conducive to breakage. Mature trees should be pruned chiefly by lightly thinning out younger shoots as needed to prevent overcrowding, by removing long, erect, wandlike shoots called water sprouts that arise from older branches, and by cutting out any older, weak wood that may be necessary to admit reasonable light. Do not cut thick branches if that can be avoided. Prune espaliered trees as for apples.

Harvest before full ripeness is attained. Unlike most fruits, pears are better if they

Harvest pears just before they are fully ripe

(c) In fruit

complete their ripening off the tree. Pick as soon as the stalk parts fairly readily from the branch when the fruit is lifted. If left on the tree much longer, the flesh becomes mealy or gritty (some varieties naturally have more gritty flesh than others) or rots at its core. Take great care when handling pears. They bruise easily and specimens so damaged soon rot. To complete the ripening process spread the fruits in layers in a cool, dark or shaded place and cover them with newspaper. Ideal conditions are a temperature of about 65°F and a relative humidity of 80 to 85 percent. At higher temperatures and in cold storage pears last much less well than apples.

Varieties of European pear (Pyrus communis) include 'Bartlett', or as it is known in Europe, 'William's Bon Chretien'. One of the most reliable croppers and a bearer of fruits of excellent quality for eating out of hand and canning, this is probably the most widely grown variety, well adapted for home as well as commercial orchards, but rather more subject than some varieties to fire blight. Another high quality variety appropriate for home orchards, 'Seckel' has small, delightfully flavored fruits and is quite resistant to fire blight. Trees of this sort are slow to come into bearing. 'Beurre Bosc' has large fruits of

Pear 'Seckel'

Pear 'Beurre Bosc'

excellent quality, but is slow to reach bearing age. 'Tyson', which produces small fruits of good quality, is markedly blight resistant.

The best keeper for winter use 'Beurre d'Anjou' is a productive variety slow to come into bearing. Another with fruits that keep well, but a tree of poor growth habit, 'Winter Nelis' is cultivated most in the Far West and little grown elsewhere.

Other varieties include 'Clapp Favorite', which has large fruits of good quality, but is notably subject to fire blight; 'Comice', perhaps the finest flavored of all pears, but a shy bearer; 'Dana Hovey', also rather a poor cropper, but otherwise very good; and 'Sheldon', which produces fine fruits but not in quantities that encourage growing it commercially.

Hybrids between the European pear and the sand pear (*Pyrus pyrifolia*), of China, are so inferior in fruit quality to straight European pear varieties that they should be planted only in warm, humid regions where the incidence of fire blight is so great that the cultivation of other sorts is not practicable. Sand pear hybrid varieties include 'Douglas', 'Garber', 'Kieffer', 'LeConte', 'Orient', 'Pineapple', and 'Waite'.

Propagation of pears is best effected by top grafting three- or four-year-old trees of the blight-resistant variety 'Old Home' with scions of the sort to be multiplied,

operating well out along the scaffold branches so that considerable lengths of 'Old Home' variety are retained. The 'Old Home' trees are obtained by budding or grafting it onto understocks of seedlings of European pears. Formerly, direct budding or grafting of desired varieties onto seedling understocks was practiced, but that is less inhibiting to fire blight disease than the method advocated.

Dwarf pear trees are obtained by grafting onto understocks of quince, the sort called 'Angiers' or 'Malling A' being especially well suited for the purpose. Not all varieties of pears graft well directly onto quinces. Among those that do not are 'Beurre Bosc', 'Sheldon', and 'Winter Nelis'. Such kinds are multiplied by grafting onto varieties of pears compatible with quinces and that have already been grafted upon them. Varieties used for the intermediate graft include 'Bartlett', 'Beurre Hardy', 'Pitmaston Duchess', and 'Seckel'.

Pests and Diseases. Among the chief pests of pears are aphids, borers, leaf blister, leaf rollers, mites, plant bugs, psyllids, and thrips. The most serious disease, fire blight, is bacterial. It quickly kills branches, is easily recognizable by the dead flowers and dead foliage turning black and remaining attached to the branches, as well as by the presence of cankers and mummified fruits. By avoiding heavy pruning and excessive fertilizing development of gross soft growth especially encouraging to this disease is discouraged. Spraying with the antibiotic streptomycin serves to check the blight. Prompt removal of affected branches is imperative. Make the cuts 6 to 8 inches below visible points of infection and sterilize the tools between each successive cut by dipping in alcohol or sodium hypochlorite (household bleach). Other diseases of pears are leaf spots and scab. For detailed information about and recommended controls for pests and diseases consult a Cooperative Extension Agent or State Agricultural Experiment Station.

PEAS. One of the most delicious and universally appreciated garden vegetables, peas are among the easiest to grow if conditions are reasonably right and if seeds are sown early enough for plants to crop before distressingly hot weather comes.

Varieties of *Pisum sativum*, a native of southern Europe and western Asia, garden or English peas as they are often called in the south, belong to the pea family LEGUMINOSAE. Highly nutritious, they are grown commercially for drying, canning, and freezing as well as for marketing fresh. Besides the more familiar sorts esteemed for their edible seeds, there are varieties called snow peas or sugar peas, the entire seed pods of which are edible.

Suitable soils for this crop include practically every type capable of supporting a vegetable garden. Ideally they should be well drained, reasonably fertile, the topsoil 8 inches deep or deeper, and from slightly acid to slightly alkaline. Peas, which generally appreciate lime, do not prosper in markedly acid soil. They need sunny sites, but for second sowings especially, north-facing slopes because they are cooler are more favorable than land tilted toward the south.

Because of the need in most parts of North America for sowing peas as early in spring as possible, it is very advantageous to ready the ground the previous fall. Spade or plow it deeply, turning under generous quantities of manure, compost, or other humus-building organic matter, and leave the surface rough over winter. If organic material is in short supply merely scratch or fork over the upper inch or two of soil in early fall and sow winter rye. Turn this under on the first occasion in late winter that the ground is dry enough to work with spade, rotary tiller, or plow. If you miss that opportunity rain is likely to make it impracticable to have the ground ready in time for the best sowing date, which in the vicinity of New York City is mid-March, at Boston, Massachusetts, about three weeks later, in other parts of the north correspondingly early.

To ensure the longest possible harvesting, the best procedure is to sow on the same early date two or more varieties that take different periods (given in seed catalogs in an approximate number of days) to reach the picking stage. Where climate allows crops from sowings later than the earliest possible to mature, successional ones may be spaced ten days to two weeks apart, but this is impracticable in most parts of the United States. In parts of the south and in other regions with winters mild enough to encourage continuous growth sowings are made from September to February to give crops for harvesting in winter and early spring.

Shortly before sowing, fork or harrow a dressing of complete fertilizer into the ground. Even though peas are legumes and so can use atmospheric nitrogen, they do not do this significantly until growth is well advanced and until then nitrogen taken from the soil is used advantageously.

Varieties of peas are grouped according to whether they have smooth or wrinkled seeds and, for convenience, according to the heights the plants attain. Smooth-seeded varieties are more cold hardy than wrinkled-seeded ones and are suitable for sowing a week to ten days earlier. Their produce, however, is not of quite such high quality. Most dwarf varieties are smooth-seeded. Tall sorts, which must be afforded supports, range from 2½ to 6 feet or higher. Dwarf or low varieties, 1 foot to about 2 feet tall, usually are grown without supports. These last come into bearing a little more quickly than tall varieties and should be included in the earliest sowings. Among the most popular varieties, which along with others are listed and briefly described in seed catalogs, are these: Dwarf sorts, 'Alaska' (smooth-seeded), 'Blue Bantam', 'Laxtonian', 'Little Marvel', and 'Progress No. 9'; tall sorts, 'Alderman', 'Freezonia', and 'Wando'. Snow or sugar pea varieties include 'Dwarf Gray Sugar' and 'Mammoth Melting Sugar'.

Peas are grown in rows spaced about as far apart as the expected height of the variety, which information is provided in the catalogs of seedsmen, up to a maximum distance between rows of about 4 feet for the tallest varieties. Because individual pea plants are slender and bear comparatively few pods, to assure satisfactory returns it is necessary to sow fairly thickly.

Two methods are most commonly used. One involves making for each row two drills or furrows about 6 inches apart and 3 to 4 inches deep, the other of making for each row a flat-bottomed trench about 6 inches wide (the width of a spade blade) and 3 to 4 inches in depth. The latter plan is often preferred by gardeners with British or other northern European experience. The seeds are covered with soil to depths of 1 inch to 2 inches, which leaves a depression along the rows. This is helpful when watering becomes necessary later. The soil covering over the earliest sowings should be shallower than for successional ones. Yet a third way sometimes employed for dwarf peas and that may prove a convenience for home gardeners, is to sow in beds 4 feet wide with paths 1½ to 2 feet wide between adjacent beds. This, which makes possible maximum harvests from minimum areas, involves shoveling out the beds to a depth of 1 inch to 2 inches, sowing the seeds, and covering them to a depth of 1½ to 2 inches with the soil taken out plus, if needed, a little shoveled from the paths. Scatter the seeds of dwarf varieties approximately 1 inch to 1½ inches apart and later if the seedlings come up too thickly

Sowing peas in a broad, flat-bottomed trench: (a) Scattering the seeds

(b) Raking soil over the seeds

thin them to an average of 1½ to 2 inches apart. Spacing between plants of tall varieties, which should be a little more generous, is achieved by sowing the seeds about 2½ inches apart and later if necessary thinning the seedlings to an average of 3 to 4 inches between individuals.

Supports of trellis, chicken wire, strings, or pea stakes or pea brush (twiggy brushwood with the bottom of each piece sharpened and thrust firmly into the ground)

must be provided for tall peas. Position the supports at the time of sowing or very shortly afterward.

Routine care consists of reasonable attention to keeping down weeds and in dry weather soaking at weekly intervals with water. It is of great advantage, too, to mulch the ground along the sides of the rows to keep it comparatively cool and uniformly moist. If the soil is rather poor in nutrients, an application of fertilizer

Pea stakes: (a) With bases sharpened, tied into bundles

(c) Peas supported by tall pea stakes

(b) Positioned to support a row of tall peas

(d) Positioned to support a row of low-growing peas

Chicken wire: (a) Installed to support tall peas

(b) Supporting rows of tall peas

when the plants are about half-grown will prove helpful.

Begin harvesting as soon as the first pods are plump and well filled with sizable peas and before these begin to show signs of toughening or becoming hard. Pick successively at intervals of a few days as long as the plants are productive. Ideally peas should be cooked within an hour of being picked. If this is impracticable keep them in a refrigerator or other cool place. In temperatures of 70°F or higher, their eating quality deteriorates in a very few hours. Harvest snow peas while the pods are yet tender and pick frequently to encourage the longest possible harvest. All peas cease to produce earlier

than otherwise if pods mature on the vines.

Pests and Diseases. The chief pests of peas are aphids, most easily controlled by spraying or dusting with rotenone or nicotine insecticides. Fungus root rots and a wilt disease can be serious especially if the soil is poorly drained or too acid or has carried crops of peas for successive years. Rotating pea plantings on a yearly basis to different parts of the garden helps to keep these troubles in check. Powdery mildew, which causes a whitening or graying of the foliage is especially likely to develop in warm, humid weather. Applications of a fungicide at its earliest appearance checks its spread.

PEAT. Peats result from the partial decay of plant remains (roots, leaves, stems, etc.) under water or in places waterlogged most of the time. They are akin to mucks, but differ in containing considerably less mineral matter and in the structure of the plant remains of which they are composed being visible, at least with the aid of a hand lens. Nevertheless, peats and mucks intergrade, there is no sharp demarcation between them. Because they contain less mineral matter and are less compact, bulk for bulk typical peats weigh much less than typical mucks. When dry they are comparatively loose and fluffy. The character and quality of peats vary depending upon the kind of plants of which they are formed, the chemical contents of the water in which they were developed, and the rate and degree of their decay.

Of the various kinds of peat available to gardeners, one of the most important is discussed separately under Peat Moss. Another commonly available type is sedge peat or reed peat, often sold as humus or peat humus. This results from the partial decay of sedges, reeds, cat-tails, certain bog grasses, often with lesser amounts of other swamp and shallow-water plants. The best qualities are dark brown to black and when dry are comparatively light in weight, loose, and fluffy. Mostly they are less acid than peat moss, their reactions ranging from pH 4.4 to 6.5. They contain more nitrogen, a total of 2 to 3½ percent, than peat moss, but like it, no appreciable amounts of other nutrients. Their ability to absorb water is from three to six times their own dry weights, as compared with from six to fifteen times for peat moss.

Sedge or reed peat is sold, after being piled in heaps and weather-dried, in a raw condition, and as a product known as cultivated peat. This last is prepared by draining peat bogs, sowing cover crops that, when they attain suitable size, are disked under and allowed to decay. The surface layer is then removed, piled in heaps to drain and partially dry, after which it is screened and bagged or packaged. Cultivated sedge peats are said to be more favorable than raw ones to plant growth, but improvement is not always apparent.

Other peats, less commercially important, but in some areas available locally, are hypnum and forest peats. The first results from the partial decay of mosses other than *Sphagnum*, chiefly species of the genus *Hypnum*. This has many of the qualities of peat moss, but is usually only slightly acid, neutral, or even slightly alkaline. Its water-absorbing capacity, and nutrient content are about the same as for peat moss. Hypnum peat is light and spongy. It varies in color from drabbish brown to brown. Forest peat, or peat mold, as its name indicates, is produced in wooded regions. It is formed chiefly of

Young peas not yet ready for picking

Sedge peat: (a) Dredged from bogs

(b) Piled in heaps

(c) Dried, it is used as a soil amendment

PEAT MOSS. Much used by gardeners as a soil amendment, mulch, propagating medium, and for other purposes, peat moss is peat (organic debris that has partially decayed under water) composed chiefly of sphagnum mosses, sometimes interspersed with smaller amounts of remains of other inhabitants of acid bogs such as cranberries, blueberries, ferns, pitcher plants, and sundews. It varies considerably in appearance and properties, depending upon its source.

For horticultural purposes the best peat mosses are fairly coarse, spongy, and yellowish-brown to rich dark brown. In comparison to their bulk they are light in weight, and the parts of the mosses of which they are composed are distinguishable. Peat moss is decidedly acid, normally having a reaction of pH 3.5 to 5.

The chief virtues of peat moss are its ability to better the structures of soils by improving aeration (important with heavy, clayey soils) and its properties of absorbing, retaining, and slowly releasing moisture (important with light, sandy soils). In addition, it supplies organic matter, which, as it decays, releases small amounts of nitrogen and nearly negligable amounts of other nutrients. The acid reaction of peat moss, as well as its structure and organic nature, are especially favorable to the growth of plants of the heath family ERICACEAE and to that of many other acid-soil, and fine-rooted plants. As a mulch, peat moss serves well to conserve moisture and inhibit weeds.

Peat moss is marketed in bales, bags, and cartons, more rarely in bulk. A bushel of good quality product dried, shredded, and loosened, weighs about eight pounds. Market packs vary considerably in the amounts of organic matter they contain, and yet that should be an important basis for comparing prices. They may also vary in the quality of the product. Brand-name peat mosses sold by reputable dealers are likely to be of high quality, the best, when dry, consisting of over ninety-five percent

the partial decay of woody material including trunks, branches, and roots, as well as bark, leaves, and other parts of trees and shrubs. It is less fibrous than peat moss and characteristically contains an abundance of identifiable particles of decayed wood. Forest peat absorbs four to eight times its own dry weight of water. It contains from 1 to 2½ percent nitrogen, and nearly negligable amounts of other nutrients.

Both domestic and imported peats are marketed in North America. The imports are peat mosses chiefly from Germany, Holland, and Ireland. Domestic peats include peat mosses, mostly from deposits north of a line drawn from southcentral Maine through northcentral New York to northcentral Minnesota and British Columbia, and sedge peats chiefly from south of that line. In the northern states some hypnum peat is extracted and marketed.

The relative values of peats for horticultural purposes depend upon the particular use it is to be put to, the total organic matter it contains, and to some extent its acidity-alkalinity rating.

Peat moss is marketed in bales or sometimes in bulk

organic matter. A typical large-sized bale measures about 36 by 23 by 23 inches, weighs about 175 pounds, and contains before compression about twenty-two bushels. When thoroughly loosened and fluffed up one such bale occupies about a cubic yard. Smaller bales, often more convenient for home gardeners to handle than the larger ones, are available. For information about related materials see the Encyclopedia entry Peat.

PEBBLE PLANTS. See Stone or Pebble Plants.

PECANS. The native American tree *Carya pecan*, of the walnut family JUGLANDACEAE, bears the delicious nuts called pecans. It is now cultivated far beyond its native range of from Indiana to Iowa, Alabama, Texas, and Mexico, and selected varieties are much more uniform in the size and quality of their produce than wild populations.

The first pecan trees recorded as cultivated were brought from the Mississippi valley by Thomas Jefferson in 1775. They were given to George Washington, who planted them at Mount Vernon, where some still exist.

Although hardy in colder climates, as trees grown for their nuts pecans are practically restricted to the south with some extension northward in the Mississippi drainage basin and to the west. Careful attention should be given to selecting planting varieties known to do well locally. Cooperative Extension Agents and State Agricultural Experiment Stations can be of great help here. In general the best paper shell varieties, such as 'Stuart' and 'Schley', are suitable only for the deep south, but newer sorts with thin-shelled nuts are available for planting further north. Not all varieties are self-fertile. Such sorts fruit sparingly or not at all unless another compatible variety is growing nearby. Varieties that are self-fertile include 'F. W. Anderson' and 'Mahan'.

Pecans respond best to deep, well-drained, fertile soil and need considerable space. Mature specimens may exceed 100 feet in height, but do not achieve that within the lifetimes of those who plant them. For orchard purposes a minimum spacing of 75 feet between individuals was formerly recommended, but present practice usually calls for 30 to 40 feet. Because their fallen leaves stain paint do not locate them near houses.

Plant only young, nursery-grown trees obtained from a reliable source, expertly dug and packed. Any serious damage to their very strong and deep taproots can only result in disappointment or failure. Fall is the best time to plant. Dig deep holes. Set the trees scarcely deeper than they were in the nursery, with the roots positioned naturally without bending or crowding and pack good soil firmly around them.

After planting, the taproot strikes deeply and within a very few years strong, shallow, horizontal roots develop and in time a dense mattress-like growth of feeder roots extends downward from about 6 inches below the surface. This makes unwise any attempt at working the soil deeply near the trees with plow or rotary tiller, but keeping weeds down by shallower cultivation is advocated. An even better practice is to keep the ground mulched. Pecans can be grown in grass sod, even in lawns, but that is less satisfactory than under mulch or clean cultivation. Established trees benefit from a spring application of a nitrogen fertilizer.

Harvesting is by picking the nuts from the ground after they drop naturally. They may be eaten at once, but are better flavored if kept for a week or more.

Propagation is best achieved by budding selected sorts onto one-year-old seedlings. It is also possible to top work old trees by budding or grafting superior varieties onto them.

PECTINARIA (Pectin-ària). Endemic to South Africa, *Pectinaria* belongs in the milkweed family ASCLEPIADACEAE. A *Stapelia* relative, it consists of seven species and bears a name from the Latin *pectinatus*, comblike, applied in allusion to the corona lobes of *C. arcuata* being toothed.

Pectinarias are succulent, leafless, tufted herbaceous perennials. Their acutely to obscurely four- to eight-angled stems are usually prostrate, in the wild they are often partly buried. They are toothed or knobby along the angles. The small blooms are solitary or in clusters along the stems between the angles, those of *P. pillansii* often developing underground. They have a five-lobed calyx and corolla, the lobes of the latter joined at their apexes, leaving spaces between at the sides so the bloom is cage-like. At the center of the bloom is a development consisting of an outer and inner corona. There are five stamens, their stalks united to form a tube surrounding the style. The fruits are paired, narrow-spindle-shaped, hairless, podlike follicles.

Curious *P. arcuata* has bluntly-four-angled stems 2 to 4 inches long or longer that form loops up to 1 inch high by arching over and burying their tips in the ground. In twos, threes, or occasionally solitary along the sides or undersides of the loops, the ½-inch-long, hairless flowers, their outsides pale yellow with purple-tinged lobes, on their insides are dark purple with whitish lobes and a yellow corona. Strongly four-angled, fat, pointed-toothed, procumbent stems, from 1 inch to scarcely over 2 inches long are characteristic of *P. tulipiflora*. In pairs, its short-stalked flowers, cylindrical to more or less egg-shaped, under ½ inch long, and lobed to about the middles or the corollas, come from the bases of the stems. They are purple-red,

hairless outside, on their insides hairy. Occasionally the tips of the corolla lobes of this species part and the bloom assumes the aspect of a tiny tulip, a characteristic acknowledged in its name. Its prostrate, conspicuously toothed stems thicker than those of the last, *P. saxatilis* develops broadly-egg-shaped, minutely-hairy, black-purple blooms, rather under ½ inch long, in clusters of four to seven on the young stems.

Garden Uses and Cultivation. Although not showy in bloom, pectinarias are prized by collectors of succulents. They respond to conditions and care that suit *Duvalia*. For more general information see Succulents.

PEDALIACEAE — Pedalium Family. Closely related to the figwort family SCROPHULARIACEAE, the pedalium family consists of fifty species of dicotyledons distributed among a dozen genera. Mostly herbaceous plants, rarely shrubs, they chiefly inhabit shores and deserts. The sorts of this family have opposite leaves and glandular hairs that emit clammy slime. The flowers, solitary or in clusters of usually three, are asymmetrical and have a five-cleft calyx and a more or less two-lipped corolla with a curved tube and five lobes (petals). There are four fertile stamens in two pairs and often a staminode (nonfunctional stamen). The style is long. There are two stigmas. The fruits are capsules or nuts frequently with hooked spines or wings. Cultivated genera are *Ceratotheca*, *Pterodiscus*, *Sesamothamnus*, and *Sesamum*.

PEDATE. This alludes to a palmate leaf the side lobes of which are two-cleft.

PEDDIEA (Peddi-ea). The twenty species of *Peddiea*, of the mezereum family THYMELAEACEAE, are natives of tropical Africa, South Africa, and Malagasy (Madagascar). The name commemorates nineteenth-century Lieutenant-Colonel Peddie, who first discovered the genus.

Shrubs or small trees, the sorts of this genus are predominantly hairless. They have alternate leaves and small, yellowish-green or green, bisexual flowers in stalked racemes or umbels. Each flower has a cylindrical four- or five-lobed calyx, no petals, eight or ten short-stalked, nonprotruding stamens, and one short style capped with a headlike or saucer-shaped stigma. The fruits are small and somewhat fleshy.

The first species described botanically, *P. africana* is native to South Africa. An erect, freely-branching, evergreen shrub with a superficial resemblance to *Daphne laureola*, from which it differs in its flowers being in umbels as well as in other ways, this species is up to 12 feet tall. Its glossy, short-stalked, elliptic to oblong-elliptic leaves, mostly 2½ to 3½ inches long by up to 1 inch wide, have a pronounced midrib.

Peddiea africana

In terminal, stalked umbels of up to sixteen, the slightly fragrant flowers are up to ½ inch long. Borne in winter, they have four or five light green, spreading, petal-like sepals, about ⅛ inch long, eight or ten stamens, and a slender style. Approximately ½ inch long, the ovate fruits are black.

Garden and Landscape Uses and Cultivation. Although little known in cultivation, the species discussed has obvious merit for gardens and other landscapes in mild, dryish, frost-free or essentially frost-free climates, such as are found in much of California, and for beds or containers in large conservatories. It prospers in well-drained soil of medium fertility and is easily propagated by cuttings taken in spring or fall and planted in a propagating bench, preferably with slight bottom heat. A tendency to become bare of foliage in its lower parts as height is gained is easily prevented by judicious pruning.

PEDICULARIS (Pedic-ulàris) — Lousewort, Wood-Betony, Elephant's Head, Indian Warrior. The botanical and the least attractive of the common names listed above allude to a former unfounded belief that animals that ate these plants became especially susceptible to infestations of lice. The derivation of *Pedicularis* is from the Latin *pediculus*, a louse. This genus belongs to the figwort family SCROPHULARIACEAE and comprises about 500 species, mostly of temperate parts of the northern hemisphere, the majority native in temperate Asia. It is also represented in the Andes of South America.

Louseworts include annuals and biennials, but are apparently mostly herbaceous perennials. Some or possibly all are partially parasitic on roots of other plants. Because of this and of our imperfect knowledge of which plants particular species parasitize, their cultivation is generally unpredictable, and often difficult. This is unfortunate because many kinds, including a high proportion of those native to North America, are sufficiently attractive to be suitable for wild gardens and similar developments. They have alternate or less often opposite, pinnate, pinnately-lobed, or toothed leaves. Their flowers, in usually spikelike, squat or more elongated racemes, are white, yellow, purple, or red. They mostly have five-, more rarely four- or two-lobed calyxes and a two-lipped, tubular corolla with the upper lip usually larger, hoodlike, and enclosing the anthers, and the lower generally three-lobed. There are four stamens in pairs of different lengths. The fruits are flattened capsules.

In North America the wood-betony (*P. canadensis*) occurs in upland woods and prairies from southern Canada to Florida, Texas, and Mexico. A sparsely-hairy perennial, its usual several stems are up to 1½ feet tall. Chiefly basal, its lanceolate to oblanceolate leaves, up to 5 inches long, are usually lobed more than halfway to their midribs. The flowers, yellow to purplish-red and about ¾ inch long, have two teeth near the apex of the upper lip. Favoring wet soils from Labrador and Quebec to Nova Scotia, and in Europe and Asia, *P. palustris* is hairless or hairy and has usually branched stems up to 2 feet in height. Its leaves, mostly on the stems, are lanceolate, lobed nearly to their midribs, and about 2 inches long. The flowers, ¾ inch long, are pinkish-purple, sometimes with purple upper lips. This is an annual or a biennial. Another wet soil species, *P. lanceolata* is up to 3 feet tall, few-branched or without branches, and has mostly opposite leaves 2 to 4 inches long, lobed less than halfway to their midribs. The yellow blooms are 1 inch long. This is indigenous from Massachusetts to Manitoba, Nebraska, North Carolina, and Missouri. It is a perennial.

Variable *P. bracteosa* is a hairless, leafy-stemmed perennial, native to woods and meadows from Colorado to British Columbia and California. From 2 to 3 feet tall, it has leaves, up to 1 foot long, divided to their midribs. The yellowish flowers are ¾ inch long. Indigenous from Alberta to British Columbia, New Mexico, and California, *P. racemosa* is a perennial 6 inches to 1½ feet in height. It has lobeless, finely-double-toothed, lanceolate leaves 2 to 4 inches long. The flowers are from a little under to a little over ½ inch long. The blooms are pink to purplish. In variety *P. r. alba* they are white to yellowish. Ranging in the wild from Labrador to British Columbia, New Mexico, and California, perennial *P. groenlandica*, hairless and about 1½ feet tall, has lanceolate leaves 2 to 10 inches long, pinnate and with toothed lobes. The flowers, from purple-pink to almost red, have the upper lip projecting as a curved, about ¾-inch-long beak suggestive of an elephant's trunk. Because of this, the species is sometimes called elephant's head and little red elephants. Endemic to dry slopes in California and Baja California, *P. densiflora*, known as Indian warrior, is a perennial up to 1½ feet in height, with basal or stem foliage hairy or nearly hairy, the leaves up to 6 inches long, and twice-pinnately-lobed. Purple-red, the flowers are ¾ to 1 inch long.

Garden and Landscape Uses and Cultivation. About all that can be said under this heading is that locations for the various species as similar as possible to their native habitats should be tried and to suggest that seeds be sown where the plants are to remain. Plants transplanted from the wild are not likely to live. Increase of established plants can be had by divisions taken in early spring and planted fairly near the mother plants.

PEDILANTHUS (Pedil-ánthus) — Redbird-Cactus or Slipper Flower or Jew Bush. Despite the fanciful name redbird-cactus applied to one species, *Pedilanthus* is not a cactus, nor is it related to cactuses. Kin rather of poinsettias, castor beans, and crotons (*Codiaeum*), it belongs in the spurge family EUPHORBIACEAE. There are fourteen species. The name, from the Greek *pedilon*, a sandal, and *anthos*, a flower, alludes to the form of the blooms. The genus is native to warm parts of the Americas.

Succulent, milky-juiced shrubs with generally cylindrical, more or less jointed stems, pedilanthuses have alternate, undivided leaves that usually soon drop. Their floral structure and the arrangement of the flowers in what botanists call cyathea are similar to those of *Euphorbia*, differing only in the involucre being asymmetrical with a protrusion at one side at the base, instead of being symmetrical and without any such outgrowth.

The redbird-cactus (*P. tithymaloides* syn. *P. carinatus*), also called slipper flower and Jew bush, is best known. Native from Florida to Venezuela, and the West Indies,

Pedilanthus tithymaloides without foliage

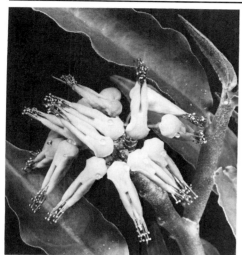

Pedilanthus tithymaloides with foliage

this has many, often zigzagged, up to finger-thick, crowded stems 3 to 6 feet tall. Its pointed, ovate to ovate-lanceolate leaves are up to 4 inches long by about one-half as wide. The prominent midrib forms a toothed keel on the underside of the leaf. Sitting atop each stem, fancifully resembling a cluster of tiny red birds, is a dense group of ½-inch-long, brightly colored flowers (technically cyathea) that are narrowly-flask-shaped and have pointed, beaklike ends from which project the stamens and style. The fruits are small capsules. Varieties are *P. t. nana-compacta*, with erect branches and closely set plain green leaves, *P. t. smallii*, with very markedly zigzagged stems, and *P. t. variegatus*,

Pedilanthus tithymaloides variegatus

with foliage prettily variegated with white and carmine-pink.

Much like the redbird-cactus, but with blunt leaves generally notched at their apexes, and having midribs that do not form keels on the under surfaces of the leaves, *P. retusus* is indigenous to Brazil. Whitish stems, tiny to minute leaves, and green flowers are characteristic of 3-foot-tall *P. macrocarpus*, of Mexico. Similar, but with the flower stalk attached toward the back of the flower instead of close to its center, *P. cymbiferus* (syn. *P. aphyllus*) is also Mexican. Bushy, 2- to 3-foot-tall *P. bracteatus*, of Mexico, has nearly stalkless, oblong leaves 2 to 4 inches in length. Usually leafless at flowering time, this bears its blooms in repeatedly forked clusters at the apexes of the shoots.

Garden and Landscape Uses and Cultivation. Pedilanthuses may be grown outdoors in areas of tropical and subtropical climates, with lengthy dry seasons, and in greenhouses and sunny windows. They associate well with other succulents, and prosper under conditions appropriate for desert cactuses. If soil drainage is excellent, the leafy kinds grow satisfactorily where humidities are higher than are suitable for many cactuses. As pot specimens pedilanthuses need coarse soil. One that contains an abundance of crushed brick, sandstone, tufa rock, or similar material to ensure porosity, and not too high an organic content, is best. Watering is needed only very occasionally or not at all in winter. At other times water often enough to prevent the soil from becoming completely dry, but not until it approaches that condition. For best results full sun is needed. Indoors, minimum winter night temperatures of 45 to 50°F are satisfactory, with higher levels maintained by day and at other seasons. Propagation is easy by seed and by cuttings planted under conditions that suit those of succulent euphorbias and cactuses.

PEDIOCACTUS (Pedio-cáctus) — Snowball Cactus or Mountain Cactus. The genus *Pediocactus*, of the cactus family CACTACEAE, considered broadly consists of seven variable species widely distributed in the western United States, or if a narrower interpretation is made, of fewer, possibly only one sort. The first arrangement is accepted here and plants segregated by some authorities at *Toumeya* and *Utahia* are included. The name, from the Greek *pedio*, a plain, and *Cactus*, a related genus, purports to allude to the habitat of some kinds.

The snowball or mountain cactus (*P. simpsonii*) has stems or plant bodies up to 5 inches in diameter and height, but occasionally slightly taller. In the active growing season approximately spherical, during the winter resting stage they usually become flatter and then broader than high. Generally they are solitary, more rarely clustered. In spirals, the conical or pyramidal tubercles that cover the surface are each tipped with a cluster of fifteen to thirty slender, white to whitish radial spines and on mature specimens up to

eleven stouter centrals up to ¾ inch long, whitish in the lower parts, brownish or reddish-brown above. The flowers, under 1 inch long, pinkish and sprouting from woolly areoles, partly close at night. This species is a native of Montana and Wyoming to Washington and Oregon.

A splendid example of plant mimicry, *P. papyracanthus* (syn. *Toumeya papyracantha*) is covered with papery spines that so closely resemble the dried leaves of the gama grass among which this species grows that finding it is often exceedingly difficult. It has cylindrical to egg-shaped stems up to 3 inches long and not over ¾ inch wide. Usually they are solitary, but in old specimens they sometimes cluster. Spiraled around them are about eight rows of cylindrical or dome-shaped tubercles. The densely arranged spine clusters each have four or fewer flat, whitish to light gray central spines, ¾ inch to 1¼ inches in length and much wider than thick, and six to eight much smaller ones that spread horizontally. The funnel-shaped flowers ¾ to 1 inch wide have white perianth segments (petals) with brownish midribs. The stamens are about one-half as long as the petals. The stigma has five or six spreading lobes. This species is native to Arizona and New Mexico.

Other sorts are these: *P. bradyi*, of Arizona, has solitary or rarely clustered plant bodies 1 inch to 1½ inches in diameter and up to 2½ inches high. They have densely-spined, conical to pyramidal tubercles. The spines, all radials, white to pinkish or tan and in clusters of eighteen to twenty-three, are not more than 1/16 inch long. The pink flowers are ¾ inch in diameter. *P. knowltonii* has solitary or clustered stems, at maturity up to 1½ inches tall and ½ to 1 inch in diameter. They have clusters of mostly eighteen to twenty-three, minute, white radial spines, but no central ones. The ¾-inch-wide pink blooms are succeeded by fruits ⅛ inch in diameter. *P. paradinei*, of Arizona, has flattened or depressed plant bodies up to 2 inches tall and 3¼ inches wide furnished with blunt-conical tubercles. The spine clusters consist of about twenty yellow radials and four to six similar centrals up to 1½ inches long. The flowers, about 1 inch wide, have white petals with pink midribs. *P. sileri* (syn. *Utahia sileri*), of Arizona, grows in the wild in well-drained gypsum soil. An attractive species, it has an almost spherical plant body up to 4 inches in diameter with thirteen to sixteen prominent ribs cleft into short, angled tubercles. At the apex of each is a cluster of eleven to fifteen stiff, white radial spines and three or four black centrals with lighter bases, and about ¾ inch long. The yellow, day-opening flowers, 1 inch across, come from the apexes of the plants. The fruits are scaly.

Garden Uses and Cultivation. Choice for inclusion in collections of succulents, pediocactuses succeed under conditions agreeable to most cactuses. They adapt best to well-drained, gritty soil containing little organic matter and for some sorts, a sprinkling of gypsum. Success with some is more certain if they are propagated by grafting onto stronger-growing cactuses. For more information see Cactuses.

PEEGEE. The peegee or p.g. hydrangea is *Hydrangea paniculata grandiflora*. The name arose from the common practice of nurserymen abbreviating the specific and varietal parts of the name and labeling plants *Hydrangea p.g.*

PEEPUL TREE is *Ficus religiosa*, significant to Buddhists, who believe that the Buddha received enlightenment under one.

PELARGONIUM (Pelar-gònium) — Geranium, Storksbill. This horticulturally important genus, of the geranium family GERANIACEAE, comprises about 280 species and a multitude of hybrids and horticultural varieties. The natural distribution of *Pelargonium* centers in South Africa, where by far the greatest number of its species are native. In addition, one each is endemic to the Canary Islands, St. Helena, Tristan da Cunha, the eastern Mediterranean region, southern Arabia, India, Australia, and New Zealand. The name comes from the Greek *pelargos*, a stork, alludes to the fruits' fanciful resemblance to a stork's beak.

Most widely cultivated are the showy red-, pink-, and white-flowered hybrids called zonal or bedding geraniums and the trailing ones known as ivy-leaved geraniums. Next in importance are the group of hybrids identified as Lady Washington or Martha Washington geraniums or pelargoniums. Then come the many species and hybrids grouped as scented geraniums or pelargoniums. A few other sorts, some more or less succulent, are grown. None belongs to the botanical genus *Geranium*, which consists of annuals and herbaceous perennials, many hardy. As applied to members of the genus *Pelargonium*, geranium is strictly a vernacular or common name, highly legitimate as such because of its long and widespread usage.

Pelargoniums are nonhardy subshrubs and shrubs, or much more rarely herbaceous perennials, annuals, or biennials frequently with aromatic or strongly-scented foliage. Their leaves are lobeless or variously lobed or dissected, those of most sorts opposite. The flowers, chiefly in umbels, have commonly, except for double and semidouble horticultural varieties, five each sepals and petals, the two upper petals frequently larger and colored differently from the others. There is a total of ten stamens and staminodes (non-functional stamens), and one pistil. The fruits are capsule-like.

The feature that most surely distinguishes *Pelargonium* from the genus *Geranium* is that the calyxes of its flowers have a spur extending backward. But unlike those of most spurred flowers, delphiniums and impatiens, for example, the spurs are not free and separate, but are united to the stalks of the blooms usually so completely that they are detectable only as a slight hump on the stalk that marks the end of the spur or by slicing across the stem and spur near the flower so that the hollow interior of the spur can be seen.

Zonal or bedding pelargoniums or geraniums (**P. hortorum**), also called fish or horseshoe geraniums, are complex hybrids, the results of over a century and one-half of crossing and selection. These are the geraniums most esteemed as flowering house and greenhouse plants, for summer beds and other temporary decorative uses outdoors, and in areas with mild, dry climates as permanent adornments of gardens. Their parentage chiefly involves *P. zonale* and *P. inquinans*, species introduced from South Africa to Europe before the end of the eighteenth and at the beginning of the nineteenth century. Other sorts have undoubtedly played parts in the development of present-day hybrids, which include miniatures only a few inches tall, and giants, which in favorable environments, exceed 12 feet in height. The majority run from 1 foot to 3 feet high and taller sorts can be kept to this size by pruning.

The kinds of this group have stout, erect, somewhat succulent, branched stems and finely-hairy foliage that when bruised emits an odor some liken to that of fish (hence the name fish geranium). Mostly alternate, and depending upon variety and cultivation from 1 inch to 5 inches across, the longish-stalked leaves, nearly circular to kidney-shaped, have slightly scalloped, more or less round-toothed edges and usually an irregular broad zone of darker green, bronzy-green, or other color paralleling the margin a little

Zonal pelargonium 'Olympic Red'

Variegated-leaved zonal pelargonium 'Wilhelm Langguth'

distance in from it (this, a legacy of the parent species *P. zonale*, gives reason for the name zonal geraniums). The flowers, produced practically continuously throughout the year and single, semidouble, or double, are in long-stalked umbels. Some novelty sorts have fringed, spotted, or otherwise distinctive petals. In the bud stage they are strongly deflexed, becoming horizontal to erect as they open. Coming in a wide range of colors, many have petals of nearly equal size or the two upper may be smaller than the three lower. Besides plain green-leaved varieties, there are many with foliage beautifully variegated with white, cream, yellow, bronze, and pink. A selection of varieties, some of which are illustrated, is given in the Encyclopedia entry Geraniums.

Variegated ivy-leaved pelargonium 'L'Elegante'

Ivy-leaved pelargoniums or geraniums (varieties. some perhaps hybrids, of *P. peltatum*) in favorable environments bloom practically throughout the year. They have weak, hairless or nearly hairless, more or less trailing or vining stems swollen at the nodes and those of vigorous sorts attaining lengths of several feet. Their distinctly alternate, slightly-fleshy leaves, 2 to 3 inches in diameter, have long stalks joined to the shallowly-five-lobed or five-angled blades well in from their toothless, hair-fringed margins. The long-stalked flower trusses are of few to many asymmetrical blooms that have hairy individual stalks and two upper petals with blotches and stripes darker than their base colors, which range from white through many shades of pink to wine-reds, purple-violets, and crimson. There are double- as well as single-flowered sorts. For descriptions of a selection of these, some of which are illustrated, see the Encyclopedia entry Geraniums.

Lady Washington pelargonium 'Mary Bard'

Lady Washington or Martha Washington pelargoniums or geraniums (**P. domesticum**) are astonishingly beautiful in bloom and come in a wide variety of colors. Their rather pansy-like flowers are frequently handsomely blotched with darker hues. Unlike zonal and ivy-leaved geraniums, these are seasonal rather than year-round bloomers. Their displays last for a few weeks in spring, during the rest of the year they are without blooms.

A hybrid complex, the result of crossing several South African species, Lady Washington geraniums are softly-hairy, somewhat woody-stemmed, stiffly-branched plants 2 to 3 feet tall or taller. From 2 to 4 inches in diameter and without the darker bands characteristic of zonal and many ivy-leaved geraniums, the leaves are ovate with heart- to almost kidney-shaped bases, somewhat angled and edged with pointed teeth of various sizes. Up to 2½ inches or more in diameter and in large trusses, the flowers have two upper petals broader than the others and richly blotched toward their bases with from dark red to almost black. The base color and that of the other petals ranges from pure white through a variety of pinks to wine-red and crimson.

Formerly these were more popular, especially in Europe, than they now are. Vigorous, large-flowered varieties were classified as show and decorative pelargoniums, compact kinds with smaller blooms as fancy pelargoniums. Descriptions of a selection of these are given in the Encyclopedia entry Geraniums.

Scented-leaved pelargoniums or geraniums include several species as well as varieties and hybrids, parentage of the latter sometimes presumed rather than precisely known. Their fragrances, discernible only after brushing or rubbing the foliage, are generally distinctive and easily recognizable, but, as perceptions and identifications of odors vary with individuals, allowances must be made for this.

The apple-scented geranium (**P. odoratissimum**) has a short main stem from which sprout many straggling branches up to 1½ feet in length, often considerably

Pelargonium odoratissimum

shorter. The hairy, pleasantly fragrant leaves have short to quite long slender stalks and thin, round-toothed, kidney-shaped blades 1 inch to 2 inches across and conspicuously to scarcely indented at their bases. The ¼-inch-long flowers, in umbels of few atop stalks 2 to 3 inches long, have individual stalks about ½ inch long with the spurred part extending for about one-half their lengths. Their whitish to white petals are not wide-spreading. From the apple geranium closely allied **P. fragrans**, not to be confused with P. crispum to which that name is sometimes misapplied, is distinguishable by the spurred part of the individual flower stalks being much longer than their basal spurless portions.

Apricot-scented P. 'Ninon', freely-branched, bushy, and rough-hairy, attains heights of 4 feet or more and has triangular, deeply-three-lobed, glandular leaves rather like those of P. graveolens. The lobes are cleft, toothed, and curled. The small and numerous flowers are white to pink or sometimes red, the upper petals with purple veins and a carmine-red spot.

Coconut-scented **P. grossularioides**, 1 foot to 2 feet tall, is a perennial, or sometimes an annual or a biennial. It has more or less trailing or straggling stems and slender-stalked, roundish leaves mostly up to 1½ inches across and shallowly-lobed and toothed. The umbels of three to ten small, magenta-pink to paler flowers come from the upper leaf axils. This is naturalized in parts of California.

Lemon-scented geranium is a name appropriately applied to P. crispum and a group of hybrids and varieties of that species. Among the hybrids are sorts for which the name P. citriodorum is often used, but that designation is inaccurately applied and must be replaced by **P. citrosum**. The hybrids often have larger leaves, not so distinctly two-ranked as those of P. crispum, and frequently bigger flowers, but identification of the sorts that belong here is often puzzling. Typical **P. crispum**, at most 2 to 3 feet tall, has many severely

Pelargonium crispum

erect branches furnished with numerous slightly grayish leaves usually or often in two ranks. Rounded and rarely over 1 inch in length, they have somewhat cleft, bluntly-toothed, crisped or crestlike edges. The flowers, from one to three at the ends of short, stout stalks and ¾ to 1 inch long, are pink with darker markings. From the typical species P. c. minor is distinguished by its much smaller, almost stalkless leaves.

Horticultural sorts with many of the characteristics of P. crispum and presumably variants, mutants, or hybrids of that species, although not all have a clearly defined lemon scent, include these: P. c. variegatum with leaves blotched with yellow and 'Lady Mary', similar to P. limoneum, but with deeper pink flowers. 'Prince of Orange' or 'Orange' has leaves up to 2 inches wide and less crisped than those of P. crispum. 'Prince Rupert' has larger, shorter-stalked leaves than P. crispum and

Pelargonium crispum variegatum

is more robust. 'Variegated Prince Rupert' is similar to the last, but its leaves have creamy-white edges. **P. limoneum,** of hybrid origin and strongly lemon-scented, has small three-lobed leaves, longer-stalked than those of *P. crispum* and toothed at their apexes.

The lime-scented geranium (**P. nervosum**) is believed to be a derivative of *P. crispum*. A bushy sort, it has small, roundish, shallowly-three-lobed, sharply-toothed leaves with slightly ruffled edges and showy umbels of lavender-pink flowers that have two upper petals broader than the others and marked toward their bases with dark veinings.

The nutmeg-scented geranium (**P. fragrans**), believed to be a hybrid between *P. exstipulatum* and *P. odoratissimum*, is somewhat shrubby, much-branched, and up to 1 foot in height. It has heart-shaped, more or less three-lobed, blunt-toothed leaves, about 1 inch in diameter, furnished with short hairs and with stalks up to 2½ inches long. The flowers are small and white with the upper petal red-veined. In umbels of four to eight, they have very

Pelargonium tomentosum

Pelargonium denticulatum

short individual stalks. The leaves of *P. f. variegatum* are irregularly brushed with white. Variety 'Snowy Nutmeg' is lower, has grayish leaves broadly bordered with creamy-white.

The peppermint-scented geranium (**P. tomentosum**) has very beautiful, velvety-hairy, rich green foliage strongly and unmistakably fragrant of peppermint. Often broader than tall, it has stems up to several feet in length. Its opposite or alternate leaves have blades up to 5 inches across with five to seven shallow lobes. The slender flowering stalks, 3 to 5 inches long, support umbels of few to twenty blooms with individual stalks ½ to 1 inch long. The flowers are white with red markings, their three lower petals longer and narrower than the upper pair. Compact *P. t. variegatum* has leaves broadly edged with creamy-white. A variety of the rose-scented geranium (*P. graveolens*) named *P. g. variegatum* has mint-scented foliage.

Pine-scented **P. denticulatum** is less common in cultivation than the frequency with which its name appears in gardens suggests. Its name is often misapplied to *P. radens* and its variety 'Dr. Livingston'. The true species, about 3 feet tall, has slender, branched stems and leaves of ferny aspect with hairless, sticky upper surfaces. They have approximately triangular blades 1½ to 3 inches long and about as wide, divided to their bases into about three major lobes cleft into secondary lobes and toothed. The flowering stalks carry one to three lilac-purple to rose-purple blooms with very short individual stalks. The two upper petals are ½ inch long and deeply notched at their apexes, the others are slightly smaller and not

notched. A variety with narrower leaves than the typical species, *P. d. filicifolium* (syn. *P. filicifolium*) is more commonly cultivated.

Pungent-scented sorts include **P. radens** (syn. *P. radula*). This has much the aspect of *P. denticulatum*, from which it differs in its leaves being rough-hairy and not sticky and in the petals of its flowers not being notched at their apexes. Shrubby and up to 4 feet tall, *P. radens* has leaves deeply cleft into toothed segments rolled under at their margins. Its lavender-pink to rose-pink flowers are marked with purple at their centers. Variety 'Dr. Livingston' (syn. 'Skeleton Rose') has lemon-scented leaves more finely cleft than those of the typical species.

Pelargonium radens 'Dr. Livingston'

The oak-leaf geranium (*P. quercifolium*) and its varieties and hybrids are also pungent-scented. Bushy and up to 3 feet tall, this species has triangular-oblong to triangular-obovate leaves with blades 2 to 4 inches long coarsely-pinnately-lobed to beyond their middles and toothed. The pale pink to deeper pink or violet-pink flowers have narrow petals with darker veinings, the two upper bigger than the others. Among the several varieties are 'Fair Ellen', rather lower and more freely-branched than the species and with rather bigger blooms; 'Giant Oak', with leaves notably bigger and flowers slightly smaller than those of the species and with red spots; and 'Skelton's Unique', a spreading sort with leaves less deeply lobed than those of the species and lavender-pink blooms.

Other pungent-scented sorts include *P. jatrophaefolium* and *P. glutinosum*. A hybrid between *P. quercifolium* and *P. denticulatum*, the sort named **P. jatrophaefolium** has sticky-surfaced leaves deeply cleft into a few narrow, finely-toothed lobes. The small flowers are light pink with darker markings. Up to 3 feet or more in height, **P. glutinosum** has erect, branched stems and triangular-heart-shaped, sticky-hairy leaves palmately slashed into five to seven pointed, pinnately-cleft, toothed lobes. The flowers, in clusters of seven or fewer, are rose-pink with each of the ½-inch-long, obovate upper petals decorated with a carmine-red spot. The other petals are smaller. **P. vitifolium**, the grape-leaved geranium, is up to 3 feet tall and shaggy-hairy. It has erect stems and blunt-heart-to somewhat kidney-shaped, bluntly-lobed leaves 1 inch to 2½ inches wide. Its pink flowers, in headlike umbels on stalks up to 4 inches long, have purple-veined upper petals slightly over ½ inch long, smaller lower ones.

Rose-scented geraniums include relatively rare *P. capitatum* and *P. graveolens* (syn. *P. terebinthinaceum*), as well as varieties and hybrids of the latter. Minty-rose-scented, **P. capitatum** has weak, straggling stems, up to 3 feet long or sometimes longer, clothed with white hairs. Its leaves have roundish-heart-shaped, toothed blades with three to five blunt, shallow lobes. The umbels of bloom on slender stalks 1 inch to 4 inches long are of eight to twenty pink flowers with ¾-inch-long, dark-purple-veined upper petals and three shorter, rose-pink lower ones. From this sort **P. graveolens**, varieties of which are sometimes misnamed *P. terebinthinaceum*, differs in its grayish-green leaves being cleft beyond their middles into three major lobes, which are again lobed and toothed. In outline they are five-sided to triangular; unlike those of *P. radens* their margins are not rolled under. Varieties that belong here include *P. g. minor*, smaller in all its parts, but otherwise similar to the species; 'Lady Plym-

Pelargonium 'Grey Lady Plymouth'

Pelargonium graveolens variegatum

outh', less vigorous than the typical species and its leaves blotched with creamy-white; 'Grey Lady Plymouth', as robust as the species, its leaves narrowly edged with white. Also believed to be varieties of *P. graveolens* are 'Camphor Rose', with bigger, slightly camphor-scented leaves and *P. g. variegatum*, which has large, strongly mint-scented leaves edged with white.

Southernwood-scented **P. abrotanifolium** is distinctive. From 2 to 3 feet tall and freely-branched, it has very finely-divided, grayish, hairy foliage. The leaves, under 1 inch across, are fan-shaped and three-cleft with the main divisions dissected into slender, blunt-linear segments. The white or pink, ¾-inch-wide flowers have two upper petals broader than the others and marked with red or purple. The plant cultivated as **P. divaricatum** (not the original hybrid to which that name was applied) is similar, but a little more vigorous and has somewhat coarser foliage. Its flowers are pink. Its botanical standing has not been determined.

Strawberry-scented **P. scarboroviae** (syn. 'Count of Scarborough'), presumably a derivative of *P. crispum*, has slender, erect, branched stems and small, firm, three-lobed, toothed leaves. The bright pink flowers have red featherings on their upper petals.

Other sorts that normally retain their foliage throughout the year include these: **P. acerifolium**, one of the ancestors of the Lady Washington geraniums, is bushy and has 3-inch-wide, toothed leaves cleft to about their middles into three to five angular lobes. The dark-streaked purple flowers, in panicles, have petals twice as long as the sepals and like the flower stalks densely-hairy. The leaves of *P. a. foliis-variegatus* are edged with creamy-white. **P. acetosum**, botanically related to

Pelargonium acetosum

P. peltatum, differs from that sort in the stalks of its slightly gray-green leaves joining the slightly-cupped blades at the bottoms of their wedge-shaped bases, not some little distance in from their margins. The spidery, salmon-pink flowers, 1¾ inches across, have spreading, narrow petals. **P. angulosum**, a parent of the Lady Washington geraniums, differs from allied *P. cucullatum* in being more harshly-hairy and having shorter-stalked leaves 1½ to 2½ inches across with wedge-shaped or slightly rounded instead of heart-shaped bases. The leaves are angled or shallowly-three- to five-lobed and toothed. The flowers have red-purple petals, the upper ones 1 inch long or longer. **P. blandfordianum**, a hybrid of *P. graveolens* and *P. echinatum*, has slender stems and slightly musky-scented, white-hairy, bluish-gray leaves deeply cleft into narrower segments than those of *P. graveolens*. The small flowers are white, veined with purple, and with the upper petals spotted with red. **P. burtoniae**, shrubby, has rather succulent stems and short-stalked, rather fleshy, somewhat glaucous, obovate to rounded, shallowly-lobed leaves toothed at their apexes. The two- to seven-flowered umbels are of blush-pink to deeper pink, spidery blooms with very narrow petals. **P. cordifolium** (syn. *P. cordatum*), erect,

Pelargonium cordifolium

Pelargonium cordifolium (flowers)

shrubby, and somewhat variable, has long-stalked, hairy to nearly hairless leaves with pointed-heart-shaped, toothed and sometimes obscurely-lobed blades up to 5 inches long. The flowers, on usually branched stalks, are purplish-pink. Their upper petals, wedge-shaped and notched at their apexes, are approximately 1 inch long. The lower petals are much smaller, but longer than the sepals. **P. cucullatum,**

Pelargonium cucullatum

a parent of the Lady Washington geraniums, is woody-stemmed, freely-branched, and softly-hairy. Its quite long-stalked leaves with blades 2½ to 3½ inches across are kidney- to broadly-heart-shaped and more or less cupped. They have slightly scalloped, finely-toothed margins, but are not lobed. The flowers, red with darker veins, have petals ¾ inch to 1¼ inches long. **P. frutetorum** is related to *P. zonale* and like that species has leaves that display a clearly evident dark horseshoe-shaped zone. Up to about 4 feet in height, it has finely-hairy stems and slightly round-lobed, round-toothed leaves. Its salmon-pink blooms, their petals broad and about ¾ inch long, are in ample umbels. **P. grandiflorum** is shrubby, hairless, and somewhat glaucous. Its long stalked leaves have five to seven deep, broad, toothed lobes. White with red or violet-purple lines on the upper pair of petals, which are much broader than the others, the flowers are generally in threes. This is a parent of the Lady Washington geraniums. **P. inquinans,** one of the parents of the zonal geraniums and largely responsible for the red coloring of the flowers of many of that hybrid complex, is about 1 foot tall and branched. Its velvety-hairy, slightly fleshy leaves, differing from those of *P. zonale* in not having a dark, horseshoe-shaped zone, are 2½ to 4 inches across, bluntly-toothed, and shallowly-seven-lobed. The red or sometimes pink flowers have petals approximately ¾ inch long, not notched at their apexes. **P. lateripes** has clambering, prostrate, or hanging slender stems, up to about 3 feet long, and hairless, five-angled, heart-shaped to roundish leaves often with a reddish zone and with a tendency to fleshiness. Closely related to *P. peltatum,* its flowers resemble those of that species. **P. papilionaceum,** up to 3 feet tall and much-branched, has hairy stems and long-stalked, hairy, roundish leaves with heart-shaped bases. The small flowers, in umbels of ten or fewer, have two red-purple-spotted pink upper petals

Pelargonium peltatum

much longer than the other petals, which scarcely exceed the sepals in length. **P. peltatum,** the variable ancestor of garden varieties called ivy-leaved geraniums, has thinnish, more or less zigzagged, trailing stems and hairless or almost hairless, slightly fleshy, toothless leaves with stalks that join the five-angled or five-lobed blades some little way in from their margins. The flowers, in long-stalked umbels of usually eight or fewer, are pink to purplish, with the two upper petals striped or blotched with purple. **P. praemorsum** (syn. *P. quinatum*) has slender, woody stems, toothed, deeply-palmately-lobed leaves, and yellow or creamy-yellow flowers lined with red that have two upper obovate petals very much larger than the others. **P. salmoneum** is much like *P. zonale,* but its slightly fleshy leaves are without dark zones. From 2 to 2½ inches in diameter and often somewhat glaucous, they are shallowly-five-lobed and toothed. The flowers are salmon-pink with the upper petals veined with red. **P. zonale,** a parent of the bedding geraniums classified as *P. hortorum,* is subshrubby to shrubby. It has thick, semisucculent stems and roundish, long-stalked leaves with heart-shaped bases, round-toothed margins, and a more or less distinct darker zone paralleling and a little distance from the margin. The flowers, typically pink, are much less symmetrical and have narrower petals than those of most *P. hortorum* varieties.

Kinds that lose their foliage completely and are dormant for a period in summer include several with tuberous roots and short to well-developed sometimes swollen stems or rarely no stems. The leaves are prevailingly pinnate. The flowers range from dull yellow to greenish-yellow and from red to almost black with yellow-edged petals. Kinds belonging here are these: **P. apiifolium** has stems much swollen at the nodes and hairless, glaucous, slightly fleshy, twice-pinnate leaves with triangular blades about 6 inches long and wide, their final divisions markedly lobed. The flowers, about ½ inch across and in umbels of twenty to thirty, have very short individual stalks and dull black-purple-maroon petals with greenish-yellow margins. **P. ardens,** a hybrid of *P. fulgidum* and *P. lobatum,* has a knobby stem with short branches and lobed, hairy leaves up to 8 inches across. Its flowers are garnet-red, their petals paling at their margins and the upper ones with darker spots. **P. bicolor** has strongly-scented, finely-hairy, trilobed leaves, heart-shaped in outline, with the center lobe again three-lobed and the side lobes cleft into two lobes. The ¾-inch-wide blooms in umbels 2½ inches across have velvety petals of deep Dubonnet-red with rose-pink margins. **P. fulgidum** has densely-silky-hairy, pinnate leaves, triangular to broadly-heart-shaped

shallow, rounded lobes. The branched flowering stalks carry blooms with petals

Pelargonium tetragonum

Succulent pelargoniums that lose their foliage for a period during the summer

elliptic, pinnate leaves with their leaflets
much divided in almost carrot-like fashion. The pink or yellow flowers in tight

must be kept dry during their period of
dormancy. At its conclusion, just as new
leaf growth begins, attend to any needed
repotting. Most sorts grow slowly and are
best served by keeping them in receptacles
rather small in relation to their sizes. If repotting does not seem desirable, pricking
away a little of the surface soil and replacing it with new will be of benefit. For these
succulent kinds be sure the earth is porous
and nutritionally slightly on the lean side.

Pests and Diseases. The pests of pelargoniums are aphids, caterpillars, mites,
black vine weevil, white fly, and root knot
nematodes. Mealybugs, scale insects, and
slugs may also cause damage. Among diseases, bacterial and fungus leaf spots,
black stem rot, root rots, and crown gall
are fairly frequent, as is a virus that causes
the leaves to pucker and another that results in mottled foliage. Destroy virus-in-
fected plants. Water-soaked spots on the
foliage are the result of edema, caused by
excessive wetness and too high humidity.

PELECYPHORA (Pele-cýphora) — Hatchet
Cactus. Two species of Mexican cactuses
make up *Pelecyphora*, a genus of the cactus
family CACTACEAE. They are small plants
resembling *Solisia*, but without milky sap
and with their flowers originating at the
tops of the stems. The name is from the
Greek *pelekys*, an axe, and *phoreo*, to bear,
and alludes to the shape of the tubercles.
The common name hatchet cactus calls attention to the tubercles (protrusions from
the plant body) being laterally compressed, fancifully like the blades of hatch-
ets. This is also a feature of *Solisia*.

The plant bodies of *Pelecyphora* are egg-
to club-shaped, with their broad ends
uppermost. Their tubercles are crowned
by spines arranged like double-edged
combs with teeth spreading in the plane
of the plant body. Bell- or funnel-shaped,
the blooms have short perianth tubes. The
small, smooth fruits contain black seeds.

With age forming clusters of grayish-
green, sometimes brown-tinged, plant
bodies each 2 to 4 inches tall and one-half
as wide, *P. aselliformis* has its tubercles in
spirals. The flowers, about 1¼ inch in diameter, are surrounded by woolly hairs.
They are rosy-purple with the outer of the
four rows of the pointed perianth segments (petals) often whitish and the inner
ones strap-shaped and toothed. The stamens and style are white, the stigma is
greenish-yellow. The fruits are soft and located among the tubercles. Differing in
having solitary rather than clustered plant
bodies, *P. pseudopectinata* is slightly bigger than *P. aselliformis*, although it may not
appear so because often much of its plant
body is buried. Its pink to rosy-purple
flowers have very pointed petals. The
plant some authorities recognize as *P. strobiliformis* is treated in this Encyclopedia as

Pelecyphora aselliformis

Encephalocarpus strobiliformis, the one called
P. pectinata as *Solisia pectinata*, and the one
grown as *P. valdeziana* as *Thelocactus valde-
zianus*.

**Garden and Landscape Uses and Culti-
vation.** These are very slow-growing
plants suitable for the same purposes and
needing the same conditions and care as
most other small cactuses. They come
readily from seed, but are often grafted on
more vigorous understocks to induce
faster growth. For more information see
Cactuses.

PELEXIA (Pel-éxia). As ornamental flowering plants the forty species of *Pelexia*, of
the orchid family ORCHIDACEAE, have little
to recommend them, but the foliage of
some is decidedly decorative. They are natives of Mexico, Central America, the West
Indies, and warmer parts of South America. The name, from the Greek *pelex*, a hel-
met, refers to the hooded dorsal sepal.

Pelexias are allied to *Stenorrhynchos* and
grow in the ground rather than perched
on trees. Their leaves are long-stalked and
spring directly from the roots or arise from
sheaths at the bases of branchless stems.
The blooms, in dense to more open
spikes, are of moderate size. The upper or
dorsal sepal is joined with the petals into
a narrow hood, the other two sepals are
linear. The lip has a spurlike blade, more
or less hidden between the spur-shaped
bases of the lateral sepals. Their column is
short. When out of bloom pelexias scarcely
resemble the conventional idea of orchids,
they look more like tropical members of
the arum family (ARACEAE).

Pelexia maculata

Native to the West Indies, *P. maculata*
forms clumps of broad-elliptic, leathery,
fleshy leaves 9 inches or so long and with
channeled stalks. Above they are lustrous
olive-green spotted with creamy-white
faintly tinted with pink. Their undersides
are dark purplish. Erect and purple-
stalked, the flower spikes have small,
greenish, pink-tipped blooms with whitish
lips.

Garden Uses and Cultivation. In the
main these orchids interest only collectors
of the unusual. As a foliage plant the species described has moderate appeal, its
blooms are not of decorative significance.
The cultural needs of the group consist of
porous soil containing abundant organic
matter, well-drained, always moderately
moist, but not overwet, and humid green-

house conditions with shade from strong sun, and a minimum night temperature in winter of 55 to 60°F. Propagation is by division at the beginning of the growing season. For additional information see Orchids.

PELICAN FLOWER is *Aristolochia grandiflora* and *Peliosanthes graminea.*

PELIOSANTHES (Pelios-ánthes) — Pelican Flower. Fifteen species of tropical Asia and Indonesia constitute *Peliosanthes,* of the lily family LILIACEAE. The name comes from the Greek *pelios,* livid, and *anthos,* a flower.

Rhizomatous, evergreen, herbaceous perennials with all-basal, elliptic leaves, peliosanthes have spikes or racemes of flowers with six tepals, six stamens, and one style. The fruits are capsules.

Native to India, *P. graminae* has linear leaves ¼- to 1-inch-wide, pale green flowers, and blue fruits. An excellent groundcover, it thrives in the tropics in ordinary soil in part shade. Propagation is by division and seed.

PELLAEA (Pel-làea) — Cliff-Brake. Cliff-brake is the common name of this genus of eighty species of ferns of the pteris family PTERIDACEAE. Its appropriateness stems from their proclivity for growing among or on rocks. The botanical name refers to the dark color of the leafstalks of many kinds. It derives from the Greek *pellaios,* dusky. The genus is widely distributed in the wild, most abundantly as to species in South America and South Africa. The plant formerly named *Pellaea densa* is *Aspidotis densa.*

Cliff-brakes, mostly small and tufted, are sometimes medium in size. They have once-, twice-, or thrice-pinnate, glossy-stalked, leathery fronds (leaves), usually all similar. More rarely the spore-bearing fronds have narrower leaflets or segments than the sterile ones. The round or oblong clusters of spore capsules are usually so close together that they form a continuous line along the margins of the frond segments and are covered by the slightly or much turned-under edges of the segments.

Hardy, and native from Vermont to British Columbia, Arizona, and Guatemala, and generally inhabiting limestone cliffs, *P. atropurpurea* has fronds with dark purple to black, hairy stalks, and long-triangular, one- to three-times-pinnate blades, up to 10 inches long by two-thirds as wide, with wide-spreading primary divisions and lanceolate to linear-oblong, sometimes lobed segments. Closely allied *P. glabella* (syn. *P. atropurpurea bushii*) has more rigid fronds with hairless or nearly hairless stalks and the margins of the fertile segments more definitely turned under to hide the clusters of spore capsules. It occurs usually on dry limestone cliffs from Vermont to British Columbia and Arizona. Its fronds have linear to broad-lanceolate, once- or twice-pinnate or deeply-pinnately-lobed blades up to 9 inches long, with oblong to linear-ovate, usually lobed or eared segments, the basal ones usually stalked. Variety *P. g. occidentalis* (syn. *P. occidentalis*) has smaller, once-pinnate, less-deeply-lobed fronds than the typical species. Resembling *P. glabella* in aspect, *P. breweri* has thicker rhizomes with generally stalkless basal segments. It is native from Utah to Washington and California.

Several nonhardy pellaeas are cultivated outdoors in warm regions and in greenhouses. One is the popular button fern (*P. rotundifolia*), a native of New Zealand,

Pellaea rotundifolia

Australia, and Norfolk Island. In the wild this most commonly inhabits dry, but sometimes moist woodlands. It has thin, wiry rhizomes and narrow, pinnate, lustrous, dark green fronds 6 inches to 1 foot or more in length. The segments (leaflets), alternate on either side of the midrib, are nearly round and up to ¾ inch in diameter. Differing from the last chiefly in its thicker rhizomes and its leaf segments

Pellaea falcata

being longer and proportionately narrower, *P. falcata* enjoys a wider natural range. It occurs, usually in dryish, stony, shady places in New Zealand, Australia, India, and Malaya. The slightly sickle-shaped leaflets are up to 2 inches long by up to one-third as broad. Native to the West Indies, *P. viridis* has fronds 1½ to 2½ feet in length, with shining black stalks and broadly-ovate, twice-pinnate blades. The segments of the barren fronds are more conspicuously and blunter-

Pellaea viridis

Pellaea viridis macrophylla

toothed than those of spore-producing fronds. This has been cultivated as *P. hastata.* Variety *P. v. macrophylla,* in gardens often misnamed *Pteris adiantoides,* has leaves with much larger and broader, but fewer segments than those of the species. Although its fronds are less leathery, young ones, which are only once-pinnate, have much the appearance of those of the holly fern (*Cyrtomium falcatum*). African *P. calomelanos* forms tufts of wiry-stalked, broadly-triangular, twice-pinnate fronds 1 foot to 1½ feet long. Their ultimate segments, up to ¾ inch long, are more or less triangular and shallowly scalloped or shaped with the leaf stalk joining the blade some distance from the margin and without an opening existing between the top of the leafstalk and edge of the leaf). It is this characteristic that distinguishes *Peltiphyllum* from *Saxifraga*.

The umbrella plant (**P. peltatum**), and here it should be noted that this common

Peltiphyllum peltatum

name is also used for the entirely unrelated *Cyperus alternifolius*, is stemless. A deciduous herbaceous perennial, from a fleshy horizontal rhizome it sends up from toward the ends of the rhizomes long-stalked, nearly round leaves, depressed at their centers and 1 foot to 2 feet across. They have five to fifteen lobes, are mostly hairless, and may be lifted on their hairy stalks to a height of 3 feet or even more. The flowers come before the leaves. They are ½ to ¾ inch across, pinkish or white, and many together in terminal panicled clusters carried in stout, pinkish-brown, hairy stalks, considerably shorter than the leaves eventually become. Each flower has five sepals, five petals, ten stamens, and red styles. The fruits are follicles. Variety *P. p. nanum* is 1 foot to 1¼ feet tall and has leaves with blades 6 to 9 inches in diameter.

Peltiphyllum peltatum nanum

Peltiphyllum peltatum (flowers)

Garden Uses. Unlike many western American plants, this thrives in the east. Perfectly hardy in the vicinity of New York City and perhaps farther north, it is best adapted for wet spots at watersides and bog gardens. If the area is large enough, a clump set beside a stream in a rock garden is appropriate. In spring its flowers attract attention and later its leaves. The latter are of a scale that contrasts sharply with the lesser foliage of most rock garden plants. The contrast can be pleasing. Even the purist rock gardener dedicated to the belief that none but mountain plants should inhabit his domain does not violate his creed by admitting *Peltiphyllum*.

Cultivation. No particular heartbreaks attend the cultivation of this plant. It is grateful for a deepish soil that contains a decent proportion of such organic matter as compost, leaf mold, peat moss, or old and well-rotted manure and that is never less than comfortingly damp. Propagation can be achieved by division in spring and by seeds sown as soon as they are ripe in soil always kept moist.

PELTOBOYKINIA (Pelto-boykínia). This segregate from *Boykinia* consists of two rare endemic natives of mountain woods in Japan, members of the saxifrage family SAXIFRAGACEAE. The separation is based on the flowers of the present genus having ten as opposed to five stamens. Also, the leaves of *Peltoboykinia* are peltate, that is the leafstalk is affixed to the blade some distance in from the margin. The latter characteristic gives reason for the name, derived from the Greek *pelte*, a shield, and the name of the related genus.

Peltoboykinias are hardy, deciduous, herbaceous perennials with creeping rhizomes. Chiefly basal and long-stalked, the large leaves are lobed in hand-fashion (palmately). The little flowers, in terminal, branched clusters, have shallowly-bell-shaped, five-lobed calyxes and five, toothed, creamy-white, glandular-dotted petals at least twice as long as the sepals. There are two separate styles. The fruits are capsules containing minute seeds.

Sometimes cultivated *P. tellimoides* (syn. *Boykinia tellimoides*) has short, thick rhizomes, stems 1 foot to 2 feet tall, one or two nearly round, basal leaves with seven to thirteen shallow, triangular-ovate, broader-than-long, toothed lobes, and two or three smaller, short-stalked to nearly

Peltoboykinia tellimoides

stalkless stem leaves. The flowers, in clusters of several, have petals about ⅓ inch long. Closely similar **P. watanabei** differs in the eight to ten longer-pointed lobes reaching to below the middle of the leaves. They are narrowly-wedge-shaped-ovate and two or three times as long as wide.

Garden and Landscape Uses and Cultivation. Peltoboykinias are suitable for damp soils containing an abundance of organic matter in woodlands and other lightly shaded places. They are increased by seed and by division.

PELTOPHORUM (Peltóph-orum)—Yellow-Caesalpinia, Yellow-Poinciana or Yellow-Flamboyant. Among the numerous genera of the pea family LEGUMINOSAE are many trees with ornamental flowers. Here belong species of *Peltophorum*, a genus native to the Old and the New World tropics that differs from *Poinciana* and *Caesalpinia* in technical details of its flower structure. All these genera belong in the subsection *Caesalpinoideae* of the LEGUMINOSAE, a group characterized by having blooms with spreading, nearly equal-sized petals rather than the pea-shaped ones typical of nearly all LEGUMINOSAE natives in temperate regions. There are about fifteen species of *Peltophorum*. The generic name, from the Greek *pelte*, a shield, and *phoreo*, to bear, alludes to the shape of the stigma.

Peltophorums have panicles of yellow flowers, each with five sepals and petals; ten, separate, down-curved stamens, pubescent at the bottoms of their stalks; and one style. Their fruits are flattish pods with narrowly-winged edges. They remain on the trees for a long time. Not the least attractive feature is the abundant foliage consisting of finely-twice-pinnate leaves divided into numerous small leaflets.

The yellow-poinciana or yellow-flamboyant (**P. pterocarpum** syns. *P. inerme*, *P. ferrugineum*), native from Malaya to Australia, must not be confused with *Poinciana*

Peltophorum pterocarpum, Hope Gardens, Jamaica, West Indies

or with the flamboyant (*Delonix regia*). One of the most glorious shade and ornamental trees of the tropics, it is in some places much used as a street tree. Up to 50 feet or more in height, it has a broad head of spreading branches and evergreen, lacy foliage. Its young shoots leaf midribs, and branches of the flower panicles are densely clothed with reddish-brown hairs. The leaves are 1 foot to 2 feet long and have even-sized, ¾-inch-long leaflets strung in opposite pairs along their secondary ribs, ten to twenty pairs to each major division of the leaf. The orange-yellow flowers, 1 inch to 1½ inches in diameter and with the odor of grapes, are attractive to bees. They are in erect panicles 10 inches to 1½ feet long. Their petals have a stripe of brown hairs on their outsides. The conspicuous, broad, flat, blunt-ended, oblong seed pods, at first light mahogany, turn dark reddish-brown as they age. They are 2½ to 4 inches long and contain one to four seeds. In many places this sort blooms twice a year.

Other species, less commonly cultivated, include these: **P. brasiliense**, of Jamaica, 35 to 45 feet tall, has leaves with six to eight pairs of elliptic leaflets 1 inch to 2 inches long, and solitary or clustered racemes of flowers. **P. dasyrachis**, of southeastern Asia and Sumatra, much resembles *P. pterocarpum*, but has shorter panicles of bloom. **P. dubium**, of Brazil, which also has much the aspect of *P. pterocarpum*, has leaves with twenty to thirty pairs of leaflets to each major division of its leaves.

Garden and Landscape Uses and Cultivation. In the humid tropics and subtropics peltophoras have much to recommend them for use on home grounds and parks and as street trees, although they are reported not to be very resistant to storm damage. They grow rapidly in a variety of soils and are easily raised from seed.

PELTOSTIGMA (Pelto-stigma). The rue family RUTACEAE includes *Peltostigma*, a genus of three species of trees of the West Indies. One is occasionally cultivated for ornament in the tropics and warm subtropics. In allusion to the form of the stigma, the name is derived from the Greek *pelte*, a shield, and *stigma*, an organ of a flower.

Native to Jamaica, **P. pteliodes** is evergreen and generally not over 25 feet in height. When crushed, its parts exude a balsamic odor. Its alternate, stalked, translucent-gland-dotted leaves have three elliptic, lanceolate, or oblanceolate leaflets; the center one, the biggest, is 2 to 4½ inches long. The creamy-white, sweetly fragrant flowers, 1¼ to 2 inches in diameter, are cupped, downy on their outsides, and in forked, long-stalked clusters from the leaf axils. They have four or rarely three sepals, the inner pair petal-like, four

Peltostigma ptelioides (leaves and flower)

Peltostigma ptelioides with fruits

petals, and many stamens. Almost stalkless, the stigma is large and eight-lobed. The symmetrical, star-shaped fruits are composed of six to ten podlike parts about ¾ inch long that spread like the spokes of a wheel. Each contains two seeds or, rarely, one seed.

Garden and Landscape Uses and Cultivation. Not much known horticulturally, this is sometimes planted as a general-purpose shrub or tree in the tropics and near tropics. It succeeds under ordinary conditions, in sun or part-day shade, and is easily increased by seed and cuttings.

PENCIL-CEDAR is *Juniperus virginiana*. The Himalayan pencil-cedar is *Juniperus macrocarpa*.

PENIOCEREUS (Penio-cèreus). The genus *Peniocereus* consists of seven species of cactuses with quite enormous, turnip- or beetlike tuberous roots and thin, climbing, clambering, or prostrate stems. It belongs in the cactus family CACTACEAE and is endemic to the southwestern United States and Mexico. The name is from the Greek *pene*, thread, and the name of the genus *Cereus*, of the same family.

The sparingly-branched stems of peniocereuses are usually four- or five-angled, less often three-angled. Somewhat wavy-edged, their ribs have areoles (potential spine-producing cushions) with comparatively few spines. The flowers, red-tinged on their outsides, are predominantly white. Very fragrant, and opening only at night, they are large, funnel-shaped, and have long, slender perianth tubes and spreading or recurved perianth segments (petals). The stamens protrude a little from the throats of the blooms. The bright scarlet fruits, ovoid, fleshy, and edible, have clusters of easily removed, small spines.

Called deerhorn cactus or desert night-blooming-cereus **P. greggii** (syn. *Cereus greggii*) has a tuber ordinarily 6 to 8 inches long by 2 to 3½ inches wide, but specimens with tubers 2 feet in diameter, weighing 60 to 125 pounds are recorded. There are one to several tubercled stems from 1 foot to 9 feet tall and ¾ to 1 inch wide. When young they are downy. The blackish, thick-based, small spines are in clusters of seven to eleven, of which one or two are centrals, the others radial spines. The solitary, slender-tubed blooms are 6 to 8 inches long and about 3 inches wide. The fruits contain dull seeds. This native of Arizona and Mexico grows among shrubs and under trees. From it, **P. johnstonii**, of Baja California, differs chiefly in its young shoots not being downy, its flowers being somewhat smaller, and its seeds shining.

Garden Uses and Cultivation. Among the most lovely of night-blooming cactuses, peniocereuses are not considered easy to grow in regions where they are not native. This is especially true of specimens on their own roots. Better results are had by grafting them onto vigorous understocks. At all times great care must be taken not to give too much water. Plants for keen collectors of succulents, peniocereuses may be grown outdoors in warm desert and semidesert regions and in greenhouses. For additional information see Cactuses.

PENNANTIA (Pen-nántia). Belonging to the icacina family ICACINACEAE, this genus of four New Zealand, Australian, and Norfolk Island species is represented in cultivation by *Pennantia corymbosa*. The name honors a Welsh naturalist, Thomas Pennant, who died in 1798.

This genus consists of shrubs or trees with alternate leaves. Individuals may be unisexual or have both unisexual and bisexual blooms. The flowers have five each sepals, petals, and stamens and are in terminal panicles. They are succeeded by small, fleshy fruits containing a three-angled stone.

Like many New Zealand woody plants, *P. corymbosa,* when young, differs markedly in appearance from mature specimens, so much so that juvenile and adult plants may appear to be different species. The juvenile stage has slender interlacing branches and leaves rarely over ½ inch in length. On mature trees, which are 20 to 30 or sometimes 40 feet tall, the leaves are 2 to 4 inches long. If an adult plant is cut back or injured it is likely to produce juvenile growth. The tiny flowers of *P. corymbosa*, waxy, white, fragrant, and produced in profusion, are on white-hairy stalks. The fleshy fruits are black.

Garden and Landscape Uses and Cultivation. This tree is worth planting for variety. It succeeds in mild climates in ordinary soils and is propagated by seed and cuttings.

PENNISETUM (Penni-sètum) — Fountain Grass, Feathertop. Consisting of about 120 species, native in many warm parts of the world, *Pennisetum* belongs in the grass family GRAMINEAE. Its name, derived from the Greek *penna*, a feather, and *seta*, a bristle, refers to the bristly flower panicles. One species, known as pearl-, African-, or Indian-millet (*P. americanum* syn. *P. glaucum*) is cultivated in many varieties in warm countries for forage and for its edible grains (seeds). Others also supply fodder. One, the kikuyu grass (*P. clandestinum*), a native of Africa, is used as a lawn grass in the tropics. In parts of California it is a pestiferous weed.

Pennisetums are tufted perennials and annuals with stolons or rhizomes. They have slender to stout stems, and usually flat leaf blades. Mostly cylindrical, their spikelike panicles consist of narrow, stalkless or nearly stalkless spikelets, solitary or in clusters of two to five. Each spikelet has two flowers, the lower infertile or male, the upper bisexual and surrounded by a collar of generally many, fine, hairlike bristles that are often feathered with short hairs. The bristles add much to the decorative effect of the flower spikes. They fall with the spikelets. The bracts that accompany the flowers are without awns (bristles).

Fountain grass (*P. setaceum* syns. *P. ruppelii*, *P. ruppelianum*) is a popular and exceedingly graceful ornamental. A native perennial of tropical Africa, southwest Asia, and Arabia, and naturalized in California, it is frequently cultivated as an annual. It forms clumps of slender, arching and erect stems, 2 to 4 feet tall, and has very narrow, pointed, flat or rolled, leaf blades 1 foot to 2 feet long. Its slightly curving to erect flower spikes are solitary and terminal. Green, coppery-colored,

Pennisetum setaceum

rose-pink, or purplish, they are up to 1 foot long or longer by 1 inch to 1½ inches wide. Their numerous straight bristles, up to 1¾ inches long, with their lower parts thickly feathered with silky hairs, are largely responsible for the elegance of the spikes. The lanceolate spikelets are in clusters of two or three. Variety *P. s. atrosanguineum* has dark reddish-purple foliage, and deep purplish-crimson flower spikes.

Feathertop (*P. villosum* syn. *P. longistylum*) is another perennial that behaves

Pennisetum villosum

satisfactorily when treated as an annual. A native of mountains in East Africa, and naturalized in North America, it is loosely tufted and 1 foot to 2 feet tall. It has folded or flat leaf blades up to ¼ inch wide by up to 6 inches long. Topping each stem is a nodding or erect, broadly-cylindrical to nearly spherical, brownish or purplish, dense flower spike 1 inch to 4½ inches long and up to 2 inches broad. The spikes are decorated with numerous spreading bristles up to 3 inches long, their lower parts are feathery with loose hairs. The spikelets are pointed-lanceolate.

South American **P. latifolium** is a perennial 4 to 9 feet tall. It has thick rhizomes and stout stems, densely-hairy at the joints, and branched toward their tops. The pointed-lanceolate leaf blades are up to 2 inches broad and 1 foot to 2½ feet long. The dense, nodding, greenish flower spikes, at the ends of the stems and branches, have solitary, lanceolate spikelets, with rough but not hairy bristles. The spikes are 2 to 4 inches long.

Native from eastern Asia to Australia, *P. alopecuroides* (syn. *P. japonicum*) forms crowded clusters of slender stems 2 to 5

Pennisetum alopecuroides

feet tall. It has pointed leaves up to ¼ inch wide by 1 foot to 2 feet long. The solitary, silvery-yellowish, greenish, or purple panicles, 2 to 8 inches long and up to 2 inches wide, are cylindrical. They terminate the stems and are of feathery appearance because of their spreading rough but not hairy bristles up to 1¼ inches long. The pointed-lanceolate spikelets are solitary or in twos. This sort is a perennial.

South Africa is home to *P. macrourum*, a perennial with clusters of slender to quite stout stems 3 to 6 feet tall and mostly basal foliage. Its rolled or sometimes flat leaf blades, ½ inch to considerably less wide, are up to 2 feet long and very slender-pointed. The cylindrical flower panicles, erect or leaning, are up to 1 foot long by ¾ inch through and brownish or purplish. They have many rough but not hairy bristles that may be ½ inch long or slightly longer and solitary, pointed-lanceolate spikelets.

Some annual pennisetums are worth cultivating for ornament. Here belong *P. pedicellatum* and *P. polystachyon*. The former is indigenous from North Africa to India, the latter in tropical America, Africa and India. Erect, and with slender to stout branching stems 1 foot to 3 feet tall, *P. pedicellatum* has pointed, flat leaf blades up to 10 inches long and ¼ to ¾ inch wide. Nodding or upright, the crowded to rather loose, slender, cylindrical panicles, whitish, tannish, to purplish or reddish,

and 2 to 6 inches in length, are very bristly, with the bristles up to 1 inch long and their lower parts furnished with silky hairs. In clusters of two to five, or solitary, the spikelets are lanceolate and without stalks. The spikelets of *P. polystachyon* are solitary and stalkless. This kind attains a height up to 6 feet, but is often lower; it has branched stems, leaf blades up to 1½ feet long, and orange-brown, purplish, or reddish, crowded, cylindrical flower panicles up to 6 inches long and nodding or upright. The lower parts of the bristles, the longest of which are up to 1¼ inches long, are silky-hairy.

Garden and Landscape Uses. The pennisetums described here are attractive ornamentals suitable for flower beds and borders and less formal landscapes. They supply excellent material for flower arrangers, suitable either fresh or dried. For drying it is important to gather the panicles before they reach full maturity, otherwise the spikelets are likely to shed. The perennials are generally not hardy in the north, but some can be grown as annuals and all respond if lifted in fall and wintered in a cool greenhouse, cellar, garage, or similar place. Pennisetums succeed in ordinary garden soil in sun.

Cultivation. Seeds of the annuals and perennials to be grown as annuals are sown in early spring where the plants are to remain, and the seedlings are thinned to allow sufficient space without harmful overcrowding. The perennials may be raised from seed or by division in early fall or spring. Although fountain grass and feathertop can be grown as annuals, superior results are had where they are not hardy by lifting plants each fall and wintering them in a cool place where they are not subjected to hard freezing (a light freeze is not harmful), and in late winter cutting back the foliage, dividing the clumps into small pieces, trimming their roots, and potting them in 4-inch pots. These starts are grown in a cool greenhouse until all danger from frost is over, then they are planted in the garden.

PENNY-CRESS. See Thlaspi.

PENNYROYAL. Two different plants are known by this name. The classic pennyroyal, of Europe, is a mint, *Mentha pulegium*. American-pennyroyal is botanically related *Hedeoma pulegioides*. They are described under Mentha, and Hedeoma. Both are appropriate for herb gardens. Their leaves and tops can be used in ways similar to mint in beverages and for garnishing, and fresh or dried they may be employed in cooking, although their flavors are too pronounced for most modern tastes.

European pennyroyal is perennial. It thrives with little care, under conditions that suit mint, in ordinary, fairly moist soil

in sun or part-day shade. It is readily increased by division in spring or early fall, or seeds may be used. Plants may be set about 6 inches apart. American-pennyroyal is an unprepossessing annual, an inhabitant of dry and moist upland woods. It is easily grown from seeds sown in spring, where the plants are to remain, in a lightly shaded or open place. Thin the seedlings sufficiently to prevent overcrowding.

PENNYWORT. This common name is applied to *Hydrocotyle* and *Umbilicus rupestris*.

PENSTEMON (Pen-stèmon) — Beard Tongue. Almost exclusively of North American provenance (one of the about 250 species is native in Central America and one occurs in northeastern Asia), *Penstemon* belongs in the figwort family SCROPHULARIACEAE. Its name, sometimes incorrectly spelled *Pentstemon*, derives from the Greek *pente*, five, and *stemon*, a stamen. It alludes to the flowers having five stamens, counting the one staminode as such.

Penstemons are herbaceous perennials, subshrubs, and small shrubs, many of considerable ornamental value. They have deciduous or evergreen leaves, the lower ones stalked, those above often stalkless, opposite or in whorls (circles of three or more). In terminal racemes or panicles or rarely solitary, the prevailingly showy flowers have a five-parted calyx, a tubular to bell-shaped corolla with a two-lobed upper lip and a three-lobed lower one, four fertile stamens, and one bearded or beardless staminode (nonfunctional stamen). The slender style is terminated by a knoblike stigma. The fruits are capsules.

Botanically this superb group is generally easy to recognize as to genus, but often puzzling to identify more precisely, this because differences between species are often based on small, sometimes recondite technical characters. Most kinds are of medium height to tall, but some are low and mat-forming or tufted. The majority have flowers in the blue-purple, blue, or lilac-blue range, but a few have whitish or yellowish and a few distinctly yellow blooms. In a not inconsiderable number of sorts the flowers are scarlet, crimson, or of similar hue.

Penstemons occur natively in a wide range of habitats. A few inhabit woodlands and meadows in the eastern and midwestern parts of North America, but the vast majority occur in the region from somewhat east of the Rocky Mountains, westward and southwestward. Their habitats range from cool, moist, mountain ones at alpine or lower altitudes to woodlands and dry, hot plains, semideserts, and deserts.

Except for the production of the *P. gloxinioides* hybrids, plant breeders have paid little attention to *Penstemon*, yet the genus appears to promise marvelous opportunity for experiment with the objective of raising superior garden plants. With such a large number of possible parental species procurable from such diverse natural habitats, it is not difficult to envisage hybrids developed from which selections could be made for gardens in most regions, sorts suitable for beds and borders and cut flowers and perhaps a few for rock gardens, although in the main the latter are better served by natural species than man-made hybrids.

Red-flowered species, all natives of western North America or Mexico include these: *P. barbatus* (syn. *Chelone barbata*), one of the most frequently cultivated species, is native from Colorado and Utah to

Penstemon barbatus

Mexico. From 3 to 6 feet tall and hairless, it has lanceolate to linear, toothless leaves and panicles of loosely arranged, bright red, tubular to funnel-shaped flowers 1 inch long or slightly longer, strongly two-lipped with the upper lip much longer than the bearded lower one. The staminode is hairless. From the typical species, *P. b. torreyi* differs in having somewhat bigger flowers, essentially beardless in their throats. *P. bridgesii*, of Colorado to Arizona and California, is subshrubby and 1 foot to 3 feet high. Hairless or sparingly-short-hairy, it has spatula-shaped to linear-oblanceolate or elliptic, toothless leaves, 1 inch to 3 inches long, and rather narrow, somewhat one-sided, glandular-pubescent panicles of scarlet to vermilion, strongly two-lipped flowers 1 inch to 1¼ inches long. The staminode is hairless. *P. centranthifolius*, commonly called scarlet bugler, which inhabits dry soils in Arizona and California, has few to several wand-like stems 1 foot to 4 feet tall and thick, glaucous, spatula-shaped to ovate-lanceolate or lanceolate, toothless, 1½ to 2½-inch-long leaves, the uppermost stalkless and stem-clasping. The narrow flowers, in wandlike spires accounting for the upper

halves of the stems, have scarlet corollas 1 inch to 1¼ inches long with short, scarcely-spreading lobes (petals). The staminode is hairless. *P. clevelandii*, native in southern California and Baja California, 1 foot to 3 feet tall, has green or somewhat glaucous, toothless or toothed, ovate to heart-shaped or triangular-lanceolate, rigid leaves, the lower ones stalked. The crimson to red-purple flowers in narrow, raceme-like panicles up to 1 foot long are ¾ to 1 inch long. Their staminodes are almost or quite hairless. *P. cordifolius*, of coastal southern California, is not hardy in the north. An evergreen shrub, it has loosely disposed, arching to semiclimbing stems up to 10 feet long. Its short-stalked, fuchsia-like, ovate leaves ½ inch to 1¾ inches in length are coarsely-toothed. In dense, glandular-hairy panicles at the shoot ends, the orange-scarlet to scarlet flowers have straight corolla tubes 1 inch to 1½ inches long and densely-hairy staminodes. *P. corymbosus*, a tufted, subshrubby Californian 1 foot to 1½ feet tall and hairless to grayish-hairy, has toothless or remotely-toothed, elliptic leaves ½ inch to 1½ inches long. Its brick-red blooms, in short, often many-flowered, glandular-hairy clusters at the stem ends, have yellow, densely-bearded staminodes. *P. eatonii*, of Utah and Colorado to California, and 1 foot to 3 feet tall, has hairless sometimes slightly-glaucous, oblanceolate to lanceolate-oblong or broad-elliptic leaves with blades up to 4 inches long, the upper ones stalkless. The tubular, not prominently two-lipped flowers, in slender, one-sided, raceme-like panicles occupy the upper halves of the plants height. About 1 inch long and scarlet, they have beardless or more or less hairy staminodes. *P. hartwegii*, of Mexico, is erect and 2 to 3 feet tall, with lanceolate to ovate-lanceolate, pointed, toothless leaves, the upper ones stem-clasping. About 2 inches long and more or less drooping, the scarlet to crimson tubular-funnel-shaped flowers have spreading perianth lobes. This is a parent of the hybrid *P. gloxinioides*. *P. isophyllus* is a minutely-hairy Mexican, 2 to 6 feet tall, with numerous elliptic to lanceolate, toothless leaves 1 inch to 2½ inches long and loose raceme-like panicles of coral-red to scarlet-crimson flowers 1½ inches to 2 inches in length, whitish lined with red on their insides, hairy in their throats. The staminodes are hairless. *P. labrosus*, of California and Baja California, a close ally of *P. barbatus*, is few-stemmed, 3 to 6 feet tall, and hairless. It has linear to oblanceolate leaves up to 4½ inches long, the upper ones much reduced in size. The scarlet flowers about 1½ inches in length are in slender, somewhat one-sided panicles. Their staminodes are hairless. *P. murrayanus*, of Arkansas and Texas, 2 to 3 feet in height, is hairless and glaucous. It has ovate to oblong leaves or the upper

Penstemon newberryi

ones, the pairs of which are united at their bases, nearly round. They are up to 4 inches long. The deep scarlet flowers, 1 inch to 1½ inches long, have hairless, hooked staminodes. *P. newberryi* (syn. *P. menziesii newberryi*), of Washington to California, is a woody-stemmed species much like *P. davidsonii*, but has proportionately longer, more pointed leaves and rosy-purple to carmine or nearly scarlet flowers about 1 inch long. Perhaps slightly more tender than *P. davidsonii*, this kind is called mountain pride. *P. puniceus*, of Arizona and Mexico, 1 foot to 6 feet tall, has thick, glaucous, oblong to obovate lower leaves up to about 5 inches long and upper ones smaller and more lanceolate with those of the pairs sometimes united at their bases. The 1-inch-long, rose-red to vermilion flowers are in panicles of many. The staminodes are hairy. *P. richardsonii*, native from Idaho to British Columbia, one of the latest penstemons to bloom, and 9 inches to 3 feet tall, has brittle stems and almost holly-like, deeply-toothed or pinnately-cleft leaves up to 3 inches long. The loosely arranged, rose-red to bright rose-lavender flowers, about 1 inch long, have slightly bearded staminodes. *P. rupicola*, of Washington to Oregon, is a pubescent, freely-branched shrublet with prostrate stems and erect branches up to 4 inches tall with ¼- to ½-inch-long, bluish-glaucous, ovate, thick, round-toothed leaves. Its abundant rose-carmine to rose-crimson or rose-purple flowers 1 inch to 1½ inches in length and bellied on their undersides are in sprays of few. They look like small red snapdragons. Their fertile stamens are longer than their usually bearded staminodes. Unfortunately this has proved difficult in eastern gardens. *P. utahensis*, of Utah, Nevada, and Arizona, is 1 foot to 2 feet tall and hairless. It has lanceolate to oblong or oblanceolate leaves up to 3 inches long embracing the stems with their bases. The ¾- to 1-inch-long flowers, attractively displayed in loose spires, have crimson or carmine corollas with slender tubes and flaring petals. The staminodes are usually beardless.

Yellow-, white-, and pink-flowered sorts native to western North America include these: *P. albidus*, widely distributed through the prairies and plains from Minnesota to Texas and New Mexico, is about 1 foot tall. Its lanceolate to oblong, toothed or toothless leaves, which are rough to the touch, are up to about 2½ inches long. The stalks of the flowering parts are downy and glandular-pubescent. Approximately ¾ inch long, the white flowers are occasionally tinged with lilac. Their staminodes are slightly bearded. This is usually short-lived. *P. ambiguus*, native from Colorado to Arizona, and Mexico, is bushy and 9 inches to 1½ feet tall, and in habit of growth and leafage, it suggests a fine-foliaged *Linum*. It has freely-branched stems and slender, linear to linear-oblong leaves up to 2½ inches long. The phloxlike flowers have corollas with very slender tubes and nearly symmetrical faces of spreading petals. About ½ inch long, they are delicate to bright pink and often purplish on their outsides. The staminodes are beardless. *P. antirrhinoides*, of southern California and Baja California, is an evergreen shrub 2 to 7 feet tall. It has stems, with many spreading branches, that like the foliage, are finely-hairy. Its toothless, linear to ovate-elliptic leaves are up to ¾ inch long, but usually smaller. In wide, leafy panicles, the slightly sticky, brownish-red-tinged, broad, bright yellow flowers are ½ to ¾ inch long. Their protruding staminodes are densely-clothed with yellow hairs. *P. confertus*, of Alberta to Idaho and Washington, is 9 inches to 2 feet tall. It has oblong to linear, hairless leaves, up to 2 inches long, and narrow, erect spires of ½-inch-long yellow flowers each with a dense tuft of brown hairs on its lower lip. The staminodes are bearded. *P. deustus* is native from Wyoming to British Columbia and California. Woody-stemmed and much-branched below, it forms hairless or sparsely-short-glandular-hairy, often sprawling clumps 8 inches to 2 feet tall. Its pointed, coarsely-toothed, ovate to oblong-lanceolate leaves are ½ inch to 1¼ inches long. The spires of bloom are of ½-inch-long, yellowish flowers with purplish lines in their throats. They come from the axils of the upper leaves. Their staminodes are hairless or have short beards. *P. grinnellii*, of California and southern Oregon, 1½ to 3 feet tall, is much like *P. palmeri*, but has usually bright green, hairless, coarsely-toothed, broadly-lanceolate leaves up to about 3½ inches long. Its pink-flushed, cream-colored, broadly-bell-shaped flowers, 1 inch long or longer are in ample panicles. They have densely-bearded staminodes.

Blue, purple, lilac, lavender, and similar flower colors, those of *P. attenuatus* sometimes varying to yellow, are characteristic of these chiefly western species: *P. acaulis*, a native of a very limited area in Montana, Wyoming, and Utah and an enchanting miniature without obvious stems, forms dense tufts 1 inch to 2 inches tall of crowded linear leaves up to ¾ inch long. The bright blue flowers with yellow-hairy throats are stalkless and nearly ½ inch across. The staminodes are bearded with golden-brown hairs. *P. acuminatus*, native from Nevada to Washington, Idaho, and Oregon, 9 inches to 1½ feet tall and hairless, has thick, bluish-green, toothless, ovate to heart-shaped leaves up to 3 inches long, the upper ones encircling the stems and sometimes nearly round. The light blue-purple flowers, about ¾ inch long and with bearded staminodes, are in several to many tiers. This is usually short-lived. *P. alpinus* is false to its name because it rarely occurs above tree level and prefers lower mountain elevations. Resembling *P. glaber* from which it differs in technical details of the calyxes of its flowers, this handsome sort, 4 inches to 2½ feet tall, tends unfortunately to be short-lived. It has lanceolate to ovate leaves 3 to 4 inches long, some with stem-clasping bases, and spikelike panicles of broad-funnel-shaped, 1- to 1½-inch-long, blue to purple-blue flowers, bellied on their undersides and with a few white hairs within. The staminodes are hairless. *P. anguineus* (syn. *P. rattanii minor*), native from Oregon to California, is 1½ to 2½ feet tall. It has elliptic to ovate basal leaves and oblongish to triangular-ovate or heart-shaped higher ones with bases that clasp the stems. About ¾ inch in length, and in long, erect, interrupted spires, the flowers have corollas with reddish-violet to purple tubes and violet to purple-blue lobes (petals). The hairless or sparingly-hairy staminode protrudes. *P. angustifolius* is a very attractive, but commonly short-lived native from South Dakota to Montana and New Mexico. From 9 inches to 1½ feet tall, hairless and glaucous, it has pointed, linear to linear-lanceolate leaves up to 2½ inches long and generous columns of ½- to ¾-inch-long, fine blue flowers. The staminodes are bearded. *P. attenuatus*, ranging from Montana to Washington, Wyoming, and Idaho and of the *P. procerus* relationship, 1 foot to 2 feet tall, is hairless except in the flowering parts. The leaves, spatula-shaped to pointed-lanceolate, are up to 1½ inches long. From deep blue-purple to light yellow, the ½- to ¾-inch-long flowers in several well-separated tiers have bearded staminodes. *P. azureus* (syn. *P. heterophyllus azureus*), of California, is a subshrub 8 inches to 2 feet tall or sometimes taller. It has blue-glaucous, hairless, oblanceolate to obovate or lanceolate, short-stalked to stalkless leaves ½ inch to 2 inches long. In narrow, erect panicles, the deep-blue-purple, gaping flowers are from a little under to a little over 1 inch long. The staminodes are usually hairless. Under favorable conditions this persists for three or four years, but is rarely longer-lived. *P. barrettiae*, of Oregon, about 1 foot tall and compact, has toothed or toothless, hairless, glaucous, ovate to lanceolate leaves up to about 3 inches long. The lilac to rose-purple, 1½-inch-long flowers, with much the aspect of those of *P. cardwellii*, have hairless staminodes. *P. caespitosus*, of Colorado, Wyoming, and Utah, forms broad, low tufts or mats of nearly prostrate, pubescent stems and narrow, spatula-shaped, toothless leaves up to ½ inch long. About ¼ inch long, the lavender-purple flowers are hairy in their mouths. The staminodes are bearded. *P. calycosus* inhabits open woodlands from Maine to Michigan, Alabama, and Missouri. Hairless to sometimes somewhat hairy and more or less glandular-pubescent in the flowering parts, it is up to 4 feet tall and has lanceolate to ovate-lanceolate, toothed or toothless leaves up to 6 inches long. Its violet-purple flowers, white on their insides and most often 1 inch to 1¼ inches long, have bearded staminodes. *P. campanulatus* is a beautiful Mexican, almost hairless and up to about 2 feet tall. It has toothed, lanceolate leaves 1 inch to 3 inches in length, and bell-shaped, rose-purple to violet or rarely white flowers approximately 1 inch long. The staminodes are bearded. *P. cardwellii* (syn. *P. fruticosus cardwellii*) is a loosely tufted shrubby kind 4 inches to 1 foot tall. Its toothed to almost toothless, short-stalked, thick, bluntish, evergreen leaves are elliptic and ½ inch to 1½ inches long. The flowers, in raceme-like arrangements of few, bright purple to deep blue-violet, are about 1¼ inches long and bearded on their insides and at the tips of the staminodes. More or less intermediate between *P. fruticosus* and *P. newberryi*, this is native from Oregon and Washington to Alberta. *P. cinereus*, of Oregon and California, is tufted and forms clumps 6 inches to 1½ feet high. It is allied to *P. humilis* and by some authorities is treated as a variety of that species. It has slender stems and firm, gray-hairy, toothless, lanceolate to lanceolate-ovate leaves mostly up to ¾ inch long. The flowers, in several tiers of few on glandular-pubescent stems, bright blue to blue-purple and up to ½ inch long, have staminodes clothed with short yellow hairs. *P. cobaea*, native from Nebraska to Missouri, Arkansas, and Texas, and often favoring limy soils, is 1 foot to 2 feet tall. One of the most splendid and showiest, this is finely-downy to somewhat glandular in its flowering parts. It has oblong to lanceolate, generally toothed, pointed leaves 4 to 8 inches long. The large panicles are of pale to violet or deep purple, bell-shaped blooms 1½ to 2 inches long. The staminodes are bearded. *P. comarrhenus*, of Colorado and Utah, 1¼ to 3 feet tall and nearly hairless, has broad-elliptic to oblong or spatula-shaped, toothless leaves up to 4 inches long. The 1-inch-long, light blue flowers have bearded staminodes and few to many long hairs from the tips of the stamens. This has usually a rather short life-span. **P. crandallii,** a native of mountains in Colorado and Utah, forms mounds or mats up to 6 inches high of almost prostrate or slightly ascending stems and linear-oblanceolate leaves up to ¾ inch long. About 1 inch long and light to dark purplish-blue, the flowers have bearded staminodes. Varieties with white and with pink flowers are known. **P. cyananthus** (syn. *P. glaber cyananthus*) is a pretty, generally short-lived native of Wyoming, Idaho, and Utah. From 1 foot to 2½ feet tall, it has broadly- to oblong-lanceolate or heart-shaped, hairless or hairy, toothless leaves, the lower ones stalked and up to 6 inches long. The ¾- to 1-inch-long, dark blue to blue-purple flowers are handsomely displayed in generous tiers, those toward the tops of the stems less separated than the lower ones. Their staminodes are bearded. **P. cyathophorus,** of Colorado and Wyoming, 9 inches to 2 feet tall, has spatula-shaped to nearly round, bluish-green, leathery, toothless leaves about 2½ inches long, the bases of the upper pairs meeting and overlapping around the stems. The ½-inch-long, light blue flowers are in dense, cylindrical spikes. Their staminodes are bearded. **P. davidsonii** (syn. *P. menziesii davidsonii*) is akin to *P. scouleri* and *P. newberryi*. Native at high altitudes from northern California to Washington, it forms mats about 3 inches high. It has hairless, but not glaucous, ovate to elliptic, toothless leaves about ⅓ inch long and blue-lavender to purple-violet flowers 1 inch to 1¾ inches long in racemes of one to five. The staminodes are hairy. White flowers are born by *P. d. alba.* The leaves of *P. d. menziesii* are without teeth. Variety *P. d. thompsonii* is bigger and larger in its parts than the typical species. **P. ellipticus** occurs at high altitudes from Alberta to Montana and Idaho. Forming loose mats of trailing stems, it has oblong-elliptic, toothed leaves ¾ inch to 1¼ inches long. In clus-

Penstemon eriantherus

Penstemon fruticosus crassifolius

ters of two to four pairs, the light violet flowers, about 1¼ inches long, have bearded staminodes. The stamens are hairy at their apexes. **P. eriantherus** is native from North Dakota to Washington, Nebraska, Colorado, and Oregon. From 9 inches to 1 foot tall and pubescent, this sort has oblong to linear, toothless leaves and short, compact panicles of 1-inch-long, wide-mouthed, usually lavender or pinkish- to rosy-lavender flowers lined with purple. The protruding staminodes are bearded with yellowish hairs. **P. euglaucus,** of Oregon, 6 inches to 1½ feet tall, and a close relative of *P. procerus,* has hairless, glaucous, firm foliage. Its oblong-lanceolate leaves are toothless, and up to 2½ inches long. Deep blue and about ½ inch long, the flowers, the lower lips of which are somewhat hairy, are clustered on the stems in well-separated tiers. The staminodes are bearded. **P. fruticosus,** native from Alberta to Washington, Wyoming, and Oregon, is a charming shrubby sort that forms dense clumps 4 inches to 1½ feet in height. Its lanceolate to broadly-elliptic leaves, toothed or toothless, are about 1 inch in length. The 1-inch-long, lavender-blue to purple flowers have bearded staminodes. Toothless leaves and rich rosy-lavender flowers are typical of *P. f. crassifolius.* White blooms characterize *P. f. alba,* hardy in sheltered places in southern New England. Variety *P. f. scouleri* (syn. *P. scouleri*), 6 inches to 1½ feet tall, has short-stalked, sharply-toothed, narrow-linear-lanceolate leaves ¾ inch to 1½ inches long. The lilac-purple, minutely-glandular flowers, 1½ to 2 inches long, are in racemes of five to twelve. **P. gairdneri,**

Penstemon fruticosus scouleri

Penstemon fruticosus scouleri (flowers)

a tufted, gray-hairy native of Idaho to Oregon, is 4 inches to 1 foot tall. It has linear to spatula-shaped leaves up to about 1 inch long, with their margins rolled inward, and lavender-purple flowers ½ to ¾ inch long with wide-spreading corolla lobes (petals). The staminodes are branched. **P. glaber** (syn. *P. gordonii*), native from North Dakota to Wyoming, is one of the most beautiful species, but rarely is long-lived. Hairless, slightly glau-

Penstemon davidsonii

cous, and 1 foot to 2 feet tall, this variable sort has glossy, toothless, broad, oblanceolate to lanceolate leaves up to 6 inches long. The rich blue to blue-purple flowers 1 inch to 1¼ inches long and bellied on their undersides, are in rather compact, one-sided spires that curve outward. Their staminodes are bearded only at their tips. Variety *P. g. roseus* has deep pink blooms. *P. glandulosus,* of Idaho, Washington, and Oregon, is sticky-hairy throughout. From 1½ to 3 feet in height, it has ovate to lanceolate, coarsely-toothed leaves, the largest up to 10 inches long. The rather washed-out purple to lilac flowers 1 inch to almost 2 inches long are in well-separated tiers. Their staminodes are beardless. A pink-flowered variant is more attractive than the typical species. Both are intolerant of much moisture and tend to be short-lived. *P. gracilentus,* a native of Oregon, Nevada, and California and allied to *P. procerus,* is 9 inches to 2 feet tall, and has linear to oblong-lanceolate leaves up to 4 inches long, mostly basal and long-stalked. Rather more than ½ inch long, the purplish-blue to reddish-purple flowers, hairy on the insides of their lower lips, have somewhat bearded staminodes. *P. gracilis,* widely dispersed throughout the Great Plains of North America, is 9 inches to 1½ feet tall and hairless. It has pointed, oblanceolate to linear-lanceolate, finely-toothed leaves, the largest basal ones up to 4½ inches long, most smaller. Its flattish, pale violet-blue to whitish flowers, up to nearly 1 inch long, are in loose, slender, sometimes one-sided spires with glandular-hairy stems. The staminodes have prominent yellow beards. *P. grandiflorus* is an astonishingly beautiful native of dry soils throughout much of the central United States. From 2 to 4 feet tall and completely hairless, it has broad-obovate-oblong to ovate, somewhat stem-clasping, toothless, bluish-green leaves up to 2½ inches long and 1½- to 2-inch-long, broadly-bell-shaped, bluish-lavender flowers in raceme-like spires about 8 inches long. The staminodes are minutely-hairy at their tips. *P. hallii,* a tufted high alpine 4 to 8 inches tall, is a native of Colorado and Utah. Hairless, it has linear, toothless leaves and bluish to violet-purple flowers about ¾ inch long. Their staminodes are bearded. *P. heterophyllus,* of California, is an erect, hairless shrub up to about 5 feet tall. It has stalkless or very short-stalked, pointed, lanceolate to linear leaves ¾ inch to 1¾ inches in length and long, loose panicles of mostly many dark blue, purple, or lilac flowers, 1 inch to 1¼ inches long, with beardless staminodes. Variety *P. h. purdyi,* selections of which are grown as *P.* 'Blue Bedder' and *P.* 'Blue Gem', is 6 inches to 2 feet tall. It has narrow, pointed leaves and flowers that vary in color from rosy-lavender to rich gentian-blue. *P. humilis* is a variable, tufted sort 6

inches to 1 foot tall or sometimes taller, usually finely-gray-hairy throughout. Closely related to *P. cinereus,* this differs in having wider corolla lobes (petals). Its mostly evergreen, basal leaves are oblanceolate to elliptic or ovate, stalked, and up to 4½ inches long. The stem leaves are smaller and most often stalkless. The wide-mouthed, blue-purple flowers usually in a few separate tiers, are approximately ½ inch long. Their staminodes are bearded. *P. jamesii,* of Colorado and Utah, 6 inches to 1½ feet in height, has downy, linear-lanceolate, sometimes toothed leaves up to 4 inches long. Its about 1-inch-long, bluish-violet flowers with white hairs inside are in narrow, one-sided, glandular-hairy racemes. Their staminodes are yellow-bearded. The plants are generally short-lived. *P. laetus,* of Nevada, Oregon, and California, 9 inches to 2½ feet tall, has minutely-pubescent stems and foliage. The leaves are lanceolate to linear and toothless. Tubular to bell-shaped, the wide-mouthed flowers, variable as to size, average about 1 inch in length. They are blue-lavender to blue-violet. The staminodes are beardless. *P. linarioides* is an extremely variable native of Colorado and Utah, with erect stems 6 inches to 1½ feet high. Its densely- to sparsely-hairy, linear to threadlike leaves, 1 to 3 inches long, are mostly crowded on short, sterile shoots near the base of the plant, others are on the flowering stems. Bright bluish-purple and ½ inch long or a little longer, the flowers, in one-sided slender spikes, have bearded staminodes. *P. monoensis,* a handsome Californian, is up to 1¼ feet high. It has leathery, finely-gray-pubescent, broadly-lanceolate leaves up to 2½ inches long, the lower ones stalked, those on the stems stalkless. The ¾-inch-long, rose-purple flowers are in often quite heavy spires up to 8 inches long. The staminodes are bearded. *P. montanus,* of Montana to Idaho and Wyoming, which forms loose clumps 4 to 9 inches high, has gray-hairy, sharply-toothed, ovate to elliptic leaves up to 1¾ inches long. Its pinkish-purple to blue flowers, about 1¼ inches in length, have staminodes without beards. *P. nemorosus* (syn. *Chelone nemorosa*) inhabits woodlands and moist, open places from British Columbia to California. From 1 foot to 2½ feet tall, it has thin, short-stalked, lanceolate to ovate, conspicuously toothed leaves 2 to 5 inches in length. Loosely clustered the pinkish-purple flowers, 1 inch to 1½ inches long, and strongly two-lipped with the lower lip much longer than the upper, have bearded staminodes. *P. nitidus* has a wide distribution in the mountains of western North America. Closely related to *P. acuminatus* and up to 1 foot tall, it has leathery, toothless, oblongish to ovate leaves. About ¾ inch long, its blue flowers, in erect panicles, have bearded stam-

inodes throughout its length and are hairless or somewhat hairy. *P. ovatus,* an

Penstemon nitidus

Penstemon ovatus

excellent native from Oregon to British Columbia, is 2 to 4 feet tall and more or less hairy. It has ovate, bright green, thinnish, toothed leaves, the uppermost stem-clasping, and loose, erect panicles of blue to purple flowers, about ¾ inch long, with bearded lower lips and staminodes. *P. palmeri,* one of the most splendid beard tongues, ranges in the wild from Utah to California and Arizona. From 2 to 4 feet in height, it has ovate to lanceolate, often sharply-toothed, hairless leaves, those of the uppermost pairs joined at their bases. The flowers, exceeding 1 inch in length, are very delicate pink or lilac marked on

Penstemon ovatus (flowers)

Penstemon procerus

stalked sprays the about 1-inch-long lavender blooms are bearded inside the lower lip and have slightly bearded, protruding staminodes. **P. saxorum,** of Colorado and Wyoming, closely resembles P. subglaber, but has slightly smaller flowers and is often somewhat lower. **P. secundiflorus,** of Wyoming to New Mexico, 6 inches to 1½ feet tall, is hairless and glaucous. Its somewhat fleshy, oblanceolate leaves, up to 3 inches long, are without teeth and commonly clasp the stems with their heart-shaped bases. The pinkish-lavender to lilac flowers, ¾ to 1 inch long, have spreading lips and hairy or hairless staminodes. The plants are usually short-lived. **P. serrulatus** is wild from Oregon to Alaska. A subshrub up to 2 feet tall, hairless except in its uppermost parts, this has elliptic to lanceolate or ovate leaves 2 to 3½ inches long and shallowly- to deeply-toothed. The 1-inch-long, blue to purple flowers have a yellow-bearded staminode. **P. speciosus** (syn. P. glaber speciosus), native from Washington to California and in cultivation generally short-lived, is 9 inches to 3 feet tall and hairless or very finely-gray-hairy. Typically it has several stout stems and firm, thick, toothless leaves, the basal ones stalked, spatula-shaped to oblanceolate or elliptic and up to 6 inches long, those on the stems, excepting the lowermost, smaller, more or less stalkless, and linear-lanceolate. The bright blue to purple-blue, 1- to 1½-inch-long flowers are in

rather loose tiers. Their staminodes are beardless or nearly so. **P. spectabilis** deserves its name. One of the showiest sorts of the southwestern United States and up to 4 feet tall or taller, this is hairless and glaucous. Its coarsely-toothed, ovate to ovate-lanceolate leaves, stem-clasping at their bases, are up to 4 inches long. The 1-inch-long, or longer, bluish-violet flowers are arranged in tall, loose, narrow-pyramidal panicles. Their staminodes are without hairs. **P. strictus,** a variable native from Wyoming to Colorado and Utah, is hairless and 9 inches to 2 feet tall. The leaves are linear to spatula-shaped or lanceolate, toothless, and up to 4 inches long. Deep blue to violet-blue, the 1-inch-long flowers, in slender, one-sided spikes, have staminodes naked of hairs, the stamens with long hairs at their tips. This in cultivation is usually short-lived. **P. subglaber,** native from Wyoming to Utah, from 9 inches to 3 feet high, and hairless, has oblanceolate to linear-lanceolate leaves up to 4 inches long. The 1-inch-long, deep blue to violet flowers are in narrow, wandlike panicles. Their staminodes are bearded. This tends to be short-lived. **P. teucrioides,** native from Colorado to Utah and up to 6 inches tall, has crowded, very slender, short-hairy leaves, up to ½ inch long, and inflorescences of few to many ½-inch-long, bluish-purple flowers with yellow-bearded staminodes. **P. venustus,** of Idaho to Washington and Oregon, 1 foot to 2½

the insides of their lips with purple lines. The staminodes are bearded. **P. procerus,** native from Saskatchewan to British Columbia, Colorado, and California, and highly variable, is most often 8 inches to 1¼ feet tall, rarely lower or higher. Essentially hairless, it has few or no basal rosettes of foliage. The leaves, the lower ones stalked, those above stalkless, are oblanceolate to elliptic or ovate, toothless, and up to 4 inches long. More or less down-pointed, the deep blue-purple flowers, ¼ to nearly ½ inch long, are in compact, ball-like clusters. Their insides and the ends of the staminodes are bearded. Basal rosettes of foliage are well developed in P. p. tolmiei, a beautiful dwarf variety with shorter, broader leaves than the species and sometimes with yellowish flowers. This species and its variety appreciate or at least tolerate dampish soils. **P. rattanii,** of Oregon to California, 1 foot to 2 feet tall, has hairless stems and foliage. Its basal leaves, up to 6 inches long, are stalked, lanceolate, and toothed, its stem leaves are much smaller, ovate-lanceolate, and stalkless. In glandular-pubescent-

Penstemon serrulatus

feet high, and nearly hairless, has lanceolate, toothed leaves up to 2 inches long and late-appearing, 1-inch-long light purple to bright blue flowers in erect, showy, uninterrupted, spikelike spires. Their staminodes are bearded. *P. virens*, an ally of *P. humilis*, is native from Colorado to Alberta and Nevada. From 6 inches to 2 feet in height, it has narrow-lanceolate to wider leaves sometimes toothed and up to 2 inches long. The blue or blue-violet, ½-inch-long flowers in slender spires of rather widely spaced tiers have glandular hairs on their outsides, a beard of hairs on their lower lips, and yellow-bearded staminodes. *P. watsonii*, native from Idaho to Colorado and Nevada, is hairless and without basal rosettes of foliage. Its several to many stems bear lanceolate leaves about 2 inches long with heart-shaped bases that embrace them. Arranged in few to many tiers, and more crowded toward the tops of the columns of blooms, the blue to blue-purple flowers are about ½ inch long. Their staminodes have yellow beards. *P. whitedii*, native from Montana to Washington and allied to *P. eriantherus*, is up to 1 foot high and slightly hairy. The leaves, linear to linear-lanceolate, lanceolate, or spatula-shaped, and up to 3½ inches long, are sparingly toothed or toothless. The blue-purple to nearly red flowers, about ¾ inch long, have bearded staminodes. *P. wilcoxii*, native from Montana to Washington, is up to 4 feet tall and hairless. It has glaucous, sharp-toothed,

Penstemon digitalis

Penstemon laevigatus

leaves, the largest 4½ to 6 inches long. In erect, more or less glandular-pubescent, ample panicles, the white flowers, usually lined with purple on their insides and sometimes suffused with pale violet, are 1 inch to 1¼ inches long. They have bearded staminodes. *P. hirsutus* inhabits dry woodlands and fields from Quebec and Maine to Michigan, Virginia, and Kentucky. Usually softly-hairy throughout, but sometimes hairless below, and glandular-pubescent in its flowering parts, this has oblong to lanceolate, toothed leaves up to 4½ inches long. Its flowers have slender-tubed, purplish or light violet corollas about 1 inch long, densely-hairy but without purple lines inside. The staminodes are bearded. Variety *P. h. pygmaeus* is only 6 inches in height. Very sim-

Penstemon wilcoxii

ovate to triangular-ovate leaves, the basal ones long-stalked, those on the stems stalkless, and airy panicles of bright blue, purple, or sometimes pink flowers slightly bearded within. The staminodes have short, dense, brown beards.

Eastern North American sorts with white to purplish flowers include these: *P. digitalis* occupies damp woodlands and prairies from Maine to Michigan, Alabama, and Texas. Up to 5 feet tall, usually hairless and sometimes somewhat glaucous, it has shining stems and ovate to narrowly-oblong or lanceolate, toothed

Penstemon hirsutus pygmaeus

ilar *P. tenuiflorus*, a native of dry limestone soils from Kentucky to Alabama, has white flowers. *P. laevigatus*, of meadows and open woodlands from Pennsylvania to Missouri and Florida, 2 to 3 feet tall, has

dull, usually minutely-hairy stems and lanceolate to narrowly-oblong, toothed leaves hairless on their undersides. The flowering parts are more or less glandular-pubescent. The pale violet blooms, ½ to 1 inch long, have bearded staminodes.

A group of nonhardy hybrid penstemons identified as *P. gloxinioides*, the re-

Penstemon gloxinioides: (a) With delicate pink flowers

(b) With red flowers

sults of mating *P. cobaea* and *P. hartwegii*, are exceptionally fine garden plants that give of their very best only in regions of reasonably cool summers, but often do moderately well under rather more torrid conditions. They include a number of splendid named varieties reproducible only by cuttings, but plants raised from seeds sown in spring make gay showings the first summer. The hybrids come in various colors and may be started indoors early and treated like other annuals.

These bushy hybrids have erect stems 1 foot to 2½ feet high, and good-looking broad leaves. Their foxglove-like flowers, in one-sided spike- or raceme-like panicles, come in a range of colors from pink, rose-pink, and carmine to scarlet, as well as white and purplish-lilac. Named varieties, popular in northern Europe, are not easy to come by in North America, but a search through the catalogs of dealers in herbaceous perennials may reveal a few.

Garden and Landscape Uses. Among the great number of penstemons that form such an important part of America's native floral heritage are kinds suitable for a variety of horticultural purposes as well as a few of little promise. We are not concerned with the latter. In making selections take into consideration the widely diverse environments under which the different sorts grow in the wild and match garden sites to native habitats as best you may. Not that you should necessarily at-

tempt to slavishly reproduce natural conditions, just be guided by them.

For native plant gardens and informal uses, nearly all are admirable in regions of their natural range and a great many adapt to naturalization or seminaturalization well away from home. The showier of the taller ones, say those 1 foot high or higher, can also be employed with good purpose more formally in groups in flower beds and borders and for supplying cut blooms. Give serious consideration to the *P. gloxinioides* hybrids for these purposes. Lower kinds delight rock gardeners, and some of those easiest to grow may be used at the fronts of beds and as edgings.

But penstemons have limitations that must be accepted and respected. Although perennial, certain kinds, especially those that do not make tufts, rosettes, mounds, or mats of basal foliage, are short-lived, that is, they tend to behave like biennials. But these ordinarily produce abundant seeds so that maintaining stocks of them is an easy matter.

Like many western American plants, a fairly large proportion of penstemons are either not sufficiently winter hardy or for other reasons do not do particularly well in eastern gardens, but a fair number do and it is often a matter of trial to determine which will accommodate to particular sites and situations. Among those likely to be most satisfactory in the east are *P. acuminatus, P. angustifolius, P. barbatus, P. confer-*

tus, P. diffusus, P. digitalis, P. fruticosus, P. glaber, P. grandiflorus, P. hirsutus, P. laevigatus, P. menziesii, and *P. ovatus.* For desert and semidesert kinds, the selection of warm, sheltered, sunny sites and provision of perfect drainage may bring success, and at least some of those from high altitudes and northern latitudes yield to blandishments well known to successful cultivators of alpines including among the most important the selection of the coolest possible locations such as are likely to be afforded by north-facing slopes.

Sunny sites perfectly drained suit most penstemons best, but those that in the wild inhabit open woodlands and similar environments prefer and some others tolerate part-day or light shade, and a few prosper in dampish soils.

Cultivation. Penstemons come very readily from seeds, which afford a convenient means of raising stocks of many species. But the method has the disadvantage that the offspring of kinds that vary considerably, and many do, may not be as desirable as the plant from which the seeds were collected. Propagation by division or cuttings overcomes this difficulty, but not all sorts are amenable to these methods of multiplication, neither lending themselves to splitting nor producing shoots suitable for use as cuttings.

Divide in early spring or in mild climates in early fall. Take cuttings in summer or early fall. Plant the cuttings in a shaded cold frame in sand, perlite, or a mixture of one of these and peat moss, or root them under mist outdoors or in a cool greenhouse.

In Europe cuttings of choice varieties of *P. gloxinioides* are usually planted in late summer 3 or 4 inches apart in sandy soil in cold frames where the resulting plants remain until the following spring when they are transplanted 8 to 10 inches apart to their summer flowering quarters. These kinds need fertile soil kept always moderately moist.

Once established in locations reasonably favorable to their individual needs penstemons demand no unusual care, but attempting denizens of high mountains, deserts, and other highly specialized environments under conditions vastly different from those to which they are accustomed in the wild can be challenging and frustrating. Difficulties can often be minimized by avoiding excessive watering and by affording kinds known or suspected to be on the borderline of hardiness the protection of a cold frame over winter.

PENTAGLOTTIS (Penta-glóttis). The plant once known as *Anchusa sempervirens*, and now as *Pentaglottis sempervirens*, is the only member of its genus. It belongs in the borage family BORAGINACEAE. The name comes from the Greek *pente*, five, and *glotta*, a tongue; it refers to the five scales in the throat of the corolla. From *Anchusa* this genus differs in technical characteristics of the fruits as well as in having broadly-ovate, conspicuously net-veined leaves with the aspect of those of *Symphytum*.

Native to Europe, *P. sempervirens* is an ornamental, hardy herbaceous, hairy, perennial up to about 2 feet in height. Its blue flowers are borne among bracts in long-stalked, coiled-branched clusters. The corollas have short tubes with five scales closing their throats and five spreading lobes (petals). The fruits, often called seeds, are technically nutlets.

Garden Uses and Cultivation. Any ordinary soil and a sunny location are suitable for this species. It is easily propagated by seed, and by division in spring or early fall. It may be used in flower beds and borders and in informal settings. No special care is needed.

PENTAPERA (Pent-ápera). Closely related to heaths (*Erica*), and belonging to the heath family ERICACEAE, the only species of this genus, *Pentapera sicula*, is endemic to Sicily. Its variety *P. s. libanotica* inhabits Cyprus, Libya, and Lebanon. The name is derived from the Greek *pente*, five, and *pera*, a pouch, and alludes to the five-celled fruits. From heaths *Pentapera* differs in having flowers with five, instead of four sepals and petals.

A small, straggling, prostrate shrub, *P. sicula* has slender, slightly hairy stems and crowded, deep green, linear leaves in circles of four. Urn-shaped, pale pink, and with dark brown anthers, the flowers,

mostly nodding, are few together in clusters. Their corolla lobes are reflexed. More erect and up to 1½ feet tall, *P. s. libanotica* is a dense shrub, more attractive than the species, with dark green leaves often tipped with cream. It blooms profusely from late winter or spring until early summer. Its flowers are white, tinged with pink.

Garden Uses. These shrubs are especially appropriate for rock gardens, but they can also be used to good effect at the fronts of borders and in other places where low, evergreen, small-leaved shrubs can be effective. They are not hardy in the north, but have proved highly successful in California.

Cultivation. Unlike most plants of the heath family these do not need acid soil and are not resentful of hard water. In the wild they grow on limestone cliffs, and in cultivation do well in well-drained neutral soil. They need full sun. Propagation is by seeds sown in spring and by summer cuttings.

PENTAPTERYGIUM. See Agapetes.

PENTAS (Pén-tas). Approximately fifty African and Madagascan species of prostrate and erect herbaceous plants and shrubs of the madder family RUBIACEAE compose *Pentas*. One is popular for outdoor flower gardens and as a greenhouse and window garden ornamental. The name, from the Greek *pente*, five, alludes to the flower parts commonly being of that number.

Pentases have opposite, hairy, stalked, ovate to ovate-lanceolate leaves. Their

usually rather small, long-tubular flowers, in heads or clusters, have four to six sepals of unequal size, a hairy corolla with a swollen tube, and generally five, spreading lobes (petals), four to six stamens, and a protruding, branched style. The fruits of pentases are capsules containing numerous minute seeds.

The best-known sort, an excellent free-bloomer cultivated in a number of varieties differing chiefly in the color of flowers, which ranges from purple-red to scarlet, pink, and white, is African *P. lanceolata* (syn. *P. carnea*). From 1 foot to 2 feet tall, and erect or spreading, this evergreen subshrub has stems more or less woody toward their bases. Its short-stalked, elliptic, lanceolate, or ovate, pointed leaves are 3 to 6 inches long by up to 2 inches wide. The nearly stalkless blooms, about 1 inch long and ½ inch wide, are in compact, bouvardia-like clusters. They have hairy throats. East African *P. zanzibarensis* is a rather loose subshrub or shrub with lanceolate leaves and heads, about 2½ inches across, of small, slightly fragrant, pale lilac flowers.

A shrub or tree, native to Malagasy (Madagascar), and up to about 15 feet in height, *P. mussaendoides* has shoots densely-brown-hairy when young and tapering, oblanceolate leaves up to about 5 inches long. Its 1-inch-long flowers are in large, terminal panicles.

Garden and Landscape Uses. Little experience has been had with the tree pentas described above, but it appears to be of decorative worth for outdoor planting in tropical and warm subtropical, frostless or

Pentas lanceolata

Pentas zanzibarensis

almost frostless climates. The other is an excellent, continuously blooming bedding and pot plant, and in warm climates, a good permanent garden ornamental. Few plants are easier to grow. Moderately fertile, well-drained soil and a sunny location suit its needs.

Cultivation. Pentases can be raised from seed, but cuttings root so easily that this is the method commonly adopted. Cuttings root readily at any time under conditions that suit geraniums, begonias, fuchsias, and other popular bedding plants. To have plants of suitable size for planting out in spring at about the time that it is safe to set out tomatoes, cuttings are taken in fall from outdoor plants or in January or February from plants wintered indoors. When rooted, they are potted into small pots, and later into bigger ones. Receptacles 3 or 4 inches in diameter usually serve until the plants are transplanted outdoors. The young plants are exposed to full sun where the night temperature is 55 to 60°F and that by day five to ten degrees higher. The soil is kept evenly moist, and the tips of the shoots are pinched out occasionally to induce branching. Before the plants are set in the ground outdoors they are hardened for a couple of weeks by standing them in a cold frame or sheltered location outside. Specimens that are to be kept in pots for indoor or patio or terrace decoration are moved into larger containers as their root growth makes necessary. When their final pots are filled with roots weekly applications of dilute liquid fertilizer are helpful.

PEONY. Peony is the common or vernacular name of the species and varieties of the botanical genus *Paeonia* described elsewhere in this Encyclopedia. In regions where winters are sufficiently cold and long enough to afford them adequate dormancy, peonies are rewarding garden plants, dependable, extremely long-lived, and easy to grow. No garden in which their cultivation is practical should be without them. Old-fashioned plants, they have been beloved by generations of American and European gardeners. They have been cultivated in China for over 2,000 years.

Peonies are classified in two chief groups, herbaceous kinds, which are the better known and die completely to the ground in fall, and tree kinds, which do not die back. Tree peonies belie their name in that they are not trees, but shrubs with much-branched, woody stems. In fall they lose their leaves, but their stems persist. Both herbaceous peonies and tree peonies bloom in early summer and have substantial foliage that remains attractive throughout the time it is in evidence.

Herbaceous peonies are displayed to their best advantage as single specimens, in groups of three to five in beds or borders of herbaceous perennials or in mixed flower beds and borders, or in greater numbers in beds and borders planted with peonies only. Because their exquisite blooms, 5 to 8 inches or more in diameter and those of some kinds fragrant, last well in water and lend themselves to flower arrangements, herbaceous peonies are also admirable for inclusion in cutting gardens. Tree peonies are choice and superb plants for shrub beds and as featured specimens in mixed flower borders and other special locations. Their blooms, because of their short stalks, are less suitable for cutting than are those of herbaceous varieties. They range from 6 to 10 inches or more in diameter.

The first herbaceous peonies to be cultivated in European and American gardens were *P. officinalis* and its varieties. The species, a native of southern France to Albania, has single blooms. Its double-flowered variety, *P. o. rubro-plena*, with deep ruby-red flowers, is the "piney" of old-fashioned gardens. As a parent, *P. officinalis* has played a significant role in the production of modern hybrids.

The most popular herbaceous peonies, those called Chinese peonies, are derivatives of *Paeonia lactiflora* (syn. *P. albiflora*), a native of China and Siberia, first introduced to cultivation in Europe in 1784. By about 1800 a number of horticultural varieties of this species had been brought from Chinese gardens to Europe and America. Since then, many thousands of varieties have been raised from the original introductions and their progeny, and,

Raised in France in 1851, *P. lactiflora festiva maxima*, its double white flowers flecked with carmine, is still a great favorite

during the present century, hybrids between Chinese varieties and species other than *P. lactiflora* have been raised and have become popular. In this breeding work, Americans played a foremost part and are still very active. Outstanding among American breeders was Professor A. P. Saunders, of Clinton, New York, who,

over a period of about thirty years and most intensively in the period between World War I and World War II, made many thousands of crosses and introduced several distinctive groups of hybrid peonies represented by numerous varieties.

For horticultural purposes, herbaceous peonies are classified into five groups according to the form of their flowers. Doubles have blooms with five or more guard

A modern double-flowered herbaceous peony

A modern single-flowered herbaceous peony

(basal) petals and a heaped, dense, center mass of apparent petals that represent transformed stamens and carpels. Semi-doubles have five or more guard petals and a center of broad petals intermixed with or encircled by pollen-bearing stamens. Japanese varieties have flowers with five or more guard petals and a large bunch of staminodes (stamens with abortive anthers that produce no pollen). Anemones, which by some catalogers are included with the doubles or with the

Penstemon digitalis variety

Penstemon fruticosus

Penstemon, undetermined species, in a rock garden

Penstemon gloxinioides

Penstemon hirsutus pygmaeus

A patriotic display of red, white, and blue petunias

Petteria ramentacea

Purple petunias with white verbenas

Pink and purple petunias with pink cannas

Phacelia, undetermined species

Phacelia, undetermined species

A modern anemone-flowered herbaceous peony

Japanese sorts, have flowers with five or more guard petals, often in more than one row, and a central bunch of petal-like transformations of stamens that may be the same color as or a different color from the petals. Singles are varieties that have blooms with five or more petals surrounding a bunch of fertile (pollen-bearing) stamens.

A well-located clump of herbaceous peonies

Herbaceous peonies in a cutting garden

Tree peonies fall into two chief groups, the Chinese or European sorts, the latter, derivatives of varieties originally brought from China to England and later to America in the nineteenth century, and Japa-

Tree peonies: (a) Single-flowered

(b) Semidouble-flowered

(c) Double-flowered

nese sorts, originally developed in Japan from varieties brought originally from China. Chinese or European varieties have fully double flowers of shaggy aspect, often somewhat hidden among the foliage, and mostly so heavy that their stalks droop. Japanese varieties have mostly single or semidouble blooms carried well above the foliage and with straight stalks. They withstand even more cold than the Chinese or European varieties. A third group of tree peonies, hybrids between *P. suffruticosa*, *P. lutea*, and *P. delavayi*, has resulted from breeding begun in the 1890s by Victor Lemoine, of France, and continued in the 1920s and 1930s by the American A. P. Saunders. These handsome hybrids have single, semidouble, and double blooms in colors ranging from white and ivory-white through pale yellow to deep yellow and from blush-pink to deep pink, scarlet, crimson, and dark maroon. The flowers of some varieties are fragrant.

The needs of peonies are simple. They prefer full sun, but tolerate part-day shade. Wind-swept locations are not to their liking; reasonable shelter is desirable. Of great importance is that the soil be suitable. Provided subsurface drainage is satisfactory, it may range from sandy to decidedly clayey. If the soil is sandy, during its initial preparation incorporate with it especially generous amounts of organic material, such as rotted manure, compost, or peat moss. Lighten clayey soil by incorporating liberal amounts of coarse sand, gritty coal cinders, or perlite, as well as some organic material. In the years following planting, the soil's ability to provide nutrients for these hearty feeders must be maintained by annual applications of fertilizer. It is important that the soil be of adequate depth. Not under 1 foot and preferably 1½ feet or more of fertile topsoil overlying a porous substratum is needed for the best results. Because established plants that are doing well are better left undisturbed, they may occupy the same site for many years without giving an opportunity for the modification of subsurface conditions. Slightly acid to slightly alkaline soil is most agreeable to peonies.

Planting and, when necessary, transplanting are best done in early fall, although if circumstances necessitate, they can be successfully done in early spring. Allow ample space for each plant. For most herbaceous peonies a circle 3 feet in diameter is not more than adequate for each plant, and tree peonies are likely to eventually need a space at least twice as wide. Make holes of ample size and fork into their bottoms generous amounts of well-rotted manure, compost, or other decayed organic material and a liberal dressing of bonemeal or superphosphate. If practicable, complete this work at least two weeks before planting, thus allowing time for the soil to settle. In planting, set the crown of the plant, from which the eyes (buds) sprout, not more than 2 inches, and in southern gardens only 1 inch to 1½ inches, beneath the surface. Work soil among and around the roots, making sure no voids are left, and make it firm by packing it with a stick or by treading. Peonies planted in cold areas and those planted late in fall elsewhere are likely to benefit from, during the first winter, a covering of salt hay, branches of evergreens, or other suitable loose material.

Routine care is not onerous. As soon as spring weather permits, remove any winter covering that has been used, apply a dressing of a complete fertilizer, and stir this shallowly into the surface soil, taking care not to damage the buds at the crowns of the plants. Control weeds throughout the season by the use of a cultivator or hoe, taking care not to disturb the soil to a depth of more than about 1 inch. Alternatively, a mulch of peat moss, ground corncobs, or some similar material may be employed. Most herbaceous peonies, and especially those with large, heavy blooms, need some support. Often used, and generally most appropriate, are circles of stout wire attached at a height of about 1 foot above the ground to three or four stout stakes driven in a circle near the periphery of the peony clump. If the largest flowers are desired, disbud by pinching out while small all lateral buds that sprout from below the chief terminal bud of each stem; for maximum garden display and a longer season of bloom, better results are had by not disbudding and, instead, relying upon a much greater number of somewhat smaller flowers. In dry weather deep soakings with water, timed so that the plants are never allowed to wilt to an appreciable extent, are very desirable. Some gardeners allow the dead foliage of peonies to remain on the plants over winter as a means of providing some protection by holding snow. However, it is wiser, after it has been killed by frost, to cut down the foliage at ground level and burn or otherwise destroy it (do not put it on the compost pile); elimination of the foliage is advisable because the quite serious botrytis disease lives over on plant parts such as these, providing sources of infection the following year.

Propagation of peonies is most commonly undertaken by vegetative means. True species, but not garden varieties or hybrids, can also be raised true to type from seeds, and this is the method employed by breeders of new varieties. If seeds are to be used, gather them promptly as they ripen and sow them without delay, or alternatively, stratify them by mixing them with slightly damp peat moss, sand, or vermiculite in a polyethylene plastic bag until they begin to

sprout. If they are allowed to dry out they will take at least two years from sowing to germinating. Sow in flats or in a ground bed in a cold frame. Keep the soil moderately moist and, until the young plants appear, shaded. When big enough to handle conveniently, transplant the seedlings about 1½ feet apart in a nursery bed, there to remain until they first bloom, which is likely to be in four to five years.

Division of the root crowns is a more usual way of increasing herbaceous peonies. To divide old plants, in early fall cut off their foliage, lift the clumps carefully, and with a stream of water from a hose flush away all soil. Stand the plants in the shade for a few hours so that the roots become less brittle, then with a sharp knife or shears cut the crowns into suitably sized divisions. Let each division retained for planting consist of three stout roots, 4 to 6 inches long by ½ to 1 inch wide, and three to five eyes (growth buds). Slice the ends of the roots slantwise so that the cut surfaces face downward and dust the cuts with powdered sulfur or other fungicide. Divisions with one or two eyes may be

A single-eyed division of a herbaceous peony

used, but these take a year or two longer to produce blooming-size plants. If sufficient material is available, save it for planting divisions made only from the outsides of the clumps.

Tree peonies are commonly propagated by grafting from mid-August to mid-September. This somewhat uncertain procedure usually results in fairly high losses among young plants during their first two years. The wedge graft is employed. The scion, a shoot 2 to 3 inches long of the current season's growth of the variety to be propagated, is cut at its base into a smooth-surfaced wedge and inserted firmly into a slit cut into the upper end of the understock. The understock is a piece of root, 4 to 6 inches long and ½ to 1 inch

wide, of a variety of herbaceous P. lacti-flora. Bind the graft tightly with a rubber grafting strip or, less desirably, soft string. Then soak for about 1 hour in water to which Clorox has been added, one tablespoon to each gallon of water. Next, lay the grafts horizontally on a 2-inch layer of slightly damp peat moss or sawdust in flats or in a cold frame. Cover them with the same material and then position another layer of grafts until, in all, there are four layers topped off with a layer of peat moss or sawdust. Never permit the peat moss or sawdust to dry out. When scion and understock have united, a process that takes three to four weeks, plant the grafts perpendicularly in a nursery bed, 4 to 5 inches apart and with the uppermost bud 2 to 3 inches beneath the surface. There they should remain for two years,

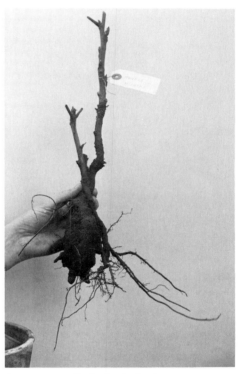

A young grafted plant of a tree peony

before being transplanted to their permanent locations.

Diseases and Pests. The chief diseases of peonies are botrytis blight, root knot or Lemoine's disease, and root rot. The first, especially prevalent during wet springs, causes rotting of the stems and flower buds, so that the latter fail to open, and finally rotting of the foliage. This nuisance is combated by planting where there is good air circulation and by sanitary measures that include the prompt removal of all affected parts and the clearing away of all foliage in fall after it has been killed by frost. Root knot results in beadlike swellings on the roots of infected plants. Probably caused by a virus, root knot has no known cure. Some infected plants con-

Peony flower buds infected with botrytis disease

tinue to bloom satisfactorily. Either destroy or segregate from other peonies specimens that are infected. Premature dying of parts of plants with rotted roots is the first indication of root rot disease. Examine the roots and if rot is found, soak them for forty-five minutes in a fungicide before replanting in a new location. The chief animal pests of peonies are ants, nematodes, rose chafers (a type of beetle), and thrips. Ants seek peonies for the sweet exudation that accompanies the flower buds. In feeding on this they may spread botrytis disease and, therefore, it is advisable to destroy them. Nematodes infest the roots, which then develop many pea-like nodules. Heavy infestations cause stunting, weak growth, and paling of the foliage. Destroy infested plants and do not plant others in the same area. Thrips, especially troublesome in the south, are a cause of buds failing to open and discoloration of the petals of those that do. Control by spraying with an insecticide.

PEPEROMIA (Peper-òmia). The genus *Peperomia*, of the pepper family PIPERACEAE, widely distributed in warm parts of the world, is represented in the native flora of the United States in southern Florida. It comprises possibly 1,000 species of chiefly low evergreen perennials and some annuals, the latter not in cultivation. The name is from the Greek *peperi*, pepper, and *homoios*, resembling. It alludes to its relationship and resemblance to the tropical genus *Piper* to which the vine that is the source of the condiment pepper belongs, but not the peppers of the vegetable garden.

Peperomias grow in the ground or sometimes perch on trees as epiphytes. They sometimes have tuberous roots or creeping rhizomes or rootstocks, or are tufted plants without these. They may have branched erect stems or short stems without branches, less commonly, they are stemless. Usually the stems, like the foliage, are more or less succulent. Alternate, opposite, or in whorls (circles of more than two), the often attractively variegated, undivided, lobeless, toothless leaves frequently have tiny translucent dots apparent if the leaf is viewed against strong light. The bisexual flowers, in dense, rarely rather showy spikes, are minute to small. Greenish to white and without sepals or petals, each consists of two stamens and one stigma. The fruits are tiny and berry-like.

Popular *P. caperata*, of Brazil, is available in several varieties. Sometimes called 'Emerald Ripple', the one that appears to be most typical of the species is some 4 inches tall by about 5 inches across. It has

Peperomia caperata 'Emerald Ripple'

a short, branched stem and, displayed in spiraled, more or less rosette fashion, strongly rippled or corrugated leaves with pink stalks up to 3½ inches long and broad-heart-shaped to ovate blades up to 1½ inches across. Pale on their undersides, above they are green to grayish-green with the valleys of the corrugations tinted chocolate-brown. The greenish-white slender, tail-like flower spikes, at maturity, have two or three antler-like points from their apexes. A smallish edition of the last, *P. c. crespa* has a short stem and rounder, blunter, green to olive-green leaves, chocolate-brown toward their centers, paler on their undersides. Miniature *P. c.* 'Little Fantasy' much resembles 'Emerald Ripple', but is dwarfer and has smaller leaves. The pink-stalked leaves of *P. c. variegata* are beautifully variegated with broad, irregular marginal bands of milky-white. Less robust *P. c. tricolor* has red-stalked, creamy-white leaves with an irregular central patch of milky-green, and a red base, that radiates partway along the veins. Also with corrugated leaves, *P. meridana* is native to Venezuela. Up to 6 inches tall, it has rich red, branched stems with along each of their three angles a wavy wing. The slightly-lobed, ovate,

Peperomia meridana

hairless leaves, ½ to ⅞ inch long, have rich green upper surfaces, paler undersides, and slightly three-winged stalks. The erect, slender, cream-colored flower spikes are up to 4 inches long.

Corrugated or quilted leaves are also characteristic of Brazilian *P. griseoargentea*. This, about as big and somewhat resembling *P. caperata*, has also been called *P. hederaefolia*; it is sometimes known as ivy peperomia. It has rosettes of pink-stalked leaves with thin, broad-heart-shaped, silvery to leaden blades with depressed, purplish veins. The flower spikes

Peperomia griseoargentea

circular, short-pointed leaves depressed at their centers and up to 8 inches long by 6½ inches wide. They are bluish-green faintly marked between the veins with silver and have red stalks. The leaves of **P. polybotrya,** a native of Colombia and Peru, sometimes 10 inches tall, are alternate and have reddish stalks. Their nearly vertical blades are round-ovate and have abrupt-pointed apexes and a clear pale spot above the junction with the leafstalk. The blades are 2 to 4 inches long. The flower spikes are in terminal panicles. Less fleshy than the sorts just discussed, **P. gardnerana,** of Brazil, has pink to reddish stems and long-stalked, pointed-ovate, glossy, quilted leaves with pale undersurfaces and wavy margins.

Peperomia polybotrya

are greenish-white. Dark olive-green to coppery, almost black leaves distinguish *P. g.* 'Blackie', a variety with small, compact rosettes of foliage. The beautiful olive-green, much-wrinkled leaves of *P. g. nigra* deepen to almost black along the veins.

Long-stalked, shield-shaped, hairless leaves with stalks joined to the blades well in from their margins are characteristic of several sorts, among them the watermelon peperomia (**P. argyreia** syn. *P. sandersii*). The leaves of this Brazilian have red stalks

Peperomia argyreia

and fleshy blades with conspicuous lengthwise bands of green and silver reminiscent of some watermelons. Nearly stemless, shapely, and full-foliaged, this sort, 6 to 9 inches tall, has leaf blades 2 to 3 inches long. Its flower spikes are in panicles. Much like it, but with decidedly bigger, concave leaves and flower spikes not in panicles, **P. arifolia** is Brazilian. Also with thick leaves the stalks of which join the blades well in from the margins are *P. peltifolia* and *P. polybotrya.* Native to Venezuela and Brazil, **P. peltifolia** has nearly

Peperomia polybotrya in bloom

Old in cultivation and popular for dish gardens, **P. obtusifolia,** native from Mexico to northern South America and in the West Indies, is cultivated in several varieties. The typical species may attain 1 foot in height, but is usually lower; except for the stalks of its flower spikes, it is hairless.

Peperomia obtusifolia

It has a fleshy stem, when old decumbent at its base, and short-stalked, succulent leaves with more or less concave upper surfaces. Obovate to broad-spatula-shaped and blunt-pointed or notched at their apexes, the 2- to 3-inch-long blades have short, red stalks. The stalks of the inconspicuous flower spikes are minutely-hairy. Varieties of this peperomia are *P. o. alba,* which has creamy-yellow stems and leafstalks marked with red, and pointed-ovate leaves, the young ones entirely creamy-yellow. *P. o. albo-marginata* is small, has thick, pointed-ovate leaves with creamy-white edges and central portions green with a milky overcast. *P. o.* 'Gold Tip' has dark green leaves marbled especially near their apexes with creamy-yellow. *P. o. lougenii* is a small edition of the typical species with blunt, ovate to obovate leaves with cream-colored variegation. *P. o. min-*

Peperomia obtusifolia variegata

ima has small, obovate, rich lustrous green leaves, without variegation, and pale undersides. *P. o. variegata* has red-blotched pale stems and light green, pointed-ovate leaves prettily variegated with milky-green and bordered with a broad, feather-edged band of creamy-white.

Peperomia clusiaefolia

Peperomia quadrangularis

With much the aspect of *P. obtusifolia*, but its leaves proportionately longer, stalkless, or very short-stalked and their bases more or less clasping the stem, *P. clusiaefolia* is indigenous to the West Indies and Venezuela. A slow-grower, this has alternate, narrow-obovate, concave leaves rarely attaining a maximum of 6 inches long by 3½ inches wide, usually considerably smaller. They have narrow, dull red edges and pale undersides with a purple midrib. Handsome *P. c. variegata* has broad, irregular, creamy-yellow borders to its leaves, which have narrow red edges. Another of this relationship, *P. magnoliaefolia* scarcely differs from *P. obtusifolia* except in technical details of its fruits. As known in cultivation it is a robust sort with obovate-elliptic leaves up to 5 inches long and with depressed veins. The stalks of its flower spikes are generally hairless. The plant cultivated as *P. tithymaloides* is apparently a horticultural variant of *P. magnoliaefolia*.

Trailing or creeping, slender-stemmed peperomias include these: *P. dahlstedtii* (syn. *P. fosteri*), of Brazil, has red stems and thick, pointed-elliptic, pale-veined leaves in twos or threes. *P. puteolata*, of Peru, is very beautiful, with slender, trailing stems and, in whorls of three, leaves with pointed-lanceolate, leathery blades 3 to 4 inches long and one-third to one-half as wide. They are adorned with five well-defined, sunken, yellowish, longitudinal veins, on the upper surfaces depressed, beneath raised. *P. quadrangularis* (syn. *P. angulata*), of the West Indies, Central America, and northern South America, is a small, trailing epiphyte with slender, four-angled stems and mostly opposite, obovate to nearly circular, very short-stalked leaves up to 1 inch long, with convex undersides. They have three chief veins, depressed and yellowish. *P. rotundifolia* (syn. *P. nummulariifolia*), very widely distributed throughout warm parts of the Americas, is a low, matting creeper with threadlike stems. It has slightly hairy, alternate leaves nearly circular and about

Peperomia quadrangularis (foliage)

¼ inch across, or broad-elliptic and up to ⅓ inch long. Variety *P. r. pilosior* (syn. *P. prostrata*) has densely-hairy young stems and young leaves. The latter, ovate-circular, green to reddish-brown with paler veining, are narrowly edged with red and fringed with hairs. *P. serpens* (syn. *P. scandens*), native from Panama to Brazil and

Peperomia rotundifolia pilosior

Peru, is small, with trailing or creeping, almost threadlike stems and alternate, triangular-roundish, pointed to bluntish leaves up to ¾ inch or occasionally 1¼ inches long, sometimes wider than long. They have short, reddish stalks. A variant with variegated leaves is cultivated. *P. trinervis*, of Bolivia, Peru, and Venezuela, is a robust creeper with red stems and fleshy, pointed-ovate leaves with three conspicuous depressed veins. *P. trinervula*, of Venezuela, has trailing stems and 1-inch-long, fleshy, ovate to broad-elliptic, slightly pubescent leaves.

The only cultivated peperomia that makes a really fair flower display is Ecuadorean *P. fraseri* (syn. *P. resedaeflora*). This has a tuberous base and erect, branched stems 9 inches to 1½ feet tall. Its

Peperomia fraseri

Peperomia fraseri (flower spike)

basal leaves more or less in rosettes, those above are opposite or, near the tops of the stems, alternate. Circular-ovate, their depressed veins responsible for their quilted appearance, the largest is 1¾ inches long by 1¼ inches wide. Most are smaller. The white flowers are in dense pyramidal spikes up to 2 inches long.

Other peperomias in cultivation include these: *P. acuminata,* of Mexico, has fleshy, more or less trailing stems and narrowly-ovate, hairy, bright green leaves with depressed veins, smaller than those of *P. glabella* and more pointed. *P. bicolor,* of Ecuador, has white-hairy, reddish-brown stems up to 9 inches high and alternate, obovate to broad-elliptic, more or less hairy leaves, the largest up to 2 inches long by 1 inch wide, with a broad center band and narrower side veins of silver. *P. blanda,* native from Bolivia to Venezuela, is erect and clothed with fine hairs. Its leaves are opposite, broad-elliptic to obovate, and green with lighter colored longitudinal veins. *P. calvicaulis,* of Costa Rica, has more or less trailing stems and fairly large, pointed-elliptic, somewhat pubescent, light green leaves with paler undersides. *P. cerea* (syn. *P.* 'Dr. Goodspeed'), of Peru, is bushy, 1 foot to 1½ feet tall with fleshy stems and leaves, the latter pointed-ovate, about 1 inch long, and mostly in whorls of three. Their slightly-cupped upper surfaces are dull green, their undersides brownish. *P. columnella,* a freely-branched succulent from northern Peru, up to about 6 inches tall, has very thick stems hidden behind five vertical rows of down-pointing, heart-shaped, stalkless leaves, with translucent, glossy, window-like upper surfaces. The tiny flowers are in short, thickish terminal spikes. This species, not easy to grow on its own roots, succeeds best grafted on *P. dolabriformis* or other thick-stemmed species. *P. cordata,* the plant known in gardens by this name, is not surely identified botanically. It has glossy, broad-heart-shaped, quilted leaves tapered to pointed apexes. *P. crassifolia,* African, has fleshy, rigidly erect stems and alternate, 3-inch-long, obovate to somewhat lozenge-shaped, fleshy, quilted, green leaves with pale midribs. *P. dolabriformis,* of Peru, has loose rosettes of succulent, spatula-shaped leaves, long relative to their widths and with the halves on either side of the midrib folded together so that their pale undersides are the most visible parts. *P. elongata,* a variable native of northern South America, in the wild perches on trees. Mostly hairless, it has alternate, lanceolate-elliptic leaves 1½ to 3 inches long by up to 1 inch wide and slightly hair-fringed toward their apexes. The flower spikes are solitary or in twos. *P. galioides,* of northwest South America, small and erect, has branched, succulent stems and very narrow, 1-inch-long leaves depressed along their midribs and in whorls of four or five. *P. glabella,* of Central America, northern South America, and the West Indies, has creeping stems with branches up to 6 inches tall. Except for a few hairs on the leafstalks it is hairless. Its ovate to elliptic-lanceolate leaves, up to 2½ inches long or a little longer, are pointed, with

Peperomia glabella variegata

three or five main veins spreading from the base. The slender flower spikes, from the upper leaf axils, are 2 to 4½ inches long. Variety *P. g. variegata* has leaves margined with creamy-white. *P. grandifolia,* of Guiana, is fleshy and has broad-elliptic to slightly obovate, somewhat cupped, fleshy, glossy, green leaves with paler midribs. *P. hirta,* of Cuba, has rather straggling, freely-branched stems and small, pointed-obovate, soft, satiny leaves clothed with short gray hairs. Their undersides are paler than their upper surfaces. *P. incana,* a succulent native of Brazil, has a rigid stem and stiff, fleshy leaves clothed with a felt of white hairs. *P. japonica,* the only peperomia native in Japan, is endemic there and in the Ryukyu Islands. It has erect, sparingly-branched stems up to 1 foot tall and whorls (circles of more than two) of three to five, elliptic to broadly-elliptic or obovate, short-stalked leaves ½ inch to 1 inch long by one-half to two-thirds as wide. The erect flower spikes are up to nearly 2 inches long. *P. maculosa,* of Central America, northern South America, and the West Indies, up to 1 foot tall, has alternate, long-stalked,

Peperomia incana

Peperomia maculosa

elliptic to elliptic-ovate, more or less hairy or nearly hairless, short-pointed leaves 3 to 8 inches long by up to 4½ inches wide, with greenish-white midribs and side veins. The terminal flower spikes are solitary or paired. *P. marmorata* 'Silver Heart', from Brazil, has thin green or bluish-green, red-stalked, taper-pointed, heart-shaped leaves brushed with silvery-gray, with bright green, depressed veins. *P. metallica,* Peruvian, has an erect stem and narrow-elliptic leaves with a coppery,

Peperomia metallica

metallic luster relieved by a silver-green band along their centers. Their silvery undersides have bright red veins. *P. moninii,* of Reunion Island, erect and branched, has opposite, small, lozenge-shaped green leaves, reddish on their undersides, pubescent above. *P. nivalis,* of Peru, is a neat sort with erect stems and alternate, hairless leaves ½ to ¾ inch long. *P. orba* (syn. *P.* 'Princess Astrid'), of unknown provenance, has erect, pubescent, much-branched, downy stems and alternate, short-stalked, elliptic leaves with blades up to 2¼ inches long that angle slightly upward from their midribs and are pubes-

Peperomia ornata

cent. **P. ornata,** of Venezuela, has a short stem and long-stalked, fleshy, elliptic to obovate, red-stalked leaves with smooth, green blades up to 5 inches in length that have prominent lengthwise veins light-colored above, purplish-red on their under surfaces. **P. pereskiaefolia,** of Brazil and Venezuela, has red, erect to sprawling stems and opposite, smallish, lozenge-shaped to elliptic or obovate, thick, waxy, pale-veined, dull green leaves 1½ to 2 inches long. **P. perrottetiana,** of Mauritius, is a hairless species with trailing or semi-trailing stems and short-stalked, broad-elliptic to obovate leaves with three main veins. From ¾ inch to 1¼ inches long, they have green upper surfaces and paler undersides. The slender, erect flower spikes are solitary. **P. pseudovariegata,** of Colombia, has erect to procumbent stems and alternate, oblong-lanceolate leaves 4

to 5½ inches long with hairless upper surfaces, pubescent lower ones. Solitary or in pairs, the 5- to 6-inch-long flower spikes have stalks 2 to 3 inches long. Variety *P. p. sarcophylla* (syn. *P. sarcophylla*), of Colombia and Ecuador, has sprawling to drooping, fleshy, broad-lanceolate, hairless leaves up to 8 inches long with greenish-ivory-white midribs bordered with gray-green. **P. rubella,** Mexican, has very slender, erect, branched red stems thickly furnished with olive-green, obovate leaves up to ½ inch long, with rich crimson undersides and upper surfaces netted with silver. **P. subpeltata,** of Java, has leaves sometimes 1 foot long that are fleshy,

Peperomia urocarpa

ovate to heart-shaped, and lustrous green with a cast of gray and with paler midveins. Their undersides are finely-hairy. **P. urocarpa,** native from Paraguay to Colombia, has semivining or trailing stems erect at their ends. The alternate, round-ovate to heart-shaped, fleshy leaves, up to 2 inches wide, have about seven principal veins spreading along shallow furrows from their bases. **P. velutina,** of Ecuador, erect and sparingly-branched, has pubescent stems and alternate, short-stalked, bronzy-green, elliptic leaves 2 to 3 inches long by up to 1¾ inches wide with seven pale longitudinal veins. They are hairless or at their bases slightly hairy or perhaps are sometimes velvety-hairy throughout. The flower spikes are terminal and from the leaf axils. **P. verschaffeltii,** probably a native of Peru, is a handsome sort with short stems and red-stalked, five- or seven-veined, ovate-elliptic, bluish-green leaves, heart-shaped at their bases and with broad, longitudinal, silvery bands. The flower spikes are white and solitary. **P. verticillata,** of Cuba, Jamaica, Mexico, and Central America, has erect, finely-hairy red stems and whorls (tiers) of four to six or sometimes pairs of obovate to ovate or nearly round leaves ¼ to 1 inch long or perhaps sometimes bigger. **P. viridis,** a robust Mexican, has erect stems and alternate, fleshy, bright green, pointed-ovate leaves.

Garden and Landscape Uses. Peperomias are best known as beautiful small fo-

Peperomia perrottetiana

Peperomia verschaffeltii

liage plants for greenhouses and terrariums, with some of the more succulent sorts, best able to flourish in or at least tolerate dry atmospheric conditions, as plants for dish gardens and growing in windows. All these purposes they serve well planted in pots, or trailing sorts in hanging baskets, and in ground beds.

In the tropics and warm subtropics selected sorts are excellent groundcovers and rock garden ornamentals. They thrive beneath trees and shrubs and in other shaded places.

Cultivation. Without exception peperomias appreciate warmth (temperatures of 65°F and higher are satisfactory), fairly high humidity, and shade from strong sun, but the degree to which the last two conditions must be met to achieve success varies considerably according to kind. Sorts with plain green, thick, fleshy stems and foliage are tolerant of much drier atmospheres and greater light intensities than thin-leaved kinds or those with highly variegated foliage.

Too much wetness and too dense shade bring trouble. Few peperomias will long stand constantly saturated soil. Under such conditions the roots and eventually the bases of the plants rot. Shade so heavy that minimum light for satisfactory growth is denied results in elongated, weak stems and leafstalks and smaller foliage. What may be described as bright indirect light, that is daylight without exposure to strong sun, is ideal. Lack of natural light can be compensated for by artificial illumination. Peperomias are very satisfactory for indoor light gardens.

About soil these plants are not unduly choosy. They prefer mixes that include rather generous amounts of partially decayed organics, such as compost, leaf mold, or peat moss, and that are fairly loose, that drain freely, and that are kept pleasantly damp but allowed to dry somewhat between waterings. Misting the foliage with water under conditions in which the moisture will dry from the leaves within an hour or two is beneficial. Well-rooted specimens respond to biweekly or monthly applications of dilute liquid fertilizer.

Propagation of trailing peperomias is easily achieved by division and cuttings, of other sorts by cuttings, leaf cuttings, and sometimes by careful division. These enterprises may be undertaken at any time, preferably in early spring.

PEPINO is *Solanum muricatum*.

PEPPER. See Capsicum, and Piper. For pepper-tree see Macropiper, Schinus, and Vitex. Pepper-grass is *Lepidium*. Pepper vine is *Ampelopsis arborea*. Sweet pepperbush is *Clethra alnifolia*.

PEPPERIDGE is *Nyssa sylvatica*.

PEPPERMINT is *Mentha piperita*. The peppermint gum is *Eucalyptus amygdalina*.

PEPPERS. The familiar condiment pepper, both black and white, is a product of *Piper nigrum*. This, discussed under Piper, is not our interest here. Instead, we are concerned with the peppers of the vegetable garden, the kinds sliced in salads, stuffed with meat and cooked, pickled, and used in other engaging ways as foods, to add piquancy to foods, and as garnishings. We shall also deal with ornamental peppers grown in pots for winter decoration. All these are of the genus *Capsicum* and are described botanically under that entry.

Peppers are of many varieties. For practical purposes they can be classified as sweet and hot. The fruits of the former are

Fruit of a pepper nearing maturity

mild, those of the other extremely pungent. Sometimes seeds from sweet peppers produce plants with hot fruits. This is because the flowers of the seed parent or mother plant were fertilized with pollen from a hot variety. The offspring take after the male parent in this matter of pungency.

Although peppers are easy to grow, they often disappoint by not cropping satisfactorily. Not infrequently they make plenty of bush, foliage, and even flowers, but few or no peppers. This has puzzled many gardeners. It has been thought that highly fertile soil containing excessive amounts of nitrogen is the cause of the trouble, and to some extent this may contribute, but there is little doubt that the chief and usually the only factor responsible is the water content of the plant. If at budding or blooming time conditions are such that the plants lose more moisture by transpiration from their foliage than they can replace through their roots, the buds and flowers drop, and the setting of fruit is reduced or prevented. Conditions that bring about such rapid loss of water are high temperatures and low relative humidity, often aggravated by wind. What the housewife hanging out laundry would call a good drying day may cripple the pepper crop. Nor can this be surely prevented by watering. A stage is reached when no matter how moist the soil is the roots simply cannot replace the loss from the foliage. Obvious aids are to select sites for peppers sheltered from sweeping winds and to make sure that the earth is kept reasonably moist. Because early-fruiting varieties are likely to bloom and set their fruits before the hottest, driest summer weather comes, they are likely to offer better chances of success than late-maturing kinds. Varieties are listed and described in seedsmen's catalogs.

The cultivation of peppers is much like that of tomatoes. Except in the subtropics and tropics, give the plants a head start by sowing the seeds in a greenhouse or under approximately similar conditions about eight weeks before it is safe to set them in the garden. Sow in pots or flats of porous soil, cover with a sheet of glass or polyethylene plastic and a piece of paper to shade the soil, and put to germinate in a temperature of 70 to 75°F. As soon as the seedlings break ground, remove the coverings, and except for giving very light shade for a few days against strong sun, grow in bright light where the night temperature is 60°F and that by day up to fifteen degrees higher. As soon as the second pair of leaves develop, transplant individually to small pots, or about 3 inches apart in flats.

Do not plant outdoors until the ground is warm and the weather is settled, a week or two later than it is safe to plant the first tomatoes. In preparation for planting,

Rooted leaf cuttings of *Peperomia argyreia*

Peppers harvested; one cut to show interior

harden the plants by standing them for a week or two in a cold frame or warm, sheltered place outdoors. Choose for this crop a sunny, preferably sheltered, location where the soil is well-drained, fertile, and in good physical condition. If possible rotate the crop so that it does not occupy the same site in successive years. Set the plants 1 foot to 1½ feet apart in rows 2 feet apart. Some gardeners prune pepper plants by shortening the branches, but there seems to be no advantage in this. It is important to keep weeds down by frequent shallow surface cultivation or, after quite warm weather comes, by mulching. Peppers are harvested either before they are fully ripe and before they have begun to color, when they are called green peppers, or after they have assumed their bright red, yellow, or black-purple coloring and are fully mature. To harvest, cut the stems so that a short piece remains attached to the fruit. When fall frost threatens, harvest all fruits that remain and store them in a cool, frostproof cellar or similar place. They will keep for up to three months or longer.

Ornamental peppers are excellent pot plants, rivaling in their usefulness Christmas-cherries. Although perennials, they are not worth keeping after their first fruiting. It is easier and more satisfactory to treat them as annuals. The kinds used have small, spherical or cone-shaped, red, purple, or creamy-white fruits that show to good advantage against their backgrounds of rich, dark green foliage. To have plants in full fruit for Christmas, sow seeds in July, in the way described above for eating peppers (as a matter of interest, the fruits of ornamental varieties are edible). Transplant the seedlings to pots rather than flats and repot as often as the

roots fill their containers into successively bigger pots until they occupy those 4 or 5 inches in diameter. Use a coarse, porous soil mix, not excessively rich in nitrogen, but nourishing. Water moderately rather than excessively. Too much water and fertilizer encourage lush instead of desirable compact growth. The plants must not, however, be permitted to wilt from dryness. Occasional applications of dilute liquid fertilizer after the final pots are filled with roots are beneficial. Until cool fall nights are at hand you may keep ornamental peppers in a sunny place outdoors with their pots buried nearly to their rims in a bed of sand, peat moss, or similar material, or they may be accommodated in a greenhouse. In any case they must be brought indoors well before frost. A sunny greenhouse where the night temperature is 60°F and that by day is five to fifteen degrees higher is to their liking. Exposure

Ornamental peppers: (a) A pot specimen

to low temperature causes yellowing and dropping of the leaves.

Pests and Diseases. Peppers are subject to a number of troubles. Aphids, flea-beetles, potato beetles, stem borers, leaf miners, pepper maggot, the white larvae of which invade the fruits, and pepper weevil, which causes the buds and small fruits to drop and the fully grown fruits to be contorted, may attack. Of diseases, anthracnose, fungus leaf spots, bacterial leaf spots, phytophthora blight, and ripe rot decay are most prevalent. Tobacco mosaic and other viruses that bring about stunting, or mottling or curling of the foliage, affect peppers, as do the physiological diseases, blossom end rot (similar to that of tomatoes), and sun scald. It is important not to smoke or handle tobacco when working with these plants.

PEPPERWORT. See Marsilea.

PERAPHYLLUM (Pera-phyllum) — Squaw-Apple. Of interest only to collectors of the botanically unusual, the solitary species of this genus of the rose family ROSACEAE inhabits dry soils from California to Oregon and Colorado. Its name, from the Greek *pera*, excessively, and *phyllon*, a leaf, alludes to the crowded foliage.

The squaw-apple (*Peraphyllum ramosissimum*) is a deciduous shrub very closely related to *Amelanchier*, the chief differences being that its flowers are in umbel-like clusters rather than definite racemes as is usually the case with amelanchiers and that they have broad, rounded petals. Also, the leaves are much narrower than those of amelanchiers. Attaining a height of 3 to 6 feet and intricately branched, the squaw-apple has oblong to oblanceolate leaves ¾ inch to 2 inches long by about ¼

(b) One with ovoid fruits

(c) One with conical fruits

inch wide, crowded toward the ends of spurlike branchlets and scattered along the new shoots. They are silky-hairy when young and may have toothed edges. The flowers, white or tinged pink and with pink centers, are two to three together or occasionally solitary. They are almost ¾ inch across and have persistent, five-lobed calyxes, five spreading, ovate petals, approximately twenty stamens, and two styles. The pendulous, spherical fruits are pomes (fruits structured like those of mountain-ashes and apples) ⅓ inch or slightly more in diameter. They are yellowish and bitter. This shrub, hardy in southern New England, is satisfied with ordinary soil. It is propagated by seed and by layers.

PEREGRINA is *Jatropha integerrima*.

PERENNIALS. Technically the word perennials encompasses all plants that normally in their natural habitats and elsewhere under favorable circumstances persist for more than two full growing seasons and so are more or less permanent in contrast to annuals that die at the end of their first, and biennials that die at the end of their second, growing season. All trees and shrubs, all ferns, practically all bulb plants, and many vines are perennials.

The group is divided on the basis of characteristics of the stem tissue into woody perennials, which include all trees and shrubs and all vines that have woody (ligneous) stems, and herbaceous perennials, which have stems without woody tissues or are stemless. There is no sharp line of distinction between these groups and some sorts of plants, often called subshrubs, have stems with a certain amount of ligneous tissue, but not sufficient to give them the firm, woody character characteristic of more typical shrubs. Perennials may be deciduous or evergreen, hardy or not.

In common garden usage, perennials is somewhat loosely employed in a more restricted sense to include only herbaceous plants and sometimes a few subshrubby sorts that persist for more than two years; it excludes trees, shrubs, and woody vines. In temperate regions its application is often still further limited to plants that are sufficiently hardy to live through winters outdoors. A more precise identification for such kinds is hardy herbaceous perennials. Many nonhardy or tender herbaceous perennials are grown as annuals and are generally known to gardeners and listed in seed catalogs as such. Here belong petunias, snapdragons, and most verbenas.

Familiar hardy herbaceous perennials include all or some sorts of achilleas, aconites, anemones, aquilegias, armerias, artemisias, asters, astilbes, campanulas, centaureas, chrysanthemums, coreopsises,

Popular hardy herbaceous perennials include: (a) Anemones

(b) Centaureas

(c) Delphiniums

delphiniums, echinaceas, echinopses, eryngiums, geraniums, geums, gypsophilas, heleniums, heliopsises, hemerocallises, heucheras, hollyhocks, hostas, *Iberis*,

(d) Eryngiums

(e) Heleniums

(f) Hemerocallises

Iris, kniphofias, liatrises, limoniums, lupines, *Lychnis*, lythrums, *Macleaya*, monardas, nepetas, oenotheras, peonies, physostegias, poppies, potentillas, rudbeckias, salvias, scabiouses, sidalceas, *Stachys*, thalictrums, tradescantias, trolliuses, verbascums, and veronicas, as well as such

(g) Hostas

Pereskia, undetermined species in Cuba

(h) Peonies

bulb plants as crocuses, hyacinths, lilies, and narcissuses. For information about the uses of hardy herbaceous perennials see the Encyclopedia entry Flower Beds and Borders.

PERESKIA (Perésk-ia) — Barbados-Gooseberry or Lemon-Vine. The genus *Pereskia*, of the cactus family CACTACEAE, is indigenous from Mexico to South America and the West Indies. It was named to honor Nicholas Claude Fabre de Peiresc, who died in 1637. There are about twenty species. The name has also been spelled *Peireskia* and *Peirescia*. Some kinds accepted as *Pereskia* here are by some botanists segregated as *Rhodocactus*.

Pereskias are among the most un-cactus-like cactuses in appearance. They have leaves with much the look of those of ordinary nonsucculent plants, and their slightly fleshy stems soon become woody and have little obvious resemblance to the fat ones generally associated with cactuses. To the casual observer, pereskias are just leafy, thorny shrubs that at times bear attractive pink, yellow, or white flowers. But the botanically alert easily detect give-away characteristics that point to membership in the cactus family. One such evidence is that the spines, branches, and flowers sprout from specialized areas on the stem called areoles. The flowers and fruits are also quite clearly cactaceous. To more or less clinch matters, other kinds of cactuses can be readily grafted upon them. Related cactus genera that bear well-developed leaves are *Pereskiopsis* and *Quiabentia*, but in these genera the areoles have glochids (small, barbed bristles) like those of *Opuntia*, and the flowers also are opuntia-like.

Pereskias include trees, shrubs, and vines. Their spines, solitary or clustered, are not barbed. Their leaves are alternate, deciduous, broad, flat, and slightly fleshy. Solitary, clustered, or panicled, in the leaf axils or terminal on the stems, the flat, wheel-shaped flowers have spreading perianth parts (sepals and petals that merge from one to the other without obvious distinction), numerous stamens, and a solitary style. The juicy, fleshy fruits, technically berries, contain thin-shelled black seeds, those of some kinds edible.

The Barbados-gooseberry or lemon-vine (**P. aculeata**), at first an erect shrub, with age becomes a vine with woody stems up to 30 feet in length. On their lower parts they have, in ones to threes, slender, straight spines. The spines above are shorter, curved, and usually in pairs. Short-stalked, and short-pointed at their apexes, the leaves are lanceolate to ovate, 2 to 4 inches long, and have prominent midribs. White, pale yellow, or pinkish, and with a somewhat unpleasant odor, the blooms, 1 inch to 1½ inches in diameter, are in clusters or panicles. They are succeeded by pale yellow fruits, at first spiny and leafy, but smooth at maturity, and ½ to ¾ inch in diameter. They are eaten out of hand and made into preserves. In some parts of South America the leaves are cooked as a vegetable. This is the only *Pereskia* with spiny fruits. Variety *P. a. rubescens* has leaves variegated with red.

A shrub or small tree with a trunk up to 4 inches in diameter, **P. grandifolia** (syn. *Rhodocactus grandifolius*), in gardens often cultivated as *P. bleo*, attains heights of 6 to 15 feet. It has heavy, very spiny stems, and short-stalked, elliptic to ovate, fleshy leaves 3 to 6 inches long and 1¼ to 1¾ inches broad. The nearly black spines, solitary or in pairs, are up to 2 inches long. Of a lovely pink hue or white, the roselike flowers, clustered at the branch ends, are 1½ to 1¾ inches wide and are followed by green, irregularly pear-shaped fruits, leafy and about 2 inches long. True **P. bleo** (syn. *Rhodocactus bleo*), not to be confused with

Pereskia aculeata

Pereskia grandifolia

Pereskia grandifolia (flowers)

the previous species, which often travels under that name, is native to Panama and Colombia. Up to about 20 feet in height, it is treelike or shrubby and has stems, reddish and spineless when young, that later become green, with clusters of five or more spines. Up to 8 inches long by 2 inches wide, the thinnish leaves have stalks approximately 1 inch long. The bright pink, short-stalked flowers, in clusters, are 1½ to 1¾ inches wide. The top-shaped, light yellow fruits are as much in diameter.

Native from Paraguay to Argentina, **P. sacharosa** is an upright shrub up to 20 feet tall. Its stems have large areoles bearing

Pereskia sacharosa

several straight spines up to 2 inches long. In clusters and very showy, the pink or white flowers are 3 to 3½ inches in diameter. The leafy, roundish fruits are 1½ inches long or somewhat longer.

Mexican **P. conzattii** is an erect shrub or tree 25 to 40 feet tall and much-branched. It has short-stalked, almost round leaves with a greatest diameter of up to 1 inch. The approximately 1-inch-long spines are in clusters of few to many. The flowers of this species are unknown. Its smooth fruits are pear-shaped and up to 2 inches long.

Garden and Landscape Uses. In the dry tropics and warm subtropics the chief landscape application of this genus is as hedge plants, for which purpose *P. aculeata* is especially popular. They are formidable barriers. The other important use to which pereskias are commonly put is as understocks on which to graft *Rhipsalis, Rhipsalidopsis, Schlumbergera,* and some other cactuses.

Cultivation. These are strong-growing plants that thrive outdoors in almost any well-drained soil in the tropics and subtropics and that endure arid conditions with extreme fortitude. This is also true when they are grown in greenhouses. They need full sun and are very easily increased from cuttings and from seed. For general suggestions regarding their cultivation see Cactuses.

PERESKIOPSIS (Pereski-ópsis). The name of this group of the cactus family CACTACEAE suggests similarity to *Pereskia* and, in fact, is derived from the name of that genus and the Greek *opsis,* resembling. Similarities in appearance between the two

genera, especially in their possession of abundant foliage of the type associated with plants other than cactuses, exist, but *Pereskiopsis* is more closely allied to *Quiabentia* and *Opuntia* than to *Pereskia*. This botanical relationship is based, of course, upon the structure of the flowers and fruits.

There are about a dozen species of *Pereskiopsis*, native from Baja California to Guatemala. They are trees and shrubs with erect, cylindrical stems and thick, somewhat fleshy, persistant leaves. The areoles (places on cactus stems from which spines develop) are in the leaf axils and have, in addition to spines, small bristle-like, barbed spinelets called glochids. These are not present in *Pereskia*. The blooms of *Pereskiopsis* resemble those of *Opuntia*. Solitary and stalkless on shoots of the previous year, they are yellow or reddish. The seeds are covered with matted hairs.

From 3 to 6 feet tall, **P. aquosa** has elliptic leaves about 3 inches long by about one-third as broad, with reddish edges. The young areoles have long white hairs; later they develop glochids and one or two spines a little over 1 inch long. The blooms are yellow marked toward their outsides with red. The yellowish-green, pear-shaped fruits are about 1 inch long. Up to 10 feet tall, **P. diguetii** has hairy stems that become reddish with age. Its obovate leaves, up to 2 inches long, have areoles with long, pendant, white hairs and later brownish wool, numerous brown glochids, and one to four, but most commonly not more than two, unequal spines, the longest of which may be 3 inches long. The blooms are yellow. Very spiny older stems are a feature of *P. porteri,* which is 3 to 4 feet in height. When young its stems are without spines or nearly so, later there are eight or fewer from each areole as well as many brown glochids. The obovate-pointed leaves are from a little under to a little over 1 inch long. The yellow flowers, about 1½ inches across, are succeeded by orange-red fruits 2 inches long. From the last named, *P. gatesii* differs in its rounder leaves, deep pink blooms, and fruits that are only ¾ inch long. The leaves of *P. rotundifolia* are nearly round. Each areole has a solitary spine. The stems are thick and woody, the blooms reddish-yellow and about 1¼ inches across. Spatula-shaped, glossy, fleshy leaves 1 inch to 2 inches long characterize *P. spathulata,* 3 to 6 feet tall and with red blooms and greenish fruits. The areoles on its gray-green stems when young have white hairs. These soon fall and are replaced by whitish wool and brown glochids. At first they have one or two spines, later up to eight. Normally 3 to 6 feet tall, *P. velutina* has stems that when young are hairy. Its velvety, lanceolate to elliptic leaves, with blades up to 2¼ inches long, become reddish-brown as they age. Its bright yellow blooms are reddish or greenish on their outsides. Their ovaries have leafy bracts.

Garden and Landscape Uses and Cultivation. These are the same as for *Pereskia.* For general information on uses and cultivation see Cactuses.

PEREZIA (Per-èzia). Native from the southwestern United States to southern South America, *Perezia* is little known horticulturally. Named after the sixteenth-century apothecary and author Lorenzo Perez, it belongs in the daisy family COMPOSITAE and comprises possibly seventy species of perennial herbaceous plants and annuals.

Perezias have tufts of all basal leaves or have erect stems with alternate, often stem-clasping, usually spine-toothed leaves. The flower heads, solitary or in panicles, are composed of disk florets (the kind that form the centers of daisies); there are no ray florets (the petal-like ones of daisies). The seedlike fruits or achenes are densely-glandular or glandular-hairy.

The kind most likely to be cultivated is the Californian perennial *P. microcephala.* This common inhabitant of dry slopes has stoutish stems about 3 feet tall and shortly-rough-hairy, minutely-glandular, toothed leaves 4 to 8 inches long, and oblong-ovate. Their bases are broad and stem-clasping. The panicles of whitish or purplish-pink small flower heads are 1 foot to nearly 2 feet long and up to 1 foot broad. The annual *P. multiflora* is a native of South America. Erect and 1 foot tall or taller, it has oblong, stem-clasping, pinnately-cut, spiny-margined leaves up to about 6 inches long. Its bluish flower heads are in crowded, flat-topped clusters.

Garden and Landscape Uses and Cultivation. The annual species described here may be used to give variety in flower gardens. Its seeds are sown in well-drained soil in spring in sunny locations where the plants are to remain, and the seedlings are thinned sufficiently to avoid overcrowding. Alternatively, the seeds may be started early in a greenhouse, and the young plants set in the garden later. The perennial described is adapted for cultivation in California and places where the climate is similar. It may be used in flower borders and less formal plantings. Its hardiness away from its home territory has not been adequately determined. It grows without difficulty in a variety of well-drained soils in full sun and is propagated by seed and by division.

PERGOLA. A pergola is a garden structure similar in purpose and design but generally proportionately longer than an arbor. Often they take the form of colonnades with the upright supports tied together with horizontal side members and with cross-ties forming an openwork roof. Pergolas are suitable for spanning paths to afford shade, and to provide support for vines and climbing roses.

PERIANTH. This term applies collectively to the calyx and corolla of a flower. It is most often used when there is no marked differentiation between calyx and corolla, between sepals and petals. Then, the perianth parts are correctly identified as tepals, but in common parlance, if all are petal-like, as they are for instance in hyacinths, lilies, and tulips, all are less accurately called petals.

PERICOME (Perícom-e). Two species of *Pericome,* of the southwestern United States and Mexico, are recognized. They are tall, branching, strongly aromatic herbaceous perennials of the daisy family COMPOSITAE. The name is from the Greek *peri,* around, and *kome,* a tuft of hairs, and alludes to the hairy edges of the seedlike fruits (achenes).

Pericomes have opposite, stalked, halberd-shaped to triangular-lanceolate, glandular leaves, and terminal, flat-topped clusters of numerous small golden-yellow flower heads composed of all disk florets (the kind in daisies that form the centers of the flower heads as opposed to those that look like petals). The florets are bisexual and have four-toothed corollas. The anthers protrude prominently and the styles have two long slender branches.

Native of dry stony places above 5,000 feet, from California to Texas, Oklahoma, and Mexico, *P. caudata* has erect stems, more or less woody at their bases and up to 6 feet tall, and long-pointed leaf blades up to 2 inches long. The involucres (collars of bracts) of the flower heads are broadly-

bell-shaped and consist of twenty to twenty-five bracts.

Garden and Landscape Uses and Cultivation. Pericomes are little known outside the regions of their occurrence as natives. Their degree of hardiness elsewhere is not fully established. Fairly ornamental, they are especially adapted to dry, exposed, sunny locations. They may be used in flower borders and less formal plantings and, in their home territory, in collections of native plants. They adapt to moist soils and are easily raised from seed and by division.

PERIDERIDIA (Perider-ídia)—Squaw Root. The tuberous roots of some members of *Perideridia,* of the carrot family UMBELLIFERAE, were important foods of the Indians. There are nine species, all North American, and all except one, western. The name comes from the Greek *peri,* around, and *derros,* a leather coat. Its application is not clear.

Perideridias are hairless herbaceous perennials with erect, branching stems, and leaves, one- to three-times-pinnately-divided, the lower ones more dissected than the upper ones. The small white or pinkish flowers are in loose umbels formed of smaller umbels. They have five sepals and five petals. The small, dry fruits are flattened and ridged. By some botanists these plants are included in *Carum.*

Squaw root (*P. gairdneri* syn. *Carum gairdneri*) has a solitary stem 1 foot to 4 feet tall. Most of its leaves are pinnately-divided into linear to lanceolate, usually undivided segments ¾ inch to 4½ inches long. The upper leaves often are not divided. The flowers are as described in the previous paragraph. This species is indigenous from California to New Mexico, British Columbia, and Alberta. Similar, but with more finely divided leaves with shorter segments, and not over 2 feet in height, *P. oregana* (syn. *Carum oreganum*) is native from California to British Columbia.

Garden Uses and Cultivation. In gardens devoted to native plants and those in which plants used by the Indians are emphasized, these plants rightly have places. They may be used also in semiwild areas. Otherwise they make little claim for the attentions of gardeners. They need moist, fertile soil and sunny locations and are increased by seed and by division.

PERILLA (Períl-la). One coleus-like kind of this group of four to six annuals native from India to Japan is cultivated as a foliage plant for summer display in garden beds. The genus *Perilla,* the name an East Indian one for *P. frutescens,* belongs in the mint family LABIATAE.

Perillas have square stems and opposite, undivided leaves. Their small, two-lipped flowers are in axillary or terminal racemes or panicles. They differ from those of *Coleus* in that the filaments of their stamens are not joined for one-third of their length from their bases to form tubes or sheaths around the styles. Each has a bell-shaped, five-toothed calyx and a short-tubed corolla with five unequal lobes (petals). There are four stamens and a two-parted style. The fruits are seedlike nutlets.

Commonly cultivated **P.** *frutescens crispa* (syn. *P. nankinensis*) differs from the species *P. frutescens,* which has escaped

Perilla frutescens

Perilla frutescens (flowers)

Perilla frutescens crispa

from cultivation in North America and often inhabits roadsides and waste places from Massachusetts to Ohio, Iowa, Florida and Texas, in having dark bronzy or purple-brown instead of green foliage. These plants, 3 to 4 feet tall and freely-branched, have broad-ovate, long-stalked, toothed leaves with blades up to 4½ inches long. Their white to reddish flowers, which make no appreciable show, appear in late summer and fall. This species is native from India to Japan. Widely distributed in the wild throughout most of the natural range of the genus, variety *P. frutescens crispa* is available in several minor variations to which seedsmen apply such names as *compacta* and *laciniata,* the latter to sorts with crimped and curled foliage. A variation with variegated foliage is sometimes grown.

Garden Uses and Cultivation. Perillas are useful for creating subtropical effects. They grow rapidly, need little care, and prosper in full sun or slight shade in any ordinary garden soil. They may be raised from seeds sown directly outdoors in early spring and the seedlings transplanted to where they are to remain, but it is more usual to sow early indoors and to raise the seedlings to planting-out size in small pots or flats in a sunny, warm greenhouse or hotbed. When the latter plan is followed the seeds are sown in a temperature of 65 to 70°F in January or February and the young plants are kept growing in a minimum temperature of 55°F. The plants are not set outdoors until it is safe to plant tomatoes. Another plan is to lift plants from the garden in fall before frost, cut them back somewhat, pot them, and house them in a greenhouse with a minimum temperature of 55°F. Cuttings taken from such stock plants in March root readily and make good planting out stock by May.

PERIPLOCA (Períplo-ca) — Silk Vine. Ten deciduous and evergreen, woody, twining vines, indigenous from southern Europe to Africa and the Orient, are included in *Periploca,* of the milkweed family ASCLE-PIADACEAE. The name is from the Greek *periploke,* an intertwining, and refers to the habit of the plants.

Periplocas have poisonous, milky juice and opposite, undivided, lobeless leaves. The small flowers are in clusters from the shoot ends or leaf axils. They have a calyx of five sepals, glandular on their upper surfaces, and a five-lobed, wheel-shaped corolla with at its base a five- or ten-lobed corona (crown). There are five very short-stalked separate stamens, the anthers of which are hairy on their backs and united at their tips, and a short style supporting a disklike stigma. The fruits are paired, podlike follicles containing numerous winged seeds.

The commonest sort cultivated is *P. graeca,* a native of southern Europe and

western Asia, and hardy in southern New England. Deciduous and up to 40 feet tall, this has glossy, green-stalked leaves, ovate to pointed-oblong-lanceolate and up to 4 inches long by about one-half as broad. They remain on the vines until late in the fall. The starlike flowers, about 1 inch in diameter, are in terminal, loose, long-stalked clusters. They have brownish-purple petals with greenish margins, green on their outsides, a central five-lobed crown, and purple stamens. The fruits, about 5 inches long and ½ inch wide, are packed with seeds about ¼ inch long with tufts of silky hairs at their ends. Native to northern China, **P.** *sepium,* lower and more slender than *P. graeca,* is hardy as a vine at New York City, and as a groundcover protected by a covering of snow in winter, much farther north. Its leaves are deciduous, lanceolate, and dark glossy-green on their upper surfaces, paler beneath. They are up to 3½ inches long by up to ¾ inch wide. The flowers, about ¾ inch in diameter, are similar to those of *P. graeca,* but in few-flowered clusters.

Garden and Landscape Uses. Silk vines are fast-growing, sun-loving climbers for pergolas, arbors, posts, walls fitted with wires around which stems can twine, trunks of trees, and other supports. Their chief attraction is their foliage. The flowers are interesting, but not highly showy.

Cultivation. Propagation of silk vines is easy by seed, cuttings, and layering. Young plants may be set in their permanent locations in spring. Succeeding in any ordinary well-drained soil, they require no special routine care.

PERISSOLOBUS BIJLII is *Machairophyllum bijlii.*

PERISTERIA (Peris-tèria)—Dove Orchid or Holy Ghost Flower. Seventeen species in the opinions of some authorities, not more than about half a dozen according to others, all of notable horticultural merit, constitute *Peristeria,* of the orchid family ORCHIDACEAE. Two or three are fairly commonly grown by orchid fanciers. The group is native to Central and tropical South America. Its name is derived from the Greek *peristera,* a dove. It alludes to a fanciful resemblance of the column and wings of the lip of the flower to the bird of peace. This comparison is made also in a vernacular name of the best-known species. Its other common name reflects imagery less mundane and less subject to direct comparison, but possibly as apt.

Peristerias are epiphytic (tree-perching) and terrestrial (growing in the ground). They have large, ribbed leaves that unfold in succession, and from the bases of the pseudobulbs, racemes of more or less spherical or cupped blooms with similar, broad, concave sepals and petals, and a three-lobed lip with the center lobe movable and the lateral ones broad, winglike, and attached to the column.

The dove orchid or Holy Ghost flower (*P. elata*), a native of Colombia, Costa Rica, and Panama, and the national flower of the last, has broad, ovoid pseudobulbs 4 to 6 inches tall, with up to five lanceolate-elliptic, deciduous leaves 2 to 4 feet in length and up to 1 foot wide. The flowering stalks, 3 to 5 feet tall, bear, usually before the foliage dies, ten to twenty 2-inch-wide, creamy-white, waxy blooms in their upper thirds. These open in succession over a long period. Fragrant, the flowers have a fleshy, broadly-obovate lip and a column with curious rose-red-spotted, large wings attached.

The leaves of *P. cerina* die before the flowers appear. A native of Brazil and perhaps northward, this has more slender pseudobulbs than *P. elata*, the largest up to 5 inches long and with three or four leaves. The racemes of up to fifteen, mostly up-facing, fragrant, fleshy blooms are about 6 inches long. About 1½ inches wide, they are medium to rich yellow, with the outer part of the lip orange. Similar, but with less compact racemes of not over about seven flowers, *P. pendula*, of Panama and the Guianas, has red-mottled, white blooms 2 inches in width. Of the same relationship, *P. guttata* has flattened-ovate-oblong pseudobulbs 3 to 4 inches long with from their summits usually three pointed, broad-lanceolate leaves

about 1 foot long. Its nearly globular, fragrant, fleshy flowers in short prostrate racemes are approximately 1½ inches in diameter. Buff-yellow to pale salmon-pink, they are freely spattered with reddish-purple or maroon spots.

Garden Uses and Cultivation. Peristerias are of interest to orchid collectors. For their successful cultivation, peristerias need plenty of warmth and humidity, they may be accommodated in intermediate- or warm-temperature greenhouses. They prosper in hanging baskets, on rafts, and in a loose rooting compost of tree fern fiber and partially rotted leaf mold, with a generous admixture of broken crocks (small pieces of broken clay flower pots) and crushed charcoal. Good light with shade from strong sun is needed. From when new growth starts in spring until the foliage begins to die away, abundant water, and regular applications of dilute liquid fertilizer are needed. When in fall the foliage starts to yellow, stop fertilizing, increase intervals between waterings, and finally permit the rooting medium to become completely dry and the plants to rest. Since peristerias dislike root disturbance, replanting should not be done more often than necessary. For further information see Orchids.

PERISTROPHE (Peris-trophe). The about thirty species of *Peristrophe* are natives of the tropics of Africa and Asia. They belong

in the acanthus family ACANTHACEAE. The name, from the Greek *peri*, around, and *strophos*, a belt, alludes to the collars of bracts that accompany the clusters of blooms.

Peristrophes are herbaceous or subshrubby plants with erect or partially prostrate stems and opposite, undivided, toothless leaves. The flowers are solitary or in groups of two or three attended by involucre-like collars of bracts generally longer than the deeply-five-cleft calyxes. The rose-pink to purple corollas have slender tubes widening toward their tops and two approximately equal-sized, wide-spreading lips (petals), the lower with three teeth or lobes, the upper essentially toothless and lobeless. There are two protruding stamens slightly shorter than the corollas, and a slender style. The fruits are four-seeded capsules.

An excellent winter-blooming greenhouse plant, and suitable for outdoors in warm, frost-free climates, *P. speciosa* is a native of India. Broad, erect, branching, and 2 to 3 feet tall, it provides a splendid display of rosy-magenta blooms over a long period beginning in fall. Woody toward its base, it has stems that narrow above the nodes and ovate, lanceolate-ovate, to elliptic, pointed leaves 4 or 5 inches long. Its flowers, on slender stalks, are 1½ to nearly 2 inches long, and slightly more across their faces. In clusters of two or three, they are borne in great profusion. The bracts are oblanceolate. Lower, laxer, and less showy in bloom, *P. hyssopifolia* (syns. *P. angustifolia*, *P. salicifolia*), of Java, has branches, downy in their upper parts, that spread more or less horizontally. The leaves are narrow-elliptic to lanceolate and 2 to 3 inches long. The terminal clusters of magenta-red flowers have collars of two unequal-sized, ovate-oblong, hairy-margined bracts. In *P. h. aureo-variegata* the centers of the leaves have a feathered variegation of yellow.

Peristeria guttata

Peristrophe hyssopifolia aureo-variegata

Peristrophe hyssopifolia aureo-variegata
(leaves and flowers)

Garden Uses. In greenhouses *P. speciosa* is grown as a pot plant. When used decoratively care must be exercised about the colors with which it is associated. Its rather harsh magenta-pink blooms clash badly with most reds and many pinks. They are at their best near whites and pale yellows. The flowers do not last when cut. The other species described is sometimes grown in pots, but is perhaps at its best in hanging baskets. The variegated variety is usually preferred.

Cultivation. Although perennials and often treated as such, peristrophes are easily grown and flowered as annuals. The best plan is to raise new plants each spring from cuttings or seeds. Both methods are easy in a moist atmosphere in a temperature of 60 to 70°F. The seedlings or rooted cuttings are transferred to small, well-drained pots and to larger ones as growth necessitates. The young plants may have the tips of their shoots pinched occasionally to promote branching. Peristrophes flourish in porous, fertile soil that contains a reasonable amount of organic material, such as leaf mold or peat moss, kept moderately moist at all times. Once established, a night temperature of 55°F with a daytime rise of five or ten degrees is satisfactory. The atmosphere should be fairly humid, but not oppressively so. On favorable occasions the greenhouse should be freely ventilated. If the plants are kept indoors during the summer, light shade is needed.

As an alternative to keeping them indoors they may, after the weather is warm and settled, be planted outside in sunny nursery beds and be dug up carefully and potted before fall frost. This works very well provided the newly potted plants are placed immediately in a shaded, humid greenhouse and for the first week or ten days their foliage misted lightly with water at frequent intervals. Once they have re-

covered from the shock of lifting and transplanting it is essential that they be exposed to full light and more airy conditions. The blooms fail to open in shade. As blooming-size plants, *P. speciosa* may occupy containers 6 to 10 inches in diameter, depending upon how early in spring the plants were propagated. Receptacles not larger than the 6-inch size are adequate for *P. hyssopifolia*.

PERIWINKLE. See Vinca. The Madagascar-periwinkle is *Catharanthus roseus.*

PERLITE. This is a type of volcanic rock expanded by heating to 1,800°F. It consists of white, gritty, porous particles as big or somewhat bigger than large grains of sand. Sterile, and essentially neutral in reaction (pH 7.0 to 7.5), when dry it weighs 6 to 9 pounds, when wet about 25 pounds, per cubic foot. It contains no plant nutrients. Perlite is very useful for including in soil mixes, especially for

Perlite is a useful soil additive

plants in flats, pots, and other containers. When so used it serves much like sand, but more effectively, to improve porosity and aeration. It is also an excellent medium in which to root cuttings. Unlike vermiculite, perlite has neither cation exchange nor buffering capacity and so does not minimize pH changes nor hold nutrients in reserve for slow release. Its benefits are entirely mechanical. Perlite does not deteriorate or decay in the soil, being porous, it holds moisture on its interior as well as exterior surfaces.

PERMANGANATE OF POTASH. See Potassium Permanganate.

PERMANENT WAVE TREE is *Salix matsudana tortuosa.*

PERNETTYA (Pernét-tya). Low, evergreen shrubs make up *Pernettya*, of the heath family ERICACEAE. There are twenty or perhaps more species, natives of Mexico, South America, New Zealand, and Tasmania. The name commemorates Antoine Joseph Pernetty, chronicler of Bougainville's voyage of discovery to South America and the Falkland Islands. Pernetty died in 1801.

Pernettyas differ from related *Vaccinium* in the ovaries of their flowers being above rather than below the sepals and petals, and from *Gaultheria* in having as fruits berries with small, dry calyxes at their bases. The hybrid between *Pernettya* and *Gaultheria* is named *Gaulthettya*. The short-stalked, usually finely-toothed, leathery leaves of *Pernettya* are alternate. Solitary or in racemes from the leaf axils, the blooms have five-lobed calyxes, urn- to bell-shaped corollas with five small lobes (petals), ten stamens, and one style. The fruits are long-persistent, nearly spherical berries. Those of some kinds are reported to be poisonous.

Highly ornamental, especially in fruit, *P. mucronata,* of southernmost South

Pernettya mucronata (flowers)

Pernettya mucronata (fruits)

America, is one of the hardiest species and the one most commonly cutivated. Spreading freely by suckers, and generally 1 foot to 1½ feet tall, but sometimes considerably higher, it has broadly-elliptic to oblong, round-based, toothed leaves up to ¾ inch long by approximately one-third as broad. Solitary from the leaf axils, the ¼-inch-long, white flowers are widely urn-shaped. They are succeeded by flattened-spherical, very long-persistent, white, pink, red, lilac, or purple berries, about ½ inch in diameter, that have associated with them the persistent membranous calyxes. Horticultural varieties differing chiefly in the color of their fruits often have varietal designations descriptive of that feature, such as *alba, rosea, coccinea, lilacina,* and *purpurea.*

A prostrate shrub, native from Costa Rica to Chile and up to 1 foot tall, **P. prostrata** has rigid stems and glossy, hairless, ovate-lanceolate leaves up to ⅝ inch long. The flowers have urn-shaped corollas a little over ¼ inch long. The fruits are blue-black. Narrow-elliptic to lanceolate leaves up to 1⅛ inch long and purplish-black fruits are characteristic of more upright *P. p. pentlandii.*

Pernettya prostrata pentlandii (fruits)

Mat-forming creepers about 3 inches high, **P. tasmanica** and **P. nana** are similar, natives, respectively, of Tasmania and New Zealand. They have leathery, commonly slightly toothed, oblong to oblong-lanceolate leaves up to ¼ inch long. Their usually solitary flowers are ¼ inch long. Those of *P. tasmanica* are bell-shaped and have blunt calyx lobes, styles longer than the filaments (stalks of the stamens), and anthers without bristles at their apexes. Its fruits are usually red. The urn-shaped, white, pink, or red blooms of *P. nana* have sharply pointed calyx lobes, styles not longer than the filaments, and anthers with minute bristles at their tips. The fruits are white, pink, or red.

Garden and Landscape Uses. Although pernettyas may survive outdoors in shel-

tered places as far north as Philadelphia or even southern New England, they do so reluctantly and are much better suited for climates more salubrious, such as those of parts of California and the Pacific Northwest. They need a sunny location; in shade they tend to become straggly. Pernettyas are admirable for rock gardens and inclusion in collections of choice shrubs, and *P. mucronata* makes a very attractive pot plant.

Cultivation. Seeds, cuttings, division, and layering are practical means of propagating pernettyas. To be sure of having *P. mucronata* fruit satisfactorily it is necessary to have growing in proximity plants that originated from two or more seedling stocks. This can be assured by interplanting varieties that have differently colored berries. Individual seedlings are usually self-sterile, they do not set fruits well to their own pollen, and plants raised from cuttings, divisions, or layers function merely as extensions of the individuals from which the propagations were taken. Routine care is not demanding. Their primary needs are a cool, moist, but not wet well-drained soil that contains an abundance of peat or other organic matter. Sun is required. A mulch of peat moss or similar organic material aids in keeping the roots cool and evenly damp. No regular pruning is required, but it helps if occasionally old, worn-out branches are removed from *P. mucronata* and the ends of any straggly shoots cut back.

PEROVSKIA (Peróv-skia) — Russian-Sage. Of nine species of *Perovskia*, of the mint family LABIATAE, indigenous from Iran to the Himalayas, about three are cultivated. The name, sometimes spelled *Perovskia,* commemorates a nineteenth-century provincial governor of Russia, Vasili A. Perovski.

These are aromatic herbaceous perennials and subshrubs that differ from *Salvia,* which they otherwise resemble, in technical details of their anthers and in the upper lips of their corollas being four-lobed. The leaves are opposite and toothed, lobed, or cleft. The flowers, in rather distantly spaced whorls (circles of more than two) form large panicles. They are asymmetrical and have two-lipped, tubular, toothed calyxes and short, funnel-shaped, two-lipped corollas, the upper lips of which are four-lobed. The lower ones are down-pointed and not lobed. There are two fertile stamens. The fruits consist of four small, seedlike nutlets.

A deciduous subshrub 3 to 5 feet in height with stiffly upright stems, foliage grayish with stellate (star-shaped) hairs, and violet-blue flowers with downy, whitish stalks, in late summer and fall, the Russian-sage (**P. atriplicifolia**) is moderately hardy in the north. It has lanceolate to narrowly-ovate, coarsely-toothed, short-

Perovskia atriplicifolia

stalked leaves 1 inch to 2½ inches long. It has in whorls of up to six ⅜-inch-long blue flowers with purplish or grayish calyxes. The blooms make no great show individually, but are sufficiently numerous that the spikes, in panicles 1 foot long or longer, are quite attractive and elegant. This is native to the Himalayas.

Lesser known species sometimes cultivated, as hardy or perhaps slightly less so than the Russian-sage, are **P. abrotanoides,** native from Turkestan to Iran, and **P. artemesioides,** native from Iran to West Pakistan. The first, 2 to 3 feet tall, has twice-pinnately-cleft, ovate leaves about 2 inches long and narrow panicles of blue-purple flowers. The other, as tall or somewhat taller, has purple-blue flowers in slender panicles.

Garden and Landscape Uses. As a garden plant Russian-sage is esteemed for its late blooms, grayish foliage, and light, graceful appearance. It may be used effectively in groups in mixed flower borders, alone in beds, and more informally in naturalistic landscapes. The other species described may be used similarly.

Cultivation. Given the kind of location indicated, no difficulty attends the cultivation of these plants. They need thoroughly well-drained soil and full sun. They propagate readily from cuttings and seed. Planting may be done in spring or early fall, spacing individuals about 2 feet apart. To encourage the best bloom, prune the plants back fairly hard in late winter or early spring and at the same time remove any dead wood and very crowded shoots. A spring application of a complete fertilizer is helpful.

PERREIRAARA. This is the name of orchid hybrids the parents of which include *Aerides, Rhynchostylis,* and *Vanda.*

PERSEA (Pér-sea) — Avocado or Alligator-Pear. The best-known member of the genus *Persea,* of the laurel family LAURACEAE, is the avocado. A few others are cultivated. The group consists of possibly 150 species of warm regions of the Old World and the New World with the greatest concentration of kinds in the Americas. The name is an ancient one for some fruit tree of Egypt.

Perseas are trees or shrubs with alternate, undivided, lobeless and toothless, often aromatic, leathery, pinnately-veined leaves. The small flowers, in clusters or panicles, have deeply-six-parted perianths; the parts, similar and in two circles of three, are best identified as tepals rather than sepals and petals. There are usually twelve stamens in four series, of which the inner three are represented by nonfertile staminodes. The style is slender, the fruits, technically berry-like, are, except in the avocado and closely related kinds, generally less than ¾ inch in diameter.

The avocado or alligator-pear (**P. americana** syn. *P. gratissima*) probably originated in southern Mexico and adjacent territory to the south. It is now cultivated throughout the tropics and subtropics. Not aromatic, and reaching a maximum height in excess of 100 feet, but usually not much over one-half as tall, it is broad-headed and has elliptic-lanceolate, broad-elliptic, or oblong leaves from 3 inches to over 1 foot long, with undersides usually more or less glaucous. The little, short-stalked, greenish flowers are in broad clusters. The fruits are green and large, globular, and egg- or pear-shaped. They are the well-known avocados of commerce. Distinct from the typical species in having shoots and foliage that when crushed are anise-scented and black fruits with reflexed, more persistent calyxes is

Persea americana in California

Persea americana (flowers)

the Mexican avocado *P. a. drymifolia*. The Trapp avocado, formerly distinguished as *P. leiogyna*, and some other variants previously accorded rank as species, are included in *P. americana*.

Red-bay or bull-bay (**P. borbonia** syn. *P. carolinensis*) is an aromatic shrub or erect-branched, symmetrical tree sometimes over 50 feet tall, but often lower, a native in swampy, moist, or sometimes drier soils from North Carolina to Florida and Texas. Its lustrous, dark green, toothless leaves, elliptic to lanceolate, and 1¾ to 5 inches long by 3 inches wide, are sparsely-coppery-hairy beneath. The small, pale yellow flowers, few to several in short-stalked clusters, are succeeded by subglobose, red-stalked, blue-black, glaucous fruits barely ½ inch long. Variety *P. b. humilis* has leaves not over 3½ inches long by 2¼ inches wide, densely-coppery-hairy on their undersurfaces. Found only in Florida, this blooms a month later than *P. borbonia*. Swamp red-bay, swamp-bay, or sweet-bay (**P. palustris** syn. *P. pubescens*) is a densely-foliaged shrub or tree rarely exceeding 40 feet in height that inhabits coastal regions from Virginia to Florida, Texas, and the Bahamas. It differs from *P. borbonia* chiefly in the hairs on its branchlets and foliage standing erect rather than lying parallel with the surface and in the stalks of the flower clusters being usually longer instead of generally shorter than those of the leaves in the axils of which they develop. Its blue-black fruits are ½ to ¾ inch long.

Cultivated in California, Florida, and elsewhere in mild climates are Chilean *P.*

Fruits of two varieties of *Persea americana*

meyeniana, a tree up to 20 feet tall or a little taller, and *P. indica,* a small tree indigenous to the Canary Islands, Madeira, and the Azores. The first is somewhat, but not strongly, aromatic. It has elliptic to obovate leaves, nearly hairless, dull above, and glaucous on their undersides. They are 2 to 4½ inches long by 1½ to 3 inches wide. The flower clusters are mostly shorter-stalked than the leaves in the axils of which they are borne. The dark-colored fruits are ellipsoid and about ½ inch long. An attractive ornamental, *P. indica* has oblong to lanceolate-oblong, leathery leaves up to 6 inches in length, pubescent on their undersides. The stalked flower clusters are of few white blooms. The scarcely fleshy fruits are ¾ inch long.

Garden and Landscape Uses and Cultivation. In addition to the cultivation of avocados for their fruits, dealt with under Avocado, the perseas described here are planted to some extent for ornament and succeed without special care in ordinary soils and locations. They are propagated by seed and by cuttings. Avocados raised from seeds are popular as houseplants. For more about these see the Encyclopedia entry Avocado.

A seedling avocado (*Persea americana*) as a houseplant

PERSIMMONS. Two species called persimmon are cultivated for their edible fruits, the most important the Japanese persimmon, Japanese date-plum, or kaki, the other the native American persimmon. The first, *Diospyros kaki* is hardy in mild

climates only; the American persimmon, *D. virginiana,* prospers as far north as New England.

The Japanese persimmon is grown commercially in California, Florida, and Texas. In the Orient it is known in hundreds of varieties, but few are cultivated in America. Most are self-sterile, which means that for them to set fruit it is necessary to have a compatible pollen-producing variety, such as 'Gailey', growing nearby. The varieties 'Fuyugaki' and 'Tane-Nashi' are self-fertile and fruit without the assistance of pollinator trees.

The fruits, which look somewhat like ripe tomatoes, have soft, sweet flesh, that of some sorts astringent before completely ripe, but less so than that of the fruits of the American persimmon.

The Japanese persimmon succeeds in a wide variety of soils except poorly drained and wet ones. Trees may be spaced 15 to 20 feet apart and kept to acceptable size and shape by judicious pruning. Propagation is by grafting or budding onto American persimmon or onto *Diospyros lotus.* Because of the long taproots of these species, great care must be taken when transplanting.

The American persimmon under forest conditions attains heights of 60 feet or more, but in the open seldom exceeds one-half that and perhaps 20 to 25 feet is more usual. Its somewhat plumlike fruits, ½ inch to 2 inches long are yellow to orange-brown when ripe and ordinarily contain one to few large seeds embedded in flesh that at full maturity is soft and usually agreeably flavored. However, a small proportion of seedling trees bear fruits that are never edible.

To be suitable for eating the fruits must be dead ripe. Before that they contain tannic acid, which makes them so extremely astringent that they pucker the

Fruits of the American persimmon:
(a) Nearing maturity

(b) Fully ripe, after exposure to frost

mouth severely. It is commonly observed that full ripeness is not attained until after frost, but this is by no means always true. In some regions and with some varieties edibility is achieved without exposure to freezing temperatures.

Because of differences in the sizes and eating qualities of the fruits of seedling trees it is important to plant only superior selections of American persimmon. Several of these have been given varietal names and are propagated vegetatively, or wild trees of proven quality may be multiplied by budding or grafting onto two- or three-year-old seedlings. The latter are easily grown from seeds taken from ripe fruits and sown immediately in a cold frame or in an outdoor bed.

American persimmons succeed in almost any fairly good soil if it is not poorly drained or wet, but prefer decidedly fertile earth. Spacing of 15 to 20 feet between individuals is satisfactory if the trees are to be kept fairly small by thoughtful pruning. Because serious damage to their long taproots is likely to cause death, these trees are not easy to transplant. Set out young, carefully dug specimens in the fall and prune their tops severely to compensate for loss of roots.

PERSOONIA (Persòon-ia)—Toru. With the exception of one endemic of New Zealand, all sixty species of evergreen trees and shrubs of this genus are Australian or Tasmanian. They belong in the protea family PROTEACEAE and, except for the New Zealander, are perhaps not in cultivation in North America. The name commemorates C. H. Persoon, a distinguished botanist, who died in 1837.

Persoonias have alternate, indistinctly-veined, usually slender, undivided leaves, of firm texture. Their bisexual, small flowers, solitary, paired, or in racemes, are symmetrical and have perianths of four yellow to whitish, curved, narrow segments and four stamens. The fruits are drupes (similar in structure to plums).

The toru (*Persoonia toru*), which together with *Knightia excelsa* are the only respresentatives in the New Zealand flora of the PROTEACEAE, a family that has numerous species in Australia and South Africa, is a rather upright tree 30 to 40 feet tall. It has minutely-hairy shoots and thick, leathery, toothless, short-stalked leaves, alternate and often crowded at the shoot ends. Pointed, narrowly-linear-lanceolate, and rather glossy, they are up to 4 inches long by ½ to ¾ inch wide. The fragrant flowers, up to ⅓ inch long, are in 2-inch-long rusty-hairy, axillary racemes, each of six to twelve blooms. The flowers have brownish-yellow, pubescent perianths not exceeding ⅓ inch in length. The fruits are reddish and ½ to ¾ inch long.

Garden and Landscape Uses and Cultivation. The toru is planted in California as an interesting ornamental. It adapts to a variety of soils, preferring those that are sandy and contain adequate supplies of organic matter. Propagation is by seed and by cuttings.

PERU and PERUVIAN. These words appear in the common names of these plants: apple-of-Peru (*Nicandra physalodes*), balsam-of-Peru (*Myroxylon balsamum pereirae*), marvel-of-Peru (*Mirabilis jalapa*), Peruvian-daffodil (*Hymenocallis narcissiflora*), and Peruvian mastic tree (*Schinus molle*).

PESCATORIA (Pesca-tòria). A group of a dozen or more species of orchids of the orchid family ORCHIDACEAE compose *Pescatoria*. Natives of Central and northern South America, they are related to *Zygopetalum* and *Huntleya*, from which they are chiefly distinguished by the forms of the lips of the blooms. The name, sometimes spelled *Pescatorea*, commemorates Monsieur Pescatore, a French orchid fancier and hybridizer, who died in 1855.

Pescatorias are epiphytes (tree-perchers). They are without pseudobulbs and have clusters of fans of fairly fleshy leaves and, from the leaf axils, on rather short, erect, horizontal, or drooping stems, solitary, fragrant, large waxy blooms.

Native to Costa Rica and Panama, *P. cerina* (syn. *Zygopetalum cerinum*), has leaves up to 1 foot long. Its white blooms, generally with citron-yellow basal blotches on their sepals, have a bright yellow lip with a large, commonly reddish-brown, semicircular, ridged crest. The column is white. About 3 inches in diameter, the flowers come in late summer and fall. More robust, with leaves up to 1¼ feet in length, *P. klabochorum* (syn. *Zygopetalum klabochorum*) blooms in summer. The flowers of this native of Ecuador and Colombia are 3½ inches wide. The sepals and petals,

Pescatoria cerina

the latter shorter, are white with dark brown-purple tips. The three-lobed, trowel-shaped, yellow or white lip has, except at its margins, rows of purple-tipped hairs, and a many-ridged, yellow callus, brown at its top. The short column is purple and brown. Much like *P. cerina* but somewhat larger, and its creamy-white flowers with green-tipped sepals, exceeding 3 inches in diameter, *P. dayana*, of Colombia, blooms in winter. The crimson- or purplish-suffused, white lips of its blooms are notched at their apexes and have a large red-violet callus.

Garden Uses and Cultivation. These are choice plants for inclusion in collections of intermediate-temperature orchids. Their needs are those of *Zygopetalum*. For more information see Zygopetalum, and Orchids.

PESTS OF PLANTS. The words pest and disease are susceptible of various interpretations. One may include diseases caused by bacteria, fungi, viruses, and other causes among pests and identify damage done by at least some creatures belonging to the animal world as diseases. The line of distinction is not always easy to draw.

In this Encyclopedia the fairly common convenient convention of listing as pests creatures of the animal world that damage plants and as diseases troubles that result from an assortment of other causes is followed.

Controlling pests, to limit as far as practicable the harm they cause, is done in various ways. The imperative need is for keen observation, early detection, accurate identification, and appropriate remedial measures taken at the most favorable times. Many of the admonitions given under Diseases of Plants in this Encyclopedia are equally valid in dealing with pests. For the best locally applicable information about the best and most up-to-date recommendations regarding problems pre-

sented by pests keep in close touch with your Cooperative Extension Agent and publications, often free, of your State Agricultural Experiment Station.

A selection of pests are discussed under these entries: Ants, Aphids, Armyworms, Bagworms, Bees, Beetles, Billbugs, Birds, Borers, Budworms and Budmoths, Bugs, Butterflies, Cankerworms or Inchworms, Casebearers, Caterpillars, Cats, Centipede (Garden), Chinch Bugs, Chipmunks, Corn Earworms, Crickets, Curculios, Cutworms, Deer, Dogs, Earwigs, Earthworms, Flies, Gophers, Grasshoppers, Greenhouse Orthezia, Hornworms, Lace Bugs, Leaf Cutters, Leaf Hoppers, Leaf Miners, Leaf Rollers, Leaf Skeletonizers, Leaf Tiers, Mealybugs, Midges, Millipedes, Mites, Moths, Nematodes or Nemas, Plant Hoppers, Psyllids, Rootworms, Sawflies, Scale Insects, Slugs and Snails, Sowbugs and Pillbugs, Spanworms, Spittlebugs, Springtails, Termites, Thrips, Tree Hoppers, Wasps, Webworms, Weevils, and Woodchucks. See also Insects, and Biological Control of Pests.

PETAL. Divisions of the corolla of a flower, petals may be quite separate, as in geraniums (*Pelargonium*) and roses, or more or less united, sometimes only at their bases, as is true of the flowers of cucumbers and primulas.

PETALOSTEMON (Petalo-stémon)—Prairie-Clover. From thirty-five to fifty species of North American herbaceous plants of the pea family LEGUMINOSAE constitute *Petalostemon*. Few are cultivated. The name, alluding to the petals and stamens being joined, comes from the Greek *petalon*, a petal, and *stemon*, a stamen.

Petalostemons have crowded, glandular-dotted, pinnate leaves with a terminal as well as lateral leaflets and dense spikes or heads of small pea-like flowers with petals joined at their bases to the stamen tube, and the banner or standard petal separate. There are five stamens and one style. The fruits are small pods.

Attractive kinds include these: *P. candidum* (syn. *Dalea candida*), up to 2½ feet high, has leaves up to 2 inches long with usually seven or nine linear to oblong leaflets. Its flowers, in cylindrical spikes ¾ inch to 3½ inches long, are white. This is native from Colorado and Saskatchewan to Mississippi and Arizona. *P. gattingeri* (syn. *Dalea gattingeri*), a native of limestone soils in Tennessee and Alabama, 1 foot to 1½ feet tall, is erect or spreading. Its leaves have five to seven linear to narrowly-oblong leaflets and are up to ¾ inch long. The short-stalked spikes of rose-purple blooms are ¾ inch to nearly 3 inches long. *P. purpureum* (syn. *Dalea purpurea*) is 1 foot to 3 feet tall. Indigenous from Indiana to Saskatchewan and Texas, this is hairless or sparingly-hairy. Its leaves, up to 2 inches long, have slender-linear leaflets. The violet or rose-purple blooms are crowded in spikes 1 inch to 2 inches long. *P. villosum* (syn. *Dalea villosa*), native from Michigan to Saskatchewan and Texas, is conspicuously silky-hairy. It has stems erect and up to 2 feet tall, or sprawling, and leaves ¾ to 1 inch long with thirteen to nineteen elliptic, oblong, or oblanceolate leaflets. In cylindrical spikes 2 to 4 inches long, the flowers are bright rose-purple or more rarely white.

Garden and Landscape Uses and Cultivation. The species described are suitable for flower beds and native plant gardens and naturalizing in sunny places where the soil is very well-drained. Because of their deep, woody roots, petalostemons greatly resent transplanting. The most satisfactory procedure is to raise plants from seeds and grow them in pots until large enough to be set out in their permanent locations.

PETASITES (Petasì-tes) — Butterbur, Winter-Heliotrope. Hardy herbaceous perennials, the cultivated kinds of *Petasites* have bold foliage and bloom in winter or early spring. Belonging to the daisy family COMPOSITAE, the genus, in the broad sense accepted here, comprises twenty species, natives of Europe, Asia, and North America. By some botanists *Petasites* is interpreted as having only five species, the North American and eastern Asian kinds being transferred to other genera. The name, from the Greek *petasos*, a broad-brimmed hat, alludes to the leaves.

These are deep-rooted plants with thick, underground, spreading rhizomes. Their chief leaves are all basal. They have often large, heart- to kidney-shaped blades, more or less felted, especially on their undersides, with white-woolly hairs. The flower heads are unisexual and resemble stubby paint brushes. They are more or less densely clustered in panicles or racemes at the tops of thick stalks beset with

Petasites fragrans

alternate, small, sometimes scalelike, leaves. They are without, or have very short, ray florets (the kind that in daisies look like petals), and are purple, white or rarely yellowish. The fruits are seedlike achenes.

Winter-heliotrope or sweet-coltsfoot (*P. fragrans*), of the Mediterranean region, displays its strongly vanilla-scented blooms on stalks 6 inches to 1½ feet long in late winter or spring. In dense clusters, they are lilac, purple, or nearly white. The female flower heads have short rays. The 5-inch-wide leaves develop at the same time as the blooms. They have roundish blades with heart-shaped bases and small marginal teeth.

Naturalized in eastern North America, the butterbur, bog-rhubarb, or butterfly-dock (*P. hybridus* syn. *P. vulgaris*) is native to Europe and Asia. Its leaves come after the flowers. They have stalks up to 2 feet long and heart- to kidney-shaped, toothed blades 6 inches to 3 feet in diameter. Their upper sides are hairless or nearly so. Beneath they are cobwebby-hairy. The all-rayless, reddish-purple flower heads are crowded in ovoid panicles lifted on stems to heights up to 1½ feet.

The alpine butterbur (*P. paradoxus* syn. *P. niveus*) differs from *P. hybridus* chiefly in its broadly-triangular leaves having two wide-spreading basal lobes and its flower heads being whitish or pale pink. Similar, *P. albus* has more conspicuously and irregularly-toothed leaves, not over 1 foot across, and yellowish-white flower heads. Both *P. paradoxus* and *P. albus* are natives of Europe.

Circumpolar in its natural distribution, and in North America extending southward to Massachusetts, Michigan, Minnesota, and California, *P. frigidus* (syn. *P. nivalis*) has long-stalked, commonly fairly-deeply five- to seven-lobed, more or less toothed, heart-shaped or triangular leaves 4 to 10 inches wide, and white-woolly beneath. Its flower stalks appear with the foliage and are from 4 inches to over 1½ feet tall. The panicles, raceme-like or looser, are of whitish flower heads, the females with short ray florets.

Wild in Japan, China, Korea, and the Ryukyu Islands, *P. japonicus* has long-stalked leaves that develop after the flowers and have roundish-kidney-shaped, short-toothed blades up to 1¼ feet across, cobwebby-white-hairy on their undersurfaces, and when young, hairy above. In panicles, the flower heads are white. Much larger, *P. j. giganteus* of Japan, Sakhalin, and the Kurile Islands, has leaves with stalks up to 6 feet tall and wavy-margined blades 3 to 4½ feet across. In the Orient both *P. japonicus* and its larger variety are cultivated for their leafstalks, which are eaten as vegetables, and for their flower buds, which serve as a condiment.

Petasites japonicus giganteus

Garden and Landscape Uses and Cultivation. These vigorous plants have the distressing habit of spreading widely and, because of their deep roots, of being difficult to contain or eradicate. They should be planted only where their exuberant territorial expansionist tendencies will not be obnoxious. Because of their early appearance their blooms are interesting, and their large leaves are effective at watersides and other places. Especially impressive are those of *P. japonicus giganteus*. As a group these are lovers of moist soils, but they will grow in drier ones, especially the rampantly spreading winter-heliotrope. Propagation is very easy by division. New plants can also be had from seed.

PETIVERIA (Petiv-èria)—Guinea Hen Weed. The only species of *Petiveria*, of the pokeweed family PHYTOLACCACEAE, is occasionally cultivated in greenhouses. A native of tropical and subtropical America, including the West Indies and Florida, it is named after James Petiver, an English botanist and apothecary, who died in 1718.

Guinea hen weed (*P. alliacea*) is a forked-branched, somewhat weedy-looking subshrub 2 to 3 feet tall that when crushed gives off a strong onion-like odor.

Petiveria alliacea

Its thin, ovate to elliptic leaves are 3 to 4 inches long by about 1½ inches wide. They are besprinkled with minute semi-transparent dots, visible when held to the light. The tiny, pink, white, or greenish flowers are distantly spaced, singly or in pairs, along slender terminal and axillary racemes. Each petal-less bloom has a persistent calyx of four unequal, lanceolate lobes, and four to eight stamens. This species is employed in native medicine and as an insect repellent.

Garden Uses and Cultivation. The Guinea hen weed is grown for interest and ornament and thrives in ordinary fertile soil watered to keep it moderately moist. A minimum night temperature of 60 to 65°F is satisfactory, with a daytime rise of five to fifteen degrees. Propagation is by cuttings of semimature shoots in a propagating case, preferably with slight bottom heat, and by seed.

PETREA (Pet-réa)—Purple Wreath, Queen's Wreath, Sandpaper Vine. To the vervain family VERBENACEAE belong the about thirty species of *Petrea*. The name of this genus commemorates Baron Petre, an English patron of botany, who died in 1743. This genus is native from Mexico to Brazil and the West Indies.

Petreas are shrubs and woody vines with opposite or whorled (in circles of three or more), undivided, usually firm, leathery leaves. The violet-purple to white flowers are in long terminal racemes. They have a brightly colored, five-lobed calyx that is commonly paler than the short-tubed corolla, which also have five lobes (petals). There are four stamens, two of which are longer than the others, and one style. The berry-like one- or two-seeded fruit is included in the persistent calyx.

The purple wreath (*P. volubilis*) is one of the most beautiful of tropical vines. Native from Mexico to Central America, it has twining stems up to 40 feet long. Its

Petrea volubilis

evergreen, sand-papery, short-stalked, opposite leaves are elliptic and 2 to 8 inches long. The pale blue to violet flowers are in terminal racemes up to 1 foot in length that superficially resemble those of wisterias, but the two genera are not botanically related. Normally the trumpet-shaped corollas are darker in color than the large, showy calyxes. The latter have tubes densely-hairy on their outsides and spreading lobes that, after the corollas drop, continue to increase in size and gradually fade in color until they become ash-gray stars that eventually serve as wings to the fruits and so aid in their dispersal. In favorable climates this vine may bloom several times a year. In variety *P. v. albiflora* the blooms are white.

From the last, the West Indian *P. kohautiana* differs mainly in its leaves being smoother, practically stalkless, and more obviously heart-shaped at their bases and in the tubes of its calyxes being less densely-hairy. A white-flowered variety, *P. k. anomala*, is cultivated. Another species known in cultivation is *P. racemosa,* of Brazil. It has toothed, more or less wavy leaves.

Garden and Landscape Uses. Petreas must be ranked with the best flowering vines for the tropics and subtropics. They are excellent in greenhouses. They respond to ordinary soil, need full sun, and give little or no trouble. Pruning may be needed to restrict them to size and shape.

Petrea volubilis (flowers)

Cultivation. Propagation is by seed, cuttings in a greenhouse propagating bench with slight bottom heat, and layering. Pruning, consisting of thinning out weak and crowded shoots and shortening others, is done in late winter or spring. In greenhouses petreas may be grown in well-drained large pots or tubs or in ground beds, with their shoots trained up pillars or along wires stretched a few inches beneath the roof glass. They are watered freely from spring through fall, more sparsely in winter. They succeed where the night temperature in winter is 50 to 55°F, and day temperatures then are five to ten degrees higher. At other seasons temperatures may be higher, but an airy rather than a dank, humid atmosphere should be maintained.

PETROCALLIS (Petro-cállis)—Rock Beauty. Closely related to *Draba*, the genus *Petrocallis* is confined to alpine heights in Europe and northern Iran. Included are two species of the mustard family CRUCIFERAE. The name comes from the Greek *petros*, rock, and *kallos*, beauty, and alludes to the habitats of the plants and their visual appeal.

These crucifers form tight, low, grayish-green mounds up to 1 foot across where conditions are to their liking, but less expansive in places less congenial to denizens of high mountains. The minute, wedge-shaped leaves, three-toothed at their apexes and with eye-lashed margins, are crowded on the many shoots, which in *P. pyrenaica* (syn. *Draba pyrenaica*) are downy, in closely similar *P. fenestrata* hairless. Both have racemes of small flowers with the four sepals, four petals, two short and four long stamens, characteristic of the mustard family. The blooms of *P. fenestrata* are white and in racemes 2 to 3 inches tall. The vanilla-scented ones of *P. pyrenaica* change from white to pale lilac, and are in racemes usually not over 2 inches tall. The fruits are small pods.

Garden Uses and Cultivation. Sun-lovers and appreciative of limestone soils, these high alpines are only for keen and reasonably skilled rock gardeners. They are most likely to succeed under moraine conditions and are propagated by seed and by division. They are ill-adapted for regions where summer temperatures run high.

PETROCOPTIS (Petro-cóptis). Endemic to calcareous rocks in the Pyrenees and other mountains in Spain, the half-dozen species of *Petrocoptis* belong in the pink family CARYOPHYLLACEAE. The name, from the Greek *petros*, rock, and *kopto*, to break, directs attention to their liking for crannies and crevices.

This genus consists of herbaceous perennials with woody bases and paired leaves forming tufts or rosettes from which arise the flower stalks. The blooms, very like those of closely related *Lychnis*, have five sepals, five lobeless, toothless petals, ten stamens, and five styles. The fruits are capsules containing black seeds each of which, unlike those of *Lychnis*, has a conspicuous tuft of hair.

Most frequent in gardens is **P. glaucifolia** (syns. *P. legascae*, *Lychnis legascae*), of the Pyrenees. From 3 to 6 inches tall, this is rather loosely tufted and has branched stems and gray-green foliage. Its profuse flowers, bright carmine with white centers, are ⅔ inch across. Superior **P. pyrenaica** (syn. *Lychnis pyrenaica*) has the same habit of growth as *P. glaucifolia* and similar glaucous foliage, but its pink or white flowers are somewhat bigger. The basal leaves of *P. pyrenaica* are spatula-shaped. Those above are broad-ovate. More compact *P. p. grandiflora* has larger, more beautiful, clear pink flowers.

Garden Uses and Cultivation. Plants for collectors of alpines, these miniature *Lychnis* relatives are suitable for rock garden moraines and for cultivating in pots in alpine greenhouses. They succeed, not always without some show of reluctance, in porous, sandy soil that contains a fairly generous proportion of leaf mold or peat moss. Propagation is by seeds, which cultivated plants produce freely, and which germinate readily.

PETRONYMPHE (Petro-nýmphe). The only species of *Petronymphe*, of the amaryllis family AMARYLLIDACEAE, was discovered in 1949 in Mexico. Its name is derived from the Greek *petros*, rock, and *nymphe*, a nymph, and alludes to the plant's habitat.

In the wild **P. decora** favors outcrops of limestone. Related to *Bessera*, *Triteleia*, and *Brodiaea*, it has corms (solid bulblike organs) from which are produced three to seven channeled, strongly-keeled, narrow-linear, more or less lax, leaves, up to somewhat more than 1½ feet long, and a slender flower stalk topped by an umbel of about a dozen blooms that dangle on long, slender stalks. Their perianths have narrow tubes and six slightly spreading, much shorter lobes (petals). The flowers are up to 2¼ inches long and pale yellow with longitudinal green stripes. The six yellow-stalked stamens do not extend beyond the mouth of the flower. The style is tipped with a globular stigma.

Garden Uses and Cultivation. A collector's item, this species may be grown outdoors and in greenhouses under conditions similar to those that suit such South African bulbs as freesias, ixias, and sparaxises. Well-drained soil and full sun are needed. Generous supplies of water are required when the plant is in foliage, none during its season of dormancy. In greenhouses the corms are potted and started into growth in fall and are rested in summer. A winter night temperature of 45 to 50°F is adequate, with a few degrees increase by day permitted

PETROPHILA (Petrò-phìla). The name of this genus of the protea family PROTEACEAE is sometimes spelled *Petrophile*, but *Petrophila* is preferred. The about forty species are endemic to Australia. The name comes from the Greek *petros*, rock, and *philos*, loving, and refers to the natural habitats of many kinds.

Petrophilas are evergreen shrubs of low to moderate height. They have rigid, leathery, alternate, undivided or pinnately-divided leaves. The flowers are crowded into dense, terminal or axillary conelike heads. The fruits are achenes contained in small conelike heads formed of the floral bracts and are often displayed along the upper parts of the shoots in spire- or spike-like groupings or in terminal or axillary rounded heads. From closely related *Isopogon*, this genus differs in having persistent instead of deciduous cone scales.

One of the better-known species, *P. biloba* is 6 to 8 feet in height and may be compact or somewhat straggly. It has flat leaves with generally three sharp-pointed, ovate to oblong segments ½ to ¾ inch long, the center, smaller one, downturned, the others point upward. The many clusters of seven to eleven slender flowers are from cones ¼ inch long. Individual blooms are about ¾ inch in length. The clusters are very many and form long, cylindrical spikelike sprays. The blooms are a lovely grayish-lavender-pink.

One of the best yellow-flowered kinds, **P. media** has upright, rigid branches and is 6 feet or so tall. Its undivided, slender, cylindrical leaves, stiff and sharp-pointed, usually about 3 inches in length, are sometimes considerably longer. The hairy flowers are about ½ inch long. Another yellow-flowered species, *P. propinqua* is erect and about 6 feet tall. This has slender branches and flat, twice-divided or twice-cleft leaves with slender segments under 1 inch long. Its flowers are small but numerous.

Other species worth seeking include *P. anceps*, 2 feet tall, with undivided, very slender, flat leaves 1 inch to 3 inches long and ovoid spikes of yellow flowers in clusters of three to five. Another, *P. divaricata*, which is about 4 feet tall, has leaves twice-divided into slender segments ½ to 1 inch long. It makes a good display of pale yellow flowers. Prostrate **P. longifolia** has ground-hugging branches and undivided, very slender, erect, cylindrical leaves 6 inches to 1 foot long. The fragrant, yellow to white flowers are borne chiefly at the circumference of the plant.

Garden and Landscape Uses and Cultivation. These pleasing shrubs are suitable for warm, dry climates such as that of California. They are useful for beds, banks, and rock gardens. They succeed in well drained, nearly neutral soils, and in general require about the same conditions and care as *Hakea*

PETROPHYTUM (Petró-phytum). Sometimes included in *Spiraea*, the three species of *Petrophytum* differ from that genus, as more narrowly interpreted, in having blooms in cylindrical, spikelike racemes instead of panicles or clusters, in their habits of growth and leaf characteristics, and in recondite botanical details. They are prostrate, mat-forming, hardy evergreen shrublets of the rose family ROSACEAE. The name, from the Latin *petros*, rock, and the Greek *phyton*, a plant, alludes to their natural habitats in rock crevices. The genus is endemic to western North America.

Petrophytums have alternate, crowded or tufted leaves, undivided and without lobes or teeth. They are oblanceolate to spatula-shaped. The tiny flowers are in crowded racemes terminating erect stalks furnished with a few bracts. They have five persistent sepals, the same number of white petals, twenty to forty slender-stalked stamens, and usually five pistils with styles short-hairy at their bases. The fruits are small podlike follicles. In general appearance species of *Petrophytum* much resemble each other.

Confined in the wild almost entirely to the crevices of shelving limestone or granitic rocks, *P. caespitosum*, a native of western North America, spreads into mats or cushions up to 3 feet wide. Its silky-hairy leaves, up to ½ inch long, have one main vein and are grayish-green on both surfaces. The flower stalks, ¾ inch to 3½ inches tall, terminate in flower spikes, sometimes somewhat branched at their bases, and up to 2 inches long. From *P. caespitosum* the other species are distinguished by their larger, hairless to silky hairy leaves having three chief veins.

Petrophytum caespitosum showing woody rootstock

Petrophytum caespitosum in bloom

Endemic to basaltic cliffs in Washington, *P. cinerascens* has leaves ½ to 1 inch long and flowers, with twenty to twenty-five stamens, in spikes that are often branched. From it, *P. hendersonii,* an endemic of the Olympic Mountains in Washington, differs in its flowers being always in branchless racemes and in having thirty-five to forty stamens.

Garden and Landscape Uses and Cultivation. Although not always easy to satisfy, petrophytums, where they do well, are splendid additions to rock gardens and dry wall plantings. They need full sun and gritty, porous soil. They are best accommodated in rock crevices. Increase is by seed and by cuttings.

PETRORHAGIA (Petror-hàgia)—Tunic Flower. Plants long familiar to gardeners as *Tunica* now are named *Petrorhagia.* They belong in the pink family CARYOPHYLLACEAE. There are twenty species, natives of the Mediterranean region; two are somewhat naturalized in the United States. The name is from the Greek *petra,* rock, and *rhage,* a crevice, and alludes to the habitats of the plants.

From closely related *Dianthus,* this genus differs in technical details of the calyxes. It comprises annuals and perennials, with wiry stems swollen at the joints, small, opposite, narrow leaves, and flowers that look like tiny dianthus blooms, solitary or in clusters. Below the five-lobed, five- to fifteen-ribbed calyx are one to three pairs of overlapping bracts. There are five spreading petals, ten stamens, and two styles. The fruits are small capsules.

The tunic flower (**P. saxifraga** syn. *Tunica saxifraga*) is a hardy, tufted perennial with much the misty aspect of a low gypsophila. A dainty, spry plant, usually under 9 inches in height, it has hairless or sparsely-hairy, branching stems, the lower parts often prostrate. The leaves are narrowly-linear and about ½ inch long. Solitary at the ends of slender branches, or

loosely clustered, the purplish-pink, pink, or white flowers are up to ½ inch in width. Their calyxes have five ribs. The blooms are very freely produced over a long summer period. A number of horticultural variants are recognized. These include *P. s. alba,* with white flowers; *P. s. carnosa* and *P. s. rosea,* with blooms deeper pink than usual with the species; *P. s. splendens,* with larger pink blooms; *P. s. flore-pleno,* which has double flowers; and a dwarf variety, *P. s. nana.*

Garden Uses and Cultivation. The tunic flower grows with little or no care and often seeds itself with such abandon that it can become a minor nuisance that must be prevented from establishing itself among choicer, less insistent, rock garden treasures. That is not an unduly onerous task; a little hand pulling does the trick. A good plant for edgings, rock gardens, and dry walls, it can with enthusiasm be recommended to beginning rock gardeners. This species and its varieties are at their best in well-drained, gritty or sandy soil of medium or even low fertility, and in full-sun. Once established they live for many years with practically no attention. The typical species is readily raised from seeds, the varieties by cuttings made in early summer from shoots taken from low on the plants, planted in a humid, shaded cold frame, in a greenhouse propagating bench, or under mist.

PETROSELINUM (Petro-selìnum) — Parsley. Of the five species of this genus of the carrot family UMBELLIFERAE, only the common parsley is of account to gardeners. Native to the Mediterranean region, *Petroselinum* has a name derived from the Greek *petra,* rock, and *selinon,* parsley. It consists of annuals, biennials, and hardy herbaceous perennials with one-, two-, or three-times-pinnately-divided leaves with their ultimate segments lobed or toothed. The tiny greenish or reddish flowers are in umbels of smaller umbels. The flowers are without sepals. Each has five petals, five stamens, and two styles. The flattened, ovate, five-ribbed, seedlike fruits consist of a pair of dry, ribbed carpels joined only at their bases and apexes. Parsley (*P. crispum*), a biennial or short-lived perennial, is too familiar to warrant description. For information about its cultivation see the Encyclopedia entry Parsley.

PETTERIA (Pet-tèria). Closely related to *Laburnum* and *Cytisus,* the only species of *Petteria* is native to the mountains of the Balkan Peninsula. It is an erect, deciduous shrub 6 to 8 feet in height, belonging to the pea family LEGUMINOSAE. Its name commemorates the Dalmatian botanist Franz Petter, who died in 1853.

The branchlets of **P. ramentacea** are green. The dull leaves have stalks ½ inch to 2 inches long and three round-ended or

Petteria ramentacea

slightly notched, elliptic to obovate, toothless leaflets ¾ inch to 2½ inches long and about one-half as wide. They are hairy at their margins and along the mid-veins on their undersides. In ten- to twenty-flowered, 1½- to 3-inch-long, crowded, erect racemes from the ends of short shoots of current season's growth, the fragrant, yellow, pea-like flowers are borne in late spring. They are ¾ inch long, and have downy calyxes with upper lips cleft completely to their bases, and three-toothed lower lips. The ten stamens are united. Brown when ripe, and containing five to nine orange-brown seeds, the fruits are somewhat inflated pods up to 2 inches long.

Garden and Landscape Uses and Cultivation. Hardy in southern New England, this little-known species is chiefly of interest for inclusion in botanical collections. Its seeds, like those of *Laburnum,* are poisonous if eaten. It is propagated from seed and succeeds in porous, well-drained soil in full sun.

PETUNIA (Petùn-ia). Almost too well known to need describing, the hybrid petunias so commonly cultivated are the offspring of species that, together with tomatoes, potatoes, and tobacco, belong in the nightshade family SOLANACEAE. So magnificent, accommodating, and varied in their colorings and forms are these man-developed hybrids that few gardeners grow the original wild kinds, yet some but by no means all of these are quite charming and worthy of cultivating for their interest, although they do not compare in size of bloom or variety of flower color with their more flamboyant progeny. The name is derived from a native South American name for tobacco. The genus *Petunia* consists of forty species, natives of South America, chiefly of the southern parts.

Single varieties of *Petunia hybrida*

These are freely-branching, rather weak-stemmed annuals and tender perennials clothed with fine, sticky hairs that cause them to feel slightly clammy. Their leaves, soft and without lobes, are mostly alternate, but the upper ones are often opposite. The solitary, stalked flowers, from the leaf axils are terminal. They have a deeply-five-cleft calyx, a funnel- or salver-shaped, more or less five-lobed corolla, five stamens in two pairs and a rudimentary, smaller one, and one style. The fruits are dry capsules containing many tiny seeds.

Two species, *P. axillaris* and *P. violacea*, both natives of Argentina, are the parents of *P. hybrida*, a name that embraces all the garden hybrid varieties of petunias. They and their offspring are tender perennials, but seedsmen have done such a good job of developing varieties and strains of ordinary garden petunias that come amazingly true to type when raised from seed that it is rare indeed for anyone to propagate from cuttings any except the double-flowered kinds, although this is quite easy to do. It is just as well, however, that seeding is the favored method of increase because petunias are susceptible to virus diseases that can be transmitted from plant to plant by knives as well as by insects. When seeds are used each new crop gets off to a disease-free start.

The large white petunia (**P. axillaris**) is a robust, thick-stemmed plant, 1 foot to 2 feet tall, with thickish, ovate-oblong leaves and dull white, long-tubed flowers, 2 to 2½ inches long, that are fragrant in the evening. The violet-flowered petunia (**P.**

violacea) is a much lower, more prostrate species, with only the tips of its more slender branches erect and then not rising higher than 6 to 10 inches. Its leaves are ovate to ovate-lanceolate, and its rose-red to violet-red flowers have tubes up to 1½ inches long and of lighter color than the flaming mouth of the flower. Self-sown seedlings of garden petunias that often persist as garden escapes commonly revert to these ancestral species or to something very like them.

The common garden petunia (**P. hybrida**) is available in a bewildering number of varieties to which new ones are added each year. They are adequately described, and often illustrated, in the catalogs of seedsmen. They come in various types, such as balcony petunias, which have long stems and are especially suitable for window boxes, porch boxes, urns, and hanging baskets, and compact, dwarf varieties, particularly adapted for summer bedding. There are single- and double-flowered

Petunia hybrida, double-flowered

of the water leaf family HYDROPHYLLA-CEAE, are natives of the Americas, the greater number of western North America. They are annuals, biennials, and herbaceous perennials. Referring to the crowded flowers of some kinds, the name comes from the Greek *phakelos,* a cluster.

Phacelias are usually hairy and often sticky-glandular. Mostly alternate, the lower sometimes opposite, their toothless or toothed leaves are undivided and lobeless or are pinnately- or twice-pinnately-divided or lobed. The few to many blooms are in clusters or branched sprays of one-sided, coiled racemes. They have deeply-five-lobed calyxes that often enlarge as the seeds form. The corollas are wheel- to saucer- or bell-shaped. They are purple, blue, white, or yellow, and may drop or remain after they wither. They have five lobes (petals). On their insides they may or may not have a pair of scales opposite the base of each stamen. There are five protruding or nonprotruding stamens. The single two-lobed or deeply-cleft style has two stigmas. The fruits are capsules.

The California bluebell or wild-canterbury-bell (*P. minor* syns. *P. whitlavia, Whitlavia grandiflora*) is a beautiful glandular-hairy annual 1 foot to 2 feet tall, and loosely-branched. It has coarsely-toothed, ovate leaves, heart- to wedge-shaped at their bases, and up to 2 inches long. The lower ones are long-stalked. Those of the upper parts of the stems have much shorter stalks. The flowers are purple or rarely white. They have tubular-bell-shaped corollas, slightly constricted in their throats, and up to about 1½ inches in length. The tubes are three times as long as the petals. The stamens protrude slightly. The appendages at their bases are hairy. This kind inhabits dryish soils in southern California and Baja California. Very similar and also a native annual of southern California, *P. campanularia* differs in having glorious blue, bell-shaped flowers with corolla tubes twice as long as the petals, not constricted in their throats. White-flowered *P. c. alba* is less attractive than the blue-flowered type.

Other glandular-hairy annuals with toothed but not divided leaves are *P. parryi* and *P. viscida* (syn. *Eutoca viscida*), the first native of southern California and Baja California, the other of southern California. From 6 inches to 1½ feet tall, *P. parryi* has ovate leaves up to 2 inches long, with heart- or wedge-shaped bases. The lower ones have long, the upper short, stalks. In loose racemes, and ¾ to 1 inch wide, the saucer-shaped, dark purple to violet flowers, with paler centers, have petals at least as long as the corolla tube and slightly protruding, hairy stamens with appendages at their bases. Somewhat taller *P. viscida* differs in having short-stalked lower leaves and stamens without appendages at their bases. Its saucer- to nearly wheel-shaped flowers are gentian-blue with purplish or whitish centers. The stamens, which do not protrude, have white anthers. When bruised the foliage has an odor of formalin. Variety *P. v. albiflora* has white flowers. Its leaves lobeless or nearly so, often sprawling, hairy *P. divaricata* is an annual native of California. It has stems 3 inches to over 1 foot long. Its rather distantly-spaced, broad-ovate to oblong leaves, the lower ones fairly long-stalked, those above gradually smaller and shorter-stalked until the top ones are stalkless, are lobeless or sometimes have a pair of small lobes or teeth at their bases. The open-bell-shaped blue flowers, in often paired curved racemes, from the branch ends, are about ½ to ¾ inch wide. They have non-protruding stamens and a two-lobed style.

Ferny-foliaged annuals with pinnate leaves include *P. tanacetifolia* and quite similar *P. congesta*. Native from Nevada to California, Arizona, and Baja California, *P. tanacetifolia* is erect, much-branched, 1 foot to 3 feet tall, and bristly-hairy. Its ovate-oblong leaves, 4 to 8 inches long, are twice- or thrice-pinnately-divided or lobed. The many blue or lavender, broadly-bell-shaped blooms, with white-bristly sepals, are in tight clusters or are crowded along the coiled branches of the flower sprays. The hairless stamens have appendages completely joined to their bases. The stamens are at least one-and-a-half times as long as the ¼-inch-long corollas, which have petals about one-half as long as their tubes. From the last, *P. congesta* differs in being scarcely as tall, softly-hairy, and in having petals about equal to the corolla tube in length and in the lower parts only of the appendages being joined to the white-anthered stamens. Its many branched stems erect, and 6 inches to 2 feet tall, annual *P. ciliata,* native to California and Baja California, has pinnate or pinnately-lobed leaves, the basal ones oblong to ovate and up to 4 inches long. Quite numerous, the nearly stalkless flowers are in terminal sprays or clusters. From 6 inches to 1½ feet in height, branched or not, *P. linearis* is hairy. It has linear, essentially stalkless leaves up to 3½ inches long without lobes or cleft into three to seven narrow ones. Its bright blue-violet, bluish-lavender, or occasionally white flowers are in terminal clusters of short, curved spikes. Their stamens scarcely protrude. This native at fairly high altitudes from the Rocky Mountains to British Columbia and California usually grows in dryish, gravelly soils.

Perennial *P. sericea, P. hastata* (syn. *P. leucophylla*), and *P. lyallii* are indigenous from the Rocky Mountains to British Columbia and California. A high mountain species, *P. sericea* is 4 inches to 1½ feet tall. It has a woody crown, and often silvery-silky-hairy, pinnately-lobed, toothed, ovate to oblong leaves 1 inch to 3 inches long. In spikelike clusters of short racemes, up to 6 inches in length, but frequently shorter, the many purple-blue to

Phacelia campanularia

white blooms are displayed. Their ¼-inch-long, broad-bell-shaped corollas have petals equaling the tubes in length. The stamens, with appendages joined to their bases, protrude conspicuously. Favoring dry, rocky places at altitudes above 2,500 feet, *P. hastata* is up to 1½ feet tall and densely-silvery-hairy. Its lanceolate to narrowly-ovate leaves are without lobes or teeth and up to 2½ inches long. The lower ones have stalks as long as the blades, the upper ones are short-stalked. In rather crowded panicles, the nearly stalkless, bell-shaped flowers are white to lavender-blue, and approximately ¼ inch long. A very attractive, low, densely-white-hairy variety is *P. h. compacta*. Up to about 8 inches tall, tufted, and woody at the base, *P. lyallii* is showy in bloom. It has fairly deeply-pinnately-lobed, elliptic to oblanceolate leaflets, up to 4 inches long, and short, crowded clusters of dark blue to deep purple flowers, about ⅓ inch long. This mountain species is found chiefly above timberline on rock slides.

Eastern North American natives include annual or biennial *P. bipinnatifida,* which grows chiefly in damp, frequently limestone soils from Virginia to Illinois, Ohio, Georgia, and Alabama. From 6 inches to 2 feet tall, in its upper parts glandular-pubescent, this has twice-pinnately-lobed leaves. Its little bluish-lavender to violet-blue flowers have petals mostly longer than the corolla tubes and protruding stamens with basal appendages. Annual or biennial, *P. purshii* ranges from Pennsylvania to Minnesota, North Carolina, Ala-

Phacelia purshii

bama and Missouri. Ordinarily this does not exceed 1 foot in height. Its leaves are cleft into five to nine lanceolate to elliptic lobes. Light blue with white centers, the small flowers have shortly-fringed petals. The stamens scarcely protrude. They have tiny basal appendages. This favors rich woodlands and thickets.

Garden and Landscape Uses. The most frequently grown phacelias are annuals. These are excellent for sunny flower beds, and in their home territories, for native

plant gardens and naturalistic areas. They do best where sheltered from strong winds. Unfortunately they do not stand torrid, humid weather well. Because of this, they are suited only for early summer display outdoors and for blooming in late winter and spring in greenhouses in many parts of North America. The perennials, challenging species for rock gardeners, are likely to prove difficult or impossible under conditions much different from those they enjoy in the wild. They need gritty well-drained soil and are impatient of winter wetness and hot, humid summer weather. Established specimens do not transplant well. It is wisest to set out young plants from pots.

Cultivation. Annual and biennial phacelias (the latter can be grown as annuals) are not choosey about soil so long as it is well drained and at least passing fertile. Sow seeds in early spring, or in places of mild winters in fall, where the plants are to remain. Cover them to a depth of about ⅛ inch. Thin the seedlings to from 6 inches to 1 foot apart depending upon the vigor of the species. Because of possible losses during the winter, defer the final thinning of fall sowings until spring. In regions of hot, humid summers, good early displays of bloom are had by sowing in a greenhouse in March in a temperature of about 55°F, transplanting the seedlings individually to pots or to flats, growing them in full sun in a temperature of 50°F at night and up to fifteen degrees higher by day, and after a short period of hardening off setting them out in the garden as soon as all danger of frost has passed. Careful transplanting, so that the roots are not unduly disturbed is necessary. Subsequent care is minimal. About all that is necessary is to keep down weeds and stake neatly to prevent storm damage. For spring blooming in greenhouses, sow in September or October and transfer the seedlings to successively larger pots as root growth makes necessary, until as finals they occupy containers 5 or 6 inches in diameter. Grow throughout where the night temperature is 45 to 50°F and that by day not over ten degrees or so higher. Avoid over watering. After the final pots are filled with roots, supply mild liquid fertilizer every week or two. Neat staking is likely to be needed.

PHAEDRANASSA (Phaedran-ássa)—Queen-Lily. The six species of *Phaedranassa,* of the amaryllis family AMARYLLIDACEAE, are bulb plants from high altitudes in South America. Their name, alluding to the beauty of the blooms, comes from the Greek *phaidros,* gay, and *anassa,* queen.

Phaedranassas have round to ovoid bulbs with one to few, stalked, elliptic, narrowly-oblong to lanceolate leaves and hollow, leafless stalks crowned with umbels of drooping, tubular or narrowly-fun-

nel-shaped, greenish-red or two-colored blooms. The six perianth lobes (petals) are united at their bases into a tube. Above, they are erect except for their out-turned tips. This arrangement gives the flowers a long, cylindrical form. There are six stamens, joined to the petals near the top of the corolla tube, and a slender style. The fruits are capsules.

Native to Costa Rica, *P. carmiolii* has short-necked bulbs 2 to 3 inches in diameter. Its one to three, blunt, oblanceolate leaves, up to 1¼ feet long by about 2 inches wide, have blades with pronounced midribs. Their stalks are channeled and 6 to 8 inches long. In umbels of a dozen or fewer atop stalks 1 foot to 2 feet tall, the flowers, about 2 inches long on individual stalks 1 inch long, are deep coral-red with green tips margined with yellow. The stamens protrude and are longer than the styles. Very like the last, but with the style extending well beyond

Phaedranassa carmiolii

Phaedranassa carmiolii (flowers)

the stamens, is *P. chloracra,* a native of Peru. Its leaves are oblanceolate to elliptic, its flowers purplish-rose-pink tipped with green. Variety *P. c. obtusa,* sometimes distinguished as *P. obtusa,* has blunt petals.

Garden and Landscape Uses and Cultivation. The species described are charming for locating permanently outdoors where winters are frostless, or essentially so, and for growing in cool greenhouses. They thrive with little care in well-drained, fertile soil in sun and bloom yearly in summer or fall. Out of doors, and in ground beds in greenhouses, the bulbs are planted with their tips beneath the surface, but in pots it is better if their upper two-thirds are above the soil. This assures maximum depth for the roots. Repotting in nutritious, loamy, porous soil is needed at intervals of a few years only. It should be done in spring at the beginning of a new season of active growth. Water is supplied in moderation when leaves are in evidence. During the resting period, when no foliage is to be seen, it is withheld entirely. Well-rooted specimens in pots benefit from occasional applications of dilute liquid fertilizer during the period of active growth. Temperatures indoors during winter should be 45 to 50°F at night and five to ten degrees more by day. At other times somewhat higher temperatures with the greenhouse freely ventilated on all favorable occasions are in order. Propagation is easily carried out by offsets, seed, and bulb cuttings.

PHAEDRANTHUS. See Distictis.

PHAENOCOMA (Phaeno-còma). The only species of *Phaenocoma,* of the daisy family COMPOSITAE, is native to South Africa. Alluding to the involucres of the flower heads, its name is derived from the Greek *phaino,* to shine, and *kome,* hair.

Phaenocoma prolifera

Distinguished from *Helichrysum,* to which it is kin, by the central florets of its flower heads being all males instead of bisexual, *P. prolifera* is a rigid-branched shrub, 1½ to 3 feet tall, with white stems and of hoary aspect. Its hairless leaves are heathlike and about ¼ inch long. The flower heads, solitary at the stem ends, are 2 inches wide and have many spreading, silvery-pink to rose-purple, pointed ray florets and centers of darker disk florets. The fruits are achenes.

Garden Uses and Cultivation. This is satisfactory for sunny rock gardens and similar intimate plantings, in warm, dry climates, and also for cool greenhouses, where it succeeds under conditions that suit succulents and other desert plants. Its flowers dry as "everlastings." It needs well-drained, peaty soil. Propagation is by cuttings and by seed.

PHAENOSPERMA (Phaeno-spèrma). The only species of *Phaenosperma,* of the grass family GRAMINEAE, is a native of open woodlands in Japan, Korea, China, and Taiwan. Its name, alluding to its seeds being exposed between the bractlike parts of the inflorescences, derives from the Greek *phaneros,* visible, and *sperma,* seed.

A handsome perennial 2½ to 5 feet tall, *P. globosum* is a graceful grass with flat,

Phaenosperma globosum

narrowly-lanceolate, pointed leaves, 1 foot to 2 feet long by 1 inch to 1½ inches wide, with finely-toothed margins. Their upper surfaces are dark green; their undersides are glaucous. The minute flowers in loose panicles 8 inches to 1½ feet long with spreading or drooping, cylindrical branches, are in one-flowered, green spikelets, that are deciduous at maturity and that gape to show the spherical seeds, up to ⅛ inch in diameter.

Garden and Landscape Uses and Cultivation. Not hardy in the north, this species is appropriate in climates where little frost is experienced for lightly shaded locations where the soil is fertile and moderately moist. Propagation is easy by division and by seed.

PHAGNALON (Phag-nàlon). About forty species constitute *Phagnalon,* of the daisy family COMPOSITAE. They resemble *Helichrysum,* but have usually long-stalked solitary flower heads. They are natives from the Mediterranean region to the Canary Islands and central Asia. The name, an anagram of *gnaphalon,* French for cotton or cottony, alludes to the woolly hairs of some sorts. The flower heads consist of disk florets (the kind that compose the eyes of daisies). There are no ray florets (the petal-like ones in daisies). The collars of bracts (involucres) immediately behind the flower heads are not brightly colored; usually they are brownish and leathery or papery. The fruits are achenes.

A subshrub, *P. rupestre* is up to 1 foot tall. It has white-woolly shoots, and oblong-lanceolate leaves with a cobweb of hairs on their upper sides and white-woolly felting beneath. Their undulating edges are rolled inward. The spherical, solitary flower heads, rather under ½ inch in diameter, on stalks up to 2½ inches long, are brownish-yellow. This is a native of rocky and stony areas in the Mediterranean region and Asia Minor.

Garden Uses and Cultivation. The precise hardiness of this rarely cultivated species is somewhat uncertain. It probably will not survive winters in the north and surely not where it is subjected to long periods of wetness. The drier Mediterranean-type climate of California and some other parts of the west suits it better. It is for well-drained, dryish soils and full sun. Propagation is by seed and perhaps by cuttings.

PHAIUS (Phài-us) — Nun's Orchid. This genus, of the orchid family ORCHIDACEAE, is wild from warm parts of Asia to Malagasy (Madagascar), East Africa, and Australia. It includes about fifty species and has a name, alluding to the flower color of the first kind described, derived from the Greek *phaios,* swarthy or dark. Hybrids between species of *Phaius* and between it and *Cymbidium,* and *Spathoglottis* exist.

Terrestrial or less commonly epiphytic (tree-perching), these have clustered, short and thick, or slender, stemlike, leafy pseudobulbs. Kinds with pseudobulbs of the first type much resemble calanthes, but differ in the lip being free from, instead of with its base joined to, the column. Characteristically erect, the flower stalks come from the sides of the pseudobulbs and terminate in racemes of many to numerous blooms opening in succession. They have three sepals, two essentially similar spreading or half-spreading petals, and a large, trumpet-shaped lip, usually pouched or spurred at its base, with side lobes enclosing the column.

The nun's orchid (*P. tankervilliae* syn. *P. grandifolius*) is beautiful and popular. Naturalized in the West Indies, Panama,

Phaius tankervilliae

Phaius tankervilliae (flowers)

Hawaii, and possibly to a limited extent in southern Florida, it is native from southern China through much of southeastern Asia and Indonesia to Australia. It has dull green, clustered pseudobulbs about 3 inches tall and as wide, each with three or four pointed, narrow-elliptic leaves 2 to 3 feet long. The thick-textured, fragrant blooms, up to about 4½ inches across, are in racemes of ten to twenty on stout, erect stalks sometimes exceeding 4½ feet in height. The stalks come from the bottoms of the pseudobulbs. The sepals and petals spread widely. They are reddish-brown, often with yellowish margins, and have opaque-white backs. The trumpet-shaped lip is generally whitish on its outside; inside it is yellowish-brown or yellow, stained with rose-purple. Native to tropical Asia, Indonesia, and the Philippines, **P. flavus** (syn. *P. maculatus*) has more or less conical pseudobulbs up to about 4 inches tall. There are eight or fewer lanceolate leaves with blades about 1½ feet long by 4½ inches wide, sometimes spotted with yellow, their bases overlapping to form a false stem 2 feet long. The flower stalks, 2 to 3 feet tall, carry many 2- to 3-inch-wide flowers, pale yellow with the lip marked with brown, hairy, and with three ridges or keels. Another with clustered, fat pseudobulbs about 3 inches long, **P. callosus** inhabits Malaya and Indonesia. Its four or fewer narrow-elliptic leaves are 1 foot to 2 feet long. Up to 4 inches wide, the fragrant flowers, in racemes of ten or fewer, are yellowish-brown with purple

markings on the lip and reddish-brown backs to the sepals and petals.

With leafy, slender, stemlike pseudobulbs 1½ feet long, **P. amboinensis** is a native of Indonesia. Its dull green leaves are elliptic. In racemes of seven or fewer, the blooms are carried to heights of about 3 feet. Pure white, with a bright yellow, nearly spurless lip, they are slightly fragrant and about 4 inches across.

Two Madagascan terrestrial species, *P. tuberculosus* (syn. *Gastorkis tuberculosa*) and *P. humblotii* (syn. *Gastorkis humblotii*) are sometimes cultivated but are not considered easy to grow. They tend to deteriorate and eventually die even under care of experienced growers. Its spindle-shaped, horizontal or slightly ascending pseudobulbs 2 to 4 inches long, **P. tuberculosus** has several pointed, oblong-lanceolate leaves up to 1¼ feet long. About 2 feet tall, the sturdy, erect flowering stems terminate in a raceme of up to seven nearly 3-inch-wide blooms. Their spreading, pointed-elliptic-oblong sepals and petals are pure white. The ample three-lobed, funnel-shaped lip, its center lobe notched at its apex, is orange-yellow freely spotted with reddish-purple. It has bristly, white hairs. Tightly clustered, subspherical pseudobulbs approximately 1½ inches in diameter are characteristic of **P. humblotii**. Each has a few pointed-elliptic leaves 1 foot to 2 feet long by 4 inches wide. The erect flowering stalks 1½ to 2 feet tall or taller terminate in racemes of up to twelve 2-inch-wide blooms. They are pale rose-

purple with suffusions of white. The widely spread sepals and petals are obovate-elliptic. The lip is large, prevailingly white edged with rosy-purple, with on the side lobes, which tend to embrace the column, patches of yellowish-brown. The center lobe is crisped at its edges and decorated with a pair of big bright yellow teeth.

Garden and Landscape Uses and Cultivation. Being ground orchids, these do well in the humid tropics and warm subtropics in very well-drained, raised beds of chiefly coarse organic material. A suitable mix consists of one-third by bulk of rich, turfy topsoil, and two-thirds, of which one-half can be dried cow manure, coarse organics, such as osmunda or tree fern fiber, leaf mold, and fir bark, the whole loose and porous enough to ensure free admission of air and passage of water. Good specimens can be grown in similar mixes in pots. High temperatures and high humidity favor good growth. In greenhouses maintain night temperatures in winter for sorts limited in the wild to Malaya, Indonesia, Malagasy (Madagascar), and other hot lands at 65 to 70°F, five to ten degrees lower for those, such as *P. tankervilliae*, that inhabit somewhat cooler regions. Let day temperatures exceed those maintained at night by five to fifteen degrees. Shade from strong sun is necessary. Repotting needs attention annually as soon as flowering is through. Every second or third year division at potting time should be done. High temperatures and high humidity favor good growth and, except for a little let-up for a three-week period following the completion of growth of the new pseudobulbs, water should be applied generously. Once the flower spikes show, regular applications of dilute liquid fertilizer are helpful. Propagation is by separating the pseudobulbs and by laying the flower stalks, after the blooms have faded, on moist sand in a propagating bench in a shaded, humid greenhouse. Plantlets soon develop from the dormant buds along the stalks, and within a few months they will be big enough to remove and pot individually. For more information see Orchids.

PHALAENOPSIS (Phalaen-ópsis) — Moth Orchid. Here belong some of the most beautiful tropical orchids. The genus, imperfectly understood botanically, contains thirty-five or more species. From some, hybridists have raised numerous splendid horticultural varieties. In the wild *Phalaenopsis*, of the orchid family ORCHIDACEAE, occurs in tropical Asia, Indonesia, New Guinea, Australia, the Philippine Islands, and Taiwan. The name comes from the Greek *phalaina*, a moth, and *opsis*, resembling. It suggests, as does the colloquial name moth orchid, a fanciful resemblance.

Moth orchids are epiphytes (plants that perch on trees without taking sustenance from them), or they sometimes grow on rocks. Mostly evergreen, but more rarely deciduous, they are without pseudobulbs. From very short, thick stems they develop a few, usually wide spreading or recurved, oblongish, often mottled, two-ranked, thick leathery leaves. The long-lasting flowers, commonly in short or long, erect, arching or pendulous panicles, more rarely are solitary. They are prevailingly white, flushed with rose-pink or rose-purple; are yellowish or yellow with brown markings; or are magenta-pink. Attractive, they are usually well displayed in graceful panicles. Their nearly equal-sized sepals spread widely or are sometimes reflexed. The petals are similar to the sepals except that they are sometimes much bigger. The three-lobed lip, its side lobes erect, is joined to the bottom of the slightly curved or straight column and in some kinds has appendages at its tip. Hybrids between *Phalaenopsis* and *Vanda* are named *Vandaenopsis*; those between *Phalaenopsis* and *Renanthera*, *Renanthopsis*; and those between *Phalaenopsis* and *Arachnis*, *Arachnopsis*.

Parent of many superior white-flowered horticultural varieties, variable **P. amabilis** was the first species discovered. Native to Indonesia, New Guinea, northern Australia, New Britain, and the Philippine Islands, it has unmottled, blunt-elliptic, ovate-elliptic, to obovate leaves 1 foot long or longer by 4 inches wide. Its fragrant blooms, up to 5 inches across and twenty

Phalaenopsis schillerana

or fewer along gracefully arching stems that occasionally attain lengths of 3 feet, are well displayed. Their sepals and petals are usually milky-white with their back surfaces tinged pink. The linear or cross-shaped lip is spotted and striped with red. It is shorter than the blunt petals and has a pair of yellow, antenna-like, appendages. Similar **P. aphrodite** (syn. *P. amabilis aphrodite*) differs chiefly from *P. amabilis* in its flowers being not over 3 inches in diameter and in having lips with a broad-triangular middle lobe with darker red markings. This native of the Philippines and Taiwan is parent of many fine horticultural varieties. Formerly considered to be a variety of *P. aphrodite*, but differing in its young leaves being mottled silvery-gray and in the shape of the callus on the lip of the flower, *P. sanderana* is endemic to the Philippine Islands.

In growth habit and foliage *P. schillerana*, of the Philippine Islands, is much like *P. amabilis*, except that its leaves are less rigid, are mottled with silvery-gray, and often have purplish undersides. Its pale rose-purple blooms, with the disk of the lip golden-yellow, differ from those of *P. amabilis* in their rather variously shaped lips having two incurved, usually short horns instead of long, tendril-like appendages. The blooms, which rarely exceed 2½ inches in diameter, are in gracefully arching, few- to many-flowered panicles up to 3 feet long. They have anchor-shaped lips with the center lobe narrowed a little below the apex, then flaring. Not quite as vigorous and smaller than the last, very variable **P. stuartiana** (syns. *P. schillerana stuartiana*, *P. s. alba*), of the Philippine Islands, much resembles it in growth and foliage, but its 2-inch-wide blooms are white and yellow with the sepals spotted with cinnamon-brown and the lip with reddish-purple.

Phalaenopsis stuartiana

Phalaenopsis stuartiana (flowers)

Easily grown **P. lueddemanniana** is one of several closely allied species. A native of the Philippine Islands, it is extremely variable in size, flower color, and other details. Its rather stiff, yellowish-green, elliptic, oblong-elliptic, or obovate leaves are up to 1 foot long by 4 inches broad. Generally not over 2 inches wide, the very fragrant, waxy, long-lived blooms, two to seven on each long, arching or pendulous stalk, ordinarily open in succession. Most

Phalaenopsis lueddemanniana

pallens, often confused with *P. lueddemanniana ochracea,* is distinguished by the more fleshy lip of the flower being differently shaped and structured.

Somewhat similar in habit and appearance are *P. cornu-cervi* and *P. mannii.* Of Malaya, Sumatra, Java, and Borneo, *P. cornu-cervi* has leathery leaves mostly under 1 foot long and about 1½ inches wide. Its flattened flower stems carry up to two dozen 2-inch-wide blooms, greenish-yellow or yellow barred and mottled with reddish-brown, and with a white or pale yellow bearded lip with orange-yellow markings and yellow, white, and violet appendages. Native to northern India, *P.*

Phalaenopsis cornu-cervi

typically they are white or yellowish, freely spotted and barred with chestnut-brown and stained with cinnamon-brown and amethyst-purple. The three-lobed lip, white and bright carmine-red with yellow at the base and on the side lobes, has a hairy callus near its apex. Variety *P. l. ochracea* (the name is often misapplied to *P. hieroglyphica*), has sepals and petals marked with ochre-yellow instead of brown and purple. Larger, quite differently patterned blooms distinguish *P. hieroglyphica* (syn. *P. lueddemanniana hieroglyphica*), of the Philippine Islands, from *P. lueddemanniana.* Its narrower, yellowish-white sepals and petals are covered with curious figures, spots, or circles of cinnamon-brown. Another Philippine Islander misnamed *P. lueddemanniana ochracea,* is *P. fasciata.* It differs from *P. lueddemanniana* in the shape and structure of the lip.

Variable *P. violacea* differs from *P. lueddemanniana* in having flowers with an ovate instead of oblong middle lobe to the lip and the callus toward its apex hairless instead of hairy. Typically the sepals and petals are magenta-pink with greenish apexes and the lip dark magenta-purple with side lobes marked with yellow. Varieties with white, white and green, and light yellow sepals and petals are known. Yet another Philippine Island species, *P.*

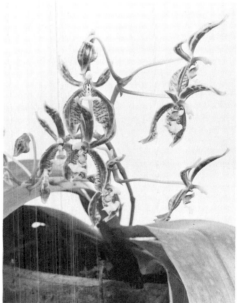

Phalaenopsis mannii

Phalaenopsis violacea

mannii has short-pointed, ovate-oblong to lanceolate leaves rather under 1 foot long by about 2 inches broad, and usually shorter flower stems than those of *P. cornu-cervi,* with up to half a dozen blooms about 1½ inches wide, all of which open at once. They are yellowish with generally plentiful spots and cross-bands of brown, but sometimes with few or no spots. The white lip is shorter than the petals.

A charming, small-flowered native of the Philippine Islands and Taiwan, **P. equestris** (syn. *P. rosea*) has leaves 6 to 8 inches long, and approximately one-half as wide. They sometimes have purplish undersides. The almost erect flower stalks, up to 1 foot tall, over a period of several months expand up to fifteen usually white and rose-red blooms about 1½ inches wide. The lip is darker than the sepals and petals and has a red-spotted, yellow crest. White-flowered varieties occur.

Other sorts cultivated include these: **P. amboinensis**, of the Molucca Islands, has elliptic leaves 8 inches to nearly 1 foot long and few-flowered racemes up to 1½ feet in length of approximately 1-inch-wide blooms with sepals and petals white with crossbars of cinnamon-red. **P. cochlearis**, of Sarawak, has thinnish oblong-ovate leaves 5 to 8 inches long, and in panicles up to about 1½ feet long, flowers with inconspicuously brown-barred, white sepals and petals a little over ½ inch long. **P. fuscata**, of the Philippine Islands, has obovate-oblong leaves up to about 1 foot long. Its flowers, yellow with brown markings, have elliptic sepals with recurved margins and shorter, obovate-oblong petals. About ½ inch long, the lip has three squarish side lobes and a flat, ovate center lobe with a callused disk. **P. gigantea**, of Borneo, has oblong-ovate, pendulous leaves 1 foot to 1½ feet long and, almost as long, racemes crowded with fleshy, aromatic, 2-inch-wide flowers with greenish sepals and petals blotched with maroon or reddish-brown. The three-lobed lip is white, blotched and lined with crimson. **P. kunstleri**, of the Malay Archipelago, has obovate, pendulous leaves 7 to 9 inches long and in often branched racemes, fleshy flowers 1½ to 2 inches across. The sepals and petals, the latter shorter than the petals, are yellow with brown or reddish-brown centers. Three-lobed, the lip is white to pale yellow with the center lobe streaked with brown. **P. parishii**, of Burma, has short stems and ovate to asymmetrically ovate leaves 2½ to 4½ inches long. Few to several 1-inch-wide flowers on zigzagged stems up to 6 inches long have white to creamy-white sepals and petals and a magenta to violet-purple lip. Variety *P. p. lobbii* has flowers with two chestnut-brown bands on each side of the center lobe of the lip. **P. pulchra** (syn. *P. lueddemanniana pulchra*), of the Philippine Islands, resembles *P. lueddemanniana* in growth habit. Its racemes are of a few, fleshy, deep rosy-purple blooms about 2 inches in diameter and with a three-lobed lip. **P. sumatrana**, of Malaya, Borneo, and Sumatra, has oblong-ovate to obovate leaves up to 1 foot long.

Its 6- to 10-inch-long stalks carry up to nine approximately 2-inch-wide flowers that have creamy-white sepals and petals more or less banded with purplish-brown and a three-lobed lip that is white with purplish or reddish streaks.

Phalaenopsis sumatrana

Phalaenopsis sumatrana (flowers)

Garden Uses and Cultivation. Species, varieties, and hybrids of *Phalaenopsis* are greatly esteemed by orchid fanciers. The finer kinds, chiefly hybrids, are much grown for cut flowers. In suitable environments they are not difficult to manage. They need considerable warmth, a minimum temperature on winter nights of 65 to 70°F, rising by day to 75 to 80°F, and higher in summer. High relative humidity is important, but when the plants are in bloom the atmosphere should be somewhat drier than at other times. Drafts are harmful and some growers advocate motionless air, but others recommend a gentle circulation by well-located fans. Success is had with various potting mixes including firmly packed osmunda and tree

fern fibers, redwood bark and fiber, and fir bark. Repotting should not be done more often than quite necessary, root disturbance being resented. Whatever the mix, it must pass water through freely yet remain moist. The plants may be grown in pans (shallow pots) with drainage holes in their sides as well as bottoms, hanging baskets, or on rafts or slabs of tree fern trunks. The roots must be kept moist at all seasons, but never excessively so. Whenever possible watering should be done in bright weather and care taken not to wet the plants. If water collects in their centers and remains overnight it is likely to cause crown rot. Misting the foliage with a light spray of water on bright days is beneficial. Shade from strong sun, rather more than most orchids need, is requisite. Light intensities in the vicinity of 1,000 foot candles are adequate, but somewhat stronger illumination is in order during the period of active growth. During the growing season monthly or semimonthly applications of dilute liquid fertilizer promote growth and good health. Propagation by division is practicable at long intervals only, since these orchids are slow in developing multiple crowns. A few, notably *P. lueddemanniana*, develop plantlets on their flower stems that afford means of increase. For more information see Orchids.

PHALARIS (Phál-aris)—Canary Grass, Ribbon Grass or Gardener's Garters. The name *Phalaris* is an ancient Greek one for an unknown kind of grass. The plants to which it now refers number about fifteen species, natives of temperate and warm-temperate climates, especially of the Mediterranean region. They belong to the grass family GRAMINEAE and include annuals and perennials. One, the canary grass, is the source of seeds popular as food for small cage birds.

Members of the group have slender or stout stems and flat leaves. The flowers are in crowded, spikelike panicles or spikes composed of short-stalked, flattened spikelets without awns (bristles). Each spikelet has a single fertile flower and two vestigial ones.

Canary grass (**P. canariensis**) is an annual 1 foot to 3 feet tall with slender to thickish stems in tufts or solitary. Its pointed, hairless, linear to lanceolate-linear leaves are 2 to 10 inches long by up to ½ inch wide. The egg-shaped to nearly cylindrical flower panicles are upright and ¾ inch to 2½ inches long by ½ to ¾ inch wide. They consist of densely crowded, obovate, whitish spikelets with green or rarely purple stripes. The seeds are shining straw-yellow. This native of the Mediterranean region is naturalized in North America. Similar to canary grass, but lower and differing in technical details of the spikelets, **P. minor**, of the Mediterranean region, is about as ornamental.

Phalaris arundinacea picta

Ribbon grass or gardener's garters (*P. arundinacea picta* syns. *P. a. variegata*, *P. a. elegans*) is a popular ornamental. It is a variety of the reed canary grass (*P. arundinacea*) distinguished by its leaves being striped longitudinally with white or cream. Another variant, *P. a. luteopicta* is similarly marked with golden-yellow. The reed canary grass and its varieties are hardy perennials 2 to 6 feet tall. They have creeping rhizomes and form vigorously spreading clumps. The variegated varieties flower infrequently, the species regularly. The stems are stout and upright. They have hairless, linear leaves up to 1 foot or more in length by up to ¾ inch in width. The dense, cylindrical or tapering flower panicles, up to 10 inches long and up to 1½ inches wide, have upright branches. Whitish, greenish, or purplish, the spikelets are up to ¼ inch long. This species is a native of North America, Europe, Asia, and South Africa.

Toowoomba canary grass (*P. tuberosa*) is decidedly ornamental, as well as being good fodder. Native to the Mediterranean region, it forms dense or open tufts 1 foot to 5 feet in height. Its stems, slender or thick, are swollen at their bases. The pointed leaves are up to 1 foot long or longer and somewhat under ½ inch wide. Cylindrical or cylindrical-egg-shaped, the crowded, pale green or purplish flower panicles are 1 inch to 4½ inches long by ½ to 1 inch wide. The elliptic-oblong spikelets of which they are composed are up to ⅓ inch long.

Garden and Landscape Uses. Ribbon grass is a useful ornamental summer foliage plant that survives and even flourishes with little or no care in sun or part-day shade. It is especially useful for moistish soil in out-of-the-way corners where little else will grow with the meager attention that satisfies it. Caution should be exercised about planting it near choice, weaker growing plants for it is decidedly invasive. It can be kept in check, however, by cutting around the clumps with a spade each spring or fall and removing the excess growth. The Toowoomba canary grass does not spread as does *P. arundinacea* and its varieties. Like the canary grass its chief ornamental value is in its attractive panicles of flowers.

Cultivation. Canary grass and *P. minor* are cultivated by sowing seeds in spring where the plants are to remain, in sunny locations in ordinary garden soil. The seedlings are thinned to 4 to 5 inches apart. The perennial kinds of *Phalaris* are propagated by division or, except the variegated varieties, by seed. They need practically no routine care other than the clearing away of dead stems and foliage in fall. A spring application of fertilizer promotes vigorous growth; sometimes the tendency of the spreading kinds to extend themselves may need checking.

PHANERA is *Bauhinia corymbosa*.

PHANEROPHLEBIA (Phanero-phlebia). Some botanists include this genus of ferns in closely related *Cyrtomium* of the Old World tropics and subtropics. Others, and their interpretation is followed here, accept *Phanerophlebia* as a separate genus of eight or more species endemic to warm parts of the Americas. It belongs in the aspidium family ASPIDIACEAE. The name, from the Greek *phaneros*, visible or evident, and *phlebos*, a vein, alludes to a feature of the fronds.

Phanerophlebias have leathery or less firm pinnate leaves with three- to four-forked veins that may or may not join toward the margins of the leaflets. It is upon the type of veining that the distinction between *Phanerophlebia* and *Cyrtomium* is based. The quite large, circular clusters of spore capsules are distributed in spotlike fashion over the under surfaces of the leaflets.

Native to Mexico and Central America, *P. macrosora* in general aspect much resembles the common holly fern (*Cyrtomium falcatum*). It has decidedly stout rhizomes and a crown of arching or semierect fronds 2½ to 4 feet long. Their leathery

Phanerophlebia macrosora showing clusters of spore capsules

blades, of thirteen to thirty-five narrowly-oblong, straight or slightly sickle-shaped, long-pointed leaflets 6 to 10 inches in length, are 1½ to 3 feet long by 9 inches to 1½ feet broad. When brushed against, the foliage gives off a delicate but definite skunklike odor.

Appropriately named, *P. juglandifolium* (the epithet *juglandifolium* means with walnut-like leaves) is an attractive native of

Phanerophlebia juglandifolium

deep shade in humid forests of Venezuela and Guatemala. A tufted plant, it has a short, curved, woody rhizome, and lustrous leaves up to about 1 foot long with five to eleven leaflets 1½ to 2 inches wide, their veins near the margins of the leaflets conspicuously joined.

Garden and Landscape Uses and Cultivation. These are as for *Cyrtomium*. For additional information see Ferns.

Phanerophlebia macrosora

PHASEOLUS (Phas-èolus)—Bean. The chief importance of *Phaseolus*, of the pea family LEGUMINOSAE, rests in the number of important food crops it embraces. It includes more than 175 species, mostly natives of tropical America, but some of other warm regions. The name is an ancient Greek one for a species of *Vigna*. For the plant sometimes named *P. caracalla* see *Vigna caracalla*.

The sorts of *Phaseolus* are mostly annual and nonwoody perennial, twining vines, with leaves of three undivided leaflets that exhibit pronounced sleep movements by drooping when darkness comes. In a few kinds the leaves have only one leaflet. The flowers, few to many together, are in clusters or racemes from the leaf axils. Pealike, they are white, yellow, red, or purple and have two sepal-like bracts, which may soon fall. An identifying characteristic is that the keel of the bloom is coiled. There are ten stamens, nine of which are joined and one separate. The style has a longitudinal beard. The fruits are pods containing several to many seeds.

The chief garden vegetables that belong in the genus *Phaseolus* are dealt with in this Encyclopedia under Beans. Here belong pole and bush snap beans (*P. vulgaris* and *P. v. humilis*, respectively), pole and bush lima beans (varieties of *P. limensis* and *P. lunatus*), the sieva, Carolina, civet, or butter bean (*P. lunatus* and *P. l. lunonanus*), and the tepary bean (*P. acutifolius latifolius*). In addition, the scarlet runner bean in some parts of the world is cultivated extensively as a vegetable.

Phaseolus coccineus

The scarlet runner bean (**P. coccineus** syn. *P. multiflorus*), much grown in Europe for its edible pods, is less well known as a food plant in the United States, but is cultivated as an ornamental. In its typical form it is a tall climber, in frost-free climates perennial, but almost always cultivated as an annual. Its leaves have three broad leaflets 3 to 5 inches long and without teeth. Its bright scarlet flowers, ¾ to 1 inch long, are in showy clusters varying from almost as long as to longer than the leaves. This native of tropical America has produced a number of varieties including nonclimbing ones and a white-flowered one (*P. c. albus*), the white Dutch runner bean.

Garden and Landscape Uses and Cultivation. As quick-growing vines for growing up strings, wires, brushwood, or other supports these plants are highly satisfactory. They flourish with little trouble in almost any fertile, well-drained soil in sun. Propagation is by seed. Those of the scarlet runner and its variety are sown outdoors in early spring where the vines are to remain. In cold climates those of the snail flower are more usually started early indoors and the plants later planted outdoors or kept in pots in greenhouses. In the tropics and subtropics they may be grown throughout in the open.

PHEASANT'S-EYE is *Adonis aestivalis*. The pheasant's eye narcissus is *Narcissus poeticus*.

PHEBALIUM (Pheb-àlium). This genus, of the rue family RUTACEAE, comprises forty species, all, except for a New Zealander, Australian. The name *Phebalium* comes from *phibale*, a classical name for the myrtle (*Myrtus*) and alludes to the appearance of the plants.

These are aromatic shrubs and small trees with alternate, undivided leaves and small white, yellow, or pink blooms, generally in terminal or axillary umbel-like clusters, but sometimes forming compact heads, or they may be solitary. The flowers have four or five each sepals and petals, eight or ten stamens. The fruits consist of five one-seeded segments or carpels but often only one or two of these develop seeds. The leaves have translucent dots, easily seen when viewed against the light. Rarely conspicuously hairy, the foliage sometimes has a few stellate (starry) hairs or may be scaly. In some kinds there are neither scales nor hairs. The wood of some sorts is used for cabinetwork and turnery.

In California and similar regions of mild climates, **P. argenteum**, of Western Australia, is cultivated. It has pointed, narrowly-lanceolate, short-stalked, evergreen leaves about 3 inches long, with prominent center veins. The flowers are in axillary and terminal, branching, loose clusters. They are about ⅓ inch wide and densely clothed with white scales.

Garden and Landscape Uses and Cultivation. This genus contains, in addition to the one described, several attractive species not yet cultivated in America. They are plants for mild, dry climates, well-drained soils, and full sun. Propagation is by fresh seeds, which are often difficult to germinate, and by cuttings of firm but not woody shoots, which root quite readily.

PHELLODENDRON (Phello-déndron) — Cork Tree. Despite its common name this group is not the source of commercial cork; that comes from an oak, *Quercus suber*. The genus *Phellodendron* belongs to a quite different family from the oaks, the rue family RUTACEAE. It consists of ten species, natives of eastern Asia. Its name, from the Greek, *phellos*, cork, and *dendron*, a tree, alludes to the bark of *P. amurense*.

Phellodendrons are hardy deciduous trees with opposite, pinnate leaves resembling those of walnuts, and with a terminal leaflet. When crushed the foliage is strongly aromatic. If held to the light the leaves show tiny translucent dots. Male and female flowers are on separate trees. Inconspicuous, they are small, yellowish-green or whitish, sometimes marked with pink, and are in terminal panicles or clusters. The blooms have five to eight each sepals and petals, the males five or six stamens longer than the petals and a rudimentary ovary, the females a short style and five vestigial stamens (staminodes). The berry-like, very dark blue-black fruits taste strongly of turpentine. They contain five seedlike stones.

The Amur cork tree (**P. amurense**) is the finest and hardiest. It survives throughout

Phellodendron amurense

Phellodendron amurense (bark)

Phellodendron amurense (fruits)

New England and well into Canada. A picturesque, stout-branched tree of rugged appearance, its most striking feature is its deeply-furrowed, corklike bark. It attains a height of about 45 feet and spreads widely. The leaves, with five to thirteen pointed, ovate to ovate-lanceolate leaflets 2 to 4 inches long, have round-toothed, hair-fringed margins and are lustrous on their upper sides. Their under surfaces are slightly glaucous and are without hairs except for possibly a few on the midribs. The finely-short-hairy flower clusters are 2½ to 3½ inches long. The fruits are not over ½ inch in diameter. This species is indigenous to Korea, China, and Japan. Also with thick, deeply-fissured, corky bark, Japanese *P. lavallei* (syn. *P. amurense lavallei*), somewhat taller than the last, has leaves with five to thirteen dull, elliptic-ovate to lanceolate-oblong, pointed leaflets 2 to 4 inches in length. Their undersides are not glaucous, but when young are pubescent; older leaves may be hairy only on the veins beneath. The flower clusters are about 3½ inches wide. The fruits are slightly more than ⅓ inch in diameter. This is hardy in southern New England.

Phellodendron lavallei

Kinds without thick, corky bark are *P. sachalinense* (syn. *P. amurense sachalinense*), *P. japonicum*, and *P. chinense*. Nearly as hardy as the Amur cork tree, but more symmetrical and less picturesque, *P. sachalinense* is up to about 45 feet in height. It has leaves with seven to eleven ovate or ovate-oblong, pointed leaflets up to 4½ inches long, and scarcely or not fringed with hairs. Their undersides are more or less glaucous and, like the flower panicles are almost or quite without hairs. The panicles are 2½ to 3½ inches in length. The fruits are a little over ⅓ inch wide. This species is indigenous to Japan.

Phellodendron sachalinense at the Arnold Arboretum, Jamaica Plain, Massachusetts

Phellodendron japonicum at the Royal Botanic Gardens, Kew, England

About 30 feet tall, *P. japonicum* (syn. *P. amurense japonicum*), of Japan, and *P. chinense*, of China, are rather rare in cultivation. The first survives about as far north as New York City, the other in southern New England. The leaves of *P. japonicum* have nine to thirteen dull, pointed, ovate to ovate-oblong leaflets 2½ to 4 inches long, and hairy on their undersides especially along the veins. The rather loose flower clusters, 2 to 3 inches broad, have hairy stalks. The fruits are under ½ inch in diameter. Unlike those of the last, the more crowded flower panicles of *P. chinense* are longer than broad; they are 2½ to 3½ inches in length and have hairy

stalks. The leaves have seven to thirteen oblong-lanceolate to oblong-ovate leaflets 3 to 5 inches in length, hairy on their undersides. The fruits are under ½ inch wide. Variety *P. c. glabriusculum* is distinguished by the undersides of the leaves being pubescent only on the veins.

Garden and Landscape Uses. Phellodendrons are more neglected than their merits deserve. Splendid landscape trees, of fairly rapid growth, they are remarkably free from pests and diseases. They scale well with small properties and their foliage is bold, rich green, and handsome; in fall it turns yellow, but this phase does not last long. When female trees are dropping their berries they are a trifle messy, but for a short period only. The rough-barked species are admirable for creating effects of picturesque age. The Amur cork tree has the massive dignity of a great oak, but on a smaller scale. Also beautiful as lawn trees, they are splendid in association with contemporary low houses. However, because of their eventual spread, which may be 50 feet, they should not be planted close to buildings. A sunny location and any fairly fertile, deep, well-drained soil suit cork trees. They thrive on limestone as well as nonlimestone soils.

Cultivation. Once established, these trees need no routine attention. As young specimens a little pruning to train or shape them may be in order, but beyond that essentially no care is needed. Propagation is very easy by seed, indeed seedlings are likely to spring up spontaneously in abundance beneath fruiting trees. Cuttings of semimature short shoots with a heel of older wood attached to their bases root readily if made in late summer and planted under mist or in a propagating bed in a cold frame or greenhouse, preferably with slight bottom heat.

PHELLOPTERUS MACRORHIZUS is *Cymopterus macrorhiza*.

PHELLOSPERMA (Phello-spérma). By many modern botanists *Phellosperma*, of the cactus family CACTACEAE, is included, doubtless appropriately, in closely related *Mammillaria*. When accepted as a distinct entity, it consists of one species. Its name, from the Greek *phellos*, cork, and *sperma*, seed, alludes to the corky bases of the seeds.

Native of sandy soils in desert regions of the southwestern United States and Baja California, *P. tetrancistra* (syn. *Mammillaria tetrancistra*) has solitary, ovoid to ovoid-cylindrical plant bodies, 3 to 6 inches high or sometimes higher by 1½ to 2½ inches wide, thickly covered with clusters of thirty to forty or perhaps sometimes more white or dark-tipped white radial spines ⅜ to ½ inch long or longer and one to four white-based, red to black principal hooked centrals ½ to 1 inch long.

Phellosperma tetrancistra

The bright pink to rose-purple flowers, 1 inch to 1½ inches in diameter, originate somewhat below the apex. The club-shaped, scarlet fruits contain large, dull black seeds with a corky appendage almost as big as the seed itself.

Garden Uses and Cultivation. A collector's item, this has generally proved difficult to grow. Best chances of success are likely to follow grafting it onto a stronger-growing cactus. For more information see Cactuses.

PHILADELPHUS (Phila-délphus) — Mock-Orange. The genus *Philadelphus*, of the saxifrage family SAXIFRAGACEAE, is important horticulturally. It contains about seventy-five species and many beautiful hybrids of mostly hardy, free-flowering, deciduous shrubs. In the wild it forms parts of the native floras of North America, Europe, and Asia. Philadelphuses are sometimes called syringas, which is confusing because *Syringa* is the botanical name of lilacs. The name commemorates Ptolemy Philadelphus, a king of the third century B.C.

Mock-oranges have many erect or arching branches, often with shredding bark, and opposite, undivided leaves, those of some kinds when crushed smelling of cucumber. The white or sometimes yellowish, often fragrant blooms are solitary or in few-flowered clusters, often arranged in racemes or in panicle-like fashion. Usually there are four, more rarely five or six petals (in double-flowered horticultural varieties more). There are twenty to forty stamens and four or less commonly three or five styles. The fruits are small capsules. The botany of *Philadelphus* is very complex, and horticultural varieties cannot always be assigned with surety to particular species. From related *Deutzia* mock-oranges

differ in having branchless rather than stellate (starlike) hairs and in their flowers generally having only four calyx lobes and petals and more than ten stamens.

Commonly cultivated *P. coronarius* is very variable and some of its variants decidedly inferior. The only species native to Europe, this occurs also in adjacent Asia. About 12 feet tall, it has distantly-toothed, ovate to ovate-oblong leaves, up to about

Philadelphus coronarius

3 inches long, hairy along the veins of their undersides and along the leafstalks. Its creamy-white blooms, about 1 inch to 1½ inches across, are in five- to nine-flowered racemes. Their calyxes are usually hairless except at their edges. Noteworthy among its many horticultural varieties are *P. c. aureus*, with bright yellow foliage that dulls as the season advances; *P. c. deutziaeflorus* (syn. *P. c. multiflorus-plenus*), a low variety that has double flowers with slender, pointed petals; *P. c. dianthiflorus*, a low variety with double flowers with round-ended petals; *P. c. duplex* (syns. *P. c. flore-pleno, P. c. nanus, P. c. pumilus*), a low variety with double or semidouble flowers, but that fails to bloom or blooms only sparingly until it is several years old; *P. c. primulaeflorus* (syn. *P. c. rosaeflorus-plenus*), with wide-petaled, double blooms similar to those of *P. c. dianthiflorus*, but the plant is somewhat taller; *P. c. salicifolius*, distinct because of its lanceolate leaves being 2 to 4 inches long and ½ to ¾ inch wide; *P. c. speciosissimus* (syn. *P. speciosissimus*), smaller-leaved and lower than the typical species; *P. c. variegatus*, the leaves of which are broadly and irregularly edged with white, and *P. c. zeyheri*, which is of upright habit and has single flowers 1 inch wide.

Lustrous rather than dull green foliage distinguishes shapely and compact *P. inodorus*. This native from North Carolina to Georgia and Mississippi is up to about 10 feet tall. It has usually toothless, ovate leaves, hairy only on their veins beneath, and up to 4 inches long. Solitary, or in twos or threes, the flowers are 2 to 2¼

Philadelphus coronarius zeyheri

inches wide. They open before those of most mock-oranges. Despite the implication of the specific name, they are not entirely without fragrance. Scentless blooms 1¾ to 2 inches wide, in twos, threes, or solitary, are borne by *P. i. grandiflorus*. Native from North Carolina to Florida and Alabama, this 10- to 15-feet-tall species has arching branches and elliptic-ovate, distantly-minutely-toothed leaves, up to about 5 inches long, with almost hairless undersurfaces.

Two small-leaved mock-oranges are *P. microphyllus*, native from Colorado to New Mexico and Arizona, and *P. pekinensis*, of China and Korea. Graceful *P. microphyllus*, about 4½ feet high, has lustrous, extremely short-stalked, toothless, pointed leaves, elliptic-ovate to oblong-lanceolate, up to ¾ inch long, with stiff hairs and glaucous undersides. The mostly solitary, 1-inch-wide blooms are deliciously pineapple-scented. They have united styles a little shorter than the stamens. From 5 to 8 feet tall, *P. pekinensis* has long-pointed, oblong-ovate, usually three-veined, gray-green leaves 1 inch to 2 inches long, with purplish stalks. They are distantly toothed, and except in the axils of the veins of their undersides, are mostly without hairs. Slightly fragrant, with short stalks, and styles about as long as the stamens, the 1-inch-wide or somewhat wider, yellowish-white blooms are in racemes of five to nine.

Similar to each other in appearance, but the first, one of the latest blooming mock-oranges, flowering two weeks after the other, *P. incanus* and *P. subcanus*, natives of China, are hardy in southern New England. About 10 feet tall and with arching branches, they have ovate to ovate-oblong leaves 2½ to 4½ inches long and with forward-pointing teeth. Their upper surfaces have few or no hairs. Their undersides are gray-hairy, the hairs of *P. incanus* softer and more plentiful than those of *P. subcanus*. The blooms, 1 inch or a little more in diameter, and in five- to nine-flowered, one-sided racemes, have hairy calyxes. They are white, scentless or slightly fragrant, those of *P. incanus* lacking the hairs usually found at the bases of the styles in *P. subcanus*. From the last two species, which it much resembles, Chinese *P. magdalenae* differs in its upper as well as lower leaf surfaces being covered with stiff hairs. Its freely produced, scented flowers, about 1 inch wide, have hairy calyxes, and are in seven- to eleven-flowered, one-sided racemes.

Creamy-yellow flowers nearly 2 inches in diameter, but unfortunately partly hidden by the foliage, are produced by *P. pubescens*, native from Tennessee to Alabama and Arkansas. This broad shrub, up to 10 feet in height, is hardy in New England. It has ovate to elliptic, pointed leaves up to 4 inches long, and generally distantly toothed. They are dark green and nearly hairless on their upper surfaces, thickly-gray-hairy beneath.

One of the earliest mock-oranges to bloom, *P. schrenkii*, native from Korea to Manchuria, and hardy through much of New England, is about 6 feet tall, and up-

right. Its leaves are ovate to ovate-lanceolate, toothed, and 1½ to 3½ inches long or occasionally longer. Pure white, about 1½ inches across, and in densely-hairy-stalked racemes of five to seven, the blooms have styles usually hairy at their bases. Variety *P. s. jackii* has leaves sparingly-hairy on their undersides, and more densely-pubescent flower stalks.

Hybrid mock-oranges are legion and include the finest of the clan. Among the oldest are *P. falconeri* and *P. nivalis*. Of undetermined parentage, *P. falconeri* is a shrub up to 8 feet tall with narrow-ovate leaves up to 2½ inches long and, in clusters of usually three to seven, slightly fragrant, single white flowers about 1¼ inches across and with narrow, pointed-elliptic petals and a style markedly longer than the stamens. *P. nivalis*, its parents *P. coronarius* and *P. pubescens*, has ovate, toothed leaves with undersides slightly hairy, and in racemes of five to nine, 1¼- to 1½-inch-wide flowers with hairy calyxes, a style divided only at its apex, and stigmas longer than the anthers. Variety *P. n. plenus* has double flowers. Especially noteworthy is the bewildering array bred in the late nineteenth century in France by the nurseryman Victor Lemoine, and his successors, and known as the Lemoine hybrids. These are grouped according to their known or conjectured parentages as follows. *P. lemoinei*, its parents *P. microphyllus* and *P. coronarius*, has very fragrant flowers. Typical varieties are 'Avalanche', 4 to 5 feet tall, with single, 1-inch-wide, very fragrant blooms; 'Belle Etoile', 4 feet

Philadelphus falconeri

Philadelphus nivalis

Philadelphus lemoinei: (a) Single-flowered variety

(b) Double-flowered variety

tall, its flowers single and about 2¼ inches in diameter; double-flowered 'Boule d'Argent', with blooms 2 inches wide and hardiest of the group; and 'Mont Blanc', 4 feet tall, with single blooms 1¼ inches wide. **P. cymosus,** a hybrid of uncertain parentage, has single or double blooms. Varieties that belong here include 'Conquete', which has very fragrant, 2-inch-wide, single blooms; 'Norma', with single flowers 1¾ inches in diameter; and 'Voie Lactee', 6 to 8 feet in height, its single flowers 2 inches wide. **P. purpureo-maculatus,** a hybrid of *P. lemoinei* and *P. coulteri,* is less hardy to winter cold than *P. lemoinei* and *P. cymosus.* Its flowers are conspicuously blotched with maroon or purple at the bases of the petals. Typical varieties are 'Nuage Rose', 'Sybille', and 'Sirene', 4 feet tall, single-flowered, and

the hardiest of the *P. purpureo-maculatus* varieties. **P. virginalis,** its parents *P. lemoinei* and probably *P. nivalis plenus,* the latter an old hybrid of *P. pubescens* and *P. coronarius,* has double or semidouble blooms generally large and of superb quality. Varieties belonging here are 'Argentine', 4 feet tall, with double blooms 2 inches in diameter; 'Bouquet Blanc', 6 feet tall, with 1-inch-wide single flowers; and 'Virginal', one of the best of the low, double-flowered kinds.

More recent hybrids raised in North America include 'Cole's Glorious', which has single, 2-inch-wide blooms; 'Frosty

Morn', extremely cold resistant, with double, fragrant flowers; 'Silver Showers', a 3-foot-tall, single-flowered variety. Other hybrids include one of the latest mock-oranges to bloom, **P. insignis** (syn. *P.* 'Souvenir de Billiard'). Its parents perhaps *P. pubescens* and *P. lewisii californicus,* this tall shrub is hardy in southern New England. It has big, leafy panicles of slightly fragrant flowers 1¼ inches across. A big shrub about as hardy as the last, **P. magnificus,** its parents *P. inodorus grandiflorus* and *P. pubescens,* has 2-inch-wide flowers in racemes or clusters of three to five. A low shrub distinct from others discussed

Philadelphus cymosus 'Conquete'

Philadelphus virginalis 'Virginal'

here, *P. pendulifolius*, its parents *P. pubescens* and presumably *P. inodorus laxus*, has drooping, ovate to elliptic leaves and short-stalked flowers 1 inch wide or a little wider, in racemes of five to seven.

Garden and Landscape Uses. Mock-oranges share with lilacs and some other commonly planted shrubs the disadvantage of being interesting only when in bloom, for about two weeks of the year. At other times they are masses of characterless foliage or leafless branches. But when in flower the best kinds are really magnificent, and the fragrances of some are as delightful as any found in gardens. These shrubs have other advantages. Most mock-oranges are hardy, and all are remarkably free of pests and diseases. They make good screens and grow in practically any ordinary, reasonably good soil with almost no care. They stand pruning well, and branches in gorgeous bloom are splendid for flower arrangements. To bloom well they need full sun. The quantity and quality of the flowers decreases with increased shade. Owners of small gardens may with good cause question the wisdom of devoting space to these short-season beautifiers of the terrain, but for larger landscapes there is no doubt that they deserve serious consideration. They may be used as boundary plantings, included in shrub beds, set singly or in groups in lawns, or against low walls they overtop.

Cultivation. Mock-oranges require little in the way of cultivation. Pruning consists of thinning out old and crowded branches as soon as blooming is through and at the same time cutting off the parts of branches that have flowered, leaving the laterals that come from below the flowering parts to grow and to bloom the following year. Never should the bushes be cut to formal shapes or in such manner that all the branches are cropped. The objective is to thin out unwanted growths without destroying the natural grace of the plant. Like most shrubs, these benefit from mulching with compost or similar suitable material and, during drought, from periodic soakings with water. In poorish soils the application of a complete garden fertilizer each spring is of benefit. Propagation is easily achieved by leafy summer cuttings planted under mist or in a cold frame or greenhouse propagating bench and by hardwood cuttings taken in fall. Seeds can be used to increase species and produce new varieties. But those taken from plants growing in mixed collections are likely to give hybrid progeny.

PHILAGERIA (Phila-gèria). The name of this bigeneric hybrid between two Chilean species of the lily family LILIACEAE is formed from those of its parent genera, *Philesia* and *Lapageria*. It was raised in the latter half of the nineteenth century by the renowned English nursery firm of Veitch and is named *Philageria veitchii*. Although exhibiting characteristics intermediate between those of its parents, the hybrid more obviously resembles *Lapageria*. It is a slender-branched, half-climbing or scrambling evergreen shrub with stalked, finely-toothed, oblong leaves about 1¼ inches long and lustrous dark green above. Borne in the leaf axils, the few, solitary, nodding blooms have six petals (correctly, tepals), the three outer light rosy-purple, the inner three bright rose-pink.

Garden Uses and Cultivation. This is only for the avid collector of rare plants. Its cultural requirements are those of *Lapageria*. It is not hardy in the north.

PHILESIA (Phil-èsia). The name *Philesia* alludes to the beauty of the blooms. It comes from the Greek *phileo*, to love. There is only one species. It belongs in the lily family LILIACEAE and is a native of southern Chile to the Strait of Magellan.

An erect, evergreen, branching shrub up to 4 feet tall in its homeland, but often considerably lower in cultivation, *P. magellanica* (syn. *P. buxifolia*) is a close relative of *Lapageria*. A hybrid between the two is named *Philageria*. The leaves of *Philesia*, alternate, leathery, and short-stalked, have recurved margins and one main vein. They are 1 inch to 1½ inches long, narrowly-oblong, and dark green on their upper surfaces and glaucous beneath. So unlike the foliage of most plants of the lily family is this that out of bloom the shrub looks much like a *Vaccinium*. Nodding, and trumpet-shaped, the lovely deep rose-pink, waxy blooms come in summer. About 2 inches long, they are solitary or few together at the branch ends. Each has a calyx of three short sepals and a corolla of three much more showy petals that are two to three times as long as the sepals. The six stamens, joined below their middles into a tube, do not protrude; neither does the solitary style. The fruits are nearly spherical berries.

Garden Uses and Cultivation. Like so many southern South American plants this choice lily relative needs specialized conditions and must be regarded as a connoisseur's item, not for casual planting. It stands neither freezing nor torrid summers. An equable, temperate, fairly humid environment meets its needs. In mild parts of the British Isles it is grown in protected places outdoors, and it may be expected to do at least as well in parts of the Pacific Northwest. It favors well-drained, moderately moist, somewhat acid, peaty soil, but will not stand stagnant wetness about its roots. Some gardeners report that decayed wood mixed with the soil is advantageous. A cool location, with dappled shade to temper the strongest sun, is most to this plant's liking. No pruning is needed. Propagation is by division, layer-

ing, and seed, and by cuttings set in a cool greenhouse propagating bench. The last root very slowly.

Greenhouses where the winter night temperature is between 40 and 50°F and day temperatures are not much higher are suitable for *P. magellanica*. In summer, shade is needed and as cool, airy conditions as can be maintained.

PHILIBERTIA. See Sarcostemma.

PHILIPPINE-TEA is *Ehretia microphylla*.

PHILIPPINE-VIOLET is *Barleria cristata*.

PHILLYREA (Philly-rea). Native of the Mediterranean and Black Sea regions, *Phillyrea* is a genus of four species of the olive family OLEACEAE. Its members are evergreen shrubs and small trees. The name is an ancient Greek one of these plants.

Phillyreas have short-stalked, opposite, undivided, leathery, toothed or toothless leaves, and clustered in the leaf axils of the shoots of the previous year, little white flowers with four-lobed calyxes and corollas and two protruding stamens. The blue-black to black, berry-like, egg-shaped to nearly spherical, one-seeded fruits are drupes (fruits of the plum type). Exerted stamens, and corolla lobes (petals) longer than the corolla tube, distinguish this genus from the hybrid between it and *Osmanthus* named Osmarea.

The hardiest and most beautiful species is *P. decora* (syn. *P. vilmoriniana*). This native of the Black Sea region lives outdoors in sheltered locations about as far north as

Phillyrea decora

New York City. Rigidly branched and dense, it is 5 to 10 feet tall. Its shoots are without hairs. The firm leaves are pointed, narrowly-ovate to ovate-lanceolate, and toothless or almost so. They are 2 to 5 inches long by ½ inch to 1¾ inches wide. The flowers are pure white, the slender-stalked fruits about ½ inch long.

A broader shrub, or small tree up to 30 feet tall, *P. latifolia* is a native of southeast Europe and Asia Minor. Its shoots are minutely-pubescent, its dark green, ovate to round-ovate, lustrous leaves 2 to 2½ inches long by 1 inch to 1½ inches broad. The dull white flowers are followed by nearly spherical fruits ¼ inch in diameter. In *P. l. spinosa* (syn. *P. !. ilicifolia*) the leaves are strongly toothed and 1 inch to 1½ inches long. This species and its variety are decidedly less hardy than *P. decora*. Very like *P. latifolia* except for its much narrower, willow-like leaves, which are linear, toothless, and 1 inch to 2½ inches long by up to ½ inch wide, is *P. angustifolia*. Dull white, its blooms are succeeded by roundish egg-shaped fruits ¼ inch long. This native of southern Europe and North Africa is not hardy in the north.

Garden and Landscape Uses and Cultivation. As single specimens and for backgrounds and screening, phillyreas, especially *P. decora*, are desirable. Their habits of growth and handsome foliage are their chief attractions. Their fragrant blooms make little display. They accommodate to ordinary well-drained soil, and do well in shade. Cuttings 2 to 4 inches long made in summer from the ends of firm shoots root readily in a propagating bed in a greenhouse or cold frame or under mist. Increase can also be had by layering and by seed. No special routine care of established specimens is needed. Pruning, if it is desired to restrain plants to size or to shape them, is done in spring. If necessary hard cutting back may be done, phillyreas recover well from such drastic treatment.

PHILODENDRON (Philo-déndron). Few botanical names are more familiar to Americans than *Philodendron*. Even city dwellers correctly recognize as such kinds commonly grown as indoor foliage plants. Yet the genus is so vast and its botany so complicated that correct identification of many kinds as to species is extraordinarily difficult, and without flowers (seldom produced by most kinds in cultivation) for examination, often impossible. In this treatment the most important cultivated kinds are accounted for, but new ones are likely to be introduced from time to time, and it must be remembered that quite startling differences in appearance, especially in leaf size and sometimes shape, may result from different environments and from the age of the plant. The number of species is approximately 275, all natives of warm parts of the Americas, including the West

Indies. The name, from the Greek *phileo*, loving, and *dendron*, a tree, alludes to the many species that in the wild are tall, tree-climbing vines. But not all philodendrons develop in that way, some grow on rocks or in the ground as free-standing, nonvining specimens.

Belonging to the arum family ARACEAE, philodendrons are evergreen perennials with branching, semiwoody or woody stems, and alternate, thick leaves with parallel side veins. The leaves may be undivided and without lobes or teeth, divided into separate leaflets, pinnately-lobed, or toothed. In outline ovate to oblong, heart-, arrow-, or halberd-shaped, they have stalks that sheathe the stems with their bases. The true flowers are borne in inflorescences commonly, but incorrectly called flowers. Each inflorescence consists of numerous tiny, unisexual flowers crowded along a spikelike organ called a spadix, at the base of which is a bract called a spathe. The female flowers are toward the base of the spadix, the males above them. As the fruits (berries) develop the spadixes thicken. In *Philodendron* the inflorescences are short-stalked, solitary or clustered, and come from the leaf axils or are terminal. Often they are fragrant. The thick, persistent spathes, as long or longer than the spadixes and variously colored, encircle them; they have boat-shaped blades. The plant called *P. pertusum* is *Monstera deliciosa*.

More or less trailing kinds with slender, weak stems include *P. scandens*, of tropical America. This has adult-type leaves with stalks shorter than the ovate, reflexed blades, which are up to 1 foot long by two-thirds as wide and have two or three pairs of lateral veins. The inflorescences have greenish spathes 4 to 6 inches in length sometimes tinged with reddish-purple toward the base inside. Juvenile-type leaves, considerably smaller, have satiny, green upper surfaces and green to reddish-purple undersides. Variety *P. s. micans* (syn. *P. micans*), of Panama, in its juvenile phase has leaves dark green above, red-purple beneath. Most familiar *P. s oxycardium* (syn. *P. oxycardium*), of Mexico, is frequently misnamed *P. cordatum*, which name properly belongs to another species. Both its juvenile and larger adult leaves are glossy-green on both surfaces. Brazilian *P. cordatum* much resembles *P. scandens*, but its leaves have stalks shorter or longer than the blades, which have about five pairs of chief lateral veins and in the adult phase are up to 1 foot long by 10 inches wide. Native to Peru, *P. grazielae*, which roots freely from its slender stems, has bright, glossy-green, heart- to kidney-shaped leaves with blades up to 3½ inches long, usually wider than their lengths, and with a ¾-inch-long, tail-like point at the apex. Costa Rican *P. microstictum*, sometimes erroneously grown as *P. pittieri*, has

Philodendron scandens oxycardium

Philodendron grazielae

glossy leaves with broad-triangular to nearly heart-shaped blades up to 9 inches long tapered to sharp points, and with stalks about equaling the blades. Small, bluish-green, heart-shaped leaves largely overcast with a leaden or silvery hue, and with the chief veins of their undersides red, are characteristic of the slender-stemmed juvenile form of *P. ornatum* (syn. *P. sodiroi*), of Brazil. The adult phase of this has broadly-ovate leaves up to 2 feet long, with reflexed, sometimes gray-blotched blades deeply heart-shaped at their bases.

Stouter-stemmed vines with leaves not divided or lobed and that even in their juvenile stages are much larger than the

Philodendron microstictum

Philodendron ornatum

Philodendron domesticum

Philodendron erubescens 'Golden Erubescens'

Philodendron erubescens

Philodendron glaziovii

kinds dealt with above include several species and hybrids. Among the most common are those now to be considered. Popular **P. domesticum,** which in cultivation is usually labeled *P. hastatum* although that designation properly belongs to a different plant not known to be cultivated, is of unknown origin. It is a vigorous grower with thickish, fresh green, arrow- to ovate- or oblong-heart-shaped, often undulate-surfaced leaves that have paler, raised veins. The inflorescences have pale green spathes, red on their insides. Handsomely variegated *P. d. variegatum* has foliage irregularly splashed with shades of green, creamy-white, and white. The waxy-looking, narrowly-heart- or arrow-shaped, bronzy-green, red-edged leaves of **P. erubescens,** of Colombia, have wine-red undersides and stalks marked with red. The variety called 'Golden Erubescens' is a vigorous vine with yellow leaves, pinkish on its undersides. A native of Brazil, **P. glaziovii** is a high climber with stems that root from the nodes and, more or less in two ranks, leathery, lanceolate to arrowhead-shaped leaves with blades up to 1½ feet long and with pale midribs. The inflorescences have spadixes and spathes 6 to

7 inches long, the latter greenish-yellow outside and straw-yellow with the interior of the tube scarlet. Colombian **P. gloriosum** has broadly-heart-shaped, predominantly silvery-green velvety leaves with narrow red margins and clearly defined white to pinkish veins. The leaves of

P. imbe are much like those of *P. erubescens,* but with the lateral veins almost at right angles to the mid-vein. Their under surfaces are reddish, their stalks marked with red. A slow grower, **P. mamei,** of Ecuador, has large, somewhat puckered or

Philodendron gloriosum

Philodendron mamei in Brazil

quilted, broadly-ovate-heart-shaped, green to grayish-green leaves splashed with silvery-gray. Hybrid **P. mandaianum,** intermediate between its parents *P. domesticum* and *P. erubescens,* is an excellent kind, the lustrous foliage of which ranges from metallic-purplish-red to wine-red. Very beautiful **P. melanochrysum** (syn. *P. an-*

dreanum), of Colombia, has heart-shaped, iridescent, dark olive-green leaves brushed with copper and of a rich velvet texture. They have stalks up to 1½ feet in length and blades 1½ to 2½ feet long, the latter with well-defined pale green midribs and lateral veins. In its juvenile state often cultivated as *P. dubium,* Mexican and Central

American **P. radiatum** is a vigorous vine, its adult broad-ovate leaves deeply cleft into deep, narrow lobes. The juvenile ones are much less dissected. Mexican **P. sagittifolium** has arrow- to halberd-shaped, wavy-surfaced leaves, the basal lobes of the adult ones wide-spreading. They have depressed veins. Indigenous to Costa Rica, **P. talamancae** is a slow-growing vine with rigid, long-stalked, triangular-lanceolate to broad-elliptic leaves, heart-shaped at their bases, with a pale mid-vein. Their blades are up to 2 feet long. Velvety, dark bronzy-green heart-shaped leaves with pinkish undersides are characteristic of **P. verrucosum,** of Central and South America. The leafstalks are clothed with red or

Philodendron radiatum

Philodendron talamancae

green hairs. Possibly of hybrid origin, *P. v. purpureum* has smallish heart-shaped, emerald-green leaves with silver-bordered pink veins and areas of wine-purple.

Stouter-stemmed vines with lobed leaves include several popular philodendrons. Here belongs *P.* 'Florida', an intermediate hybrid between *P. pedatum* and *P. squamiferum.* This has leaves, brownish-red on their undersides, mostly deeply-cleft into five chief lobes, and with the veins on their upper surfaces depressed. Its parents *P. pedatum palmatisectum* and *P. squamiferum*, variety *P.* 'Florida Compacta' is similar. The leaves of *P.* 'Florida Varie-

Philodendron 'Florida Variegata'

gata' are variegated with creamy-yellow. Adult leaves of West Indian *P. lacerum* are deeply cleft into narrow lobes. Very juvenile ones have wavy, lobeless and toothless margins, and intermediate-type leaves are coarsely-toothed. All are broadly-ovate and lustrous green with paler veins. The long-stalked leaves of *P. pedatum,* of Venezuela, northern Brazil, and adjacent territory, have oblong to heart-shaped blades with five or seven deep lobes some of which may be shallowly-lobed. Variety *P. p. palmatisectum*, of Brazil to Surinam, has olive-green leaves divided almost or quite to their bases into three or more lobes or leaflets that are again lobed. The plant that has been cultivated as *P. panduraeforme* is *P. bipennifolium.* Native to Brazil, this has fiddle- or horse-head-shaped leaves, dull olive-green and with the middle of the five lobes much the largest and narrowed to its base. Native to northern South America, *P. squamiferum* much resembles *P. pedatum,* but its pale-veined leaves have more broadly-ovate center lobes and two pairs of pointed side lobes. The leafstalks are bristly.

Shrub-type, nonvining, or self-heading philodendrons, some of which in their native lands attain the dimensions of small

Philodendron bipennifolium

Philodendron squamiferum

trees, were little known in the United States before 1950, although a few were being grown in botanical collections. The chief reason for their scarcity was that propagating them by vegetative means is extremely slow and seeds were not available. In an article published in 1949 in the *National Horticultural Magazine,* a technique employed successfully in Florida that caused *P. bipinnatifidum* to produce seed was described. This stirred interest and other breeders and growers adopted it. Not only did this make possible the rapid production of young plants of species, it made the development of hybrids between species practicable.

Shrubby philodendrons include several giant kinds, chiefly natives of southern Brazil and adjacent territory. The most

massive become small trees or broad evergreen shrubs, some up to 20 or 30 feet in diameter with stout, self-supporting stems and impressively bold foliage. Their spread is attained by their stems leaning or bending under the weights of their leafy tops as they age until they touch the ground. There, they take root then grow upward again with branches leaning in all directions. The new branches repeat the same growth pattern. In addition to the really big shrubby philodendrons, all of which in cultivation belong to the botanical subgenus *Meconostigma*, there are a number of self-heading forms of normally tree-perching (epiphytic) species that behave in the same way and serve the same purposes, but are generally smaller.

Largest and most magnificent of cultivated shrubby philodendrons, Brazilian *P. eichleri* has drooping, boldly veined, deeply scallop-edged leaves with arrow-shaped blades 4 to 7 feet long. Native to

Philodendron eichleri in the Fairchild Tropical Garden, Miami, Florida

Paraguay, *P. undulatum* when mature is not over 3 to 4 feet tall. It has long-stalked leaves up to 2 feet long and 1¼ feet wide with lobeless, broad-arrow-shaped blades. Its somewhat cupped, wavy and lobed leaves are smaller than those of kinds previously discussed. An intermediate hybrid between *P. eichleri* and *P. undulatum* has leaves that approximate 3 feet in length; it is unnamed.

Other giant shrubby philodendrons include *P. bipinnatifidum* and *P. selloum.* Similar in aspect and both natives of Brazil, these are among the most cold-resistant kinds. In Florida mature specimens when dormant have survived temperatures as low as 22°F, but younger plants are severely damaged by even a few degrees of frost. Up to about 15 feet in height, these have leaves with stalks 1 foot to 3 feet long or sometimes longer and more or less heart-shaped, twice-pin-

Philodendron bipinnatifidum, Montreal
Botanical Garden, Montreal, Canada

Philodendron selloum

nately-lobed blades 2 to 3 feet long by two-thirds as broad. The chief differences between these species are that *P. bipinnatifidum* is usually more leafy than *P. selloum*, its leafstalks are more slender, and its leaf blades have inconspicuous, opaque, lateral veins, whereas those of *P. selloum* are more visible and translucent. Also, the terminal lobes of the leaves of *P. bipinnatifidum* are proportionately longer than those of *P. selloum*. In the last, the side lobes exceed the terminal one in length. The foliage of *P. s. variegatum* is variegated with creamy-yellow or pale green. Similar to *P. selloum*, but its leaves flatter, less cupped, and with lobes more frilled, *P.* 'Sao Paulo', of Brazil, is popular and satisfactory. An intermediate hybrid between it and *P. selloum* is named *P.* 'Jungle Gardens'.

Impressive **P. speciosum,** of Brazil, 6 feet or so tall, has leaves with somewhat corrugated, pointed-heart-shaped blades 2 to 2½ feet long by 1¼ to 1½ feet wide that hang vertically from the tops of long, erect stalks. Another Brazilian, **P. cymbispathum** (syn. *P.* 'Species No. 1') when young

has cupped, ovate-arrow-shaped, wavy leaves. Those of older specimens are lobed, but much less deeply than those of *P. bipinnatifidum*, which in general this species resembles. It is more compact than *P. bipinnatifidum*.

Several good hybrids involving kinds just described are cultivated. Among these **P. fosteranum** has as parents *P. bipinnatifidum* with *P. cymbispathum*. From the first the offspring differs chiefly in its firm-textured leaves having shorter stalks and less deeply cut blades. Of the same parentage, **P. macneilianum** has large, wavy, deeply-lobed leaves broadly-triangular-ovate in outline. The parents of excellent **P. evansii** are *P. selloum* and *P. speciosum*. The hybrid

has lustrous leaves with elephant-ear-shaped, lobed, wavy blades up to 3½ feet long. It is less compact than many self-headers. Robust **P. barryi,** the parents of which are *P. bipinnatifidum* and *P. selloum*, has lustrous leaves similar to that of *P. bipinnatifidum*, but with wider lobes.

Smaller self-heading philodendrons include **P. longistylum**. This has much the aspect of *P. wendlandii*, from which it differs most obviously in producing creeping runners. Wine-red on their undersides, the short-stalked, usually abruptly-pointed, leathery, oblanceolate to oblong leaves, glossy-green above and with a clearly defined midrib, are 1½ feet long or longer. The undersides of older leaves are red-

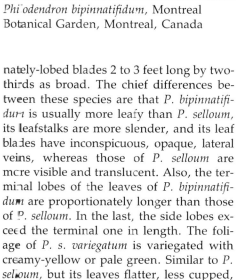

Philodendron speciosum, Rio de Janeiro,
Brazil

Philodendron longistylum

dish-purple. Another native of Brazil, *P. martianum* (syn. *P. cannaefolium*) has distinctive, lobeless, smooth-edged, lanceolate leaves with swollen, channeled stalks. Native to Guiana, *P. melinonii* has triangular-ovate, lobeless, pale-veined, green leaves with channeled, red stalks. Indigenous to Brazil and Venezuela, *P. pinnatifidum* has metallic-green foliage, the leaves pinnately-lobed and with depressed veins. Its channeled leafstalks are spotted with red. Native to Costa Rica and Panama, *P. wendlandii* has rosettes of 2-foot-long, thick, long-obovate leaves with short, spongy stalks. Its variety, *P. w. variegatum*, has foliage variegated with yellow. There are several hybrids of *P. wendlandii*. An especially attractive one, *P.*

Philodendron wendlandii

'Lynette', its other parent *P. elaphoglossoides*, forms a rosette of 1-foot-long, bright green, leathery leaves with conspicuously depressed lateral veins.

Garden and Landscape Uses. Philodendrons, of wide diversity of growth habits and leaf sizes and shapes, constitute one of the most important groups of tropical foliage plants. Their calla-lily-like inflorescences ("flowers") also have interest and beauty, but for these, which develop only on mature specimens in favorable environments, the plants are not primarily grown. In the tropics and warm subtropics where these plants thrive the vining kinds are magnificent, ascending tree trunks, walls, and other supports, the shrubby ones serving as underplantings and lawn specimens. The former prefer partial and will stand considerable shade. The shrubby kinds do best in open locations with some shade from the middle-of-the-day sun. In the United States they are suitable for outdoor cultivation in Florida, southern California, and Hawaii.

Besides their values as outdoor landscape ornamentals in suitable climates, they are handsome furnishings for greenhouses devoted to tropical plants. They are also well adapted for growing in pots, tubs, and other containers as houseplants and for other interior decorative uses.

Cultivation. The chief need of philodendrons is for a fertile, fairly loose soil that contains an abundance of organic matter, drains freely, and is kept moist, but not waterlogged. They withstand dryish atmospheres fairly well, but are much more luxurious in humid ones. Specimens that have filled their containers with roots benefit from regular applications of dilute liquid fertilizer. Shade from strong sun is needed. Indoors a winter night temperature of 60 to 70°F is satisfactory. By day, and during the warm part of the year at night also, temperatures considerably higher are in order.

Propagation of vining kinds is most commonly by cuttings and air-layering, but seed may also be used. Bushy, self-heading philodendrons are most easily and rapidly raised from seed, but it is possible to root cuttings, each consisting of a short piece of stem with one leaf attached.

A seedling of *Philodendron selloum*

PHILYDRACEAE—Philydrum Family. This group of monocotyledons consists of four genera totaling five species. Its members are evergreen with rhizomes and, in two ranks, narrow leaves with sheathing bases. The small flowers, in spikes or panicles have three- to five-parted or -cleft perianths, one stamen, and one style. The fruits are capsules. The only genus treated in this Encyclopedia is *Orthothylex*.

PHLEBODIUM (Phle-bòdum)—Hare's Foot Fern. By some authorities included in *Polypodium*, the genus *Phlebodium*, of the polypody family POLYPODIACEAE, consists of ten species or according to some authorities one highly variable species, of ferns native to tropical America. Its best-known sort, *P. aureum*, is commonly cultivated in several varieties. The name derives from the Greek *phlebos*, a vein, and alludes to the many veins and veinlets of the fronds.

Phlebodiums are tree-perchers (epiphytes) with thick, creeping, scaly rhizomes. Spaced along them are usually

hairless, often glaucous fronds (leaves) with broad blades cleft nearly to their winged midribs. This genus differs from *Polypodium* in the reticulated patterns formed by the veins of its leaves.

The hare's foot fern (*P. aureum* syn. *Polypodium aureum*) is a vigorous, highly variable species with densely-scaly rhizomes that creep over the soil surface or

Phlebodium aureum

the trunks or branches of trees. Its somewhat distantly-spaced, long-stalked, arching to drooping, green to glaucous-blue-green, more or less oblong fronds are 1½ to 5 feet long. Toward their bases the blades are often of separate oblong, wavy-edged leaflets 6 inches to 1 foot long by 1 inch to 2 inches broad, pointed at their apexes. The upper parts of the fronds are cleft nearly to the midrib into segments or lobes similar to the leaflets. The clusters of spore capsules are large and conspicuous.

Among the best-known varieties of the hare's foot fern are these: *P. a. araneosum* has smaller, more deeply-incised fronds with narrower lobes than the typical species. The undersides of the fronds are blue-green, their upper surfaces glossy. *P. a. areolatum* (syn. *P. sporadocarpum*) has gray rhizomes with few scales and grayish-stalked, bluish fronds, smaller than those of the typical species and with silvery-blue undersides. *P. a. glaucum*, somewhat smaller than the typical species, has fronds that, especially on their undersides, are glaucous-blue. *P. a. mandaianum* has crested or crisped, bluish-green fronds. *P. a. undulatum* (syn. *P. mayii*), compact, has deeply-lobed, bluish fronds with broad, distinctly wavy lobes.

Garden and Landscape Uses and Cultivation. The hare's foot fern and its varieties are handsome ornamentals well suited for outdoors in the humid tropics and subtropics and for growing in greenhouses. Indoors they appreciate a winter night temperature of 60°F, a humid atmosphere, and good light with some shade from strong sun.

The potting mix should consist chiefly of such organic material as peat moss, half-decayed leaves, or fir bark of the sort used for orchids, with perhaps the addition of a small amount of half-decayed grass sod from which much of the soil has been shaken. To this may be added some coarse sand or perlite, crushed charcoal, and dried cow manure. It is very important that the texture of the mix be coarse enough to permit free entry of air and rapid drainage of excess moisture.

Repotting is best done in late winter or early spring, just before new growth begins. Keep the soil evenly damp, but not constantly saturated. Specimens that have filled their containers with roots benefit from regular applications of dilute liquid fertilizer. Propagation is easily achieved by division at the start of the growing season and by spores. Sporelings, however, are likely to exhibit considerable variation and not reproduce the parent plant true to type. For more information see Ferns.

PHLOMIS (Phlò-mis)—Jerusalem-Sage. In excess of 100 species are accounted as belonging to *Phlomis*, of the mint family LA-BIATAE. Comparatively few are of garden merit, but not all such are cultivated. Natives of temperate parts of the northern hemisphere in the Old World, they have a name, applied by the ancient Greeks to the mullein (*Verbascum*), that alludes to the vague similarity of the woolly-hairy stems and foliage of some species.

Evergreen shrubs, subshrubs, and deciduous herbaceous perennials, often with woolly hairs, phlomises have very distinctly four-angled shoots, and opposite leaves, the upper ones sometimes reduced in size and more or less bractlike. The flowers are in whorls (tiers) of many, that open in succession from below upward. Yellow, purple, or white, they have very short-tubed, strongly two-lipped corollas with the top lip laterally compressed, hairy, and notched or not, and the lower one spreading and three-lobed. There are four stamens in pairs of different lengths. The fruits are capsules that split into four parts, each containing one seed. Besides the kinds discussed below several Asian species not now cultivated would be worth introducing to gardens.

For alpine plant enthusiasts **P. rotata**, of western China, may be expected to have special appeal. It forms a ground-hugging rosette of nearly round leaves, and has 2-inch-tall spikes of purple-blue blooms. Western Asian kinds likely to thrive in California-type climates, but not presently available, include *P. armeniaca* and *P. anisodonta*.

Jerusalem-sage (**P. fruticosa**), an evergreen, broad shrub 2 to 4 feet tall, has densely-hairy shoots and oblongish to ovate leaves up to 5 inches long and wrinkled much like those of common sage. They are green and hairy on their upper side and much more densely-white- or yellowish-hairy beneath. The dusky yellow flowers, about 1¼ inches long, are in single or paired whorls that form globose clusters at and near the tops of the stems. The floral bracts are ovate. This old-time garden plant is a native of the Mediterranean region.

Also yellow-flowered, herbaceous **P. russeliana** is often in gardens misidentified as *p. viscosa*. Native to Asia Minor, it is 3 to 5 feet in height and has ovate to oblong-lanceolate leaves about 4 inches long, wrinkled, green above and hairy on their undersides. The blooms are in superimposed, well-spaced whorls of forty to fifty. The floral bracts are pointed-linear or awl-shaped.

Dullish purple blooms characterize **P. tuberosa,** a species native of southern Eu-

Phlomis fruticosa

Phlomis fruticosa (flowers)

Phlomis russeliana

Phlomis russeliana

Phlomis tuberosa

Phlomis tuberosa (flowers)

rope and Asia often misnamed *P. alpina,* a circumstance that may trap the unwary into acquiring it on the assumption it is a low mountain plant suitable for rock gardens. On the contrary, it is a vigorous, deciduous, herbaceous perennial with strong tuberous roots and erect stems 4 to 6 feet tall or taller that have coarse, wrinkled, long-stalked, heart-shaped to obovate, round-toothed leaves up to 8 inches long. The flowers are in fairly distantly spaced tiers of thirty to forty. The floral bracts are awl-shaped. True *P. alpina* is a Siberian species, 1 foot to 2 feet in height, with broadly-heart-shaped leaves up to 8 inches long, purple blooms in whorls of twenty to thirty, and awl-shaped floral bracts.

Other species sometimes cultivated include the lampwick plant (*P. lychnitis*), so called because its leaves were once used as lampwicks. Subshrubby, about 2 feet tall, and hoary, this has narrowly-linear, stem-clasping leaves 2 to 3 inches long, with densely-white-hairy undersides. Its flowers are yellow. Cream-colored flowers tinged with green, and pinkish within, and reddish floral bracts are borne by *P. samia,* of North Africa. This grows 2 to 3

Phlomis italica

feet tall and has pointed, ovate-heart-shaped, wrinkled leaves. A native of the Mediterranean region, *P. herba-venti,* 1½ feet tall and much branched, has hairy stems. Its toothed, green leaves sometimes have grayish undersides. In whorls of twenty or fewer, the flowers are violet-purple. Subshrubby *P. italica,* up to about 1 foot tall, has stems and foliage densely clothed with a felt of white hairs. The longish-stalked, bluntish leaves, oblong to slightly triangular-oblong and 1½ to 2 inches long, have margins with shallow, rounded teeth. The about ¾-inch-long, pale pink to rose-pink flowers are in six-flowered, distantly-spaced whorls assembled in terminal spikes. This is native of the Balearic Islands.

Garden and Landscape Uses and Cultivation. Except *P. tuberosa* and *P. alpina,* the species discussed above are not reliably hardy in the north, but are well adapted to areas with slightly warmer climates. They need sunny locations and, again excepting the two mentioned, which prefer more moisture, dryish soil of low to moderate fertility. No special care is required other than the removal of faded flower stalks and any cutting back necessary to promote tidiness. The latter is best done just before new growth begins. Propagation is easy by seed, cuttings, and division. The yellow-flowered kinds discussed above may be accommodated at the fronts of shrub borders and in perennial beds and more informal areas. They look well at the bases of walls and other places in association with masonry. Tall and somewhat spindling *P. tuberosa* is best adapted for grouping in semiwild, naturalistic areas.

PHLOX (Phlóx) — Moss-Pink, Wild-Sweet-William. Nearly seventy species constitute the important horticultural genus *Phlox.* Except for *P. sibirica,* of Siberia, all are natives of North America. In addition, there are numerous natural variants, a host of horticultural varieties, and a few hybrids. In their classification and identification phloxes present perplexing problems, yet because they embrace a high percentage of extremely desirable kinds gardeners should try to understand their relationships The most important group of the phlox family POLEMONIACEAE, the genus is named from the Greek *phlox,* a flame. in allusion to the brilliant flower colors of some kinds. For night-phlox see Zaluzianskya, for prickly-phlox, Leptodactylon.

Phloxes include annuals, deciduous and evergreen herbaceous perennials, and subshrubs. Their leaves are undivided, stalkless or short stalked, and mainly opposite, but those near the tops of the stems may be alternate Commonly they have a prominent midrib. The flowers are showy, in branched clusters called cymes, in panicles, or solitary. They have slender,

five-lobed or five-toothed, persistent calyxes and white, pink, red, lavender, blue, purple, or yellowish corollas with narrowly-cylindrical tubes and five spreading lobes (petals). The petals, rounded to obovate, are sometimes notched or cleft. There are five short-stalked, unequal-sized stamens that generally do not protrude and a slender style branching into three stigmas. The fruits are capsules that open along three lines to discharge the seeds. Botanically phloxes are classified primarily according to the lengths of their styles relative to the stamens and by their habits of growth.

From the gardeners' point of view it is convenient to group them as spring-blooming perennials, summer-blooming perennials, annuals, and alpine kinds. Inevitably the allocation of species and varieties to these categories is somewhat arbitrary.

Spring-blooming phloxes of low stature include some of the most useful and ornamental garden perennials. Many can be grown with little or no trouble, others are more demanding. They include lovers of sun-drenched, dryish locations and kinds that prosper in light or dappled shade where the soil is damper. Among the easiest and most satisfactory of the sun-lovers are *P. subulata* and *P. bifida.* These hybridize freely and garden varieties intermediate between them are common. Both have styles as long as or longer than the longest stamens. The first, called moss-pink and rock-pink, has many prostrate, branching, rooting stems, woody toward their bases and numerous, crowded, sharp-pointed, awl-shaped leaves, ¼ to ¾ inch long, and mostly with smaller leaves in their axils. The few-flowered clusters of bloom, on branches up to ¾ inch long, are so plentiful that often the entire plant is completely hidden by them. The flowers are ½ to ¾ inch wide and come in many hues of pink, magenta, and rose-purple, as well as white. Their petals are notched up to one-quarter of their lengths. This

Phlox subulata

Phlox bifida

Phlox nivalis 'Camla'

Phlox adsurgens

Phlox divaricata

species is wild from Ontario to Michigan, New York, North Carolina, and Kentucky, usually occupying poor, gravelly, sandy, or rocky soils. Differing in having longer leaves and more deeply notched petals, *P. bifida* is typically noncreeping and looser in habit. Of rather erect growth, it rarely has clusters of smaller leaves in the axils of the main ones. Its blooms, ½ to ¾ inch across and pale blue-violet to white, have petals notched for one-quarter to one-half of their lengths. This species ranges in the wild from Michigan to Iowa, Tennessee, and Arkansas. A variant, *P. b. stellaria*, has more shallowly notched petals, and glandless hairs, or none.

Hybrids of *P. subulata* and *P. bifida* are often listed as *P. stellaria*, but are distinct from *P. bifida stellaria* mentioned above. They show characteristics intermediate between the parents but commonly those of *P. subulata* predominate. Some are especially fine. The plants known in gardens as *P. frondosa* are presumably hybrids of *P. subulata* and *P. nivalis*. Of the same parentage is the beautiful, compact, bright-pink-flowered *P.* 'Vivid.'

Superficially resembling *P. subulata*, but botanically markedly different by reason of its styles being shorter than the shortest stamens, *P. nivalis* inhabits dry, open woodlands from Virginia to Florida and Alabama. Its persistent, procumbent, much-branched stems are crowded with awl-shaped to linear-lanceolate leaves, up to ¾ inch long and usually with smaller ones clustered in their axils. The flowering stems are 3 to 6 inches high. The blooms, light purple, pink, or white, and ¾ to 1 inch across, have petals sometimes slightly jagged at their apexes. Their calyxes are glandular-pubescent. Variety *P. n. hentzii* is 6 inches to 1 foot tall and more coarsely-glandular. There are several very good horticultural varieties of *P. nivalis* including the beautiful pink-flowered 'Camla', and 'Avalon White' and 'Gladwyne', both

white-flowered. Several showy phloxes offered as hybrids of *P. subulata* are variants of that species; Alexander's "subulata hybrids" belong here. Large-flowered *P. henryae* is a hybrid between *P. subulata* and *P. bifida*.

Native of rich damp woods in the Appalachian Mountains and the Piedmont, *P. stolonifera* is a hairy plant that each spring sends slender creeping stems from the tops of those of the previous year in all directions over the ground surface. These are furnished along their lengths with, and terminate in, rosette-like clusters of stalked, obovate to spatula-shaped leaves ¾ inch to 2½ inches in length. From the terminal clusters are developed in spring erect flowering stems, 6 inches to 1 foot tall, with a few pairs of leaves and topped with few-flowered, loose clusters of round, pink to reddish-purple blooms, with yellow anthers. The flowers are a little over 1 inch wide and have styles ¾ to 1 inch long. For long this was the only cultivated phlox not known to have a white-flowered variant, but in the 1960s such a plant was discovered and will undoubtedly become known as *P. s. alba*.

Hybrids between *P. stolonifera* and *P. subulata* are correctly named *P. procumbens.* In gardens they have frequently been miscalled *P. amoena*, a designation that rightly belongs to an entirely different plant, a species. The hybrids are attractive for sun or light shade, and are intermediate between their parents. They form clumps of prostrate shoots with persistent, oblanceolate to spatula-shaped leaves up to 2 inches long. In spring they produce erect stems, 6 inches to 1 foot tall, ending in clusters of bright purple blooms ¾ inch in diameter. An especially good variety, *P. p.* 'Millstream', has pink flowers with a white ring and a star of deep red at their centers.

Closely related to *P. stolonifera* is *P. adsurgens,* a charming native of open acid woodlands in California and Oregon. Its nearly circular to narrowly-ovate, stalkless leaves, usually up to 1 inch long, are without hairs, but the stalks of the flower clusters are hairy. The blooms, ½ to ¾ inch

across and few together, are chiefly in tones of clear pink, paling at their centers and with a dark stripe extending upward from the bottom of each petal. Variants with pure white blooms occur. The anthers are golden-yellow. This species is less hardy to cold than *P. stolonifera* and does not prosper outdoors in the northeast, although it succeeds there in alpine greenhouses. Several variants of *P. adsurgens* have been selected and named as horticultural varieties. Hybrids between *P. stolonifera* and *P. adsurgens* are reported to have been raised.

The wild-sweet-william or blue phlox (*P. divaricata* syn. *P. canadensis*), of rich, slightly acid, woodland soils, is a short-styled species of great garden merit. As a wildling it occurs from Quebec and New York to Michigan, Illinois, South Carolina, and Alabama. Its equally lovely variety *P. d. laphamii*, distinguished from the type by

Phlox divaricata (flowers)

Phlox paniculata variety

Phlox paniculata 'Norah Leigh'

having petals not notched at their apexes, is found westward and southward to Wisconsin, Minnesota, Georgia, Mississippi, and Texas. The variety does better in sunny locations than the species. Both have persistent, partly evergreen, more or less prostrate, rooting stems from which in spring arise many erect flowering shoots. The leaves are ovate-lanceolate to oblongish and 1¼ to 2 inches long. The blooms, which range from lavender-blue to pale violet and white, are in loose-branched, glandular-pubescent clusters. They are ¾ inch to 1¼ inches across. White-flowered forms are sometimes named *P. d. alba*. Hybrids of *P. divaricata* and *P. paniculata* are cultivated as *P. arendsii*.

Much like *P. divaricata* is **P. pilosa,** a variable kind that botanists divide into several geographical subspecies. From the wild-sweet-william it differs in its nonflowering shoots being erect instead of prostrate, in its leaves being proportionately narrower and linear to ovate-lanceolate or ovate, and in its flowers tending to pinkish rather than a bluish shade of lavender or purple. Its foliage is usually hairy, and often the corolla tubes have glandular hairs and the sepals bristly tips. Native to upland woods and prairies chiefly to the south and west of the range of *P. divaricata*, and often occurring in drier soils, *P. pilosa* favors sunnier, less moist locations in gardens.

Summer-flowering perennial phloxes of taller growth are familiar to gardeners as named horticultural varieties listed and often beautifully illustrated in color in catalogs of dealers in hardy herbaceous perennials. Their numbers are legion and new ones are introduced almost yearly. In flower color they range from purest white to deepest crimson and include many variants of pinks and reds, lavenders and purples. Some have enormous trusses of blooms. These are among the finest contributions to gardens derived from the native flora of North America. The chief progenitor of these border phloxes is *P. paniculata,* a native of moist, fertile soils from New York to Indiana, Kansas, Georgia, and Arkansas. The kinds grouped as *P. arendsii* are hybrids between it and *P. divaricata*. Contrary to statements commonly made the garden phloxes called *P. decussata* are not of hybrid origin, but are direct derivatives of *P. paniculata*. In the wild *P. paniculata* has erect stems 3 to 6 feet tall, with pairs of lanceolate to nar-

A summer-flowering hybrid phlox

rowly-oblong or elliptic leaves 3 to 6 inches long. Its long-styled flowers, most commonly of a magenta hue that makes little appeal to the discriminating, but varying to white, are in often quite large panicles. They are about 1 inch in diameter in the wild, often considerably larger in garden varieties. Except for inclusion in native plant gardens, the wild species will be neglected by most gardeners in favor of its much more gorgeous garden varieties. One of these last, *P. p.* 'Norah Leigh' is notable for its attractive white-variegated foliage.

The earliest summer-flowering perennial phloxes are chiefly garden varieties of the thick-leaved phlox (*P. carolina*). Often hybrids between it and *P. maculata* are cultivated as *P. suffruticosa*. The old and very good, pure white variety 'Miss Lingard' belongs here; it may be a hybrid between *P. carolina* and *P. maculata*. As a wild plant **P. carolina** inhabits light woodlands from Maryland to Ohio, Illinois, Florida, and Mississippi. It is quite variable and at its extremes approaches *P. glaberrima* and *P. ovata*. Typically it differs from the former in having calyxes, including their lobes, over ½ inch long, and from the latter in having at least eight nodes (joints) on the stems below the flower clusters. Up to 3 feet in height, and usually hairless, this phlox has linear to ovate-lanceolate leaves up to 4 inches long, and rounded clusters of pinkish-purple blooms up to 1 inch wide, with styles ¾ to 1 inch long.

Other summer-blooming eastern North Americans, suitable for including in gardens of native plants, are *P. glaberrima, P. ovata, P. pulchra,* and *P. maculata*. The distinctions between the first two and *P. carolina* are given in the previous paragraph. The leaves of **P. glaberrima** are linear to narrowly-lanceolate. The flowers, about ¾ inch wide, are reddish-purple. This species is up to 4 feet in height. The stems of **P. ovata** are 1 foot to 2 feet tall and at

Phlox ovata

Phlox drummondii at the front of a border of annuals

blooming time rarely have more than three pairs of leaves, the lower comparatively long-stalked. A few joints at the base are without leaves. The flowers are ¾ inch to 1¼ inches across and reddish-purple to, rarely, white. Very like *P. ovata*, but with longer, prostrate non-flowering shoots, and short-stalked lower leaves, is **P. pulchra**, a rare native of Alabama that has beautiful, large, soft pink flowers. Somewhat variable, with pink or red blooms, **P. maculata**, a plant of dampish soils, resembles *P. paniculata*, but differs in its leaves being essentially smooth-edged instead of having minute teeth and hairs and in their secondary veins being obscure instead of evident. Usually its stems are purple-streaked. Blooming in late spring or summer, this and *P. carolina* are parents of garden kinds called *P. suffruticosa*.

Annual phloxes grown in gardens are derivatives of **P. drummondii**, a native of Texas widely naturalized in the Gulf states. Summer-bloomers, they are available in many flower colors and combinations, including buff-yellow, and in varieties with fringed and variously dissected petals. In seedsmen's catalogs they are offered under many fancy and latinized names. They range in height from 6 inches to about 1½ feet and are erect, much-branched, and glandular-hairy. Oblong to broad-ovate or lanceolate, their leaves, the lower ones paired, the upper alternate, narrow to their bases or are stem-clasping. They are 1 inch to 3 inches long. The flowers, about 1 inch across, are borne profusely in rounded to flattish clusters. They have long, slender, spreading calyx lobes and stamens and styles shorter than the corolla tubes.

Alpine phloxes is a convenient horticultural designation for those mainly western North American species that form low, compact mounds greatly resembling those of many high mountain plants. As a group name it is something of a misnomer because, although many of the species do inhabit high mountains or similar environ-

Cut flowers of *Phlox drummondii* displayed in a container

ments in subarctic or arctic regions, others are plants of dry foothills and arid plains. The group includes several gems. Unfortunately many are not easy to grow and some verge on the impossible. One of the easiest is **P. alyssifolia**, a tufted species up to 4 inches in height, from Nebraska and Wyoming to Montana, and Saskatchewan. It has linear to oblong leaves about ¾ inch long and hairy along their edges. The bluish, pink, or rarely white flowers, slightly over ½ inch wide, have corolla tubes shorter than the petals. Variety *P. a. abdita* is taller and fuller, variety *P. a. collina* is smaller and not glandular.

Two closely related species are *P. multiflora*, indigenous from Montana to Colorado, and *P. andicola*, native from North Dakota to Colorado. Up to 6 inches tall, **P. multiflora** has linear leaves up to an inch long, with or without hairy margins. The

Phlox drummondii 'Twinkle' has flowers, starry in effect, because of their variously-toothed petals

lilac, pink, or white, solitary flowers are up to ¾ inch across. Variety *P. m. patula* has longer leaves and flower stalks, and *P. m. depressa* is smaller than the typical species. Quite different is *P. andicola,* a native of the Great Plains and foothills of the Rocky Mountains. This forms patches of "treelike" stems, 2½ to 4½ inches tall, with stiff, awl-shaped leaves up to ¾ inch long, with spreading hairs. Its flowers are one to five at the tops of the stems. They are ½ inch or a little more in diameter and white, yellowish, or purplish.

A name frequently misapplied in gardens is *P. douglasii.* The true species forms conspicuously glandular-pubescent clumps 4 to 8 inches in height. Named

Phlox douglasii

after its discoverer, the botanist-explorer David Douglas of Douglas-fir fame, who first found it in the Rocky Mountains in 1827, it inhabits the Columbia Plateau and adjacent Rockies. It has awl-shaped leaves ¼ to ¾ inch long, more or less furnished with glandular hairs, and pale lavender to white blooms somewhat over ½ inch across, and solitary or in twos or threes. Variety *P. d. rigida* is 2 to 3 inches tall and has stiff, sharp-pointed, glaucous-green leaves up to ⅓ inch long and solitary, pink to white blooms. The variety is indigenous from California to Washington. Even more compact is *P. d. hendersonii,* native at high altitudes in the Cascade Mountains. Very similar to *P. douglasii,* but having distinctly longer, linear to linear-lanceolate leaves, **P. missoulensis** is a beautiful cushion plant about 4 inches in height, a native of Montana. Its solitary flowers are white, pinkish, or lavender and about ¾ inch in diameter. This has been more amenable to cultivation than many Western phloxes.

Somewhat resembling *P. douglasii,* but looser, and with larger flowers and nonglandular hairs, **P. diffusa** is native from California to Oregon. Its prostrate stems,

up to 9 inches long, are furnished with thinly-hairy, linear-awl-shaped, yellowish-green leaves about ½ inch long. At the ends of short branches the usually solitary, pink, lilac, or white flowers are ½ to ¾ inch in diameter. Variety *P. d. subcarinata* differs in technical details of the calyx, *P. d. longistylis* in having styles much longer than normal for the species, and *P. d. scleranthifolia* in having very narrow leaves. Some of the forms of this variable species have proved fairly easy to grow, others are much more difficult.

Another variable species highly tempting to alpine gardeners is *P. hoodii,* native from the Great Plains to the Rocky Mountains, and represented by varieties to the Sierra Nevada and Cascade Mountains. This and its variants are characteristically covered to a greater or lesser degree with cobwebby white hairs. They form compact mounds with short, sharp-pointed leaves, about ⅓ inch long, and usually have attractive lavender, pink, or white blooms less than ½ inch in diameter. Varieties of *P. hoodii* are *P. h. bryoides,* with markedly four-sided, hairy stems, and solitary flowers; *P. h. glabrata,* hairless except at the bases of the leaf edges; *P. h. canescens* hairy to hairless, and with blooms solitary or up to three together, and usually taller than the typical species; *P. h. muscoides* forming mats of woolly foliage less than 2 inches high and with solitary white flowers; and *P. h. viscidula* characterized by its glandular pubescence.

Garden and Landscape Uses. Spring-flowering, perennial phloxes easy to grow include moss pinks, wild-sweet-william, and other such kinds. They are splendid for furnishing the fronts of flower borders, edging paths, brightening rock gardens, and other uses. For partial shade *P. divaricata* and its variety *P. d. laphamii* are admirable. The latter is rather more tolerant of sun than the former. These are at their best in fertile soils generously laced with organic matter, and although not wet, not lacking moisture. Trailing *P. stolonifera* and *P. procumbens* also succeed in shade or part-shade and when out of bloom are excellent flat carpets of greenery. If the soil contains abundant humus and is not parched the last two may also be grown in sunny locations. The kinds that revel in sun, however, and are quite wonderful for planting on slopes, in rock gardens, wall gardens, and like places where they are fully exposed, are *P. subulata, P. vifida, P. nivalis,* their varieties and hybrids.

Summer-blooming perennial phloxes are among the glories of temperate-region gardens. They flower when their profusion of white and brilliantly colored blooms are especially welcome and, provided varieties are chosen to include both early- and late-blooming sorts, are attractive for several weeks. In addition to decorating gardens they are useful as cut

Summer-blooming phloxes are dominant in this perennial border

flowers, although as such they are not long lasting. These phloxes are magnificent in great clumps in borders as well as in less formal, semiwild surroundings, such as at the fringes of woodlands and at watersides, where the ground is a foot or more above water level. It is important that they are placed where they have good air circulation, otherwise they are likely to be much affected with mildew.

Annual phloxes are superb in flower beds, window and porch boxes, garden urns, and similar containers, and as cut flowers. Full sun and ordinary garden soil suit their needs.

Alpine phloxes by and large are strictly for skilled rock gardeners who enjoy very real challenges and are not discouraged by failures. They may be accommodated in rock gardens, and in pans (shallow pots) in alpine cold frames and greenhouses.

Cultivation. As is to be expected from as diverse a group as phloxes, the cultural needs of phloxes vary considerably. Here we consider them according to the four groups established in our previous discussion. Low, perennial, spring-blooming kinds are easy to satisfy. Given reasonably good earth, porous, well-drained and not overrich for the sun-lovers, damper, but not wet, and containing a decent proportion of organic matter for those that favor shade, success is almost assured. Once established these are likely to go for many years with little or no attention. A light shearing after flowering may be advisable. Their propagation is by division or by removing small rooted pieces, without digging up entire plants in early fall, spring, or after flowering; by summer cuttings in a cold frame or similar environment; and by seeds, but it must be remembered that seeds of garden varieties and hybrids do not reproduce their parents true to type.

Summer herbaceous perennial phloxes, taller than spring-flowering kinds, often survive for long periods with little or no

with a male on either side but often parts of the flower cluster bear blooms of only one sex. The fruits, red at maturity, are ovoid and about ⅓ inch long.

Garden and Landscape Uses and Cultivation. This is a handsome palm, but only under intensely tropical and decidedly humid conditions can it be expected to thrive. Except possibly in southern Florida, it is not adapted for outdoor cultivation in the continental United States. In greenhouses it needs a minimum winter night temperature of 70°F and night temperatures at other seasons a few degrees higher. Day temperatures should be higher than those maintained at night. High humidity, shade from strong sun, fertile, well-drained soil, and generous supplies of water are requisites. Well-rooted specimens may be given dilute liquid fertilizer at intervals of two weeks from spring through fall. Seeds, which retain their germinating power for a short time only, are the only means of increase. They should be sown in sandy peaty soil in a temperature of 80 to 90°F. For other information see Palms.

PHOENIX (Phoè-nix) — Date Palm, Wild-Date Palm. Most important of this group of seventeen species is the date palm, but there are as well other kinds that as ornamentals interest horticulturists. They belong in the palm family PALMAE and are natives of the tropics and subtropics of the Old World. The ancient Greek name for the date palm is phoenix.

These plants have solitary or clustered trunks conspicuously roughened by the remains of leafstalks and the scars of fallen leaves that spiral around them. A characteristic feature of their pinnate leaves is that the lower leaflets are often modified into spines. The branched flower clusters are among the foliage, male and female flowers usually on separate trees. Male flowers commonly have six stamens. Fe-

males, after being fertilized by pollen from the males, develop oblong-oval fleshy fruits each with a solitary, elongated, grooved seed.

The date palm (*Phoenix dactylifera*) has been cultivated since prehistoric times, for so long that we do not know its country of origin. Most probably it is a native of North Africa and western Asia. In any case it has been of tremendous importance to the inhabitants of those lands since time immemorial and we know that it has been cultivated there for at least 5000 years. One of the earliest representations of a palm extant is that of this species carved in bas-relief on the terrace walls of the temple of Queen Hatshepsut, across the Nile River from Luxor (Thebes) in Egypt. The Queen died in 1481 B.C., so this date palm in stone is more than 3500 years old. The many biblical references to palms undoubtedly refer to date palms. According to the scriptures (1 Kings 6 : 29 and 32), Soloman ornamented his Temple with carved figures of palms and (John 12 : 13) Christ was welcomed to Jerusalem by the people bearing branches (leaves) of palm trees.

The date is a tree of deserts and semi-deserts. It thrives in arid lands in oases and other spots where underground water is available and withstands brilliant sun and burning heat by day and comparatively low temperatures by night better than almost any other plant except certain cactuses and succulents.

The date palm (*P. dactylifera*) has a massive trunk up to 100 feet in height and a great crown of stiff arching leaves. Often the trunk is more or less leaning, and from its base secondary trunks or offsets are produced. The gray-green leaves, 10 to 20 feet long, are covered with a thin waxy coating. The upper leaflets form two ranks, the lower ones four. Toward the base of the leaf they grade into stiff spines. The old dead leaves remain hanging beneath the crown of living foliage for several years. The flower clusters are

A plantation of *Phoenix dactylifera* in California

branched and each may bear 10,000 blooms. Very rarely male and female flowers are on the same tree. The cylindrical-ovoid fleshy fruits are the nutritious edible dates of commerce.

To the peoples of the dry lands the date palm inhabits, this tree represents life itself. In many areas its fruits are the only available food for man for long periods of the year, and many animals live on those alone. So highly was the tree regarded that Mahomet admonished the Arabs "Honor the date palm for it is your mother." Besides its service as a provider of food its leaves and wood are used for huts, fences, and construction, and from its leaf fibers ropes, cordage, and baskets are made. Mixed with camel hair, the fibers are fabricated into cloth for tents. Most commercial dates are produced in Iraq, where it is estimated there are 20,000,000 trees. They are also grown in Arizona and California. For successful fruit production a long period of summer heat without rain or high humidity is necessary. From very early times it has been known that female date palms must be pollinated to assure fruits, and the common practice since antiquity has been to cut branches of flowers from male trees and secure them over or between the receptive female flower clusters.

The wild-date palm (*P. sylvestris*) differs from the true date palm in having a solitary trunk up to 50 feet in height and fruits with thin, very astringent, inedible flesh about ¾ inch long. A native of India, in its homeland this kind is used as a source of sugar, which is obtained from the sap or toddy. Palm wine is also made from the sap and the leaf fibers are used for ropes. The wild-date palm is fast growing and has a crown of grayish-green leaves. It is planted as an ornamental in many warm parts of the world. This species hybridizes with the Canary-Island-date palm (*P. canariensis*) as well as with the true date palm, and it is not always easy to distinguish between the hybrids and the parent species. Another Indian species is *P. rupicola*, a slender, graceful tree about 25 feet in height with two rows

Phoenix dactylifera in Baja California

A handsome hybrid *Phoenix* of unknown parentage at the Fairchild Tropical Garden, Miami, Florida

Phoenix sylvestris, the Huntington Botanical Garden, San Marino, California

A hybrid *Phoenix*, one parent probably *P. sylvestris*

Phoenix rupicola (at right), the Huntington Botanical Garden, San Marino, California

Phoenix canariensis, the Fairchild Tropical Garden, Miami, Florida

Phoenix canariensis, New Orleans, Louisiana

of soft, pliable, leaflets in a single plane. Its fruits are bright yellow and about ¾ inch long. This is a very lovely decorative tree. One of the most popular palms is *P. canariensis,* as its name indicates, a native of the Canary Islands. Up to 60 feet in height and with a solitary stout trunk, this kind has a large crown of bright green, stiff leaves 15 to 20 feet long with the leaflets spreading in many directions and the lower ones represented by spines, which like the leafstalks are yellowish. Yellow to reddish when ripe, the globose to ellipsoid, somewhat pulpy fruits, up to 1 inch in length, hang in large clusters. This phoenix is highly regarded and much planted as an ornamental in Florida, California, Hawaii, and other warm regions. A native of Africa and Madagascar, *P. reclinata* usually has several trunks and attains a height of about 25 feet, but may become considerably taller if restricted to one trunk by removal of the offsets or suckers while they are small. The long leaves, curved downward at their ends, have soft fluffy hairs beneath, especially when young. The leaflets are quite stiff, sharp-

Phoenix reclinata, Disneyland, Anaheim, California

Phoenix roebelenii

pointed, and about 1 foot long. Brown or reddish, the ¾-inch-long fruits are ovoid-ellipsoid. A very ornamental species from Laos is *P. roebelenii.* This usually multiple-stemmed palm is much prized by horticulturists because of its low stature and the fine, feathery appearance of its foliage. Its trunks are from 3 to 9 feet in height, its leaves up to 6 feet long. They have numerous narrow, dark green, soft, gracefully drooping leaflets that are gradually replaced toward the base by orange spines. Not well understood botanically and sometimes confused with the last, *P. loureiri* is native from India to China. Up to 15 feet tall, but often lower, and with solitary or clustered trunks or sometimes practically trunkless, *P. loureiri* has more or less glaucous, arching leaves, the leaflets of which are in groups spaced along the midrib. In clusters up to 3 feet long, the ½- to ¾-inch-long fruits are red.

Garden and Landscape Uses. These palms are much esteemed as ornamentals. Several are planted freely outdoors in Hawaii, California, Florida, and other tropical and subtropical regions. Provided their roots have access to reasonable supplies of

Photinia beauverdiana

Photinia beauverdiana (flowers)

Photinia beauverdiana (fruits)

toothed. They have eight to fourteen veins angled outward from both sides of the midrib. The flower clusters are 2 inches across; the nearly spherical fruits ¼ inch in diameter. In *P. b. notabilis* the leaves are elliptic and 3½ to 4½ inches long, and the clusters of bloom are nearly or quite 4 inches wide.

Garden and Landscape Uses. In the south and on the Pacific Coast evergreen photinias are excellent for general purpose landscaping. Their foliage, flowers, and fruits are pleasing, and they succeed with minimum care in sun or part-day shade. The deciduous kinds are also good for landscaping and can be used to excellent effect as single specimens and in mixed shrub plantings. They prefer sun. The best soil for photinias is deep, well drained, and reasonably fertile.

Cultivation. The old-time practice of propagating photinias by grafting onto understocks of hawthorn or quince is not a wise one. Plants raised from seed, layers, or summer cuttings rooted under mist or in a cold frame or greenhouse propagating bench are far superior. No regular pruning is necessary, but any needed to shape or contain the plants to size may be done in early spring.

PHOTINOPTERIS (Photin-ópteris). The only species of *Photinopteris*, of the polypody family POLYPODIACEAE, is a medium-sized evergreen fern native from Java to Malacca and the Philippine Islands. Its name is a combination of the Greek *photos*, light, and *pteris*, a fern. The application is not clear.

Usually epiphytic (tree-perching), but not uncommonly growing in the ground, **P. horsfieldii** (syn. *P. speciosa*) has creeping rhizomes at first scaly, later naked and

Photinopteris horsfieldii

glaucous, from which arise rather distantly spaced pinnate fronds (leaves). The lower leaflets, not spore-producing, are pointed-ovate to elliptic and hairless. The upper leaflets are fertile and much narrower than the barren lower ones. Their spore capsule clusters are in rows.

Garden Uses and Cultivation. Of interest to collectors, this species responds to conditions and care suitable for such tree-perching tropical ferns as *Aglaomorpha* and *Drynaria*. For further information consult entries under these names and under Ferns.

PHOTOPERIODISM. See Light.

PHOTOSYNTHESIS. This function of chlorophyll-containing plants is basic to all life. The food supplies of plants and animals, including man, are directly or indirectly dependent upon it, as is the presence of nearly all the oxygen in the atmosphere. All animals and all parasitic and saprophytic plants derive their foods from plants or from animals that live on plants capable of photosynthesis.

The word photosynthesis, from the Greek *photos*, light, and *synthesis*, putting together, is aptly descriptive. It is the process, carried out exclusively by plant cells containing green chlorophyll (sometimes, as in certain coleuses, codiaeums, cordylines, and other plants, the green is masked by red, yellow, or other colors). Employing the energy of light, the plant combines carbon dioxide from the air with hydrogen from water (or in bacterial photosynthesis, other substances) to produce the sugar called glucose, which chemically stores the transformed light energy. This first simple product is then built into more complex foods, such as fats and proteins.

Besides the typical photosynthesis carried out by the vast majority of plants, called green-plant photosynthesis, a much less significant amount is attributable to a few sorts of bacteria that obtain the hydrogen they use in the process from substances other than water.

Environmental factors that affect photosynthesis are light intensity, temperature, and the availability of water and carbon dioxide. Inadequacies of any of these, and with light and temperature these may include duration at particular levels, slow or halt the photosynthetic process. Increases up to optimum levels, which vary considerably for different plants, speed the rate of photosynthesis.

Optimum light intensity for photosynthesis in a large number of plants runs from about one-tenth maximum summer sunlight for shade-loving or shade-enduring sorts to one-third to one-fourth maximum summer intensity for sun-loving kinds. Artificial light may substitute for sunlight to the extent that its intensity and duration are satisfactory, and it is commonly used indoors as a supplement to or a substitute for natural daylight.

The provision of adequate supplies of water is of prime concern to growers of plants. Shortages reduce the rate of photosynthesis, partly as a result of the stomata closing and reducing the availability of carbon dioxide to the plant, partly because when a plant wilts because of inadequate water supply it may be some hours after the water balance is restored before photosynthesis functions fully again.

Carbon dioxide averages approximately three percent of the air, but varies in different habitats from one-half to several times that amount. It often serves as the factor limiting the rate of photosynthesis. If other conditions are favorable, increasing the carbon dioxide content of the air up to several times its average boosts photosynthesis. This is sometimes done in greenhouses, but too high or too long concentrations can be damaging rather than helpful.

PHRAGMIPEDIUM (Phragmi-pèdium) — Lady Slipper. The sorts of *Phragmipedium*, of the orchid family ORCHIDACEAE, cultivated are frequently misnamed *Cypripedium* and sometimes *Selenipedium*. The latter, a genus of three South American species probably not in cultivation, has flowers that after they fade do not drop their corollas. Unlike cypripediums, phragmipediums are of tropical provenance, have evergreen foliage, and have flowers with a three-celled rather than a one-celled ovary. There are about twelve species of *Phragmipedium* (syns. *Phragmopedilum*, *Phragmipedilum*). Because of the shapes of the lips of their blooms, they share with *Cypripedium* and *Paphiopedilum* the vernacular name lady slipper. The generic name, from the Greek *phragmos*, a fence, alludes to the structure of the ovary.

Natives of tropical America from southern Mexico to Brazil, Bolivia, and Peru, phragmipediums mostly grow in the ground, but sometimes perch on rocks or trees. They are without pseudobulbs and have evergreen, leathery, strap-shaped leaves, much longer and narrower than those of paphiopedilums. The racemes or panicles of flowers are of several blooms that open in succession and, after the flowers fade, drop their corollas. The blooms have two lateral sepals that are united and lie behind the lip, the other (the dorsal sepal) is uppermost and behind the column. There are two similar lateral petals and a pouched or slipper-shaped lip with reflexed or inturned margins.

One of the most astonishing orchids, epiphytic *P. caudatum* is graceful, highly variable, and has a natural range approximating that of its genus. It has tightly clustered fans of about six leathery, strap-shaped leaves that are 1 foot to 2 feet long and 1¼ to more than 2 inches wide. Their apexes are unequally two-lobed. The flowers, the largest of all phragmipediums, are six or fewer on stalks sometimes exceeding 2 feet in length. They have brownish-crimson or purplish petals with yellow bases; these hang like slender ribbons and may be 2 feet to over 2½ feet in length. The sepals are narrow, about 6 inches long, and curve forward. They are pale yellow to whitish with yellowish-green veins, and at the apexes brownish-crimson. Their back sides are pubescent. The lip, which projects forward, is bronzy-green with darker veining and 2 to 2½ inches long. Many variants of this species have identifying varietal names.

Narrower leaves are characteristic of *P. longifolium*, of Central America and Colombia. This has six to ten blooms on stalks 2 or 3 feet tall, but they lack the immensely elongated petals of *P. caudatum*. The crowded, two-ranked tufts of foliage consist of pointed, linear to linear-strap-shaped leaves that may exceed 2½ feet in length and are up to 1¾ inches in width. The several, nearly 8-inch-wide, long-lasting flowers on each stalk open in succession over a protracted period. The ovate-lanceolate, white-margined dorsal (upper) sepal is pale green with rosy-purple veining; the much broader lower sepals ovate, and green with darker green veining. Spreading nearly horizontally, usually slightly twisted, and yellowish-green with pink margins that shade to white below, the 3½- to 6-inch-long petals are linear-lanceolate. The 2-inch-long lip is yellow-green shaded with bronze or dull purple, with pink-purple dots on its infolded side lobes. A native of Costa Rica, Panama, and Colombia, this blooms chiefly in fall. Many variants have identifying varietal names.

Other species sometimes find places in collections of orchid fanciers. With tufts of leaves up to 1½ feet long by ½ inch wide spaced along creeping rhizomes, *P. caricinum*, of Peru and Bolivia, has flower stalks up to 2 feet tall with seven or fewer blooms approximately 6 inches across. They have whitish sepals veined with green; narrower, pink-tipped, white, twisted, pendulous petals; and a dark-veined, yellow-green lip with infolded, green- and purple-spotted, white side

lobes. The leaves of *P. lindleyanum*, of Venezuela and the Guianas, are up to 2 feet long by 2½ inches wide. On pubescent stalks up to nearly 4 feet tall the seven or fewer 3-inch-long blooms are light green veined with red or red-brown. Sepals, petals, and lip are of much the same coloration. The petals, narrower than the sepals, are about 2 inches long. Native of Colombia and in habit much like the last, *P. schlimii* has leaves about 1 foot long by ¾ inch wide. The flowers of each often-branched, hairy-stalked, raceme or panicle are eight or fewer. The dorsal (upper) sepal and the petals are similar. Whitish or greenish, stained with pink or pale lilac, they are about 1 inch long. The lower sepals are white with green veins. The lip is rose-carmine with a whitish underside and white- and pink-streaked, infolded side lobes.

Hybrids between species of phragmipediums are numerous and frequently cultivated. Most, as well as some horticulturally significant nonhybrid variants of certain species, have fancy rather than Latin-form names. These are described in dealers catalogs and in specialized orchid literature, including periodicals and books.

Phragmipedium hybrids: (a) *P. sedenii*

Phragmipedium schlimii

(b) *P. schroederae*

Garden Uses and Cultivation. Generally easy to satisfy, phragmipediums accommodate well to intermediate-temperature greenhouses where the atmosphere is humid and sufficient shade, but no more, is available to protect the foliage from scorching. Containers rather small for the sizes of the specimens and extremely well drained give the best results. Fill the pots to one-half their depths or more with crocks, and pot so that the surface of the rooting medium is mounded well above the rims of the containers. These orchids grow satisfactorily in a variety of rooting mediums that admit air freely and do not retain stagnant water. For most a mixture of turfy loam, tree fern fiber or osmunda fiber, with some crocks (small pieces of clay flower pot) and crushed charcoal serves well. Osmunda fiber alone or mixed with chopped sphagnum moss is recommended for *P. caudatum*. Watering is done to keep the compost moist at all times, but long periods of wetness at the roots are not tolerated. Well-rooted specimens benefit from regular applications of dilute liquid fertilizer. For more information see the Encyclopedia entry Orchids.

PHRAGMITES (Phragmì-tes)—Reed Grass. Of the three or four species of perennials that compose *Phragmites*, of the grass family GRAMINEAE, only the common reed grass is well known. The name *Phragmites* is derived from the Greek *phragma*, a screen or fence, and alludes to the visual effect of these grasses where they border rivers and streams.

Phragmites have stout, spreading rhizomes; tall, erect stems; flat, broad leaf blades; and large freely-branched panicles of three- to eleven-flowered spikelets. Common throughout North America and in South America, Europe, Asia, Africa, and Australia, they occupy swamps and wet soils, usually almost or quite to the exclusion of other plants, and often cover great areas as is the case in the Jersey Meadows adjacent to New York City.

The common reed grass (**P. australis** syn. *P. communis*), deciduous and 6 to 12 feet tall, has numerous reedlike stems. Its grayish-green, rough-edged leaf blades are slightly under to slightly over 1 inch wide and may be 2 feet long or longer. The brownish or purplish, silky-hairy, plumy panicles of bloom, dense or loose and usually nodding, are ½ foot to 1½ feet long. They mature in late summer. They very rarely produce fertile seeds. Natural spread of this grass is mostly dependent upon its amazingly vigorous rhizomes, which under favorable circumstances extend for as much as 30 feet from the parent clumps. Pieces of these, carried by currents, floods, birds, and animals, result in the start of new colonies, which, under favorable conditions, quickly establish themselves and proceed with their relentless

Phragmites australis

takeover of territory occupied by weaker species. Variety *P. a. striopictus* (syn. *P. a. variegatus*), less robust than the typical kind and with leaves striped with yellowish-white, is sometimes cultivated.

The dried stems of common reed grass are sometimes used for thatching, temporary screens and fences, and for making mats to protect cold frames from frost.

Garden and Landscape Uses and Cultivation. Only a bold or foolish gardener would introduce the plain green-leaved type of this aggressive grass to a site that he did not want to abandon to it. Once well established it is virtually indestructible. In some places natural stands serve usefully in the landscape picture, and in some places erosion is controlled by their presence. The variegated-leaved variety, *P. a. striopictus*, is less robust and less rapidly invasive. Nevertheless it is wise to confine its roots to wooden or concrete tubs rather than to plant them directly in the mud or soil at pool or other waterside margins. This hardy grass thrives in any fertile, wet soil and needs no particular care other than to be divided and replanted, in spring, when the containers it occupies become crowded.

PHRYNIUM (Phryn-ium). Belonging in the maranta family MARANTACEAE, the Old World tropical genus *Phrynium* comprises thirty species. Its name, from the Greek *phryne*, a toad, alludes to these plants inhabiting marshes. The plant sometimes grown as *P. variegatum* and *P. micholitzii* is *Maranta arundinacea variegata*.

Phryniums are evergreen herbaceous perennials with much the aspect of *Calathea* and *Maranta* from which they differ technically in the ovaries of their flowers having one instead of three compartments. They have creeping rhizomes from which arise stems with, near their bases, long-stalked, parallel-veined leaves and terminating in a usually much-branched spike of flowers that, because of the place-

ment of a single leaf that often accompanies it, may appear to be lateral. The leaves have essentially elliptic blades, sometimes variegated, sometimes with purple undersides. The bracts in the axils of which the two to several pairs of white or purple-and-white flowers arise are arranged spirally. The blooms have three sepals, three petals united at their bases into a tube, one fertile stamen, and nonfertile stamens (staminodes). The fruits are capsules.

Native to tropical Asia, **P. dracaenoides** has stiff, erect stems and fleshy, green to bluish-green, pointed-lanceolate leaves with channeled stalks. Some of the leaves are basal, others are in tufts high on the erect stems. These tufts can be removed and used for propagation.

Garden and Landscape Uses and Cultivation. These are as for *Calathea*.

PHUOPSIS. See Crucianella.

PHYCELLA (Phy-cèlla). By some authorities included in *Hippeastrum*, the genus *Phycella*, of the amaryllis family AMARYLLIDACEAE, consists of about seven species, natives of South America.

Phycellas are bulb plants with all basal, narrow-linear leaves and hollow flowering stalks surmounted by an umbel of a dozen or fewer, more or less drooping, funnel-shaped, usually short-tubed flowers. Each has six petals (or more correctly, tepals), six stamens in two series of three, and one style capped with a headlike or three-lobed stigma. The fruits are capsules containing black, flat seeds.

Native to Chile, **P. phycelloides** (syns. *Hippeastrum phycelloides*, *Amaryllis phycelloides*) has glaucous leaves up to 1 foot in length and developing with them, stalks carrying up to six bright red blooms with yellowish interiors.

Garden and Landscape Uses and Cultivation. These are as for *Hippeastrum*.

PHYGELIUS (Phy-gèlius) — Cape-Fuchsia. Two South African subshrubs or shrubs, not related to *Fuchsia* but having flowers of similar aspect or perhaps more resembling those of *Penstemon*, constitute *Phygelius*, of the figwort family SCROPHULARIACEAE. They are useful ornamentals for mild climates, such as that of California. The name comes from the Greek *phyge*, flight or avoidance, said to refer to the plant having escaped the attention of botanists for so long.

Cape-fuchsias are bushy and nonhairy. They have angled or winged stems and mostly opposite, although the upper ones may be alternate, undivided, stalked, toothed leaves. The graceful, pendulous blooms are in loose terminal panicles. They have five-parted calyxes and long, tubular corollas with five short, rounded lobes (petals). There are four stamens that, like the slender style, protrude a long way

Phaedranassa carmiolii

Phalaenopsis lueddemanniana

Pale blue *Phlox divaricata* with yellow *Aurinia saxatilis* and grape-hyacinths

Phlox drummondii

Phlox procumbens

A pink-flowered *Phlox paniculata* variety behind pink petunias

Phyllodoce empetriformis

Phlox paniculata varieties in a cut flower garden

Pink-flowered varieties of *Phlox subulata* in a rock garden

from the mouth of the bloom. The fruits are capsules.

Most common in cultivation, *P. capensis* attains a height of 3 to 6 feet and has ovate or lanceolate-ovate leaves up to 5 inches long. In candelabra-like panicles, its showy, 1½- to 2-inch-long blooms, with slightly curved, narrowly-trumpet-shaped corolla tubes, are borne profusely over a

Phygelius capensis

Phygelius aequalis

long period. Somewhat variable as to color, they are characteristically scarlet. From this species *P. aequalis* differs in being up to 3 feet tall and in having shorter-stalked, crimson to dull salmon-red flowers, with nearly straight corolla tubes, in more crowded panicles.

Garden and Landscape Uses and Cultivation. Cape-fuchsias are attractive for fronting shrub beds, for foundation plantings, and for including in perennial borders. They make no difficult demands of the gardener. Although in general widely adapted only to warm climates, the common Cape-fuchsia has been successfully grown permanently outdoors in very sheltered locations at the base of south-facing walls in the vicinity of New York City. Cape-fuchsias respond to well-drained,

fertile, light, loamy soil and full sun or at most a little part-day shade. Average moisture is to their liking, but they withstand hot, dry conditions well. In late winter or early spring pruning is done by cutting out weak shoots and shortening strong ones. In cold climates a heavy winter mulch is advisable. This protects the roots by reducing the depth to which the ground freezes.

As well as being useful outdoors, Cape-fuchsias are attractive when grown in pots or tubs in cool greenhouses. They respond to conditions that suit chrysanthemums and require the same care as *Buddleia asiatica*. Propagation is very easy by cuttings and by seed.

PHYLA (Phy-la)—Fog Fruit or Frog Fruit. A variety of one of the ten species of *Phyla*, of the vervain family VERBENACEAE, is planted as a groundcover in California and other mild-climate regions. The genus, chiefly a native of tropical and subtropical America, but represented by one or two species in the Old World, consists of procumbent or creeping, sometimes woody-based, herbaceous plants. Its name, alluding to the dense heads of blooms, is from the Greek *phyle*, a tribe or clan. By some authorities *Phyla* is included in *Lippia*, and under that name is often grown in gardens. As a segregate it is differentiated by its flowers usually being in four ranks in spikes that elongate conspicuously as the fruits, which divide into two seedlike nutlets, develop.

Native in the United States from Virginia to California and southward, and in many other warm regions of the New World and the Old World, *P. nodiflora* (syn. *Lippia nodiflora*) is very variable. It has widely spreading, rooting stems, somewhat woody at their bases, with procumbent or upright branches. Its stalkless or very short-stalked, hairy or hairless leaves are opposite or whorled, spatula-shaped, oblong or lanceolate, toothed toward their apexes, and up to ¾ inch long. The long-stalked, subcylindrical to egg-shaped, crowded flower heads, ¼ to ½ inch wide, are of tiny, whitish to purplish blooms. They terminate stalks up to 4½ inches long. Variety *P. n. canescens* (syns. *Lippia canescens*, *L. nodiflora canescens*) has grayish-hairy foliage and flower spikes that lengthen and become cylindrical as they age. Variety *P. n. reptans* (syns. *Lippia reptans*, *L. nodiflora reptans*) has ovate to obovate-wedge-shaped leaves and ovoid flower heads. Variety *P. n. rosea* (syns. *P. rosea*, *Lippia nodiflora rosea*) has smaller leaves than the typical species and forms dense mats. Its flowers are white to pink.

Garden and Landscape Uses and Cultivation. In California and other areas with warm, dry climates, *P. n. rosea* is used as a lawn grass substitute, often under the name *Lippia repens*. It is suitable for slopes

Phyla nodiflora canescens

and other difficult areas in sunny locations. It succeeds in a variety of soils, even those low in nutrients, but does better in moderately fertile ones. It stands walking upon and mowing and soon forms dense mats. Propagation is usually by planting sods of about 2 square inches at distances of 1 foot to 2 feet apart. Water to encourage them to start growing, but after they are established, water at less frequent intervals than for lawn grass or most lawn grass substitutes.

PHYLICA (Phyl-ica). There are approximately 150 species of *Phylica*, of the buckthorn family RHAMNACEAE. Most are shrubs, a few small trees. They are evergreens, chiefly natives of South Africa, but occurring also in Madagascar and Tristan da Cunha. The name comes from the Greek *phyllikos*, leafy. It is in allusion to the abundant foliage.

Phylicas have alternate, commonly rigid, leathery, often hairy, short-stalked, mostly small, crowded leaves that have toothless and often rolled-under margins. The flowers may be axillary or terminal. They are solitary or in heads, spikes, or racemes, often associated with conspicuous bracts. The blooms are small and have usually cup-shaped, five-lobed, persistent calyxes, five small or sometimes no petals, and five stamens. The fruits are little capsules.

In the wild frequently growing near the sea. South African *P. ericoides* is a usually compact, freely-branched, rather heathlike shrub up to 2 feet tall. It has sparsely-gray-hairy shoots and closely set, short-stalked, linear to awl-shaped leaves, hairy on their undersides, about ⅓ inch long, and with revolute margins. The tiny, minute-petaled flowers are in hemispherical heads about ⅓ inch wide.

Garden and Landscape Uses and Cultivation. For rock gardens and similar locations in California and elsewhere where little or no frost is experienced and the climate is dryish, the species described is useful. It succeeds near the sea and needs well-drained soil and an open, sunny location. It is raised from seed and from cuttings taken in summer and planted under mist, or in a propagating bed in a greenhouse or cold frame.

PHYLLAGATHIS (Phyllá-gathis). This genus, belonging in the melastoma family MELASTOMATACEAE, in the wild is confined to tropical southeast Asia. About twenty species are recognized, but very few are cultivated. The name *Phyllagathis*, from the Greek *phyllon*, a leaf, and *agetheos*, divine, alludes to the beauty of the foliage.

These plants have large, mostly opposite, prominently veined, roundish leaves that may or may not be toothed. Sometimes the terminal leaf is solitary. The flowers, in crowded, short-stalked heads, have usually four petals and twice as many stamens as petals. The fruits are top-shaped capsules.

A highly ornamental foliage and flowering plant, *P. rotundifolia* is native to Sumatra. It is 1 foot to 2 feet tall and has a

Phyllagathis rotundifolia

Phyllagathis rotundifolia (flowers)

short, stout stem, four-angled like the branches, and dark purple. Its broadly-ovate to nearly round leaves are 6 to 9 inches across. They have seven or nine prominent longitudinal veins curving from base to apex and corrugated or pleated between by a pattern of spreading lateral veins that link those running lengthwise. The foliage is glossy metallic green above with overtones of red; the undersides of the leaves are dark red. In densely crowded, spherical heads, each with a collar (involucre) of bracts, the small pink to reddish flowers are borne in summer.

Garden and Landscape Uses and Cultivation. Chiefly, these are plants for tropical greenhouses. Only in the humid tropics can they be cultivated outdoors. They flourish in coarse, rich soil in well-drained containers and need good light with only sufficient shade to protect their foliage from scorching. A greenhouse minimum night temperature of 60 to 65°F is most to their liking. This may be increased by five to fifteen degrees during the day, and at other seasons should be still higher. Repotting is done in late winter. Water is applied freely from spring through fall, rather less plentifully in winter. Except in winter, applications of dilute liquid fertilizer may with advantage be made to well-rooted specimens at weekly intervals. At all seasons high humidity should be maintained and the plants protected from cold drafts. Propagation is by cuttings of moderately firm young shoots and by leaf cuttings laid flat on the sand, or other propagating material, in a tropical greenhouse propagating bench supplied with bottom heat.

PHYLLANTHUS (Phyl-lánthus) — Emblic or Myrobalan, Otaheite-Gooseberry or Gooseberry-Tree. This very diversified group of the spurge family EUPHORBIACEAE consists of about 600 species of nonsucculent, herbaceous plants, shrubs, and trees, predominantly natives of the tropics of the Old World, but well represented in the native floras of the warmer parts of the Americas, and with a few species indigenous to the United States. The name, from the Greek *phyllon*, a leaf, and *anthos*, a flower, alludes to the blooms of some kinds being on branches that have the form of leaves. Plants previously segregated as *Cicca*, *Emblica*, and *Xylophylla* are here included in *Phyllanthus*. Other kinds commonly known in gardens as *Phyllanthus* belong in *Breynia* and *Glochidion*.

Phyllanthuses have alternate, lobeless and toothless leaves in two ranks that resemble the leaflets of pinnate leaves or are arranged spirally around the stems, or they may be without leaves and instead have flattened, leaflike branches called phyllodes. Their flowers are unisexual, most commonly with both sexes on the same plant. They come, generally in com-

pact clusters, sometimes singly, from the leaf axils or from little notches along the edges of the phyllodes. They are without petals. The calyx is four- to six-lobed. Most often male blooms have three to five, but may have only two or up to fifteen stamens, with their stalks united or not. Female flowers very rarely have abortive stamens (staminodes). They have three, more rarely two or from four to twelve, styles, separate or joined, and more or less lobed or branched. The fruits are berries or capsules.

The emblic or myrobalan (*P. emblica*) is an evergreen shrub or tree of tropical Asia, in cultivation up to 30 feet tall, but in the wild attaining twice that height and, exceptionally, 100 feet tall. It has a graceful, feathery crown, with the narrow-linear leaves, up to 1 inch long, closely placed alternately along twigs 6 to 9 inches in length to look much like pinnate leaves. When they first expand the leaves are pink. The tiny, inconspicuous, pale green flowers are along the undersides of the leafy sprays. The sour fruits, greenish-yellow when ripe, and spherical, are ¾ to 1 inch in diameter. They are cooked to make a sour relish.

The Otaheite-gooseberry or gooseberry-tree (*P. acidus* syns. *Cicca acida*, *C. disticha*), a sparsely-branched, often crooked,

Phyllanthus acidus

evergreen tree, is 10 to 25 feet in height; a native of tropical Asia, it is naturalized in the West Indies and other warm regions. Its slender leafy branchlets, with much the appearance of pinnate leaves, and 9 inches to 1 foot long, are clustered at the ends of the branches. The leaves are 1 inch to 3 inches long by one-half as wide. They are ovate to heart-shaped or nearly round and when young are pink. The solitary or clustered racemes of little pink or red flowers are 1 inch to 3 inches long. The short-stalked, flattened-spherical, six- to eight-ridged fruits, ¾ inch in diameter, when ripe are greenish, yellowish, or waxy white. They hang in little bunches. They are cooked to make relishes.

Native to Java, *P. arborescens* (syn. *Glochidion arborescens*) is a tree up to 40 feet tall. It has short-stalked, pointed-elliptic to obliquely-ovate leaves 3½ inches to 1 foot long and 2 to 6 inches wide. Young specimens are attractive as pot plants. Another

Phyllanthus arborescens

Phyllanthus pulcher

native of Java, *P. pulcher* is a small shrub with ½- to 1-inch-long, short-stalked, broad-oblong, blunt, hairless leaves tipped with a tiny point, with glaucous undersides. Its yellow flowers, red toward their bases, hang on bright red, 1-inch-long stalks. The females are solitary from the axils of the upper leaves, the males are solitary or few together from those of the lower leaves.

A group or subgenus of *Phyllanthus*, by some botanists segregated as the genus

Xylophylla, is normally without leaves and has capsular fruits. The parts that look like and function as leaves are phyllodes, along the edges of which the tiny flowers are displayed. Very rarely, small true leaves are borne at the ends of the phyllodes. To this group of about ten species belong *P. arbuscula* (syn. *Xylophylla speciosa*) and *P. angustifolius* (syn. *Xylophylla angustifolia*), natives of Jamaica, and *P. epiphyllanthus* (syns. *P. falcatus*, *Xylophylla falcata*), of the West Indies.

A tree up to about 20 feet tall, *P. arbuscula* is quite variable. Its phyllodes, carried in two ranks on deciduous branchlets, are lanceolate, 1½ to 3 inches long by ⅜ to ¾ inch wide. The whitish blooms are quite close together and concentrated toward the apexes of the phyllodes. From this, shrubby *P. angustifolius* differs in being not over about 10 feet in height and having linear-lanceolate to lanceolate phyllodes 2 to 4 inches long and generally under ¾ inch wide. They are two-ranked along deciduous branchlets. Its reddish to cream-colored flowers, usually more distantly spaced than those of *P. arbuscula* are from deeper little notches in the phyllode

Phyllanthus epiphyllanthus

Phyllanthus epiphyllanthus (flowers)

margins. In the wild this sort favors dryish limestone soils. A shrub generally not exceeding 6 feet in height, *P. epiphyllanthus* has pointed, somewhat sickle-shaped phyllodes, each a modified branchlet borne directly from the stem, and 3 to 8 inches long by ¼ to ¾ inch wide. They are not in two ranks, but radiate in all directions around the stem. The pink to red flowers come from small notches along the margins of the phyllodes, most abundantly above their middles.

Garden and Landscape Uses and Cultivation. In the tropics and warm subtropics phyllanthuses are planted as ornamentals primarily for their foliage, and the emblic and Otaheite-gooseberry to some extent for their fruits. They are easily maintained in ordinary soil in sun or part-day shade and need no special care. In greenhouses that shelter choice tropicals, phyllanthuses, especially those of the *Xylophylla* group, are grown for their distinctive, graceful appearance and for the interest of the manner in which their blooms are borne. They succeed in fertile, porous, peaty soil in well-drained pots under conditions that suit crotons, dracaenas, and other firm-leaved tropicals. The soil should be kept moist, but not excessively wet. Care must be taken not to give them too large containers. They do best when their roots are slightly crowded. Propagation is by cuttings, air-layering, and seed. For their best growth a minimum winter night temperature of 60°F and warmer conditions during the day are needed. A moderately humid atmosphere and shade from strong sun are required. Repotting is best done in early spring.

PHYLLITIS (Phyll-ītis)—Hart's Tongue Fern. Although visually very different, botanically the eight or fewer species of hardy, evergreen ferns, of temperate and subtropical parts of the northern hemisphere including North America, that constitute this genus, of the asplenium family ASPLENIACEAE, are so closely akin to *Asplenium* that by some authorities they are included there. Horticulturally, it seems better to follow those who recognize two genera. The distinction, a technical one, concerns the arrangement of the clusters of spore capsules, which in *Phyllitis* are paired, but so close together that ultimately each pair appears to be one. Derived from the Greek *phyllon*, a leaf, the name was given because the fronds (leaves), unlike those of most ferns, are undivided and not what is commonly thought of as fernlike in appearance.

Mostly small, phyllitises have thickish, more or less wavy, tongue- or strap-shaped, toothless, bright green leaves, usually indented at the base to form two conspicuous lobes or ears. The lateral veins, pinnately disposed and twice forked, diverge at nearly right angles from the midrib. The spore-containing bodies are in long narrow clusters that parallel the lateral veins.

Hart's tongue fern (*P. scolopendrium* syn. *Scolopendrium vulgare*) is a beautiful, and in many parts common, native of shady places in Europe. It has short, erect rhizomes, and leaves 1 foot to 2 feet in length, their stalks up to one-half as long as the blades, which are 1½ to 3 inches broad and without basal lobes. Differing scarcely except for its smaller size, *P. s. americana* is an extremely rare native of limestone rocks and rubble in restricted areas in Ontario, New York, and Tennessee. Its leaves attain a maximum length of about 1½ feet and a width of up to 1½ inches, but they often are smaller.

Phyllitis scolopendrium

Numerous horticultural varieties of the European hart's tongue fern are recognized and named, and are prized by specialist collectors. Most are characterized by having fronds forked or crested or both, to varying degrees.

Garden Uses and Cultivation. Hart's tongue ferns are delightful for shaded, sheltered spots in woodland gardens, wild gardens, rock gardens, and other shaded places, and the American kind for native plant gardens. They are also successful in pots in cool greenhouses. They need loose, porous soil, which contains an abundance of limestone and leaf mold or peat moss, and is moist but not excessively wet. Propagation is by spores and by division. The latter method is the only practical one with the horticultural varieties. A greenhouse shaded from bright sun, with a humid atmosphere, and a winter night temperature of 40 to 50°F is a suitable environment for potted hart's tongue ferns. On all favorable occasions the structure should be ventilated freely. These plants can also be grown in shaded cold frames, with their pots buried nearly to their rims in peat moss or sand. Pot specimens are repotted in spring, just as new growth begins. For additional information see Ferns.

PHYLLOCACTUS. This is an old and discarded name for *Epiphyllum*.

PHYLLOCARPUS (Phyllo-cárpus) — Monkey Flower Tree. Two species of medium- to large-sized trees constitute this tropical American genus of the pea family LEGUMINOSAE. One, the monkey flower tree, is cultivated in Florida. The name is from the Greek *phyllon*, a leaf, and *karpos*, a fruit. It alludes to the winged seed pods.

Phyllocarpuses have leaves with an even number of paired leaflets and flowers in short, often clustered racemes from the nodes of leafless branches of the previous year. The blooms are red or purple. The short-tubed calyxes are four-lobed. There are three obovate petals and ten stamens that, except at their tops, are joined into a sheath split down one side. The slender style ends in a small stigma. The fruits are curved, flat pods, winged along one side, and containing usually one shining seed.

The monkey flower tree (*Phyllocarpus septentrionalis*), a native of Guatemala, known there as *flor de mico*, is 60 feet tall or taller. It has leaves with four to six pairs of lustrous, obovate, broad-elliptic, or oblong, toothless leaflets 1½ to 2¾ inches long. The flowers, which come before the leaves, are in short racemes often assembled in large panicles. They are brilliant red and about 1 inch wide. The fruits are flat pods, 2 to 2½ inches long by about 1 inch wide.

Garden and Landscape Uses and Cultivation. Although the monkey flower tree grows well in Florida and attains spreads of 60 feet or more, specimens very rarely bloom there. In Guatemala flowering is reliable and abundant in January and February. This may be associated with the fact that there the tree drops its leaves and rests for a period each year, whereas in Florida it is evergreen. A disadvantage of the monkey flower tree is that it is subject to storm damage. It cannot be recommended for planting in Florida, but is worth trying elsewhere in the tropics and subtropics. In its homeland, it occupies dry, rocky areas at altitudes of 1,000 to 2,000 feet and is reported to bloom most freely following dry falls and early winters. It is propagated by seed.

PHYLLOCEREUS. See Epiphyllum.

PHYLLOCLADUS (Phyllócla-dus). This genus of seven curious evergreen trees and shrubs of New Zealand, Tasmania, the Philippine Islands, the Molucca Islands, Borneo, and New Guinea has a name derived from the Greek *phyllon*, a leaf, and *klados*, a branch. It was applied because the apparent leaves are really flattened branches (cladophylls) and the true leaves are reduced to tiny scales borne along their edges. The genus *Phyllocladus* be-

longs in the podocarpus family PODOCARPACEAE. It is not common in North America, but may be grown in such mild areas as parts of California and the Pacific Northwest.

The branches of these plants are usually whorled (in tiers). The lateral cladophylls spiral around the branches and are undivided, but the terminal ones are deeply lobed so that they resemble pinnate leaves and are in whorls. Male and female flowers may be on the same or separate trees. The former are in clusters at the ends of the shoots, the latter, solitary or several together in conelike structures, are borne along the margins of the cladophylls. The seeds, small and nutlike, are seated in miniature cups in the manner of acorns. Some species are exploited for their lumber and for their bark, which is used for tanning and dyeing.

The celery-top-pine (*P. asplenifolius* syn. *P. rhomboidalis*), of Tasmania, receives its vernacular name from the celery-leaf appearance of its terminal cladophylls. In its native land it ranges in size from a bush a few feet tall at high altitudes to a tree up to 100 feet tall with a trunk diameter of 3 feet. Its native climate is cool, humid, and equable, and often this species is subjected to snowfalls. Better than any other Tasmanian tree it tolerates wet, acid soils. Its wood is used for various purposes including boats, flooring, and doors. The branches of the celery-top-pine are stout, and its glaucous cladophylls vary in outline, being diamond-shaped, fan-shaped, or irregularly-lobed. They are 1 inch to 2 inches long and up to ¾ inch broad. The cones, crimson at maturity, are about ¼ inch long and wide and are borne on the terminal cladophylls.

The tanekaha (*P. trichomanoides*), a native of the North Island of New Zealand, produces wood with the same uses as that of the celery-top-pine. Its bark is used for tanning and from it the Maoris obtain a red dye. This species attains a maximum height of about 70 feet and a trunk diameter of 3 feet. Its branches are tiered and its slender branchlets have fan-shaped, ovate, or nearly round cladophylls ¼ to 1 inch in length, the young ones reddish-brown. Male and female flowers are on the same plant. The toatoa (*P. glaucus*) is another species native to the North Island of New Zealand. It attains a height of about 40 feet and a maximum trunk diameter of 2 feet. Its short, stout branches are usually in tiers. The cladophylls of the main stems are solitary and fan-shaped, with toothed margins, the others are in whorls and resemble pinnate leaves, with the terminal division larger than the others. Male and female flowers of this species are usually on separate trees. From the Philippine Islands, New Guinea, and Borneo comes variable *P. hypophyllus*, a tree up to 35 feet in height with a trunk diameter of up to 2 feet, that in its homelands is restricted to high elevations. Its cladophylls, the largest 3½ inches long by 1½ inches broad, vary much in shape and size and are very glaucous.

Garden and Landscape Uses. The sorts of this interesting genus are worth testing in regions of mild winters. They are especially suitable for arboretums and other special plantings.

Cultivation. Few data are available regarding the cultivation of phyllocladuses. In the south of England, where they grow slowly, they prosper in well-drained, sandy, loamy soils not subject to drought. For other information see Conifers.

PHYLLODOCE (Phyllódo-ce). Low, evergreen shrublets of heathlike aspect compose *Phyllodoce,* of the heath family ERICACEAE. There are seven species, natives of high latitudes and mountains in the northern hemisphere. The name is that of a sea nymph of Roman mythology.

Phyllodoces have prostrate or ascending branches and small, crowded, alternate, linear leaves with rolled-under margins. In terminal umbels or sometimes solitary, the nodding blooms have commonly five-, less often four- or six-parted calyxes and little urn- to bell-shaped corollas with generally five, sometimes four or six, small lobes (petals). There are eight to twelve stamens and one style. The fruits are capsules.

Wild in northeastern North America, Europe, and Asia, *P. caerulea* achieves a height of about 6 inches. Diffusely-branched, it has minutely-toothed leaves rarely more, and often less than, ⅓ inch long. The urn-shaped, rosy-purple flowers are ⅓ inch long or slightly longer.

Native from Alaska to Wyoming and California, *P. empetriformis* has upright stems about 6 inches tall. Its hairless leaves are up to ½ inch long. Its bell-shaped, rosy-purple flowers, about ⅓ inch long, have blunt sepals, and corolla lobes much shorter than the corolla tube. The stamens do not protrude. A hybrid between this and *P. glanduliflora* has pink, urn-shaped blooms with pointed sepals. The sulfur-yellow flowers of *P. glanduliflora,* a 1-foot-high species native from Alaska to Montana and Oregon, are urn-shaped, on their outsides pubescent, and approximately ⅓ inch in length.

Garden and Landscape Uses and Cultivation. These charming shrublets are delightful for rock gardens, wild gardens, and similar purposes in the cool north. They will not stand hot summers. Because they are somewhat difficult to transplant, specimens taken from the wild are likely to die. Better results are had by setting out young plants from pots. A peaty, moist, but well-drained soil is to their liking, as

is a sunny or partly shaded location. No special care is needed by established specimens. Shearing off the faded flowers is all the pruning needed. Maintenance of a mulch of peat moss is helpful. Increase is by seed, by cuttings about 1 inch long taken in August and planted in a propagating bed in a cold frame or cool greenhouse, and by layering in early fall.

PHYLLOPODIUM (Phyllopòd-ium). The annuals, perennial herbaceous plants, and subshrubs that constitute *Phyllopodium,* of the figwort family SCROPHULARIACEAE, are natives of South Africa. They are usually sticky-hairy and have opposite lower leaves, but upper ones that are alternate. The small subcylindrical blooms are most commonly in terminal spikes and have five spreading corolla lobes of nearly equal size. The name of the genus is derived from *phyllon,* a leaf, and *podium,* a little foot.

Only one of this genus of fifteen species appears to be cultivated, *P. capitatum.* This is an attractive, free-flowering annual, up to 7 inches in height, that tends to become woody below and is covered with white hairs. Its toothed leaves, up to 1 inch long, are lanceolate-elliptic to oblanceolate. The brilliant orange-yellow flowers, each ¼ inch long, are produced in such profusion that they make a very creditable and pretty display throughout the summer.

Garden Uses. The best uses for this little plant are as edgings to paths and flower beds or borders and for planting in drifts in rock gardens. Its flowers can be cut and used effectively in small arrangements such as table decorations.

Cultivation. Like most South African annuals, *P. capitatum* gives of its best only where summers are fairly cool; it abhors exceedingly hot, humid weather. It thrives in rather poor, sandy soil and needs a sunny location. For the most satisfactory results the seeds should be sown in a greenhouse in a temperature of 60 to 65°F eight to ten weeks before it is considered safe to transplant the young plants to the garden, which can be done as soon as the weather is warm and settled and there is no further danger of frost. The seedlings are transplanted 2 inches apart in flats of porous soil and grown in a sunny greenhouse where the night temperature is 55 to 60°F and the day temperature is five to ten degrees higher. For a week or two before the plants are set in the garden, they are hardened by standing the flats in a cold frame or sheltered place outdoors. A planting distance of about 4 inches between individuals is satisfactory.

PHYLLOSTACHYS (Phyllò-stachys). One of the most important genera of bamboos, *Phyllostachys,* of the grass family GRAMI-

NEAE, contains about thirty species. It is indigenous from Japan to the Himalayas. Its name, derived from the Greek *phyllon,* a leaf, and *stachys,* a spike, alludes to the flowers being in leafy spikes.

Some of the hardiest bamboos, kinds that survive in sheltered locations outdoors in southern New York and southern New England, belong in this genus. From most cultivated bamboos its sorts are recognizable by their canes being distinctly flattened or channeled lengthwise on one side, the flattened area changing alternately at each node from side to opposite side. The same characteristic occurs in *Shibataea,* but in that genus the branches from the nodes about the centers of the canes are slender, short, and typically three to five, whereas those of *Phyllostachys* are stout and usually in pairs, although sometimes a smaller third branch develops between the two major ones. The rhizomes of *Phyllostachys* are slender, the leaf sheaths soon fall. The flowers have three stamens.

The golden or fish pole bamboo (*P. aurea*), of Japan and China, and one of the hardiest sorts, is up to 20 feet tall. It has

Phyllostachys aurea

prominently grooved, about 1½-inch-thick canes, at first green, but when mature yellow and with conspicuously swollen nodes. Toward the bases of the canes the nodes are very close together. They provide a good grip if that part of the cane is fashioned into the handle of walking cane or umbrella. This species has short-pointed leaves with eight- to ten-veined blades up to 4 inches long by ¾ inch wide, fringed with hairs on one margin and a portion of the other. They are light green on their upper surfaces, glaucous beneath. Not a rapid spreader, this handsome bamboo is suitable for planting even where space is fairly limited. It forms a good hedge. Believed to bloom every fifteen to thirty years, unlike many bamboos this sort does not die after flowering.

The yellow groove or stake bamboo (*P. aureosulcata*) is a 30-foot-tall native of China. Perhaps the hardiest of the genus, this has dull green canes about ½ inch in diameter with above each a section striped with yellow and green. Usually three to five on each branch, the leaves, up to 6 inches long by ¾ inch wide, are densely-hairy at their bases.

The giant timber bamboo or madake (*P. bambusoides* syn. *P. quilioi*), of China, has been cultivated there and in Japan for centuries and in both countries is the largest and commercially most valuable kind. Naturalized in India and Burma and relatively hardy, this attains heights of up to 70 feet, but often is considerably lower. The canes are up to 5 inches or more in diameter. It forms open clumps of glossy, bright green, often arching canes free of any powdery coating between the nodes but when young purplish at the nodes and with a waxy band there. As they age they become yellow to brown. The branches are usually in pairs. The leaf blades, 6 to 7½ inches long and about 1¼ inches wide, dark green above, sea-green on their undersides, have short-pointed apexes. One margin is completely, the other partially, fringed with fine hairs and at the base of the leaf blade there is a circle of long, bent hairs. Distinct and handsome P. b. 'Castillon' (syn. *P. b. castillonii*) has golden-yellow to orange-yellow canes with one side bright green and grooved. This commonly attains heights of 15 to 20 feet. Quite often the leaves are variegated with yellow. Similar to the last, *P. b.* 'Allgold' differs in its canes lacking the green stripe up one side. Rare *P. b.* 'Castillon Inversus' has green canes with yellow grooves. In Japan called the wrinkled bamboo, *P. b. marliacea* has green canes with the nodes at their bases so close together that a gnarled or wrinkled effect results. The branches, usually solitary, are sometimes in twos or threes. The leaves are bright green above, gray-green on their undersides.

The black bamboo (*P. nigra*) is especially handsome. A native of China long cultivated in Japan, it has running rhizomes and forms open rather than compact clumps. Its mature canes, up to about 25 feet tall and 1¼ inches in diameter, doubly grooved on alternate sides between successive nodes, are a beautiful black. First-year canes are olive-green, second-year canes green with black blotches. Young canes have a white powdery band beneath each node. The thin leaves are usually not over 3½ inches long but sometimes attain 5 inches. About ½ inch wide, they have one margin bristly and the other partially so. Elegant *P. n.* 'Henon' (syn. *P. n. henonis*) has arching canes up to 50 feet tall and 3 inches in diameter that, when young, are bright green and rough to the touch, but become brownish-yellow at maturity. Mostly this sort has three branches

at each node. The leaves, up to 4 inches long by ¾ inch wide, are fringed with hairs on both margins. Markedly tessellated, they have bright green upper surfaces and pale grayish-green lower ones. Variety *P. n.* 'Bory' (syn. *P. n. boryana*) has broader leaves than either *P. nigra* or *P. n.* 'Henon'. It resembles the latter, but its canes are golden-yellow splashed with brown, dark purple, or black, except that when young they are green. There are usually three branches at each node.

The chief edible bamboos of Japan and China (the young shoots of many others including all described here may also be eaten) are *P. dulcis*, *P. pubescens*, and *P. viridis*. The sweet-shoot bamboo (*P. dulcis*), of China, has hairless, more or less ribbed canes up to 40 feet high and 2½ inches thick coated with meal between the joints. The leaves, mostly two or three on each short branch, with linear to narrowly-triangular blades up to about 5 inches long and almost 1 inch wide, are generally densely-hairy toward their bases. Native to China, the moso bamboo (*P. pubescens* syn. *P. edulis*) under ideal conditions may be 75 feet or more in height and 5 inches in diameter; in warm parts of the United States it has attained a height of 60 feet. A distinguishing feature is the marked velvety-pubescence of the young canes, which at maturity are golden- or orange-yellow. The nodes are not prominent. Beneath each node the cane is encircled with a waxy band. The leaf blades, up to 5 inches long and slightly over ½ inch wide, have both margins fringed with fine hairs. Their upper surfaces are green, their undersides paler. This is the largest of the running-type bamboos (sorts that do not form compact clumps). In the Orient its canes are used for household articles and for paper pulp. In warm regions attaining heights of up to almost 50 feet, *P. viridis* differs from *P. pubescens* by having minutely-dimpled young canes, bright green when young, which later become greenish-yellow. Up to 3¼ inches in diameter, they have nonprominent nodes, each with usually two branches. The leaf blades are up to 5 inches long by ¾ inch wide, or sometimes larger on new canes. Their upper sides are bright green, beneath they are grayish-green. One margin is edged with fine bristles, the other partly so. The leaf sheaths are not persistent. The canes are widely spaced so that the plant forms groves that one can walk through rather than compact clumps. A variety named *P. v.* 'Robert Young' is an attractive ornamental with canes at first light green, but later golden with green stripes.

Other sorts cultivated include these: *P. flexuosa*, Chinese, has glaucous-green, often zigzag canes up to 30 feet high by 2¾ inches wide. The eight- to ten-veined slender-pointed leaf blades, up to 6 inches long by ¾ inch wide, dark green above,

have glaucous undersides and one margin finely-toothed. *P. meyeri*, of China, up to 30 feet tall and with canes up to 2¾ inches in diameter has, except for the closeness of the nodes toward the bases of the canes, much the aspect of *P. aurea*. *P. viridiglaucescens*, also of China, has straight, somewhat mealy-coated canes up to 35 feet tall by 2 inches in diameter. Its leaves have blades up to 4 inches long by ¾ inch wide with eight to fourteen rather obscure veins. *P. vivax*, a robust Chinese, sometimes attaining 50 feet in height, has glaucous-green, ribbed canes up to almost 5 inches in diameter. The drooping leaves have blades up to 8 inches long by ¾ inch wide.

Garden and Landscape Uses and Cultivation. For this information see Bamboos.

PHYMATIDIUM (Phy-matídium). The genus *Phymatidium*, of the orchid family ORCHIDACEAE, contains some half dozen species, inhabitants of Brazil. The name, derived from the Greek *phyma*, a swelling or bladder, perhaps alludes to the bladder-like pouch at the bottom of the lip of the flower.

Diminutive epiphytes (tree-perchers) with ample roots and small leaves, phymatidiums are without pseudobulbs. The flowers are pale and tiny.

In aspect *P. tillandsioides* suggests a close tuft of hairlike grass 1½ to 2 inches

Phymatidium tillandsioides

tall out of which in summer sprout slender flowering stalks scarcely exceeding the leaves in length and bearing several stalked, translucent-white blooms under ½ inch across.

Garden Uses and Cultivation. Of interest chiefly to orchid fanciers, phymatidiums, rare in cultivation, may be expected to respond to conditions and care appropriate for *Ornithocephalus*. For more information see Orchids.

PHYMOSIA (Phy-mòsia). The Mexican, Central American, and West Indian genus *Phymosia*, of the mallow family MALVA-

CEAE, consists of about seven species. The name, derived from the Greek *phyma*, a tumor, alludes to the somewhat inflated carpels of the first species described.

Phymosias are nonhardy shrubs and small trees with stems and leaves clothed with stellate (star-shaped) hairs. The leaves are undivided and are lobed in palmate (handlike) fashion. The flowers are in loose, umbel-like clusters from the axils of the upper leaves. They have a five-cleft calyx and beneath it three bracts that often drop early. There are five rose-red to mauve petals and a column of many stamens with the lower parts of their stalks united, the upper ends free. The stigmas are terminal. The dry fruits consist of many two- to three-seeded carpels.

A shrub or tree 3 to 20 feet tall, Mexican *P. umbellata* (syn. *Sphaeralcea umbellata*) in gardens is often misnamed *Sphaeralcea vi-*

Phymosia umbellata

tifolia, which is correctly a synonym of *P. rosea*, from which *P. umbellata* can be distinguished by the bracts below the calyxes of its flowers being separate. The shoots, long leafstalks, and to a greater or lesser extent leaf blades of *P. umbellata* are clothed with starry hairs. The leaves are broadly-ovate, 2½ to 9 inches long, and somewhat seven-lobed; they look like woolly maple leaves. Mostly in long-stalked clusters of three, more rarely of twos or fives, the more or less bell-shaped blooms, up to 1½ inches long, have white-based, blood-red or crimson petals, a column of white stamens, and a pink style and stigma with each of the several carpels. Much larger, somewhat bell-shaped blooms, their petals 2¼ to 2¾ inches long, are borne by *P. rosea* (syns. *Sphaeralcea rosea*, *S. vitifolia*), a shrub or tree up to 25 feet tall and native to Mexico and Guatemala. The lobes of the leaves of this kind are mostly longer and more sharply pointed than those of *P. umbellata*. The

very handsome blooms, ranging from pink to deep red, are in long-stalked clusters. The bracts below the calyxes are united from their bases to their middles.

Garden and Landscape Uses and Cultivation. The species described here are decidedly attractive for use in beds and borders and for planting as single specimens on lawns. They need a sunny location and well-drained, moderately fertile soil, being very intolerant of wet soils. Because of their long taproots, well-established specimens rarely transplant well. It is better to set out young specimens from containers. Routine care is minimal. Seed and cuttings afford ready means of increase.

PHYODINA. See Cuthbertia.

PHYSALIS (Phýs-alis) — Chinese Lantern Plant or Winter Cherry, Cape-Gooseberry, Husk-Tomato or Strawberry-Tomato or Ground-Cherry or Dwarf Cape-Gooseberry, Tomatillo. Cultivated species of *Physalis*, a genus of 100 species of annuals and herbaceous perennials of the nightshade family SOLANACEAE, include some grown for ornament and others for their edible fruits. The group is a native of warm parts of the world, chiefly of the Americas. Its name, from the Greek *physa*, a bladder, alludes to the inflated calyxes.

Physalises are erect or straggling, their stems often somewhat woody toward their bases. They have alternate or sometimes seemingly opposite, undivided, stalked, and often angled, usually soft leaves that, like the stems, may be hairy or hairless. The white, greenish-yellow, or yellow flowers, often with darker centers, make no effective display. They are solitary or few together from the leaf axils or stems between the leaves. They have five-toothed calyxes that become large, papery, and bladder-like and, except sometimes for a small aperture at the apex, completely enclose the fruits. The wheel- to shallowly-bell-shaped corollas have five lobes or teeth (petals) and are generally purple-spotted at their centers. There are five stamens and a slender style terminated by a somewhat two-lobed stigma. The fruits are spherical, greenish or yellow berries.

The Chinese lantern plant (*P. alkekengi* syn. *P. franchetii*), a native from southeast Europe to Japan, earns its common name because of the handsome, ribbed, orange-scarlet to scarlet calyxes of its flowers. Also called winter-cherry, this perennial, sometimes grown as an annual, spreads vigorously by means of long, subterranean stems. Its hairy or hairless aboveground stems, usually branchless, are more or less zigzagged and 1 foot to 2 feet tall. The stalked, short-pointed, ovate, often angular leaves, 2 to 3 inches in length, are hair-fringed. About ¾ inch across, the whitish flowers have yellow anthers. The glories

Physalis alkekengi (flowers)

Physalis alkekengi (fruits)

of this species are its brightly colored calyxes at fruiting time. These, up to 2 inches long and nearly as wide, hang in abundance from the stems and look like little Chinese paper lanterns. The stems, cut with the lanterns attached and dried, make long-lasting decorations.

The Cape-gooseberry (*P. peruviana*) is a partially erect, 1½- to 3-foot-tall perennial. It has broadly-ovate to ovate-lanceolate, softly-hairy leaves, sometimes with a few irregular teeth, and with asymmetrically heart-shaped, rounded, or squared bases. The shallowly-bell-shaped blooms, ½ inch or slightly more wide, are pale yellow blotched and veined inside with purple, with dark purple anthers. The edible yellow fruits are surrounded by somewhat hairy, husklike calyxes. This is a native of tropical South America.

The husk-tomato, strawberry-tomato, ground-cherry, or dwarf Cape-gooseberry (*P. pruinosa*), native from Massachusetts to Ontario, Iowa, Florida, and Tennessee, is a densely-softly-gray-hairy annual, much like *P. peruviana*, but lower and widely-branching from the base. It has ovate to heart-shaped leaves with wavy-toothed margins. They are usually markedly-unequal-sided at their bases. The flowers, marked on their insides with five brown spots, have yellow or purple-tinged anthers. The edible fruits are yellow, sweeter than those of *P. peruviana,* and about ¾ inch in diameter. The hairy calyxes surrounding the fruits are much like those of the last species. Very similar *P. pubescens* is perhaps grown under the same common names.

The tomatillo (*P. ixocarpa*) is a branching, erect or spreading annual 3 to 4 feet tall, hairless or nearly so except on its minutely-downy youngest parts. It has long-stalked, pointed, ovate to lozenge-shaped, toothed or toothless leaves 2 to 3 inches long. Its flowers, ¾ inch wide or wider, are bright yellow, with five very dark brown spots inside. The anthers are purplish. The purplish, very sticky fruits are enclosed in tight-fitting, purple-veined, husklike calyxes. This is native to Mexico.

Garden and Landscape Uses and Cultivation. The only kind grown as an ornamental, for garden display and for cutting for use in dried arrangements, is the Chinese lantern plant. This vigorous, hardy spreader grows without difficulty in ordinary soils of various types in sun or light shade. Often, it is raised as an annual from seeds sown early, but it is quite susceptible to increase by division. When needed for drying for indoor decoration, the stems must be cut before the lanterns have been damaged by fall rains, tied in loose bundles, and hung upside down in a dry, airy place. When the leaves dry they are removed, leaving the fruits and their colorful calyxes on naked stems. The other kinds described above are grown for their edible fruits. Their cultivation is discussed under Husk-Tomato.

PHYSARIA (Phy-sària)—Bladderpod. Moderately showy, yellow-flowered mountain plants of dryish soils in western North America constitute *Physaria,* of the mustard family CRUCIFERAE. There are about fourteen species, rather similar and related to *Lesquerella.* Alluding to the seed pods, the name derives from the Greek *physa,* a bellows. The common name bladderpod, also applied to *Lesquerella,* refers to the same feature.

Physarias are hardy herbaceous perennials with basal rosettes of undivided, toothless or toothed, longish-stalked leaves and usually short flowering stems, with smaller, short-stalked leaves. Stems and foliage are clothed with little, stellate (star-shaped) hairs. The flowers are in racemes and, typical of their family, have four petals that spread to form a cross. There are four erect sepals, and six stamens, two of which are shorter than the others. The fruits are more or less inflated

pods, often broader than long, more or less heart-shaped, and conspicuously notched at the apex, where the prominent style is retained.

Silvery-foliaged *P. alpestris* and *P. didymocarpa* have much-inflated seed pods. Their basal leaves are spatula-shaped to obovate, and up to about 3½ inches long, those of the first sort usually toothless, those of the other often toothed. The flower stems, about 4 inches long in *P. alpestris* and up to 6 inches in *P. didymocarpa,* have smaller, oblanceolate leaves. The blooms, almost or quite ½ inch long, are in fairly compact racemes.

Differing from the kinds discussed above in having seed pods slightly or not inflated are *P. oregana* and *P. geyeri,* both grayish plants with little starry hairs on stems and foliage. The main stem of the first is often, that of the second never, branched. Their basal leaves are up to about 2 inches long, with blades obovate or oblanceolate to ovate. Those of *P. oregana* are toothed to toothless, those of *P. geyeri* usually without teeth. The leaves of the flowering stems are smaller and oblanceolate. The flowers are ¼ to nearly ½ inch long. In *P. geyeri purpurea* the blooms are purplish or with age become purplish.

Garden Uses and Cultivation. Only in rock gardens can these plants be managed and displayed to advantage. They make no great shows of bloom, but are pretty in spring when they flower, and throughout the season their foliage is neat and attractive. Scree or moraine conditions (described under Rock and Alpine Gardens) or stony or gravelly, thoroughly well-drained soil suit them best. Full sun is needed. Excessive watering must be avoided. Seeds afford a ready means of raising new plants, or this can be done by careful division in spring or immediately after blooming, and by summer cuttings.

PHYSIANTHUS ALBENS is *Araujia sericofera.*

PHYSIC NUT. This name is applied to *Jatropha curcas* and *J. multifida.*

PHYSOCARPUS (Physo-cárpus) — Ninebark. Ninebarks are hardy deciduous shrubs of the rose family ROSACEAE. All but one of the ten species are natives of North America; the other is Asian. They look much like, and are closely related to *Spiraea,* but differ in their fruits being small inflated pods (follicles) and in their leaves having at the bases of their stalks conspicuous appendages called stipules. The name, from the Greek *physa,* a bladder, and *karpos,* a fruit, is of evident application.

The bark of *Physocarpus* shreds or peels in strips. The leaves, much resembling those of currants (*Ribes*), are alternate, undivided, lobed, and toothed. In umbel-like

clusters at the ends of short branchlets that come along the shoots of the previous year, the small white or pinkish flowers are displayed in early summer. They have five sepals, the same number of spreading petals, twenty to forty stamens, and one to five styles. If more than one, the styles are more or less joined at their bases.

Common ninebark (*P. opulifolius* syn. *Spiraea opulifolia*), up to 10 feet tall, is vigorous. Its basically ovate, toothed leaves, usually three-lobed, are 1 inch to 3 inches long. The white to pinkish blooms are in clusters up to 2 inches wide. They have hairless or nearly hairless stalks and calyxes and three to five hairless follicles that become the seed pods. This is native from Quebec to Michigan, Virginia, and Tennessee. The natural variety *P. o. intermedius* (syn. *P. intermedius*) is distinguished by its leaves being more shallowly- and bluntly-lobed than those of the typical species and by its pods being hairy. The plant is lower than *P. opulifolius* and often less shapely. *P. o. luteus* has leaves at first bright yellow that change to a bronzy hue. A dwarf, small-leaved variety is *P. o. nanus.* Asian *P. amurensis* much resembles common ninebark, from which it differs in its somewhat larger leaves and in the follicles of its flowers and its seed pods being densely-downy. The white flowers, with reddish-purple stamens, are ½ inch or slightly more in diameter.

Western American species include *P. monogynus, P. bracteatus, P. capitatus,* and *P. malvaceus.* Distinguished from common ninebark by its lower stature, being normally not over 3½ feet tall, and by its flowers having usually two densely-hairy follicles that later are the seed pods, *P. monogynus* has ovate to kidney-shaped, mostly three-lobed, toothed, hairless or nearly hairless leaves from 1 inch to 1½ inches long. In clusters of few, its white to pinkish blooms are ½ inch in diameter and have hairless or nearly hairless stalks and calyxes. Similar to the last, but showier, *P. bracteatus* is up to 6 feet tall or

Physocarpus capitatus

taller. In outline its leaves are broadly-ovate and three-lobed. Its white flowers, almost ½ inch wide, have hairy stalks and calyxes. Closely related to common ninebark, but clambering to heights of 12 to 20 feet and having the stalks and calyxes of its flowers densely-downy, **P. capitatus** inhabits stream banks and moist soils. Its ovate to heart-shaped, toothed, three- or five-lobed, sparsely-hairy to hairless leaves are mostly 2½ to 3½ inches in length. The white flowers, about ½ inch wide, occur in crowded clusters. Their three to five follicles are hairless. Smaller than the last, **P. malvaceus** usually favors drier soils. About 6 feet tall, it has leaves averaging smaller than those of P. capitatus and blooms in fewer-flowered clusters. Each flower has usually two, sometimes more, follicles. They are hairy. The flowers are white and approximately ½ inch wide.

Garden and Landscape Uses. Although less showy in bloom and fruit than many popular deciduous shrubs, ninebarks are by no means virtueless. They can be put to good uses, especially in fairly large plantings where it is less necessary that each plant contribute a substantial display than is often the case with smaller ones. They are hardy, the common ninebark extremely so, and are remarkably free from pests and diseases. Their foliage blends well with neighbor plants and they make good foils for other ornamentals. Ninebarks adapt readily to a variety of soils and locations, preferring earth of reasonable fertility, and sun. They stand pruning and shearing well. The variety *P. opulifolius nanus* makes very good low hedges. Other ninebarks can be used for taller hedges.

Cultivation. Except for an occasional thinning out of crowded old branches and regular shearing of hedges, ninebarks need little attention. If they become too ungainly they can be cut as far back as deemed necessary and will renew themselves with new shoots. They can be increased by division, and easily by summer leafy cuttings planted under mist, or in a cold frame or greenhouse propagating bed. Hardwood cuttings also root readily. The species come readily from seed.

PHYSOSIPHON (Physo-sìphon). Not frequent in cultivation, *Physosiphon*, of the orchid family ORCHIDACEAE, consists of twenty species. It is native from Mexico to Brazil. Its name, from the Greek *physa*, a bladder, and *siphon*, a tube, alludes to the form of the blooms.

In habit much like *Pleurothallis*, and with clustered, erect, one-leaved stems in place of pseudobulbs, physosiphons are tree-perchers (epiphytes). Their small to minute blooms are in one-sided racemes, generally about twice as tall as the foliage, that come from the junctions of the leaves and pseudobulbs. Their sepals which are the showy parts of the blooms, are joined

into a bell-shaped tube that includes the minute petals and lip.

Most often cultivated, *P. tubatus*, of Mexico and Guatemala, has fleshy, elliptic to oblanceolate leaves 2½ to 6 inches long. Its usually arching or spreading, many-flowered racemes, often several from one leaf axil, are 5 inches to 1 foot long or somewhat longer. The nodding blooms, up to ¾ inch but usually less in length, are greenish-yellow to yellow, or brick red. Mexican *P. lindleyi* has oblong-elliptic leaves 2½ to 4 inches long by up to ¾ inch wide. Its arching or spreading, slender racemes of many rich orange-red flowers are about ½ inch long by nearly as wide across their faces.

Physosiphon lindleyi

Garden Uses and Cultivation. Physosiphons are attractive orchids for inclusion in collections and pose no great difficulties to the grower. The species described here does well in intermediate- and warm-temperature greenhouses, but kinds from higher altitudes are likely to need cooler environments. They may be grown attached to slabs of tree fern fiber or potted in containers rather small for the sizes of the specimens in osmunda or tree fern fiber with which some chopped sphagnum moss has been mixed. Shade from strong sun is needed. The rooting medium is kept fairly moist at all times, more so when active growth is being made. Constant saturation must, however, be avoided. For more information see Orchids.

PHYSOSTEGIA (Physo-stègia) — False-Dragonhead, Obedient Plant. The genus *Physostegia*, of the mint family LABIATAE, consists of nine species, all North American. The name, derived from the Greek *physa*, a bladder, and *stege*, a covering, refers to the inflated calyxes of the developing fruits.

Hairless or nearly hairless herbaceous perennials, false-dragonheads form clumps of erect, slender, four-angled stems, with paired, lanceolate to oblongish, toothed

leaves evenly disposed along them. The flowers, interspersed with small leafy bracts usually shorter than the equally-five-toothed calyxes, are in stiff, terminal, spikelike clusters. They are paired in the axils of the bracts and range in color from purplish-pink to white. Their corollas are asymmetrical, with the tube increasing in diameter toward its mouth and its lobes forming two short lips, the upper erect, concave and sometimes slightly notched, the lower spreading, three-lobed, and about as long as the upper. There are four stamens in pairs of two lengths, and a cleft style. The fruits, commonly called seeds, are three-angled nutlets.

The obedient plant (*P. virginiana* syn. *Dracocephalum virginianum*) is the principal kind cultivated. Its common name alludes

Physostegia virginiana

Physostegia virginiana (flowers)

to the fact that its flowers, in four vertical rows, if moved so that they point in other than their normal direction, remain as placed. This is a rigidly erect plant about 3 feet in height with neat foliage and dense flower spikes. Its leaves are 2 to 4½ inches long, the upper ones smaller than those below. The flowers, most commonly purplish-pink, are 1 inch to 1¼ inches long. This species inhabits moist woods and prairies from Vermont to Ohio, Illinois, Oklahoma, Tennessee, and Alabama. Variety *P. v. alba* has white flowers. Vigorous *P. v. gigantea* is up to 7 feet tall. A horticultural variety of considerable merit, *P. v.* 'Vivid', about 2 feet tall, has rich rosy-pink flowers. A good ivory-white-flowered variety, 'Summer Snow' spreads less vigorously than most sorts. Variety 'Summer Glow' blooms earlier than the typical species and has rosy-crimson blooms. Such appellations as *superba*, *splendens*, *rosea*, and *rubra* have been used by gardeners and nurserymen to identify slightly superior or supposedly superior forms selected for cultivation; most are not appreciably better than the wild species. A variety with green leaves abundantly variegated with white is also cultivated. Other species of false-dragonheads are sometimes grown in gardens, but they do not differ sufficiently from *P. virginiana* in details of horticultural significance to warrant detailed description.

Garden and Landscape Uses. Discriminating gardeners are likely to have mixed emotions about false-dragonheads. On the one hand they are accommodating, easy to grow, and bloom in late summer when good hardy herbaceous perennials in bloom are none too plentiful, on the other they spread vigorously, often to the point of being invasive, if not periodically curbed, and their flower color range is distressingly limited. The blooms last well as cut flowers. On the whole the balance sheet totes up in favor of these plants, but it behooves the gardener to assiduously seek the best color forms, not to be content with the more washy hues that are all too common, and to take the spade occasionally and dig out and restrict unwanted increase. When so selected and controlled, these plants are legitimate for naturalizing in informal areas, for grouping in borders, and for including in cutting and native plant gardens. They are especially adaptable to damp soils, but stand drier ones well and flourish with unconcern in full sun or light shade. Too much shade results in weak stems and pallid blooms. Full sun and dryish soils checks their tendency to spread too rapidly.

Cultivation. Division is the simplest means of increasing desirable kinds. This may be done in early fall or spring. Cuttings taken in early summer may also be used successfully. Seeds sown in spring germinate readily and produce plants that bloom in their second, or sometimes first, year, but such plants are likely to show considerable variation and include a fairly high proportion of nondescript color forms. Routine cultivation calls for no special effort. For the best results the plants should be divided and replanted every year or every other year. Divisions should be fairly small and planted about 9 inches apart in not too fertile soil.

PHYTELEPHAS (Phytél-ephas) — Tagua Palm, Vegetable Ivory or Ivory-Nut Palm. This curious genus differs from all others in the palm family PALMAE, except *Nypa*, which is similar in many respects, but has male and female flowers in the same clusters; those of *Phytelephas* are on separate plants. The name, from the Greek *phyton*, a plant, and *elephas*, elephant, alludes to its seeds supplying the vegetable ivory of commerce. This is an extremely hard, white, bonelike cellulose used for making billiard balls, buttons, chessmen, knobs, inlays, and similar purposes.

The genus here considered includes fifteen species of trunkless or short-trunked tropical American palms that grow naturally along river banks and have large feather leaves. Their male flowers, minute and in long, pendulous, sausage-shaped clusters, have numerous stamens, in some species as many as a thousand. The female flowers are much bigger and in erect clusters that form large, rounded, more or less dense heads. The fruits, each containing several seeds, are very big. Actually they are compound fruits, the results of the fertilization of several flowers. Their outer coats are hard and covered with spinelike protuberances so that in appearance they resemble fruits of the durian (*Durio zibethinus*).

The species most exploited for vegetable ivory is **P. macrocarpa.** This is prostrate or has stems that may rise to a height of 6 feet. Its leaves, 15 to 20 feet long, arch gracefully upward and are rich dark green.

Garden and Landscape Uses and Cultivation. These are decidedly collectors' plants, subjects for growing in special palm collections. Little is recorded about their horticultural uses and cultivation, but they quite certainly need a humid, tropical climate and moist soil, or equivalent conditions in a greenhouse. They are appropriate for including in collections of plants of use to man, such as are sometimes assembled in botanical gardens. It is to be expected that they would grow under conditions suggested for *Verschaffeltia*. For more information see Palms.

PHYTEUMA (Phy-tèuma) — Horned-Rampion. Native to Europe and temperate Asia, *Phyteuma*, of the bellflower family CAMPANULACEAE, consists of forty species of mostly low, erect, hardy herbaceous perennials. Its name, a classical Greek one meaning "the plant," was used by Dioscorides for *Reseda phyteuma*, reputed to have aphrodisiac properties.

Horned-rampions have undivided, toothless or shallowly-toothed leaves. The basal ones, tufted or more or less in rosettes, are long-stalked. Those of the stems are alternate, smaller, usually narrower, and shorter-stalked to stalkless. The little flowers, often without individual stalks, are crowded in hemispherical to spherical heads or longer spikes. They have five-lobed calyxes, and a corolla cleft almost to its base into five linear lobes (petals) that remain for a long time joined at their apexes but later separate and spread. There are five stamens and one style, ending in two or three projecting, slender stigmas. The fruits are capsules. Other plants sometimes included in *Phyteuma* belong in *Asyneuma*.

Choicest is **P. comosum,** a tufted mountain gem 2 to 6 inches high that inhabits sheer limestone cliffs in the European Alps. This has thickish, glossy leaves, the basal ones coarsely-toothed, ovate-heart-shaped to nearly round. The leaves of the

Phytelephas macrocarpa in the botanic garden, Rio de Janiero, Brazil

Phyteuma comosum

stems are smaller, short-stalked, pointed-ovate-lanceolate. The briefly-stalked, flask-shaped, bulbous-based, tubular flowers, ½ to ¾ inch long, are in dense semispherical heads of fifteen to twenty. They are blue or purple with paler lavender or pink lower portions.

Others with flowers in globular heads are *P. orbiculare*, *P. scheuchzeri*, and *P. hemisphaericum*, all of the mountains of Europe. A variable kind 6 inches to 2 feet tall, *P. orbiculare* has round-toothed leaves, the basal ones lanceolate to more or less heart-shaped, those of the stems linear-lanceolate, the upper ones stalkless. The heads of dark blue blooms, ½ to 1 inch in diameter, have at their bases lanceolate to heart-shaped bracts shorter or longer than the flowers. In the wild this sort favors dryish soils. In general appearance much like the last, but usually not over 1 foot tall, *P. scheuchzeri* is a finer kind that differs in its basal leaves being saw-toothed instead of round-toothed and the bracts underneath the flower heads being much

Phyteuma scheuchzeri

longer, linear, and often recurved. In loose rosettes, the grasslike basal leaves of 2- to rarely 6-inch-tall *P. hemisphaericum* are linear to narrowly-spatula-shaped. The few stem leaves of this high alpine kind are broader. Its blue flowers are in flattish heads up to ¾ inch in diameter, with at their bases long-pointed, hair-fringed, broad-elliptic bracts about one-half as long as the blooms.

Flower heads at least twice as long as wide are featured by some horned-rampions, among them *P. betonicaefolium*, *P. spicatum*, and *P. ovatum*. Native to mountains in Europe, *P. betonicaefolium* usually does not exceed 1 foot in height. It has blue or lilac flowers in heads at first egg-shaped, later cylindrical. The bracts beneath the flower heads are shorter than the blooms and linear. The basal leaves are heart-shaped to broad-elliptic, and double-toothed. Those of the stems are narrower. Less attractive than the last, and 1 foot to 3 feet tall, *P. spicatum* has usually whitish, yellowish, or less commonly blue flowers in cylindrical heads with linear bracts, some longer than the blooms. This is

Phyteuma spicatum

widespread through Europe. From it, *P. ovatum* (syn. *P. halleri*) differs in having dark blue-purple flowers in heads with leafy, lanceolate bracts beneath them. As wide as long, the blades of the basal leaves are heart-shaped and strongly-toothed. The stems are leafy with the upper leaves lanceolate. This native of European mountains attains heights of up to 3 feet.

Other kinds include *P. humile*, of the European Alps. A coarser version of *P. hemisphaericum*, this is 3 to 6 inches tall and has crowded, linear-lanceolate, faintly-toothed, often hairy basal leaves, few stem leaves, and blue to dark violet flowers in flattish heads, with long bracts at their bases; *P. michelii*, 1 foot to 2 feet tall, a native of southern Europe, with ovate-heart-shaped basal leaves, linear-lanceolate stem leaves, and light to dark blue or rarely white blooms in ovoid to cylindrical heads with reflexed bracts; *P. nigrum*, na-

tive to central Europe, up to 1 foot tall, with blunt, heart-shaped basal leaves, oblong-ovate, toothed or toothless stem leaves, and seldom blue, more commonly dark violet, flowers in ovoid heads; *P. siebeni*, a kind from the European Alps, from 3 to 9 inches in height, with roundish-ovate to somewhat heart-shaped, round-toothed basal leaves, toothed lanceolate stem leaves, and globose heads of deep blue flowers; and *P. vagneri*, of Hungary, 1 foot tall or taller, with toothed, heart-shaped basal leaves, lanceolate to linear stem leaves, and globular heads, that elongate as they age, of deep violet-blue flowers.

Garden and Landscape Uses. The taller horned-rampions may be grouped at the fronts of flower beds or used informally in less tended areas. None is astonishingly showy, and those with very dark blooms, such as *P. nigrum*, or very pale ones, such as *P. spicatum*, may prove too somber or too insipid for the tastes of those who esteem brilliance of flower before botanical interest and variety. Dwarf phyteumas may appeal more and can, with good conscience, be given places in rock gardens and alpine greenhouses.

Cultivation. Except for *P. comosum*, *P. siebeni*, *P. hemisphaericum*, and other dwarfs from very high altitudes, phyteumas domesticate without special care. They mostly prefer limestone soil, but commonly adjust to any that is moderately fertile, well drained, and not excessively dry. For alpine kinds, the rooting medium should be very porous. A very gritty one that permits moisture to drain from the crowns of plants and yet assures moisture to the roots is ideal. Such combinations may be had in rock garden moraines and screes and can be provided for plants in pots or pans (shallow pots) in alpine frames or greenhouses. Phyteumas are in no sense shade plants, but where hot summers prevail they are grateful for a little relief, such as may be offered by a not-too-close tree or a nearer large rock, from heat of the middle of the day. Phyteumas come readily from seed and may be increased by division in early spring.

PHYTOLACCA (Phyto-lácca) — Pokeweed or Scoke, Ombú. Best known of this genus of the pokeweed family PHYTOLACCACEAE is the common pokeberry, pokeweed, or scoke of eastern North America. A rather striking plant in foliage and fruit, it must be regarded with suspicion. Its roots are extremely poisonous and serious trouble has resulted when they inadvertently have been used with or in place of horse-radish. The attractive berries are also toxic. Children have died after eating them. Interestingly, the young shoots that push up in spring are quite harmless when cooked, and by some people, they are esteemed as a substitute for asparagus. Very different, the ombú is a nonhardy, evergreen tree of South America, planted in California and other mild-climate regions for ornament and interest.

Chiefly American, but represented also in the native floras of Africa and Asia, *Phytolacca* consists of thirty-five species of hairless or nearly hairless herbaceous plants, shrubs, and trees. They have alternate, usually stalked, undivided, toothless, ovate, elliptic, or lanceolate leaves and erect or pendulous racemes, terminal or opposite the leaves, of small flowers. The blooms are succeeded by fleshy or juicy berries or by aggregate fruits of several berry-like parts or achenes. The flowers are without petals. They have four- or five-parted calyxes, six to thirty-three stamens, and five to sixteen pistils and styles. The name is from the Greek *phyton*, a plant, and the French *lac*, the color crimson lake. It refers to the red juice of the berries.

Pokeberry, pokeweed, or scoke (*P. americana* syn. *P. decandra*) grows wild from Maine to Florida and Texas. A robust, rather fetid-smelling, deciduous,

Phytolacca americana (fruits)

herbaceous perennial, under favorable conditions it may attain heights of 12 feet, but is often lower. From 4 inches to 1 foot in length, its pointed leaves are ovate-lanceolate to oblong. The bisexual, ¼-inch-wide, whitish flowers, in slender racemes up to 8 inches long, at first are erect, but become pendulous as fruits form. The glossy berries change from green to rich black-purple as they ripen.

The ombú (*P. dioica*) is a rapid-growing evergreen tree that develops an immense trunk and has a huge crown to a height of 60 feet or more, usually broader than high. From the base of the trunk develop irregular growths with the aspect of bulky roots. These may occupy a circle 60 feet in diameter and in places be tall enough to serve as seats. The trunk of the ombú is of loose fibrous tissue with large voids. It contains such a high percentage of water that when green it will not burn. Because

Phytolacca dioica, Huntington Botanical Garden, San Marino, California

Phytolacca dioica showing basal development of trunk, Huntington Botanical Garden, San Marino, California

of this, the tree is highly resistant to grass fires that occur where it grows natively. The elliptic to ovate leaves have prominent mid-veins and are 4 inches long or longer. Male and female flowers are on separate trees. They are white, and in somewhat erect or drooping racemes rarely longer than the leaves. Male blooms have twenty to thirty stamens, females ten staminodes (nonfunctional stamens) and an ovary of seven to ten carpels. The berries have their pistils joined at their bases. In Argentina and other parts of South America, the ombú is highly regarded and the subject of many stories, songs, and legends.

Species less well known in gardens include *P. octandra*, of Central and northern South America. A herbaceous or subshrubby perennial 2 to 3 feet tall, this has elliptic to ovate-lanceolate leaves up to 8 inches long. Its racemes of white, pink, or red flowers are erect and remain so in fruit. The fruits are purple. Ranging in the wild from Mexico to Central America, and naturalized in California, *P. heterotepala*

is a broad evergreen subshrub or shrub about 4 feet tall. It has elliptic to ovate-elliptic leaves, up to 8 inches in length, and green flowers in long drooping racemes. They are succeeded by black-purple berries.

Native to China, and in aspect much like American pokeberry, *P. esculenta* (syn. *P. kaempferi*) is a herbaceous perennial up to about 3 feet tall. It has nearly round to ovate-elliptic leaves up to 6 inches long. Its white flowers are in erect racemes sometimes up to 1 foot long that do not droop after the purple-black berries form. In the Orient this is sometimes cultivated as a vegetable. Also Chinese, *P. clavigera* differs from the American pokeberry chiefly in its purplish-pink flowers

Phytolacca clavigera (flowers)

being in more densely-crowded, erect, spikelike racemes and in each having twelve instead of twenty or more stamens. Its fruits are black.

Garden and Landscape Uses. Native American pokeweed may sometimes serve as a decorative in naturalistic areas and for inclusion in collections of native plants, but its poisonous qualities must always be seriously considered before permitting it in gardens. A splendid shade tree, the ombú is adapted to southern California, Florida, and other regions with warm, essentially frostless climates. It is of great interest because of its massive appearance, curious trunk development, and rapid growth. The other species described above are sometimes grown in special plant collections and in plantings to provide variety. Whether they are poisonous does not seem to be recorded.

Cultivation. In climates adapted to their growth, phytolaccas thrive with little care and in a variety of soils. They appreciate full sun or at most part-day shade and are easily raised from seed and cuttings. Ordinary soil suits.

PHYTOLACCACEAE — Pokeweed Family. Most plentiful in native species in tropical and subtropical America and South Africa, this family of dicotyledons consists of 100 species of herbaceous plants, shrubs, and trees accommodated in a dozen genera. Few are cultivated. Most familiar to North Americans is the native poke or pokeweed (*Phytolacca americana*).

Plants of the PHYTOLACCACEAE have alternate, undivided, lobeless, toothless leaves and, mostly in racemes from the leaf axils or terminal, bisexual or unisexual flowers with four- or five-cleft persistent calyxes, usually no corollas, three to many stamens and rarely petal-like staminodes (nonfertile stamens), and one to many pistils each with a short style or none. The fruits are berry-like drupes, small nuts, or less often capsules. Genera cultivated are *Agdestis, Ercilla, Petiveria, Phytolacca, Rivina,* and *Trichostigma.*

PIARANTHUS (Piar-ánthus). Low succulent plants of the milkweed family ASCLEPIADACEAE constitute the exclusively South African genus *Piaranthus.* There are sixteen species. The name, from the Greek *piar,* fat, and *anthos,* a flower, alludes to the fleshy blooms.

Leafless, and with watery juice, piaranthuses look much like stapelias, but differ in the coronas of their flowers being without outer lobes. Their stems are thick and prostrate or more or less upright. From their middles or near their tops the flowers develop in pairs or clusters. They have five-parted calyxes, corollas with five lobes that spread like the rays of a starfish and are wheel-shaped, sometimes with depressed centers. Generally the corollas are velvety on their inner surfaces. A corona or crown of a single circle of five lobes, each with a toothed or tubercled crest along its back, arises from the short stamen column that comes from the base of the corolla. The lobes of the crest are rarely erect or may or may not have erect tips. The fruits are podlike follicles.

Kinds cultivated include *P. cornutus* and *P. foetidus.* Its bluntly four-angled, glaucous-green stems ½ inch to 1½ inches long and ½ inch or a little more in diameter, with three to five tubercle-like projections or teeth along each angle, *P. cornutus* has flowers in pairs. They are without definite corolla tubes and are 1 inch to 1¼ inches in diameter. The deep-purple-dotted, yellowish or whitish lobes of the corolla are pointed-lanceolate. Like some stapelias, *P. foetidus* has blooms that emit a penetrating, carrion-like odor. Wheel-shaped, without a definite corolla tube, they have broad petals handsomely cross-marked with purple bars or spots on a yellowish background. Often in pairs, but

sometimes solitary or in clusters of up to six, the blooms are about ¾ inch wide. Their coronas are orange-yellow marked with purplish-brown. This species has obscurely four- or five-angled stems ½ inch to 2½ inches long, oblong, ovoid, or nearly spherical. Grayish-green, they become purplish where exposed to strong sun.

Other sorts in cultivation are these: *P. globosus,* not known as a wild plant, has ovoid to spherical stems under 1 inch long and solitary or paired flowers about ½ inch wide. The velvety-hairy corolla is pale greenish-yellow sprinkled with red or lavender dots. The yellow corona has a red-spotted crest. *P. pallidus* has bluntly-four-angled, spherical to oblong stems and, in clusters of four or fewer from near their apexes, essentially tubeless, 1-inch-wide, wheel-shaped velvety-pubescent, yellow flowers. *P. parvulus* has 2-inch-long, ovoid to oblong-ovoid, bluntly-four-angled stems. Its flowers are in clusters of up to a dozen near the apexes or at the middles of the stems. Wheel-shaped, ½-inch-wide, velvety-pubescent, and pale yellow, they have conspicuously tubercled corona lobes. *P. pillansii* has stems subcylindrical or with four or five blunt, toothed angles. Chiefly in pairs near the apexes of the stems, the velvety-pubescent, greenish-yellow to yellow flowers are about 1½ inches in diameter. *P. pulcher* has small-toothed, obscurely-four-angled stems and near their tops or middles solitary or paired, ¾-inch-wide greenish-yellow, velvety-pubescent flowers marked with purple-brown.

Garden Uses and Cultivation. These are much admired plants for inclusion in choice collections of succulents. Their cultural needs are those of stapelias.

PICEA (Pi-cea) — Spruce. The fifty species that comprise *Picea* include many of our most important coniferous trees as well as a number of cultivated kinds no bigger than shrubs. They belong in the pine family PINACEAE. The name is an ancient Latin one derived from *pix,* pitch, in allusion to the resinous qualities of the trees.

Spruces are confined as natives to the northern hemisphere predominantly to temperate and cold regions. They are pyramidal evergreens, often of great heights that frequently form forests clothing reaches of the northlands and mountains of North America, Europe, and Asia. The greatest number of species are Asian, the fewest European.

In the popular mind spruces (*Picea*) are often confused with firs (*Abies*), and they do superficially resemble each other, both having the appearance of conventional Christmas trees. But botanically they are quite distinct and once certain pertinent facts are known easily told apart. The fruiting (female) cones of spruces are pen-

dulous or reflexed and are at the ends of the branchlets, whereas those of firs are upright and are lateral on the branchlets. Also, the cones of spruces remain intact after they shed their seeds, whereas those of firs disintegrate, the scales breaking away individually from the axis on which they are borne. The leaves of spruces are attached at their bases to tiny cushion-like pegs that stand out from the branches and remain attached after the leaves fall and give to the older branchlets a rough grater-like character quite different from the smooth surfaces of firs from which the leaves break off cleanly leaving circular scars flush with the surface of the twig. The branches of spruces are usually whorled (in tiers) and the needle-like leaves are generally four-angled and not compressed as they are in most firs. This last, however, is not a completely reliable distinguishing characteristic because some spruces have flattened needles and some firs four-angled ones. When branches of spruces dry the leaves soon drop. Because of this these conifers are less satisfactory than firs as Christmas trees.

Prevailingly symmetrical, stately, and often somewhat somber looking, spruce trees have solitary, tapered trunks. Their bark is usually thin and scaly, but may be more or less furrowed toward the bases of the trunks on old specimens. The winter buds are usually not resinous. Densely clothing the branchlets, the needle-like leaves are arranged spirally. They are four-angled and have evident lines of white stomata (tiny pores) on all sides or are flat with stomatic lines only on the side facing the ground (really the upper surface, but because the leaf is twisted it appears to be the lower one). Male and female cones are borne on the same tree, the former in the axils of the leaves, the latter at the ends of the branchlets. The leaves of spruces are generally stiffer and more sharply pointed than those of firs, and for this and other reasons are less well adapted for making fragrant pillows such as are made from balsam fir and some other kinds of *Abies.*

Spruces are important timber trees. Their wood is highly esteemed for a wide variety of purposes and is generally lighter, stronger, and more elastic than that of firs. Vast amounts are used for paper pulp and plywood and for light construction—interior trim and mill products as well as for boxes, crates, and packing cases. The wood of the Norway spruce (*P. abies*) is valued above all others for making the bodies of violins and the sounding boards of pianos, this because of its remarkable resonance. It is the so-called Swiss-pine wood of violin makers. The violins of Stradivari and Guarneri were constructed of spruce. It is believed that those old masters and others searched the European Alps long and lovingly for trees that would supply lumber of the quality needed to serve the highest expressions of their craft.

Native American spruces, excluding those restricted to Mexico, are seven in number, of which four are endemic to the west. Two of these, the Colorado spruce and the Engelmann spruce are generally the most satisfactory American spruces for landscaping. They prosper in the northeastern and northcentral states as well as in the west. The other westerners, the Sitka spruce and *P. brewerana*, are less adaptable. The remaining three North Americans include the red spruce, with its native range restricted to the east, and the white spruce and black spruce, which are distributed across the northern part of the continent from Labrador to Alaska. Except in the northern parts of the regions of their natural occurrence, none of the last three is satisfactory at low elevations. Because of this, their uses for landscaping are limited. A variety of the white spruce called the Black Hills spruce is better suited for that purpose. This is very hardy and more likely to flourish away from its native habitat than the white spruce.

The Colorado spruce (*P. pungens*) is most popular in its blue-foliaged phases, known collectively as the Colorado blue spruce (*P. p. glauca*). Selected varieties are

Picea pungens glauca, Arnold Arboretum, Jamaica Plain, Massachusetts

given identifying names. Symmetrical and broad-pyramidal, the Colorado spruce occasionally reaches a height of 150 feet, but more usually 100 feet is its maximum. It has deeply-furrowed bark and tiers of horizontal branches. Its green to bluish-green, rigid, prickly, sharp-pointed, four-angled leaves, ¾ inch to 2¼ inches long, point outward from all around the hairless branchlets. The cones, cylindrical and 2 to 4 inches long by 1 inch to 1¼ inches broad, have thin, flexible scales. When mature they are light brown. The Colorado spruce is native from Colorado to

New Mexico, Utah, and Wyoming. When raised from seeds its progeny vary considerably in foliage color from green to glaucous-blue, or less often silvery-blue. Varieties include these: *P. p. argentea* has intensely silvery-bluish-white foliage; *P. p. aurea* has yellow foliage; *P. p. bakeri* has rather long, rich blue leaves; *P. p. compacta* is a dwarf, dense, flat-topped, shrubby kind; *P. p. hoopsii*, densely-foliaged, py-

Picea pungens argentea

Picea pungens hoopsii

ramidal, and with spreading branches, is perhaps the most glaucous variety of *Picea pungens*; *P. p. hunnewelliana*, low, shrubby, and broadly-pyramidal, has light green, comparatively flexible leaves; *P. p. 'Koster'*, the Koster blue spruce, very symmetrical and with clearly whorled branches, has lightly curved, silvery-blue leaves that retain their color throughout the year. It differs markedly from *P. p. pendula*, which was once named *P. kosterana*; *P. p. moerheimii* has glaucous-blue foliage and is compact; *P. p. 'Montgomery'* with grayish-blue leaves ½ to ¾ inch long, is dwarf, compact, and very slow-growing; *P. p.*

Picea pungens pendula

Picea pungens 'Montgomery' (the original plant at The New York Botanical Garden)

pendula, markedly asymmetrical in outline and with drooping branches, has branchlets that vary from pendulous to erect; *P. p. procumbens*, with spreading or prostrate branches and bluish foliage, is low and shrubby; *P. p. prostrata* is a prostrate dwarf, with glaucous-blue foliage, that occasionally develops an erect leader that

Picea pungens prostrata

may attain a height of 20 feet; and *P. p. viridis* has green foliage.

The Engelmann spruce (**P. engelmannii**), native from New Mexico and Arizona to Oregon and Alberta, in favorable environments may attain a height of 150 feet. Like the Colorado spruce it has quadrangular leaves, but unlike that species its shoots are clothed with minute-glandular hairs. The leaves, which have a disagreeable odor when crushed, are bluish-green and up to 1 inch long. The cones, cylindrical and up to 3 inches long, before ma-

Picea engelmannii, Arnold Arboretum, Jamaica Plain, Massachusetts

turity are green tinged with red and later light brown. The Engelmann spruce, even to its ill-scented foliage, is in many respects similar to the white spruce, but differs in having hairy shoots and softer leaves. Intermediate hybrids occur. Horticultural varieties of *P. engelmannii* are *P. e. argentea*, with silvery-gray foliage; *P. e. fendleri*, which has pendulous branchlets and slender leaves arranged radially around the shoots; *P. e. glauca*, with blue-green foliage; and *P. e. microphylla*, a

Picea glauca (cones)

dwarf, rounded, shrublike kind with leaves shorter than those of the species.

The white spruce (**P. glauca**) is native from Labrador to Alaska and southward to New York, Minnesota, and Montana. It may attain a height of 100 feet, but is usually shorter. It has ascending branches and usually drooping, hairless branchlets clothed with more or less glaucous, bluish-green, four-angled leaves about ¾ inch long that have a strong mousey odor when crushed. The cones are 1½ to 2 inches long. As may be expected of such a widely dispersed species this is somewhat variable. A very hardy variety, the Black Hills spruce (*P. g. densata*) is distinguished by its dense habit, slow growth, and bright green to bluish-green foliage. Other varieties include the Alberta spruce (*P. g. albertiana*), which has more crowded leaves and cones not more than 1½ inches

Picea glauca albertiana

long. As a native this variety is confined to the western part of the range of the white spruce; at its tallest, it may exceed 150 feet in height. Variety *P. g. aurea* has yellow foliage. Variety *P. g. caerulea* has bluer foliage than most sorts and is of dense habit. Similar, but with horizontal young shoots and the old ones drooping, is the one known horticulturally as *P. g. hendersonii*. A very fine dwarf variety, *P. g. conica* is a low-growing, compact, densely-pyramidal edition of *P. g. albertiana*, with slightly hairy shoots and thin, spiny-pointed, slender leaves up to ½ inch long that spread in all directions. Another dwarf, *P. g. echinaeformis* has bluish-green, forward-pointing leaves about ³⁄₁₆ inch long. Other dwarf variants include *P. g. compacta*, *P. g. nana*, and *P. g. parva*, the last a natural-occurring variant at alpine elevations and in exposed places.

The black spruce (**P. mariana**) differs from the white spruce in having densely-pubescent branchlets. Rarely 100 feet tall and often much lower, this is native from Labrador to Alaska, in the mountains

Picea mariana (foliage)

southward to Virginia, and to Michigan and Wisconsin. It is narrowly-pyramidal with its top often irregular and rather open. Its branchlets are usually pendulous and are clothed with four-angled, dull dark green or bluish-green leaves up to ¾ inch long that have broader white bands on their down-facing than on their up-facing sides. The ovoid cones, which when young are dark purple, are up to 1½ inches long. Varieties to be preferred to the typical species for landscape planting are *P. m. doumetii*, which grows more slowly and is denser than the species, and *P. m. beissneri*, which is similar to the last, but broader and has lighter bluish-green foliage.

The red spruce (**P. rubens**), often confused with the black spruce, differs from it in having lustrous green leaves and cones that, when young are green or purplish-green, and that are about 2 inches long when mature. The leaves are ½ inch long or slightly longer and four-angled. This sort is narrowly-pyramidal and may attain a height of 100 feet. It is native from Nova Scotia to, in the high mountains, North Carolina.

Picea rubens (cones)

The Sitka spruce (*P. sitchensis*) and *P. brewerana* are not well suited for growing east of the Rocky Mountains and, although hardy in the northcentral and northeastern states, in general are useful for landscaping only in their home regions and where climates are similarly cool and humid. Native from Alaska to California, *P. sitchensis,* in the wild sometimes attaining a height of 200 feet, has red-brown bark and hairless branchlets. Its winter buds are resinous and its spiny-pointed, flattened leaves, ½ to 1 inch long, have a slight keel (longitudinal ridge) on their up-facing side and whitish bands beneath. Cylindrical and 2 to 4 inches long, the fruiting cones are yellow to reddish-brown, the male cones dark red. Native to northern California and southern Oregon, *P. brewerana* is quite distinct because of its slender, whiplike branchlets that are often 6 to 8 feet in length and hang from wide-spreading branches, the lower of which tend to droop. Its shoots are hairy, its buds resinous. The dark green leaves,

gracefully. Specimens thirty years or so old are likely to become disreputable in appearance and at about forty years their tops often die. Until they begin to fail they are decidedly handsome. Dwarf varieties of this species do not behave in this way. The Serbian spruce is unquestionably one of the best looking of the genus and increases in beauty with age. For landscape planting it is to be preferred to the Norway spruce. Of equal merit is the Oriental spruce. This grows rather more slowly than the Norway and Serbian spruces, which depending upon location and the objective of the planter, may or may not be a virtue.

The Norway spruce (*P. abies*) inhabits the mountains of central and northern Europe and extends eastward to the Volga River. In Lapland and eastern Russia it occurs further north than any other tree. Pyramidal and sometimes attaining a height of 200 feet, it is heavily-branched and densely-foliaged. The branches spread widely and the branchlets usually droop.

Picea abies (cones)

The twigs may be covered with minute hairs or be hairless. The four-sided leaves, dark green or olive-green and ½ to 1 inch long, terminate in a horny blunt point. The cylindrical fruiting cones, 4 to 6 inches in length, are green or purple before maturity, but are light brown when fully ripe. There are a bewildering number of varieties of the Norway spruce; at least 140 have been described. As may be readily imagined, correct identifications of these is not only a matter of extraordinary difficulty, it is often quite impossible to accomplish. A few of the more important of this vast number are listed here. Among plain green-leaved tree forms of merit are *P. a. columnaris*, which has short, horizontal branches and is narrow and columnar; *P. a. nigra*, with exceptionally dark green foliage and very densely-branched; and *P. a. pyramidata*, which forms a narrow pyramid and has markedly ascending branches. Two kinds of interest because of the un-

Picea brewerana in Ireland

Picea abies, Arnold Arboretum, Jamaica Plain, Massachusetts

1 inch or so long, are flattened and slightly convex on both surfaces. They may be somewhat pointed or blunt and spread in all directions. The fruiting cones are cylindrical with narrowed ends. Purple before they mature, and ripening to light russet-brown, they are 2½ to 5 inches long. This spruce, which occurs in the wild in quite limited, isolated areas, is rare in cultivation.

Europe, or Europe and nearby western Asia, are the native territories of three species of special interest to landscapers. These, the Norway, Serbian, and Oriental spruces, thrive in the cooler parts of North America including the northeastern and northcentral states. By far the most widely planted is the Norway spruce, an impressive conifer that unfortunately has the disadvantage of frequently failing to age

Picea abies with lower branches forming a well-developed low "skirt" extending outward from the base of the tree

Picea abies pendula at the Arnold Arboretum, Jamaica Plain, Massachusetts

A group of *Picea abies pendula*

Many have arisen as branch sports or mutations, some as seedlings, and yet others as "witches'-brooms." Discovered by observant horticulturalists, many of these atypical kinds have been propagated and perpetuated. Most, and perhaps all in time, revert to types of growth more normal for the species and produce some vigorous shoots without much evidence of dwarfness. Such shoots must be cut out if the dwarf habit is to be encouraged and preserved. Of the better known dwarf varieties those here mentioned are among the most distinct. A common kind of rounded, compact habit, with conspicuously reddish buds and leaves up to ½ inch long, is *P. a. clanbrasiliana*. Orange-colored branchlets and stiff, dark green leaves about ¾ inch long are characteristics of the dwarf, broadly-conical *P. a. eliwangerana*. The variety *P. a. gregoryana*, a low, dome-shaped plant, has crowded, spreading branchlets and narrow leaves, up to ½ inch long that spread in various directions. Low and mound-like, *P. a. maxwellii* becomes twice as broad as high

and has short branchlets clothed with bright green leaves. Often not over 1 foot in height, *P. a. nana* is compact and cushion-like. Somewhat uneven in outline, but pleasing in its irregularity, is *P. a. parsonii*, which at the Arnold Arboretum, Jamaica Plain, Massachusetts, is 5 feet tall. Having a spread up to 15 feet, attractive *P. a. procumbens* does not exceed 3 or 4 feet in height and is very uniform. One of the dwarfest and most compact varieties, usually up to 1 foot in height, is *P. a. pygmaea*.

Picea abies parsonii at The New York Botanical Garden

usual color of their foliage are *P. a. argenteo-spica*, in which the young shoots are creamy-white, and *P. a. finedonensis*, which has pale yellow young foliage that changes to bronzy-green. Kinds with pendulous branches are *P. a. pendula*, noteworthy because of its "weeping" branches close to the trunk and sometimes trailing on the ground, and the curious *P. a. inversa*, in which these characteristics are intensified. Even more unusual, sometimes to the point of being grotesque, is *P. a. virgata*, which has a few long snakelike branches, straight or crooked and frequently down-turned and nearly, or sometimes completely, destitute of branchlets. The leaves of this abnormal kind spread radially all around the shoots. It is of interest that this variety occurs spontaneously in the wild and has been recorded from places as distant from each other as Norway, Sweden, Bohemia, and Poland. Seedlings raised from *P. a. virgata* vary considerably, but a proportion duplicate the parent in their curious and distinctive habit of growth.

Dwarf varieties of Norway spruce are numerous and very confusing to identify.

The Serbian spruce (**P. omorika**), an endemic of southeastern Europe, is narrow-pyramidal and attains heights up to 100 feet. Its dense head is constructed of branches that spread or angle upward or downward and have short, drooping, pubescent branchlets. The buds are dark brown and pubescent, but not resinous. From ⅓ to ¾ inch long and flat, but with keels on both surfaces, the leaves display a pair of broad white bands separated by the green midrib on their down-facing sides. Above they are lustrous dark green.

Picea abies clanbrasiliana at the Arnold Arboretum, Jamaica Plain, Massachusetts

Branchlets and cones of *Picea abies virgata*

Picea abies gregoryana at The New York Botanical Garden

Picea omorika

The cones are glossy, oblong-egg-shaped, up to a little over 2 inches long, and cinnamon-brown. From the Norway spruce it is distinguished by its hairy shoots and prevailingly shorter leaves. The latter are up to ⅔ inch long. Also, its cones are only 3 to 4 inches long, whereas those of the Norway spruce are 4 to 6 inches. There are two varieties, *P. o. alpestris*, which has densely-pubescent twigs and bluish or grayish-green leaves slightly longer than those of the typical kind. This variety, intermediate between *P. obovata* and the Norway spruce, is slow-growing and compact. Variety *P. o. fennica* has dark green foliage and rounded, finely-toothed cone scales.

The Oriental spruce (*P. orientalis*) is a native of the mountains of Asia Minor and the Caucasus. In the wild it is sometimes

Picea orientalis (center) and *P. pungens moerheimii* (right), Arnold Arboretum, Jamaica Plain, Massachusetts

180 feet in height. Graceful, pyramidal, and densely-foliaged, it is distinguished by its leaves being shorter than those of any other spruce except certain dwarf horticultural varieties, such as variants of the Norway spruce. The trunk of the Oriental spruce is straight and slender and its branches are short, with the result that the top is narrow and spirelike. The lower branches are often somewhat pendulous. Its shoots are densely-hairy. The glossy-green, flattened leaves, up to ½ inch long and keeled (with a longitudinal ridge) on both sides, have two broad white bands facing the ground. They do not spread radially, but are in more or less comblike rows; those on the upper sides of the shoots overlapping and pointed forward. The lustrous, cinnamon-brown fruiting cones, ovoid-oblong and up to 2¼ inches in length, before maturity are blue-black. The variety *P. o. pendula* has drooping branchlets.

Asian spruces total more species than are indigenous to Europe and America to-

gether. About one-half the known species of *Picea* inhabit the rugged mountains of central and western China, and the genus is abundant throughout the colder, humid, northern and mountainous regions from Sakhalin Island, Japan, and Taiwan westward across the vast reaches of continental Asia until Asian and European species meet and overlap. Some Asian spruces occur over vast regions, others are more local. Comparatively few are in general cultivation, but the collections of living trees in the arboretums and botanical gardens of America, Europe, and elsewhere in temperate regions contain good representations obtained as a result of the efforts of a few hardy and intrepid plant explorers who tramped the mountains, plateaus, and plains of distant and almost inaccessible Asia during part of last century and the early part of this and sent home seeds.

The tigertail spruce (*P. torana* syn. *P. polita*) is the tallest Japanese spruce. Attaining a height of 130 feet at its maximum, but usually lower, and stiffly-

A group of *Picea torana*

pyramidal, it has rigid, sickle-shaped, spine-tipped leaves about ¾ inch long that stand at right angles to the twigs, which features provide easy means of recognizing this species. The leaves are quadrangular, slightly compressed, and surround the shoots except for a V-shaped channel along their undersides. The cones, 2½ to 4 inches long, are cinnamon-brown at maturity. This spruce is hardy in southern New England.

The Saghalin spruce (*P. glehnii*), a handsome kind, forms a narrow head and attains a maximum height of about 120 feet. Its reddish-brown bark is a distinctive feature. Its branchlets are furnished with short hairs, often confined to the furrows. Slightly compressed, quadrangular, and slender, the leaves, up to ½ inch long, terminate in short, horny points. Because of their shortness and arrangement they give

to the branchlets much the appearance of those of the Oriental spruce. The cones are cylindrical, about 2½ inches long, and shining brown when ripe. This species is hardy as far north as Newfoundland.

The Himalayan spruce (*P. smithiana*) is comparatively tender, but in sheltered localities survives in southern New England. In its native Himalayas it grows 200 feet tall or sometimes taller and forms a stately specimen with conspicuously pendulous branches. Its shoots are hairless and its incurving leaves, up to 1½ inches long, spread all around them. The winter buds are resinous. The slender, quadrangular leaves, tapered to fine horny points, are angled toward the tips of the drooping branchlets. The cylindrical cones, which narrow at their ends, are 4 to 7 inches long. At first bright green, they become brown at maturity. Because this species starts into growth early it should not be located where late frosts are apt to be damaging.

The dragon spruce (*P. asperata*) is the most vigorous and probably the best Chinese sort. It has special merit as being one of the most satisfactory spruces for seaside planting. In appearance it resembles the Norway spruce. In western China it attains a height of 100 feet, but since it was not introduced into America or Europe until 1910, specimens there are considerably smaller. The shoots of this species are usually, but not always, without hairs. The rigid, prickly-pointed, quadrangular leaves are ½ to ¾ inch long and spread all around the shoots. The cones, 3 to 5 inches in length, are gray to brownish. This is a variable species and varietal names have been applied to several natural variations.

Additional kinds, unless otherwise noted, all hardy to winter cold at least as severe as that of southern New England, include these: *P. alcoquiana* (syn. *P. bicolor*), a Japanese, hardy through most of New England. Up to 80 feet tall, it has quadrangular leaves with white lines on all sides and cones about 4 inches long. *P. a. acicularis* has more densely-crowded, mostly incurved, bluish-white leaves. *P. a. reflexa* has cones with reflexed tips to their scales. *P. jezoensis*, the Yeddo spruce, occurs over a wide territory in Japan and continental Asia. A flat-leaved kind, attaining 150 feet in height, it is spirelike. The buff-colored branchlets are without hairs. The leaves are crowded and overlapping on the upper sides of the shoots, and below spread and curve upward to expose the lower sides of the shoots. The apparent undersides of the leaves have two broad bands of silvery-white. The cylindrical cones are 2 to 3 inches long. *P. j. hondoensis* has shorter leaves without conspicuous white bands. *P. koyamae*, about 60 feet tall, is a native of Japan. It has hairless or hairy shoots, dark green, crowded leaves, and conspicuous, cylindrical, resinous cones 2 to 4½ inches long. *P. likiangensis*, of western China, may attain a height of 100 feet or more and has usually hairy shoots and quadrangular, compressed leaves that on the upper sides of the shoots point forward and overlap and beneath spread more or less in two opposite rows. The cones are 2 to 3¼ inches long. *P. l. balfourana* (syn. *P. balfourana*) differs in having densely-hairy twigs and cones that are violet-purple when young. At maturity the cones are 3½ inches long. It is usually a small, bushy tree. *P. l. purpurea* (syn. *P. purpurea*) has leaves about ½ inch long and cones 1½ to 2½ inches long, purple when young. *P. maximowiczii*, the Japanese bush spruce, is usually 40 to 50 feet in height and densely branched. It has hairless shoots and quadrangular, radially spreading, rigid, dark green leaves about ½ inch long. The cones are 2½ inches long. *P. meyeri* is closely related to *P. asperata*. It has yellowish, usually pubescent branches and bluish-green, often curved, four-angled leaves. The cones are up to 3 inches long. *P. montigena* is closely related to and perhaps only a variant of *P. likiangensis*. It is a native of western China. *P. morrisonicola*, native to Taiwan, is related to *P. glehnii*, but has hairless shoots. Its four-sided leaves are up to ¾ inch long, its cones 2 to 2½ inches long. *P. obovata*, the Siberian spruce, rare in cultivation, is a close relative of the Norway spruce (*P. abies*). A native of from northern Europe to Kamchatka, it is up to 100 feet tall. From the Norway spruce the Siberian spruce differs in having duller, usually shorter leaves and shorter cones, under 3½ inches long. The leaves, four-angled and pointed, are often bluish-green. *P. schrenkiana* is a native of central Asia that attains a height of 100 feet or more and somewhat resembles *P. smithiana*, but does not have resinous winter buds. It is also hardier. The shoots are hairy or without hairs and bear

dull green, four-sided leaves ¾ inch to 1¼ inches long that overlap on the upper sides of the shoots and spread below. The cones are 3 to 4 inches long. *P. spinulosa*, the Sikkim spruce, exceeds 200 feet in height in its native Himalayas. Its branches droop and it has long pendulous branchlets. The flattened, slender, sharp-pointed leaves spread more or less radially. They are ¾ inch to 1¼ inches long. This is a tender kind adaptable only for regions of mild winters. *P. wilsonii*, of central China, attains a height of about 40 feet and has slender branches and hairless shoots. The dark green, four-angled, sharp-pointed leaves are ½ to 1 inch long. The cones are 2 to 2½ inches long.

Garden and Landscape Uses. Where conditions are favorable spruces are among the most satisfactory and beautiful evergreen conifers, but in unsuitable environments they are likely to become bedraggled and of little decorative value or die. Like firs (*Abies*) they dislike excessively high temperatures, arid atmospheres, polluted air, and dry soils and so are not adapted for city conditions. Nevertheless, as a group they are less finicky than firs and several, including *P. abies*, *P.*

A dwarf variety of *Picea abies* in a rock garden

glauca densa, *P. omorika*, and *P. orientalis*, resist heat and drought fairly well. Spruces withstand exposure to wind better than firs and are good windbreak or shelter trees. At their best they are shapely, beautiful, and highly ornamental. They can be used effectively as single specimens on lawns and other places where their symmetry can be displayed to advantage, and in groups. They are especially useful as screens and backgrounds and make good hedges. The dwarf varieties are excellent in rock gardens and as specimen plants in formal gardens and elsewhere. Spruces appreciate deep, fertile, fairly moist soils. Although very definitely sun-lovers, they tolerate some shade and are very appropriate for planting on north-facing slopes.

Cultivation. Whenever practicable spruces should be propagated from seed. When this is not possible, as with horticultural varieties, grafting, cuttings, or layering must be resorted to. Grafting is done in winter or very early spring in a greenhouse, the veneer graft being used. It is important that the scions be prepared from leading rather than lateral shoots, otherwise asymmetrical plants unlikely to develop a central leader, result. Cuttings should also be made from leading shoots. These are taken in late summer or fall and are planted under mist or in a greenhouse propagating bench where a very humid atmosphere is maintained. A mixture of sand and peat moss is a good rooting mixture and mild bottom heat to keep the rooting medium about five degrees warmer than the air promotes root formation. It is a good plan to treat the cuttings with a hormone rooting powder before they are planted. Seeds, stored from the previous fall in a cool dry place, are sown in late winter or spring in a cool greenhouse or cold frame, in sandy, peaty soil. The seed pots, flats, or beds must be kept evenly moist. Under favorable conditions seeds germinate readily. The young seed-

Picea pungens argentea as a lawn specimen

A hedge of *Picea pungens glauca*

Picea schrenkiana, Royal Horticultural Society's Garden, Wisley, England

lings should be lightly shaded from strong sun. As soon as they are big enough to handle easily they are transplanted individually to small pots or to flats or cold frames. Spruces form compact masses of roots and can be transplanted safely even when large. Early spring, before new growth begins, and early fall are the best times for this operation. Routine care includes any measures necessary to control diseases or pests and watering very thoroughly in extended periods of drought. The plants benefit if the ground is kept mulched with compost, peat moss, pine needles, or other organic material. Except when grown as hedges, spruces need no pruning. Hedges are trimmed when the new shoots are in ''candle'' form, before their leaves spread.

PICK-A-BACK PLANT is *Tolmiea menziesii.*

PICKEREL WEED. See Pontederia.

PICKERINGIA (Picker-íngia) — Chaparral-Pea. Related to lupine (*Lupinus*), from which it differs technically in its stamens being separated to their bases, and to *Thermopsis*, from which it differs in being woody and having purple flowers, the only species of the genus *Pickeringia* is endemic to California. A rigid, spiny evergreen shrub up to 7 feet in height, it belongs to the pea family LEGUMINOSAE. Its name commemorates Charles Pickering, who explored California in 1841.

The chaparral-pea (**P. montana**) has firm, nearly stalkless leaves of one to three leaflets that, if more than one, arise from a common point; they are palmately-arranged. The leaflets are obovate to oblanceolate and up to ½ inch long. The pea-like purple flowers, ¾ inch long, are solitary and almost stalkless. The fruits are linear, straight, flat pods, somewhat constricted between the several black seeds. The chaparral-pea is a native of dry slopes and ridges. In the wild it rarely produces seeds, but spreads by underground stems; this it is especially likely to do after fires. A variety, *P. m. tomentosa*, is distinguished by its young shoots and leaves being hairy.

Garden and Landscape Uses and Cultivation. The chaparral-pea is not hardy in the north. It has limited use as a landscape shrub in its native range and in similar climates and may be grown under conditions approximating those under which it occurs naturally. It may be increased by division and by seed.

PICRASMA (Picrás-ma). A close relative of the tree of heaven (*Ailanthus*), and like it belonging in the quassia family SIMARU-BACEAE, the genus *Picrasma* is confined in the wild to Asia, mostly to the warmer parts, although one of its six species extends well to the north. Its name is from the Greek *picrazein*, having a bitter taste, and alludes to a well-marked quality of the bark and other parts.

Picrasmas are deciduous trees with alternate pinnate leaves, each with a terminal leaflet, crowded toward the ends of the branches and branchlets. Unisexual and bisexual flowers are on the same tree. These are small and in loose, stalked clusters from the leaf axils. They have four or five petals, the same number of stamens as petals, and a slender style that is two- to five-branched at its apex. The fruits are one-seeded, dry, and berry-like.

Only one species appears to be cultivated, and that rarely. It is **P. quassioides** (syn. *P. ailanthoides*), a kind hardy as far north as New Hampshire and reported to have grown there to a height of 20 feet in as many years. The maximum height of this tree is perhaps 40 feet. It has rather stiff branches angling upward at about forty-five degrees, and leaves 10 to 15 inches in length of nine to fifteen short-stalked, pointed, sharply-toothed leaflets with lustrous upper surfaces and paler undersides. They are devoid of hair except on the mid-veins beneath when young. The younger shoots are reddish-brown conspicuously marked with yellow spots. The leaf buds are cinnamon-brown. Without decorative merit, the greenish flowers, ⅓ inch across, hang in loose clusters. The

Picrasma quassioides

Picrasma quassioides (leaves and flowers)

round-ovoid fruits to which the persistent calyxes remain attached, are red and pea-sized. In fall the foliage assumes handsome shades of orange and scarlet. All parts of this native of northern India, China, Korea, Japan, and Taiwan are very bitter.

Garden and Landscape Uses. The chief attractions of *P. quassioides* are its rarity, its autumn foliage, and that it is not known to attract pests or diseases. It may be used to best advantage as a specimen where it has sufficient room to develop without being crowded.

Cultivation. Any ordinary soil is satisfactory. New plants may be raised from seed, and root-cuttings also provide a very ready means of increase.

PICRIDIUM VULGARE is *Reichardia picroides.*

PICRIS (Píc-ris). Natives of temperate parts of the Old World, the about fifty species of *Picris* belong to the daisy family COMPOSITAE. The name, from the Greek *pikros*, bitter, alludes to the foliage.

Picrises are annuals, biennials, and herbaceous perennials, with alternate, usually toothed leaves, and flower heads in loosely-forking-branched clusters, which, like those of dandelions, are composed of all similar strap-shaped, yellow ray florets. The fruits are achenes.

Very variable **P. hieracioides** is a bristly biennial or perennial, 6 inches to 3 feet tall. Its lower leaves are oblanceolate, toothed or toothless, and up to 9 inches long. Those above are smaller and lanceolate. The few to many flower heads are 1 inch to 1¼ inches across. Annual or biennial **P. echioides**, of Europe and North Africa, 1 foot to 3 feet tall, has oblong-lanceolate to oblanceolate, toothed, bristly-hairy leaves up to 1 foot long. Its flower heads are ¾ to 1 inch across.

Garden Uses and Cultivation. The chief use for these plants is to add variety to flower gardens. They are satisfied with any ordinary garden soil. Sow the seeds in spring where the plants are to bloom and thin the seedlings to 6 to 9 inches apart. Alternatively, sow earlier indoors and set the young plants in the garden later. No special care during the growing season is needed.

PIE PLANT is Rhubarb.

PIERIS (Pìe-ris) — Japanese-Andromeda, Mountain-Andromeda. Although segregated from *Andromeda* as a distinct and separate entity as long ago as 1834, plants of the genus *Pieris* are still often known as andromedas in gardens. The ten species differ from the two that constitute *Andromeda* in that their anthers are reflexed rather than upright and their leaves are toothed instead of being smooth-edged.

Belonging in the heath family ERICACEAE and named for *Pieris*, of Greek mythology, the genus *Pieris* consists of evergreen shrubs or small trees native to North America, Cuba, and eastern Asia. Its members have alternate, short-stalked leaves and small, short-stalked, fat-urn-shaped flowers in terminal clusters or axillary racemes. The flowers have five small, recurved corolla lobes and ten stamens. The seed capsules are not thickened along the lines that split to release the tiny seeds. Some species previously included in *Pieris* now belong in *Lyonia*.

The two commonest species in American gardens are the Japanese-andromeda (*P. japonica*), a native of Japan, and the mountain-andromeda (*P. floribunda*), a native of the southern Appalachian Mountains. Hardy as far north as southern New England, **P. japonica** has dark green, lustrous, ovate to oblong-lanceolate leaves up to 3½ inches long with margins fringed with bristly hairs. They are of a bronzy hue when young. Its white flowers, ¼ inch long and not angled, are in terminal, drooping, branched clusters, 3 to 6 inches long, that form in fall and open in spring. Under favorable conditions this sort be-

Pieris japonica

Pieris japonica (flowers)

Pieris japonica variegata

Pieris japonica variegata (flowers)

Pieris floribunda

comes a tree up to 30 feet in height, but more often does not exceed shrub dimensions. Variety *P. j. variegata* has smaller, white-margined leaves. *P. j. pygmaea* is a dwarf variety with narrower leaves. From the above, **P. floribunda** is readily distinguised by the upright flower clusters that

Pieris floribunda (flowers)

terminate its shoots and by its shoots and leafstalks being covered with stiff hairs lying flat on the surface. It does not exceed 6 feet in height and is often lower. Its leaves, fringed with hairs, and glandular-dotted on their lower surfaces, are ovate to oblong-lanceolate and up to 3 inches in length. Its flowers, about as large as those of the last species, are white and conspicuously five-angled; they form in fall and expand in spring. This is the hardier of these two species; it survives winters outdoors well north in New England.

Especially lovely because of the flaming red brilliance of its young foliage, which remains colorful for a long time, **P. forrestii** is unfortunately not hardy north of Washington, D.C. Where it does grow well, in the Pacific Northwest and other mild-climate regions, it is one of the choicest of evergreen shrubs. A native of western China, and 6 to 12 feet in height, it has elliptic-lanceolate to oblanceolate leaves 2 to 4½ inches long and about one-half as wide. The pure white flowers, about ⅜ inch long, have white calyx lobes

Pieris forrestii

Pieris forrestii (young brilliant red

Pieris nana

Pieris forrestii (flowers)

Pieris nana (flowers)

and are in drooping, branched clusters. Some botanists regard *P. forrestii* as merely a variety of **P. formosa**, which differs chiefly in that its young leaves are less fiery red than those of *P. forrestii* and its calyx lobes are green, or sometimes tinged with red where exposed to sun; also its flower clusters are more erect and its leaves are often somewhat larger. Although in cultivation this is rarely more than 12 feet in height, in its homeland it is reported to sometimes grow up to 20 feet. It is not hardy in the north. Both *P. forrestii* and *P. formosa* spread by suckers.

Other kinds sometimes cultivated include these: **P. nana** (syn. *Arcterica nana*), of Japan, Kamchatka, and nearby islands, is an extremely hardy, wiry-stemmed shrublet 2 to 4 inches tall, with 1-inch-long leaves in threes or sometimes twos that in winter assume pleasing tones of bronze and red, and arching racemes or clusters of three little nodding, white or pearly-white fragrant flowers. **P. phillyreaefolia,** of the southeastern United States, inhabits bogs and wet places. There, it may become 2 feet tall, but it often assumes the habit of a vine and grows as an epiphyte

(a plant that lives on other plants, but does not take nourishment from them) on the trunks of the pond-cypress (*Taxodium ascendens*). In cultivation it succeeds quite well in shrub fashion in the ground. Its flowers are in axillary racemes. It is not hardy in the north. **P. taiwanensis,** a native of Taiwan, is up to about 10 feet tall. It has pure white flowers and is distinguishable from *P. japonica* by its spreading or upright rather than drooping flower clusters and by the outsides of the sepals being smooth instead of minutely-hairy. This kind is less hardy than *P. japonica*.

Garden and Landscape Uses. The plants of this genus include some of the loveliest and most satisfactory of garden evergreen shrubs for acid to neutral soils. They will not tolerate alkalinity. Tiny *P. nana* is a gem for rock gardens and other special collections, and the others serve well for a wide variety of landscape purposes. They associate splendidly with other evergreens of all kinds and especially with those belonging in the heath family ERICACEAE, such as rhododendrons, mountain-laurels,

and azaleas. For shrub beds and foundation plantings they are superb and they can be employed effectively near watersides, provided their roots are well above the water level, and in open woodlands and informal areas. At their best where somewhat sheltered, they do not tolerate windy locations well. Light shade is desirable, although they will grow in full sun if the soil does not dry; in part-shade the pesky lace bug is less troublesome.

Cultivation. The cultivation of these plants is about the same as that which assures good results with rhododendrons. The soil should be somewhat acid and well-drained, yet retentive enough so that the roots never suffer from lack of moisture; a high organic content is favorable, and so when preparing planting sites it is well to incorporate to a depth of a foot or more very liberal amounts of good compost, leaf mold, peat moss, or other decayed organic matter to serve as a sponge and to provide nourishment and a congenial habitat for the roots. Pierises transplant well provided a good unbroken ball of soil is retained about their roots; *P. floribunda* is a little more sensitive to root disturbance than *P. japonica*. Spring, late summer, or early fall are the best times for this work. No regular pruning is needed, but ill-placed branches may be removed at any time. Should the plants become overgrown and straggly, they may be renewed by pruning them back drastically in early spring, just before new growth begins. The cutting may be well back into old thick trunks and branches and must be followed by fertilization. Care must be taken that the soil does not become dry during the ensuing summer or in the fall. Such severe pruning encourages the production of new shoots from low down on the old wood and eventually a new top is generated. Like many other plants of the heath family, these root near the surface, and it is very harmful to hoe or dig beneath them or close to them. Much benefit results from maintaining a permanent organic mulch, such as peat moss or compost, around them. Water applied should not be alkaline.

Propagation is usually by seeds sown on the surface of finely sifted, sandy, peaty soil or milled sphagnum moss and scarcely or not covered. The sowing medium is kept evenly moist by immersing the containers almost to their rims and permitting the moisture to seep from below. Pieces of shaded glass are placed over the seed containers until germination takes place. A cool greenhouse or cold frame provides suitable conditions for germination. Cuttings may also be rooted. These may be taken in late summer and inserted in a propagating bed in a cool greenhouse, or somewhat earlier if placed under mist. Softer cuttings taken from plants that have been forced into early growth in a greenhouse often root better than those taken from outdoors. Treating the cuttings with a root hormone preparation before insertion is advisable. Layering also may be employed to secure increase.

Diseases and Pests. Sometimes a fungus, for which at present there is no effective control, attacks these plants; it enters the roots and destroys them so that the upper parts die back and eventually the entire plant perishes. In wet seasons fungus leaf spot diseases may be prevalent. Pests of pierises are lace bugs, scale insects, and mites.

PIGEON. The word pigeon forms parts of the common names of these plants: pigeon berry (*Duranta repens* and *Rhamnus californica*), pigeon-pea (*Cajanus cajan*), pigeon-plum (*Coccoloba diversifolia*), and pigeon wood (*Hedycarya arborea*).

PIGGY-BACK PLANT is *Tolmiea menziesii.*

PIGNUT is *Carya glabra.*

PIKAKE is *Jasminum sambac.*

PILEA (Pi-lea) — Artillery Plant, Creeping Charlie, Panamigo, Aluminum Plant. Possibly 400 species of tropical and subtropical annuals and herbaceous perennials or less commonly subshrubs of varied aspect are contained in widely distributed *Pilea*, of the nettle family URTICACEAE. A few are common in cultivation; many are too weedy to attract gardeners. The name, alluding to the shape of one segment of the perianth, comes from the Latin *pileus*, a cap.

Pileas have opposite, undivided leaves with or without three, or sometimes five, prominent longitudinal veins. Their tiny to minute, unisexual flowers, with the sexes on the same or different plants, are in loose clusters or panicles or in stalked or stalkless heads from the leaf axils. Male flowers have perianths with four or more or rarely fewer, female flowers with three segments. In male blooms stamens, and in female flowers staminodes (nonfunctional stamens), equal the perianth segments in number. Female flowers have a brushlike, stalkless stigma. The fruits are achenes with the persistent perianth segments attached.

The artillery plant (*P. microphylla* syn. *P. muscosa*) earned its common name because of the smokelike clouds of pollen that are discharged with some force from male flowers located in sunny places. This native from southern Florida to tropical South America is variable, bushy, much-branched, and of varied stature, from 4 inches to 1 foot or a little over. Of ferny aspect, it has succulent stems and numerous fleshy, two-ranked leaves, typically bright green, and of two sizes, the larger shortly-stalked and with a blade about ¼

Pilea microphylla

Pilea serpyllacea

Pilea nummulariaefolia

inch long. Individual plants carry one or both sexes of minute, brownish flowers in short-stalked clusters not as long as the leaves. Similar to the artillery plant and by some botanists considered synonymous

with it, but having stouter branches and nearly spherical leaves, is Mexican *P. serpyllacea.*

Creeping Charlie (*P. nummulariaefolia*) shares its vernacular name with entirely different *Lysimachia nummularia*. A hairy perennial with trailing or creeping, rooting stems and bright green, nearly circular, round-toothed, stalked leaves up to 1 inch in diameter, this is native from Panama to Peru and in the West Indies. Its flowers, the sexes usually on separate plants, are in very small, axillary clusters.

The panamigo (*P. involucrata*), native in Panama, northern South America, and the West Indies, is upright and branched. From 4 to 6 inches tall, it has stalked, blunt, ovate to obovate, round-toothed, puckered leaves, purplish-tinged, and ½ inch to 2 inches long. The tiny, brownish flowers are many together in flattish, spreading clusters. Sometimes called blackleaf-panamigo, *P. repens* is a low, spreading Mexican species. It has wrin-

Pilea involucrata

Pilea repens

Pilea cadierei

kled, nearly round, coarsely-toothed, lustrous, coppery brown, stalked leaves with blades about 1¼ inches long that are purplish and hairy beneath. The greenish-white flowers are in long-stalked small heads. Known as silver-panamigo, **P. pubescens,** of Cuba, has brown hairy stems and lustrous silvery or leaden-colored, short-stalked leaves wedged shaped at their bases and with coarsely toothed margins. Their gray-green undersides are hairy along the veins.

The aluminum plant (**P. cadierei**), a native of Indochina, rates its common name because the distinct variegation of its foliage suggests that the leaves have been splashed or brushed with aluminum paint. An interesting fact about this variegation is that is is not, as is the case with many variegated-leaved plants, the result of absence of chlorophyll (readily proved by viewing a leaf against strong light), but by the epidermis of the leaf being separated in blister fashion from the underlying tissue by an air pocket. The aluminum plant, erect, branched, and bushy, attains a height of about 1 foot. It has four-angled stems and beautifully marked, ovate leaves up to 3½ inches long by 2 inches broad, toothed toward their apexes, and with 1-inch-long stalks. The long-stalked white or pink-tinged, spherical flower clusters are freely produced and quite decorative. A miniature edtion, *P. c. minima* is dwarfer and smaller in all its parts than the typical kind.

Several other pileas are cultivated. A free-branching, stem-rooting creeper, **P. depressa,** of Puerto Rico, has succulent, ¼-inch-long, roundish, obovate, fresh green leaves, toothed at their apexes. Largest-leaved of commonly cultivated pileas, **P. grandifolia,** of Jamaica, is upright, branched, and 2 to 3 feet tall or sometimes taller. It has long-stalked, wrinkled or quilted, coarsely-toothed, glossy green or bronzy-green, essentially hairless leaves with pointed-ovate blades 4 to 8 inches

Pilea depressa

Pilea grandifolia: (a) Showing male flowers

long, with three prominent longitudinal veins, and panicles of small, whitish to purplish blooms, the males in small, spherical clusters on long stems, the females in flattish panicles. Also from Jamaica, **P. crassifolia** attains the same

(b) Showing female flowers

height, and except for its smaller, narrower leaves (they are up to 4 inches long by 2 inches wide), much resembles the last. West Indian **P. nigrescens** becomes about 1 foot tall and has very dark green, pointed-ovate, wrinkled leaves, blotched with gray-green, and up to 5 inches long. *Pilea* 'Silver Tree', seemingly unidentifed as to species, is an upright grower with white-hairy stems and wrinkled, pointed-long-ovate leaves, very sparsely-hairy above, more densely-hairy and reddish beneath, with sunken veins and round-toothed margins. Except for a broad central band of silvery-white and dots of the same color along the sides, the leaves are bronzy-green. Another trailing kind with rooting stems is known in cultivation as *P.* 'Black Magic'. This has ½-inch-wide, puckered, roundish, slightly-toothed leaves of a rich metallic-bronzy-green hue. It is said to be a native of Colombia. With

Pilea nigrescens

(b) Flowers

Pileostegia viburnoides

Pilea 'Silver Tree'

Pileostegia viburnoides (foliage and flowers)

Pilea 'Coral': (a) A well-grown plant

minutive enough to be used in terrariums, dish gardens, and bottle gardens. Outdoors in warm regions they are splendid rock garden subjects, and *P. grandifolia* can be used effectively as a groundcover beneath trees and shrubbery. In the main they appreciate some shade, but *P. microphylla* and *P. serpyllacea* prosper in sun and can be used very effectively as narrow edgings to paths and flower beds.

Cultivation. Among tropical plants, pileas are as easy to cultivate as any. They like warmth, and revel in high humidity, even though fleshy-leaved *P. microphylla* and *P. serpyllacea* will succeed where the air is drier than that tolerated by other kinds. Cuttings root with such ease that they are a usual means of propagation. The creeping kinds are readily increased by division, and when available seed may be used. Any moderately fertile, well-drained soil with a reasonable organic content suits. It should be kept moderately moist but not constantly wet.

PILEOSTEGIA (Pileo-stègia). This genus of hydrangea relatives occurs wild from India to China and Taiwan. It belongs in the saxifrage family SAXIFRAGACEAE and consists of three species. The only one cultivated is a prostate or climbing evergreen shrub, which, as its botanical name *Pileostegia viburnoides* suggests, superficially resembles a viburnum. For its introduction to cultivation we are indebted to the great plant collector E. H. Wilson, who sent seeds from China to the Arnold Arboretum in 1908. The name is derived from the Greek *pilos*, felt, and *stege*, a roof, in allusion to the corolla.

Attaining a height of 15 feet, *P. viburnoides* has scurfy shoots and opposite, pointed, lobeless, toothless leaves, narrowly-elliptic to ovate or obovate, and narrowing gradually at their bases. They are 2½ to 6 inches long by ¾ inch to 2½ inches broad and are scurfy when young. Their veins are strongly evident. The un-

der leaf surfaces are minutely-pitted. The creamy-white flowers, which appear in fall, are crowded in terminal clusters 4 to 6 inches broad and about as long. Each bloom is about ⅜ inch in diameter and has a four- or five-lobed calyx, four or five petals, and eight or ten stamens, the latter constituting the showiest part of the flower. The fruits resemble those of hydrangeas; they are small, dry, and top-shaped.

Garden and Landscape Uses. An attractive self-clinging evergreen vine, *P. viburnoides* is useful for clothing walls, tree trunks, and other surfaces to which it can attach itself; it is not appropriate for growing against wooden houses or other surfaces that must be painted periodically. In the wild it rambles over cliffs and trees, and in gardens it is suitable for covering large rocks and tree stumps.

Cultivation. Deep, fertile, well-drained soil that is never excessively dry best suits this vine, which grows satisfactorily in sun or part-day shade. Routine care is minimal. After blooming the faded flowers should be removed. The only pruning needed is any necessary to confine the

somewhat the aspect of *P. grandifolia* but more refined and compact, *P.* 'Coral' is a bushy sort with pointed-elliptic, dark bronze to purplish-bronze, toothed leaves up to 3½ inches long by 1½ inches wide. Distinctly glossy and of quilted appearance, the leaves have three prominent longitudinal veins.

Garden and Landscape Uses. The pileas described here are charming for outdoor gardens in the tropics and warm subtropics, for greenhouses, and as houseplants. All, except perhaps *P. grandifolia*, are di-

plant to an allotted space. Propagation is easy by cuttings and by seed.

PILGERODENDRON (Pilgerodén-dron) — Alerce. The only member of this genus is a rarely cultivated conifer previously included in *Libocedrus*. It is native to southern Chile, chiefly to the west of the Continental Divide, and in its home territory is exploited for lumber. From other members of the former *Libocedrus* complex, *Pilgerodendron* differs technically in the number of its pollen sacs. It belongs in the cypress family CUPRESSACEAE. Its name, honoring a Director of the Botanical Garden, Berlin, Germany, Dr. Robert Knud Friedrich Pilger, who died in 1953, is based on his name and the Greek *dendron*, a tree.

In the wild sometimes 160 feet tall, but usually lower, *P. uviferum* (syns. *Libocedrus cupressoides*, *L. tetragona*) is narrowly-conical. It has flat sprays of quadrangular branchlets clothed with four rows of small scalelike leaves that clasp the stems for much of their length, but spread widely at their tips. The spreading parts are under ¼ inch long. Male cones are nearly cylindrical. At maturity female cones, up to ½ inch long, are short-stalked and consist of four scales, the upper pair fertile, each containing one, or rarely two, seeds. This species, sometimes confused with *Fitzroya cupressoides* and like it called alerce, is easily distinguished from *Fitzroya* by the arrangement of its leaves, which are in twos rather than threes. Also, those of *Fitzroya* are broadest toward their apexes, whereas the leaves of *Pilgerodendron* are widest at their bases. The cones are quite different.

Garden and Landscape Uses and Cultivation. This rare tree is not likely to be met with away from its native home except in collections of unusual plants. Little known in North America, it is considerably less hardy than the incense-cedar and is suitable for trial only in regions of mild winters. It may be expected to have the same ornamental uses and the same cultural needs as the incense-cedar (*Calocedrus decurrens*). For further general information see Conifers.

PILOCARPUS (Pilo-càrpus). Consisting of twenty-two species of shrubs and small trees of tropical America and the West Indies, *Pilocarpus*, of the rue family RUTACEAE, has a name, alluding to the shape of the fruits, derived from the Greek *pilos*, a cap, and *karpos*, a fruit.

These plants have usually alternate, pinnate leaves of four or fewer pairs of leaflets and a terminal one. The small flowers, in long racemes, have four or five petals, and the same number of stamens. Some species, including the one described here, are sources of the medicinal drug jaborandi.

Pilocarpus pennatifolius

Pilocarpus pennatifolius (flowers)

Up to 10 feet tall or taller, *P. pennatifolius* has alternate, leathery, evergreen leaves 1 foot to 1½ feet long with two or three pairs and a terminal one of elliptic to obovate leaflets 3 to 9 inches long. The drooping, spikelike racemes up to 1½ feet long or somewhat longer are of very many reddish-brown flowers with stamens conspicuously tipped with yellow anthers; they have a sourish odor.

Garden and Landscape Uses and Cultivation. A handsome foliage shrub or small tree, the species described is useful for outdoor landscaping in the tropics and subtropics. Reported to be hardy wherever lemons can be grown, it is sometimes cultivated in greenhouse collections of plants useful to man. Adaptable to any satisfactorily drained, reasonably fertile

soil, it is propagated by seed and by cuttings.

PILOSOCEREUS (Pilóso-cereus). Treelike, bushy, and prostrate species numbering about sixty constitute *Pilosocereus*, of the cactus family CACTACEAE. By conservative botanists included in *Cephalocereus*, this genus inhabits Florida, the West Indies, and Central and South America. Its name, derived from the Greek *pilos*, hair, and the name of the related genus *Cereus*, refers to the abundant hair of some kinds.

Pilosocereuses have mostly stout, distinctly ribbed stems with areoles (specialized areas from which spines and flowers arise) with few to many woolly hairs (the areoles from which the flowers come are usually very woolly) and spines that are generally needle-like. The funnel-shaped blooms open at night. The fruits are without scales or spines.

Kinds cultivated include these: *P. chrysacanthus* (syn. *Cephalocereus chrysacanthus*), of Mexico, has columnar stems, branched low, up to 15 feet tall and 3½ to 4 inches thick. They have nine to twelve ribs, areoles with long white hairs, and twelve to fifteen yellow spines 1 inch to 1½ inches long. The 3½-inch-long flowers are light pink to rose-red. *P. glaucescens* (syn. *Cephalocereus glaucescens*) is a beautiful Brazil-

Pilosocereus glaucescens

ian. Up to 20 feet tall and 4 inches thick, its glaucous-blue-green stems have seven to ten ribs closely furnished with clusters of thirteen to eighteen ½- to ¾-inch-long, light yellow radial spines and five to seven yellow centrals about as long. The flowering areoles have white hairs. The 3-inch-long blooms are white. *P. glaucochrous* (syn. *Cephalocereus glaucochrous*), of Brazil, up to 12 feet tall, has 2- to 3-inch-thick, very blue-glaucous stems with five to nine notched ribs. The spine custers are of nine to twelve pale yellowish to grayish radials ½ to ¾ inch long and three or four stouter, up to 2-inch-long centrals. The whitish to light pink flowers are up to 1 inch in length, the bluish-green to reddish fruits 1½ to 2 inches in diameter. *P. luetzelburgii* (syn. *Cephalocereus luetzelburgii*), of Brazil, is distinctive. It has dark green stems at first spherical, later ovoid, eventually decidedly narrowed toward their tops and flask-shaped. Up to 3 feet tall, they have thirteen to sixteen ribs. The areoles have white wool and the upper ones, from which the flowers arise, curly white hairs up to ¾ inch in length. The clusters of yellowish to gray spines are of fifteen to eighteen needle-like radials up to about ½ inch long and four or five about 1-inch-long centrals. Approximately 2 inches in length, the flowers have olive-green outer petals, white inner ones. The flattened-spherical fruits are a little over 1 inch wide. *P. palmeri* (syn. *Cephalocereus palmeri*), of Mexico, has erect, glaucous-blue, columnar stems up to about 20 feet tall that branch above in candelabra fashion and at their ends are clothed with white, woolly hairs. They have seven to nine prominent ribs and woolly areoles with clusters of eight to twelve 1-inch-long radial spines and one to four longer centrals.

Pilosocereus palmeri

About 2½ inches long, the flowers are brownish to purplish. *P. royenii* (syn. *Cephalocereus royenii*) is West Indian. From 6 to 25 feet tall, its numerous glaucous, blue to green stems branch from their bases, are 9 inches to 1 foot thick, and have seven to eleven ribs. From ½ inch to 2½ inches long, the very variable spines are ¾ inch to 2¼ inches long and yellow. Approximately 2 inches in length, the flowers, which come from areoles with long, white hairs, are greenish-yellow to purplish, with the inner petals white.

Garden and Landscape Uses and Cultivation. Pilosocereuses thrive in warm, desert and semidesert climates such as suit the majority of tree-type and other large cactuses and many other succulents. They are also suitable for inclusion in greenhouse and conservatory displays and collections. Of vigorous growth and considerable adaptability, they prosper in porous, well-drained soil in full sun and where they receive part-day shade. They are easily propagated by cuttings and seed. For more information see Cactuses.

PILULARIA (Pilu-lària) — Pillwort. About six species of aquatic and subaquatic ferns constitute *Pilularia*, of the Marsilea family MARSILEACEAE. The genus is native to temperate North America, Europe, Australia, and New Zealand. Its name, derived from the Latin *pilula*, a little ball or pill, refers to the sporocarps.

Pilularias have creeping, very slender stems and threadlike or grasslike leaves without developed blades. As with related *Marsilea* and *Regneilidium*, the spores are in hard organs called sporocarps that grow on or near the bottoms of the leafstalks. The sporocarps of *Pilularis* are spherical.

Native to Europe and North America, *P. globulifera* has long-creeping stems that root from the nodes, and bright green leaves up to 3 inches long or sometimes a little longer and ³⁄₁₆ inch wide. Essentially stalkless and ⅛ inch or less in diameter, the sporocarps are clothed with short hairs.

Garden Uses and Cultivation. The species described here is sometimes grown in aquariums and pools. It prospers in soil covered shallowly with water and is easily propagated by division.

PIMELEA (Pi-mèlea) — Rice Flower. Evergreen, erect to prostrate shrubs of the mezereum family THYMELAEACEAE constitute *Pimelea*, a genus confined in the wild to Australia, New Zealand, Timor, and Lord Howe Island. Referring to the fleshy seeds, the name is derived from the Greek *pimele*, fat. There are eighty species.

Pimeleas have alternate or opposite, undivided, lobeless, toothless leaves, Usually those immediately beneath the clusters of small white, pink, red, or yellow flowers

are bigger than those below and form involucres (collars) upon which the flower heads rest. The unisexual or bisexual blooms are without petals. Their showy parts are the corolla-like, tubular calyxes with four spreading, petal-like lobes. There are two stamens, and a long style tipped with a headlike stigma. The fruits are small drupes (fruits structured like plums).

The best known species is *P. ferrruginea*. This Australian, fairly dense and up to 4 feet tall, has opposite, ovate to oblong leaves up to ½ inch long, with rolled-un-

Pimelea ferruginea

der margins. Its rose-pink, hairy flowers are in nearly spherical, pin-cushion-like heads 1 inch to 1½ inches in diameter at the ends of the numerous branchlets. Another Australian, *P. ligustrina*, 4 to 8 feet in height, has opposite, ovate to oblong leaves, 1 inch to 2 inches long, and quite showy, globular terminal heads of silky, white flowers. In its native Australia called bunjong or banjine, *P. spectabilis* is a slender shrub 2 to 4 feet tall with starry, white, pale yellow, or pink flowers in pin-cushion-like heads that before they open have pink centers. They are 2 to 3 inches across. The crowded leaves are opposite, linear to lanceolate, and up to 1½ inches long.

A good rock garden species for mild-climate regions, *P. prostrata* (syn. *P. coarctica*), of New Zealand, has ground-hugging, woody stems and forms wide, gray-green carpets an inch or two high. The closely set, almost stalkless, spreading to down-pointing leaves, ovate to elliptic-oblong and often red-margined, are up to ¼ inch long. The three- to ten-flowered clusters of tiny, fragrant, creamy-white blooms make a pleasing, but not extravagant show. The heads of bloom are about

Pimelea prostrata

¾ inch wide. The berry-like, ovoid, white or red fruits are up to ¹⁄₁₀ inch long. This kind, which has a liking for limestone soils, is a good cover for small bulb plants. It is very variable.

Other species cultivated include these: **P. graciliflora,** of Australia, is up to 2½ feet tall. It has opposite, lanceolate leaves ½ to ¾ inch long and spherical heads of white flowers. **P. humilis,** a shrublet 4 to 8 inches high, is a native of Australia and Tasmania. It has hairy stems and overlapping, blunt, oblong to ovate-oblong leaves up to ¼ inch long. Its white flowers are in heads ¾ inch to 1¼ inches across. **P. tomentosa,** of New Zealand, is a slender shrub 1 foot to 1½ feet tall with wandlike white- or grayish-hairy stems and linear to lanceolate leaves, hairy on their undersides, hairless above, up to 1½ inches long. A dozen or fewer small flowers compose each head.

Garden and Landscape Uses and Cultivation. As outdoor plants Australian pimeleas are successful only in regions of Mediterranean-type climates, that is where winters are mild, summers warm and dry. In the United States such conditions are found only in the far West and parts of the Southwest. In addition, they can be grown as pot plants or in ground beds in cool greenhouses under conditions that suit Australian acacias and leptospermums, South African heaths, and similar plants. The New Zealand species stand cooler, moister environments than the Australian kinds. All need neutral or slightly acid soil, well drained and containing always enough moisture to preclude the possibility of desiccation and death of the plants, but never for long periods wet. Exposure to full sun, or at most slight part-day shade, is needed. Propagation is easy by seed and by cuttings.

PIMENTA (Pi-ménta)—Allspice, Bay Rum Tree, Pimento. A tropical American group of eighteen species of aromatic trees or shrubs of the myrtle family, MYRTACEAE constitutes *Pimenta.* Its best-known mem-

bers are allspice, so called because its dried immature fruits, used as a condiment, are thought to impart the combined flavors of cloves, nutmeg, and cinnamon, and the bay rum tree, the leaves of which are distilled to obtain an oil used in bay rum and perfumery. The name derives from the Spanish *pimento,* allspice.

Pimentas are closely related to *Myrtus* and *Eugenia,* differing in technical details of their fruits. They have large, leathery, stalked leaves with the veins angling outward from the midribs, and undersides finely dotted with black. Borne in three-branched clusters at the ends of the branches or from the leaf axils, the numerous little white flowers have top-shaped calyx tubes, four or five sepals, four or five petals, and numerous stamens. The small berry-like fruits contain one or two seeds.

Allspice (**P. dioica** syn. *P. officinalis*), native to the West Indies and Central America, 30 to 40 feet tall, has oblong-elliptic leaves 2 to 7 inches long with ½-inch-long stalks. About ¼ inch across, its clustered flowers have four each sepals and petals. The purple fruits, brown after they dry, are ¼ inch in diameter. Especially abundant in Jamaica, the source of commercial allspice, this species favors limestone soils. An oil distilled from its leaves is employed as an adulterant of bay rum. Its hard wood is used for walking canes and similar purposes.

Bay rum tree (**P. racemosa** syns. *P. acris, Amomis caryophyllata*) is native to the West Indies and northern South America. A shrub or tree up to 45 feet tall, and much like allspice, this is easily distinguished by its blooms having five each sepals and petals. Its elliptic to obovate leaves are up to 6 inches long. The fruits are about ⅓ inch in diameter.

Garden and Landscape Uses and Cultivation. None of these species is of significant horticultural importance in North America. They are suitable only for the tropics. Allspice yields best in dry climates. Pimentas are occasionally included in greenhouse collections of plants useful to man, and adapt easily to pot and tub cultivation. They succeed in well-drained, fertile soil in humid greenhouses with a minimum winter temperature of 55 to 60°F. The soil should be kept moderately moist. Pruning to shape, and repotting, is done in late winter. Increase is easily had by cuttings and seed.

PIMPERNEL. See Anagallis. The water-pimpernel is *Samolus parviflorus.*

PIMPINELLA (Pimpin-élla)—Anise. Of the about 140 species of *Pimpinella,* of the carrot family UMBELLIFERAE, only one is of horticultural significance. Chiefly Mediterranean, this genus is native from Greece to Egypt. Its name is of uncertain derivation.

Pimpinellas are perennial herbaceous or rarely annual plants with usually once- or more pinnately-divided leaves and umbels of small white, yellowish, pink, or purplish five-petaled flowers with five stamens and two styles. Their tiny fruits (commonly called seeds) are compressed and ovate or sometimes broader than long.

Anise (**P. anisum**) is a pubescent, branched annual 1½ to 2½ feet tall, native from Greece to Egypt. It has long-stalked, coarsely-toothed basal leaves up to 2 inches long and stem leaves divided pinnately or into three narrowly-wedge-shaped, toothed or toothless leaflets. The flowers, in large loose umbels, are small and yellowish. The fruits, flattened-ovate, have lengthwise ribs.

The very agreeable odor of anise is especially attractive to dogs and has been used by burglars, thieves, and dog thieves to allay the suspicions of those animals. A bag of anise dragged across country leaves a scent that hunting dogs will follow as they would that of a fox. Extracts of anise are much used in medicines, and the leaves and seeds are employed for flavoring cheeses, cakes, cookies, candies, and salads. It is, of course, responsible for the flavor of the liqueur anisette.

A nearly hairless perennial, European **P. major,** 1½ to 3 feet tall, has brittle, prominently-ribbed or angled stems and leaves of seven to thirteen usually undivided, pointed, ovate to lanceolate lobes up to 1½ inches long. The tiny white or pinkish flowers are in flat, terminal umbels up to 2½ inches across. The flowers of *P. m. rubra* are pink.

Garden Uses and Cultivation. An appropriate plant for herb gardens or for a corner of the vegetable garden, anise is so strongly flavored that a few plants are ample for most home gardens. They are best grown in well-drained fertile soil in full sun. The seeds are sown in spring in rows 2½ to 3 feet apart and the seedlings are thinned to 1½ feet in the rows. Summer care consists of suppressing weeds. The crop is harvested by cutting whole seed heads after they are ripe, but before they begin to shatter, spreading them on paper in a dry, airy place, and, when they are thoroughly dry, rubbing the heads and winnowing the seeds free of bits of stalk and other extraneous matter. They may be stored in tight jars or other containers. They retain their flavoring properties for many years. The other species described and its variety succeed under the same conditions as anise.

PINACEAE — Pine Family. This important family of gymnosperms, which formerly included kinds now segregated as *Cupressaceae* and *Taxodiaceae,* comprises ten genera totaling 250 species of bisexual, cone-bearing, resinous trees or much less often shrubs. It has a wide natural distribution and is especially abundant in temperate parts of the northern hemisphere. Many of its sorts are esteemed as ornamentals; a goodly number are sources of valuable lumber and pulpwood. Canada balsam, pitch, turpentine, rosin, and edible seeds (pinon nuts) are products of pines.

Members of this family, except *Larix* and *Pseudolarix*, are evergreens. They have needle-like, clustered or solitary leaves arranged in spirals. The primitive flowers, to the nonbotanical scarcely recognizable as such, are in cones with flattish, spiraled scales and separate bracts. Female cones, in all genera except *Abies* and *Keteleeria* pendulous, become woody as they mature, and remain tightly closed until the winged seeds, usually two to each scale, are ripe. Cultivated genera include *Abies*, *Cedrus*, *Keteleeria*, *Larix*, *Picea*, *Pinus*, *Pseudolarix*, *Pseudotsuga*, and *Tsuga*.

PINANGA (Pinán-ga). A hundred and fifteen low to moderately tall, feather-leaved palms with solitary or multiple, slender, bamboo-like trunks are included in *Pinanga*, of the palm family PALMAE. They are natives from India to New Guinea and the Philippine Islands. The name is a modification of a local Malayan one, *pinina*, for these palms.

Pinangas have leaves with usually short, often broad leaflets, the upper ones frequently much wider than those lower on the midrib. The bases of the leafstalks may be sheathing and form a crownshaft or false trunk that looks like a continuation of the true trunk or, depending upon species, may be without crownshafts. The short flower clusters come from beneath the leaves and have a single spathe. The flowers are in threes, the central one female, the others males. The males have from six to numerous stamens. The ellipsoid fruits are usually yellow to deep red.

Native to Java and Sumatra, *P. kuhlii* has several stems up to 30 feet in height and 3- to 4-foot-long leaves with three to

Pinanga kuhlii

six pairs of leaflets 1 foot to 2 feet long and up to 3 inches wide. The branched flower clusters are about 1 foot in length. The fruits are almost ½ inch long. Not over 9 feet in height, *P. patula*, of Sumatra, has stems thickened at their bases and leaves 4 to 5 feet long with sixteen to thirty-six leaflets up to 1 foot long by 2 inches wide. The upper ones are often united. The sheathing leafstalks form a distinct crownshaft. The branched flower clusters are short. The fruits are ⅔ inch long and orange-red. Malayan *P. disticha* (syn. *Ptychosperma disticha*) usually has a cluster of trunks 2 to 6 feet tall. Its 1- to 1½-foot-long ovate-wedge-shaped leaves are undivided or may have a few lateral leaflets.

Garden and Landscape Uses. These palms are attractive as individual specimens and in groups and associate well with architectural features, such as buildings. They are adapted to humid, tropical climates where little or no frost is experienced and are excellent greenhouse plants.

Cultivation. Pinangas are easy to grow. Outdoors they prefer part-shade and thrive in any ordinary garden soil not excessively dry. In greenhouses they need a minimum winter temperature of 60 to 65°F. From spring through fall the lowest temperature at night should be 70°F. At all seasons day temperatures should exceed night ones by five to ten degrees. Let the soil be coarse, fertile, and porous, and the pots, tubs, or ground beds in which they are planted well drained. Shade from strong sun and a humid atmosphere are essential, and watering must be adequate to keep the soil from ever being really dry. In winter rather less water is needed than at other times. Biweekly applications of dilute liquid fertilizer from spring through fall are very helpful.

Propagation is by seeds sown in sandy peaty soil in a temperature of about 80°F. Cluster-stemmed kinds can also be increased by very careful division, but this is a rather tricky operation. Divisions taken with as many roots as possible and planted in sandy peaty soil are placed for a period of six to eight weeks in a very humid, shaded greenhouse where the temperature is 70 to 90°F. These conditions favor the reestablishment of their root systems. For more information see Palms.

PINCHING. A form of pruning, pinching, or pinching back as it is also called, refers to nipping out with finger and thumb the soft growing tip of a shoot. Chiefly done to promote branching, it is also practiced to keep specimens shapely, limit their size, and influence the time of blooming. When small side shoots (laterals) are nipped out completely to prevent branching, as is done when tomatoes are grown to single stems, the operation is called pinching out, but gardeners also refer

Pinching the shoots of a chrysanthemum plant

to pinching back as pinching out the tips. Pinching is also sometimes called stopping.

PINCUSHION. See Leucospermum. The blue pincushion is *Brunonia australis*, the pincushion flower *Scabiosa atropurpurea*.

PINE. For true pines see Pinus. Other plants with common names that include the word pine are these: Australian-pine (*Casuarina equisetifolia*), Australian black-pine (*Podocarpus amarus*), Australian brown-pine (*Podocarpus elatus*), celery-top-pine (*Phyllocladus asplenifolius*), Chilean-pine (*Araucaria araucana*), cypress-pine (*Callitris*), dammar-pine (*Agathis dammara*), ground-pine (*Lycopodium obscurum*), hoop-pine (*Araucaria cunninghamii*), kauri-pine (*Agathis*), King-William-pine (*Athrotaxus selaginoides*), New-Caledonian-pine (*Araucaria columnaris*), New Zealand black-pine (*Podocarpus spicatus*), New Zealand white-pine (*Podocarpus dacrydioides*), Norfolk-Island-pine (*Araucaria heterophylla*), pine drops (*Pterospora andromedea*), red-pine (*Dacrydium cupressinum*), running-pine (*Lycopodium clavatum*), screw-pine (*Pandanus*), and umbrella-pine (*Sciadopitys verticillata*).

PINEAPPLE. See Ananas. The false-pineapple is *Pseudananas sagenarius*, the pineapple flower *Eucomis*, the pineapple-guava *Feijoa sellowiana*, the pineapple sage *Salvia elegans*, and the wild-pineapple *Tillandsia fasciculata*.

PINELLIA (Pin-éllia). Seven species of eastern Asia constitute *Pinellia*, of the arum family ARACEAE. The name commemorates Giovanni Vincenzo Pinelli, of the botanical garden of Naples, Italy, who died in 1601. The group is closely related to jack-in-the-pulpit (*Arisaema*), differing in that one side of the lower part of the spadix is joined to the inside of the spathe, so that flowers develop only along one side of that portion of it, and in that each ovary contains only one ovule.

Pinellias are tuberous herbacious perennials with leaves divided into three to seven leaflets or not so dissected. They are lobed or lobeless. The solitary flower stalk terminates in a typical calla-lily-like flower structure, a spadix (spike crowded with minute flowers), from the base of which arises a large bract. In *Pinellia*, as in *Arisaema*, the lower part of the spathe curves to form a tube completely surrounding the spadix. But the latter does not stand stiffly and neatly beneath the overhanging top of the upper part of the spathe as in *Arisaema triphyllum* "jack" does in his "pulpit." Instead, the spadix ends in a long, slender appendage or tail and protrudes like that of the dragon root (*A. dracontium*). The lower portion of the spadix, the part attached to the spathe, has only female flowers, the males are above and are separated from the females by a ringlike protrusion from the inside of the top of the tubular portion of the spathe.

Native to Japan, China, and Korea, *P. ternata* is naturalized in New Jersey and southern New York. It has small tubers and a few deciduous, long-stalked leaves that have three stalkless or almost stalkless

Pinellia ternata

ovate-elliptic to oblong leaflets 1½ to 4½ inches long by up to 2 inches wide, hairless and without teeth. At some little distance from their bases and at their apexes, the leafstalks develop small bulbils. Carried atop slender stalks 8 inches to 1 foot long or longer, the green floral structures look like small, narrow jack-in-the-pulpits with a slender, cylindrical tongue curving upward and outward from their mouths. The spathe is 2 to 2½ inches long, the spadix with its appendage 2½ to 4 inches long. The fruits are small green berries.

Garden Uses and Cultivation. Of interest to lovers of the unusual rather than of

outstanding beauty or charm, this species should be not be introduced casually to gardens. Unless placed where its natural spread can cause no inconvenience, nor interfere with choicer plants, it may become a troublesome weed. It grows in partial shade in ordinary soils and, spontaneously, often beneath rhododendrons. Increase is by division, bulbils, and seed.

PINESAP is *Monotropa hypopithys*. Sweet-pinesap is *Monotropsis*.

PINEWOODS-LILY is *Eustylis purpurea*.

PINGUICULA (Pinguíc-ula) — Butterwort. The names *Pinguicula* and butterwort used for the thirty-five species of this genus of the bladderwort family LENTIBULARIACEAE allude to the greasy appearance of the thick leaves. The botanical one is derived from the Latin *pinguis*, fat. Butterworts are carnivorous plants that inhabit wet soils and boggy places throughout much of the northern hemisphere and along the spine of the Andes to southern South America. They are occasionally cultivated by lovers of the interesting and unusual, but are less well known to gardeners than pitcher plants (*Sarracenia*), Venus' fly trap (*Dionaea*), and some other insect-trapping kinds.

Butterworts are small herbaceous perennials, some hardy in the north, others not. They form basal rosettes of undivided, toothless, soft leaves from the centers of which arise slender stems, naked of foliage, that lift pretty purple, blue, yellow, or white, solitary flowers. The leaves commonly exude a sticky secretion and are clammy or slimy to the touch. The blooms, somewhat suggestive of violets, have a four- or five-parted calyx and a two-lipped, long-spurred corolla, the five lobes (petals) of which spread widely. There are two stamens and a pistil with a short style or none. The fruits are capsules.

Like other carnivorous plants, butterworts ordinarily fill part of their nitrogen needs by digesting the bodies of creatures they catch, but this source of nourishment is not essential to their well-being. Their method of entrapment is similar to that of sundews (*Drosera*). Their leaves are clothed with glandular hairs that secrete a sticky, dewlike substance. Insects and other tiny creatures that come into contact with it become entangled. Then the leaf very slowly rolls over on itself, and special glands excrete a ferment. After the digestible parts of the prey are absorbed the leaf gradually unfolds. Laplanders use the leaves of *P. vulgaris* to curdle milk.

Wild in Europe and Asia and in North America from Labrador to Alaska, New England, New York, Michigan, Minnesota, and Washington, *P. vulgaris* has ground-hugging, yellowish-green, ovate or elliptic leaves up to 2 inches long. The

flower stalks, 2 to 6 inches long, carry violet blooms with a white patch in their throats. Including the spur, they are ½ to ¾ inch long and nearly as wide. Western European *P. grandiflora* is similar, but has longer blooms, the lower lips of which are broader than long, and the spurs are less slender. The alpine butterwort, of European mountains, *P. alpina* has whitish, rarely reddish- or violet-flushed flowers ⅓ to nearly ½ inch long, with one or two yellow spots in their throats. Its leaves are elliptic to lanceolate. From the last, *P. lusitanica*, of Europe, differs in having smaller, lavender flowers with cylindrical instead of conical spurs. Up to 1 foot in height, *P. elatior* (syn. *P. australis*) ranges in the wild from North Carolina to Florida. Its approximately 1-inch-wide blooms vary from purple to white.

Bright yellow, nearly symmetrical blooms distinguish *P. lutea*. This native from North Carolina to Florida and Louisiana has ovate to oblong-ovate leaves and flowers ½ inch to 1½ inches long and wide at the tops of stalks up to 1 foot or sometimes a little more in length. The throats of the blooms are marked with red.

Mexican *P. caudata* (syn. *P. bakeriana*) is especially worthy. It has two types of leaves, those during the early part of the

Pinguicula caudata

Pinguicula caudata with insects trapped on its leaves

growing season are long and slender, the later leaves are fewer, larger, and broad-ovate. The long-stalked, deep carmine-red blooms, with red-lined, paler throats, are up to 2 inches long and almost as wide. Their spurs greatly exceed the corolla tubes in length. A smaller Mexican, **P. gypsicola** has broad-based, linear, early summer leaves about 2 inches in length

Pinguicula gypsicola

and later oblong-spatula-shaped ones that form dense rosettes. The two-lipped, purple blooms have narrow petals and a slender, purplish spur much longer than the short corolla tube, with a pair of teeth at its end.

Garden Uses and Cultivation. The hardiness of these decidedly interesting plants may be deduced from the climates of the regions they inhabit in the wild. They are suitable for bog gardens, wet sites in rock gardens, and for cultivation in greenhouses. They need a sunny site, a humid atmosphere, and always-moist, sandy peaty soil. For greenhouse cultivation pans (shallow pots) 6 inches in diameter are suitable receptacles. Three plants of larger kinds are enough in each pan. To allow for the spread of the foliage they should be planted near the edge of the container. This is done in February just before new growth begins. No repotting is needed afterward. Watering is done by keeping the pans standing in filled saucers, not by overhead sprinkling. In October the plants are rested by putting them where the night temperature is 50°F and that by day only a few degrees higher. The

soil is not allowed to dry. The leaves then gradually die and dormant rosettes or resting buds form. Butterworts can be raised from seeds sown in peaty soil kept constantly moist, but an easy and more common method is by leaf cuttings. These consist of small, firm leaves broken off cleanly at the stem and laid flat on a greenhouse propagating bed or on the surface of a pan of peaty soil kept standing in a saucer of water, and covered with a bell jar or tent of transparent polyethylene plastic film to ensure a highly humid atmosphere.

PINK. Common names of plants that contain the word pink include these: cushion-pink (*Silene acaulis*), fire-pink (*Silene virginica*), Indian-pink (*Lobelia cardinalis* and *Silene californica*), marsh-pink (*Sabatia*), moss-pink or rock-pink (*Phlox subulata*), mountain-pink (*Centaurium beyrichii*), mullein-pink (*Lychnis coronaria*), pink-and-white shower (*Cassia nodosa*), pink-broom (*Notospartium carmichaeliae*), pink-jacaranda (*Stereospermum kunthianum*), pink shower (*Cassia grandis*), sea-pink (*Armeria*), swamp-pink (*Helonias bullata*), and wild-pink (*Silene caroliniana*).

PINKROOT is *Spigelia marilandica*.

PINKS. As a common or vernacular name, pinks is sometimes used to include practically all dianthuses except carnations and sweet williams and among natural species of *Dianthus* are sorts known by such names as maiden pink and cheddar pink. Here the word is employed in a more limited way to a few groups of highly horticulturally developed varieties of *Dianthus* for which the designation pinks is more commonly reserved.

Cottage pinks, or as they are often called in Great Britain just pinks, have been bred from *D. plumarius*, a species brought to England from eastern Europe before the middle of the seventeenth century and there, and more especially in Scotland, treasured and carefully nurtured since. It is probable that modern varieties of this group are not all pure derivatives of *D. plumarius*, but that some represent hybrids between that species and the carnation (*D. caryophyllus*) and perhaps other kinds. Botanical evidence of this probability is found in the absence of beards in the throats of the flowers and in other details. This also may account for the greater tenderness to cold of some varieties than others. Sorts that exhibit this relationship to *D. caryophyllus* were classified by Dr. L. H. Bailey as hortulan cottage pinks

Cottage pinks form low, dense mounds of glaucous-blue foliage above which rise in late spring or early summer flowering stems 1 foot to 1½ feet tall so numerous and prolific of blooms that the foliage is almost completely hidden. The deliciously

A cottage pink

fragrant blooms are 1 inch to 1½ inches across, single, semidouble, or double, with smooth, toothed, or fringed margins to the petals. The color range includes pure white and various shades of pink. Commonly the centers of the flowers are darker, often wine-red. Named and choice varieties of cottage pinks are propagated vegetatively, but plants raised from seed provide charming, free-flowering specimens with considerable variation among individuals as to color of bloom and other characteristics. The flowers of seedlings are usually single or semidouble.

A button pink

Button pinks are an interesting and quite lovely hybrid group to which the name *D. latifolius* is applied. Their parents are the sweet william and either the rainbow pink or cottage pink. Plants of this hybrid complex are ½ foot to 1½ feet high, with green leaves up to 4 inches long by ½ inch wide or slightly wider. The branched stems have two to four blooms at the end of each branchlet of loose flower clusters. Each bloom is up to 1 inch in diameter. When raised from seeds the flowers are mostly dark red or purple-red

Rainbow, Indian, or Chinese pinks

to dark crimson, but there are white-flowered and pink-flowered sorts. Some have double blooms. Varieties 'Beatrix', with double pink flowers, and 'Silvermine', with double pure white flowers, belong here and are especially lovely. Button pinks are perennials, although often short-lived ones.

The rainbow, Indian, or Chinese pink (*D. chinensis*) is a biennial or short-lived perennial. Garden varieties bloom the first year from early sown seeds and are often grown as annuals. A native of China and other parts of eastern Asia, in the wild it attains a height of 6 inches to 2½ feet and has erect stems obviously thickened at the nodes and branchless or branched only at their tops. The leaves are green, the basal ones usually dried by the time the plant is in bloom. The very narrow stem leaves are up to 3 inches long. The scentless flowers, borne in loose clusters of up to fifteen, are ½ to 1 inch across and rosy-lilac with a purple eye. The petals are toothed at the margins.

Horticultural interest in the rainbow pink centers in its magnificent garden varieties that are available in a great range of forms and flower colors, which have been cultivated for centuries in the Orient. The date of their first introduction to Europe is not known, but great interest in them developed as a result of an importation to St. Petersburg, Russia, from Japan shortly after the middle of the nineteenth century. Undoubtedly the varieties brought to Europe represented the results of selecting and breeding for desirable forms by Chinese and Japanese gardeners over a long period of time. Two varietal names applied to the kinds grown at St. Petersburg were *D. chinensis heddewigii*, for those with toothed petals, and *D. c. laciniatus*, for those with deeply-dissected, fringed petals. Since then, cross-breeding has so merged the two that no clear differences exist and intermediates are common. In addition, new forms have been developed, including kinds with double flowers.

Modern rainbow pinks are highly ornamental hardy plants 6 inches to 1 foot tall, and bushy, with green foliage and a plentitude of beautiful flowers 2 to 4 inches across that range in color from white to pink, lavender, and red, and many combinations in which the colors form attractive and often bizarre patterns. They bloom continuously from mid-summer to frost, but are at their best when nights are moderately cool.

Garden and Landscape Uses. Cottage and button pinks are delightful for the fronts of flower beds and borders and as cut blooms. Rainbow pinks, treated as annuals, serve similarly. All revel in full sun and need porous, preferably neutral to slightly alkaline, soil, but tolerate slight acidity. Good drainage is exceedingly important. These plants abhor constantly wet soil.

Cultivation. Make ready for planting by spading and mixing into the ground generous amounts of compost, decayed manure, or other suitable organic matter, a dressing of bonemeal or other fairly lasting fertilizer, and if available a heavy sprinkling of unleached wood ashes. If the soil is more acid than pH 6.5, fork into its surface ground limestone at the rate of about half a pound to 10 square feet or about one-half that amount of hydrated lime.

Early fall and early spring are the best seasons to plant cottage pinks and button pinks. Space them 9 inches to 1 foot apart, taking care not to set the plants appreciably deeper than they were previously. Routine care calls for little beyond shearing off old flowering stems after blooming is through and in protracted spells of dry weather watering deeply periodically. This last should not be overdone, however; pinks stand dry conditions remarkably well.

Propagation of selected varieties of cottage and button pinks may be by cuttings (sometimes called pipings) taken in late spring or early summer and planted in a bed of firmly packed sand or mixture of sand and peat moss in a cold frame located on the north side of a wall or otherwise lightly shaded. Water well immediately after planting; rather sparingly but not to the extent that the cuttings suffer from insufficient moisture, from then on. After rooting begins gradually increase ventilation of the frame until the sash can be left off entirely. By fall the young plants will be ready for lining out in a nursery bed or this can be delayed until spring. At the end of another year they will be nice specimens for planting in their permanent locations. As an alternative to rooting cuttings, layering affords a practical means of securing increase and seeds may also be employed. These last germinate readily if sown in a cold frame or in a protected bed outdoors in April or May or in a greenhouse earlier, but seedling plants exhibit much variation and inevitably a greater or lesser percentage are much inferior to the best of the named varieties.

Rainbow, Indian, or Chinese pinks are invariably raised from seeds usually sown early indoors and the seedlings transplanted to flats or small pots in the manner appropriate for many summer-blooming annuals and grown in these until the weather has moderated sufficiently to plant them in their flowering quarters, spaced 7 to 9 inches apart.

Alternatively, seeds may be sown directly outdoors as soon as the ground is readily workable in spring and the seedlings thinned out to the desired distance. If lifted carefully the thinnings can be successfully transplanted. Yet a third possibility, less commonly employed, is to sow in a cold frame in August to give plants for transferring to their flowering locations in early spring.

Pests and Diseases. Among pests sometimes troublesome are aphids, caterpillars, cutworms, red spider mites, slugs, snails, and thrips. Diseases that may occur in-

Physalis alkekengi

Picea glauca albertiana

Picea pungens 'Montgomery'

Picea pungens glauca

Picea pungens variety

A path bordered with *Pilea microphylla*

Pinguicula caudata

Pieris japonica

Picea pungens variety

clude rots, rust, and wilt. Despite these possibilities, unless planted in distinctly unfavorable places, pinks are usually relatively immune to these troubles.

PINNATE. This means with parts, like those of a feather, in two rows that spread outward from a central axis. A pinnate leaf has leaflets arranged in this fashion, a pinnately-veined leaf, side veins that diverge in this manner from a mid-vein. Compare palmate.

PINUS (Pi̇n-us)—Pine. The genus *Pinus*, of the pine family PINACEAE, is the most important one of the great group of plants called conifers. It also contains the most species, upward of a hundred, the exact number depending upon the point of view of the botanical authority accepted. The natural distribution of pines is confined almost entirely to the northern hemisphere; only in Sumatra does one species, *P. merkusii*, cross the equator. The generic name is an ancient Latin one.

Pines are predominantly inhabitants of temperate and warm-temperate climates. In the tropics they are generally confined to high altitudes. They are most abundant as to species in North America, especially in the western part of the continent and in Mexico. More than half the known sorts are endemic to the New World. A dozen kinds are indigenous from the European Alps to North Africa and the Canary Islands, and twice as many in eastern Asia from the Himalayas to Japan and Kamchatka and southward. Northern Europe and northern Asia are poor in native pines. Three species only occur there in the vast territory that extends from the Atlantic to the Pacific.

Geologically, pines are an ancient group. They first appeared in the Mesozoic, more than 60,000,000 years ago, but did not become dominant factors in the major floras of the earth until the end of the Tertiary, less than 1,000,000 years ago. Since, they have been highly successful in competition with other plants and are believed to be still advancing southward. In many regions they form continuous, one-species forests, in other areas they grow in scattered groves or as individual trees intermixed with other kinds, or alone. The oldest living thing is possibly a pine. In 1954 the annual rings in the trunk of a specimen of a bristle-cone pine (*P. aristata*) growing in eastern California were found to number 4,100, indicating an age of that many years.

Pines are handsome, evergreen, resinous trees, or very rarely shrubs, with branches usually in whorls (tiers) and needle-like leaves. Their primitive flowers are unisexual with both sexes on the same tree. The males are located at the bases of the new shoots in yellow, orange, or red, catkin-like clusters. They produce pollen

Clusters of catkin-like spikes of male flowers of a pine

Female flowers are contained in the small, scaly structures evident at the tips of these pine shoots

so abundantly that if a branch bearing ripe flowers is shaken it is distributed in sulfur-yellow clouds. The female flowers are in structures that usually develop at or near the shoot ends, or more rarely, at irregular intervals along young shoots. These structures become the familiar cones containing the seeds.

It must be understood that the flowers of pines are flowers in a technical sense only. Reduced to the barest essentials to justify the application of that term, they scarcely conform to the popular conception of a flower. Females consist only of ovules, two to each cone scale, males of anthers only, also two to each scale. The ripe pollen is dispersed by the wind. The scales of young female cones are open, but close immediately after they receive the pollen. About a year elapses until fertilization (the uniting of the male and female reproductive cells) takes place. When this is accomplished the female cones rapidly increase in size. In most species they ma-

ture their seeds at the end of their second year, but those of some not until they are three years old.

Seed-bearing cones, ovoid to cylindrical and in some species of large size, have woody scales, usually noticeably thickened at their apexes, and until ready to discharge the seeds, tightly pressed together. The exposed, thickened end of each scale ends in an umbo or boss, usually terminated by a spine or a prickle. The seeds of most species are conspicuously winged.

The cones of some pines remain on the branches without shedding their seeds for many years after they mature. This is notably true of certain western American species, the cones of which in the wild stay intact until subjected to the heat of a forest fire. In some cases unopened cones drop to the ground where the seeds are liberated as the result of the scales rotting or the activities of squirrels or other animals.

As young trees, pines are almost always symmetrical and pyramidal, but with age many develop highly picturesque crowns, more or less flat-topped, rounded, or pyramidal, according to species, and with wide-spreading branches. The primary leaves of seedlings and young trees are solitary and temporary. From their axils arise the secondary, more permanent leaves or needles. Almost always the secondary leaves are in groups of two to five, but in *P. monophylla* and in some varieties of other species, they are solitary, and in *P. durangensis*, a Mexican species not known to be in cultivation, there are six to eight needles in each cluster. The bases of the needle clusters are enclosed in sheaths, which may be deciduous and soon fall, or permanent. Some pines shed their secondary needles at the end of the second year, others retain them for three to five, rarely up to fourteen or even more years.

The usefulness of pines extends far beyond their importance as ornamentals. They serve industry in many ways and many species are esteemed for forestry planting. For this they are widely employed in the southern as well as the northern hemisphere. They occupy somewhat the same relative position of importance among temperate region trees that palms do among tropicals. They are sources of lumber, plywood, pulpwood, turpentine, rosin, pitch, tar, and essential oils. The seeds of some are used as foods. The Scots pine is cultivated for Christmas trees.

Native American pines with five leaves to each bundle include the Eastern white pine, the mountain or Western white pine, the whitebark pine, the sugar pine, the Mexican pine, the torrey pine, the bristle-cone or hickory pine, and the limber pine, all except the first and the Mexican pine natives of the western part of the continent.

The Eastern white pine (**P. strobus**), is especially noteworthy. Its maximum height is 200 feet. It has horizontal branches, young shoots with some hairs at first, and soft, flexible, gray-green needles 2 to 4½ inches long. Its spindle-shaped cones, usually curved, are 3 to 8 inches in length. They mature in their second year. This magnificent tree, highly valued for its lumber, once covered vast areas of northeastern North America, but is now uncommon in really large sizes. It occurs from Newfoundland to Iowa and Georgia and is the only pine native to the eastern United States and eastern Canada with its needles in clusters of five. Much used as an ornamental and for reforesting, it grows quite rapidly, especially in its early years. In Great Britain it is known as the Weymouth pine because, following its introduction into that land in 1705, it was much planted by Lord Weymouth. A handsome, compact, rounded variety that seldom exceeds 6 feet in height, P. s. um-

Pinus strobus umbraculifera

braculifera (syn. P. s. nana) has leaves ¾ inch to 1½ inches long. A prostrate variety with trailing branches that closely follow the contours of the ground is P. s. prostrata. The young foliage of P. s. variegata (syn. P. s. aurea) is yellowish. A variety in which the five leaves are joined for much of their length so that they appear as one is P. s. monophylla. Narrower than the typ-

Pinus strobus

Pinus strobus (cone)

Pinus strobus fastigiata

ical species and with erect branches, P. s. fastigiata breeds remarkably true from seeds.

Native chiefly in Montana and Idaho, but extending to California and British Columbia, the mountain or Western white pine (**P. monticola**) somewhat resembles its eastern relative, but is usually but not always a smaller, narrower tree of heavier appearance, with downy young shoots and leaves, more rigid than those of P. strobus, in bundles of five, and up to 4 inches long. They persist for three or four years. Its slender, cylindrical, slightly curved cones are 4½ inches to 1 foot in length; they have more scales than the cones of P. strobus. This species is hardy in southern New England. Minature P. m. pygmaea, possibly identical to a variety

named P. m. minima in 1888, is a compact sort with crowded, short, dark green leaves. A specimen of this attained a height of 1 foot in seven years.

Pinus monticola pygmaea

Another five-needled species is the whitebark pine (**P. albicaulis**), which occurs in the Rocky Mountains and from California to British Columbia. A high-mountain, very hardy kind, rarely exceeding 60 feet in height, it is often shrublike. Its trunk and wide-spreading branches are often contorted and, on young trees, have whitish bark. On older specimens the bark sheds in small patches. The leaves are up to 2½ inches long and dark green. Its cones, up to 3 inches in length, do not shed their seeds as soon as they are ripe.

Most imposing of all pines, the sugar pine (**P. lambertiana**), native from Oregon to Baja California, is occasionally over 225 feet in height (a height of 246 feet is recorded). It may have a trunk diameter in excess of 10 feet. The sugar pine is a five-needled species with pubescent branchlets and stiff, spirally-twisted, sharp-pointed leaves 2 to 4 inches long that are dark green with white lines on their backs. They fall in their second or third year. The stalked, cylindrical cones are 10 to 20 inches long. This species is greatly esteemed for its lumber. It may live for 500 years. It is the only five-needled pine with deciduous sheaths to the leaf clusters that has downy shoots. It is hardy in southern New England, but grows slowly there. The colloquial name refers to the sugary exudation that occurs from the wood.

The Mexican pine (**P. ayacahuite**), closely related to the last, also produces splendid lumber. A graceful, five-leaved sort, this attains a height of 100 feet and has leaves 4 to 8 inches long and cones up to 1¼ feet long. It is native from northern Mexico to Guatemala and Honduras, but is nowhere abundant. It is not hardy in the north.

Pinus ayacahuite in the botanic garden at Mexico City

Pinus aristata

Pinus torreyana in a native stand near San Diego, California

The torrey pine (**P. torreyana**), now native of only two very limited localities in southern California, in past geologic ages extended as far north as British Columbia. A crooked tree, rarely over 45 feet high in the wild, it grows considerably taller in cultivation and develops an interesting candelabra-like top of quite massive branches. Its leaves, up to 1 foot or somewhat more in length, dark green, rigid, and in clusters of five, form tufts at the ends of the branches. They remain for several years before they fall. The cones are 4 to 6 inches long; their scales have short spiny tips. This pine is not hardy in the north.

Possibly the oldest of all living things, the bristle-cone or hickory pine (*P. aristata*), attains a maximum age of over 4,000 years. Up to 50 feet in height and bushy, it sometimes does not exceed the dimensions of a shrub. It grows slowly. Its dark green leaves, made grayish by encrustations of resin are up to 1½ inches long and

in bundles of five. Its cylindrical-ovoid cones, up to 3½ inches long, have scales that have umbos with an incurved spine. The bristle-cone pine is native from California to Colorado. In the east it is hardy as far north as Massachusetts.

The limber pine (*P. flexilis*), slender-pyramidal when young, becomes broadly-

Pinus flexilis

Pinus flexilis (foliage)

round-topped with age. A tree 50 to 80 feet in height, it has remarkably pliant shoots, sometimes downy when young, and dark green leaves 2 to 3 inches in length and in clusters of five. They remain without falling for up to fourteen years. The ovoid cones are up to 6 inches long. This species is indigenous from Texas and California to Alberta. It, *P. albicaulis*, and Asian *P. pumila* are the only five-needled pines with leaves not finely-toothed along their edges. Unlike *P. albicaulis*, the limber pine sheds its seeds as soon as they are ripe. It is much taller than *P. pumila*, which, in contrast to *P. flexilis*, has densely hairy shoots. Variety *P. f. reflexa* is taller and has longer leaves. Variety *P. f. albo-variegata*, has many of its leaves white. Variety *P. f. nana* is dwarf and bushy. The limber pine is hardy about as far north as New York City.

American pines with always three needles to each bundle are the longleaf pine, the loblolly pine, and the pitch pine, all natives of the eastern part of the continent, and the digger pine and the big cone pine, endemics of California.

The longleaf pine (**P. palustris**) justifies its colloquial name by having leaves on young trees up to 1½ feet long, on mature specimens up to one-half that length, in

A young specimen of *Pinus palustris*

tufts at its branch ends. They remain for two years. A handsome species, indigenous from Virginia to Florida and Missouri, it attains a height of 120 feet and has an open head of ascending branches and almost stalkless cones up to 10 inches long with a short reflexed spine terminating each umbo. Very characteristic of this pine are the white-fringed scales of its winter buds. The most important timber tree of the southeastern United States, it is also a much valued source of rosin and turpentine.

The tallest pine of the southern United States, the loblolly pine (**P. taeda**) sometimes exceeds 150 feet in height. Native

Pinus taeda

Pinus rigida

Pinus rigida (trunk with tufts of leaves)

Pinus rigida (cones)

Pinus sabiniana (branching habit)

from New Jersey to Florida and Texas, it has reddish bark, a dense, round-topped head, and bundles of three rigid, sharp-pointed, rather light green leaves 5 to 10 inches in length that are shed when three or four years old. Its lower branches are spreading, its upper ones more erect. The stalkless cones are ovoid-oblong and 2 to 5 inches long, with umbos terminating in a stout, triangular spine.

The pitch pine (*P. rigida*), up to 80 feet tall, has an open, irregular head of horizontal branches. The dark green, wide-spreading, stiff leaves, 3 to 5 inches long and in groups of three, last two years. Standing out at right angles from the branchlets, the egg-shaped cones are 2 to 3½ inches long. They remain for many years after their seeds are dispersed. At maturity this is picturesque with its trunk and major branches often sprouting short tufts of foliage. After felling it often produces shoots from the stump, but these never develop into trees and are not long-lived. This species is native from Maine to Tennessee and Georgia, in the southern

part of its range confined to the mountains.

The digger pine (*P. sabiniana*) forms a loose, sparsely foliaged, rounded head of distinctive appearance. It is occasionally 80 feet, but usually not much more than 50 feet in height. Its branches are short and crooked, its pale bluish-green leaves, in threes, are rather slender and 8 inches to 1 foot long. They last three years. The egg-shaped, slightly lopsided, deflexed cones are 6 to 10 inches long and have strongly pointed umbos. The wings of the edible seeds form rims around them and are shorter than the seeds. The cones remain for several years after the seeds are dispersed. Native only to California, the digger pine is tender, but less so than the other endemic of California with leaves in threes, the big-cone pine.

The big-cone pine (*P. coulteri*), up to 80 feet in height, has a pyramidal, open head and thick, stiff, bluish-green leaves 6 to 8 inches long. Its down-turned, slightly lopsided cones are egg- to oblong-egg-shaped and 10 inches to somewhat over 1 foot long. Their scales have large umbos with a strong, curved spine. The wings of the seeds are decidedly longer than the seeds. From all other pines, *P. coulteri* and *P. sabiniana* are distinct in having both very large cones and seeds with wings that form rims around them.

American pines with leaves invariably in twos include the red pine, scrub pine, and jack pine of the northeast, the lodgepole pine of the Rocky Mountains, and the shore pine and the bishop pine of California.

The red pine (*P. resinosa*) is also called Norway pine. This suggests alien origin, but the Norway to which reference is supposed to be made is a village in Maine, not the European country. Native from New-foundland to Manitoba, Pennnsylvania, and Minnesota, this species often inhabits gravelly and sandy soils too poor to support the Eastern white pine. It occasionally attains a height of 150 feet, but more usually does not exceed 70 feet. The red pine has reddish-brown bark and a broad, pyramidal head of spreading, sometimes drooping branches. Its glossy-green, flexible leaves, in pairs, are up to 6 inches long, the longest of any pine native in northeastern North America. Its nearly stalkless, ovoid cones are 1½ to 2½ inches long and without prickles. This is decidedly ornamental. Variety *P. r. globosa* is dwarf and approximately spherical. In general appearance the red pine resembles the Austrian pine (*P. nigra*), but its leaves are much more pliant, the sheaths surrounding the bases of its leaves are usually longer (½ to ¾ inch), and its cones fall before they are fully mature. A striking feature is the bright red color of the male flowers.

The scrub pine (*P. virginiana*) may attain a height of 100 feet, but more commonly is not over one-half as tall and has a rather scrubby or straggly top. It has slender, horizontal, or drooping branches

Pinus virginiana (leaves and cone)

and purplish, glaucous young shoots, which serve to distinguish this species from all other two-leaved pines. The leaves are twisted, rigid, and about 3 inches long. Up to 3 inches long, the cones are conical-ovoid and nearly stalkless. They persist on the branches for long periods. The umbos of their scales end in a prickle. The scrub pine is indigenous from New York to Georgia and Alabama. It grows well in clayey soils.

The jack pine (*P. banksiana*) is usually considerably lower than its maximum height of 70 or more feet. It has a rather open, broad top of crooked branches and rigid, twisted, diverging leaves ¾ inch to

Pinus banksiana

Pinus banksiana (leaves and cone)

1½ inches long in pairs. The usually curved and lopsided cones, 1½ to 2 inches long, are conical-ovoid with umbos without prickles. They remain on the tree for long periods, releasing their seeds gradually and irregularly. This, the northernmost pine of eastern North America, is indigenous from New York to Minnesota and almost the Arctic Circle. It grows even where the soil is underlaid with permafrost.

The shore pine (*P. contorta*) has a natural range from California to Alaska, extending eastward and gradually merging into its variety the lodge-pole pine (*P. c. latifolia*), the most abundant conifer of the Rocky Mountains. The latter differs from the shore pine, which is of scrubby appearance, in being more imposing, slenderer, pyramidal, and taller, occasionally up to 150 feet tall, but more commonly not exceeding one-half that height. The shore pine is round-headed and 20 to 30 feet tall. Unlike the lodge-pole pine, it is not hardy in the northeastern United States. Both have rigid needles, twisted and in pairs. Those of the shore pine are up to 2 inches

long, those of the lodge-pole pine somewhat longer. The stalkless cones are conical-ovoid and lopsided, the last-mentioned characteristic being more pronounced in the shore pine than in the other. They persist on the trees and often remain closed without discharging their seeds for years. The umbos of their scales have a fragile prickle.

Indigenous to California and Baja California, the bishop pine (*P. muricata*) has 4- to 7-inch-long, stiff, dark green leaves in pairs that form tufts at the branch ends.

Pinus muricata, Royal Botanic Gardens, Kew, England

Pinus muricata with female flowers

Attaining a height of 50 to 90 feet, it is round-headed or flattish-topped, with stout, spreading branches. Its lopsided, stalkless cones are conical-ovoid and 2 to 3½ inches in length; they remain closed without discharging their seeds for many years. Their umbos have a stout, triangular spine. The seeds are black. This handsome species is not hardy in the north.

American native pines inconstant in the number of leaves in each bundle include several of importance. In the eastern part of the continent are the shortleaf pine, table mountain pine, and slash pine. Western species in this group are the Monterey pine, knob-cone pine, the Mexican stone pine, the nut pine, the Western yellow pine, and the Jeffrey pine.

The shortleaf pine (*P. echinata*) ranges from New York to Illinois, Florida, and Texas. A broad-ovoid-headed species 75 to 125 feet in height, and often with drooping branches, its leaves are slender, flexible, bluish-green, and 3 to 5 inches long. Most commonly they are in twos, sometimes in threes. Its conical-egg-shaped, symmetrical cones are about 2 inches long. The umbos of the cone scales are furnished with a short spine. This handsome tree is hardy in southern Massachusetts.

Pinus pungens (cones)

The table mountain pine (*P. pungens*) is indigenous from New Jersey and Pennsylvania to Georgia and Tennessee. It rarely is 60 feet, more usually not more than about 30 feet tall, and forms a broad, often wide, open head. Most commonly its stiff, twisted leaves, 1½ to 3 inches long, are in twos, more rarely in threes. They are dark green. The conical-egg-shaped, symmetrical cones, 2 to almost 4 inches long, have scales with umbos that end in a strong, curved spine.

The slash pine (*P. elliottii*), not hardy in the north, is native from South Carolina to Florida and Louisiana. This species has been confused with tropical American *P. caribaea*, a species not indigenous to the United States. Sometimes exceeding 100 feet in height, it typically develops a long bare trunk with a crown of branches at its top. Its dark green leaves are crowded and 8 inches to 1 foot long. They are in twos

or threes. The conical-oblong, symmetrical cones, 3 to 6½ inches long, have scales with umbos furnished with a tiny, recurved prickle.

The Monterey pine (*P. radiata* syn. *P. insignis*) is too tender for the northeastern United States, but is highly esteemed for planting in comparatively mild climates. It is much used for forestry in New Zealand,

Pinus radiata

Australia, South Africa, and parts of South America. It is handsome and has an irregular open head of stout, spreading branches and luxurient, grass-green foliage. Its leaves, in twos or threes, are slender and 4 to 6 inches long. The lopsided, short-stalked or stalkless, down-pointed cones are conical-egg-shaped, 3 to 6 inches in length, and in clusters. The umbos of their scales have a minute spine. The cones often remain on the branches for many years without dispersing their seeds. The Monterey pine is native in limited areas in California and Baja California. The leaves of *P. r. binata* are in pairs.

Another Westerner with two or three leaves in each bundle, is the knob-cone pine (*P. attenuata*). This tender species, which in the wild ranges from California to Oregon, is not hardy in the north. Ordinarily about 30 feet in height, it occasionally is up to three times as tall. Usually its yellowish-green leaves are slender, rigid, and 3 to 7 inches in length. The cones, narrowly-egg-shaped and 3 to 6 inches long, are short-stalked and lopsided. They are persistant on the branches and remain for years without dispersing their seeds. The popular name of this pine alludes to the conical knoblike projections of the cone scales, each of which has a stout, incurved spine.

The Mexican stone pine or pinon pine (*P. cembroides*) and the nut pine (*P. edulis*) also have leaves in twos or threes. The first is a tender kind, native from Arizona and New Mexico to Mexico. The other hardy in southern New England, is native

from New Mexico to Wyoming. The Mexican stone pine, up to 25 feet tall, has spreading branches and slender, dark green leaves 1 inch to 2 inches long, strongly incurved and mostly in pairs. The almost spherical cones, 1 inch to 2 inches in diameter, have few scales and contain edible, dark brown, narrowly-winged seeds ½ to ¾ inch long. The umbos of the cone scales are broad and blunt. The leaves of the nut pine, mostly in pairs, are ¾ inch to 1½ inches long and rigid. The tree, larger than the Mexican stone pine, may attain a height of 45 feet. The scales of its broad-ovate cones have umbos with a tiny incurved spine. The nut pine, bushy when young, round-topped in age, has horizontal branches. Its seeds were an important food of the Indians. The cones are ¾ inch to 1½ inches long and almost stalkless.

The Western yellow or ponderosa pine (*P. ponderosa*), one of the giants of its race, has leaves usually in threes, but ranging from two to five in a cluster. This

Pinus ponderosa (cones)

rather variable species is indigenous to a vast area from British Columbia to the Rocky Mountains, South Dakota, Nebraska, Texas, southern California, and possibly northern Mexico. It has the widest natural distribution of any western North American pine and is the second tallest, being exceeded only by the sugar pine (*P. lambertiana*). It grows under widely varying conditions and kinds of soil and is hardy in southern New England. Attaining a maximum height of 230 feet, the Western yellow pine typically develops a spirelike outline with spreading or more or less pendulous branches, but sometimes is broader and has a shorter trunk. From *P. coulteri* it differs in its more slender winter buds and smaller cones without strongly hooked spines, and from closely related *P. jeffreyi* in its darker bark, resinous winter buds with the tips of their scales not free, and the leaves not being bluish-green. There are other microscopic technical differences. The Western yellow pine hybridizes naturally with both *P. coulteri* and *P. jeffreyi*. Its rigid, spreading, sharp-pointed leaves, which last three years, are 5 to 10 inches long, curved, and densely crowded. The solitary or clustered, stalkless or nearly stalkless, egg-shaped cones are 3 to 8 inches in length and have the umbos of their scales furnished with a minute prickle. When they fall they often leave a few of the lower scales attached to the branchlets. The Rocky Mountain form of the species, distinguished as *P. p. scopulorum*, has usually shorter needles and more drooping branches than the more western typical kind, and its cones, about 3 inches long, are shorter. Variety *P. p. arizonica* has leaves 4 to 7 inches long, in clusters of three, four, or five, and slightly lopsided cones 2 to 3 inches long and almost as broad. Other varieties are *P. p. crispata*, with curved leaves; *P. p. pendula*, with markedly drooping branches; *P. p. tortuosa*, with contorted branches and stout, twisted, glaucous green leaves; and *P. p. scopulorum* 'Koolhaas', a compact variety with pendulous branches the lower ones of which are prostrate on the ground, and a nodding leading shoot.

The Jeffrey pine (*P. jeffreyi*) is similar to the Western yellow pine and has been considered a variety of that species. The chief differences are detailed above under Western yellow pine. Up to 180 feet tall and chiefly Californian, it extends into Baja California, Nevada, and Oregon. It hybridizes naturally with *P. ponderosa* and *P. coulteri*.

The curious single-leaf pine (**P. monophylla**) is the only species of pine with usually solitary leaves (occasionally they are paired). There are horticultural varieties of other species, however, that have this characteristic. It is closely related to, and by some botanists considered to be a variety of, the Mexican stone pine (*P. cembroides*). It is also similar to the nut pine (*P. edulis*). From both it differs chiefly in its solitary leaves. The single-leaf pine, hardy as far north as southern New England, grows slowly and may attain a height of 50 feet, but often does not exceed more than one-half that. Its rigid, dark green leaves are ¾ inch to 1½ inches long. Its nearly stalkless, broadly-egg-shaped cones are 1½ to 2 inches in length. The flattened umbo of each cone scale has a minute tiny recurved spine.

Another maverick species of the same botanical relationship is **P. quadrifolia** (syn. *P. parryana*). A rare native of southern California and Baja California, its stiff, light glaucous-green leaves are most commonly in bundles of four, more rarely in

threes or fives, and are 1½ to 1¾ inches long. This species attains a height of about 40 feet and is pyramidal. Its cones are nearly spherical and have scales with a tiny recurved spine to the umbo. This is not hardy in the north.

Old World pines with five leaves in each cluster include five of considerable ornamental value. Three are completely Asian, the Swiss stone pine (*P. cembra*) is indigenous from northern Asia to the Alps of central Europe, and the Macedonian pine (*P. peuce*) to the Balkans.

The Japanese white pine (*P. parviflora*) is a wide tree that attains a maximum height of 90 feet, but in cultivation is often not over 30 to 50 feet tall. Pyramidal when young, it is flat-topped when aged. It has horizontal, slender branches with crowded, usually rather rigid, curved, bluish-green leaves that are markedly white on their inner surfaces and are in clusters of five. In brushlike tufts at the branch ends and 1 inch to 2½ inches long, they do not fall until they are three or four years old. The nearly stalkless, egg-shaped cones are 2 to

Pinus parviflora

Pinus parviflora (cones)

3 inches long and have a few rounded scales. They are in clusters of three to four and remain on the branches for six or seven years. Variety *P. p. brevifolia* has leaves 1 inch long. The leaves of *P. p. glauca* are stiffer and more glaucous than those of the typical species. The Japanese white pine is hardy in southern New England.

The Korean pine (*P. koraiensis*) differs from the Japanese white pine in having leaves mostly 2½ to 4½ inches in length. They are white-lined and in bundles of five. From the Eastern white pine (*P. strobus*), of North America, it is distinguishable by its young shoots being decidedly pubescent, and from the Swiss stone pine

Pinus koraiensis

(*P. cembra*), by its usually longer leaves and longer cones. The Korean pine grows slowly and, although in its homeland it attains a height of 75 to 100 feet or more, it is much lower as known in cultivation in North America and is well adapted for use where space is fairly limited. It has a pyramidal head. The cones, 3½ to 6 inches long, are ovoid-conical and have blunt scales recurved at their tips. The seeds are edible. This species, native to Japan, Korea, and Manchuria, is hardy in New England and southern Canada.

One of the most beautiful and elegant of pines, the Himalayan white pine (**P. wallichiana** syns. *P. excelsa*, *P. griffithii*, *P. nepalensis*) is native from western China to Afghanistan and in places covers great areas as one-species forests. Among Himalayan conifers this is second only to the deodar cedar (*Cedrus deodara*) in its importance as timber. It is up to 150 feet in height and forms a broad, open, pyramidal head of wide-spreading, horizontal to slightly ascending, branches. A conspicuous feature is its gracefully drooping, slender leaves 5 to 8 inches long, in bundles of five, and grayish or bluish-green. In section they are triangular and are usually abruptly bent close to their bases. The cy-

A young specimen of *Pinus wallichiana*

Pinus wallichiana zebrina (foliage)

shaped, contain edible seeds. Its young shoots are very downy. It is indigenous in the mountains of southern Europe from the Alps to the Carpathians and is hardy through most of New England. A closely related, five-needled kind previously known as *P. c. sibirica* is the Siberian pine (*P. sibirica*). This is taller and faster growing and is confined as a native to the northern part of European Russia and Siberia. It is very hardy, but not important horticulturally. In Russia its seeds are used for food.

The Macedonian pine (*P. peuce*), sometime 100 feet in height, is slow-growing and narrowly-pyramidal and has ascending branches. Its leaves, in groups of five,

Pinus peuce

Pinus canariensis in California

Pinus canariensis (foliage)

lindrical cones, 6 to 10 inches long, are on stalks 1 inch to 2 inches long. Variety *P. w. monophylla* has single leaves (apparently the result of the five leaves that are normal for the species being joined into one). Variety *P. w. nana*, dwarf and bushy, has shorter leaves. In variety *P. w. zebrina*, the leaves are horizontally banded with yellow and green. This species is hardy in southern New England. In favorable climates it grows rapidly. From *P. ayacahuite* and *P. armandii* the Himalayan white pine is distinguished by its shoots being completely hairless, and from the Macedonian pine (*P. peuce*) by being much broader and having longer, more flexible leaves.

The Swiss stone pine (*P. cembra*), up to 100 feet high, has leaves in fives and is most closely related to the Korean pine, but differs in being narrower, denser, and in having cones 2½ to 3½ inches in length. This sort, pyramidal until mature, then assumes a rounded outline. Its soft, gray-green leaves are 2 to 5 inches long. Its cones, shortly-stalked and bluntly-egg-

which remain for three years, are slender, sharp-pointed, and 3 to 4¼ inches long. The cones, cylindrical and curving, are 4 to 6 inches long and have scales very noticeably hollowed below their tips. The Macedonian pine is much like the Himalayan pine (*P. wallichiana*), but slenderer, with shorter leaves. It somewhat resembles the Swiss stone pine (*P. cembra*), but has hairless young shoots. It is hardy through most of New England.

Three-leaved pines of the Old World include three of importance as ornamentals, the Canary Island pine, the chir pine, and the lacebark pine. They are very beautiful and quite different from each other. The Canary Island pine (*P. canariensis*), native of the islands its name indicates, resembles the chir pine but obviously belongs with the pines that inhabit the Mediterranean region and adjacent areas. Attaining a height of 80 feet and developing a broad, round-topped head of slender branches and drooping branchlets, this species has pendulous and spreading light green leaves in bundles of three, and 9 inches to 1 foot in length. The glossy cones, cylindrical-ovoid, are 4 to 9 inches long and have blunt umbos. Its seeds are ½ inch long. Trunk and branches are usually fur-

nished with short leafy branchlets and its winter buds have conspicuous, reflexed, white-fringed scales. This is hardy in mild climates only.

The chir pine (*P. roxburghii*), not hardy in cold climates, is cultivated in California. Native to the Himalayas, it has drooping leaves in bundles of three, 9 inches to 1 foot long, and is especially handsome when young. In its homelands it is important as a timber tree and a source of rosin. Its cones, 4½ to 8 inches long, are egg-shaped. They differ from those of *P. canariensis* in that the exposed parts of the scales are elongated and reflexed.

The lacebark pine (*P. bungeana*) is named in allusion to its most striking feature, the character of the bark of mature specimens. This flakes and shows dappled patches of grayish-green, light gray, and chalky-white, the white areas increasing in size and merging as the tree ages. The branches are grayish-green. The lacebark pine, a rare native of the mountains of central China, is planted by the Chinese near temples. In cultivation it is normally a bushy tree up to 50 feet in height, often branching and producing a number of sec-

Pinus bungeana

Pinus bungeana (bark)

Pinus mugo mugo

Pinus sylvestris in Scotland

Pinus sylvestris (branch system)

Pinus sylvestris (leaves and cone)

ondary trunks from near the ground. In the wild it may be 80 to 100 feet tall. Its foliage is rather sparse, the leaves, in threes, stiff, sharp-pointed, two-edged, and 2 to 3 inches long. They persist for four or five years. The conical-ovoid, nearly stalkless cones, 2 to 3 inches long, have umbos ending in a recurved triangular spine. The lacebark pine is one of the loveliest of its race. It grows as a native on limestone soils and is hardy through most of New England. Except for the Himalayan *P. gerardiana* it is the only three-leaved pine with sheaths at the bottoms of the leaf bundles that are deciduous. Because individuals vary greatly in the intensity of the whiteness of their bark, whenever possible propagation of the lacebark pine should be by grafting scions taken from a tree of known high quality, rather than by raising plants from seeds.

Two-leaved pines of the Old World include several of the most important cultivated species. Here belong the Swiss mountain pine, the Scots pine, the Austrian pine, the Italian stone pine, the Japanese black pine, and the Japanese red pine, to name only some of the better known.

The Swiss mountain pine (*P. mugo* syn. *P. montana*) includes several, not always easy to differentiate varieties. The most familiar is the dwarf, bushy, mugo pine (*P. m. mugo*), popular for use in foundation plantings and for other places where an evergreen shrub rather than a tree is more appropriate. Selected forms of this have been given identifying names such as *compacta*, 'Gnom', and *slavinii*. The Swiss mountain pine, 40 feet in height, is pyramidal. The mugo pine, not often over 3 to 4 feet in height but sometimes 10 feet or more, is rounded or billowy in outline. The leaves of the Swiss mountain pine are stiff, bright green, and paired, 1 inch to 3 inches long and twisted. They persist for five or more years. Its almost stalkless, egg-shaped cones are ¾ inch to 2½ inches long. Their scales have umbos that end in a spine. Variety *P. m. pumilio* differs from *P. m. mugo* only in minor technical details of the cones. Although identified as the Swiss mountain pine, this species has a much wider natural distribution than its name suggests. It occurs in the mountains from the Pyrenees to the Carpathians, but is nowhere common. At lower altitudes it gradually mingles with, and perhaps hybridizes with, the Scots pine (*P. sylvestris*). The Swiss mountain pine and the Scots pine are closely related, differing in anatomical details of their leaves and in the Scots pine having longer-stalked cones and lighter green foliage, as well as being taller. The Swiss mountain pine and its varieties are very hardy.

The Scots or Scotch pine (*P. sylvestris*) is one of the most familiar conifers of the Old World and is planted considerably in North America both for ornament and the commercial production of Christmas trees. For the last purpose it is well adapted, but as an ornamental, in most parts of the east where it may be grown, it is not as good as many other pines. Its orange bark is certainly attractive, but the tree tends to become unkempt and not sightly after thirty or forty years. In the wild the Scots pine inhabits a tremendous range, throughout northern Europe and Asia from the Atlantic to the Pacific and extending in pockets even to the Mediterranean. It exhibits considerable variation, and during the centuries it has been in cultivation many variants have been recognized by botanical and horticultural varietal names. The Scots pine is extremely hardy and will grow almost as far north as it is possible for trees to survive. Commonly 70 to 100 feet in height, it sometimes grows up to 150 feet. As a mature tree it usually has a long clear trunk that branches at the top to form an irregular flat crown; as a young tree it is pyramidal. Its stiff, glaucous-gray-green, twisted leaves, in pairs, are 1 inch to 4 inches long. They remain for about three years. The cones are mostly conical-egg-shaped and are solitary or in clusters of two or three. They have short stalks and are 1 inch to 3 inches in length. The umbo of each scale terminates in a short prickle. From the closely related Swiss mountain pine (*P. mugo*), the Scots pine differs in being much taller and having the tips of its bud scales free.

For the most part the numerous botanical variations of the Scots pine have little or no horticultural significance, and even the named horticultural varieties are not very commonly cultivated. Among varieties recognized are *P. s. argentea*, with very glaucous leaves and silvery cones; *P. s. aurea*, a slow-growing bushy kind with yellowish foliage; *P. s. beuvronensis*, an extremely dwarf, dome-shaped shrub suitable for rock gardens; *P. s. compressa*, a dwarf, narrow, columnar tree with glaucous, blue-green foliage and tiny cones; *P. s. fastigiata*, similar in shape to the last named, but faster growing and not a dwarf; *P. s. nana*, similar to *P. s. beuvronensis* but less compact; *P. s. pendula*, which has drooping branches; *P. s. variegata*, with leaves variegated with yellowish-white; and *P. s. viridis-compacta*, a loose, pyramidal bush with bright grass-green foliage.

The Austrian pine (**P. nigra**) is an outstanding ornamental, much esteemed for landscape planting and hardy through

Pinus nigra (bark)

most of New England. It is dense and pyramidal when young, round-topped when aged. A rapid grower, this pine has very rigid dark green leaves, usually 3 to 4 inches long, but sometimes more, which it retains for three years. The stalkless, egg-shaped cones, 2 to 3½ inches long, have scales with a flattened umbo, usually with a short spine. This species is native to Europe and western Asia. Variety *P. n. austriaca*, described as having shorter needles, does not differ significantly from the typical species. The Crimean pine (*P. n. caramanica* syn. *P. n. pallasiana*), up to 100 feet or more in height, is oval in outline and has many stout branches, the lower ones of which are ascending as are the branchlets. The Pyrenees pine (*P. n. cebennensis*) is 70 to 80 feet tall and has a narrow-pyramidal, rather loose crown of ascending branches. Its leaves are flexible. Variety *P. n. hornibrookiana* is a dwarf, compact bush with leaves 2 to 2½ inches long. It originated as a witch's broom on an Austrian pine at Rochester, New York. The Corsican pine (*P. n. laricio* syn. *P. n.*

poiretiana), up to 120 feet tall, has fewer and shorter branches than the typical Austrian pine. When aged it is flat-topped. A dwarf variety, *P. n. monstrosa* has contorted short branches and crowded leaves. Curious, but not very attractive, *P. n. pendula* has drooping branches. A rare, prostrate variety is *P. n. prostrata*. Variety *P. n. pygmaea* is slow growing and forms a dense, globose shrub. Characterized by its ascending branches and slender outline, *P. n. pyramidalis* was first found at Rochester, New York.

From the Mediterranean region come two fine two-needle pines of rather limited hardiness, the Italian stone pine (*P. pinea*) and the cluster pine (*P. pinaster*). The former has been so long cultivated for its edible seeds that its precise native home is a matter of conjecture. Some think it originated in southwestern Europe, others that it was brought westward by the Etruscans from the eastern Mediterranean area, and yet others that its original home was Crete. These are three of several theories. Be it as it may, this species is now a familiar inhabitant of Mediterranean lands. Up to about 80 feet tall, **P. pinea** has a flattish, umbrella-like crown. Exceedingly picturesque and of asymmetrical outline, it has stiffish, sharp-pointed bright green leaves, slender and about 8 inches long. The cones, egg-shaped to nearly globular, are 4 to 6 inches long. Their scales have

Pinus pinea in Italy

Pinus nigra

Pinus nigra laricio, Royal Botanic Gardens, Kew, England

Pinus pinea planted in 1861 at the Royal Botanic Gardens, Kew, England

flattened umbos. The seeds are edible and ½ to ¾ inch long. This pine is hardy in California and in similar climates, but not in regions appreciably colder. The cluster pine (**P. pinaster**), or maritime pine as it is also called, is considerably hardier. It may be expected to grow as far north as Virginia. It is suitable for seaside locations, but has the disadvantage of being difficult to transplant successfully except when quite young. It is a pyramidal tree up to 100 feet tall, with sometimes drooping branches. Often twisted, and glossy-green, its rigid needles are 5 to 9 inches long. The cones, in clusters, are conical-egg-shaped, short-stalked, and 4 to 7 inches long. They persist on the branches for long periods. Their scales have a spined umbo.

The Aleppo or Jerusalem pine (**P. halepensis**) has leaves in twos or sometimes threes. Of the Mediterranean region species, it has the widest natural distribution.

Pinus halepensis

It occurs from the Atlantic coast of Spain and France to Israel, Jordan, and Asia Minor, and is indigenous in North Africa. It is not native to Aleppo. This species, which is commonly planted in Mediterranean lands, is hardy in mild climates only. It is 50 to 80 feet in height and typically pyramidal, although in cultivation sometimes distinctly round-headed. Its leaves are 2½ to 4½ inches in length and very slender. The short-stalked, conical cones, 2½ to 3½ inches long, point backward along the branches and have scales with spineless umbos. The backward pointing cones and stiffer, usually shorter leaves distinguish the species from P. h. brutia (syn. P. brutia), a less attractive Mediterranean pine. These are the only pines that usually have their needles in pairs and have non-resinous winter buds with recurved scales. A variety of the Aleppo pine, P. h. pityusa, has leaves 1½ to 2 inches long. Variety P. h. stankewiczii differs from the typical kind only in technical details.

Especially well adapted for seashore planting is the Japanese black pine (**P.**

Pinus thunbergiana

thunbergiana syn. P. thunbergii). A native of Japan, and southern Korea, it is hardy throughout much of New England. Dense, spreading, and usually irregularly and rather open-branched, it attains an eventual height of almost 100 feet. Its dark green leaves are 3 to 5 inches long. Serving to distinguish it from many pines are its grayish-white winter buds with fringed scales. The conical-egg-shaped cones are short-stalked and 2 to 3 inches long. The umbos of their flattened scales sometimes end in a small spine.

The Japanese red pine (**P. densiflora**) is a native of Japan, Korea, and China. Up to 100 feet tall, it has orange-red bark, an irregular head of horizontal branches, and

Pinus densiflora

slender bright green leaves 3 to 5 inches in length. The conical cones are short-stalked and 2 inches long. The umbos of their scales sometimes end in a spine. An interesting variety is the tanyosho or Japanese umbrella-pine (P. d. umbraculifera), a low-growing tree with a distinctive umbrella-shaped top. Another variety, sometimes called the dragon's eye pine (P. d. oculus-

Pinus densiflora umbraculifera

Pinus densiflora oculus-draconis (foliage)

draconis), has leaves banded with two yellow lines. More varieties are cultivated in Japan.

Other species in cultivation include these: **P. armandii**, native of western China and up to 60 feet tall, has horizontal spreading or pendulous branches, leaves 4 to 6 inches long in fives and white-lined on their inner surfaces, and stalked, cylindrical cones 4 to 7 inches long. It resembles P. griffithii, but has stouter cones with broader scales and leaves with a distinct bend near their bases. It is hardy in southern New England. **P. balfourana**, the fox-tail pine of California, is a rare mountain species up to 90 feet tall. Pyramidal, it has short, incurved leaves with sheaths partly deciduous, which distinguishes it from all other five-needled species except P. aristata. Its cones, 3½ to 5 inches long, are bigger than those of the last named, and its leaves are without resinous incrustations. It is hardy in southern New England. **P. caribaea**, a name once applied to the slash pine (P. elliottii), is now restricted to a species native to the West Indies and Central America. From the slash pine it differs in having its needles in threes, fours, or less commonly fives. Up to 100 feet tall, it has a rounded or irregular crown, leaves crowded at the branch ends,

Pinus caribaea (trunk)

Pinus caribaea (young specimens)

and reflexed conical cones 2 to 4¾ inches long, with a minute prickle ending the umbo. This is not hardy in the north. *P. clausa,* the sand pine, from Alabama to Florida, is spreading and up to 20 feet tall. Its dark green leaves, in pairs or triplets, are up to 3 inches long. The conical-egg-shaped cones, 2 to 3½ inches long, are in clusters. They remain, often without opening, for many years. This is not hardy in the north. *P. gerardiana* is distinguished from its near ally, the lacebark pine (*P. bungeana*), by its denser foliage, usually longer, slenderer leaves, and larger cones with conspicuously reflexed scales. It attains heights up to 80 feet and sheds its bark, as does the lacebark pine. Its leaves are 2 to 4 inches long, its oblong-egg-shaped cones 6 to 8 inches long. The seeds of this endemic of the Himalayas are an important article of diet in its native lands. This species is not hardy in the north. *P. glabra,* the cedar pine, a scarce native of the southeastern United States from South Carolina southward, is a low-

land, two-needled species up to 120 feet in height with twisted leaves 1½ to 3 inches long and usually solitary, egg-shaped cones up to 2 inches long with a weak spine to each scale. This pine is not hardy in the north. *P. heldreichii,* of the Balkans, is closely related to the Austrian pine (*P. nigra*) and is hardy in southern New England. Up to 80 feet in height, it has bright green leaves in pairs. They are 2½ to 3½ inches long. The cones are 3 inches long, each scale with a short prickle. *P. insularis* (syn. *P. khasyana*), the benguet pine, native of mountains in the Philippine Islands, India, Burma, Thailand, and Vietnam, gradually merges with *P. tabuliformis yunnanensis.* Up to 100 or 150 feet tall, this species has leaves usually in threes, rarely in twos. Bright green, slender, and flexible, they are up to 10 inches long. The symmetrical ovoid-conical cones are 2 to 4 inches long. The benguet pine is hardy only in the tropics and subtropics. *P. leiophylla* is Mexican and not hardy in the north. A tree of moderate size, it has slender branches and leaves in clusters of five. They are 4 to 5 inches long, slender, and gray-green. The umbos of the scales of the ovoid, 1½- to 2½-inch long cones, end in a minute prickle, which usually falls early. The cones do not ripen until their third season and often remain for several years without opening. *P. leucodermis* (syn. *P. heldreichii leucodermis*) inhabits dry, limestone soils in mountains from Italy to Greece and the Balkans. Up to 90 feet tall, it differs from *P. heldreichii* in having grayish-white shoots with leaves only at their ends. The bark is flaky. The rigid leaves, in pairs, are up to 3½ inches long. The glossy cones are 2 to 3 inches long. This pine is hardy in southern New England. Dwarf horticultural varieties are known. *P. luchuensis* is native to the Ryukyu Islands, including Okinawa. Attaining 100 feet in height, it has an umbrella-shaped head. Its leaves, in pairs, are 6 to 8 inches long. The cones are conical-egg-shaped, symmetrical, and up to 2 inches in length. This is not hardy in cold climates. Closely similar, and possibly specifically identical, is *P. taiwanensis,* of Taiwan. *P. massoniana,* a two-leaved pine of China, is sometimes confused in cultivation with the Japanese black pine (*P. thunbergiana*). It differs in having slender leaves 6 to 8 inches long, cone scales with markedly thickened ends, and in technical details. It is not hardy in the north. From the related Japanese red pine (*P. densiflora*) it may be told by its longer leaves and nut-brown instead of gray or brownish cones. *P. merkusii,* the tenasserim pine, is a tropical species with the distinction of being the only pine that occurs naturally south of the Equator, in one small area in Sumatra. Reports that it grows natively in Borneo, Java, and Timor are erroneous, the specimens there were planted by the Dutch. It also is native to

the Philippines Islands, Vietnam, Cambodia, Thailand, and Burma. A two-needled kind, it attains a height up to 100 feet. Its leaves are 7 to 10 inches long. Its cones, solitary or paired and narrowly cylindrical and often curved, are 2 to 3 inches long. *P. montezumae,* a Mexican and Central American species, has bluish-green leaves 7 to 10 inches long, usually in fives, but varying from three to eight in a cluster. Up to 100 feet or more in height, this has egg-shaped to cylindrical, stalked cones, 2½ to 10 inches long, with a minute spine to each scale. It is not hardy in the north. *P. oocarpa,* of Mexico and Central America, has its needles usually in clusters of five, sometimes in fours. Up to 60 feet tall, it forms a compact, rounded crown of bright green foliage; the leaves are 10 to 12 inches long. The egg-shaped cones, 2 to 3½ inches long, are persistent. This pine extends as a native further south than any other New World species. A variant, *P. o. trifoliata* is distinguished by its leaves being in clusters of three. *P. pumila,* the dwarf stone pine of northern Asia and Japan, is a hardy species closely related to the Swiss stone pine (*P. cembra*) and to *P. sibirica.* It is sometimes regarded as a variety of *P. cembra.* A shrub, often prostrate, but up to 10 feet tall, its leaves, in clusters of five, are 1½ to 2 inches long. Its very short-stalked cones, about 2 inches long, do not open. *P. serotina,* the pond pine, is closely related to, and by some botanists is accepted as a variety of, the pitch pine (*P., rigida*). It is a smaller tree with longer leaves, shorter cones, and more resinous winter buds than the latter and inhabits wetter soils. It is native from South Carolina to Florida. *P. tabulaeformis,* the Chinese pine, native of a vast region in northern China, is hardy in southern New England. It varies much from a symmetrical specimen up to 80 feet tall to a flat-topped low, scrubby plant. Its leaves, in pairs or triplets, are crowded, sharp-pointed, and 2 to 6 inches long. The egg-

Pinus tabulaeformis

Pinus tabulaeformis (leaves and cone)

shaped, lopsided cones, are persistent and up to 2 inches long, with the scales barely prickle-pointed. Variety *P. t. yunnanensis* (syn. *P. yunnanensis*) has leaves up to 10 inches long in bundles of three and cones up to 3½ inches in length. From the Japanese black pine (*P. thunbergiana*) the Chinese pine is distinguished by its winter buds being light brown instead of whitish, and from the Japanese red pine (*P. densiflora*) by its cones changing as they mature from pale yellowish-brown to dark nut brown, instead of being grayish or brownish throughout. *P. teocote* is widely distributed in Mexico and Central America and is somewhat variable. It is not hardy in the north. From 30 to 90 feet in height, it has stiff leaves in clusters of from two to five, most commonly three. They last for three years and are 4 to 7 inches long. The cones, about 2¼ inches long, are ovoid-oblong. They mature in their second year, which distinguishes this species from the related *P. leiophylla*. Variety *P. t. macrocarpa* has bigger cones. *P. uncinata* (syn. *P. mugo rostrata*), except for its much greater height, closely resembles *P. mugo*. Up to 75 feet high, this native of Europe has leaves in clusters of two and cones up to 2¼ inches long. Variety *P. u. rotundata* (syn. *P. mugo rotundata*) is shrubby.

Hybrid pines are not numerous and are not of great horticultural importance. Generally their characteristics are intermediate between those of their parents. Hybrids that have been given names are *P. attenuradiata* (*P. attenuata* × *P. radiata*), *P. halepensi-pinaster* (*P. halepensis* × *P. pinaster*), *P. holfordiana* (*P. ayachuite* × *P. griffithii*), *P. hunnewellii* (*P. parviflora* × *P. strobus*), *P. murraybanksiana* (*P. contorta latifolia* × *P. banksiana*), *P. rhaetica* (*P. mugo* × *P. sylvestris*), *P. schwerinii* (*P. griffithii* × *P. strobus*), *P. sondereggeri* (*P. palustris* × *P. taeda*), and *P. wettsteinii* (*P. mugo* × *P. nigra*).

Garden and Landscape Uses. Although their importance as landscape ornamentals is overshadowed by their tremendous use-

fulness to man in other ways, pines must be rated highly as decoratives; at least that is true of many species. In addition to their beauty of form and evergreenness and their delightful "piney" fragrance so noticeable on still warm days, they appeal because of their quite general ability to thrive in soils and situations ill adapted to most evergreens. Basically they are plants of dry or dryish soils of rather low fertility. Few tolerate wet feet. They are lovers of openness. Full sunshine favors them, and indeed is essential to the well-being of practically all. Wind-swept sites are especially to the liking of many. Pines are frugal plants, well designed to secure and conserve to their best use meager supplies of water and nutrients. To these ends their roots range widely and their leaves expose minimum surface, and that protected by a thick and often waxy cuticle. Despite their addiction as natives to soils of low fertility, they respond gratefully to those nearer the gardeners' ideal. They can with confidence be planted in any ordinary soil where drainage presents no unusual problems.

Many, indeed most, pines are extremely picturesque when old. They develop a ruggedness of character and beauty of outline, often asymmetrical, perhaps unexcelled and surely rarely equaled in the plant world. There is a brooding quality about a grove of ancient pines, a dignity to a lone specimen that has weathered many years. Even as younger trees they are handsome, although perhaps less distinctive in their youth than when quite young or quite old, but perfection is not an impressive characteristic of adolescence.

Particular uses of pines that have wide appeal are as windbreaks, shelter belts, and screens, as lawn specimens, and for planting in groves and clumps. They may be fittingly employed in association with buildings and other architectural features. They make splendid backgrounds for shrub and flower beds. Pines can also be successfully grown as hedges. They are used for training as bonsai (Japanese-style dwarfed trees), and some kinds are admirable for planting near the sea. The low-growing mugo pine is a favorite for foundation plantings and rock gardens.

Not all pines are best suited for all purposes, and not all are adapted to every part of North America. Local experience must be used as a guide. Arboretums, botanical gardens, state agricultural experiment stations, and regional nurseries are equipped to advise more specifically regarding selections; here, however, are some general suggestions.

Among the most rapid growing kinds are the Eastern white pine, Austrian pine, Scots pine, and Cuban pine. The red pine and longleaf pine also grow quite quickly. Much slower in attaining size are the lim-

ber pine and the various scrub pines. Among kinds most adaptable to seashore conditions are the Japanese black pine, Italian stone pine, pitch pine, Aleppo pine, shore pine, and the Monterey pine. The Austrian pine also does well near the sea. Of those especially suitable for dry soils are the Canary Island pine, pitch pine, scrub pine, and jack pine. Among the best for the dry atmospheric conditions of the Middle West are the Eastern white pine, Austrian pine, and mugo pine. Kinds that succeed in limestone soils are the Himalayan white pine, Austrian pine, Aleppo pine, and Italian stone pine.

Cultivation. By far the best and most practical way to propagate most pines is by seed. But this method will not do, of course, for horticultural varieties, and cannot be exploited in the case of kinds for which seeds are not available. Then, the propagator must resort to grafting. Fortunately this is a relatively easy and certain way to achieve increase provided it is

A good stand of seedling pines in a cold frame

done by a skilled operator who has a suitable greenhouse available. Understocks are best if of the species to which the pine to be increased belongs, or one that is botanically closely related. Grafting is done in late winter, the side graft, or veneer graft, being the kind used. Seeds sown in fall or spring in well-drained, sandy peaty beds outdoors or in cold frames and protected from the depredations of mice, birds, and other disturbances germinate without difficulty. They may also be sown in pots or flats in a greenhouse in winter in a temperature of 50 to 60°F. Cones of pines that do not when mature naturally open their scales to discharge the seeds may be induced to do so by the judicious application of fire heat.

Pines are light lovers. Some stand a certain amount of shade in their early years, but, except possibly as small seedlings, none is benefited, and after the seedling stage exposure to full sun is ideal. Generous spacing should be allowed between young plants so that they do not crowd or unduly shade each other. The first transplanting from the seed beds should be when they are one or two years old depending upon how closely the plants stand and how large they are. At that time deformed seedlings and runts should be discarded. It is important not to permit the roots to dry. Although many pines grow well in loose sandy, gravelly, and rocky soils, such media are not desirable in nurseries. Except when very small, intact balls of earth must be retained about the roots of pines that are transplanted and it is difficult or impossible to dig such balls in the kinds of soils mentioned. More binding, loamy earths, which do not favor such wide root ramification and which hold together better as root balls, are desirable for pine tree nurseries.

The best planting times are early spring and late summer or early fall. Not all pines are easy to transplant successfully after they are more than a foot or two high, especially from the wild or from sites

A balled and burlapped, nursery-grown Austrian pine delivered for planting

where they have not been transplanted or root pruned at intervals of three to four years as should be done in nurseries. But some kinds, such as the Austrian pine, Eastern white pine, and others commonly employed for landscaping, move without undue difficulty if carefully handled. An increasingly common nursery practice, especially in the West, is to grow young pines in containers. Such stock can be successfully planted out at almost any time.

Pruning pines calls for nice judgment. They do not respond as well as hemlocks, cryptomerias, and certain other conifers, but if handled judiciously the operation can be beneficial. The best way of controlling growth is by shortening the new shoots in spring when they are in the "candle" stage, that is before their leaves begin to spread. If cut back then to from

Pruning a pine by shortening the "candle" of new growth

one-half to one-third their length, the rate of annual extension is very much diminished. It is at this stage that hedges of pines should be pruned or sheared; this should be done yearly. Except when hedge effects are desired, every effort should be made to preserve intact the central leading shoot. If it is injured or removed vigorous specimens may respond by producing several new leading shoots. In such cases it is necessary to remove all except one, early. Some pines tend, even without injury to occasionally develop double or triple leading shoots. Usually all except one should be removed, but with kinds known to be of bushy habit, such as the Chinese lacebark pine (*P. bungeana*) and the mugo pine (*P. mugo mugo*), more than one may be retained. The removal of larger branches from pines is not something to be done without careful thought. If they are merely shortened they rarely make sufficient new growth to repair and hide the results of the operation and an ugly stubbed-back condition is likely to be apparent. Most usually it is better to remove entire branches than to shorten them. However, if this becomes necessary, it is often wise to do it gradually so that the bark of the trunk and of branches that was shaded is not too precipitously exposed to full sun.

Established pines normally need little attention other than any necessary to control pests and diseases. Their fallen needles make a perfect mulch and wherever possible should be allowed to accumulate beneath them. These can, however, be a fire hazard in places where carelessly tossed lighted cigarettes or other sources of conflagration are possibilities. In such areas it is advisable to rake and remove the needles and replace them with a compost of other less flammatory material.

Pests and Diseases. As is to be expected of a group so widely dispersed and so nu-

merous as the pines, they are subject to a number of pests and diseases. Some are geographically comparatively local, others of more general occurrence. If in doubt, the safest plan is to consult a Cooperative Extension Agent, State Agricultural Experiment Station, or other competent authority familiar with local conditions, regarding diagnosis of troubles and their controls. Among diseases that may attack seedlings are damping off and fungus dieback or tip blight. The use of sterilized soil for seed sowing is recommended. Older trees may be infected with blister rusts, cankers, twig blight, needle blight, rusts, and wood decays. Insects that may be troublesome are aphids, bark beetles, borers, caterpillars of the pine shoot moth and other moths, sawflies, false webworm, scale insects, leaf miners, spittle bugs, and weevils.

PINXTERBLOOM. The pinxterbloom or pinxter flower is *Rhododendron periclymenoides*. The Florida pinxter is *Rhododendron canescens*. See Azaleas.

PIP. The seeds of apples, oranges, pears, and some other fruits are called pips and so are single growth buds with roots attached of lily-of-the-valley. The latter, specially grown for forcing out of season and kept in storage until about a month before they are required to bloom, are known as forcing pips.

PIPER (Pi-per) — Pepper, Betel Pepper. Here belongs the tropical vine of which the fruits are peppercorns, ground to produce the familiar spice pepper. Peppers of vegetable gardens belong to the genus *Capsicum*. Their cultivation is dealt with under Peppers. The genus *Piper* belongs to the pepper family PIPERACEAE. It comprises possibly as many as 2,000 species of herbaceous plants, shrubs, small trees, and vines from many warm parts of the world. The name is an ancient one.

Pipers, often aromatic, have alternate leaves, and tail- or catkin-like spikes of minute flowers, usually unisexual, with the sexes on separate plants. The blooms are without calyxes or corollas, and their parts are too small to see easily without a lens. The stamens number one to four, the stigmas two to four. The fruits are dry or fleshy berries.

Pepper of commerce consists of the finely ground, dried fruits of *P. nigrum*. If the skins and pulp are removed and only the seeds ground, white pepper results, black pepper if the skins and pulp are retained and ground with the seeds. Pepper, in terms of crop value is the most important of all species. Twenty-five thousand tons are imported into the United States yearly. Since ancient times, this spice has been one of the most sought products of tropical Asia. The Greeks and Romans took tribute in the form of pepper. Later European nations established the spice trade to the Indies and fought to gain access to and control of the disposition of pepper and other spices.

Common pepper (*P. nigrum*) is a tall, woody, handsome-foliaged, evergreen vine that roots from its stems. Its thickish, broadly-ovate to almost round, stalked, dark green leaves, usually asymmetrical at their rounded bases and 4 to 6 inches long, have five to nine distinct veins. The flowers are usually unisexual. The ripe fruits are red.

Piper nigrum

Piper betle

Betel pepper (*P. betle*) is an evergreen that somewhat resembles the last, but commonly has broader leaves. A tall vine or trailer, native from India to Malaysia, this is the source of betel leaves used in the eastern tropics to wrap betel nuts together with a little powdered lime and selected flavorings, in preparation for chewing. The dark green leaves, ovate to broadly-heart-shaped, are from 3 to 7 inches long by 1½ to more than 3 inches

wide. Their bases are asymmetrical. The flowers are in slender spikes.

A beautiful, hairless foliage vine, *P. ornatum,* of the Celebes and New Britain islands, attains heights of 10 to 15 feet. It has short-pointed, ovate to broadly-heart-

Piper ornatum

shaped, seven-veined leaves, 3 to 5 inches long, with stalks attached to the blades some distance in from their margins. When young, the glossy leaves are intricately traced with slender lines of silvery-pink and dotted with the same color. Later, their luster diminishes and the etchings and spots become whitish. Sometimes confused with the last, *P. crocatum* (syn. *P. ornatum crocatum*), of Peru, has thin, vining stems and longer-pointed, rather narrower, glossy leaves of blackish-olive-green hue clearly marked along the veins with broader bands of silvery-pink and with spots of the same color. The undersides of the leaves are dark purple. Another variegated-leaved vine, *P. porphyrophyllum* is sometimes misidentified in gardens as *Cissus porphyrophyllum*. This, one of the loveliest of foliage vines, is native to the East Indies. It has rows of white bristles along its stems. Its broadly-heart-shaped leaves, quilted in appearance, are 3 to 6 inches long with wine-red undersides. Above, they are moss-green, with pink markings mostly along the yellow veins, and most clearly evident at their junctions. A native of northern India and Burma, *P. sylvaticum* has prostrate stems and erect branches. Its five- to seven-veined gray-green leaves, stipled with silver between the veins and with a pinkish glow, are oblong-lanceolate to broad-ovate or heart-shaped, the upper ones narrower and shorter-stalked than those below. These last have stalks up to 4 inches long and blades 3 to 4 inches long. The male flowers are in threadlike spikes 2 to 3 inches long, the females in shorter, erect spikes. Plain green-leaved *P. kadzura* (syn. *P. futokadsura*) is a trailing vine native

Piper kadzura

in woodlands near seashores in southern Korea, Japan, and the Ryukyu Islands. It has ovate, or on young specimens rounded-heart-shaped leaves 2 to 3½ inches long by up to 1½ inches wide, generally with five prominent veins, and long-pointed at their apexes. Their undersides, paler than the upper ones, often have scattered, soft hairs. The flowers are unisexual with the sexes on separate plants. The spherical, bright red fruits are approximately ⅙ inch in diameter.

Piper auritum

A weak-stemmed shrub, *P. auritum,* native from Mexico to Panama, is 3 to 6 feet tall or sometimes taller. It has broadly-heart-shaped leaves 8 inches to 1¼ feet long with a short stalk winged in its lower part and a pronounced mid-vein with several side veins angling from it in pinnate fashion. Both surfaces, at least along the veins, are furnished with minute hairs. The flowers are in slender, pendent spikes 4 to 9 inches long. In its homelands the seeds and fruits of this species are used for seasoning foods and the plant is employed medicinally as a diaphoretic, diuretic, and stimulant. Another shrubby kind, impressive *P. magnificum* (syn. *P. bicolor*), of Peru, has corky-barked stems, and glossy, bluntly-round-apexed, oblong to ovate, markedly corrugated leaves up to 6 inches in length or sometimes larger, one-half or more as broad and with winged stalks. Their upper surfaces are green, their undersides wine-red to purple. A nearly hairless, broad shrub 4 to 12 feet tall, *P. methysticum* (syn. *Macropiper methysticum*) has prominently jointed, green stems and heart-shaped leaves 5 to 8 inches long by nearly as broad, with from their bases eleven to thirteen strongly evident veins. The sexes are on separate plants, the flowers are in slender spikes usually shorter than the leaves. From the roots of this species an intoxicating beverage called kiva is made. Other shrubby kinds sometimes encountered in cultivation are *P. macrophyllum*, of Mexico, which has heart-shaped, rich glossy green leaves up to 1 foot in length, with a paler midrib and sunken veins, and tropical American *P. peltatum*, a kind with slender stems and smooth, dark green, heart-shaped leaves.

Garden and Landscape Uses and Cultivation. In humid, tropical environments, outdoors and in greenhouses, pipers are among the easiest plants to grow. Horticulturally, they are esteemed as foliage vines and shrubs, and the common pepper and betel pepper are often included in displays of economic plants (plants of commercial importance). All grow luxuriently in fertile, well-drained, moist soil, and appreciate some shade. Indoors, a minimum winter night temperature of 60°F or higher is best for most kinds, but the Japanese species does well at 50°F or even lower (outdoors it even survives light frosts). Temperatures by day and at other seasons may with advantage considerably exceed those maintained on winter nights. Young plants are easily raised from cuttings of firm young shoots set in a greenhouse propagating bench or under approximately similar conditions, in sand, sand and peat moss, vermiculite, perlite, or other suitable rooting medium. Pipers do well in ground beds and in pots and other containers. Wires or other supports must be provided for the vines, or they may be allowed to trail. They also do well in hanging baskets. Occasional pruning or trimming to keep the plants in bounds and from becoming straggly may be needed. This is best attended to in late winter or early spring. Then, too, any repotting needed should be done. From spring to fall, regular applications of dilute liquid fertilizer to specimens that have filled their containers with roots do much to stimulate vigorous growth. In addition to their usefulness in tropical gardens and greenhouses, some pipers, *P. kadzura*, *P. nigrum*, and *P. betle*, for example, offer possibilities as houseplants.

PIPERACEAE — Pepper Family. This family of dicotyledons comprises nine genera totaling 3,000 species of vining or less frequently erect, often more or less succulent, often aromatic herbaceous plants and evergreen woody sorts, some trees. Their stems are generally thickened at the nodes (joints). The undivided, lobeless, and toothless leaves are chiefly alternate, rarely opposite or whorled (in circles of more than two). The minute, bisexual or unisexual flowers are most commonly densely crowded in fleshy, tail- or catkin-like spikes sometimes arranged in umbels. Without calyxes or corollas, they have one to ten stamens and usually one to four stigmas. The fruits are berries. Cultivated genera include *Macropiper*, *Peperomia*, and *Piper*.

PIPEWORT. See Eriocaulon.

PIPSISSEWA. See Chimaphila.

PIPTADENIA (Pipta-dènia). Fewer than a dozen species of trees, shrubs, or rarely climbers are included in *Piptadenia*, of the pea family LEGUMINOSAE. Native from Mexico to tropical South America, the group is of minor garden importance. The name, from the Greek *pipto*, to fall, and *aden*, a gland, alludes to the glands dropping.

Most piptadenias have spines or prickles. The primary divisions of their alternate, twice-pinnate leaves are in opposite pairs and are composed of several to many broad leaflets. The pea-shaped blooms are in long spikes from the leaf axils. They have a five-toothed calyx, a five-lobed corolla, and ten stamens scarcely or not joined. The fruits are straight or slightly curved pods.

A tree or shrub, native of Brazil, *P. rigida* has leaves of three to six pairs of primary divisions, each with numerous narrowly-sickle-shaped leaflets ⅓ inch long. The spikes of white flowers are 1 inch to 1½ inches long. The seed pods are linear and up to 5 inches in length.

Garden and Landscape Uses and Cultivation. Occasionally planted as an ornamental in the tropics and frost-free or essentially frost-free subtropics, the species described here succeed in ordinary soils and sunny locations. It is increased by seed.

PIPTANTHUS (Piptán-thus). Although rarely cultivated in America, the deciduous and partially evergreen shrubs of China and the Himalayas that constitute *Piptanthus*, of the pea family LEGUMINOSAE, appear to be well suited for the milder parts of the United States. In sheltered locations the hardiest kinds probably succeed as far north as Washington, D.C. There are eight species. The name, from the Greek *piptos*, to fall, and *anthos*, a

flower, was applied because the blooms soon drop. This genus is closely related to *Baptisia* and *Thermopsis*, but is readily distinguished by its stipules (appendages at the bases of the leafstalks) being joined together rather than separate or wanting.

Piptanthuses have very pithy young shoots, alternate, stalked leaves of three stalkless leaflets and erect, short, terminal spikes of yellow, pea-shaped flowers. The fruits are flattened, pea-like pods.

The best known sort, *P. nepalensis* (syn. *P. laburnifolius*), from 8 to 12 feet high, has downy young shoots and leaves 3 to 6 inches long. In mild climates much of its

Piptanthus nepalensis

foliage remains through the winter, but toward the northern limits of its hardiness it is deciduous. The leaves, dark green above and glaucous beneath, at first have silky hairs, but soon lose them. The blooms, about 1½ inches long and in stiff, hairy, racemes 2 to 3 inches long and broad, and furnished with hairy bracts, are produced in April or May. This species is native from Nepal to Sikkim and Bhutan.

Much hardier than the last, *P. tomentosus* is a native of China. A slender shrub about 7 feet tall, its young branches are hairy and its leaves, green on both sides, when young are reddish-hairy beneath and conspicuously silky-hairy above. With age they lose some of their hairiness. The flowers are similar to those of *P. nepalensis*, but have calyxes covered with long silky hairs instead of down. In bloom this species is even more beautiful than its Himalayan relative.

Probably the hardiest sort is *P. concolor*, of western China. Attaining a height of about 6 feet and with white-pubescent young branches, this has leaves green on both sides. They are slightly pubescent only when young. The flowers, about 1 inch long, have silky-hairy calyxes. Variety *P. c. yunnanensis*, from southwest China, is distinguished by its young branches being only slightly hairy or hairless, its leaves being glaucous beneath, and by its slightly bigger flowers and narrower seed pods.

Garden Uses. Piptanthuses are attractive, showy shrubs for early bloom in sunny locations and well-drained soils. They can be used effectively in shrub borders and other plantings.

Cultivation. Because these plants usually suffer from transplanting it is advisable to grow them in pots until they are big enough to plant in their permanent locations. They are usually raised from seeds sown in a cold frame or outdoors in a protected place as soon as they are ripe or in spring, or they may be grown from summer cuttings made so that the basal cut passes through the solid part of the stem at a node and does not expose a large area of pith. The young plants grow quickly and are ready for setting where they are to remain when about one year old. If larger specimens for planting are desired, they can be maintained in pots until they are two years old. No regular pruning is needed, but any necessary to keep the plants shapely should be done as soon as flowering is finished.

PIQUERIA (Piquèr-ia) — Stevia. Gardeners and florists invariably use stevia, which is the name of a related genus, as the common name for the only species of *Piqueria* that appears to be in cultivation. The genus *Piqueria* belongs in the daisy family COMPOSITAE and consists of twenty species of opposite-leaved, tender shrubs and herbaceous perennials, natives from Mexico to the Andes and the West Indies. Its name commemorates the eighteenth-century Spanish botanist, A. Piquer.

A nonhardy herbaceous perennial, *P. trinervia* is often misnamed *Stevia serrata*. It is 3 to 4 feet tall, and has oblong-lanceolate, toothed leaves and large loose clusters of small, fluffy heads of creamy-white flowers without ray florets. It is a native of Mexico. In addition to the typical species there is a dwarfer, more compact variety

Piqueria trinervia

and one with double flowers. The fruits are seed-like achenes.

Garden Uses. This plant can be grown outdoors as a perennial in frost-free and nearly frost-free climates and is cultivated in greenhouses to supply flowers for cutting during fall and winter. Its blooms last well in water and are especially useful for associating with more massive flowers, such as chrysanthemums, carnations, daffodils, and tulips; they serve much the same purpose in flower arrangements as baby's breath (*Gypsophila*). It can also be used as a decorative pot plant for embellishing conservatories and display greenhouses.

Cultivation. When grown in greenhouses this plant is propagated each year from cuttings, which old plants, cut back after flowering, produce in abundance. The cuttings, made and inserted in a propagating bench in a cool greenhouse in spring, root readily and are then potted in 2½-inch pots. When about 3 inches high their tips are pinched out and one or two later pinchings may be done to encourage bushiness. The plants may be transplanted 10 inches to 1 foot apart in July to greenhouse benches or beds filled with moderately fertile porous soil, or they may be planted in outdoor nursery beds to be lifted in fall before frost and set then in greenhouse beds or benches. If this latter practice is followed, they should be dug with as little damage to the roots as possible, be well watered immediately after planting, and if practicable be lightly shaded for a few days. Spraying the foliage with water several times on sunny days assists in preventing wilting during the time the roots are becoming reestablished. If stevias are to be grown as pot plants, they are repotted, as growth demands, until they occupy containers 6 to 9 inches in diameter and are either grown on in the greenhouse or are stood outdoors or in a deep cold frame for the summer. Whichever mode of cultivation is followed stevias need full sun and, without maintaining the soil in a constantly saturated condition, ample supplies of moisture. After their containers are well filled with healthy roots, pot-grown specimens benefit from weekly applications of dilute liquid fertilizer.

This is an easy crop to grow in a sunny, airy greenhouse with a winter night temperature of 45 to 50°F and which is ventilated freely when the day temperature is higher by five to ten degrees. Excessive humidity is to be guarded against in winter. When grown in pots piquerias are likely to need staking. When grown outdoors in mild climates as a perennial this plant needs a sunny location, ordinary fertile, reasonably moist garden soil; it may be increased by division in spring.

Diseases and Pests. Basal rotting may occur in cuttings in propagating benches;

this is prevented by using sterilized sand, vermiculite, or perlite as a rooting medium. The plant is also subject to aster virus yellows. Pests that sometimes infest it are aphids and white fly.

PISONIA (Pi-sònia). This genus of about fifty species of the four o'clock family NYCTAGINACEAE, widely dispersed in the tropics and subtropics of both hemispheres, consists of trees, shrubs, and rarely woody climbers. The name *Pisonia* commemorates the Dutch naturalist and physician William Piso, who died in 1648.

Pisonias are sometimes spiny. Their leaves are stalked, and alternate, opposite, or more or less whorled (in circles of more than two). The small flowers, in terminal or lateral clusters, are usually unisexual with the sexes on different plants, less often the sexes are on the same plant; rarely the blooms are bisexual. They are without petals, but have a four- or five-lobed, bell-shaped calyx. The stalks of the six to ten stamens unite to form a tube. The style is slender. The fruits are technically achenes, partly embedded in the calyxes. Often they are extremely sticky.

The para-para or bird-catching tree (*P. umbellifera* syn. *Heimerliodendron brunonianum*) is a native of Australia, New Zealand, the Bonin Islands, and Mauritius. A tree sometimes over 20 feet in height, it has short-stalked, oblong to oblong-elliptic leaves up to 1¼ feet long and 4 inches wide that are opposite or whorled (in circles of more than two). The inconspicuous pinkish, yellowish, or greenish flowers are in terminal, hairy clusters 2 to 4 inches across. The ribbed fruits 1 inch to 1½ inches long have persistent calyxes. They are covered with a sweet, sticky substance, for which reason the early settlers of New Zealand named it the bird-catching tree. The Maoris knew it as the para-para. In Hawaii, where it inhabits dry and semidry regions and was called papala kepau, the fruits were employed to catch birds, the feathers of which were used to make

Pisonia umbellifera variegata

cloaks and helmets for the chiefs. A very handsome, variegated-foliaged variety, *P. u. variegata* has leaves marbled with two shades of green and edged with creamy-white. The young leaves are tinged red or pink along their midribs.

Garden and Landscape Uses and Cultivation. In tropical and subtropical climates, this evergreen and its variety are handsome garden ornamentals. They thrive in any fairly good soil in sun or partial shade. They are also attractive for setting in ground beds in large conservatories and for growing in containers for the decoration of greenhouses and as houseplants. When cultivated indoors they respond to what gardeners term intermediate temperatures. This means that the minimum winter night temperature is about 55°F and the daytime temperature is five to ten degrees higher. In spring and summer warmer conditions are appropriate. A moderately humid atmosphere is desirable, and from spring to fall, shade from strong sun. A fertile, porous, coarse potting soil, freely drained, suits them best. It should be maintained in an evenly moist, but not wet condition. In winter, rather drier soil conditions than those maintained at other seasons are recommended. Specimens that have filled their pots with roots can be maintained in good condition for a long time by fertilizing regularly from spring through fall with dilute liquid fertilizer. Repotting or top dressing is done in late winter or spring, and at that time any pruning needed to shape the plant or limit its size should be done. Cuttings and air layerings are satisfactory methods of propagation. The cuttings are planted in a mixture of sand and peat moss or other favored propagating medium in a humid, shaded, propagating bench in a tropical greenhouse.

PISTACHE. See Pistacia.

PISTACHIO NUT is *Pistacia vera.*

PISTACIA (Pis-tàcia) — Pistachio or Pistache. The pistachio nut of commerce is a familiar product of one species of this genus of ten of the cashew family ANACARDIACEAE. A native chiefly of the Mediterranean region and warm, dry regions in Asia, *Pistacia* is represented also by one species that inhabits the Canary Islands, and one species the warm parts of North and Central America. The name, pronounced pistashia, is an adaptation of the Latin one for the pistachio nut tree.

The first known source of turpentine, used by early painters in oils, was the terebinth tree (*P. terebinthus*). Because most came from the Mediterranean island of Chios it was called, and still is, Chian turpentine. Mastic, a product of *P. lentiscus*, is used in the Orient for chewing and to flavor wine. More widely it is employed as

a cement for jewels and theatrical beards, and is a component in gilt varnishes; in industry it is used in photomechanical reproduction and for other purposes.

Pistacias are small to medium-sized, aromatic, evergreen or deciduous trees and shrubs with alternate, pinnate leaves with or without a terminal leaflet. The small, petal-less flowers are in racemes or panicles from the leaf axils or branch ends. They are unisexual, the males with a five-lobed or five-parted calyx and five stamens, the females with a calyx three- or four-parted or lobed, and with a three-lobed style. The fruits are dry drupes (fruits structured like plums). Pistachio nuts are the kernels or seeds of the drupes. In preparing them for market, the soft outer flesh that surrounds the nuts is removed and the nuts are dried or soaked in brine. Often their shells are dyed bright, attractive colors.

The pistachio tree (*P. vera*), a native of the Mediterranean region and adjacent Asia, is an evergreen up to about 30 feet tall. It has spreading branches, and leaves, at first hairy, later hairless, with up to five pairs of bluntly-ovate, nearly stalkless leaflets, but no terminal one. The ovoid to oblongish, wrinkled, reddish fruits contain seeds with tasty pale green or yellow kernels. There are several commercial varieties of this species.

The mastic tree (*P. lentiscus*), of the Mediterranean region, is an evergreen shrub or tree up to about 15 feet in height. Its winged-stalked leaves have six, eight, or ten glossy, leathery, blunt leaflets about 1 inch long, with the undersurfaces paler than the upper ones. The spherical fruits, about 1 inch in diameter and at first reddish, become black when fully ripe. Another Mediterranean species, *P. terebinthus* is a small, deciduous tree. Its leaves have slightly winged stalks and nine to thirteen leaflets. The flowers, in axillary panicles, have purplish stamens and reddish stigmas. The slightly flattened and wrinkled, roundish fruits are dark purple.

Pistacia chinensis

An ornamental, *P. chinensis* is a deciduous tree of China, with foliage rather resembling that of an ash (*Fraxinus*) that colors attractively before it falls; it is often represented in Chinese paintings. Up to about 60 feet in height, it has leaves with four to six pairs, without a terminal one, of lanceolate leaflets. The fruits change as they mature from scarlet to purple. They are the size of peppercorns.

American *P. mexicana* is an evergreen shrub or short-trunked tree up to 30 feet in height. Its leaves have an uneven number, nine to twenty-nine, of blunt, ovate to wedge-shaped leaflets. Its flowers are in panicled spikes from the leaf axils. The somewhat flattened, dryish, purplish fruits, up to ⅕ inch in diameter, contain edible seeds. This occurs as a native from Texas to Mexico and Guatemala.

Garden and Landscape Uses and Cultivation. Pistacias are best suited to warm, dry climates and generally are satisfied with poorish, dryish soils. The pistachio tree prospers under conditions that suit olives, but is slightly hardier. It is grown chiefly for its nuts, which are produced only if the female flowers are fertilized with pollen from a male tree. To assure this, it is usual when planting orchards to set male trees in the proportion of one to five to seven females. The trees are spaced about 25 feet apart. Chinese *P. chinensis* is a very good ornamental, suitable for planting as a specimen or in company with other trees and shrubs. It is also used as an understock on which to graft the pistachio nut tree. The hardiest species, it survives outdoors at Washington, D.C.

PISTIA (Píst-ia)—Water-Lettuce. Only careful examination of its flowering parts reveals that the water-lettuce belongs in the arum family ARACEAE. Even then, the observer must be versed in botany. Without such understanding it is about as easy to accept the water-lettuce as kin to the completely unrelated salad lettuce as to believe that it is close kin of calla-lilies, jack-in-the-pulpits, and philodendrons. The name *Pistia* may be derived from the Greek *pistillum*, the female organ, alluding to the form of the spathe or from the Greek *pistos*, watery, referring to the habitat. There is only one species, *P. stratiotes*, a native of many warm parts of the world, including the United States from Florida to Texas.

The water-lettuce is beautiful. Normally free-floating, but in very shallow water rooting into mud, it has rosettes of grooved, shell-like, velvety-scurfy, light green, spongy leaves 4 to 8 inches in length. In much the manner of a waxed surface they shed water freely. Most gardeners never see the inflorescences (flowers and associated parts) that develop in the leaf axils. The small spathe, which represents the petal-like organ that in the

Pistia stratiotes

Pistia stratiotes (foliage)

Pistia stratiotes (flowers)

calla-lily envelops the central columnar yellow spadix, is white and leaflike. The spadix (the equivalent of the center spike in a calla-lily) is joined to it and is shorter. The minute unisexual flowers are on the spadix and both sexes are on the same plant. The water-lettuce multiplies freely by offsets.

Garden Uses and Cultivation. This is one of the prettiest of plants for decorating tropical pools. It does not thrive in aquariums nor can it be grown well if the temperature of the water and of air above it is less than 70°F. Higher temperatures are advantageous. Slightly acid, soft water, preferably rain water, over a soil bottom that supplies nutrients to the water, is most to the liking of the water-lettuce. Good light is essential.

Propagation is by offsets and by seeds sown in spring or summer in pots or pans (shallow pots) of sandy peaty soil. Cover the seeds with ¼ inch of sand, then stand the containers with the sand surface 1 inch above the water. In bright light and a temperature of 82°F, the seeds soon germinate and within two months the plants will be big enough to be set floating.

PISTIL. The female part of a flower consisting of an ovary, a stigma, and usually between them a style. The pistil occupies the center of the bloom and may consist of one carpel or of two or more carpels that are united. If there is more than one separate carpel, each is called a pistil. In male flowers the pistil is absent or is rudimentary and nonfunctional.

PISUM (Pi-sum) — Pea. Half a dozen species, of which only the common edible pea has garden importance, belong in this European and western Asian genus of the pea family LEGUMINOSAE. The name is the ancient Latin one for the pea.

The species of *Pisum* are annuals and perennial herbaceous plants with pinnately-divided leaves of up to three pairs of leaflets, and ending in branching tendrils. At the bases of the leaves are large leaf-life appendages called stipules. The flowers are solitary or in few-flowered racemes from the leaf axils. White or variously colored, they have ten stamens, nine of which are joined in a tube around the style, and one separate. Down one side of the style runs a row of hairs. The fruits are pods of the well-known pea type.

The garden pea (*P. sativum*) is a vining annual (some dwarf horticultural varieties have little tendency to climb) that attaches itself by tendrils. It is hairless and more or less glaucous. Its leaves have one to three pairs of leaflets and stipules mostly bigger than the leaflets. Solitary to two to three together, the white to purple flowers have their wing petals joined to the keel. They are succeeded by pods up to 4 inches long containing smooth or wrinkled seeds. Variety *P. s. elatius* has lilac or purple blooms, in racemes longer than the leaves, and granular seeds.

From prehistoric times the pea has been cultivated for human food and fodder. Its blooms are what are thought of as typically pea-shaped, which means that they have a large upper, erect petal, the standard or banner petal; two horizontal or wing petals; and two forward-pointing, more or less joined petals that form a keel. The exact origin of the garden pea is lost in antiquity. In the wild it is known only as an escapee from cultivation. Cultivated varieties are grouped as *P. s. humile*, early, dwarf varieties; *P. s. macrocarpon*, the edible-podded kinds; and *P. s. arvense*, which has smaller pods and seeds and is grown for forage and as a cover crop. The garden pea is of particular interest because it was with it that the classic studies of heredity of Gregor Mendel were achieved. For cultivation see Pea.

PIT. The seeds of apples, cherries, oranges, peaches, pears, and some other fruits are sometimes called pits.

PIT FRAME and PIT GREENHOUSE. These are garden structures often simply referred to as pits and so constructed that their floors are considerably below the level of the ground outside. Pits are most commonly used for propagating and forcing and for accommodating and overwintering plants too tall for ordinary cold frames. They are less expensive to construct than conventional greenhouses, re-

A pit frame or pit greenhouse

quire less artificial heat to maintain required temperatures, and are appropriate for a wide variety of plants, especially sorts that appreciate a fairly humid atmosphere and, in some cases, that thrive best when close to the roof glass.

PITANGA is *Eugenia uniflora*.

PITCAIRNIA (Pit-cáirnia). Species of *Pitcairnia*, of the pineapple family BROMELIACEAE, very rarely adopt the tree-perching habit so common to the family. More often they grow in the ground, sometimes on rocks. Except for West African *P. feliciana*, restricted in the wild to warm parts of the Americas, there are about 260 species. The name commemorates William Pitcairn, a physician of London, England, who maintained a botanical garden. He died in 1791.

Evergreen or deciduous, mostly stemless herbaceous perennials compose this genus. Stalked or stalkless, their linear to lanceolate or sometimes broader leaves are in clusters or tufts or in many ranks with their bases overlapping along the stems. Their edges may be smooth, toothed, or spiny. Their undersides are often conspicuously covered with scales. Sometimes some of the lower leaves are reduced to little more than stout spines. The flowering stalks, branched or not, bear often showy, slightly asymmetrical flowers in heads, spikes, racemes, or panicles. The individual blooms are stalked or nearly stalkless. They have three sepals, three petals, six stamens, often much shorter, sometimes slightly longer than the petals, and one slender, three-parted style about as long as the petals. The fruits are capsules.

Most frequently cultivated, *P. corallina*, of Colombia, is stemless. It has pleated, smooth-edged, long-stalked leaves 2 to 3 feet long by 2 to 4 inches broad, and with white scurf on their undersides. The very showy, arching or pendulous, red flower stalks are 1 foot to 1½ feet long. The blooms have 1-inch-long brilliant scarlet sepals and about 3-inch-long coral-red petals edged with white.

Other big to medium-sized sorts include these: *P. albiflos*, of Brazil, has tufts of many linear, spineless leaves up to 2 feet long by ½ to ¾ inch wide, and branchless flowering stalks up to 2 feet tall with white blooms that have petals about 2 inches long. *P. atrorubens* is a native of humid forest habitats at fairly high altitudes in Costa Rica and Panama. A beautiful stemless species, this has stalked, lanceolate leaves about 2 feet long by 2 to 3 inches broad, with prickly edges. The white to yellowish blooms with 2- to 3-inch-long petals, are many together in spikes up to 1 foot in length, handsomely decorated with blood-red bracts. *P. carinata*, a Brazilian, is a bulbous-based sort with few spineless, hairless, dark green leaves up to 2 feet long by about 1 inch wide. Its bright red blooms are in spikes up to 9 inches in length. *P. echinata*, from Colombia, attains heights of 4 feet or more, has stems with twelve to twenty lanceolate leaves 3 to 4 feet in length by 1 inch to 2 inches wide, spiny toward their bases, and clothed with white scurf on their undersides. The branched flowering stalks, 2 to 4 feet tall, have white-petaled blooms with yellow sepals with orange-red bases. Variety *P. e. villensis* has pinkish-orange petals. *P. flammea* is Brazilian. A variable inhabitant of wet woodlands and rocks, this grows erectly, has stalkless, spineless, pointed-sword-shaped leaves white-scurfy on their undersides, and is 2 to 3 feet long by 1 inch to 1½ inches wide. The flowers, in racemes up to 1 foot or sometimes more in length, have bright red to sometimes white petals. The bracts are green. *P. heterophylla* is a clump-forming native of dry and humid habitats from Mexico to northern South America and the West Indies. Its rosettes, bulbous at their bases, are of deciduous, grassy, 2-foot-long, inner arching leaves mostly over ½ inch wide, and outer ones reduced to persistent spiny bases. The showy, pink to red flowers, in nearly stalkless headlike racemes, with green bracts, develop in spring before the grassy foliage. *P. integrifolia*, of Trinidad and Venezuela, has 2- to 3-foot-long, hairless, linear leaves about ½ inch long, minutely-spiny near their bases and white-scurfy on their undersurfaces. In

Pitcairnia heterophylla

Pitcairnia heterophylla (flowers)

pyramidal, about five-branched panicles of loose racemes, the flowers have 1-inch-long, yellow-based, bright red petals. *P. maidifolia*, of Central America and northeastern South America, perches on trees and moist, shaded rocks. A robust species, it has lanceolate, spineless leaves 2 to 3 feet long by 2 to 2½ inches wide, with channeled stalks. The outermost leaves are represented by blackish sheaths. Erect and up to 2 feet long, the flowering stalks have green or yellowish bracts and a one-sided spikelike raceme of blooms with greenish sepals and 2-inch-long, greenish-white to white petals. *P. samuelsonii* is endemic to Hispaniola. The outside leaves of its rosettes are dark-colored and spinelike. The others, green and up to more than 2 feet long, are clothed on their under surfaces with white scales. The branchless or few-branched, erect flowering stalks are white-woolly. The blooms are cream-colored to yellow. *P. staminea*, of Brazil, has stems with up to thirty stalked, soft, grasslike leaves up to 2 feet long by ¼ to ½ inch wide, hairless above, with a thin covering of whitish scurf on their undersides. The flowers, in loose panicles or racemes up to 2½ feet in length, have slender, bright red petals over 2 inches long and long-protruding stamens. *P. wendlandii*, native from Mexico to Guatemala and Costa Rica, is a robust sort up to 5 feet tall. Its short-stalked, spineless or slightly spiny leaves have elliptic-lanceolate blades up to 3 feet long by 3 inches wide. The sulfur-yellow flowers are in erect, cylindrical spikes about 1 foot long terminating longer stalks. The bracts are claret-brown. *P. xanthocalyx* is a Mexican species. From a bulblike base arch twenty or fewer evergreen, lanceolate leaves 2 to 3 feet long and dusted with whitish scurf on their undersides. The loosely-arranged, 2-inch-long, primrose-yellow flowers are, atop a 2-foot-long stalk, in racemes 1 foot to 2 feet in length. The bracts are green.

Smaller pitcairnias likely to be cultivated include these: *P. andreana*, of Colombia, 8

Pitcairnia xanthocalyx

Pitcairnia xanthocalyx (flowers)

inches to 1 foot tall, has a few pendulous, bright green, lanceolate leaves 1 foot to 1½ feet long and white-scaly on their undersides. The flowers, with green sepals and yellow-tipped, bright orange-red petals, are in short racemes of few. *P. aphelandraeflora*, native from Panama to Brazil, has 1-foot-tall, slim stems with numerous slender, erect or recurved, minutely-toothed, spine-tipped leaves about 8 inches long. Not over 6 inches long, the flowering stalk terminates in a raceme of short-stalked, bright coral-red blooms 2 to 2½ inches long. *P. beycalema* is a Brazilian about 1 foot tall. It has several to many grassy leaves, green on their upper surfaces and white-scaly beneath, and is 6 to 9 inches long. The flowers, in erect racemes up to 9 inches in height, have greenish-red sepals and bright red petals, the latter about 2 inches long. The bracts are brilliant red. *P. punicea*, endemic in Mexico and Guatemala, reportedly often grows on limestone cliffs. Under 1 foot in

height, its many leaves are about 1 foot long by ⅓ inch wide The racemes of bright red flowers approximately 9 inches long, are lifted just above the foliage. *P. tabuliformis*, of Mexico is distinct in aspect. It has flat rosettes of thin, almost papery, spreading, elliptic leaves up to 6 inches long by 2 to 3 inches broad and green on both surfaces, with darker longitudinal veins above. Low in the hearts of the rosettes the brilliant red flowers are in dense heads of up to forty surrounded by a collar of broad, green bracts. *P. tuerckheimii*, a native of Guatemala, attains heights of up to 2 feet. The basal leaves overlap to form spiny, bulblike structures. The upper ones, which soon fall, are up to 8 inches long by ½ inch wide. Rising above the foliage, the flowering stalk carries a 6-inch-long loose raceme of crimson blooms.

Garden and Landscape Uses. In tropical and subtropical climates pitcairnias are suitable for lightly shaded or even sunny locations. They are useful as underplantings for palms and can be displayed in other ways. They are also satisfactory in greenhouses. The smaller ones can be used as houseplants Some are adaptable for hanging baskets and for growing on rafts.

Cultivation. So long as the rooting mix is coarse and porous, admitting air fairly readily and permitting the free drainage of water, the character of the soil is not of first importance. One containing generous amounts of organic material and some turfy topsoil with the admixture of coarse grit or perlite and some dried cow manure is satisfactory. Repot at the beginning of the growing season. Indoor winter night temperatures of 50 to 55°F suit most kinds, with an increase by day of up to fifteen degrees. Water moderately, allowing the rooting medium to become dryish between applications. Moister and warmer conditions in summer than in winter are in order. Fertilize well-rooted specimens at about ten-day intervals from spring to fall with dilute liquid fertilizer Propagation is by division in spring and by seed.

PITCH-APPLE is *Clusia rosea*.

PITCHER PLANTS. Plants belonging to several genera that have leaves modified into more or less pitcher-shaped organs are called pitcher plants. All are carnivorous. See Nepenthes, and Sarracenia; for the Australian pitcher plant, Cephalotus, for the California pitcher plant Darlingtonia. See also Carnivorous or Insectivorous Plants.

PITCHER-SAGE is *Lepechinia calycina*.

PITHECELLOBIUM (Pithecel-lòbium)—Manila-Tamarind, Texas-Ebony, Cat's Claw or Black Bead. The possibly 200 species of

Pithecellobium are warm-country trees, shrubs, and occasionally woody vines, belonging in the mimosa group of the pea family LEGUMINOSAE. The name comes from the Greek *pithecos*, an ape, and *lobos*, a lobe, and refers to the fanciful earlobe appearance or earring-like look of the coiled pods of some kinds. By some authorities treated as *P. saman*, the rain tree or monkey pod is in this Encyclopedia dealt with as *Samanea saman*.

Pithecellobiums have alternate, twice-pinnate leaves of few to many leaflets, pompon or mimosa-like heads or spikes of flowers, and seed pods that in some kinds are much contorted or twisted. They are natives of the tropics and warm subtropics of the Americas, including the United States, and of the Old World, and are sources of useful lumbers, tanning materials, dyes, and other products. The fruits of some kinds are used as food for animals and to some extent man, and for making beverages.

The Manila-tamarind (*P. dulce*) is also known as guaymochil and huamuchil. Despite its colloquial name, its original home is from Mexico to Colombia and Venezuela. Now it is planted in many warm countries for shade and ornament, and in Hawaii it has become naturalized and occurs spontaneously. There its seeds are made into leis. Its blooms attract bees and it is considered a honey plant. Animals feed on its pods and the pulp surrounding the seeds is edible and is used to make a lemonade-like beverage. In Mexico the bark is employed for tanning and as the source of a yellow dye.

Usually not exceeding 50 feet in height and often lower, the Manila-tamarind frequently develops a more or less crooked trunk and limbs and has a wide-spreading crown with low-hanging, switchlike young branches. Evergreen or almost so, it has slender-stalked leaves divided into two parts, each with two slightly asymmetrical elliptic leaflets ½ inch to 2 inches long. Their undersurfaces are paler than their dull green upper ones. The densely-hairy, whitish flowers, each about ⅛ inch long and with numerous threadlike white stamens and a slender red style, are many together in short-stalked, globular, fuzzy heads distantly spaced in narrow, erect panicles at the branch ends. Slightly flattened, much curved or coiled, and constricted between the seeds, the pods are 4 to 5 inches long by about ½ inch wide. They are greenish suffused with pink or red, and split along both edges to expose nine or ten glossy-black seeds surrounded by sweet, whitish or pinkish pulp. The seeds are suspended on short pink stalks. A variety with leaves variegated with white, at least for part of the year, is reported from Hawaii.

A handsome native of Java, *P. junghuhnianum* is distinctive and is planted for ornament in southern Florida and elsewhere. A small to medium-sized tree, it has cream to yellow flowers in brushlike, axillary, long-stalked heads. Its leaves, 6 inches to 1 foot long or longer, have one to three pairs of primary divisions each with five to twelve, mostly alternate, rather distantly-spaced, mostly elliptic leaflets, 1 inch to 4 inches long by ¼ inch to 1¾ inches broad. The largest leaflets are at the ends of the leaf divisions. The inside linings of its seed pods are red.

Species native to the United States are the Texas-ebony (*P. flexicaule* syn. *Ebenopsis flexicaulis*), the cat's claw or black bead (*P. unguis-cati*), and *P. guadelupense*. Not a relative of the true ebony (*Diospyros ebenum*), **P. flexicaule** is a neat-foliaged

Pithecellobium flexicaule

shrub or tree from about 20 to 50 feet in height with zigzagged branchlets beset with pairs of sharp spines ¼ to ½ inch long. The small, twice-pinnate, dark green leaves consist of an even number, usually two or three pairs, of primary divisions up to 1 inch long, each with two to six pairs of nearly stalkless, opposite, obovate to elliptic, leaflets mostly under ½ inch long. The flowers, fragrant, yellowish, and about ⅛ inch long, are in slender, dense spikes 1½ inches in length, and clustered. The fruits are slightly curved, dark brown, flat pods up to 7 inches long by up to 1¼ inches broad. The approximately ten seeds are surrounded by pulp. The Texas-ebony ranges as a native from Texas to Yucatan.

The cat's claw or black bead (**P. unguis-cati**) and the closely similar **P. guadelupense** occur as natives from Florida to northern South America, and in the West Indies. From the cat's claw, *P. guadelupense* differs in rarely having spines, in its leafstalks being shorter than the stalks of the individual leaflets, and in having pubescent ovaries. The cat's claw is a twiggy shrub or small tree mostly not more than 15 feet tall. It has bright green foliage and slender-stalked racemes of fuzzy heads of

greenish-yellow to pinkish blooms that are fragrant and have hairless ovaries. The leaves have few, usually four, asymmetrically broadly-ovate to nearly round leaflets under ½ inch to 2¼ inches long, with stalks shorter than the main leafstalks.

Garden and Landscape Uses and Cultivation. In tropical and subtropical regions, the pithecellobiums described are appreciated as ornamentals and the taller sorts as shade trees. The Manila-tamarind, popular on both counts, is esteemed for planting in public places, on home grounds, and along roadsides. It withstands dry conditions well and responds to shearing. It makes good hedges. Its fallen leaves are reported to so acidify the soil that the cultivation of grass and other plants may become difficult, but as with the monkey pod, it may well be that the deprivation of the soil of moisture and nutrients is partly responsible for this. Although less well known than the monkey pod and Manila-tamarind, *P. junghuhnianum* also promises well as a shade and ornamental tree.

The cat's claw, its near relative *P. guadelupense*, and the Texas-ebony are useful as shrubs and trees of mostly small dimensions. They withstand a few degrees of frost. Their growth habits and small, neat foliage are attractive, and they prosper in a variety of soils, including sandy ones. However, they grow best in fertile earth, and the Texas-ebony, although it does well where the atmosphere is dry and is a good species in the southwest, needs ample soil moisture.

Cultivation. Soil preferences are indicated above. Provided with acceptable earth and a warm, essentially frost-free climate, pithecellobiums grow without any special care other than whatever pruning or shearing may be considered desirable to limit them to size or to influence their shape. Propagation is usually by seed, but sometimes cuttings are used.

PITHECOCTENIUM (Pithecoc-tènium) — Monkey's Comb. Inhabiting warmer parts of the Americas from Mexico to Argentina and the West Indies, the seven species of *Pithecoctenium* belong in the bignonia family BIGNONIACEAE. The name, from the Greek *pithekos*, a monkey, and *ctenion*, a comb, presumably refers to the spiny fruits. One or two species are cultivated, but not commonly.

These are evergreen woody vines with opposite leaves of three leaflets or of two leaflets and a slender, three-branched tendril. The white or violet flowers, in terminal racemes or panicles, have bell-shaped calyxes sometimes with five small teeth. The curved, bell-shaped corollas, enlarged above their bases, have five rounded, spreading lobes (petals) that form a somewhat two-lipped face to the bloom. The stamens do not protrude. The slender style ends in a two-lobed stigma. The

flowers are succeeded by large prickly fruits, which technically are capsules.

Monkey's comb (**P. cynanchoides**), native to Uruguay and Argentina, is a slender vine with angled, gray-felty shoots and leaves with ovate, 1- to 2-inch-long leaflets, of which there are three, or two with a tendril between. The two lowest flowers of each raceme are long-stalked. The corollas are leathery, about 2 inches long, and downy on their outsides. They are white on their outsides, yellow within. Covered with yellow bristles, the broad, flattish seed pods are abut 2½ inches long. Rarer in cultivation, **P. echinatum** (syns. *P. muricatum*, *Bignonia echinata*), native from Mexico to Brazil, has ovate leaflets 2 to 4 inches long and 2-inch-long flowers at first white with yellow throats, but changing to yellow as they age. The seed pods, up to 8 inches in length, are covered with sharp, short, spiny projections.

Garden Uses and Cultivation. These are as for *Clytostoma* and *Allamanda*.

PITOMBA Is *Eugenia luschnathiana*.

PITTOSPORACEAE — Pittosporum Family. Trees, shrubs, and woody vines sometimes spiny and classified in nine genera totaling 200 species constitute this family of dicotyledons. They are natives of tropical, subtropical, and warm-temperate parts of the Old World. Many are handsome. They have leathery or somewhat fleshy, undivided, lobeless and toothless leaves, alternate or in whorls (circles of more than two). The bisexual or rarely unisexual flowers, solitary and in panicles or other branched formations, wheel- to bell-shaped, have five each sepals and petals sometimes united at their bases, five stamens with stalks shorter than the anthers, and one short style. The fruits are capsules or berries. Genera cultivated include *Billardiera*, *Bursaria*, *Hymenosporum*, *Marianthus*, *Pittosporum*, and *Sollya*.

PITTOSPORUM (Pittós-porum) — Victorian-Box, Mock-Orange. This is an important group of nonhardy, evergreen trees and shrubs of which several species are greatly admired for outdoor landscaping and a few for growing in containers. It belongs to the pittosporum family PITTOSPORACEAE and occurs natively in Australia, New Zealand, islands of the Pacific, including Hawaii, Asia, and Africa. Of the 150 or more species, a large proportion are endemic to limited geographical regions. None of the twenty-six New Zealand species, for instance, occurs elsewhere. Only one of the more numerous Australian kinds extends beyond that continent. One species each are restricted to Lord Howe Island and Norfolk Island and so on. A few kinds enjoy wide distributions. Especially in New Zealand and Hawaii the species intergrade and easy identification is not always possible. The name *Pittosporum* comes from the Greek *pitta*, pitch, and *spora*, seeds, in allusion to the resinous coatings of the seeds.

Pittosporums frequently have leaves clustered toward the branch ends, sometimes in apparent whorls (circles of more than two). Except occasionally on young seedlings, they are undivided and toothless or are more or less sinuately toothed; the leaves of seedlings may be lobed or even pinnately-divided, but this phase soon passes. The small flowers, often functionally unisexual, each have five sepals, petals, and stamens, and a short style. The petals are usually united toward their bases. The flowers may be solitary at the branch ends or in the leaf axils, but more commonly are in terminal clusters or panicles. The fruits are spherical, subspherical, or obovoid capsules, often flattened laterally and containing two to many seeds. Some kinds, for example, *P. kirkii* and *P. cornifolium*, of New Zealand, are epiphytic; they perch on other trees without taking nourishment from their hosts.

Apart from its contribution to ornamental horticulture the usefulness of *Pittosporum* is limited. The woods of some kinds are sometimes used for handles of golf clubs, billiard cues, and for other special purposes. Many species are or have been employed in native medicine and some as fish poisons. Other kinds have local uses as condiments. In drier parts of Australia, *P. phillyraeoides* is fed to stock.

Tallest of cultivated kinds, the eastern Australian diamond-leaf pittosporum (*P. rhombifolium*) in the wild sometimes attains 100 feet in height, but often is less than one-half that. It has a rounded symmetrical head and alternate leaves, sometimes clustered near the branch ends. They may be coarsely-toothed or toothless and up to 4 inches long and one-half to three-quarters as broad. The many flowers, ¼-inch-long, in umbel-like clusters at the branch ends, have spreading, white petals. The fruits are bright orange and about ¼ inch long. A tree 25 to 60 feet in height, *P. ferrugineum* ranges from eastern Australia to Malaysia. When young its shoots, like its young leaves, are rusty-hairy. The stalked, elliptic to obovate, alternate leaves, often crowded toward the shoot ends, are up to 4½ inches long and are about one-half as broad. In umbel-like clusters with rusty tomentose stalks, at the ends of the branches the yellow flowers, tubular with recurving petals, develop. The globose fruits are ⅓ inch in diameter.

Victorian-box or orange pittosporum (*P. undulatum*) is horticulturally one of the most useful species. From 15 to 40 feet tall, it is a broad shrub or tree well clothed with alternate, lustrous, elliptic-oblong to oblanceolate, leathery leaves up to 6 inches in length by one-third as wide. Usually

Pittosporum undulatum in California

Pittosporum undulatum (leaves and flowers)

their margins are wavy. The clusters of four to fifteen fragrant, white flowers, with petals joined at their bases and spreading or recurved above, are terminal. Each bloom is about ½ inch long, and the yellow to brown fruits are about ½ inch wide. Victorian-box is native of eastern Australia. Called tarata and lemonwood, in its native New Zealand. *P. eugenioides* is up to 40 feet tall. It has spreading branches and slender-stalked, alternate or nearly opposite leaves, often crowded at the branch ends. They are oblong-elliptic to elliptic and 2 to 6 inches long by one-half to three-quarters as wide. Their upper sides are glossy-green, beneath they are paler. Commonly their edges are much waved. In umbel-like clusters the fragrant, ¼-inch-long flowers, with yellowish petals that spread from their bases, are borne at the branch ends. The green to black fruits are about ⅓ inch long. Variety *P. e. variegatum* has gray-green leaves with wavy margins attractively variegated with creamy-white.

Native to Indonesia, *P. moluccanum* is a small to medium-sized, broad-crowned, evergreen tree with grayish bark. Its wavy-margined, glossy-green, obovate leaves are about ⅓ inch long. Yellowish

Pittosporum eugenioides variegatum

Pittosporum moluccanum (fruits)

and honey-scented, its flowers are succeeded by egg-shaped, orange fruits. About ⅓ inch long, they split to show a scarlet mass of pulpy seeds.

Small trees or tall shrubs ordinarily 15 to 30 feet in height are numerous among *Pittosporum* species; several are cultivated. One of the most popular and distinctive, the narrow- or willow-leaved pittosporum (*P. phillyraeoides*), has much the appearance of a weeping willow. Widespread in its native Australia, it has pendulous branches and alternate, linear-oblong, toothless leaves 1 inch to 5 inches long by up to ½ inch, but usually under ¼ inch wide. Very leathery, when young they are tomentose. At the ends of leafy branchlets the pale yellow or white flowers are clustered. They are ⅓ to ½ inch long and tubular for two-thirds of their lengths, with spreading or reflexed lobes (petals). The fruits, up to ¾ inch long, are dark red to orange. From the last, *P. bicolor*, also Australian, is readily distinguished by having upright branchlets and leaves decidedly hairy on their undersides. They are oblong-lanceolate to linear and ¾ inch to 3 inches long by ⅛ to a little over ½ inch wide. Clustered at the ends of leafy branches the yellow flowers, up to ½ inch long, are veined with red or reddish-purple. Their petals spread from above their middles. The subspherical fruits, ⅓ to ½ inch in diameter are more or less hairy.

New Zealand species of small tree dimensions include popular **P. tenuifolium** (syn. *P. nigricans)*, which is called tawhiwhi in New Zealand. The tawhiwhi has alternate, short-stalked leaves, often crowded at the branch ends, and generally with wavy margins. They are obovate to elliptic, ¾ inch to 2¼ inches long by ⅓ inch to 1¼ inches broad. Above they are green sometimes marked with purple; their undersides are paler. When young they are sparsely-hairy. The dark purple, maroon, pink, or white flowers, ⅓ to ½ inch long, have petals separate to their bases and spreading above their middles. The subspherical fruits are ½ inch in diameter and more or less hairy. Variety *P. t. colensoi* (syn. *P. colensoi)*, in its native land called mountain tawhiwhi, differs from the typical species in having leaves 1¾ to 4½ inches long by ⅓ inch to 2 inches broad, usually without wavy margins and not marked with purple. Horticultural varieties are *P. t. argenteum* (syns. *P. t.* 'Silver Matipo' and perhaps *P. t.* 'Silver Queen'), which has silvery-gray foliage; *P. t. garnettii*, with leaves margined with white and flecked with red; *P. t. purpureum*, with leaves deeply suffused with purple; and *P. t. variegatum*, with leaves edged with white or cream.

Another popular New Zealander, called karo, **P. crassifolium** may be a small tree, but sometimes does not exceed shrub dimensions. It has upright branches, with downy younger parts, and alternate leaves frequently clustered toward the branch tips. Obovate to oblanceolate, they have thickened, revolute, toothless margins and are 1¼ to 3½ inches long by ¾ to 1 inch wide. When young, both surfaces are densely-hairy, their undersides remain so. Male flowers are in terminal umbels of five to ten, females are solitary or in twos. The blooms are dark red or purple-red and have petals, separate to their bases, with recurved tips. The fruits are hairy, subspherical capsules ¾ inch to 1¼ inches long. An inhabitant of coastal regions in New Zealand, **P. umbellatum,** about 20 feet tall, has branches in whorls (circles of more than two), their young parts clothed with hairs. The alternate or clustered, toothless, leathery leaves, elliptic to obovate-wedge-shaped, are 2 to 4 inches long and about one-half as wide. The dull red or pink blooms a little under ½ inch long are in many-flowered terminal clusters. Their petals, joined below, spread from above their middles. The green to black fruits, less than ½ inch across, are subspherical to nearly four-angled, and sparsely hairy.

Endemic to Hawaii, **P. hosmeri** inhabits dry lava slopes. About 20 feet tall, it has shiny green, somewhat wrinkled, oblanceolate leaves 4 to 10 inches long by 1 inch to 2½ inches wide, woolly-hairy on their undersides. The flowers are in dense, short-stalked clusters from the leaf axils and along the leafless parts of the shoots. They are nearly ½ inch long and cream. The egg-shaped fruits are 2 to 3 inches long; when young they are hairy, at maturity they are orange. In *P. h. longifolium,* the leaves are up to 1¼ feet long by 3½ inches wide. Sometimes 30 feet in height, but often not more than a tall shrub, **P. adaphniphylloides,** a native of China, has slightly downy young shoots and under leaf surfaces. The dark green leaves have oblong to obovate blades 4 to 8 inches long by 1¾ to 3½ inches wide. In terminal panicles of globose clusters, the greenish-yellow flowers are ¼ inch long. The spherical fruits are up to ⅓ inch in diameter. Closely related **P. daphniphylloides,** of Taiwan, is up to 10 feet tall, with smaller, shorter-stalked leaves.

The Cape pittosporum (**P. viridiflorum**) is a South African native of excellent decorative appeal. It has much the aspect of *P. tobira*. A tree 30 feet tall, it is often lower and shrubby. Its obovate, wavy-edged, toothless leaves are 1 inch to 4 inches long and up to 1 inch wide. They are leathery, lustrous, and when crushed, strongly scented. The ¼-inch-long, yellowish-green flowers are in crowded terminal clusters. The hairless fruits are about ¼ inch long.

Shrubby pittosporums, those that never, or rarely, attain the forms or sizes of trees, include a few very familiar to gardeners. Here belongs perhaps the most widely grown member of the genus, Japanese, Chinese, and Taiwanian **P. tobira**. This sort is sometimes called mock-orange. Normally 6 to 10 feet tall, but sometimes exceeding 20 feet, this beautiful species is excellent both in foliage and bloom. Its blunt, obovate, thick leaves 2 to 3½ inches long, and nearly or quite as wide as their length, are hairless and have rolled-under margins. They are clustered in almost ro-

Pittosporum tobira

sette-like whorls at the shoot ends. The white or yellowish, very fragrant blooms, nearly ½ inch long, are in quite showy terminal umbels. The angled, egg-shaped, densely-hairy fruits, about ½ inch long, have spreading petals. Variety *P. t. variegatum* has leaves beautifully variegated with creamy-white. Very low *P. t. wheeleri* is appropriate for use as a groundcover. Chinese **P. heterophyllum** is a shrub 3 to

Pittosporum tobira variegatum

Pittosporum tobira wheeleri

12 feet tall. Its leaves vary in shape from lanceolate to ovate-lanceolate and obovate, and are 1 inch to 3½ inches long, leathery, and without marginal teeth. The fragrant, yellow flowers, about ⅓ inch long, are in umbel-like pubescent clusters at the branch ends. The fruits are globular, brown, and ¼ to ⅓ inch in diameter. Variety *P. h. sessile* is a prostrate shrub with stalkless leaves.

Lonely Lord Howe Island northwest of New Zealand is the only place where **P. erioloma** is native. Much like *P. tobira*, it is 6 to 15 feet tall, and has thick oblanceolate to obovate, thick-margined leaves crowded at the branch ends and 1¼ to 2 inches long by ⅓ to ⅔ inch wide. Their upper sides are dark green, their undersurfaces paler. In small terminal clusters, the yellowish flowers with reddish bases are about ½ inch long. Their petals spread from above their middles. The rounded fruits are ½ to ¾ inch in diameter. Endemic to islands off the New Zealand coast, *P. fairchildii*, from 10 to 15 feet in height, has obovate to elliptic-oblong leaves often crowded at the shoot ends. Toothless, they are up to 3 inches long by one-half as broad, pale green above and lighter on their undersides. The purple flowers, solitary or in clusters of two to four at the branch ends, have petals that spread above their middles. The leathery fruits, up to 1 inch in diameter, are subglobose. Very similar to *P. crassifolium* and like it native of New Zealand, *P. ralphii* differs in being a shrub not over 12 feet tall and in having leaves that narrow abruptly rather than gradually to their stalks and fruits scarcely over ½ inch long.

Australian **P. revolutum,** a variable shrub about 10 feet tall, has alternate, elliptic-ovate to elliptic-oblong leaves 1¾ to 8 inches long by one-third to one-half as wide. They are reddish-hairy on their undersides and have thickened, rolled-under, sometimes wavy margins. Mostly the foliage is crowded at the shoot ends. The light yellow flowers, in clusters of up to a dozen, but sometimes solitary, have brown-hairy stalks. They are up to a little over ½ inch long and have petals with spreading or reflexed tips. The subglobose to ellipsoid, green to brown fruits are few-to six-lobed and ¾ inch to 1¼ inches long.

Garden and Landscape Uses. Pittosporums are handsome landscape furnishings that can be put to many good uses. As single specimen trees and shrubs, well located, they are remarkably effective. They look well when grouped and are adapted to foundation plantings, backgrounds, and use for screens and hedges, both informal and sheared. They stand some shade and prosper in sun. Any moderately good soil, even a dryish soil, is satisfactory. In general, pittosporums do well near the sea and are also satisfactory in city gardens. The foliage of some kinds

Pittosporum tobira, a young plant

A hedge of *Pittosporum tobira*

makes good cutting for use in flower arrangements.

Because they have sufficient character to associate well with masonry and suchlike architectural features, *P. tobira, P. undulatum,* and some others are very suitable for tubs and planters, which in mild climates can be left outdoors the year around, but elsewhere must be wintered indoors. These are attractive plants for conservatories and large greenhouses; as small specimens they are to some extent used as room plants.

Cultivation. Little skill is needed to manage pittosporums. The only pruning necessary, except for an annual shearing of formal hedges, is an occasional shortening of an unruly shoot, or somewhat more drastic cutting to shape or keep to size specimens that need this attention. Such work is best done in spring. Plants in containers need repotting from time to time in their early years, and top dressing annually after they have attained the largest receptacles they are intended to occupy. They must be watered freely from spring to fall, more moderately in winter. In greenhouses a winter night temperature of 40 to 50°F is high enough and by day at that season no more than five to fifteen more is needed. It is necessary that on all favorable occasions the greenhouse be freely ventilated. These plants benefit from being stood outdoors in summer. Seed, and cuttings of firm but not hard shoots, are easy methods of propagation. Layering is also satisfactory.

PITYOPSIS (Pity-ópsis). Eight species of the daisy family COMPOSITAE constitute *Pityopsis.* Endemic to the eastern and southeastern United States and Central America, the genus is by some authorities included in *Chrysopsis.*

The sorts of this genus are herbaceous perennials, which usually spread by underground stolons. They have leafy, solitary or clustered stems. The linear-oblanceolate to narrower leaves, alternate and with parallel veins, are often grasslike,

and generally hairy. The daisy-form, yellow flower heads are small and in clusters. The fruits are seedlike achenes.

Native in dry, sandy soils chiefly in coastal regions from Massachusetts to New Jersey, **P. falcata** (syns. *Chrysopsis falcata, Heterotheca falcata*) is compact, leafy, and from 4 inches to over 1 foot tall. It forms clumps of white-woolly stems, branched above and furnished with curved, rigid, parallel-veined, linear leaves 1 inch to 4 inches long and mostly under ¼ inch wide, but the lowermost sometimes wider. The individual flower heads are ¾ inch across. Ranging in the wild from Delaware to Ohio, Florida, and Louisiana, **P. graminifolia** (syns. *Chrysopsis graminifolia, Heterotheca graminifolia*) has stolons and solitary or loosely grouped stems 1 foot to 3 feet tall. The leaves, like the stems, are silky-hairy. The basal ones, long-linear and in rosettes, are 4 inches to 1½ feet long. Those on the stems are shorter. The flower heads are about ½ inch across. Native to North Carolina and Georgia, **P. pinifolia** (syns. *Chrysopsis pinifolia, Heterotheca pinifolia*), except for the leaves that form the basal rosette, is nearly hairless. It has stolons and leafy stems, usually in clumps, 8 inches to 1¼ feet tall. The basal leaves are up to 1½ inches long, those of the stems up to 3 inches long. The flower heads are about ¾ inch wide.

Garden and Landscape Uses and Cultivation. These plants are suitable for naturalizing and for inclusion in native plant gardens. They thrive in well-drained, acid soil and need a sunny location. Propagation is easy by division and by seed.

PITYROGRAMMA (Pityro-grámma)—Gold Fern, Silver Fern. Once highly prized as greenhouse ornamentals, gold and silver ferns are less commonly grown than formerly, but are still found in the collections of specialists and in botanical gardens. About fifteen species of the pteris family PTERIDACEAE, they are interesting and beautiful natives chiefly of the Americas, but with a few in Africa, Madagascar, and the Mascarene Islands. They have also been named *Ceropteris* and *Gymnogramma.* The name *Pityrogramma* comes from the Greek *pityron,* chaff or husk, and *gramme,* a line. It alludes to a characteristic of the groups of spore capsules.

Pityrogrammas have clusters of erect or arching, twice- or more-times-pinnate leaves, those of many kinds attractively covered on their undersides, and young fronds often wholly, with a dense layer of yellow or white, waxy powder. Very occasionally parts of a frond may be white- and the remainder yellow-coated. Horticultural variants with crested or forked fronds are known. The linear clusters of spore capsules are along the veins.

The identification of these ferns is especially difficult because of the freedom with which they hybridize in cultivation and in the wild. The best-known tropical species is *P. calomelanos,* a variable kind indigenous to the West Indies, tropical America, and tropical Africa. This has leathery, twice- or thrice-divided fronds up to 3 feet long by as much as 10 inches wide. Their nearly black stalks are as long as the typically ovate-lanceolate blades. The ultimate segments of the latter are sharply-lobed or cleft. Usually the leaves are densely-coated on their undersides with white, more rarely pinkish or pale yellow powder. Occasionally this is absent. In *P. c. aureoflava* the undercoating is bright yellow to orange-yellow.

Merging and perhaps hybridizing with *P. calomelanos,* and native of tropical America from Mexico and the West Indies southward, *P. tartarea* has twice- or rarely

Pityrogramma chrysophylla heyderi

Pityrogramma chrysophylla farinifera

Pityrogramma tartarea

thrice-divided, long-triangular fronds 1 foot to 2 feet in length by up to 6 inches wide, covered on their undersides with white or more rarely cream powder, and with their ultimate segments bluntly-lobed or cleft. In *P. t. aurata* the undercoating is bright yellow.

The gold fern (*P. chrysophylla*) has leaves coated on their undersides with golden-yellow, or less commonly white, powder. Its leafstalks are reddish-brown to blackish. This is a native of the Lesser Antilles and Puerto Rico, and is naturalized in Samoa. The undersides of the leaves of *P. c. heyderi* are of an even richer golden-yellow than those of typical *P. chrysophylla* and those of *P. c. farinifera* are mealy on the upper sides and silvery-white beneath. The Jamaican gold fern (*P. sulphurea*) inhabits Jamaica and some other West Indian islands. Its leaves, up to 1 foot long and not over 5 inches wide, have stalks considerably shorter than their blades. The undercoating of the leaves is always sulfur-yellow. More luxuriant and with larger leaves than its parent *P. chrysophylla*, the hybrid *P. hybrida* is intermediate between that species and its other parent *P. calomelanos*. Its leaf margins,

Pityrogramma hybrida

barely turned under, are doubly-toothed. This kind tolerates winter night temperatures as low as 40°F.

The California gold fern (*P. triangularis*), with its varieties, ranges from California and Baja California to Arizona, Nevada, Utah, and British Columbia, favoring shaded, rocky places. It differs from other kinds in having leafstalks quite round instead of being grooved on their topsides and in the scales on its rhizomes having a dark central stripe. Its fronds, triangular-pentagonal in outline and up to 1¼ feet long, have blades about as broad as long that account for one-third or slightly more of the total length of the frond. The pow-

der covering the undersides of the leaves is pale yellow to orange-yellow. Variety *P. t. viscosa* has leaves sticky on their upper sides and covered with white meal beneath. In *P. t. pallida* the fronds are powdered with white on both surfaces. Those of *P. t. maxonii* have yellowish glands on their upper sides and are coated with pale yellow or whitish powder beneath.

From Peru, and imperfectly understood botanically, comes *P. pearcei* (syn. *P. decomposita*), a vigorous grower with thrice-pinnate fronds with 1-foot-long stalks and three- or four-times-divided blades up to 1½ feet in length. Their undersides are coated with bright yellow meal. Another botanically poorly understood species is *P. pulchella,* of Venezuela. This is character-

Pityrogramma pulchella

Pityrogramma pulchella showing underside of one leaf

ized by having strongly-toothed segments to its mature leaves and much-dissected juvenile ones. Of upright growth, its fronds, up to 1 foot long and dark green above, are coated beneath with white powder, and are two- or three-times-divided.

Garden and Landscape Uses and Cultivation. Gold and silver ferns give little trouble to gardeners. They are easy to grow in greenhouses, and where climates are similar to those they know in the wild, outdoors. Their fullest beauty is seen only by raising the leaves and inspecting their undersides, or by growing them in baskets suspended above eye level. As greenhouse plants, those of tropical and subtropical origin succeed under rather drier atmospheric conditions than many ferns, but they still need moderate humidity. The winter night temperature for most kinds should be 55 to 60°F and that by day five to fifteen degrees higher. Gold and silver ferns succeed in well-drained pots or pans (shallow pots) in rather coarse, fertile, porous soil that contains a goodly proportion of organic matter, but is distinctly loamy and is kept always moist. They are seriously harmed if the soil is allowed to dry. When watering, care should be taken not to wet the foliage. Indoors shade from strong sun is needed. In warm weather the greenhouse must be ventilated to avoid a dank, stagnant atmosphere. Repotting is done in late winter or early spring. Well-rooted specimens are benefited by applications of dilute liquid fertilizer. Because young specimens are usually better looking than old ones it is advisable to raise new stocks from spores regularly, so that old specimens that have lost some of their beauty may be discarded. In southern Florida P. calomelanos succeeds in full sun outdoors. For more information see Ferns.

PLAGIANTHUS (Plagi-ánthus). Fifteen species of Australian trees and shrubs constitute *Plagianthus*, a genus of the mallow family MALVACEAE. The name derives from the Greek *plagios*, oblique, and *anthos*, a flower, and alludes to a characteristic of the blooms.

Plagianthuses have alternate, undivided leaves and small, unisexual or bisexual flowers, solitary or in clusters, in the leaf axils or terminal. The flowers sometimes have small bracts on the leafstalks below their five-toothed calyxes. There are five small petals and several to many stamens, which for most of their lengths are joined to form a tube that surrounds the one to five styles. The fruits consist of one to five dry capsule-like carpels. Plagianthuses are closely related to *Hoheria*, differing chiefly in the flowers having one instead of several carpels and in their stigmas being linear instead of rounded. The plant formerly known as P. lyallii is Hoheria lyallii.

There are two New Zealand species, both endemic. One, *P. regius*, is a tree with flowers in large clusters, the other, *P. divaricatus*, is a shrub with blooms solitary or few together. Like so many New Zealand woody plants, these show much variation between the foliage typical of young specimens and older specimens, but on mature plants shoots having juvenile foliage quite often develop. Deciduous or evergreen, **P. regius** (syn. *P. betulinus*), up to 50 feet tall, sometimes retains its juvenile phase a long time and is then an elegant, intricately branched, non-flowering shrub up to 6 feet tall. As a juvenile its leaves are very short-stalked and rather distantly spaced. Broad-ovate to ovate-lanceolate, they are deeply-toothed and from ⅓ to ¾ inch long by about two-thirds as wide. As the plant assumes the adult stage, successive leaves change until they have stalks 1 inch or more in length and broad-ovate to ovate-lanceolate, irregularly-coarsely-toothed blades ½ inch to 3 inches long and up to over 1 inch broad. The mostly unisexual flowers, the males yellowish-white, the females greenish, have slender stalks and are in panicles up to 10 inches long. Not exceeding ⅙ inch in diameter, they are white with red anthers. The seeds are solitary. Variety *P. r. chathamicus* never has juvenile-type foliage.

Shrubby, semievergreen *P. divaricatus*, up to 6 feet tall, but sometimes prostrate, is an inhabitant of seashores. It has slender, often pendulous, more or less flexible, generally interlacing branches and toothless leaves clustered on short branchlets. Those on young plants are short-stalked, linear- to narrowly-spatula-shaped, and from ½ to slightly over 1 inch long by up to ⅕ inch wide. The leaves of adult plants are ¾ inch to under ¼ inch long and not over ⅙ inch wide. Occasionally an adult plant will produce a branch with juvenile leaves up to 1½ inches long. The inconspicuous, yellowish, mostly unisexual, very short-stalked flowers are ⅕ inch across. The fruits, spherical and downy, have one to three seeds.

Australian *P. pulchellus* is an evergreen, summer-flowering shrub or small tree with heart-shaped, coarsely-irregularly-toothed leaves, often with two basal lobes. The leafstalks are slender and 1 inch to 2 inches long; the leaf blades are 2½ to 4½ inches long. Solitary, or in brief racemes, the white flowers are ¼ inch in diameter.

Garden and Landscape Uses and Cultivation. These southern hemisphere species are not hardy in the north, but are attractive for mild climates. They make little floral show, but are shapely and pleasing. They are best satisfied with well-drained, fertile, loamy soil and sunny locations. Under favorable conditions growth is rapid. Except to shape or restrain the size of the plants, no pruning is needed. Propagation is by seed, and by summer cuttings 3 to 5 inches long made of lateral shoots, taken with a heel of older wood at their bases, and planted under mist or in a greenhouse propagating bench. Layering is also a means of multiplication.

PLANCHONELLA (Plan-chonélla). Approximately 100 species are included in *Planchonella*, of the sapodilla family SAPOTACEAE. The genus is native from Hawaii and the Ryukyu Islands south of Japan to Malaysia, Indochina, Australia, and New Zealand. Its name honors Jules Emile Planchon, a French botanist, who died in 1888.

Planchonellas are trees or shrubs with milky sap and alternate, undivided, lobeless, toothless leaves. Their flowers, solitary or clustered, have a four- or five-lobed calyx, four or five each petals, stamens, and staminodes (abortive stamens), and one style. The fruits are berries.

One species, **P. costata** (syns. *P. novozeylandica*, *Sideroxylon novo-zeylandicum*), native to New Zealand and Norfolk Island, is the only representative of its family indigenous there. Sometimes cultivated in California and places with similar mild climates, this is a tree up to 45 feet tall. It has evergreen, leathery, elliptic to obovate leaves from 2 to 5 inches long. Their upper surfaces are lustrous. Except for the midribs on their undersides, they are hairless. Solitary or in pairs, the tiny flowers are of little ornamental merit. The fruits are about 1 inch long.

Garden and Landscape Uses and Cultivation. The species described has merit as an ornamental evergreen that adapts to ordinary garden conditions. It may be propagated by seed and by cuttings.

PLANE TREE. See Platanus.

PLANERA (Plan-èra)—Water-Elm. A relative of the true elms (*Ulmus*), and like them belonging in the elm family ULMACEAE, the only species of *Planera* is sufficiently distinct to form a separate genus. From elms it differs in having some of its flowers unisexual, a characteristic shared with *Hemiptelea* and *Zelkova*, which also belong in the elm family. The fruits of those genera, however, are neither symmetrical nor roughened with prominent, fleshy spinelike points. The name *Planera* commemorates a German professor of medicine, Johann Jakob Planer, who died in 1789.

The water-elm (*P. aquatica*), native from Kentucky to Florida and Texas and not hardy in the north, is a deciduous tree up to 40 feet tall, broad-topped, and with spreading branches. Its young shoots are clothed with short hairs. Forming two ranks, the short-stalked leaves are ovate to ovate-oblong, asymmetrical at their bases, and irregularly-toothed. They have roughish upper surfaces and pinnate veins, well defined on their undersides. At maturity they are hairless. There are both bisexual and unisexual flowers, both small and appearing in spring before or with the leaves. They have a greenish, deeply 4- or 5-lobed calyx, no petals, four or five stamens, and the bisexuals and females a two-parted style. The males are in clusters at the bases of the new shoots. The bisexual and female blooms are solitary or in twos or threes in the axils of the young leaves. The ovoid fruits, about ⅓ inch long, are drupes. They mature in spring.

A lover of wet soils, the water-elm in its home territory often favors locations inundated for long periods each year and too wet for most trees.

Garden and Landscape Uses and Cultivation. The water-elm has little to recommend it horticulturally and is rarely planted except in botanical collections. It succeeds in moist soils and can be propagated by seeds, layering, and grafting onto seedling elms.

PLANNING GARDENS AND HOME GROUNDS.

Designing and developing home landscapes as well as those that surround institutional and industrial buildings and others such as parks and similar developments of a public nature, calls for careful planning, competent installation, and orderly follow-up procedures. Public, institutional, and industrial landscape design is usually entrusted to professional landscape architects, the installation to contractors supervised by the landscape architects or to other professionals, and the aftercare to gardeners.

Home gardeners, unless the property is of estate size, usually proceed on a do-it-yourself basis so far as planning is concerned; they employ perhaps a local nursery or landscape contractor to plant some trees and shrubs and install lawns and supplement this by planting they do themselves. Maintenance is likely to be their own concern perhaps with the aid of a little help hired as needed by the day.

Good landscaping adds to the cash value of a home and to the joy and pleasure of its owners. Lawns, trees, shrubs, and flowers are the components of garden pictures. Their quality, arrangement, and standard of upkeep reflect upon those responsible for them as much as do the interiors of the owners' homes or the clothes the owners wear.

More and more gardens are regarded as extensions of the home, places to be lived in for at least a large part of each year instead of merely looked at. So modern landscaping calls for developing the property practically as well as beautifully and always with an eye to ease and economy of maintenance.

Every year many tens of thousands of new homeowners begin making gardens where none existed before. They accept the task of transforming a piece of natural landscape, or more often a plot devastated to a greater or lesser extent by builders, into a pleasing complement to their homes. Others face the job of renovating neglected or overgrown gardens or remaking their old ones to fit current needs.

All too often inexperienced garden makers dive into the task without giving the matter adequate thought, or they engage professional planning help when they could achieve equally as good or better results themselves and save what is often a not inconsiderable expense.

The garden that you plan and develop should be *your* garden and your family's; it should express your preferences and make provision for your way of life and the things you want to do outdoors. The landscape design appropriate for a young couple with growing children is likely to be quite different from one for older folks without a family at home. How much entertaining you expect to do outdoors must be taken into consideration and, of course, whether or not you enjoy working in a garden as a hobby and growing flowers and vegetables or whether you just want a good-looking, landscape to set off your home to advantage and to enjoy.

Unfortunately, most amateurs who landscape homes must make their most important decisions at the time of their greatest ignorance. Only with the passing years do they realize their mistakes. It is so much easier to landscape a second garden than a first. The thing to do is grasp basic principles, proceed slowly, and exercise restraint. Overplanting is the greatest bugaboo of good landscaping, even for professional landscape architects.

The designs of houses and gardens today are simpler than in many past periods. Functionalism is considered good. So is originality, if it is restrained. Superficial decoration has been discarded. Along with the gingerbread and curlicues of late nineteenth- and early twentieth-century architecture have gone geometrical flower beds, tortuous paths, elaborate fountains, complicated rustic work, gazing

A small lawn backed by an attractive foundation planting of mostly coniferous evergreens complements this house

globes, and other features that once cluttered gardens. The best gardens are lovely and livable.

To begin, you must think of your place as a whole. Forget detail until later. When you do this, you will find that certain parts of your grounds serve special functions and must be given particular characters. In front of the house, leading down to the street or road, is a more or less public area. Unless you screen it with a wall or fence or hedge, it is likely to be visible to passersby. This is the setting for your house as strangers see it. This is the front that serves as an introduction to visitors. This is the part of your garden that, if well done, contributes to the beauty and landscaped effect of your community. Nothing

A shade tree and a flowering tree set in a well-kept lawn that extends to the sidewalk, together with a foundation planting of mostly low evergreens, and pyracanthas espaliered on the walls, compose this charming landscape

Palms of several sorts are thoughtfully located to provide this pleasing setting for a house in Florida

Pyramidal yews with heucheras at their bases flank this door

Here a large specimen juniper, placed to justify a curve in the road, dominates, while taller trees to the left and right frame the house

Symmetrical balance is achieved by the use of a specimen boxwood and a vine on each side of this door

A low post and rail fence, its base attractively planted with herbaceous flowering plants, here separates a front lawn from the public sidewalk

is better than a well-kept lawn as a main feature here. Appropriately placed shade trees and discreetly located shrubbery may frame the house and define the boundaries of the lot. A foundation planting that really weds the house to the ground is usually a good addition. Dignity and charm achieved by restraint and good relation of mass to mass and line to line should keynote the landscaping in front of

An asymmetrical doorside planting employs, at the left, a tall evergreen shrub to give height, and at its base and at the right of the door, lower plants; a rose bush in a container blooms in summer

Massed evergreens achieve a pleasing moundy effect here

a house. Do not spot single bushes and flower beds indiscriminately in the lawn; well-located examples can, however, be employed to advantage.

The private garden, the terrace, outdoor living room, play area, and so on are usually at the back, or sometimes the side, of

A Japanese influence is clearly evident in the landscaping of the front of this Californian home; the plants employed include a fruit tree, bird-of-paradise, cycads, and pines pruned in bonsai-like cloud fashion, all fronted by a perfect lawn

Terraces, which make delightful sitting areas, adjacent to the house: (a) Level with the surrounding land

(c) If the terrain makes it desirable, lower than the surrounding land

(b) A little higher than the surrounding land (two figures above)

Evergreen trees and shrubs provide pleasant screening in this California garden; a border of large-leaved ivy (*Hedera canariensis*) defines the lawn

A substantial planting of tall evergreens and deciduous trees masks a boundary wall; container plants add interest to the foreground

the house. Livability and usefulness should be stressed here. If there are children, play space for them may be included. The private area should be screened to provide reasonable privacy

and to block undesirable views. Background plantings of trees and shrubs, as well as walls and fences, must seem to belong, to be part of the picture, to have purpose. They should be married to the earth and to buildings and other features so that unity is achieved. Do not screen out favorable views from the garden. Preserve them, frame them with appropriate planting, use them as focal points. These are "windows" through which you look from your garden to the outside world. Focal points are important. If there are no pleasing views to provide reason for outward-looking vistas perhaps you should completely screen your garden (not necessarily

formally) at its margins. Then create inside the garden one or more focal points, points of interest to which the eye is led by clever design and planting. A pool, a seat, a gateway, or an interesting tree or evergreen may serve to center attention. Use discretion here; strongly competing points of interest create unrest. Only one distinct focal point should be evident in any one view.

When planning the private area, consider especially the views from the major windows of the house, and be sure to include the kitchen window, near which the woman of the house is likely to spend some time.

Small flowering trees, such as the dogwood here associated with rhododendrons and other evergreens, are often appropriate near the house

The small pool and statue in the middle of a broad grass path flanked by two flower borders adds interest here

A bold clump of *Phormium tenax* is a focal feature here

A lawn, with a small pool with a fountain and four low statues at its center, trees and flowering shrubs at its borders, and with a seat and chairs at its rear, creates this peaceful garden

An inviting gate encourages exploration beyond this border of tall shrubs

A wall, softened by appropriate planting, provides enclosure and privacy for this garden in California; the flowering cherry tree and bed of marigolds are well related to each other and to the house

A statue, with two stone urns planted with geraniums in the foreground, give character to this garden

A border of mixed annuals and hardy perennials, backed by a paling fence, encircles the lawn of this suburban New York home

Views of private areas in gardens: (a) A formal flower bed decorates this tiny plot

(b) A spacious lawn, screened with evergreens, is a feature of this New Orleans garden

(c) A neat flower border backed by a tall deciduous tree, a flowering dogwood, and a dark evergreen complement a well-kept lawn

A fairly spacious lawn near the house is nearly always desirable. Define it in some way, by a hedge or fence or shrubbery, so it gives a desirable sense of enclosure and an outdoor living room effect. The back lawn should be an outdoor extension of the interior of your home, approached, if

(d) A low dry wall of fieldstone with an irregular planting of perennials along its top supports this informal terrace

(e) A charming herb garden reveals the interest of the owner of this home

(f) A lush planting of palms and other appropriate plants gives character to a swimming pool in this Hawaiian garden

possible, by a porch or terrace from the living room. One or more well-placed shade trees that cast a shadow where it is

appreciated when the sun is at its hottest, from midday until late afternoon, make good sense here. Flower borders at the margins of the lawn may be used to give color and interest.

On small lots the back garden must, in effect, be one room. It may be skillfully and charmingly planned to seem larger than it is. Formality may be dispensed with by achieving asymmetrical rather than symmetrical balance. Perspectives and scale can create certain illusions. But it must remain one room. Cutting a small lot into too many smaller parts destroys simplicity and charm.

With the larger lot, say one more than 50 by 100 feet, the private part of the garden may then include not only the outdoor living room adjacent to the house, but areas that extend beyond it to the rear and the sides. These may feature special gardens, such as ones devoted to roses, rock gardens, herbs, cut flowers and vegetables, as well as naturalistically landscaped areas with trees, shrubs, and perhaps spring bulbs and other flowers growing beneath them. Here your problem as a designer is to tie the various "rooms" of this larger area into one satisfying, congruous whole. Plan so that the entire area is not seen from any one place. Inviting paths may lead the visitor to unexpected views and places of special interest, but transitions must be easy and natural. Above all, do not stick patches of flower beds about like postage stamps on a letter. The garden that consists of a few beds imposed on a lawn without relation to other features in the general picture is, it is hoped, as dead as a dodo.

The service area is necessary and must be utilitarian, but it may also be reasonably attractive and integrated into the overall plan. This part may include the garage and all or part of the drive leading to it, facilities for drying laundry, garbage containers, fuel and other delivery facilities, storage space for garden tools, and, perhaps, a play place for children. Often the kitchen door opens into it. The service area should be of adequate size, but not larger than necessary. It is usually a good plan to screen or partially screen it from other parts of the garden and perhaps from the road, which usually forms at least one boundary of it. If a vegetable and berry patch are included in the plan it may form a transition from the service to the private area.

Prepare plans for your garden before planting. Errors made on paper are easier to correct than those made in plantings. A garden plan need not be elaborate, but it should clearly show, *in scale*, the area and what you propose to do with it. Except for gardens of considerable size and varied grades, it is not necessary to show contours. If such are needed, have a skilled person make the plan. In most cases, a

Pinus strobus nana

Pinus bungeana (trunk)

Pinus strobus fastigiata

Pinus densiflora umbraculifera

Pistia stratiotes

Platanus occidentalis (trunk)

Pittosporum tobira

Platycodon grandiflorus

Pleurothallis truncata

Plumbago indica

large sheet of graph paper, a pencil, ruler and compass are all that are needed.

On the paper locate the boundaries of the lot, the house, driveway and such other permanent features as trees, shrubs, and outcropping rocks. Before you put anything new on paper, give your terrain several good, hard lookings-over. Consider the particular purposes that different areas must serve, and plan with the idea of saving whatever good, satisfactorily placed trees and shrubs are there and of clearing away any that are not good or do not fit into your landscape scheme. It is just as important to be ruthless with the worthless as to be careful and considerate with the worthwhile.

Remember, when drawing your plan, that you will not be looking at your garden from above; therefore, geometrical designs that seem good on paper may disappoint when transferred outdoors. The secret for the beginner is to work from the ground to the paper in the first place rather than the reverse. Here's how.

Go out on your lot with stakes and a ball or two of string. Set a stake wherever you propose to plant a tree, a row of stakes with string connecting them where you propose a wall or fence or hedge. Outline beds and borders that you think you want with stakes and string. In a similar way, lay out paths, drives, steps, and other features. Leave them and live with them for a week or longer. Walk around the lot and consider the stakes from every angle and means of approach. Change them as you see possible improvements. When you have them approximately as you want them, prepare your planting plan based on the location of the stakes. The result, to an untutored eye, may not look as balanced and pleasing as a more theoretical plan dreamed up at a drawing table, but it is likely to make more sense and be far more workable.

Beware of providing for too many plants. Remember, they grow. Even the most wispy tree, four or five years of age, will heighten and broaden considerably in ten or twelve years. If set without regard for its growth, it may crowd its neighbors, to its and their detriment, well before that. Of course, you must choose suitable plants, kinds that are likely to thrive in your climate and conditions, kinds that will serve the purposes they are intended to even after years have passed. It's no good planting young forest evergreens in a foundation planting or towering, easily storm-damaged poplars near a house.

In an area as extensive and varied as North America the kinds of plants it is practical to use varies greatly from region to region. Those best adapted for the deep south are mostly totally unsuited for New England; those that prosper in the humid Pacific Northwest are unlikely to grow well in the drier and hotter Midwest. Be-

Avoid planting specimens likely to become too big: (a) False-cypresses

(b) Rhododendrons

Unless chosen wisely with regard for the ultimate height they are likely to attain, the evergreens on both sides of this door will become too large for their locations

fore you choose plants for your own garden, consider local conditions. Drive around a little and notice which kinds are thriving. Visit nurseries and consult your Cooperative Extension Agent (the modern

equivalent of what was formerly the County Agricultural Agent) or your state agricultural experiment station.

Do not plant trash. There are too many really good plants available to make room in your garden for inferior varieties. It's true that choice kinds often cost more, but they are worth it. If you must economize, buy smaller specimens than you otherwise would, but get good kinds. You may be able to save by setting out fewer plants than you think you need. Makers of new gardens are often so anxious for immediate effect that they overplant, forgetting that the plants grow and soon crowd each other if they are not adequately spaced. Yet another possibility is to propagate at least some of your own plants. This is not practicable with all kinds, but it is easy to start with a few groundcover plants, for instance, and multiply them so that before long you have many times the original number.

Beware of friends' and neighbors' offerings when you are setting out a garden. With the best intentions in the world they will want to share with you plants from their own gardens. Some may be well worth having and will fit into your garden scheme admirably, but others are likely to be invasive kinds that spread disastrously.

Plant the kind of garden that pleases you, one that provides privacy if you wish, one more open if you prefer not to be closed in, one full of color or one in which green predominates, one that contains few kinds of plants or a collector's type garden rich with variety. There are endless variations you can play. Choose the one that suits your site, purse, and inclination or, if these are incompatible, one that is at least a satisfactory compromise.

Your land may be flat, tilted in this direction or that, or it may include various eminences, hollows, or other irregularities. It may boast existing trees, shrubs, outcropping rocks, wet spots, even a pond, streamlet, or stream. Give all these careful consideration in making your plan and well before you begin to plant. Aim to take advantage of existing grades and features. Work with what you have. Do not fight the natural landscape unless for some particular purpose you must.

Rock, outcropping naturally or bared in the course of grading, may with appropriate simple planting become a prized feature of a garden or perhaps can be developed into a charming rock garden. Low-lying wet spots frequently lend themselves to becoming bog gardens or water-lily pools.

Take stock of existing trees and shrubs and identify them by kind. You will want to remove any that are so impossibly located that they cannot be worked into the garden plan, are obviously too decrepit to save, or are of "weed" types. Sorts in this last category vary in different geographical regions. They are likely to be troublesome because they are hosts to pests and diseases, because they self-sow too freely, or for other reasons. Good (or bad) examples in many areas are wild cherry and tree-of-heaven.

Existing trees and shrubs may need thinning out, pruning, or other rehabilitation work. You may find it worthwhile to transplant some, but your success in this (with other than quite small specimens) is likely to be less certain than with nursery-grown trees that have been periodically root-pruned to make transplanting surer. Save every tree and shrub that can make a legitimate contribution to the garden landscape you are developing.

The contours or surface grades are of immense importance in establishing a feeling that the garden is in harmony with its surroundings, that it fits the landscape. This appearance of rightness, of belonging, cannot be attained if grades are wrong.

Many beginners assume that a lawn should be flat, and their efforts at grading are directed toward attaining this end. If the location is too steep, they are likely to attempt a series of flat or nearly flat terraces separated by banks, walls or other devices making severe changes of grade. That is, they are likely to do this if their pocketbooks permit.

This is wrong. Level areas of lawn have their useful place in many garden plans, but to assume that the more level the turf is, the better, is sheer nonsense. Unless there is good need for a lawn to be flat, every effort should be made to have it otherwise. A perfectly level lawn often indicates lack of imagination.

Flatness is a restrictive landscape feature. It calls for formal or semiformal plantings. It does not permit the easy use of the beautiful and seemingly casual informal planting that goes so splendidly with gentle slopes and flowing contours.

Poorly landscaped, a flat lot can be a horror. Straight lines of paths and plantings cross it without apparent purpose, or, worse still, meaningless, silly curves may be introduced to produce "artistic" effects.

This is not to say that perfectly level panels of well-kept turf are not grand when well located or that flat terraces in the immediate vicinity of the house and at "overlooks," for example, are not in good taste, but that they should be accepted only after careful thought and that in many places contours are preferable. Too-steep grades present their own difficulties, and contoured ground, badly landscaped, can be pretty awful, too; but it is harder to do a bad job of landscaping it.

If your lot is not level, develop it in such a way that its natural grades are retained wherever feasible and let any necessary modifications be in keeping with them.

The surface to try for should roll or flow in smooth, pleasing slopes that merge im-

perceptibly without sudden changes of grade or direction. But be practical about it. Arrange the grades so that they present no very special difficulties, as, for example, extraordinary steep ones may do. Let the lawn slope gently away from the house for at least 10 or 12 feet so that surface water drains away (a matter of particular importance when the ground is frozen). Arrange minor valleys for paths, or, alternatively, let them follow natural depressions.

These recommendations are not to be taken to preclude the possibility of having paths leading to high points of vantage; the point to remember is that they should follow the apparently easiest way to their objectives. Curves or turns made without obvious reason or a hill climbed when an easier way is apparent are bad. Functionalism in landscape grading brings its own beauty as it does in so many forms of art.

A flat lot in flat country is natural, and a perfectly level garden in a naturally flatland region never looks out of place, as such gardens may look when artificially created in hilly or rolling country.

Interest can often be added to a level lot by contouring it slightly, but such efforts must not be extreme. Err by doing little rather than too much. Avoid hills and scooped-out depressions that are obviously the work of an enthusiastic bulldozer operator. Aim for gentle rises and barely perceptible hollows, always with outlets so that surface water does not collect. By having the higher land where you will plant trees and tall shrubbery and the lower where free sweeps of lawn and low-growing plants are to be, you will accentuate and improve the effect.

PLANT BREEDING. Plant breeding is based on controlling the sexual opportunities and activities of plants with the objective of securing progeny superior to their parents in one or more ways. Empirically and with conspicuous success it has been engaged in almost since the beginning of plant domestication. The earliest agriculturalists undoubtedly observed that certain individuals among their crops were better suited for their purpose, usually of serving as food, than others.

Soon the giant step forward was taken of saving for planting instead of eating some of the seeds of superior plants. By following this practice through successive generations remarkable changes in cultivated plant populations were accomplished. Before the dawn of recorded history, the major cereal grains and some other basic food crops were well established as different in ways favorable to man from sorts known in the wild. Such progress was made that many cultivated forms became dependent upon the attentions of man to survive and perpetuate their kinds. Unable to successfully meet the competition of wild populations unless

tended by agriculturists, they died out or reverted to primitive types. Cultivated forms of cereals and some other food crops were so modified that even today many cannot with certainty be related to wild ancestors.

Scientific plant breeding based on an understanding of genetic principles is a much more recent development. It dates from the experimental work with peas begun in 1857 by Gregor Mendel, a monk at Brunn in Austria (now Brno in Czechslovakia), but it was not until the beginning of the twentieth century that much attention was given to this activity. Since then, tremendous strides have been made in the improvement of agricultural crops and many garden ornamentals.

The successful plant breeder sets a goal, one that emphasizes as many desirable characteristics as it seems practicable to attain, but often with particular emphasis on one or few. The special qualities sought may include greater uniformity, higher yields, superior flavor or color, more favorable times of maturing, different plant forms, better resistance to diseases and pests, and improved tolerance of low or high temperatures. Once the objective is established it is important to keep it clearly in mind and work purposefully toward its accomplishment.

Controlled mating as well as careful selection of plants to be retained plays an important part in modern plant breeding. It is effected by manipulating pollination, the transfer of pollen from anther to stigma. When this occurs within the same flower or between flowers of the same plant (and in this context individuals of the same clone count as one plant) the flower is self-pollinated; if the transfer is between different plants, it is cross-pollinated. Naturally and without interference by humans some kinds of plants, most obviously those in which male and female flowers are borne by separate individuals, are cross-pollinated, whereas with others self-pollination is usual.

Preventing unwanted pollen from reaching the stigmas of flowers with which he or she is working is as important to the plant breeder as is assuring the arrival of the desired sort. Bisexual flowers selected for seed production must be emasculated by removing their anthers well before they develop ripe pollen. This is generally done with scissors or forceps. Equally as important is protecting the stigma from contamination with unwanted pollen from other flowers. This is usually accomplished by covering the flower selected to produce seed with a paper or plastic bag well in advance of the stigma becoming receptive.

Pollination is done as soon as the stigma is receptive, usually by breaking a ripe anther over it or by transferring ripe pollen with a fine-hair brush from anthers of a flower that have been "bagged" to prevent foreign pollen from lighting upon them. As soon as the transfer of pollen is accomplished, the flower is again covered with a paper or plastic bag.

Self-pollination as a rule results in more uniform progeny than cross-pollination. Selection of the most desirable of the progeny as parents of the next generation repeated for a number of generations, a method called mass or phenotypic selection, results in a greater adherence to the standards selected.

Pure line breeding of self-pollinated plants is a refinement likely to give more uniform results. It involves segregation of superior individuals as seed parents, evaluating and making selections from their progeny, usually for several generations, and then conducting trials to establish as certainly as practicable the virtues of the populations so secured, which are called pure line varieties.

Hybridization or cross-fertilization between selected individuals of normally self-pollinated plants is much employed as a means of developing through pedigree breeding progeny superior to the parents that will breed true to type. Pedigree breeding involves elimination of inferior types and selection of superior ones over several generations with careful records kept and final stringent tests made of the results achieved.

Hybrid varieties of corn and some other plants are not stable in the sense that their progeny breeds true to type. They are recreated each season by cross-pollinating selected parents. Called F_1 hybrids these commonly exhibit desirable hybrid vigor as well as considerable uniformity.

Selective breeding of plants that normally cross-pollinate may involve mass or phenotypic breeding, production of hybrid varieties, and the development of what are called synthetic varieties. These last result from crossing a number of individuals of proved superiority as parents and with various genetic constitutions. They frequently exhibit hybrid vigor as well as the ability to breed true for more than one generation.

Back-crossing is a technique employed by plant breeders to effect improvement by imparting to a desirable variety a trait possessed by some other that it lacks. Here, the varieties are crossed and the progeny is bred to or back-crossed on the desirable variety. This is repeated for a few generations and when a plant with all the desired characteristics appears it is propagated vegetatively or is self-pollinated and plants of the succeeding generations rigorously selected.

Many horticultural plants are reproduced vegetatively instead of from seeds. With such, the aim of plant breeders is to develop hybrids or varieties worthy of being maintained in these ways. Whether or not they breed true from seeds is of little or no significance. Beginning plant breeders must remember that crosses are possible only between fairly closely botanically related kinds of plants and that the closer the relationship, in general, the better the chance of success. Crosses between varieties of the same species are more common than between different species, those between species of the same genus are very much more frequent than those between different genera. It is also important to bear in mind that comparatively rarely do first generation, F_1 seedlings from a cross exhibit all the potentials of the mating. Only when these are self-pollinated and the next generation, the F_2, is grown does the full range of variability become apparent.

PLANT HOPPERS. These include sucking insects called lantern-flies and mealy flata. Much resembling leaf hoppers, but bigger, they hop in lively fashion when disturbed. The most destructive, the corn plant hopper, also called corn leaf hopper, can be controlled by dusting or spraying before damage is done with sulfur, pyrethrum, or rotenone. Less destructive is a conspicuous plant hopper called mealy flata, the mature insect, ¼ inch long or longer, in late summer congregates in large numbers on branches and twigs of a wide variety of shrubs and woody vines which they clothe with white strands that hide the immature insects. Control is not important, but if deemed desirable can be had by spraying with pyrethrum, rotenone, or malathion.

PLANT LICE. See Aphids.

PLANT NAMES. Like all names, those of plants serve as means of reference. They enable us to communicate impressions and observations in a minimum number of words and with more or less precision. It is far simpler and less susceptible of misinterpretation to say "I have in my garden *Caltha palustris*" than "I have in my garden a hardy, deciduous, spring-flowering herbaceous perennial" and follow that with a more or less recognizable description, and it is more precise than saying "I have cowslips in my garden," because cowslips as a name is used for both *Caltha palustris* and *Primula veris*, and these are unrelated and very different plants.

The simplicity of *Caltha palustris* stems from it consisting of two instead of many words, its exactness from it referring to one particular kind of plant and no other. This last is true also of some, but by no means all vernacular plant names. London plane alludes only to *Platanus acerifolia*, but African-violet applies to several species of *Saintpaulia* and hybrids between them, and bluebell or bluebells is used for a number of completely unrelated plants; in eastern North America *Mertensia virginica*, in England *Endymion nonscriptus*, in Scotland *Campanula rotundifolia*, in Texas *Eustoma grandiflorum*, and in Australia *Sollya*

fusiformis is called bluebell-creeper. There are undoubtedly more, so although the names bluebell and bluebells are simple they are not precise.

Another great merit of scientific names is that, unlike common ones, they indicate relationship. All true lilies have obviously much in common, are closely related, and share the generic name *Lilium*, which no other sort of plant does. But the common names Amazon-lily, ginger-lily, mountain-lily, yellow pond-lily, and lily-of-the-valley indicate no close affinities, and indeed belong to species all of different plant families. And, unlike vernacular names in English and other modern languages, botanical names have international currency, being intelligible to informed peoples of all tongues.

Common names, when sufficiently distinctive and clearly understandable, can and should be used. They are frequently apt, often beautiful, and many are part of the rich heritage of the English language. But to employ vernacular names when they do not adequately convey exactly what is meant is frustrating and defeating of purpose. Then botanical and recognized horticultural names should be employed.

A disturbing tendency, more usual in the United States than in most countries where English is spoken, is to invent "common" names for plants that have none. The catalogs of some dealers are replete with such names. Mostly they are without much value for conveying information and are likely to be found in few or perhaps only one such publication.

Botanical names are mostly no more difficult to learn and remember than common ones, only their unfamiliarity when first encountered makes it seem so. Almost everyone is likely to be acquainted with a considerable number of such names at least so far as genus is concerned. Who for instance has not heard of *Camellia*, *Canna*, *Chrysanthemum*, *Gladiolus*, and *Rhododendron*, perhaps even of *Ageratum*, *Caladium*, *Eucalyptus*, *Fuchsia*, *Ginkgo*, and *Lantana*. All of these are botanical, scientific, or "Latin" names that do double duty as English ones. And they are few of many. In other instances, the botanical name differs only slightly from the vernacular one. Roses for example belong to the genus *Rosa*, true lilies to *Lilium*, hyacinths to *Hyacinthus*, heliotropes to *Heliotropium*, and tulips to *Tulipa*. But frequently there is no such similarity.

The names just discussed are those of plant genera, not of such lesser categories as species or varieties. They are somewhat analogous to the family names of people. But, as there may be more than one person in the Smith family, so there frequently is more than one species in a genus of plants. We identify the various Smiths by a given name. We may for example have John Smith, Mary Smith, and William Smith. In like manner we add a "specific epithet" to the generic names of plants to identify particular species, but instead of placing it before the group designation, as is done with people naming, it goes after it. Thus instead of the form John Smith, Mary Smith, and William Smith we use *Lilium candidum, Lilium longiflorum,* and *Lilium regale* respectively for Madonna, Easter, and regal lilies. Note specific names differ from people names in not designating one particular individual, but in being applicable to all those of a group sufficiently alike to be accepted as a species. Sometimes minor differences exist between members of a species and may be of sufficient importance to warrant recognition. This is done by appending to the specific name a third term that converts it to a more discriminating designation. The segregations recognized by these finer splits are, in horticultural practice, called varieties or cultivars. Botanists employ a series of terms, such as subspecies, variety, and forma, to distinguish more precisely between them.

The present system of naming plants scientifically is based on the work of the great Swedish botanist Carolus Linnaeus, who was born in 1707 and who died in 1778. His "Genera Plantarum" (Genera of Plants), published in 1737, and his "Species Plantarum" (Species of Plants), published in 1753, represent benchmarks in the practice of plant nomenclature.

In these works, Linnaeus established three categories, genus, species, and varietas (variety), as warranting recognition in the application of names. As examples of how this now universally accepted system operates we may consider three flowering dogwoods. All belong to the genus *Cornus*. That one word is the generic name of each of these dogwoods and of all other members of the same genus. To more precisely identify the dogwoods we are considering, each is given a specific name consisting of *two words*, the generic name plus a specific epithet (this last is not by itself, as it is often loosely called, a specific name). The specific name of the eastern North American flowering dogwood is *Cornus florida*, that of the western species *Cornus nuttallii*, and that of the kind native in Japan *Cornus kousa*. Individuals of the eastern American flowering dogwood that have the red- instead of white-bracted flower clusters are distinguished by the variety name *Cornus florida rubra*, formed by adding a third term to the specific name. Populations of *Cornus florida* or *C. f. rubra* that have resulted from propagating selected individuals, so that all individuals of the sort are genetical duplicates of the original plant, are clones, also distinguished by varietal or cultivar names. Examples are *Cornus florida pendula, C. f.* 'Cherokee Chief', *C. f.* 'White Cloud', and *C. f. xanthocarpa*.

Despite the orderliness of the rules for applying scientific names to plants many often bewildering problems arise in practice. From the gardeners' point of view, not the least of these is the frequency, and to the uninformed, apparent capriciousness with which botanists change names of plants long known under others. It is difficult for many to appreciate why the asparagus fern they have known as *Asparagus sprengeri* must become *A. densiflorus* or the name *Helxine soleirolii* for baby's tears must become *Soleirolia soleirolii*.

The most frequent reasons for such changes are the need to comply with the *International Code of Botanical Nomenclature* and to reflect the outcome of new research.

Under the priority rule of the botanical code, the correct name of a plant (except for certain generic names that are "conserved") relates to the first one under which it was recognizably described. This makes necessary a change of name each time (and this happens frequently) a name older than the one current is discovered in botanical literature. Theoretically, an end will come to changes of this sort when all needed corrections have been made.

Changes in names that result from studies of the significance of differences between sorts of plants and the relationships between them of necessity reflect subjective opinions of the research workers. A population that one authority considers distinct enough to be worthy of a specific name another may treat as only worthy of recognition as a variety of a species, and the relatively inclusive genera of some botanists may by others be split into more discrete genera. Because plant taxonomy (the study of the kinds of plants and their relationships) is a living science with new discoveries constantly being made and old concepts reviewed in the light of additional knowledge by researchers with different outlooks, name changes are bound to continue to be made and the intelligent gardener and others concerned with plants will accept this fact.

To be valid a botanical name must be published in a printed or similarly reproduced book, journal, or periodical of acceptable wide distribution accompanied by a description (since 1936 in Latin) or, in rare instances, in place of a description a sufficiently detailed illustration. These provisions eliminate from botanical nomenclature many Latin-form names used in horticultural literature. Provision for the treatment of the latter is made in the *International Code of Nomenclature for Cultivated Plants*.

Botanical names irrespective of their derivation, and many come from Greek, English, and other sources in addition to Latin, are given Latin forms and reflect the rules of Latin grammar. Generic names, always written with a capital initial, are nouns or are treated as such and may be masculine, feminine, or neuter. Specific epithets may be uniformly begun with a small (lowercase) letter, the recommended procedure, or by giving capital or small initials to different ones according to certain rather involved rules. Specific epithets may be adjectives or nouns. If adjectives they must agree in case and gender with the name of the genus, if nouns no such agreement is required. The same rules govern the application of terms designating botanical varieties. In scientific usage it is the practice to append after the specific name the name or an abbreviation of the name of the person who first described the plant under the name employed, thus: *Rosa rugosa* Thunb. (first described by the botanist Carl Pehr Thunberg); *Acer negundo* L. (first described by the great Swedish botanist Linnaeus).

Many specific names honor or commemorate people. These are usually in the genitive (possessive) case, for example *Lilium henryi* (the *Lilium* of Mr. Henry), *Lilium willmottiae* (the *Lilium* of Miss Willmott), *Lilium bakeranum* (the *Lilium* of the Bakers), and *Clematis davidiana* (the *Clematis* of David). Less often specific names are adjectives. Then their epithet endings take the gender and case of the genus. Thus we have *Ceanothus veitchianus* (the Veitch *Ceanothus*), a masculine ending in *us*; *Begonia lindleyana* (the Lindley *Begonia*), a feminine ending in *ana*; and *Sedum middendorffianum* (the Middendorf *Sedum*), a neuter ending in *um*.

Specific epithets of names honoring or commemorating men are formed by adding to the person's name *ii* if its last two letters are not *er* and it ends in a consonant other than *y*. Otherwise the masculine specific epithet is formed by adding one *i* to the name. Thus we have *Gentiana andrewsii*, but *Gentiana farreri, Gentiana parryi,* and *Gentiana makinoi*. Specific epithets of names honoring or commemorating women are made by adding to the person's name the letters *ae* or *iae*, as in *Primula julianae* and *Lilium sargentiae*.

Not all specific names are commemorative. Many refer to geographical regions, which usually but not invariably indicate the nativity of the plants. Here for example belong *Platystemon californicus* (Californian *Platystemon*), masculine; *Lonicera americana* (American *Lonicera*), feminine; and *Sedum anglicum* (English *Sedum*), neuter. Other specific names refer to characteristics of the plants themselves. Here for example belong *Thymus hirsutus* (the hairy *Thymus*), masculine; *Campanula persicifolia* (the peach-leaved *Campanula*), feminine; and *Viburnum odoratissimum* (the fragrant *Viburnum*), neuter. Less common are specific names that include obsolete or current genus names as epithets as is true of *Liriodendron tulipifera* and *Diervilla lonicera*, and those, such as *Ligustrum ibota* and *Podocarpus totara*, which are derived from vernacular names.

Hybrids between genera, in a sense, artificial genera, are given identifying group names. If only two or sometimes if three parents are involved, these are formed by combining parts of the names of the parent genera provided the result does not exceed more than eight syllables. Thus *Mahoberberis* is the name of hybrids between *Mahonia* and *Berberis*, *Laeliocattleya* of hybrids between *Laelia* and *Cattleya*, and *Sophrolaeliocattleya* of hybrids between *Sophronitis*, *Laelia*, and *Cattleya*.

Hybrids resulting from combining four or in some cases only three genera, and which mostly occur in the orchid family, are given names formed by adding *ara* to the end of the name of a person, usually one prominently identified as a collector, student, or cultivator of the group. Examples are *Yamadara*, for hybrids involving all four genera *Laelia*, *Brassavola*, *Cattleya*, and *Diacrium*, and *Sanderara* for hybrids involving *Odontoglossum*, *Brassia*, and *Cochlioda*.

The *International Code of Nomenclature for Cultivated Plants*, first published in 1958, and since revised, has as its objective the promotion of uniformity, accuracy, and fixity in the naming of plants in cultivation for which provision is not made under the Botanical Code. Its chief concern is with varieties (cultivars). These are defined as assemblages of "cultivated individuals which are distinguished by any characters (morphological, physiological, cytological, chemical, or others) significant for the purposes of agriculture, forestry, or horticulture, and which, when reproduced (sexually or asexually) retain their distinguishing features."

Such varieties or cultivars differ from assemblages to which botanists apply the word variety (or more explicitly *varietas*) in that they do not occur as natural populations, being dependent upon cultivation for permanent survival. According to this horticultural code, the names of cultivars must consist of that of a genus or species followed by a cultivar term that unless established prior to 1959 must be in "fancy" rather than Latin form, thus the cultivar term whether in Latin form or not is given with initial capitals to the words that compose it, except where this is contrary to national custom, and preceded by the abbreviation "cv." or enclosed in single quotation marks; minor variations of these rules apply to groups of very similar cultivars. In this Encyclopedia the names of cultivars or horticultural varieties are not indicated in this fashion. Instead, those in Latin form appear in italics without a capital initial, those in non-Latin form are enclosed in single quotation marks and with capital initials.

The meanings of the epithets of specific names are often of interest. Here is a selection of those frequently encountered among cultivated plants, omitting names commemorative of people.

abrotanifoli-us, -a, -um, with leaves resembling southernwood

abysinnic-us, -a, -um, native of Ethiopia (Abyssinia)

acanthifoli-us, -a, -um, with leaves resembling those of *Acanthus*

acaul-is, -e, stemless or almost so

acephal-us, -a, -um, headless

acer, acris, acre, sharp-pointed or sharp or pungent to the taste

acerifoli-us, -a, -um, with leaves like those of a maple (*Acer*)

aceroides, resembling a maple (*Acer*)

achilleifoli-us, -a, -um, with foliage like that of yarrow (*Achillea millefolium*)

acicular-is, -e, needle-like

acidissim-us, -a, -um, extremely acid or sour

acidos-us, -a, -um, acidus, acid or sour

aconitifoli-us, -a, -um, with leaves resembling those of monkshood (*Aconitum*)

aculeat-us, -a, um, prickly

aculeatissim-us, -a, -um, very prickly

acuminat-us. -a, -um, tapered to a long, narrow point

acuminatifoli-us, -a, -um, with leaves tapered to long, narrow points

acutangul-us, -a, -um, with sharp angles

acutifoli-us, -a, -um, with sharp-pointed leaves

acutilob-us, a, -um, with sharp-pointed lobes

acutipetal-us, -a, -um, with sharp-pointed petals

acut-us, -a, -um, sharply pointed

acutissim-us, -a, -um, very sharply pointed

adiantifoli-us, -a, -um, with foliage like that of the maidenhair fern (*Adiantum*)

adiantoides, resembling the maidenhair fern (*Adiantum*)

adnat-us, -a, -um, united or joined together

adonidifoli-us, -a, -um, with foliage like that of *Adonis*

adpress-us, -a, -um, pressed together

adscendens, ascending

adsurgens, rising in upright fashion

aegyptiac-us, -a, -um; aegyptic-us, -a, -um, Egyptian

aequal-is, -e, equal

aequilob-us, -a, -um, with equal lobes

aequitrilob-us, -a, -um, with three equal lobes

aesculifoli-us, -a, -um, with leaves like a buckeye or horsechestnut (*Aesculus*)

aestival-is, -e, of summer

aestiv-us, -a, -um, developing or ripening in summer

aethiopic-us, -a, -um, African

aetnens-is. -e, of Mount Etna, in Sicily

affin-is, -e. related or similar to

african-us, -a, -um, African

agavoides, resembling an *Agave*

ageratifoli-us, -a, -um, with leaves like *Ageratum*

ageratoides, resembling *Ageratum*

aggregat-us, -a, -um, grouped or clustered

agrari-us, -a, -um, of the fields

agrest-is, -e, of the fields

agrifol-us, -a, -um, with rough leaves

aizoides, resembling *Aizoon*

alabamens-is, -e, from Alabama

alat-us. -a, -um, winged

albescens, whitish

albicans, off-white, becoming white

albicaulis, with white stems

albid-us, -a, -um, whitish

albifrons, with white fronds

albiplen-us, -a, -um, with double white flowers

albispin-us, -a, -um, with white spines

albomaculat-us, -a, -um, spotted with white

albopict-us, -a, -um, painted with white

albopilos-us, -a, -um, white-hairy

alboplen-us, -a, -um, with double white flowers

albovariegat-us, -a, -um, variegated with white

alb-us, -a, -um, white

aldenhamens-is, -e, originated at Aldenham, a garden near London, England

aleppic-us, -a, -um, of Aleppo (Haleb), Syria

algeriens-is, -e, of Algeria

alleghaniens-is, -e, of the Allegheny mountains

alliace-us. -a, -um, onion-like in flavor, scent, or appearance

alnifoli-us, -a, -um, with alder-like leaves

aloides or alooides, resembling *Aloe*

aloifoli-us. -a, -um, with leaves like *Aloe*

alpestr-is, -e, of mountains at altitudes usually below timberline

alpicola, a mountain dweller

alpin-us, -a, -um, of mountains at altitudes usually above timberline

amar-us, -a, -um, bitter

amazonic-us, -a, -um, of the Amazon river region

ambigu-us, -a, -um, doubtful, uncertain

ambrosioides, resembling *Ambrosia*

amelloides, resembling *Amellus*

american-us, -a, -um, of North or South America

amethystin-us, -a, -um, amethyst- or violet-colored

ammophil-us, -a, -um, sand-loving

amoen-us, -a, -um, pleasing

amphibi-us, -a, -um, growing on land and in water

amplexicaul-is, -e, stem-clasping

amplexifoli-us, -a, -um, leaf-clasping

amurens-is, -e, from the region of the Amur river

amygdaliform-is, -e, almond-shaped

amygdalin-us, -a, -um, almond-like

amygdaloides, resembling an almond

anacanth-us, -a, -um, thornless

anacardioides, resembling the cashew nut tree (*Anacardium*)

anagyroides, resembling *Anagyris*

angular-is, -e, angular

angulat-us, -a, -um, angular

angulos-us, -a, -um, with many corners or angles

angustifoli-us, -a, -um, with narrow leaves

anisat-us, -a, -um, anise-like

anisodor-us, -a, -um, scented of anise

anisophyll-us, -a, -um, with pairs of leaves, one bigger than the other

annular-is, -e, ringlike

annulat-us, -a, -um, with rings

annu-us, -a, -um, annual

antarctic-us, -a, -um, of south polar regions

anthemoides, resembling chamomile (*Anthemis*)

anthyllidifoli-us, -a, -um, with leaves like *Anthyllis*

antiquorum, of the ancients

antirrhiniflor-us, -a, -um, with flowers like those of snapdragon (*Antirrhinum*)

antirrhinoides, resembling snapdragons (*Antirrhinum*)

apert-us, -a, -um, bare, open, or exposed

apetal-us, -a, -um, without petals

aphyll-us, -a, -um, without or apparently without leaves

apiculat-us, -a, -um, with a brief, usually sharp point

apiifoli-us, -a, -um, with celery-like foliage

appendiculat-us, -a, -um, with appendages

appenin-us, -a, -um, of the Appenine mountains

appress-us, -a, -um, pressed against

apric-us, -a, -um, sun-loving

apter-us, -a, -um, without wings

aquatic-us, -a, -um; aquatil-is, -e, growing in or beside water

aquilegiifoli-us, -a, -um, with leaves like columbine (*Aquilegia*)

arabic-us, -a, -um; arab-us, -a, -um, Arabian

arachnoides; arachnoide-us, -a, -um, with hairs suggesting a spider's web

araliifoli-us, -a, -um, with leaves like those of *Aralia*

arborescens; arbore-us, -a, -um, more or less treelike

arbuscul-us, -a, -um, resembling a small tree

arbutifoli-us, -a, -um, with leaves resembling those of *Arbutus*

arctic-us, -a, -um, from the north polar region

arcuat-us, -a, -um, arched or bent like a bow

ardens, glowing

arenari-us, -a, -um, sand-loving

argenteoguttat-us, -a, -um, silver-spotted

argenteomarginat-us, -a, -um, edged with silver

argenteovariegat-us, -a, -um, variegated with silver

argente-us, -a, -um, silvery

argentin-us, -a, -um, of Argentina

argut-us, -a, -um, with sharp teeth or notches

argyrae-us, -a, -um, silvery

argyrocom-us, -a, -um, with silvery hairs

argyroneur-us, -a, -um, with silvery veins

argyrophyll-us, -a, -um, with silvery leaves

arid-us, -a, -um, inhabiting dry places

arifoli-us, -a, -um, with leaves like *Arum*

ariifoli-us, -a, -um, with leaves like *Sorbus aria*

aristat-us, -a, -um, with a beard or bristles

arizonic-us, -a, -um, of Arizona

armat-us, -a, -um, thorny or spiny

armeniac-us, -a, -um, of Armenia

arnoldian-us, -a, -um, of the Arnold Arboretum, near Boston, Massachusetts

aromatic-us, -a, -um, aromatic or fragrant

artemisioides, resembling *Artemisia*

articulat-us, -a, -um, having joints

arundinace-us, -a, -um, reedlike

arvens-is, -e, of cultivated fields

asarifoli-us, -a, -um, with leaves like those of wild-ginger (*Asarum*)

ascendens, sloping upward

asiatic-us, -a, -um, Asian

asper, asper-a, -um, rough

asperat-us, -a, -um, roughened

aspericaul-is, -e, with rough stems

asperifoli-us, -a, -um, with rough leaves

asperrim-us, -a, -um, very rough

asphodeloides, resembling the asphodel (*Asphodelus*)

asplenifoli-us, -a, -um, with leaves resembling those of spleenwort (*Asplenium*)

assurgens, ascending

assurgentiflor-us, -a, -um, with flowers in ascending clusters

asteroides, resembling *Aster*

astilboides, resembling *Astilbe*

asturic-us, -a, -um; asturiens-is, -e, of Asturia, in Spain

atlantic-us, -a, -um, from near the Atlantic Ocean or from the Atlas Mountains, in North Africa

atrat-us, -a, -um, blackened

atriplicifoli-us, -a, -um, with leaves like those of *Atriplex*

atropurpure-us, -a, -um, dark purple

atrorubens, dark red

atrosanguine-us, -a, -um, dark blood-red

atroviolace-us, -a, -um, dark violet

atrovirens, dark green

attenuat-us, -a, -um, narrowed to a point

aubrietioides, resembling *Aubrieta*

augustissim-us, -a, -um, very majestic or notable

august-us, -a, -um, majestic or notable

aurantiac-us, -a, -um; auranti-us, -a, -um, orange-colored

aurantifoli-us, -a, -um, with leaves resembling those of the orange (*Citrus aurantium*)

aurat-us, -a, -um, ornamented with gold

aureomaculat-us, -a, -um, spotted with gold

aureomarginat-us, -a, -um, edged with gold

aureoreticulat-us, -a, -um, with gold veins

aureovariegat-us, -a, -um, variegated with gold

aure-us, -a, -um, golden

auricom-us, -a, -um, with golden hairs

auriculat-us, -a, -um, with an earlike appendage

australiens-is, -e, Australian

austral-is, -e, southern

austriac-us, -a, -um, Austrian

autumnal-is, -e, of autumn

axillar-is, -e, borne in axils

azaleoides, resembling azaleas

azoric-us, -a, -um, of the Azores

azure-us, -a, -um, sky-blue

babylonic-us, -a, -um, of Babylonia

baccans, berry-bearing or berry-like

baccat-us, -a, -um, berry-like

baccifer, baccifer-a, -um, berry-bearing

bacillar-is, -e, sticklike

balcanic-us, -a, -um, of the Balkan Peninsula

baldens-is, -e, of Monte Baldo, Italy

balearic-us, -a, -um, of the Balearic Islands

balsame-us, -a, -um, suggesting balsam

balsamifer-us, -a, -um, balsam-bearing

baltic-us, -a, -um, of the Baltic Sea region

bambusoides, resembling bamboo

banatic-us, -a, -um, of Banat, Romania

barbadens-is, -e, of Barbados, West Indies

barbat-us, -a, -um, with a beard of long, weak hairs

barbiger-us, -a, -um, having barbs or beards

barbinerv-is, -e, with barbed or bearded veins

barbulat-us, -a, -um, lightly bearded or with a beard of short hairs

baselloides, resembling *Basella*

basilar-is, -e, relating to the base

basilic-us, -a, -um, royal or princely

batatas, the Carib Indian name of the sweet potato

bavaric-us, -a, -um, of Bavaria

belgic-us, -a, -um, of Belgium, sometimes of the entire Netherlands

belladonna, meaning beautiful lady, this alludes to a former use of the plant for enhancing the beauty of the eyes

bellidifoli-us, -a, -um, with leaves like *Bellis*

bellidiform-is, -e, having the form of a daisy (*Bellis*)

bellidioides, resembling *Bellium*

bell-us, -a, -um, beautiful

benedict-us, -a, -um, blessed, of good repute

bengalens-is, -e, of Bengal, India (sometimes spelled *benghalensis*)

bermudian-us, -a, -um, of Bermuda

berolinens-is, -e, of Berlin, Germany

bessarabic-us, -a, -um, of Bessarabia

betace-us, -a, -um, resembling beets

betonicifoli-us, -a, -um, with leaves like betony (*Stachys betonica*) betulifoli-us, -a, -um, with leaves like a birch (*Betula*)

betulin-us, -a, -um; betuloides, resembling birch (*Betula*)

bicolor, of two colors

bicorn-is, -e; bicornut-us, -a, -um, with two horns

bidentat-us, -a, -um, having two teeth

bienn-is, -e, biennial

bifid-us, -a, -um, cleft into two parts

biflor-us, -a, -um, with twinned flowers

bifoli-us, -a, -um, with twinned leaves

bifurcat-us, -a, -um, forked into two usually nearly equal branches

bignonioides, resembling *Bignonia*

bijug-us, -a, -um, with two pairs united

bipinnat-us, -a, -um, twice-pinnate

bisect-us, -a, -um, in two equal parts

biserrat-us, -a, -um, double-toothed

biternat-us, -a, -um, with three divisions each of three parts

bivalv-is, -e, with two valves

bland-us, -a, -um, mild, pleasing

blepharophyll-us, -a, -um, having leaves fringed like eyelashes

bolivian-us, -a, -um, of Bolivia

bombycin-us, -a, -um, silky

bonariens-is, -e, of Buenos Aires, Argentina

borbonic-us, -a, -um, of Réunion Island, at one time called Ile Bourbon or in honor of the Bourbon kings of France

boreal-is, -e, northern

borinquen-us, -a, -um, of Puerto Rico (at one time called Borinquén)

borneens-is, -e, of Borneo

botryoides, like a bunch of grapes

brachiat-us, -a, -um, branches at approximately right angles

brachyanth-us, -a, -um, with short flowers

brachybotrys, short-clustered

brachycarp-us, -a, -um, with short fruits

brachycer-us, -a, -um, short-horned

brachypetal-us, -a, -um, short-petaled

brachyphyll-us, -a, -um, with short leaves

brachysiphon, with short tubes

bracteat-us, -a, -um, having bracts

bracteos-us, -a, -um, with conspicuous bracts

brasiliens-is, -e, of Brazil

brassicifoli-us, -a, -um, with leaves like cabbage (*Brassica*)

brev-is, -e, short

brevifoli-us, -a, -um, with short leaves

brevipedunculat-us, -a, -um, with a short flower stalk (peduncle)

breviscap-us, -a, -um, with a short flowering stalk (scape)

brevistyl-is, -e, with a short style

britannic-us, -a, -um, of Great Britain

briziform-is, -e; brizoides, resembling quaking grass (*Briza*)

bronchial-is, -e, used for treating bronchitis

bryoides, mosslike

buccinatori-us, -a, -um; buccinat-us, -a, -um, shaped like a crooked horn

buddleoides, resembling *Buddleia*

bulbifer, bubifer-a, -um, bearing bulbs

bulbiform-is, -e, bulb-shaped

bulbos-us, -a, -um, bulbous or conspicuously swollen

bulgaric-us, -a, -um, of Bulgaria

bullat-us, -a, -um, blistered or puckered (bullate)

burmanic-us, -a, -um, of Burma

buxifoli-us, -a, -um, with leaves like boxwood (*Buxus*)

byzantin-us, -a, -um, of Istanbul (Byzantium)

cachemiric-us, -a, -um, of Kashmir

caerulescens, becoming blue or bluish

caerule-us, -a, -um, dark blue

caesi-us, -a, -um, bluish-gray

caespitos-us, -a, -um, clump-forming

calabric-us, -a, -um, of Calabria, Italy

calamifoli-us, -a, -um, having reedlike foliage

calathin-us, -a, -um, basket-like

calcarat-us, -a, -um, with spurs

calcare-us, -a, -um, lime-loving

calcicola, growing in limy soil

calendulace-us, -a, -um, orange-colored like flowers of *Calendula*

californic-us, -a, -um, of California

callianth-us, -a, -um, with beautiful flowers

callicarp-us, -a, -um, with beautiful fruit

callimorph-us, -a, -um, beautifully formed

callistachy-us, -a, -um, having beautiful spikes

callistegioides, like *Calystegia*

callizon-us, -a, -um, with beautiful bands or zones

callos-us, -a, -um, calloused or thick-skinned

calocephal-us, -a, -um, with a beautiful head

calophyll-us, -a, -um, having beautiful leaves

calycin-us, -a, -um, calyx-like

cambric-us, -a, -um, of Wales (Cambria)

camelliflor-us, -a, -um, having flowers like *Camellia*

campaniflor-us, -a, -um, having bell-shaped flowers

campanulari-us, -a, -um; campanulat-us, -a, -um, bell-shaped

campanuloides, resembling *Campanula*

campestr-is, -e, of the fields

camphorat-us, -a, -um, resembling or pertaining to camphor

campylocarp-us, -a, -um, having curved or bent fruits

camtschatcens-is, -e; camtschatic-us, -a, -um, of Kamchatka

canadens-is, -e, of Canada

canaliculat-us, -a, -um, grooved or channeled

canariens-is, -e, of the Canary Islands

cancellat-us, -a, -um, latticed or cross-barred

candelabrum, candelabra-like

candicans, shining or woolly-white

candidissim-us, -a, -um, intensely white

candid-us, -a, -um, shining or pure white

canescens, having off-white or ashy-gray hairs

canin-us, -a, -um, pertaining to dogs, thus by inference inferior

cannifoli-us, -a, -um, with leaves like *Canna*

cantabric-us, -a, -um, of Cantabria, Spain, or the Cantabrian mountains

cantabrigiens-is, -e, of Cambridge, England

capens-is, -e, of the Cape of Good Hope, South Africa

caperat-us, -a, -um, wrinkled

capilliform-is, -e, hairlike

capitat-us, -a, -um, having dense heads

cappadocic-us, -a, -um, of eastern Asia Minor (Cappadocia)

capreolat-us, -a, -um, with tendrils

capre-us, -a, -um, relating to goats

capsular-is, -e, like capsules

cardaminifoli-us, -a, -um, with leaves like *Cardamine*

cardinal-is, -e, cardinal-red

carduace-us, -a, -um, like a thistle

carduncul-us, -a, -um, like a small thistle

caribae-us, -a, -um, of the Caribbean region

carinat-us, -a, -um, keeled

carinthiac-us, -a, -um, of Carinthia (Austria)

carmine-us, -a, -um, carmine

carne-us, -a, -um; carnicolor, flesh-colored or deep pink

carnos-us, -a, -um, fleshy

carolinian-us, -a, -um; carolinens-is, -e; carolin-us, -a, -um, of North or South Carolina

carpatic-us, -a, -um, (sometimes spelled carpathicus) from the Carpathian Mountains

carpinifoli-us, -a, -um, having hornbeam-like leaves

carthusianorum, of the monks of the Carthusian Monastery of Grande Chartreuse near Grenoble, France

cartilagine-us, -a, -um, suggesting cartilage

caryophyll-us, -a, -um, with the aromatic smell of walnut leaves

cashmerian-us, -a, -um, of Kashmir

castane-us, -a, -um, chestnut-colored

catalpifoli-us, -a, -um, having leaves like *Catalpa*

catarractae; catarractarum, of a waterfall or waterfalls

catawbiens-is, -e, of the Catawba region of the Blue Ridge Mountains of eastern North America

cathayan-us, -a, -um, of China (Cathay)

cathartic-us, -a, -um, having purgative qualities

caucasic-us, -a, -um, of the Caucasus

caudat-us, -a, -um, with a tail or tails

caulescens, stemmed

cauliflor-us, -a, -um, bearing flowers on the trunk or stem

cav-us, -a, -um, hollow

centifoli-us, -a, -um, many-leaved

centranthifoli-us, -a, -um, with leaves like *Centranthus*

cephalonic-us, -a, -um, of the Greek island of Cephalonia

cerasifer, cerasifer-a, -um, bearing cherries or cherry-like fruits

cerasiform-is, -e, shaped like cherries

cerifer, cerifer-a, -um, waxy

cerinthoides, resembling *Cerinthe*

cernu-us, -a, -um, nodding or drooping

chalcedonic-us, -a, -um, of Chalcedon (Asia Minor)

chamaedrifoli-us, -a, -um, having leaves like *Chamaedrys*

chasmanth-us, -a, -um, with gaping flowers

cheilanth-us, -a, -um, with lipped flowers

chelidoniodes, resembling *Chelidonium*

chilens-is, -e, of Chile

chiloens-is, -e, of Chiloe Island, off the coast of Chile

chinens-is, -e, Chinese

chionanth-us, -a, -um, with snow-white flowers

chloranth-us, -a, -um, having green flowers

chlorochilon, having a green lip

chrysanthoides, resembling *Chrysanthemum*

chrysanth-us, -a, -um, having golden flowers

chrysocarp-us, -a, -um, having golden fruit

chrysocom-us, -a, um, with golden hair

chrysolep-is, -e, with golden scales

chrysoleuc-us, -a, -um, gold and white

chrysophyll-us, -a, -um, golden-leaved

cichoriace-us, -a, -um, resembling chicory (*Cichorium*)

cicutifoli-us, -a, -um, with leaves like water-hemlock (*Cicuta*)

cistiflor-us, -a, -um, with flowers like *Cistus*

cistifoli-us, -a, -um, with leaves like *Cistus*

citrat-us, -a, -um, resembling *Citrus*

citrifoli-us, -a, -um, with leaves resembling *Citrus*

citriniflor-us, -a, -um, with lemon-yellow flowers

citrin-us, -a, -um, lemon-colored, or citron-like

citriodor-us, -a, -um, lemon-scented

citroides, resembling *Citrus*

clandestin-us, -a, -um, hidden

claus-us, -a, -um, closed

clavat-us, -a, -um, club-shaped

clavellat-us, -a, -um, shaped like a small club

clematide-us, -a, -um, resembling *Clematis*

clethroides, resembling *Clethra*

clypeat-us, -a, -um, having the shape of a Roman shield

clypeolat-us, -a, -um, somewhat shield-shaped

coccifer-us, -a, -um, berry-bearing or host to berry-like scale insects

coccine-us, -a, -um, scarlet

cochlearifoli-us, -a, -um, with leaves like *Cochlearia*

cochlear-is, -e, spoon-shaped

cochleat-us, -a, -um, spiraled like the shell of a snail

coelestin-us, -a, -um; coelest-is, -e, sky-blue

coerulescens, bluish, becoming blue

coerule-us, -a, -um, blue

cognat-us, -a, -um, closely related

colchic-us, -a, -um, of Colchis, a region near the Black Sea

collin-us, -a, -um, of the hills

colorat-us, -a, -um, colored

columbari-us, -a, -um, pertaining to doves, or dovelike

columbian-us, -a, -um, of British Columbia or the Columbia River region

columnar-is, -e, columnar

comat-us, -a, -um, with a tuft

commixt-us, -a, -um, mixed

commun-is, -e, common or communal

commutat-us, -a, -um, changed or changing

comos-us, -a, -um, having a tuft

compact-us, -a, -um, compact

complanat-us, -a, -um, flattened

complex-us, -a, -um, encircled or complex

complicat-us, -a, -um, complicated

composit-us, -a, -um, compound

compress-us, -a, -um, compressed

concav-us, -a, -um, hollowed

conchifoli-us, -a, -um, with leaves like seashells

concinn-us, -a, -um, neat or elegant

concolor, of one uniform color

condensat-us, -a, -um; condens-us, -a, -um, crowded

confertiflor-us, -a, -um, with crowded flowers

confert-us, -a, -um, crowded

conform-is, -e, conforming to type or similar to related sorts

confus-us, -a, -um, confusing

congest-us, -a, -um, congested

conglomerat-us, -a, -um, crowded

conjugat-us, -a, -um; conjugal-is, -e, united in pairs

conjunct-us, -a, -um, united

connat-us, -a, -um, twinned or having opposite leaves joined at their bases

consanguine-us, -a, -um, related

consolid-us, -a, -um, solid or stable

conspers-us, -a, -um, scattered

conspicu-us, -a, -um, conspicuous

constrict-us, -a, -um, constricted

contort-us, -a, -um, twisted, irregularly bent

contract-us, -a, -um, contracted

controvers-us, -a, -um, controversial

convallaroides, like lily-of-the-valley (*Convallaria*)

convolvulace-us, -a, -um, resembling *Convolvulus*

copallin-us, -a, um, gummy or resinous

corallin-us, -a, -um, coral-red

cordat-us, -a, -um, heart-shaped

cordifoli-us, -a, -um, having heart-shaped leaves

cordiform-is, -e, heart-shaped

corean-us, -a, -um, of Korea

coriace-us, -a, -um, thick and leathery

coriari-us, -a, -um, like leather

corniculat-us, -a, -um, with small horns

cornut-us, -a, -um, horned or horn-shaped

corollat-us, -a, -um, resembling a corolla

coronans; coronat-us, -a, -um, crowned

coronari-us, -a, -um, used for or relating to garlands

coronopifoli-us, -a, -um, with leaves like *Coronopus*

corrugat-us, -a, -um, wrinkled

corsic-us, -a, -um, of Corsica

cortusoides, resembling *Cortusa*

coruscans, glittering

corylifoli-us, -a, -um, with leaves like *Corylus*

corymbiflor-us, -a, -um, with flowers in corymbs

corymbos-us, -a, -um, having corymbs

costat-us, -a, -um, ribbed

cotinifoli-us, -a, -um, with leaves like *Cotinus*

cotinoides, resembling *Cotinus*

crassicaul-is, -e, with thick stems

crassifoli-us, -a, -um, thick-leaved

crassipes, thick-stemmed, or thick-footed

crass-us, -a, -um, thick or fleshy

crataegifoli-us, -a, -um, having leaves like hawthorn (*Crataegus*)

crataegoides, resembling hawthorn (*Crataegus*)

crenatiflor-us, -a, -um, with scalloped flowers

crenat-us, -a, -um, with rounded teeth or scallops

crenulat-us, -a, -um, somewhat scalloped

crepitans, rustling or crackling

cretace-us, -a, -um, chalky or pertaining to chalk

cretens-is, -e; cretic-us, -a, -um, of Crete

crinit-us, -a, -um, with long, usually weak hairs

crispat-us, -a, -um; crisp-us, -a, -um, crisped or closely curled

cristat-us, -a, -um, crested or with tassel-like tips

crithmifoli-us, -a, -um, with leaves like *Crithmum*

crocat-us, -a, -um; croce-us, -a, -um, saffron-colored or yellow

crotonifoli-us, -a, -um, with leaves like *Croton*

cruciat-us, -a, -um, in the shape of a cross

cruent-us, -a, -um, blood-colored

crystallin-us, -a, -um, crystal-like or crystalline

ctenoides, comblike

cucullar-is, -e; cucullat-us, -a, -um, hoodlike

cucumerifoli-us, -a, -um, with cucumber-like leaves

cultrat-us, -a, -um; cultriform-is, -e, having the shape of a knife blade

cuneat-us, -a, -um, wedge-shaped

cuneifoli-us, -a, -um, having wedge-shaped leaves

cuneiform-is, -e, wedge-shaped

cupreat-us, -a, -um; cupre-us, -a, -um, copper-colored or coppery

cupressifoli-us, -a, -um, with leaves like cypress (*Cupressus*)

cupressiform-is, -e; cupressin-us, -a, -um; cupressoides, resembling cypress (*Cupressus*)

curassavic-us, -a, -um, of Curaçao, Netherlands Antilles

curt-us, -a, -um, shortened

curvat-us, -a, -um, curved

curvifoli-us, -a, -um, having curved leaves

cuspidat-us, -a, -um, with stiff, sharp points

cuspidifoli-us, -a, -um, having leaves with a stiff, sharp point

cyananth-us, -a, -um, blue-flowered

cyane-us, -a, -um, blue

cyanocarp-us, -a, -um, having blue fruits

cyanophyll-us, -a, -um, blue-leaved

cyatheoides, resembling *Cyathea*

cyclamine-us, -a, -um, resembling *Cyclamen*

cylindrace-us, -a, -um; cylindric-us, -a, -um, cylindrical

cymbiform-is, -e, boat-shaped

cymos-us, -a, -um, having flowers in cymes

cynaroides, resembling *Cynara*

cypri-us, -a, -um, of *Cyprus*

cytisoides, resembling broom (*Cytisus*)

dacrydioides, resembling *Dacrydium*

dactylifer, dactylifer-a, -um, fingered or finger-like

dactyloides, resembling fingers

dahuric-us, -a, -um; dauric-us, -a, -um; davuric-us, -a, -um, of Dahuria

dalmatic-us, -a, -um, of Dalmatia

damascen-us, -a, -um, of Damascus

danaeifoli-us, -a, -um, with leaves like *Danae*

daphnoides, resembling *Daphne*

dasyacanth-us, -a, -um, thick-spined

dasyanth-us, -a, -um, with shaggy flowers

dasycarp-us, -a, -um, having hairy fruits

dasyclad-us, -a, -um, with shaggy branches

dasyphyll-us, -a, -um, shaggy-leaved

dasystemon, with hairy stamens

daucifoli-us, -a, -um, having leaves like a carrot (*Daucus*)

dealbat-us, -a, -um, whitened, with a coating of white powder

debil-is, -e, weak or frail

decandr-us, -a, -um, having ten stamens

decapetal-us, -a, -um, having ten petals

decaphyll-us, -a, -um, having ten leaves

decidu-us, -a, -um, deciduous

decipiens, deceptive or cheating

declinat-us, -a, -um, declined or bent downward

decomposit-us, -a -um, divided more than once

decorat-us, -a, -um; decor-us, -a, -um, decorative or becoming

decorticans, with shedding bark

decuman-us, -a, -um, huge, immense

decumbens, with trailing stems, their tips erect

decurrens, running down the stem

deflex-us, -a, -um, bent downward

deform-is, -e, deformed

deject-us, -a, -um, dejected or debased

delect-us, -a, -um, chosen

delicatissim-us, -a, -um, most delicate

delicat-us, -a, -um, delicate

delicios-us, -a, -um, delicious

delphinanth-us, -a, -um, with flowers like *Delphinium*

delphinens-is, -e, of Dauphine, France

delphinifoli-us, -a, -um, with leaves like *Delphinium*

deltoides; deltoide-us, -a, -um, triangular

demers-us, -a, -um, submerged

demiss-us, -a, -um, hanging, weak

dendroide-us, -a, -um, treelike

dendrophil-us, -a, -um, tree-loving

densat-us, -a, -um; dens-us, -a, -um, dense, compact

densiflor-us, -a, -um dense-flowered

densifoli-us, -a, -um, densely-leaved

dentat-us, -a, -um; dentifer, dentifer-a, -um; dentos-us, -a, -um, toothed

denticulat-us, -a, -um, slightly toothed

denudat-us, -a, -um, naked

dependens, hanging

depress-us, -a, -um, flattened

desertorum, of deserts

deust-us, -a, -um, burned

diabolic-us, -a, -um, devilish

diacanth-us, -a, -um, with paired spines

diandr-us, -a, -um, with paired or two stamens

dianthiflor-us, -a, -um, with flowers like *Dianthus*

diaphan-us, -a, -um, transparent

dichotom-us, -a, -um, repeatedly forked

dichrom-us, -a, -um; dichro-us, -a, -um, with two distinct colors

dictyophyll-us, -a, -um, having leaves conspicuously netted with veins

didym-us, -a, -um, paired or twofold

difform-is, -e, of unusual form

diffus-us, -a, -um, loosely spreading

digitat-us, -a, -um, shaped like an open hand

dilatat-us, -a, -um; dilat-us, -a, -um, expanded, spread out

dimorph-us, -a, -um, with two forms of flowers, leaves or fruit on the same plant

dioic-us, -a, -um; dioecious, with male and female reproductive organs on the same plant

dipetal-us, -a, -um, with two petals

diphyll-us, -a, -um, having two leaves or leaflets

diplotrich-us, -a, -um, with two kinds of hair

dipterocarp-us, -a, -um, with two winged fruits

dipter-us, -a, -um, two-winged

disciform-is, -e, disk-shaped

discoide-us, -a, -um, disklike, without ray florets

discolor, of two different colors

dispers-us, -a, -um, scattered

dissect-us, -a, -um, deeply cleft

dissimil-is, -e, unlike kinds typical of the genus

dissitiflor-us, -a, -um, with flowers loosely arranged

distachy-us, -a, -um, two-spiked

distans, widely separated

distich-us, -a, -um, two-ranked

distort-us, -a, -um, misshaped

distyl-us, -a, -um, with two styles

diurn-us, -a, -um, day-flowering

divaricat-us, -a, -um, spreading

divergens, spreading widely from the center

diversicolor, with diverse colors

diversiflor-us, -a, -um, diversely-flowered

diversifoli-us, -a, -um, diversely-leaved

diversiform-is, -e, of various forms

dodecandr-us, -a, -um, having twelve stamens

dolabrat-us, -a, -um; dolabriform-is, -e, hatchet-shaped

domestic-us, -a, -um, domesticated, employed as houseplants

doronicoides, resembling *Doronicum*

drabifoli-us, -a, -um, having leaves like *Draba*

dracaenoides, resembling *Dracaena*

dracocephal-us, -a, -um, dragon-headed

dracunculoides, resembling tarragon (*Artemisia dracunculus*)

dracunculus, a small dragon

drupace-us, -a, -um; drupifer, drupifer-a, -um, bearing drupes (fleshy fruits)

drynarioides, resembling the fern genus *Drynaria*

dryophyll-us, -a, -um, with leaves like those of oaks

dubi-us, -a, -um, doubtful, not conforming

dumos-us, -a, -um, bushy or shrubby

duplex; duplicat-us, -a, -um, double

durabil-is, -e, lasting

dysenteric-us, -a, -um, thought to be effective in the treatment of dysentery

ebenace-us, -a, -um, ebony-like

eben-us, -a, -um, ebony-black

ebracteat-us, -a, -um, bractless

eburne-us, -a, -um, ivory-white

echinat-us, -a, -um, hedgehog-like, covered with prickles

echinocarp-us, -a, -um, having prickly fruits

echinosepal-us, -a, -um, having prickly sepals

echinosperm-us, -a, -um, having prickly or spiny seeds

echioides, resembling *Echium*

edul-is, -e, edible

effus-us, -a, -um, straggly or loosely spreading

elaeagnifoli-us, -a, -um, with leaves resembling those of *Elaeagnus*

elastic-us, -a, -um, elastic or containing an elastic substance

elatior, taller

elat-us, -a, -um, tall

elegans; elegantul-us, -a, -um, elegant

elegantissim-us, -a, -um, very elegant

ellipsoidal-is, -e, ellipsoid

elliptic-us, -a, -um, elliptical

elongat-us, -a, -um, elongated

emarginat-us, -a, -um, slightly notched at the apex

emetic-us, -a, -um, causing vomiting

eminens, prominent or eminent

empetrifoli-us, -a, -um, with leaves like those of *Empetrum*

enneacanth-us, -a, -um, having nine spines

enneaphyll-us, -a, -um, having nine leaves or leaflets

ensat-us, -a, -um, sword-shaped

ensifoli-us, -a, -um, with sword-shaped leaves

ensiform-is, -e, like a straight, pointed sword or a typical iris leaf

epigae-us, -a, -um, growing close to the earth

equestr-is, -e, having to do with horses or horsemen

equin-us, -a, -um, of horses

equisetifoli-us, -a, -um, with leaves like horsetail (*Equisetum*)

erect-us, -a, -um, upright

eriacanth-us, -a, -um, woolly-spined

erianther-us, -a, -um, with woolly anthers

erianth-us, -a, -um, with woolly flowers

ericae-us, -a, -um, relating to heaths (*Erica*)

ericifoli-us, -a, -um, with leaves like a heath (*Erica*)

ericoides, resembling heath (*Erica*)

erigen-us, -a, -um, born in Ireland (Erin)

erinace-us, -a, -um, resembling a hedgehog

eriobotryoides, resembling *Eriobotrya*

eriocarp-us, -a, -um, woolly-fruited

eriocephal-us, -a, -um, woolly-headed

eriophor-us, -a, -um, wool-bearing

eriostachys, with a woolly spike

eriostemon, with a woolly stamen

erosus, -a, -um, with a jagged margin

erratic-us, -a, -um, unusual or sporadic

erubescens, blushing

erythrocalyx, having a red calyx

erythrocarp-us, -a, -um, having red fruit

erythrocephal-us, -a, -um, red-headed

erythropter-us, -a, -um, having red wings

erythrosor-us, -a, -um, having red spore cases

esculent-us, -a, -um, edible or to do with eating

etrusc-us, -a, -um, from Tuscany (Etruria), Italy

eucalyptoides, resembling *Eucalyptus*

euchlor-us, -a, -um, good green

eugenioides, resembling *Eugenia*

eupatorioides, resembling *Eupatorium*

euphorbioides, resembling *Euphorbia*

europae-us, -a, -um, European

evect-us, -a, -um, extended

exaltat-us, -a, -um, tall or lofty

exasperat-us, -a, -um, roughened

excavat-us, -a, -um, hollowed

excellens, excellent or excelling

excels-us, -a, -um, tall

excis-us, -a, -um, cut out

eximi-us, -a, -um, distinguished

exoniens-is, -e, of Exeter, England

exotic-us, -a, -um, foreign

expans-us, -a, -um, expanded

exsert-us, -a, -um, exserted

extens-us, -a, -um, extended

exudans, exuding

fabace-us, -a, -um, resembling the broad bean (*Vicia faba*)

fagifoli-us, -a, -um, with leaves like the beech (*Fagus*)

falcat-us, -a, -um; falciform-is, -e, sickle-shaped

falcifoli-us, -a, -um, having sickle-shaped leaves

fallax, false or deceptive

farinace-us, -a, -um, mealy, floury, containing starch

farinos-us, -a, -um, mealy or powdery

fascicular-is, -e; fasciculat-us, -a, -um, clustered or bundled

fastigiat-us, -a, -um, of columnar habit with many erect branches

fastuos-us, -a, -um, proud

fatu-us, -a, -um, insipid, not good

febrifug-us, -a, -um, dispelling fever

fenestral-is, -e, with window-like openings

ferox, very thorny, ferocious

ferrugine-us, -a, -um, rust-colored

fertil-is, -e, fruitful

festal-is, -e; festin-us, -a, -um, gay, festive

ficifoli-us, -a, -um, with leaves like a fig (*Ficus*)

ficoides; ficoide-us, -a, -um, resembling a fig (*Ficus*)

filamentos-us, -a, -um; filari-us, -a, -um, with threads or threadlike filaments

filicaul-is, -e, having a threadlike stem

filicifoli-us, -a, -um, with fernlike leaves

filiform-is, -e, threadlike

filipendul-us, -a, -um, resembling meadowsweet (*Filipendula*)

fimbriatul-us, -a, -um, having a small fringe

fimbriat-us, -a, -um, fringed

firm-us, -a, -um, strong

fissil-is, -e; fissurat-us, -a, -um; fiss-us, -a, -um, cleft or fissured

fistulos-us, -a, -um, hollow, pipelike

flabellat-us, -a, -um, fanlike

flabellifer, flabellifer-a, -um, fan-bearing

flabelliform-is, -e, fan-shaped

flaccid-us, -a, -um, weak or soft

flagellar-is, -e; flagelliform-is, -e, whiplike

flamme-us, -a, -um, flamelike or flame-colored

flavens, yellow

flaveol-us, -a, -um, yellowish

flavescens, yellowish, becoming yellow

flavicom-us, -a, -um, yellow-haired

flavid-us, -a, -um, yellowish

flavispin-us, -a, -um, with yellow spines

flavissim-us, -a, um, intensely yellow

flav-us, -a, -um, yellow

flexicaul-is, -e, with a flexible stem

flexil-is, -e, flexible

flexuos-us, -a, -um, zigzag or tortuous

floccos-us, -a, -um, woolly

flocculos-us, -a, -um, somewhat woolly

flore-albo, having white flowers

florentin-us, -a, -um, of Florence, Italy

flore-pleno, having double flowers

floribund-us, -a, -um; florid-us, -a, -um; florifer, florifer-a, -um, bearing flowers abundantly

floridan-us, -a, -um, of Florida

fluitans, floating

fluminens-is, -e, of Rio de Janeiro (Flumen Januarii), Brazil

fluvial-is, -e; fluviatil-is, -e, of rivers or running water

foemina, feminine

foeniculace-us, -a, -um; foeniculat-us, -a, -um, like fennel (*Foeniculum*)

foetid-us, -a, -um, ill-scented

foetidissim-us, -a, -um, very ill-scented

foliace-us, -a, -um, leaflike

foliat-us, -a, -um, with leaves

foliolat-us, -a, -um; foliolos-us, -a, -um, with leaflets

folios-us, -a, -um, leafy

follicular-is, -e, having follicles

fontan-us, -a, -um; fontinal-is, -e, of springs or fountains

formosan-us, -a, -um, of Taiwan (Formosa)

formos-us, -a, -um, beautiful

formosissim-us, -a, -um, very beautiful

fourcroides, resembling *Furcraea*

foveolat-us, -a, -um, slightly pitted

fragariflor-us, -a, -um, with flowers like those of strawberries or of the color of strawberries (*Fragaria*)

fragarioides, resembling a strawberry (*Fragaria*)

fragil-is, -e, brittle or quick to wilt

fragrans, fragrant

fragrantissim-us, -a, -um, very fragrant

fraxine-us, -a, -um, resembling the ash (*Fraxinus*)

fraxinifoli-us, -a, -um, with leaves like those of ash (*Fraxinus*)

frigid-us, -a, -um, of cold regions

frondos-us, -a, -um, leafy

fructifer, fructifer-a, -um, fruitful

frutescens; fruticans; fruticos-us, -a, -um, shrubby

fucat-us, -a, -um, painted or dyed

fuchsioides, resembling *Fuchsia*

fulgens; fulgid-us, -a, -um, shining

fulvescens, becoming yellowish-brown

fulv-us, -a, -um, reddish-orange

fumariifoli-us, -a, -um, having leaves like those of fumatory (*Fumaria*)

funebr-is, -e, funereal

funiculat-us, -a, -um, resembling a slender cord

furcans; furcat-us, -a, -um, forked

furfurace-us, -a, -um, mealy or scurfy

fuscat-us, -a, -um, brownish

fusiform-is, -e, spindle-shaped

galacifoli-us, -a, -um, having leaves like *Galax*

galegifoli-us, -a, -um, having leaves like those of goat's rue (*Galega*)

gallic-us, -a, -um, French

gandavens-is, -e, of or relating to Ghent, Belgium

gangetic-us, -a, -um, of the region of the Ganges River, India

garganic-us, -a, -um, from Monte Gargano, Italy

geminat-us, -a, -um, paired

geminiflor-us, -a, -um, having paired or several flowers

gemmat-us, -a, -um, jeweled

gemmifer, gemmifer-a, -um, with buds

general-is, -e, usual or prevailing

genevens-is, -e, of Geneva, Switzerland

geniculat-us, -a, -um, bent like a knee

genistifoli-us, -a, -um, with leaves like *Genista*

geometric-us, -a, -um; geometrizans, with formally arranged markings

georgian-us, -a, -um, from Georgia, U.S.A.

georgic-us, -a, -um, from Georgia, U.S.S.R.

geraniifoli-us, -a, -um, with leaves like *Geranium*

geranioides, resembling *Geranium*

germanic-us, -a, -um, of Germany

gibberos-us, -a, -um, with a hump on one side

gibbiflor-us, -a, -um, having flowers with a hump on one side

gibbos-us, -a, -um; gibb-us, -a, -um, swollen on one side

gibraltaric-us, -a, -um, of Gibralter

gigante-us, -a, -um, very tall or very large

gigas, giant

glabell-us, -a, -um; glabrat-us, -a, -um; glabrescens; glabriuscul-us, -a, -um, somewhat hairless

glaber, glabr-a, -um, hairless

glaberrim-us, -a, -um, completely hairless

glacial-is, -e, from icy-cold regions

glandiform-is, -e, glandlike

glandulifer, bearing glands

glanduliflor-us, -a, -um, with glands on the flowers

glandulos-us, -a, -um, glandular

glaucescens, gray, grayish-green, or bluish-green because of a thin coating of easily removable, often waxy particles

glaucifoli-us, -a, -um, with foliage as described above under glaucescens

glauciifoli-us, -a, -um, with leaves resembling those of *Glaucium*

glaucophyll-us, -a, -um, having leaves coated as described above under glaucescens

glauc-us, -a, -um, gray, grayish-green, or bluish-green because of a thin coating of easily removable, often waxy particles

globifers, globifer-a, -um, with more or less spherical clusters

globos-us, -a, -um, spherical

globular-is, -e, referring to a small sphere

globulifer, globulifer-a, -um, having clusters of small spheres

globulos-us, -a, -um, small and spherical

glomerat-us, -a, -um, clustered in approximately spherical heads

glorios-us, -a, -um, glorious

gloxinioides, resembling *Gloxinia*

glumace-us, -a, -um, having glumes (chaffy floral bracts of grasses and sedges)

glutinos-us, -a, -um, sticky or tacky

glycinioides, resembling the soybean (*Glycine*)

glyptostroboides, resembling *Glyptostrobus*

gnaphaloides, resembling *Gnaphalium*

gracilent-us, -a, -um, slender

gracil-is, -e, slender, graceful

graciliflor-us, -a, -um, having slender or graceful flowers

gracilior, more graceful

gracilipes, having a slender stalk

gracilistyl-us, -a, -um, having a slender style

gracillim-us, -a, -um, most graceful

graec-us, -a, -um, of Greece

gramine-us, -a, -um, grasslike

graminifoli-us, -a, -um, with leaves resembling those of grass

grand-is, -e, large

grandiceps, with a large head

grandicusp-is, -e, with big points

grandidentat-us, -a, -um, with big teeth

grandiflor-us, -a, -um, with large flowers

grandifoli-us, -a, -um, with large leaves

grandiform-is, -e, large

granitic-us, -a, -um, inhabiting granite or granite-like rocks or cliffs

granulat-us, -a, -um, with little grainlike tubercles or knobs

granulos-us, -a, -um, granular or seemingly covered with granules

gratissim-us, -a, -um, very pleasing

grat-us, -a, -um, pleasing

graveolens, strongly fragrant

grise-us, -a, -um, gray

groelandic-us, -a, -um, of Greenland

guianens-is, -e, of Guiana, South America

gummifer, gummifer-a, -um, gum-producing

gummos-us, -a, -um, gummy

guttat-us, -a, -um, speckled or spotted

gymnocarp-us, -a, -um, with naked fruits

gyrans, going around in circles

haemanth-us, -a, -um, having blood-red flowers

haematodes, blood-red

halimifoli-us, -a, -um, with leaves like *Atriplex halimus*

halophi-us, -a, -um, salt-loving

hastat-us, -a, -um, shaped like a halberd or arrowhead

hebephyll-us, -a, -um, with downy leaves

hederace-us, -a, -um, like ivy (*Hedera*)

hederifoli-us, -a, -um, with ivy-like leaves

helianthoides, resembling *Helianthus*

hellenic-us, -a, -um, of Greece

helvetic-us, -a, -um, of Switzerland

helvol-us, -a, -um, light brownish-yellow

hemisphaeric-us, -a, -um, hemispherical

hepaticifoli-us, -a, -um, with leaves like those of *Hepatica*

heracleifoli-us, -a, -um, with leaves like those of *Heracleum*

herbace-us, -a, -um, herbaceous, not woody

hesper-us, -a, -um, of the West

heteracanth-us, -a, -um, variously spined

heteranth-us, -a, -um, variously flowered

heterocarp-us, -a, -um, variously fruited

heterolep-is, -e, variously scaled

heteromorph-us, -a, -um, of varying form

heteropetal-us, -a, -um, variously petaled

heterophyll-us, -a, -um, variously leaved

hexagon-us, -a, -um, six-angled

hexapetal-us, -a, -um, with six petals

hexaphyll-us, -a, -um, with leaves in sixes

hians, gaping

hibernal-is, -e, pertaining to winter

hibernic-us, -a, -um, of Ireland (Hibernia)

hibiscifoli-us, -a, -um, with leaves like those of *Hibiscus*

hiemal-is, -e, of the winter

himalaic-us, -a, -um; himalayens-is, -e, of the Himalayas

hippophaeoides, resembling *Hippophae*

hirsut-us, -a, -um, hairy

hirsutissim-us, -a, -um, very hairy

hirsutul-us, -a, -um, somewhat hairy

hirtell-us, -a, -um, rather hairy

hirt-us, -a, -um, hairy

hispanic-us, -a, -um, of Spain (Hispania)

hispid-us, -a, -um, bristly or bristly-hairy

hollandic-us, -a, -um, of Holland

holocarp-us, -a, -um, having whole fruits, neither lobed nor split

holochrys-us, -a, -um, wholly golden

hololeuc-us, -a, -um, wholly white

hondoens-is, -e, of Hondo, Japan

horizontal-is, -e, spreading horizontally

horrid-us, -a,-um, very prickly

hortens-is, -e; hortorum; hortulan-us, -a, -um, of gardens

humifus-us, -a, -um, sprawling

humil-is, -e, low or dwarf

humulifoli-us, -a, -um, with leaves like those of hops (Humulus)

hungaric-us, -a, -um, of Hungary

hupehens-is, -e, of Hupeh, China

hyacinthin-us, -a, -um, dark purplish-blue, or resembling a hyacinth (Hyacinthus)

hyalin-us, -a, -um, transparent or partially so

hybrid-us, -a, -um, hybrid

hydrangeoides, resembling Hydrangea

hyemal-is, -e, of winter

hypericifoli-us, -a, -um, with leaves like those of Hypericum

hypericoides, resembling Hypericum

hypnoides, resembling the moss Hypnum

hypochondriac-us, -a, -um, of somber aspect

hypogae-us, -a, -um, underground

hypoglauc-us, -a, -um, glaucous beneath

hypoleuc-us, -a, -um, white beneath

hypophyll-us, -a, -um, under the leaf

hyssopifoli-us, -a, -um, with leaves like those of hyssop (Hyssopus)

hystrix, bristly

ianthin-us, -a, -um, violet-blue

iberic-us, -a, -um, of the Iberian Peninsula or of Georgia, U.S.S.R.

iberide-us, -a, -um, resembling Iberis

iberidifoli-us, -a, -um, with leaves like those of Iberis

idae-us, -a, -um, of Mount Ida, Asia Minor

ignescens; igne-us, -a, -um, fiery-red

ilicifoli-us, -a, -um, with leaves like those of holly (Ilex)

illecebros-us, -a, -um, enticing

illustrat-us, -a, -um, pictured

illustr-is, -e, brilliant

illyric-us, -a, -um, of the region of ancient Illyria

imbricat-us, -a, -um, overlapping like the scales of a fish or tiles on a roof

immaculat-us, -a, -um, without spots

immers-us, -a, -um, growing under water

impedit-us, -a, -um, tangled or hindered

imperial-is, -e, imperial or showy

impress-us, -a, -um, depressed or sunken

impudic-us, -a, -um, shameless or lewd

inaequal-is, -e, unequal

inapert-us, -a, -um, closed

incan-us, -a, -um, hoary

incarnat-us, -a, -um, flesh-colored

incert-us, -a, -um, doubtful

incisifoli-us, -a, -um, having cut leaves

incis-us, -a, -um, cleft deeply and irregularly

inclinat-us, -a, -um, bent downward

incomparabil-is, -e, incomparable

inconspicu-us, -a, -um, inconspicuous

incurvat-us, -a, -um; incurv-us, -a, -um, bent inward

indic-us, -a, -um, of India

indivis-us, -a, -um, not divided

indurat-us, -a, -um, hard

inebrians, intoxicating

inerm-is, -e, without prickles

infectori-us, -a, -um, colored or dyed

infest-us, -a, -um, troublesome or dangerous

inflat-us, -a, -um, swollen

inflex-us, -a, -um, bent inward

infundibuliform-is, -e, funnel-shaped

ingens, enormous

innoxi-us, -a, -um, harmless

inodor-us, -a, -um, not scented

inquinans, stained or flecked

inscript-us, -a, -um, inscribed

insign-is, -e, remarkable

insipid-us, -a, -um, insipid

insulan-us, -a, -um; insular-is, -e, of an island or islands

intact-us, -a, -um, intact

integer, integr-a, -um, entire

integrifoli-us, -a, -um, having entire or undivided leaves

intermedi-us, -a, -um, intermediate

interrupt-us, -a, -um, not continuous

intertext-us, -a, -um, intertwined

intort-us, -a, -um, twisted

intricat-us, -a, -um, tangled

intrors-us, -a, -um, turned inward

inundat-us, -a, -um, growing in ground likely to be flooded

involucrat-us, -a, -um, having a circle of bracts surrounding a cluster of flowers or florets

involut-us, -a, -um, rolled inward

ioens-is, -e, of Iowa

ionanth-us, -a, -um, with violet-colored flowers

iric-us, -a, -um, of Ireland

iridescens, iridescent

iridiflor-us, -a, -um, with flowers like those of Iris

iridifoli-us, -a, -um, with leaves like those of Iris

iridoides, resembling Iris

irritans, irritating

irrorat-us, -a, -um, minutely spotted, as though sprinkled with dew

isabellin-us, -a, -um, yellowish

islandic-us, -a, um, of Iceland

isophyll-us, -a, -um, having leaves of equal size

istriac-us, -a, -um, of Istria, Italy, Yugoslavia

italic-us, -a, -um, of Italy

ixioides, resembling Ixia

ixocarp-us, -a, -um, with sticky fruits

jamaicens-is, -e of Jamaica, West Indies

japonic-us, -a, -um, of Japan

jasmine-us, -a, -um; jasminoides, resembling jasmine (Jasminus)

javanic-us, -a, -um, of Java

junce-us, -a, -um, resembling rushes (Juncus)

juniperifoli-us, -a, -um, with leaves like those of juniper (Juniperus)

juniperin-us, -a, -um, juniper-like

kalmiiflor-us, -a, -um, with flowers like those of mountain-laurel (Kalmia)

kamtschatic-us, -a, -um, of Kamchatka

kansuens-is, -e, of Kansu, China

kashmirian-us, -a, -um, of Kashmir

kermesin-us, -a, -um, carmine

kewens-is, -e, of the Royal Botanic Gardens, Kew, England

kiusian-us, -a, -um, of Kyushu, Japan

korean-us, -a, -um; koriaens-is, -e, of Korea

kousa, Japanese name of Cornus kousa

labiat-us, -a, -um; labios-us, -a, -um, with a lip

laburnifoli-us, -a, -um, with leaves like those of Laburnum

lacer, lacer-a, -um, lacerated

laciniat-us, -a, -um; lacinios-us, -a, -um, shredded or cleft into narrow divisions

lactescens, becoming milky

lacte-us, -a, -um; lacticolor, milk-white

lactifer, lactifer-a, -um, having milky sap

lactiflor-us, -a, -um, with milk-white flowers

lactucifoli-us, -a, -um, with leaves like those of lettuce (Lactuca)

lacustr-is, -e, of lakes

laetiflor-us, -a, -um, with bright flowers

laetivirens, bright green

laet-us, -a, -um, bright

laevicaul-is, -e, with smooth stems

laevigat-us, -a, -um; laev-is, -e, smooth

lagodechian-us, -a, -um, of Lagodechi, the Caucasus

lamellat-us, -a, -um, layered

lanat-us, -a, -um, woolly

lanceolat-us, -a, -um; lance-us, -a, -um, lanceolate (spear-shaped)

laniger, laniger-a, -um; lanos-us, -a, -um; lanuginos-us, -a, -um, woolly

lapponic-us, -a, -um, of Lapland

laricin-us, -a, -um, resembling larch (Larix)

lasiacanth-us, -a, -um, woolly-spined

lasiandr-us, -a, -um, woolly-stamened

lasiocarp-us, -a, -um, woolly-fruited

lasiopetal-us, -a, -um, woolly-petaled

lenticular-is, -e; lentiform-is, -e, lens-shaped

lent-us, -a, -um, tough and pliant

leonur-us, -a, -um, resembling a lion's tail

leopardin-us, -a, -um, spotted like a leopard

lepidot-us, -a, -um, scaly

leptocaul-is, -e, slender-stemmed

leptoclad-us, -a, -um, slender-branched

leptolepis, with thin scales

leptopetal-us, -a, -um, thin-petaled

leptophyl-us, -a, -um, thin-leaved

leptosepal-us, -a, -um, with thin sepals

leptostachys, leptostachy-a, -um, with slender spikes

leucanth-us, -a, -um, with white flowers

leucocaul-is, -e, with white stems

leucocephal-us, -a, -um, with white heads

leucochil-us, -a, -um, with white lips

leucoderm-is, -e, with white skin

leuconeur-us, -a, -um, with white veins

leucopetal-us, -a, -um, with white petals

leucophyll-us, -a, -um, with white leaves

leucostachys, leucostach-a, -um, with white spikes

leucotrich-us, -a, -um, with white hairs

libani; libanotic-us, -a, -um, of Mount Lebanon, Lebanon

liburnic-us, -a, -um, of Croatia (Liburnia)

lignos-us, -a, -um, woody

ligular-is, -e; ligulat-us, -a, -um, straplike

ligusticifoli-us, -a, -um, with leaves like those of lovage (*Ligusticum*)

ligustrifoli-us, -a, -um, with leaves like those of privet (*Ligustrum*)

ligustrin-us, -a, -um, resembling privet (*Ligustrum*)

likiangens-is, -e, of the Lichiang Mountains, China

lilacin-us, -a, -um, lilac-colored

liliace-us, -a, -um, resembling a lily (*Lilium*)

liliflor-us, -a, -um, with flowers like those of a lily (*Lilium*)

lilifoli-us, -a, -um, with leaves like those of a lily (*Lilium*)

limens-is, -e, of Lima, Peru

limnophil-us, -a, -um, of swamps

limoniifoli-us, -a, -um, with leaves like those of sea-lavender (*Limonium*)

limos-us, -a, -um, of marshlands or wet places

linariifoli-us, -a, -um, with leaves like those of *Linaria*

linearifoli-us, -a, -um, with linear leaves

linear-is, -e, narrow, with nearly parallel sides

lineat-us, -a, -um, striped or lined

linguiform-is, -e; lingulat-us, -a, -um, shaped like a tongue

liniflor-us, -a, -um, with flowers like those of flax (*Linum*)

linifoli-us, -a, -um, with leaves like those of flax (*Linum*)

littoral-is, -e; littore-us, -a, -um, of seashores

livid-us, -a, -um, bluish-gray, lead-colored

lobat-us, -a, -um, lobed

lobelioides, resembling *Lobelia*

lobulat-us, -a, -um, having small lobes

lomariifoli-us, -a, -um, with leaves like those of *Lomaria*

long-us, -a, -um, long

longebracteat-us, -a, -um, with long bracts

longependunculat-us, -a, -um, with long peduncles (flower stalks)

longicaul-is, -e, with long stalks

longicom-us, -a, -um, with long hairs

longicusp-is, -e, long-pointed

longiflor-us, -a, -um, with long flowers

longifoli-us, -a, -um, with long leaves

longihamat-us, -a, -um, with long hooks

longilob-us, -a, -um, with long lobes

longipes, with long stalks

longipetal-us, -a, -um, with long petals

longisepal-us, -a, -um, with long sepals

longispin-us, -a, -um, with long spines

longissim-us, -a, -um, very long

longistyl-us, -a, -um, with long styles

lophanth-us, -a, -um, with crested flowers

louisian-us, -a, -um, of Louisiana

lucens; lucid-us, -a, -um, bright or shining

ludovician-us, -a, -um, of Louisiana

lukiangens-is, -e, of Lukiang, China

lunat-us, -a, -um; lunulat-us, -a, -um, crescent-shaped

lurid-us, -a, -um, dusky-yellow or sallow

lusitanic-us, -a, -um, of Portugal (Lusitania)

luteol-us, -a, -um, yellowish

lutescens, becoming yellow or yellowish

lute-us, -a, -um, yellow

luxurians, luxuriant

lychnidifoli-us, -a, -um, with leaves like those of *Lychnis*

lycopodioides, resembling club-moss (*Lycopodium*)

lydi-us, -a, -um, of Asia Minor

lyrat-us, -a, -um, fiddle-shaped

lysimachioides, resembling *Lysimachia*

macedonic-us, -a, -um, of Macedonia

macracanth-us, -a, -um, having large spines

macraden-us, -a, -um, having large glands

macrandr-us, -a, -um; macranther-us, -a, -um, with large anthers

macranth-us, -a, -um, having large flowers

macrobotrys, with large grapelike clusters

macrocarp-us, -a, -um, with large fruits

macrocephal-us, -a, -um, with large heads

macrodont-us, -a, -um, with large teeth

macrophyll-us, -a, -um, with large leaves

macrorrhiz-us, -a, -um, with large roots

macrosperm-us, -a, -um, with large seeds

macrostachy-us, -a, -um, with large spikes

maculat-us, -a, -um; maculifer, maculifer-a, -um; maculos-us, -a, -um, spotted

madagascariens-is, -e, of Madagascar

magellanic-us, -a, -um, of the region of the Straits of Magellan

magnific-us, -a, -um, magnificent

majal-is, -e, May-flowering

majestic-us, -a, -um, majestic

major; maj-us, -a, -um, bigger

malabaric-us, -a, -um, from Malabar, India

malacoides, soft or mucilaginous, like mallow

maliform-is, -e, apple-shaped

malvace-us, -a, -um, resembling a mallow (*Malva*)

malviflor-us, -a, -um, with flowers like those of a mallow (*Malva*)

mammiform-is, -e, formed like a nipple

mammillat-us, -a, -um; mammillar-is, -e; mammos-us, -a, -um, breastlike or nipple-like

mandshuric-us, -a, -um, of Manchuria

manicat-us, -a, -um, having long sleeves

manipurens-is, -e, of Manipur, India

margaritace-us, -a, -um; margarit-us, -a, -um, pearly or pertaining to pearls

margaritifer, margaritifer-a, -um, pearl-bearing

marginal-is, -e; marginat-us, -a, -um, margined

marilandic-us, -a, -um, of Maryland

maritim-us, -a, -um, of the sea

marmorat-us, -a, -um; marmore-us, -a, -um, marbled or mottled

maroccan-us, -a, -um, of Morocco

mas; mascul-us, -a, -um, masculine

matronal-is, -e, pertaining to March 1st (Roman festival of the matrons)

mauritanic-us, -a, -um, of North Africa (Mauretania)

mauritian-us, -a, -um, of Mauritius

maxillar-is, -e, pertaining to jaws

maxim-us, -a, -um, biggest

medic-us, -a, -um, medicinal

mediopict-us, -a, -um, striped down the middle

mediterrane-us, -a, -um, from the region of the Mediterranean Sea or from far inland

medi-us, -a, -um, intermediate

medullar-is, -e; medull-us, -a, -um, pithy

megacalyx, having a large calyx

megacanth-us, -a, -um, having large spines

megacarp-us, -a, -um, having large fruits

megalanth-us, -a, -um, having large flowers

magalophyll-us, -a, -um, having large leaves

megapotamic-us, -a, -um, of the big river (usually the Amazon)

magarrhiz-us, -a, -um, with big roots

megasperm-us, -a, -um, having big seeds

megastachy-us, -a, -um, with a big spike

megastigm-us, -a, -um, with a big stigma

megaseifoli-us, -a, -um, with leaves like *Bergenia* (*Megasea*)

meleagr-is, -e, spotted like a guinea fowl

meliodor-us, -a, -um, honey-scented

mellit-us, -a, -um, honey-sweet

meloform-is, -e, melon-shaped

membranace-us, -a, -um, membranous

meridian-us, -a, -um; meridional-is, -e, of midday

metallic-us, -a, -um, metallic

mexican-us, -a, -um, Mexican

micans, glittering

micracanth-us, -a, -um, with small thorns

micranth-us, -a, -um, with small flowers

microcarp-us, -a, -um, with small fruits

microcephal-us, -a, -um, with a small head

microchil-us, -a, -um, with a small lip

microdasys, small and shaggy

microgloss-us, -a, -um, with a small tongue

microlep-is, -e, with small scales

micropetal-us, -a, -um, with small petals

microphyll-us, -a, -um, with small leaves

microsepal-us, -a, -um, with small sepals

microsperm-us, -a, -um, with small seeds

militar-is, -e, suggesting or pertaining to soldiers

millefoliat-us, -a, -um; millefoli-us, -a, -um, with many leaves or leaflets

mimosifoli-us, -a, -um, with leaves like those of *Mimosa*

mimosoides, resembling *Mimosa*

miniat-us, -a, -um, bright red

minim-us, -a, -um, smaller

minut-us, -a, -um, very small

minutiflor-us, -a, -um, with minute flowers

minutifoli-us, -a, -um, with minute leaves

minutissim-us, -a, -um, most minute

mirabil-is, -e, wonderful

missouriens-is, -e, of Missouri

mit-is, -e, mild, spineless

mitrat-us, -a, -um, mitered or turbaned

mitriform-is, -e, miter-like

mixt-us, -a, -um, mixed

modest-us, -a, -um, modest

moldavic-us, -a, -um, of the Danube Basin

molle, a Peruvian native name

mollicom-us, -a, -um, with soft hairs

moll-is, -e, soft or with soft hairs

mollissim-us, -a, -um, very soft

moluccan-us, -a, -um, of the Molucca Islands

monacanth-us, -a, -um, one-spined

monadelph-us, -a, -um, having the filaments of the stamens united

monandr-us, -a, -um, with one stamen

mongolic-us, -a, -um, of Mongolia

monilifer, monilifer-a, -um, having a necklace

moniliform-is, -e, necklace-like

monocephal-us, -a, -um, with one head

monogyn-us, -a, -um, with one pistil

monopetal-us, -a, -um, with one petal

monophyll-us, -a, -um, with one leaf

monosepal-us, -a,-um, with one sepal

monosperm-us, -a, -um, with one seed

monostachy-us, -a, -um, with one spike

monstros-us, -a, -um, monstrous or abnormal

montan-us, -a, -um, of mountains

monticola, inhabiting mountains

morifoli-us, -a, -um, with leaves like those of mulberry (*Morus*)

mosaic-us, -a, -um, having a mosaic pattern

moschat-us, -a, -um, musk-scented

moupinens-is, -e, of Pooksing (Mupin), China

mucronat-us, -a, -um, with short terminal points

mucronulat-us, -a, -um, with a short, hard point

multibracteat-us, -a, -um, having numerous bracts

multicaul-is, -e, with many stems

multicav-us, -a, -um, with many hollows

multiceps, with many heads

multicolor, many-colored

multifid-us, -a, -um, divided many times

multiflor-us, -a, -um, with many flowers

multilineat-us, -a, -um, with many lines

multinerv-is, -e, with many veins

multiplex, doubled, much folded

multiradiat-us, -a, -um, having many rays

multiscapoide-us, -a, -um, with many naked flower stems

mural-is, -e, inhabiting walls

muricat-us, -a, -um, roughened, with firm points

musaic-us, -a, -um, having a mosaic pattern

muscipil-us, -a, -um, fly-catching

muscitoxic-us, -a, -um, poisonous to flies

muscoides, resembling flies

muscos-us, -a, -um, resembling moss

mutabil-is, -e, changeable, usually as to color

mutat-us, -a, -um, changed

mutic-us, -a, -um, blunt

myosotidiflor-us, -a, -um, with flowers like those of forget-me-not (*Myosotis*)

myriacanth-us, -a, -um, having numerous thorns

myriocarp-us, -a, -um, having many fruits

myriophyll-us, -a, -um, having many leaves

myriophylloides, resembling *Myriophyllum*

myrsinifoli-us, -a, -um, with leaves like those of *Myrsine*

myrsinoides, resembling *Myrsine*

myrtifoli-us, -a, -um, with leaves like those of myrtle (*Myrtus*)

mysorens-is, -e, of Mysore, India

nankinens-is, -e, of Nanking, China

nan-us, -a, -um, dwarf

napiform-is, -e, turnip-shaped

narbonens-is, -e, of Narbonne, France

narcissiflor-us, -a, -um, with flowers like those of *Narcissus*

narcissifoli-us, -a, -um, with leaves like those of *Narcissus*

natalens-is, -e, of Natal, South Africa

natans, floating

navicular-is, -e, boat-shaped

neapolitan-us, -a, -um, of Naples, Italy

nebulos-us, -a, -um, cloudlike

neglect-us, -a, -um, neglected or overlooked

neilgherrens-is, -e, of the Nilgiri Hills, India

nelumbifoli-us, -a, -um, with leaves like those of lotus (*Nelumbo*)

nemoral-is, -e; nemoros-us, -a, -um, of woodlands or groves

nepalens-is, -e, of Nepal

nepetoides, resembling *Nepeta*

neriiflor-us, -a, -um, with flowers like those of oleander (*Nerium*)

neriifoli-us, -a, -um, with leaves like those of oleander (*Nerium*)

nervos-us, -a, -um, having conspicuous veins

nevadens-is, -e, of the Sierra Nevada, Spain; the Sierra Nevada, California; or the state of Nevada

nidus, a nest

niger, nigr-a, -um, black

nigrat-us, -a, -um; nigrescens; nigricans, blackish

nilotic-us, -a, -um, of the valley of the Nile River

nipponic-us, -a, -um, of Japan

nitens; nitid-us, -a, -um, shining

nival-is, -e; nive-us, -a, -um; nivos-us, -a, -um, snow-white, or of snowy regions

nobil-is, -e, noble or notable

noctiflor-us, -a, -um; nocturn-us, -a, -um, flowering at night

nodos-us, -a, -um, with conspicuous nodes (joints)

nodulos-us, -a, -um, with small nodes (joints)

nonscript-us, -a, -um, without markings

nootkatens-is, -e, of the region of Nootka Sound, British Columbia

norvegic-us, -a, -um, of Norway

notat-us, -a, -um, spotted or marked

novae-angliae, of New England

novae-caesareae, of New Jersey

novae-zelandiae, of New Zealand

novaeboracens-is, -e; novi-belgii, of New York

nucifer, nucifer-a, -um, bearing nuts

nudicaul-is, -e, naked-stemmed

nudiflor-us, -a, -um, naked-flowered

nummulari-us, -a, -um, resembling a coin

nutans, nodding

nyctagine-us, -a, -um, night-blooming

obconic-us, -a, -um, having the shape of an inverted cone

obes-us, -a, -um, fat or succulent

oblat-us, -a, -um, flattened at the end

obliqu-us, -a, -um, oblique

oblongat-us, -a, -um, oblong

oblongifoli-us, -a, -um, with oblong leaves

oblong-us, -a, -um, oblong

obovat-us, -a, -um, egg-shaped, with the broadest end uppermost

obscur-us, -a, -um, indistinct, dark or dusky

obsolet-us, -a, -um, rudimentary

obtusifoli-us, -a,-um, with blunt leaves

obtus-us, -a, -um, blunt

occidental-is, -e, western

ocellat-us, -a, -um, with eye-like spots or patches

ochrace-us, -a, -um, ochre-colored

ochroleuc-us, -a, -um, yellowish-white

ocimoides, resembling basil (*Ocimum*)

octandr-us, -a, -um, with eight stamens

octopetal-us, -a, -um, with eight petals

oculat-us, -a, -um, having an eye or eye-like spot or patch

oculirose-us, -a, -um, with a rose-colored eye

ocymoides, resembling basil (*Ocimum*)

odorat-us, -a, -um; odorifer, odorifer-a, -um; odor-us, -a, -um, fragrant

odoratissim-us, -a, -um, very fragrant

officinal-is, -e, having or thought to have medicinal virtues

oleifoli-us, -a, -um, with leaves like those of the olive (*Olea*)

oleoides, resembling the olive (*Olea*)

olerace-us, -a, -um, of vegetable gardens

olifer, olifer-a, -um, oil-bearing

olitori-us, -a, -um, having to do with culinary herbs

olivace-us, -a, -um, greenish-brown

olympic-us, -a, -um, of one of several mountains named Mount Olympus

omeiens-is, -e, of Mount Omi, China

ophioglossifoli-us, -a, -um, with leaves like those of adder's tongue fern (*Ophioglossum*)

oppositifoli-us, -a, -um, having opposite leaves

opuliflor-us, -a, -um, with flowers like those of *Viburnum opulus*

opulifoli-us, -a, -um, with leaves like those of *Viburnum opulus*

opuloides, with leaves resembling those of *Virburnum opulus*

orbicular-is, -e; orbiculat-us, -a, -um, disk-shaped

orchide-us, -a, -um; orchioides; orchoides, orchid-like

orchidiflor-us, -a, -um, having flowers resembling those of orchids

oregan-us, -a, -um; oregon-us, -a, -um, of Oregon

oreophil-us, -a, -um, lover of mountains

oriental-is, -e, of the Orient

origanifoli-us, -a, -um, with leaves like those of marjoram (*Origanum*)

origanoides, resembling marjoram (*Origanum*)

ornat-us, -a, -um, showy

ornithocephal-us, -a, -um, shaped like the head of a bird

ornithopod-us, -a, -um; ornithopus, resembling the foot of a bird

orthobotrys, with erect clusters

orthocarp-us, -a, -um, with erect fruits

orthoclad-us, -a, -um, with straight branches

orthogloss-us, -a, -um, with a straight tongue

orthopter-us, -a, -um, with straight wings

orthosepal-us, -a, -um, with straight sepals

oval-is, -e, broadly-elliptic or oval

ovat-us, -a, -um, egg-shaped with a wide end at the base

ovifer, ovifer-a, -um; oviger, oviger-a, -um, having egg-shaped structures

ovin-us, -a, -um, having to do with or resembling sheep

oxyacanth-us, -a, -um, with sharp spines

oxygon-us, -a, -um, sharp-angled

oxylob-us, -a, -um, with sharp-pointed lobes

oxyphil-us, -a, -um, of acid soils

oxyphyll-us, -a, -um, with sharp-pointed leaves

pachyanth-us, -a, -um, having thick flowers

pachycarp-us, -a, -um, with thick seed coats

pachyphloe-us, -a, -um, having thick bark

pachyphyll-us, -a, -um, thick-leaved

pachypod-us, -a, -um, with thick-based stems

pacific-us, -a, -um, of the Pacific Ocean

palaestin-us, -a, -um, of Palestine

pallens; pallid-us, -a, -um, pale

palmar-is, -e, a hand's breadth, high or wide

palmat-us, -a, -um, shaped like a hand with outstretched fingers

palmifoli-us, -a, -um, with palmlike leaves

paludos-us, -a, -um; palustr-is, -e, of marshes

pandurat-us, -a, -um, fiddle-shaped

paniculat-us, -a, -um, with flowers in panicles

pannos-us, -a, -um, tattered or shredded

papaverace-us, -a, -um, resembling a poppy (*Papaver*)

papilliger, papilliger-a, -um; papillos-us, -a, -um, having tiny, soft protuberances

papyrace-us, -a, -um, papery

papyrifer, papifer-a, -um, of use for making paper

paradisi; paradisiac-us, -a, -um, of Paradise

paradox-us, -a, -um, paradoxical

parasitic-us, -a, -um, parasitic

pardalin-us, -a, -um; pardin-us, -a, -um, spotted like a leopard or related to leopards

parnassi; parnassic-us, -a -um, of Mount Parnassus, Greece

parnassifoli-us, -a, -um, with leaves like those of *Parnassia*

partit-us, -a, -um, parted

parvibracteat-us, -a, -um, with small bracts

parv-us, -a, -um, small

parviflor-us, -a, -um, with small flowers

parvifoli-us, -a, -um, with small leaves

pastoral-is, -e, having to do with shepherds, hence of pastures

patagonic-us, -a, -um, of Patagonia

patens; patul-us, -a, -um, spreading

pauciflor-us, -a, -um, having few flowers

paucifoli-us, -a, -um, having few leaves

paucinerv-us, -a, -um, having few veins

pavonin-us, -a, -um, peacock-blue or with an eye-shaped patch like those on a peacock's tail

pectinat-us, -a, -um, resembling a comb

pectinifer, pectinifer-a, -um, having a comb

pedatifid-us, -a, -um; pedat-us, -a, -um, cleft like the foot of a bird

pedemontan-us, -a, -um, of Piedmont, Italy

peduncular-is, -e; pedunculat-us, -a, -um, having distinct flower stalks (peduncles)

pedunculos-us, -a, -um, having many or prominent flower stalks (peduncles)

pellucid-us, -a, -um, translucent or transparent

peltat-us, -a, -um, shaped like a shield and with the stalk attached in from the margin of the blade

pelviform-is, -e, like a shallow cup

pendulin-us, -a, -um; pendul-us, -a, -um, hanging

peninsular-is, -e, of a peninsula

pennat-us, -a, -um, pinnate or feathered

pensil-is, -e, hanging

pensylvanic-us, -a, -um, of Pennsylvania

pentagon-us, -a, -um, having five angles

pentagyn-us, -a, -um, having five pistils

pentandr-us, -a, -um, having five stamens

pentaphyll-us, -a, -um, having five leaves, or leaflets

pentapter-us, -a, -um, with five wings

peregrin-us, -a, -um, exotic or foreign

perennans; perenn-is, -e, perennial

perfoliat-us, -a, -um; perfos-us, -a, -um, perfoliate, with the stem apparently piercing the leaf

perfora-us, -a, -um, with or apparently with small holes

persicifoli-us, -a, -um, having leaves like those of a peach (*Prunus persica*)

persic-us, -a, -um, of Persia

persistens, persistent

pertus-us, -a, -um, perforated

peruvian-us, -a, -um, of Peru

petaloide-us, -a, -um, petal-like

petiolar-is, -e; petiolat-us, -a, -um, having leaves with distinct stalks

petrae-us, -a, -um, rock-loving

phaeocarp-us, -a, -um, having dark fruit

philadelphic-us, -a, -um, of Philadelphia

phoenice-us, -a, -um, of Phoenicia, or purple-red

phyllomaniac-us, -a, -um, producing abundant leafy growth

picturat-us, -a, -um, variegated

pict-us, -a, -um, brightly colored or brightly painted

pileat-us, -a, -um, having a cap

pilifer, pilifer-a, -um, having short hairs

pilos-us, -a, -um, clothed with long soft hairs

pilular-is, -e; pilulifer, pilulifer-a, -um, having small spherical fruits

pimpinellifoli-us, -a, -um, having leaves like those of *Pimpinella*

pinetorum, of pine forests

pinifoli-us, -a, -um, with leaves like those of a pine (*Pinus*)

pinnatifid-us, -a, -um, pinnately-cleft

pinnatifoli-us, -a, -um, having pinnate leaves

pinnatinerv-is, -e, with pinnate veins

pinnat-us, -a, -um, feather-like

piperit-us, -a, -um, pepper-like, having a sharp, hot taste

pisifer, pisifer-a, -um, pea-bearing

planiflor-us, -a, -um, having flat flowers

planifoli-us, -a, -um, having flat leaves

planipes, having a flat stalk

plan-us, -a, -um, flat

platanifoli-us, -a, -um, with leaves like those of a plane tree (*Platanus*)

platanoides, resembling a plane tree (*Platanus*)

platyacanth-us, -a, -um, having broad spines

platyanth-us, -a, -um, having broad flowers

platycarp-us, -a, -um, having broad fruits

platycaul-is, -e, having a broad, flat stem

platycentr-us, -a, -um, having a broad, flat spur

platyclad-us, -a, -um, having flat branches

platygloss-us, -a, -um, having a flat tongue

platypetal-us, -a, -um, having broad petals

platyphyll-us, -a, um, having broad leaves

platypod-us, -a, -um, with broad stalks

platyspath-us, -a, -um, with a broad spathe

platysperm-us, -a, -um, with broad seeds

pleniflor-us, -a, -um, having double flowers

plenissim-us, -a, -um, very double

plen-us, -a, -um, double

plicat-us, -a, -um, pleated

plumari-us, -a, -um; plumat-us, -a, -um, plumed or feathered

plumbaginioides, resembling *Plumbago*

plumos-us, -a, -um, feathery

pluriflor-us, -a, -um, many-flowered

podagric-us, -a, -um, gouty or swollen at the base

podophyll-us, -a, -um, having leaves with stout stalks

poetic-us, -a, -um, pertaining to poets

polifoli-us, -a, -um, with leaves gray like those of *Teucrium polium*

polit-us, -a, -um, elegant or neat

polyacanth-us, -a, -um, having many thorns

polyandr-us, -a, -um, having many stamens

polyanthemos; polyanth-us, -a, -um, having many flowers

polybotry-us, -a, -um, having many clusters

polycarp-us, -a, -um, having many fruits

polycephal-us, -a, -um, having many heads

polychrom-us, -a, -um, of many colors

polygaloides, resembling *Polygala*

polylepis, having many scales

polymorph-us, -a, um, having many forms

polypetal-us, -a, -um, having many petals

polyphyll-us, -a, -um, having many leaves

polyrrhiz-us, -a, -um, having many roots

polysepal-us, -a, -um, having many sepals

polystachy-us, -a, -um, having many spikes

pomeridian-us, -a, -um, of the afternoon

pomifer, pomifer-a, -um, bearing apple-like fruits

ponderos-us, -a, -um, ponderous or heavy

pontic-us, -a, -um, of the region bordering the southern shore of the Black Sea

populifoli-us, -a, -um, with leaves like those of a poplar (*Populus*)

populne-us, -a, -um, relating to poplars (*Populus*)

porcin-us, -a, -um, food for pigs or relating to pigs

porophyll-us, -a, -um, having or seeming to have holes in the leaves

porphyre-us, -a, -um, of a warm reddish hue

porphyrophyll-us, -a, -um, having purple leaves

porrifoli-us, -a, -um, having leaves like those of leeks (*Allium porrifolium*)

portulacace-us, -a, -um, resembling *Portulaca*

poteriifoli-us, -a, -um, having leaves like those of *Poterium*

praealt-us, -a, -um, exceedingly tall

praecox, very early

praestans, distinguished

praevern-us, -a, -um, in advance of spring

pratens-is, -e, of meadows

primuliflor-us, -a, -um, with flowers like those of primroses (*Primula*)

primulifoli-us, -a, -um, having leaves like those of primroses (*Primula*)

primulin-us, -a, -um, primrose-yellow

primuloides, resembling primroses (*Primula*)

princeps, the most distinguished

prismatic-us, -a, -um, angled like a prism

proboscide-us, -a, -um, snoutlike

procer-us, -a, -um, tall

procumbens, prostrate

profus-us, -a, -um, abundant

prolifer, prolifer-a, -um, flowering freely or with many side shoots or buds adapted for propagation

prolific-us, -a, -um, free-fruiting

propinqu-us, -a, -um, related

prostrat-us, -a, -um, prostrate

protrus-us, -a, -um, protruding

provincial-is, -e, of Provence, France

pruhonician-us, -a, -um, of Pruhonice, Czechoslovakia

pruinat-us, -a, -um; pruinos-us, -a, -um, glistening as though frosted

prunifoli-us, -a, -um, with leaves like those of plums (*Prunus*)

pruriens, causing itching

psittacin-us, -a, -um, parrot-like

psittacorum, of parrots

psycodes, butterfly-like

pteridoides, resembling ferns of the genus *Pteris*

pubens; pubescens; pubiger, pubiger-a, -um, downy

pudic-us, -a, -um, bashful

pulchell-us, -a, -um; pulcher, pulchr-a, -um, pretty

pulverulent-us, -a, -um, dusted with powder or meal

pulvinat-us, -a, -um, cushion-like

pumil-us, -a, -um, dwarf

punctat-us, -a, -um, spotted

pungens, having sharp points

punice-us, -a, -um, reddish purple

purgans, purgative

purpurascens, purplish

purpurat-us, -a, -um, made purple

purpure-us, -a, -um, purple

pusill-us, -a, -um, very small

pustulat-us, -a, -um, of blistered appearance

pygmae-us, -a, -um, very small or tiny

pyramidal-is, -e; pyramidat-us, -a, -um, pyramidal

pyrenae-us, -a, -um; pyrenaic-us, -a, -um, of the Pyrenees

pyrifoli-us, -a, -um, with leaves like those of pears (*Pyrus*)

pyriform-is, -e, pear-shaped

pyxidat-us, -a, -um, having a lid

quadrangular-is, -e; quadrangulat-us, -a, -um, having four angles

quadrat-us, -a, -um, in fours

quadricolor, four-colored

quadrifid-us, -a, -um, cut into four parts

quadrifoli-us, -a, -um, with leaves in fours

quercifoli-us, -a, -um, having leaves like those of an oak (*Quercus*)

quinat-us, -a, -um, in fives

quinqueflor-us, -a, -um, with flowers in fives

quinquefoli-us, -a, -um, with leaves in fives

quinquenerv-is, -e, five-veined

quinquepunctat-us, -a, -um, five-spotted

quitens-is, -e, of Quito, Ecuador

racemiflor-us, -a, -um; racemos-us, -a, -um, having flowers in racemes

radiat-us, -a, -um, radiating or with rays

radicans, having stems that root

radula, suggesting a rasp or file

ramiflor-us, -a, -um, having flowers in branched arrangements

ramosissim-us, -a, -um, much-branched

ramos-us, -a, -um, branched

ranunculoides, resembling buttercups (Ranunculus)

rapace-us, -a, -um, relating to turnips (Brassica rapa)

rapunculoides, resembling Rapunculus, a group now included in Campanula

rariflor-us, -a, -um, having scattered flowers

reclinat-us, -a, -um, bent backward

rect-us, -a, -um, erect

recurvat-us, -a, -um; recurv-us, -a, -um, curved backward

rediviv-us, -a, -um, returned or returning to life

reduct-us, -a, -um, reduced or made small

reflex-us, -a, -um; refract-us, -a, -um, bent sharply backward

refulgens, shining brightly

regal-is, -e, regal

reginae, of the queen

regi-us, -a, -um, royal

religios-us, -a, -um, sacred, or used in religious ceremonies

remot-us, -a, -um, scattered

reniform-is, -e, kidney-shaped

repandus, with somewhat wavy margins

repens; reptans, creeping

resediflor-us, -a, -um, with flowers like those of mignonette (Reseda)

resedifoli-us, -a, -um, with leaves like those of mignonette (Reseda)

resinifer, resinifer-a, -um; resinos-us, -a, -um, resinous

reticulat-us, -a, -um, netted

retroflex-us, -a, -um; retort-us, -a, -um; retrofract-us, -a, -um, twisted back

retus-us, -a, -um, with a rounded and slightly notched apex

revolut-us, -a, -um, rolled backward

rex, king

rhamnifoli-us, -a, -um, with leaves like those of Rhamnus

rhamnoides, resembling Rhamnus

rhizophyll-us, -a, -um, having leaves that produce roots

rhodanth-us, -a, -um, with rose-pink flowers

rhombic-us, -a, -um; rhomboide-us, -a, -um, diamond-shaped or rhomboidal

rhytidophyll-us, -a, -um, having wrinkled leaves

ricinifoli-us, -a, -um, with leaves like those of the castor-bean (Ricinus)

ricinoides, resembling the castor-bean (Ricinus)

rigens; rigid-us, -a, -um, rigid

rigidifoli-us, -a, -um, having rigid leaves

ringens, gaping

ripari-us, -a, -um, of river banks

rival-is, -e, of streamsides

rivular-is, -e, loving brooks

robustispin-us, -a, -um, having strong spines

robust-us, -a, -um, strong or stout

roman-us, -a, -um, of Rome

rosace-us, -a, -um, roselike

rose-us, -a, -um, rose-colored

rosmarinifoli-us, -a, -um, with leaves like those of rosemary (Rosmarinus)

rostrat-us, -a, -um, beaked

rosular-is, -e, with rosettes

rotat-us, -a, -um, wheel-shaped

rotundat-us, -a, -um; rotund-us, -a, -um, rounded

rotundifoli-us, -a, -um, having round leaves

rubell-us, -a, -um; rubescens, reddish

rubens; ruber, rubr-a, -um, red

rubiginos-us, -a, -um, rosey

rubioides, resembling Rubia

rubricaul-is, -e, red-stemmed

rufescens, becoming reddish

rugos-us, -a, -um, wrinkled

rupestr-is, -e, loving rocks

rupicola, living among rocks

rupifrag-us, -a, -um, a breaker of rocks

ruscifoli-us, -a, -um, with leaves like those of the butcher's broom (Ruscus)

rustican-us, -a, -um; rustic-us, -a, -um, of the country

ruthenic-us, -a, -um, of Ruthenia, U.S.S.R.

rutilans, reddish

saccat-us, -a, -um, baglike

saccharat-us, -a, -um, sweet, or appearing as though dusted with sugar

saccharifer, saccharifer-a, -um, a source of sugar

saccharin-us, -a, -um, sugary

saccharoides, resembling sugar cane (Saccharum)

saccifer, saccifer-a, -um, bearing bags

sachalinens-is, -e, of Sakhalin Island, U.S.S.R.

sacrorum, of sacred places

sagittal-is, -e, shaped like an arrowhead

sagittifoli-us, -a, -um, with leaves shaped like the head of an arrow

salicifoli-us, -a, -um, with leaves like those of willows (Salix)

salicin-us, -a, -um, willow-like

salicornioides, resembling Salicornia

salign-us, -a, -um, willow-like

salin-us, -a, -um, of salty places

salsuginos-us, -a, -um, of salt marshes

saluenens-is, -e, of the Salween River, Burma and China

salvifoli-us, -a, -um, having leaves like those of Salvia

sambucifoli-us, -a, -um, with leaves like those of elder (Sambucus)

sanct-us, -a, -um, holy

sanguine-us, -a, -um, blood-red

sapid-us, -a, -um, of agreeable taste

sapientum, pertaining to wise men

saponace-us, -a, -um, soapy

sarcodes, fleshlike

sarmentos-us, -a, -um, having runners

sarniens-is, -e, of Guernsey (Sarnia), Charnel Islands

sativ-us, -a, -um, cultivated

saxatil-is, -e; saxicola, inhabiting rocks

scaber, scabr-a, -um, rough

scabiosifoli-us, -a, -um, having leaves like those of scabious (Scabiosa)

scandens, climbing

scapiger, scapiger-a, -um; scapos-us, -a, -um, having scapes (naked, flowering stalks)

scarios-us, -a, -um, shriveled

scelerat-us, -a, -um, wicked, capable of hurting

schipkaens-is, -e, of the Shipka Pass, Bulgaria

schizopetal-us, -a, -um, with cut petals

schizophyll-us, -a, -um, with cut leaves

scholar-is, -e, relating to school

scilloides, resembling Scilla

sclerocarp-us, -a, -um, having hard fruits

scopari-us, -a, -um, brooklike

scopulorum, of cliffs or crags

scorpioides, scorpion-like

scotic-us, -a, -um, of Scotland

secundiflor-us, -a, -um, with flowers on one side

secund-us, -a, -um, one-sided

segetal-is, -e; segetum, of grain fields

selaginoides, resembling Selaginella

semperflorens, everblooming

sempervirens, evergreen

sempervivoides, resembling Sempervivum

senecioides, resembling Senecio

senescens, aging

senil-is, -e, having white hairs

sensibil-is, -e; sensitiv-us, -a, -um, quickly responding to touch or other stimuli

sepiari-us, -a, -um, of hedges or used for hedges

septangular-is, -e, seven-angled

septemfid-us, -a, -um, with seven cuts

septemlob-us, -a, -um, seven-lobed

septentrional-is, -e, northern

sericanth-us, -a, -um, with silky flowers

serice-us, -a, -um, silky

sericifer, sericifer-a, -um; sericofer, sericofer-a, -um, bearing silk

serotin-us, -a, -um, blooming or ripening late

serpens, creeping

serpentin-us, -a, -um, relating to snakes or to serpentine rocks

serpyllifoli-us, -a, -um, with leaves like those of Thymus serpyllum

serratifoli-us, -a, -um, having saw-toothed leaves

serratulat-us, -a, -um, having little saw-like teeth

serrat-us, -a, -um, saw-toothed

sessil-is, -e, without stalks

setace-us, -a, -um, with bristles

setifer, setifer-a, -um; setiger, setiger-a, -um; setos-us, -a, -um, bristly

setifoli-us, -a, -um, with bristly or bristle-like leaves

sexangular-is, -e, six-angled

siame-us, -a, -um, of Thailand (Siam)

siculiform-is, -e, dagger-shaped

sicul-us, -a, -um, of Sicily

signat-us, -a, -um, clearly marked

silvatic-us, -a, -um; silvestr-is, -e, of woodlands

simil-is, -e, similar

simplex, branchless

simplicicaul-is, -e, with branchless stems

simplicifoli-us, -a, -um, without compound leaves

simulans, resembling

sinens-is, -e; sinic-us, -a, -um, of China

sinuat-us, -a, -um; sinuos-us, -a, -um, having wavy margins

sitchens-is, -e, of Sitka, Alaska

smaragdin-us, -a, -um, emerald-green

smilacin-us, -a, -um, relating to *Smilax*

sobolifer, sobolifer-a, -um, having creeping, rooting stems

social-is, -e, forming colonies

solar-is, -e, of sunny places

soldanelloides, resembling *Soldanella*

solid-us, -a, -um, solid or dense

somnifer, somnifer-a, -um, inducing sleep

sorbifoli-us, -a, -um, with leaves resembling those of the mountain-ash (*Sorbus*)

sordid-us, -a, -um, dirty

spars-us, -a, -um, few or scattered

spathulat-us, -a, -um, resembling a spatula

specios-us, -a, -um, showy

spectabil-is, -e, spectacular

speculat-us, -a, -um, mirror-like

sphacelat-us, -a, -um, dead

sphaeric-us, -a, -um, spherical

sphaerocarp-us, -a, -um, having spherical fruits

sphaerocephal-us, -a, -um, having spherical heads

spicifer, spicifer-a, -um, bearing spikes

spiculiflor-us, -a, -um, having flowers in small spikes

spinescens; spinifer, spinifer-a, -um; spinifex; spinos-us, -a, -um, spiny

spinulifer, spinulifer-a, -um, with little spines

spiral-is, -e, spiral

splendens; splendid-us, -a, -um, splendid

spuri-us, -a, -um, false

squalens; squalid-us, -a, -um, dirty-looking

squamat-us, -a, -um, having small scale-like leaves or bracts

squamos-us, -a, -um, having abundant scales

squarros-us, -a, -um, having parts spreading or with recurved ends

stachyoides, resembling *Stachys*

stamine-us, -a, -um, having conspicuous stamens

stellar-is, -e; stellat-us, -a, -um, starlike

stenocarp-us, -a, -um, having narrow fruits

stenopetal-us, -a, -um, having narrow petals

stenophyll-us, -a, -um, having narrow leaves

stenostachy-us, -a, -um, with narrow spikes

steril-is, -e, sterile

stipulace-us, -a, -um; stipular-is, -e; stipulat-us, -a, -um, having well-developed stipules

stolonifer, stolonifer-a, -um, having stolens

stramineus, straw-colored

streptocarp-us, -a, -um, having twisted fruits

streptopetal-us, -a, -um, having twisted petals

streptophyll-us, -a, -um, having twisted leaves

streptosepal-us, -a, -um, having twisted sepals

striat-us, -a, -um, striped

strict-us, -a, -um, erect

strigillos-us, -a, -um, having bristly hairs lying flat with the surface and pointing in one direction

strigos-us, -a, -um, having stiff bristles

strobilifer, strobilifer-a, -um, bearing cones

strumari-us, -a, -um; strumos-us, -a, -um, having cushion-like swellings

stylos-us, -a, -um, having prominent styles

suaveolens, sweetly fragrant

suav-is, -e, sweet

subacaul-is, -e, with a short stem

subalpin-us, -a, -um, of lower alpine regions

subauriculat-us, -a, -um, somewhat eared

subcaerule-us, -a, -um, somewhat blue

subcan-us, -a, -um, graying

subcarnos-us, -a, -um, rather fleshy

subcordat-us, -a, -um, somewhat heart-shaped

subdentat-us, -a, -um, almost toothless

subdivaricat-us, -a, -um, somewhat spreading

subelongat-us, -a, -um, somewhat lengthened

suberect-us, -a, -um, nearly upright

subglauc-us, -a, -um, somewhat glaucous

subhirtell-us, -a, -um, somewhat hairy

submers-us, -a, -um, submerged

subpetiolat-us, -a, -um, having short leafstalks

subscandens, somewhat climbing

subterrane-us, -a, -um, underground

subulat-us, -a, -um, awl-shaped

subvillos-us, -a, -um, with rather soft hairs

succulent-us, -a, -um, fleshy

suecic-us, -a, -um, Swedish

suffrutescens; suffruticos-us, -a, -um, somewhat shrubby

sulcat-us, -a, -um, furrowed

sulfure-us, -a, -um; sulphure-us, -a, -um, sulfur-yellow

sumatran-us, -a, -um, of Sumatra, Indonesia

superb-us, -a, -um, superb

supin-us, -a, -um, prostrate

surculos-us, -a, -um, having suckers or shoots

suspens-us, -a, -um, hanging

sutchuenens-is, -e, of Szechwan, China

sylvatic-us, -a, -um; sylvester, sylvestr-is, -e; sylvicola, of forests

syriac-us, -a, -um, of Syria

syringanth-us, -a, -um, having flowers like those of lilacs (*Syringa*)

syringifoli-us, -a, -um, having leaves like those of lilacs (*Syringa*)

tabular-is, -e, flat or table-like or of Table Mountain, South Africa

tabuliform-is, -e, flat or table-like

taiwanens-is, -e, of Taiwan

taliens-is, -e, of the Tali Mountains, China

tamariscifoli-us, -a, -um, with leaves like those of tamarisk (*Tamarix*)

tanacetifoli-us, -a, -um, with leaves like those of tansy (*Tanacetum*)

tangutic-us, -a, -um, of Kansu, China

taraxacifoli-us, -a, -um, with leaves like those of a dandelion (*Taraxacum*)

tardiflor-us, -a, -um, late-flowering

tardiv-us, -a, -um; tard-us, -a, -um, tardy or late

tartaric-us, -a, -um, of Central Asia

tasmanic-us, -a, -um, of Tasmania

tatsienens-is, -e, from Tatsienlu, China

tauric-us, -a, -um, of the Crimea

taxifoli-us, -a, -um, with leaves like those of yew (*Taxus*)

tectorum, of roofs

tenax, strong or matted

tenuicaul-is, -e, having slender stems

tenuiflor-us, -a, -um, having slender flowers

tenuifoli-us, -a, -um, having slender leaves

tenuipetal-us, -a, -um, having slender petals

tenu-is, -e, slender

terebinthinace-us, -a, -um; terebinthinin-us, -a, -um, relating to terpentine

teres, cylindrical

terminal-is, -e, terminal or relating to boundaries

ternat-us, -a, -um, in clusters of three

terrestr-is, -e, of the ground

tessellat-us, -a, -um, checkered

testace-us, -a, -um, brick-colored

testicular-is, -e; testiculat-us, -a, -um, resembling testicles

tetracanth-us, -a, -um, with spines in fours

tetragon-us, -a, -um, having four angles

tetrandr-us, -a, -um, having four stamens

tetranth-us, -a, -um, with flowers in fours

tetraphyll-us, -a, -um, with leaves in fours

tetrapter-us, -a, -um, four-winged

teucrioides, resembling *Teucrium*

texan-us, -a, -um, of Texas

textil-is, -e, used in weaving

thalictroides, resembling *Thalictrum*

theifer, theifer-a, -um, tea-bearing or tea-scented

thuyoides, resembling *Thuja*

thymifoli-us, -a, -um, having leaves like those of thyme (*Thymus*)

thymoides, resembling thyme (*Thymus*)

thyrsiflor-us, -a, -um, with flowers many together in arrangements called thyrses

tibetic-us,-a, -um, of Tibet

tigrin-us, -a, -um, striped or spotted like a tiger or jaguar, or tiger-toothed

tiliace-us, -a, -um, resembling a linden (*Tilia*)

tilifoli-us, -a, -um, with leaves like those of a linden (*Tilia*)

tinctori-us, -a, -um, used in dyeing

tinctorum, of dyers

tingitan-us, -a, -um, of Tangiers

tirolens-is, -e, of the Tyrol

titani-us, -a, -um, very big

tomentos-us, -a, -um, having dense, woolly hairs

torrid-us, -a, -um, of hot, dry places

tortil-is, -e; tort-us, -a, -um, twisted

toxicari-us, -a, -um; toxic-us, -a, -um; toxifer, toxifer-a, -um, poisonous

translucens, translucent

transparens, transparent

transylvanic-us, -a, -um, of Transylvania, Romania

trapeziform-is, -e, having four unequal sides

tremuloides, resembling the poplar (*Populus tremula*)

tremul-us, -a, -um, trembling

triacanth-us, -a, -um, three-spined

triandr-us, -a, -um, having three stamens

triangular-is, -e; trangulat-us, -a, -um, three-angled

tricaudat-us, -a, -um, with three tails

tricephal-us, -a, -um, three-headed

trichocalyx, having hairy calyxes

trichogyn-us, -a, -um, having hairy ovaries

trichophyll-us, -a, -um, having hairy leaves

trichosperm-us, -a, -um, having hairy seeds

trichotom-us, -a, -um, three-branched

tricocc-us, -a, -um, having fruits with three deep lobes

tricolor, of three colors

tricorn-is, -e, having three horns

tricuspidat-us, -a, -um, with three points

tridens; tridentat-us, -a, -um, three-toothed

trifid-us, -a, -um, cut into three parts

triflor-us, -a, -um, having flowers in threes

trifoliat-us, -a, -um; trifoli-us, -a, -um, having leaves or leaflets in threes

trifurcat-us, -a, -um; trifurc-us, -a, -um, three-forked

trilobat-us, -a, -um, three-lobed

trimestr-is, -e, of three months

trinerv-is, -e, three-veined

tripetal-us, -a, -um, three-petaled

triphyll-us, -a, -um, with leaves in threes

tripter-us, -a, -um, three-winged

trisperm-us, -a, -um, with seeds in threes

tristachy-us, -a, -um, having spikes in threes

triternat-us, -a, -um, three times in threes

trist-is, -e, dull or sad

triumphans, splendid or triumphant

trivial-is, -e, ordinary

trolliifolius, with leaves like those of globe flower (*Trollius*)

truncat-us, -a, -um, cut squarely across

tubat-us, -a, -um, trumpet-shaped

tuberculos-us, -a, -um; tuberculat-us, -a, -um, covered with little warts (tubercles)

tuberos-us, -a, -um, tuberous

tubifer, tubifer-a, -um; tubulos-us, -a, -um, tubular

tubiflor-us, -a, -um, having tubular flowers

tulipifer, tulipifer-a -um, having flowers like those of tulips

tumid-us, -a, -um, swollen

turbinat-us, -a, -um, top-shaped

turgid-us, -a, -um, inflated, turgid

typhin-us, -a, -um, resembling cat-tails (*Typha*)

typic-us, -a, -um, typical of a group

uliginos-us, -a, -um, of swamps

ulmifoli-us, -a, -um, having leaves resembling those of elms (*Ulmus*)

ulmoides, resembling elms (*Ulmus*)

umbellat-us, -a, -um, bearing umbels

umbraculifer, umbraculifer-a, -um, branched in umbrella-like fashion

umbros-us, -a, -um, shade-loving

uncinat-us, -a, -um, hooked at the ends

undat-us, -a, -um; undulat-us, -a, -um, wavy

unguicular-is, -e; unguiculat-us, -a, -um, having claws contracting to a long, slender basal part

unicolor, self-colored (one-colored)

unidentat-us, -a, -um, with one tooth

uniflor-us, -a, -um, having one flower

unifoli-us, -a, -um, having one leaf

unilateral-is, -e, one-sided

uninerv-is, -e, one-veined

uniseriat-us, -a, -um, in one row

univittatus, having one stripe

urban-us, -a, -um; urbic-us, -a, -um, of towns

urceolat-us, -a, -um, urn-shaped

urens, stinging

urophyll-us, -a, -um, having long tail-like apexes to the leaves

ursin-us, -a, -um, suggesting a bear or sometimes, in allusion to the Great Bear. northern

urticifoli-us, -a, -um, having leaves like those of a nettle (*Urtica*)

urticoides, resembling a nettle (*Urtica*)

usitatissim-us, -a, -um, most useful

ustulat-us, -a, -um, burned or scorched

util-is, -e, useful

utriculat-us, -a, -um; utriculos-us, -a, -um, bladder-like

uva-ursi, bear's grape

uvifer, uvifer-a, -um, bearing grapes or grapelike fruits

vaccinifoli-us, -a, -um, having leaves resembling those of *Vaccinium*

vaccinioides, resembling *Vaccinium*

vacillans, variable

vagans. wandering or widely distributed

vaginal-is, -e; vaginat-us, -a, -um, sheathlike or sheathed

valdivian-us, -a, -um, of Valdivia, Chile

valid-us, -a, -um. well-developed or strong

variabil-is, -e; varians; variat-us, -a, -um, varying or variable

variegat-us, -a, -um, variegated

veget-us, -a, -um, vigorous

velutin-us, -a, -um, velvety

venenat-us, -a, -um, poisonous

venenos-us, -a, -um, exceedingly poisonous

veros-us, -a, -um, conspicuously veined

ventricos-us, -a, -um, swollen on one side

venust-us, -a, -um, charming, beautiful

verbascifoli-us, -a, -um, having leaves like those of *Verbascum*

veris. of the spring

vermicular-is, -e; vermiculat-us, -a, -um, wormlike

vernal-is. -e, of the spring

vern-us, -a, -um, of the spring

verrucos-us, -a, -um, warty

verruculos-us, -a, -um, having small warts

versicolor. colored variously

verticillar-is, -e; verticillat-us, -a, -um, having parts in whorls (tiers)

ver-us, -a, -um, true to type

vespertin-us, -a, -um, of the evening

vestit-us, -a, -um, clothed, generally with hairs

vexans, irritating, wounding

vexillar-is, -e, having flags or standards

viburnifoli-us, -a, -um, having leaves like those of *Viburnum*

viciifoli-us, -a, -um, with leaves like those of vetch (*Vicia*)

villos-us, -a, -um, clothed with soft hairs

viminal-is. -e; vimine-us, -a, -um, having long, wandlike shoots

vinifer. vinifer-a, -um, wine-producing

vinos-us, -a, -um, wine-red

violace-us, -a, -um, violet-colored

violascens, becoming or somewhat violet-colored

virens, green

virescens, becoming green

virgat-us, -a, -um, wandlike

virginal-is, -e; virgine-us, -a, -um, white (virginal)

virginian-us, -a, -um; virginic-us, -a, -um; virginiens-is, -e, of Virginia

viridescens, becoming green

viridiflor-us, -a, -um, having green flowers

viridifoli-us, -a, -um, having green leaves

virid-is, -e, green

viridissim-us, -a, -um, intensely green

viridul-us, -a, -um, somewhat green

viscidifoli-us, -a, -um, having sticky leaves

viscid-us, -a, -um; viscos-us, -a, -um, viscid or sticky

vitace-us, -a, -um, resembling a grape vine (Vitis)

vitellin-us, -a, -um, suggesting the yolk of an egg

vitifoli-us, -a, -um, having leaves like those of a grape (Vitis)

vittat-us, -a, -um, striped longitudinally

volubil-is, -e, twining

vomitori-us, -a, -um, emetic

vulgar-is, -e; vulgat-us, -a, -um, common

warleyens-is, -e, of Warley Place Gardens, Essex, England

wolgaric-us, -a, -um, of the Volga River region

xanthacanth-us, -a, -um, with yellow spines

xanthin-us, -a, -um, yellow

xanthocarp-us, -a, -um, with yellow fruits

xantholeuc-us, -a, -um, yellowish-white

xanthonerv-is, -e, with yellow veins

xanthophyll-us, -a, -um, having yellow leaves

xanthorrhiz-us, -a, -um, having yellow roots

yedoens-is, -e, of Tokyo (Yedo), Japan

yunnanens-is, -e; yunnanic-us, -a, -um, of Yunnan, China

zebrin-us, -a, -um, with zebra-like stripes

zeylanic-us, -a, -um, of Ceylon

zonal-is, -e; zonat-us, -a, -um, banded, or striped horizontally

PLANT PATENTS. Although the legal rights of individuals, institutions, and corporations to patent inventions and discoveries in mechanical, chemical, processing, and related fields is generally recognized and fairly well understood, the public is less familiar with the existence of similar rights, protected by appropriate legislation, to patent plants. This is partly because of the comparatively recent establishment of plant patent laws. It was not until 1931, following the signing on May 23, 1930 by President Hoover of the Townsend-Purnell Plant Patent Act, an amendment to the general patent law, that the first plant patent was granted in the United States. The plant patent law, the first such in the world, has been followed by similar legislation in many countries. United States plant patent #1 was granted to the rose 'New Dawn'. Since then the vast majority of plant patents (more than 2,800 had been granted in the United States by 1969) have been for roses.

A United States plant patent is a document called a letters patent testifying that the "invention," as the protected kind of plant is called, has been registered with the Patent Office of the United States Department of Commerce. It grants the inventor (breeder or discoverer) for a period of seventeen years certain rights to control the production, use, and sale of the invention. At the end of the seventeen-year period the invention becomes public property.

To be patentable a plant must be new in the sense that it possesses a novel feature or features or a novel combination of features, that it is useful, and that it is capable of being propagated vegetatively by methods other than seed or spores. A plant is not deemed new if it has been sold, publicly shown, or described more than one year before the filing of the application for the patent. Furthermore, if a United States patent is desired for a plant for which similar protection of any type is applied for in another country, the United States application must be made within one year of the date of the foreign filing.

A patent application consists of a specification, a drawing, and an oath by the applicant that he believes himself to be the original and first inventor of the invention for which the patent is sought. The specification should state the objectives that led to the invention, how it was made, and how the plant for which application is made differs from its parents and similar kinds. Descriptive detail should be in botanically and horticulturally accurate and acceptable terms, with a standard color chart used to define colors. It should end with a statement calling attention to and claiming as the invention the particular features considered to be unique. The drawing in the case of a plant patent may consist of one or more photographic color transparencies. It is better that they be not smaller than 4 by 5 inches. The practical way of going about obtaining a plant patent is to engage the services of an attorney who specializes in plant patents.

The rights of a patent owner are "to exclude others from asexually reproducing the plant or selling or using the plants so reproduced for a period of seventeen years." The owner may license others to propagate, use, or sell the invention, or to engage in any combination of those activities. Arrangements of this kind are common. Remedy of infringement of a plant patent is obtained by civil action. The judge may award to the owner of an infringed patent triple damages and not less than a reasonable royalty together with interest and costs to be determined by the court.

PLANTAGINACEAE — Plantain Family. Consisting of 270 species accommodated in three genera, this family of dicotyledons is, except for some sorts of plantains (Plantago) troublesome in lawns and other places, of very minor horticultural importance. Its kinds are herbaceous perennials, or rarely subshrubs, prevailingly with basal rosettes of alternate or rarely opposite, often parallel-veined leaves. In heads or spikes, the minute flowers are usually bisexual. Their calyxes and papery corollas are typically four-toothed or four-cleft, or the corollas are sometimes three-lobed. There are four or less often one or two protruding stamens and one pistil. The fruits are capsules or tiny nuts enclosed in the persistent calyxes. Only Plantago is cultivated. The plantain family is widely represented in the native floras of many parts of the world.

PLANTAGO (Plan-tàgo) — Plantain. Best known of the genus Plantago are common kinds that grow so luxuriently and exasperatingly as weeds in lawns and waste places. Few of the approximately 265 species are cultivated. Plantains belong in the plantain family PLANTAGINACEAE. The genus consists almost exclusively of annual and perennial herbaceous plants and is distributed in temperate regions throughout the world. The botanical name Plantago is an ancient Latin one.

Plantains grown for ornament or curiosity include colored-leaved and other unusual horticultural varieties of weedy kinds. From the annual P. psyllium, native from southern Europe to India, psyllium seeds used in medicine are obtained. In times past, other kinds, including P. major, P. media, and P. coronopus, were employed medicinally. The first was one of the nine sacred herbs of the ancient Saxons. Another distinction belongs to P. major. Because it followed human migration from Europe and became established as a pernicious weed in practically all parts of the temperate world, it became known as "Englishman's foot" and "white man's foot," a fact referred to by Longfellow in "Hiawatha." The common name plantain, in addition to being used for species of Plantago, is applied in the tropics to a kind of banana (Musa paradisiaca). The two are not botanically related.

Except for a few subshrubby kinds, in which the leaves are alternate or rarely opposite, plantains have all basal foliage arranged in rosettes. Their tiny, incon-

Plantago major atropurpurea

Plantago major rosularis

spicuous flowers are slender, erect spikes or globose heads. Male and female flowers occur on the same plant; sometimes the blooms are bisexual. They have four-parted calyxes and corollas, typically greenish or brownish, and two or four stamens. The fruits are capsules containing two to several seeds.

Plantains occasionally cultivated include two varieties of *P. major,* a species native or freely naturalized throughout the United States and Canada, Europe, and Asia. Bronzy-purple, broad-elliptic leaves about 7 inches in length are characteristic of *P. m. atropurpurea.* Its slender flower spikes are about as long. Called the rose plantain, *P. m. rosularis* has been cultivated as a curiosity for centuries. It is distinguished by having, instead of the slender flower spikes typical of the species, stalks terminating in rosettes, up to 3½ inches in diameter, of blunt green leaves. A variegated-leaved variety of the narrow-leaved *P. lanceolata,* **P. l. marginata** has leaves, up to 1 foot long, edged and blotched with white. This kind apparently originated in France. Much smaller and rarely exceeding 3 inches in diameter is **P. nivalis,** a silvery-hairy-leaved species of Spain that has tiny spherical green flower heads atop stalks 2 to 3 inches in height. An evergreen subshrub, **P. cynops** is interesting, but of little beauty. A native of central and southern Europe, it has slender, linear leaves up to 2½ inches long and yellowish-white flower heads. Quite attractive in bloom, **P. reniformis,** of the Balkan Peninsula, is a perennial with usually one rosette of stalked, softly-hairy, ovate-heart-shaped to nearly circular leaves with blades 2 to 6 inches long and conspicuously toothed in their lower parts. Somewhat exceeding the leaves, the flowering stalks terminate in a dense spike of flowers with white stamens and white anthers.

A branched annual up to 2 feet tall, **P. psyllium,** of the eastern Mediterranean region, is naturalized in parts of North America. It has opposite, linear leaves up to 3 inches long and glandular-hairy. The flowers are in dense spikes up to ½ inch

Plantago nivalis

long. Perennial **P. media,** of Europe and temperate Asia, has elliptic to obovate or oblanceolate leaves 4 to 8 inches long. Its flowers are in slender-conical to cylindrical spikes up to 4 inches long.

Garden Uses and Cultivation. Admittedly limited in their acceptance as garden decoratives, horticultural varieties of plantains are only likely to find favor with lovers of the unusual and bizarre. The species *P. major, P. media,* and *P. psyllium* may rightly be included in herb gardens, and *P. nivalis* is worth a modest place among collections of rock garden plants. None is difficult to cultivate. All succeed in any ordinary soil in full sun. Propagation of the species is by seed or division, of horticultural varieties by division, which may be done in early fall or spring.

Plantago reniformis

PLANTAIN. This is the common name of *Plantago* and certain varieties of *Musa.* Mud-plantain is *Heteranthera,* rattlesnake-plantain *Goodyera,* water-plantain *Alisma,* wild-plantain *Heliconia bihai.* The plantain-lily is *Hosta.*

PLANTERS. These, containers in which plants are displayed for effect, are popular decorations for indoors and for terraces, patios, and similar places. They are the modern equivalent of the jardinieres popular half a century and more ago. It is not always possible to draw sharp lines of distinction between planters and tubs in which plants are grown for display, nor is there any great need to do so for in some of their uses tubs unquestionably function as planters. Window and porch boxes, long popular, are in fact planters.

A tall dieffenbachia, a variegated rubber plant, a dracaena, and a trailing philodendron furnish this planter

A monstera is featured in this planter arrangement, with trailing philodendron at its base

An effective planter arrangement of dieffenbachias and trailing episcias

A planter filled with tulips

Planters are employed as integral parts of furnishing and decorating schemes. They are used for such purposes as window decorations, screens, space dividers, traffic directors, and as reliefs against blank walls. They fit especially well with many contemporary styles of architecture as well as such older traditional ones as Spanish, Mexican, and Early American.

Planters may be portable or built-in, at floor level or raised on legs, stands, tables, or shelves. Sometimes they are fitted with small wheels or large swivel casters so they can be rolled from place to place. They may be of wood, brick, terra-cotta, stone, fiberglass, or a number of other suitable materials. If wood is used it should be a rot-resistant kind, such as cypress or redwood, or be treated with a wood preservative or lined with metal, such as zinc. However, zinc, unless coated with asphaltum paint, is harmful to the roots of some plants.

Sizes and designs of individual planters are as various as space permits, imagination, and good taste suggest. Obviously they should fit their surroundings, and not compete too strongly for attention with the plants they contain. Barrels cut to suitable heights make very satisfactory planters for some locations, especially outdoor ones.

Good effects can be achieved where space admits by grouping planters of similar or complementary designs, sizes, and shapes. If built as portable modules they can be rearranged from time to time to give variety to the planter garden.

There are two ways of planting. One, in view of the name of these containers the most honest, is to remove the plants from the pots in which they come and plant them in soil or a substitute mix with which the planter is filled after being adequately crocked to assure drainage. The other, involving a little cheating perhaps, is to leave the plants in their pots and bury them to just above the rims of these in perlite, vermiculite, or peat moss filled into the planter. Either way, one or more kinds of plants may be employed in each container, spaced and arranged to achieve the most pleasing effects. If more than one sort is chosen be sure all will be satisfied with the same environment.

PLANTING and TRANSPLANTING. In its broadest sense, planting alludes to all deliberate introductions of plants or plant parts into soil or other rooting mediums with the objective of having them grow. Sowing seeds, as illustrated by the common expressions "planting corn" and "planting cotton," is surely included and so is putting into the ground such portions of plants as potato tubers, dahlia roots, and tulip bulbs. Filling window boxes, hanging baskets, and such receptacles as decorative urns with plants is also called planting.

More specific terms are used for some planting operations. Gardeners speak of sowing seeds or of seeding, and when plants are set in pots or tubs, potting or tubbing. Even more limiting terminology is sometimes employed, for instance sprigging and plugging in reference to methods of planting lawns.

In this Encyclopedia, planting seeds is dealt with under Seeds, Propagation By, planting in pots and tubs under Potting and Repotting, planting hanging baskets under Hanging Baskets, and sprigging and plugging under Lawns, Their Making and Renovation. Here the discussion is limited to techniques employed to set plants and plant parts other than seeds in the ground outdoors and in greenhouse beds and benches indoors.

The words planting and transplanting are to some extent interchangeable. In the sense that the plant or part involved is transferred from one location to another or is dug and reset, all transplanting is planting. Yet there are subtle differences in the employments of these terms. Generally transplanting is reserved for operations that include both lifting (digging) plants from the ground and replanting them in new locations. For example, one *transplants* a rose bush from one part of the garden to another, but *plants* one purchased from a nursery. This last operation does not include the lifting (done previously by the nurseryman).

Ideal times for planting and transplanting are those most conducive to speedy recovery from the operation and, in the case of crop plants, those most likely to assure well-timed harvests and good returns. Of necessity compromises must sometimes be made and the judgments of even the most experienced gardeners are subject to miscalculations regarding weather and sometimes other factors.

Very often the period just before new growth begins, which means late winter or early spring for many but not all plants, is most favorable. The urge to grow that succeeds a period of partial or complete dormancy encourages newly set plants to become established with minimum delay.

But substantial new root development takes place with many plants, notably deciduous and evergreen trees and shrubs, hardy herbaceous perennials, and spring-flowering bulbs, at times other than immediately before top growth starts, especially in late summer and fall after the production of shoots and leaves has finished and the ever-increasing demands on the root system for water and nutrients typical of the spring season is not operative.

Fall then is highly favorable for planting and transplanting a great variety of plants. In regions of cold winters, complete the work sufficiently early for new root development to take place before the ground freezes sufficiently to halt root growth, but in mild climates the installation of most hardy trees and shrubs can be continued with every prospect of success whenever weather permits throughout the winter. Where extremely cold winters are usual, it may be best to delay most or all planting until spring.

Late spring and summer are considered favorable seasons to transplant certain herbaceous perennials, notably irises, which move well immediately after they are through flowering, and Oriental poppies, which can be conveniently transferred during their summer period of dormancy. Moving and if needed dividing English and polyanthus primroses is easily accomplished as soon as they have ceased blooming, the transfer of narcissuses from place to place in the garden after their foliage has died and before it has been removed.

Convenience often dictates some departure from what are generally considered ideal times for transplanting. For instance, in dealing with a border of mixed perennials it is usually better to replant all or all of a section of it at one time in fall or early spring, than to move each sort at what may be considered the ideal time for it. When this is done irises, peonies, primroses, narcissuses, and the like receive the same treatment as other occupants and if properly handled suffer no appreciable harm.

Out-of-season planting has been made practicable by the modern practice of selling well-established, actively growing young trees, growing shrubs, roses, and

herbaceous perennials in containers. These lend themselves to setting out in full leaf and even in bloom. They may require somewhat more aftercare in the way of watering than nearly dormant stock, but they have the great advantage of making possible a considerable extension of what otherwise would be short planting seasons.

When the nursery practice of selling hardy plants in containers was first promoted in the northeast and midwest, experienced gardeners regarded it with suspicion. They thought such plants were bound to suffer permanent harm from their roots having been confined and particularly from having been twisted in the containers. This despite the fact that in California and other mild, dry regions planting from cans had long been as standard as elsewhere had been setting out nonhardy bedding plants and small

Modern nurseries sell plants in various types of containers for planting outdoors:
(a) Pots

(b) Composition containers

specimens of other sorts from pots. If properly done, planting from containers has everywhere proved perfectly feasible as well as highly convenient.

(c) Peach baskets

(d) Wooden boxes

(e) Roofing paper girdled with wire mesh

To plant a rose in full leaf and flower from a composition container: (a) Remove the container

(b) Set the plant in a large hole and at the correct depth, taking care not to break the root ball

(c) Add fertile soil around the root ball

(d) Pack the soil firmly with a wooden stick

(e) Before the hole is completely filled, soak with a slow stream of water

(f) Finish by leveling the soil and spreading a mulch around the newly set-out plant

Setting out plants in leaf from containers, and this applies to specimens from pots as well as larger cans and plastic or composition receptacles, calls for different techniques to those employed for bare-root and balled and burlapped specimens. To make sure the soil in which the plants are growing is moist at planting time soak it thoroughly a couple of hours before. Remove the plants from the containers, or more explicitly unless they are clay or reusable plastic pots, the containers from

around the plants, without breaking the root ball. This is often best accomplished by slicing down the side of the container. For doing this most easily, special tools are available. As for all planting, dig holes of ample size, do not break the root balls, firm the soil around them, and then soak the soil with water and perhaps mulch around the newly set plants.

Bare-root planting is usual with young deciduous trees, shrubs, and roses, and sometimes is used for very young and small evergreens. Young herbaceous perennials are also on occasion transplanted with little or no soil about their roots, as are certain young vegetables, those of the cabbage tribe, for example. Precautions for all bare-root planting include being sure when lifting the plants to retain as many roots as possible, to take care they are not allowed to dry while out of the ground, and unless the soil is decidedly moist, to water thoroughly immediately after plant-

To plant a leafless bare-root deciduous tree: (a) Dig a hole of ample size to accommodate the roots and leave some space around them

(b) Add manure, compost, or other organic matter

(c) With a fork, mix it thoroughly with the soil at the bottom of the hole

(f) Tread the soil to make it quite firm

To plant a bare-root rose: (a) Prune back the top as needed

(d) If a single stake is to be used, drive it into the center of the hole, then set the tree in place, taking care that it is at the correct depth and that its roots are spread evenly in their natural positions

(g) Finish by leveling the surface soil

(b) Cut the ends of broken roots cleanly across

(e) Fill in with fertile soil and work it among the roots

ing. To assure the roots being kept moist keep them covered with wet burlap, paper, straw, leaves, or similar material, or with sheets of plastic while out of the ground. Pruning the tops to such an extent that the amount of leafage they develop will not make undue demands upon the roots for water is usually a wise procedure with deciduous trees and shrubs, and to a lesser degree, is sometimes practicable with small evergreens.

Dig holes of adequate size to easily accommodate the roots without crowding, and if the soil is inferior considerably wider than the spread of the roots. Be sure the earth forming the bottoms of the holes is of encouraging quality. If unsatisfactory fork into it considerable amounts of compost, rotted manure, or peat moss and some bonemeal or a dressing of superphosphate, or remove poor, infertile subsoil and replace it with topsoil. In any case make loosened soil in the bottom of holes for trees and shrubs reasonably firm by tamping or treading.

(c) If at all dry, soak the root for a few hours in a pail of water

(d) Set the plant in a hole big enough to spread the roots in their natural directions

To plant small bare-root evergreens (here *Ilex crenata*) in nursery rows: (a) Dig holes of ample size

To plant a balled and burlapped evergreen (here a mountain-laurel): (a) Dig a hole of ample size and fork compost, peat moss, or other decayed organic material into its bottom

(e) Fill in good soil between and around the roots and tamp it firm

(b) Without allowing the roots to dry, set the plants in place, work good soil between and around the roots, and make it firm

(b) Position the plant and cut away and remove as much of the burlap as possible without breaking the ball

(f) Finish with the rose set at the correct depth and the surface soil level

(c) Flood the depression with water, then level and finish the surface neatly

Before setting, trim any broken roots with a sharp knife. Then position the plant. Correct depth is important. Too deep, or too shallow, planting is frequently responsible for indifferent results and failures. Generally a soil line visible on the trunks of trees and shrubs indicates the depth at which they have been growing. It is usually safest not to set plants

deeper than they were previously, or not with their upper roots more than 2 or 3 inches beneath the surface. Never plant too deeply just to anchor a specimen securely. If support is needed drive a stake

in the center of the hole before positioning the young tree and after planting is completed tie its trunk to this.

Spread the roots carefully in their natural postions and work soil between them so they are in layers instead of being clumped and crowded as is likely to happen if earth is just shoveled into the hole without care for the positions the roots are forced to assume. When working soil among the roots pack firmly each layer as covered. Complete the operation by bringing the soil to surface level and making it firm. If waterings are likely to be necessary, erect a rim of earth around the periphery of the root area so that a saucer to hold water is formed. In any case, if the soil is dryish, it should be soaked as soon as planting is finished.

Balled and burlapped evergreens and fairly big to very large deciduous trees and shrubs as well as clumps of herbaceous perennials that are to be moved with big

(c) Fill in with good soil to within 2 or 3 inches of the surface and tamp it firm

(d) Soak with water two or three times, fill with soil to grade, and then spread a mulch around the bush

Planting a large balled and burlapped tree (here a willow in leaf): (a) The tree delivered by the nursery, the lacing that tied the base of the ball to the wooden platform removed

(b) The tree moved to the planting site

(c) The tree planted

(d) Soaking the newly planted ball with water

(e) The tree already pruned to thin out the branches and reduce the foliage

balls of earth, those of the perennials usually without being wrapped, generally transplant most satisfactorily in early fall because then they have maximum time to grow new roots before being faced with the summer stress of supplying the tops with the increased supplies of water they need at that season. But spring planting is also satisfactory and for a few sorts with thick, fleshy roots, such as magnolias, is often preferred.

Primary concerns with balled and burlapped specimens are that the balls are big enough and are not broken. As a rough guide, with specimens of most deciduous trees the root balls should be 1 foot in diameter for each inch of trunk diameter measured at a height of about 4 feet. With evergreens the diameter of the balls should usually equal at least two-thirds the spread of the branches. But these are only approximations. Actual ball sizes must be tailored to such circumstances as whether the roots are compact or wide-ranging, the type of soil, and particularly whether the specimens have been transplanted within the last two to four years, as young nursery-grown specimens usu-

ally will have been. It all adds up to how big a ball is necessary to ensure taking enough roots to adequately support the tops. With deciduous trees and shrubs and some evergreens, the demand of the tops can be lessoned by reducing their size at planting time by fairly severe pruning.

When purchasing balled and burlapped trees and shrubs, be sure the balls are of soil in which the roots have been and are growing. The all too common practice of selling plants with "manufactured" balls as balled and burlapped is reprehensible. Such balls are made by packing earth around bare roots and wrapping the whole in burlap or plastic. Specimens so treated are not superior to bare-rooted ones if their roots have not been allowed to dry.

The technique of planting balled and burlapped trees and shrubs involves digging holes of adequate size, in most cases 2 feet or more wider than the diameters of the balls. It is often advantageous to do this two or three weeks in advance of planting so that any loose earth in the bot-

toms of the holes has time to settle and installation of plants from nurseries can proceed without undue delay.

When digging the holes, put the topsoil in one heap, the subsoil in another. If the subsoil is decidedly infertile remove some of it and replace it with topsoil. Fork into the bottoms of the holes generous

Successfully transplanting London plane trees 25 feet tall and with a 25-foot spread in early fall at Aqueduct Raceway, New York City: (a) Before transplanting

(b) Pruning to thin out the tops and slightly reduce their spread

(c) Digging a root ball

(d) Wrapping a ball in heavy burlap

(e) Lacing a ball with rope

(f) The lacing completed

(g) Pulling a tree from its hole up a slope dug for the purpose and onto a wooden platform

(h) Towing to the planting site

(i) The trees, guyed to deadmen buried in the ground and with their trunks wrapped with burlap after planting, prosper in their new locations the following summer

amounts of compost, manure, or other organic material, then pack the loosened earth firmly by tamping or treading. If it is at all clayey, do not do this when it is wet and sticky.

Correct planting depth is very important. Inexperienced and careless planters often set plants too shallowly, or worse, too deeply. In most cases it is satisfactory to have them 1 inch to 2 inches or with big specimens up to 3 inches deeper than they were previously, which can usually be determined from the position of a soil line on the trunk or stems, but with azaleas, rho-

dodendrons, camellias, and other sorts known to abhor having their upper roots covered with material more compact than a loose mulch, it is important not to more

Transplanting large London plane trees, in early fall, from New Jersey to a Manhattan site: (a) A specimen dug, balled and burlapped, pruned, and with its branches tied together ready for removal from the nursery

(c) Arriving in New York City

(e) Positioning a tree in a hole carefully prepared as to depth and width; planting is completed by back-filling with good topsoil, tamping it firm, and drenching with water

(b) The ball of a tree, with a wooden platform laced to its base, on a flat-bed truck ready for transportation

(d) Off-loading, after removing the platform and the ties that held in the branches

A newly planted young tree, supported by three stakes, with a "saucer" around its base to hold water

Protect trunks of newly planted trees form sunscald: (a) Wrap them with strips of burlap or special tree-wrap paper, winding the strip around the base of the trunk, tying it securely, and then winding it spirally upward

than barely cover the tops of the balls with soil or to have them even with the surface and rely upon a mulch to keep them moist and cool.

When positioning the plants remember that if the bottoms of the holes were loosened by spading or forking, even though they were afterward moderately consolidated by tamping, some further settling may take place and the balls may sink a little after planting. Make allowance for this in positioning them.

After the plant is in place, cut the ties that hold the burlap or substitute material and without breaking the ball slice away some of the wrapping and fold the remainder into the bottom of the hole. Some gardeners cut the ties but leave the covering intact, a practice satisfactory with loosely woven burlap, but not with plastic substitutes that do not permit roots to grow through them readily.

Next fill good soil around the ball and tamp it firmly. Should the soil taken from

the hole be of poor quality, mix with it a generous amount of compost, peat moss, or other suitable decayed organic material, including if procurable a proportion of rotted manure, as well as a liberal dressing of bonemeal or other long-lasting fertilizer. When about two-thirds of the backfill has been shoveled around the ball and tamped some gardeners soak it with water before filling in the remainder, but if the soil is at all clayey, it is better to wait until the hole is completely filled before watering. Packing wet clayey soil destroys its structure, making it unfriendly to the growth of roots. In any case complete the job by making a saucer around the periphery of what was the hole to hold water applied immediately after planting and later. Construct the saucer by erecting as its rim a ridge of soil that stands a few inches above normal ground level, not by creating a depression.

If support is needed, as it often is with newly planted trees, provide it by driving

(b) Finish by giving it one or two horizontal turns around the trunk and tying it securely

A newly planted tree secured by three stakes and wires passing through short pieces of hose

A newly planted tree secured by wires passing around the trunk through pieces of hose and strained at ground level to sturdy stakes

Planting with a trowel: (a) A young chrysanthemum

(b) Firming the soil about the roots of the chrysanthemum

(c) Divisions of iris

(d) A broccoli planted with soil around its root

(e) Bare-rooted lettuce plants

two or three stout stakes outside the periphery of the root ball and securing the trunk to these by wires that where in contact with the trunk pass through short pieces of rubber hose to prevent damage to the bark. Alternatively, and especially with big trees, use three guy wires passed in similar fashion around the trunks a few feet above the ground and attached to "dead men." For more information see the Encyclopedia entry Staking and Tying.

Setting out plants of sizes that can comfortably be held in one hand is done somewhat differently. Instead of concentrating on individual holes make ready the entire area to be planted. Spade, fork, rotary till, and mix in organic matter and any other amendments deemed desirable. Do not pack the earth and as far as practicable avoid walking or stepping on it.

A trowel is most convenient for planting small specimens with balls of soil, such as bedding plants from pots or flats or lifted from cold frames or nursery beds. A spade may prove more convenient for planting clumps of herbaceous perennials and small evergreens being moved with balls of soil not burlapped. When dealing with bare-rooted small plants, such as cabbages and leeks, a dibber may be the preferred tool to employ.

Aftercare of newly set plants can play a very important part in determining success. Immediate concerns are to encourage root growth and, if the plants are in foliage, to prevent excessive loss of moisture by transpiration from the leaves.

The first to a large extent depends upon keeping the ground sufficiently moist, but not so constantly saturated that the roots are denied adequate supplies of air. If dry

Planting a dormant herbaceous perennial: (a) Set the plant in a hole made with a trowel or spade

(b) Fill the hole with soil and firm by treading around the plant

(c) Rake the surface smooth

weather follows planting, thorough soakings to the full depth of the roots at five- to ten-day intervals are likely to suffice. Such drenchings are much more satisfactory than more frequent shallow wettings. With trees and shrubs, it is desirable to pay attention to watering throughout the entire first summer following planting, but after the first month or so applications can be less frequent than just suggested. Mulching is of immense benefit in conserving moisture and in maintaining equable soil temperatures.

Several courses are followed to limit excessive loss of moisture by transpiration. Pruning at planting time does this by less-

Planting cabbage with a dibber (dibble): (a) Push the tool into the ground

(b) Wiggle it from side to side to enlarge the hole

(c) Hold the plant with its roots in the hole and with the dibber push soil against the roots

ening the amount of foliage the roots are called upon to supply. The same result comes from the removal of leaves or parts of leaves. Those of divisions of iris and polyanthus primroses, for example, are usually cut back one-third to one-half at planting time, and it often helps hollies and other broad-leaved evergreens that one does not want to prune back if up to one-half their leaves are picked off when they are transplanted.

Spraying with an antitranspirant or antidesiccant that reduces loss of moisture from aboveground parts by covering them with a thin film of plastic or other material is a favorite and practical way of reducing water loss, most commonly used with evergreens, but sometimes with other trees and shrubs.

Shading from bright sun, sheltering from wind, and misting fairly frequently with water are routine methods of discouraging excessive transpiration. In most cases these procedures need be done only for a week or two, until the foliage is able to stand up to normal exposure without wilting.

To settle the soil around their roots and supply moisture, water plants with leaves immediately after they are planted: (a) With a hose

(b) With a stream from a watering can

(c) With a watering can fitted with a spray

(c) Lift the plants out

(b) Hyacinths

To remove plants from flats: (a) Slice between them two weeks before planting

(d) Separate them carefully to prevent damaging the roots

(c) Regal lilies

(b) Tap the flat on the ground to gain space to insert fingers

Planting bulbs with a trowel: (a) Crocuses

(d) Tulips

Because plants of these sorts are generally in full leaf at planting time it is especially important to preserve as much of their root systems as possible and to water thoroughly as soon as planting is completed. The shock of separating plants crowded in flats can be minimized by slicing between them with a knife about two weeks before they are to be removed from the flat so that each plant stands in its own small rectangle of earth. So far as practicable, choose dull, humid weather for planting, but not when the ground is sodden. Make holes large enough that the roots are not cramped, and firm the soil against them.

Planting bulbs, tubers, corms, and the like is usually most conveniently accomplished with a trowel. For small ones a dibber is sometimes used, and for planting in grass turf a special tool called a bulb planter is convenient. A common mistake is planting too shallowly, although with a few sorts, such as Madonna lilies, too deep planting is more likely. Another frequent error that brings poor results is

Podophyllum hexandrum

Plumeria rubra

Plumeria rubra acutifolia

Podophyllum peltatum

Podophyllum peltatum as a groundcover

Polemonium carneum

Polygonum affine

Pogonia ophioglossoides

Polygonum bistorta

Polygala californica

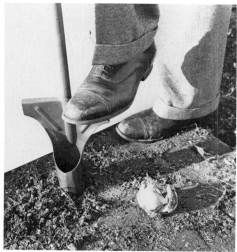

Using a bulb planter: (a) Push it into the ground

(b) Stop at the full depth of the planter's cylinder

(c) Withdraw the planter with a plug of soil; a bulb is then dropped into the hole and the plug replaced on top of it and pushed down with the foot

planting with their bottoms almost or quite sitting on hard, infertile subsoil impossible for roots to penetrate. All bulb plants, even stem-rooting lilies, need at least a few inches of agreeable soil beneath

them. Make sure subsurface drainage is satisfactory and have the soil fertile and in a satisfactory crumbly condition.

Transplanting involves lifting plants from sites they occupy and installing them in new ones. Except for sorts with bulbs, corms, or tubers that have no permanent roots and can be moved when their annual ones have died, a chief concern is with preserving sufficient roots to support the aboveground parts. This generally presents no difficulty with herbaceous perennials that die to the ground each year and are moved when dormant, or with trees and shrubs that have compact masses of plentiful, much-branched roots. But unless handled carefully, success is less certain with trees and shrubs that have deep taproots or a few, wide-spreading main roots and a large proportion of their feeder roots toward the ends of them and at considerable distances from the trunk. These and sometimes other reasons are often responsible for failure when specimens of such trees as dogwoods, magnolias, sour gums, and sweet gums are transplanted from sites where they have been long established.

In well-conducted nurseries, trees and shrubs, especially those known to resent root disturbance, are transplanted every two or three years. Each time roots are cut, and this causes them to branch and develop a more compact mass containing a much greater proportion of the total roots than would be the case without such interference. Because of this, final moves to their permanent locations can be made with much greater prospect of success than with specimens taken from locations where they have been growing undisturbed for many years.

Moving trees and shrubs from the wild or other places where they have been growing for a long time can be facilitated by root pruning them (see the Encyclopedia entry Pruning) at least a year before they are transplanted. Choose times when the ground is reasonably moist for transplanting. If the work must be done during a spell of dry weather, soak the soil to the full depth of the root ball the day before digging.

Besides careful digging, and with balled and burlapped specimens secure lacing to prevent the root ball breaking, every care must be taken when transplanting to prevent the roots from drying. With this in mind protect them from exposure to sun and wind. This may be done by keeping them covered with leaves, hay, straw, burlap, or other suitable material kept moist or by heeling them in (planting them temporarily closely together with loose soil, peat moss, or the like covering the roots).

PLATANACEAE — Plane Tree Family. This family of dicotyledons consists of only the

genus *Platanus*, described in the following entry.

PLATANUS (Plát-anus)—Plane Tree. Sycamore or Buttonwood or Buttonball. Species of *Platanus* are so similar to each other and so different from all other trees that botanists group them in a family by themselves, the plane tree family PLATANACEAE. There are ten species, all natives of the northern hemisphere, their chief center of distribution the southwestern United States and Mexico. The name is derived from *platanos*, the Greek name of the oriental plane. At an earlier stage in the Earth's development, the genus was more widely dispersed and there were more species. Fossils of extinct kinds are abundant in North America, Greenland, central Europe, and eastern temperate Asia, although in the last three regions no plane trees now grow natively. The indication is that plane trees have been part of the Earth's flora for at least 100,000,000 years.

Plane trees are deciduous. They have alternate leaves that typically are palmately-lobed, palmately-veined, and somewhat maple-like. One species only, *P. kerri*, of Laos, has lobeless, pinnately-veined, ovate-lanceolate leaves that somewhat resemble large beech leaves. The bases of the leafstalks of all sorts completely conceal the axillary winter buds, fitting over them like a candle snuffer over a candle flame. The minute unisexual flowers are in quite large, dense, spherical heads attached to pendulous stalks. The number of heads on each stalk is an important factor in identification. It varies from mostly one, in *P. occidentalis*, to usually ten or twelve, in *P. kerri*, a species not in cultivation. The heads of flowers are either completely male or completely female, with both sexes on the same tree. The females are succeeded by seeds packed tightly together in balls that remain long after the leaves have fallen. A very characteristic feature of these trees is their scaling bark. The outer covering of the trunk and larger branches peels in big patches, exposing smooth new surfaces lighter colored than the older parts. This gives a more or less piebald appearance to trunk and limbs.

Plane trees are chiefly esteemed for shade and ornament. In addition, the tough, difficult-to-split wood of the American plane is used for boxes, crates, furniture, interior trim, and butchers' blocks, and that of the oriental plane for inlay work and wood pulp.

The American plane, buttonwood, or sycamore (*P. occidentalis*) occurs spontaneously from Maine to Ontario, Iowa, Florida, and Texas, most commonly near the banks of streams and other waters. It is the most massive, but perhaps not the tallest deciduous tree indigenous to the continent. In the fertile bottom lands of

Platanus occidentalis

Platanus occidentalis (bark)

Platanus occidentalis (branching habit)

Platanus occidentalis (fruits—seed balls)

Platanus racemosa in southern California

Platanus orientalis in Kashmir

the basins of the Mississippi and the lower Ohio rivers it attains heights of up to 175 feet and may have a trunk 10 to 14 feet in diameter.

Sometimes the trunk is single, but often the main axis divides into two or three stout, upright secondary trunks that support the dense framework of branches of the rounded, oblongish, or wide-spreading head. The bark, except that of the lower part of the trunk, which is fissured and dark brown, is smooth and very light colored, often creamy-white. The leaves, up to 9 inches across with mostly three, but sometimes five shallow lobes, are as broad or broader than they are long and toothed or not. The clusters of flowers and smoothish 1-inch-wide seed balls are long-stalked, usually solitary, less often paired. Variety *P. o. glabrata* has usually firmer-textured, smaller leaves with the clefts between the leaf lobes extending to about one-third the depth of the blade.

The California plane tree, buttonwood, or buttonball (*P. racemosa* syn. *P. californica*) differs from the eastern American species in having two to seven flower clusters on each stalk followed by bristly or smooth seed balls, and in its more deeply three- to five-lobed leaves, which are usu-

ally toothless. As a native confined to California and Baja California, this is sometimes 120 feet tall, but more usually does not exceed 80 feet. Its main trunk is often very short and divided into a few secondary trunks that diverge erratically. Much like *P. racemosa* and sometimes treated as a variety of it, the Arizona sycamore (*P. wrightii*) is a handsome native of Arizona, New Mexico, and northern Mexico. From its California relative it differs chiefly in its remotely-toothed or toothless leaves being even more deeply-cleft into three or five lobes and its fruiting heads being usually stalked, but intergrades between this and *P. racemosa* occur in the wild.

The oriental plane (*P. orientalis*) grows spontaneously from southern Europe to Kashmir, but in some parts of this territory may not be an original native, having been introduced by man. Certainly it has been cultivated and cherished for shade, fuel, and lumber for many centuries. Herodotus writes of it; Xerxes dallied in its shade; Pliny and Aristotle discoursed beneath it. It was brought from Greece to Italy in 390 B.C. and soon became a favorite of the Romans. That it is aboriginal in southeastern Europe and Asia Minor there is no doubt, but elsewhere in the Mediterranean region where it is now spontaneous, especially where hot summers prevail, the desire and efforts of travelers and conquerors to establish the noble tree they had seen elsewhere may be responsible for its presence.

The famous Chenar trees, of Shalimar garden and so abundant elsewhere in Kashmir, are oriental planes. In North America this species is little known. Few if any authentic specimens occur, but its name is widely applied to selections of the hybrid London plane. It is believed that the oriental plane is one of the parents of this last, and forms of the hybrid that most resemble it are the ones frequently mislabeled.

The oriental plane differs from native American *P. occidentalis* in usually having three or four, but sometimes as many as five or six, heads of flowers (or later fruits) on each stalk although a few stalks may only have two. It also differs in its leaves having five to seven deeper lobes more coarsely-toothed and sharper-pointed than those of *P. occidentalis*. In *P. orientalis*, the clefts between them extend halfway or more to the junction of leaf blade and stalk. The oriental plane may have a single central trunk or may branch a few feet above the ground into several massive, spreading limbs. Its bark is less milky-white than that of *P. occidentalis*. The oriental plane is very long-lived, specimens may persist for many centuries. Under favorable conditions it may be the longest-lived of European trees.

The London plane (**P. acerifolia** syn. *P. hybrida*) is probably more familiar to residents of cities in the temperate regions than almost any other tree. It has been planted in vast numbers in London, Paris, New York, Philadelphia, Buenos Aires, Nanking, and countless other urban communities around the world, and everywhere it endures difficult environments, minimal care, and drastic pruning better than almost any other tree. Yet the origin of the London plane is not surely known. It grows nowhere in the wild. But there can be no reasonable doubt that it is a fertile hybrid between the eastern American buttonwood (*P. occidentalis*) and the oriental plane (*P. orientalis*) that originated in Europe before 1666. By that year it was in cultivation at the Oxford Botanic Garden in England, but it seems improbable that it originated in England, since its American parent does not thrive there and is not known to bear flowers in the British Isles.

It is much more likely that Portugal or Spain was the birthplace of the London plane. In the Iberian Peninsula its presumed parents thrive and reach flowering size. The tree at Oxford may have been imported into England as a cutting or a young specimen. Be that as it may, the

Platanus acerifolia at The New York Botanical Garden

Platanus acerifolia (fruits—seed balls)

Platanus acerifolia at the Royal Botanic Gardens, Kew, England

Platanus acerifolia at Oxford University, England; this is a propagation from the original tree

London plane is intermediate in all respects between its supposed parents. Notably its seed balls are mostly in strings of two. Rarely a few are solitary or in threes or sometimes even more. The surfaces exposed by the flaking of the bark, like those of *P. orientalis*, are more yellowish and more varicolored than those of *P. occidentalis*. The five-lobed leaves are less deeply cut than those of *P. orientalis*, but more deeply cut than those of *P. occidentalis*, and the center lobe is narrower than is usual in the latter species.

Actually there is considerable variation in the leaves of different "strains" of the

London plane, and seedlings exhibit quite noticeable differences. It is quite apparent to the keen observer that London planes in America have a different aspect from those of Europe. They more closely resemble native American *P. occidentalis*. The not unlikely suggestion has been made that the American trees represent back-crosses between the original London plane and its presumed parent, the eastern American buttonwood. Varieties of *P. acerifolia* are *P. a. keiseyana*, with leaves variegated with yellow; *P. a. suttneri*, which has white blotches on its leaves; *P. a. pyramidalis*, which does not have drooping lower branches and usually has three-lobed leaves mostly broader than long; and *P. a. hispanica*, which usually has leaves up to 1 foot across with five-toothed lobes. It is of interest to note that although this tree was widely planted in London shortly before 1838 and from then onward, the name London plane does not appear to have been applied to it much before 1915. The London plane characteristically has a single trunk, a broad, round head, and somewhat drooping lower branches. It attains a maximum height of about 150 feet.

Garden and Landscape Uses. Plane trees are too big for most modern gardens. They are primarily subjects for parks, parkways, and other large-scale landscape developments and as street trees. Because of its great susceptibility to anthracnose disease, the American buttonball (*P. occidentalis*) is much less suitable for planting than the much more resistant London plane. In warm, dryish climates, such as that of southern California, *P. racemosa* is useful for the same purposes as the London plane serves in cooler regions.

Cultivation. Planes thrive best in deep, moderately moist, but not wet, soils. They transplant readily and stand hard pruning well, but this should not be done unless limitations of space or other good reason make it necessary or desirable. Propagation is by seeds sown in spring and covered with soil to their own diameter and by hardwood cuttings of leafless shoots made in fall. The oriental plane is much more difficult to propagate by cuttings than other cultivated kinds.

Diseases and Pests. Anthracnose is by far the most serious disease of plane trees. In addition, they are susceptible to fungus leaf spots, but these are of minor importance. The chief insect pests are aphids, scales, and the sycamore plant bug.

PLATYCARYA (Platycàr-ya). Two species have been described in *Platycarya*, of the walnut family JUGLANDACEAE. The name comes from the Greek *platys*, broad, and *karya*, a nut. It alludes to the compressed fruits. From all other genera in the walnut family this is distinct in its female flowers and fruits being in erect conelike catkins. This genus is endemic to China.

Platycarias are small to medium-sized deciduous trees with much the aspect of walnuts, hickories, and wingnuts. As with hickories the pith of the twigs is solid, not in thin transverse plates like that of walnuts and wingnuts. The leaves are alternate and pinnate, with a terminal leaflet. The inconspicuous unisexual flowers, without perianths, consist of stamens or pistils. The females are in the axils of terminal conelike structures of overlapping bracts, the males in slender, cylindrical, usually pendulous catkins originating just below the females. The fruits are winged

nutlets that including the wings measure ⅛ inch or slightly more across.

A rare and fairly handsome tree up to 40 feet tall or sometimes a large shrub, *P. strobilacea* is not hardy in severe climates, but in sheltered locations may succeed as far north as southern New England. Its leaves, 6 inches to 1 foot long, have five to fifteen, stalkless, long-pointed, toothed or double-toothed, ovate-lanceolate leaflets 1½ to 4½ inches in length. When young they are slightly hairy, but are glabrous later. This is true also of young shoots. The species that has been described as *P. sinensis* is perhaps not sufficiently distinct to be accepted as more than a variety of *P. strobilacea*.

Garden and Landscape Uses and Cultivation. Graceful-foliaged *P. strobilacea* is suitable for use as a lawn specimen and similar purposes. It succeeds in soils of medium fertility. It may be propagated by seed and by layering and by grafting onto seedling hickories.

PLATYCERIUM (Platy-cèrium) — Staghorn Fern, Elkhorn Fern. The seventeen species of *Platycerium*, of the polypody family POLYPODIACEAE, constitute an unusual and easily recognizable group. They are native to tropical Africa, Asia, South America, and warm-temperate Australia. Its name comes from the Greek *platys*, broad, and *keras*, a horn, and like the common name was applied because of the antler-like appearance of the fronds (leaves) of most kinds.

Staghorn ferns, of noble aspect, are in the main too large for indoors except in public conservatories and roomy greenhouses, but are impressive outdoor ornamentals in tropical and subtropical places such as Florida, California, and Hawaii. They are epiphytes. Like most orchids and bromeliads in the wild, they perch high on trees, but unlike parasites, take no nourishment from their hosts. Their nomenclature is much confused, a situation aggravated by the abundance of horticultural varieties and some hybrids of natural species.

To the nonbotanical, platyceriums may not look much like ferns. They lack the lacy appearance commonly associated with that group. But their sexual reproduction, by spores instead of seeds, is clearly that of non-flowering plants, and technical details place them surely with the ferns. The spores are in tiny capsules in large patches on the undersides of the fronds.

Two very distinct kinds of fronds are produced. Barren ones, usually comparatively small, and shield-, disk-, or fan-shaped, or more rarely forked, bear no spores and are located at the bases of the plants near the roots. The much larger, usually forked, fertile ones angle downward or upward and bear spores.

Most commonly cultivated, easy to grow, and because it stands lower temperatures than other kinds, best adapted for outdoor cultivation in southern California and Florida, *P. bifurcatum* is native to Australia, New Guinea, New Caledonia, and Lord Howe Island. Very variable, in some manifestations it resembles *P. hillii*, *P. veitchii*, and *P. willinckii*. In all of these the patches of spores extend from or almost from the tips to the bases and sometimes further of the ultimate segments of the fronds. The fertile fronds of *P. bifurcatum*, up to somewhat more than 3 feet long, and twice- or thrice-divided into strap-shaped segments densely-hairy on their undersides, droop only on very old specimens. More typically they are erect to nodding. Their undivided, unexpanded basal portions are 2 inches long or longer. Frequently the patches of spore capsules extend around the bottoms of the clefts (sinuses) between the final divisions of the fronds. The light to dark brown barren fronds with a darker central stripe and often fringed margins, are linear to lanceolate. Varieties of *P. bifurcatum* are numerous. Here belong *P. b. subrhomboideum*, in which the ultimate frond segments are not

Platycerium bifurcatum variety at Montreal Botanical Garden

strap-shaped, but broaden markedly from their bases, and *P. b. lanciferum*, in which the fronds are deeply-forked into segments not over ¾ inch wide. Horticultural varieties differing in various details from the typical species are *P. b. majus*, *P. b.* 'Netherlands', *P. b.* 'Roberts', *P. b.* 'San Diego', *P. b. bloomei*, and *P. b.* 'Ziesenhenne'.

Very similar to some variants of *P. bifurcatum* is Australian *P. veitchii*. It differs chiefly from *P. bifurcatum* in its very stiff, always erect fronds, which in typical examples are silvery-white, especially on their undersides. The fertile fronds are erect, up to 2 feet long or longer. The barren ones are deeply-cut along their upper edges into finger-like lobes.

Pendulous fertile fronds, their unexpanded basal portions not over ½ inch

Platycerium veitchii at the Royal Botanic Gardens, Kew, England

Platycerium hillii at The New York Botanical Garden

Platycerium hillii showing patches of spore clusters

Platycerium willinckii at Montreal Botanical Garden

Platycerium hillii showing platelike basal fronds

Platycerium ellisii, of gardens

Platycerium willinckii lemoinei at The New York Botanical Garden

long, are characteristic of **P. willinckii.** Its patches of spore capsules, except when the ultimate segments of the fronds are very short, extend around the bases of the clefts between the segments. Varieties of

P. willinckii are *P. w. lemoinei*, *P. w* 'Payton', and *P. w* 'Scofield'. Erect fertile fronds, hairless or nearly hairless on both surfaces, are typical of **P. hillii.** They have wedge-shaped bases. Their upper thirds are forked one or more times into ultimate segments up to 8 inches long by 2¼ inches wide. The patches of spore capsules frequently extend from the tips of the ultimate frond segments to around the bases of the clefts between them, but may be less extensive. The barren fronds are roundish to kidney-shaped and more or less shallowly-lobed. This is a native of Australia. In *P. h.* 'Drummond', the shorter, suberect fronds have spore patches limited to the margins of the ultimate segments, or, if completely across them, notched at both ends. Plants commonly cultivated as **P. ellisii** are mostly variants of *P. hillii* 'Drummond'. The name *P. ellisii* belongs to another species.

Patches of spore capsules occupying long central areas of the fertile fronds characterize **P. andinum,** of the mountains of Bolivia and Peru. These fronds droop, are 6 to 9 feet or more long, and divided

in antler fashion into slender lobes. The erect, barren fronds, up to 3 feet long, are irregularly lobed along their upper margins. They have rounded bases. Patches of spore capsules limited to special stalked roundish to kidney- or rarely wedge-shaped, convex lobes up to 6 inches long by 10 inches wide are typical of **P. coronarium.** The round-bottomed barren fronds, erect and round-lobed, are up to 2 feet long or longer. Hanging limply, the fertile fronds, much cut into strap-shaped lobes, are up to six feet long or longer. This is native in tropical Asia, Indonesia, and the Philippine Islands.

The plant long known as *P. alcicorne* is **P. vassei,** of Africa and Madagascar. This has tightly overlapping barren fronds presented as lustrous green, net-veined hemispheres from the apexes of which sprout the erect, repeatedly forked fertile fronds. The patches of spore capsules are at or below the ends of the ultimate lobes. Crescent- or V-shaped patches of spore capsules around the bottoms of the clefts between the lobes of the drooping fronds are typical of **P. stemmaria.** As known in cultivation, this native of Africa has two- to four-times-forked fertile fronds up to 1½ feet long, with broadly-wedge-shaped divisions. Variants with narrower divisions occur in the wild. The sterile fronds are erect, oblong, 1 foot or somewhat

Platycerium stemmaria

more long by about one-half as broad. They have wavy margins.

Bold and handsome *P. grande*, of Malaysia, Java, and Australia, has erect, lobed, fan-shaped barren fronds up to 2 feet or more across. The fertile fronds, usually in pairs, are pendulous, 1 foot to 6 feet in length, the two first (main) branches of similar size and several-times branched into strap-shaped lobes. One or rarely two usually semicircular areas of spore capsules are borne on the undersurfaces of the broad, wedge-shaped basal parts of fronds. Variety *P. g. tamburinense* has fronds with shorter, wider, blunter lobes. Much like *P. grande*, but its smaller fertile fronds densely-downy and with two, rather than usually one, patches of spore clusters, *P. wallichii* is a native of Malaya, Burma, and Thailand. Another much like *P. grande* is *P. wilhelminae-reginae*, of New Guinea. This is distinguished by the margins of its barren fronds being fringed near their bases and by the first (main) division of the fertile fronds being of two very unequal parts, one short and wedge-shaped, the other with a wedge-shaped base, then much cleft and recleft into narrow lobes, and up to 6 feet in length.

Sporelines of *Platycerium wilhelminae-reginae*

Fertile fronds not lobed in staghorn fashion, but broad-ovate, smooth-edged, and spreading, are characteristic of the cabbage or elephant ear fern (*P. angolense* syn. *P. velutinum*). Each has a patch of spore clusters near its apex. The barren fronds are large, erect, and fan-shaped. They have rounded bases and wavy upper edges. This is a native of tropical Africa. Another without antler-like fertile fronds, *P. madagascariense*, of Malagasy (Madagascar), is recognized by its round to kidney-shaped barren fronds being, at least when dry, honeycombed with depressions that produce a waffle-like pattern. The margins are more or less irregularly-lobed. The down-sweeping fertile fronds, up to 1 foot long and broad, are triangular. Their broad apexes are shallowly-lobed and sometimes have one or two deeper clefts. The spore capsules cover most of the upper halves of the fronds without quite reaching the apexes of the lobes.

Garden and Landscape Uses. Staghorn ferns are magnificent ornamentals for outdoors, where climates permit, and for exhibiting in large conservatories and greenhouses. Of bold appearance and noble aspect, they can be used to good effect as focal points and featured pieces. They add beauty and interest wherever they are displayed.

Cultivation. The hardier platyceriums, those native of Australia, are cultivated outdoors in Florida and southern California, and in greenhouses where a minimum night temperature of 50 to 55°F is maintained. More tropical kinds prosper in greenhouses with a minimum night temperature about ten degrees higher. Temperatures by day are increased over those maintained at night by five to fifteen degrees. At other seasons considerably higher temperatures both by day and night than those provided in winter are beneficial. A fairly humid but not oppressively moist atmosphere and good light with shade from strong sun are needed. Dimly lit or dank locations are unsuitable for staghorn ferns. Perfect drainage of the rooting medium is essential. This is fairly assured for specimens attached to tree trunks, sheets of cork, slabs of tree fern trunk, and suchlike supports. Make certain of it for pot specimens by installing a deep layer of crocks in the bottom of the container. Water carefully. Never allow the rooting medium to become dry, but do not have it constantly sodden. Excessive wetness, especially in winter, soon results in an unhealthy state, first evidenced by spotting of the barren fronds.

The rooting compost must be porous, largely organic, and capable of retaining moisture. Osmunda or tree fern fiber with some half-decayed leaves (oak leaves are excellent) and a little crushed charcoal mixed in serves well. These ferns are started on their supports by affixing them

with wire or with nylon thread. Some rooting compost is packed between the backs of the barren fronds and the support. In time roots develop and attach the plants firmly. Once established do not disturb them, but each spring pick away as much of the old compost as can be removed without damage to the roots or fronds and top-dress with new. To establish in pots, take a piece of cork bark, slab of tree fern trunk, or section of decay-resistant wood, such as locust, cedar, cypress or redwood, about twice as long as the depth of the container. Center this in the pot and fill around it nearly to the rim crocks or other drainage material. Cover these with a layer of the rooting compost, and attach the fern to the support in the way described above.

Propagation of nearly all of these ferns is most often by removing the small rooted plantlets that develop from roots or rhizomes near the barren fronds and pegging these with hairpin-like pieces of wire onto the surface of sifted compost of the type used as a rooting medium for mature plants or one consisting of peat moss and coarse sand or perlite. When the young plants have rooted well and are of suitable size, they are fixed to supports. Do not detach the plantlets until they have formed several small sterile fronds of their own. Then cut them away carefully, keeping with the young plants as many of these as possible. New plants can also be raised from spores, but this is a slow and rather tedious business. Unfortunately it is the only way to increase *P. grande*, which does not produce offsets. For more information see Ferns.

PLATYCLADUS (Platy-clàdus) — Oriental Arbor-Vitae. Formerly included in *Thuja*, the only species of *Platycladus*, of the cypress family CUPRESSACEAE, is native to China and Korea. Its name, derived from the Greek *platys*, broad, and *klados*, a branch, alludes to the branchlets being two-ranked in a vertical plane, a feature that distinguishes this genus from closely related *Thuja*. The name *Biota* was formerly used for this genus.

The oriental arbor-vitae (*P. orientalis*, syn. *Thuja orientalis*) is a densely-branched evergreen shrub or tree up to 40 feet or occasionally more in height. Its trunk, covered with reddish-brown bark that peels in thin flakes, usually forks near its base into several secondary trunks. The branches are more or less erect, the branchlets very slender. The leaves, scalelike and of nearly the same bright green on both sides, up to ⅛ inch long, have tiny glands. The cones, when young glaucous-blue, are ¾ to 1 inch long and consist of usually six fleshy scales, each with a strongly developed, hooklike process at its apex. Except for the upper two, which are united, each cone scale has one or two wingless seeds.

Platycladus orientalis variety

Platycladus orientalis aureus

A selection of better known varieties of oriental arbor-vitae includes these: *P. c. argenteus* has young shoots tipped with creamy-white; *P. o. aureus* (syn. 'Berckman's Golden'), broad pyramidal, has bright golden young foliage that later becomes green; *P. o. azureus* has glaucous-blue foliage; *P. o. bakeri*, pale green, tolerates hot, dry locations; *P. o. beverleyensis*, pyramidal, has golden-yellow foliage at its branchlet tips; *P. o.* 'Bonita', similar to *P. o. aureus* but has less bright yellow foliage, and the plant is more ovoid; *P. o. columnaris*, narrowly-columnar, has green foliage; *P. o. conspicuus*, very dense and slender-pyramidal, has golden-yellow young foliage; *P. o. decussatus*, a dwarf, has all-juvenile bluish-green foliage; *P. o. elegantissimus*, slow-growing, stiffly erect, and narrowly-pyramidal, has yellow young growth that changes to green before winter; *P. o. flagelliformis* has pendulous, threadlike branchlets; *P. o. funiculatus*, with drooping branchlets, has two types of foliage; *P. o. globosus* is dwarf and spherical; *P. o. intermedius*, with pendulous branches, has two kinds of foliage; *P. o. maurieanus* forms a green, slender col-

umn; *P. o. meldensis*, low and irregularly-narrow-pyramidal, has bluish-green, needle-like leaves; *P. o.* 'Rosedale', which grows slowly, is an ovoid bush with all-juvenile foliage that in summer is bluish-green, but becomes bronzy-purple in winter; *P. o. sieboldii*, a dense, rounded shrub, has light green foliage and *P. o. strictus* (syn. *P. o. pyramidalis*), a compact, pyramidal tree, has bright green foliage.

A hedge of *Platycladus orientalis*

Garden and Landscape Uses and Cultivation. The oriental arbor-vitae and its varieties are considerably less hardy than the American arbor-vitae (*Thuja occidentalis*) and somewhat less hardy than the giant arbor-vitae (*T. plicata*), but in climates to their liking their uses and cultural requirements are as for *Thuja*.

PLATYCLINIS. See Dendrochilum.

PLATYCODON (Platy-còdon) — Balloon Flower. Consisting of one well-known attractive, variable species, *Platycodon*, of the bellflower family CAMPANULACEAE, is a native of northeastern Asia. The name is derived from the Greek *platys*, broad, and *kodon*, a bell, and alludes to the flowers. From related *Campanula* it differs in its seed capsules opening by valves at their tops.

The balloon flower (*P. grandiflorus*) is a deciduous, herbaceous, hairless perennial with erect stems branched in their upper parts and 1½ to 2½ feet tall. The ovate to ovate-lanceolate, short-stalked, sharply-toothed leaves are 1 inch to 3 inches long. The upper ones are solitary, the lower in whorls (circles of more than two). Mostly solitary at the branch ends, the flowers in the bud stage are inflated and approximately balloon-shaped, which explains the common name. Varying in color from dark blue-purple to white, when open they are 2 to 3 inches across. They have five narrow calyx lobes and a bowl-shaped corolla with five or sometimes more, broad, pointed lobes. There are five stamens with

Platycodon grandiflorus

stalks much thickened at their bases and five styles. Among the best known varieties are *P. g. albus*, with white blooms; *P. g. japonicus*, with ten-lobed flowers; *P. g. mariesii*, a low grower with flowers about 2 inches across; *P. g. roseus*, with pink flowers; and *P. g. semi-duplex* and *P. g. semi-plenum*, with blooms that are semi-double.

Garden Uses. This old-time favorite ranks high among hardy herbaceous perennials. It thrives with minimum care in a wide variety of soils and in late summer produces over a long period a wealth of choice blooms, valuable alike for garden display and for cutting for indoor decoration. A sunny location and fertile soil suit it best. The balloon flower is remarkably free of pests and diseases.

Cultivation. Because it starts into growth very late in spring, great care must be taken not to damage the shoots before they emerge. Transplanting is done early in spring or in early fall, but need not be frequent. Balloon flowers remain vigorous, often for many years, without root disturbance. A planting distance of 9 inches to 1 foot between individuals is satisfactory. When they are divided, this is done, although not very easily, in spring, before growth is much advanced. A sharp, heavy knife and some deftness are needed to section the compact crowns expeditiously. Seeds sown in a cold frame or outdoors in May, or indoors earlier, are an alternative and usually preferable means of propagation. Seedlings bloom in their second year. Routine care consists of applying a complete fertilizer in spring, controlling weeds, necessary minimum staking, removing faded blooms, and cutting down and carrying away old tops after they have been frosted in fall.

PLATYCRATER (Platy-cràter). One Japanese species constitutes this near relative of *Hydrangea*, of the saxifrage family SAXIFRAGACEAE. Not hardy in the north, it is of minor horticultural value. Its name derives from the Greek *platys*, broad, and *crater*, a bowl, and refers to the calyxes of the sterile flowers.

Sparsely furnished with coarse hairs, *Platycrater arguta* is a deciduous, prostrate shrub with opposite, stalked, undivided, coarsely-toothed, sparsely-hairy, broadly-lanceolate leaves 4 to 8 inches long by 1½ to 2 or rarely 3 inches wide. The blooms, in five- to ten-flowered, lax terminal clusters, are ¾ to 1 inch across and are of two kinds. The majority are bisexual and have four sepals, four white petals, numerous yellow stamens, and two styles. The few sterile blooms are without petals, stamens, and styles. They consist of only a calyx with its parts joined to form a flat, shallowly-three- or four-lobed disk. The fruits are slender, many-seeded capsules. Variety *P. a. hortensis* has smaller flowers, three to five in a cluster, and usually is without sterile blooms.

Garden Uses and Cultivation. About as far north as Virginia this shrub succeeds outdoors in shaded places and dampish soils. Of interest only to collectors of botanical novelties, it is propagated by summer cuttings and seed.

PLATYLOBIUM (Platy-lòbium). Endemic to Australia and Tasmania, *Platylobium*, of the pea family LEGUMINOSAE, consists of possibly six species. Its name, derived from the Greek *platys*, broad, and *lobus*, a pod, alludes to the fruits.

Platylobiums are evergreen shrubs, most with opposite leaves, but one species not known to be in cultivation, *P. alternifolium*, with alternate leaves. The leaves are undivided, lobeless, and toothless. The pea-like, yellow flowers, solitary in the leaf axils, have a large standard or banner petal, smaller wing petals, and a small keel. There are ten united stamens and one style. The fruits are broad, flat pods winged along one edge.

A straggling or procumbent shrub 1 foot to 1½ feet tall, *P. angulare* has very short-stalked, conspicuously-veined, triangular leaves, spine-tipped at each angle, and up to 1¼ inches long and wide. The standard petal, notched at its apex, is a little more than ½ inch wide. A nearly hairless shrub 4 to 5 feet tall, *P. formosum* has very short-stalked, conspicuously-veined, heart-shaped to ovate leaves 1 inch to 2 inches long. Its solitary, terminal and axillary, conspicuously-stalked flowers have a standard petal 1 inch wide, notched at its apex, and bright yellow with at its base a dark reddish blotch. The fruits are up to 1½ inches long. Variety *P. f. parviflorum* has narrower leaves and smaller flowers. A hairless to hairy shrub 3 to 4 feet tall or prostrate, *P. obtusangulum* has short-stalked, triangular to ovate-heart-shaped leaves up to 1¼ inches long and wide with a bristle at each angle. Solitary on the leaf axils, the very short-stalked flowers have a densely hairy calyx and a standard petal

¾ to 1 inch long, orange-yellow with red markings at its base and deeply-notched at its apex. The pods are up to 1¼ inches long.

Garden Uses and Cultivation. Little known in contemporary gardens and with little published about their cultivation in North America, platylobiums should prove welcome additions to gardens in California and other places with similar Mediterranean climates. In general they respond to conditions that suit acacias and many other Australian trees and shrubs. Propagation is by seed and perhaps by cuttings.

PLATYMISCIUM (Platy-míscium) — Roble. This genus of thirty species of Central and South American, nearly deciduous trees and shrubs belongs to the pea family LEGUMINOSAE. *Platymiscium* has a name derived from the Greek *platys*, wide, and *misches*, a stalk or stem.

Platymisciums are yellow-flowered trees and shrubs, often with hollow branchlets that, in the wild, are frequently inhabited by ants. Their leaves are opposite or in threes or fours. Each has three, five, or seven large leaflets, the lateral ones opposite. The pea-like blooms are in racemes from one-year-old branches and appear usually just before new foliage sprouts. They have a short-toothed calyx and ten stamens united into a tube split down one side, or rarely with one stamen free from the others. The fruits are one-seeded, flattened pods.

The roble (*P. pinnatum* syn. *P. polystachyum*) is a tree 45 to 60 feet tall or taller, but frequently lower and often quite small and shrublike. It has hairless leaves with three- to five-stalked, ovate to elliptic leaflets 2½ to 6 inches long. The ½-inch-wide, fragrant, bright yellow to orange-yellow flowers are produced in abundance in stalked racemes 2 to 4 inches long. The seed pods are thin and about 2½ inches long by 1 inch wide. The wood of this native of northern South America, Trinidad, and Panama is durable, hard, and heavy. It is used for turnery, knife handles, backs of brushes, and veneers.

Garden and Landscape Uses and Cultivation. A useful addition to the many beautiful flowering trees of the pea family that come from the tropics, the species described above can serve for general purpose landscape planting in warm, frostless and practically frostless climates. It succeeds in sunny locations in ordinary soils and is propagated by seed.

PLATYSTEMON (Platystèm-on) — Cream Cups. Botanists differ in their interpretations of *Platystemon*. Some admit as many as sixty species, others regard these as merely segregates of one variable species. The latter view prevails among conservative taxonomists and is adopted here. Belonging to the poppy family PAPAVERA-

CEAE, this genus has a name derived from the Greek *platys*, broad, and *stemon*, a stamen. It refers to the flattened filaments of the stamens.

Cream cups (*P. californicus*) is an attractive native from California to Arizona and Utah, usually growing in open, grassy places. It is a much-branched, lax-stemmed annual from 4 inches to 1 foot tall. It has opposite, undivided, narrowly-lanceolate, softly-hairy, grayish-green leaves and solitary upturned, usually cream-colored, slender-stalked flowers with three sepals, six (in garden varieties sometimes more) petals, many stamens, and six to numerous pistils. The blooms, which resemble miniature poppies, are about 1 inch in diameter.

Garden Uses. The chief garden use of cream cups is for edging flower beds and borders. It may also be used appropriately in drifts in rock gardens. In very hot and humid weather cream cups tends to do poorly and sometimes dies off, but usually recovers after the most torrid of summer weather has passed and makes a good show in the fall.

Cultivation. Cream cups needs a porous soil and an open, sunny location. Sow the seeds where the plants are to bloom as soon as the soil is workable in spring. Cover them to a depth of about 1⁄10 inch and thin out the young plants so that those remaining are about 4 inches apart. Where winters are mild seeds sown outdoors in fall result in early-blooming plants that provide a colorful display beginning in late spring.

PLATYTHYRA (Platy-thỳra). One of the many segregates from the vast complex of succulent plants once included in *Mesembryanthemum*, the genus *Platythyra* belongs in the carpetweed family AIZOACEAE. Its only species is native to South Africa. The name, from the Greek *platys*, broad, and *thyra*, a door, presumably alludes to the construction of the seed capsules.

Mats or cushions of creeping stems and fleshy, somewhat pointed, lanceolate leaves that narrow gradually to their stalks are formed by *P. haeckeliana*, a lush-growing close relative of *Aptenia*. The leaves are 1¼ to 2 inches long by up to almost ½ inch broad. The pale yellow blooms are on stalks approximately ½ inch long. About ⅓ inch in diameter, and daisy-like in aspect, they are entirely different in structure from daisies. Each is a single bloom, not a head of florets. The fruits are capsules.

Garden Uses and Cultivation. These are as for *Aptenia*.

PLEACH. To pleach is to train a row of closely planted trees to form a continuous narrow wall or hedge of strictly formal aspect. It is accomplished by interlacing their branches and keeping their sides tightly pruned or sheared. A narrow vista bor-

Hornbeam trees pleached to form an arbor

dered on each side by trees persuaded in this fashion is called a pleached allee. Pleaching can be used effectively to form arches, arbors, screens, and backings.

Because of the several years necessary to achieve impressive effects and the considerable effort that must be expended annually on maintenance, pleaching is seldom done on the grand scale of the past, but it is effective when employed more modestly to produce pleasing features in formal gardens.

For best results, trees to be pleached should be planted as young specimens 6 to 8 feet apart. Many sorts of trees are suitable. Among those most favored in the past are beeches, hornbeams, lindens, and plane trees.

PLECTRANTHUS (Plect-ránthus). Several excellent species and varieties of these *Coleus* relatives are cultivated, though none has the brilliant colored foliage of the most popular coleuses. Instead, the sorts of *Plectranthus* are admired for their blue, purple, or white flowers, for their creamy-white-margined foliage, or for their trailing, vinelike habits. They belong in the mint family LABIATAE. The name, from the Greek *plektron*, a spur, and *anthos*, a flower, was given because the flowers have pouches or spurs at the bottoms of their corolla tubes. The 250 species are widely distributed in the wild through the warmer parts of Asia, Africa, Australia, and islands of the Pacific.

Plectranthuses are chiefly herbaceous perennials and subshrubs, less commonly shrubs. From *Coleus* nearly all differ in the stalks of the stamens being separate instead of joined near their bases into a short tube. They have four-angled stems, and opposite, undivided leaves, which are sometimes ill-scented when bruised. Often stalked, the smallish, asymmetrical blooms are in whorls (tiers) arranged in loose panicles or in spikelike fashion. The blooms have five-toothed calyxes, tubular,

two-lipped corollas, with the lower lip plain and the upper one cleft to give three or four lobes, four stamens, and one style with two stigmas. The fruits consist of four seedlike nutlets.

Sometimes called Swedish-ivy, *P. oertendahlii* is probably a native of South Africa. A trailer with rooting stems, it has thickish, shallowly-round-toothed, broadly-ovate to nearly round, hairy leaves with blades 1 inch to 1¾ inches long. Dark

Plectranthus nummularius

green sometimes tinged with bronze and with a clearly defined network of white veins on their upper surfaces, they have purplish undersides. The short-stalked, pale lavender flowers, about ¾ inch long in usually branchless spikes 2½ to 6 inches long, make quite elegant displays. The bases of their corolla tubes are swollen. In *P. o. variegatus* the leaves are variegated, especially at their margins, with milky-white. Another trailer, South African *P. nummularius* in gardens is not infrequently misnamed *P. australis*. It has sprawling or prostrate stems, often rooting from the nodes and, like the foliage,

Plectranthus oertendahlii

with slender hairs. Nearly circular, somewhat fleshy, and rather coarsely-toothed, the leaves have blades up to 2½ inches in diameter. The delicate lavender flowers in loose racemes 6 inches to nearly 1 foot long have a cylindrical corolla tube nearly ½ inch long, scarcely swollen at its base. A trailer, in bloom up to 1 foot tall, South African *P. purpuratus* has fleshy, stalked, broad-ovate to nearly circular, distinctly-veined, scallop-toothed, grayish to dark green, velvety-pubescent leaves 1 inch to 2 inches in diameter. Its little white to lavender flowers are in loose, erect, narrow panicles.

Plectranthus purpuratus

Plectranthus 'Variegated Mint-leaf', of gardens

A charming sort known as *Plectranthus* 'Variegated Mint-leaf' is thought to be a variety of *P. madagascariensis,* a native of southeastern Africa and Malagasy (Madagascar). Especially suited for hanging baskets, it has long, slender, trailing or pendent, hairy stems and somewhat fleshy, nearly circular, round-toothed leaves from 1 inch to 1½ inches wide, and milky-green edged with white. When brushed against they are strongly mint-scented. The little flowers are white flushed with lilac. This plant has also been grown as *Iboza*.

Erect, bushy and up to 4 feet tall, *P. fruticosus* was the first plectranthus to be discovered. It inhabits damp, shaded places in South Africa. A herbaceous perennial, its stems become woody as they age. This has thickish, stalked, broad-ovate leaves, with blades up to 4 inches long and three-quarters as wide, coarsely-toothed and thinly-hairy. The blue-mauve flowers, approximately ⅓ inch in length, and many together in long spikes or panicles of spikes, look much like those of coleuses. They have long-protruding stamens. The largest-flowered cultivated plectranthus, *P. saccatus*, of South Africa, is an erect or somewhat loose subshrub 1½ to 4 feet tall. It has stalked, more or less hairy, broadly-triangular-ovate leaves with blades up to 2 inches long, with a few coarse teeth along their sides. In terminal racemes 2 to 3½ inches long are mauve, blue, or rarely white flowers, which sometimes exceed 1 inch in length. Quite delightful in bloom, and well suited for adding winter color to greenhouses, and in tropical and subtropical climates for growing outdoors, *P. chiradzulensis*, of East Africa, has clear blue flowers in rather distantly spaced whorls on slender-branched panicles. An erect, bushy plant 2 feet tall or taller, this has triangular leaves slightly hairy on their upper surfaces, and clammy, which emit a strongish odor when bruised. They are from 1 inch to 3½ inches long and have round-toothed margins. This sort resembles *Coleus* in that its stamens are united for a short distance at their bases. Beautiful variegated-leaved *P. coleoides marginatus* is a cultivated variety of a green-leaved species native of India that does not seem to be in cultivation. Erect, bushy, and 1 foot or so tall, the variety has green and grayish-green, ovate leaves 2 to 3 inches long, with creamy-white, scalloped margins. The flowers are white and purple. A sort recently introduced to cultivation in North America as *P. forsteri* is obviously misnamed. The newcomer, erect and bushy, somewhat resembles *P. fruticosus* and *P. coleoides marginatus*, but differs from both in being decidedly velvety-pubescent. Its leaves, larger and less pointed than those of *P. coleoides marginatus*, are irregularly-crenately-toothed and margined with creamy-white.

Other sorts cultivated include these: *P. australis*, a native of Australia, is erect and 2 to 3 feet high. It has broad-ovate, fleshy, round-toothed leaves 1 inch to 1½ inches long and racemes up to 8 inches in length of light purple flowers in whorls (tiers) about ½ inch apart. *P. ciliatus* is tropical African. A subshrub, it has densely-hairy stems and sparingly-hairy, pointed-ovate to pointed-elliptic, toothed leaves up to 3 inches long. In racemes or panicles with few branches, the ½-inch-long or somewhat longer flowers have corollas with tubes pouched above their bases. *P. coeruleus*, a rare aromatic native of rocky areas in Kenya, is a low, succulent trailer with small, stalkless, pubescent, very fleshy, toothed, ovate-elliptic leaves thickly

Plectranthus forsteri, of gardens

crowded along its stems. Its blue flowers are in ascending panicles. *P. glaucocalyx* is Chinese. From 1 foot to 3 feet tall, it has coarsely-toothed, pointed-ovate, plain green leaves 2 to 2½ inches long and hairy on their undersides. The light purple to bluish flowers up to ¼ inch long are in loose panicles. *P. myrianthus*, of tropical Africa, is erect and has 3-inch-long, broadly-ovate, somewhat hairy, toothed

Plectranthus myrianthus

leaves. In raceme-like spires up to 6 inches long, the down-pointing flowers, a little over ¼ inch in length, are blue. *P. tomentosus*, of South Africa, is bushy and has blunt-broad-ovate, round-toothed, hairy leaves up to 3½ inches long and racemes or panicles of ½-inch-long or a little longer, purple flowers.

Garden and Landscape Uses. Plectranthuses are not hardy. For outdoors they are adapted only to warm, frost-free regions. There, they can be used effectively to ornament flower beds and the trailing kinds, rock gardens and similar places. In most parts of North America, it is as greenhouse and houseplants that they appeal. The trailers are well suited for hanging baskets and pots, the upright kinds for pots. Of the latter, *P. coleoides marginatus* is of a size that accommodates to window gardens, the other upright kinds described, generally too tall for that use, are best suited for greenhouses.

Cultivation. Plectranthuses respond to the general conditions and care that suit *Coleus* and are easily propagated from cuttings and seed. Not particular as to soil so long as it is well drained, they prefer a fertile one kept moderately moist without being constantly saturated. They differ from the familiar colored-leaved coleuses in appreciating just a little shade from strong summer sun. Well-rooted specimens are benefited by regular applications of dilute liquid fertilizer. To induce branching and so produce desirable bushy specimens it is important to pinch the tips out of the shoots of erect-growing kinds

Plectranthus coleoides marginatus

Plectranthus coeruleus

two or three times during their early development.

PLECTRITIS (Plectrì-tis). To *Plectritis*, of the valerian family VALERIANACEAE, belong fifteen species of annuals, natives of western United States and Chile. The genus is closely related to *Valerianella*, but has more congested flower clusters and differs in botanical details. Its name is derived from the Greek *plekto*, to plait, and refers to the complexity of the flower clusters.

These plants are annuals with erect or straggling stems and opposite, undivided, toothless or few-toothed leaves. The flowers, in heads or interrupted spikes, are small. Without calyxes, they have five-lobed, two-lipped, usually spurred corollas, three stamens, and usually a two-lobed stigma. The fruits are dry and capsule-like.

Probably the only sort cultivated, *P. congesta* is an erect, bushy plant some 2 feet in height. Hairless, it has opposite,

Plectritis congesta

mostly toothless leaves ½ inch to 2 inches long. The flowers, ⅓ inch long and rose-pink, are spurred and conspicuously two-lipped.

Garden Uses. The species described is useful for flower beds and borders. It begins blooming in summer from seeds sown in spring and in late spring from fall-sown seed. In regions of moderately cool summers, it flowers continuously until fall, but usually ceases well before where the summers are very hot and humid.

Cultivation. No special problems attend the cultivation of this pretty annual. It needs a sunny location and well-drained, reasonably fertile soil. Sow the seeds where the plants are to bloom, in early spring, or in regions of mild winters, in fall, and cover them to a depth of about ¹⁄₁₀ inch. Thin out the seedlings so that they stand about 6 inches apart.

PLEEA (Ple-èa)—Rush Featherling. Native to pineland swamps in the coastal plain from North Carolina to Florida, the only species of this genus of the lily family LILIACEAE is a slender, rushlike, herbaceous perennial from 1 foot to 2½ feet tall. Its name honors Auguste Flée, author of a flora of Paris, who died in 1825.

The rush featherling (*Pleea tenuifolia*) has a few erect or nearly erect leaves 1 foot to 2½ feet long, the lower ones with long slender blades. Its flowers, in slender, terminal racemes of three to nine, are white, tinged green on their undersides. The six, firm-textured, spreading petals, or more properly tepals, are lanceolate and ½ to ⅔ inch long. There are six to twelve, most commonly nine, stamens with yellow anthers and three styles. The fruits are small capsules.

Garden Uses and Cultivation. An interesting, but not showy plant for use in bog gardens and other wet-soil areas, the rush featherling is appropriate for native plant gardens in the southeastern United States. It needs conditions similar to those it is accustomed to in the wild, and is increased by seeds, which should be sown while they are fresh and before they have dried, and by division. The extent of its hardiness outside its natural range is not determined.

PLEIOBLASTUS. See Arundinaria.

PLEIOCARPA (Pleio-carpa). This genus of the dogbane family APOCYNACEAE comprises three species endemic to tropical Africa. Its name is derived from the Greek *pleios*, many, and *karpos*, fruits.

Pleiocarpas are small trees or shrubs with hairless stems and foliage. Their leathery leaves, opposite or in threes, are undivided. The flowers, most often in stalkless, often opposite clusters in the leaf axils, are much more rarely in compact panicles or false umbels. They have five sepals, a tubular corolla with five spreading lobes (petals), five stamens, and one style. The fruits are berry-like.

Pleiocarpa mutica

An attractive ornamental, *P. mutica* is an evergreen shrub 5 to 6 feet tall with short-stalked, pointed-elliptic leaves 3 to 7½ inches long by 1 inch to 2½ inches wide. Clustered in the leaf axils, its richly fragrant, white, starry flowers are about ¾ inch across. They are borne freely by quite young plants as well as by older ones.

Garden and Landscape Uses and Cultivation. These are as for *Ixora*.

PLEIOGYNIUM (Pleio-gýnium) — Burdekin-Plum or Queensland-Hog-Plum. The tree known by the above colloquial names is planted in Florida, California, Hawaii, and other warm regions. A genus of two species of Australia, the Philippine Islands, New Guinea, and some Pacific islands, *Pleiogynium* belongs in the cashew family ANACARDIACEAE. It is thus cousin to the mango, cashew nut, and poison-ivy. Derived from the Greek *pleion*, many, and *gyne*, female, the generic name probably alludes to the female flowers.

The Burdekin-plum or Queensland-hog-plum (*P. cerasiferum* syn. *P. solandri*), 40 to 60 feet tall and often thick-trunked and irregularly shaped, has alternate, pinnate leaves with an odd number (seven to thirteen) of blunt, asymmetrically ovate, nearly stalkless leaflets 2 to 3 inches long. Male and female blooms are on separate trees. Tiny and yellowish, and in many-flowered narrow panicles or racemes, those composed of males are up to 8 inches long; the females are in shorter clusters. The edible, tomato-shaped, purple fruits are about 1½ inches in diameter and contain a solitary large stone surrounded by white to reddish, acid-sweet pulp. It is used for jams and jellies.

Garden and Landscape Uses and Cultivation. This moderately ornamental species is planted in warm climates for its interest and its fruits. It grows under ordinary conditions of soil and exposure and is propagated by seed.

PLEIONE (Pleiò-ne). So closely related is this genus of the orchid family ORCHIDACEAE to *Coelogyne* that some botanists include it there. When treated separately, *Pleione* consists of ten species, natives of Asia. Its name is that of the ancient Greek mythological character Pleione, mother of the Pleiades. The chief difference between *Pleione* and *Coelogyne* is that the pseudobulbs of the latter are perennial.

Pleiones grow natively in mosses and in shallow accumulations of organic debris at the bases of tree trunks and on fallen logs rather than as true epiphytes perched on trees like many other orchids. They have small pseudobulbs (bulblike organs) that live for only one season. Each develops one or two broad, thin leaves 4 inches to 1 foot long that die after the new pseudobulbs mature. The showy flowers are solitary or in twos on short stalks that come from the bottoms of the pseudobulbs, just before or together with the new foliage. They have similar sepals and petals, not united at their bases. The comparatively large lip is three-lobed and has several longitudinal crested ridges. Its side lobes usually curve around and sheathe the column. The roots are annual; they wither and die when the leaves fade.

The hardiest species is *P. bulbocodioides,* of western China and Taiwan. Highly variable, it includes kinds grown in

Pleione bulbocodioides

gardens as *P. delavayi, P. formosana, P. henryi, P. limprichtii, P. pogonioides,* and *P. pricei.* Its flask-shaped pseudobulbs gradually narrow above to a terminal beak. Its flowers develop with the young foliage. They range from deep mauve to much paler mauve-pink or, rarely, white. They are 2 to 2½ inches across and the lips, paler than the sepals and petals, are irregularly marked with brick-red to magenta. Occasionally the lip is white with yellow markings. There are two to seven wavy, white or yellow ridges on the lip.

Also blooming when in leaf are *P. hookerana, P. grandiflora,* and *P. scopulorum.* All have pseudobulbs that taper gradually toward their tips and end in a pointed beak. Native to India, *P. hookerana* (syn. *P. laotica*) has blooms 2 to 2½ inches across, with white or pink-flushed sepals and petals, pale yellow throats, and white to pink lips, blotched near their ends with brownish-purple, and with six or seven fringed ridges. The flowers of *P. grandiflora,* of western China, are large and pure white and have broad-elliptic lips with four to five irregularly-crested ridges. The lips of the usually bright pink blooms of *P. scopulorum* are kidney-shaped, have four to five irregularly-crested ridges, and are usually darker than the sepals and petals. Rarely its flowers are white.

Leafless when in bloom are *P. humilis, P. forrestii,* and *P. yunnanensis.* Their pseudobulbs narrow gradually to beak-tipped apexes. Several varieties of *P. humilis* have been named. The flowers, 2 to 3 inches across, have white or mauve-pink sepals, petals, and lips, the lips marked at

their ends with brownish-purple, and with six or more fringed ridges alternating with violet, red, or yellow-brown stripes. The throats of the blooms are yellow. Hailing from Burma and Yunnan, *P. forrestii* has flowers that range from pale yellow to light orange-yellow and are blotched on their lips with reddish-brown. The blooms of *P. yunnanensis,* a native of India, Burma, and western China, have bright magenta-pink sepals and petals and paler lips marked with red or purple.

Two kinds have barrel-shaped pseudobulbs, tipped with short, sharp points or beaks, instead of gradually sloping flask-shaped ones like those of the others here discussed. With white sepals and petals that have a few red spots at their tips, and white to yellow lips streaked with purple and furnished with five fringed ridges, the blooms of *P. maculata* are about 2 inches across. This species is native in India, Burma, and Thailand. From northern India and Burma, *P. praecox* has flowers 2 to 3 inches in diameter with bright rosy-purple, rarely paler or white, sepals and petals, and a paler pink lip marked at its base with yellow, and having five fringed ridges. The plants previously named *P. lagenaria, P. reichenbachiana,* and *P. wallichiana* belong here.

Garden Uses. Pleiones are beautiful low orchids for cultivating in pans (shallow pots) in greenhouses, and outdoors in rock gardens in those few places in North America where such treatment is practicable. They need cool conditions (they are mountain plants), but will not survive much frost. In favored parts of the British Isles they are grown successfully outdoors. A cool greenhouse is likely to afford the best conditions for pleiones. They bloom in winter and spring.

Cultivation. Although botanically related to coelogynes, pleiones have different horticultural needs. In growing pleiones one may discard all preconceived notions of the need for special composts for orchids and, above all, put aside any ideas that all orchids are denizens of the tropics that pine if lacking considerable warmth and high humidity. These are definitely not desiderata of pleiones. In greenhouses a winter night temperature of 50°F is adequate. Pleiones prosper in any good ordinary potting soil porous enough to drain readily, admit air, and encourage rooting. It should be coarse and fibrous rather than finely sifted; a mixture of equal parts turfy loam, coarse peat moss, and gritty sand or perlite, to which a little bonemeal has been added is satisfactory. The pseudobulbs may be planted about 3 inches apart, not deeply, but with their upper two-thirds projecting above the soil. Following planting, which is done each year either just before flowering or immediately afterward, water carefully at first to avoid soggy soil. As the roots take posses-

sion of the new soil more frequent watering will be necessary. The plants must not suffer from lack of moisture when in active growth. During the growing season biweekly applications of dilute liquid fertilizer are agreeable. A fairly, but not oppressively, humid atmosphere should be maintained and shade from strong sun provided. At the end of the summer growing season, when the foliage begins to die naturally, intervals between waterings should be gradually lengthened and the soil permitted to become progressively drier between applications. Finally, it is allowed to dry completely. Then the crop of young oatlike bulbils that develop about the mother pseudobulbs may be harvested, placed in polyethylene bags, and, together with the pans containing the larger pseudobulbs, stored in a temperature of 40 to 50°F until time for a new cycle of growth arrives. This is indicated by the swelling of the sides of the pseudobulbs caused by developing flower buds. For additional information see Orchids.

PLEIOSPILOS (Pleios-pìlos). These stone plants, so called because their leaves closely resemble in appearance small chunks of granite, are favorites of fanciers of dwarf nonhardy succulents. They belong in the *Mesembryanthemum* division of the carpetweed family AIZOACEAE and are natives of South Africa. The name alludes to the dotted surfaces of the leaves. It comes from the Greek *pleios,* full, and *spilos,* dotted.

A desert genus, *Pleiospilos* enjoys wide distribution in its native land, and comprises about thirty-eight species. These are stemless or may have short stems that branch with age. Each growth consists usually of one or two, occasionally more, pairs of leaves, alternate pairs being at right angles to each other. From gray-green to dark green, sometimes suffused with reddish-brown, and copiously sprinkled with translucent dots, they have flattish upper surfaces and lower rounded ones. The leaves are blunt or pointed. Appearing in late summer or fall and opening in the afternoons, the flowers, those of many kinds coconut-scented, are reminiscent in general appearance of daisies, but in structure they are very different. Each is a single bloom not, as is a daisy, a head composed of numerous florets. The fruits are capsules.

Living rock is the imaginative name under which *P. bolusii* often appears in catalogs of dealers. It is highly descriptive and appropriate. The two angular leaves, gray-green with darker green dots and sometimes tinged reddish, and granular and rough surfaced on their outer sides, resemble nothing so much as chunky rocks. This is especially true when the plants are dormant. Usually there is only one pair of leaves to each growth. These have upper smooth sides wider than their 1½- to 3-inch length and lower semicylindrical surfaces that project at their apexes to form prominent chins. From between the pairs of leaves in late summer or fall develop one to few fragrant, golden-yellow flowers 1¼ to 3 inches or a little more across.

Similar to *P. bolusii* and producing fertile hybrids with it, is **P. simulans.** The most obvious difference is that the lower, keeled surfaces of its leaves, of which each shoot may have two pairs, never extend forward to form chinlike apexes. The leaves, up to about 3 inches in length, are almost as broad as they are long and about ½ inch thick. They have flat or slightly hollowed upper sides often recurved toward their tips. The deliciously fragrant, pale yellow to orange, nearly stalkless, flowers, one to few together, are of the same size as those of *P. bolusii*.

Pleiospilos magnipunctatus

Pleiospilos nelii

More globose and less angular than those of *P. bolusii*, the leaves of **P. nelii** have well-developed, rounded chinlike extremities. Their upper or inner surfaces face each other and are quite often quite close together, or they may gape. Their undersides are rounded, but are not warted like those of *P. bolusii*, and the green dots are smaller. About 2 inches in diameter, the longish-stalked flowers, are white toward their centers, then light orange-yellow with pale yellowish tips. Their undersides may be suffused with pink.

A clump-forming kind, **P. magnipunctatus** has usually growths of one or two pairs of spreading, thick leaves, united slightly at their bases. Gray-green, green, or brownish, sometimes tinted bluish, and sprinkled with darker dots, they are 1½ to 3 inches long, and at their widest, above

their middles, about ½ inch broad. The slightly rounded, hollowed or flat upper leaf surfaces are blunt-margined and recurved at the apexes. The obscurely three-angled undersides are bluntly-keeled and somewhat rough-surfaced.

Very beautiful, **P. purpusii** has growths with one or two pairs of slightly incurving, tapering, pointed leaves 2 to 3 inches in length and from ½ inch to 1¼ inches wide at their middles. They are green or yellowish-green with conspicuous dark green dots. Their upper sides are flattish, their under surfaces round-keeled, but not drawn out as chins at the leaf ends. The yellow flowers are up to 3½ inches in diameter.

Superficially resembling *Lithops* and very different from other species of *Pleiospilos* considered here, **P. hilmari** has plant bodies of usually a single pair of 1-inch-long leaves, which have slightly rounded upper surfaces and rounded lower ones that project forward to give chinlike ends to the leaves. They are green tinged with red and conspicuously furnished with darker translucent dots. An interesting feature is the more or less distinct translucent window at the apex of each leaf. One inch in diameter, the flowers are golden-yellow.

Other kinds likely to be cultivated include **P. dekenahii,** which develops several growths, each with a pair of spreading, long-pointed, waxy-coated, gray-green leaves, roughened with conspicuous green dots, reddish at their edges, and about 1¼ inches long by 1 inch wide at their middles. The flowers are pale yellow and about 1¼ inches across. Leaves of unequal length characterize **P. willowmorensis.** Each shoot has one pair or two. They have flattish upper surfaces and partially keeled

lower ones and are up to 2½ inches long by ¾ inch wide and thick. They are purplish-green with many prominent dots. The solitary yellow flowers, paling to white at the bottoms of their petals, are up to almost 3 inches in diameter.

Garden Uses. Because these astonishing plants are easier to grow than many of their relatives among the great assemblage of *Mesembryanthemum*-like plants that inhabit South Africa they can with confidence be recommended to beginners as well as to more experienced collectors and fanciers of succulents. Except in frostless, desert regions they cannot be grown outdoors, but they are well adapted for greenhouse and window garden cultivation, and in or out of bloom are of interest to observe and to display, especially to visitors not familiar with these "stones that bloom."

Cultivation. Because they have deep roots pleiospiloses are better accommodated in regular pots than in the shallower ones called pans. Sharp drainage is essential and the soil must be porous and not too nutritious. Excessive fertility, like too much watering, causes the plants to grow out of character and to become less appealing than when they are slightly starved; it also encourages soft growth that may be subject to rot. The growing season of these plants is late spring and summer and then they should be watered moderately. During their winter season of rest they are kept dry. Full sun is necessary for the best development of their coloring, and for their most prolific blooming. Propagation is most simply accomplished by seeds, which are easily obtained by cross-pollinating; plants do not set seeds to their own pollen. Because these plants hybridize freely, if true-to-type seedlings are wanted, flowers to be fertilized should be prevented from chance pollination by other species. For additional information see Succulents.

PLEIOSTACHYA (Pleio-stáchya). The tropical American genus *Pleiostachya*, of the maranta family MARANTACEAE, consists of two species. Its name, alluding to its manner of flowering, comes from the Greek *pleios*, many, and *stachys*, a spike.

Evergreen herbaceous perennials in the wild inhabiting swamps and forests, pleiostachyas resemble marantas from which they differ in technical details. They have stout rhizomes from which arise clusters of long-stalked, pinnately-veined leaves with oblong-lanceolate to paddle-shaped blades. The heavily bracted spikes of paired flowers are in panicles. Each bloom has three sepals, a tubular, three-lobed corolla, one fertile stamen, and one staminode (nonfertile stamen). The fruits are capsules.

Native from Honduras to Panama, vigorous *P. pruinosa* is 3 to 9 feet tall. Its leaves have pubescent stalks longer than the blades, which are lanceolate and up to 2 feet long by 8 inches wide. Their dark green upper surfaces have many lateral veins, the undersurfaces are deep purple. Markedly flattened, the flower spikes are 3 to 6 inches long. The flowers have white sepals and petals, and a blue or deep-violet staminode.

Garden and Landscape Uses and Cultivation. These are as for *Calathea*.

PLEOMELE. See Dracaena.

PLEOPELTIS (Pleo-péltis). About forty species including the kinds previously named *Lepisorus* constitute *Pleopeltis*, of the polypody family POLYPODIACEAE. Some botanists include them, at least those native to the western hemisphere, in *Polypodium*. The name, from the Greek *pleos*, full, and *pelte*, a small shield, refers to the shield-shaped scales that often clothe the fronds (leaves).

Mostly small, these ferns, widely distributed in the tropics and subtropics, have scaly rhizomes and leathery fronds jointed where they meet the rhizome. Their blades, lobeless and toothless or very rarely pinnately-lobed, have scales on both or one surface or sometimes are nearly naked. The nearly round, less often elongated, clusters of spore capsules are at the junctions of the several veinlets.

Brazilian *P. percussa* (syn. *Polypodium percussum*) has long, thin rhizomes furnished with well-separated, leathery, shortish-stalked, evergreen fronds with blades 6 inches to 1 foot long by ¾ inch to 1½ inches wide that taper to points at their apexes. They are scaly on their under surfaces. The large, circular clusters of spore capsules are in longitudinal rows

Pleopeltis percussa

one on each side of the midrib and midway between it and the leaf margin.

Native to Japan, Korea, China, Indochina, and the Philippine Islands, *P. thunbergiana* (syn. *Lepisorus thunbergianus*) has long, slender, creeping rhizomes densely-clothed with erect, linear to awl-shaped, minutely-toothed, brown scales. Hairless, lobeless, and toothless, the fronds, 6 inches to 1 foot long, linear and ¼ inch to slightly over ½ inch wide, narrow to both ends and have somewhat recurved margins. Their upper sides are dark green, the undersides paler. The clusters of spore capsules, almost touching each other when mature, are in two rows, one on each side of the midrib on the upper halves of the undersides of the fronds. From the last, *P. clathrata* (syn. *Lepisorus clathratus*), of Japan, Taiwan, and from China to India, differs in having fronds with veins that show clearly in dried specimens (those of *P. thunbergiana* are indistinct). The leaves of *P. clathrata*, strap-shaped and narrowed to both ends, sometimes have slightly wavy margins. Rarely exceeding 6 inches in length, they are ¼ to ½ inch wide. When young they are slightly scaly, later becoming naked.

Garden and Landscape Uses and Cultivation. Pleopeltises are attractive for inclusion in collections of ferns and other foliage plants that succeed outdoors in mild, essentially frostless, fairly humid climates, and for greenhouses. In places favorable to their outdoor cultivation, they may be placed in the crotches of trees or attached to trunks of tree ferns, rough-trunked palms, or other trees that provide root holds. In greenhouses where the winter night temperature is 50 to 55°F, they succeed in well-drained pots or pans or attached to pieces of tree fern trunks. Their needs and methods of propagation are as for *Drynaria*. For additional information see Ferns.

PLEURISY ROOT is *Asclepias tuberosa*.

PLEUROSPA (Pleur-óspa). This is the name of a genus of two species of the arum family ARACEAE, formerly known as *Montrichardia*. They are natives of coastal swamps, margins of rivers, and other wet places in tropical America and the West Indies. The name, presumably alluding to the flowers being confined to one side of the spadix, is derived from the Greek *pleura*, side.

Pleurospas are remarkable among aquatic and semiaquatic aroids in having woody, sometimes sparsely-branched, bamboo-like stems or trunks that rise to a height of 9 to 10 feet. They are often spiny, and frequently develop supporting prop roots. At the top of each stem is a loose cluster of broadly-arrow-shaped, evergreen leaves, with long stalks that with their bases clasp the stems, and basal lobes longer or shorter than the center one. The flowers, as is characteristic of the arum family, are in calla-lily-like inflorescences, commonly called "flowers." Each of these consists of a clublike spadix (spike) studded with the tiny true flowers and from the base of which comes a leaf- or petal-like spathe (bract). In *Pleurospa* the spathe is obliquely-funnel-shaped, and enfolds the lower part of the spadix. Male and female flowers are closely packed on the spadix, the former along the upper part, the latter below, with no intervening naked portion of spadix. Male flowers have up to six stalkless stamens, the females ovaries with spherical, stalkless stigmas. The fruits are large, spongy, one-seeded berries.

Native to the West Indies, Panama, and northern South America, *P. arborescens* (syn. *Montrichardia arborescens*) is 3 to 10 feet tall. It has usually prickly stems supported at their bases by prop roots. The stems, about ¾ inch in diameter for most of their lengths, toward their bases are much thicker. The leaves have stalks up to 1 foot or longer, and deeply-arrow-shaped blades 1 foot to 1½ feet long, with backward-pointing basal lobes. The "flowers" have spathes, white or cream-colored, their bases rosy on their insides and greenish on their outsides. They are 4 to 6 inches long by up to 3 inches wide. The thick spadices are slightly shorter than the spathes. The berries are ⅓ to ½ inch in diameter.

Garden and Landscape Uses and Cultivation. In the tropics and warm subtropics occasionally planted by watersides and in other wet soils for bold effects, these impressive aroids grow without difficulty in muddy earth and tolerate brackish water. They are vigorous colonizers and when well established may be difficult to restrict to space. They need sunny locations and are easily increased by division, offsets, and by fresh seed sown before it has dried in soil kept muddy and in a temperature of 70 to 80°F. They may be grown in large containers in tropical greenhouses.

PLEUROTHALLIS (Pleuro-thállis). This vast genus of the orchid family ORCHIDACEAE comprises approximately 1,000 species, occurring wild from Florida and Mexico to Argentina and the West Indies with the majority of its sorts in Central America and tropical South America. The name is derived from the Greek *pleuron*, a side or rib, and *thallos*, a branch. It alludes apparently to the flowers. Plants treated in this Encyclopedia as *Restrepia* are by some authorities included in *Pleurothallis*.

Nearly all tree-perchers (epiphytes), a few inhabitants of cliffs and rocks, the sorts of this genus, because of the small sizes and relatively dull coloring of their flowers, are of minor horticultural importance, although one or more sorts are likely to be found in the collections of orchid fanciers of catholic interest. Of very diverse growth forms and sizes, these plants have rhizomes and clustered stems, but never pseudobulbs. Some sorts attain heights of several feet, others are so diminutive they are almost mosslike. Nearly always terminal, rarely lateral, the racemes or clusters of flowers or less often long-stalked solitary ones are extremely variable in form in the different kinds, but most are so small that a magnifying glass is needed to fully appreciate the intricacy and beauty of individual flowers. Mostly the two petals are smaller than and often are more or less enclosed by the three often variable sepals. The lip usually resembles the petals, but is three-lobed.

Representative kinds include these: *P. calyptrostele*, of Costa Rica and Panama, is a 1-inch-tall creeper with fleshy, oblanceolate leaves up to ½ inch long and, few together on slender stalks, minute flowers. *P. cardiothallis*, native from Mexico to Costa Rica, attains heights of nearly 2½ feet. Its slender stems may exceed 1½ feet in length, its leaves are leathery, lanceolate- to ovate-heart-shaped, and 4 to 9 inches long by up to 4 inches wide. The flowers, varying from deep red to greenish-yellow, are ½ inch long or slightly longer. They do not open widely. *P. car-*

Pleurothallis cardiothallis

Pleurothallis carnosa

nosa, of unknown provenance, a foot or so tall, has oblong-heart-shaped, brownish-green to reddish-green leaves 3 to 3½ inches long by up to 1½ inches wide. The short-stalked flowers are dull red. *P. foliata* is a tropical American with 1- to 2-inch-tall stems in tufts. Up to ½ inch long, its leaves are ovate. Taller than the foliage, the flowering stalks carry few to several pale yellow, minute blooms. *P. fulgens*, of Costa Rica, forms tufts of short stems and up to 5-inch-long, fleshy, oblanceolate leaves. Shorter than the leaves, the flowering stalks have mostly one ⅜-inch-long, red-orange bloom. *P. gelida*, native from the southernmost tip of Florida (where it blooms only following mild winters) and southern Mexico through Central America and the West Indies to northern South America, 4 inches to 1½ feet tall, has nearly always solitary, oblong-elliptic leaves 3 inches to 1 foot long by 3 inches wide, and slender, one-sided racemes of tiny creamy-white, delicately scented flowers. *P. macrophylla* (syn. *P. roezlii*), of Colombia, is from 1½ to 2 feet tall. Up to about 9 inches long by nearly one-half as wide, the fleshy leaves are elliptic to oblong-elliptic. Arching flower stalks carry a dozen or fewer ill-scented, purple to wine-colored, fleshy-lipped blooms sometimes over 1¼ inches across, which do not open fully. *P. quadrifida*, native from Mexico to Panama and the West Indies, is very variable. From 4 inches to 2 feet tall, it has slender stems and oblong-elliptic, oblanceolate, or linear leaves up to 7 inches long by 1¼ inches wide. The nodding, fragrant, yellow to greenish-yellow flowers, many together on stalks up to 1¼ feet long, are ¼ to ½ inch across. They do not open fully. *P. saurocephala*, a Brazilian, up to 1½ feet tall, has fleshy, elliptic to elliptic-oblong leaves 4 to 6 inches long and, longer than the leaves, flowering stalks with many ⅜-inch-long green or greenish-brown blooms. *P. schiedei*, of Mexico, is tufted and 2 to 3 inches tall. Dotted with greenish-purple, its oblanceo-

Pleurothallis sclerophylla

late leaves are fleshy. The white-fringed, blackish-brown little flowers are few on each stalk. *P. sclerophylla* (syn. *P. stenopetala*), of Brazil, has crowded clumps of stems 2 to 4 inches tall with pointed-elliptic, 2- to 3-inch-long leaves. Not much exceeding the foliage, the erect, slender, one-sided flower spikes carry many about ½-inch-long blooms that have very slender pale green to yellowish sepals and petals and a lip with often a central yellow mark. *P. tonduzii*, of Costa Rica, up to a

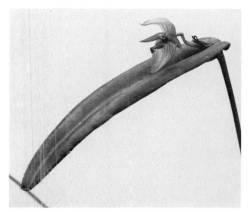

Pleurothallis tonduzii

little over 1 foot tall, has lanceolate leaves up to about 1 foot long by 1¼ inches wide. The solitary flowers, about 1¼ inches long, have pink-tinged, tan sepals and petals and a light brown lip. *P. truncata*, of the Andes of Ecuador, is 5 to 10 inches tall. It has slender, erect stems and pointed-lanceolate leaves 3 to 5 inches tall. The tiny orange flowers are many together in slender spikes up to about 4 inches long.

Garden Uses and Cultivation. Known commonly as "botanicals," the species of this genus are generally of interest only to collectors of orchids. Most thrive without special attention, but as can be imagined, the optimum needs of the members of a genus as widely dispersed as this vary according to species, and some few kinds do not adapt readily to cultivation.

Depending upon growth habit, they may be accommodated in pots, small in comparison to the sizes of the plants, or on rafts in osmunda or tree fern fiber, or be attached to slabs of tree fern trunks. Their temperature requirements are related to the natural habitats of the various sorts. There are kinds that are best suited for cool, intermediate, and warm or tropical greenhouses, respectively. All need moderate shade from strong sun and a fairly humid atmosphere. Those described here prosper in intermediate greenhouse conditions.

Being evergreen and without pseudobulbs, the sorts of this genus have no season of complete dormancy and thus require watering throughout the year, but less abundantly in winter than at other times. Well-established specimens benefit from regular fertilizing, less frequently in winter than from spring to fall.

A notable characteristic of these orchids is their intolerance of root disturbance. Do not repot them more often than quite necessary. This must, of course, be done if there is any indication that the rooting medium is becoming sour or stagnant and unkindly to growth. For additional information see Orchids.

PLUCHEA (Plùch-ea) — Marsh-Fleabane. This chiefly tropical and subtropical genus of strongly scented shrubs, herbaceous perennials, and annuals is little known horticulturally. Comprising more than thirty species, some indigenous to the United States, Pluchea belongs in the daisy family COMPOSITAE and has a name commemorating the Abbé Pluché, a French naturalist, who died in 1761.

Plucheas have alternate leaves, and small pink, white, or creamy heads of florets, all of the disk type, in clusters. The outer florets of each head are female, the inner ones bisexual. The fruits are achenes.

Native of saltwater and brackish-water and sometimes freshwater marshes through much of the United States and the West Indies, **P. purpurascens** is a leafy, more or less glandular-hairy annual up to 4 feet tall. Its toothed, short-stalked or sometimes stalkless, pointed leaves are lanceolate to ovate and mostly up to 4 inches long by under 3 inches wide. Forming rounded or flattish, often leafy clusters, the flower heads are pinkish-purple and have involucres (collars) of pink- or purplish-tipped bracts. Similar, but inhabiting only fresh water wet places and growing up to 6 feet in height, **P. camphorata** is less hairy than P. purpurascens. It is indigenous from Delaware to Illinois, Florida, and Texas.

Garden and Landscape Uses and Cultivation. For wet soils and in native plant gardens, the species described have modest merit. They are grown by scattering seed in fall or spring where the plants are to remain.

PLUGS. These are small pieces of grass sod cut from established lawns or other cultivated turf and used for planting new lawns. Only a few grasses, notably zoysias, are adaptable to this method of establishment, a procedure more common in the south than the north.

PLUM. Besides its use as a common name for some kinds of the genus Prunus, the word plum forms parts of the common names of these plants: batoko-plum or governor's-plum (Flacourtia indica), Burdekin-plum or Queensland-hog-plum (Pleiogynium cerasiferum), coco-plum (Chrysobalanus icaco), date-plum (Diospyros lotus), ground-plum or prairie-plum (Astragalus crassicarpus), Guiana-plum (Drypetes lateriflora), hog-plum (Spondias mombin and Ximenia americana), jambolan-plum or Java-plum (Syzygium cumini), Kafir-plum (Harpephyllum caffrum), marmalade-plum (Pouteria sapota), Natal-plum (Carissa grandiflora), Orleans-plum (Chrysophyllum pruniferum), pigeon-plum (Coccoloba diversifolia), plum-yew (Cephalotaxus harringtonia), and Spanish-plum (Spondias purpurea). See also Plums.

PLUMBAGINACEAE — Plumbago Family. There are approximately 500 species contained in the ten genera of this geographically widespread, but chiefly Old World family of dicotyledons, several of considerable value as ornamentals. The family consists of shrubs, sometimes more or less vining, and stemmed or stemless herbaceous plants, many natives of semiarid and arid climates, and frequently of limestone soils.

The leaves are alternate or in basal rosettes. The symmetrical flowers are displayed in panicles, spikes, or heads. They have a five-toothed or five-lobed, often persistent calyx, usually with five or ten angles, ribs, or wings, and a five-lobed corolla, tubular or its petals united at their bases only. There are five each stamens and styles, the former frequently hairy or glandular. The fruits, often enclosed in the calyxes, are capsules or utricles.

Cultivated genera include Acantholimon, Armeria, Cerastostigma, Goniolimon, Limonium, Plumbago, and Psylliostachys.

PLUMBAGO (Plumbà-go) — Leadwort. A few attractive ornamentals in this genus of a dozen warm region species are grown in mild climates and greenhouses. Other plants cultivated under this name belong in Ceratostigma. Leadworts belong in the plumbago family PLUMBAGINACEAE. The meaning of the name Plumbago, derived from the Latin plumbum, lead, is obscure.

Leadworts are mostly perennials and include herbaceous and shrubby kinds. They have alternate leaves with eared or stem-clasping bases. Their flowers, which look much like those of phloxes, and are blue, red, or white, are in spikes or racemes. They have bristly-glandular-hairy, five-lobed calyxes, slender-tubed corollas with five spreading lobes (petals), five stamens, and a five-branched style. The fruits are capsules. In Asia and South America, beggars use the juices of these plants to induce blisters and sores to excite pity.

The best-known kind is **P. auriculata** (syn. P. capensis), a native of South Africa.

Plumbago auriculata

This upright, straggling or partly climbing shrub bears a profusion of azure-blue, or in variety P. a. alba white flowers almost continually. In California and elsewhere in warm climates, it attains heights of 15 to 20 feet, but it can be kept much lower by pruning. It blooms when quite small. Except for its flower trusses, this species is devoid of hairs. Its leaves are scattered along the stems and are long-ovate to rather spatula-shaped, their blunt ends tipped with a short point. They are up to about 2 inches long. The flowers, in large

Plumbago indica

rounded clusters, are about 1½ inches long and approximately 1 inch across. Very different winter-blooming *P. indica* (syns. *P. coccinea, P. rosea*), of tropical Asia, tends to climb. It has thin stems that, like the leaves, are hairless, and long, erect, slender racemes of pink to red flowers with corolla tubes about 1 inch long. The ovate-elliptic leaves are up to 4 inches in length. Native of tropical and subtropical America and ranging into the southern United States, shrubby *P. scandens* is a climbing or trailing plant with ovate-lanceolate to oblong-lanceolate leaves up to 5 inches long. Its white flowers have corolla tubes ¾ inch long. The face of the flower is up to ½ inch across. Another New World species is annual *P. caerulea,* of Peru. An erect, freely-branched plant up to 1½ feet in height, this has smooth, ovate or elliptic leaves with winged stalks and terminal spikes of rich violet-blue flowers.

Garden and Landscape Uses. In climates where little or no frost is experienced, *P. auriculata* and its white variety are very useful for training against walls, pillars, posts, and fences. They make attractive informal hedges and can be grown in containers to decorate patios, steps, and other architectural features. They are also excellent for greenhouses. In humid, tropical climates and in tropical greenhouses *P. indica,* is an excellent decorative. Annual *P. caerulea* is a pretty item for summer outdoor beds and as a greenhouse pot plant.

Cultivation. Outdoors and in greenhouses *P. auriculata* and *P. scandens* are very easy to grow. They need full sun and well-drained, reasonably fertile soil. Indoors, abundant moisture must be supplied from spring through fall, less in winter. A winter temperature of 50°F at night and slightly higher during the day is adequate. Whenever weather permits, the greenhouse should be ventilated freely. The plants are pruned to size and shape in late winter or spring. Greater skill is required to grow *P. indica* well. It needs more tropical, more humid conditions. A minimum temperature of 60 or 65°F should be maintained, and the atmosphere should always be very humid. Good light with a little shade from the strongest sun of summer is favorable. The soil must be rich, porous, well-drained, and always moist, a little less so for a month or six weeks after flowering than during the season of active growth. The kinds discussed above, if their containers are filled with healthy roots, benefit from weekly applications of liquid fertilizer during summer. Propagation of shrubby leadworts is usually by cuttings, but root cuttings afford a reliable method of increasing *P. indica.* Seeds of *P. caerulea,* sown in February or March in a temperature of 60 to 65°F, give plants that, potted singly in

small pots as soon as they are large enough to handle easily and grown in a sunny greenhouse with a night temperature of 55°F, are suitable for planting outdoors about the time that geraniums are set out, or they can be transferred to 5- or 6-inch pots and used for summer bloom in the greenhouse. In their early stages they should be pinched once or twice to induce bushiness. This leadwort can also be flowered from seeds sown directly outdoors in spring. Red spider mites and mealybugs are the chief pests of plumbagos.

PLUMCOT. Of slight interest as curiosities, plumcots are hybrids between plums and apricots originated early in the twentieth century by Luther Burbank. Little known, they are without horticultural importance.

PLUME, PLUMED, and PLUMELESS. These words are used as parts of the common names of these plants: Apache plume (*Fallugia paradoxa*), Idaho plume (*Holodiscus discolor*), plumed-poppy (*Macleaya cordata*), prince's plume (*Stanleya pinnata*), plumed thistle (*Cirsium*), plumeless thistle (*Carduus*), and scarlet plume (*Euphorbia fulgens*).

PLUMERIA (Plum-èr-a) — Frangipani or Temple Tree. Frangipanis, sometimes called temple trees, are familiar to most visitors to warm countries. Planted freely throughout the tropics and subtropics, their distinctive forms, fragrant, showy, waxy blooms, and extended flowering season make them difficult to overlook. In Hawaii their long-lasting flowers are much used in leis. In the Americas and elsewhere they are employed as church decorations and in Asia are favored offerings in Buddhist temples. The name honors Charles Plumier, a French botanist, who died in 1704. The eight species of *Plumeria,* a native of tropical America and the West Indies, belong in the dogbane family APOCYNACEAE.

These are small trees or shrubs with comparatively few, thick, succulent branches, stiffly and often rather awkwardly arranged, and with scars marking the places from which leaves have fallen. The large, alternate leaves are crowded near the branch ends. They are undivided, and pinnately-veined. The lateral veins of some kinds are joined to a vein paralleling the edge of the leaf. Twenty to sixty together, the large, fragrant flowers are in stalked, branched, flattish, terminal clusters. They are white, pink, red, yellow, or combinations of these hues. Each bloom has a small five-parted calyx, a slender corolla tube, and five spreading corolla lobes (petals) that overlap on one side at their bases in propeller-like fashion. There are five stamens and a short, two-lobed stigma. The fruits are paired, leathery

pods (technically follicles) with numerous winged seeds. All parts of frangipanis contain abundant, caustic, milky sap that flows freely from wounds. This is reported to be poisonous, but has been used in folk medicines.

The kinds principally cultivated are *P. rubra* and *P. obtusa* and varieties and probably hybrids of them. From 15 to 25 feet tall, *P. rubra* has pubescent young branches and elliptic-oblong to elliptic-ovate, hairless leaves, shortly pointed at both ends, and 6 inches to 1¼ feet long. They have rather distantly spaced lateral veins at nearly right angles to the midrib and joined to a vein that parallels the leaf margin. Their stalks are up to 2½ inches long. The red, rose-pink, or purplish flowers 2 to 2½ inches in diameter, are in drooping panicles. They have slender perianth tubes up to 1 inch long. The seed pods are 6 to 10 inches long by 1 inch wide. Varieties of this species include 'Emma Bryant', with yellow-tinged, rose-red blooms, and 'Hilo Beauty', with currant-red flowers. Predominantly yellow flowers often blushed with pink on their outsides are characteristic of *P. r. lutea.* The blooms of *P. r. tricolor* are white with a yellow center, and the edges of the petals are rose-pink.

Plumeria rubra variety

Very fragrant, yellow-centered white flowers are borne by *P. r. acutifolia* (syns. *P. acutifolia, P. acuminata*) on trees up to 35 feet tall. The leaves are oblong, tapered at both ends, and up to 1¼ inches long by 3 inches wide. The blooms, 3 to 3½ inches in diameter, have obovate petals longer than the corolla tubes. The seed pods are 8 inches long by 1 inch wide. Popular derivatives of this variety grown in Hawaii are 'Common Yellow' or 'Graveyard Yellow', which has white flowers with lemon-yellow eyes; 'Gold', with white-tipped yellow petals; 'Sherman', with white blooms with deep yellow centers; and 'Samoan Fluff', with white flowers with canary-yellow centers.

The young shoots of **P. obtusa** are hairless. Attaining a height of 12 to 20 feet, this species blooms freely while quite small. It has obovate, oblanceolate, or oblong leaves 3 to 8 inches in length, and with rounded or notched ends. At their bases they narrow to stalks 1 inch to 3 inches long. The nearly straight lateral veins spread widely. In few- to several-flowered clusters, the flowers are white with yellow centers. They are 1¼ to 1¾ inches in diameter, with perianth tubes ½ to ¾ inch long and rounded, obovate petals. The seed pods are 3 to 5 inches long by ½ inch wide. Variety 'Singapore', with white flowers with yellow centers, belongs here.

Less ornamental kinds are *P. alba* and *P. bahamensis*, limited in the wild to the West Indies. **P. alba** has long-pointed, linear-oblong to oblong-lanceolate leaves, with turned-under margins not parallelled by a vein joining the lateral veins. They are 6 inches to 1 foot long by ½ inch to 3 inches broad and are minutely-hairy on their undersides. The slightly fragrant blooms, white with yellow centers, have obovate petals longer than the corolla tubes. They are 1 inch or more in diameter. Up to 12 feet high, *P. bahamensis* has lanceolate or linear-lanceolate leaves up to 1 foot long by 1 inch to 1½ inches wide. The many lateral veins angle forward and outward from the midribs. The flowers are white, ¾ inch across, and have perianth tubes about as long as the petals. The seed pods are 4 inches long by ½ inch wide.

Garden and Landscape Uses. Frangipanis are excellent as lawn specimens, and for other locations where small flowering trees can be displayed advantageously. They bloom abundantly over a long period, in Hawaii almost throughout the year, in Florida and southern California in summer. In climates with a definite dry season they usually flower when they are leafless, but in constantly moist climates they are likely to be evergreen and bear flowers and foliage at the same time. Frangipanis are not hardy where the temperature goes below 25°F for more than very brief periods. Both foliage and blooms last well on branches cut and stood in water and are practicable for flower arrangements. Frangipanis thrive in full sun or part-day shade and in a wide variety of soils including dry, rocky ones. They are good seaside plants. In greenhouses they are chiefly restricted to botanical collections.

Cultivation. Among the easiest of plants to grow, frangipanis can be transplanted successfully even when quite large with comparatively small balls of roots. They are propagated very easily by cuttings consisting of terminal pieces of stem. After these have had their bases sliced cleanly across with a sharp knife, they are air-dried for a day or two to allow the cuts to heal before planting. During the rooting process, which is likely to take about a month, the sand, soil, or other medium in which they are planted is kept dryish, but not completely dry. Seeds may be used to raise new plants, but selected varieties cannot be reproduced true to type in this way.

In sunny greenhouses, frangipanis succeed in well-drained containers or ground beds in porous soil watered moderately from spring through fall, sparsely in winter. Airy, dryish atmospheric conditions, such as are maintained for cactuses and other succulents, suit them. The winter night temperature may be 45 to 50°F, with a few degrees increase by day. During other seasons they are kept at warmer temperatures.

PLUMS. Geographically, the most widely grown of all pomological fruits except grapes, plums come in numerous varieties, some of which adapt to cultivation in every one of the contiguous continental United States and adjacent Canada. They belong to the genus *Prunus*, of the rose family ROSACEAE. In addition to kinds esteemed for their edible fruits, which are our concern here, there are sorts called flowering plums, which are grown purely as ornamentals. Those are treated in this Encyclopedia under Prunus.

Plum varieties belong in three groups based on the geographical origins of the species from which they are derived. Most important are the European plums (*Prunus domestica* and *P. insititia*). In addition there are Japanese plums (*P. salicina*) and native North American plums based on *P. americana* and other species. There are also hybrids between *P. salicina* and *P. americana* known as Japanese-American varieties.

A variety of European plum

European plums have been cultivated in North America since the days of its earliest settlement. Commercial production is chiefly confined to California, Oregon, Washington, and Idaho, with a very much smaller contribution from the Great Lakes region of Michigan, New York, Ohio, and Ontario. For home use they may be successfully grown over a much wider territory. To this group belong the prunes, sorts the fruits of which have a high sugar content and are suitable for drying, and the varieties of *Prunus insititia* called damsons and mirabelle plums.

Damson plums

Japanese plums vary considerably in their tolerance of low temperatures. Some varieties are hardier than European plums, others more tender to cold than peaches. They have red or yellow fruits, and are cultivated commercially in California and Ontario. Hybrids between these and American *Prunus americana*, successful in regions too cold for European plums, have mostly large, red fruits that, although inferior in quality to European varieties, are decidedly acceptable and are superior to most native American varieties.

Native American plums, scarcely grown commercially, are cultivated for home use. Those derived from *Prunus americana*, a species native east of the Rocky Mountains, are hardier than European and Japanese varieties, those from *P. nigra*, of eastern Canada even hardier. The wild goose plum (*P. munsoniana*), adaptable to regions of higher summer temperatures than other kinds, is a native of the lower Mississippi valley, and *P. hortulana*, the fruit of which is chiefly used for jams and jellies, of somewhat further north. The beach plum (*P. maritima*), a very hardy native of eastern North America, is planted to a limited extent for its fruits, chiefly in the east.

Sites for plums, other than sorts especially adapted to harsher conditions, should be selected with thought to avoidance of low-lying places into which cold air drains on still nights and which can be particularly damaging in spring when the trees are blooming. The middle parts of slopes are to be preferred to either hollows or hilltops. The nearby presence of lakes or other large bodies of water is beneficial because their effect on air temperature tends to prevent too early bloom. This same advantage accrues from planting on north-facing slopes. Such sites are especially suitable for varieties of Japanese plums.

Soils for plums may be of various types, but in general those of a slightly clayey nature are preferred to lighter ones. But success can be had on relatively sandy land if it is fertile and not too dry. It is important that subsurface drainage be good. Although plums will succeed in moister ground than cherries and peaches, they will not tolerate wet feet.

Planting may be done in reasonably mild climates in fall and on the West Coast through winter, but in regions of harsher conditions it is better to wait until spring. Choose one- or two-year-old trees for planting, and space them 20 to 25 feet apart after first preparing the soil in the manner recommended for apples.

Pruning during the first few years following planting should be directed toward producing a good head. Because plums vary considerably in their growth habits, some attention must be given to this in deciding where to cut, taking into account, for example, the natural tendency of varieties of the European plum, including damsons, and some Japanese plum varieties to branch erectly, and of other sorts of Japanese plums to develop wide-spreading branches.

The type of tree known as the modified leader is usually preferred for plums. To achieve this, begin forming the head at planting time by cutting out all except three or four well-spaced branches. During the next several years prune no more than necessary to keep the center of the tree open and to check the development of crossing branches and narrow, weak crotches.

Once the cropping stage is reached, pruning, especially for varieties of the European plum in most regions, should be even lighter and consist of no more than a little thinning to prevent overcrowding, and the cutting out of any excessively vigorous, erect shoots known as water sprouts. The warm, dry summers of the Pacific Coast region dictate the need for more severe pruning. There, head back or thin out shoots made the previous season in addition to thinning out the smaller fruiting branches. If this is not done the fruits will be undersized and of poor quality. Where winters are severe delay pruning until there is no longer danger of cold weather.

Thinning out young fruits to the extent that the trees are not called upon to carry more than they can mature adequately is very important with most plums, especially the Japanese varieties. It is not needed with damsons and prunes. If not done with kinds that benefit from thinning

Thinning out young fruits of plums

the result will be large crops of undersized fruits. Besides improving the quality of the fruit, thinning reduces the incidence of brown rot disease and the danger of branches breaking through overloading.

Attend to thinning immediately following the natural fall of young fruits called the June drop. Remove sufficient fruits so that those left do not touch each other (are 2 to 3 inches apart).

Routine care involves, in addition to pruning and thinning, soil management and, of course, pest and disease control. This last will depend upon the particular threats, which are likely to vary somewhat in different regions. Consult the local Cooperative Extension Agent or authorities at your State Agricultural Experiment Station about this. Plums may be grown in grass sod chopped up occasionally with a disk harrow to prevent it from becoming too dense or under a system of clean cultivation until midsummer followed by a cover crop to be turned under later. A third alternative, and one often most beneficial for the home orchard, is to keep the ground mulched with hay, coarse compost, or other suitable material.

Fertilizing may be needed to maintain desirable vigor, but mulching, where practiced, is likely to provide adequate nutrients. The element most likely to be in short supply, nitrogen, can be given by applying to trees three years old or younger up to ½ pound of nitrate of soda (or enough of some other fertilizer to supply an equivalent amount of nitrogen) in spring. For trees four or five years old, increase the amount up to a maximum of 2 pounds of nitrate of soda and for still older specimens up to 4 pounds, always adjusting the actual amount used to vigor and apparent need of the tree. Sometimes potash deficiency causes the outer leaves of 'Italian Prune' to die at their edges by midsummer. If this occurs, heavy applications of unleached wood ashes or of a fertilizer supplying potash will, over a period of a year or two, bring relief.

Harvesting should be delayed until the fruits are fully ripe because little or no improvement takes place once they are picked, and only the ripest fruits are of highest quality. Great care must be exercised in handling because at this stage they are very subject to bruising. If they must be kept for a while store at 33 °F, a little higher if the fruits are not fully ripe.

Varieties should be chosen not only for adaptability to locality, but with full awareness that many are self-sterile, that is, they will not crop unless another sort satisfactory as a cross-pollinator is planted nearby. Pollinators should be provided for all American and Japanese varieties and hybrids of them, although a few of each are partially self-fertile. Of the European types 'Agen', 'California Blue Egg', 'California Yellow Egg', 'Italian Prune', 'Reine Claude', 'Stanley', and the damson varieties 'French' and 'Shropshire' are self-fertile, others are generally self-sterile.

Popular varieties, the Europeans presented according to the broad groups in which they are classified, include the following. The Damson group is of very hardy trees with small fruits chiefly used for jams and culinary purposes. Those called damsons have tart, blue-purple fruits and include 'French Damson' and 'Shropshire', those called mirabelle plums are sweet and yellow-skinned. Best known of the last is 'American Mirabelle'. The 'Green Gage' or 'Reine Claude' group has yellowish-green to golden, sweet fruits of superb eating quality. Here belong 'Golden Transparent Gage', 'Green Gage', 'Imperial Gage', 'Jefferson', 'Reine Claude', and 'Washington'. The 'Lombard' group of varieties has medium- to large-sized, red, purple, or blue-purple, yellow-fleshed, oval fruits, with more or less distinct necks. To this group belong the red-fruited varieties 'Lombard' and 'Pond', neither of high quality, and the superior blue- or blue-purple-fruited varieties 'Albion', 'California Blue', 'Grand Duke', 'Pacific', and 'President'. The Prune group has red to reddish-purple fruits, with a high sugar content, suitable for drying as well as for canning and eating out of hand. Here belong 'Agen' or 'French Prune', 'Imperial Epineuse', 'Stanley', and 'Sugar'. The 'Yellow Egg' group includes yellow-fleshed, yellow- and purple-fruited varieties, the fruits large, oval, and with more or less obvious necks. The chief varieties are 'Golden Drop' and 'Yellow Egg'. Japanese varieties having red or yellow fruits include 'Beauty', 'Burbank', 'Formosa', 'Gaviota', 'Inca', 'Kelsey', 'Santa Rosa', 'Shiro', and 'Wickson'. Japanese-American hybrids have mostly large, red fruits superior to those of the American species, but not as high in quality as the best varieties of European plums. The hybrids include 'Ember', 'Fiebing', 'Kaga', 'Kahinta', 'Monitor', 'Pipestone', 'Redcoat', 'Red Glow',

'Superior', 'Surprise', and 'Waneta'. Varieties of native American plums include 'Hawkeye' and 'DeSoto' derived from *Prunus americana*, 'Cheney' from *P. nigra,* 'Golden Beauty', 'Miner', and 'Wayland' from *P. hortulana,* and 'Eastham', 'Hancock', and 'Premier' from the beach plum (*P. maritima*). The wild goose plum (*P. munsoniana*) is also planted to some extent.

Pests and Diseases. These are essentially the same as with cherries and peaches, but curculigos are likely to be more troublesome and so is the fungus disease called black knot, which causes spindle-shaped galls on twigs and branches. As a deterrent to its spread, prune out affected parts as soon as noticed. Consult a Cooperative Extension Agent or State Agricultural Experiment Station for more details and for recommended spray schedules.

PLUNGE. In gardeners' language, to plunge is to sink potted plants to the rims of their containers in a bed of soil, sand, coal cinders, peat moss, sawdust, or similar material or to bury and completely cover to depths of a few inches in such beds pots of bulbs, such as hyacinths, narcissuses, and tulips intended for forcing later. The purposes of plunging are to assure the roots more uniform moisture and temperatures than if the pots were standing on the surface of the ground or in other exposed positions and to reduce the need for frequent watering.

Plunging perennials planted in composition containers

Many houseplants and some greenhouse occupants benefit from being plunged outdoors during the summer, some in full sun, others in shade or partial shade. When plunging in soil, select a well-drained location and if the ground is clayey put a layer of gravel or sand under each pot. As a precaution against earthworms entering the pots, place a piece of slate or flat stone beneath the drainage hole of the pot.

Potted chrysanthemums plunged outdoors for the summer

POA (Pò-a)—Kentucky Blue Grass, Meadow Grass, Canada Blue Grass. Chiefly natives of temperate and cold regions, with a few at high elevations in the tropics, the more than 250 species of *Poa* belong to the grass family GRAMINEAE. The genus is indigenous to all hemispheres. Its name is an ancient Greek one for grass or fodder. Several poas are esteemed for pasture and hay, and some, notably Kentucky blue grass, for lawns. Regrettably a few, including annual meadow grass (*P. annua*), which invades lawns, gravel paths, and other garden areas, and Canada blue grass or wire grass (*P. compressa*), are weeds.

Poas are annuals and perennials of low to medium stature, often with rhizomes, and mostly sod-forming. Their generally flat or folded, rather narrow leaf blades have boat-shaped, blunt, or pointed ends. The flower panicles, loose or compact, and with branches in groups of two or more, are of two- to ten-flowered, stalked, flattened spikelets.

Kentucky blue grass (*P. pratensis*) is doubtfully native in North America. Certainly its occurrence, except in Canada and along the northern boundary of the United States, represents colonization from Europe. A splendid sod-former and premier cool-climate lawn grass, this sort has slender rhizomes and bright green leaves with soft blades up to 8 inches long by up to ⅕ inch wide. The flowering stems, which are 1 foot to 3 feet tall, have usually nodding, ovoid, rather dense, purplish or green panicles mostly 3 to 4 inches long by one-half as wide, but occasionally much larger. This grass dislikes acid soils and shade.

Wood meadow grass (*P. nemoralis*) is shade-tolerant. Because of this it is used in grass seed mixtures for shaded lawns. Native to Europe, it is naturalized in moistish soils in eastern North America. A loosely tufted rather than creeping perennial 1 foot to 3 feet in height, it has hairless leaf blades up to 5 inches long by not over ⅛ inch broad. The usually nodding, loose to fairly dense, narrowly-ovoid to nearly cylindrical, greenish to purplish flower pan-

icles are up to 8 inches long. Their branches are in clusters of about five.

Rough-stalked meadow grass (*P. trivialis*), another European species naturalized in North America, is used to some extent in lawn grass seed mixtures for shady areas. A moist-soil perennial up to 3 feet tall, it has stems that flop at their bases and then become erect. The leaf sheaths that enclose them are usually rough-hairy. The green or purplish leaf blades are soft, hairless, and up to 6 inches long by up to ¼ inch wide. The loose to fairly crowded, greenish, reddish, or purplish, ovoid or cylindrical flower panicles, up to 8 inches long, have erect branches in groups of three to eight.

Canada blue grass or wire grass (*P. compressa*) may be distinguished from Kentucky blue grass by its flat stems, bluish foliage, and more compact flower panicles. It is sometimes used in lawn seed mixtures for poor, acid soils and shady areas. Native to Europe, and naturalized in North America, this sod-forming perennial has long rhizomes and erect, markedly flattened, stiff stems up to 2½ feet tall. Its bluish-green, hairless leaf blades are up to 4 inches long and slender. Short-branched and narrow, the erect, dense panicles, up to 3 inches in length, are mostly brownish. This is sometimes a persistent weed in cultivated land.

Garden Uses and Cultivation. These are discussed under Lawns, Their Making and Maintenance.

POACHED-EGGS-DAISY is *Myriocephalus stuartii.*

POD. In its strict sense, a pod is a dry, one-compartment fruit that splits to release its seeds. Horticulturally, the term is often employed less exactly to include various more or less podlike fruits.

PODACHAENIUM (Podac-haènium). The genus *Podachaenium,* of the daisy family COMPOSITAE, is limited in its natural distribution from Mexico to northern South America. Its name comes from Greek *podos,* a foot, and *achene,* a type of fruit characteristic of the daisy family. It alludes to the fruits, seedlike achenes, being slimmed at their bases into two-winged footstalks.

Podachaeniums are shrubs with large, stalked, toothed or angularly-lobed leaves most of which are opposite, but the upper ones sometimes alternate. They have daisy-type flower heads with yellow centers of disk florets encircled by white ray florets, arranged in large panicled clusters.

Grown outdoors in California and similar mild-climate regions, *P. eminens* (syn. *Ferdinanda eminens*), of Mexico, is up to 25 feet tall. It has hairy shoots and ovate to nearly round leaves, toothless or with up to seven angular lobes, and up to 1 foot long. The leaves are velvety-gray-hairy on their undersides, less hairy above. The flower heads, about 1 inch across, are in panicles up to 8 inches or more in diameter. When bruised the plant has a strong odor.

Garden and Landscape Uses and Cultivation. A vigorous grower and quite showy, this shrub succeeds in ordinary well-drained soil in open locations, and is a good decorative for general purpose landscaping. Any pruning needed to restrain or shape the plant is best done after flowering. Propagation is easy by seed and by cuttings.

PODALYRIA (Podalý-ria). Named after Podalyrius, the physician who accompanied the Greek army to Troy, and son of Aesculapius, *Podalyria*, of the pea family LEGUMINOSAE, comprises twenty-five South African species of evergreen shrubs. They have alternate, undivided, more or less silky-hairy leaves. The stalked flowers are solitary or in clusters of two to four from the leaf axils. They are pea-like, with the standard and lateral petals of nearly equal size. The fruits are swollen, egg-shaped, to oblong, pubescent pods.

Greatly beloved in its homeland, where it is called keurtjie and its opening blooms herald spring, handsome *P. calyptrata* may attain a height of 6 to 10 feet and produces great masses of pink blooms that are especially lovely when seen in association with the silver tree (*Leucadendron argenteum*). Its shoots are slightly downy. Its blunt, obovate to broad-elliptic leaves are 1 inch to 2 inches long, up to 1 inch wide, and are slightly hairy. The flowers, freely produced near the shoot ends, are solitary or in pairs on stalks 1 inch to 1½ inches long. Deeply-two-lobed and reflexed, the banner or the standard petal is 1 inch or more wide.

Podalyria calyptrata in South Africa

White-flowered *P. biflora* (syn. *P. argentea*), up to 6 feet tall, has elliptic leaves with rust-colored margins. The flowers

Podalyria biflora in South Africa

have a large, reverse-heart-shaped standard petal, shorter wing petals. and an even shorter keel. Usually lower than *P. biflora*, procumbent *P. sericea* occasionally attains a height of 6 feet. Remarkable for its silvery, silky-downy foliage, it has short-stalked leaves, obovate to ovate, not over 1 inch long, with short-pointed, recurved tips. On ¼-inch-long stalks, the solitary flowers are in the upper leaf axils. They are pale pink and comparatively small, with the standard petal notched and ⅜ inch across.

Very handsome *P. burchellii*, 2 to 3 feet tall, has wandlike stems and rather thickish, ovate to elliptic, ¾- to 1-inch-long leaves, densely-silky-hairy on their undersides, more sparsely so above. Solitary or less often in pairs on stalks much shorter than the leaves, the numerous flowers are rosy-purple to white.

Podalyria burchellii

Garden and Landscape Uses and Cultivation. The outdoor cultivation of these handsome shrubs in North America is confined to essentially frost-free parts of California and places with similar climates. They are pleasing as single specimens and in groups. As cool greenhouse plants, they are attractive. Podalyrias respond to well-drained peaty soils and sunny locations. Seeds afford the most

satisfactory method of increase, but cuttings made from short side shoots with a heel (sliver) of older wood attached can be rooted in greenhouse propagating benches and under mist. In greenhouses the winter night temperature should be 45 to 50°F with a daytime rise of five to ten degrees allowed. At other seasons the structure should be ventilated freely and kept as cool as practicable. Airy conditions favor the best growth. Pruning to shape and repotting may be done after flowering is through. At all times the soil should be moderately moist. Well-rooted specimens appreciate biweekly applications of dilute liquid fertilizer from spring through fall.

PODANGIS (Pod-ángis). The one species of *Podangis*, rare in cultivation, belongs to the orchid family ORCHIDACEAE, and is a native of tropical Africa. Its name, from the Greek *podos*, a foot, and *angas*, a vessel, refers to the footlike spur of the lip of the flower.

Some 3 to 5 inches tall, *P. dactyloceras*, without pseudobulbs, has fans of very fleshy, bluish-green, linear, ¼-inch-wide leaves. Its long-spurred, translucent, white flowers, in short racemes from the base of the plant, and about 1 inch long, have a green-tipped column.

Podangis dactyloceras

Garden Uses and Cultivation. Of considerable interest to collectors of orchids, this species succeeds under conditions that suit tropical angraecums. For further information see Orchids.

PODOCARPACEAE — Podocarpus Family. Half a dozen genera of resinous evergreen coniferous trees and shrubs totaling 125 species, chiefly natives of the southern hemisphere, but extending northward to Central America, the West Indies, and Japan, constitute this family. They have alternate or opposite, scale- or needle-like or lanceolate to ovate leaves or phylloclads (flattened branches that look and function like leaves). The flowers are unisexual with the sexes usually on separate plants, the males typically with many stamens and in spikes or catkin-like structures at the ends of leafy shoots or arising from the axils of leaves, the females solitary, axillary or terminal, or in conelike structures. The fruits are one-seeded, usually berry-like or drupelike, rarely conelike. Genera cultivated are *Dacrydium, Phyllocladus, Podocarpus,* and *Saxegothaea.*

PODOCARPUS (Podocár-pus) About 100 species of more or less resinous evergreen trees and shrubs, chiefly natives of the southern hemisphere, are included in this important genus of the podocarpus family PODOCARPACEAE. Because of their flat and sometimes fairly broad leaves they do not on casual inspection look like other conifers. Their appearance is more suggestive of angiosperms than gymnosperms. The name *Podocarpus* comes from the Greek *podos,* foot, and *karpos,* fruit, and alludes to the fact that the fruit stalks of many kinds are thick and fleshy.

Podocarpuses have linear to ovate or rarely scalelike leaves that usually are alternate, rarely opposite. Their flowers, from the leaf axils or sometimes at the ends of brief leafy shoots, are mostly unisexual with the sexes generally on separate trees, the males in catkin-like clusters, the females solitary or in groups, sometimes in spikes. The one-seeded, berry-like or plumlike fruits are on stalks usually red or purple and in most kinds fleshy and conspicuously swollen as a result of the thickening and fusing of the upper part of the stalk and one or more sterile scales of the flowering complex. The swollen fruits stalks are edible. Some botanists segregate kinds without swollen fruit stalks as the sepatate genus *Prumnopitys,* but that is not done here.

Podocarpuses are of ancient lineage. Plants closely related to them were abundant in the Jurassic era 130 to 175 million years ago. The genus includes many species that produce valuable lumber and is remarkable because one of its members, *P. ustus,* native to New Caledonia, is the only parasitic conifer. A shrub up to 3 feet tall, it lives on *Dacrydium taxoides,* an evergreen tree up to 50 feet tall.

New World natives include about one-quarter of the known species. They occur from Mexico to southern Chile and in the West Indies. Several are exploited for their lumber, among them *P. andinus, P. salignus,* and most importantly, *P. nubigenus.* Native to Chile and Patagonia, **P. nubigenus** grows to a height of 80 feet with a trunk diameter of 3 feet. Its leaves, in two opposite rows or spirally arranged, are leathery, up to 1¾ inches long by ⅙ inch wide, and green above and glaucous beneath. The fruits have swollen, fleshy stalks. Southern Chilean **P. andinus** is ordinarily up to about 45 feet tall, but a specimen exceeding 60 feet in height is

Podocarpus andinus, the Royal Botanical Garden, Edinburgh, Scotland

recorded in southern England. This species is very like a yew (*Taxus*) in gross appearance and in cultivation is often shrub-like with several trunks or upright main branches developing from close to the ground and with lateral branches that hide the trunks. Its linear leaves up to 1 inch in length are more or less in two ranks and point toward the tips of the shoots. Their upper sides are bright green and their lower sides have two broad glaucous bands. Usually male and female flowers are on separate plants. The fruits resemble small plums and are yellowish-white. In its native Chile, **P. salignus** attains a height of 70 feet, but in cultivation is lower and often bushlike. It has slender, pendulous branchlets and lustrous-green, narrowly-lanceolate leaves up to 6 inches long by ¼ inch wide. The fruits, about ⅓ inch long, are on swollen, fleshy stalks.

Asian kinds most common in cultivation are the Japanese, Chinese, and Taiwanian **P. macrophyllus** and **P. nagi** and their varieties. Most frequent in the United States, **P. macrophyllus** is reported to grow up to

Podocarpus macrophyllus as a pot plant

60 feet tall in Japan, but in cultivation is generally considerably lower and sometimes does not exceed the dimensions of a shrub. Its spirally-arranged, leathery, bright green leaves are up to 5 inches long or sometimes longer by ½ inch wide. Their undersides are glaucous. The fruit stalks are swollen and purple, the fruits about ⅓ inch long. Varieties are *P. m. angustifolius,* with comparatively narrow leaves; *P. m. argenteus,* with silver-variegated leaves; and *P. m. maki,* a shrubby kind with upright branches and leaves under 3 inches long and ⅓ inch wide (this is much used in containers). An endemic of Taiwan, *P. m. nakaii* is a tree of medium size with a trunk up to 2 feet in diameter and leaves up to 4½ inches long by ½ inch wide.

Podocarpus macrophyllus maki in bloom

In Japan up to 90 feet high, **P. nagi** has purplish, smooth bark. Its comparatively broad leaves, green above and with paler undersides, resemble those of an *Agathis.* They are up to 2 inches long by one-half as wide and opposite or nearly so. The round fruits have a glaucous bloom. The leaves of *P. n. angustifolius* are about ½ inch long and proportionately narrower than those of the typical species. The leaves of *P. n. rotundifolius* are broader than those of the species. Variety *P. n. variegatus* has comparatively short, broad leaves variegated with yellow.

Ranging in its several geographical varieties from China to New Guinea, **P. neriifolius** at its maximum is 100 feet or more in height and has spreading branches arranged more or less in tiers. Its leaves vary greatly in size, from 1½ to 9½ inches long by ⅕ inch to 1⅛ inches wide. The egg-shaped fruits, up to ½ inch long, are on stalks that have two fleshy bracts. An interesting horticultural variety is *P. n. variegatus,* which has foliage variegated with yellow, sometimes to such an extent that only the midribs of the leaves are green.

Australia and New Zealand are the homelands of many podocarpuses including the Australian brown-pine and the Australian black-pine, the latter endemic to Australia, but the former also indigenous to the Philippine Islands and Java, the kahikatea or New Zealand white-pine, the miro, the matai or New Zealand black-pine, the totara, and the thin-bark totara.

The Australian brown-pine (*P. elatus*) inhabits the rain forests of New South Wales and Queensland, where it attains a height of 100 feet and a trunk diameter of about 3 feet. Its leaves vary from 2 to 6 inches in length on mature specimens, up to as much as 9 inches on young trees. The fruits are on fleshy, swollen stalks. The wood is employed for carpentry and cabinetmaking and because of its freedom from resin, for making boxes in which foods are packed.

The tall Australian black-pine (*P. amarus*) has lustrous green leaves with paler under than upper surfaces. Those of adult trees are up to 6 inches long and from slightly under to slightly over ½ inch wide. The reddish, glaucous fruits are up to 1 inch in length. The lumber is used for carpentry and interior trim. Probably the most cold-resistant of podocarpuses, *P. alpinus,* of Tasmania, a densely-branched shrub from 1 foot to 12 feet high, has narrow leaves up to ⅓ inch long arranged more or less in two rows. The very tiny fruits have fleshy stalks. This, which in the wild grows at high altitudes, may be expected to succeed in the Pacific Northwest.

The kahikatea or New Zealand white-pine (*P. dacrydioides*) is up to 200 feet tall, but more often does not exceed 120 feet. Its trunk is 2 to 5 feet in diameter and clear of branches for a long distance from the ground. Those of specimens growing in wet soils are usually prominently buttressed. The kahikatea has pendulous, bronzy-green branchlets and two types of foliage, juvenile and adult. The leaves of young trees, in two rows, up to ⅓ inch long, are soft, flat, and pointed. Leaves of mature trees, green or bronzy-green and arranged spirally around the shoots, overlap. Both types of foliage occur on trees of intermediate age. This is an important source of lumber for general carpentry and for making barrels, boxes, and packing cases. It is endemic to New Zealand.

The miro (*P. ferrugineus*), of New Zealand, is especially abundant in the South Island and is an important timber tree. Its strong, hard, often beautifully figured wood is used for buildings and for marine pilings. Ranging from 50 to 90 feet in height, this species has scaling bark. Its leaves, close together in two rows, are up to 1¼ inches long by under ¹⁄₁₀ inch wide on young trees. On mature trees they are about one-half as long. Male and female flowers are on separate trees. The fruits are bright red covered with a thin coating of bluish wax.

The matai or New Zealand black-pine (*P. spicatus*), one of the most important lumber trees of its homeland, has bluish-black bark. It attains a maximum height of 80 feet with a trunk diameter of 2 to 3 feet. When young it has slender, drooping branches and small, narrow, bronzy-green leaves up to ½ inch in length, but at maturity the trees develop rounded crowns with erect branches. The fruits are globular and black with a bluish waxy bloom, their stalks are not swollen.

The totara (*P. totara*) in New Zealand is second in importance only to the kauri-pine (*Agathis australis*) as a lumber producer. It is widely distributed in its native islands and under good conditions exceeds 100 feet in height with a trunk almost or quite 3 feet in diameter and free of branches for a considerable distance from the ground. Its leaves, in two ranks or scattered irregularly, vary from a little under to a little over ½ inch long by ⅛ inch wide or slightly wider on mature specimens, and may be twice as large on young trees. The globular fruits are on fleshy, crimson stalks. The wood is esteemed for building, cabinet work. and for making poles, fencing, railroad ties, and pilings.

Podocarpus totara, Huntington Botanical Garden, San Marino, California

The thin-bark totara (*P. hallii*), as its colloquial name implies, has very thin, papery bark. It grows to a height of 65 feet and has slender branches; those of young trees tend to droop. Its brownish-green leaves on younger specimens are 1 inch to 2 inches long and slightly under ¼ inch broad, on mature trees they are somewhat smaller. The fruit stalks are fleshy and usually red. This species is particularly abundant on Stewart Island and is common in the South Island. Hybrids between it and *P. totara* are believed to occur.

South African podocarpuses are among the most magnificent of native forest trees. They and *Widdringtonia* are the only conifers indigenous to South Africa, where the podocarpuses are known as yellow-woods.

The upright yellow-wood (*P. latifolius*) is widely distributed and is exploited for its lumber, which is used for a wide variety of purposes including interior trim, flooring, boxes and barrels, and railroad ties. The maximum height of this species is about 100 feet and its largest trunk diameter about 4 feet. It has thin, peeling bark and when mature, stiff, erect branchlets with leaves 1 inch to 2 inches long and up to ¼ inch wide, those of younger trees are bigger. The fruits are globose, their stalks fleshy and usually green. Of similar habit, but with narrower leaves, is *P. elongatus,* also a large tree. Its fleshy fruit stalks carry globular fruits and are usually red or purple.

The Outeniqua yellow-wood (*P. falcatus*) has been confused with *P. latifolius* and *P. elongatus,* but its fruit stalks are not fleshy and there are other differences. Specimens considerably over 100 feet tall have been reported. One measured 127 feet in height, had a girth of 21 feet, 6 feet above the ground, and was clear of branches for a distance of 63 feet from its base. This tree was estimated to be not less than 1,500 years old. The Outeniqua yellow-wood has thin, brown, peeling bark and leaves either more or less in two rows or spiraled around the shoots. On mature trees they range from ¾ inch to 2 inches long and up to ⅛ inch wide, those of younger specimens are bigger. The round fruits are glaucous-green. The wood is used for a wide variety of purposes such as buildings, interior trim, flooring, furniture, boxes, and railroad ties. Another South African, *P. henckelii,* produces useful lumber used for the same purposes as that of *P. latifolius,* to which it is closely related. This sort has drooping branches, and leaves, on mature trees, that are up to 2½ inches long and slightly over ⅛ inch broad. Those of young specimens may be considerably larger. The fleshy, glaucous-green fruit stems bear globose fruits.

Native to high elevations in Abyssinia, Uganda, and Kenya, *P. gracilior* may exceed 60 feet in height with its trunk free of branches for a considerable distance from its base. The branches and foliage of mature trees are crowded with leaves smaller than those of young specimens, which are up to 2½ inches long by almost ¼ inch wide. The fruits, purplish, glaucous and ½ to ¾ inch long, are borne at the ends of short leafy twigs. This podocarpus is greatly esteemed for its lumber, which is used for buildings, flooring, interior trim, and furniture. One of the largest species is *P. usambarensis,* a native of East Africa, which attains heights of 180 to 250 feet and produces useful lumber used in general carpentry. Its leaves are up to 3 inches long by up to ¼ inch wide. The globular fruits, about 1 inch in diameter, are on slender stalks.

Podocarpus gracilior in California

Garden and Landscape Uses. As far as outdoor cultivation is concerned, podocarpuses are mild climate evergreens. The hardiest is *P. alpinus,* which may be grown in sheltered places outdoors perhaps as far north as Philadelphia. They are esteemed chiefly for their ornamental foliage, but the male flowers of some are quite pretty. They are easy to grow in conservatories and greenhouses and are adaptable for tubs and other containers. Kinds commonly grown in that way for decorating large rooms, banks, stores, offices, and similar places are *P. elongatus, P. gracilior, P. macrophyllus, P. nagi,* and *P. neriifolius,* and their varieties. In Japan *P. nagi* is popular for training as bonsai. Outdoors, podocarpuses are handsome when given adequate room to develop without crowding. Among sorts esteemed as hedge plants are *P. andinus* and *P. macrophyllus.* Other kinds would prove equally satisfactory for the purpose.

Cultivation. If the climate is suitable, podocarpuses make no special demands of the gardener. They thrive in any fairly good garden soil that is well drained, but not likely to be excessively dry at any time, and in sun or part-shade. For best results, generous amounts of compost, peat moss, leaf mold, or other decayed organic material should be incorporated with the soil before planting, and it is helpful to keep a mulch of some such material on the soil at all times. The most satisfactory times for planting are shortly before new leaf growth begins in spring, or in early fall. Pruning to shape the plants as needed can be done at any time when they are not in active growth, but no regular pruning is necessary unless the plants are to be grown as hedges or other formal shapes. Propagation is best accomplished, whenever they are obtainable, by seeds sown in porous soil in well-drained containers in a temperature of about 60°F. The seeds are covered with soil to a depth equal to their own diameter and the soil is maintained in an evenly moist condition. They may also be increased by cuttings

taken in summer and inserted under mist or in a propagating bench in a very humid greenhouse or cold frame.

PODOLEPIS (Podó-lepis). Confined in the wild to Australia, this comparatively little known genus consists of twenty species. It belongs to the section of the daisy family COMPOSITAE that has flower heads of all ray florets like a dandelion rather than a central disk encircled by ray florets like a daisy. The name *Podolepis,* derived from the Greek *podos,* a foot, and *lepis,* a scale, has reference to the scales of the involucre (collar of bracts surrounding the flower head) that narrow to footstalks or claws. Although in the wild some kinds are herbaceous perennials, even in Australian gardens these plants thrive better in cultivation when treated as annuals.

Species of *Podolepis* have undivided, linear to lanceolate leaves, those of the stems alternate. When young they are woolly. The yellow, pink, or purple flower heads are solitary atop erect, branchless stems or are few to many together in loose inflorescences with branching stems. The fruits are seedlike achenes.

Its flower heads yellow and dandelion-like, *P. jaceoides* (syn. *P. acuminata*), 1 foot to 2½ feet tall, has soft-green, linear to oblanceolate, basal leaves 3 to 7 inches long and smaller stem leaves. Also yellow-flowered, *P. robusta,* up to 2 feet tall, has white-woolly, spatula-shaped basal leaves up to 8 inches long, often with crinkled margins, and smaller, stalkless, broadly-linear stem leaves. The flower heads are 1 inch wide. Pink-flowered *P. rosea,* 1 foot to 2 feet tall, has wiry stems and thick, stem-clasping, pointed-linear leaves up to 2½ inches long by ½ inch wide. Their margins are rolled back and both surfaces are webbed with white hairs. The flower heads are about ¾ inch wide.

Podolepis rosea

Garden and Landscape Uses. These plants are suitable for massing in groups at the fronts of flower borders and, their

flowers, for drying as everlastings. For this purpose they should be cut just before they reach maturity, tied in small bundles, and hung upside down in an airy place to dry.

Cultivation. Porous, well-drained soil and full sun best suit these plants. Seeds may be sown in spring where they are to bloom and the seedlings thinned to 6 to 8 inches apart, or they may be sown indoors about ten weeks before it is expected that the plants are to be planted in the garden, and be grown in the interim in a sunny greenhouse with a night temperature of 50°F and day temperatures five to fifteen degrees higher, depending upon the intensity of the light. Seeds germinate satisfactorily in a temperature of 60°F. The seedlings are transplanted, as soon as they are large enough to handle, individually to small pots or are spaced 2 inches apart in flats (shallow boxes). They are planted outdoors after all danger of frost has passed. No special care is afterward needed. Faded flower heads should be removed.

PODOPHYLLUM (Podophýll-um) — May-Apple. One of the ten species of *Podophyllum* is a native of eastern North America, the others are indigenous from the Himalayas to eastern Asia. Some botanists include them in the barberry family BERBERIDACEAE, by others they are segregated, along with *Diphylleia, Podophyllum,* and three other genera, in the separate May-apple family PODOPHYLLACEAE, a group considered to be somewhat intermediate between the barberry family and the buttercup family RANUNCULACEAE. The name, from the Greek *podos,* a foot, and *phyllon,* a leaf, perhaps refers to the stout stalks of the basal leaves.

Podophyllums are deciduous herbaceous perennials with horizontal rhizomes and large palmately-lobed leaves, the stalks of which are attached to the centers of their blades. The flowers are solitary and have six deciduous petal-like sepals, six to nine petals, and as many or twice as many stamens as petals. Commonly the flowers are white, but sometimes pink, purple, or brown. The fruits are large, fleshy, egg-shaped, many-seeded berries.

Medicinal uses of *Podophyllum* are based on resins extracted from *P. peltatum* and *P. hexandrum.* These are active cathartics and have been seriously investigated for their possible usefulness in the control of skin cancers. They are extremely harmful if they come into contact with the eyes. Commercial supplies of medicinal American podophyllums are collected chiefly in Virginia, Kentucky, North Carolina, Tennessee, and Indiana. Although the rhizomes, leaves, and seeds of the May-apple are poisonous the pulp of the ripe fruits may be eaten freely and without serious harm, although possibly with cathartic ef-

Podophyllum peltatum in a woodland

Podophyllum hexandrum (flowers)

Podophyllum peltatum (flower)

Podophyllum peltatum (fruits)

Podophyllum hexandrum (leaf and fruit)

fects. They have a sweetish, subacid, peculiar flavor, which some people find agreeable, but others not.

The May-apple (**P. peltatum**) is sometimes called mandrake, but that name more properly belongs to the European *Mandragora*. The May-apple is a native of moist, open woods and moist soils at roadsides and other places from Quebec to Minnesota, Florida, and Texas. It has rhizomes that extend horizontally for several feet underground and from which arise two kinds of stems, sterile ones without blooms, and flowering ones. Each flowerless stem, 1 foot to 1½ feet tall, terminates in an umbrella-like leaf up to 1 foot across, with seven to nine wedge-shaped, toothed lobes. The flowering stems each bear two half-round leaves at their tops, similarly lobed and toothed, with the number of lobes ranging from five to seven. From the crotch formed by the leaf stems arises a stalked, nodding, fragrant flower 1½ to 2 inches across, cup-shaped, and with six to nine white petals delicately traced with transparent veins. The ovoid fruits are lemon-yellow when ripe and almost or quite 2 inches long.

Native to India, *P. hexandrum* (syn. *P. emodi*) blooms later than the American kind. From 1 foot to 1½ feet tall, it has three- to five-lobed leaves up to 10 inches in diameter, often spotted with purple-brown and when they first expand, bronzy. The white to pale pink flowers are 1½ to 2 inches across; the bright red fruits 1 inch to 2 inches long. Pink flowers characterize *P. h. major*.

Garden Uses and Cultivation. The only species much cultivated in North America is the May-apple (*P. peltatum*). The Asian kinds have the same landscape values and require the same cultural conditions, but they may be less cold-tolerant; this is certainly true of *P. hexandrum*. The May-apple is a splendid plant, of noble appearance because of its rather massive foliage, for furnishing undercover in woodlands and along shady paths and in other places where filtered sunlight seeps through the overhead canopy or where good side light is available. It makes its best display when planted in generous sweeps and drifts and where there is room for it to extend itself without hindrance. For best results, a deep, dampish to quite wet soil that contains an abundance of organic matter, such as leaf mold, peat moss, or compost, is best. Planting may be done in very early spring or in early fall. Propagation is by division, by cuttings from the underground rhizomes, and by seeds sown as soon as they are ripe in sandy peaty soil in a cold frame or protected bed outdoors. The seed soil must be kept in an always moist condition.

PODRANEA (Podrán-ea)—Queen of Sheba Vine. From nearly related *Pandorea* this African genus of two species differs most obviously in the conspicuously inflated calyxes of its flowers. It belongs in the bignonia family BIGNONIACEAE. The name *Podranea* is an anagram of *Pandorea*.

Podraneas are woody vines with opposite, pinnate leaves with terminal and lateral leaflets. The pink or lilac blooms are in terminal panicles. They have an inflated, bell-shaped, regularly-five-toothed calyx and a tubular corolla, cylindrical below, but bell-shaped in its upper part. There are four nonprotruding, paired stamens, a slender style, and two stigmas. The fruits are scarcely compressed capsules.

Sometimes called Queen of Sheba vine, **P. brycei**, of Rhodesia, is a vigorous evergreen up to 25 feet tall or taller, which prospers in California and elsewhere in subtropical and tropical climates. Its leaves are up to 10 inches long. Each consists of seven, nine, or eleven short-stalked, pointed-lanceolate, usually toothless leaflets about 2 inches long. The light pink flowers have yellow throats and are striped with deep pink or red. They are about 1¼ inches long and 2 inches across. A native of South Africa, **P. ricasoliana** has leaves with more abruptly-pointed, broader, toothed leaflets that number seven or nine and are up to 1 inch long. Its 2-inch-long flowers, in loose panicles, are pale pink striped with red.

Garden and Landscape Uses. Appropriate for covering large wall spaces, pergolas, arches, lattice screens, tall pillars, and other supports outdoors in warm climates, podraneas are also suitable for large greenhouses and conservatories. They need full sun and fertile soil. Often they are bare of foliage in their lower parts and for good effect must be screened below by suitable shrubs.

Cultivation. No special care is needed to grow podraneas successfully. In greenhouses they respond to the conditions and care that suit *Allamanda*. Pruning is best done in late winter or spring, sufficient to keep the vines within bounds and to prevent undue overcrowding of the stems. These vines are subject to infestations of scale insects and mealybugs.

POELLNITZIA (Poellnít-zia). Previously known as *Apicra rubriflora*, the only species of the genus *Poellnitzia* is *P. rubriflora*. The name honors the German botanist Karl von Poellnitz, student of succulent plants, who died in 1945. Native to South Africa, this plant belongs in the lily family LILIACEAE.

Closely related to *Astroloba*, **P. rubriflora** differs in its flowers being bigger, about 1 inch long, orange-red, and having incurved tips to the perianth segments (petals). The stem attains a height of up to 9 inches and has sharp-pointed, blue-green leaves crowded in five vertical rows. Very thick, they are ovate-triangular, much rounded beneath and slightly on their upper surfaces, 1 inch to 1½ inches long by up to 1 inch wide. The blooms are in racemes up to almost 2 feet in length.

Garden Uses and Cultivation. These are the same as for *Haworthia* and *Gasteria*. For general suggestions see Succulents.

POGONIA (Pog-ònia)—Snake Mouth. The genus *Pogonia*, of the orchid family ORCHIDACEAE, occurs wild in temperate and warm parts of the Americas and Asia. Its name, from the Greek *pogonias*, bearded, was given because of the bearded lips of the flowers. There are fifty species, all ground orchids. The whorled-pogonia is *Isotria*.

Pogonias are herbaceous perennials. They have fibrous roots, a short rhizome, and an erect stem with one or more alternate leaves. The solitary or rarely twin blooms have somewhat spreading sepals and petals, not united, and similar in color. The petals are rather shorter and broader than the sepals. The down-pointing lip, lobed or lobeless, is bearded. The club-shaped column extends forward over the lip.

Its flowers fragrant, the snake mouth (**P. ophioglossoides**) is a deciduous inhabitant of bogs and other wet places from Newfoundland to Minnesota, Florida, and Texas. It has horizontal roots, and stalked,

Pogonia ophioglossoides

lanceolate to narrowly-ovate basal leaves. The slender stem, 8 inches to 1½ feet tall, has a solitary lanceolate to narrow-elliptic leaf up to 4 inches long by 1 inch wide near its middle, and a smaller one of similar shape below the usually single bloom. The latter is rose-pink. Its lip, with red veins and a beard of yellow or white hairs, is fringed at its margins. Sepals, petals, and lip are ¾ inch to nearly 1 inch long. The sepals are lanceolate, the petals elliptic, the lip spatula-shaped, with its base enclosing the column, but not joined to it. White flowers are borne by *P. o. albiflora*. The plant sometimes called *P. verticillata* is *Isotria verticillata*.

Garden Uses and Cultivation. The choice orchid described may be grown under conditions that simulate as closely as possible those under which it grows in the wild. It is appropriate for native plant gardens, bog gardens, and rock gardens. For more information see Orchids.

POGOSTEMON (Pogo-stèmon) — Patchouli. This genus, which consists of about forty species of the mint family LABIATAE, is native from India to eastern Asia. Its name, from the Greek *pogon*, a beard, and *stemon*, a stamen, alludes to the stalks of its stamens usually being bearded at their centers. An important Oriental perfume called patchouli is the product of a species of *Pogostemon*. It is popular in India, where it is known as pucha-pat, but is not held in general esteem by Occidentals, although it is used to scent soaps and is the source of the characteristic perfume of cashmere shawls.

Opposite-leaved shrubs, subshrubs, and herbaceous plants compose *Pogostemon*. Their flowers, in whorls (tiers) in the upper leaf axils, have tubular, five-toothed calyxes, tubular corollas with four nearly equal lobes (petals), four stamens, and a single style with two stigmas. The fruits are four seedlike nutlets.

The source of oil of patchouli, **P. patchouly** (syn. *P. heyneanus*) is native to India and Burma. A subshrubby species about 3 feet in height, it has soft, stalked, broadly-ovate leaves 3 to 4 inches long that when bruised emit the characteristic odor. Its terminal and lateral spikes of small purplish-tinged, white flowers are in panicles.

Pogostemon patchouly

In its homeland the crop is harvested two or three times a year, and the fragrant oil is distilled from its fresh or dried leaves.

Native to the East Indies, **P. plectranthoides**, 2 to 3 feet tall, has ovate leaves 2 to 3 inches long, double-toothed along their margins. In somewhat one-sided spikes of roundish clusters, the small, white flowers have long-protruding stamens furnished with long, pale lilac hairs.

Garden Uses and Cultivation. Only in educational displays of plants useful to man and sometimes in herb gardens is *P. patchouly* likely to be found in North America. The other species is grown outdoors in warm climates and sometimes in greenhouses for its floral display. Both

Pogostemon plectranthoides

A Christman display of poinsettias

sorts respond to temperature and other conditions that suit *Coleus*, reveling in full sun and ordinary, fairly nutritious soil of moderate moisture content. In the north, *P. patchouly* flourishes in outdoor beds in summer, but must be wintered in a cool greenhouse or equivalent accommodation. To have plants for this use, take cuttings in late summer, winter the young plants in a cool greenhouse or equivalent accommodation and plant them outdoors the next spring after the weather is warm and settled. Root cuttings of *P. plectranthoides* in a greenhouse in spring. Pot the rooted plants in well-drained, moderately fertile soil. Pinch out the tips of their shoots two or three times during the growing season to encourage branching. When they have filled the pots in which they are to bloom with roots, give biweekly or weekly applications of dilute liquid fertilizer. Both species can also be raised from seed sown indoors in late winter or spring.

POINCIANA. Plants formerly known by this generic name belong in *Caesalpinia*. The royal poinciana is *Delonix regia*, the yellow-poinciana, *Peltophorum pterocarpum*.

POINSETTIA. Besides its use as the common name of *Euphorbia pulcherrima*, treated in the next entry, the word poinsettia forms parts of the common names of these plants: annual poinsettia (*E. heterophylla*) and wild-poinsettia (*Warszewiczia coccinea*).

POINSETTIA. Botanically *Euphorbia pulcherrima*, of the spurge family EUPHORBIACEAE, this popular ornamental has a common name commemorating its discoverer, J. R. Poinsett, first United States Ambassador to Mexico, the native home of the poinsettia.

About 1825, Poinsett introduced the species to his garden at Charleston, South Carolina. Since then it has made great strides horticulturally. Not only is it much appreciated as a flowering shrub for outdoor landscape uses in parts of California, the deep south, and elsewhere in the subtropics and tropics, millions of plants are grown in greenhouses to satisfy the com-

mercial florists' Christmas season demand; it is also grown by amateurs in greenhouses and to some extent, although usually with considerably less success, as window plants.

Modern varieties are very different from the original introduction. Besides sorts with the familiar brilliant red bracts there are others with pink or creamy-white ones and double-flowered ones with heads with many more bracts than usual. These last for many weeks.

Since the early years of the twentieth century, the Californian family of nurserymen and plant breeders named Ecke has tremendously enriched the choice of varieties available. The emphasis in their breeding work has been toward the pro-

Modern poinsettias: (a) A red-bracted variety

(b) A pink-bracted variety

duction of dwarfer plants with larger, longer-lasting, firmer-textured bracts, and foliage that keeps better.

The showy parts of poinsettias are not flowers (the true flowers are the little yellow developments in branched clusters at the centers of what are more commonly called "flowers"), but assemblages of large, spreading, petal-like bracts that together with the true flowers form what are technically inflorescences. For details about these see Euphorbia.

A white-bracted poinsettia showing the true flowers clustered at the centers of the inflorescences

As outdoor shrubs, poinsettias succeed with minimum care in regions of warm to hot summers and little or no frost. They adapt to a variety of soils if well drained, preferring those slightly acid. Full sun is necessary. In localities subject to occasional light frosts choose sheltered locations or plant against south-facing walls. In frost-free regions, poinsettias can be used effectively as informal hedges.

Up to 10 feet tall or taller, and left to their own devices showing a great tendency to become leggy and ungainly, poinsettias can be improved greatly by judicious pruning, but even so it is often best to screen the lower parts of their stems with such lower plants as the Natal-plum (*Carissa*) or the dusty miller (*Senecio cineraria*).

Once each year, at the beginning of the new growing season, prune poinsettias severely, and when new shoots appear, thin them out to a number the plant may be reasonably expected to develop in good condition. Further compacting, but most likely at the cost of smaller flower heads, can be done by one or two later prunings at intervals of two months. When the bracts begin to show color, to become red, pink, or white according to variety, apply a fertilizer that supplies nitrogen in quickly available form every two weeks.

For greenhouse cultivation, many commercial and some amateur growers start

Propagating poinsettias: (a) Fill a flat or greenhouse propagating bench with damp coarse sand

(b) Pack the sand firmly

(c) Make holes in the sand with a dibber and set the cuttings so that their bases touch the bottoms of the holes

(d) With the dibber, firm the sand against the cutting

(e) Water with a fine spray and place in a warm, humid greenhouse under mist or lightly shaded from direct sun

(f) When the cuttings have sufficient roots, pot them individually into small pots

their plants from rooted cuttings purchased from specialists. Others buy field-grown stock plants produced in southern California and plant them in greenhouses as sources of cuttings. Still others, chiefly amateurs, obtain cuttings from plants of the previous year kept over from the time when they passed out of bloom.

Whether of one's own raising or purchased, in April or May cut the dormant stock plants back to a height of a foot or more (cut weak stems farther back than stout ones), repot the plants in fresh soil, water thoroughly, and put them in a sunny, humid greenhouse where the temperature is 65 to 70°F at night, a few degrees warmer by day. Spray the tops frequently, but lightly with water. When new shoots are well started reduce the night temperature to 60°F and maintain daytime levels five to fifteen degrees higher depending upon the brightness of the weather.

Make the cuttings in successional batches from May to September from terminal portions of shoots developed from the stock plants. Except for the last batch, always let the shoots become long enough to leave a piece of stem with at least two good leaves after the terminal piece, which is to be the cutting, is removed. It is necessary to retain this foliage so that the next shoots will be strong ones. Thin, weak cuttings do not produce strong, vigorous plants.

Early morning, when their tissues are turgid with water, is the best time to take the cuttings; these should be about 4 inches long. Many gardeners favor making the basal cut just beneath a node, but with poinsettias this is not necessary. Remove only the bottom leaf. Plant the cuttings in sand, vermiculite, perlite, or one of those mixed with a little peat moss in a propagating bench in full sun and under mist. If not under mist maintain high humidity and shade the cuttings heavily until rooting begins and they no longer wilt when exposed to sun. In planting the cuttings, do not set them so closely that their foliage overlaps too much. About 2 inches apart in rows 5-inches apart is about right.

Rooting takes place most satisfactorily if the medium in which the cuttings are set is maintained at 70°F, and if by day, unless the weather is warmer, the air temperature is about the same with a drop to 60°F at night permitted. Under these conditions the cuttings will have roots ½- to 1-inch long in two to four weeks. Then pot them individually in 2½- or 3-inch pots, shade for a few days, and then expose to full sun in a humid greenhouse.

Plants from early cuttings may have the tips of their stems pinched out to induce branching with the result that each carries two or three heads of bloom, but in commercial practice it is more usual not to pinch, instead allowing each individual to

develop only one head of bracts and flowers. The latest date for pinching should be mid-August to September 1st. Most often, except when tall specimens in large pots or tubs are desired, the final containers are pans (shallow pots) rather than deeper receptacles and if these are bigger than 6 inches in diameter it is usual to plant three or more plants in each.

Whatever the final containers, pot the young plants into them early in October, selecting for each pan plants of uniform size. Use fertile, free-draining, loamy soil. From then on grow in full sun in a humid greenhouse with a night temperature of 60 to 62°F and by day five to fifteen degrees warmer. Water to keep the soil evenly moist, and after the containers are filled with roots give dilute liquid fertilizer regularly at one- to two-week intervals. Commercial growers often use chemical growth regulators, of which several are available as sprays or soil drenches to limit the heights to which the plants will grow. These must be applied according to the manufacturer's directions and with some judgment.

Timing flowering to have plants in optimum condition when needed, generally for the Christmas holiday season, is effected by various manipulations. Plants propagated from early cuttings, not pinched, and grown in normal daylight usually come into bloom a little too early. Reducing the night temperature gradually to 52°F or even 50°F beginning in late November compensates for this tendency. Plants propagated from late cuttings naturally bloom somewhat later. A commonly used timing method is to manipulate day length, or more correctly the duration of darkness in each period of twenty-four hours, for a period in fall. By using artificial light to reduce the length of the nights to 10 hours beginning soon after mid-September and continuing through the first five to ten days of October, blooming is delayed. Under normal, unassisted daylight, buds begin to develop in late September, but with longer days provided artificially, bud production does not start until the lighting is discontinued.

Poinsettias as houseplants are not often highly successful, yet many people like to attempt them. Those that do usually try to keep over for flowering the following year plants bought for Christmas. Rooting new plants from cuttings is rarely practicable under house conditions. If you want to try this, here is what to do. After your plant drops its leaves, commonly in January or February, but sometimes not until March or even later, cut its stems about halfway back and quit regular watering. Put the plant in a cellar or an equivalent place where the temperature is 55 to 60°F or thereabouts. To keep the stems from shriveling, it will probably be necessary to water the soil every two to four weeks, but in the main it must be kept dry.

In early May take the plant out of its pot and remove as much old soil as possible. Scrub the pot clean and let it dry thoroughly, then replant the poinsettia in it in new, loamy, fertile, porous soil. Water thoroughly and stand the plant in a sunny window in a room with a temperature of 60 to 70°F. Keep the soil evenly moist.

As soon as nights are warm enough, in climates approximating that of New York City in early June, put the plant outdoors in full sun with its pot buried to the rim in earth. A piece of slate or similar material placed under the drainage hole will prevent earthworms entering. In early July pinch out the tips of the branches and if it seems desirable repot into a larger container, but without disturbing the roots. Water regularly and unless you have repotted, fertilize lightly every two or three weeks. Lift the pot from the ground occasionally to break any roots that may be reaching into the outside soil.

In early fall before night temperatures drop below 60°F, bring the plant into a sunny window where it is not subject to drafts, chilling, or escaping gas from furnaces or other sources. Never allow the soil to become dry, but avoid constant saturation. Sudden temperature changes are highly detrimental. A night level of 60°F, with a rise of five to ten degrees by day, is ideal, with at least moderate humidity. Leaf dropping commonly follows any se-

To grow on poinsettias a second year: (a) After the blooms have faded and all or most of the leaves have dropped, cut the stems partway back and store the plants in a dry place

(b) In May, cut the stems further back to a length of about 6 inches, repot in fresh soil, move to a sunny, warm location, and resume watering

rious departure from the environment recommended above.

Nonflowering of house-grown poinsettias is likely to be caused by exposing them to artificial light. These are short-day plants that bloom only when nights are fourteen hours long or longer. Exposure to light for brief periods or of low intensity during the night periods condition poinsettias not to bloom. If fluffy white insects (mealybugs) appear, destroy them by touching each with a swab dipped in alcohol, taking care not to get this on the foliage or stems.

Pests and Diseases. Poinsettias are relatively free of troublesome pests, mealybugs, scale insects, and whitefly being the most common. It is important to free the plants of these well before the bracts begin to develop, since insecticides are likely to bleach or in other ways mar them. Several fungus root rots and stem rots can cause problems. These are encouraged by inad-

(c) Allow one to three strong shoots to grow from each plant

equate soil drainage and excessive watering.

Two diseases for which there are no controls sometimes appear. One, bacterial, causes stems to crack, ooze yellowish sap, and die; the other, called scab, occurs chiefly in the tropics and causes cankers that encircle and kill the stems and distort, by crinkling, leaves local to the affected parts. Early identification and prompt destruction of affected plants is the best procedure if these diseases occur.

POISON. This word forms parts of the common names of the following: Bushman's poison (Acokanthera oppositifolia), crow poison (Nothoscordum bivalve), fly poison (Amianthium muscaetoxicum), poison bulb (Crinum asiaticum), poison-camas (Zigadenus nuttallii), poison-hemlock (Conium maculatum), poison-ivy (Rhus radicans), poison-oak (Rhus diversiloba), and poison sumac (Rhus vernix).

POISON-IVY, POISON-OAK, and POISON SUMAC. These are common names of pestiferous North American and West Indian species of Rhus, of the cashew family ANACARDIACEAE. None is cultivated, but all present hazards to those who work or play where they grow. A nonvolatile, gummy oil contained in all parts of the plants is capable upon coming in contact with the human skin of causing severe, painful irritation and blistering. Sensitivity varies greatly with individuals and some people are immune or seemingly so, whereas the slightest exposure by others causes severe dermatitis. But even individuals who have considered themselves not susceptible, and on numerous occasions over many years have experienced contact

Poison-ivy (*Rhus radicans*)

without untoward results, may, after massive exposure, be affected. If this happens they become sensitized so that in the future even slight exposure results in development of symptoms.

Poisoning comes only from actual skin contact with the active principle, but does not necessarily depend upon the plant being touched. Numerous well-authenticated instances make clear that handling dogs and other animals, or shoes, clothing, tools, golf clubs, and the like that have made contact with these plants can cause poisoning. It is known, too, that minute droplets of the causative substance carried in the smoke from fires involving poison-ivy, poison-oak, or poison sumac can cause severe affliction. It is probably even possible for sensitive individuals to suffer from being near without actually touching plants of these kinds when they are in flower. Then enough pollen blown short distances may cause trouble.

Avoiding contact is the surest way of keeping free of this form of dermatitis. If contact is made, immediate and thorough washing with strong laundry soap will frequently prevent development of symptoms. Should a rash result, soothing lotions sold by drugstores afford the best relief. In severe cases, consult a physician. Exceptionally, hospitalization may be required.

Elimination of these pestiferous weeds from gardens and other domestic areas may be achieved by digging them out, the work to be done by nonsusceptible individuals clothed to prevent skin contact, or by employing chemical weed killers of which ammonium sulfamate is one of the most effective.

POISONOUS PLANTS. Plants that upon contact or when eaten cause discomfort, pain, or death may fairly be described as poisonous. One group, those the spores or pollen of which are responsible for hay fever and kindred ills, are beyond the scope of this treatment, which is limited to con-

sideration of certain sorts that poison in other ways.

Dermatitis or irritation of the skin results from contact with some plants, among the best known poison-ivy and poison-oak, which are discussed separately under their genus names in this Encyclopedia. Belonging to the same botanical family, the cashew has fruits (nuts) that unless heat-treated, as are those sold for eating, cause similar distress, and so may, although usually less severely, fruits of that other well-known relative, the mango. Familiar as a greenhouse pot plant, *Primula obconica* can trigger serious dermatitis, although modern varieties seem less likely to do so than older ones.

Many euphorbias and other plants of their family, including poinsettias, contain sap, usually milky, that upon contact with the skin can cause inflammation and blistering. These juices are especially harmful to the eyes. Should any enter, clear it promptly by repeated washing with water, and consult a doctor without delay.

Contact with nettles, laporteas, and other stinging plants brings discomfort, sometimes severe and long-lasting, as a result of injection by hypodermic-needle-like hairs of a chemical irritant.

Solar dermatitis (phytophotodermatitis) may be more common than generally thought, its symptoms often perhaps being attributed to poison-ivy. It occurs when skin, moistened by perspiration or water, has been in contact with certain plants and then is exposed to sunlight. The effect is reddening and development of a burning sensation within twenty-four hours of exposure and continuance of the reddening for several months.

Plants that may poison as a result of eating parts of them are very numerous and no attempt is made here to discuss more than some of the more common. Pets as well as humans can be harmed by ingesting such plants.

In all cases where poisoning is suspected, consult a physician without delay or take the person to a hospital emergency department or clinic or call the local Poison Control Center (number in the telephone book) for advice. If possible collect for identification and preserve by pressing between sheets of newspaper good specimens of the suspected plant.

Mushrooms and toadstools other than the domesticated mushroom sold for eating should be shunned by all except knowledgeable specialists with a good grounding in mycology. Some kinds, it is true, are harmless and even agreeable to the palate, but the possibility of collecting dangerous or deadly sorts along with or instead of others is too great to take chances. By far the most common cause of death from mushroom poisoning is caused by poisonous amanitas. Extremely small amounts of these can be fatal.

Many plants other than fungi contain poisonous principles that may be confined to or be more concentrated in some parts than others, that may be more harmful under certain conditions or at particular seasons than others, and in a few cases that may be rendered innocuous by cooking, although this is not generally true.

Poisoning has occurred from cooking and eating green rhubarb leaves but the familiar red leafstalks are harmless and healthful. Potatoes that have developed chlorophyll and become green as a result of long exposure to light contain a poisonous substance. The seeds contained in the berries of yew are poisonous, but not the red flesh that surrounds them. The fruits of the May-apple (*Podophyllum*) are edible when fully ripe, but dangerous to eat before then, whereas those of the tropical akee (*Blighia*) are poisonous both before and after full ripeness, and harmless at their prime. Young shoots of pokeberry (*Phytolacca*) may be cooked and eaten with impunity, older parts and berries are poisonous.

Berries and other fruits and seeds that are poisonous may be eaten by accident or design and are often attractive to children. Other parts of the same plants may or may not be toxic. Kinds with poisonous berries include balsam-apple and balsam-pear (*Momordica*), baneberry, cohosh (*Actaea*), black locust (*Robinia*), black nightshade (*Solanum nigrum*), blue cohosh (*Caulophyllum*), broad or fava bean (*Vicia fava*) (here only a small percentage of people are affected), buckeye or horse-chestnut (*Aesculus*), castor-bean (*Ricinus*), chinaberry (*Melia*), Chinese lantern (*Physalis*), corn cockle (*Agrostemma*), Christmas-cherry or Jerusalem-cherry (*Solanum*), coontie (*Zamia*), crab's eye or rosary-pea (*Abrus*), deadly nightshade (*Atropa*), English ivy (*Hedera*), four o'clock or marvel-of-Peru (*Mirabilis*), golden chain tree (*Laburnum*), golden dewdrop or sky flower (*Duranta*), henbane (*Hyoscyamus*), holly (*Ilex*), hyacinth-bean (*Dolichos*), jetbead (*Rhodotypos*), jimsonweed and related species (*Datura*), Kentucky-coffee tree (*Gymnocladus*), lantana (*Lantana*), lily-of-the-valley (*Convallaria*), May-apple (*Podophyllum*), mescal-bean (*Sophora*), moonseed (*Menispermum*), oleander (*Nerium*), physic nut and related species (*Jatropha*), pokeweed (*Phytolacca*), prickly-poppy (*Argemone*), snow-on-the-mountain and other euphorbias (*Euphorbia*), spurge-laurel (*Daphne mezereum*), tung oil tree (*Aleurites*), wild cherry (*Prunus serotina*), wisteria (*Wisteria*), woody nightshade (*Solanum*), and yew (*Taxus*).

Bulbs, tubers, roots, and other underground parts of some plants are poisonous, and other parts of the same sorts may be. Kinds with poisonous underground parts include amaryllis (*Hippeastrum*), autumn-crocus (*Colchicum*), black snakeroot or death camas (*Zigadenus*), crinum-lily

(*Crinum*), daffodils or narcissuses (*Narcissus*), gloriosa-lily (*Gloriosa*), hyacinth (*Hyacinthus*), and star-of-Bethlehem (*Ornithogalum*).

Stems, foliage, or flowers of certain plants are toxic if chewed or eaten or if "tea," which may be made by children from them, is imbibed. Other parts of the same plants may also be dangerous. Among kinds with poisonous stems, foliage, or flowers are bleeding heart (*Dicentra*), bloodroot (*Sanguinaria*), boxwood (*Buxus*), Carolina yellow jessamine (*Gelsemium*), dumb cane (*Dieffenbachia*), false-hellebore (*Veratrum*), foxglove (*Digitalis*), greater celandine (*Chelidonium*), hydrangeas (*Hydrangea*), Indian-tobacco and related species (*Lobelia*), jessamine (*Cestrum*), larkspur (*Delphinium*), monkshood (*Aconitum*), philodendron (*Philodendron*), rhubarb, green leaves only (*Rheum*), tansy (*Tanacetum*), tobacco (*Nicotiana*), poison- or water-hemlock (*Cicuta*), and yellow-oleander (*Thevetia*).

POKEBERRY or POKEWEED is *Phytolacca americana*.

POKER PLANT or RED HOT POKER. See Kniphofia.

POLASKIA (Pol-áskia). One species of the cactus family CACTACEAE constitutes *Polaskia*. Its name honors Charles Polaskia, a twentieth-century American cactus enthusiast.

Native to Mexico, treelike **P. chichipe** (syns. *Lemaireocereus chichipe*, *Cereus chichipe*) is about 15 feet tall. It has a short trunk, up to 3 feet in diameter, and thick, erect branches with nine to twelve well-defined ribs. Its clusters of 2- to 4-inch-long spines are of six to nine radials and one central. The small, white flowers are succeeded by edible red fruits, ¾ to 1 inch in diameter, containing red flesh and small black seeds. They are sold in Mexican markets.

Garden and Landscape Uses and Cultivation. This is an attractive species for outdoor landscaping in warm desert and semidesert regions and for including in greenhouse collections of cactuses. It succeeds without difficulty in reasonably fertile, porous soil and full sun and responds to conditions and care appropriate for most tree-type desert cactuses. For more information see Cactuses.

POLEMONIACEAE — Phlox Family. Important horticulturally as a source of many fine ornamentals, the phlox family comprises fifteen genera, totaling 300 species of dicotyledons. Chiefly North American, it is represented also in the native floras of South America, Europe, and Asia. Consisting mostly of annuals and herbaceous perennials, it includes a few subshrubs, shrubs, twining vines, and small trees.

Plants of this family have alternate or opposite, undivided or palmately- or pinnately-divided leaves. Their symmetrical or nearly symmetrical flowers, mostly in terminal heads or branched clusters, less often solitary from the leaf axils, have five-lobed calyxes and corollas, the latter usually with a well-developed tube and wide-spreading lobes (petals), but sometimes bell-shaped. There are five stamens and a usually three-branched or less often two-branched style. The fruits are capsules. Genera cultivated include *Cantua*, *Cobaea*, *Collomia*, *Eriastrum*, *Gilia*, *Ipomopsis*, *Langloisia*, *Leptodactylon*, *Linanthus*, *Loeselia*, *Phlox*, and *Polemonium*.

POLEMONIUM (Polemò-nium) — Jacob's Ladder or Greek-Valerian or Charity. This genus includes hardy herbaceous perennials and a few annuals and biennials. Most are natives of western North America, but *Polemonium* is represented also in the eastern part of the continent and in the natural floras of Europe, temperate Asia, and South America. Treated conservatively, as is done here, it consists of about twenty species. Some botanists split it more finely into as many as fifty. It belongs in the phlox family POLEMONIACEAE. The name is an ancient one based on that of the Greek philosopher Polemon.

Polemoniums have pinnately-divided or lobed leaves, with narrow to much broader leaflets undivided, or divided in pinnate or in palmate (handlike) fashion. The flowers, solitary, in headlike or loose clusters, have five-toothed, bell-shaped calyxes that increase markedly in size after the flowers fade, and a funnel-, bell-, or broadly-wheel-shaped, blue, purple, pink, yellowish, or white corolla with five obovate lobes (petals). There are five stamens and a style with three stigmas. The fruits are few- to many-seeded capsules.

Jacob's ladder, Greek-valerian, or charity (**P. caeruleum**), an old-time garden favorite, is wild from the mountains of

Polemonium caeruleum

North America, Europe, and Asia to the Arctic. A number of subspecies or varieties of this variable kind are recognized. Characteristically it has erect, glandular-pubescent stems 1 foot to 3 feet tall, with pinnate or occasionally twice-pinnate leaves becoming progressively smaller upward. The leaves have nineteen to twenty-seven lanceolate to elliptic leaflets up to 1½ inches long. The terminal leaflet is quite separate from the others. The flowers, in elongated terminal clusters, are blue or rarely white, and up to 1 inch long and wide. Their petals are about twice as long as the corolla tube. The stamens may or may not protrude. The capsules, without stalks, contain seeds that do not become mucilaginous when wet. From the typical species, *P. c. van-bruntiae* (syn. *P. van-bruntiae*) differs in its stamens being one-and-a-half times as long, instead of only

Polemonium caeruleum van-bruntiae

slightly longer than the corolla. The flowers of *P. c. amygdalinum* (syn. *P. occidentale*), at most slightly over ½ inch long, have stamens that do not protrude and an exerted style.

Closely allied to Jacob's ladder is **P. carneum** (syn. *P. amoenum*). It differs in its stems being less rigidly erect and becoming decumbent with age, and its leaves often having the terminal three of their thirteen to twenty-one ovate to ovate-lanceolate leaflets more or less joined. This species is 1 foot to 2½ feet tall and minutely-hairy. Its saucer-shaped flowers, ½ to 1 inch wide, are salmon- or flesh-colored, aging to blue or purple. The style is longer than the corolla. It is native from the San Francisco Bay region to the Olympic Peninsula in Washington.

The name **P. foliosissimum** is given populations previously recognized as *P. albiflorum*, *P. archibaldiae*, *P. filicinum*, *P. molle*, and *P. robustum*. This variable species ranges through much of the Rocky Mountains, and in Nevada and Arizona.

From 8 inches to 2½ feet tall, its stems have leaves, not much reduced in size upward, that have eleven to twenty-five narrowly-lanceolate leaflets with at least the upper five extended along the midrib. The blue, violet, cream, or white flowers, from slightly less to a little more long than broad, have stamens shorter than the corollas. The seeds when wet are mucilaginous.

Excellent perennials, less than 1 foot in height, are *P. reptans*, wild in damp soils from New York to Kansas and Alabama; *P. pulcherrimum* (syn *P. haydenii*), which ranges from Alaska and the Yukon to the Rocky Mountains and California; and *P. boreale* (syns. *P. richardsonii*, *P. humile*), an inhabitant of far northern regions. The first has slender, leafy stems, the foliage of the others is chiefly basal. Hairless or hairy, the leaves of *P. reptans* have seven to nineteen broadly-lanceolate to ovate leaflets, usually with three conspicuous longitudinal veins. The loose clusters are of blue blooms with petals only a little

Polemonium elegans

Polemonium reptans

longer than the corolla tube, and stamens not much exerted. The seed capsules are stalked. From 3 to 9 inches tall, tufted *P. pulcherrimum* has leaves with eleven to thirteen elliptic to broad-ovate leaflets sparse with glandular hairs. The terminal leaflets are not joined. The bell-shaped flowers, up to ⅓ inch long and broad, and with nonprotruding stamens, are in loose clusters on few-leaved, branched or branchless stalks. Arctic *P. boreale*, erect and up to 1 foot tall, has leaves of thirteen to twenty-three elliptic to nearly round leaflets. Its broadly-bell-shaped flowers, ½ to 1 inch wide, in loose heads, have stamens shorter than the corolla. Similar to *P. pulcherrimum*, from which it differs mainly in its sepals being longer, narrower, and pointed, is *P. delicatum*, a native of high mountains in Colorado, Utah, Arizona, and California. Asian *P. pulchellum* differs from *P. pulcherrimum* in the three terminal leaflets of its leaves being joined and in its flowers being more funnel-shaped.

Dense heads rather than loose clusters of flowers are borne by *P. viscosum* (syn. *P. confertum*), *P. eximium*, and *P. elegans*. Instead of being in two ranks the leaflets of the mostly basal leaves of the first two are usually three- to five-parted and appear to be in tufts. Sometimes 1½ feet tall but often lower, *P. viscosum*, an inhabitant of alpine-arctic regions from the Rocky Mountains westward, has blue to rarely white flowers with stamens shorter than the corolla. Variety *P. v. mellitum* (syn. *P. mellitum*) is distinguished by its looser heads of yellow blooms. Differing from *P. viscosum* but slightly, *P. eximium* has flower clusters that, especially as they pass into the seed stage, are more congested and ovoid rather than cylindrical. Also, the apexes of its sepals are rounded rather than sharply pointed. The flowers are blue. The leaves of dwarf *P. elegans* are in two ranks. This kind is endemic to peaks of the Sierra Nevada, California.

Garden and Landscape Uses. The species and varieties described above are perennials. The tall ones are agreeable, easy-to-grow flower garden plants, the blooms of which are useful for cutting as well as garden ornament. Low *P. reptans* is an excellent, easily managed groundcover as well as a very acceptable addition to rock gardens and similar sites. Alpine and arctic polemoniums are harder to satisfy, and for the most part are adapted only to rock gardens and alpine greenhouses where the special attentions needed by plants from high altitudes and latitudes can be given.

Cultivation. The more easily grown polemoniums flourish in sun or part-day shade in fertile, well-drained, reasonably moist, but not wet, mellow soil. Fertilize annually in spring with a complete garden fertilizer. Except for having their faded flowers removed, little attention is required. Every third or fourth year they need lifting, dividing, and replanting. More finicky alpine species are most likely to give satisfaction in very gritty, not over-rich, moist, but well-drained soils or in a rock garden moraine. A little light shade from the most intense sun is appreciated, and where warm summers are the rule as cool a location as can be given. All polemoniums are easily raised from seed. Division in spring or early fall is also generally successfully practiced.

POLIANTHES (Poli-ánthes)—Tuberose. One scarcely associates the fragrant tuberose with the century plant, yet the botanical relationship is fairly close. Both are included in the amaryllis family AMARYLLIDACEAE, the former in the Mexican genus *Polianthes*, the latter in *Agave*. The name *Polianthes* is probably derived from the Greek *polios*, shining or white, and *anthos*, a flower, in allusion to the blooms of the common tuberose. There are thirteen species.

Herbaceous perennials with fibrous roots, and thick, often bulbous, rootstocks constitute *Polianthes*. Hairless, they have more or less fleshy leaves, smooth-edged or minutely-toothed, and clustered in more or less rosette fashion at and near the bases of the branchless flower stalks. The longest leaves are below, above they become progressively smaller until they are merely bracts. The flower stalks are erect and have several to many long-tubed, funnel-shaped blooms in spikelike racemes. They have six persistent perianth parts (more in double-flowered tuberoses) commonly called petals, but more correctly tepals, six stamens, and a three-lobed style. The fruits are capsules.

The tuberose (*P. tuberosa*) has never been found wild, but it is much cultivated, especially in its double-flowered variety. It is closely related to Texan *P. runyonii*, from which it differs in having white instead of greenish to brick-red petals, and in the margins of its leaves being smooth instead of finely-toothed. The tuberose has bulb-like, tuberous rootstocks, long-pointed,

Polianthes tuberosa: (a) Single-flowered

(b) Double-flowered

narrow, stem-clasping leaves, and flower stalks 2 to 3½ feet tall. Its waxy-white, heavily fragrant flowers are in loose spikes. They have perianth tubes, bent near their bases, 1 inch to 1½ inches long.

The faces of the flowers are up to 2½ inches in diameter. The history of the common tuberose is interesting. It was, it is believed, cultivated in Peru by the Aztecs in pre-Colombian times. The single-flowered type was brought from Mexico to a monastery in France in 1530 and was grown secretly there until 1594 when it was released for cultivation elsewhere. The double-flowered variety appeared in Holland some centuries after the introduction of the single-flowered species. It is *P. t. plena.*

The charming Mexican twin flower (*P. geminiflora* syn. *Bravoa graminiflora*) attains a height of 1 foot to 2 feet. Its sword-shaped basal leaves approximating the flower stalks in length, are up to ½ inch wide. Nodding and in pairs along the graceful, loose racemes, the ¾- to 1¼-inch-long, red or orange, long flowers have a sharp downward bend near their bases.

Garden and Landscape Uses and Cultivation. For this information about *P. tuberosa* see Tuberose. The Mexican twin flower is suitable for well-drained, porous soils in sunny locations. In mild climates it behaves as a permanent perennial. Elsewhere success may be had by planting in spring and lifting after fall frost, and then storing the tubers as recommended for tuberoses. Propagation is by natural increase of the tubers and by seed.

POLIOTHYRSIS (Polio-thýrsis). The only species of *Poliothyrsis*, a native of China, belongs in the flacourtia family FLACOURTIACEAE. It is a deciduous tree related to *Idesia*, from which it differs in having as fruits capsules instead of berries. Its name, in appropriate allusion to the large panicles of bloom, comes from the Greek *poiios*, grayish-white, and *thyrsos*, a panicle.

Not hardy in the north, *P. sinensis* is a narrow tree 30 to 45 feet tall, with alternate, stalked, ovate to ovate-oblong, slender-pointed, toothed leaves 4 to 7 inches long by up to 5 inches wide. They have three to five prominent veins extending from their bases, with lateral veins branching from them. Their undersides and stalks, like the shoots, are conspicuously downy when young. The flowers are unisexual, with the sexes intermixed in terminal panicles. At first greenish-white, they soon become yellow. About ⅓ inch across and without petals, they have five sepals. The males have many stamens and rudimentary ovaries, the females functional ovaries, three styles, and vestigial stamens (staminodes). The fruits are ellipsoid capsules containing many seeds each surrounded by a broad wing. They are ½ to ¾ inch long.

Garden and Landscape Uses and Cultivation. This uncommon species, first brought into cultivation about 1908, is unlikely to be planted except in arboretums

and other special collections. Probably not hardy in climates harsher than that of Virginia, it thrives in ordinary well-drained soil and is propagated by seed, summer cuttings, and root cuttings.

POLLARD. To pollard is to practice a severe type of training and pruning fairly commonly done in parts of Europe, but rarely done in North America. It consists of cutting the tops off young trees when they are a few feet tall, allowing branches to grow only from near the apexes of the shortened trunks, and at intervals of a few years cutting back the branches practically to their bases.

Sometimes pollarding is done as a means of restricting the size of trees, more often as a means of obtaining long, straight shoots or branches of diameters suitable for basket making, bean poles, and other purposes. Among trees most commonly pollarded are beeches, hornbeams, lindens, and willows. In North America, *Catalpa bignonioides nana* grafted onto *C. bignonioides* is pollarded to produce rather ugly specimens with globular heads supported on tall, branchless trunks.

POLLEN. Usually dustlike and granular, less commonly, as in orchids and milkweeds, adhering in masses called pollinia, pollen consists of spores produced by the anthers of flowers. The spores contain the male reproductive cells or gametes necessary to fertilize the female sexual elements or ovules. See Pollination.

POLLIA (Pól-lia). Sixteen species constitute *Pollia*, of the Old World tropics, subtropics, and Japan. They belong to the spiderwort family COMMELINACEAE. The name commemorates Jan van der Poll, burgomaster of Amsterdam, who died in 1781.

Pollias are herbaceous perennials with upright stems from sometimes creeping bases. Near their tops the stems, which terminate in dense or loose panicles of small, white or pink blooms, are furnished with largish leaves. The flowers have three persistent sepals, the same number of petals, six stamens or three stamens and three staminodes (nonfunctional stamens). The fruits are berry-like capsules.

Native to damp forests in tropical Africa, *P. condensata* has thick stems, 2 to 6 feet in length, and pointed, lanceolate-obovate, nearly hairless leaves up to 1 foot long by one-quarter as wide, narrowed to their stem-clasping bases. The greenish-white flowers, in dense panicles up to 2 inches long, have each three fertile stamens and three staminodes. The shining, dark blue fruits have white stalks. Japanese, Chinese, and Taiwanian *P. japonica* has long, creeping rhizomes and stems 1 foot to 3 feet long or in some forms perhaps considerably longer. Each carries up to about ten narrowly-oblong to broadly-

Pollia japonica

Pollia japonica (flowers)

oblanceolate leaves 8 inches to 1 foot long, tapered to both ends. In erect loose panicles, the ¼-inch-wide, white flowers, with six fertile stamens, are succeeded by blue fruits ¼ inch in diameter.

Garden and Landscape Uses and Cultivation. Rare in cultivation, *P. japonica* may not be hardy in the north. Where winters are not too severe, it is suitable for woodland gardens. The African species described needs conditions suitable for *Dichorisandra*. Propagation is by seed and by division.

POLLINATION. This is the transfer of pollen from the anthers to the stigmas of flowers, with flowering plants a necessary preliminary to fertilization and usually, but not invariably, seed formation. It may be accomplished between anthers and stigmas of the same plant or clone (self-pollination) or between different plants (cross-pollination). In many plants, there are mechanisms that make self-pollination difficult or impossible. Some plants, notably certain fruit trees, are sterile to their own pollen. Plant breeders frequently take steps to prevent self-pollination and also chance cross-pollination.

Common agencies by which pollen is transferred are bees, other insects, and wind. Birds, bats, and flowing water also serve as pollinators, and man purposefully engages in pollination as a technique of plant breeding.

POLYANDROCOCOS (Polyandrocó-cos). One unisexual feather-leaved palm is the only species of *Polyandrococos*, of the palm family PALMAE. Its name, in reference to the numerous stamens (male parts of the flower), is derived from the Greek *poly*, many, *aner*, man, and *Cocos*, the name of the coconut palm.

Native to Brazil, *P. caudescens* has a solitary, smooth trunk up to about 20 feet in height and a large dense crown of stiff leaves up to 12 feet in length, with many narrow, sword-shaped leaflets each with a prominent midrib. The branchless flower clusters, which develop among the foliage, have male flowers in their upper parts, females below. The latter have bracts that enlarge as the fruits develop and form close, cylindrical spikes. Each male bloom has a hundred or more stamens. The ellipsoid or obovoid fruits, about ¾ inch long, concave at their apexes, are hairy within the cavity.

Garden and Landscape Uses and Cultivation. This rare and handsome palm, primarily a collectors' item, is not frequent in cultivation and little is known of its possibilities as an ornamental or its cultural needs, but it may be expected to thrive outdoors in humid tropical and warm subtropical climates and tropical greenhouses. It is probably adaptable to cultivation in southern Florida and Hawaii and may be expected to grow under conditions suitable for *Areca*. For additional information see Palms.

POLYANTHUS is *Primula polyantha*.

POLYCALYMMA STUARTII is *Myriocephalus stuartii*.

POLYGALA (Polý-gala)—Milkwort, Seneca Snakeroot. Only a few of the 500 to 600 species of annuals, herbaceous perennials, subshrubs, and shrubs of *Polygala*, of the milkwort family POLYGALACEAE, are cultivated. The genus is widely dispersed in the wild through temperate and warm regions. Its name, used by Dioscorides, comes from the Greek *polys*, much, and *gala*, milk. The plants were believed to stimulate milk secretion.

Polygalas have alternate, or rarely opposite or whorled (in circles of more than two), undivided, toothed or toothless leaves. Their flowers in aspect strangely resemble pea-shaped ones of the family LEGUMINOSAE. They have usually five sepals, the two colored, petal-like side ones much bigger than the others, and three or seldom five petals united at their bases and joined to the slit tube formed of the eight stamens. The bottom petal is keel-shaped and usually carries a prominent crest on its upper side. The side petals are small and sometimes cleft into two lobes. The upper petal is often wanting. The style is upturned. The fruits are capsules.

Fringed polygala or flowering-wintergreen (*P. paucifolia*) is a charming, but difficult-to-grow native from New Brunswick to Saskatchewan, New York, and Wisconsin, and in the mountains to Georgia. A low, creeping, evergreen perennial, this inhabits rich, organic, acid soils. It has 3- to 5-inch-tall, erect stems with ovate to oblong leaves clustered in their upper parts and smaller, almost scalelike, more distantly spaced ones below. The magenta-pink or rarely white blooms, in clusters of up to four, have conspicuously fringed crests. More interesting than showy, Seneca snakeroot (*P. senega*) is a herbaceous perennial about 1½ feet tall, with usually from near its base several branchless stems, clothed with lanceolate to oblong-lanceolate leaves up to 2 inches long, often increasing in size from below to the upper parts of the stems. The tiny, white or greenish flowers are in crowded spikes about 2 inches long. Native to Oregon and California, *P. californica* has slender stems 2 inches to 1 foot tall and short-stalked, elliptic leaves up to 1½ inches long. Two kinds of flowers are produced, petal-less ones from near the base of the plant and, in loose, terminal racemes, bright rose-pink to paler blooms with petals nearly ½ inch long.

Polygalas native to Europe occasionally cultivated include charming *P. chamaebuxus*, a creeping, evergreen shrublet up to 6 inches tall and hardy in favored places in southern New England. Its leathery leaves are ovate to linear-lanceolate and ½ inch to a little over 1 inch long. Solitary or in pairs from the leaf axils, the white, yellow, or purplish-pink blooms have keels shorter than the upper petals, ⅓ to ½ inch long. The wing petals are spreading. This is chiefly a mountain species that favors pastures, rocky slopes, and light woodlands. Native to limestone and chalk soils in Europe, *P. calcarea* is a tufted herbaceous perennial with decumbent stems, usually leafless except for rosettes at their ends. The leaves, spatula-shaped to obovate, are at most sparsely-hairy, often hairless. The nearly erect flower stalks have leaves smaller than those of the rosettes, and linear-lanceolate. The generally blue or white, rarely pink flowers are in racemes of six to twenty. From the last, *P. amara* differs in its rosettes being basal, with a naked portion of usually prostrate stem below them, and in the leaves being bitter. This is a native of the mountains of southern Europe. Native to the Pyrenees, *P. vayrediae* resembles *P. chamaebuxus*. It differs in having linear to linear-lanceolate leaves. The flowers have pinkish-purple upper petals, wings, and corolla tubes.

A rather densely-branched shrub 3 to about 8 feet tall, *P. myrtifolia* is a native of South Africa. It has somewhat glaucous, ovate-oblong leaves up to 1¼ inches long and one-third as broad. Few together in short, terminal, leafy racemes, the greenish-white flowers have wing petals margined and veined with rosy-purple and a purple keel petal with a conspicuous white, lacy crest of three narrow lobes. Variety *P. m. grandiflora* has larger, rich rosy-purple blooms, about 1 inch long. A

Polygala myrtifolia grandiflora

presumed hybrid between this and *P. oppositifolia* of South Africa, the last unusual in having opposite leaves, *P. dalmaisiana*, possibly is only a variety of *P. grandiflora*. A fine ornamental shrub much resembling *P. d. grandiflora*, it has large rosy-magenta blooms with the bases of the keels white. Another South African, *P. virgata* is a hairless shrub 6 to 15 feet in height, but often very much lower. It has wandlike stems, linear to narrow-elliptic leaves, and flesh-pink to purple flowers, over ½ inch long, many together in leafless terminal racemes 3 to 4 inches in length. Native to Baja California, *P. apopetala* is a shrub up to 15 feet tall, but commonly considerably lower. It has slender, pubescent stems and ovate to lanceolate leaves 1 inch to 2 inches long. Its flowers, in terminal racemes 3 to 8 inches long, are pinkish-purple. They have four sepals and are ½ inch long or a little longer.

Annual or biennial species of North America that may occasionally be included in collections of native plants or grown for interest in rock gardens and similar places, include the following. About 1½ feet tall, *P. alba* has linear leaves about 1 inch long and spikelike racemes of white flowers. It is native from North Dakota to Montana, Texas, and Arizona. Wild from Maine to Nebraska, Minnesota, and Florida, *P. cruciata* has linear to spatula-shaped leaves,

usually in whorls (circles of more than two) of four, and dense, stalkless, cloverlike spikes of rose blooms. Of tufted growth, and indigenous from southern New York to Florida and Louisiana, *P. lutea* is a tufted species with 1-inch-long, oblong-lanceolate leaves and 1½-inch-long, spikelike racemes of orange-yellow flowers. Loose racemes of magenta-pink to purple flowers are borne by *P. polygama*, native from Nova Scotia to Florida and Texas. Up to 1½ feet tall, it has spatula-shaped to oblong leaves about 1 inch long. Rose-purple to greenish or white flowers in ½-inch-wide, spherical heads are borne by *P. viridescens*. This native from Nova Scotia to Louisiana has 1-inch-long, oblong to linear-oblong leaves.

Garden and Landscape Uses. The shrub milkworts discussed above are excellent general-purpose outdoor flowering plants in warm, dryish, frost-free or nearly frost-free climates. They are commonly planted in California and other regions of mild climates. They are also good furnishings for cool greenhouses and conservatories in containers or ground beds. The lower perennials, such as *P. paucifolia*, *P. chamaebuxus*, and *P. calcarea*, are best suited for rock gardens and like locations where they can be afforded conditions not too dissimilar from those they prefer in the wild. Seneca snakeroot and other American species are appropriate in native wild gardens.

Cultivation. The requirements of milkworts differ from species to species. It would be hazarding too much to expect acid-soil *P. paucifolia* to prosper under conditions favorable for lime-loving *P. calcarea*. Some inquiry into the environments favored by the plants in the wild, or a little judicious trial and error testing, may be necessary before you find the best garden locations and conditions for them.

In greenhouses *P. myrtifolia* and *P. dalmaisiana* are attractive pot plants. In large conservatories they do well in ground beds. They thrive in fertile, peaty, porous soil kept evenly moist, but not wet, in full sun. In summer, container specimens benefit from being put outdoors, their pots buried to their rims in a bed of sand or peat moss. They must be brought inside before frost. In winter a night temperature between 45 to 50°F is adequate. Daytime temperatures may be five to fifteen degrees higher. The greenhouse should be ventilated freely on all favorable occasions. To train these as shapely specimens it is necessary to pinch the tips out of their shoots two or three times during their early stages. To keep them shapely, prune them in late winter or spring, back close to the bases of the previous year's growth. At that time, too, attend to repotting.

Propagation of polygalas can be by seed, and depending upon the amenability of the kind, by division, cuttings, or layering.

POLYGALACEAE—Milkwort Family. Some 800 species contained in 12 genera constitute this family of dicotyledons; a few are cultivated as ornamentals. The group, of widespread natural distribution, does not occur in New Zealand, Polynesia, or in arctic zones. It includes herbaceous plants and shrubs, some with vining stems, and small trees. Its leaves, sometimes scalelike, are alternate, opposite, or in whorls (circles of more than two) and undivided and without lobes or teeth. Solitary or in spikes, racemes, or panicles, the flowers are asymmetrical and often superficially resemble those of the pea family. They have persistent calyxes of generally five separate or more or less united sepals, two of which are often larger than the others and are winged or petal-like. There are three or five petals, the two upper ones joined together or to the stamens and the lower one concave and frequently with a fringed crest or keel. There are three to ten, but most commonly eight stamens most often united to form a split sheath enclosing the style, which usually supports two stigmas. The fruits are capsules or less often samaras, drupes, or nuts.

Cultivated genera include *Comesperma*, *Polygala*, and *Securidaca*.

POLYGONACEAE — Buckwheat Family. Some 800 species allocated between about 40 genera constitute this family of dicotyledons, which is most prolific of kinds in temperate parts of the northern hemisphere; it is represented much less abundantly in the tropics and south of the equator. Among its best-known sorts are buckwheat and rhubarb.

Members of the buckwheat family include a few shrubs and trees, but the great majority are annual, biennial, and perennial herbaceous plants. Some are vines. They have stems conspicuously swollen at the nodes and alternate or very rarely opposite or whorled (in circles of more than two), undivided leaves, with the bases of their stalks usually encircling the stems as clearly evident sheaths. The small flowers, in spikes, racemes, panicles, or other arrangements are most commonly bisexual, or if unisexual, with the sexes on the same or on different plants. Without petals, they have generally three or six often petal-like sepals, six, nine, or rarely more stamens united or not at their bases, and a two- or four-cleft style. The fruits are three- or less often two-sided, small winged nuts. Among genera cultivated are *Antigonon*, *Atraphaxis*, *Chorizanthe*, *Coccoloba*, *Eriogonum*, *Fagopyrum*, *Homalocladium*, *Muehlenbeckia*, *Oxyria*, *Polygonum*, *Rheum*, *Rumex*, *Ruprechtia*, and *Tripiaris*.

POLYGONATUM (Polygón-atum) — Solomon's Seal. Northern hemisphere deciduous herbaceous perennials of the lily family LILIACEAE constitute *Polygonatum*. There are perhaps fifty species. The name, used by Dioscorides, and from the Greek *polys*, much, and *gony*, a knee, refers to the many-jointed rhizomes. The common name alludes to the prominent scars on the rhizomes resembling seals of the sort applied to official documents.

Solomon's seals have thick, knotty, horizontal, creeping rhizomes from which come erect or gracefully arching, branchless stems with along their upper reaches alternate, opposite, or rarely whorled (in circles of more than two), ovate, lanceolate, or linear leaves. The pendulous or nodding white, yellowish, greenish, or rarely pinkish flowers are solitary or in clusters of four to several from the leaf axils. They are more or less bell-shaped, with the perianth segments united into a tube with six short lobes (petals). There are six stamens and a slender style tipped with an obscurely-three-lobed stigma. Neither stamens nor style protrude. The fruits are black, blue-black, or red berries.

North American species number four that are not always clearly distinct. All have hairless stems and alternate leaves that, except those of **P. pubescens,** which have minute, white hairs on the veins on their undersides, are hairless. The lowest leaf, a bract, on the stems of *P. commutatum* and *P. biflorum* and its varieties, is green and persistent. In the other American species, *P. pubescens* and *P. cobrense*, it is papery and soon falls.

Great Solomon's seal (**P. commutatum**) is 3½ to 6 or 7 feet tall. The upper, leafy parts of its stout stems exceed the lower naked portions in length. There are from about twelve to twenty-four stem-clasping, elliptic-lanceolate to broadly-elliptic leaves, up to 6½ inches long by 4 inches wide. They have seven to nineteen veins prominent throughout their lengths. Solitary or in groups of up to fifteen, the yellowish-green to greenish-white blooms are

Polygonatum commutatum (fruits)

from ¾ to nearly 1 inch long. The dark blue berries are ⅓ to ½ inch long. This species is native from New Hampshire to Manitoba, Georgia, and northeastern Mexico. Except that in its typical phase it is generally less vigorous, of daintier aspect, and commonly has fewer and smaller flowers, small Solomon's seal (**P. biflorum** syn. *P. canaliculatum*) differs in no constant characters from the last. It is variable, three varieties being recognized by botanists. Small Solomon's seal rarely exceeds 2 feet in height but sometimes attains 6 feet. Of its generally one to five, but up to nine, leaf veins, only the center one is usually conspicuous for the full length of the leaf. Its flowers are commonly solitary or in twos or threes, or sometimes more together. They are greenish or in one variant, deep yellow. This species occurs in usually sandy, moist to dry woodlands from New Hampshire to Manitoba, Florida, and Texas.

ers ¾ to 1 inch long. The last more closely resembles European *P. odoratum* than it does any American species. It is native to mountains from New Mexico to Arizona.

Plants commonly cultivated as *P. multiflorum* are hybrids of that species and *P. odoratum*, both natives of Europe, including the British Isles, and of temperate Asia. These hybrids, for which the correct name is **P. hybridum,** have characteristics intermediate between those of the parents, and presumably include the double-

Polygonatum hybridum

flowered and variegated-leaved kinds previously considered to be varieties of *P. multiflorum*, and named *P. m. flore-pleno* and *P. m. striatum*, respectively. True **P. multiflorum** has cylindrical stems 2 to 4 feet tall, with alternate, very short-stalked, stem-clasping, pointed-oblong leaves 3 to 5 inches long, with up to nine principal veins. The white flowers, evidently con-

Polygonatum commutatum

Polygonatum biflorum

The blooms of *P. pubescens*, a native of rich, moist woods from Nova Scotia to Manitoba, Georgia, and Indiana, are mostly not over ½ inch long. Its stems are 1 foot to 3 feet tall. From it *P. cobrense* differs in having hairless leaves and flow-

Polygonatum multiflorum at the Royal Botanic Gardens, Kew, England

stricted at their middles and about ¾ inch long, are in clusters of two to five. The stalks of their stamens are hairy. Angular rather than cylindrical stems 1 foot to 2 feet tall distinguish **P. odoratum** (syn. *P.*

Polygonatum odoratum thunbergii

Polygonatum falcatum

officinale) from *P. multiflorum*. More robust than typical *P. odoratum*, Japanese *P. o. thunbergii* (syn. *P. japonicum*), up to 3½ feet in height, has leaves up to 6 inches in length and flowers nearly or quite 1 inch long. Leaves variegated with longitudinal, white stripes are characteristic of *P. o. variegatum*.

Other Solomon's seals in cultivation include these: *P. falcatum*, of Japan and Korea, has stoutish, cylindrical stems 1 foot to 2 feet tall and alternate, stalkless, lanceolate to elliptic leaves 3½ to 4½ inches

Polygonatum odoratum variegatum

long, often with a longitudinal center band of white. Usually in clusters of three to five, but sometimes solitary, the ¾-inch-long, greenish-white flowers have practically hairless stalks. *P. hookeri*, of the Himalayas and western China, is a charming miniature 1 inch to 3 inches tall. From rhizomes it produces erect stems with alternate, elliptic leaves ½ inch to 1½ inches long. Solitary in the axils of the upper leaves, the up-facing, cream to pale yellow or lavender-pink, lilac, or purple flowers are ½ inch wide or a little wider. *P. latifolium*, a European species naturalized to some extent in New England, up to 4 feet tall, has angled stems and alternate, ob-

Polygonatum hookeri

long leaves, pubescent on their undersides and up to 6 inches long. The pubescent, green-lobed, white flowers are up to ¾ inch long and solitary or in clusters of up to five. *P. sibiricum*, of northern Asia and the Himalayan region, 2 to 4 feet tall, has linear leaves coiled at their tips, up to 6 inches long, in whorls. The ½-inch-long, greenish-white to purplish flowers in clusters of two to four have stamens with hairy stalks. *P. verticillatum*, of Europe and eastern Asia, has angled stems up to 4 feet tall and whorls of linear-lanceolate leaves up to 4½ inches in length, not coiled at their apexes. In clusters of up to four or solitary, the greenish-white flowers, narrowed at their middles and a little under ½ inch long, have hairy-stalked stamens. The fruits are red.

Garden and Landscape Uses. Solomon's seals are gracious plants for open woodlands and other lightly shaded sites where the soil is decently nourishing, deep, and moderately moist without being wet. The kinds described above are hardy and are elegant for providing flowers for use in arrangements. Because the foliage of necessity is taken with the blooms, care must be exercised not to cut too many stems from any one clump, otherwise it will be seri-

ously weakened. Another good use for Solomon's seals is to force them into early bloom in pots in greenhouses or even in windows.

Cultivation. Few plants are easier to grow than these. They are commonly increased by division, which may be done in early spring or early fall, but they may also be raised from fresh seeds sown in sandy peaty soil kept evenly moist without being for long periods saturated. Established clumps benefit from mulching with compost, leaf mold, or peat moss. They can remain undisturbed for long, but when they become crowded to the extent that the bloom production or quality declines they need digging up, dividing, and replanting in deeply spaded soil enriched with generous amounts of decayed organic matter such as compost or well-rotted or dried manure, and bonemeal.

To have plants early, strong clumps are dug in early fall and planted in rich soil in 6- or 7-inch pots, which are put in a cold frame or are plunged (buried nearly to their rims) in a bed of sand, peat moss, or some similar material outdoors. Early in the new year or later, the pots are brought into a light, cool (night temperature 50 to 55°F, day temperature five to ten degrees higher) greenhouse, window, or similar place and are watered to keep the soil evenly moist. New growth soon starts and elegant decorative plants result. After blooming is over, watering is continued and the plants are kept growing under cool conditions until there is no longer any danger of frost; then they are taken from the pots and planted outdoors. The same plants are not suitable for forcing in successive years.

POLYGONUM (Polý-gonum) — China Fleece Vine or Silver Lace Vine, Knotweed, Prince's Feather. Several excellent ornamentals, as well as a great number of weedy or otherwise unattractive kinds, are included in the about 300 species of *Polygonum*, of the buckwheat family POLYGONACEAE. The group is widely distributed in most parts of the world from frigid regions to the tropics. It includes annuals and perennials, mostly herbaceous, but a few woody, ranging from lowly spreaders to upright kinds and tall vines. A few are aquatics. The conspicuously swollen-jointed stems characteristic of most polygonums give reason for their name, which comes from the Greek *poly*, many, and *gony*, a knee.

Polygonums have undivided, alternate, or whorled (in circles of more than two), opposite leaves. The appendages (stipules) at the bases of the leafstalks usually sheathe the stems. Mostly bisexual, but rarely unisexual with the sexes on the same or separate plants, the small flowers, commonly in spikes, racemes, or heads, are often colorful and showy. They have white, pink, or red perianths of usually five petal-like lobes or segments, from three to nine, but most commonly five stamens, and a two- or three-parted style. The fruits are angled achenes, with the persistent perianth parts attached.

Popular hardy vines are the China fleece or silver lace vine (**P. aubertii**), a native of China, and closely related **P. baldschuanicum,** of Bukhara, which is distinguished from *P. aubertii* by its mostly drooping racemes of pink blooms ¼ inch wide or wider. The flowers of *P. aubertii* are white to greenish-white, rather less than ¼ inch wide, and mostly in erect panicles. These vigorous, hairless species climb by twining stems to heights of about 20 feet. They have slender-stalked, thin, ovate to ovate-oblong leaves, shallowly-heart-shaped at their bases, bronzy when they first unfold,

Polygonum aubertii

Polygonum baldschuanicum

with blades 1½ to 2 inches long. The fragrant blooms are in loosely-branched, showy panicles.

Mexican-bamboo (**P. cuspidatum** syns. *P. sieboldii, Reynoutria japonica*), of Japan, and the closely similar sacaline (**P. sachalinense** syn. *Reynoutria sachalinensis*), of Sakhalin Island, are viciously aggressive spreaders that form forest-like clumps of

Polygonum cuspidatum

erect, few-branched stems. They should never be introduced where the slightest chance exists that they will crowd other plants or take possession of areas needed for other purposes. Their roots extend to depths of 2 to 3 feet or more and once established are extremely difficult to eradicate. These are robust, hardy herbaceous perennials, the Mexican-bamboo up to 8 feet tall, the sacaline sometimes one-half as tall again. The first has short-pointed, ovate to nearly circular leaves, square-cut or wedge-shaped at their bases, and up to 6 inches long. The leaves of the other, which may reach 1 foot in length, are ovate-oblong and have, at least the lower ones, shallowly-heart-shaped bases. In both, the racemes of white or greenish-white flowers are in quite showy panicles from the upper leaf axils. A dwarf, alpine variety, *P. c. compactum,* spreads much less aggressively than *P. cuspidatum.* It is often grown under the name *P. reynoutria.* From 1 foot to 2 feet tall, it has leaves 1 inch to

Polygonum cuspidatum compactum

2 inches long and roots much less deeply than the typical species. The foliage of *P. c. spectabile,* a less vigorous grower than the typical species, is prettily marbled with white, red, and green.

Polygonum cuspidatum spectabile

Much less aggressive, hardy or at least moderately hardy, upright herbaceous perennials include certain natives of the Himalayas. Here belongs **P. campanulatum.**

Polygonum campanulatum

From 3 to 4 feet tall, this has slender, erect stems, branched freely above, and lanceolate, elliptic, or ovate leaves mostly 3 to 4½ inches long. In loosely branched, terminal panicles the pink flowers are bell-shaped and about ½ inch long. Variety *P. c. lichiangense* (syn. *P. lichiangense*), of western China, has leaves with grayish undersides and white flowers. Generally similar to *P. campanulatum,* but with leaves mostly over 4½ inches long and white flowers that open more widely, **P. polystachyum** is native to the Himalayas. Another native of that region, **P. amplexicaule** is up to 3 feet tall. It has ovate to lanceolate leaves, and rose-red blooms in spikes up to 6 inches long. Variety *P. a. album* has white flowers, variety *P. a. atropurpureum* dark red flowers. Himalayan **P. molle** (syn. *P. rude*) is a compact, bushy perennial 2 to 3 feet high with hairy stems and stalked, elliptic-lanceolate leaves, hairy on their undersides. Its white flowers are in large, hairy, terminal panicles.

Lower herbaceous perennials, hardy or moderately so, are *P. vaccinifolium* and *P. affine,* both of the Himalayas. About 1 foot tall, and with trailing stems, **P. vaccinifolium** has pointed-elliptic leaves ½ to ¾ inch long, and deep rose-pink flowers in erect spikes 2 to 3 inches long. From 1 foot

Polygonum molle

Polygonum coriaceum

Polygonum viviparum

Polygonum vaccinifolium

Useful for watersides and moist soils, snakeweed (**P. bistorta**) is a 1- to 1½-foot-tall, hardy European and Asian knotweed with chiefly basal, oblong-ovate, wavy leaves 3 to 6 inches long, the lower ones with broadly-winged stalks. The crowded, cylindrical spikes of pink to white flowers

Polygonum bistorta

Polygonum capitatum

to 1½ feet high, and with oblanceolate leaves 2 to 4½ inches long, **P. affine** has pink or red blooms in erect spikes up to 3 inches long. From 1 foot to 2 feet tall and a native of western China, **P. coriaceum** is attractive. It has elliptic to ovate-elliptic leaves, the lower ones stalked, the upper ones stalkless. They have a prominent mid-vein and are 2 to 5½ inches long by up to 2 inches wide. Carried well above the foliage on slender, erect stalks, the dense, cylindrical spikes of pink flowers are 1¾ to 2 inches long by ½ to ¾ inch wide.

are 1½ to 3 inches long. The bright pink flowers of *P. b. superbum* are in conical spikes. Differing from *P. bistorta* chiefly in its leaves being longer and narrower, **P. bistortoides** is a native of western North America. Favoring moist, frequently calcareous soils, **P. viviparum** is a perennial up to 1 foot tall or slightly taller. Widely distributed in arctic and subarctic regions and on mountains in temperate regions in North America, Europe, and Asia, it has erect stems. Its lower leaves, long-stalked and linear-oblong, are 1½ to 3½ inches long; the leaves on the stems are smaller and narrower. Pink to white, the flowers are in racemes 1 inch to 3½ inches long that in their lower parts bear tiny purple bulbils.

A pretty, nonhardy, mat-forming perennial, **P. capitatum**, of the Himalayas, is a good low groundcover in mild climates, and it also makes an interesting pot plant.

From 1 inch to 3 inches high, it has slender, trailing stems up to nearly 1 foot long and elliptic, short-stalked leaves ½ inch to 1½ inches long, each with a dull purple, V-shaped band. The spherical heads of pink flowers, lifted above the foliage on short, erect stalks, are up to ½ inch in diameter.

A handsome tropical African knotweed hardy only in mild regions, **P. senegalense albotomentosum**, often grown as *P. lanigerum*, has branched stems 2 to 6 feet tall and silvery white-hairy, long-pointed, recurved, wavy-edged, lanceolate leaves 4 to

Polygonum affine

Polygonum senegalense albotomentosum

6 inches long, and panicles of slender racemes 1 inch to 2 inches long of white, coppery-pink, or reddish flowers. Frost-tender, this sort is good for flower borders and naturalizing in the tropics and subtropics, and in the north for temporary summer displays.

Prince's feather (**P. orientale**) is an annual, a native of India naturalized in parts of North America. It has branched, pubescent stems, and finely-hairy, ovate leaves, the larger lower ones 4 to 10 inches long.

Polygonum orientale

The large panicles of rose-pink to crimson flowers are of crowded, cylindrical, generally drooping racemes 2½ to 3½ inches long. Typically 4 to 8 feet tall, this has produced horticultural variants usually listed as *P. o. pumilum*, of lower stature.

Garden and Landscape Uses. Appropriate uses for knotweeds vary greatly according to species. The vines are admirable for covering pergolas, arbors, fences, and other supports that supply holds for their twining stems. The taller, upright, herbaceous perennials, with the tall Mexican-bamboo and the sacaline notable exceptions, are suitable for perennial borders and for groups in naturalistic settings. The Mexican-bamboo and the sacaline, despite their decorative qualities, should never be planted in gardens. Their only possible uses are to furnish out-of-the-way places where their rapid and complete takeover of adjacent ground cannot possibly be objectionable. Dwarf *P. cuspidatum compactum* is a useful groundcover for banks and other difficult places, but it, too, spreads quite rapidly and may require curbing. Low-growing *P. affine* and *P. vaccinifolium* lend themselves to use in rock gardens and the fronts of flower borders. In mild climates, *P. capitatum* is a good rock garden plant and prostrate groundcover. It is also pretty for growing in pans (shallow pots) and in hanging baskets in cool greenhouses. At watersides and in wet soils, *P. bistorta* and *P. bistortoides* are successful.

Cultivation. Polygonums are generally of very easy culture. Some, but not all, root readily from cuttings. Division provides an easy alternative means of increasing the perennials, or they can be raised from seed. Polygonums are not particular about soil, except that they commonly prefer reasonable moisture. A few need damp or wet earth. Too rich soil is likely to result in excessively coarse growth. Leaner diets are better. Full sun or at most a little part-day shade are to the liking of polygonums. The vining kinds may be restricted to size and shape by shearing or pruning in late winter or spring. The annual prince's feather is raised from seeds sown where the plants are to remain, and the young plants are thinned to about 1½ feet apart, or seeds may be sown indoors early and the young plants set out later. Plants of *P. lanigerum* needed for temporary summer displays are usually raised from seeds sown early indoors. The young plants are handled like those of annual bedding plants and are set in the garden after all danger from frost is past.

POLYPODIACEAE—Polypody Family. Cosmopolitan in its natural distribution and by far the largest family of ferns, this comprises 7,000 or more species, many esteemed as ornamentals. They have creeping or upright, branched, scaly or hairy rhizomes and usually pinnately-divided, but sometimes undivided, stalked fronds (leaves) coiled in their early stages and with numerous veins. The sterile and fertile fronds may be similar or dissimilar. The spore capsules, borne on the undersides or at the margins of the fronds, are in circular or elongate clusters (sori), which may or may not be covered or surrounded by an indusium. Cultivated genera include *Aglaomorpha*, *Campylcneurum*, *Crypsinus*, *Drymoglossum*, *Drynaria*, *Drynariopsis*, *Lemmaphylum*, *Merinthosorus*, *Microgramma*, *Microsorium*, *Niphidium*, *Philebodium*, *Photinopteris*, *Platycerium*, *Pleopeltis*, *Polypodium*, *Pseudodrynaria*, and *Pyrrosia*.

POLYPODIUM (Poly-pòdium)—Polypody or Wall Fern, Resurrection Fern. The extent of *Polypodium*, the type genus of the polypodium family POLYPODIACEAE, is interpreted variously by different authorities. Some include as subgenera sorts that others assign to as many as twenty different genera, leaving only about seventy-five species in *Polypodium*. In this Encyclopedia, without prejudice to *Goniophlebium* being retained as the name of certain Old World ferns, New World natives previously known by that name are included in *Polypodium*, but *Campyloneurum*, *Microgramma*, *Microsorium*, *Niphidium*, *Phlebodium*, and *Pleopeltis*, all by some authorities accepted in *Polypodium*, are treated as separate genera. Other sorts at one time included in *Polypodium* now belong in *Aglaomorpha*, *Arthropteris*, *Crypsinus*, and

Drynaria. The name *Polypodium*, alluding to the branched rhizomes, comes from the Greek *polys*, many, and *pous*, a foot.

Of nearly cosmopolitan distribution in the wild, *Polypodium* includes kinds that always grow in the ground as well as many tropical and subtropical sorts that commonly live as epiphytes perched on trees. Mostly evergreen, they have creeping, branched rhizomes with fronds (leaves) jointed to them in such a way that distinct scars remain after the fronds are detached. Pinnate, pinnately-lobed, or without separate leaflets, lobes, or teeth, the fronds have branched veins with the ends of the branches free (separate) or joining those of others. The clusters of spore capsules, dotted on the backs of the fronds or toward their apexes, are without coverings (indusia).

The common polypody or wall fern of Europe (*P. vulgare*) is seldom cultivated in North America, although a few of its many variants, including *P. v. bifidum*, in which the lower or sometimes all of the leaflets end in fish-tail forks, and *P. v. longicaudatum*, distinguished by its fronds having long, tail-like terminal segments, are grown. Inhabiting banks and rocky places or occasionally perching on trees, *P. vulgare* has mats of thick scaly rhizomes and linear-lanceolate, leathery fronds. The latter, 9 inches to 1¼ feet long and up to 3 inches wide, have stalks about one-half as long as the blades, which are deeply-cleft into ten to twenty pairs of sometimes slightly-toothed, usually curved, bluntish lobes or segments up to ½ inch wide. The spore clusters are in rows, one on each side of the midrib.

Polypodium vulgare

European species closely similar to and previously included in *P. vulgare* are **P. australe** and **P. interjectum**. The three hybridize among themselves and some confusion results. The second differs from *P. vulgare* in having softer, broad-ovate to triangular fronds. The third, believed to be a stable hybrid between *P. vulgare* and *P. australe*, is intermediate between its putative parents. Of these three species there are many varieties with crested, plumed, or dissected fronds, but it is not always possible to say with certainty to which species a particular variety belongs.

Native North American species include a group closely related to the common polypody or wall fern of Europe and by some authorities considered to be varieties of that variable kind. Here belongs the American wall fern of the eastern part of the continent and several species that are natives of the west.

The American wall fern (*P. virginianum*) differs from *P. vulgare* in botanical details including its rhizomes having smaller scales and the midribs of its leaf segments not curving inward at their bases. Inhabiting rocks, rocky banks, and bases of

Polypodium virginianum

trees, this evergreen native from Newfoundland and Nova Scotia to British Columbia, Georgia, Tennessee, and Arkansas has slender, much-branched, stringlike rhizomes. Green on both sides and hairless, its leathery, oblong-lanceolate to triangular fronds up to 10 inches long and 3½ inches wide are deeply-pinnately-lobed. The clusters of spore capsules, at the ends of veinlets, form single rows near the margins of the leaf segments. Rare varieties occur that differ from the typical species in having less leathery leaves or differently shaped or lobed ones or in having blades without lobes. Most extreme in the dissection of its leaves is *P. virginianum cambricoides*.

The Western polypody (*P. hesperium* syn. *P. vulgare columbianum*), ranging from Alaska to Baja California, South Dakota, and New Mexico, chiefly inhabits crevices and rock ledges. It has slender, densely-scaly rhizomes and rather closely set 6- to 8-inch-long fronds with triangular-oblong to linear-oblong blades pinnately-cleft almost to their midribs. The bluntish, narrow-oblong to elliptic leaflet-like segments, usually under 1 inch long, have round-toothed margins. The clusters of spore capsules are in single rows alongside the main veins of the leaflets.

Restricted in the wild to California and Baja California where it inhabits ledges, moist banks, and sometimes exposed sea bluffs, *P. californicum* (syns. *P. intermedium*, *P. vulgare intermedium*) is a deciduous sort with slender, creeping rhizomes and membranous fronds 4 inches to 1 foot long, with oblong to narrowly-ovate blades cleft nearly to their midribs into linear-oblong, blunt, or somewhat pointed segments up to 2¼ inches long and with a single line of spore capsule clusters along both sides of the mid-veins. Similar, the licorice fern (*P. glycyrrhiza* syn. *P. vulgare occidentale*) grows on rocks, logs, and mossy tree trunks from California to Alaska. From *P. californicum* it differs in having more slender rhizomes and leaves with mostly lanceolate blades.

Native from California to British Columbia, where it inhabits cliffs, slopes, and mossy logs, *P. scouleri* has creeping rhizomes with chaffy scales when young, naked later. Its few leathery fronds are 6 inches to 2 feet long or somewhat longer. They have triangular-ovate blades longer than the stalks, with two to fourteen pairs of linear to narrowly-oblong, round-toothed lobes or segments. The clusters of spore capsules on the undersides of chiefly the upper leaflets are crowded against the mid-veins.

The resurrection fern (*P. polypodioides*) is an evergreen terrestrial or epiphytic sort native from Maryland to Illinois, Florida, and Texas and southward to and throughout tropical and subtropical South America. This has slender, cordlike rhizomes and fronds 3 inches to 1 foot long, with oblong blades of a maximum width of 2½ inches cleft into eight to twenty pairs of linear to somewhat spoon-shaped lobes up to ¼ inch wide and rounded at their apexes. Their upper surfaces are smooth, their lower ones have a scurf of roundish scales. The clusters of spore capsules are in little pits near the edges of the leaf segments, close to their tips. In dry weather the segments curl markedly, to expand again when humid conditions return. This is reason for the vernacular name resurrection fern.

Other New World polypodiums in cultivation include natives of the West Indies, Mexico, and Central and South America. One, *P. thyssanolepis*, occurs as far north as Arizona. Belonging here are these kinds: *P. brasiliense*, of tropical South America, has stout rhizomes with distantly spaced, pinnate fronds 1½ to 2½ feet long. They have many oblong-lanceolate leaflets, 5 to 7 inches long, tapered at their apexes, and two or three or less often one or four longitudinal rows of closely spaced clusters of spore capsules on each side of the midvein. *P. fimbriatum*, of tropical South America, is a handsome sort with creeping, hairy rhizomes and erect and spreading, lanceolate, pinnate fronds 6 inches to 1¼ feet long, thickly felted with silvery- to

Polypodium fimbriatum

leaden-gray hairs on their upper surfaces and rust to brownish hairs on their undersides. The clusters of spore capsules are in two rows. *P. kuhnii*, of Central America, has creeping rhizomes and membranous fronds, 1 foot to 1½ feet long, with many rather widely separated, straight to sickle-shaped, tapering leaflets up to about 9 inches long by ½ inch wide. The clusters of spore capsules are in single rows, one on each side of and close to the mid-veins of the leaflets. *P. lepidopteris*, of tropical South America, has stout rhizomes and pinnate, linear, hairy fronds, up to 2 feet

Polypodium lepidopteris

long by 1¼ to 3 inches wide, cleft into many toothless leaflets that spread at right angles from the midvein. The clusters of spore capsules are in two rows paralleling the mid-veins of the leaflets. *P. lepidotrichum*, native of Mexico to South America, has very thick, creeping rhizomes closely covered with slender scales. Its fronds, 1 foot to 2 feet long, have ten to seventeen pairs of pointed, linear, minutely-scaly leaflets up to about ½ inch wide. The clusters of spore capsules are in single rows, one each side of the mid-veins of the leaflets. *P. loriceum*, of the West Indies, Mexico, and Central America, has creeping rhizomes and well-spaced fronds 1½ to 2 feet long or longer. Their elliptic-oblong to triangular blades, which narrow to pointed apexes, have numerous, slightly sickle-shaped, 2- to 4-inch-long, pointed leaflets wider at their bases because the margin on the side toward the tip of the leaf is expanded to form a little triangle. The clusters of spore capsules are in single rows on each side of the mid-veins of the leaflets. **P. maritimum,** of Mexico and Central America, grows on trees or in the ground. It has straggling rhizomes with, spaced along them, fronds 1 foot to 2 feet tall with pinnate, oblong or triangular-oblong blades. The leaflets, spread at nearly right angles to the blades, are bluntish-oblong with at their bases a small expansion of the margin pointing to the apex of the frond. The spore capsule clusters are in one or two rows on each side of the mid-veins of the leaflets. **P. menisciifolium,** of Brazil, in cultivation often misidentified as *P. fraxinifolium,* has stout, spreading rhizomes along which are spaced fronds 1 foot to 2½ feet long. They have many sometimes somewhat sickle-shaped, pointed-oblong leaflets 3½ to 8 inches long by ½ to 1 inch wide. The clusters of spore capsules are mostly in one or two rows on each of the mid-veins of the leaflets. **P. mosenii,** of Brazil, a close ally of *P. brasiliense* and *P. lacerum,* in gardens is often misnamed *P. latipes.* It has scaly rhizomes with, spaced along them, fronds 2 to 3 feet long that have many straight or slightly sickle-shaped, pointed-linear leaflets up to 8 inches long by ¾ inch wide with the upper margin of each dilated a little at its base and joined to the midrib. The clusters of spore capsules are in two or three rows on each side of the mid-veins of the narrow leaflets. **P. pectinatum,** of Brazil, has stout rhizomes and pointed, oblong to strap-shaped fronds 1½ to 2 feet long by 2 to 2½ inches wide, that because of their numerous narrow leaflets of approximately equal length have, as the botanical name implies, a comblike aspect. The leaflets widen slightly where they join the midrib. There is one row of spore capsule clusters on each side of the mid-veins of the leaflets. **P. plebejum,** of tropical America, has thick rhizomes and fairly widely-spaced fronds 6 inches to 1½ feet long. The clusters of spore capsules are in single rows on each side of the mid-veins of the narrow leaflets. **P. ptilorhizon,** of Costa Rica, has slender, often glaucous rhizomes and rather widely-spaced fronds 6 inches to 1 foot long by 2½ to 3½ inches wide. The blunt or pointed leaflets have on their undersides clusters of spore capsules in single rows on each side of their mid-veins. The margins of the leaflets facing the apexes of the fronds widen appreciably at their bases. **P. rhodopleuron,** of Mexico and Central America, and reportedly difficult to grow, has scaly rhizomes with rather distantly spaced, triangular-lanceolate fronds 9 inches to 1¼ feet long by up to 4

Polypodium triseriale

inches wide, with many narrow, pointed-lanceolate leaflets. The clusters of spore capsules are in single rows on each side of the mid-veins of the leaflets. **P. thyssanolepis** ranges as a native from Arizona through Mexico, Central America, South America, and the West Indies. It has densely-scaly rhizomes and fronds 4 inches to 1 foot long, with ovate blades accounting for about one-half their lengths. They are cleft deeply into comparatively few rather widely spaced lobes or segments that are thickly clothed with a felt of soft, sometimes hairlike scales. The clusters of spore capsules are in single rows on each side of the mid-veins of the lobes. **P. triseriale** (syn. *Goniophlebium triseriale*), of tropical South America, has stout rhizomes. Its firm, pinnate fronds, 1 foot to 2 feet long and up to 1 foot wide, have linear to narrow-elliptic toothless leaflets 2 to 6 inches long and up to ¾ inch wide. The clusters of spore capsules are in two to six rows paralleling the mid-veins of the leaflets.

The jointed or golden polypody (**P. subauriculatum**), native from tropical Asia to Australia, has stout, scaly rhizomes and spaced along them evergreen, arching to pendulous fronds exceptionally up to 8 feet long, but more often 3 to 4 feet long by about 1 foot wide. Their very numerous ¼- to ½-inch-wide leaflets, up to 6 inches long, may be toothed or toothless. Some are irregularly-pinnately-lobed and some repeatedly less irregularly-lobed. The clusters of spore capsules are in single rows,

one each side of the mid-veins of the leaflets. Variety *P. s. knightiae* is especially esteemed for hanging baskets. A large fern with pinnately-divided fronds with crested margins, this, when grown outdoors in

Polypodium subauriculatum knightiae

Florida and southern California, loses its leaves for a brief period each year. **P. formosanum,** of Taiwan, has slender, wide-creeping, bluish-glaucous rhizomes from which sprout well-separated, pinnate or very deeply-pinnately-lobed fronds with fairly long stalks and oblongish blades up to 1 foot long or sometimes longer by up to 4 inches wide, with usually hairs along the chief veins. The clusters of spore capsules are in single rows on each side of the mid-veins of the leaflets.

Garden and Landscape Uses. Hardy polypodiums are delightful furnishings for rock, wild, and other naturalistic gardens where light or dappled shade shields from the fiercest sun. They are especially appropriate for planting in crevices and at the bases of rocks in slightly acid soil that contains abundant organic matter and is not excessively dry.

In the humid tropics and subtropics nonhardy sorts can be displayed similarly. Some are appropriate for planting in wads of coarse organic debris packed into the crotches and crevices of rough-barked trees. They are also splendid in pots and hanging baskets or on rafts or in ground beds in greenhouses.

Cultivation. If location and soil suit, no special problems attend the cultivation of polypodiums. They respond best to fairly high humidity and to the soil being damp, but not constantly saturated.

Indoors, the temperature for tropicals should not be under 58°F at night, and a few degrees higher is better. By day increases of five to fifteen degrees above night levels, depending upon the brightness of the weather, are in order. Good growth is promoted by giving well-rooted specimens dilute liquid fertilizer at about two-week intervals from spring to fall. Increase is easy by division in spring and by spores. For more information see Ferns.

POLYPODY. See Polypodium.

POLYPOGON (Poly-pògon)—Beard Grass. About ten species of annuals and perennials, mostly of warm-temperate regions, constitute *Polypogon*, of the grass family GRAMINEAE. The name is from the Greek *polys*, many, and *pogon*, a beard. It alludes to the bristly panicles of bloom.

Polypogons have slender, erect stems and narrow, flat leaves. Their flowers are in spikelike panicles of one-flowered, short-stalked spikelets.

Annual beard grass (**P. monspeliensis**), a native of Europe, Asia, and Africa, and naturalized in North America, is up to 2 feet tall, with stems solitary or in tufts. Its leaves are hairless and up to 6 inches long by under ⅓ inch broad. The dense, cylindrical, light green or yellowish flower heads may be 6 inches long by 1½ inches wide or considerably shorter and proportionately narrower. The silky bristles, largely responsible for the pleasing appearance of the panicles of bloom, are up to ⅓ inch long.

Garden and Landscape Uses. The attractive grass described above is useful for fronts of flower beds and for inclusion in fresh and dried flower arrangements. For the latter purpose, it should be cut while the panicles are fairly young, otherwise the spikelets are likely to shatter.

Cultivation. This is simple. Seeds are sown thinly in spring in freely drained soil of reasonable quality, in a sunny location. If seedlings sprout too thickly they are thinned to 2 to 4 inches apart. The only other care needed is that necessary to discourage weeds.

POLYPTERIS. See Palafoxia.

POLYRRHIZA. See Dendrophylax.

POLYSCIAS (Polý-scias)—Wild-Coffee or Coffee-Tree, Angelica. Cultivated members of this genus are often grown under the names of two related genera, *Aralia* and *Panax*. They are tropical and subtropical shrubs and small trees admired for their foliage. Belonging in the aralia family ARALIACEAE, there are about eighty species of *Polyscias*, none native to the Americas. The name comes from the Greek *poly*, many, and *skias*, shade, and alludes to the dense foliage.

These are spineless, generally hairless plants. Their leaves sometimes aromatic, often show considerable variation in form, sometimes on the same plant. They are mostly once-, twice-, or more-times-pinnately-divided. Several horticultural varieties have variegated or dissected foliage. In umbels, heads, or more rarely spikes, usually disposed in panicles, the tiny green or whitish flowers have no appreciable decorative value, nor do the berry-like fruits. The flowers have usually four-toothed, sometimes five-toothed, or toothless calyxes, four or five petals, the same number of stamens, and five to eight styles. From *Aralia* this genus differs in that in the bud stage the petals of its flowers meet without overlapping, from *Panax* in its leaves not being palmate. Despite the common names applied to some kinds, *Polyscias* is not botanically related to coffee or to the herb angelica.

Wild-coffee, or coffee-tree as it is sometimes called, **P. guilfoylei** (syns. *Aralia guilfoylei*, *Nothopanax guilfoylei*) is a favorite ornament in tropical gardens. A stout shrub or small tree 10 to 20 feet tall, this native of Polynesia has upright branches, and once-pinnate leaves 1 foot to 1½ feet in length, with five to seven or rarely nine well-separated, stalked, elliptic-ovate to nearly round, sometimes obscurely-lobed leaflets, 3 to 5 inches in length, with a few teeth at their apexes, and wedge- or at least not heart-shaped at their bases. Most commonly the leaves of this variable species are blotched with gray or edged with white. The umbels of flowers are in large, loose panicles. In *P. g. monstrosa* the leaflets are jagged-toothed, margined with white, and splashed with gray. The twice-pinnate leaves of *P. g. laciniata* have white-edged margins to their more or less drooping, prong-toothed leaflets. Their green surfaces are obscurely marked with light olive-brown. Sometimes called celery-leaved panax, *P. g. quinquefolia* has dark coppery-

Polyscias guilfoylei quinquefolia

Polyscias guilfoylei victoriae

green leaves, with the leaflets irregularly-and coarsely-lobed. Very beautiful *P. g. victoriae* is smaller and more compact than other varieties. Its much-divided leaves are white-edged.

Equally as handsome, **P. balfourana** (syn. *Aralia balfourana*) can be distinguished from *P. guilfoylei* by its long-stalked leaves having usually three but sometimes only one prominently stalked leaflets with heart-shaped bases. Up to 25 feet or more in height, this native of New

Polyscias balfourana

Caledonia has foliage with round to kidney-shaped, blunt leaflets, 3 to 4 inches in diameter, and coarsely-round-toothed at their margins. The slender-stalked umbels of flowers are clustered on the stalks of large panicles. Variety *P. b. marginata* has grayish-green leaves strikingly and irregularly margined with white. The leaves of *P. b. pennockii*, commonly of one leaflet, are predominantly of a slightly sickly pale green hue tinted with creamy-white and irregularly-edged with dark green.

Polyscias balfourana marginata

Polyscias balfourana pennockii

Smaller-growing **P. fruticosa** (syn. *Aralia fruticosa*) and **P. filicifolia** (syn. *Aralia filicifolia*) attain heights of 6 to 8 feet. The former, native from India to Polynesia, can be distinguished from the latter, which is often known as angelica, by its leaves being three- or more-times, instead of only once, pinnately-divided. The leaflets have freely-cleft, spiny-toothed margins. The flowers are in short-stalked umbels from the leaf axils. Variants are *P. f. elegans*, which is similar to and possibly identical with *P. f. plumata*. These are more compact than typical *P. fruticosa*. The South Sea islands are home to *P. filicifolia*, the leaves of which in young plants, are dissected in

ferny fashion and are bright green with purplish midribs. Those of old specimens are likely to have much wider, even broadly-ovate leaflets with less or no dissection or toothing.

Native to Mauritius, **P. paniculata** has lustrous, pinnate leaves, generally with seven stalked, broad-elliptic to oblong, toothed leaflets, the terminal one of which is the largest, up to 7 inches in length, with rounded or tapering bases. The flowers are in spikelike racemes up to 4 inches long. The leaflets of *P. p. variegata* are generously blotched with cream and greenish-white. The plant grown in Hawaii as **P. scutellaria** may not strictly represent that species. It is a shrub 6 to 12 feet tall, with leaves of one to five nearly round, stalked leaflets up to 5 or 6 inches in diameter and with shallow, rounded teeth.

Garden and Landscape Uses. In the humid tropics the members of this genus are much esteemed for general landscaping. The tall, erect growers, such as *P. guilfoylei* and *P. balfourana*, are much used for hedges and barriers. These and other kinds are grown as ornamentals in tropical greenhouses and conservatories and as houseplants. They prosper under conditions that suit crotons (*Codiaeum*), dracaenas, and other leathery-leaved tropicals and are content with ordinary soil that is fairly drained, reasonably nourishing, and not excessively dry. Outdoors they stand part-day shade or full sun, but are not happy if exposed to sweeping winds.

Cultivation. No unusual care is needed by these plants. Any pruning to keep them shapely or restrict them to size may be done at the start of a new growing period. In greenhouses they are satisfied where the minimum winter night temperature is about 60°F and that by day five to fifteen degrees higher. At other seasons both night and day temperatures may be considerably higher. A humid atmosphere is required and, indoors, some shade from bright summer sun. Watering to keep the soil evenly moist but not saturated is practiced, and the health of pot-bound specimens is promoted by occasional applications of dilute liquid fertilizer. Propagation is by cuttings, air-layering, or rarely by seed.

Pests. The chief pests are mealybugs, red spider mites, scale insects, and root nematodes.

POLYSTACHYA (Poly-stàchya). Widely distributed *Polystachya*, of the orchid family ORCHIDACEAE, is represented in the native floras of warm parts of the Americas from Florida to the West Indies and Brazil, in those of tropical Asia, Indonesia, and China, but most abundantly in those of Africa. About 200 species are recognized. The name, from the Greek *polys*, many, and *stachys*, a spike, alludes to the branched spikes of some species.

Not much cultivated, polystachyas are epiphytes (tree-perching plants that take no nourishment from the trees they live upon) of varied growth forms and flower colors. The flower stalks come from the tops of the small pseudobulbs. They carry small to medium-sized blooms, usually hooded, and with their lips uppermost. As is usual in orchids, the flower parts consist of three sepals, two petals, a lip, and a column representing the united male and female parts.

Having one of the widest natural ranges among orchids, *P. flavescens* (syn. *P. luteola*) is native from Florida to Mexico, throughout tropical America, and through much of the Old World tropics. Its small pseudobulbs clustered, each has one to several leaves 2 inches to 1 foot long and ¼ inch to 1½ inches wide. The many-flowered racemes or panicles with their stalks are erect and 1 foot to 1½ feet long

Polystachya flavescens

or longer. The pale, yellowish-green, fragrant blooms have sepals much wider than the petals. The middle lobe of the three lobes of the lip has wavy or crisped margins and a disk with little glandular hairs. *P. adansoniae*, of tropical Africa, frequently perches on baobab trees. It has small, oblongish pseudobulbs each with two to four spreading, narrowly-elliptic to linear leaves 1½ to 2½ inches long by about ½ inch wide. In erect, narrow spikes, its ¼-inch-long flowers, which do not open fully, are white or greenish with brown- or purple-tipped sepals and petals. Golden-yellow to orange-yellow blooms more or less striped with brown, hairy on their outsides, and not opening widely are borne by *P. affinis* (syn. *P. bracteosa*), of West Africa. About ½ inch wide, they are in arching or pendulous, many-flowered, loose racemes, together with their hairy stalks about 1 foot long. This has closely

Polystachya adansoniae

Polystachya cultriformis

Polystachya leonensis

clustered pseudobulbs, about 2 inches in diameter, each with a pair of pointed, elliptic-lanceolate, thin, leathery leaves up to 8 inches long, and usually purple on their undersides. **P. cucullata** (syn. *P. galeata*), of tropical West Africa, has nearly cylindrical, clustered pseudobulbs, 2 to 3 inches long, each topped by a solitary linear-lanceolate to oblong, blunt or pointed leaf up to 6 inches long. In ones or twos atop stalks mostly shorter than the leaves,

Polystachya cucullata

the flowers, which do not open widely, are 1 inch to 1½ inches long. They are pale green with purplish spots. **P. cultriformis,** a native of tropical Africa, Malagasy (Madagascar), the Comoro Islands, and the Mascarene Islands, is a somewhat variable species from 4 inches to 1 foot tall. Its leaves are strap-shaped. The small, fragrant flowers, ranging from white through cream to deep yellow and from pink to mauve-purple, are in slender-stalked, narrow racemes. **P. hislopii,** of Zimbabwe (Rhodesia), has ovoid to oblong-spindle-shaped pseudobulbs about 2 inches long. Each has three or four lanceolate-strap-shaped leaves 2 to 6 inches long. In hairy, erect or arching, few-flowered racemes, the hooded blooms are ¾ inch to 1¼ inches long and hairy on their outsides.

Polystachya hislopii

They have pale green sepals and petals and a white lip spotted and sometimes veined with purple or violet. **P. laxiflora,** of Sierra Leone, has creeping rhizomes with, strung closely together along them, small, thickened, stemlike, two-leaved pseudobulbs. The narrow-elliptic to oblongish leaves are 6 to 9 inches long. Borne in panicles of sometimes up to as many as fifty, the buff-yellow flowers,

Polystachya laxiflora

with an orange lip or a yellow lip streaked with red, are about ⅝ inch across. **P. leonensis,** a native of Sierra Leone, has small pseudobulbs spaced closely along a creeping rhizome. Each has three or four pointed-linear leaves 3 to 4 inches long. In rather loose, erect racemes, the small flowers have pale green sepals and petals and a white lip with the undersurfaces of its side lobes light purple and the middle lobe white-mealy. Indigenous to southeast Africa, **P. pubescens** has small, crowded pseudobulbs each with two or three oblong-lanceolate leaves 3 to 4 inches long. The flower stalks and racemes are together about 5 inches long. The up to twenty blooms, about ¾ inch wide, are bright yellow. The lip, smaller than the sepals and petals, and with fuzzy-hairy side lobes, like the sepals is streaked with red. Its center lobe has a reflexed apex. **P. shirensis,** of East Africa, has small pseudobulbs and linear-strap-shaped leaves. Its tiny yellowish-green flowers, glossy on their

Polystachya shirensis

outsides, are crowded in short erect spikes spaced 2 to 3 inches apart along long, erect, slender stalks. **P. transvaalensis,** of South Africa, is up to 7 inches tall or sometimes taller. It has slender, erect

Polystachya transvaalensis

stems and numerous aerial roots. Its stem-clasping leaves are strap-shaped and up to 4 inches long by ¾ inch wide. The about 2-inch-long panicles are of a few small, down-pointing, greenish-white flowers tinged or spotted with purple. **P. vulcanica,** of tropical Africa, up to 5 inches tall, has clustered, slender, canelike pseudobulbs each surmounted with a solitary, thickened, slender, linear leaf up to 3½ inches long. Usually in twos or solitary, the attractive flowers, ½ inch or slightly more wide, are cream or cream tinged with lavender, with a violet lip and a column tipped with violet.

Polystachya vulcanica

Garden Uses and Cultivation. Belonging to the assemblage known as "botanical" orchids as contrasted with showier kinds grown commercially, many members of this genus are delightful and well suited for inclusion in fanciers' collections. They are generally easy to manage and so possess appeal for beginners as well as more experienced orchid growers. for more information see Orchids.

POLYSTICHUM (Polýs-tichum) — Christmas Fern, Holly Fern. This genus of about 135 species of ferns, almost cosmopolitan

in its natural distribution, is most abundant in mountains in the tropics. It belongs in the aspidium family ASPIDIACEAE, or according to those who do not accept that segregate, in the polypodium family POLYPODIACEAE. Its name, from the Greek *polys,* many, and *stichos,* a row, alludes to the clusters of spore capsules of some sorts being in many rows. The plant sometimes called *Polystichum aristatum* is *Arachniodes aristata.*

Polystichums have usually more or less erect or short-creeping rhizomes and clustered fronds (leaves) with blades one- or more-times-pinnate or pinnate with the leaflets pinnately-lobed. The ultimate segments generally end in brief points. The veins mostly fork once. The round clusters of spore capsules are on the veins on the undersides of the fronds.

Christmas fern or dagger fern (**P. acrostichoides**), a beautiful evergreen native from Nova Scotia to Wisconsin, Florida, Texas, and Mexico, has slender, creeping rhizomes and pointed, lanceolate-linear,

Polystichum acrostichoides

Polystichum acrostichoides (two fertile fronds and one sterile frond)

once-pinnate leaves with stalks about one-quarter as long as the blades, with chaffy scales. They are 1 foot to 3 feet or somewhat more in length by 2 to 5 inches wide and have twenty to thirty-five pairs of alternate, pointed-linear-oblong, spine-

toothed leaflets that spread at right angles, with a sharp earlike projection at the base of the edge faced to the apex of the frond. Their undersides are scaly, their upper surfaces without scales. The fertile (spore-bearing) portions of fertile fronds consist of several to many pairs of leaflets from the tip of the frond down that are markedly smaller and narrower than the lower leaflets that are without spores. The closely set spore capsules are mostly in two rows on each side of the mid-vein of the leaflets.

Northern holly fern (**P. lonchitis**), of mostly limestone soils and shaded, cool locations across North America and in northern Europe and Asia, has short, erect rhizomes and once-pinnate, usually evergreen, linear-lanceolate, leathery leaves 9 inches to 2 feet long by up to 3 inches wide with twenty-five to forty pairs of leaflets, mostly lanceolate, but the lowermost reduced in size and more or less triangular. They spread at right angles from the midrib and have a prominent earlike lobe on the side toward the tip of the frond. From the Christmas fern this differs in the fertile and sterile leaflets being similar, instead of the fertile being markedly smaller and narrower, and in the spore capsules being mostly in single rows on each side of the mid-vein.

Giant holly fern or Western sword fern (**P. munitum**) is a native chiefly of damp woodlands from Montana to Alaska and California. Evergreen, it has stout, suberect rhizomes and clumps of coarse, leathery, once-pinnate, linear-lanceolate fronds 1 foot to 4 feet long by 2 to 10 inches wide with scaly stalks and numerous pointed, sharp-toothed, slightly sickle-shaped leaflets, eared at their bases and usually with clearly evident, three-branched

Polystichum munitum

lateral veins. The clusters of spore capsules are big and set closely together in two or sometimes more rows.

American natives with fronds at least in their lower parts twice- or more-times-pinnate include *P. braunii, P. californicum,* and *P. dudleyi.* One of the loveliest of American ferns, called shield fern, a name it shares with species of *Dryopteris*. **P. braunii** occurs in the wild from Newfoundland to Pennsylvania and Wisconsin. It has suberect rhizomes and deciduous or sometimes partially evergreen fronds with scaly stalks and elliptic blades. Up to 3 feet long by 3½ to 8 inches wide, they have thirty to forty pairs of primary leaflets, each with many small leaflets margined with fine, spiny teeth. The basal one of these on the edge toward the tip of the frond is biggest. The clusters of spore cases are in rows, one on each side of the mid-veins of the ultimate segments. Endemic to California, **P. californicum** has stout, suberect, scaly rhizomes. Its fronds are 1 foot to 4 feet in length. They have linear-lanceolate to linear-oblong blades 2 to 8 inches wide with many broad-based, linear, pinnately-lobed leaflets, the ultimate segments tipped with spines. Similar **P. dudleyi**, also of California, differs in having leaflets mostly pinnate and with the lowest divisions pinnate or pinnately-cleft.

A rather rare native of South Africa, **P. luctuosum**, in its homeland, occurs in deep shade beside streams. Its crown has many large, black scales. Its leathery, twice- or thrice-pinnate, triangular fronds are 1 foot to 3 feet long and at their bases 5 to 10 inches wide. Each lobed or toothed leaflet ends in a bristle point. Widely variable **P. setiferum** is an inhabitant of most temper-

Polystichum luctuosum

Polystichum setiferum

ate and warm parts of the world, except North America. Its 1- to 2-foot-long fronds, very shaggy with chaffy, cinnamon-brown scales along their stalks and usually most of their midribs, have pinnate blades 3 to 6 inches wide with numerous leaflets that are pinnate or pinnately-lobed, with ultimate segments ending in slender, curved points. The closely set clusters of spore capsules cover most of the undersurfaces of the outer ends of the leaf blades. A variety that produces plantlets freely on its fronds, *P. s. proliferum* (syn. *P. s. viviparum*) is com-

Polystichum setiferum proliferum

monly cultivated. Native to Japan, Taiwan, Korea, and China, **P. tsussimense** has broadly-lanceolate to oblong-ovate fronds 1 foot to 1¾ feet long by 4 to 8 inches wide, with very shaggy stalks and lanceolate leaflets. Their lower leaflets are pinnate, the upper ones deeply-pinnately-cleft. The ultimate leaf segments are margined with short, spiny teeth. The large clusters of spore capsules are in single rows on both sides of the mid-vein.

Polystichum tsussimense

Garden and Landscape Uses and Cultivation. Polystichums are attractive for outdoors and greenhouse cultivation. The natural geographic range of species gives a fair indication of their probable hardi-

ness. Several, but not all described here, are hardy in climates not colder than that of New York City. Moderately moist soil of a woodland type suits these plants. Shade from strong sun is needed. Propagation is by division and by spores. For more information see Ferns.

POMADERRIS (Poma-dérris). The buckthorn family RHAMNACEAE contains *Pomaderris*, a wholly southern hemisphere genus of evergreen trees and shrubs, some of which are planted for ornament in the south, in California, the Pacific Northwest, and in similarly salubrious places. None of the about forty-five species is hardy in the north. The name, given in allusion to the membranous covering of the seed capsules, comes from the Greek *poma*, a cover or lid, and *derris*, a skin.

The plants that belong here have alternate leaves generally more or less clothed with whitish or rust-colored, stellate (star-shaped) hairs, and from species to species varying greatly in form and size. In clusters or panicles, the little flowers have five sepals, five or no petals, and five stamens. There is a more or less divided style and three stigmas. The fruits are capsules.

Kinds that have flowers without petals include, as its name indicates, **P. apetala**, of Australia, Tasmania, and New Zealand. This somewhat variable shrub or tree has round-toothed, broadly-ovate to ovate-lanceolate leaves, hairless above and white- or gray-hairy on their undersides. They are 2 to 4 inches long. Its tiny pale-yellow to pale green flowers are in terminal and lateral clusters. Australian **P. phylicaefolia**, also with petal-less flowers, is represented in New Zealand by *P. p. ericifolia*, a densely-branched shrub about 3 feet tall. Its young shoots and undersides of its foliage are white-hairy. The almost needle-like leaves are 2 to 4 inches long. Freely produced, the pale yellow flowers are in clusters of few, mostly along leafy twigs, sometimes terminal.

A New Zealand variety of another Australian species, **P. prunifolia edgerleyi** (syn. *P. edgerleyi*) differs from the typical species in being not over about 3 feet tall, and more or less straggling. Its broadly-elliptic to elliptic-oblong, slightly-toothed leaves are ½ to 1 inch long by ¼ to ½ inch wide. Their margins are not recurved. Their upper surfaces are scratchy-hairy, their lower ones covered with white hairs, and along the veins with brown hairs. Without petals, the pale flowers are in many axillary and terminal clusters. New Zealand **P. rugosa** is narrowly erect and up to 12 feet tall. Its blunt leaves, ½ inch to 2 inches long by ¼ to ½ inch wide, are elliptic to oblong-lanceolate. Their undersides are thickly clothed with white hairs, and have brown hairs along the veins. The pale, petal-less flowers are in numerous terminal and axillary clusters.

Flowers with petals are characteristic of the kinds now to be described. Tasmanian *P. elliptica* and New Zealand *P. kumeraho* are similar. The first differs from the second in having on the veins of its leaves and on its calyx tubes stellate (starlike) hairs with long, soft rays. Up to about 9 feet tall, these shrubs have oblong to broad-elliptic leaves up to 2 to 2½ inches long and white-hairy on their undersides. The bright yellow flowers, ¼ inch wide, are in round-topped clusters up to 4 inches across. Related *P. hamiltonii*, of New Zealand, differs in having leaves that taper at both ends, with only their main veins obvious, and in its flowers having white petals. Australian *P. lanigera*, a shrub up to 10 feet tall, has shoots and under leaf surfaces densely-clothed with often rust-colored down. Pointed and ovate-lanceolate to oblong, the leaves are 3 to 5 inches long and from a little under to somewhat over one-half as wide. The many small yellow-petaled flowers, in rounded clusters 2 to 4 inches wide, are near the ends of the shoots.

Garden and Landscape Uses and Cultivation. Not hardy in the north, in milder climates pomaderrises are attractive shrubs for general ornamental purposes. They prosper in ordinary to poorish soils, in sun or part-day shade, and are increased by cuttings of firm, half-ripened, but not hard and woody, young shoots and by seed.

POMATO, POTOMATO, or TOPATO. These names refer to plants obtained by grafting tomatoes onto potatoes and vice versa. Such specimens are easily achieved, but, except perhaps as teaching aids, are curiosities without practical merit. When the potato is the understock and the tomato the scion the grafted specimen may produce both potatoes and tomatoes, but not in worthwhile amounts or sizes. Neither potatoes nor tomatoes are borne by potatoes grafted onto tomatoes.

POMEGRANATE is *Punica granatum*. The pomegranate melon is *Cucumis melo dudaim*.

POMETTE BLEUE is *Crataegus brachyacantha*.

POMME BLANCHE is *Psoralea esculenta*.

POMPELMOUS is *Citrus maxima*.

POMPON. Some double-flowered varieties of chrysanthemums, dahlias, zinnias, and certain other plants are classified as pompons. The flower heads of these, also known as pompons, are small and buttonlike and have their florets arranged regularly and compactly.

PONCIRUS (Ponci-rus)—Trifoliate-Orange. The one species of *Poncirus*, a native of

northern China, is closely related to the orange and the lemon, which belong in the genus *Citrus*, but from *Citrus* it differs in having deciduous leaves each of three leaflets, flowers borne on shoots older than those of the current year, and other technical details. A member of the rue family RUTACEAE, it has a name derived from the French *poncire*, a kind of citron.

This species is much hardier than any member of the genus *Citrus*; in sheltered locations it thrives outdoors in the vicinity of New York City. Because of its hardiness it is much used as an understock for grafting citrus fruits and has been hybridized with *Citrus sinensis* to obtain hardier citrus fruits called citranges. Highly attractive as an ornamental the trifoliate-orange does not have edible fruits.

The trifoliate-orange (*P. trifoliata* syn. *Aegle sepiaria*) is a small tree or tall shrub densely- and intricately-branched and with long, stout, very sharp and strong spines that, like the branches, are green and impart to the plant something of the appearance of an evergreen, even in winter. The leaves, often in tufts from old wood, have slightly-winged stalks and three elliptic to obovate leaflets, the central one 1½ to 2½ inches long, the side ones 1 inch to 2 inches long. The flowers, borne in spring, are white, deliciously fragrant, and 1½ to 2 inches in diameter. Their pet-

Poncirus trifoliata (flowers)

Poncirus trifoliata (fruits)

als are conspicuously narrowed toward their lower ends, and their stamens are quite separate and not joined at their bases. Sometimes some of the stamens are more or less petal-like, but when this occurs the flowers are commonly smaller and less handsome. A highly decorative feature of this unusual shrub or small tree is the fruits that develop freely even as far north as Long Island and other areas near New York City. They are unmistakably small oranges, but with skins as fuzzy as a peach and dull, but pleasingly deep lemon-yellow. Characteristically they are spherical and 1½ to 2 inches in diameter; less often they are lemon-shaped. The peel is strongly, disagreeably flavored, but nicely orange-scented. The pulp is scanty, dryish, and contains many seeds.

A curious variety, *P. t. monstrosa* is cultivated in Japan particularly as a bonsai (dwarfed, container-grown specimens). This is naturally a dwarf with twisted branched, curved spines and very small leaves, with the side leaflets often merely filaments with nodelike thickenings that are oil glands.

Garden and Landscape Uses. This rigid shrub or small tree is decorative at all seasons, but especially in spring when in bloom and in fall when its fruits ripen. It is excellent as a single specimen on a lawn or in a shrub border and forms an effective

A hedge of *Poncirus trifoliata*

hedge. Care should be taken, however, to locate it where passersby are unlikely to be harmed by its formidable thorns. It needs a sunny location and is best suited to well-drained, but reasonably moist, neutral or somewhat acid, loamy soils. It does not prosper on sandy or alkaline soils. For garden decoration, large-flowered individuals should be chosen. Cut branches bearing flowers or fruits can be used with good effect in floral arrangements.

Cultivation. The trifoliate-orange is easily raised from seeds taken from the fruits as soon as they are ripe and sown immediately in a protected bed outdoors, in a cold frame, or in a pot or flat indoors, in sandy, peaty soil. It may also be propagated by summer cuttings. Little or no pruning is needed when the plant is grown as a free-standing specimen, but it stands well any cutting back or shearing that is needed, as is the case when it is grown as a restricted hedge or if it becomes desirable to reduce an overgrown and lanky specimen. Pruning may be done any time, but immediately after flowering is probably best.

POND. The word pond forms parts of the common names of these plants: pond-apple (*Annona glabra*), pond-cypress (*Taxodium distichum nutans*), pond-lily (*Nymphaea*), pond nut (*Nelumbo lutea*), pond spice (*Litsea*), and yellow pond-lily (*Nuphar*).

PONDWEED. See Potamogeton. The Cape pondweed is *Aponogeton distachyus*.

PONGAMIA (Pon-gàmia) — Poonga Oil Tree or Poona Oil Tree. There is only one species of *Pongamia*, of the pea family LEGUMINOSAE. It is a deciduous or semideciduous tree native of seashores and river banks in the Old World tropics and subtropics from Asia to Australia. Its botanical designation is a Latinized form of its Malabar name, *pongam*. The colloquial names allude to its seeds being the source of poonga or poona oil, once extensively employed in India and elsewhere in Asia for illumination and medicinally. From its roots a fish poison is obtained and its foliage is said to make good cattle fodder. In Ceylon this tree is used to shade tea plantations and there and elsewhere its young stems and foliage are used to fertilize tea and rice.

Pongamia pinnata at the Fairchild Tropical Garden, Miami, Florida

The poonga oil tree (*P. pinnata*) has a spreading, moderately dense crown and attains a maximum height of about 70 feet. Its hairless, shining leaves, 6 to 12 inches long, have five or seven short-stalked, ovate to elliptic leaflets 2 to 5 inches long, arranged in opposite pairs on a slender midrib that ends in a leaflet. When bruised they emit a strong odor. The expanding new leaves are pink. Pea-shaped, the pale lilac, pink, or sometimes white blooms are in loose racemes up to 5 inches long. Individuals are about ½ inch long. They have a broad standard or banner petal and a blunt keel of petals that cohere at their tips. The ten stamens are united. The fruits are somewhat sickle-shaped, woody pods about 2½ inches long by one-half as broad, each containing one flat seed. The pods do not open naturally to free the seeds, which are released only when the pods rot.

Garden and Landscape Uses. Among tropical shade trees this is one of the most ornamental. Shapely, and agreeable both in and out of bloom, it has the advantage of being so deep-rooted that grass grows well beneath it. For planting near the sea the poonga oil tree is especially well adapted. It is also excellent beside streams, lakes, and ponds. Although in its natural habitat the poonga oil tree invariably grows near water, it succeeds when planted under much drier conditions; in India it is a favorite roadside tree even in fairly arid regions. The poonga oil tree is appropriate for avenues and as a lawn specimen. Within its home territory it is often planted as a street and shade tree and for these purposes it is employed in other warm climates, including the southernmost parts of the United States. It grows in any ordinary soil.

Cultivation. The care of this tree makes no particular demands of the gardener. It is propagated by seed and by cuttings. In India, a common method of increase is to stick branches into damp ground, where they root without trouble.

PONTEDERIA (Ponted-èria) — Pickerel Weed. The name of these western hemisphere freshwater aquatics, of which there are about eight species, commemorates the Italian botanist Gulio Pontedera, who died in 1757. They belong in the pickerel weed family PONTEDERIACEAE, which also includes the water-hyacinth (*Eichhornia*) and *Reussia*.

Unlike water-hyacinths, the sorts of *Pontederia* are not free floating, but root into the bottoms of shallow waters and into marshes. From creeping rhizomes arise basal leaves and flowering stems that have a solitary complete leaf and, higher up, a bladeless sheathlike leaf. The two-lipped flowers are in spikelike panicles. From those of *Reussia* they differ in both lips being three-lobed. They are predominantly blue, varying to white, with the uppermost perianth lobe marked with yellow. There is no clear distinction between calyx and corolla, hence all the petal-like parts are referred to as perianth lobes. Each flower has six stamens, three of which protrude. There is one style. The fruits are achene-like.

The common pickerel weed (*P. cordata*) is a handsome summer-bloomer indigenous from Nova Scotia to Ontario, Minnesota, Florida, and Texas. It has many upright or nearly upright stems and forms compact clumps of considerable size. Up to 3½ feet in height, it has lower stem leaves similar to those that spring directly from the thick rootstocks. They have long fleshy stalks and broadly-heart-shaped to lanceolate blades that may be 1 foot long

Pontederia cordata, a native stand

Pontederia cordata (flowers)

or longer, but often are smaller. The handsome spires of rich violet-blue blooms, 3 to 6 inches long, are displayed to advantage well above the foliage. Crowded in spikes, the blooms are funnel-shaped, with perianth lobes about ⅓ inch long. Variety *P. c. angustifolia* (syn. *P. montevidensis*) has lanceolate to linear-lanceolate leaves with tapered bases.

Garden Uses. As an ornamental, pickerel weed ranks high. It has quite lovely foliage and beautiful flowers of a most attractive hue. A sturdy grower, it spreads satisfactorily, but not so rampantly that it is likely to become a pest. It provides height and so contrasts well with water-lilies and other floating-leaved aquatics. It blooms over a long summer season. Pickerel weed accommodates as well to tub culture as to mud bottoms in shallow water.

Cultivation. A fertile, loamy soil, such as suits water-lilies, and locations in full sun are highly satisfactory. Tubs 1 foot or more deep are appropriate containers. Planting is done in spring, the most suitable depth is for the roots to be covered with 3 or 4 inches of water. After fall frosts blacken the foliage, the stems are cut off at water level and removed. Container-grown clumps that become crowded and show signs of deterioration should be divided and replanted in new soil in spring. Propagation is easy by division, also by seeds kept moist from the time of gathering until they are sown in pots of peaty, loamy soil. After the seeds are sown they are covered with 1 inch of sand and their containers submerged under about 2 inches of water.

PONTEDERIACEAE — Pickerel Weed Family. The thirty species of monocotyledons that constitute this family belong in six genera. The family is native to tropical, subtropical, and warm-temperate regions, but not Europe. Its members are fresh-water aquatics that float, or are erect and root into soil bottoms of ponds, lakes, and other sluggish, fresh waters.

Herbaceous perennials, the sorts of this family have floating or submersed leaves, the latter sometimes reduced to leafstalks. The flowers, usually in spikes or spikelike arrangements and more or less asymmetrical, have three each sepals and petals, three or six stamens, one long style, and a sometimes slightly three-lobed stigma. The fruits are capsules or small nuts. Cultivated genera include *Eichhornia*, *Heteranthera*, *Pontederia*, and *Reussia*.

PONTHIEVA (Pon-thieva). The genus *Ponthieva*, of the orchid family ORCHIDACEAE, is native to tropical, subtropical, and warm-temperate parts of the Americas. It comprises about twenty-five species. Its name commemorates Henri de Ponthieu, an eighteenth-century French botanist.

Ponthievas are mostly ground orchids, but a few species perch on trees as epiphytes. Characteristically, they have rhizomes, a cluster of basal leaves, and an erect raceme of small flowers.

Native in wet woodland soils from Virginia to the West Indies, Mexico, Central America, and South America, *P. racemosa* has fleshy, oblong-elliptic to nearly lanceolate leaves up to 7 inches long, but often smaller, and a flowering stalk 6 inches to 2 feet tall. The whitish-green flowers, often with bright green veins, and up to a little over ¼ inch long, open in succession over a long period. Usually epiphytic, *P. maculata,* of Colombia and Venezuela, is softly-hairy throughout. It has generally two elliptic-lanceolate leaves and a flowering stalk 1 foot to 1½ feet tall with up to twenty nearly 1¼-inch-wide flowers, with a reddish dorsal sepal, violet- or green-spotted white lateral sepals, and brown-striped, golden-yellow petals and lip.

Ponthieva maculata

Ponthieva maculata (flowers)

Garden Uses and Cultivation. The sorts of this genus, probably none easy to grow and with little information regarding their cultural needs available, are likely to appeal only to fanciers of rare orchids. For ground-inhabiting species, such as *P. racemosa*, treatment that satisfies *Spiranthes* and *Habenaria* is suggested. Epiphytes, such as *P. maculata*, may respond best to the conditions and care appropriate for *Cynorkis*.

PONY TAIL is *Beaucarnea recurvata*

POONA OIL OR POONGA OIL TREE is *Pongamia pinnata.*

POOR-MAN'S-ORCHID. See Schizanthus.

POOR MAN'S WEATHERGLASS or SCARLET PIMPERNEL is *Anagallis arvensis.*

POPINAC is *Acacia farnesiana*. The white-popinac is *Leucaena glauca.*

POPLAR. See Populus. The Queensland-poplar is *Homalanthus populifolius.*

POPPY. Besides members of the genus *Papaver*, which are correctly identified as poppies, other plants have the word poppy as parts of their common names. Among such are these: blue-poppy (*Meconopsis betonicifolia*), bush-poppy or tree-poppy (*Dendromecon*), California-poppy (*Eschscholzia californica*), celandine-poppy (*Stylophorum diphyllum*), flaming-poppy or wind-poppy (*Stylomecon heterophylla*), harebell-poppy (*Meconopsis quintuplinervia*), horned-poppy or sea-poppy (*Glaucium*), Matilija-poppy (*Romneya*), Mexican tulip-poppy (*Hunnemannia fumariaefolia*), plume-poppy (*Macleaya cordata*), poppy anemone (*Anemone coronaria*), poppy-mallow (*Callirhoe*), prickly-poppy (*Argemone*), snow-poppy (*Eomecon chionantha*), water-poppy (*Hydrocleys nymphoides*), Welsh-poppy (*Meconopsis cambrica*), and yellow Chinese-poppy (*Meconopsis integrifolia*).

POPPY. True poppies belong to the genus *Papaver*, and their species are described under that entry in this Encyclopedia. Other plants that have poppy as a part of their common name, such as California-poppy, prickly-poppy, and blue-poppy, are discussed under their generic names, which for those just mentioned are *Eschscholzia*, *Argemone*, and *Meconopsis*, respectively. Here, we shall deal with the garden and landscape uses and cultivation of true poppies. They include some of the most beautiful and easily grown flower garden ornamentals.

Poppies present colorful displays of bloom. Some kinds, notably oriental poppies and Iceland poppies, are excellent cut flowers. Others have blooms that drop their petals so quickly that they are of little use in flower arrangements. The tall kinds are admirable for sunny beds where the soil is freely drained. The dainty alpine poppy (*P. alpinum*) responds to similar conditions in rock gardens. There are annual, biennial, and perennial poppies.

Brilliant; single, semidouble, and double; pink, salmon, carmine, scarlet, crimson, and white flowers, without black at their centers and without black stamens, are produced in abundance by Shirley poppies, a horticultural strain of *Papaver rhoeas*, the poppy of Flander's fields. From 1 foot to 2 feet tall, these have blooms 3 inches or more in diameter. They were developed by an English amateur gardener, the Reverend W. Wilks, from a single aberrant plant of *P. rhoeas* that he found growing in a field.

The Shirley poppy is the only annual kind commonly cultivated. This resents transplanting. For the best results sow

Oriental poppies: (a) In a garden

(b) Flowers

seeds in early spring where the plants are to stay, and rake them into the surface soil so that they are covered to a depth of about ⅛ inch. Before the seedlings become crowded thin them to 9 inches to 1 foot apart. Cultivate the surface soil between them shallowly to admit air and discourage weeds. If a little support is needed this can be given by inserting twiggy brushwood stakes between the plants as inconspicuously as possible. With the coming of hot, humid weather flowering is reduced and finally ceases. Prompt removal of faded flowers prevents seed formation and prolongs the blooming season.

Oriental poppies are among the showiest and most stately hardy herbaceous perennials. They are admired for their foliage and gorgeous blooms, the latter lifted well above the leafage to heights of 2 or 3 feet from the ground. Unfortunately, the leaves die down for a period in high summer and leave what can be unsightly gaps in flower beds. This can be circumvented, at least to some extent, by planting, as neighbors, plants that will sprawl or cascade over the vacant spots or will grow tall enough to at least partially hide them. Suitable for these purposes are perennial baby's breath (*Gypsophila paniculata*), sealavender (*Limonium*), obedient plant (*Physostegia*), tall veronicas, and *Salvia azurea*. Oriental poppies flower in June and for a comparatively short period, along with bearded irises and perennial lupines. Then, their great crepe-paper-like blooms are among the outstanding glories of gardens. Many varieties offered by dealers in hardy perennials are described in catalogs.

In color they vary from deepest blood-red to mahogany-red, claret-red, orange-red, exquisite rose-pinks, salmon-pink, and white. Some kinds have double flowers. White-flowered varieties are generally less robust than others. In size, the blooms range from 5 to 8 inches in diameter.

For the best effects locate oriental poppies singly or in groups of three some little distance back from the front of the border. They are not well adapted for planting in large groups. Before planting, prepare the soil thoroughly. Make it agreeable to a depth of at least 1 foot. Do this by spading it deeply and mixing in liberal amounts of compost, peat moss, or very well-rotted manure, and some bonemeal. Plant in summer when the poppies are without foliage, not in spring or fall. Space the plants about 1½ feet apart. Newly planted oriental poppies take hold rather slowly, and usually it is the second summer before they bloom well. They have thick, fleshy roots and resent being transplanted. Once established and doing well, unless transplanting becomes quite necessary, it is best to leave them undisturbed. Routine care is not arduous. A spring application of a complete garden fertilizer encourages good growth. Neat staking before the blooms open may be needed to forestall storm damage. In cold climates, a protective winter cover of salt hay or branches of evergreens is desirable.

To raise new plants, old ones can be dug up in early fall or spring and divided, but root cuttings afford a more convenient means of increase. Make these in summer as soon as the foliage has died. Cut thick roots into pieces 3 to 4 inches long. Plant

these vertically (with the end of the root that was originally nearest the crown of the plant up) or horizontally, covered to a depth of ½ to 1 inch, in sandy soil in a cold frame or nursery bed outdoors. Keep the soil moderately moist, but not wet. Through the winter protect from heavy freezing with a mulch of branches of evergreens, salt hay, or other suitable material, and in spring plant in rows in a nursery bed where the young propagations can complete a season's growth before being transferred to their permanent locations. Oriental poppies are also easily raised from seeds, but seedlings of horticultural varieties must not be expected to duplicate their parents. The majority are likely to have orange-red flowers. Sow seeds shallowly and thinly in a cold frame or outdoors in finely pulverized soil in spring. Do not transplant until fall. Then, either set the seedlings where they are to remain permanently or transfer them to a nursery bed for a year. The last procedure gives the opportunity to weed out less ornamental individuals before planting in the display garden.

Iceland poppies are among the daintiest of the clan, admirable for garden decoration, in beds by themselves or grouped in mixed flower borders, and for cut flowers. Modern strains come in a wide variety of delicate and rich colors in the yellow, orange, apricot, and pink range, and white, some with double flowers. They have wiry stems and blooms 4 to 5 inches in diameter. Technically, Iceland poppies are perennials, but they often give the best results when treated as biennials. Sow seeds thinly and shallowly in late spring or early summer in sandy soil in a cold frame or outdoors, and as soon as the seedlings are big enough to handle transplant them 6 inches apart, in rows about 1 foot apart, in a sunny, well-drained nursery bed where the soil is porous, but nourishing. In fall

Iceland poppies

or the following spring transfer the plants to their blooming stations, making sure that they will receive full sun and that the soil is fertile and decidedly porous. An alternative method is, instead of transplanting the seedlings to a nursery bed, to thin them out, leave those that remain undisturbed until fall, and then plant them in their final locations.

Perennial, usually rather short-lived, or sometimes biennial poppies of the *P. atlanticum* relationship, including *P. lateritium*, *P. rupifragum*, *P. pilosum*, and *P. apokrinomenon*, prevailingly have long-stalked, crinkly-petaled blooms in brick-red to orange-red, apricot, tangerine, and umber-yellow shades, smaller than those of Shirley poppies, but not less fragile. These flourish in a variety of soils, provided they are not excessively wet, in full sun. In the main they give of their best where the earth is lean rather than rich in nutrients. Too fat a diet results in too lush growth and a shortened life span. Often, these poppies self-sow with some degree of abandon. Use them in informal areas, in higher, more distant parts of rock gardens, in bays in front of shrub borders, and with other plants to achieve flowery meadow effects.

The alpine poppy (*P. alpinum*) is in a class by itself. In effect a miniature Iceland poppy, it belongs very definately in rock gardens and perhaps nowhere else, unless it be atop a planted wall or between the crevices of flagstone paving where its roots can reach to a porous stratum beneath. This kind appreciates limestone soils, but is not so finicky that the satisfaction of this liking becomes a must. Nevertheless it is all to the good to mix peanut-size chips of limestone liberally with the soil in which it is to root. You will get the best results with this one by sowing seeds where the plants are to remain and pulling out surplus seedlings. It does not take kindly to transplanting.

POPULUS (Pópu-lus)—Cottonwood, Poplar, Aspen. Together with willows (*Salix*), poplars constitute the willow family SALICACEAE. Unlike willows, the majority of which are shrubs, some evergreen, poplars are all deciduous trees. From willows they differ in their catkins being pendulous. Thirty-five species of north temperate regions comprise *Populus*, which name is its ancient Latin one. In addition, there are numerous natural hybrids and some man-made ones bred to secure superior trees for paper pulp and other commercial purposes. The prevalence of hybrids and the fact that poplars are nearly always unisexual and bloom when the trees are leafless, add to the complexity of identifying the sorts of this genus.

Poplars have alternate, undivided leaves and tiny, petal-less flowers in separate catkins of all males or all females. The males have many stamens, the females two to four stigmas. The fruits are small capsules containing seeds surrounded by tufts of white cottony hairs that aid in their dispersion by wind. This cottony covering is especially noticeable in kinds known in North America as cottonwoods. Rapid growers, poplars are exploited for their lumber, which is used for paper pulp, matches, excelsior, boxes, crates, and other purposes. It is of interest that the "willow trees" of Psalms 137 : 2 upon which the Israelite captives in Babylon hung their harps and wept in their discomfort were quite surely poplars (*P. euphratica*). A mistranslation of the Bible into English is the cause of the error.

The kinds of poplars called cottonwoods have deeply-furrowed, grayish bark, leaves with very flattened leafstalks that allow the blades to dance with the slightest movement of the air, and seeds with conspicuous amounts of cottony hairs. The sorts called aspens also have quaking leaves, but their bark is smooth and grayish or greenish. Balsam poplars are distinguished by the strong balsamic odor of their large and very sticky winter buds. White poplars have coarsely-toothed or lobed leaves with a dense felt of white hairs on their undersides.

The best known cottonwood (*P. deltoides*) is an open-headed, very hardy tree, native from Quebec to North Dakota, Kansas, Florida, and Texas. Attaining a height of about 90 feet, this has triangular-ovate or broad-ovate leaves with flattened stalks and margins coarsely-toothed and fringed with hairs. They are bright green on both sides. This species is commonly planted in the Midwest for shade and windbreaks, and, provided its roots have access to moisture, it withstands high temperatures, drying winds, and winter cold better than most trees. Because the cottony seeds of female specimens create considerable litter the planting of males only is suggested. Short-lived, this cotton-

Populus deltoides

Populus deltoides (trunk)

Populus deltoides (leaves and young fruits)

wood cannot be recommended for planting where superior trees prosper, but it is useful in regions too dry for most.

The black poplar (*P. nigra*) belongs to the same section of the genus as *P. deltoides*. Native to Europe and western Asia and long cultivated, it generally has a short trunk with deeply-fissured bark, a pyramidal head of wide-spreading branches, and orange twigs. Its ovate-lozenge-shaped, long-pointed leaves are without lobes and have very flattened stalks; they flutter in the slightest breeze. Attaining a height of 100 feet, this tree is extremely hardy.

The Lombardy poplar (*P. nigra italica*) is the best known of several variants of the black poplar. A narrow tree of almost exclamation mark outline, it has an erect,

Populus nigra italica, a group of three

rigid trunk and branches. It was first brought to the United States in 1784. Although long a favorite for screens and vertical accents, it is so subject to a serious die-back disease that it is not recommended as a permanent tree, but is sometimes useful as a quick-growing screen to last for twenty years or so. A rare variant of the black poplar, *P. n. thevestina*, looks much like the Lombardy poplar, but has bark as white as that of a birch. Little known in America or the British Isles, it is common in Kashmir and Algeria. Columnar *P. n. elegans* (syn. *P. n. plantierensis*), with downy twigs and leafstalks, is probably a hybrid of *P. nigra* and the birch-leaved poplar (*P. n. betulifolia*). This last differs from the typical black poplar in having smaller leaves and downy young branches and leafstalks.

The Carolina poplar (*P. canadensis eugenei*) has botanical and common names that suggest American origin. Actually this, a male, is one of several forms of a hybrid between *P. deltoides* and *P. nigra* or one of the latter's varieties, the first of which is believed to have originated in France about the middle of the eighteenth century. The Carolina poplar is narrower than other members of this hybrid complex, to which the name *P. canadensis* is applied. Despite the fact that the Carolina poplar is very hardy and has been widely planted as a street tree, it cannot be recommended. It has all the faults associated with poplars mentioned earlier, causing

considerable litter by dropping catkins, leaves, and twigs. The Carolina poplar grows to a height of 100 to 150 feet and has smooth, triangular, long-pointed, glossy leaves about 4 inches long, sparsely-fringed with hairs and reddish when they first appear.

The Berlin poplar (*P. berolinensis*), a hybrid between *P. laurifolia* and the Lombardy poplar, very hardy, has a columnar head of upright branches. It has lozenge- or ovate-lozenge-shaped, bright green leaves paler on their undersides than above and with round stalks. This is one of the best trees for the northern prairies.

The white poplar or abele (**P. alba**) is a Eurasian with an irregular, open, wide-spreading head and up to 100 feet in height. It has whitish bark on its younger branches and ovate leaves, lobed or

Populus alba: (a) In summer

(b) In winter

coarsely-toothed, glistening white beneath, grayish-green on their upper surfaces. In fall its foliage turns reddish or red. The Bolleana poplar (*P. a. pyramidalis*) is a handsome narrow variety with somewhat the aspect of the Lombardy poplar. Because it is less subject to disease than

Populus alba (flowers)

Populus alba (leaves)

Populus alba pyramidalis

the last it can be used advantageously as a substitute for it. Variety *P. a. nivea* has leaves even more intensely white beneath than the typical white poplar. The leaves of *P. a. richardii* have yellow upper surfaces. The white poplar and its varieties withstand seaside conditions well and hot, dry summers and cold winters. They produce sucker growths for some distance around the trunk and these can be something of a nuisance.

The balsam poplar or tacamahac (*P. balsamifera* syn. *P. tacamahacca*), of North America, is an ornamental inferior to certain of its Asian close relatives. Ranging in the wild from Labrador to Alaska, New York, Michigan, and Oregon, it attains a height of 100 feet. It has rather thick, ovate to ovate-lanceolate leaves. Allied to the last and one of the handsomest of poplars, *P. maximowiczii*, of Japan and the nearby Asian mainland, has a broad open head up to 90 feet in height and dull green elliptic or nearly round leaves, whitish beneath and up to 5 inches long. It is the first poplar to leaf out in spring. Another balsam poplar, a native of China, *P. simonii* is a slender, dense-headed tree up to 35 feet in height with rhombic-ovate leaves up to 5 inches long, whitish or pale green beneath. Its variety *P. s. fastigiata* is narrower than the type; *P. s. pendula* has drooping branches. Yet a third beautiful Asian is western Chinese *P. lasiocarpa*, which has ovate leaves 6 inches to 1 foot long, with red stalks and midribs and light green, pubescent undersides. It attains a height of 60 feet.

Balm of Gilead (*P. gileadensis*), of which only female trees are known, is probably a hybrid between *P. balsamifera* and *P. deltoides*, although some authorities believe it to be a selected form of *P. balsamifera subcordata*. Attaining a height of about 60 feet and producing suckers freely around its base, this has a wide crown and thick, angled, brown-hairy twigs. Its leaves, 4 to 6½ inches long and densely-hairy along the veins of their undersides, are triangular-ovate with usually heart-shaped bases.

The American quaking aspen (*P. tremuloides*) has small, ovate to nearly round, flat-stalked leaves that tremble with every breath of wind. This, which probably has the widest natural distribution of any tree in North America, is seen at its best in groves. It does not make a good solitary specimen. In fall its foliage changes to a fine yellow.

Other poplars include these: *P. canescens*, the gray poplar of Eurasia, much resembles *P. alba*, but has smaller leaves with gray undersides. *P. fremontii*, a cottonwood of western North America, is up to 90 feet tall and similar to *P. deltoides*. It is adapted to dry alkaline soils and desert conditions. *P. grandidentata*, the large-toothed aspen of eastern North America, attains heights up to 75 feet, but has a rather narrow head. It is similar to *P. tremula*, with larger, more coarsely-toothed leaves. *P. laurifolia*, of Siberia, 45 feet tall, has lanceolate to elliptic-ovate leaves with grayish undersurfaces. *P. sieboldii*, the Japanese aspen, which closely resembles *P. tremula*, is up to 70 feet tall. *P. tremula*,

Populus grandidentata

the European aspen, which closely resembles *P. tremuloides*, is indigenous to Eurasia and North Africa. *P. trichocarpa*, the Western balsam poplar, and one of the tallest American trees, ranges from Alaska to California. Specimens 225 feet in height have been recorded. This is similar to *P. balsamifera*.

Populus trichocarpa, a small specimen in southern California

Garden and Landscape Uses. As a group poplars cannot be highly recommended for home landscaping except that a few sorts are useful in regions where better trees will not thrive. Their chief asset, besides the adaptability of some to difficult climates, is their rapid rate of growth. Disadvantages include relatively short lives, brittle branches, and roots that range widely and are given to lifting pavements and clogging drains.

Cultivation. Poplars prefer dampish soil or at least sites where their roots can reach moisture. They are usually propagated by hardwood cuttings, which root without

difficulty; indeed pieces of dormant shoots, planted outdoors in fall or early spring with just the tips protruding from the ground and kept watered, will often root where set. Trees can be raised from seeds sown as soon as ripe, for they soon lose their vitality, but seeds are often produced rather sparingly and because of hybridity may give rise to a variable progeny. In the early years, pruning consists of shaping the young tree by removing lower branches to establish a clear trunk and of encouraging the development of a shapely head of well-placed major limbs.

Diseases and Pests. Poplars are subject to several serious canker diseases and some to an equally serious die-back disease. They may suffer from a branch gall, leaf blister, and various leaf spot diseases as well as from rust and powdery mildew. The chief insect pests are aphids, caterpillars, scale, borers, and willow leaf beetle.

PORANA (Porán-a) — Christmas Vine or White-Corallita or Snow Creeper. This genus of fifteen species of the morning glory family CONVOLVULACEAE contains one sort popular in Florida and other warm regions, as well as some lesser known kinds of horticultural merit. Restricted as a native of tropical and subtropical parts of Africa, Asia, and Australia, *Porana* has a name of obscure origin, perhaps derived from a native East Indian name. The common name white-corallita is somewhat misleading because *Porana* is not botanically related to the true corallita (*Antigonon*).

Poranas are twining vines with alternate, usually heart-shaped, lobeless leaves and panicles or clusters of small flowers with calyxes of five sepals, some or all of which enlarge after the blooms fade, and white, blue, or purple, bell- or funnel-shaped, five-lobed corollas. There are five stamens and a solitary, sometimes two-lobed style. The fruits are capsules.

Most commonly cultivated, the Christmas vine, white-corallita, or snow creeper (*P. paniculata*), of India, is a robust, silvery-hairy, freely-branching evergreen with stems 20 to 30 feet long and pointed-heart-shaped leaves 3 to 6 inches long. Its white, funnel-shaped blooms up to ⅓ inch across, with lobeless styles, are in panicles from the leaf axils. They are borne in such profusion that they suggest blanketing snow. In this species only three of the sepals enlarge as the fruits develop. The latter are hairy. Another kind, *P. volubilis*, of Burma and Malaya, is similar to *P. paniculata*, but its flowers have two-lobed styles and all five of the sepals enlarge in fruit.

The annual snow creeper (*P. racemosa*) is rare in cultivation. Native to India and Burma, it has slender-pointed, hairy or smooth, heart-shaped leaves 3 to 4 inches long and small, white, starry flowers with spreading corolla lobes, in leafy, loose panicles.

Garden and Landscape Uses and Cultivation. These are excellent vines for covering surfaces and supports where there is opportunity for their stems to twine. They are useful as porch screenings and fence covers and grow without difficulty in ordinary soils in sunny locations. The Christmas vine is usually propagated by cuttings and layering, and so is *P. volubilis,* but if seeds are available they could undoubtedly be used to secure increase. The annual *P. racemosa* is raised from seeds handled in the same manner as those of morning glory (*Ipomoea*).

PORCELAIN BERRY is *Ampelopsis brevipedunculata.*

PORCUPINE SHRUB is *Barleria lupulina.*

PORFIRIA (Por-firia). One Mexican species of the cactus family CACTACEAE, by conservative botanists included in *Mammillaria* and intermediate between that genus and *Ariocarpus,* constitutes *Porfiria.* The name commemorates Jose de la Cruz Porfirio Diaz, President of Mexico, who died in 1915.

The plant bodies or stems of *P. coahuilensis* (syns. *P. schwartzii, Mammillaria coahuilensis*) are flattened-spherical. Solitary and approximately 1¾ inches in diameter, they have fleshy taproots, contain milky sap, and have sprouting from them bluegreen nipple-like protrusions or tubercles nearly 1 inch long and with triangular bases. At the tip of each tubercle is a starry cluster of about sixteen slender, graywhite, ¼-inch-long radial spines and a brown-tipped, stouter central one. The bell- to funnel-shaped blooms come from near the tops of the plants. About 1¼ inches wide and open by day, they have corolla tubes, ovaries, and fruits naked of scales or bristles. Their petals are white or pinkish with a deeper pink central band. The stamens are whitish, the style pink. The stigma is five-lobed, the fruits berry-like.

Garden Uses and Cultivation. These are as for *Mammillaria.* For additional information see Cactuses.

PORO-PORO is *Solanum aviculare.*

PORTEA (Pòrt-ea). There are six species of *Portea.* Endemic to eastern Brazil, they are evergreen herbaceous perennials of the pineapple family BROMELIACEAE. The name honors the nineteenth-century French naturalist Dr. Marius Porte, who first brought *Portea* into cultivation.

Porteas have rosettes of scaly, strap-shaped, toothed leaves. Their branched panicles, from the centers of the rosettes, have brightly colored bracts, and slender-stalked flowers, the three asymmetrical sepals of which are more or less united, and end in long points. Longer than the six stamens and style, the three petals are not united to each other, but each is joined to one stamen. At the bottom of each petal is a pair of fringed scales. The style is three-cleft. The fruits are fleshy berries.

Largest and showiest of the genus, **P.** *leptantha* has rigid leaves with broadly-elliptic sheathing bases, and spine-toothed margins. They are up to 3 feet long by 4 inches wide, tapered to a long spine at the apex. Their upper sides are green and essentially smooth, beneath they are furnished with grayish scales. The stout, much-branched, red flower stalk carries its broad panicle of numerous ¾- to 1-inch-long blooms to heights of 4 feet or more. The flowers have orange-yellow ovaries and yellow or perhaps sometimes brick-red petals. Also cultivated, *P. petropolitana* in bloom is 3 to 4 feet tall. This has rosettes of rigid, spiny-edged, strap-shaped leaves, and lifted on stalks above them, rather compact panicles 1 foot to 1½ feet long of many small flowers with pink-orange, spiny sepals, lavender-tinged white petals, and a lavender style. More graceful and with softer, yellowish-green, black-spined leaves, *P. p. extensa* has looser panicles of bloom. The lavender petals contrast with the bright green ovaries. When fully mature the fruits are dark purple.

Garden and Landscape Uses and Cultivation. The porteas discussed here grow well in Florida, thriving, as in the wild, near the sea and in full sun. They are splendid ornamentals for gardens in the tropics and warm subtropics and may be grown on rocks, attached to trees, or in containers. Unlike those of most bromeliads, their flower stalks remain long after the blooms have gone. If considered objectionable they must be cut off as they cannot be pulled free. For more information see Bromeliads or Bromels.

PORTIA TREE is *Thespesia populnea.*

PORTLANDIA (Port-lándia). Two attractive species of the twenty-five of *Portlandia* are occasionally cultivated. The group consists of tropical evergreen shrubs or small trees of the madder family RUBIACEAE and is native to Mexico and the West Indies. Its name honors a Duchess of Portland, who died in 1785.

Portlandias have thick, leathery, shiny, opposite, undivided leaves, with broad, joined basal appendages (stipules) and large white, purple, or red, often fragrant blooms, solitary or two or three together on stalks from the leaf axils. The calyxes are four- or five-lobed, the corollas funnel- to bell-shaped, with five lobes (petals). There are five stamens. The fruits are more or less egg-shaped leathery capsules.

Probably native to Mexico, *P. platantha,*

up to 3 feet in height, has pointed, elliptic-ovate leaves with broadly-triangular stipules. The white blooms, up to 6 inches long by one-half as wide across the face of the flower, have four calyx lobes and a five-lobed, nearly bell-shaped corolla.

The largest-flowered species is the West Indian *P. grandiflora.* From 6 to 15 feet in height, it has short-stalked, pointed, elliptic-oblong to ovate leaves about 8 inches long by 3½ inches wide with stipules that soon fall. When young, the foliage is reddish. The blooms, often pinkish in bud, open pure white and are funnel-shaped and 6 to 8 inches long by 3 inches wide; they have five corolla lobes. The stamens protrude. The fragrant flowers expand early in the evening and remain attractive for several days. They are reminiscent of Easter lilies or daturas and are attractive to sphinx moths, hummingbirds, and some other birds. In the tropics this species often flowers several times a year.

Portlandia grandiflora

Garden and Landscape Uses. Portlandias are adapted only to warm, frost-free climates and for cultivation in greenhouses. They are resistant to dryish conditions and *P. grandiflora,* at least, thrives in limestone soil. They grow well in full sun or part-day shade. Because their large flowers are easily damaged by wind it is advisable to afford these plants sheltered locations.

Cultivation. Propagation is easy by seeds sown in a temperature of about 70°F. Cuttings planted in a greenhouse propagating bench with bottom heat or under mist also afford means of increase. In greenhouses a minimum winter night temperature of 60°F is needed, and higher temperatures by day and at other seasons. Rich, porous soil kept evenly moist, but not wet, and a humid atmosphere promote good growth. Some shade from strong sun is required. Well-established specimens benefit from regular applications of dilute liquid fertilizer.

PORTUGAL-LAUREL is *Prunus lusitanica*.

PORTUGUESE-SUNDEW is *Drosophyllum lusitanicum*.

PORTULACA (Portulàc-a). Very few of the 200 species of *Portulaca*, of the purslane family PORTULACACEAE, are worthwhile horticulturally. Those of most concern to gardeners are the rose-moss and purslane. The meaning of the name of the genus is uncertain, but it is of Latin derivation. This genus is native to many warm and temperate regions.

The rose-moss (**P. grandiflora**) is a well-known, easy-to-grow annual with prostrate or ascending stems that have tufts of hairs at the joints and are sometimes 1 foot tall but usually lower. The leaves are thick, fleshy, and mostly alternate but sometimes are paired or clustered. The flowers of cultivated forms are 1 inch or more in diameter, single to double, and come in a wide range of bright colors and white, including pale to deep yellow, orange, pink, red, magenta-purple, and variously striped mixtures. Immediately below each bloom is a collar of leaves. Individual flowers are short-lived, but the plants bloom profusely and continuously. The flowers open fully only in sun, in dull weather they remain closed. This species is a native of Brazil.

Portulaca oleracea

Portulaca grandiflora: (a) Single-flowered

(b) Semidouble-flowered

Purslane or pussley (**P. oleracea**) is best known as a pestiferous trailing annual weed that concerns gardeners only because it must be eliminated or controlled. It is, however, edible and may be cooked as "greens" and as a potherb. For this purpose the French upright-growing variety (*P. o. sativa*), which differs markedly in appearance from the wild species, is preferable. Another variety, *P. o. giganthes*, which has double yellow flowers 1 inch in diameter, is sometimes grown as an ornamental. The flowers of purslane are of interest because their sensitive stamens move when touched. Of uncertain provenance, and now widely naturalized, *P. oleracea* is believed to be an original native of western Asia.

Other species worth cultivating as decorative annuals are **P. marginata,** of Venezuela, and a variety of **P. pilosa,** of the southeastern United States and Mexico. The former has thick, red stems and red-margined, spatula-shaped leaves about ¾ inch long, and yellow blooms. The latter has cylindrical leaves ½ inch long, tufts of hairs at the stem joints, and red-purple flowers up to ½ inch in diameter. Variety *P. p. hortualis,* with flowers ¾ inch across, is cultivated.

Garden and Landscape Uses. The French variety of purslane is appropriate for herb gardens and vegetable gardens. The rose-moss and the other kinds discussed here are admirable for edgings, banks, rock gardens, beds, window boxes, porch boxes, and other places, where an easily grown, showy annual fills the need. Full sun and porous, well-drained, not necessarily very fertile soil are needed.

Cultivation. Seeds of the rose-moss are sometimes started indoors and the resulting plants set in their flowering quarters after all danger of frost has passed, but unless some special reason, such as the convenience of setting out plants rather than sowing seeds in window or porch boxes, is relevant, there is no particular advantage in sowing indoors. Usually seeds are broadcast, where the plants are to remain and bloom, by scattering them thinly and raking them lightly into the surface soil. Sowing is not done until the ground is fairly warm and cold weather is past, about the time the first corn is planted. The resulting plants should be thinned to 6 inches to 1 foot apart depending upon the fertility of the soil. French purslane should be sown about the same time as corn in rows 1½ feet apart, and the young plants are thinned to stand 8 to 10 inches apart.

PORTULACACEAE—Purslane Family. Nineteen genera totaling 350 species constitute this cosmopolitan family of dicotyledons. The majority are annuals, some are herbaceous perennials, a few are subshrubs. Most are more or less succulent and hairless or nearly so.

Members of the purslane family, prostrate to erect, have alternate or opposite, undivided, lobeless leaves; when opposite those of each pair sometimes joined at their bases. The flowers, symmetrical or asymmetrical, are in branched clusters, more or less panicle-like arrangements, or sometimes are solitary. They most often have two sepals and commonly four or five, rarely more petals, often notched at their apexes and sometimes joined at their bases. They have few to numerous stamens and a two- or three-parted style. The fruits are capsules. Cultivated genera include *Anacampseros, Calandrinia, Calyptridium, Ceraria, Claytonia, Lewisia, Montia, Portulaca, Portulacaria,* and *Talinum.*

PORTULACARIA (Portulacàr-ia). One of the two species of this South African genus of the purslane family PORTULACACEAE is commonly cultivated. It bears no obvious similarity to portulacas of flower gardens or to purslane or pussley weed, both which belong in the genus *Portulaca*, but the relationship is acknowledged in the name *Portulacaria*, which means resembling *Portulaca*. The plant sometimes named *P. pygmaea* is *Ceraria pygmaea*.

Portulacarias are nonhardy, succulent shrubs with opposite, obovate, fleshy leaves and, in leafy panicles, minute pink flowers. The blooms have two sepals, four or five petals, four to seven stamens, and a stalkless stigma. The fruits are tiny capsules.

The sort cultivated, *P. afra*, 2 to 12 feet tall or sometimes taller, has grayish stems and many spreading and interlacing red-brown, cylindrical, nearly horizontal branches. The leaves, ¼ to ½ inch long,

Portulacaria afra: (a) In South Africa

(b) As a pot plant

are rich shining green, flat above, and rounded on their undersides. The flowers are without decorative importance. Variety *P. a. variegata* has leaves prettily edged with creamy-white and with a thin red line around their margins. Attractive *P. a. tricolor* has pendulous stems and pale green leaves, with conspicuous creamy-white variegation. Their edges are suffused with pink. In *P. a. aurea*, the center of the leaf is yellow and the underside pinkish. Other varieties are *P. a. macrophylla*, with

Portulacaria afra tricolor

Portulacaria afra tricolor in a hanging basket

leaves up to 1 inch long, and *P. a. microphylla*, with leaves much smaller than those of the typical kind. In the wild *P. afra* inhabits dense thickets and provides forage for wild and domestic animals, including elephants.

Garden and Landscape Uses. This shrub and its varieties are excellent for outdoors in warm dry climates where most other succulents thrive and for indoor cultivation in pots and hanging baskets in greenhouses and window gardens. Small specimens are often planted in dish gardens. Where hardy outdoors, *P. afra* is useful for hedges.

Cultivation. Portulacarias thrive in porous, well-drained soil in full sun. They abhor stagnant water about their roots. Indoors they succeed in a wide range of temperatures. Winter minimums of 45 or 50°F at night are sufficient, but higher ones are acceptable. Day temperatures should always be somewhat higher than night ones. Water moderately from spring through fall, never letting the soil remain dry for long periods. In winter, drier soil conditions, but never complete dryness, are in order. Propagation is easy by cuttings. After they are made allow them to

dry for a few days in an airy place out of direct sun before planting them in sand, perlite, or vermiculite.

POSOQUERIA (Poso-quèria) — Needle Flower. Fifteen species of small trees and shrubs constitute *Posoqueria*, native to warm parts of North, Central, and South America, and the West Indies. One is popular in Florida. The group, which belongs to the madder family RUBIACEAE, has a name derived from a native one of Guiana.

Posoquerias have opposite, undivided, hairless leaves and terminal clusters of white, pink, or red, fragrant blooms. The flowers have five-toothed calyxes and long, slender corolla tubes with five spreading lobes (petals). There are five stamens. The fruits are rather large, many-seeded, fleshy berries.

Needle flower (*P. latifolia*) attains heights of 15 to 45 feet. Its lustrous, short-stalked, broad-elliptic to oblong, or ovate, leathery leaves are 3 to 7 inches long. The pendulous clusters of heavily-scented, white blooms, produced abundantly in spring from the branch ends, have been likened in their general effect to giant honeysuckles (*Lonicera*). Each consists of a dozen or more flowers spraying outward from the meeting point of two leaves. Individuals have extremely slender corolla tubes 3 to 6 inches long, from the ends of which the petals spread like spokes of a wheel 1 inch to 1¾ inches in diameter. The translucent, orange-yellow fruits, 1½ to 3 inches in diameter and containing several seeds, are edible, but scarcely palatable. This species is indigenous from Mexico to South America.

Garden and Landscape Uses and Cultivation. The very lovely shrub or small tree described thrives in the tropics and subtropics. Tender to frost, in the United States it is reliably hardy only in Hawaii and parts of Florida. It is beautiful for home gardens and for the ornamentation of parks and suchlike landscapes. For its best satisfaction it needs fertile soil that is well drained. It succeeds under rather dry conditions. Propagation is by seed and by cuttings.

POSSUM-HAW is a vernacular name of *Ilex decidua*, *Viburnum acerifolium*, and *V. nudum*

POT BOUND or ROOT BOUND. Plants that have filled their pots or similar containers with such masses of roots that further growth is restricted and health and vigor can only be maintained, if indeed this is possible, by regular fertilizing are said to be pot bound or root bound.

Some plants, if adequately fertilized, prosper for many years, sometimes indefinitely, and may even bloom more freely when pot bound. Illustrative of the many that thrive in such a condition are agapanthuses, aspidistras, clivias, and numerous ferns and palms. But many other plants, especially those grown as one-season crops, such as cinerarias, chrysanthemums, cyclamens, and greenhouse primulas, suffer serious harm from being allowed to become pot bound before they have undergone their final repotting into containers large enough to satisfy them through the flowering period.

POT MARIGOLD is *Calendula officinalis.*

POT MARJORAM. See Origanum.

POT OFF. The transfer of small plants from pots, pans, or flats in which several to many have been growing to individual pots is called potting off. In a common sequence, seeds are sown indoors, the seedlings are pricked off into community pots, pans, or flats from which later they are potted off.

POT ON. Transferring plants from smaller to larger pots or pans is called potting on.

POTAMOGETON (Potamo-gèton)—Pondweed. Pondweeds are cosmopolitan in their natural distribution. They are aquatic perennials, or perhaps sometimes annuals, normally rooting in the bottoms of ponds and slow-flowing streams and sometimes inhabiting brackish or saline water. They belong in the pondweed family POTAMOGETONACEAE and number about 100 species. The name *Potamogeton* is a modification of an ancient Greek name of some water plant, *potamogeiton,* and is derived from *potamos,* river, and *geiton,* a neighbor.

Pondweeds produce leaves on the underwater parts of their stems and, if they reach the surface, some floating leaves. The latter often differ markedly from the submersed ones. In deep water they have fewer floating leaves than in shallow water. Flowering is often erratic; colonies that have failed to bloom for years are likely to produce freely for one season then lapse into another long non-blooming period. Because they vary greatly in response to different environmental conditions, especially changed light, and because of the prevalence of hybrids, they are not botanically well understood and identification as to species is often very difficult.

Potamogetons have slender rhizomes that in many kinds develop tubers at their ends, branched or branchless stems, and mostly alternate (the uppermost may be opposite) leaves. The tiny inconspicuous flowers are above water or submersed. They are in one or more stalked axillary whorls (circles surrounding the stems). If more than one, the whorls form headlike clusters or interrupted or continuous

spikes. The blooms have neither sepals nor petals. Each consists of four stamens and four pistils.

Several pondweeds found wild in America are cultivated, chiefly in aquariums. Among them is **P. crispus,** a kind without floating leaves, native of Europe and naturalized from Massachusetts to Minnesota, Virginia, and Missouri, often in brackish water. Sparingly-branched, it has 1½- to 3-inch-long, stalkless, linear-oblong leaves with wavy margins. The flowers are in dense spikes ⅓ inch long. The color of its stems and leaves vary, depending upon the kind of water and the light intensity, from emerald-green to brownish-red. Of annual duration, at least in cultivation, this plant propagates freely by scaly resting buds that form at the ends of the stems.

The slender-stemmed, much-branched **P. gramineus** is an exceedingly variable native from Quebec to Alaska, New York, and California, and in Europe. Typically, its stems are slightly flattened and its submersed, stalkless, linear, linear-lanceolate, or obovate leaves are 1½ to 3½ inches long and up to ⅓ inch broad. The floating leaves, elliptic to egg-shaped, are 1 inch to 2 inches long and one-quarter to one-half as wide. The dense, cylindrical flower spikes are ½ to 1 inch or slightly more in length.

Distinct among the species considered here is the totally submersed **P. filiformis,** native from Greenland to Alaska, Pennsylvania, Michigan, Minnesota and Arizona, and in Europe. Much branched from the base, it has erect, narrow-linear or threadlike leaves 2 to 4½ inches in length. Its spikes of bloom are 1 inch to 2 inches in length, with the lower whorls (circles) of flowers distinctly separated. Widely distributed throughout the northern hemisphere, **P. natans** occurs in North America from Quebec to Alaska, Pennsylvania, Indiana, Iowa, Colorado, and California. Its stems are sparsely or not at all branched and have their underwater leaves represented by narrow phyllodes (leafstalks without blades attached). The chief leaves float. Elliptic or egg-shaped, they are 2 to 4 inches long and one-half as broad; their stalks are usually longer than the blades. The flower spikes, dense and cylindrical, are 1 inch to 2 inches long. Also very distinct among pondweeds here considered is **P. perfoliatus,** which ranges as a wildling from Newfoundland to Quebec to Florida, and in Europe. It has slender stems, mostly short and freely-branched, and rather widely-spaced, submersed leaves, oblong-lanceolate, elliptic, or nearly round; their bases clasp the stem, often in such a way that they unite and completely surround it, giving the impression that the stem passes through the leaf blade. There are no floating leaves. The flower spikes are ½ to 1 inch long.

Pondweeds not native to continental North America include *P. gayi,* of southern South America; *P. coloratus,* of the West Indies, North Africa, and warm parts of Asia and Australia; *P. lucens,* of Europe, Asia, Africa, and Australia; and *P. densus,* of Europe, temperate Asia, and North Africa. When grown in good light, **P. gayi** has brownish-red stems and leaves. The stems are slender and freely-branched, especially in their upper parts. The linear leaves are 1½ to 3 inches long. Also usually reddish is **P. coloratus.** Its lower leaves are lanceolate, but those above are elliptic and plantain-like. The floating ones are egg-shaped and up to 4 inches long by nearly one-half as wide. The flower spikes are very short. Completely submersed, **P. lucens** is a strong grower, with freely-branching stems and translucent, short-stalked, lanceolate to broadly-elliptic leaves 2 to 10 inches long by up to 4 inches wide. The flower spikes are up to 2 inches or a little more in length. The attractive, completely submersed **P. densus** has crowded, stalkless leaves in pairs. They are up to 1½ inches long by one-half as wide and are often recurved. The flowers are few together in short spikes.

Garden Uses. The cultivation of pondweeds is chiefly restricted to aquariums. Strangely, many, for example, *P. filiformis,* are rather difficult to grow under such conditions, although in outdoor pools most flourish to the extent of becoming troublesome weeds if they are not carefully restricted to tubs or other containers. Undoubtedly insufficient light is a factor in this failure to thrive indoors. Another unfavorable circumstance for hardy kinds may be too high water temperatures, especially in winter. None makes any floral display, and those with floating leaves are the only ones that can be clearly seen in outdoor pools. The underwater kinds are pleasing decorations for aquariums.

Cultivation. Propagation in cultivation is invariably by division and by removing parts of the stems and planting them as cuttings. They grow in mud or in sand with a slight mud content. Exposure to strong light is essential for the best results, without this they soon weary, become bedraggled, and finally die. The hardy kinds should be grown in unheated water. Best adapted for tropical aquariums are *P. gayi* and *P. coloratus.* Some pondweeds, notably *P. crispus, P. filiformis, P. gayi,* and *P. perfoliatus,* do best in water that is alkaline because of a fairly high lime content.

POTAMOGETONACEAE—Pondweed Family. Interpreted narrowly, this is a cosmopolitan group of 100 species of dicotyledons divided between two genera of chiefly submerged or floating aquatics or much less commonly bog plants. Conservative botanists include about twenty-five additional species that others treat in six separate small families. Members of the family have usually creeping stems or rhizomes with branches extending upward in the water and bearing alternate or opposite leaves in two ranks; those that float are often very different from submersed ones. The minute flowers are bisexual or unisexual, with the sexes on the same or sometimes different plants. They are without perianths or have vestigial ones. There are one to four stamens, a short style or none, and one to four stigmas. The fruits are nutlets or drupelets. Only *Potamogeton* is ordinarily cultivated.

POTASSIUM. Essential for plant growth, potassium is a metallic element the chemical symbol for which is K. Its salts, potassium chloride, potassium nitrate, potassium sulfate, and potassium phosphate, are used in commercial fertilizers and the final figure of the three (as in 5-10-5) that by law must appear on every container of fertilizer sold in the United States indicates the percentage of potassium. Unleached wood ashes contain potash, a crude form of potassium oxide. They are of considerable value as a fertilizer.

Although the proportion of potassium in plants is small, its significance is great and not yet fully understood. It is known to be essential to the proper functioning of photosynthesis and respiration.

Symptoms of potash deficiency may include stunting, poorly developed root systems, weak stems, and browning, bronzing, scorching, or curling of the margins and apexes of leaves. These symptoms are most likely to show in beets, carrots, potatoes, sweet potatoes, and in pineapples, tomatoes, and other fruits that store sugar or starch (products of photosynthesis) in quantity.

The application of fertilizers containing potassium to soils lacking adequate supplies promotes stamina and disease resistance. It also has the effect of improving the color and flavor of fruits. Potassium tends to delay maturity and so in hot, dry seasons fertilizers containing it may be used to extend the growing period of crops that would otherwise end their growth before reaching their best development.

Because of their high solubility, potassium salts leach rapidly from sandy soils of low organic content. Clay is deflocculated by them and becomes pasty and sticky. This can be avoided or corrected by judicious application of ground limestone or lime.

POTASSIUM CHLORIDE. Also called muriate of potash, this is an important fertilizer. See Fertilizers.

POTASSIUM MAGNESIUM SULFATE. Known as double manure salts, this is a fertilizer. See Fertilizers.

POTASSIUM NITRATE. Also called nitrate of potash, this is an important fertilizer. See Fertilizers.

POTASSIUM PERMANGANATE. A mild fungicide and disinfectant, potassium permanganate or permanganate of potash has also some fertilizer value as a source of potassium. It consists of dark purple crystals that appear rich red by transmitted light and dissolve readily in water. A solution of one ounce in six gallons of water, which is harmless to plants, may be used as a spray to discourage some leaf spot and other fungus diseases and to partially disinfect soil prior to sowing seeds. Earthworms in soil in pots are brought to the surface by standing the pots to their rims for an hour in a solution of potassium permanganate.

POTASSIUM SULFATE. Also known as sulfate of potash, this potash fertilizer contains 48 to 52 percent water-soluble potash. Rate of application is ½ to 1 ounce per square yard.

POTATO. In addition to being the name of the familiar vegetable (see next entry), the word potato forms parts of the common names of these plants: air-potato (*Dioscorea bulbifera*), devil's-potato (*Echites umbellata*), Eskimo-potato (*Fritillaria camschatcensis*), potato-bean (*Apios americana*), potato-tree (*Solanum crispum* and *S. macranthum*), potato yam (*Dioscorea bulbifera*), sweet-potato (*Ipomoea batatas*), and wild-sweet-potato vine (*Ipomoea pandurata*).

POTATOES. This popular vegetable is more commonly grown as a field crop than in gardens, but even where lack of space or practical economics preclude its extensive cultivation, a small home planting can bring delights to the table generally unattainable from bought supplies. Vegetable gardens afford no more flavorful products than freshly cooked, newly dug potatoes.

One of the New World's great contributions to mankind's basic food supplies, the others include corn, string beans, lima beans, and tomatoes, potatoes (*Solanum tuberosum*) belong to the nightshade family SOLANACEAE. They are natives of the Andean region of South America.

Potatoes thrive only in comparatively cool, humid conditions. They are not well adapted to long, hot summers. Ground for them should be sunny, well-drained, fertile, and have a pH reading of 6 or lower. A higher pH encourages scab disease. Because of this, liming ground for potatoes is usually detrimental. There should be at least 9 inches of topsoil. If on the heavy or clayey side, it is important that it be managed so that it remains crumbly, not sticky and pasty. This is encouraged by plowing or spading in fall and leaving the surface

Near Cuzco, Peru: (a) Indian women preparing land for planting potatoes

(b) The harvest

rough over winter, or if a rotary tiller is used, by sowing a cover crop of winter rye in fall and turning it under in late winter or spring. Plowing or spading sandy and sandy-loam soils may be done in spring.

Fertility is promoted by supplying fairly generous amounts of such organic matter as partly rotted manure or compost (seaweed, excellent for the purpose, may be had in some localities for the trouble of collecting) supplemented by fertilizers. It is usual to strew the organic matter along the bottom of the trenches in which the potatoes are planted, rather than mix it with the entire upper layer of soil, and to apply the fertilizers either just before planting or chiefly as side dressings later.

For planting, "seed" potatoes are used. These are not seeds, but are small-sized tubers selected for the purpose. The smallest may be planted whole, but it is more usual to use somewhat bigger ones cut into chunky pieces called sets each weighing 1¼ to 2 ounces and containing at least one and preferably two eyes from which sprouts develop. It is of great importance to use only clean, disease-free "seed." To assure this, purchase "certified seed potatoes" or "certified seed sets." "Certified" means that the potatoes were inspected by government officials at least twice during

Cutting potatoes into sets for planting

Planting potatoes

Potatoes in active growth

their growing season and once in storage for trueness to variety and freedom from disease. It is cheap insurance to buy "certified" instead of relying upon home-grown potatoes as planting stock.

It is usual to sprout the seed of early and midseason varieties before planting. This is done by standing them with their ends with the most eyes pointing upward in shallow trays or boxes and keeping them in a light place where the temperature is 50 to 60°F for two to three weeks so that by planting time well-developed young shoots are clearly in evidence. If the seed potatoes are of sufficient size to cut into sets, do this a day or two before planting and dust the cut surfaces with sulfur or some other fungicide.

Potato varieties are grouped as early, midseason, and late. The first planting, of an early variety, may be made in a very sheltered location, such as one protected by a hedge or windbreak or occupying a south-facing slope, almost as soon as the ground is first workable in spring, three to four weeks before the last frost may come. In more exposed locations wait two to three weeks longer. On heavy soils, planting dates for early potatoes should be slightly later than on sandy ground. Two to three weeks after the first planting a second one of an early variety and, if a long season of supply is desired, a first one of a midseason variety may be made.

Late varieties to give crops for storing are planted about six weeks after the first earlies, but because of the considerable attention to spraying needed to produce good crops of these it is generally advantageous for home gardeners to concentrate on early and midseason sorts. Among satisfactory earlies are 'Irish Cobbler', 'Early Gem', and 'Chippewa'. For later crops 'Katahdin', 'Kennebec', and 'Burbank' are popular. If in doubt, before making selections consult a Cooperative Extension Agent as to varieties best suited to your locality.

Plant the seed potatoes or sets in furrows (trenches) 1 foot to 1½ feet apart, 4

Hilling up potatoes

to 5 inches deep. Set them 1¼ to 1½ feet apart and cover to a depth of a couple of inches with soil. Keep the soil shallowly cultivated so the surface is always loose and weeds are destroyed before they attain significant size.

When the shoots are about 3 inches high, hill soil up to them to form a ridge along each row. Do this by pulling with a hoe soil from along each side of the row, in this way creating a shallow trench or furrow there. A second and perhaps third hilling will be needed at the tops lengthen.

This piling of loose soil encourages rooting from the lower parts of the stems, supports them, and facilitates digging the crop. It also, because of repeated disturbance of the earth, does much to eliminate weeds. For this reason potatoes are a good "cleaning" crop to plant on weed-infested ground as part of the preparation for other kinds of plants.

Harvest early and second early potatoes as needed for the table, beginning as soon as tubers big enough for the purpose have formed and continuing at intervals of a few days or longer. Allow late varieties intended for storage to remain until the vines (tops) have turned quite brown either because they are fully matured or because they have been killed by frost.

Harvesting potatoes

Lift the tubers with a fork, taking great care not to spear or otherwise damage them. Allow those intended for storage to lie on the ground for an hour or more, but not overnight, then put them in a dark, frost-free place where the air is fairly humid and the temperature remains as near 35 to 40°F as possible.

POTATO-VINE. This colloquial name is used for *Solanum jasminoides*, *S. seaforthianum*, and *S. wendlandii*.

POTENTILLA (Poten-tílla)—Cinquefoil, Five Fingers. As wildlings, the perhaps 500 species of *Potentilla*, of the rose family Ro-SACEAE, are widely distributed through temperate and subarctic regions of the northern hemisphere. They include common weeds of meadows, waysides, waste places, and lawns, as well as lovely alpines and a few worthwhile sorts from lower altitudes. The majority are herbaceous perennials, some are annuals, and a few are subshrubs or shrubs. From among this varied assortment of natural species, fine garden plants can be gleaned and there are some attractive hybrids. The name, alluding to supposed medicinal qualities, derives from the Latin *potens*, powerful. The vernacular names cinquefoil and five fingers allude to the forms of the leaves of many kinds.

Potentillas have leaves composed of leaflets arranged palmately (spreading from the top of the leafstalk like the fingers of a hand) or pinnately (spreading from both sides of a central axis or midrib). Usually they are toothed. In most cases, the shrubs excepted, the basal leaves are much bigger than those of the stems. Solitary or in branched clusters or sprays, the flowers have calyxes of five spreading lobes (sepals) with bractlets alternating with them. Except in a few double-flowered horticultural varieties, which have more, the petals number five. Those of most sorts are yellow but white-, pink-, and red-flowered potentillas occur. There are ten to numerous stamens and, sprouting from a more or less hairy receptacle, many easily detachable styles. The fruits are heads of small seedlike achenes usually enclosed in the persistent calyxes that mature on the dry receptacles.

Shrub potentillas or bush cinquefoils cultivated are derivatives of what under the name P. fruticosa was long accepted as a single variable species inhabiting northern North America, Europe, and Asia. More recent evaluations appraise this concept a complex of three or more variable species of which the one that retains the name P. fruticosa is indigenous to North America, northern Europe, and western Asia. Central and eastern Asian populations formerly included in P. fruticosa are segregated as P. davurica and P. parvifolia. In addition there are natural and artificial hybrids as well as selections to which names have been given. Most cultivated sorts are based on the eastern Asian species, although some hybrids have P. fruticosa in their parentage. We now consider this group of species.

With age a loose and somewhat straggly deciduous shrub, **P. fruticosa** is commonly a rounded bush 2 to 4 feet tall and as wide or wider. It has erect stems, peeling brown bark, and more or less hairy, pinnate leaves of usually five, less often three or seven toothless, pointed-lanceolate leaflets ½ to 1 inch long by up to ¼ inch wide, the three upper ones sometimes joined at their bases. From 1 inch to 1½ inches in diameter and with club-shaped styles, the bright yellow blooms are borne chiefly in one flush and do not provide as long a succession as those of many garden varieties.

Native to northern China and Siberia, **P. davurica** (syns. P. arbuscula, P. glabrata) is highly variable. Typically not over 1½ feet tall, it has upright stems with pendulous twigs. Its hairless leaves have five stalkless, oblong-ovate leaflets up to ½ inch long, the three terminal ones united at their bases. The usually solitary white flowers have slender, 1-inch-long hairy stalks. Leaves densely-glandular on their

Potentilla fruticosa: (a) A single plant

(b) A spray of flowers

(c) Flowers and leaves

undersides are characteristic of P. d. albicans (syn. P. d. farreri; dwarf P. d. beesii is a low sort with silvery foliage and golden-yellow blooms. From the typical species, P. d. rhodocalyx is distinguished by its more congested growth and the calyxes of its white, cup-shaped blooms being stained with crimson. A variant with leaves of always three leaflets is P. d. r. ternata. Variety P. d. subalbicans (which like P. d. rhodocalyx has in the past been misnamed P. fruticosa veitchii) is well distinguished by its leaves having a thin covering of white hairs on their upper surfaces

and a much denser growth on their undersides. This has comparatively large, white blooms. Variety P. d. mandschurica (syn. P. fruticosa mandschurica) is an excellent low, grayish-leaved variety with white flowers. Chinese **P. parviflora**, seldom over 3 feet high, typically is denser-foliaged and has smaller leaves than P. fruticosa and P. davurica, with mostly seven leaflets. Its leaves are rarely more than ½ inch long, their leaflets about one-half that. Also, its yellow flowers have a threadlike instead of club-shaped style. Varieties include P. p. 'Gold Drop' (syn. P. p. farreri), with leaflets ¼ to ⅜ inch long; P. p. pumila, extremely dwarf, and with silky-hairy leaves with leaflets ¼ inch or less long; and P. p. tenuiloba, the leaves of which are narrower, and with more hairy leaflets than those of the typical species.

Compact, low, and sometimes semi-prostrate, **P. parvifolia**, of the Himalayas and western China, is distinguished by its more or less hairy, but never silvery foliage and comparatively large, deep orange blooms. Its narrowly-oblong leaves are under ½ inch long by about ⅕ inch wide. Himalayan **P. ambigua** makes neat, flat, spreading mats of grayish-green or green foliage above which are displayed on stems 1 inch to 2 inches long, solitary,

Potentilla ambigua in a rock garden

golden-yellow blooms ¾ to 1 inch wide. The leaves have three broad-obovate to wedge-shaped leaflets ¼ to ½ inch long and three-toothed at their apexes.

Garden varieties, selections or hybrids of the above shrubby species, include these: **P. beanii**, supposedly of hybrid origin, is a dwarf with dark green foliage, white flowers. P. 'Farrer's White', akin to P. davurica, is small, compact. **P. friedrichsenii** (syn. P. 'Berlin Beauty') is a vigorous hybrid 6 feet tall with gray-green foliage and light yellow blooms. **P. grandiflora**, which grows robustly to 5 feet high, has sage-green leaves and large, canary-yellow flowers. P. 'Kathryn Dykes' produces an

Potentilla friedrichsenii

Potentilla tridentata: (a) As a groundcover

Potentilla 'Longacre'

(b) Flowers

3 to 4 inches high. It has long-stalked, palmate leaves of three or five obovate leaflets, toothed at their apexes, green and hairless above, white-silky-hairy beneath. The largest, the center ones, are 1 inch to 1½ inches long by ½ inch wide. Freely-borne and two to several on stalks that are pubescent, but not with silvery-silky hairs, the ¾-inch-wide white blooms are often partly hidden beneath the foliage. They have petals longer than the sepals. This accommodating plant, which thrives in sun or part-shade in a variety of soils, blooms in early spring and often again in fall. It is a native of central and eastern Europe. From the last, *P. alchemilloides,* of the Pyrenees, differs in its stems and flower stalks as well as the undersides of its foliage being silvery-silky-hairy. Its palmate leaves are of five or seven oblong-elliptic leaflets up to 1 inch long and usually with three small teeth at their apexes. The many ¾-inch-wide white flowers, in loose sprays 4 inches or more tall, have petals longer than the sepals, notched at their ends. As its name indicates this in foliage has much the aspect of *Alchemilla alpina.*

Native to the Balkan Peninsula, *P. apennina,* in bloom, is up to 8 inches tall. It has leaves of three obovate leaflets up to ½ inch long, toothed at their apexes, usually silvery-silky-hairy on both sides, and less often hairless above. The white blooms, ½ to ¾ inch across, are in sprays of up to seven. Variety *P. a. stoianovii* has broader leaflets and pale pink blooms. Somewhat glandular-hairy, *P. rupestris,* of Europe and adjacent Asia, is 1 foot to 2 feet tall. Its basal leaves are pinnate and of five to seven ovate to roundish, round-toothed leaflets ¾ inch to 2 inches in length. The upper leaves have three leaflets. Pure white, ½ inch to 1¼ inches wide, and with a central bunch of yellow stamens, the blooms are in loose, branched clusters. Variety *P. r. pygmaea,* neat and 3 to 4 inches tall, has flowers a little over ½ inch wide.

abundance of primrose-yellow blooms on somewhat silvery-foliaged bushes about 6 feet tall. P. 'Longacre' is a dwarf, dense-mat-forming variety with bright, almost sulfur-yellow blooms. P. 'Manelys' (syn. P. 'Moonlight'), with leaves similar to but a little smaller than those of P. vilmoriniana, is a small shrub with pale yellow blooms. P. 'Mount Everest', up to 5 feet tall and compact, has white flowers. **P. ochroleuca** is a hybrid resembling P. friedrichsenii, but its flowers are cream-colored. P. 'Primrose Beauty', with yellow flowers with deeper yellow centers, is small and has arching branches and gray-green leaves. **P. rehderana,** about 4 feet tall, has very small leaves and light yellow flowers. P. 'Red Ace', a remarkable variety with tomato-red blooms, was developed in England and introduced in 1976. P. 'Tangerine' is low, has wide-spreading branches, and, if grown in light shade, coppery-yellow to orange blooms. On plants in full sun they are yellow. **P. vilmoriniana,** 6 feet tall and with very silvery foliage, has cream-colored flowers. It is a superior variety.

Tufted **P. tridentata,** a low, carpeting evergreen subshrub, native from Greenland to Minnesota and Connecticut and in the mountains south to Georgia, is a

charming sort for rock gardens and similar places. Its stems, woody at their bases, are 2 inches to 1 foot tall. The leaves, mostly basal, have three palmately-disposed, oblanceolate, leathery leaflets ½ to 1 inch long, squarish and three-toothed at their apexes, dark green, glossy and hairless above, paler and with obscure bristly hairs on their undersides. The white flowers, about ⅓ inch wide, are in loose clusters.

White-flowered herbaceous perennial cinquefoils include **P. alba,** which makes pretty, slowly-widening mounds in bloom

Potentilla alba

Potentilla rupestris pygmaea

Yellow-flowered herbaceous perennial cinquefoils worthy of cultivation are fairly numerous, but many are so similar that comparatively few will satisfy most gardeners. Among the best are these: **P. argyrophylla** is a Himalayan with scarcely-branched, leafy stems and long-stalked leaves, silky-hairy above, white-hairy on their undersides, and with usually three stalkless, coarsely-toothed, broad-obovate leaflets 1½ to 2½ inches long. Its long-stalked, 1-inch-wide, yellow flowers are in loose clusters. **P. aurea,** of the mountains of Europe, favors non-limestone soils. Much like *P. crantzii,* but more matting and about 4 inches high, it has leaves of usually three, less often five, palmately-arranged, oblanceolate to nearly round leaflets up to ¾ inch long. They have silky hairs along their margins and on the veins beneath and at their ends are toothed,

Potentilla aurea

Potentilla aurea plena

Potentilla crantzii

with the terminal tooth much smaller than the others. The flowers, ½ to ¾ inch wide, are in sprays with stalks silky-hairy above. Blooms of *P. a. plena* are nearly double. **P. crantzii** (syn. *P. alpestris*). a native of much of Europe, closely resembles *P. aurea,* but the center tooth of the few at the apex of each leaflet is not markedly smaller than those on either side of it. Approximately 3 inches high, it is sometimes taller. **P. fragiformis** is Siberian. From 6 to 8 inches tall, it has long-stalked, softly-hairy leaves, rounded in outline and of three deeply-toothed leaflets ½ inch to 2 inches

Potentilla fragiformis

long. The flowers are golden-yellow, 1 inch to 1¾ inches in diameter, and have an orange blotch at the base of each petal. **P. nevadensis** inhabits dry rocks and screes in the Spanish Sierra Nevada. In bloom up to 1 foot, but as known in cultivation usually not exceeding 3 or 8 inches in height, and downy, it has more or less hoary-looking leaves of five linear to oblong-lanceolate, palmately-arranged leaflets ¼ to ½ inch long with round-toothed margins and silky-hairy undersurfaces. The many yellow flowers, in clusters of up to four or solitary and ½ to ⅛ inch in diameter, have sepals slightly longer than the bracts behind them. **P. recta,** of Europe and Asia and naturalized

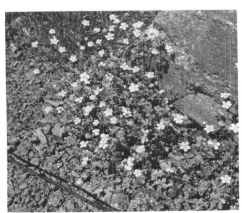

Potentilla nevadensis

Potentilla recta warrenii

in North America, in its naturalized form is scarcely admissible as a garden plant, but superior **P. r. warrenii** (syn. *P. r. macrantha*), an Asian variety, surely is. Somewhat hairy, this has erect, freely-branched stems 1½ to 2 feet tall with leaves of five or seven palmately-arranged, oblongish, coarsely-toothed leaflets 2 to 4 inches long. Like the stems these are hairy. Its clear buttercup-yellow, freely-produced blooms are 1½ inches wide. The variety comes true from seeds. **P. tabernaemontani,** has been commonly grown as *P. verna.* A very variable, mat-forming, more or less hairy sort, this has rooting, prostrate stems with upright branches up to 4 inches tall. Its palmately-divided leaves are of five or seven oblanceolate to obovate leaflets up to 1½ inches long by ½ inch wide, but often smaller. Solitary or in clusters of up to a dozen, the bright yellow blooms, ½ to almost 1 inch wide, have the bracts behind the calyx much shorter than the sepals. This sort, possibly of hybrid origin, is native to Europe and adjacent Asia. Presumably the very dwarf plant grown as *P. verna nana* belongs here. **P. tonguei** (syn. *P. tormentilla-formosa*), a hybrid between *P. anglica* and *P. nepalensis,* has trailing stems up to 1 foot long and leaves with 3- to 5-inch-long, obovate, coarsely-toothed leaflets. The flowers, about ½ inch in diameter, are buff-yellow to apricot-yellow, with a small red-brown blotch at the base of each petal.

Pink- and red-flowered herbaceous perennial cinquefoils include these: **P. atrosanguinea,** of the Himalayas, resembles *P. napalensis,* but the three leaflets of its strawberry-like leaves usually have brief stalks and are silky-hairy on their undersides. Also, its blooms are deep purple. Variety *P. a.* 'Gibson's Scarlet' has beautiful blood-red blooms. **P. nepalensis,** of the Himalayas, differs from the last in its long-stalked, somewhat hairy basal leaves having five leaflets. They are oblong-obovate, coarsely-toothed, green on both surfaces, and 2 to 3 inches long. The stems are erect and branched. About 1 inch in diameter,

Potentilla atrosanguinea 'Gibson's Scarlet'

the rich rose- to cherry-red flowers are in loose clusters. They have petals deeply notched at their apexes. Lower and especially free-blooming, *P. n. willmottiae* has rose-pink flowers. Native to limestone rocks and screes in the Alps of Europe, *P. nitida* ordinarily has pink flowers, much more rarely white ones. Unfortunately, in cultivation, it frequently fails to bloom. Nevertheless it is worth growing for its foliage. From 1 inch to 2 inches tall, this sort has leaves densely-silvery-silky-hairy above as well as on their undersides. They have usually three leaflets, under ½ inch long, obovate to oblanceolate, and often toothed at their apexes. The ¾-inch-wide flowers have petals notched at their ends.

A splendid group of at least three dozen hybrid varieties derived from crosses made in the nineteenth and early twentieth centuries, chiefly in France, between *P. argyrophylla*, *P. nepalensis*, and perhaps *P. atrosanguinea* are little known in America, yet they are quite stunning flower garden plants and are useful as cut blooms. Unfortunately these beautiful hybrids have not proved reliably hardy in the vicinity of New York City, but in somewhat milder climates they should be satisfactory. From 1½ to 2 feet tall, they include both single-, semidouble-, and double-flowered sorts in a considerable range of colors and with blooms up to 1½ inches across. Among varieties offered in England are 'Arc en Ciel', its flowers blended tones of orange and red; 'Etna', with crimson blooms; 'Flamenco', which has intensely red single flowers; 'Glory of Nancy', the orange-crimson blooms of which are semidouble; 'Jupiter', with double crimson flowers; 'Mons. Rouillard', its very large flowers crimson with an orange blotch on the petals; 'Star of the North', which has rich crimson flowers; 'William Rollisson', its nearly double blooms of an orange-flame hue; and 'Yellow Queen', the semidouble flowers of which are bright yellow.

Garden and Landscape Uses. Although in most parts of North America shrub po-

tentillas cannot be accounted among the finest flowering shrubs, they should by no means be ignored by gardeners. When at the height of their first flush of bloom they are unquestionably attractive, having something of the appearance of small-flowered single roses, but their often too-strongly-touted successions of flowers are usually too sparse to be really effective. Their foliage shows no fall color. They are without showy fruits. That presents the negative side. Positively they are thoroughly hardy, succeed in almost all soils, are remarkably free from pests and diseases, are long-lived, and need practically no care. They can be usefully employed in sunny sites in mixed shrub plantings or as single specimens or groups.

Of other kinds, *P. tridentata* and the lower herbaceous sorts are ideal for rock gardens and similar areas and the taller ones for the fronts and middle reaches of flower beds and borders.

Cultivation. As a group, these plants are not difficult, indeed some sorts make themselves so much at home that they reproduce by self-sown seeds. Most adjust well to a variety of soils, but advantage is sometimes had by supplying lime to known calciphiles and withholding it from calcifuges. The majority are not too finicky and get along perfectly well in approximately neutral earth. If in doubt experiment a little. But the soil should not be overfertile, the dwarf alpine and subalpine species especially do best on a somewhat spartan diet. Gritty earth well-drained is to the best liking of most. The taller flower garden sorts respond to somewhat richer, sandy soils. Good drainage is important. Primarily sun-loving plants, some potentillas stand a little shade and some in regions of hot, bright summers are probably better for a little such protection during the hottest part of the day. Increase is by seed and division, early spring or early fall being the preferred seasons to undertake this last operation.

POTERIUM (Po-tèrium)—Salad Burnet or Garden Burnet. About twenty-five species closely related to *Sanguisorba* and by some authorities included in that genus constitute *Poterium*, of the rose family ROSACEAE. Natives of Europe, western Asia, and North Africa, they differ from *Sanguisorba* in all or some of the flowers being unisexual. The name is a Greek one for another kind of plant.

Poteriums are herbaceous perennials or subshrubs with pinnate leaves with toothed or lobed, opposite leaflets. The tiny flowers, in dense heads or spikes, have four petal-like sepals joined at their bases, four to numerous or rarely only two stamens, one, two, or less often three carpels and styles. The fruits are achenes.

Salad burnet or garden burnet (*P. sanguisorba* syn. *Sanguisorba minor*) is a hardy

perennial European and Asian species naturalized in North America. From 8 inches to about 2 feet tall, it has leaves of up to a dozen toothed, ovate leaflets up to ¾ inch long. The nearly spherical to egg-shaped, green or brown flower spikes, ½ to ¾ inch long, are composed of bisexual and unisexual flowers. They have numerous stamens and two styles.

A subshrub 2 to 3 feet tall, *P. spinosum* (syn. *Sarcopoterium spinosum*), of Asia Minor, has hairy branches that usually end in sharp thorns. Its leaves are of nine to fifteen, sharply-toothed, ovate leaflets densely-hairy on their undersides and barely ½ inch long. The flower spikes are greenish, cylindrical to egg-shaped, and 1 inch to 1¼ inches long.

Garden and Landscape Uses and Cultivation. Salad burnet or garden burnet is used to some extent as a salad green, for flavoring drinks, and for garnishing. It and *P. spinosum* are also grown for ornament. They are easy to manage, thrive in ordinary, reasonably fertile garden soil in full sun or where shaded for only a small part of each day. They are suitable for grouping in beds and borders and for planting in naturalistic surroundings. Propagation is by division in spring or early fall, and by seed. In the north, *P. spinosum* is not reliably hardy.

POTHERB. This term covers a variety of herbs added, chiefly for flavoring, to soups and other foods cooked in pots. Black potherb is *Smyrnium olusatrum*.

POTHOIDIUM (Pothòid-ium). The only species of *Pothoidium*, of the arum family ARACEAE, is an interesting native of the Philippine Islands, the Celebes Islands, and the Molucca Islands. Its name, in reference to a relationship and similarity, comes from that of *Pothos*, and the Greek *oides*, resembling.

A vine, in the wild up to 50 feet tall or taller and of distinctive appearance, *P. lobbianum* has slender, branching, angled stems and more or less two-ranked,

Pothoidium lobbianum

Potentilla tabernaemontani variety (syn. *P. verna nana* of gardens)

Primula cortusoides

Primula japonica

Poncirus trifoliata (fruits)

Portulaca grandiflora

Protea cynaroides

Primula malacoides

Primula vulgaris variety

Primula vialii

Primula polyantha variety

pointed, narrow-linear to narrowly-oblong leaves 3 to 8 inches long by up to ½ inch or a little more wide. The apical one-quarter to one-third of each leaf appears to be jointed to the lower portion, with an evident constriction indicating the junction. As is usual in the arum family, the tiny flowers are clustered on spikelike spadixes that have a petal-like bract called a spathe at the base. In *Pothoidium*, the flowers are restricted to approximately the upper one-half of the spadix, the lower portion is stalklike and without flowers. The spadixes and spathes, together called an inflorescence, are in terminal racemes. The fruits are berries.

Garden and Landscape Uses and Cultivation. These are as for vining philodendrons. See Philodendron.

POTHOS (Pò-thos). Few of the about seventy species of *Pothos*, of the arum family ARACEAE, are cultivated, but the name is often misapplied to *Epipremnum aureum* and *Scindapsus pictus* and its varieties. In the wild restricted to the tropics of the Old World, *Pothos* has a name adapted from its Sinhalese one, *potha*.

Evergreen vines that cling by aerial roots, pothoses have lobeless leaves in two ranks, with flattened, often wide-winged stalks. The inflorescences, commonly referred to as "flowers," have a stalked, usually ovoid spadix furnished with small flowers with six-parted perianths. The spathe is small. The fruits are berries.

Native to the Philippine Islands and Indonesia, *P. hermaphroditus* is a high climber. Its leaves have winged stalks approximately 3½ inches long and lanceolate to linear-lanceolate blades about 1 inch wide and up to 4½ inches long. From it *P. seemannii*, of China and Taiwan, differs in the blades of its elliptic to oblanceolate leaves being slightly shorter and their stalks seldom exceeding 1 inch in length.

Pothos seemannii

Garden and Landscape Uses and Cultivation. These are as for *Philodendron* and *Scindapsus*.

POTOMATO. This name, as well as pomato and topato, have been used for tomatoes grafted onto potatoes and vice versa. Such plants are of no value except as curiosities.

POTS and PANS. Also called flower pots and flower pans, these are usual and convenient containers in which plants are grown more or less permanently or until ready for transplanting. Pans differ from pots only in their proportions. Standard pots are circular and taper outward from their bottoms to their tops, where they are as wide as their heights. Pans are shallower. Those called azalea pans are three-quarters as high as their widths, bulb pans

Standard earthenware (clay) pots

Standard earthenware (clay) pans

are proportionately less tall, seed pans shallower still. To give added strength and to make possible stacking one inside the other without jamming, pots and pans usually have rims. Holes for drainage are provided in their bottoms and for those in which orchids are grown sometimes in their sides as well.

Until plastics became available, these containers were generally made of porous earthenware. Some still are, but the use of plastic is now more common. Each has advantages and disadvantages. Earthenware is heavier and more easily broken, important considerations when plants are to be shipped. But the additional weight provides greater stability for specimens with tops large in relation to the sizes of the containers they occupy

A decorative earthenware pot

Gardeners accustomed to clay pots sometimes assert that plants grow better in them than in plastic, but this is not true if appropriate adjustments are made in watering practices.

Because loss of moisture through plastics is nil, plants in containers of such materials need less frequent applications of water than those in pots of porous earthenware. In dry climates the evaporation of moisture through the sides of clay pots lowers the temperature of the soil, which in hot climates is generally advantageous.

POTTING and REPOTTING. Installing plants in pots and later transferring them to others often but not invariably larger, are garden operations known, respectively, as potting and repotting. They are forms of planting and transplanting and the principles important to success with those procedures are equally important here.

A potting mix or rooting medium containing soil or not, and suited to the particular needs of the plants, must be provided (see the Encyclopedia entry Potting Soils and Potting Mixes). Soil-based mixes vary from those containing large proportions of organic matter, such as are suitable for the majority of begonias, ferns, gesneriads, and many other plants that in the wild grow in woodlands and other humus-rich places, to rooting mediums consisting chiefly of inorganic or mineral type soil that suit most succulents and other inhabitants of desert and semidesert regions. A great many plants, geraniums and chrysanthemums, for example, do best in in-between-type, loamy potting soils.

For certain plants, for instance, azaleas and heaths, the mix must be decidedly acid, for a few, including Martha Washington geraniums and some succulents and alpines, one with an alkaline reaction, higher than pH 7, is desirable. For the vast majority of plants, slightly acid to neutral soil is conducive to satisfactory results.

Prepare potting mixes to suit the needs of particular plants: (a) For ferns, begonias, and some others, one containing much organic matter

Potting an azalea in an acid soil mix

(c) Packing them firmly with a potting stick

(b) For cactuses and other succulents, a coarse, porous mix containing little organic matter

(c) For many plants, such as sansevierias, a loamy, intermediate-type mix

The sizes of the containers must be suited to the plants, their expected rates of growth, and the purposes for which they are being grown. All this calls for some Many orchids, bromeliads, and other epiphytes are potted in osmunda fiber, chips of bark, or other loose materials without admixture of soil.

knowledge and judgment. Many amateurs make the mistake of overpotting, of putting plants in too-large receptacles. Do not do this. It is best to transfer from small to big containers in a series of graduated shifts, spaced to allow the plants to fill with healthy roots each size in which they are potted before being transferred to the next larger. Except when repotting big specimens, which may justify larger shifts, a move into a pot 1 inch to 2 inches larger

Osmunda fiber is often used for bromeliads and orchids: (a) Cutting the fiber into small pieces

(b) Positioning the pieces around the roots of an orchid

in diameter than the one previously occupied is in most cases adequate.

When to pot or repot depends upon a number of circumstances. Some kinds of plants once they have attained receptacles

A group of plants assembled for repotting

of sizes suitable for their needs, succeed best if left undisturbed for several years, at least until they begin to show some evidence of deteriorating. Examples are eucharises, haemanthuses, hippeastrums, and nerines, among bulb plants. Aspidistras, clivias, dracaenas, many ferns, rubber plants, sansevierias, most cactuses and other succulents, and aroids and palms are examples of other types. Big specimens of aucubas, bay trees, oranges and other citrus fruits, pandanuses, tree ferns, and the like in large pots or tubs will live more or less permanently without repotting or retubbing. Instead, each spring they may be top-dressed by pricking away 2 to 3 inches of the surface soil and replacing it with new.

Other plants need repotting annually, or in the case of quick-growing sorts such as chrysanthemums, cinerarias, and poinsettias and young specimens of many others, more frequently.

Examine permanent plants, those retained for more than a year, at the beginning of each growing season to determine

Bulb plants with permanent roots do not
need repotting every year:
(a) Haemanthuses

(b) Hippeastrums

(c) Nerines

Pot plants that are commonly potted and
later repotted one or two times within
one season include: (a) Cinerarias

(b) Poinsettias

(c) Primulas, which complete their
growth in one season and are then
usually discarded

whether or not repotting is needed. With
the majority of kinds this means late winter or early spring, but the seasonal cycles
of some few sorts begin at other times,
that of Lady Washington geraniums, for
example, in high summer, that of nerines
in early fall. Depending upon kind and
often upon whether the specimens are
young and you want them to grow as rapidly as reasonably practicable to larger
sizes or are at a stage when increase in size
is not especially desirable, further repotting may be needed during the season of
active growth.

If a plant is clearly suffering because its
roots are in unsuitable soil, perhaps the
result of poor drainage or excessive watering, the wisest course, even though it is
not the usual time, is to repot immediately. When engaging in such out-of-season potting, use the smallest container
that will easily accommodate the roots
after as much of the old, unsuitable soil as
practicable has been pricked away. Provide excellent drainage and by careful attention to watering, maintenance of encouraging temperatures and suitable

humidity, and such shade as may be
needed to temper strong sun, nurse the
repotted specimens back to health and
vigor.

Potting and repotting procedures differ
depending upon circumstances. In general,
harm results to leafy specimens if their roots
are seriously disturbed without leafage

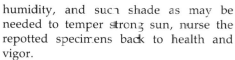

To repot a leafy plant, such as this
geranium, without reducing its foliage:
(a) Soak the roots very thoroughly one to
two hours before repotting

(b) Pick off all flower buds

being adequately reduced by compensatory
pruning. This is especially true of plants in
active growth. But it is quite practicable and
frequently desirable to prick away or shake
off some, at times most or even all of the
old soil from roots of plants just emerging
from a period of dormancy and without
leaves, and this may also be done with
plants you have cut back more or less severely, as for instance, fuchsias, geraniums,

To repot a leafless plant: (a) Such as this drastically pruned geranium

(b) Prick away much of the old soil with a pointed stick

(c) Leave all or most healthy roots intact

(d) Repot in new soil in a well-drained pot

(e) A pruned-back geranium starting into new growth

or perlite than for subsequent repottings. Press the soil lightly rather than firmly, water immediately, and return to an environment similar to that from which the propagations came, to be kept there at least until new root growth is well begun.

Pot rooted cuttings and other small bare-rooted plants into pots only just big enough to accommodate the roots

and lantanas in late winter. Sometimes, as with a palm that has wound roots around the bottom of its pot to such an extent the soil ball is raised and watering becomes difficult, it is even desirable to cut away part of the roots. If this is done, keep the plant in a highly humid atmosphere for a few weeks afterward.

Plants potted for the first time, as distinct from those being repotted, include rooted cuttings and other propagations, larger specimens lifted from flats, cold frames, or outdoors, and bulbs and similar plant parts without roots.

Pot cuttings and other propagations into pots just big enough to accommodate their roots in a mix containing no fertilizer, but much more generous proportions of sand

During this period avoid excessive watering, keep the atmosphere agreeably humid, provide light shade if that seems desirable, and protect from drafts and other drying influences.

Lift annuals, biennials, and herbaceous perennials to be potted with as large balls of roots and soil as can conveniently be taken. The annuals will usually come from flats or perhaps be in peat pots into which they were pricked out. In either case, they will normally be ready for transfer to containers 4 inches in diameter. The biennials and perennials, dug from cold frames or outdoor nursery beds, are likely to need containers 5 to 8 inches or perhaps even more in diameter.

For seedlings that have been growing in soil, use a potting mix that contains a much higher proportion of soil (loam) and less sand or perlite than would be appro-

To repot a palm: (a) Prick away old, compacted soil

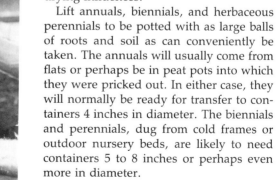

(b) Lower the plant, after some basal roots have been cut off, into its new pot

To pot asparagus "ferns": (a) Transfer them from the seed pot to small individual pots

(b) Press the soil lightly about the roots

priate for newly rooted cuttings. Proportion the ingredients so that it is agreeable to the particular kind of plant and include a little bonemeal or other slowly available fertilizer. Have the mix moderately coarse, but passable through a screen, depending upon the size of the pots to be used, of ¾- or 1-inch mesh.

Again depending upon the sort of plant, pack the soil moderately to quite firmly then drench it with water applied as a fine spray. If the plants have much foliage, take steps to prevent it being damaged and to forestall leaf dropping. Do this by shading from strong sun, sheltering from drafts and wind, and maintaining a moist atmosphere at least until the plants have recovered enough from the shock of the operation to stand exposure without wilting.

Do not water so frequently that the soil is constantly saturated, but neither allow it to dry to the extent the foliage wilts. Misting or lightly spraying the tops of the plants with water when it is expected that it will dry within an hour is beneficial.

Roses and small shrubs are sometimes forced in pots or tubs for early bloom in greenhouses. Pot bare-root specimens of these immediately after leaf drop in fall. See that they have substantial amounts of roots, and do not let these dry. Select pots just big enough to comfortably accommodate the roots with a little manipulation perhaps to fit them, but not the extent that they are tightly cramped. Trim the ends of broken roots and prune the tops, too, if this is thought desirable. Use coarse, fertile, porous soil and pack it firmly. Then put the plants in a cold frame, water them well, and keep them cool.

Bulb plants, and here we include those with tubers, corms, and other bulblike parts, as candidates for potting or repotting fall into two groups, those at potting time without and those with permanent roots. Use porous, fertile soil. Set the bulbs one to several in each pot depending upon kind and results desired. Plant them at appropriate depths and provide subsequent treatment according to their needs, as indicated in the discussions of the various kinds under their appropriate entries in this Encyclopedia.

Repotting bulb plants that have permanent roots is also done at or immediately before the beginning of their new season's growth. These, however, which include amaryllises (Hippeastrum), Amazon-lilies, crinum-lilies, ornithogalums, and such semibulbous kinds as agapanthuses and clivias, ordinarily do not require attention more often than every three years and many, if in good health, can remain undisturbed for longer. Because they are to stay in their containers for long periods it is especially important to use nourishing soil that will not soon break down and become impervious to air and water. To minimize the likelihood of this include in the mix generous amounts of coarse sand, grit, perlite, or similar mineral particles.

If the plants are without foliage at potting time, prick away with a pointed stick as much old soil from among the roots as possible. Follow a similar procedure with sorts with evergreen foliage, but leave more of the old soil ball intact. Select pots of sizes that will accommodate the roots with 1 inch or with large specimens 2 inches of additional space all around and pack the soil firmly. Upon completion of the task water well with a fine spray and place the plants in environments considered, according to the needs of different kinds, encouraging to new growth.

Basic to all potting and repotting is the use of clean, dry containers. If they are new clay pots, they are likely to be so dry that tiny particles of soil packed into them will be sucked into their interior walls and this will make removal of the plant from the pot difficult later. To obviate this, submerge new pots for two or three minutes (not longer) in water. Clean old pots by washing or scrubbing them thoroughly in water, without soap or detergent, and air-drying before use.

To assure adequate drainage: (a) Place a large crock hollow side down over the drainage hole

(b) Then add a layer of smaller crocks

(c) Finish with a layer of old leaves, straw, or a piece of nylon stocking

Good drainage is necessary and is best promoted by placing over the hole in the bottom of the pot a piece of crock (broken flower pot), hollow side down, or something that serves similarly to allow water to escape, and covering this with a layer of smaller crocks or other drainage material and finally some coarse leaves, moss, or the like to stop soil washing down and clogging the drainage.

Remove a geranium from its pot by tapping the pot rim on the edge of a table

Specimens being repotted must first be removed from their old containers. If these are pots of a size easy to handle, this is usually best accomplished by turning them upside down, spreading one hand over the surface soil, holding the bottom of the pot in the other, and tapping its rim on the edge of a solid bench or table. With large pots or tubs it may be necessary to lift them an inch or two off the ground and

To handle uncomfortably spiny cactuses and other succulents conveniently:
(a) Use tongs

(b) Or wrap a piece of cloth around them

tap their rims with a mallet or other fairly massive piece of wood. Employing tongs or a piece of cloth wrapped around the plant so that its two ends serve as a handle afford convenient alternatives to using clumsier gloves when handling small cactuses and other succulents with sharp spines.

Potting is begun by placing a little soil on top of the drainage, setting the plant so it is centered and is at the right depth in the container. In doing this have the finished surface of the soil sufficiently below

To repot a well-rooted leafy plant:
(a) After taking it from its pot, pick out and discard the old drainage material

(b) Loosen the outer roots slightly with a pointed stick

(c) Cover the drainage in the new pot with a little new soil

the top of the pot to allow for watering. A sound rule is to leave space for enough water that will, in one filling, saturate the entire ball of soil. This obviously means leaving a greater depth when potting into big than small containers, but it also involves some adjustment to the firmness with which the soil is packed. Because it will sink somewhat in response to repeated watering, loosely pressed soil may be left higher in the pot than may soil packed firmly.

Moderns generally favor packing soil for

(d) Center the plant with the top of the root ball appropriately below the rim to leave space for watering

(e) If the plant is large, pack new soil around the root ball with a potting stick

(f) If the plant is small, pack new soil with the fingers

(g) After potting is completed, the plant is ready for watering with a fine spray

potted plants less firmly than old-time gardeners, who for such sorts as chrysanthemums, Lady Washington geraniums, and such woody-stemmed plants as heaths, citruses, and bay trees, frequently rammed it to almost the hardness of a much used dirt road. Still, for these and other kinds known to prefer firm potting it is well to have the earth compressed enough that no appreciable dent can be made by pressing a finger firmly into it. To achieve such solidity with pots above the 5-inch size, it is usual to tamp the soil with a potting stick, using the wedge-shaped end around the sides, the blunt end over the surface. With smaller pots, adequate firmness can be achieved by pressing the soil with the fingers.

For plants that prefer looser root runs, such as African-violets and other gesneriads, begonias, and ferns, and many other plants particularly those that favor soil containing large proportions of organic matter, press the soil less firmly, so that it gives a little when its surface is pressed firmly with a finger.

Avoid leaving voids (gaps or holes not

To avoid disturbing the surface soil of newly potted plants, water with a fine spray

filled with soil) and finish with a surface that is level and roughed slightly so that marks of the fingers or potting stick are not evident.

Water newly potted plants immediately if they are leafy and their roots have been much disturbed or if the weather is warm and dry, but not until the next day perhaps or after even a longer wait if the foliage is sparse or absent and if the root ball has been left intact or if dull, humid weather prevails. Under these last conditions, lightly spraying the tops with water without drenching the soil is likely to suffice for a day or two, but do not wait until the soil is really dry before saturating it. When you do water, apply the water in a spray fine enough not to disturb the surface and give enough to thoroughly soak the whole mass of the soil, then no more until good judgment proclaims need. Light shade for a few days following repotting may benefit normally sun-loving plants by hastening their recovery from shock that sometimes results from the operation. Shade is essential of course for kinds that normally need protection from strong sun.

POTTING SOILS and POTTING MIXES.

For plants in pots and other containers, it is usual to prepare special soils or mixes. No matter how well suited to the needs of outdoor plants soil is, without modification it is rarely as well adapted for potting and repotting as could be wished. But it can easily be made so. One reason for its unsuitability is that packing in pots compacts it, with the result that free admission of air and passage of water are impeded. Furthermore, under the influence of repeated waterings and because often for much of the year temperatures higher than normal outdoor ones are maintained indoors, the organic material in the soil breaks down, becoming more or less pasty, which further interferes with drainage and the supply of air to the roots. And lastly, because of the limited amount of soil available to plants in pots it is often helpful to have it somewhat more nutritious than is usual with outdoor soils.

Until approximately the middle of the twentieth century, practically all potting mixes, except for tree-perching orchids and other epiphytes, such as bromeliads, consisted chiefly of soil, but now various soil-less mixes, usually based on peat moss or related organic products, have come to the fore and have generally proved satisfactory. Despite this, except in regions where suitable topsoil is not available, soil-based potting mixes are still the most widely employed.

The basic ingredients of potting soils are topsoil (loam), organic matter, such as leaf mold, peat moss, or humus, and inorganic materials, such as sand, perlite, broken crocks, broken bricks, or vermiculite. To

these are frequently added, depending upon the needs of individual plants, dried manure, bonemeal, wood ashes, charcoal, and sometimes other ingredients. If the topsoil, organic material, or, less likely, any of the other ingredients are suspected of harboring disease organisms or pests, sterilize them before adding them to the mix. See the Encyclopedia entry Soil Sterilization.

Although plants vary as to the types of soil they thrive best in, it is by no means necessary to prepare a special formula for each species and variety. In their needs they fall into a few groups—those, such as cactuses and other succulents, that require a coarse, gritty, medium that contains a comparatively small amount of organic material and through which water passes with great ease; those, such as ferns, begonias, and African-violets, that give of their best only when grown in a soil that is extremely rich in decayed organic matter and that revel in the evenly moist root conditions that such a soil provides; those, such as geraniums and chrysanthemums, that succeed best in a fairly heavy (moderately clayey) soil; those, such as gardenias and camellias, that prefer acid soil conditions; and those, such as Martha Washington geraniums, that respond best in a slightly alkaline soil. Some plants have a wider range of tolerance for soils than others. Many will grow in any reasonably good earth provided it is well drained—others are more finicky, you must give them a soil pretty much to their liking. This is particularly true of plants that favor acid soils.

City dwellers and others may find it difficult to obtain necessary ingredients for compounding their own soils or inconvenient to mix them. These people can get along quite well with prepared mixes sold by garden centers, department and dime stores, and mail-order houses. Such mixes are free of pests, diseases, and weed seeds. Because they are usually compounded to keep shipping weight at a minimum, they commonly contain less topsoil than would normally be used in home mixes. Except African-violets, ferns, and others known to prefer loose earths containing very abundant organic matter (humus), it is often helpful, but not essential, to add to commercial mixes ten to twenty percent by bulk of good topsoil. City folk may be able to acquire this from a friend's garden or from a vacant lot in the suburbs or country, or even from a friendly contractor engaged in planting street trees. Florists who operate greenhouses are other possible sources of topsoil.

Let the topsoil be the best you can obtain. For preference, cut grass sods 4 to 5 inches thick from a lush meadow or field and pile them (with a 3-inch layer of manure, if this is obtainable, between 8- to

Chop soil for use in potting mixes from a pile of alternate layers of grass sods and manure

10-inch layers of sod) grass-side down out of doors for six months to a year, until the grass is dead, but not until its fibrous roots have completely decayed. Then chop it with a spade or break it with the fingers, but do not remove the fibrous portion. This gives "life" to the soil. Good loam

prepared in this way should be pleasant to handle, slightly springy, and have a delightfully sweet earthy smell. If you lack turf soil made ready in this way, use instead topsoil taken from a rich vegetable garden, cultivated field, or fertile meadow. Soil that has grown good corn is excellent.

The sand used must be coarse and free of fine silty particles. That from a river or sand bank is usually better than sea sand, although the latter may be used provided it is coarse and if it has been well washed to free it of all traces of salt. To do this, leave it outdoors exposed to normal rains for a few months, or alternatively, stick the end of a hose into the bottom of a pail or barrel, fill the pail or barrel with sand and run water through the hose. Let the water overflow for ten minutes or so. Strain off the surplus water and let the sand dry. City dwellers can obtain coarse sand from pet shops dealing in aquarium supplies, or sometimes from building sites.

An admirable substitute for sand, and indeed in some ways superior to it, perlite consists of particles of a porous, heat-treated, volcanic rock. It is much used by

professional and amateur growers of indoor plants. It has the great virtues of weighing very much less than sand and of having porous particles. In some ways similar, vermiculite is sometimes employed as a sand substitute. It holds moisture well and is light in weight, but unlike perlite its particles are compressible and in time lose much of their porosity. Because of this, vermiculite is generally useful only in soils in which plants will remain for a short while before being again potted or transplanted, for those used in the first potting of cuttings, and for those into which small seedlings are transplanted.

Coarser than sand, perlite, or vermiculite, broken crocks, broken brick, crushed sandstone, crushed clam shells, oyster shells, or even egg shells are useful for increasing the porosity of potting soils. The various shells should only be included in mixes for plants that do not object to lime. They are unsuitable for acid-soil plants.

A good general purpose potting soil mix for most strong-rooted plants, such as chrysanthemums, English ivy, fuchsias, geraniums, palms, and sanseverias, consists of topsoil four parts, leafmold, peat

To prepare a general-purpose, soil-based mix, assemble: (a) Damp but not wet topsoil

(c) Coarse sand or perlite

(e) Dried cow manure may be used also

(b) Leaf mold or peat moss

(d) Add bonemeal or other slow-release fertilizer

(f) Mix thoroughly by turning it two or three times with a shovel

To test the finished mix: (a) While slightly damp, squeeze a handful tightly

(b) If on opening the hand, the soil, after being tapped lightly with the finger, remains in a clodlike lump, more sand or perlite and perhaps more leaf mold or humus is needed

(c) If, when the hand is opened, the soil falls apart, or if in a lump, when lightly tapped, it disintegrates, it is in suitable physical condition

moss, or humus two parts, dried cow manure one part (or one-third as much dried sheep manure), coarse sand or perlite two parts (this may be partly replaced by finely broken crocks or brick or crushed oyster or clam shells), bonemeal a pint to each bushel of the mix, wood ashes two quarts to each bushel of the mix, and a complete garden fertilizer, such as a 5-10-5, half pint to each bushel.

For special-purpose mixes for particular plants other additives are used: (a) Crocks of bricks broken into small pieces

(b) Broken charcoal

For plants that need a soil with a high organic content, such as African-violets, begonias, ferns, and gloxinias, a good mix is topsoil two parts, leaf mold, peat moss. or humus two and one-half parts. coarse sand or perlite one-half a part, broken crock or broken brick one part, crushed charcoal one-half a part, dried cow manure one part, and bonemeal a pint to each bushel of the mix.

A mix for succulent plants, including most cactuses, is topsoil two parts, leaf mold, peat moss. or humus two parts, coarse sand or perlite two parts, broken crocks, broken bricks, or broken oyster or clam shells two parts, bonemeal a pint to each bushel of the mix, ground limestone a pint to each bushel of the mix, and wood ashes two quarts to each bushel of the mix. If the topsoil is alkaline omit the limestone. For such strong-growing plants as aloes and agaves, add one-tenth part by bulk of the mix of dried cow manure. For acid-soil plants, such as azaleas, camellias, gardenias, and heaths, use topsoil two parts, leafmold or humus one part, peat moss two parts, coarse sand or perlite two parts, and dried cow manure one part.

For the first potting of newly rooted cuttings and seedlings, use a mix of a type known to be agreeable for later pottings of the same kind of plant, but double or treble the proportion of sand or perlite and omit all fertilizers. Also, sift the ingredients through a ½-inch screen.

For epiphytes, such as orchids and bromeliads, use soil-less mixes based on chips of bark of firs, Douglas-fir, redwood, or other kinds known to be agreeable. The chips are graded to uniform size and are sterilized before being sold commercially. Other ingredients employed alone or in various proportions in mixes for epiphytes are osmunda fiber, tree fern fiber, coconut fiber, and sphagnum moss. To any of these may be added perlite, chicken grit,

and crushed charcoal, the last to help keep the mix from souring, to, as gardeners say, keep it sweet. Some growers include small amounts of such organic fertilizers as steamed bonemeal and dried blood with mixes for epiphytes and some even add inorganics such as superphosphate, but many prefer to omit all such and to rely on satisfying the nutrition of the plants by supplemental fertilizing later.

More important than the actual ingredients or their proportions is the texture of the potting mix. When slightly damp, as it should be when used, a handful squeezed tightly should be sufficiently crumbly that when the hand is opened and the soil mass is tapped lightly it falls apart. If it remains in a tight clod the need for more mineral amendments or organic matter or both is clearly indicated. The proportions of the various ingredients necessary to achieve desirable texture will, of course, depend considerably on the basic soil. If that is sandy and porous less mineral amendments will be needed than if it

Add perlite to bark chips to make a potting mix for epiphytes

is somewhat clayey. If its organic content is low, more organic additive will be needed than if it is naturally rich in such substances.

The coarseness of the mix is important. Do not make the common mistake of sifting potting soils too finely. It is a good rule to have them as coarse as can conveniently be worked among the roots and between them and the sides of the pot. For fine-rooted sorts, such as heaths, and for seedlings, rooted cuttings, and other plants of small size, sifting through a sieve with a ½-inch mesh may be desirable, but for larger and fairly coarse-rooted specimens a mix passed through a ¾- or even a 1-inch screen is sufficiently fine, and for really big plants in tubs and other large containers even more lumpy soil may be advantageous.

As noted soil-less potting mixes for plants other than epiphytes became increasingly popular from mid-century on and are now widely used, exclusively by many commercial growers, and by some amateurs. Their advantages are that they are more easily standardized, that they are much lighter than soil, that they require less labor to prepare, that they are simpler to store and handle; they are also free of pest and disease organisms. Their chief disadvantage is that they have less "buffering" capacity than soil. This means that unless fertilizing is fairly carefully controlled marked and rapid changes in nutrient levels can occur.

Commercially prepared potting mixes come in conveniently sized packages

The stimulus to develop satisfactory soil-less mixes, and techniques for their employment, came from the increasing difficulty commercial growers in many regions experienced in obtaining adequate supplies of suitable topsoil, and from the possibilities soil-less mixes seemed to offer for reducing the amount of labor required for pot plant production and for standardizing procedures to the extent that surer results could be had from less experienced labor.

As early as the late 1920s, experimental work was under way at Ohio State University to determine the practicability of using mixtures of peat moss and sand in place of soil-based potting mixes, but the middle of the century had passed before any considerable use of soil-less mixes was established.

A giant step forward was the development, in the late 1950s, at the University of California (Los Angeles) of what became known as the U.C.L.A. or U.C. mixes. These consisted of fine sand or peat moss used alone or in various proportions, fortified with one of half a dozen prescriptions for nutritive additives. Two of the most popular U.C.L.A. mixes are those designated D and E. The first contains by volume seventy-five percent peat moss and twenty-five percent sand with, added to each cubic yard, five pounds of dolomitic limestone, four pounds of calcium carbonate, two pounds of superphosphate, and four ounces each of potassium nitrate and potassium sulfate, or as an alternative that supplies more nitrogen, some in slow-release organic form, five pounds of dolomitic limestone, two pounds each of calcium carbonate and superphosphate, two and one-half pounds of horn and hoof meal, and four ounces each of potassium nitrate and potassium sulfate.

Peat moss without sand forms the bulk of the U.C.L.A. mix D. To each cubic yard is added five pounds of calcium carbonate, two and one-half pounds of dolomitic limestone, one pound of superphosphate, and six ounces of potassium nitrate, or alternatively, five pounds of calcium carbonate, two and one-half pounds of dolomitic limestone, one pound each of superphosphate, horn and hoof meal, and six ounces of potassium nitrate. This second prescription for nutrient additives supplies more nitrogen, some in slow-release organic form.

Peat-lite mixes developed at Cornell University are among the best known and most widely used soil-less mixes. They are based on peat moss and vermiculite or peat moss and perlite. Several formulations have been devised. A particular feature of these mixes is that, to each cubic yard, three fluid ounces of a non-ionic wetting agent is incorporated, either by adding it to five to ten gallons of water or to a smaller amount of vermiculite and mixing it in.

Peat-lite mixes for pot plants are identified as A and B. The first consists of equal parts by volume of sphagnum peat moss and vermiculite with, added to each cubic yard, five pounds of dolomitic limestone, one and one-half pounds of calcium nitrate or potassium nitrate, one pound of superphosphate, and two ounces of fritted trace elements (FTE 503). Peat-lite B mix differs from the A mix in that perlite is substituted for the vermiculite, the amount of superphosphate is doubled, and potassium nitrate, not calcium nitrate, must be used.

Cornell foliage plant mix, for plants that respond best to a rooting medium with fairly high moisture retention characteristics, consists of, by volume, two parts of sphagnum peat and one part each of No. 2 grade vermiculite and medium-grade perlite. With each cubic yard is incorporated eight and one-half pounds of dolomitic limestone, two and three-quarter pounds of 10-10-10 fertilizer, two pounds of superphosphate, one pound of potassium nitrate, twelve ounces of iron sulfate, and two ounces of fritted trace elements (FTE 503).

Cornell epiphyte mix consists of equal parts by bulk of sphagnum peat moss passed through a one-half-inch screen, bark chips (⅛- to ¼-inch size) of white fir, red fir, or Douglas-fir, and medium-grade perlite. With each cubic yard is incorporated seven pounds of dolomitic limestone, four and one-half pounds of superphosphate, two and one-half pounds of 10-10-10 fertilizer, one pound of potassium nitrate, eight ounces of iron sulfate, and two ounces of fritted trace elements (FTE 503).

Other soil-less potting mixes have been devised, and more undoubtedly will be. Several offered under trade names are available in small or large quantities from dealers in garden supplies. Some amateurs report success with mixes prepared at home. One such consists of a bushel each of coarse sphagnum peat moss and perlite or medium-grade vermiculite with added to the whole five tablespoons each of dolomitic limestone and 5-10-5 fertilizer. Here is a field for home experiment and testing.

POTTING STICK. Used to firm the soil when potting, potting sticks are tools, usually homemade, fashioned from sections of broom handles or similar pieces of a smooth-grained hard wood with little tendency to splinter. Depending upon the size of the pot or tub, lengths of 9 inches

A potting stick in use

to 2 feet are convenient. From below the upper few inches by which the tool is grasped, potting sticks are tapered as wedges to a squared base. They are rarely needed when potting into containers less than 6 inches in diameter. Metal potting sticks available from commercial sources are especially useful for the special technique of potting orchids and other epiphytes in osmunda fiber.

POUTERIA (Pout-èria) — Sapote or Marmalade-Plum or Marmalade Fruit, Canistel or Egg Fruit. The fifty species of *Pouteria*, natives of tropical America, belong in the sapodilla family SAPOTACEAE. The name is a native one.

Pouterias are milky-juiced trees with large, thin, alternate, undivided, toothless leaves. Their nearly stalkless, white, yellow, or greenish flowers, in clusters of few to a dozen, arise from leaf scars on the naked parts of the branches below the leaves. They are symmetrical and have four to ten sepals and tubular corollas with usually four to six lobes (petals) that exceed the tubes in length. There are five fertile stamens and five non-functional slender staminodes, which sometimes are petal-like. The fruits, technically berries, are egg-shaped or oblongish.

The sapote, red sapote, marmalade-plum, or marmalade fruit, has at various times been named *Achras zapota, Lucuma mammosa, Calocarpum mammosum, C. sapota,* and *Pouteria sapota* (syn. *P. mammosa*). The last is accepted here. Native to Central America and widely cultivated in the tropics, *P. sapota* is an evergreen sometimes 100 feet tall, but more often not much more than one-half that height. It has obovate to oblanceolate, hairless leaves 4 inches to 1¼ feet in length, with the veins conspicuous and parallel from the midvein outward. The cup-shaped, inconspicuous flowers are white and about ½ inch in diameter. The thick-skinned, pointed-egg-shaped to ellipsoid fruits have scurfy, russet-brown exteriors; 3 to 6 inches long, they contain a single large seed. They have slightly sticky, sweetish flesh that to those unaccustomed to it is not particularly agreeable raw, but when made into jelly or marmalade is palatable. From the kernels of the seeds a tasty confection is prepared in Costa Rica. The green sapote (**P. viride**), also native to Central America, is similar, but has smaller leaves, downy on their undersides, and thin-skinned fruits of superior eating quality. They are not over 4 inches long and have smaller seeds than those of *P. sapota*.

The canistel or egg fruit (**P. campechiana** syns. *P. c. nervosa, Lucuma nervosa*) is a slender tree up to 25 feet in height with oblong-ovate, oblanceolate or elliptic-lanceolate, pointed, bright green leaves 4 inches to 1 foot long, without hairs, and with distinct, parallel lateral veins. The

greenish-white flowers, in twos to fives in the leaf axils, are succeeded by nearly globose, ovoid, or top-shaped, orange-yellow fruits, pointed at their apexes, and 2 to 6 inches long. They contain, usually, one to three brown seeds ¾ to 1 inch in length and marked on one side with a white blotch. The flesh of the fruits is orange-yellow and has been described as having the "texture of a cooked, mealy sweet potato" and being "sweet with a slight musky taste." Opinions differ widely as to their palatability. By some they are well liked, by others not. The fruits have a high carbohydrate content. They are eaten out of hand or sliced and served with cream and sugar. They are used in salads, pies, puddings, and jams, and are added to ice cream mixes. When eaten raw they are improved by the addition of a little butter or lime or lemon juice. This native of Central America has established itself as a naturalized citizen in the Florida Keys and is cultivated elsewhere in that state, chiefly in warmer, nearly frost-free parts. It is grown in other warm countries. Quite variable, it forms a broad or narrow head. Its leaves and fruits are of diverse shapes and sizes.

Garden and Landscape Uses and Cultivation. Pouterias are grown only in the tropics and warm subtropics. In Florida the canistel endures light frost for short periods. The sapote does well in clayey soil, but it must be well drained. Flooding of the land for even a few days results in the death of the trees. The canistel adapts easily to a wide variety of soils, including shallow, limestone ones as well as those of a sandy character. It is distinctly wind-resistant and is suitable for planting near the sea. Increase of these trees is often by seeds, which should be freed of their surrounding husks and planted shallowly. Those of the sapote germinate in about a month, but seeds of the canistel take three to five months. Alternatively, new plants can be had by grafting (using side grafts) especially desirable kinds onto seedling understocks. Cuttings root slowly. The young plants are transferred to pots or cans in which they are grown until big enough to set out permanently.

POWDER PUFF TREE is *Calliandra haematocephala*.

POWDERY MILDEW. Powdery mildews are funguses, some of which are parasitic on living plants and thus regarded as disease organisms. Their characteristic appearance is that of a white to light grayish, felty or weblike layer covering shoots, foliage, flowers, or other parts and frequently causing curling or dwarfing. Beginning as small spots they develop into patches and may eventually cover the whole surface.

Unlike downy mildews, which invade the host tissues deeply and display above

Powdery mildew on lilac

their surfaces only reproductive organs, powdery mildews are entirely superficial, except for the haustoria (absorbing organs) that penetrate the cells of the host. Powdery mildews affect an extraordinary variety of plants and are common on asters, calendulas, roses, lilacs, and zinnias. They are most common in damp places where air circulation is poor, on plants that are crowded, and when warm days are followed by cool nights; for these reasons they are most prevalent in late summer and fall.

In most cases these funguses are more unsightly than seriously harmful. Preventative measures include avoiding planting susceptible plants in humid locations where air circulation is poor, spacing to prevent overcrowding, and refraining from sprinkling with water in late afternoons or evenings. Dusting or spraying with sulfur or Karathane when temperatures are below 85°F are recommended treatments.

PRAIRIE. This word appears as parts of the common names of these plants: prairie-clover (*Petalosepalum*), prairie-dock (*Silphium terrebinthinaceum*), prairie flax (*Linum lewisii*), prairie-gentian (*Eustoma grandiflorum*), prairie-lily (*Cooperia*), prairie-mallow (*Sphaeralcea coccinea*), prairie-plum (*Astragalus crassicarpus*), prairie rose (*Rosa setigera*), prairie star (*Lithophragma*), prairie sunflower (*Helianthus petiolaris*), and queen-of-the-prairie (*Filipendula rubra*).

PRATIA (Prà-tia). The genus *Pratia* is closely related to *Lobelia*, from which it differs in having succulent fruits. It belongs in the bellflower family CAMPANULACEAE and comprises thirty-five species distributed in Australia, New Zealand, some Pacific islands, South America, tropical Africa, and tropical Asia. Very few of its members are cultivated. The name honors Ch. L. Prat-Bernon, of the French Navy, who died in 1817.

Pratias are usually creeping, but sometimes erect herbaceous plants with alternate, usually broad and toothed leaves and solitary, axillary blooms, mostly unisexual and rather small. The flowers have a five-parted calyx, and a corolla tube, like that of *Lobelia*, split to the base along the back. The corolla is two-lipped with the upper lip two- and the lower three-lobed. There are five stamens, the two lower of which are bristle-tipped. The fruits are berries.

Best known is *P. angulata treadwellii*, a large-flowered variety of a trailing species that normally has small blooms. In some places in Great Britain, notably at the

Pratia angulata treadwellii

Royal Botanic Garden, Edinburgh, *P. angulata* is a weed in lawns. Its variety is attractive in rock gardens where summers are cool and moist, and winters mild, a rare combination in the United States except in the Pacific Northwest.

Endemic to islands off the coast of Tasmania, *P. irrigua* was first discovered in 1803. So far as is known, it was not seen again by botanists until its rediscovery in 1970, which resulted in it being brought into cultivation. A prostrate, matted plant that creeps over wet ground, *P. irrigua* has crowded, somewhat fleshy, short-stalked leaves of variable shapes, often bluntly-

Pratia irrigua

toothed, and up to ⅙ inch long. The very slightly larger, nearly stalkless, starry flowers, the males and females on separate plants, are white or bluish-white with purple anthers.

Garden Uses and Cultivation. The sorts described are attractive for growing in pans (shallow pots) in greenhouses where the night temperature in winter is 40 to 50°F and by day a few degrees higher. They succeed in well-drained, gritty soil kept moderately moist and are easily increased by division.

PRAYER PLANT is *Maranta leuconeura kerchoveana*.

PRAYING MANTIS. These unusual-looking, grasshopper relatives that at rest hold their forelegs in an attitude of prayer are considered friends of gardeners. Some twenty species occur in North America, the native sorts chiefly in the south. Most abundant, largest, and most widely distributed, the Oriental mantis, as its name implies, is an immigrant from Asia, whence it was brought and liberated in the vicinity of Philadelphia, Pennsylvania, about 1896.

Egg masses of the praying mantis

Voracious eaters of other insects, praying mantises make no distinction between foes and friends of gardeners. They relish honeybees and ladybugs as much as other sorts and even consume their own kind when opportunity presents itself. The young, particularly, are cannibalistic. Eggs laid in the fall, as frothy masses of 200 or more that harden into walnut-sized egg cases, hatch in late spring to give rise to active young miniatures of the adult insects.

PREMNA (Prém-na). The plants that constitute *Premna* are natives of the African, Asian, and Pacific tropics. They belong to the vervain family VERBENACEAE and number about 200 species of trees, shrubs, and subshrubs, sometimes climbing. The

name, from the Greek *premnon*, a tree stump, refers to the short trunks of many species.

Premnas have opposite, toothed or toothless leaves. Their small white or greenish flowers are in terminal panicles or spikelike arrangements of opposite clusters. They have small lobed or toothed calyxes, and two-lipped corollas with short, cylindrical tubes, four or five spreading lobes (petals), and four stamens in pairs of unequal lengths. The fruits are berry-like drupes (fruits similar in structure to plums).

Endemic to the Philippine Islands, *P. odorata* is common there. A spreading shrub or tree up to 25 feet in height, it has shoots covered with yellowish, velvety hairs, and variable, longish-stalked, broad-elliptic to ovate or nearly heart-shaped, soft, toothless leaves, finely-hairy, especially on the veins, stalks, and undersides. Their blades are up to about 7 inches long by 5 inches wide. When crushed they have an aromatic odor. The large panicles of tiny blooms are green except for the whitish petals, of which the upper one is erect, the lateral ones reflexed. The flowers have a peppery odor, and are succeeded by bitterish, purplish-black, one-seeded berries, about the size of peppercorns, and much esteemed by birds.

Garden and Landscape Uses and Cultivation. In the tropics and warm subtropics this species is planted as an ornamental. It thrives in ordinary soils and is increased by seed and by cuttings.

PRENANTHES (Pre-nánthes)—Rattlesnake Root. Of minor importance horticulturally, *Prenanthes*, of the daisy family COMPOSITAE, comprises forty species. It inhabits North America, Africa, the Canary Islands, and Asia. Its name derives from the greek *prenes*, drooping, and *anthe*, a flower. It alludes to the nodding flower heads.

Erect, and often tall, but sometimes more or less sprawling, the species of this group are of rather weedy appearance. They contain milky juice, and have alternate leaves, the lower heart- to arrow-shaped, deeply-lobed, and usually stalked, the upper narrower, stalkless, with eared bases, and often stem-clasping. The dullish, purplish to yellowish-white, pendulous, often slender flower heads, without ray florets (those petal-like in appearance such as surround the eyes of daisies), are in panicles or clusters. The seedlike fruits are achenes.

Any of the ten or so native American species may be occasionally planted in native plant gardens where conditions approximate those the plants know in the wild. Among those likely to be so accommodated are *P. aspera* and *P. autumnalis* (syn. *P. virgata*), both about 4 feet tall. The first inhabits grasslands from Ohio to Nebraska, Louisiana, and Oklahoma, the other usually moist, sandy soils from New Jersey to Florida. These hardy herbaceous perennials are easily raised from seed.

PRENIA (Prèn-ia). The South African genus *Prenia* consists of four or five species of low, succulent shrubs, annuals, or biennials of the *Mesembryanthemum* relationship. It belongs in the carpetweed family AIZOACEAE and, like its near relatives, has blooms daisy-like in appearance, but constructed very differently. What is commonly called the flower of a daisy is a head of numerous florets, each technically a flower. The blooms of *Prenia* are single flowers. The name is from the Greek *prenes*, prostrate. It refers to the habit of the plants.

Prenias have short stems with a central cluster of leaves and prostrate or curving flowering branches with alternate leaves that are lanceolate to elliptic, and flat. White, yellow, pink, or purplish, the comparatively large blooms are solitary or in groups of up to five. The fruits are capsules.

A hairless annual or biennial, *P. sladeniana* (syn. *Synaptophyllum sladenianum*) has glaucous, reddish-edged, broad-elliptic leaves, joined at their bases and hollowed on their upper sides, which with age become reflexed. They are up to 2 inches long. The blooms, solitary, or in twos or threes, are 1 inch to 1½ inches across. They are white.

Garden Uses and Cultivation. Prenias are chiefly for collectors of choice succulents. They need very well-drained, dryish soil and full sun. Propagation of the annual or biennial kind is by seed, of others by seed and cuttings. None is frost-hardy.

PRESERVING-MELON. This name is used for *Benincasa hispida* and *Citrullus lanatus citroides*.

PRESTOEA (Prestò-ea). Twelve species of palms closely related to *Euterpe* and by some botanists included in that genus constitute *Prestoea*. They are natives of the West Indies and tropical Central America and belong in the palm family PALMAE. Their name commemorates Henry Prestoe, Government Botanist and Superintendent of the Botanic Garden, Trinidad, from 1864 to 1886.

Prestoeas may be trunkless or small to medium-sized trees. They have pinnate leaves that commonly have much longer stalks than those of *Euterpe* and branched flower clusters that arise from the leaf axils. Each cluster has two bracts of markedly different size, and the flowers, unlike those of *Euterpe*, do not nestle in depressions in the branchlet that bears them, but sit directly on it. The lower parts of the leafstalks may or may not, according to species, sheath each other to form a crownshaft. The fruits are small and globular.

Native to the West Indies, *P. montana*, often called *Euterpe globosa*, commonly grows in limestone soils. Up to 40 or 50 feet tall, from the base of its trunk it develops aerial prop roots covered with tubercles. The leaf blades, about 6 feet long and 3 to 5 feet wide, have many arching,

Prestoea montana

drooping narrow leaflets. The white flowers are in big, once-branched clusters. In Puerto Rico this species grows at higher altitudes than any other native palm. Its glossy-black fruits are a staple food of the native parrot there.

Garden and Landscape Uses and Cultivation. Prestoeas, rare in cultivation, are usually grown only in special palm collections, such as those of botanic gardens. They have the same landscape uses and need the same cultural conditions as *Euterpe*. For other information see Palms.

PRESTONIA (Pres-tòn-ia). Belonging to the dogbane family APOCYNACEAE, the sixty-five species of *Prestonia* are endemic to tropical America, including the West Indies. They are milky-juiced, perennial, more or less woody vines related to *Echites*, in which genus by some authorities they have been included. The name commemorates Charles Preston, professor of botany at Edinburgh, Scotland, who died in 1711.

Prestonias have cylindrical stems and opposite, undivided, lobeless, toothless, pinnately-veined leaves. Nearly always the umbels, clusters, or racemes of flowers come from the leaf axils rather than from the branch ends. The blooms have five-parted calyxes, tubular corollas with five wide-spreading or sometimes reflexed lobes (petals), five stamens, their anthers adherent to the stigma, and one style. The fruits are paired, many-seeded, podlike follicles.

Native to Brazil, *P. coalita* (syn. *Echites coalita*) has slender stems bearing short-stalked, oblong-lanceolate to broad-elliptic leaves 2 to 6 inches long, with pointed tips. Hairless above, they are somewhat short-hairy on their undersides. In racemes or clusters of eight to twenty, the light yellow to greenish-yellow blooms are from somewhat under ½ to about ¾ inch long.

Its stems like the undersides of its leaves, calyxes of its flowers, and seed pods, thickly covered with a golden-yellow to brownish-yellow velvet of hairs, *P. tomentosa* has pointed-broad-ovate leaves 3½ to 8 inches long by up to 4½ inches broad. Its waxy-yellow flowers, in clusters of up to twenty, have hairy corollas the tubes of which are a little over ½ inch long. The pointed seed pods, those of each pair widely divergent, are 2½ to 3¾ inches long. A native of the West Indies and northeastern South America, *P. quinquangularis* (syn. *Echites rubrovenosa*) has pointed, oblong to ovate-elliptic, hairless or nearly hairless leaves up to 6 inches long, veined when young with red or purple, when older with white. The greenish-yellow flowers, ½ to ¾ inch long, are in racemes of six to twenty. The seed pods, the pairs united at their apexes, may exceed 1 foot in length.

Garden and Landscape Uses and Cultivation. These vines are suitable only for the tropics and warm subtropics. They succeed in ordinary soils under conditions that suit *Trachelospermum*, *Mandevilla*, and *Allamanda*. Propagation is by seed and by cuttings.

PRETTY FACE is *Triteleia ixioides*.

PRICKING OFF and PRICKING OUT. These are gardeners' terms for the first transplanting of seedlings from pots, flats, cold frames, and beds to other containers or beds. The purpose is to afford more growing room and often more nourishing soil.

If the soil or other medium in which seedlings are growing is dry, water it thoroughly an hour or two before starting to prick the seedlings off. When lifting the little plants, preserve as many roots as possible and do not allow them to dry during the period, which should be brief, they are out of the soil.

Set the seedlings in holes made with a dibber (a pointed stick) or with a finger, big enough to accommodate the roots without crowding or without their ends being turned up, and push the soil gently against them, taking care not to bruise delicate tissues. Seedlings of dicotyledons (the first or seed leaves of these are a pair of similar ones) that develop a dominant central root with branches from it are best positioned so that the seed leaves just rest on the soil surface. Those of monocotyle-

To prick off seedlings: (a) Fill a flat level to its brim with soil

(b) Press the soil moderately firmly with the fingers

(c) Lift the seedlings carefully from the seed flat

(d) Separate them and set each into a hole made with a dibber

(e) Or with a finger

(f) Press the soil with dibber and fingers against the root

(g) Water with a fine spray

dons (these have a solitary, first or seed leaf and develop from their bases a cluster of equal roots) should be planted with only their roots and perhaps a tiny portion of the bottom of the stem part in the soil.

Complete the operation by watering with a fine spray. It is often helpful to shade newly pricked off seedlings for a few days, and with tender sorts in greenhouses, hot beds, and cold frames, to keep their environment a little warmer and more humid for as long.

PRICKLY. The word prickly is part of the common names of these plants: prickly-ash (*Zanthoxylum americanum*), prickly comfrey (*Symphytum asperum*), prickly-myrtle (*Clerodendrum aculeatum*), prickly-pear (*Opuntia*), prickly-phlox (*Leptodactylon californicum*), prickly-poppy (*Argemone*), and prickly-thrift (*Acantholimon*).

PRICKLY-POPPY or ARGEMONY is *Aregmone*.

PRIDE-OF-CALIFORNIA is *Lathyrus splendens*.

PRIDE-OF-INDIA is *Melia azedarach*.

PRIDE-OF-TENERIFFE is *Echium pininana*.

PRIMROSE. This is the common name of members of the genus *Primula*. It also forms parts of the common names of these plants: Arabian-primrose (*Arnebia cornuta*), Cape-primrose (*Streptocarpus*), evening-primrose (*Oenothera*), and primrose-willow (*Jussiaea*).

PRIMULA (Prím-ula)—Primrose. Cowslip, Oxlip, Auricula. The 400 to 500 species of *Primula*, of the primrose family PRIMULA-

CEAE, are mostly natives of the northern hemisphere, chiefly of mountainous and hilly regions, but some few, including the common primrose, are found at altitudes down to sea level. A scattering of kinds occur south of the equator, one in the vicinity of the Strait of Magellan. The genus is poorly represented in the native flora of North America. Its kinds are much more abundant in the flora of Europe, but the greatest concentration of sorts is in temperate Asia. The generic name, alluding to the early blooming of some sorts, is a diminutive of the Latin *primus*, first.

A few kinds of primulas are well known, but by far the greater number of cultivated sorts are familiar only to specialists and fanciers of alpine plants. In the British Isles and some other parts of Europe, more are grown than in North America, but even there a practical concentration on kinds that perform well and make a good show of bloom has largely replaced a former willingness to fuss over almost any plant that bore the name *Primula*. This is healthy, for even enthusiasts must admit that the genus includes many species wanting in garden worthiness because they lack quality of bloom and often garden permanence. This in no way denigrates kinds that are beautiful and well worth the attentions of gardeners, and among such can be found a few easy to grow as well as sorts that test the skills of experienced cultivators.

Primulas are herbaceous perennials or, in a few cases, perhaps biennials. Most are hardy, a few kinds are not. Typically they have rosettes of all basal, stalked or stalkless, lobed or lobeless, toothed or toothless leaves, and flowers solitary, in umbels, or in superimposed whorls (tiers). Flower colors range from white through cream to yellow and orange, from pale pink to deep red, and from delicate lavender to purple, violet-purple, and blue. The blooms have a tubular, funnel- or bellshaped, five-parted, persistent calyx and a corolla with a slender-cylindrical or funnel-shaped tube and five spreading or less often more or less erect lobes (petals) often notched at their apexes. There are five short-stalked stamens and one style. The relative lengths of stamens and style differ with individual plants. In some, referred to as "pin-eyed," the stamens are only one-half as long as the corolla tube and the style reaches to the mouth of the tube, in others, called "thrum-eyed" the stamens are as long as the tube and the style only about one-half as long. The fruits are capsules.

The genus is classified in thirty botanical sections, not all represented by sorts in cultivation. Gardeners are more given to grouping them according to the horticultural purposes they serve best and the kinds of environments they need. Here both points of view will be considered.

The *Vernales* section of *Primula* is preeminent in gardens because of the showiness, adaptability, and popularity as spring bedding plants of hybrid polyanthus primroses and the ease with which the demure English primrose and almost as tractable *P. juliae* and their hybrids can be grown. Also the European cowslip and oxlip belong here. Sorts of this section, natives often of lowlands in Europe and Asia, bloom in spring, have thinnish, wrinkled leaves generally with wedge-shaped bases, and flowers solitary or in umbels. The common or English primrose (**P. vulgaris** syn. *P. acaulis*), of Europe, is perennial and hardy. It has rather short-stalked, blunt, oblongish to obovate-oblong, roundtoothed, wrinkled leaves 2 to 3 inches long or sometimes longer and solitary blooms 1 inch to 1½ inches in diameter, on stems up to 6 inches in length. In the wild they nearly always are a beautiful soft primrose-yellow, but garden selections with purple and blue blooms are available and come fairly true from seeds, and there are double-flowered sorts. The polyanthus primrose (**P. polyantha**), most familiar and one of the hardiest and easiest to grow of the clan, is of hybrid origin, its parents the common primrose, cowslip, and oxlip. Magnificent strains of this perennial have

Primula vulgaris: (a) Yellow-flowered

(b) Blue-flowered

Primula polyantha

been developed, including the Munstead strain, which originated in England, and the usually slightly less hardy magnificent strains that have been bred in the Pacific Northwest. Polyanthus primroses have robust rosettes of round-toothed, obovate, blunt, wrinkled leaves 4 to 6 inches long, their blades tapered to short, narrowlywinged stalks. In ample, usually stalked but sometimes nearly stalkless umbels, the flowers, up to fully 2 inches in diameter, come in a very wide range of colors. In addition to the usual single-flowered kinds, there are varieties with double

Primula polyantha in a crevice in a dry wall

flowers, some called hose-in-hose, in which the flowers have one corolla set inside another, the Jack-in-the-greens, which sport a ruff of small green leaves around each flower, the lovely and rare gold-laced varieties, and other quaint and unusual forms bearing such Old World names as gallygaskins, pantaloons, and jackanapes. The cowslip and oxlip (**P. veris** and **P. elatior**, respectively) are nearly alike native perennials of Europe, with the oxlip's range extended as far east as Iran. The cowslip, not to be confused with *Caltha palustris*, which is known by that name in parts of North America, has rosettes of softly-hairy, ovate to ovate-oblong, wingedstalked, round-toothed leaves 2 to 3 inches long and erect flowering stalks 4 to 8 inches long topped with many-flowered umbels of delicately fragrant, yellow or much more rarely purplish flowers ½ to 1 inch wide. The blooms, with slightly cupped or saucer-like faces, are contracted a little at their mouths or centers, where

Primula veris

there are scalelike folds. These two characteristics serve to distinguish the cowslip from the oxlip, the flowers of which are flatter, without such folds, and not contracted at their mouths. Also, the seed capsules of the oxlip are as long or longer than the calyx, in contrast to those of the cowslip, which are only one-half as long. Brilliant magenta flowers with yellow throats are borne by *P. juliae,* of Transcaucasia. A close relative of the common primrose, this has been hybridized with it and other sorts to produce many lovely hybrids. Smaller than *P. acaulis,* this spreads slowly by creeping stems to form mats rather than rosettes of foliage. Its red-stalked, roundish, coarsely-toothed, hairless leaves have blades up to 1 inch long. The flowers are solitary and are borne in profusion. They have hair-fringed calyx lobes and petals deeply-notched at their apexes. Hybrids between *P. juliae,* the common primrose, and other species of the *Vernales* group are given the name *P. pruhoniciana* (syn. *P. juliana*). Typically intermediates between their parents, they have blooms, according to variety, ranging from rich crimson-purples through pinkish-orange to pure white.

The *Auricula* section of *Primula* comprises *P. auricula* and several allied species, native to the moutains of Europe, together with numerous delightful varieties and natural and artificial hybrids. Typically these sorts have thick, long, deep roots, short, fat stems, and somewhat fleshy or leathery leaves; the bases of the bracts of the umbels of flowers are usually pouched. The wild form of *P. auricula* has rosettes of fleshy, obovate to oblanceolate,

Primula auricula

frequently densely-mealy, toothed or toothless, rather horny-edged, blunt or pointed leaves 2 to 4 inches long, with tapering bases and sometimes hair-fringed margins. Often delightfully fragrant, the yellow, 1-inch-wide blooms are in many-flowered umbels. They have calyxes cleft to their middles, petals notched at their apexes. Natives of the Alps and Pyrenees, *P. rubra* (syn. *P. hirsuta*) and *P. viscosa* are close allies of *P. auricula.* With a short stem that with age branches, *P. rubra* has broad-elliptic, obovate or roundish, densely-glandular-hairy, short-stalked leaves toothed in their upper parts and 1

inch to 3½ inches long. The bell-shaped flowers in clusters of up to fifteen or occasionally solitary atop stalks 2 to 3 inches tall, are rose-pink, lilac, or mauve and ½ to 1 inch wide. The leaves of *P. viscosa* are broad-elliptic to oblanceolate, blunt, and glandular-hairy. From 3 to 6 inches long, they are usually irregularly-toothed in their upper halves and wedge-shaped at their bases. The flowering stalks, 2 to 5 inches tall, are topped by umbels of many fragrant, narrowly-bell-shaped, violet blooms a little over ½ inch wide. One of the choicest of the *Auricula* section, *P. marginata,* of the European Alps, as it ages develops thick, branched stems at the ends of which are displayed rosettes of blunt, oblongish to obovate, short-stalked, glandular-dotted leaves 1 inch to 4 inches long with scallop-toothed, white-mealy margins. In umbels, of up to twenty atop stalks 2 to 5 inches long and with white-mealy bracts, the fragrant, lavender, lavender-blue, lilac, rosy-lilac, or violet flowers, ¾ to 1 inch wide, have mealy calyxes cleft to their middles and notched petals. Hybrids of *P. auricula, P. rubra,* and *P. viscosa* are correctly identified as *P. pubescens,* but in practice those that most clearly resemble *P. auricula* are usually known as auriculas and only the ones that unmistakably reveal the characteristics of the other parents and in which those of typical *P. auricula* are subjugated are referred to *P. pubescens.* Cultivated auriculas include numerous varieties of often fantastic, almost unbelievable beauty and charm. Formerly, in the British Isles especially, they were extremely popular and fanciers exhibited at special flower shows and concentrated on raising ever more perfect varieties. Many beautiful old prints reveal the perfection of the achievements of these old-time breeders and growers, but few of the sorts they developed have survived two world wars and the changes in horticultural fashion that emphasized greater informality than the strongly stylized "florist's flowers," such as old-time carnations, pansies, and auriculas, possessed. A revival of interest in auriculas developed after the middle of the twentieth century, again chiefly in the British Isles, but to some extent in the Pacific Northwest and elsewhere where climates are favorable to their cultivation and breeders have been busy raising new and lovely varieties. As cultivated plants, auriculas have a long and strange history. Flemish weavers who fled their country in the latter half of the sixteenth century are reported to have brought them to England, where they found a congenial environment, but they were undoubtedly treasured and grown on the continent of Europe much earlier. The first importations to England had flowers of various attractive colors and combinations, but their petals were pointed, which gave to them a starry as-

Primula auricula, horticultural varieties

pect. It was not until the eighteenth century that sorts with rounded petals were developed, sorts with flowers of circular outline with scalloped margins. In the middle of the century, a remarkable development occurred when a completely new type of auricula came into being, one in which the petals of the flowers were replaced by organs that structurally are leaves (although to the ordinary observer they look like petals). Surrounding the central eye of each bloom was a patch of shining white "meal" (really microscopic glandular hairs), whereas the edges of the flowers were white, gray, or green depending upon the presence or absence of meal and its density. By the nineteenth century, the growing of auriculas and the breeding of new varieties had reached a high state of perfection and numerous shows where fanciers displayed their creations and achievements were held regularly. Many of the exhibitors were working men—cotton mill operatives, miners, and others—for whom growing auriculas was the only diversion from daily toil. As was usual in that period, very exacting standards of excellence were established and specimens for exhibition were expected to meet these very closely. In old botanical books many of the best are beautifully illustrated in color. Three chief types are cultivated, show, alpine, and border varieties. Show auriculas, their name a little misleading because in regions where they are grown other sorts are also exhibited at flower shows, are the most intriguingly beautiful of all, but are adapted for cultivation only in alpine greenhouses. Their foliage is more or less dusted with white meal and at the center of their flowers is a prominent ring of meal called the "paste." These sorts are divided into two groups, selfs, with flowers except for the white paste uniformly colored and usually yellow, red, dark maroon, or violet, and edged sorts in which the blooms are rimmed with green, gray, or white, and the zone between this and the paste is almost black. Alpine auriculas are also best suited for alpine greenhouses. They are compact and have little or no meal on their foliage. Their flowers, without paste, come in a wide range of colors, including crimson, scarlet, maroon, purple, and almost black, with a center eye of yellow or less often white. Border auriculas are the best adapted for outdoor cultivation. From alpine sorts they differ in being larger and more robust and in having a dusting of meal on their foliage and flowers, on the latter confined to the center eye and usually extremely light except in the throat. The blooms come in shades of red, purple, brown, yellow, buff, and white, as well as a variety of undesirable muddy tones.

The *Candelabra* section of *Primula* consists of kinds with bold, mostly erect foliage, and flowers in several whorls (tiers) on erect stalks. The floral bracts are small and usually inconspicuous, and according to kind the flowering parts are or are not mealy. Best known is the Japanese primrose, but the greatest number of kinds are natives of the Himalayan region. Generally robust, these respond to fertile, moist or wet soil and partial shade. China and Burma are home territories of *P. anisodora*, which has all its parts scented of anise. The leaves, up to 10 inches long, hairless, and without waxy meal, are blunt-obovate, toothed, and narrow to winged stalks. The flowers are tubular-funnel-shaped, a little over ½ inch in diameter, and brownish-purple with greenish or yellow centers. They are in five or fewer eight- to ten-flowered whorls. Native to western China, *P. aurantiaca* has rosettes of oblanceolate to obovate, toothed leaves up to 8 inches long, and on stalks about 1 foot high two to six tiers of six to twelve reddish-orange flowers about ½ inch long and wide. Rose purple to claret-crimson, slightly fragrant flowers with yellow eyes are borne freely by robust *P. beesiana*, of China. This has irregularly-toothed, ovate-lanceolate leaves 5 inches to nearly 1 foot long and up to 2 inches wide that have winged stalks, rounded or pointed apexes, and slightly hairy undersides. The flowering stalks, 1½

Primula aurantiaca

to 2½ feet tall and white-mealy only in their upper parts, carry several tiers of ¾-inch-wide blooms with calyxes cleft to their middles and like the individual flower stalks covered with white meal. A hybrid swarm of great charm, *P. bullesiana* is the outcome of crossing *P. beesiana* and *P. bulleyana*. In general aspect the offspring resemble the parent species. They come in a wide range of flower colors from creamy-white through buff-yellow and orange to lilac, pink, crimson, and purple. Deep apricot to apricot-orange blooms are characteristic of *P. bulleyana*, a Chinese kind. Its ovate-lanceolate, irregularly-toothed leaves, which narrow to winged stalks, except for sometimes a few hairs on

Primula bulleyana

their undersides are hairless. From 1½ to 2½ feet tall, the flowering stalks are white-mealy below each of the several many-flowered tiers of ¾- to 1-inch-wide blooms that have rounded, notched petals and calyxes cleft to their middles. Native to Burma and China, *P. burmanica* is somewhat like *P. beesiana*, but the calyxes and stalks of its individual blooms are not

white-mealy. Its blunt, oblanceolate, toothed, wrinkled leaves tapered at their bases to winged stalks are up to 1 foot long by about 2 inches wide. The yellow-eyed, reddish-purple flowers, ½ inch or slightly more in diameter, are in six or fewer whorls of ten to eighteen. Usually short-lived *P. cockburniana*, of China, is a handsome sort, with blunt, obovate-oblong, minutely-toothed leaves tapered at their bases and 2 to 5 inches long. At first somewhat hairy, they later become hairless. From 6 inches to 1½ feet tall, the flowering stalks carry tiers, with only tiny bracts, of brilliant orange, 1-inch-wide flowers that have white-mealy calyxes and blunt, slightly-notched petals. An attractive Chinese, *P. helodoxa* has blunt, oblanceolate, toothed leaves narrowed to winged stalks and 4 inches to over 1 foot

Primula helodoxa

long by 1 inch to 3 inches wide. From 1½ to 3 feet tall, the erect flowering stalks carry up to about five tiers of ¾-inch-wide, clear yellow flowers, with calyxes lobed about one-third of their lengths and heavily powdered with yellow meal, and petals sometimes slightly notched at their apexes. The Japanese primrose (*P. japonica*), one of the most amiable of Asian

Primula japonica

sorts, as its name implies is a native of Japan. Vigorous, easy to grow, and hairless, under favorable conditions, it makes great rosettes of leaves 4 to 8 inches long by up to 2½ inches wide. Oblong-obovate to spatula-shaped, blunt and irregularly-toothed, they have tapered bases and winged stalks. Typically bright claret-crimson with a yellow eye, but varying to purplish-pink, brownish-pink, pink, and white, the blooms, 1 inch or more in diameter, are in up to six many-flowered tiers on stout stalks 9 inches to 2 feet tall. The calyxes are mealy on their insides. The apexes of the petals are notched. Chinese **P. pulverulenta,** very fine, looks much like a refined version of the Japanese primrose. It has obovate to oblanceolate, irregularly-toothed leaves 6 inches to 1¼ feet long that narrow gradually to long, winged stalks. Its about 1½-foot-tall flowering stalks have several tiers of rich claret-crimson, 1-inch-wide blooms with orange-brown eyes. Their calyxes are heavily powdered with white meal, their petals have notched apexes. The 'Bartley' strain, which comes true from seeds, has beautiful pink flowers.

Primula pulverulenta

The *Sikkimensis* section of *Primula* consists of kinds that in habit of growth and environmental preferences are much like *Candelabra* primulas. From those they differ most obviously in their flowers being usually bell-shaped and the stalks that carry them generally having only a single umbel of blooms. Sometimes a second tier develops, but never more. The vigorous, primroses of this group revel in damp or wet, fertile soil and partial shade. The type species of the section, **P. sikkimensis,** of the Himalayas, has blunt-obovate, toothed, hairless, crinkled leaves 3 to 6 inches long by up to 1¾ inches wide. Its umbles of clear yellow, drooping, bell-shaped flowers are on stalks 9 inches to 1½ feet tall. The blooms, about 1 inch wide, have individual stalks approximately 1 inch long.

Primula sikkimensis

Primula sikkimensis (flowers)

Tibetan **P. alpicola** (syn. *P. microdonta alpicola*), in effect, is a small edition of *P. sikkimensis*. It has elliptic to oblong-elliptic, blunt, round-toothed, nearly-hairless, crinkled leaves 3 to 6 inches long by up to 3 inches wide. On stalks 1 foot to 1½ feet tall, the mealy umbels are of fragrant, yellow or less commonly creamy-white, bell-shaped flowers ¾ inch across with petals with notched apexes. The blooms are flatter than those of *P. sikkimensis.* Those of

Primula alpicola

Primula florindae

P. a. violacea are purple or violet. Very vigorous *P. florindae* suggests a giant *P. sikkimensis*. Native to Tibet, it develops rosettes of hairless, ovate, toothed, glossy leaves markedly heart-shaped at the bases of their blades, which are up to 9 inches long by two-thirds as wide. Their stalks are long, channeled, and reddish. From 1 foot to 4 feet in height, the sturdy flowering stalks support umbels of up to sixty fragrant, pendulous, sulfur-yellow, bell-shaped blooms ½ inch wide and longer than wide. The bracts of the umbels, dusted with white meal, are lanceolate and about ½ inch in length. In aspect much like a dwarf *P. sikkimensis*, but with distinctive foliage, Chinese **P. secundiflora** is about 1 foot tall. It has hairless, pointed or blunt, oblong to oblong-lanceolate, finely-round-toothed leaves up to about 5 inches long and abruptly contracted to a short stalk. Its bell-shaped, reddish-crimson flowers, about ¾ inch wide, are in one-sided umbels of up to about a dozen. Their calyxes are dusted with white meal. At first the blooms droop, but before they fade face upward.

The *Cortusoides* section of *Primula* is composed of woodland sorts with generally long-stalked, usually broad, lobed leaves without a trace of waxy meal. The flowers, in from one to three whorls (circles of several), are purplish, rosy-purple, white, or rarely yellowish. These sorts spread slowly by underground runners. After their seeds mature the foliage dies and the plants enter a period of dormancy. Typical of this group, **P. cortusoides,** of western Siberia, softly-hairy, has ovate-oblong leaves 2 to 4 inches long with more or less heart-shaped bases to the irregularly-lobed and toothed blades. From 6 inches to 1 foot tall, the slender flowering stalks are topped by umbels, furnished with linear bracts, of rose-pink flowers ½ to ¾ inch wide and with notched petals. Each bloom has an individual stalk about

½ inch in length and about as long as the calyx. Very similar *P. saxatilis*, of northern Asia, differs most noticeably from *P. cortusoides* in the much longer stalks of its individual flowers. These greatly exceed the calyx lobes in length. An inhabitant of high mountains in central and southern Europe, *P. halleri* (syn. *P. longiflora*) has lanceolate-elliptic to oblanceolate, toothed or nearly toothless leaves 1 inch to 5 inches long, heavily dusted on their undersides with yellow meal. In umbels of up to a dozen atop mealy stalks 3 to 7 inches tall, the 1-inch-long, ¾-inch-wide,

Primula halleri

violet flowers are deeply-notched at the apex of each petal. Himalayan *P. mollis* has softly-hairy, broadly-heart-shaped, slightly-lobed and toothed leaves 3 to 5 inches across, and in loose tiers on slender stalks up to 2 feet tall, ¾-inch-wide dark-centered, pink to crimson flowers. Chinese *P. polyneura* (syns. *P. veitchii*, *P. lichiangensis*) in growth habit suggests *P. sinensis*. It has long-stalked, lobed and toothed leaves up to 4 inches in diameter, white-hairy or hairless on their undersides and stalks and in outline from oblong-triangular to nearly circular. Up to 1 foot tall, the slender flowering stalks carry one or often

Primula mollis

two superimposed loose umbels of rose-pink to magenta blooms, 1 inch or more across, and with hairy bracts markedly shorter than the stalks of the individual flowers. Each bloom has a small yellow eye and notched petals. Native to Japan and of agreeable disposition, *P. sieboldii* adapts well to gardens in northeastern North America and lasts well. In aspect it suggests *P. sinensis*, but unlike that sort is quite hardy. In Japan it is cultivated in innumerable varieties, and special flower shows are held at which fanciers display their achievements in competition much

Primula sieboldii

as growers of auriculas once did in the British Isles. Softly-hairy, *P. sieboldii* forms clumps with long-stalked, ovate-oblong, crinkled leaves 2 to 4 inches long, heart-shaped at their bases, and shallowly-lobed and toothed; they die down about midsummer. In many-flowered, loose umbels on stalks 4 to 8 inches tall, the white, pink rose-purple, or red flowers 1½ to 2 inches in diameter have hairless calyxes and notched, sometimes frilled petals.

The *Farinosae* section of *Primula*, named after one of its best-known species, is of wide geographical distribution. It consists of kinds native in alpine, subarctic, and arctic regions in many parts of the northern hemisphere, including North America, and is represented south of the equator in the floras of Chile, Patagonia, Tierra del Fuego, and the Falkland Islands. With few exceptions, of which *P. rosea* is the most notable, the sorts of the *Farinosae* section have hairless or at most minutely-hairy foliage powdered with white or light-colored meal. Nearly always the bracts that accompany the flowers are more or less pouched. The birdseye primrose (*P. farinosa*), native of cool parts of Europe including Great Britain, inhabits damp upland meadows. It has lanceolate to obovate-lanceolate, toothed to almost toothless leaves, ½ inch to 3 inches long, tapered to their bases and very white-mealy on their undersides. The ½-inch-wide, lilac flowers, in many-flowered um-

Primula farinosa

bels that top stalks 4 to 6 inches tall, have blunt calyx lobes, deeply-notched petals, and yellow throats with distinct scales. The floral bracts are lanceolate. Close relatives of *P. farinosa* and by some authorities considered varieties of it, *P. laurentiana* and *P. mistassinica* are endemic to North America. Occurring on wet rocks and cliffs from Labrador to Nova Scotia and Maine, *P. laurentiana* has oblanceolate to spatula-shaped leaves up to about 4 inches long and densely dusted on their undersides with white or yellow meal. The umbels of up to fifteen ⅓- to ½-inch-wide, white to pink or lilac flowers top stalks up to 1¼ feet in length. Except for being smaller, its leaves 2 to 3 inches long and its flowering stalks rarely more than 9 inches long, *P. mistassinica* is much like the last. It is native on moist rocks, cliffs, and gravelly lake shores from Labrador probably across the continent and southward to northern New England, New York, and Illinois. One of the most satisfactory garden primroses, *P. frondosa* is a native of the Balkan Peninsula. From *P. farinosa* this is distinguishable by its about 1-inch-long, obovate, toothed leaves having distinctly winged stalks and its flowers having

Primula frondosa

pointed calyx lobes and being without or at most having vestigial scales in their throats. Like those of *P. farinosa,* the leaves are white-mealy on their undersides. About ½ inch in diameter, the yellow-eyed, rosy-lilac flowers are many together in loose umbels with collars of lanceolate bracts, atop mealy stalks 2 to 4 inches tall. They have notched petals. Native to China, Burma, and Tibet, **P. yargongensis** (syn. *P. wardii*) has ovate to elliptic, finely-toothed or toothless leaves 1 inch to 4 inches long and without waxy meal. Up to about 1 foot tall, its flowering stalks terminate in solitary umbels of a few fragrant, white-eyed, rose-pink to violet flowers about 1 inch wide and with petals notched at their apexes. The floral bracts are furnished with long appendages. Closely related **P. involucrata,** of high altitudes in the Himalayas, differs from the last most obviously in its flowers being white. Something of a maverick among primulas of the *Farinosa* persuasion, lovely **P. rosea** is remarkable for having foliage devoid of any trace of waxy meal. This moisture-loving Himalayan alpine adapts well to domestication. It forms dense tufts of very short-stalked, toothed, ovate-oblong to oblanceolate, hairless leaves 2 to 2½ inches long by up to ¾ inch wide that do not attain full size until the flowers have faded. The latter, bright rose-pink, nearly ¾ inch wide, and with deeply-notched petals, are in umbels with narrow bracts topping stalks 2 to 8 inches tall. Variety *P. r. grandiflora* is taller and has somewhat larger flowers than the typical species.

The *Denticulata* section of *Primula* is remarkable for its flowers being in dense spherical heads perched atop erect stalks in drumstick-like fashion. The blooms differ from those of the *Capitatae* section in more or less facing upward instead of being pendulous. Depending upon kind, the undersides of the foliage, the flowering stalks, and other parts are or are not dusted with meal. The sorts of this section overwinter as large, plump, scale-covered buds from which in late winter new foliage and flowers break out. The type species of its section, **P. denticulata,** of the Himalayas, has blunt, oblong-obovate to spatula-shaped, sharp-toothed, hairless leaves narrowed to winged stalks and at most slightly mealy. At flowering time they are usually only partly developed. The ½-inch-wide flowers, in crowded heads atop stalks 6 inches to 1 foot tall and of a pleasing soft lavender to lavender-violet hue, each have a small yellow eye. The blooms of *P. d. alba* are white with a yellow eye. Larger and more robust than the typical species, *P. d. cachemiriana* (syn. *P. cachmeriana*) has leaves usually almost fully developed at flowering time and conspicuously coated with yellowish meal. Its flowers are violet-purple with a yellow

Primula denticulata

eye. In addition to the varieties mentioned other selections are grown as named horticultural varieties.

The *Capitatae* section of *Primula* is distinguished from *Denticulata* primulas most obviously by the flowers of the crowded, spherical or more disk-shaped heads being more or less pendulous instead of erect. The undersides of the leaves may be mealy or not. These sorts do not have the stout winter buds of primulas of the *Denticulata* section. The sorts discussed here tend not to be long-lived and prefer damp soils. Dense, globular heads of stalkless, purplish-blue flowers and densely-white-mealy, lanceolate bracts are characteristic of **P. capitata** and its variety *P. c. mooreana,* both of the Himalayas. The latter differs from the other in being more robust, in having rather bigger leaves, white-mealy on their undersides but bright green above, and in having slightly larger flowers. The leaves of *P. capitata,* 4 to 5 inches long and oblong-lanceolate, have toothed margins and taper to winged stalks. The upper surfaces of the leaves are more or less powdered with, their undersides densely coated with, white meal. The ½-inch-wide, fragrant flowers, bell-shaped and nodding, are in spherical heads atop

Primula capitata

stems 6 to 9 inches tall, which like the calyxes, are dusted with white meal.

Section *Parryi* of *Primula* is confined in the wild to mountains in North America. Not easy to grow, its sorts bear a strong resemblance to those of the *Nivales* section, from which they are distinguished by their toothless or nearly toothless leaves being when young folded inward instead of outward. Endemic to the Rocky Mountains, beautiful **P. parryi** inhabits moist rock crevices, meadows, and stream banks at alpine altitudes. It has slightly sticky, erect, fleshy, oblanceolate, toothed leaves up to 1 foot long by 2¼ inches wide, but frequently smaller. On stalks often longer than the leaves, the umbels are of up to fifteen yellow-eyed, bright purplish-red flowers ¾ to 1 inch in diameter. Native at high altitudes in Arizona and New Mexico, **P. rusbyi** rivals *P. parryi* in beauty and is as reluctant to accept domestication. Its thin, oblanceolate, toothed leaves, 2 to 3 inches long, taper at their bases to narrowly-winged stalks. Its slender flower-bearing stalks, 4 to 6 inches tall, carry umbels of up to ten bright rose-pink flowers with notched petals forming concave faces about ¾ inch across. Unlike other parts, the calyxes of the blooms, which are cleft nearly to their middles, are powdered with white meal.

Primula rusbyi

The *Nivales* section of *Primula* contains a large number of species many untested in cultivation; most that have been attempted were found difficult or impossible to grow. Typically, they have thick necks above the crown of the roots, undivided, lanceolate, usually mealy leaves tapered to flattened stalks, and generally large, cylindrical seed capsules. The kind here discussed does best in well-drained dampish soil that contains an abundance of organic matter. Most tractable of *Nivales* primulas, delightful **P. chionantha** is a native at high altitudes in China. It has rather fleshy, broad-lanceolate to oblong-elliptic, smooth leaves, up to almost 1 foot long and 2 inches wide, tapered to winged stalks and heavily dusted on their undersides with yellow meal. The flowering stalks, 1 foot to 1½ feet tall, bear two or three tiers with yellow-mealy bracts of ¾-inch-wide, white blooms with densely-yellow-mealy calyxes and hair-fringed, notchless petals.

The *Bullatae* section of *Primula* takes its name from its leaves being bullate, that is, having the veins on their upper surfaces depressed and the areas between them bulging upward. Its few sorts, all Chinese, have woody rhizomes and lobeless, evergreen leaves. The flowers are yellow, lilac, mauve, or white. These sorts resent excessive moisture, need light shade. Most accommodating of the *Bullatae* section, **P. forrestii** develops dense clusters of finely-hairy, ovate-elliptic, toothed leaves 2 to 4 inches long, and atop stalks 6 to 9 inches tall, umbels of brilliant orange-yellow, scented flowers with darker centers.

Primula forrestii

The *Muscarioides* section of *Primula* is distinguished by its individually stalkless, down-pointing flowers being in slender stalked spikes that in miniature more or less suggest those of red hot poker plants (*Kniphofia*), but are very much smaller and are colored differently. Only one sort is at all frequent in cultivation. Distinctive **P. vialii** (syn. *P. littoniana*), of China, has fragrant flowers ¼ to ½ inch across in narrow, erect, rat-tail-like spikes 2 to 5 inches long topping stalks mealy toward their apexes, 9 inches to 1½ feet in length. The upper part of the spike consists of the bright orange-red calyxes that contrast strongly with the violet-blue, open flowers that crowd the lower portions of the spikes. The broad-lanceolate, soft-downy leaves narrow gradually to winged stalks.

The *Soldanelloidae* section of *Primula* includes choice **P. nutans,** of western China, which dies after its first flowering, but usually produces abundant seed. This has a rosette of softly-hairy, elliptic to oblanceolate leaves 4 to 8 inches long and, topping mealy stalks up to 1 foot tall or taller, crowded heads of five to fifteen fragrant,

Primula vialii

Primula vialii (flowers)

Primula nutans

1-inch-wide, nodding, wide-funnel-shaped, violet to lavender flowers dusted with whitish meal.

The *Obconica* section of *Primula* consists of a group of closely allied nonhardy species, native mostly at low elevations from China to the Himalayas, of which only *P. obconica* is horticulturally important. Its members are remarkable for the calyxes of the flowers gradually developing into what is described as a fleshy cone or cup. The long-stalked leaves, which have

Primula obconica variety

roundish blades, are completely free of meal or farina. Popular as winter- and spring-blooming greenhouse and florists' gift plants, horticultural varieties of *P. obconica*, especially those identified as *P. o. grandiflora* and *P. o. gigantea*, have larger flowers in clearer and more diverse colors than the typical wild species. There are varieties with semidouble flowers and some with blooms with frilled petals. Like the species, these have hairy, roundish-oblong, scalloped-edged leaves 3 to 5 inches across. The blooms, up to 1½ inches or more in diameter, and of various shades of pink, purple-red, and red, as well as white, are handsomely displayed in large, sturdy-stalked umbels carried well above the foliage. They come in succession over a long period in winter and spring and as window plants remain longer in bloom than varieties of *P. sinensis* and *P. malacoides*. A disadvantage of *P. obconica* is that contact with the foliage causes susceptible individuals to develop a skin rash not unlike that induced by poison-ivy. However, modern varieties are much less likely to trigger this than those of half a century more ago, and many more people are immune to primula than to poison-ivy poisoning.

The *Malacoides* section of *Primula* is a small one that includes the fairy and baby primroses. Its members resemble *Candelabra* kinds in their flowers being in several tiers, but differ in botanical details of greater significance. All are natives of Asia; none is hardy. Characteristically these sorts have long-stalked, thinnish, obscurely-lobed, toothed, hairy leaves and many stalks carrying yellow-eyed, pink, lavender, red, or white blooms. The flowering parts are more or less powdered with white meal. The seed capsules are spherical and enclosed by the calyxes. The fairy primrose (*P. malacoides*) is a graceful Chinese, much grown in its improved horticultural varieties as a winter- and spring-blooming greenhouse pot plant and in regions, such as parts of California, with Mediterranean climates for outdoor winter

Primula malacoides, single-flowered

Primula malacoides, double-flowered

and spring bedding. This has ovate to oblong-ovate, shallowly six- to eight-lobed, toothed leaves with stalks much longer than the blades; the latter hairy on their undersides, hairless above. The white, lilac-pink, rose-pink, or crimson flowers, ½ inch to 1½ inches across, in horticultural varieties are in several to many tiers decorating slender to fairly stout, erect stalks. There are double- as well as single-flowered varieties. The bracts accompanying them, like the calyxes and frequently the undersides of the leaves, are most often coated with a white meal. A miniature fairy primrose, the baby primrose (**P. forbesii**), also Chinese, differs most obviously from its larger relative in its leafstalks not exceeding in length the heart-shaped-ovate blades. The leaf blades, ordinarily not over 2 inches long, are slightly lobed and scarcely toothed. The pink or lavender-pink flowers have shorter individual stalks than those of *P. malacoides*.

The *Sinensis* section of *Primula* has flowers with bladdery calyxes that have broad, flat bases. All its kinds are Chinese; none is hardy. The sorts that belong here have long-stalked leaves and umbels of showy

blooms. Among the earliest Oriental primulas to be introduced to Europe were varieties of **P. sinensis** (syn. *P. praenitens*) brought from Chinese gardens. Softly-hairy, these varieties have leaves with long, brittle stalks and almost circular to broadly-triangular blades 3 to 5 inches across, cleft into several irregularly-toothed lobes, and at their bases heart-shaped. From 1 inch to 1½ inches wide or wider, the blooms, which have notched or fringed petals, range in color through a considerable assortment of pinks and reds as well as lavender, blue, purple, and white. They are in one or more whorls (tiers) each of up to ten blooms. A distinct group of *P. sinensis* varieties differ from earlier sorts in having smaller, more starry blooms in several tiers. These are often grown as *P. s. stellata*.

The *Verticillata* section of *Primula* comprises three or possibly four evergreen species, none hardy and all with yellow flowers that come chiefly in late winter and spring. The short-stalked leaves are in tufts or rosettes. Freely produced, the blooms are in whorls (tiers) furnished with large, leafy bracts. The buttercup primrose (**P. floribunda**), an altogether delightful native of the Himalayas, is glandular-pubescent and completely devoid of meal. It has loose rosettes of rather thin, elliptic to obovate, irregularly-toothed leaves 3 to 5 inches long. The 4- to 8-inch-tall flowering stalks carry several well-spaced tiers of delicately fragrant blooms mostly ½ to ¾ inch in diameter, but sometimes smaller,

Primula floribunda

accompanied by leafy, ovate to lanceolate bracts. The petals are rounded or slightly-notched at their apexes. Pale, sulfur-yellow flowers distinguish *P. f. isabellina*. Arabian **P. verticillata**, more robust and bigger than *P. floribunda*, differs in not being glandular-hairy and in its foliage, bracts, and calyxes being coated with a white meal. It forms loose rosettes of lanceolate to ovate-lanceolate, irregularly-

Primula floribunda isabellina

Primula verticillata

toothed leaves 4 to 8 inches long, with short, winged stalks. The flowering stalks, up to 2 feet tall, but usually lower, have several well-spaced tiers of delicately fragrant, clear yellow blooms ¾ to 1 inch wide and with slightly notched petals of a less golden hue than those of *P. floribunda*. The leafy bracts of the umbels up to 3 inches long, are linear-lanceolate. The Kew primrose (**P. kewensis**), an intermediate hybrid between *P. floribunda* and *P. verticillata* that originated as a chance seedling at the Royal Botanic Gardens, Kew, England, in 1897 and since has been reproduced by deliberate crossing, in its original sterile form is extremely rare in cultivation, since it can only be propagated by division. Very rarely, perhaps only once, has it produced seeds. From those seeds were raised the freely seeding, tetraploid plant, now commonly grown as *P. kewensis*, but which is deserving of another name to distinguish it from the sterile hybrid to which the name *P. kewensis* was first applied. The chief differences between the two, besides their sterility or

Primula kewensis, sterile form

Primula kewensis, fertile form

Polyanthus primroses in a decorative planter

fertility, are the greater size of foliage and flowers and more vigorous growth of the seed-bearing sort, and also its variability in the amount of the white, mealy coating on the leaves, bracts, and other parts. True *P. kewensis* in aspect resembles a robust *P. floribunda* with some of the characteristics of *P. verticillata*. The amount of meal on the foliage and other parts varies greatly between individuals.

Garden and Landscape Uses. Besides the many choice alpine or rock garden primulas that challenge the skills of experienced growers and those that under favorable conditions prosper in woodlands and at watersides, there are hardy sorts suitable for spring bedding or more permanent residence in flower beds and more informal plantings and nonhardy kinds used similarly in mild Mediterranean climates, such as that of California, and grown as pot plants in greenhouses. English and polyanthus primroses are also excellent as greenhouse pot plants for forcing for late winter and spring bloom. Alpine primulas, low kinds from high altitudes and far northern latitudes, are for the most part lovers of cool, humid summers. These are for keen devotees of rock

gardening and operators of alpine greenhouses.

Cultivation. Primulas need shade from strong sun, cool, humid environments, and dampish to wet soil with a fairly high organic content. Beyond these simple basics, the needs of different kinds vary considerably and so do procedures employed to grow them. Because of this, it is convenient to group them with reference to their environmental preferences and the methods of cultivation.

English primroses, polyanthus primroses, cowslips, and oxlips are the easiest to grow and the most adaptable. They are hardy and succeed in all temperate climates in average soils that, if low in organic matter, are fortified by spading in rotted manure, leaf mold, humus, or peat moss; they must never become excessively dry, but these primroses will not stand swamp conditions. Nor do they like exposure to wind or to heat reflected from walls or other surfaces. True, as spring bedding plants to be moved to other locations or discarded after blooming, polyanthus primroses endure considerable exposure, but if they are to be retained as permanent inhabitants of the garden, more genial sites are necessary. In regions of hot summers a chief trouble is their marked susceptibility to infestations of red spider mites. To combat these it is necessary to spray regularly through the hottest months. If this is not done the plants are greatly weakened, grow poorly, and are likely to succumb.

Primulas of this group are easily increased by division of old plants as soon as they are through blooming and by seed. Division is simply accomplished by pulling the clumps apart so that each division consists of a single crown with some roots. Shorten the leaves to about one-half their length and plant the divisions in a agreeable place outdoors or in a cold frame where they will benefit from a fairly humid environment and shade.

Seeds of these primulas may be sown in fall in pots plunged (buried) to their rims in sand or peat moss in a cold frame, in spring with the pots plunged or not, or although this is rarely done, seeds may be sown in a sheltered, shady spot outdoors in spring. But if sizable plants of polyanthus or English primroses are needed for spring beds, an earlier start that allows for some growth to develop indoors before the seedlings are set outdoors must be made.

The usual procedure is to sow in February in a greenhouse where the night temperature is 55 to 60°F, to transplant the seedlings, as soon as they are big enough to handle easily, 2 inches apart in flats containing soil well laced with organic matter and to keep them growing in a night temperature of 50°F with an increase by day of five to fifteen degrees until there is no longer danger of frost. The next move, after hardening the plants by standing the flats outdoors for two or three weeks, is transplanting them to a shaded nursery bed or cold frame to make their summer growth. Then in fall or the following spring they are transferred to their flowering sites.

Bog primulas, as the designation suggests, are lovers of wet soils. Nevertheless they will not do well in stagnant swamps; for their best growth they need water containing more oxygen and less accumulated organic acids. Pond sides, lake sides, and stream sides where there is some flow of water through the soil are best to their liking. Most bog primulas can be grown with notable success in rich soil that is not boggy if it is made water retentive by mixing in generous amounts of leaf mold, peat moss, or similar organic material and if it is watered enough to keep it always moist. Shade is needed in summer, but not so dense that the plants do not receive broken or dappled sun.

Rock garden and alpine greenhouse sorts of generally low stature, and excluding kinds previously dealt with that are also grown in rock gardens, need care often adjusted to the special needs of individual kinds. Some, such as *P. juliae* and the galaxy of hybrids developed from it labeled *P. pruhoniciana*, are about as easy to grow as the English primrose and respond to the same conditions. Others can be exasperatingly recalcitrant and there are intermediates of all degrees of difficulty.

If generalization is to be useful, the most that can be said is see that the soil contains ample organic matter and is well drained, but not allowed to become really dry and that except in early spring there is enough shade to mitigate heat and prevent yellowing or scorching of the foliage.

Greenhouse primulas, nonhardy sorts grown primarily as pot plants, but some in regions, such as California, that have Mediterranean climates, employed as winter and spring bedding plants, include *P. malacoides*, *P. forbesii*, *P. obconica*, and *P. sinensis*, all with white, pink, or red flowers, and *P. kewensis*, *P. floribunda*, and *P. verticillata*, with yellow blooms. With the exception of the sterile form of *P. kewensis*, all are readily raised from seed and the yellow-flowered kinds lend themselves also to increase by division immediately flowering has finished.

All these nonhardy sorts respond to approximately the same care and management. Lovers of cool, humid environments with good air circulation, they find summers in many parts of North America distressing. Then, unless an air-cooled greenhouse is available, they are best accommodated in a freely-ventilated, shaded cold frame; one located on the north side of a wall, fence, or hedge is likely to be ideal. Have the surface on which pots stand of earth, sand, cinders, or other material that when wetted absorbs moisture that gradually evaporates and humidifies the air.

In late September, or earlier if there is danger of frost, transfer the plants to a sunny greenhouse where, except for *P. sinensis* and its varieties that do better with temperatures about five degrees higher, whenever outdoor conditions permit, the indoor temperature is kept at 45 to 50°F and daytime levels, depending upon the brightness of the weather, are five to ten degrees higher.

Sow seeds of greenhouse primulas from March to May to obtain large plants that will bloom from December to April, or in late August or September to have smaller specimens. Use well-drained pots or pans (shallow pots) and a porous soil mix containing an abundance of peat moss or leaf mold. Pass this through a ½-inch screen before filling the containers, then press it moderately firm and level its surface about ½ inch below the edge of the pot. Top off with a ¼-inch layer of the same mix sifted through a finer screen and press lightly. Then water thoroughly with a fine spray or by standing the pot or pan to part of its depth in water and leaving it until moisture seeps to the surface.

Scatter the seeds thinly, press them lightly into the surface, and cover with the slightest sprinkling of soil or sand, or omit this. Put a piece of glass or polyethylene plastic film over the pot or pan, and keep it shaded in a temperature of 55 to 60°F, or if seasonal temperatures are higher than this, keep it in as cool a location as is practicable.

When the seedlings are big enough to handle conveniently, transplant them 2 inches apart in flats or individually to small pots in soil similar to that used for seed sowing, but coarser. Keep them growing in a shaded greenhouse or cold frame. Later pottings, their timing dependent upon the amount of growth the plants make, will be needed. As final containers, pots 5 to 7 inches in diameter are satisfactory. For these pottings use a porous, fertile mix containing abundant organic matter, including some dried cow manure, if available, with a generous dash of bonemeal or other fairly slow-acting fertilizer included.

Be careful when potting not to set the plants too deeply or not deeply enough. With *P. sinensis* this calls for special care because as they grow they have a tendency to develop short stems and may become "wobbly" and top-heavy. With them, it is advisable to pot at such a level that the bases of the stalks of the lowest leaves are slightly embedded in the soil.

Watering to keep the soil always damp but not constantly saturated is needed. Never allow the soil to become so dry that the foliage wilts. Because rot is apt to develop if water collects in the centers of the rosettes it is unwise to spray the foliage. Instead, promote a humid atmosphere by keeping the surfaces on which the pots are standing constantly moist.

Other care includes picking off any flower buds that develop prematurely and if the plants begin to crowd each other of spacing them to admit more light and ensure freer air circulation. As soon as the final pots are filled with roots, begin applications of dilute liquid fertilizer, at first on a biweekly basis, in late winter and spring more often.

Propagation by division is a satisfactory means of multiplying the yellow-flowered greenhouse primulas *P. verticillata*, *P. floribunda*, and *P. kewensis*. All except the sterile form of the last also come easily from seed. Dividing is done in May. A simple process, it involves pulling apart plants that have finished flowering into pieces each of one rosette of leaves with roots attached and potting them individually in small pots. From then on treat them as newly potted seedlings.

To force English and polyanthus primroses into bloom well in advance of their outdoor season in a sunny greenhouse or window of a cool room, lift strong plants in early fall from a cold frame, nursery bed, or the garden and pot them in containers just big enough to hold the roots without crowding. Use porous soil containing an abundance of compost, old rotted manure, leaf mold, or peat moss. After potting water well and sink the pots to their rims in a bed of sand, sawdust, or peat moss in a cold frame or sheltered place outdoors. In February move them indoors where the night temperature is about 50°F and that by day not more than five to ten degrees higher. Keep the soil evenly moist, and give a little liquid fertilizer every week or two. After flowering is through the plants may be planted outdoors where they will recover and bloom the following year.

PRIMULACEAE — Primrose Family. Approximately 1,000 species, distributed among twenty genera, constitute this family of dicotyledons, the majority of which inhabit north temperate regions. Most sorts are herbaceous perennials, many with rhizomes, some with tubers. They may be stemless or have erect or trailing stems. The leaves are opposite or alternate. The flowers have a five-lobed, persistent calyx, a corolla of five separate or united petals or rarely no corolla, five stamens and sometimes five staminodes (nonfunctional stamens), and one style. In some genera, including *Androsace* and *Primula*, all the flowers of individual plants either have the styles shorter or longer than the stamens. The fruits are capsules. Genera cultivated include *Anagallis*, *Androsace*, *Cortusa*, *Cyclamen*, *Dionysia*, *Dodecatheon*, *Douglasia*, *Hottonia*, *Lysimachia*, *Omphalogramma*, *Primula*, *Samolus*, *Soldanella*, and *Trientalis*.

PRINCE-ALBERT-YEW is *Saxegothaea conspicua*.

PRINCE'S FEATHER. This is a common name used for *Amaranthus hybridus erythrostachys*, *Polygonum orientale*, and *Saxifraga umbrosa*.

PRINCE'S PLUME is *Stanleya pinnata*.

PRINSEPIA (Prinsép-ia). This genus of three or four species of deciduous, spiny shrubs of China, the Himalayan region, and Taiwan belongs to the rose family ROSACEAE. Its name commemorates botanist James Prinsep, who died in 1840.

Species of *Prinsepia* have stems with pith divided into horizontal plates and alternate, often toothed leaves. The flowers are one to four together in the axils of the previous year's shoots or in racemes. They have five spreading petals, ten to numerous stamens, and one style. The juicy, plumlike, single-seeded, edible fruits are in the Orient gathered as articles of diet.

Native to Manchuria, hardy through much of New England, and about 6 feet tall, *P. sinensis* has ovate to lanceolate, slender-stalked, bright green leaves that appear in earliest spring, well before those of almost all other hardy shrubs. They are sparingly-toothed and are fringed with hairs. The yellow flowers, ½ to ¾ inch across and with ten stamens, are in axillary groups of three or four. The purple fruits are ovoid or nearly globular and ½ to ¾ inch in diameter. Native to northwest China, *P. uniflora* differs in having hairless, narrow-oblong leaves 1 inch to 2½ inches long, with few or no teeth, and solitary or in twos or threes, white flowers, ½ to ¾ inch across, with ten stamens. This sort is hardy in southern New England. It leafs out early, but later than *P. sinensis*, and blooms later. Its globose

Prinsepia uniflora

Pritchardia pacifica, a young specimen

fruits, dark wine-red, covered with a waxy bloom, are about ½ inch in diameter. Variety *P. u. serrata* differs from *P. uniflora* in having leaves that widen at their middles and usually have cut margins. Himalayan *P. utilis*, up to 12 feet in height, has elliptic to ovate, toothed leaves and creamy-white, many-stemmed, fragrant flowers in racemes. They have numerous stamens. This is usually not hardy in the north.

Garden and Landscape Uses. The chief merit of prinsepias is their early leafing habits. Their floral displays are modest, and in cultivation they do not fruit heavily enough for this to be a feature of importance. A possible reason for this is that they flower before many pollinating insects are about. Prinsepias are useful for hedges and when so employed need little trimming. A pleasing combination results from planting *P. sinensis* in association with early-blooming *Rhododendron dauricum*. The prinsepia provides a foil of delightful greenery for the rosey-purple blooms of the rhododendron, which detracts from the gaunt appearance of its naked branches.

Cultivation. Prinsepias prosper in any ordinary, well-drained soil and are best in full sun, although they stand slight shade. They need no special care beyond a little thinning out of branches that are overcrowded. This may be done in late winter or very early spring.

PRITCHARDIA (Pritchár-dia) — Loulu Palm. Here belong, except for the coconut, the only native palms of the Hawaiian Islands. Of the about thirty-five species of *Pritchardia*, of the palm family PALMAE, thirty occur there, the others are indigenous to Fiji and other islands of the Pacific. The name commemorates W. T. Pritchard, British Consul at Fiji in 1860. The name *Eupritchardia* has also been used for this genus.

Pritchardias are extraordinarily handsome, fan-leaved palms with solitary, ringed trunks, smooth at maturity. Their large, rigid, strongly-pleated, usually broadly-wedge-shaped leaves, with non-prickly stalks, are cut to about their centers into many segments with slightly cleft tips and solitary strong mid-veins. The erect or drooping flower clusters arise from among the leaves and at their bases are protected by tubular, sheathing bracts. The bisexual flowers, in clusters toward the ends of the branches, have six stamens and are succeeded by one-seeded, nearly spherical fruits. The unripe seeds, called hawane or wahane are eaten by Hawaiians and the ripe ones are relished by tree rats, wild pigs, and certain insects. The leaves are made into hats and fans and formerly were used for thatching

One of the most common kinds in cultivation is *P. pacifica*, a native of Fiji. Up to 30 feet in height, it has round leaves, up to 5 feet in diameter, that are white-tomentose when young and slightly scaly beneath, green on both sides, and with segments about one-third the depth of the blades. Their stalks are covered with white scurfy hairs. The fruits, up to ½ inch in diameter, are in large ball-like clusters. The other native of Fiji, *P. thurstonii*, rarely exceeds 15 feet in height and is slenderer. The undersides of its leaves are slightly glaucous-gray and have minute elliptic scales. The leaf segments extend from one-third to one-half the depth of the blade and the flower clusters, up to 6 feet in length, are longer than the leaves. The fruits are about ¼ inch in diameter.

The native Hawaiian *P. gaudichaudii* often does not exceed 6 feet in height and has short-stalked leaves about 2½ feet across, somewhat silvery or covered with brownish-woolly hairs beneath. Its fruits are up to 1¾ inches in diameter. A native of mountains near Honolulu, *P. martii*, 10 to 15 feet tall, has a stout trunk, and leaves with stalks and blades 3 feet long with brown felty hairs on their lower sides. Its greenish, egg-shaped fruits are 1½ to 1¾ inches long. A taller Hawaiian native, *P. hillebrandii* sometimes exceeds 20 feet in height and has leaves 4 feet across with downy stalks and undersides with a light, powdery coating.

Garden and Landscape Uses. These magnificent palms, of striking appearance because of their large, handsome leaves displayed in large globular crowns, are especially effective when planted as solitary specimens uncrowded by nearby plants. They associate fittingly with such architectural features as terraces, steps, and buildings. Pritchardias succeed in any average garden soil in sun or light shade and are splendid tub plants. They can be grown outdoors in the tropics and subtropics, where not subjected to freezing, and in large greenhouses and conservatories.

Cultivation. Pritchardias are among the easiest of palms to grow if they have reasonable supplies of water. In greenhouses, a minimum winter night temperature of 60 to 65°F and a constantly humid atmosphere should be maintained. The soil must never be allowed to dry. Shade from strong summer sun is requisite. Specimens that have filled their containers with healthy roots benefit from biweekly applications of dilute liquid fertilizer from spring through fall. Propagation is by seeds sown in sandy, peaty soil in a temperature of 80°F. For additional information see Palms.

PRIVET. See Ligustrum. Jamaica-privet is *Lawsonia inermis*, New Zealand-privet, *Geniostoma ligustrifolium*.

PROBOSCIDEA (Proboscíd-ea) — Unicorn Plant, Proboscis Flower. Two rank-growing annual members of this group of nine species of annuals and perennials of the warmer parts of the Americas are cultivated. The genus is closely allied to *Martynia* from which it differs in each flower having four instead of two fertile anthers and in the calyx being split to the base on one side. The name *Proboscidea* is from the Greek, *proboskis*, an elephant's trunk, and alludes to the form of the fruits. The genus belongs in the martynia family MARTYNIACEAE.

The kind commonly cultivated, often under the untenable name of *Martynia fragrans*, is **P. louisianica** (syns. *P. jussieui*, *P. proboscidea*). Indigenous to the southwestern United States, it occurs as a garden escape outside its native range.

Proboscidea louisianica

This somewhat sprawling, softly-hairy, thick-stemmed, clammy annual forms a low mound 3 feet in diameter and about one-half as high. Its branches, in pairs, are opposite to each other. The undivided, mostly opposite, wavy-edged, long-stalked leaves are broadly-ovate to nearly circular and up to 1 foot in diameter. The asymmetrical, funnel-shaped flowers are ivory-white to purplish-violet or are mottled with purple or yellow inside. They have three larger lower petals and two smaller upper ones. They are in short, loose, terminal clusters. Each is 1½ to 2 inches long and almost as broad. The fruit capsules, 4 to 8 inches long, are boat-shaped with a pair of strongly up-curved, slender, horn-like beaks or prolongations at one end that are longer than the body of the capsule and, along the center of the capsule body, a fringed crest. The plant cultivated as *P. fragrans* is often *P. louisianica*. True **P. fragrans** differs only slightly. It is a native of Mexico and has fragrant, reddish or wine-purple flowers and more or less lobed leaves. The plant known as *P. lutea* is *Ibicella lutea*.

Garden Uses and Cultivation. These plants are attractive flower garden ornamentals and are of interest because of their peculiar fruits which, when dried, can be used as decorative curiosities; the young fruits may be included in mixed pickles. The plants are of lush appearance and produce something of a tropical effect. In the south, where the growing season is long, the seeds may be sown outdoors as soon as it is time to sow cucumbers and melons, but in the north they should be started indoors in a temperature of 70 to 75°F. The young plants are potted individually and set out in the garden from 4- or 5-inch pots when it is safe to plant peppers and eggplants. Seeds may be sown indoors seven or eight weeks before outdoor planting time. Unicorn plants respond to fertile soil and need full sun. They should be spaced 2 to 3 feet apart. Summer care is of the simplest; the plants are vigorous enough to smother out most weeds. In dry periods they need watering, and mulching the soil around them with compost or other organic material is helpful.

PROBOSCIS FLOWER. See Proboscidea.

PROMENAEA (Pro-menaèa). Belonging to the group of orchids commonly called "botanicals," which distinguishes them from the usually larger-flowered and showier commercial kinds and hybrids, *Promenaea* is a genus of six species related to *Zygopetalum*. All are natives, mostly at fairly high altitudes, of Brazil, and epiphytes (tree-perchers that take no nourishment from their hosts). They belong to the orchid family ORCHIDACEAE. The name is derived from that of a Greek priestess of Dodona.

Promenaeas are mostly low and compact. They have clustered pseudobulbs, each with one to three, thinnish, often glaucous leaves. The flower stalks, originating from the bottoms of the pseudobulbs, have usually one relatively large bloom with three sepals similar to the two petals and a three-lobed lip, its side lobes comparatively narrow and erect.

The species cultivated resemble each other in habit. Possibly the most common, **P. microptera** has somewhat flattened, roundish pseudobulbs not over 1 inch tall, with usually three strap-shaped, grayish-green leaves about 2 inches long by ½ inch wide. The fragrant, waxy, sometimes red-spotted, pale ochre-yellow to whitish blooms are about 2 inches in diameter. The lip, yellowish streaked with red or purple, has an oblong-lanceolate middle lobe and small side ones. The 1½- to 2-inch-wide, bright citron-yellow blooms of **P. xanthina** (syn. *P. citrina*) are very fragrant. The middle lobe of the lip is obovate, the side ones erect. The latter and the base of the center lobe are dotted with red. This kind has one or two glaucous-green leaves 2 to 4 inches long and ½ inch wide from each pseudobulb. Pale yellow flowers 1½ to nearly 2 inches wide, their lips dotted with deep violet-purple are characteristic of **P. rollinsonii**. The dark green leaves, two or three from each pseudobulb, are 3 to 4 inches long by up to 1 inch wide. The blooms of **P. stapelioides** approach 2 inches in diameter.

Promenaea xanthina

They are greenish-yellow to green, abundantly spotted, blotched, and barred with dark purple. The middle lobe of the lip is nearly round. The one to three leaves of each pseudobulb are up to 4 inches long by 1 inch wide.

Hybrid *P. crawshayana,* its parents *P. stapelioides* and *P. xanthinum,* has nearly spherical pseudobulbs with two or three oblong-lanceolate leaves. Its 2¼-inch-wide flowers, creamy-yellow spotted with reddish-brown, have a lip with an ovate middle lobe and lanceolate side lobes.

Garden Uses and Cultivation. Promenaeas, attractive and easy to grow, are well suited for inclusion in beginners as well as more advanced orchid fanciers' collections. For their best comfort, they should be accommodated in suspended small baskets or pans (shallow pots). They succeed in tree fern or osmuda fiber, one of these mixed with sphagnum moss, and in fir bark. Because they dislike any suspicion of the rooting medium being stale and stagnant, repotting should be done every second year. Fairly high humidity and sufficient shade to prevent the foliage being scorched must be supplied. Except for a period of three weeks to a month following fading of the blooms, water is given generously. Frequent mild applications of fertilizer while the plants are in active growth are in order. A minimum winter night temperature of 60°F is appropriate with an increase of five to fifteen degrees by day permitted. For more information see Orchids.

PROPAGATION. The multiplication of plants constitutes propagation. Fundamental to horticulture, controlled propagation is in a larger sense, basic to civilization. Since mankind first emerged from the hunter-gatherer phase of his development, he has, to a large extent, depended upon his ability to propagate plants to supply food and to satisfy some other needs.

Methods of plant reproduction fall naturally into two categories, sexual and asexual or vegetative. The first involves fertilization of a female egg cell by a male sperm cell, the other does not. Plants propagated sexually are in the fullest sense of the word new, the result of a new combination of male and female elements. Because of this they generally exhibit to a greater or lesser degree genetic differences. Plants resulting from vegetative propagation are essentially extentions of the old ones, having a separate physical existence, but identical genetically. A very few sorts of plants are capable of developing seeds without sexual involvement by a process called apomixis. Raising plants from such seeds is a form of vegetative rather than sexual propagation but it is not of horticultural significance.

Seeds afford the most obvious means of sexual propagation. All true annuals and biennials, most vegetables and some herbs, and many herbaceous perennials are commonly raised from seed; the majority of trees and shrubs may be.

With many plants, seed sowing is the least expensive and readiest means of increasing stock, with annuals and biennials it is usually the only way. But seed propagation is not always practicable. Not all flowering plants produce seed and those that do not always regularly or abundantly. Furthermore only sorts in fairly wide demand are generally available from commercial sources, and gardeners seeking seeds of rare plants are likely to suffer frustrations and disappointments.

Even more importantly, the seeds borne by most horticultural varieties of perennials, shrubs, and trees do not produce offspring true to the parent type. Usually the progeny is inferior, at best it is likely to be highly variable.

Propagation by seed in garden practice is generally limited to multiplying species rather than horticultural varieties of herbaceous perennials, trees, and shrubs, and to raising annual and biennial plants, including most vegetables. Varieties or strains of seeds of popular flower garden annuals and biennials and vegetables that come remarkably true to type have been developed by plant breeders, and are available commercially. For details of methods of raising plants from seeds consult the Encyclopedia entry Seeds, Propagation By.

Spores, minute reproductive bodies borne by ferns, selaginellas, club mosses, mosses, and many other non-flowering plants including funguses, many of which cause plant diseases, are asexual, and thus not the result of any sexual process. Those of ferns, selaginellas, and club mosses, the only kinds likely to be employed in purposeful propagation, germinate to produce tiny plants that develop egg cells and sperm cells. The latter fertilize the former and, as a result of this sexual activity, plants of the type that bore the spores develop. And so, although spores are asexual, the horticultural procedure of raising new plants from them may fairly be regarded as sexual propagation. For information about growing plants from spores consult the article Ferns.

Vegetative or asexual propagation takes many forms. Details of special techniques employed are discussed in the Encyclopedia entries Air-Layering, Budding, Cuttings, Division, Grafting, Inarching and Approach Grafting, Layering, Meristem Culture, Runners, and Separation. Our concern here is with the general aspects of vegetative propagation, including the parts of plants that are used.

Dividing plants into two or more pieces, each usually including both roots and aboveground parts or growth buds of the original, and replanting these to develop as new individuals, is one of the simplest means of vegetative propagation. It is called division. Often, for example, with aspidistras, Boston ferns, chrysanthemums, hostas, and peonies, considerable force is needed to pull apart or to cut or chop into pieces the specimen to be divided. In other instances, and this is especially true of many bulb plants, for example narcissuses, old clumps are readily separable and the operation of dividing is then known as separating. The removal and transplanting of offsets, suckers, and plantlets formed on runners may all be regarded as types of division.

Stems and modified stems supply the plant parts most commonly employed in vegetative propagation. The most frequent way in which they are used is as cuttings or slips, but stems also provide material for layering, including air layering, and for grafting and budding. Tubers and rhizomes, both modified stems, are also much employed as starts for new plants. They are sometimes planted whole or, as is often done with the tubers of potatoes and rhizomes of achimenes, are cut into pieces first.

Leaves of some plants possess the ability to generate new plants. Those of a few, for instance, *Asplenium bulbiferum* and certain kinds of kalanchoes, develop plantlets spontaneously and these, dropping to the ground or being brought into contact with it as the leaf ages and falls over, root and become established as new individuals. In horticultural practice, leaves of many other sorts of plants are employed as cuttings. Among kinds easily increased in this way are African-violets and most or perhaps all other gesneriads, many kinds of begonias, hyacinths, lachenalias, and sansevierias, as well as crassulas, kalanchoes, sedums, and a goodly number of other succulents.

Sections of roots of some plants are convenient means of securing increase. This is especially true of sorts with thick roots, such as anchusas and horseradish, but some others, such as Japanese anemones and phloxes that have much thinner roots, also lend themselves to multiplication by root cuttings.

Vegetative propagation usually results in progeny identical with the plant propagated. The offspring in effect are extensions of the original plant and form one clone. This is not true of populations raised from seeds or spores. Individuals produced from these usually exhibit slight or sometimes greater variations and are distinct genetic entities, rather than clones.

Vegetative or asexual propagation nearly always gives plants essentially identical with the mother plant, but not invariably. Very rarely mutations (genetic changes) occur that result in some deviation, but more frequently observable variation comes from other causes.

A striking example is furnished by the popular snake plant *Sansevieria trifasciata laurentii*. If cuttings are made of sections of its broadly-yellow-edged leaves, the young plants all have plain green foliage. This is because this plant is a chimera consisting of two genetically distinct tissues and the buds that produce the young plants develop from only one of these.

Variations in growth habits of plants multiplied vegetatively sometimes depend upon the part of the mother plant selected.

Only cuttings of terminal shoots of araucarias and many other conifers produce symmetrical specimens. Those made from side branches are asymmetrical and ungainly. Although plants of yews derived from cuttings made from lateral branches are shapely, they do not develop the strong, erect leader shoot characteristic of seedlings or plants raised from cuttings of leader shoots. They are less treelike, more shrubby.

PROPHET FLOWER is *Echioides longiflorum*.

PROSERPINACA (Proser-pináca) — Mermaid Weed. Closely related to *Myriophyllum*, and like it a member of the water-milfoil family HALORAGACEAE, the genus *Proserpinaca* is indigenous from Canada to Guatemala and Cuba. Its name is an ancient one used by Pliny for some unknown plant. It comprises three species of aquatic and wet soil herbaceous perennials that differ from *Myriophyllum* in having the calyx three- instead of four-parted and in having normal rather than bractlike underwater leaves. Its small greenish or purplish, stalkless flowers are without petals. They are solitary or in twos or threes in the axils of above-water leaves. The leaves are alternate, the submersed ones, at least, deeply-pinnately-lobed or toothed. The fruits are three-angled.

Often forming large colonies of prostrate rooting stems from which arise erect flowering branches 4 inches to 1¼ feet tall, *P. palustris* occurs in the wild over the natural range of the genus. The submersed leaves are deeply-cut into slender lobes; they are smaller than above-water leaves, which are linear-oblong to linear-lanceolate and 1 inch to 3 inches long.

Other kinds are *P. pectinata* and *P. intermedia.* The former is similar to *P. palustris*, but its above-water leaves are ovate-oblong and deeply-pinnately-divided, the latter is intermediate between *P. palustris* and *P. pectinata* and may be a hybrid with these species as its parents. Both range from Nova Scotia southward, *P. pectinata* to Florida, *P. intermedia* to Virginia.

Garden Uses and Cultivation. Mermaid weed is grown in aquariums. It may be planted also in pools and bog gardens, but is less decorative than the best myriophyllums. As an aquarium plant it grows rather slowly. A satisfactory rooting medium is coarse unwashed sand, with some mud or clay content, and slightly alkaline water is best. Increase is easily achieved by cuttings. This plant needs strong light.

PROSOPIS (Pro-sòpis)—Mesquite, Screw-Bean or Tornillo. The genus *Prosopis*, of the mimosa section of the pea family LEGUMINOSAE, consists of forty species native to the Americas, two to western Asia, and one to Africa. None is hardy in the north. Some of its members give much character to desert regions in the southwest and are of importance in providing nutritious food (seeds and young shoots) for range animals and pasture for bees. Their lumber is used for firewood, fence posts, novelty articles, and trinkets. It takes a high polish. The name, of Greek origin, is of obscure meaning.

Prosopises are trees and shrubs, thorny or not, with twice-pinnate leaves, with one or two pairs of main divisions, each with usually many, small, toothless leaflets. The small, greenish flowers are in cylindrical or spherical spikes from the leaf axils. The individual flowers have only ten stamens, which distinguishes them from those of *Acacia*. The fruits are linear, leathery pods that do not split to release their seeds. The kinds known in North America as mesquites have straight pods, and spines not joined to the leafstalks; those called screw-beans have pods that are tightly spiraled ringlets, and spines that are joined to the leafstalks.

Mesquite (*P. juliflora*) is a variable species of which botanists recognize several varieties, one or more as natives of dry regions of the southwestern United States, Mexico, and the West Indies. Often not more than a much-branched shrub up to 10 feet tall, mesquite under favorable conditions becomes a tree 60 feet in height. It is pubescent or hairless. Its leaves have one or two pairs of primary divisions, each with five to twenty-one pairs of small leaflets. In cylindrical spikes 2 to 3½ inches long, the creamy-yellow flowers are succeeded by seed pods 3½ to 8 inches long.

Screw-bean or tornillo (*P. pubescens*) is a shrub 3 to 15 feet tall or, under favorable conditions, may become a tree 35 feet in height. Its greenish flowers are in spikes 1½ to 2 inches long. The pods are tight cylindrical coils 1 inch to 2½ inches long, that indeed suggest carpenters' screws.

Garden and Landscape Uses and Cultivation. Only in desert and semidesert regions are these interesting shrubs and trees likely to find favor as landscape features. Native stands can sometimes be employed to advantage by allowing them to remain in developed areas. Sometimes mesquites are planted, but because of their extensive and often extraordinarily deep root systems they do not transplant well from the wild. It is better to set out young specimens that have been raised in containers. They need well-drained, dryish soil and desert or semidesert environments. Propagation is by seed.

PROSTANTHERA (Prost-anthèra) — Australian Mint-Bush. Entirely Australian, *Prostanthera* comprises fifty species of shrubs or rarely small trees of the mint family LABIATAE. Some are cultivated in California and other mild-temperate and subtropical regions. They are usually strongly aromatic, which gives reason for their common name. The botanical designation comes from the Greek *prostheke*, an appendage, and the Latin *anthera*, an anther, and alludes to the spurlike projections on the anthers.

Prostantheras have opposite leaves and numerous small, axillary flowers often forming leafy racemes, or flowers in terminal panicles or racemes. The blooms have two-lipped calyxes and corollas. The calyx lobes are without teeth. The upper corolla lip has two, the lower three, lobes. There are two pairs of stamens, their anthers usually with one or two spurs. The fruits consist of four seedlike nutlets surrounded by the persistent calyx. From some species essential oils are obtained.

The popular *P. rotundifolia* is an evergreen shrub up to 15 feet tall, but often lower. It has scarcely-toothed, broad-ovate leaves up to ½ inch in length, and lilac to purple blooms, about as long, in terminal panicles. This species blooms freely in spring. Sometimes called Australian-lilac,

Prostanthera rotundifolia

P. lasianthos attains 20 to 30 feet in height. It has elliptic to lanceolate, toothed leaves 1 inch to 2½ inches long, and great quantities of ½-inch-long, purple-spotted, pinkish white, hairy flowers, in terminal racemes or panicles. From 3 to 6 feet tall, *P. nivea* is hairless or nearly so. Its linear to linear-lanceolate leaves have rolled-back

Prostanthera nivea

Protea cynaroides

margins and are up to 1½ inches long. Its pure white or blue-tinted blooms are solitary in the leaf axils of short leafy shoots. They are about ¾ inch across. A shrub up to 15 feet in height, **P. sieberi** has very slender shoots and ovate-wedge-shaped leaves up to 1 inch long, with a few coarse teeth or none. Its blue-purple flowers are four to eight together in terminal racemes and are about ⅓ inch across. Described as being one of the most exquisite shrubs of Australia, the crimson-throated mint-bush (**P. striatiflora**) grows under semidesert conditions. About 3 feet tall and compact, it has small leaves and crimson-throated, pure white blooms produced abundantly.

Garden and Landscape Uses and Cultivation. None of the Australian mint-bushes survive severe winters, but *P. rotundifolia*, which seems to be the hardiest, prospers in northern California and is grown successfully outdoors in the southwest of England. They are attractive as single specimens and for grouping, and they may be espaliered against walls. They respond to porous, somewhat peaty soils that drain well. They need full sun. Prune only to keep them shapely, except in the case of espaliered specimens, which must be pruned annually. Prune immediately after blooming. Propagation is easily effected by cuttings and by seed.

PROTEA (Pro-tea). Until recently, this genus of 130 species of African shrubs practically defied the efforts of American horticulturists to grow them, but extraordinary good results are now had with a few species in various parts of California, notably near San Diego, where they are grown commercially as cut flowers. The genus belongs in the protea family PROTEACEAE. Its name is a modification of that of the Greek sea-god *Proteus*, who possessed the ability to assume a wide variety of shapes. The allusion is to the amazingly varied forms the flower heads of the different species of *Protea* exhibit.

Proteas are evergreen shrubs, all natives of Africa, with the majority of species concentrated in South Africa. Their leathery, toothless leaves are alternate and may or may not be hairy. The flowers are tightly clustered in usually stalkless, generally solitary, cup- or goblet-shaped heads with involucres (collars) of overlapping, often beautifully colored, bracts. The individual flowers that compose the heads are bisexual and asymmetrical. They have tubular perianths with four segments, one of which is separate, and the other three joined. There are four stamens and one pistil, with a hairy ovary. The persistent styles remain attached to the densely bearded fruits, which are technically nuts.

The king protea (*P. cynaroides*) is the largest flowered and one of the most beautiful. Rarely exceeding 3½ feet, but sometimes nearly twice as tall, it has long-stalked, green leaves ranging from nearly round to oblong, with blades 2 to 5 inches long by 2 to 3 inches broad. The flower heads, 5 to 8 inches in length and as wide or wider, terminate the shoots. They resemble great artichokes and are white, pink, or red, with a covering of fine silvery hairs. The flowers open from the outside of the head inward.

The woolly-bearded protea (*P. barbigera*) occasionally is 8 feet tall, but is generally lower. When young, it often tends to sprawl. It has gray-green, oblong-lanceolate leaves 6 to 8 inches long by about 2½ inches wide. The flower heads, only a little smaller than those of the king protea, have the scales of their involucres prominently eyelashed with soft white hairs. The flowers forming the centers of the heads are also covered with hairs, white with dark tips, that lean inward to form a nearly black peak at the center of the head. The bracts are usually clear pink, but may be cream or greenish-white.

Especially handsome is *P. grandiceps*, a rounded shrub 4 to 5 feet tall, with crowded, broadly-elliptic, bluish-green leaves finely edged with red, 3½ to 5 inches long by 1½ to 2 inches wide. About 4½ inches long and broad, the flower heads have coral-pink bracts, the inner circles of which are fringed with pale, soft hairs.

Linear, hairless leaves 3 to 7 inches long by under ½ inch wide characterize *P. longifolia*, an erect, freely-branching kind 5 to 10 feet tall. The flower heads are up to 5 inches long and about 4 inches wide. In

Protea barbigera

Protea grandiceps in southern California

A flower head of *Protea grandiceps*

bud they are inversely conical, but when fully open their greenish-white or light pink bracts, tipped black, spread widely. The inner ones are long, slender, slightly spoon-shaped, and loosely arranged, the outer, shorter and ovate.

Other sorts cultivated include these: *P. aristata,* one of the rarest and most distinctive of the genus, is up to 6 feet tall. It has slender, linear leaves up to 4 inches long and without a distinct midrib. The stalkless heads of flowers, up to 5½ inches

Protea aristata

long by 4½ inches wide, have wine-red to brownish-red outer bracts and inner ones that shade to rose-pink. *P. longiflora* is a shrub from 6 to 10 feet tall with stalkless, elliptic leaves up to 4 inches long. Its flower heads, also stalkless, 3 to 4 inches long, are greenish-white to pink and have greenish-white bracts, the inner ones hair-fringed. *P. mellifera,* the sugar bush or honey flower, 6 to 9 feet tall, has hairy shoots and narrowly-oblong leaves up to 6 inches long. Borne at the shoot ends, and white, pink, and red, the stalkless, sticky flower heads are up to 5 inches long. *P. nana,* 2 to 3 feet tall, has slender-linear, spine-tipped leaves ½ to 1 inch long. Its nodding, cup-shaped heads of bloom are about 1½ inches wide. They have a crowded conical center of reddish

Protea nana

flowers fringed with reddish hairs, surrounded by bright rose-red to crimson bracts about 1 inch long by ⅓ inch wide. *P. neriifolia,* the oleander-leaved or pink mink protea, 6 to 10 feet tall, has narrowly-oblong leaves up to 6 inches long. The stalkless flower heads, at the ends of the shoots, up to 5 inches long, are salmon-pink to deep rose-pink tipped with a black beard. *P. susannae* is a com-

Protea neriifolia

pact bush 4 to 6 feet tall with blunt, lanceolate to oblanceolate leaves that have a distinct midrib, and are up to 5 inches long. Surrounded by the upper leaves, the short-stalked flower heads are pink with brownish-pink bracts. Because the foliage of this is disagreeably scented, it is advisable to strip the leaves from stems of flowers cut for arrangements.

Garden and Landscape Uses. The really successful cultivation of proteas in North America is such a recent development that much remains to be learned about procedures and, especially, about the needs and tolerances of individual kinds. They are decidedly plants for Mediterranean-type climates (several kinds are successful in Sicily), responding to warm dry summers and mild, moister winters. They are very definitely not suitable for humid tropics and subtropics. Sunny locations where summer breezes assure good air circulation are best, and freely drained, moderately acid soil is needed. Regions of frequent heavy summer fogs are not to their liking. Proteas are beautiful shrubs for garden ornament and for supplying long-lasting, lovely heads of bloom for cutting. They are not likely to prosper as lawn specimens because of the frequent irrigation needed by grass. A location where they can be alone or with kinds of plants needing similar conditions is best.

Cultivation. Proteas are raised from seeds sown in seed beds or flats in the open, not in greenhouses, and preferably in fall. The medium in which they are sown must drain well. It may consist of equal parts of soil, sand, and peat moss. The seeds are covered with a thin layer of coarse sand, and the beds or flats protected from birds and mice with a covering of wire mesh. Normally, germination takes place in four to six weeks, but sometimes more time is needed. Until the seeds sprout and later, watering must be done sparingly so that the soil is not constantly wet, yet never dries completely. If frost is expected, a covering of burlap or similar material is placed over the seed beds at night and removed promptly the next morning. The seedlings are transplanted individually into 4-inch pots as soon as their first true leaves begin to show, using a soil similar to that in which the seeds were sown, but coarser. They are set deeply. Later they are transferred to larger pots or gallon cans and from these to the planting sites. Free air circulation and good light are at all times important, but during their first year a little shade from very strong sun is appreciated. That afforded by a lath house is appropriate. Success with proteas largely depends upon having them survive their first year. During that period they are highly vulnerable to fatal fungus diseases. To circumvent these, the soil should be watered periodically with a fungicide. Established proteas are irrigated by applying water to the soil only, not by overhead spraying Pruning consists of shortening shoots that have bloomed. This is done automatically if the flowers are cut for decoration. Young plants may have their centers cut out to induce first branching.

PROTEACEAE—Protea Family. Mostly trees and shrubs, rarely somewhat woody herbaceous perennials, the approximately 1,200 species of this family of dicotyledons are accommodated in sixty-two genera. The greatest number are natives of the southern hemisphere, but in South and Central America, Africa, Indonesia, and Asia some occur north of the equator. None is native to North America or Europe. Some species are sources of useful lumber. Edible nuts are a product of *Macadamia*. Many ornamentals belong in the family.

Characteristically, members of the *Proteaceae* have leathery, undivided or variously divided leaves, alternate, rarely opposite, or in whorls (circles) of three or more. The flowers, bisexual or unisexual, the sexes sometimes on separate plants, are in raceme-like arrangements or in heads, the latter often with involucres (basal collars) of leafy bracts. The blooms, without petals, have petal-like sepals, four stamens, and one style. The fruits are nuts, drupes, follicles, or capsules. The seeds are often winged. Cultivated genera include *Banksia, Dryandra, Embothrium, Gevuina, Grevillea, Hakea, Hicksbeachia, Isopogon, Knightia, Lambertia, Leucadendron, Leucospermum, Lomatia, Macadamia, Mimetes, Oreocallis, Orothamnus, Paranomus, Persoonia, Petrophila, Protea, Roupala, Serruria, Stenocarpus,* and *Telopea.*

PROTECTION FOR PLANTS. The successful upkeep of plants and gardens depends upon establishing and maintaining encouraging environments. This involves, besides promoting favorable conditions for example, by watering and fertilizing, countering unfavorable ones, thus, providing protection. Threats come from many sources, among the more obvious insects and other small pests and disease organisms. For these consult the entries in this Encyclopedia titled Insects, and Diseases of Plants.

Protection implies anticipation, the need for taking precautions before damage is done. To anticipate, one must be knowledgeable about possibilities, about what may happen. To know one's enemies is a long step toward defeating them.

Trespass by children or others and invasion of property by domestic and sometimes wild animals may necessitate installation of fences or hedges. Chosen with regard for appearance as well as practicability, these can be handsome and even charming as well as effective. Among ani-

A chicken wire guard protects this young tree from animals that gnaw

Positioning wire mesh to protect a bed to be planted with bulbs

mal nuisances, dogs and deer can be especially destructive, the former by trampling seed beds, breaking plants, and urinating on them, the latter by browsing on delectable sorts, including yews of which they are particularly fond, and to some extent by trampling.

Young trees may be harmed, especially in winter when other food is scarce, by mice and rabbits gnawing their bark. Surrounding the trunks with girdles of ½-inch-mesh chicken wire or galvanized-wire hardware cloth extended to 6 inches below the ground surface and sufficiently high that even from atop a thick layer of snow the animals cannot reach the bark is a practical means of frustrating them.

Some bulb plants, notably crocuses and tulips, are susceptible to damage by mice, chipmunks, and moles. An effective protection is to surround the bed or portion of the bed in which such bulbs are planted with wire hardware cloth set vertically in the ground to a depth of 8 or 9 inches and extending to about 1 inch above the surface or, where only a few bulbs are involved, to plant them in baskets formed of the same material and set these in the ground with their rims flush with its surface.

To protect against rodents, set in the ground a wire basket to be filled with soil and planted with bulbs

Birds, more frequently in urban and suburban than rural localities, sometimes cause trouble by feeding on newly planted seeds and taking dust baths in finely raked soil. Some kinds damage ripening fruits. In the main, however, the good done by birds greatly outweighs any harm they do, and only in extreme cases should their destruction be considered.

Scares of various kinds sometimes deter birds; more often they do not, at least for long. Where it is important to give protection, the best insurance is had, where it is practicable, by covering with netting plants likely to be damaged or, with bush fruits such as blueberries, to grow them in a walk-in height cage made of a light, wooden or metal frame covered with fine-mesh chicken wire.

Other animal damage may necessitate the employment of poison baits, gas "bombs," traps, or even shooting the marauders, which may include mice, moles, chipmunks, rabbits, woodchucks, and birds such as crows, pigeons, and English sparrows. If baits or traps are employed, take great care that animals, domestic or wild, other than the culprits, and that people, especially children, are not endangered Use only humane traps. Shooting should be done only by people experienced with the use of guns and in strict accordance with local laws.

Shelter from wind is a form of protection that often makes possible the cultivation of a much wider selection of plants on sites where otherwise many would fail or at best grow poorly. It may be provided on a permanent basis by walls, fences, hedges, or more informal belts or by groups of resistant trees or shrubs, preferably evergreens. Provision of such shelter is often of critical importance in gardens near the ocean (see the Encyclopedia entry Seaside Gardens).

Give consideration to the possibility of wind damage when choosing and siting plants for foundation plantings. Both exposed and sheltered spots are common

Simple, but rarely effective, ways of scaring birds: (a) A scarecrow

A seaside garden with glass-walled fences that give protection from wind

(b) Fluttering strips of cloth

Bush fruits, such as blueberries and currants, can be protected from birds by growing them within a fine-mesh chicken wire cage

near buildings and future trouble may be averted if the planter selects for drafty corners and the like wind-tolerant sorts and restricts more sensitive kinds to sheltered nooks and similar locations.

Temporary shelter from wind such as may be given by a screen of burlap is often of help to newly planted trees and shrubs, especially evergreens that have been moved later in the season than is ideal and

that must face wintry blasts before their root systems are adequately reestablished.

Shade is another protection often provided, its purposes to reduce light intensity and moderate temperatures. The glass of greenhouses and cold frames may be

Temporary shade for young plants: (a) Wood-lath shades

(b) Pots tilted over newly transplanted seedlings

(c) A thin covering of salt hay, weighted along its edges with strips of wood

sprayed or painted with whitewash or other suitable material or shades of lath or cloth may be placed over them. Lath or shade houses are greenhouse-like structures without glass. They consist of a wood or metal pipe framework covered with suitably spaced wood or metal laths, special shade cloth, palm leaves, Spanish-moss or other material to provide the necessary shade. Temporary shade for a few days or perhaps even a week or two often benefits newly transplanted and potted plants, especially if they are leafy and their roots have been disturbed appreciably.

The trunks of newly transplanted trees may be damaged on their south sides by sunscald, especially if they were previously growing in fairly dense stands and were shaded by neighbor trees or if they have been pruned heavily and are without shade that branches removed previously afforded. As protection against this sort of damage, which occurs in winter as well as summer, it is well to wrap the trunks and sometimes the lower parts of branches

Pseudolarix kaempferi (fall foliage)

Prunus serrula (trunk)

Prunus persica, double-flowered

Prunus serrulata variety

Prunus subhirtella pendula

Ptychosperma elegans

Pyracantha coccinea lalandei

Pyracantha coccinea lalandei espaliered

Pyxidanthera barbulata

Puschkinia scilloides

Inside a lath house

The trunk of a recently transplanted tree wrapped in burlap

Mulches protect roots from extreme changes in temperature and drying:
(a) Bark chips

(b) Salt hay

(c) A young rhododendron mulched with salt hay

"pockets" that interfere with free air drainage and where, on winter nights, cold air collects, and be aware that damage is more prevalent on poorly drained than on well-drained ground. Sites swept by winds are more likely to bring grief to trees, shrubs, and woody vines than sheltered ones, but this is as likely to result from desiccation as from exposure to low temperatures. Evergreens, other than many pines and some other needle-leaved conifers, are especially likely to suffer from this cause and also from full exposure to winter sun. In cold regions north- or west-facing slopes or partially shaded places are generally better for these kinds than sunny southern or eastern exposures.

Temporary protection against cold winds and cold nights is often desirable for such early-planted warm-weather vegetables as cucumbers, melons, and squash. It can be provided by inverting over individual plants or hills small tentlike devices made of waxed paper and sold as Hotkaps and Hottents. Gallon-sized glass cider bottles, with their bottoms cut out and their necks left uncorked, are also suitable for the purpose.

The vigorous growth of this tomato, covered by a hotcap, made slitting the top of the hotcap necessary to permit the plant to emerge

The same results can be had by covering entire rows of young seedlings with continuous, low, tunnel-like tents of clear polyethylene plastic film supported on hoops of wire and with the edges of the plastic weighted to the ground with soil, stones, or boards. Make a few holes in the plastic for ventilation. Such long tents also afford excellent protection for rows of lettuce, endive, corn salad, and other crops nearing maturity against early fall frosts. By employing them the harvesting season can be extended for two to four weeks or more.

Little known in North America, cloches (the word is French in origin) are devices used to protect young plants, and particularly to secure early crops of salads and

that were previously shaded with strips of burlap or of wrapping paper made especially for the purpose and to keep these in place for a year or two.

Mulching in summer does much to promote conditions favorable to roots. By protecting the soil from the direct rays of the sun, it minimizes danger of its surface attaining temperatures inimical to growth and greatly reduces the likelihood of the soil drying and the roots near the surface becoming desiccated.

Winter protection against hazards peculiar to that season are commonly employed in northern gardens. They make possible or at least more probable the survival without appreciable harm of plants that without such attentions would likely suffer or perhaps be killed.

Excessive cold (exposure to damaging low temperatures) is the danger that comes first to mind when winter protection is considered. Although not the only hazard, it is certainly an important one. For all plants there is a low temperature that inevitably causes death and more or less serious harm is likely at a temperature somewhat above the critical minimum. This last is not constant, but varies with a number of circumstances, including the

condition of the plant tissues, the period in winter when the low is reached and its duration, the type of soil, availability of moisture, and other, often difficult to assess factors. With some plants the roots survive and send up new shoots even though the tops are killed.

Certainly careful selection of planting sites plays an important part in saving from harm plants known to be susceptible to cold injury. Avoid hollows or "frost

Continuous tents of polyethylene plastic (shown here with one side raised) provide protection for lettuce and some other crops against light frosts

Common in Europe, cloches (continuous little "greenhouses" of glass or rigid plastic fitted into wire frames) protect salad and vegetable crops

certain vegetables. The original type, much used in French market gardens managed intensively to assure maximum cropping, were large glass bells, open at their bottoms and with a solid knob at the apex. Modern cloches are really continuous tents that fit readily over a row of seedlings or larger plants and are constructed of separate panes of glass or transparent plastic that fit comfortably into specially designed wire frameworks. The ends of each row of cloches are closed by standing a single sheet of glass or plastic against them. Cloches of this type are popular in Europe, including the British Isles.

A blanket of snow throughout the winter is one of the best protections for hardy herbaceous plants and low shrubs. It keeps them evenly cold and not exposed to alternate freezing and thawing or dehydration. In places where such continuous cover can be depended upon, none other is needed, but in cold regions where the ground is bare all winter, or between snowfalls, substitute protection is highly desirable.

Winter covering or temporary mulching with loose material, such as salt hay, corn stalks, branches of evergreens (discarded Christmas trees are a likely source of these), or dry leaves, is an effective method of protecting certain plants against the vagaries of winter. Generally its purpose is not to prevent exposure to excessively low temperatures but to keep the aboveground parts of the biennials, such as pansies, foxgloves, and sweet williams, and herbaceous perennials, subshrubs and low shrubs, such as basket-of-gold, dianthuses, evergreen candytuft, and helianthemums, from suffering winter-burn caused by exposure to strong sun and drying winds when the ground is frozen. Another important purpose of winter covering is to keep the ground uniformly frozen and so prevent roots from being torn and young plants heaved out of the soil by alternate freezing and thawing. When these are the objectives it is important, especially with plants that retain foliage through the winter, not to cover too heavily. Unless assured a free circulation of air, aboveground plant parts are likely to rot.

Salt hay is an excellent winter cover for deciduous herbaceous perennials: (a) Spread it in loose layers, 3 to 5 inches thick

(b) Keep it in place with shrub or tree branches

Protection from excessive cold is, however, sometimes a chief function of winter covering and then the cover may be applied to plants without persistent aboveground parts in thicker layers than when its purpose is mainly to moderate sun and wind and to prevent alternate freezing and thawing. Many deciduous bulb plants on the borderline of hardiness or definitely not hardy in regions of cold winters survive and prosper if steps are taken to prevent the bulbs themselves, which may be 6 inches or more beneath the surface, from freezing. This can be done by covering the ground with a layer 6 inches to 1 foot thick of salt hay, cornstalks, dry leaves, or branches of evergreens. Among sorts that in southern New York can be overwintered in this way are the spring starflower (*Ipheion uniflorum*), *Crinum longifolium*, dahlias, gladioluses, and montbretias. Narcissuses planted in soil bare of cover also benefit from a 4- or 5-inch covering of this type, but it is not necessary for narcissuses planted in meadows or other grassed areas.

Do not install temporary winter covering too early. Wait until the ground has frozen to a depth of at least a couple of inches. Otherwise, mice and other rodents may be encouraged to establish winter quarters under the mulch and are likely to burrow among or otherwise damage the plants. In locations where wind is apt to disturb loose coverings, such as salt hay and dry leaves, they may be kept in place by laying over them a few pieces of brushwood or chicken wire weighted with stones.

And do not uncover too early or take too much covering off at one time in spring. To do so is likely to result in serious harm by exposing tender shoots and other parts to late freezes or, too suddenly, to strong sun and wind. Choose if possible dull, humid weather for uncovering and if the cover is at all thick remove only part of it at first, the remainder a week or ten days later.

With taller shrubs and small trees, other methods of preventing harm by winter sun and wind are adopted. These are especially important for boxwoods, camellias, and other evergreens in regions where they are on the borderline of hardiness. Here again the chief concern is to make certain that moisture is not lost from the foliage more rapidly than it can be replaced by the roots. Sometimes all that is necessary is to shade and shelter the plants by closely surrounding them with cut branches of pines or other evergreens stuck into the ground and tied around, but with important specimens it is usually better to erect screens or boxlike shelters of burlap or Saran cloth tacked to wooden frameworks. The precautions recommended for the spring removal of other temporary winter coverings apply here also. Protections of these types are most

Protect boxwoods from winter damage by: (a) A wooden frame covered with burlap

(b) Burlap sewn or stapled to frame

(c) The resultant boxlike structure

effective when used in conjunction with ground mulches.

Spraying with an antidesiccant (antitranspirant) of a kind compounded and sold especially for this purpose can, especially if combined with the use of a mulch, afford substantial protection against winter harm to evergreens. In cold climates, antidesiccants are commonly used on recently transplanted specimens, but in sunny and windy locations, they can be helpful, to some extent at least, to others. Generally two or three applications a month apart, the first given during the latter part of December, give good results.

Deciduous trees and shrubs with tops not surely hardy if exposed, frequently come through safely if guarded against the severest cold by wrapping with insulating material, that, incidentally, also prevents desiccation. Good examples are fig trees in the vicinity of New York City and *Hydrangea macrophylla* in somewhat colder climates, but the practice can be adopted successfully with most borderline shrubs and small trees that lose their leaves in winter.

To provide this sort of protection, well after leaf fall, but before danger of killing temperatures, pull together the branches of the specimen and tie them as compactly as possible without danger of breakage. Then wrap the entire bundle in a thick layer of straw, cornstalks, hay, newspaper, old blankets, or other insulation and encase it in a layer of waterproof building paper or polyethylene plastic film. If the latter, leave a smallish opening at the top and two or three around the base to allow overheated air to escape and to prevent the inside temperatures from rising too high on sunny days.

A fig tree near New York City wrapped for winter protection

Permanent mulches of materials not removed in spring but left to rot and nourish the roots afford substantial winter protection to roots near the surface and to the crowns of many shrubs, the tops of which in cold climates are killed to the ground but that renew themselves from the base each spring. Mulches of these sorts especially benefit evergreens by limiting frost penetration into the ground and so making it more surely possible for the roots to replace moisture transpired from the foliage. Such mulches, installed in fall, are in fact a substitute for the natural protection afforded plants in the wild by fallen leaves and the dead tops of grasses and other herbaceous plants. Materials satisfactory as permanent mulches include rotted manure, compost, leaves, peat moss, and bagasse. A layer 3 to 6 inches deep is commonly sufficient.

Hilling soil around the bases of trees and shrubs that, if their tops are killed, produce new shoots is an effective method of preserving some plants. In cold regions, it is commonly practiced with roses, but it is useful, too, with some other plants. The soil may be drawn up with a hoe from immediately around the plant or brought from elsewhere. The latter procedure involves more work bringing it in and removing it in spring, but has the advantage of not reducing the thickness of the layer of earth above roots that reach beyond the hills. In any case, in cold regions, defer hilling until the surface inch of the soil is frozen.

Soil for winter protection hilled up to roses

The principle involved in hilling is that of assuring transfer of sufficient heat from the ground to the heap of soil with the result that its interior never falls to the critical level at which the trunks or stems of the protected plant are killed. For example, a rose may have stems that die if exposed to 0°F, but even though the air temperature falls many degrees below that level the covered parts of its stems survive because heat from the ground, even though itself frozen, transfers to the soil that surrounds the stems and its temperature does not drop to below perhaps 20, 18, or 10°F. There are the added benefits of the covered stems not being subjected to alternate freezing and thawing or to the desiccating effects of sun and wind.

Because in severely cold climates success with hilling depends upon transfer of heat from the ground to the hill, the latter must be of material that permits heat flow, that is, it is not markedly insulating. Ordinary soil fulfills this requirement best. Such loose insulating materials as salt hay, straw, and dry leaves will not do and even materials such as peat moss are less satisfactory. A layer of some such insulating material spread over the hills of soil after they are frozen to a depth of an inch or two is very helpful, however, in maintaining their interior temperatures above the

Salt hay spread over soil hilled up to roses serves as insulation

Remove heavy accumulations of snow from evergreens by pushing upward with a rake

critical killing level. Taking down the hills in spring, done before new shoot growth is advanced, is best accomplished in dull, humid weather.

An adaptation of hilling consists of releasing from their supports the long canes of climbing roses and sometimes other plants with fairly pliable stems, laying them along the ground, heaping soil over them and weighting it down by placing boards on top of the ridges of earth.

Mechanical damage caused by snow slides from roofs must sometimes be anticipated and protection provided, especially for evergreens and sometimes deciduous shrubs in foundation plantings. It may be achieved by fixing snow guards on roofs or by erecting temporary platforms supported on posts over threatened plants. Small specimens can be saved by inverting bushel baskets or large boxes over them. If these are used on evergreens, see that there are openings in their sides to admit some light.

Serious breakage can result from accumulations of snow on branches, especially those of certain evergreens. Wet snow because it is much heavier than the light, fluffy kind is especially damaging. Free branches of accumulations as soon as possible after the snow has fallen. Do this by shaking them gently or by pushing upward with a broom or rake. Pulling downward with such tools adds to the strain on the branches and may fracture them.

Even if breakage does not occur, the branches of some evergreens, boxwoods, for example, are likely to spread outward under the weight of heavy snow with the result that the shrub is "opened up" in unsightly fashion. Susceptible specimens may be made less so by wiring their branches together, taking care of course to do this in such a way that the wires will not cut into the bark.

Ice is a potential hazard to trees, shrubs, and sometimes other plants. Water that collects and freezes around their bases or crowns can cause serious losses. These can

be largely avoided by making sure subsurface drainage is satisfactory and by establishing favorable surface grades.

Accumulations on branches and twigs resulting from ice storms or from rain freezing on them frequently result in serious breakage. Unfortunately, there is no

Additional winter protection for plants in cold frames can be provided: (a) Covering them on cold nights with mats

(b) Spreading a layer of salt hay inside the frame over deciduous perennials

practical way of preventing or lightening the deposits. Sound pruning practices help to develop sturdy frameworks of branches less subject to such breakage.

Wintering in cold frames is a highly satisfactory way of affording many sorts of plants seasonal protection. Besides mitigating excessive cold, this provides shelter from drying winds and excessive rain and makes it simple to give sorts with evergreen foliage light shade. The frames, of course, need a little attention, particularly in the matter of ventilating. For more about this see the Encyclopedia entry Garden Frames. When plants in pots are to be overwintered in frames, it is advisable to sink the containers to their rims in a bed of sand, peat moss, sawdust, or similar material.

Additional protection is often given by covering cold frames on cold nights with heavy mats of straw or other insulating material. Those that contain plants of slightly doubtful hardiness may be further insulated by banking their sides with soil or by erecting around and 9 inches to 1 foot from them a supplementary wooden

(c) Surrounding the frame with an outer framework and stuffing the space between with straw or other insulating material; top it off with waterproof paper or plastic to keep rain out

framework with the space between filled with straw, hay, cornstalks, dry leaves, or similar material, topped off with a sheet of plastic or waterproof building paper. A light covering of salt hay strewn *inside* a frame over plants that benefit from shade in winter also gives some protection from cold.

PRUNELLA (Prunél-la). Except for one or two kinds, the genus *Prunella* is undistinguished, consisting chiefly of rather weedy hardy herbaceous perennials. They belong to the mint family LABIATAE and number seven species, natives of Europe, Asia, northwest Africa, and North America. The origin of the name, which is sometimes written *Brunella*, is doubtful. It has been suggested that it is derived from the German *braune*, quinsy, for which malady these plants were thought to be a remedy.

Prunellas have slender root systems, tufts of basal leaves, and mostly branchless, four-angled stems with opposite, stalked leaves. The flowers, interspersed with leafy bracts, are in dense spikes or heads. They have a two-lipped calyx, a two-lipped corolla, with the upper lip two-lobed, the lower three-lobed. There are four stamens, one style, and two stigmas. The fruits consist of four seedlike nutlets. The very asymmetrical flowers, three of which arise in the axil of each bract, distinguish members of this group from those of the nearly-related false dragon-heads (*Physostegia*).

The most familiar, but not most decorative species is the highly variable self-heal or heal-all (*P. vulgaris*), represented in the spontaneous flora of North America by two native varieties and one introduced from Eurasia, and common in many temperate and warm-temperate parts of the world. This often is a weed in lawns, waste places, and waysides. Its stems, erect or prostrate, may attain a length of 1½ feet, but in poor, dryish soils often do not exceed 2 or 3 inches. The ovate to ovate-lanceolate leaves are toothed or toothless. The flowers, which are violet-purple, rarely magenta-pink or, in *P. v. alba*, white, have little decorative appeal. This plant is cultivated in herb and medicinal gardens for its historic interest.

Prunella vulgaris alba

Quite superior European *P. grandiflora* is more erect and 6 inches to 2 feet in height, with flower spikes 2½ to 3 inches long and flowers ¾ to 1 inch or a little more in length. Typically, they are reddish-purple, but variety *P. g. alba* has white blooms, and *P. g. carminea*, *P. g. rosea*, and *P. g. rubra*, pink or red flowers. The leaves of this species and its varieties are usually toothed. Those of *P. g. pinnat-*

Prunella grandiflora

Prunella grandiflora rosea

ifida are pinnately-lobed, those of *P. g. pyrenaica* (syn. *P. hastifolia*) are halberd-shaped (they resemble an arrowhead, with the two lower parts spreading outward). The plant grown in gardens as *P. webbiana* and of which there are purple-, pink-, and white-flowered forms is closely similar.

Garden Uses. The decorative-flowered kinds discussed here are suitable for the fronts of perennial beds and for rock gardens and can be used to advantage in informal, naturalistic places. They grow well in slight shade, or if the soil is not excessively dry, in full sun.

Cultivation. Prunellas are easily raised from seed, by division, and from cuttings. They often multiply by self-sown seed, and seedlings that establish themselves among choice, weaker growing plants, as they may easily do in rock gardens, can prove troublesome if not weeded out while small.

PRUNING. The deliberate cutting off or shortening of stems or roots to render a plant more appropriate for its purpose or location, to improve its chance of survival, or to stimulate growth constitutes pruning. The term is generally restricted to such operations performed on shrubs,

trees, and woody vines. Shortening stems or roots of herbaceous perennials, biennials, and annuals is more often called pinching or cutting back. The term pinching is also used for the removal, usually by nipping between finger and thumb, of the soft extremities of young shoots of woody plants, and pruning trees and shrubs to the extent that their above-ground parts are more or less severely and uniformly shortened is often referred to as cutting back. When properly done pruning is decidedly beneficial, but unfortunately it is one of the least understood of gardening operations and much plant butchery is performed in its name.

The pruner should have in mind a specific, attainable objective or objectives. It is important to know with reasonable accuracy how the plant will respond to each cut made. Such knowledge may be based on experience, recommendations of reliable teachers or writers, or upon careful examination and observation of the plant itself. In any case the last procedure is of great importance as a supplement to experience and the suggestions of others. Sometimes it must of necessity be relied upon alone. Certainly there is nothing mysterious or esoteric about pruning. It is an art any intelligent person can learn.

The tools to use, the choice depending upon the character of the plant and thickness and hardness of the wood, may include a heavy pruning knife, regular short-handled pruning shears, long-handled lopping shears, a pole pruner and pole saw, and a regular short-handled pruning saw. Because their teeth are designed to cut on the pull stroke rather than the push stroke and are widely set, pruning saws are better adapted for the purpose than carpenters' saws and most models offer the advantage of a curved blade. Hedge shears, manual or powered, will be needed for some types of trimming. When pruning roses and other thorny plants, the protection of a pair of stout gauntlet-type gloves is highly desirable.

Precautions to take when using such potentially dangerous tools include maintaining them in excellent condition and storing them safely, out of reach of children. Unless these are in sheaths do not hang them on pegs or suspend them in such other ways that they may pose danger if they fall. It is usually safest to lay such tools on a flat surface.

Be constantly aware of possible dangers. Unless you have professional qualifications, do not climb trees or prune from ladders. Avoid like the proverbial plague unsubstantial or wobbly stepladders and such makeshift supports as chairs and boxes. The best advice for amateur pruners is to keep one's feet on the ground.

If ladders must be employed, wooden ones are to be preferred to metal ones,

Equipment for pruning: (a) Pruning shears   (b) Lopping shears   (c) Pole pruner

(d) Pole saw   (e) Detail of upper portion of pole pruner

(f) Detail of upper portion of pole saw

(g) Hedge shears   (h) Heavy duty gloves

at their ends, and to get extra leverage you hold them there, when the blade snaps suddenly through the stem the ends of the handles are likely to come together with great force and pinch the ball of your thumb. This will often produce a painful blood blister.

Precise pruning, which as the term is used here does not include shearing, should be done with careful regard for where every cut is made. Whenever practicable, cut just beyond a bud or lateral branch and close enough so that no long stubs are left. Cut slantwise rather than at right angles, and have the base of the cut on the opposite side from and slightly above the bud or branch.

Legitimate reasons for pruning are many and various, but do not include the common vague belief of many tyro gardeners that almost every woody plant benefits from this attention. That is not so. The great majority of trees and shrubs thrive with little or no pruning, and surely need no annual cutting. Whether or not pruning is desirable often depends as much upon the purpose for which the plant is being grown and the location it occupies as upon its kind. Age, vigor, and health are also important considerations.

especially in the vicinity of electric power lines or if electrically-powered tools are being used. Position ladders with great care to avoid slipping and for added safety have someone stand on the lowest rung.

Take particular care when using electrically powered shears not to accidently cut the cable and be ever alert to potential danger of their rapidly reciprocating blades. Added safety is had by wearing rubber-soled shoes or heavy rubbers or by standing on a dry plank. Always discon-

nect electrically powered tools when they are not in use.

Manual shears and knives can easily inflict serious injury unless they are handled with respect and care. When grasping a shoot to be pruned in one hand with shears held in the other be careful to keep fingers of the holding hand well tucked in and out of reach of the cutting blade. And do not strain to cut through a too-thick or too-tough shoot. If you do, using shears with handles that curve inward and meet

With pruning shears, make slanting cuts just above a growth bud

Ill-considered cutting can defeat its objectives. For example, excessive removal of branches in an effort to "make the tree flower" often results in exuberant new top growth at the expense of the bloom. Cutting at the wrong time can bring similar unsatisfactory results. Wisterias pruned only when dormant illustrate this: they are likely to produce lush foliage and few or no flowers. In its most restrictive forms, pruning imposes certain and often severe limitations upon growth. Examples are formal hedges, topiary, and espaliers. Hedges and topiary are maintained by regular shearing, espaliers by more selective cutting, operations performed one or more times a year. Because pruning of this kind normally involves the removal of foliage at times when it is actively manufacturing food from elements obtained from the soil and atmosphere, it has a weakening effect. Sheared hedges may be killed by cold that leaves naturally grown specimens of the same species unharmed. This was clearly seen in the vicinity of New York City in the severe winter of 1933–34, when privet hedges were killed to the ground, but unsheared plants of privet came through intact.

At the other extreme we have the type of pruning that calls for no more than the removal of an occasional dead, diseased, or misplaced branch. Its effect on new growth is minimal. Between this and hard annual pruning all intermediates occur. Certain it is that there is no simple answer to the question: How should one prune an apple tree (or holly or wisteria)? One might as well ask: How often, with what, and with how much should one feed a person? The answer must be: It depends upon the person. Is it a tiny baby, a growing youngster, someone in vigorous middle age, or one declining? What work is this person called upon to do? Are they in good health or poor? Is, perchance, the person recovering from a serious operation? (And so on.) And so with pruning a plant. Is the tree a young one that must

be trained to shape and style with major thought given to forming a good head of well-placed branches? Is it already formed and mature and needing only to be maintained in good health and productive? Or is it in need of restoration because of ill health or neglect? Is it just recovering from the severe operation of transplanting? Only when these and other factors are considered can pruning be intelligently done.

Pruning is, of course, done to restrict size—to confine plants to allotted dimensions, but this can be done only within sensible limits commonly violated by thoughtless and inexperienced gardeners, who seek to correct the evils of overcrowding by using the shears. When shrubs have been set much too closely together in the first place as is often the case with foundation plantings and other home landscape features, often the only practical correction is to take out some to give those that remain more space. An overplanted border of shrubs hacked back each year to prevent them becoming a miniature jungle is a sorry travesty of fine landscaping and good gardening. Even plants limited to size by pruning need a minimum of growing room if they are to develop pleasing character and form and are to display themselves to suitable advantage. It is even possible to "prune plants to death." For instance, the mighty hemlock (*Tsuga canadensis*), which naturally becomes a tree of 70 to 100 feet tall, may be sheared to form a hedge 8 or 10 feet tall, but any attempt to restrict it to a height of 1 foot or 2 feet, which can easily be done with the edging box (*Buxus sempervirens suffruticosa*), soon results in its death. Different kinds of plants vary greatly in the amount of pruning they will stand with impunity.

Development pruning carried out in the early years of the life of a tree or shrub is frequently very important. Neglect or improper attention then may be irreparable later. This is especially true of specimens that are to have a permanent trunk and branches, as do trees, treelike shrubs, and many vines, but is of somewhat less importance with shrubs that renew themselves by sending up abundant new shoots from their bases. Unless trees are to be trained to obviously artificial shapes, as are espaliers, for example, it is important to establish branch patterns that preserve the natural habits of the individual kinds. It is characteristic of some species, the pin oak (*Quercus palustris*), for example, to develop a single central trunk with decidedly subsidiary branches, whereas the trunks of other kinds, such as the American elm (*Ulmus americana*) and the horsechestnut (*Aesculus hippocastanum*), normally divide fairly low down into several massive branches or secondary trunks. Any tendency of naturally single-trunked kinds to produce more than one

leader (main central shoot) calls for corrective pruning by the removal of the weakest or least well-placed of the competitors as early as possible.

Pruning large trees calls for special techniques. If it involves climbing, it is beyond the purview of amateurs and should be left to professionals, and only to those adequately insured against accidents. Even working from high ladders or dealing with very heavy branches located above easy reach from the ground is no job for an amateur or the ordinary hired gardener. For those without experience and special skills such work is too dangerous. A broken arm, leg, back, skull, or worse is too steep a price to pay to doctor a tree. For such work hire a reliable tree surgeon.

When removing an entire limb, cut as close to the main trunk as practicable, but not necessarily absolutely flush with it. If the branch flares (thickens) rapidly and conspicuously where it joins the trunk, the cut may be made an inch or so out from the plane of an absolutely flush cut. This exposes less surface and encourages more rapid healing. The important point is not to leave stubs. Such short pieces of branch prevent the wound being covered with callus tissue. They die, and permit the

Pruning that involves climbing should be left to experienced professionals

Stubs left when large branches are removed often die and transmit rot to the trunk

To remove a large branch: (a) First make, a few inches from the branch's point of origin, a cut into its underside

(b) Then, a few inches beyond, saw downward from the upper side until the branch falls

growth of rots that are likely to continue into the trunk and eventually destroy it.

When branches are cut part way back, the cut should be made just beyond a vigorous side branch or, in trees that are known to develop new branches readily from old ones, at a point just beyond that from which a new branch is likely to develop.

To eliminate the danger of the weight of a falling branch tearing bark from the trunk, it is advisable to make at least three cuts (in the case of very big limbs, the branch may be first reduced in length by cutting off sections, and then three cuts used to remove the final section). The first of the three cuts is an undercut made in an upward direction from the underside of the branch and extending inward until the cut begins to bind on the saw and make it difficult to pull and push. The undercut should be located several inches outward along the branch from the point where the final cut is to be made. The second cut, out several more inches from the trunk than the undercut, is made from above and extends right through the branch. The third cut, the final one, is carefully made

(c) The undercut prevents the falling branch from stripping bark beyond it

and removes the stub that is left after the second cut has severed the main part of the branch.

It is advisable to pare the margins of the saw cut with a sharp knife. This results in cleaner slicing of the cambium layer (located just beneath the bark) from which new callus tissue grows and promotes rapid and satisfactory healing.

All cuts over 1 inch in diameter should be given a protective coating of tree wound paint. When necessary, out-of-reach-by-hand wounds can be coated with tree wound paint with a paint brush tied firmly to the end of a long pole. Excellent products may be purchased for this purpose or a paint may be prepared at home. One such consists of equal amounts of white lead and powdered sulfur mixed with enough boiled linseed oil to make a thickish paint and enough carbon black to color it dark gray. Another recommendation is three or four pounds of dry bordeaux mixture stirred into a gallon of linseed oil and enough carbon black to darken the mixture. Yet a third tree wound paint is made by stirring zinc oxide into linseed oil and adding lamp black for color.

(d) Finally, saw off the stump

Rapid healing is promoted if the exposed ring of cambium tissue, which lies just under the bark, is painted with shellac dissolved in alcohol before applying the tree wound paint. In the case of large wounds that do not heal in a single year, it is advisable to renew the coat of paint once a year, but it is not necessary to renew the shellac.

Paring the edges of large cuts encourages rapid healing

A good tree wound paint can be made from a combination of: (a) White lead

(b) Powdered sulfur

To treat large pruning cuts: (a) Coat the
rim of the wound with shellac

(c) Carbon black

(b) Then coat the entire surface with tree
wound paint

(d) Wounds completely healed and
covered with new bark

(d) Boiled linseed oil

(c) A vigorous new callus scar grows
over the wound; until it completely
covers the exposed wood, renew the
paint once or twice a year

branches meet, and to cut out promptly
shoots that if allowed to remain would result in crossed or otherwise ill-placed
branches.

The modified leader-type of tree is often
adopted for apples, apricots, cherries,
peaches, and some other fruits. It is
achieved by cutting the top off a one-year-
old tree to encourage the development of
side branches as well as of a new leader,
followed by the selection of a few
branches for retention as scaffolds (permanent framework limbs) and the early
removal of all others. Two or three years
later, the new leader is pruned to just
above a strong side branch. Subsequent
pruning is done to prevent the development of a dominant central leader.

(e) Stirred to paintlike consistency

Fruit trees are often pruned to become
specimens without central leaders, to have
frameworks of few to several branches of
approximately equal importance spaced to
permit free circulation of air and admission of light between them, and to facili-
tate harvesting. Pruning to achieve these
ends must begin early. Trees so managed
are usually developed as modified leader
or open center specimens. Whichever
form is adopted, care must be taken to select for retention shoots so located that
weak crotches will not develop where

Removing a vigorous shoot that, if
allowed to remain, would develop into an
ill-placed branch

The open center form is sometimes preferred for apples and some other fruits. Trees of this type have no leader, instead they branch low and the branches form a vaselike, open-centered head. To achieve this, cut back a one-year-old tree at a height of about 3 feet. From branches that develop select just enough well-spaced ones to form a shapely head and remove all others. Future pruning includes the prompt removal of any shoot that seems disposed to become a new leader.

Formative pruning of trees, shrubs, and vines to be developed as stylized specimens, such as espaliers and standards (examples with clear trunks crowned with mophead-like tops), must be closely attuned to training procedures, to the selection and development of suitably placed shoots and branches and of tying them into position, and to removal of all unwanted shoots or parts of shoots. With sorts such as apples and pears that bear flowers and fruits on spurs, it is extremely important to make sure from the beginning that pruning is done to develop these along the branches at suitably spaced intervals. For more about this consult the entry Espalier in this Encyclopedia. Winter pruning of apples, pears, and some other

fruits when grown as espaliers or as bush-type trees grafted onto dwarfing stocks, and of some ornamentals, notably wisterias, when trained in similar fashions, must be supplemented by systematic summer pruning. This consists of cutting off the tips of the current season's shoots just above the fifth or sixth leaf as soon as that leaf is about half grown and of shortening secondary shoots that develop just beyond the first leaf.

Standards, formal specimens with a clear trunk 2, 3, or more feet tall crowned with a rounded, moplike head of branches and foliage, are developed by formative pruning. A favorite way of training bay trees, fuchsias, geraniums, heliotropes, hibiscuses, lantanas, and other plants in containers, this is sometimes applied to outdoor specimens. With a few sorts, *Catalpa bignonioides nana* and the Christmas cactus, for example, standard specimens are achieved by grafting onto tall understocks of related plants, but more frequently they are the result only of training and pruning.

(c) Lantana

The usual procedure is to begin with a rooted cutting and to keep this growing without damage to its tip until it is almost as tall as the trunk the finished specimen is to have. During this time, nip out with finger and thumb, at as early a stage as practicable, all side shoots that develop and keep the main shoot neatly tied to a stake. When it attains a satisfactory height nip out the tip of the main shoot. Select few to several of the resulting side shoots to develop as framework branches of the head and remove all others. When 5 to 6 inches long, pinch out the tips of the framework branches and repeat this procedure with other branches that form until a head of desirable size is achieved.

Hedges need special pruning in their formative stages. All too often eagerness to achieve height interferes with the best development of the hedge as a dense, uniformly compact wall without thin areas or bare spaces, especially near its base. Prune newly planted hedges as reasonably ruthlessly as you dare without danger of inflicting permanent damage. Cutting back, involving height reduction of one-third to much more, is generally advisable with deciduous hedge plants, much less severe cutting is best with most evergreens, such as hemlocks, hollies, spruces, and cherry-laurels, but if necessary, for instance if their lower parts are thinly branched, kinds such as boxwoods and yews known to respond to cutting by sending out an abundance of new shoots may be pruned more severely.

Besides initial pruning at planting time, hedges need special attention during the years they are attaining their ultimate heights. Then prune or shear them once or with fast-growing kinds twice a year in such a way that the total increase in height or width gained in any year is not more than a few inches, or with very vigorous growers perhaps up to 1 foot. By limiting annual growth in this way, repeated

Summer pruning to shorten current year's shoots: (a) Apple

Standard (tree-form) specimens developed by formative pruning: (a) Fuchsia

(b) Wisteria

(b) Geranium

To renovate a top-tall, straggly privet hedge: (a) In winter or early spring, cut it back to a 1- to 2-foot height

(b) When new growth is 6 inches long, and two or three times yearly afterward, shear its sides

(c) And shear its top, using the string stretched between stakes as a guide

branching of the shoots and consequently a dense hedge is assured. Bear in mind the advantage of having the sides of the hedge slope inward slightly from base to top is so that its lower parts receive adequate light to keep the foliage healthy. In regions where there is danger of damage from accumulations of snow, it is advisable to prune hedges to pointed or rounded tops rather than flat ones.

Compensatory pruning, the reduction in size of the tops of trees, shrubs, and woody vines at transplanting time, is frequently of critical importance to their successful and speedy reestablishment. No matter how carefully done, digging plants involves the loss of a considerable proportion of root systems that until then were adequate to supply the aboveground parts with water. Unless measures are taken to reduce demands, it may become impossible for the roots that remain to adequately supply the tops, with the result that parts of branches, whole branches, or the entire tree, shrub, or vine dies. To forestall this, whenever practicable, prune severely enough to make certain that the foliage that is left or that the foliage that will develop when growth begins will not be more than the roots can supply with water.

The extent to which it is wise to prune at planting time depends upon a number of circumstances, among the most important, the kind of plant and the proportion of feeding roots that have been lost. Usually this will be greater with specimens dug from the wild or other locations where they have been established for many years than with nursery-grown stock that has been transplanted at regular intervals.

Often it is advantageous to reduce the top by one-quarter to one-half, sometimes more. This rarely involves shortening all the branches to that extent. More often the result is achieved by selective cutting. Some branches can perhaps be eliminated

and some or all others shortened. Depending upon what kind, it may or may not be advisable to cut back leading shoots. With many sorts of evergreens, it is better not to cut into old wood, but to remove only some of the previous year's growth by shearing or equivalent pruning.

A great advantage of compensatory pruning is that it allows the gardener to

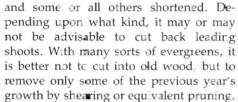

Sucker shoots: (a) Growing from the base of a tree or shrub

(c) Should be cut off

select the most advantageously placed branches for retention, whereas if it is not done some of those may be the very ones that die as a result of inability of the roots to supply the moisture they need.

Maintenance pruning of trees grown in more or less natural forms without strict training to shape varies with sorts and sometimes space limitations. A great

(b) Growing from the trunk or branches

(d) If not yet woody, broken off

many shade trees and flowering trees need no regular attention, but with all the prompt removal of broken and dead branches and sometimes of badly diseased ones is important. Also, an occasional, ill-placed branch may need removing, an excessively vigorous one shortening, or a certain amount of trimming of branches that overhang a path or otherwise interfere with the well-being of the garden or its occupants may need doing. With some trees, hawthorns and magnolias for example, sucker-like shoots called water sprouts sometimes grow from the trunk or main branches. Remove them promptly. For information about maintenance pruning of fruit trees consult the entries under their names in this Encyclopedia.

Flowering trees and shrubs fall rather neatly into three groups, those that need little or no regular pruning, those that may with advantage be pruned routinely, often annually, and bear blooms on shoots of the previous year or older, on old wood as gardeners say, and those that respond to regular pruning and carry their blooms on shoots of the current season's growth, on young wood.

Sorts that need little or no pruning include such deciduous kinds as azaleas, cherries, crab apples, daphnes, dogwoods, hawthorns, magnolias, silverbells, and viburnums. Most evergreens, notably camellias and rhododendrons, belong here.

Deciduous shrubs that bloom on previous year's wood and may, but not necessarily must, be pruned annually or perhaps at intervals of two or three years include a wide selection of sorts that bloom in spring and early summer. Among them are *Buddleia alternifolia*, *B. globosa*, deutzias, forsythias, hortensia-type hydrangeas, *Kerria japonica*, lilacs, mock-oranges, shrub and climbing roses, early-flowering spireas, *Tamarix pentandra*, and weigelas.

Prune a spring-blooming mock-orange (*Philadelphus*) by cutting out old flowering branches as soon as blooming is through

Prune shrubs in this category immediately when they are through flowering, not in winter or early spring. Earlier cutting results in a reduction in the amount of bloom. Generally the operation consists of thinning out enough old, more or less worn-out branches and weak and crowded younger ones to assure that those that remain will receive adequate light and free circulation of air. It may be expedient also to shorten overlong branches. Aim to preserve the natural habit of the plant and not to mar it by indiscriminate cutting back.

Remember, a shortened branch, one cut partway back, ordinarily gives rise to several shoots that become new branches. Therefore shortening is no cure for overcrowded growth; it merely aggravates the situation. To bring relief to bushes densely crowded with branches it is generally desirable to cut some out entirely and to shorten others by cutting back to where they join other branches.

Shrubs that bloom on current season's wood and may, but not necessarily must, be pruned annually include butterfly bush (*Buddleia davidii*), crape-myrtle, peegee hydrangea, hybrid tea and floribunda and grandiflora roses, rose-of-Sharon, *Spiraea bumalda* varieties, *Tamarix parviflora*, and vitexes.

Prune these sorts in late winter or spring before new growth begins or in mild climates in late fall or winter. In most cases the operation consists of cutting the shoots that grew the previous year back to within an inch or so of their bases, which may be at or close to the ground or considerably higher on branches that form a permanent framework. When specimens pruned in this manner become too crowded, thin out some of the old shoots that have become knobby as a result of repeated pruning. With roses the shortening of the previous season's shoots is usually less severe and some older wood may be taken out entirely. Ornamental-fruited trees and shrubs, or as they are often called, berried trees and shrubs, often present the problem that whenever cutting is done the display of fruits is reduced.

Broad-leaved evergreens, unless grown as hedges or in other formal shapes maintained by regular use of hedge or pruning shears, or accommodated as vines or trained as espaliers, need little or no cutting other than perhaps the removal of an occasional unwanted branch or the shortening of a maverick one that pokes out too far. But, if necessary or desirable, many sorts, including aucubas, barberries, boxwoods, citruses, cotoneasters, hollies, laurels (*Laurus*), privets, and the like, can be limited to size by cutting back annually the shoots of the previous year. This of course must be done with espaliered specimens and vine types, such as English ivy. It is generally best done in late winter or

Pruning a peegee hydrangea (*Hydrangea paniculata grandiflora*) in late winter:
(a) Beginning the job

(b) The result

spring before new growth appears, but with hollies and others suitable for use as Christmas greens it may be done just before the holiday season.

With large-leaved sorts, such as aucubas, laurels, and *Viburnum rhytidophyllum*, it is better to use pruning shears than hedge shears because clipping with the latter results in many leaves being sliced through and these are visually mildly disturbing, especially after their cut edges turn brown, until new growth hides them. Some large-foliaged, broad-leaved evergreens, notably rhododendrons do not lend themselves to this sort of pruning.

Conifers or needle-leaved evergreens of many sorts do not respond satisfactorily to hard pruning, but can be contained to size by annual shearing or cutting of shoots not over 1 year old. There are a few exceptions. You may cut yews, plum-yews, podocarpuses, and torreyas back severely, if necessary, with the full expectation that new shoots will sprout from the stumps of old wood, and if done with some degree of caution and without excessive butchery this is also true of junipers.

With firs, pines, spruces, and other conifers that do not produce replacement shoots from cut-back branches, it is practicable, if deemed necessary to remove entire branches by sawing flush with the trunk or, if they have fairly good side branches, to shorten them by cutting back to one of those.

Annual pruning beginning at a fairly early age is a more practical means of containing to size most coniferous evergreens, including those such as yews and junipers that may if occasion demands be dealt with more severely. With some, including the kinds just mentioned and arborvitaes, cypresses, false-cypresses, and hemlocks, this may be done before new growth begins in spring or in late summer or fall after the completion of the season's growth. The cutting back may be to within as close as ½ inch of the bases of last year's shoots or less severe depending upon whether you wish an increase in size of the plants or not.

The best way with firs, pines, and spruces is to shorten the candles of new growth in late spring before their leaves begin to spread and while they are still soft. Then they may be cut back to from two-thirds to one-third of their bases with every expectation that they will sprout secondary shoots that will be much shorter than the original ones would have been if left unpruned.

Rejuvenation pruning is done to restore to desirable size and shape and to stimulate into healthy growth trees, shrubs, and vines that have become too big or unshapely, that are badly overgrown, or that are leggy and bare at their bases. Often necessary when dealing with old, neglected gardens, it involves drastic cutting back and is by no means workable with all kinds of woody plants. It may be successfully employed to restore much-neglected hedges of plants, such as hollies, lilacs, and privets, that are known to withstand severe pruning well, but not, of course, with such sorts as hemlocks and spruces, which do not respond satisfactorily to hard pruning.

Sorts that respond are those capable of developing new shoots from really old and thick cut-back branches or trunks. If unsure about a particular specimen, head back one or two thick branches severely and observe the result through one growing season, that is, whether or not it sprouts new growth. This is not always necessary. An examination of the trunk or low parts of the branches may reveal new shoots arising spontaneously from the old wood, an indication that capacity for renewal following drastic pruning exists.

In its severest form, rejuvenation pruning consists of cutting the entire plant down in late winter or early spring to within a foot or less of the ground and following this by fertilizing generously, mulching, and making sure that in dry spells during the following summer the plant is watered thoroughly and regularly.

Limit the growth of pines by:
(a) Shortening the shoots while in the "candle" stage

(b) New growth beginning the following year

(c) The new growth of the following year completed

Obviously responsive to this treatment are shrubs such as deutzias, forsythias, mock-oranges, and a host of others that naturally produce from their bases a plentitude of stems. But many sorts that normally have a single trunk or at most two or three perhaps, may also be treated in this way. Here belong camelias, crapemyrtles, hollies, lilacs, mountain laurel, sumacs, rhododendrons, wisterias, and yews.

For surest and best results it is essential that pruning of this kind be done before new growth begins and that it be really drastic. Do not be tempted to leave any trunk or stem over 1 foot long. With grafted specimens, however, avoid cutting below the graft union, otherwise the sprouts that come will be those of the understock rather than of the superior sort grafted onto it.

If, as a result of drastic rejuvenation pruning, the number of new shoots that develop is obviously too many, thin them out early, leaving only enough of the strongest that will have the opportunity to develop without undue competition with others for light. Bear in mind, too, that if the plant you pruned became excessively tall and leggy from being crowded by neighbor plants or from other cause being denied adequate light or space, unless the adverse condition is corrected the new top that develops will follow the same pattern.

Heading back or dehorning is a less severe mode of rejuvenation pruning frequently applied to old apples, oranges, and peaches, as well as to shade and ornamental trees, and in somewhat modified form to vigorous woody vines such as wisterias. It involves severe cutting back of main branches, but retaining a skeleton framework consisting of their lower parts and of the trunk. The operation is done in

A plane tree headed back

late winter or early spring. Use a saw to make each cut wherever practicable just above a side branch rather than at a place that leaves a long branchless stub. Pare the edges of the cuts with a sharp knife and coat the cuts with tree wound paint.

A more gradual approach to rejuvenation is often advocated; instead of cutting back the entire plant to near ground level in one operation, spread the procedure over two or three years, cutting back one-half or one-third of the branches or trunks

A linden tree in Switzerland restrained in size by a type of pollard pruning

each spring. Although this is sometimes satisfactory, and with rhododendrons and a few other sorts it may sometimes be advantageous, more often the bolder treatment is to be preferred.

Root-pruning is done to shorten long, wandering roots and cause them to branch and form a denser, more compact root ball. There are two chief reasons for it. The most frequent is to prepare trees and shrubs, especially large ones, for transplanting. By root-pruning before they are moved, a much greater proportion of the total root system can be taken and chances of survival are greatly increased. It is of special advantage with trees such as dogwoods, sour gums, and sweet gums that are known to resent transplanting, especially from the wild or from elsewhere where they have been established for many years. Well-grown nursery stock that has been transplanted regularly may be moved without preparatory root-pruning.

The second purpose of root-pruning is to check excessively vigorous vegetative growth and so improve the chances of flower and fruit production. For this it can be employed with fruit trees, such as apples, pears, and plums, especially fairly young ones grafted or budded onto robust understocks or growing in rich soils, and with such ornamentals as trumpet vines and wisterias. Severely top pruning such specimens simply encourages further rank growth and inhibits flower production and subsequent fruiting. But root-pruning, properly done and with care taken to sever taproots checks vigor, encourages more balanced growth, and makes more likely the production of flowering and fruiting wood.

In preparation for transplanting, root-prune at least one full year ahead. Dig a trench so that its outer wall coincides with what will be the outside circumference of the root ball when it is dug and deep enough to sever all roots encountered. Backfill with fertile soil packed firmly.

During the next growing season young feeder roots will invade the new soil and will form part of the root ball that is transplanted.

To promote flowering or fruiting, root-prune only after careful thought. Consider whether inadequate performance may not be the result of too much shade, excessive use of nitrogenous fertilizer, faulty top pruning, or of the plant having not yet attained flowering age.

If none of these seem relevant, root-pruning may be in order. Its objectives are to cut taproots and strong, wide-spreading laterals that are without many feeding roots reasonably close to the trunk and to retain as many as possible of the fine fibrous roots.

With trees not planted for over four or five years and not too big to handle conveniently, the simplest procedure is to lift them out of the ground, shorten the offending roots, trim all cut roots with a sharp knife, and replant immediately.

A different procedure is necessary with older, bigger specimens. Instead of removing them from the ground dig a deep trench completely around them at a distance from the trunk equal to or slightly less than would be appropriate for digging a ball for transplanting. So far as practicable, save fibrous roots encountered in the upper layers of soil and tie them to one side in bundles. To cut the taproots with spade or saw, and this is important to success, it is necessary to tunnel beneath the ball. Before back-filling with soil, remove from the trench any cut pieces of roots. Use poorish rather than rich earth and pack it firmly. Because taproots that served as anchors have been severed, stake or guy root-pruned specimens as a precaution against disturbance by wind.

Root-pruning large trees may be spread over a period of two years, which results in less shock than if all is done at one time. When this plan is adopted, mark out the location of the trench and divide it into four equal parts. Root-prune two opposite quadrants the first year, the other pair a year later.

PRUNUS (Prùn-us). Of major horticultural importance, *Prunus*, of the rose family RO-SACEAE, in the broad sense is generally accepted as consisting of approximately 450 species, some hybrids, and innumerable varieties. It includes the stone fruits, almonds, apricots, cherries, nectarines, peaches, and plums, esteemed for their edible bounty, as well as species and varieties of the same groups cultivated primarily for their magnificent floral displays. Included also are the bird and choke cherries, blackthorn or sloe, cherry-laurels, and Portugal-laurel. Some botanists have treated almonds separately as *Amygdalis*, apricots as *Armeniaca*, cherries as *Padus* and *Cerasus*, cherry-laurels as *Pseudocera-*

sus, and peaches as *Persica,* but it is now more usual to accept these as subgenera or sections of *Prunus.* The name is the ancient Latin one of the plum and the cherry.

The kinds of *Prunus* are trees and shrubs chiefly natives of the northern hemisphere, mostly of temperate parts. The great majority of cultivated deciduous kinds are hardy, but most evergreen sorts will not survive winters appreciably harsher than those of Washington, D.C. Prunuses have alternate, usually toothed leaves, frequently with a few tiny knoblike glands on their stalks or at the bases of the leaf margins. In the bud stage, they may be conduplicate, that is with the two halves folded along the midrib and pressed flat together like the leaves of a closed book, or convolute, with the halves of the leaves in the bud stage rolled inward from their edges. This is often of importance in determining to which section or group of *Prunus* a particular sort belongs. The flowers, white, greenish, pink, or red, are generally in umbel-like clusters, racemes, or less commonly are solitary. Those of many deciduous sorts are displayed in spring before new foliage develops. They have a calyx of five spreading sepals, a corolla of five spreading petals or many more in double-flowered varieties, many stamens, and ordinarily one pistil. The fruits are drupes. The stone is usually a single seed enclosed in a hard covering or shell surrounded by a layer of usually soft, juicy flesh and a thin outer skin. In this Encyclopedia the kinds of *Prunus* grown chiefly as orchard trees for their edible fruits are discussed in more detail in the entries Almond, Apricots, Cherry, Nectarines, Peach, and Plums. The emphasis here is on ornamental kinds, with some descriptive notes of the species from which the orchard fruits have been derived. In the treatment that follows the sorts are grouped and presented in the following order:

Almonds, peaches, and nectarines are deciduous and have leaves in bud conduplicate, flowers and fruits with very brief stalks, the fruits except those of nectarines covered with a fuzz of velvety down.

Cherries of the subgenus *Cerasus* are deciduous and have leaves in bud conduplicate, flowers solitary or in clusters of few or in short racemes with usually conspicuous bracts, and fruits lacking a groove or furrow down one side, without a bloom (a thin, waxy coating), and containing a nearly spherical stone.

Cherries of the subgenus *Padus* are distinguished from those of the subgenus *Cerasus* by having small flowers in elongated, tail-like, usually leafy-stalked racemes of a dozen or more, usually with small bracts. Except for *P. salicifolia* those cultivated are deciduous.

Old World plums are deciduous and

have leaves in bud convolute, flowers solitary or in clusters of two or rarely three, and fruits with a groove or furrow down one side and usually with a thin waxy coating or bloom.

Native American plums are deciduous, have leaves in bud mostly conduplicate, those of a very few sorts convolute, flowers usually in clusters of three or more or rarely solitary, and fruits with a groove or furrow down one side and generally with a thin waxy coating or bloom.

Apricots have leaves convolute in bud and very short-stalked flowers and fruits, the latter covered with velvety down. They are deciduous.

Cherry-laurels are evergreens with leathery foliage and from the axils of the leaves of the previous year elongated racemes of small flowers, with leafless stalks, and little bracts. The fruits, without a groove or furrow down the side, lack a bloom (a thin waxy coating) and contain an approximately spherical stone.

The common almond (**P. dulcis** syn. *P. amygdalus*), probably Asian, but perhaps native of the Mediterranean region, is one of the earliest and most beautiful of spring-blooming trees, hardy about as far north as New York City. Deciduous and 20 to 30 feet tall, it has long-pointed, oblong-lanceolate, finely-toothed leaves 3 to 5 inches long, broadest below their middles and usually with glands on their stalks. The stalkless, solitary or paired pink flowers, which appear well before the leaves, are 1 inch to 2½ inches wide. The laterally-flattened, oblong-ovoid, velvety-downy fruits 1½ to 2½ inches long are not quite as wide as long. Unlike the fruits of most prunuses, their flesh is hard, dry, and splits at maturity to reveal the smooth, but pitted stone. Orchard almonds grown for their fruits are of two types, the sweet or edible varieties with seeds either hard- or soft-shelled, and bitter almonds (*P. d. amara*), the seeds of which contain significant amounts of deadly prussic acid, for which they are cultivated. Varieties of *P. dulcis*, esteemed for their blooms rather than their fruits, are attractive ornamentals. Here belong *P. d. alba*, with single white flowers; *P. d. albo-plena*, with double white blooms; *P. d. erecta*, of upright growth, flowers pink; *P. d. pendula*, with drooping branches; *P. d. praecox*, blooming about two weeks earlier than others, its flowers pale pink; *P. d. purpurea*, with rose-purple flowers; *P. d. roseo-plena*, with light pink double blooms; and *P. d. variegata*, with variegated foliage.

Dwarf Russian almond (**P. tenella** syn. *P. nana*), a very hardy deciduous shrub 3 to 4½ feet tall, is native from southeastern Europe to Siberia. It has long slender shoots and thickish, lanceolate to oblong-obovate or oblanceolate, sharply-toothed, short-stalked leaves 1¼ to 3 inches long, and stalkless, rosy-red blooms ½ to ¾

inch wide, solitary or in twos or threes. They have toothed sepals. The egg-shaped fruits, nearly 1 inch long, are pubescent. Varieties are *P. t. alba*, with white flowers; *P. t.* 'Fire Hill', which has erect stems and brilliant rose-red blooms; *P. t. georgica*, up to 6 feet tall, flowers pale pink, and *P. t. gessierana*, with deep pink flowers, 1 inch in diameter, that are darker in the bud stage than when open.

Flowering almond, although a designation obviously applicable to other kinds, is commonly particularly associated with *P. triloba*, a Chinese shrub or small tree

Prunus triloba

hardy in southern New England. The natural wild species correctly named *P. t. simplex* up to 15 feet in height but often lower, has broad-elliptic to obovate, short-stalked leaves sometimes three-lobed at their apexes, 1¼ to 2½ inches long and with coarsely-toothed margins. From ¾ to 1 inch across and solitary or in twos, the flowers are pink. The red fruits are subspherical, hairy, and approximately ½ inch in diameter. Variety *P. t. multiplex* (syn. *P. t. plena* and the sort first named *P. triloba*) has excellent double pink blooms. Another species, often called flowering almond, although botanically it belongs with the cherries and is discussed below

Prunus triloba multiplex

under the more appropriate name of Chinese bush cherry, is *P. glandulosa*.

Peaches and nectarines belong botanically in the same group of *Prunus* as almonds. The common peach (**P. persica**), from which are derived orchard peaches and nectarines as well as varieties grown as ornamentals and called flowering peaches, is a native of China, having been cultivated since ancient times. Hardy through most of New England, it is a tree up to about 25 feet tall with toothed, hairless, elliptic-lanceolate to oblong-lanceolate, pointed leaves broadest at or just above their middles, 3½ to 6 inches long, with glands on their brief stalks. Pink and usually solitary, the very short-stalked flowers, 1 inch to 1½ inches across, have sepals pubescent on their outsides. The downy fruits are subspherical, 2 to 3 inches in diameter, and have deeply-furrowed, pitted stones. Nectarines (*P. p. nucipersica*) differs from peaches in having rather smaller fruits without a fuzz of hairs and leaves usually more coarsely-toothed.

Flowering peaches cultivated as ornamentals include among older varieties: *P.*

The orchard peach: (a) In bud

(b) Flowers

Prunus persica albo-plena pendula

Prunus persica 'Prince Charming': (a) As an espalier

(b) Flowers

p. albo-plena, with double, white blooms; *P. p. albo-plena pendula*, similar but with pendulous branches; *P. p. camelliaeflora*, with semidouble, deep red blooms; *P. p. dianthiflora*, with pink, semidouble flowers; *P. p. pendula*, with pendulous branches and pink flowers; *P. p. pyramidalis*, of narrow, erect growth and with pink flowers; and *P. p. rubro-plena*, its flowers red and semidouble. Among the several splendid newer varieties of flowering peaches are these: 'Aurora', flowers rose-pink, double, with frilled petals; 'Cardinal', flowers double, bright red; 'Crimson Cascade', branches pendulous, flowers crimson; *P. p. foliis-rubis*, young foliage purplish-red, flowers pink; 'Helen Borchers', flowers large, pink, semidouble; 'Iceberg', flowers large, white, semidouble; 'Klara Mayer', flowers double, peach-pink; 'Prince Charming', a small upright tree, flowers rose-red, double; 'Russell's Red', flowers crimson, double; and 'Windle

Weeping', with pendulous branches, broad leaves, and cup-shaped, purplish-pink flowers. The flowering nectarine (*P.*

p. nucipersica 'Alma Stultz'), about 20 feet tall and wide, has fragrant, 2- to 2½-inch-wide pink blooms that deepen in color as they age and white-fleshed fruits.

Two other flowering peaches are cultivated, *P. davidiana* and *P. mira*, both natives of China. A tree up to 30 feet high, **P. davidiana** differs from *P. persica* in the sepals of its flowers being completely hairy. It has slender, erect branches and narrowly-ovate-oblong, finely-toothed leaves, 2 to 2½ inches long, broadest near their bases, tapered to long points, and with glands on their stalks. The 1-inch-wide, solitary, light pink flowers have very short stalks. The spherical fruits, their pitted stones free from the surrounding flesh, are yellowish, about 1¼ inches in diameter. The blooms of *P. d. alba* are white, those of *P. d. rubra*, rosy-red. Lustrous ovate-lanceolate leaves and ovoid fruits are distinguishing characteristics of *P. d. potaninii*. From other peaches **P. mira** differs in its fruits having quite smooth stones. About 30 feet tall and with slender branches, this has lanceolate leaves 2 to 4 inches long, tapered to pointed apexes, toward their bases distantly round-toothed, hairy on their undersides along the midrib, and with stalks with glands. Solitary or in pairs, the very short-stalked white flowers, ¾ to 1 inch in diameter, have sepals hairy along their margins. The densely-velvety-hairy, fleshy fruits are subspherical, about 1¼ inches in diameter.

Cherries of the subgenus *Cerasus* include all grown as orchard trees as well as the popular flowering cherries and bush cherries. These are now presented.

The sweet cherry, mazzard, or gean (**P. avium**), the progenitor of the orchard varieties of sweet cherries, is a native of Europe and adjacent Asia. Hardy into Canada, it includes several varieties worth growing as ornamentals. Pyramidal, up to 70 feet in height, but frequently lower, this is a deciduous tree with glossy bark that peels in horizontal strips. Pointed-ovate and with irregular blunt teeth, the 3- to 6-inch-long leaves are somewhat downy on their undersides. The white, cupped flowers 1 inch to 1½ inches across are in mostly stalkless umbels of several, without bracts at their bases. The fruits, sweet or at least not acid, are subspherical to ovoid and about 1 inch long. Those of orchard varieties (treated in this Encyclopedia under Cherries) are bigger. Varieties grown for ornament include *P. a. aspleniifolia*, which has leaves with deeply-cleft margins. The branches of *P. a. pendula* droop rather stiffly and awkwardly. Especially lovely *P. a. plena* has pendulous, double white blooms. It rarely if ever fruits.

The sour cherry (**P. cerasus**), the parental stock of sour cherry varieties cultivated for their fruits, differs from the sweet

Prunus persica 'Helen Borchers'

cherry in having hairless leaves, usually a few leafy bracts at the bases of the flower clusters, and red or black acid fruits. Native to Europe and temperate Asia, and hardy into Canada, this is a deciduous, suckering shrub or round-headed tree 10 to 30 feet tall with spreading and drooping branches and fine-toothed, elliptic-obovate to ovate leaves 2 to 3½ inches long. The white blooms, ¾ to 1 inch wide, are succeeded by fruits about ¾ inch in diameter. Those of orchard varieties, treated in this Encyclopedia under Cherries, are larger. A good ornamental, *P. c. flore-pleno* has semi-double blooms. The very showy, double white flowers of *P. c. rhexii* are 1 inch to 1½ inches across. Everblooming or All Saints cherry (*P. c. semperflorens*) bears white flowers sporadically through spring and summer.

The mahaleb or St. Lucie cherry (**P. mahaleb**), a deciduous, green-twigged tree up to 40 feet high, is lovely in bloom. It has broad-ovate to nearly round, short-pointed or blunt, finely-round-toothed leaves, 1½ to 2½ inches long, and usually with one or two glands on their stalks. The very fragrant, white flowers, ½ to ¾ inch wide, are in umbel-like, short racemes with bracts or small leaves at their bases. The ovoid fruits, black or less often yellow, are about ¼ inch long. This variable species, the wood of which is much esteemed for making tobacco pipes and walking sticks, is naturalized in parts of North America. It has been hybridized with the sweet cherry. Variety *P. m. pendula* has elegantly arching branches.

The wild red or pin cherry (**P. pensylvanica**), native from Newfoundland to British Columbia, North Carolina, and Colorado, is a less ornamental botanical ally of the mahaleb cherry. A shrub or tree up to 25 feet tall, with short-stalked, hairless, pointed-ovate-lanceolate, finely-sharp-toothed leaves 2 to 4 inches long, this has clusters of two to five ½-inch-wide, white flowers. Its fruits, spherical, red, and about ¼ inch in diameter, attract birds.

Japanese or Oriental flowering cherries are deciduous trees that include a few species and a large number of varieties, many of which have been cultivated in Japan for centuries. Earliest to bloom, the lovely rosebud or Higan cherry (**P. subhirtella**) is unknown in the wild. It produces, before its leaves expand, vast quantities of 1- to 1½-inch-wide, light pink blooms. Round-headed and up to 30 feet tall, this has short-pointed, lanceolate to ovate, toothed leaves, the veins of their undersides hairy. The blooms, ¾ inch in diameter, have very delicate to deeper pink petals notched at their apexes. Graceful *P. s. pendula* has crooked, pendulous branches and small single blooms; *P. s. pendula flore-plena*, pendulous branches and double flowers. Displays of semidouble white or pink blooms are presented by *P. s. autum-*

Prunus subhirtella

Prunus subhirtella pendula

nalis in spring and again in fall. A splendid hybrid between *P. subhirtella* and *P. yedoensis*, 'Hally Jolivette', about 10 feet tall, develops a dense, rounded head. Its long-lasting, double white blooms, 1¼ inches wide, are pink in the bud stage and expand before the new foliage comes.

Another early and exceedingly free bloomer, long cultivated in Japan and famed as the most plentiful of the Japanese cherries around the Tidal Basin, Washington, D.C., the Yoshino cherry (**P. yedoensis**) is believed to be a hybrid between *P. speciosa* and *P. subhirtella*. It may become nearly 50 feet high. It has a broad,

Prunus yedoensis

Prunus yedoensis (flowers)

flattish-topped head of arching branches, and resembles *P. serrulata*, but the veins on the undersides of the leaves are more or less hairy. Its white to pink flowers, about 1 inch across, come before the leaves and are faintly scented of almonds. Variety *P. y.* 'Shidare Yoshino' (syn. *P. y. purpendens*) has horizontal and arching branches that often reach to the ground, and pale pink flowers.

Prunus yedoensis 'Shidare Yoshino'

The source of more horticultural varieties than any other Asian species of flowering cherry, *P. serrulata*, of Japan, China, and Korea, is the ancestral stock of probably fifty varieties cultivated in the United States and of many more grown only in Japan. In its native territory, this may become 75 feet high, but its horticultural varieties rarely exceed 25 feet. The branches of all are usually erect. The leaves are ovate to narrow-ovate, long-pointed and somewhat glaucous on their undersides, with bristle-toothed margins. The flowers of the typical species are white, up to 1½ inches wide, and without fragrance. They are in umbels with fringed bracts. The fruits are black, about the size of peas. Variety *P. s. lannesiana* is distinguished by its leaves having longer bristly teeth and its

Prunus serrulata variety

Prunus serrulata, single-flowered variety

Prunus serrulata, double-flowered variety

flowers being fragrant and pink. Formerly regarded as a separate species, *P. s. 'Takasago'* (syn. *P. sieboldii*) has double, pink flowers, about 1¼ inches in diameter. The sort identified as *P. s. spontanea* is a natural form with white or pink flowers.

Among the most beautiful and satisfactory horticultural varieties of *P. serrulata*, others are to be found listed and described in nursery catalogs, are these: 'Amanogawa', columnar, has strictly erect branches and light pink, semidouble blooms. 'Fugenzo' (syns. 'Kofugen', 'James H. Veitch') has double, 2½-inch-wide, rosy-pink blooms that become paler as they age. 'Kwanzan' (more correctly 'Sekiyama', but the synonym is too well established in common usage to be lightly discarded), of erect habit when young but broadening with age, has large clusters of pendulous, deep pink, very double blooms displayed along with bronzy young foliage. 'Shirofugen' (syn. 'White Goddess') has double flowers up to 2½ inches across, pink at first, soon fading to white. 'Shirotae' has semidouble to nearly double, fragrant, white blooms, their petals with slightly ruffled margins. 'Shogetsu' has semidouble to double pink blooms often white at their centers. 'Ukon' displays its pendulous, delicate yellow, semidouble flowers as a nice contrast to its bronzy very young foliage.

The hardiest and one of the most beautiful Japanese cherries, *P. sargentii* succeeds throughout most of New England. Native to Japan, Sakhalin Island, and Korea, and in its homelands attaining a maximum height of 75 feet, this round-headed, vigorous sort charms not only

with its spring blooms, but also with the brilliant orange, scarlet, and crimson hues of its foliage in fall. Its sharply-toothed, hairless leaves, purplish when they unfold, elliptic-obovate to oblong-obovate, are 3 to 4½ inches long. Appearing very early, the deep rose-pink flowers, 1¼ inches wide, are in umbels of four or fewer. The purple-black, spherical-ovoid fruits are under ½ inch long. Variety *P. s. columnaris* is much narrower than the typical species, but tends to broaden as it ages.

Other Asian flowering cherries of tree dimensions include these: *P. campanulata,* the Taiwan cherry, a lovely round-headed native of southern Japan and Taiwan, and hardy in mild climates only, is up to 25 feet tall. It has ovate to elliptic-ovate or ovate-oblong, hairless or practically hairless leaves 1½ to 4 inches long, with short, forward-pointing teeth. Its deep rose-pink, slender-stalked, ¾-inch-long, bell-shaped blooms are in dense, pendulous clusters. The fruits are red, a little over ½ inch in length. *P. cerasoides,* of the Himalayas, much like the last, differs in having leaves proportionately broader, more leathery, and more sharply-toothed. Variety *P. c. rubra* has deep rose-pink blooms, red in the bud stage. *P. conradinae,* of China, hardy about as far north as southern New York, is an elegant sort up to 25 feet tall. It has narrow-elliptic to oblong-obovate, toothed leaves 2 to 4 inches long, when young hairy along the veins on their undersides. In clusters of up to four, its whitish to pinkish flowers are about ¾ inch in diameter. The red fruits are under ½ inch long. Variety *P. c.*

semiplena has longer-lasting, semidouble, fragrant blooms 1 inch in diameter. *P. lobulata* is Chinese. Hardy in southern New England and up to 30 feet tall, this has obovate to oblong-lanceolate, strongly-toothed leaves, 1½ to 3½ inches long, hairy along the veins on their undersides. Solitary or in twos or threes, the flowers are white. The red fruits are subspherical and less than ½ inch long. *P. nipponica,* a native of Japan and hardy in southern New England, is 10 to 20 feet tall, dense, and bushy. It has the distinction of its fall foliage assuming handsome shades of yellow and orange. This has long-pointed, ovate, coarsely-toothed leaves 1½ to 3½ inches long, pubescent when young, and white to light pink flowers up to 1 inch wide in twos or threes or solitary. The black fruits are spherical, about ⅓ inch in diameter. *P. n. kurilensis* (syn. *P. kurilensis*) has somewhat larger blooms. The outstanding feature of *P. serrula* is its highly polished, flaky, red-brown bark. Hardy in southern New England and about 30 feet tall, this Chinese species has pointed-lanceolate, small-toothed leaves, 1½ to 4 inches long, with the veins on their undersides pubescent and tufts of hair where the side veins join the center one. Appearing with the foliage, the white flowers are mostly in threes. The ½-inch-long, spherical to ovoid fruits are red.

Bush cherries, deciduous shrubs rarely over 10 feet high and often considerably lower, include a number of species native to North America and some to Asia. The first considered here, although botanically a cherry, is widely known as the dwarf flowering almond.

The Chinese bush cherry (**P. glandulosa**), native to China and Japan and not reliably hardy in climates more severe than that of New York City, is up to 4½ feet tall. It has ovate-oblong to oblong-lanceolate, roundish-toothed leaves up to about 3½ inches long, hairless or slightly hairy on the midribs of their undersides. Its pink to white, solitary or paired flowers are prettily displayed all along its numerous, slender, erect stems. The red fruits are spherical, up to ½ inch in diameter. The most popular varieties are *P. g. alboplena*, with double white blooms, and *P. g. sinensis* (syn. *P. sinensis*), the flowers of which are pink and double.

Prunus glandulosa sinensis

The sand cherry and Western sand cherry (**P. pumila** and **P. besseyi**, respectively) are similar. The first is native from New York to Wisconsin and Illinois, the other from Wyoming to Manitoba, Kansas, and Colorado. Up to about 8 feet tall, but with its old branches often procumbent, extremely hardy *P. pumila* has oblanceolate, hairless, toothed, grayish-green leaves up to 2 inches long, and whitish on their undersides. About ⅓ inch in diameter, the white flowers are in clusters of two to four. Scarcely edible, the subspherical, glossy, red-purple fruits barely exceed ⅓ inch in diameter. The Western sand cherry differs in having elliptic to elliptic-lanceolate leaves that spread widely instead of standing rather erectly, and sweet, agreeably flavored fruits ½ inch or a little more in diameter. It is the source of improved varieties cultivated, chiefly in the Middle West, as Hanson bush cherries. The purple-leaved sand cherry (*P.* 'Cistena'), a hybrid between *P. pumila* and *P. cerasifera atropurpurea* that attains a height of 5 to 7 feet, is esteemed chiefly for its red-purple

Prunus 'Cistena'

foliage. It has white or pinkish flowers and small blackish-purple fruits.

Other bush cherries include these: *P. concinna* is a beautiful Chinese about 6 feet tall and hardy in southern New England. It has narrow-elliptic to obovate, finely-toothed, sparingly-hairy leaves, purplish when they first unfold. In clusters of four or fewer or sometimes solitary, the white flowers are ¾ to 1 inch wide. The fruits are subspherical. *P. fruticosa*, of from central and southern Europe to Siberia, is known as the ground cherry. A spreading shrub up to about 3 feet tall, it has elliptic-ovate to oblong-obovate leaves ¾ inch to 2 inches long, and usually in stalkless umbels of two to four, white flowers a little over ½ inch in diameter. The dark red, spherical fruits are somewhat under ½ inch across. Variety *P. f. pendula* has slender, drooping branches. In Europe this species is grafted high onto understocks of *P. avium* to give standard (tree-form) specimens. *P. incana*, the willow cherry of southeastern Europe and adjacent Asia, is hardy in southern New England. Erect-branched and of loose, open habit, this has oblong-ovate to lanceolate leaves 1¼ to 2¼ inches long, grayish- or white-woolly on their undersides, dark green and hairless above. Solitary or paired, the rose-pink flowers are a little over ⅓ inch across. The red fruits are approximately ¼ inch in diameter. *P. incisa*, the Fuji cherry, in Japan much used for bonsai, is usually a shrub, but sometimes a small tree that blooms very freely in spring before its leaves appear. Unfortunately the flowers are short-lived. This, a native of Japan and hardy in southern New England, has ovate to obovate, toothed leaves, purplish when very young, 1¼ to 2½ inches long, and in fall assuming bright colors. The flowers are pink in bud, white when open. The fruits are egg-shaped, purple-black, and about ⅓ inch long. Variety *P. i. serrata* has leaves with larger teeth. *P. jacquemontii*, of the Himalayas, is a slender-branched, loose shrub, 8 to 12 feet tall, and hardy about as

Prunus incisa

far north as southern New York. Usually in pairs, its rose-pink flowers are a little under ½ inch wide. The red subspherical fruits are approximately ½ inch long. *P. japonica* is an extremely hardy native of China, very like *P. glandulosa*, but differing in its leaves being sharply-double-toothed, ovate, and broadest below their middles. The pink to almost white flowers are in twos or threes. The fruits are subspherical, wine-red, and about ½ inch long. *P. tomentosa*, native from China to Korea and the Himalayas, is an extremely hardy, variable handsome shrub or less often a small tree up to 12 feet tall. It has obovate to elliptic, wrinkled, toothed leaves, pubescent on their upper surfaces, densely-hairy beneath. The white or pinkish flowers, ½ to ¾ inch wide, are solitary or in pairs. The bright red, edible fruits are subspherical, a little under ½ inch in diameter.

Prunus tomentosa

Cherries of the subgenus *Padus*, which bloom after the foliage is well developed, are less showy in flower than most sorts of the subgenus *Cerasus*. The ones now to be considered belong in *Padus*.

The European bird cherry (**P. padus**), notable for being one of the earliest trees

Prunus padus (cut sprays)

Prunus serotina

Prunus serotina (flowers)

Prunus serotina (fruits)

to leaf in spring, is native to Europe, northern Asia, Korea, and Japan. Hardy into Canada, this is an open-headed tree up to 45 feet tall. Its leaves have glandular stalks, abruptly-pointed blades elliptic to oblong-ovate or obovate and 2½ to 4½ inches long. White, fragrant, and ⅓ to ½ inch across, the flowers, which appear much later than the foliage in pendulous racemes 3 to 6 inches long, are succeeded by black fruits ¼ inch in diameter. Blooming much earlier than other varieties, *P. p. commutata* has flowers fully ½ inch in diameter. Excellent *P. p. plena* has double blooms larger than those of the typical species. The flower clusters of *P. p. spaethii* are more or less drooping. The racemes of blooms of *P. p. watereri* are 8 inches long. Similar to the European bird cherry, but less attractive and more horribly subject to infestations of tent caterpillars, the eastern American choke cherry (*P. virginiana*) should not be admitted as a garden ornamental. Because of its extreme hardiness, adapted to regions too cold for other cherries, the Amur choke cherry (*P. maackii*) scarcely warrants planting in warmer climes. Native to Korea and Manchuria and up to 45 feet tall, this has yellow, flaking, birchlike bark and a rounded head. Its elliptic to oblong-obovate leaves, with blades 2 to 4 inches long, have usually glandular stalks and are dotted with glands on their undersides. The little white flowers in racemes 2 to 3 inches long, unlike those of other sorts of the *Padus* group, come from shoots of the previous year. The black or rum cherry (*P. serotina*) is a noble species up to 90 feet tall, the lumber of which is greatly esteemed for furniture and other uses. A native of eastern and central North America, this has somewhat pendulous branches and thickish, lustrous, peachlike, oblong-ovate to oblong-lanceolate, pointed leaves, 2 to 4½ inches long, with glandular stalks and on their undersides often hairy along the midribs. In freely-borne racemes 4 to 5½ inches long, the small white flowers are followed by showy fruits, at first red,

but at maturity black. Varieties include *P. s. aspleniifolia*, with leaves deeply, irregularly incised, and *P. s. pendula*, with drooping branches. Native to tropical America and hardy in warm climates only, the capollin (*P. salicifolia* syns. *P. serotina salicifolia*, *P. capuli*) is a large tree closely allied to the black or rum cherry, but more or less evergreen. It has narrow, long-

pointed leaves, stout racemes of small white flowers, and edible fruits up to 1 inch in diameter.

Plums agree with apricots and differ from cherries and other sorts of *Prunus* in their fruits being conspicuously grooved down one side. From most apricots they can be distinguished by their flowers having longer, more slender stalks and their fruits being smooth, usually with a waxy bloom rather than clothed with a fuzz of short hairs, and containing stones without prominent furrows along their margins. Orchard varieties are dealt in the Encyclopedia entry titled Plums. Here our concern is with natural species and varieties of ornamental merit.

The common or European plum (*P. domestica*), of uncertain, but probably southwest Asian provenance, occasionally becomes established and reproduces outside cultivation. Characteristically, this robust small tree is hardy throughout most of New England and, except occasionally in specimens that have "gone native," without thorns. Its shoots when young are sometimes sparingly pubescent. The thick, wrinkled, coarsely-irregularly-toothed, dull leaves 2 to 4 inches long, are conspicuously hairy on their undersides, less densely so above. White or cream-colored and with pubescent stalks, the ½- to 1-inch-wide flowers are mostly in clusters from short spurs, sometimes solitary or in twos or threes. The fruits, which vary considerably, are generally large, most often purple or blue-purple. They have nearly smooth stones easily separated from the flesh.

The damson or bullace (*P. insititia*) differs from the common plum in being smaller and in having smaller leaves. Also, its young shoots are decidedly hairy, its flowers usually have pubescent stalks, and its fruits are generally smaller and have flesh that clings to the nearly smooth stone. Cultivated since before recorded history, this is a native of eastern Europe and western Asia. The wild form of the damson or bullace is spiny, but cultivated sorts are only slightly so or are spineless.

The sloe or blackthorn (*P. spinosa*), native to Europe, North Africa, and western Asia, is a freely-branched shrub or occasionally small tree, hardy through most of New England. It has more or less pubescent shoots and blunt, elliptic-ovate to oblong-obovate, toothed leaves up to 1½ inches long. Produced before the leaves, the usually solitary white flowers are from somewhat under to a little over ½ inch across. The blue-black, nearly spherical, astringent fruits up to ⅝ inch in diameter, have a waxy bloom. Variety *P. s. plena* has double flowers, those of *P. s. purpurea*, a less spiny shrub with purplish foliage, are pink.

The Japanese plum (*P. salicina*), up to about 30 feet tall and long cultivated in Japan, but native to China, is extremely hardy. It has dark, glossy shoots and differs from the common plum in its oblong-obovate to elliptic-obovate, bluntly-toothed leaves being lustrous and having undersides without hairs except for tufts where side veins join the mid-vein, and in its fruits being deeply dimpled at their attachment to the stalk. Mostly in threes, the white flowers are ½ to ¾ inch in diameter. The fruits are spherical-ovoid, often with a pointed apex, 2 to 3 inches long, yellow, light red, or pale green.

The cherry plum or myorbalan plum (*P. cerasifera*), one of the most decorative species, a very hardy native of western Asia and the Caucasus, is most familiar to gardeners in its purple-leaved form. Round-headed, up to 25 feet tall, slender-branched, and sometimes spiny, this has ovate to obovate leaves 1½ to 2½ inches long. Mostly solitary, but sometimes in twos or threes and frequently crowded on short spurs to form close clusters, the pure white flowers are ¾ to 1 inch across. The cherry-like, red fruits, up to 1¼ inches in diameter, are deeply dimpled where the stalk joins them.

The best-known variety, *P. c. atropurpurea* (syn. *P. c. pissardii*) has claret-red to deep purple foliage, single, light pink blooms, and red-purple fruits. A weeping or pendulous form of *P. c. atropurpurea* is known as *P. c. a. pendula*. Other variants

Prunus cerasifera atropurpurea

Prunus cerasifera atropurpurea (flowers)

are 'Krauter Vesuvius', a somewhat smaller tree with purple-black foliage the darkest of any plum, light pink flowers, and little tendency to fruit, and 'Thundercloud', which has a more rounded head than *P. c. atropurpurea*, dark coppery foliage, pale pink to white flowers, and red fruits.

Hybrids of *P. c. atropurpurea* include *P. blireiana* (syn. *P. c. blireiana*) the other parent of which is believed to be *P. mume*. This is similar to *P. c. atropurpurea*, but has broader leaves and fragrant, semidouble pink flowers. Its foliage becomes greenish-bronze in summer. It rarely fruits. A hybrid between *P. c. atropurpurea* and the Japanese plum variety 'Duarte' is named 'Hollywood'. It has leaves, green when they first open, later becoming dark green above and purple-red on their undersides. It produces red fruits 2 to 2½ inches in diameter of good eating quality. Another hybrid, 'Oregon Trail' has as parents *P. c. atropurpurea* and the Japanese orchard plum 'Shiro'. This has leaves bright red in spring, later bronzy-green above and red-purple on their undersurfaces. The flowers are blush-white, the fruits red.

The apricot plum (*P. simonii*), not known in the wild, but of Chinese origin, is hardy in southern New England. A narrow-pyramidal tree with upright branches, this has thickish, dull, oblong-lanceolate to oblong-obovate, finely-blunt-toothed, hairless leaves 3 to 4 inches long. Solitary or in twos or threes, the short-stalked, white flowers are ¾ to 1 inch wide. The fragrant, tomato-shaped fruits, 1 inch to 2 inches in diameter and with a deep groove down one side, are dull maroon-red and have yellow flesh that clings to the stone. A hybrid, *P. sultana*, between this and *P. salicina* is represented by the horticultural variety 'Wickson'.

Native American plums include several from which orchard varieties have been derived. One such, *P. americana*, is native from Massachusetts to Manitoba, Georgia, New Mexico, and Utah. From 20 to 30 feet tall or sometimes scarcely more than a high shrub, this is often somewhat spiny and sprouts from the roots. It has hairless shoots and thick, dull, obovate to oblong-obovate, pointed, sharp-toothed, hairless or nearly hairless leaves 2½ to 4 inches long. The white flowers, in clusters of two to five, are ¾ to 1 inch or a little more in diameter. The fruits are red or occasionally yellowish, subspherical, and ¾ inch to 1¼ inches in diameter. Closely allied, but with usually broader, more bluntly-toothed leaves the Canada plum (*P. nigra* syn. *P. americana nigra*), native from New England and New York to Ohio, Illinois, and Canada, has usually oblongish orange-red fruits.

The hortulan plum (*P. hortulana*), native from Oklahoma and Iowa to Tennessee and Kentucky, and hardy in southern New England, rather resembles *P. americana* and *P. nigra*. It is from 20 to 30 feet tall, it does not sprout from the roots, and it has oblongish to ovate or lanceolate leaves 3 to 4 inches long and with finely-blunt-toothed margins. Their dullish or slightly lustrous upper surfaces are without hairs, their undersides at most are sparingly hairy. The white flowers, in groups of two to four, are about ½ inch in diameter. The nearly spherical to ellipsoid, red or yellow fruits, up to a little over 2 inches long, have at most a slight waxy bloom.

The wild goose plum (*P. munsoniana*), native from Tennessee and Kentucky to Kansas and Texas and hardy in southern New England, up to 25 feet tall, develops suckers from its roots. It has lustrous, oblong-lanceolate to elliptic or lanceolate often troughlike, finely-toothed leaves 2½ to 4 inches long, thinner than those of the hortulan plum and generally slightly hairy on the veins on the undersides. The flowers, in clusters of two to four, are white and ½ inch or more in diameter. The fruits spherical to ovoid, are about ¾ inch long and red or yellowish, with a slight waxy bloom.

The Pacific plum (*P. subcordata*), a tree or shrub native from California to Oregon and hardy in mild climates only, is up to 25 feet tall, and sometimes spiny. It has blunt, broad-ovate to nearly round leaves, convolute in bud. With generally somewhat heart-shaped bases, they are sharply-toothed, 1 inch to 3 inches long, and when young pubescent on their undersides. Approximately ¾ inch wide and in groups of two to four, the flowers are white, becoming pinkish as they age. The dark red or yellow, spherical to oblong-ovoid fruits are mostly 1 inch long or longer. The flesh clings to the stones. The Sisson plum (*P. s. kelloggii*) has larger yellow or red fruits of superior eating quality. A more slender tree than the typical species, it has leaves usually without heart-shaped bases.

The chickasaw plum or mountain-cherry (*P. angustifolia*) is a bush or tree up to 18 feet tall that sprouts freely from the roots. It has 1- to 2-inch-long, markedly trough-like, lanceolate to oblanceolate, finely-toothed, lustrous leaves sometimes slightly hairy on the veins of their undersides, and convolute in bud. The flowers, white and about ⅓ inch across, are in clusters of two to four. Cherry-like, and thin-skinned, the red or yellow fruits have a slight waxy bloom and flesh that clings to the stone. They are about ½ inch in diameter. The sand plum, *P. a. watsonii*, 3 to 6 feet tall, has markedly zigzagged twigs, smaller leaves less conspicuously toothed, and smaller flowers and thicker-skinned fruits than the typical species. Variety *P. a. varians*, of Oklahoma and Texas, more robust and bigger than the typical species, has longer leaves and longer-stalked flowers.

The beach plum (**P. maritima**), a native of coastal areas from Maine to Virginia, is typically a rather straggling, occasionally spiny, 3- to 6-foot-tall shrub with often prostrate lower branches that when planted inland sometimes becomes a small tree. It has mostly ovate to elliptic, dull leaves, 1½ to 2½ inches long, with hairless upper surfaces, softly-hairy undersides. The white flowers, in clusters of two or three, are approximately ½ inch wide. The spherical to subspherical, dull purple to red or in variety *P. m. flava* yellow fruits are covered with a waxy bloom. Approximately ½ inch in diameter, they have agreeably flavored flesh that does not cling to the stone. Several varieties with fruits of superior quality for eating out of hand and for preserves have been developed. Among the best are 'Eastham', 'Hancock', and 'Premier'.

Prunus maritima

The hog plum (**P. reverchonii**), of Oklahoma and Texas and hardy in southern New England, is a thicket-forming shrub 4 to 6 feet tall with lanceolate to lanceolate-ovate, round-toothed, markedly trough-like leaves 2 to 3 inches long, their undersides sometimes densely-hairy at first, less conspicuously so later. In clusters of two to four, the white flowers are under ½ inch wide. Spherical or ellipsoid, ¾ to 1 inch long, and with a slight waxy bloom, the fruits are red or less commonly yellow.

The common apricot (**P. armeniaca**) is a native of China esteemed for its fruits since ancient times and cultivated in many orchard varieties. Typically, it is a round-headed tree up to about 30 feet in height and hardy in southern New England. It has blunt-toothed, broad-to roundish-ovate leaves 2 to 4 inches long, short-pointed at their apexes, and, except sometimes for tufts in the axils of the undersides of the leaves, hairless. White or pinkish, the solitary, 1-inch-wide flowers are succeeded by spherical, nearly hairless, very short-stalked fruits about 1¼ inches across (larger in orchard varieties).

Yellowish with one red cheek, they contain a smooth stone with a thick furrow along one edge. Variety *P. a. flore-pleno* has semidouble, pink blooms darker in the bud stage than when expanded; *P. a. pendula* has drooping branches; and *P. a. variegata* has variegated foliage. Variety *P. a. ansu* (syn. *P. ansu*), a small tree with rounded leaves and pink blooms, is sometimes misidentified as *P. mume*. From that species it differs in its shoots being purplish and its flowers being bigger, with their sepals pointing strongly backward.

Siberian apricot (**P. armeniaca sibirica** syn. *P. sibirica*) somewhat resembles the common apricot, but has much longer-pointed leaves and scarcely edible fruits. A native of northern China, Manchuria, and Siberia, this survives through most of New England. An erect shrub or tree up to about 15 feet tall, this has finely-toothed, ovate leaves 2 to 3½ inches long, hairless except for tufts in the axils of the veins on the lower sides, reddish when young, and with reddish stalks. The short-stalked, white to pink flowers, 1¼ inches across, are mostly solitary. The ¾-inch-wide, spherical, yellow fruits, red-cheeked on the side exposed to the sun, contain a sharp-edged, smooth stone.

Manchurian apricot (**P. mandshurica**), of Manchuria and Korea, is a tree up to about 15 feet tall with wide-spreading or slightly drooping branches and broad-elliptic to ovate, sharply-toothed leaves 2 to 4½ inches long, with tufts of hair in the vein axils on their under surfaces. The solitary, pinkish flowers, approximately 1¼ inches wide and darker in bud than when open, are succeeded by 1-inch-wide, spherical, yellow fruits.

Japanese apricot (**P. mume**) differs from the common apricot in the stones of its fruits being dotted with tiny pits and in its leaves generally having wedge-shaped instead of rounded or somewhat heart-shaped bases. Up to 30 feet tall, but often lower, this native of China and Japan is hardy in climates not harsher than that of New York City. Its long-pointed, ovate to broad-ovate, sharp-toothed leaves 2 to 4 inches long, are hairy on the veins beneath and sometimes on both surfaces. The leafstalks are glandular. Very short-stalked and fragrant, the light pink blooms, solitary or in pairs, are succeeded by greenish or yellow fruits, ¾ inch to 1¼ inches in diameter, the flesh of which adheres tightly to the pitted stone. They are not suitable for eating. The flowers of *P. m. alba* are white; those of *P. m. albo-plena*, white and double; those of *P. m. alphandii*, pink and double. Double, fragrant, madder-pink, cupped blooms are borne by *P. m.* 'Beni-shi-don'; cupped, semidouble, white, white and pink, or occasional pink ones by *P. m.* 'O-moi-no-wac'. Pendulous branches and single or semidouble pale pink flowers are typical of *P. m. pendula*;

nearly hairless, usually broadly-wedge-shaped leaves, of *P. m. tonsa*. The sort sometimes named *P. m. flore-pleno* is *P. armeniaca ansu flore-pleno*.

Purple or black apricot (**P. dasycarpa**) is an attractive ornamental that flowers freely, but rarely fruits. A hybrid of the common apricot and the cherry plum (*P. cerasifera*), it is a tree about 20 feet tall with purplish shoots and dull green, elliptic-ovate to ovate, coarsely- and finely-toothed leaves 1½ to 2¼ inches long, hairy along their veins on their under surfaces, with or without glands on their stalks. The flowers are white, long-stalked, and ¾ inch across. Minutely-hairy and dark purple, the fruits are spherical, about 1¼ inches in diameter.

Cherry-laurels are attractive, densely-foliaged evergreen shrubs or trees mostly unsuitable for climates appreciably harsher than that of Washington, D.C. The European cherry-laurel (**P. laurocerasus**), typically a shrub or tree up to 20 feet in height, has short-stalked, pointed, oblong to obovate-oblong, toothed or toothless, lustrous, hairless leaves up to 6 inches long. Approximately ⅓ inch wide, the creamy-white flowers, many together in racemes 2 to 4½ inches long, are succeeded by small black-purple fruits. Several varieties distinguishable by their habits of growth

Prunus laurocerasus as a standard

Prunus laurocerasus schipkaensis

Prunus laurocerasus schipkaensis (flowers)

Prunus caroliniana

Prunus lusitanica as a standard

and leaf shapes are cultivated. Of these, *P. l. schipkaensis*, a compact variety 4 feet or so tall appears to be the hardiest. It survives outdoors as far north as New York City.

Portugal-laurel (*P. lusitanica*), an evergreen shrub or tree up to 60 feet tall, has pointed-oblong-ovate, shallowly-toothed to toothless, hairless leaves 2½ to 5 inches long. Its white flowers, approximately ⅓ inch wide, are in racemes longer than the leaves. About ⅓ inch long and pointed-ovoid, the fruits are purple. *P. l. angustifolia* (syn. *P. l. myrtifolia*), a dense, conical shrub up to 15 feet tall, has much smaller, neater foliage than the typical species. *P. l. azorica*, native to the Azores, has larger, thicker leaves than the typical species, in their unfolding stage reddish. *P. l. variegata* has leaves margined with white, sometimes tinged pink in winter.

The Carolina cherry-laurel (*P. caroliniana*), also known as wild-orange and mock-orange, is not hardy in the north. Useful for landscaping in mild regions, this is a tree 20 to 40 feet tall with pointed-oblong-lanceolate, toothless or nearly toothless leaves 2 to 4 inches long. Cf insignificant decorative appeal, its small, creamy-white blooms in 1-inch-long spikes are succeeded by glossy black fruits up to

½ inch long. Compact varieties are *P. c. compacta* and *P. c* 'Bright 'n Tight'.

Native from southern Florida to the West Indies, Mexico, and Brazil, *P. myrtifolia* (not to be confused with the variety of Portugal-laurel named *P. lusitanica myrtifolia*), up to 40 feet tall, has hairless shoots and leaves, the latter elliptic to ovate and 2 to 4 inches long. The yellowish-white flowers, about ⅛ inch across, are succeeded by subspherical, black-purple fruits ½ inch in diameter. The West Indian cherry-laurel (*P. occidentalis*), endemic to Jamaica, Cuba, and a few other Caribbean islands, is a tree up to 50 feet in height with pointed-oblong to pointed-elliptic, toothless leaves 4 to 8 inches long. The small creamy-white, fragrant flowers, in crowded racemes shorter than the leaves, are succeeded by 1-inch long, purple, egg-shaped fruits.

The California-cherry, mountain-holly, or islay (*P. ilicifolia*) and the Catalina-cherry or Islands-cherry (*P. lyonii* syn. *P. integrifolia*) are closely related evergreens, the first native of southern California and Baja California, the other of islands off the coast of California. A dense shrub or small tree rarely up to 25 feet tall, *P. ilicifolia* has lustrous, leathery, ovate to roundish, coarsely-spiny-toothed, crisped, holly-like leaves ¾ inch to 2 inches long. Its small white flowers, in slender racemes of few to many, rarely exceed 2 inches in length. The red or much more rarely yellow fruits, ovoid-ellipsoid, are approximately ½ inch long. The more treelike *P. lyonii* differs in being up to 45 feet tall, and also has darker green, more narrowly-ovate leaves, mostly without teeth and not crisped. The flowers are white and many together in racemes 2 to 4½ inches long. The fruits are almost black.

Garden and Landscape Uses. The possible employments of the members of a genus of trees and shrubs as rich in sorts of horticultural interest as *Prunus* are obviously various. The importance of some as orchard fruits is well known and those as well as others that produce no such

bounty or at least are not regularly planted as sources of edible fruits are effective and attractive ornamentals.

The great majority of the sorts of *Prunus* are deciduous and blossom freely in spring before, along with, or after leaves appear, according to kind, and sometimes influenced by local climate. Most of these lend themselves for grouping or for using as single specimens in tree and shrub borders, on lawns, and in the vicinity of buildings. Those that flower before foliage develops show to special advantage when located in front of evergreens.

Some few of these deciduous sorts serve special purposes. The beach plum, for example, is excellent in exposed locations and sandy soils near the sea, but of minor importance elsewhere. The purple-leaved sand cherry is especially useful for Midwestern gardens, and the sloe or blackthorn, especially its double-flowered variety, is well adapted for poor soils; it is a good hedge plant, for which latter purpose *P. tomentosa* also serves well. A few especially hardy sorts of *Prunus* include the mazzard cherry, the western sand cherry, the purple-leaved variety of the myrobalan plum, the double-flowered sour cherry, the Amur chokecherry, the beach plum, the double-flowered European bird cherry, and the black or rum cherry.

Among the most handsome and popular spring-blooming small trees, Japanese or Oriental cherries are available in a splendid choice of varieties, but except *P. sargentii*, are not generally hardy north of southern New England. Many are comparatively short-lived, beginning to fail when twenty to thirty years old. Double-flowered varieties retain their blooms for decidedly longer periods than single-flowered sorts.

Other popular and worthy ornamentals include the purple-leaved plum, more esteemed for its foliage than its floral display, and flowering almonds and apricots. Flowering peaches, although many varieties have been raised and distributed, seem less adaptable to permanent domestication, and although lovely in bloom, often prove short-lived.

Evergreen prunuses are less hardy than most deciduous sorts and serve quite different purposes. Their chief asset is their handsome foliage, which assures their usefulness as screening and hedge plants as well as free-standing specimens. They also do well in containers. For this last purpose the European cherry-laurel and the Portugal-laurel are especially suited and make good substitutes for the true laurel (*Laurus nobilis*). The California-cherry and Islands-cherry are little grown except in California, but there they are highly esteemed for a wide variety of uses.

Cultivation. The cultural needs of orchard fruits of the genus *Prunus*, stone fruits as they are called, are treated in the Encyclopedia entries Almond, Apricots, Cherry, Nectarines, Peach, and Plums, and ornamental sorts of the same group respond to similar care. To bloom satisfactorily, practically all deciduous kinds need full sun. Evergreen types are more tolerant of shade, and the cherry-laurel in particular prospers even where it gets little or no direct sun, but except in regions of intense sun does equally as well fully exposed. The Portugal-laurel, California-cherry, and Catalina-cherry are more tolerant of full exposure than the cherry-laurel.

Soil requirements of ornamental prunuses are not very demanding, but good subsurface drainage is a must, and for most kinds sandy earths and those of low fertility are less suitable than loamy, reasonably nourishing ones that are porous enough to ensure good aeration. For most sorts moderately moist, but not constantly damp or wet ground gives the best results. The Carolina cherry-laurel, the California-cherry and the Catalina-cherry do well under dryish conditions. Specimens in acid soils generally respond favorably to liming to bring the soil up to or nearly up to neutral (pH 7), and cherries and plums in particular do well on limestone soils. Fertilizing encourages specimens that need a little extra "push," but if done to excess may increase susceptibility to disease and reduce the floral display. General-purpose complete fertilizers applied in early fall or spring are satisfactory.

Prune deciduous sorts, if such attention is needed, with some caution. Large wounds resulting from the removal of big branches heal slowly and are likely to afford entry for wood rot funguses. In the early years, pruning to train tree specimens to shape may be needed, but no more pruning than quite necessary should be done thereafter. Some bush types need thinning out regularly to keep them from becoming overcrowded. Do this immediately after they are through blooming.

Pruning evergreen kinds may be done without qualms to any extent deemed desirable. When these are trained as hedges, espaliers, or in other formal ways, if available labor makes the procedure practicable, it is better to trim with pruning shears than hedge shears because the latter slice through leaves, leaving cut edges that become brown and unsightly until new growth covers them. Any severe pruning required is best done in spring. Lesser cutting may be done in summer.

Propagation of deciduous species may be by seeds sown outdoors or in a cold frame as soon as they are ripe, or after stratifying by mixing them with slightly damp peat moss and keeping them in a temperature of 40°F for four months and then sowing them in a greenhouse, cold frame, or outdoors. If more convenient, the seeds may be kept for up to a year in a cool, dry place before stratifying.

Horticultural varieties and hybrids that do not come true from seeds, and sometimes kinds that do if seeds are not available, are propagated by budding, less frequently by grafting onto closely related species, but with most sorts it is believed that cuttings, rooted in summer under mist or in a propagating greenhouse, give superior results. It is not improbable that the comparatively short life spans of many cultivated specimens are the result of budding or grafting on not completely compatible understocks. Evergreen species also come readily from seeds but they and their varieties are more often increased by cuttings taken in late summer and rooted under mist outdoors or in a greenhouse or cold frame.

Pests and Diseases. Aphids, Asiatic garden beetle, Oriental fruit worm, pear slug, peach borers, scale insects, and tent caterpillars may infest sorts of *Prunus*, some limited to a few kinds only. Tent caterpillars are especially partial to wild chokecherries. Unless these serve usefully as ornamentals, it is well to eliminate them. The water-lily aphis migrates in late spring and fall to ornamental cherries located near pools where water-lilies grow. Spraying with a contact insecticide controls aphids. The chief diseases of prunuses, not all a threat to all kinds, include bacterial and fungus leaf spots, twig blight, and powdery mildew.

PSAMMOPHORA (Psam-móphora). There are four species of the South African genus *Psammophora*, of the carpetweed family AIZOACEAE. The name, from the Greek *psammos*, sand, and *phorein*, to bear, alludes to the foliage of specimens in the wild being coated with sand and dust. The plant previously named *P. pillansii* is *Arenifera pillansii*.

Psammophoras are low and tufted. They have nearly-woody stems crowded with very succulent, more or less three-angled to semicylindrical, bluish-green leaves with sticky epidermises that scale off. The sand and dust that in their native haunts adhere to the gummy surfaces serve as protection against desiccation by the fierce desert sun. The flowers, like those of others of the family, suggest daisies, but are quite different. They are not, as are daisies, conglomerations of florets forming single heads, but solitary flowers. The fruits are capsules.

White-flowered *P. longifolia* has on each branch four or five very rough leaves, when young olive-green with reddish bases, later light gray-green to brownish. Narrowly-oblong and from 1¼ to 1¾ inches long, they have flat upper sides, below they are rounded, and keeled near the apex. A bushlet about 2 inches tall, *P. modesta* has gray-green leaves about ½ inch long by one-half as broad, and roundish-triangular in section. The solitary flowers are pale lilac to violet. The branches of

P. nissenii are, in the wild, generally buried in the ground with only two or three pairs of leaves showing. The latter, united at their bases and ½ inch to 1½ inches long are semicylindrical to triangular in section. The blooms are white to violet.

Garden Uses and Cultivation. These are as for *Arenifera*. For additional information see Succulents.

PSEUDANANAS (Pseud-anánas). False-pineapple is the literal translation of the name *Pseudananas*. It derives from the Greek *pseudos*, false, and *Ananas*, the genus of the pineapple. There is only one species, a native of Brazil, Paraguay, and northern Argentina and a member of the pineapple family BROMELIACEAE.

Having much the appearance of the pineapple (*Ananas comosus*), the false-pineapple (*P. sagenarius* syn. *P. macrodontes*) differs in not producing suckers from its base, but instead sending out long, underground stolons, and in its fruits being without a large leafy crown. It forms a bold rosette of spreading or recurved leaves up to 3 feet long by about 2 inches wide, commonly longer than those of the pineapple, and with sharp-spined margins. The head of flowers, about 6 inches long by one-half as wide, tops an erect stem that exceeds the leaves and is composed of spiny, red, lanceolate bracts and flowers. The latter, abut 1 inch long, have three sepals, three petals, six stamens, and a three-parted style.

Garden and Landscape Uses and Cultivation. The fruits of the false-pineapple are edible, but unlike those of the pineapple, are not of commercial importance. The plants are attractive in collections of bromeliads. They respond to conditions and care that suit pineapples. For more information see Bromeliads or Bromels, and Pineapple.

PSEUDERANTHEMUM (Pseud-eránthemum). These plants sometimes travel under the name of the allied genus *Eranthemum*, from which they differ in not having large and conspicuous floral bracts and in technical details of their pollen. There are 120 species. The name is from the Greek *pseudos*, false, and the name of the related genus. The group belongs in the acanthus family ACANTHACEAE and is indigenous in many warm parts of the world. A few kinds of *Pseuderanthemum* are commonly grown in the tropics and subtropics and in greenhouses.

Pseuderanthemums are shrubs or somewhat woody herbaceous perennials with opposite, smooth-edged or toothed leaves that in cultivated kinds are usually highly colored, and spikes, racemes, or clusters, of white, blue, purple, or red blooms sometimes marked with yellow. The calyxes have five slender lobes. The corollas are tubular and have five spreading lobes (petals) nearly equal in size, or two distinctly smaller than the others. There are two stamens, two staminodes (nonfunctional stamens), and a slender style. The fruits are capsules normally containing four seeds.

Frequently cultivated in warm parts of the Americas, **P. atropurpureum** (syn. *Eranthemum atropurpureum*) is probably native to Polynesia. It is a shrub 4 to 6 feet tall, hairless, and with short-stalked, ovate to broad-elliptic leaves 3 to 6 inches long and about two-thirds as wide. In color they vary considerably on different seedlings. Sometimes they are green, occasionally spotted with yellow, but more often they are deep purple or deep purple variously patched with pinkish-purple, pink, green, and white. The short-stalked, ½-inch-long flowers in terminal and axillary narrow spikes are ¾ to 1 inch across and purplish or white with a rose-purple eye and spots of the same hue. They have a short corolla tube and spreading petals. Variety *E. a. tricolor* has metalic-purple leaves liberally splashed with green, pink, and white.

Another popular kind also probably Polynesian, **P. reticulatum** (syn. *Ernthemum reticulatum*) is 2 to 3 feet tall. This has angled branches and short-stalked, ovate-lanceolate, green leaves enlivened with a tracing of clear yellow veins. They are 4 to 10 inches long, somewhat wavy-margined, but toothless. The flowers, in dense spikes, are 1 inch to 1½ inches in diameter and white, with one petal spotted with rosy-purple, and their throats reddish-purple. The corolla tubes are ½ inch long.

Pseuderanthemum reticulatum

Malayan **P. lilacina** is a minutely-hairy shrub 3 to 4 feet tall. It has 4- to 10-inch-long lanceolate leaves, long-tapered to their apexes. The flowers, about 1½ inches long and wide, have slender-tubed corollas, delicate lavender specked with red on the center lobe of the lower lip. Probably a native of the Solomon Islands, **P. kewense** is a shrub with short-stalked to nearly stalkless, pointed, lanceolate-elliptic to ovate leaves 4 to 6 inches in length,

Pseuderanthemum ilacina

Pseuderanthemum kewense

with glossy, purple upper surfaces and green undersides. The white flowers, about 1 inch long and wide and with narrow petals fringed with hairs, are in erect, spikelike racemes.

A low, bushy sort believed native to New Caledonia and cultivated as **P. sinuatum,** although the name may not be admissable botanically, has red-purple stems and linear, olive-green leaves mottled with gray above, purplish on their undersides, and deeply-scalloped along their margins. The white asymmetrical flowers, with pur-

Pseuderanthemum sinuatum of gardens

ple-spotted lower petals, are in terminal racemes. About 1½ inches in diameter, they are attractive. Native to tropical East Africa, **P. seticalyx** has ovate, short-stalked leaves, hairy when young, and up to 4½ inches long by almost one-half as broad. In crowded panicles 2 to 3 inches long, the 1-inch-long, white flowers measure about one-half as much across their faces.

A low herbaceous perennial, **P. alatum** is Mexican. As known in cultivation by the name chocolate plant, it has thin, coppery-brown, wing-stalked, ovate leaves, with irregular blotchings of silver along their midribs, and small purple blooms in slender, erect racemes. Wild plants are up to 1½ feet tall and have coppery-brown or green foliage. Their leaves have long, winged stalks, the wings widening from the base of the stalk upward, and broad-ovate blades from 3 to 6 inches long, with short-pointed apexes.

Pseuderanthemum alatum

Garden and Landscape Uses. The first two kinds discussed are attractive shrubs for the tropics and subtropics. They grow with little trouble in full sun or part-day shade in ordinary soil and can be used as hedges, especially *P. atropurpureum*, and for other garden purposes. The kind last mentioned, *P. alatum*, is effective as a groundcover and for use at the fronts of beds and shrub plantings. The others described may be planted in beds and at the fronts of shrub borders. All are appropriate for growing in tropical greenhouses, in ground beds, or in containers.

As temporary occupants of summer beds, *P. atropurpureum* and *P. reticulatum* are excellent, and for this purpose can be used in the north. They look well associated with acalyphas, coleuses, eucalyptuses, grevilleas, and other plants of tropical aspect.

Cultivation. Easily raised from cuttings and from seeds, pseuderanthemums are grateful plants that make considerable display and need little attention. Outdoors, in warm climates, they need occasional pruning to shape them, and little more. Even when cut severely back, they renew themselves with vigor from near the base.

In greenhouses they grow well where the minimum winter temperature is 55 to 60°F, and at other seasons higher. A humid atmosphere is appreciated and good light with a little shade from strong summer sun. During their early stages, the tips of the shoots should be pinched out occasionally to promote branching. The soil must be watered to maintain it always moist, but not constantly saturated. Well-rooted specimens benefit from applications of dilute liquid fertilizer. Repotting is done in late winter at the beginning of the growing season, and in summer if needed. With *P. sinuatum* the best results are had by starting new plants from cuttings each spring. When plants of *P. atropurpureum* or *P. reticulatum* are needed for temporary summer beds, the cuttings should be rooted in August or September and the young plants kept growing throughout the winter and spring in a greenhouse with a minimum temperature of 55°F.

PSEUDOBOMBAX (Pseudo-bómbax) — Shaving Brush Tree. Deciduous trees and shrubs, mostly without thorns or spines, to the number of twenty species constitute *Pseudobombax*, of the bombax family BOMBACACEAE. They are inhabitants of the American tropics. Their name is from the Greek *pseudos*, false, and *Bombax*, the name of a related genus.

The young stems of pseudobombaxes are usually coated with a whitish bloom. The leaves, sometimes undivided, much more commonly consist of three to nine or rarely eleven leaflets radiating from the end of a common leafstalk. The leaflets do not drop individually from the stalk; the leaf falls intact. The flowers are in clusters of two to five or solitary, but grouped near the branch ends. They have a distinctly five-lobed to nearly lobeless, persistant calyx that does not fall with the petals and stamens, five fleshy, short-lived petals with hairs in tufts, and from one hundred and fifty to ten times that number of stamens, apparently in one circle, united only at their bases, and a slender style. The fruits are large capsules containing many small pear-shaped seeds surrounded by considerable amounts of long, whitish- to reddish-woolly, kapok-like fibers.

The shaving brush tree (**P. ellipticum** syns. *Bombax ellipticum*, *Pachira fastuosa*), in cultivation often misnamed *Pachira insignis* and *Pachira macrocarpa*, is a beautiful deciduous ornamental tree up to about 30 feet tall and of striking appearance. Native to Mexico and Guatemala, it has a smooth green or gray trunk and long-stalked leaves that have three to six, but commonly five round-ended, broad-elliptic leaflets 4 inches to 1 foot in length. The

Pseudobombax ellipticum at Fairchild Tropical Garden, Miami, Florida

abundant deep pink, or in a rare variant, white flowers displayed before the leaves appear develop from tall, columnar, uppointing, finger-like buds with calyxes that resemble the cups of acorns. When its time arrives, the bud one evening suddenly bursts open, and the five strap-shaped petals, 3 to 6 inches long, purple-brown outside and white-downy within, recurve like the skin of a partly peeled banana to reveal a generous brush of rose-pink stamens about three-quarters as long as the petals and tipped with yellow anthers.

Less frequent in cultivation than the shaving brush tree, **P. grandiflorum,** of Brazil, attains heights up to 25 feet or sometimes more. Its leaves are of five to nine obovate to elliptic leaflets up to 1 foot long. Flowers with linear petals, up to 6 inches long, are borne close to the shoot ends. Their petals are deep purple-red on their outsides, paler on their insides. The stamens are numerous. The pointed-oblong fruits are 6 inches to 1 foot long.

Garden and Landscape Uses and Cultivation. These are splendid ornamentals for areas of warm climates where little or no frost occurs. They succeed in any fairly good, deep soil in sunny locations. They may be grown from seed, but are often raised from cuttings.

PSEUDOBULB. The bulblike, aboveground stems that are features of many orchids are called pseudobulbs. They differ from true bulbs in being solid, instead of being constructed of layers in the manner of an onion.

PSEUDOCALYMMA (Pseudo-cálymma)— Garlic Vine. One of several tropical American genera of handsome woody vines of the bignonia family BIGNONIACEAE, this genus is less well known than some, for example, *Clytostoma* and *Pyrostegia*. There are four species of *Pseudocalymma*, the name of which is a modification of *Adenocalymma* (sometimes spelled *Adenoca-*

Pseudobulbs: (a) Slender ones of a *Cattleya*

(b) Plump ones of *Coelogyne cristata*

lymma), a related genus in which these plants were previously included.

Pseudocalymmas have leaves of three leaflets or of two regular leaflets with a branchless tendril between them representing the third. The funnel- to trumpet-shaped flowers, in racemes or panicles, have five spreading corolla lobes (petals), four stamens, a slender style, and a two-lobed stigma. The seed pods are long and woody.

Although by no means common, the garlic vine (**P. alliaceum** syns. *Adenocalymma alliaceum*, *Bignonia alliacea*) is occasionally cultivated. All its parts are strongly onion- or garlic-scented. The leaves commonly have two oblong-elliptic leaflets 4 to 6 inches long. The flowers, 2 to 3 inches in length, open violet-purple, but become lavender or whitish as they age. The narrow seed pods are flat, up to 1 foot long by about 1 inch wide. This is a native of northern South America.

Garden Uses and Cultivation. These are as for *Clytostoma* and *Allamanda*.

PSEUDOCYMOPTERUS (Pseudo-cymópterus)—Mountain-Parsley. Belonging to the carrot family UMBELLIFERAE, the genus *Pseudocymopterus* is restricted in the wild to western North America. It consists of seven species of hairy or hairless herbaceous perennials with long taproots. The leaves are once-, twice-, or thrice-divided into threadlike or broader segments. The tiny white, yellow, or purple flowers are in umbels, formed of lesser umbels. The fruits are flattened and seedlike. The name is from the Greek *pseudos*, false, and the name of the related genus *Cymopterus*.

Mountain-parsley (*P. montanus*) is wild at high altitudes from Wyoming and Utah to Arizona, Texas, and Mexico. Up to 2½ feet tall, but often at high elevations much dwarfer, it has ovate-oblong to broadly-ovate leaves, one- to three-times-pinnately-divided and up to 7 inches long by 6 inches wide. The ultimate segments are very narrow to broadly-lanceolate. The flowers are pale yellow.

Garden and Landscape Uses and Cultivation. Except perhaps in regions where it is native, this genus is little known to gardeners. Its members may be included in collections of native plants under conditions that approximate those under which they grow in the wild. Propagation is by seed.

PSEUDODRYNARIA (Pseudo-drynària). The only species of this genus, *Pseudodrynaria coronans* is sometimes known as *Aglaomorpha coronanas*. A large fern of the polypody family POLYPODIACEAE, it is indigenous from India to Taiwan. The name comes from the Greek *pseudos*, false, and the name of another genus of ferns, *Drynaria*.

Pseudodrynaria coronans

An epiphyte, that is a plant that grows on trees or other plants without taking nourishment from them, this fern has stout creeping rhizomes covered with a dense thatch of pale brown scales, and stalkless leaves with moderately broad bases that serve to collect and hold humus-forming material. The fronds (leaves) are pinnately-deeply-divided into lanceolate segments. They are bright green, pebbly surfaced, and 2 to 4 feet long by 1 foot

to 1½ feet in width. Their lower midribs are reddish.

Garden and Landscape Uses and Cultivation. These are as for *Aglaomorpha*. For other information see Ferns.

PSEUDOESPOSTOA (Pseudo-espostòa). By conservative students, of the cactus family CACTACEAE, the only species of *Pseudoespostoa* is included in nearly related *Espostoa* from which it differs, if the latter is considered narrowly, in having stems branched from ground level, markedly lateral pseudocephalums (long masses of bristly hairs from which the flowers come), and fruits with shining seeds. The name comes from the Greek *pseudos*, false, and that of related *Espostoa*. The common name snowball cactus is used for this.

Native to Peru, *P. melanostele* (syn. *Espostoa melanostele*) has erect stems up to 6 feet in height, with eighteen to twenty low ribs. The stems are covered with matted white hairs, which hide the clusters of forty to fifty short radial spines, but not the solitary central one of each cluster, which is up to 2 inches long and projects beyond the wool. At first yellowish the centrals become black as they age. The pseudocephalium, up to about 1½ feet long by 4 inches wide, is of crowded yellowish or brownish, woolly hairs. The flowers, which open at night, are funnel-shaped, white, and about 2 inches long. Their perianth tubes and ovaries and the fruits are covered with fine white hairs. In *P. m. inermis* the central spines of the spine clusters are lacking, and the plants tend to be lower and have stouter stems.

Garden and Landscape Uses and Cultivation. One of the most beautiful cactuses, this grows rather slowly as compared with espostoas. It responds to the conditions and care that suit espostoas, succeeding in full sun in well-drained soil containing little organic matter. For further information see Cactuses.

PSEUDOLARIX (Pseudolà-rix)—Golden-Larch. The golden-larch is the only species or according to some authorities one of two species of its genus. Native to coastal mountains in China, it was discovered by the British plant collector Robert Fortune and introduced by him into European cultivation in 1853. Fortune had seen dwarfed specimens in Chinese gardens a decade earlier. The wild specimens, some 130 feet tall, he found growing near a mountain monastery. Belonging to the pine family PINACEAE, and one of few genera of deciduous conifers — the others are *Glyptostrobus*, *Larix* (larch), *Metasequoia* (dawn-redwood), and some species of *Taxodium* (swamp-cypress) — *Pseudolarix* is most closely related to *Larix*. This is reflected in its name, derived from the Greek *pseudos*, false, and *Larix*, the larch.

From larches, the golden-larch differs in

its male catkin-like cones being in clusters and its fruiting cones disintegrating as soon as the seeds are ripe. The cones of *Pseudolarix* are much bigger than those of *Larix*, the leaves larger and wider, and the short lateral shoots that bear them club-shaped and longer.

The golden-larch (*P. kaempferi* syns. *P. amabilis*, *Chrysolarix amabilis*) is a very beautiful tree hardy even north of Boston, Massachusetts. Excellent specimens at the Arnold Arboretum have lived there since 1871 and set seed abundantly every three or four years. In cultivation in America

Pseudolarix kaempferi at the Arnold Arboretum, Jamaica Plain, Massachusetts

Pseudolarix kaempferi (leaves and flowers)

Pseudolarix kaempferi (female cones)

and Europe, the mature height is likely to be 70 or 80 feet. The golden-larch is broadly-pyramidal and has whorls (tiers) of horizontal branches, the ends of which tend to be pendulous and the lowermost of which may sweep almost to the ground. Specimens with trunks 3 feet in diameter are reported as growing in China. The shoots are of two kinds, terminal ones that make considerable growth each season and along which leaves are scattered in spiral fashion, and short, spurlike, lateral branches that increase in length, but a fraction of an inch each year and have fifteen to thirty leaves radiating from their ends like the ribs of miniature parasols. Most of the foliage is borne on the spurlike shoots, which are distinctly marked with annual rings left by previous crops of leaves and are conspicously constricted between the rings. The leaves are 1 inch to 2 inches long and under ¹⁄₁₂ inch wide. When the feathery foliage first appears in spring it is a soft yellow-green and before it sheds in fall it assumes a rich golden hue. Through the summer it is a pleasing light green. Male and female cones are borne on the same tree, the former catkin-like and clustered at the ends of leafless spurs, the latter solitary on short leafy branches from the ends of spurs. The fruiting cones rather resemble miniature artichokes or at maturity when their triangular scales spread widely, rosettes of house-leeks (*Sempervivum*). They are then 2 to 3 inches in diameter. Variety *P. k. nana* is low and spreading.

Pseudolarix kaempferi nana

Garden and Landscape Uses. Because the golden-larch branches so widely that in its middle years it is often as broad as it is high, it is not suitable for small gardens, but for parks and other landscaped areas where space limitations are not a problem it is one of the finest exotic trees in America. It has grace and that indefinable quality of choiceness that recommends it to discerning plantsmen. Beautiful at all seasons, but especially so in spring when a haze of fresh green leafage envelops its branches and in fall when the soft green of its feathery summer foliage turns to bright gold, this remarkable Asian blends well with the native flora of temperate North America without any suggestion of being offensively exotic. It needs well-drained, reasonably moist, fairly fertile soil that is acid or neutral in its reaction (it responds poorly to limestone soils) and a location in full sun where it will not be crowded by other trees or buildings. In its youth and middle years, good specimens are often as broad at the base as they are tall, a 50-foot specimen is likely to have a branch spread of 50 feet. The golden-larch is also suitable for training as bonsai.

Cultivation. No special care is needed. The golden-larch transplants without difficulty and needs no regular pruning. The best method of propagation is by seeds sown in sandy peaty soil in a sheltered bed outdoors, in a cold frame, or in a cool greenhouse. Grafting rarely is satisfactory because grafted plants do not grow as vigorously as seedlings or produce as symmetrical a tree. The golden-larch is remarkably free of pests and diseases. For other information see Conifers.

PSEUDOPANAX (Pseudó-panax)—Lancewood. The genus *Pseudopanax*, of the aralia family ARALIACEAE, is indigenous to New Zealand and temperate South America. Its name comes from the Greek *pseudos*, false, and the name of the related genus *Panax*. The kinds described below are all natives of New Zealand.

Pseudopanaxes are evergreen trees and shrubs with alternate leaves, those of adult plants remarkably different from those of juvenile specimens, and those of plants in intermediate stages of growth still different. The small, dull-greenish flowers are in umbels or in umbels or panicles of smaller umbels. The males have five petals and five stamens, the females are without petals and have a five-compartmented ovary and five stalkless or short-stalked stigmas. The fruits are small, spherical, and berry-like.

Lancewood (*P. crassifolius*) is a tree 20 to 60 feet tall with very variable foliage. Young seedlings have leaves up to 2 inches long, ovate-lanceolate, and coarsely-toothed. Later leaves are up to 2 inches wide, 1½ to 3½ feet long, and distantly spiny-toothed. They are glossy-black-green, and have yellowish midribs prominently raised on both surfaces. At this stage they are very rigid, average ½ inch in width, and hang downward. At fifteen to twenty years of age, when the trees begin to branch, the leaves have three to five long-stalked leaflets 8 to 10 inches in length. At a still later stage, oblanceolate leaves 3 to 8 inches long and 1 inch to 1½ inches broad are produced. The tiny flowers are in loose terminal umbels, up to 4 inches in diameter, composed of smaller umbels. The black, five-seeded fruits are under ¼ inch in diameter. In its native land, the wood of this species is used for fence posts, piles, railroad ties, and other purposes. In *P. c. unifoliolatus*, the stage of development in which leaves of several leaflets are produced is omitted.

A shrub or slender-trunked tree 15 to 25 feet in height, *P. ferox* has, at different stages of growth, three distinct leaf forms. The leaves of young seedlings are narrowly-linear to lanceolate, small, pointed, and toothed. At the next stage, before the plants branch, the leaves are 1 foot to 1½ feet long by ½ inch wide and have strongly downturned apexes. Then they resemble leaves of *P. crassifolius* on specimens at the same stage of development, but the marginal spines are closer together and are hooked. Adult trees produce thick, linear-obovate, pointed leaves 3 to 5 inches long by ³⁄₈ inch wide. The male flowers have four each petals and stamens and are in umbels of up to ten smaller umbels. The female blooms are in dense umbels. The fruits are one-seeded. Hairless, and a shrub or tree up to 20 feet tall, *P. lessonii* goes through fewer leaf changes than the kinds described above. Its adult foliage is of shallowly- or blunt-toothed leaves, with three to five obovate or oblong-lanceolate, toothed or toothless, stalked, leathery leaflets, the longest up to 4 inches long by one-half as broad. The leaves of juvenile plants are larger. The tiny flowers are in terminal umbels of smaller umbels. The fruits are about ¼ inch long. Somewhat smaller, much-branched *P. discolor* has leaves of three to five leaflets, broader than those of *P. lessonii*.

With juvenile and adult foliage very different from each other, *P. edgerleyi* is a tree 20 to 40 feet tall. Its umbels of flowers are arranged in raceme fashion from the leaf axils. The purplish-black fruits contain three or four seeds. On young specimens the leaves have three to five pointed, lobed leaflets, purplish on their undersides. Mature plants bear undivided, oblong-lanceolate to obovate, glossy leaves 3 to 9 inches long. The juvenile leaves of *P. lineare* are short-stalked, 6 to 9 inches long by up to ⅓ inch wide, spreading or erect, and pointed. Those of older plants are clustered near the branch ends. They are short-stalked, leathery, 1½ to 3½ inches long, pointed or blunt and linear-lanceolate. Urn-shaped fruits, three- to five-seeded, succeed the flowers, which are in terminal umbels.

Garden and Landscape Uses and Cultivation. Not hardy in the north, these trees and shrubs are occasionally cultivated in greenhouses and conservatories. In climates not subject to severe freezing, they are planted permanently outdoors, chiefly as conversation pieces and something of curiosities. They grow without trouble in sun or part-shade in well-drained soil. In greenhouses they succeed where winter night temperature are 45 to 55°F and daytime ones a little higher. Rather dryish, airy atmospheric conditions are more to their liking than heavy humidity. Light shade from strong summer sun is appropriate. These plants should be watered moderately, in winter even sparingly. Propagation is by seed and by air layering.

PSEUDOPHOENIX (Pseudophoè-nix) — Cherry Palm, Wine Palm. Four species of this genus of pinnate-leaved palms, of the palm family PALMAE, are recognized, all except one endemic in Hispaniola. The exception inhabits southern Florida and other parts of the Caribbean region as well as Hispaniola. The name *Pseudophoenix* is from the Greek *pseudos*, false, and *Phoenix*, the name of another genus of palms. It alludes to a resemblance.

Cherry palms, of medium to large size, have erect, solitary trunks distinctly banded with leaf scars and waxy gray-green leaves with bases that sheath the trunk. The leaf bases fall cleanly, leaving the trunk smooth. From the leaf axils, and three or four times branched, the flower clusters contain bisexual and male blooms. The approximately spherical, often two- or three-lobed fruits are waxy-red when ripe. Cherry palms were used as sources of food and beverage long before Europeans discovered their native lands. In the wild they occupy well-drained soil overlying alkaline or saline subsoil in dry areas.

Two species are cultivated, the commonest, **P. sargentii** of the Florida Keys, the Bahamas, and southward, often grows in places periodically inundated with salt water. Rarely exceeding 30 feet in height,

Pseudophoenix sargentii, Fairchild Tropical Garden, Miami, Florida

it is usually much lower. This has a trunk under 1 foot in diameter and stiff, arching leaves, 3 to 8 feet long, regularly-pinnate, and green above and silvery on their undersides. The flower buds are dark green, the fruits ½ to 1 inch in diameter, spherical or pear-shaped and sometimes lobed.

The wine palm (**P. vinifera**), up to 75 feet in height, has a trunk usually sharply

narrowed upward from about 10 feet above the ground. In youth the trunk is bottle-shaped. The waxy gray-green leaves are lax and up to 12 feet long. The flower clusters are pendulous, the buds dark green and thickly coated with wax. The fruits, borne in dense clusters, are red when ripe, spherical or lobed, and about 1 inch in diameter. This species inhabits limestone hills in regions of little rainfall in Hispaniola. Its fruits provide livestock feed, its leaves are used for thatching, and from the sugary pith of its trunk wine is made.

Garden and Landscape Uses and Cultivation. These palms, useful for planting as single specimens or in groups, thrive in widely diverse soils and climates and are especially adaptable to alkaline and saline earths. They withstand drought, but grow well in regions of substantial rainfall if the soil is well drained. Probably the most cold-resistant is *P. sargentii*, which has survived temperatures of 25°F in Florida. Not quite as hardy, *P. vinifera* is reported to have withstood 28°F, but not without severe injury to its foliage.

Pseudophoenixes prosper in sun or shade, but are most attractive in sunny locations. In greenhouses they need good soil drainage, a fairly humid atmosphere, and shade from strong sun. They may be watered copiously from spring through fall, moderately in winter. Regular applications of dilute liquid fertilizer are helpful to specimens that have filled their containers with healthy roots. A minimum night temperature of 60°F is favorable. The daytime temperature should be a few degrees higher than that maintained at night. Propagation is by seeds, which retain their germinating power longer than those of most palms (under good storage conditions up to two years). Sow the seeds in a temperature of 85 to 90°F. The chief pests of cherry palms are scale insects, mealybugs, and red spider mites. For further information see Palms.

PSEUDORHIPSALIS (Pseudo-rhípsalis). Three species of the cactus family CACTACEAE, by some authorities included in *Disocactus*, are treated by others as the separate genus *Pseudorhipsalis*. The name, alluding to a similarity in aspect, comes from the Greek *pseudos*, false, and *Rhipsalis*, the name of an allied genus. As a native, *Pseudorhipsalis* occurs from Mexico to Costa Rica and in Jamaica.

Pseudorhipsalises live on trees as epiphytes. Leafless, they have long, jointed, flattened, leaflike stems, at first erect, but soon prostrate or drooping, with shallowly-scalloped or toothed margins furnished with areoles from which the many solitary flowers originate.

Jamaican **P. alata** (syn. *Disocactus alatus*) has stems up to 15 feet in length, with branches, toothed at their edges, 8 inches

to 1¼ feet long and 1 inch to 2 inches wide. The yellowish-white flowers are ⅝ inch across, the yellowish-green fruits ⅜ inch long. Native to Costa Rica, **P. himantoclada** (syn. *Disocactus himantocladus*) has arching or erect stems up to 1½ feet long or slightly longer, ⅜ to 1 inch wide, and bluntly-toothed. White with purplish outsides, the flowers are about 1 inch in length. Southern Mexican **P. macrantha** (syn. *Disocactus macranthus*) has slender, arching or drooping stems up to 3 feet long and 1¾ inches wide and shallowly-scalloped along their margins. Opening at night and strongly and sweetly fragrant of lemon, they are about 2½ inches wide and pale yellow except for the backs of the outer ones, which are yellow suffused with red. The red stamens are tipped with cream-colored anthers.

Pseudorhipsalis macrantha

Garden and Landscape Uses and Cultivation. These are as for *Rhipsalis*. For more information see Cactuses.

PSEUDOSASA (Pseudosá-sa). By some botanists *Pseudosasa*, which comprises a few species of eastern Asian bamboos belonging to the grass family, GRAMINEAE, is included in *Sasa*, from which others segregate it on the basis that its flowers usually have three, rarely up to five stamens instead of six, and on other botanical details. The leaf sheaths are peristent. The name, from the Greek *pseudos*, false, and the name of the genus *Sasa*, refers to the similarity.

Native to Japan, China, and Korea, **P. japonica** (syns. *Sasa japonica*, *Arundinaria japonica*) is sometimes known by its native name metake, and in Japan for some recondite reason it is referred to as the female bamboo. This has no reference to its sex for, like all bamboos, the metake is bisexual. Of elegant appearance, it is one of the hardiest bamboos, surviving outdoors in sheltered locations in southern New York. It is well adapted for growing in containers as well as in the open garden.

Pseudosasa japonica, in winter, in a New Jersey garden

Pseudosasa japonica as a pot plant

It thrives under city conditions and forms a good hedge or screen.

From 10 to 15 feet tall, this species has arching, waxy, green, round canes, about 1 inch in diameter, with generally only one branch from each joint or node. The leaves are long-pointed, conspicuously tessellated, and up to 1 foot long by up to 2 inches broad. Their upper sides, dark green and glossy, have yellow mid-veins. Beneath, the leaves are grayish-green and downy with whitish hairs except for a green band. One leaf margin is completely fringed with hairs, the other only at its top and base. Usually the clumps do not die after blooming.

Garden and Landscape Uses and Cultivation. For information on these subjects see Bamboos.

PSEUDOTSUGA (Pseudotsù-ga) — Douglas-Fir, Big-Cone-Spruce. Undoubtedly the Douglas-Fir is the best known of the seven species of this genus of conifers of the pine family PINACEAE. It and the big-cone-spruce are the only American representatives of *Pseudotsuga*. Despite their common names, these are neither firs (*Abies*) nor spruces (*Picea*), but constitute the entirely

separate genus *Pseudotsuga*, the name of which, from the Greek *pseudos*, false, and *Tsuga*, the generic name of the hemlocks, alludes to a not very striking similarity in appearance. From firs pseudotsugas differ in having pendulous cones that do not shatter as soon as they have dispersed their seeds. From spruces and hemlocks they are distinguished by the long, conspicuous three-lobed bracts protruding from between the cone scales. The genus is endemic to North America and eastern Asia.

Pseudotsugas are pyramidal evergreen trees with branches in irregular whorls (tiers) and flattened, narrow-linear leaves arranged spirally on the twigs, but so twisted as to appear to be approximately in two rows. The upper sides of the leaves are green and have depressed midribs, the undersides are marked with two longitudinal white bands. The buds, quite different from those of nearly related groups, are spindle-shaped, sharp-pointed, and nonresinous. The fruiting cones are in the axils of the upper leaves and consist of many overlapping scales shorter than the bracts. They mature in their first season.

The Douglas-fir (**P. menziesii** syns. *P. douglasii*, *P. taxifolia*) is one of America's most important timber trees and is a highly ornamental and desirable landscape subject. Its strong and durable wood is used for many purposes including general construction, building, interior trim, furniture, boxes, poles, railroad ties, plywood, and paper pulp. The great flagstaff at Kew Gardens, England, is a solid spar of Douglas-fir that after trimming measured 225 feet from base to summit. Imported from British Columbia in 1958, it was fashioned from the trunk of a tree estimated to be 370 years old. A favorite for forestation in Europe, the Douglas-fir is one of the most rapid growing conifers. It

Pseudotsuga menziesii

Pseudotsuga menziesii (trunk)

Pseudotsuga menziesii (foliage)

Pseudotsuga menziesii (fruiting cones)

makes good Christmas trees, holding its foliage well after the trees are cut.

Including its variety *P. m. glauca*, the Rocky Mountain form of the species, the natural range of the Douglas-fir extends from British Columbia to California, New Mexico, Texas, Montana, and Colorado. Its common name honors one of the most famous nineteenth-century British plant explorers, David Douglas, who collected seeds and in that way introduced the tree to England in 1827, thirty-four years after its original discovery by Archibald Menzies, whose name is commemorated in the botanical name of one species.

At its mightiest the Douglas-fir is truly imposing. Narrow-pyramidal, it may attain a height of 300 feet or more and have a trunk up to 15 feet in diameter. Specimens that reach such dimensions are comparatively rare, but 200-footers, with trunks 6 feet in diameter, are not uncommon and occur in pure stands or mixed with other conifers. Exceptionally fine examples inhabit the region between the foothills of the Cascade Mountains and the Washington coast and on Vancouver Island and nearby mainland. Typically, when grown in the open, the upper branches spread horizontally and the lower ones angle downward and often reach the ground. Under forest conditions, however, the trees are commonly so close together that they lose their lower limbs early and their immense perpendicular trunks rise, bereft of branches, to great heights. The deeply-fissured bark is very thick and corky. The twigs are clothed with minute hairs. The narrow, dark green leaves, 1 inch to 1¼ inches long, are in two comblike rows that spread upward from the shoots with a V-angle between them. When crushed the foliage is fragrant. The cones, 3 to 4 inches long by one-half as broad, consist of thin, light brown scales and bracts. The central lobes of the bracts are longer than the lateral ones.

One of the most important varieties of Douglas-fir is that native to the Rocky Mountains (*P. m. glauca*). This, sometimes called Rocky Mountain Douglas-fir and sometimes blue Douglas-fir, rarely exceeds 120 feet in height and is often lower. It grows more slowly than the coastal form of the species, is more compact, and has shorter, more or less bluish-green leaves and cones up to 3 inches long. Of tremendous importance to those who garden in cold climates, the Rocky Mountain variety is considerably hardier than the typical species of the Pacific Coast. For planting in the northeast and northcentral states, it should always be preferred. It is hardy through most of New England. Other varieties are *P. m. anguina*, a curious form with long branches with few branchlets and leaves about 2 inches long; *P. m. brevifolia*, a shrub or small tree, with leaves up to ½ inch long, that grows slowly; *P. m. caesia*, an intermediate form between the coastal *P. menziesii* and *T. m. glauca* of the Rocky Mountains; *P. m. fastigiata*, compact, pyramidal with ascending branches; *P. m. fretsii*, with exceptionally short, broad leaves; and *P. m. pendula*, with drooping branches.

The big-cone-spruce (*P. macrocarpa*), as its name indicates, has cones larger than those of any other kind; they are 3½ to 7 inches long by 2 to 2½ inches wide and consist of numerous scales, between which the bracts project from, although slightly as compared with those of the

Pseudotsuga menziesii pendula at the Arnold Arboretum, Jamaica Plain, Massachusetts

Douglas-fir. The big-cone-spruce is indigenous to California and Baja California, growing on mountain slopes and attaining a maximum height of about 80 feet with a trunk diameter up to 3 feet. Its branches are downswept, its young shoots smooth or slightly hairy, its foliage pale green to bluish-green, the leaves 1 inch to 1¼ inches long and usually sharp-pointed.

The Asian species of *Pseudotsuga* are little known in cultivation. A rare native of Japan, *P. japonica* reaches a maximum height of about 100 feet. From the American species it differs in its leaves being notched at their tips. Its young shoots are quite hairless, its leaves about 1 inch long, and its cones, up to 1¾ inches long, have reflexed bracts. The species *P. sinensis* is a rare large tree of limestone soils in western China. It has finely-hairy young shoots and leaves notched at their apexes, and up to 1½ inches long. Its cone bracts are reflexed. Indigenous to China and Taiwan, *P. wilsoniana*, up to 80 feet in height, has glabrous or minutely-hairy young shoots, leaves up to 2 inches long and notched at their tips, and reflexed cone scales with long central lobes.

Garden and Landscape Uses. The only members of this genus employed to any extent for decorative landscape planting are the Douglas-fir and its varieties; others are rarely grown in special collections, such as those maintained by botanical gardens. The Douglas-fir rates highly as an ornamental and can be used with good effect as a single lawn specimen, in groups, and as a screen and tall hedge plant, but for its best development it must be in an open location where it receives light from all sides and is protected from sweeping cold winds. It prospers in any ordinary well-drained soil of a noncalcareous nature, preferring, perhaps, reasonably fertile sandy loams to soils of a clayey character.

Cultivation. Pseudotsugas are mostly raised from seeds sown in cold frames or beds outdoors where they are protected

from disturbance by rodents or other creatures; they may also be sown indoors in pots or flats in cool greenhouses. Varieties and selected trees may be increased by veneer grafting onto seedling understocks in a greenhouse in winter. Even when quite large these trees transplant without difficulty. They benefit from having the ground around them kept mulched with compost, peat moss, or other appropriate material. In dry weather, periodical deep watering is very helpful. Shearing, necessary when the trees are to be grown as hedges, is done just before new growth begins in spring. Cut only to near to the bases of the previous season's shoots; the cutting back should not involve older wood.

PSEUDOWINTERA (Pseudo-wíntera). From *Drimys*, with which it was formerly included, but to which it does not appear to be very closely botanically related, *Pseudowintera* differs in its petals in the bud stage being exposed rather than enclosed by the calyx which in *Pseudowintera* is small and cup-shaped. The genus, endemic to New Zealand, comprises three species. It belongs in the magnolia family MAGNOLIACEAE, or according to those who separate the families, to the drimys family WINTERACEAE. The name comes from the Greek *pseudos* false, and *Wintera*, a discarded name of *Drimys*.

Pseudowinteras are shrubs or small trees with alternate, obviously gland-dotted, undivided, lobed or lobeless leaves. The flowers, in the leaf axils, are clustered, paired, or solitary. Their persistent calyxes have toothed or toothless margins. There are five or six spreading petals and five to fifteen stamens. The berry-like fruits do not cohere.

An upright shrub or tree up to 25 feet in height, *P. axillaris* (syn. *Drimys axillaris*) has slender-stalked leaves with elliptic-oblong to elliptic-obovate or obovate-oblong blades 2¼ to 4 inches long by 1¼ to 2½ inches wide. Their upper surfaces are green and lustrous, their undersides glaucous. Less than ½ inch in diameter, the greenish-yellow blooms have more or less lobed calyxes and narrow-oblong to narrow-obovate petals. Usually red, the slightly fleshy fruits are about ¼ inch in diameter. A shrub, erect and up to 6 feet tall or rarely taller, *P. colorata* (syn. *P. axillaris colorata*) is distinguished from the last by its smaller, broadly-elliptic to elliptic-obovate, dull, light green leaves flushed with pink, with their upper surfaces blotched with red, and its fruit dark red to black.

Garden and Landscape Uses and Cultivation. These are interesting and handsome furnishings for mild-climate gardens, such as those of many parts of California and the Pacific Northwest. They need moderately moist, lime-free soil and prefer lightly shaded locations. No special cultural care is needed. Propagation is by seed and by cuttings.

PSIDIUM (Psíd-ium)—Guava, Strawberry Guava or Cattley Guava. Cultivated kinds of *Psidium*, of the myrtle family MYRTA-CEAE, are popular in the tropics and warm subtropics as producers of excellent fruits especially esteemed for making jellies and pastes. The genus of about 140 species of trees and shrubs, is native to tropical America, including the West Indies. Its name is adapted from *psidion*, the classical Greek name of the pomegranate.

Psidiums have opposite, pinnately-veined, hairy or hairless leaves and flowers produced laterally on the shoots, either singly or in twos or threes. The white or whitish blooms have bell- to pear-shaped, four- or five-lobed calyxes, four or five spreading petals, numerous stamens, and a branchless slender style. The fruits, technically berries, are yellow, red, or green, globular or pear-shaped, with the persistent calyx lobes at their apexes. The pineapple-guava is *Feijoa sellowiana*, the Para-guava, *Britoa acida*.

The common guava (**P. guajava**) is an evergreen shrub or tree up to about 30 feet tall, with its trunk usually divided near the ground. Its young shoots are green and four-angled. The longish-stalked, oblong-elliptic to broadly-elliptic leaves, 3 to 6 inches long by almost or quite one-half as broad, are finely-hairy on their under surfaces. The veins are raised on the undersides of the leaves and depressed on the uppersides. Solitary or two or three together, the slender-stalked flowers are about 1 inch in diameter. The spherical,

Psidium guajava

egg- or pear-shaped, usually greenish-yellow fruits, 1 inch to 4 inches in length, have white, yellow, or pink flesh. They are made into preserves and by those who do not find their musky odor disagreeable are eaten out of hand. Cooking, to a large degree, eliminates the odor. The common

guava is indigenous from Mexico to northern South America and is naturalized in southern Florida and Hawaii. There are many horticultural varieties. Varieties of the common guava have been distributed as *P. guineense*.

The yellow strawberry guava or yellow Cattley guava (**P. littorale** syn. *P. lucidum*) is a dense evergreen bush or tree up to about 25 feet in height, and native to Brazil. It has cylindrical young shoots and short-stalked, hairless, elliptic to obovate, thick, leathery, somewhat lustrous leaves 2 to 3 or sometimes 4 inches long. The flowers, about 1 inch in diameter, are solitary. From 1 inch to 1½ inches long, the obovate to spherical, yellow fruits are acid when ripe. The purple strawberry guava or purple Cattley guava (*P. l. longipes*) is similar to the last, but has purplish-red fruits, sweet when ripe and somewhat strawberry-flavored.

Psidium littorale longipes

Brazilian guava (**P. guineense**) is a large evergreen shrub. It has hairy branchlets and large broad-elliptic to oblong leaves, hairy beneath and with somewhat velvety upper surfaces. They have slightly raised veins. The flowers are solitary or in twos or threes. Egg-shaped to cylindrical, the greenish-yellow fruits, 1½ inches long, are sweet when ripe.

The Costa Rican guava (**P. friedrichsthalianum**), a Central American tree about 25 feet tall, with four-angled shoots, has pointed, elliptic leaves 1½ to 3 inches in length. The solitary blooms, 1 inch in diameter, are succeeded by white-fleshed, sulfur-yellow fruits up to 2½ inches long.

Garden and Landscape Uses and Cultivation. In addition to their value as fruit producers, psidiums may be used as landscape evergreens. They are adaptable to a fairly wide range of soils and environments and are easily propagated by seed, cuttings, root sprouts, and superior varieties by patch budding. The hardiest kind, the strawberry guava, succeeds wherever oranges can be grown, the others need warmer, more humid conditions.

PSILOCAULON (Psilo-caùlon). Very rare in cultivation, *Psilocaulon*, of the carpet-weed family AIZOACEAE, consists of seventy-five species of small shrubs, subshrubs, and annuals of South Africa. Like other members of the *Mesembryanthemum* relationship its kinds are succulents with flowers that resemble daisies, but differ markedly from them in structure. They are single blooms, instead of heads of many florets. The fruits are capsules. The name, from the Greek *psilos*, bare, and *kaulon*, a stalk, alludes to the stems being mostly naked of foliage.

Psilocaulons have opposite, very early deciduous, little leaves, and small, white, yellow, or reddish flowers. This genus differs from *Mesembryanthemum* in its flowers having petals joined at their bases into a short tube and in technical characteristics of the fruits, which are capsules.

A freely-branched subshrub about 1 foot tall, **P. granulicaule** (syn. *Mesembryanthemum granulicaule*) has rough-hairy, jointed, succulent stems. Its leaves are ½ inch long. The whitish blooms, solitary or in pairs at the branch ends, are about ¼ inch across.

Garden Uses and Cultivation. The species described, and others when available, are of great interest to keen collectors of succulent plants. They may be planted outdoors in frost-free, desert climates, but are generally better suited for cultivation in sunny greenhouses devoted to collections of choice succulent plants. Little has been reported about their cultivation, but it may be taken for granted that they require extremely porous, freely-drained soil, kept moderately moist during their summer growing period, drier when they are not in active growth. A winter night temperature of 50°F is appropriate, with an increase of up to about ten degrees by day. Dry air conditions such as suit cactuses must be maintained. Propagation is by seed and cuttings. For additional information see Succulents.

PSILOTACEAE — Psilotum Family. The members of this family of fern allies constitute two genera of primitive, nonflowering, green plants. Without true roots or leaves, they have fork-branched stems bearing small bractlike or leaflike appendages and solitary, large organs (sporangia) containing spores. The only genus cultivated is *Psilotum*.

PSILOTUM (Psilò-tum) — Whisk-Fern. Chiefly of interest to students of botany, *Psilotum*, of the psilotum family PSILOTA-CEAE, belongs to a group of primitive, rootless, leafless, non-flowering plants that in past geological ages was a much more prominent element of the world's flora than now. It consists of two very variable species, chiefly of the tropics and subtropics of both the Old World and the

New World. Its name comes from the Greek *psilos*, naked, and alludes to the nearly hairless character of the genus.

The whisk-fern (**P. nudum**), a widely occurring native of warm regions, including South Carolina to Florida, is up to 2½ feet high, but frequently lower. Of dense, tufted habit and brushlike aspect, this species, which spreads very slowly by underground runners, has flattened or angled, rigid, forked stems. Its globose, spore-bearing organs are solitary in the axils of lateral bractlike organs.

Psilotum nudum

Psilotum nudum (stems and spore-bearing organs)

Garden Uses and Cultivation. Psilotums are for collectors of the botanically unusual. In Japan, enthusiasts cultivate a number of distinct varieties. They prosper in greenhouses where the night temperature in winter is 50 to 60°F and that by day five to fifteen degrees higher. Some shade from strong sun and a humid atmosphere are desirable. Well-drained pots containing coarse peat moss mixed with pieces of tree fern trunks or chips of fir bark (of the type used for orchids), coarse sand, and a little soil are appropriate for psilotums. They can also be grown attached to pieces of tree fern trunk in the fashion in which some orchids are cultivated. Whatever the medium, it should be kept uniformly moderately moist. Propagation is usually by division, but like ferns, psilotums can be raised from spores.

PSOPHOCARPUS (Psopho-cárpus)—Asparagus-Pea or Goa-Bean or Winged-Bean. Best known of this genus of ten species, several of which have edible pods, is the asparagus-pea or goa-bean. The genus *Psophocarpus*, of the pea family LEGUMINOSAE, inhabits warm parts of Africa and Asia. The name comes from the Greek *psophos*, a rattling sound, and *karvos*, a fruit, because of the noise made by the fruits when they burst.

Tuberous-rooted, twining herbaceous vines, psophocarpuses have leaves of three leaflets, blue or lilac pea-like flowers in spikes or racemes, and strongly four-angled or four-winged seed pods. The flowers have rounded petals and an incurved keel, their stamens are united by their stalks in one group. For another asparagus-pea see Lotus.

The asparagus-pea, Goa-bean, or winged-bean (**P. tetragonolobus**) is an annual with tuberous roots, and stems up to 15 feet long or longer. Native to India, its leaves have ovate leaflets 3 to 6 inches in length, the center one long-stalked. The bright blue, 1½-inch-long flowers are succeeded by jagged-winged pods up to 9 inches long by about ¾ inch wide. These, when young and tender, are cooked and eaten like snap beans. The mature seeds are eaten after roasting, and in some parts of the tropics the tubers and young foliage are used as food. For cultivation see Asparagus-Pea.

PSORALEA (Psor-élea)—Scurfy-Pea, Indian Breadroot or Pomme Blanche, Leather Root. Belonging to the pea family LEGUMINOSAE and inhabiting temperate, subtropical, and tropical regions of the Old World and the New World, *Psoralea* comprises 130 species. Its name, alluding to the glandular dots that cover the plants, is from the Greek *psoraleos*, scabby.

Psoraleas are shrubs, subshrubs, and herbaceous perennials with divided leaves of three or more leaflets that spread fingerwise from the top of the leafstalk. Infrequently, there are additional leaflets arranged pinnately. Sometimes the leaves have single, undivided blades. Rarely solitary, the blue, purple, pink, or white flowers are more often in heads, spikes, racemes or clusters. They have calyxes with five nearly equal lobes, the two upper often united, an ovate or round standard or banner petal, and side petals as long or shorter than the keel. There are ten stamens, and a style incurved above and slender throughout or with a thickened base. The fruits are ovate, one-seeded pods.

Indian breadroot or pomme blanche (**P. esculenta**) owes its names to its roots having been used as food by Indians and early European settlers in North America. Native from Saskatchewan to Montana, this herbaceous perennial attains heights of from 4 inches to 1½ feet. It has a large turnip- or thick spindle-shaped tuber, and erect, branchless or sparsely branched stems clothed with long hairs. The leaves, clustered chiefly near the summits of the stems, have long stalks. They have five hairy, oblong leaflets up to about 2 inches long by 1 inch broad. Bluish, the fairly large flowers are crowded among silky-hairy bracts in dense racemes up to 3½ inches in length. Much like the last except that it is almost or quite stemless, tuberous-rooted **P. hypogaea** is decidedly attractive. Its long-stalked leaves have five to seven silky-hairy, lanceolate to ovate leaflets up to 2 inches long by ⅓ inch wide. Clustered at the centers of the plants, the numerous, short-stalked, crowded racemes are of bluish flowers a little under ½ inch long, accompanied by conspicuously silky-hairy bracts. This is native from Nebraska to New Mexico. Similar in habit and just as pleasing, rather rare **P. californica**, native of the state after which it is named, has tuberous, spindle-shaped roots. Up to about 8 inches tall, its lower branches are often prostrate. The leaves, hairy on both sides, have five obovate leaflets up to 1¼ inches long, wedge-shaped at their bases, and with rounded apexes. The ½-inch-long, white and purple blooms are among silky-hairy bracts in stalked, clover-like heads. Yet another tuberous-rooted kind, **P. cuspidata** has leaves of five, broad-elliptic leaflets. Its bluish flowers are in lupine-like spikes. This native from South Dakota to Texas attains a height of 1 foot to 2 feet.

Leather root (**P. macrostachya**) is a herbaceous perennial up to 10 feet tall. It has leaves with three ovate to elliptic leaflets 3½ inches long by about 2 inches wide or frequently smaller. They are velvety-hairy or nearly hairless. The 2- to 4½-inch-long racemes have densely-pubescent stalks. About ⅓ inch long and purplish, the flowers are crowded in long-stalked spikes or heads. This Californian often grows in salt marshes. Its roots were used by Indians as a source of strong fibers.

A native of the Caucasus, **P. acaulis** is a stemless herbaceous perennial, about 9 inches high, with hairy leaves with three elliptic to ovate, toothed leaflets. The solitary, clover-like heads of cream flowers are on stalks that lift them just above the foliage.

South African shrubs sometimes cultivated are **P. pinnata** and **P. aphylla**. Softly-hairy **P. pinnata** is 4 to 12 feet in height. Its leaves have usually three, sometimes four or five pairs of pinnately-arranged, narrow-linear leaflets and a terminal one. The flowers, whitish and light blue, with a dull blue tip to the keel, are clustered in

Psoralea acaulis

Psoralea pinnata

the leaf axils toward the ends of the branches. Quite different *P. aphylla* is 3 feet tall or taller. It has erect, wandlike branches, usually without foliage except for rudimentary scalelike leaves. The solitary blue and white flowers, their keels blue-tipped, are in long, terminal racemes that frequently bend under the weight of the blooms.

Garden and Landscape Uses and Cultivation. Perhaps because the very deep root systems of many kinds make them exceedingly difficult to transplant, psoraleas are little known in gardens. Where they can be grown, which means chiefly in distinctly dry and semidesert climates, the low ones can be used to advantage in rock gardens and all the more attractive American kinds in native plant gardens. The South Africans described above are useful for warm, dry climates. All need deep, very well-drained soil, and sun. Propagation is by seed. The young plants should be grown in pots until they are planted in their permanent locations.

PSOROTHAMNUS. See Dalea.

PSYCHOTRIA (Psych-otria)—Wild-Coffee, False-Ipecac. Some botanists include in this genus, of the madder family RUBIACEAE, plants treated in this Encyclopedia as *Cephaelis*. In its limited sense, *Psychotria* consists of about 700 species, natives of warm regions around the world. The

name, from the Greek *psyche*, life, alludes to the medicinal properties of some kinds.

Psychotrias are trees, shrubs, and more rarely herbaceous perennials, sometimes climbing. Their undivided, usually ovate, oblong, or obovate, generally thin leaves are opposite or sometimes in whorls (circles of more than two). The small white, greenish, yellow, or pink blooms are in clusters or heads from the leaf axils. They have short-tubed, four- to seven-toothed calyxes, and corollas with straight, funnel- or nearly bell-shaped tubes and usually five, rarely four or six, lobes (petals). There are as many stamens as corolla lobes and a two-branched style. The fruits are small, berry-like drupes containing two seedlike stones.

Wild-coffee is a name used for *P. nervosa* (syn. *P. undata*), and *P. sulzneri*. Native from Florida to the West Indies and Central America, *P. nervosa* is a much-branched shrub or small tree with elliptic-lanceolate to broad-elliptic leaves, 2½ to 6 inches long, and little white flowers. Its small fruits are red or sometimes yellow. From it, *P. sulzneri* differs in having hairy instead of hairless shoots and leaves, the latter narrowly-oblong to elliptic-lanceolate and 3½ to 6 inches long. The tiny, clustered, green flowers are succeeded by currant-like, red, or yellow fruits. This is native in Florida and the West Indies.

Two West Indian species cultivated in Florida are *P. pubescens* and *P. ligustrifolia*, both usually shrubs up to 8 feet tall, but the first sometimes a small tree. The leaves of *P. pubescens*, elliptic to oblong-lanceolate and up to 6 inches long, are usually finely-hairy. Its small, yellow, whitish, or pinkish flowers, many together in stalked, terminal panicles, are succeeded by tiny black, subspherical fruits. The foliage of *P. ligustrifolia* is nearly or quite hairless. Lanceolate to oblanceolate, its leaves are mostly smaller than those of the last species. The little white flowers, in stalked, terminal panicles, are followed by red, ellipsoid fruits up to ¼ inch long.

South African, *P. capensis* (syn. *Grumilea capensis*) is a shrub 10 feet or so tall, with lanceolate, elliptic, or obovate leathery leaves 2 to 5 inches long, their blades with tapered bases. The fragrant, bright yellow, ½-inch-wide blooms, in branched clusters, have slightly protruding stamens. The fruits are spherical and black.

False-ipecac (*P. emetica*), a source of an inferior grade of the drug ipecac (the best source is *Cephaelis ipecacuanha*), is a subshrub up to 1½ feet tall or perhaps sometimes a shrub and taller. It has malodorous roots and pointed, elliptic to elliptic-oblong leaves 4 to 5 inches long, with hairless upper surfaces and finely-hairy undersides. In little racemes from the leaf axils, the tiny white flowers are succeeded by ¼-inch-long fruits, which are blue when ripe.

Garden and Landscape Uses and Cultivation. Despite its vast number of species, *Psychotria* is of minor horticultural importance. A few of its members are planted for ornament in the humid tropics and subtropics and false-ipecac is occasionally grown in collections of medicinal plants, outdoors where climate permits, or in greenhouses. Psychotrias, which succeed under conditions suitable for *Ixora*, are propagated by seed or by cuttings.

PSYLLIDS. Akin to aphids and sometimes called jumping plant lice, psyllids are very active sucking insects, mostly up to ¼ inch long. Some exude a sticky substance called honeydew upon which grows a disfiguring black fungus mold. When disturbed, psyllids jump rapidly. They are serious pests of many plants, including acacias, apples, blackberries and related fruits, boxwood, pears, potatoes, and tomatoes. In some cases they cause distortion and stunting. Controls must be tailored to the various sorts. Consult Cooperative Extension Agents, State Agricultural Experiment Stations, or other authorities about these.

PSYLLIOSTACHYS (Psyllio-stáchys). Formerly included in *Limonium* and, like other members of that genus commonly known by the botanically discarded name *Statice*, the seven or eight species of *Psylliostachys* belong in the plumbago family PLUMBAGINACEAE. They are natives from Israel and Syria to Iran, Afghanistan, and central Asia. The name, alluding to the spikes of bloom, derives from *Psyllium*, the name of a subgenus of *Plantago*, and the Greek *stachys*, a spike.

The plants belonging here are annuals. Their undivided, pinnately-lobed or lobeless leaves are all basal. The tiny flowers, in spikelets of two to four, are densely aggregated in branched or branchless spikes. Each has a five-lobed calyx, a tubular corolla with five spreading lobes (petals), five nearly separate stamens, and five separate styles. The dry fruits are enclosed in the persistent calyxes.

Most frequently cultivated is *P. suworowii* (syns. *Limonium suworowii*, *Statice suworowii*). This native of Iran and central Asia has spreading, essentially hairless, oblanceolate to oblong-obovate, thinnish, usually shallowly-wavy-lobed, sometimes more deeply-lobed, short-stalked, light green leaves up to 6 inches long by 2 inches wide. Two to three times as long as the leaves, the slender flower stalks terminate in rat-tail-like spikes, usually branched near their bases, of densely crowded, tiny pink flowers. The central spike, bigger than the others, is generally 4 to 8 inches long. From the last *P. spicata* (syns. *Limonium spicatum*, *Statice spicata*) differs in the stalks and midribs of its oblanceolate, deeply-pinnately-lobed leaves

Psylliostachys suworowii

being rather densely clothed, the leaf blades less thickly so, with long, crisp hairs. This is a native of sandy and saline soils in Iran and central Asia. A natural hybrid between *P. suworowii* and *P. leptostachya*, named **P. myosuroides** (syns. *Limonium myosuroides*, *L. superbum*, *Statice superba*), has spikes of white to pink flowers. It differs from *P. suworowii* in its leaves being deeply- and regularly-pinnately-lobed.

Garden Uses and Cultivation. These are delightful, easily grown annuals for flower beds and greenhouses. They enjoy fairly warm conditions and should not be planted outdoors until about the time tomatoes and dahlias are set out. They succeed in any ordinary well-drained, moderately moist soil. They abhor excessive wetness. Light, middle-of-the-day shade is beneficial. Seeds may be sown where the plants are to stay, but in the north it is preferable to sow indoors eight to ten weeks before it is safe to set the young plants outdoors; grow the seedlings in flats or small pots in a greenhouse where the night temperature is about 55°F, and that by day five to fifteen degrees higher, until shortly before they are set outdoors. Then harden them in a cold frame or sheltered place outside for a week or two.

As greenhouse plants these are attractive in 4- or 5-inch pots. Sow seeds in late summer for spring display, in late winter for summer, in a temperature of 60 to 65°F. Transplant individually to small pots and to larger ones as growth necessitates. Grow with light shade from the strongest sun, in a fairly humid atmosphere, where the winter night temperature is 55°F and that by day up to fifteen degrees higher. Water with care to avoid constant wetness. When the final pots are filled with roots give occasional applications of a dilute liquid fertilizer.

PSYLLIUM. See *Plantago psyllium*.

PTELEA (Pte-lea)—Hop-Tree or Wafer-Ash. Botanists differ as to the number of species they recognize as composing the North American genus *Ptelea* of the rue family RUTACEAE. The more conservative accept three, those favoring more refined dissection of genera admit up to ten, differentiated by technical characteristics of no appreciable horticultural significance. The name *Ptelea*, used by the Greeks for the elm (*Ulmus*), was applied to the American plants because of the similarity in appearance of their fruits to those of elms.

Pteleas are deciduous small trees and shrubs with strongly scented foliage pocked with tiny translucent dots that can be seen most readily when a leaf is viewed against the light. The leaves are usually alternate and of three almost stalkless leaflets. Borne in terminal clusters, the small, greenish-white or yellowish-white flowers are mostly unisexual. They have generally four or five each sepals and petals and four stamens, those of the females sterile. The style is short. The dry, thin fruits (technically samaras) have conspicuous, broad encircling wings.

The species most often cultivated is the hop-tree or wafer-ash (**P. trifoliata**). Native from Connecticut to Ontario, Michigan, Iowa, Florida, Texas, and northern Mexico, this is a shrub or round-headed

Ptelea trifoliata (flowers)

Ptelea trifoliata (fruits)

tree, up to 25 feet tall, that grows in woods and thickets where there is moist, fertile soil. It exhibits considerable variation, especially in the degree of its hairiness. The long-stalked leaves have three ovate, ovate-oblong, or elliptic, sometimes toothed leaflets 2½ to 4½ inches long. The two outer of each trio are somewhat lopsided. The flower clusters are 1½ to 3 inches wide. The pale greenish fruits hang in conspicuous clusters and when crushed have an odor of hops. Like other parts of the tree they are bitter and are said to have been used as substitutes for hops. Each fruit is ⅗ to 1 inch in diameter. The wing is conspicuously netted with veins. In variety *P. t. aurea* the foliage is yellow. Variety *P. t. fastigiata* has upright branches and a comparatively narrow outline. The young branches and the undersides of the leaves of *P. t. mollis* (syn. *P. deamiana*) are densely-hairy. In *P. t. pubescens*, the leaves are dull green above and pubescent beneath. The leaves of *P. t. pentaphylla* have three or five leaflets narrower than those of the typical species.

Native to California, **P. crenulata** (syn. *P. baldwinii crenulata*), from 6 to 15 feet tall, has leaves of three ovate, obovate, or lanceolate, sometimes toothed leaflets. It is not hardy in the north, but is planted to some extent in mild climates.

Ptelea crenulata

Garden and Landscape Uses and Cultivation. The hop-tree or wafer-ash (*P. trifoliata*) and the other species, although without striking merit, are pleasing enough to warrant admittance to landscaped areas and gardens. They are interesting and mildly attractive when carrying their great clusters of fruits and do well in partially shaded locations in well-drained, moderately moist, fertile soils. Specimens raised from seeds collected in the south are likely to be tender in the north. For northern use trees raised from seeds collected in the north should be sought. Propagation is by seeds sown in fall in a cold frame or protected place outdoors.

Cuttings root fairly easily and selected varieties can be increased in that way, by layering, or by grafting in winter in a greenhouse onto seedlings.

PTERETIS PENSYLVANICA is *Matteuccia struthiopteris*.

PTERIDACEAE. This family consists of ferns that typically grow in the ground, rather than on trees as epiphytes, and have creeping, ascending or erect rhizomes. Their leaves (fronds) are one- or more-times-pinnately-divided, or sometimes undivided. The clusters of spore capsules along the leaf margins parallel the veins or are distributed over considerable under surfaces of the fronds. Genera of the pteris family dealt with separately in this Encyclopedia include *Acrosticum, Actiniopteris, Adiantum, Anogramma. Anopteris, Aspidotis, Cheilanthes, Coniogramme, Cryptogramma, Dennstaedtia, Doryopteris, Hemionitis, Histiopteris, Hypolepis, Microlepia, Onychium, Pellaea, Pityrogramma, Pteridium, Pteris,* and *Sphenomeris*.

PTERIDIUM (Pteríd-ium) — Bracken or Brake. Of cosmopolitan distribution in the wild, bracken (*Pteridium aquilinum* syn. *Pteris aquilina*) is a well-known coarse fern of the pteris family PTERIDACEAE. It is the only representative of its genus. Its name is from the Greek *pteris*, a fern.

Bracken or brake (***P. aquilinum***) has vigorous, wide-spreading, blackish, nonscaly rhizomes and twice- or thrice-pinnate or pinnately-lobed leaves with the

Pteridium aquilinum

divisions opposite or nearly so. The leaves are scattered along the rhizomes rather than in tufts. The ultimate leaf segments are oblong to linear and have rolled under margins and twice- or thrice-branched veins. The spore-bearing organs are in lines along the margins of the leaflets.

Bracken is variable, and botanists recognize several geographical varieties. It ranges in height from 1 foot to 6 feet or more and grows in broad patches in open woods, on moorlands, and on mountain slopes, often in light shade. Under favorable conditions it is an invasive plant, difficult to eradicate.

Although mature fronds included in hay are reported to be poisonous to livestock, and the plant is generally avoided by browsing animals, many peoples have employed it as a source of food. American Indians ate it, drying and grinding the rhizomes to make a kind of meal. In Norway and Russia, a beer is brewed from the young shoots. In Japan, the young fronds are boiled, dried, and stored for winter use and an edible starch is prepared from the rhizomes. All in all as a food, bracken is best regarded as for emergency use only. It is not likely to appeal to Americans as a regular article of diet.

Garden Uses and Cultivation. Except occasionally in collections of native plants, bracken is rarely cultivated, but it may occur spontaneously in wild or semiwild areas. It favors sandy, peaty, acid soils. It is easily propagated by spores. Division as a means of increase is less satisfactory because of the difficulty of securing a reasonable proportion of its widely ramifying, deep roots. If attempted, division is best done in late winter or early spring before new growth begins. For further information see Ferns.

PTERIDOPHYLLUM (Pterido-phýllum). A single species, a native of coniferous woods in Japan, and rare in the wild, is the only one of this genus. From other cultivated members of the poppy family PAPAVERACEAE, to which it belongs, it is distinct in having all basal, fernlike, deeply-pinnately-cleft leaves. Their appearance suggested the generic name, derived from the Greek *pteris*, a fern, and *phyllon*, a leaf.

A nearly hairless herbaceous perennial, ***Pteridophyllum racemosum*** has short, thickish rhizomes and deep green, blunt, broadly-oblanceolate leaves cut in comb-like fashion into many slender, linear-oblong, short-toothed segments. The leaves are 4 to 8 inches long by 1 inch to 1¼ inches broad. Their upper sides are sparsely furnished with stiff hairs. The leafless flower stalks, rising to a height of 6 to 10 inches, bear nodding blooms about ½ inch wide in loose racemes 4 to 6 inches long. The stalks of the flowers are slender. The blooms have two small, broadly-ovate sepals that soon drop, four white petals, four short-stalked stamens, and a slender style ending in a cleft stigma. The fruits are two-seeded capsules.

Garden Uses and Cultivation. Not very hardy, but possibly able to survive outdoors in sheltered locations as far north as Philadelphia or perhaps New York City, this interesting species is suitable for rock gardens, open woodlands, and similar sites where moist soil containing generous amounts of humus, and shade are assured. Propagation is by seed and by division.

PTERIS (Ptèr-is) — Brake. A cosmopolitan genus of the polypody family PTERIDACEAE, consisting of about 250 species, *Pteris* includes a few popular as cultivated plants. One well-known species formerly included, the bracken is now separated as the genus *Pteridium*. It, too, is called brake. The name *Pteris*, the "p" silent, comes from the Greek *pteris*, a fern, which, in turn, relates to *pteron*, a wing, and alludes to the feathery or winglike aspect of some sorts.

These ferns have fronds (leaves) one- or more-times-pinnately-divided. The spore capsules are in lines or narrow bands running along the margins of the leaflets and protected by their rolled-under edges, which serve as a cover (an indusium).

Among the commonest sorts cultivated are three not always easy to distinguish from each other, *P. cretica, P. ensiformis,* and *P. multifida*. Highly variable, ***P. cretica*** is widely dispersed through the tropics and subtropics of the Old World. From 9 inches to 2 feet tall, it has nearly similar fertile and sterile fronds. They have slender, pale, wiry stalks and once-pinnate blades with a few narrow-lanceolate to narrow-strap-shaped leaflets, the lower

Pteris cretica

ones cleft nearly to their bases into two or three lobes. Among the many varieties recognized horticulturally are these: *P. c. albolineata* has leaves with broader segments than those of the typical species, with an obvious whitish band down the center of each. *P. c. alexandrae* is similar to the last, but the tips of its leaf segments are prominently crested. *P. c. childsii* has lively green foliage with the edges of the leaflets lobed, waved, or frilled, *P. c. cristata* has leaves with slender leaflets more or less coarsely- and irregularly-toothed, some with crested tips. Its fertile fronds are comparatively small. *P. c. 'Distinction'*

Pteris cretica albolineata

Pteris cretica wimsettii

Pteris ensiformis evergemiensis

Pteris cretica cristata

Pteris multifida

guished by its slender, few-lobed leaflets, crested at their tips.

A chief difference between **P. ensiformis,** a 1- to 2-foot-tall native of eastern Asia and Australia, and *P. cretica* is that the former has fertile fronds that differ markedly from the much shorter sterile ones. They have long, naked stalks, nearly linear leaflets not over ¼ inch wide, with the lower ones five- to seven-cleft, and much taller than the sterile fronds. The latter have short, blunt, comparatively broad, deeply-lobed or divided leaflets that sometimes develop spores near their apexes. A favorite variety *P. e. victoriae,* has a jagged-edged band of white down the center of each leaflet. Raised in Belgium in 1957,

Pteris ensiformis victoriae

P. e. evergemiensis is very much like *P. e. victoriae,* differing chiefly in its fronds being even more conspicuously variegated with white. Less vigorous than *P. cretica* and with the upper leaflets of its leaves continued as wings down the stalks at least along those portions between the upper leaflets, **P. multifida** (syn. *P. serrulata*) otherwise much resembles *P. cretica.* Native to China and Japan, and naturalized in the southern United States, this is represented in cultivation by many varieties,

has lacy leaves with the upper leaflets lobed and all of the leaflets forked and crested at their apexes. *P. c. gauthieri,* compact, resembles *P. c. wimsettii* but has broader, more freely-, irregularly-toothed leaflets. *P. c. magnifica* has narrow leaves with slender lobes, light yellow-green at their centers. They are crested at their apexes. *P. c. major* is a natural variety, a native of the Mediterranean region. About 1 foot tall, its leaves have up to six pairs of plain, stalkless, linear leaflets, the terminal one long. The sterile leaves are finely-toothed. *P. c. mayii* is a dwarfer edition of *P. c. albolineata,* with narrower leaf segments crested at their tips. *P. c. ouvardii,* which attains heights of 2 to 3 feet, has long-stalked, dark green leaves with narrow-linear leaflets. *P. c. parkeri,* robust, has lustrous foliage with broad-lanceolate, finely-toothed leaflets with wavy margins. *P. c. rivertoniana* has leaves with four or five pairs of side leaflets and a terminal one, all cleft into numerous deep lobes of various sizes. *P. c. wilsonii,* low and compact, has fresh green foliage with at the end of each leaflet a wide crest. *P. c. wimsettii* is popular. Of vigorous growth, it has firm-textured leaves with erratically-lobed or toothed, slender leaflets some with crested apexes. *P. c. w. multiceps* is distin-

among them *P. m. cristata,* a low, bushy sort with slender leaflets crested at their tips. Still dwarfer and more compact, *P. m. cristata-compacta* has much-crested sterile fronds scarcely exceeded in height by the fertile ones. In *P. m.* 'Voluta' the fronds have very slender, drooping leaflets, some crested at their ends.

Handsome and popular **P. tremula** has lacy, bright green, arching fronds with blades 1 foot to 3 feet long or longer by 6 inches to 2 feet wide. It is a variable native of Australia and New Zealand. Popular in cultivation, it has fronds with smooth, shining stalks and triangular blades, their lower parts two- or three-times-pinnate, the margins of the segments finely-toothed. Widespread as a native of the tropics, **P. quadriaurita** is a robust, rather coarse species with arching fronds 2 to 4 feet long, their stalks usually with chaffy scales. The blades, twice- or thrice-pinnate in their lower parts, are elliptic to ovate. From those of *P. tremula* they differ in their ultimate segments not being toothed. In *P. q. argyraea* the leaflets are marked with a whitish lengthwise band.

Other species in cultivation include these: **P. dentata,** of tropical and southern Africa, has pinnate, triangular fronds 1 foot to 3 feet long or longer with triangular leaflets lobed almost to their midribs, and

Pteris quadriaurita

Pteris dentata

Pteris vittata

Self-sown sporelings of *Pteris vittata* prospering in a greenhouse with cactuses

finely-toothed. **P. longifolia,** of the American tropics, is scarcely distinguishable from Old World *P. vittata,* which is more commonly grown (often as *P. longifolia*). The leaflets of the fronds of the last diverge at right angles to the midrib. **P. muricata,** of the West Indies and tropical America is very large and vigorous. Each frond has three or more twice-pinnate leaflets with their divisions deeply-lobed. **P. tripartita** (syn. *P. marginata*), a robust native of the Old World tropics, is naturalized in Florida. It has erect rhizomes and is 4 to 10 feet tall. Its huge leaves are pinnately-three-times-divided into blunt-oblong ultimate segments 1 inch to 1½ inches long. The main axis or midrib of the leaf is winged between the leaflets. **P. umbrosa,** of Australia, in aspect is remindful of an extra large *P. cretica*. Its pinnate leaves, the lower pair deeply-cleft, are up to 3 feet in length. The leaflets, up to 6 inches in length, are linear-lanceolate, toothed or toothless. Unlike those of *P. cretica,* the midribs are winged between the leaflets. **P. vittata** is remarkable because of its ability to thrive under arid conditions. Often grown as *P. longifolia,* and widespread through the tropics and subtropics of the Old World, it is naturalized in Florida. This has erect to spreading, pinnate fronds up to 2½ feet long with leaflets up to 6 inches long by usually not

over ⅓ inch wide that usually diverge from the midrib at angles less than right angles. The fertile ones are narrower than the sterile.

Garden and Landscape Uses. In the tropics and subtropics these ferns are useful, mostly in shaded, sheltered locations. The larger ones are noble ornamentals, chiefly for moistish soils. Indoors pterises are easy to grow in greenhouses, and some are esteemed as houseplants. Small specimens of *P. cretica* and *P. quadriaurita* and their varieties are popular for dish garden and indoor planters. Amazingly different from the great majority of ferns, *P. vittata* thrives in the dry atmosphere of cactus and succulent greenhouses even in sunny locations and in such places will spontaneously reproduce from spores. This suggests it as a possibility as a houseplant.

Cultivation. Little difficulty is experienced in growing ferns of this group. Most are satisfactory indoors where the night temperature in winter is 55 to 65°F, and by day is a few degrees higher. At other seasons more warmth is advantageous. A moist, but not excessively humid atmosphere is needed for the majority of sorts, but those with firm leathery leaves, such

as *P. cretica,* stand drier air, and *P. vittata* is resistant to low humidity as cactuses. All should be afforded as strong light as they can take without the foliage scorching. This means that for practically all, *P. vittata* is an exception, some shade must be provided from spring to fall.

Soil for pterises should be well drained and nourishing. Any ordinary potting soil that contains a fair amount of organic matter is likely to suit. Some sorts, notably *P. cretica* and *P. vittata,* do well in limestone earths, but for most one that is neutral or slightly acid is probably best. Water sufficiently often to keep the roots always moderately moist, and stimulate well-rooted specimens by applying dilute liquid fertilizer at two-week intervals from spring to fall. Division affords a convenient method of increase with some kinds, but others, such as *P. cretica,* do not lend themselves well to this means of increase and it is better to rely upon spores. After a few years, sorts of this kind in pots tend to become woody and hard at their crowns and less productive of good foliage. Then discard and replace them with young vigorous stock. For more information see Ferns.

PTEROCACTUS (Ptero-cáctus). Six South American species, relatives of prickly-pears (*Opuntia*), comprise *Pterocactus,* of the cactus family CACTACEAE. The name, from the Greek *pteron,* a wing, and cactus, alludes to their seeds having wings, a characteristic that distinguishes this group not only from *Opuntia,* but from all other members of the cactus family.

Pterocactuses are low plants with often very large tuber-like roots and cylindrical stems branched in their upper parts. They bear minute leaves on their younger shoots. These are quickly deciduous. The areoles (areas from which spines, bristles, flowers, etc., develop in cactuses) produce several weak, flexible spines as well as easily detachable glochids (minute barbed spines). The symmetrical flowers are without perianth tubes. Their several perianth segments (petals) are erect. The stamens and style are shorter than the petals. The fruits are dry capsules.

Native to Patagonia, *P. fischeri* is up to 4 inches in height. From a thick root it develops very warty stems up to 6 inches tall, with spherical to egg-shaped segments up to ¾ inch in diameter. The spines are yellow and up to ¾ inch in length.

Having large tuberous roots, solitary or clustered, *P. kuntzei* (syn. *P. tuberosus*) is a native of Argentina. From the tops of its roots emerge erect, low-branched stems from 1½ inches to over 1 foot long, and brownish-green or purplish in their upper parts. Above, ⅓ inch in diameter and rather club-shaped, the stem segments are 4 to 8 inches long. The numerous, closely set areoles have small white, hairlike spines flattened against the stems. From a little under to a little over 1 inch long, the flowers have lanceolate, yellow perianth segments (petals). The fruits are pear-shaped.

Garden Uses and Cultivation. Not difficult to cultivate, pterocactuses are intriguing plants for the cactus fancier. They may be grown on their own roots or grafted onto *Opuntia*. Because of their very large roots the latter plan is the better when they are to be kept in pots. They require porous, sandy soil and full sun. Their general care is that of *Opuntia*. For further information see Cactuses.

PTEROCARPUS (Ptero-càrpus). Approximately 100 species of the Old World and the New World tropics constitute *Pterocarpus*, of the pea family LEGUMINOSAE. The name, derived from the Greek *pteron*, a wing, and *karpos*, fruit, alludes to a feature of the fruits.

The sorts of *Pterocarpus* are trees and vines with alternate, pinnate leaves with a terminal leaflet and alternate or nearly opposite side leaflets. In often showy racemes or panicles, the smallish, pea-shaped flowers are yellow or, less often, white or violet and white. The fruits are flattish, more or less circular pods surrounded by a broad wing.

A handsome, large tree, *P. indicus* is a native of southeastern Asia, Malaysia, and the Philippine Islands. Its leaves, of seven to eleven ovate leaflets 2 to 4 inches long, are 6 inches to 1 foot long. The numerous ½-inch-long, fragrant, yellow flowers are in panicles from the leaf axils. The circular, flat, one- or two-seeded pods are 1½ to 2½ inches in diameter. The red, yellow, or white, rose-scented wood is extensively used for high quality furniture. A native to India and Sri Lanka (Ceylon), the bibla (*P. marsupium*) is valued for its excellent lumber, esteemed for cabinetwork, and for a gum called kino, employed medicinally and for tanning, that is derived from the tree. Up to 60 feet tall, this species has leaves of five or seven alternate, elliptic to broad-elliptic leaflets, often notched at the apex, and 2 to 4 inches long. In showy terminal panicles, the flowers are light yellow or white. Native to the West Indies and Central America, *P. officinalis* (syn. *P. draco*) is a tree 30 to 60 feet tall with leaves that have five to nine glossy, elliptic or oblong-elliptic leaflets 2 to 6 inches long. The yellow to orange-yellow flowers are in short, loose panicles. Broad-winged and roundish, the fruits are 1½ to 2 inches in diameter.

Garden and Landscape Uses and Cultivation. In Hawaii, Puerto Rico, and other tropical lands these trees are planted for ornament. They are also sometimes included in demonstration collections of economic plants (kinds exploited for products

Pterocarpus officinalis, Jamaica, West Indies

useful to man) in tropical greenhouses. For their best development they require high temperatures and high humidity. Propagation is usually by seed.

PTEROCARYA (Ptero-càrya)—Wingnut. Ten species of deciduous Asian trees related to walnuts and hickories comprise *Pterocarya* but few are in cultivation. They belong to the walnut family JUGLANDACEAE. The name is derived from the Greek *pteron*, wing, and *karya*, the Greek name of the walnut, the allusion being to the winged fruits. From hickories (*Carya*), wingnuts are easily distinguished by the pith of their branchlets being, like that of walnuts (*Juglans*), in thin horizontal plates with spaces between. The piths of hickories and of nearly related *Platycarya* are solid. From walnuts, wingnuts differ in their fruits being strung several to many together on pendulous stalks 8 inches to 1½ feet long.

Pterocaryas have alternate, pinnate leaves with a usually terminal leaflet. The flowers, insignificant from a decorative point of view, are in drooping unisexual catkins, those of males about one-third as long as the females. The males have one to four sepals and six to three times that number of stamens. The females have a four-pointed involucre of united bracts and a short style with two stigmas. The fruits are technically nutlets, each with two wings, those of *P. paliurus* united.

The Caucasian wingnut (*P. fraxinifolia*) often develops more than one trunk and attains a height of up to 90 feet. In gross aspect much resembling the black walnut (*Juglans nigra*), it has deeply-creviced bark and forms a broad, spreading, open crown. Its leaves, 8 inches to 1½ feet long, consist of seven to twenty-five dark green, stalkless leaflets, 2 to 4½ inches long. Conspicuous in summer, the roundish, light green fruits hang in racemes 1 foot to 1½ feet long. Including the wings, they are about ¾ inch in diameter. Native from the Caucasus to Iran, this species is hardy in southern New England. Variety *P. f. dumosa* is shrubby and has yellowish-brown

Pterocarya fraxinifolia

Pterocarya fraxinifolia (young fruits)

branchlets, and leaflets up to 3 inches long. Native to China, *P. stenoptera* is slightly less hardy than the Caucasian wingnut and differs in the wings of its fruits being oblong instead of nearly round and in the midribs of its leaves being furnished between the leaflets with conspicuous toothed wings. Quite often the terminal leaflet is missing, so that there are an even instead of an odd number of leaflets. Normally the leaflets number eleven to twenty-five. A hybrid between *P. fraxinifolia* and *P. stenoptera*, named *P. rehderana*, is reportedly hardier than either parent. It is intermediate in most respects and has, at least on vigorous branches, leaves with slightly winged stalks, but the wings are not toothed. This thrives at the Arnold Arboretum, Jamaica Plain, Massachusetts, where it was originally raised. It extends itself vigorously by suckers that develop freely from the roots.

Less commonly cultivated sorts include these: *P. hupehensis* grows 90 feet tall and has leaves of five to nine leaflets. The nuts, each with a pair of roundish wings, are 1 inch or slightly more in diameter. About as hardy as *P. stenoptera*, this is native of China. *P. paliurus*, also of China and about as hardy as the last, is distinct because its nuts are winged all around, so that they look like small cymbals. This attains a height of about 60 feet. *P. rhoifolia*, native to Japan, hardy in New England, is 90 feet tall and distinct because its winter buds have two or three brown scales that fall during the winter. The winter buds of the other kinds discussed here have no scales.

Garden and Landscape Uses. Although by no means common, wingnuts must be ranked with the better ornamental deciduous trees. They have very handsome foliage and are decorative as lawn specimens and in landscape groups. In Shanghai and other Chinese cities, *P. stenoptera* is used as a street tree. In California it is chiefly appreciated for its suitability for playgrounds and other areas of compacted, poorly aerated soil. Its roots are generally too aggressive for it to serve satisfactorily in small gardens.

Cultivation. For their most satisfactory growth, wingnuts need deep, reasonably moist, fertile soil and a sunny location. Given such conditions no special care is needed. They are propagated by seed and sometimes by suckers. Root cuttings afford another means of securing increase.

PTEROCEPHALUS (Ptero-céphalus). Twenty-five species of scabious-like plants of the teasel family DIPSACEAE are included in *Pterocephalus*, which inhabits the Mediterranean region, with extensions into tropical Africa. It comprises annuals, herbaceous perennials, and a few shrubs. Its name comes from the Greek *pteron*, a wing, and *kephale*, a head, and was applied because, after the flowers fall the flower heads assume a feathery appearance. Plants of this genus have opposite leaves and crowded, flattish, or concave flower heads with involucres (collars) of bracts. The fruits are achenes.

Native to the mountains of Greece, *P. parnassi* (syn. *Scabiosa pterocephala*) is a deeply-rooting, carpeting subshrub 3 to 4 inches in height. It forms broad patches. Its ovate to fiddle-shaped leaves, ⅓ to ⅔ inch long, and toothed, and the basal ones usually pinnately-lobed, are silvery-gray-

Pterocephalus parnassi

pubescent. Their stalks may be nearly as long as their blades. Their pale lilac-pink, saucer-shaped flower heads, on stalks 1 inch to 2 inches long, are attractive both before and after the blooms fade. They are ¾ inch to 1¼ inches across and are borne in summer. The individual flowers are tiny, those forming the central disk almost symmetrical, the outermost decidedly two-lipped with the upper lip of two, and the lower of three, lobes. The persistent calyx consists of a dozen to twice as many bristles.

Garden Uses and Cultivation. This species is a satisfactory rock garden plant. It is hardy about as far north as New York, but does not like hot, humid summers. Although it survives at The New York Botanical Garden, it does not really prosper there as well as in regions of more temperate summers. It is best suited for well-drained slopes and crevices between rocks and may be displayed advantageously in dry walls. It is also delightful for growing in pans (shallow pots) in alpine greenhouses. Exposure to sun is needed. Propagation is by division, cuttings, and seed.

PTERODISCUS (Ptero-díscus). This is a genus of fifteen species of the pedalium family PEDALIACEAE, native to tropical and southern Africa. The name *Pterodiscus*, alluding to the winged fruits, comes from the Greek *pteron*, a wing, and *diskos*, a circular plate.

Members of this group are perennial, succulent herbaceous plants or occasionally small subshrubs, with branched or branchless stems, tuberous at their bases, and opposite or alternate leaves, rarely smooth-edged, generally coarsely-toothed or pinnately-lobed. The short-stalked, yellow or purple flowers come from the leaf axils. They have a small, five-parted calyx, a slightly two-lipped, tubular corolla with five rounded lobes (petals), two pairs of nonprotruding stamens, and a slender style with a two-lobed stigma. The laterally compressed, spineless fruits have four longitudinal wings.

Sometimes cultivated by fanciers of succulent plants, *P. aurantiacus*, of South West Africa, has flask-shaped stems up to 1 foot tall, and branched near their apexes. Its alternate pairs of opposite, lanceolate to ovate-spatula-shaped, wavy-margined, bluish leaves are set at right angles to each other. The brilliant yellow blooms are 2 inches long or slightly longer.

Garden Uses and Cultivation. Suitable for growing outdoors in frostless desert and semidesert regions only, these plants are most often grown in sunny greenhouses devoted to succulents. They succeed in well-drained, loamy-sandy soil, kept moist during their fall-to-spring growing season, dry in summer. Seed affords the usual means of increase. For additional information see Succulents.

PTEROSPERMUM (Ptero-spérmum). One large evergreen tree of the forty species of trees and shrubs that comprise *Pterospermum*, of the sterculia family STERCULIACEAE, is sparingly cultivated in the warmest parts of the continental United States and elsewhere in the subtropics and tropics. The name, derived from the Greek *pteron*, a wing, and *sperma*, a seed, alludes to the seeds.

Entirely Asian, *Pterospermum* has its younger shoots, foliage, and other parts furnished with scales or star-shaped (stellate) hairs. The lobed or lobeless leaves are alternate, leathery, and in two ranks. The flowers, solitary or few together and terminal or axillary, have five-parted calyxes, five petals, and both fertile and infertile stamens, the latter staminodes. The fruits are angled, woody capsules with winged seeds.

Handsome *P. acerifolium*, its name meaning with leaves resembling those of a maple, is not well named. Its leaves are not maple-like. They are asymmetrically roundish, oblongish, or obovate and usually irregularly- or coarsely-toothed. They have stout stalks 1 inch to 3 inches long and blades 9 inches to 1 foot long by 6 inches to almost 1 foot broad. Their leafstalks commonly join the blade some distance in from its margin, with no opening from the stalk to the edge of the blade. Their undersides are densely covered with whitish or rusty hairs. The upper leaf surfaces are bright green and hairless. Fragrant, and solitary or in twos or threes from the leaf axils, the quite handsome blooms open at night and fall the following morning. They are pollinated by bats. In bud, the flowers are long, slender and cylindrical. When they open the five yellowish, 6-inch-long, sepals, woolly on their outsides and silky-hairy on their insides, curl backward and reveal the narrowly-funnel-shaped, white corolla composed of five petals, slightly shorter than the sepals and enclosing the five fertile and fifteen sterile stamens and the style. The football-shaped fruits, densely covered with woolly hairs and 4 to 6 inches long, have five strong ribs or angles. They contain numerous seeds with large thin wings.

Garden and Landscape Uses and Cultivation. As a shade and ornamental tree, *P. acerifolium* has much to recommend it. In Florida it blooms in December and January and has proved hardy at Orlando, although there sometimes damaged by frost. In regions where it is sometimes frozen back, unless corrective pruning is done, it is likely to develop as a multi-trunked specimen. This tree prospers in a variety of soils and is propagated by seed.

PTEROSPORA (Pteró-spora)—Pine Drops. One species that lives as a parasite on soil fungi that, in turn, obtain their nourishment from decayed organic matter is the only member of this genus, which is native under coniferous trees in the United States and Mexico. This plant belongs in the heath family ERICACEAE or, according to some botanists, to the monotropa family MONOTROPACEAE. The remarks as to growth habits and garden possibilities made under *Monotropa* apply here also.

Pine drops (*Pterospora andromedea*), 1 foot to 3 feet tall and glandular-pubescent, has erect, branchless, brown or purplish stems with scalelike leaves that do not overlap. The many nodding flowers are in slender racemes. They have a densely-glandular-pubescent, five-lobed calyx and an urn-shaped corolla with five small, recurved lobes (petals). There are ten stamens enclosed in the corolla. Each has two long, tail-like appendages. The short style has a slightly five-lobed stigma. The fruits are capsules. The name is from the Greek *pteron*, a wing, and *spora*, a seed, and refers to the winged seeds.

PTEROSTYRAX (Pteró-styrax) — Epaulette Tree. Closely related to the silver bell (*Halesia*), yet differing in obvious ways, the Asian genus *Pterostyrax* ranges from Japan to the Himalayas and comprises seven species. It belongs in the storax family STYRACACEAE. The name, from the Greek *pteron*, a wing, and *Styrax*, a related genus, alludes to the winged or ribbed fruits. Easily observed differences between *Pterostyrax* and *Halesia* are that in the former the pith of the stems is solid rather than chambered (seen as a ladder-like pattern when the shoot is split lengthwise), the parts of the flowers are in fives instead of fours, and the stamens protrude. Additionally, the flowers are many together in panicles instead of being in clusters of few as in *Halesia*.

Other characteristics of *Pterostyrax* are that its members are deciduous trees and shrubs with stellate hairs and alternate, toothed leaves. The flowers have calyxes and corollas divided almost to their bases. There are ten stamens, with a slender style slightly longer than them. The fruits, technically nuts, contain one or two seeds.

The epaulette tree (*P. hispidus*), hardy as far north as southern New England, is the usual cultivated kind. Vigorous and 40 to 50 feet tall, it forms a broad, open head of slender branches. Its short-stalked, pointed, ovate to oblong leaves, 3 to 8 inches long by 1½ to 4 inches broad, are pale green above and on their undersides grayish-green and hairy or nearly hairless. The prominent, drooping, downy-stalked panicles, 5 to 10 inches long by 2 to 3 inches wide, and often with two or three leaves at their bases, of creamy-white, fragrant blooms, are carried in June. Their branches, well separated, spread widely; the flowers hang from one side and are shaped like shoulder epaulettes worn by

Pterostyrax hispidus

military men, which gives reason for the common name. The individual blooms are about ⅓ inch long and look rather like those of deutzias. Their petals are pubescent on both sides. The spindle-shaped fruits, ½ inch long, are five-ribbed and densely covered with long, bristly hairs. Differing from the above in being somewhat more tender and in having shorter, comparatively broader flower panicles and distinctly winged fruits with short, soft hairs, *P. corymbosus* is a tree or tall shrub much rarer in cultivation. The other species described here is sometimes grown under its name.

Garden and Landscape Uses and Cultivation. These rather scarce trees are excellent for shade and ornament. They are especially handsome in bloom. They thrive best in deep, well-drained, fertile, moderately moist soil and should be allowed ample room to spread their branches, which may cover an area as wide as the tree is tall. Propagation is best by seed, but is also by layering and by summer cuttings planted in a greenhouse propagating bench or under mist.

PTERYGODIUM (Ptery-gòdium). Eighteen species of East Africa and southern Africa constitute *Pterygodium*, of the orchid family ORCHIDACEAE. The name derives from a diminutive of the Greek *pteryx*, a wing. It probably alludes to the somewhat winglike leaves.

Pterygodiums are terrestrial orchids with subterranean tubers, and stems with oblong to lanceolate leaves, the uppermost bractlike. They have loose or dense racemes of small, yellow or white flowers.

Native to South Africa, *P. catholicum* is 6 inches to 1 foot tall. Its two or rarely three stalkless, oblong to elliptic-oblong leaves are up to 5 inches long. About ¾ inch wide, the flowers are pale yellow or sometimes have orange-red petals and an orange-red lip. The lip is wavy, obscurely-three-lobed, and at its apex reflexed.

Garden Uses and Cultivation. The sorts of this genus are attractive to fanciers of

rare orchids. Unfortunately, little information is available about their needs in cultivation. It is suggested that they be planted in well-drained pots in a mix of shredded tree fern fiber, leaf mold, coarse sand, and a little loamy soil and that they be afforded cool greenhouse treatment such as suits many paphiopedilums. Water to keep the roots always moist from the time new growth begins until the foliage dies naturally. Refrain from watering during the resting season.

Pterygodium catholicum

PTERYGOTA (Ptery-gòta)—Tattele. One of the twenty species, chiefly natives of the Old World tropics, that constitute *Pterygota*, of the sterculia family STERCULIACEAE, is grown in Florida and California. It is the tattele, of India. The name comes from the Greek *pterygotos*, wing-shaped, and refers to the seeds, which being conspicuously winged, resemble one-half of a maple key. This distinguishes *Pterygota* from closely related *Brachychiton* and *Sterculia*.

The tattele (*P. alata*) is a handsome, straight-trunked, smooth-barked, large deciduous tree. Its young shoots are thickly clothed with stellate (star-shaped), yellow hairs. Crowded toward the ends of the branches, the short-stalked, heart-shaped leaves may be almost 1 foot long and about about two-thirds as broad. Both unisexual and bisexual flowers are borne. About 1 inch in diameter and few together in racemes from parts of the shoots below the lowest leaves, they are on short, very hairy stalks. They have five, six, or rarely seven fleshy, rusty-downy calyx lobes. The male blooms have their stamens joined in a column with the anthers at the apex. The female flowers have three to five stigmas crowning an urn-shaped ovary. They are succeeded by hard, woody, somewhat globose, podlike, brown fruits, 5 inches in diameter. Each contains about forty seeds that, with their large wings, are 3 inches long by one-half as wide. In Burma, the seeds are eaten.

Garden and Landscape Uses and Cultivation. For shade and ornament, this species has much to recommend it for landscape planting in warm climates where there is little or no frost. It succeeds in ordinary well-drained soil and is propagated by seed.

PTILOTRICHUM. See Alyssum.

PTILOTUS (Ptil-òtus). The plants previously cultivated as *Trichinium* belong here. The genus *Ptilotus,* of the amaranth family AMARANTHACEAE, consists of 100 species confined in the wild to Australia and Tasmania. The name, from the Greek *ptilotos,* winged, refers to the membranous bracts.

This genus comprises annuals, herbaceous perennials, and subshrubs, with alternate leaves, and flowers usually in crowded spherical, conical, or cylindrical spikes. The blooms have a short perianth tube and five extraordinarily hairy segments (petal-like parts). There are five stamens of which some are usually without anthers. The little one-seeded fruits are technically utricles.

Little known to American gardeners, some of these plants are worthwhile ornamentals, certainly worthy of trial; they are likely to prove most adaptable to warm, semidesert regions. Quite delightful are *P. exaltatus* (syn. *Trichinium exaltatum*), *P. manglesii* (syn. *Trichinium manglesii*), and *P. spathulatus* (syn. *Trichinium spathulatum*), all perennials. With erect stems usually branched in their upper parts, *P. exaltatus* has thickish leaves, the lower ones long-stalked and 3 to 5 inches long. The upper leaves are shorter and stalkless or nearly so. The flower spikes, ovoid-conical, lengthening as they age to become cylindrical, are atop long stalks. They are about 3½ inches long by one-half as wide and yellowish, tinged with pink or dull red. More richly colored, the flower heads of *P. manglesii* are lavender-pink to violet-purple; they suggest oversized fuzzy clovers and are 3 to 4 inches long by about two-thirds as wide. This species varies much in height, depending perhaps on the conditions under which it grows. It

Ptilotus manglesii

has erect or spreading stems 4 inches to 1 foot long. The lower leaves are long-stalked; 1 inch to 3 inches long, they are broad-ovate to linear. The upper ones are smaller and without stalks. The stems of *P. spathulatus* are up to 8 inches long. Its basal leaves, spatula-shaped to ovate, are about 1 inch long. The stem leaves are narrower and more pointed. The yellowish flowers are in cylindrical heads up to 4 inches in length by 1 inch or a little more in width.

Garden Uses and Cultivation. Little information is available regarding the cultivation of these plants in North America. In Great Britain they are sometimes grown in cool greenhouses, a protection needed not only against winter cold, but against over-abundant rainfall. They would be charming additions to rock gardens in warm, dry climates and may be expected to succeed in sunny locations in well-drained soils. It is possible that *P. manglesii,* and perhaps other kinds, could be grown as annuals. Seed seems to be the most satisfactory means of propagation.

PTYCHORAPHIS. See Rhopaloblaste.

PTYCHOSPERMA (Ptycho-spérma). Thirty-eight species of the palm family PALMAE, natives of northern Australia, New Guinea, and the Bismark, Solomon, and Kei Islands, constitute *Ptychosperma.* They have solitary or multiple trunks and pinnate leaves. Some botanists segregate certain multiple-trunked kinds as *Actinophloeus.* The name is derived from the Greek *ptychos,* folded, and *sperma,* a seed. It alludes to the grooved seeds of some kinds.

Of small to medium size and with ringed trunks, ptychospermas have leafstalks with sheathing bases that form a columnar crownshaft that looks like a continuation of the trunk. The blunt leaflets, toothed or ragged at their ends, are arranged regularly or irregularly according to species. The branched flower clusters, with papery bracts that fall early, have flowers in threes, the males with numerous stamens. Single-seeded, and usually red to black, the small egg-shaped or globose fruits are about ¾ inch long.

One of the best known and commonly grown is *P. elegans,* a slender-stemmed native of Australia that normally has a solitary trunk about 20 feet tall and a few-leaved, feather-duster crown of gracefully arching, bright green, short-stalked leaves 3 feet or so long. Its bushy flower clusters, about 1 foot long, arise from the trunk below the crownshaft. The ovoid-globose fruits are red. This palm somewhat resembles the Christmas palm (*Veitchia merrillii*), but has a straighter trunk, smaller fruits, and five-grooved seeds. It is naturalized in southern Florida. Another very handsome species is *P. macarthuri,* of New Guinea, which forms clumps of many slender,

greenish-gray stems and is 10 to 20 feet in height. Its leaves, up to 9 feet long, but often shorter, have twenty to thirty arching leaflets on each side of the midrib. The flowers, in clusters about 1½ feet long, develop from below the foliage. This species has somewhat the appearance of *Chrysalidocarpus lutescens,* but its stems, leafstalks, and midribs are not yellow as in that species. Very like *P. macarthuri* is New Guinean *P. nicolai.* It differs most noticeably in its young leaves and spathes being purplish-red or red. Other kinds and probably some hybrids are sometimes cultivated.

Garden and Landscape Uses. Among the best and most decorative of small to moderate-sized palms, and among the easiest to grow, ptychospermas have considerable appeal for use in home landscapes and other ornamental plantings, especially where space is limited. They are also extremely useful for cultivation in containers. They succeed in not-too-dry ordinary garden soil in sun or part-shade. Excellent *P. macarthuri* serves well as a free-standing lawn specimen and can be used with good effect to line driveways, and for screening. Its foliage makes a good background for lower plants and fits well near buildings. Usually seen to best advantage when planted in groups, *P. elegans* is excellent for high accents among lower plants. These palms are suitable for outdoor cultivation only where very little or no frost occurs. They are attractive in greenhouses and as florists' decorative plants.

Cultivation. Propagation is by fresh seeds sown in sandy peaty soil in a temperature of about 80°F. Container-grown specimens need good drainage and coarse, fertile, porous soil watered often enough to keep it always moist, but not constantly saturated. Well-rooted specimens in pots or tubs respond favorably to biweekly applications of dilute liquid fertilizer from spring through fall. In greenhouses they need shade from strong sun, and a humid atmosphere. The winter minimum night temperature should be 60°F with the day temperature some five to ten degrees higher. At other seasons, night and day temperatures may be considerably above the winter minimums. For other information see Palms.

PUBESCENT. Downy, clothed with short, soft hairs.

PUCCOON. See Lithospermum. The red-puccoon is *Sanguinaria canadensis.*

PUDDING PIPE TREE is *Cassia fistula.*

PUDDLING. This is the name of procedures used when transplanting to encase exposed roots in wet soil. It is employed with cabbages and related vegetables, as well as other plants that when young are dug bare-rooted from seed beds and are likely to be exposed for some appreciable time before planting.

To puddle such plants, dip their roots in a thick slurry of clayey soil and water. Some gardeners include a little cow manure in the mix. Keep the puddled plants covered and shaded until they are planted.

A different procedure, mostly used with larger plants including shrubs and trees, is also called puddling. Here, after the plant is set in place and the hole is partly filled with soil, the soil is drenched with water before filling in more soil to complete the planting operation.

PUERARIA (Puer-ària)—Kudzu Vine. The well-known kudzu vine must, it would seem, have provided inspiration for the famous vegetable described in *Jack and the Beanstalk*. No other climber outside the tropics makes such vigorous and rapid growth. Its stems may extend to a length of 40 to 50 feet in a single season. This *Pueraria* is one of a genus of about thirty-five species of the pea family LEGUMINOSAE, indigenous from Japan and southeast Asia to the Himalyas, and in some Pacific islands. The name commemorates the European botanist M. N. Puerari, who died in 1845.

Puerarias have thick, woody roots, herbaceous or woody twining stems, and leaves with large, sometimes lobed, leaflets. The blue to purple or rarely white, pea-like flowers are in erect racemes from the leaf axils. They have more or less two-lipped calyxes, and corollas twice or less as long, with the wing petals somewhat fused to the keel. There are ten stamens forming a single group. The incurved, hairless style is tipped with a small stigma. The fruits are more or less flattened, slender, many-seeded, beanlike pods.

The kudzu vine (*P. lobata*), the only species commonly grown, has very big tuberous roots and hairy, somewhat woody, loosely twining, slender stems. Its coarse-hairy, beanlike leaves have three round-ovate to lozenge-shaped hairy leaflets, 3 to 6 inches long and sometimes slightly lobed, but not toothed. Fragrant, violet-purple, and in dense racemes, the flowers, ½ to ¾ inch long, develop in late summer and are succeeded by flat, hairy seed pods, 2 to 4 inches long. This species is hardy about as far north as southern New York, although there its stems kill to the ground each winter and are renewed the following spring. In addition to its horticultural uses, the kudzu vine is used as forage. In the Orient, starch is obtained from its roots and cloth is made from the tough fibers of the inner bark of its stems.

Garden and Landscape Uses. The blooms of this vine are largely hidden beneath the foliage and so are not showy. Its impact as a plant for landscaping rests in its foliage effects and rapidity of growth. It is suitable to covering arbors and similar structures and as a groundcover on banks and other difficult places where rampant growth is an advantage In the north the stems mostly do not live over winter, although they may do so in sheltered places even at Philadelphia. In parts of the south, this vine, unless controlled, may become something of a pest.

Cultivation. Provided the soil is well drained the kudzu vine is easily grown. To secure even coverage of its supports a certain amount of pruning and training of the shoots is desirable. Cutting back may be necessary to restrain its exuberance. Propagation is usually by root division and cuttings, but seeds may also be used.

PUKA is *Meryta sinclairi*.

PUKATEA is *Laurelia novae-zelandiae*.

PULICARIA (Pulic-ària)—Fleabane. Called fleabanes, although that name is also applied to *Erigeron*, of the same daisy family COMPOSITAE, the sorts of *Pulicaria* have rightful claims to the designation. In the first place their botanical name comes from the Latin *pulex*, a flea, and second, the dried, powdered leaves of *P. dysenterica* were ground into an unpleasantly scented powder used to kill fleas and other insects, and the dried leaves were burned as a fumigant against such creatures. There are fifty or sixty species, natives of Europe and Africa. They are closely related to *Inula*, from which they are separated because the fruits (technically achenes but usually called seeds) have an outer row of scales in addition to one of hairs.

Pulicarias are herbaceous plants with alternate leaves and yellow, daisy-type flower heads with both disk and ray florets. The name *P. dysenterica* refers to an old belief that this species was helpful in the treatment of dysentery. It is no longer used medicinally. This kind is a gray-hairy, hardy perennial, about 2 feet tall, with branching stems and wavy-edged, oblong-lanceolate, toothed leaves 1½ to 2½ inches long. The upper ones are lanceolate and have conspicuous basal lobes. Its showy, golden-yellow flower heads, 1 inch or slightly more in diameter, have a single row of many ray florets. They are in more or less flat-topped clusters. Common in many parts of Europe, this species favors moist meadows and the banks of rivers, streams, and ditches. It spreads vigorously by underground stolons. Similar, but not spreading by stolons and the upper oblong leaves without conspicuous basal lobes, is *P. odora*, of the Mediterranean region. Its flower heads, usually few together in clusters, are occasionally solitary.

Garden Uses and Cultivation. Although not without merit as garden ornamentals,

these plants are more likely to be represented in gardens by *P. dysenterica* included in collections of herbs of historical medical interest than as regular flower garden decoratives. They grow without trouble in moist soils in full sun and are multiplied by division in early spring or fall and by seed.

PULMONARIA (Pulmon-ària)—Lungwort, Jerusalem-Sage or Blue Lungwort, Bethlehem-Sage. This genus belongs in the borage family BORAGINACEAE. There are ten species, native to Europe and Asia. Derived from the Latin *pulmo*, a lung, the name *Pulmonaria*, like its Anglo-Saxon equivalent lungwort, alludes to *P. officinalis* having been considered a remedy for diseases of the lungs. There is no valid basis for the belief, which is part of the once-popular doctrine of signatures that held that the forms and appearances of plants indicated their medicinal virtues. The leaves of *P. officinalis* were thought to resemble diseased lungs, therefore, the argument ran, the plant was a specific for pulmonary troubles.

Pulmonarias are more or less hairy, hardy herbaceous perennials of low stature. Their creeping rootstocks spread rather slowly. From them arise basal foliage and few-leaved flowering stems. The basal leaves are long-stalked, those of the stems alternate and stalked or stalkless. The purple-blue, blue, or whitish blooms are in forked clusters with curved branches, most, and always the lower ones, in the axils of leafy bracts. The calyx is five-lobed. The corolla has a bugle-shaped tube with generally tufts of fine hairs in its throat and five, spreading, blunt lobes. There are five stamens included in the corolla tube. The fruits, commonly called seeds, are small smooth nutlets. From the related genus *Mertensia*, lungworts differ in having less deeply-lobed corollas and stamens that do not protrude.

Jerusalem-sage or blue lungwort (*P. officinalis*) is up to 1 foot tall and has attractively white-spotted leaves. Those from the roots are distinctly stalked and ovate

Pulmonaria officinalis

with obviously heart-shaped bases. They are 2 to 4 inches long. The stem leaves are without stalks and broadly-ovate. Changing as they open from purplish-rosy-red to violet or sometimes remaining reddish, they are ½ to ¾ inch long. Variety *P. o. immaculata* has unspotted leaves.

Bethlehem-sage (*P. saccharata*), up to 1½ feet in height, has decidedly decorative white-spotted lower leaves that taper to both ends and oval bases and slightly winged stalks. The stem leaves, short-stalked or stalkless, are ovate-oblong. This species has whitish to reddish-violet blooms.

Pulmonaria saccharata

Pulmonaria saccharata (flowers)

The best flower color is found in good forms of the plain green-leaved *P. angustifolia,* but alas, when raised from seeds even its progeny commonly includes individuals with blooms that verge toward, or arrive at, an undistinguished reddish-purple. Such seedlings are sometimes propagated and given enticing names by nurserymen. In the main it is well to pass up offerings of *rubras, roseas,* and suchlike sly suggestions of worthwhile reds and pinks; however, there is a quite choice coral-pink flowered variety named *P. a.* 'Salmon Glory' that is worth acquiring. But the forms most desirable are the purest blues, those sometimes cultivated as *P. a. azurea* and sometimes under fancy

Pulmonaria angustifolia

names such as 'Johnston's Blue'. This species and its varieties have spotless linear to oblong-lanceolate leaves that gradually taper at their bases into narrow wings that extend along the stalks. The few stem leaves are linear-lanceolate to narrowly-elliptic and more or less stem-clasping.

Garden and Landscape Uses. These are good garden plants, easy to grow and attractive from spring through fall. In summer and later they please with their foliage, in spring both leaves and flowers are decorative. They are plants for partial shade and cool, reasonably moist soils that have a fairly high organic content. Although they will survive in hotter, drier locations, they do so only with a struggle, and then through much of the summer look limp and unhappy. They are well suited for use beneath trees and shrubs where fair light is available and root competition is not too strong. They are appropriate for woodland paths, fronts of flower borders, the north sides of buildings, and some other of those more difficult spots for which the selection of plants that can be expected to thrive is quite limited. Planted in generous expanses they make useful and interesting groundcovers. They may be used effectively in combination with daffodils, yellow-flowered primroses, forsythias, *Corylopsis,* and *Cornus mas* and *C. officinalis.*

Cultivation. Ease of cultivation is a virtue of lungworts. No demanding care is required. When flowering is over, tidiness is had by cutting off the dead flower stalks, unless it is planned to collect seeds. When, as a result of overcrowding, the plants begin to show signs of deterioration, they should be divided; this will not be necessary oftener than about every fourth year. The best time to divide and plant is early fall, but very early spring is satisfactory; if care is exercised, it is possible to transplant undivided specimens even when in bloom. Following transplanting, lungworts must be kept well watered until they have established new roots. Seasonal attention calls for watering during droughty spells. A mulch of com-

post or peat moss spread in fall or very early spring is beneficial, and a light dressing of a complete fertilizer each spring brings reward in larger and lusher foliage. Division is usually the most satisfactory means of securing additional plants. Seeds, sown in spring, germinate readily enough, but the resulting plants are likely to show much variation.

PULTENAEA (Pult-enaèa). Known only from Australia and Tasmania, where they are called bush-peas, ninety or more species of *Pultenaea* belong in the pea family LEGUMINOSAE. Their generic name commemorates Dr. Richard Pulteney, an English botanical historian, who died in 1801. These plants are small and large shrubs with undivided, generally alternate leaves and stalkless, pea-shaped blooms, yellow, orange, purplish, or red, solitary and axillary, or in terminal heads. The upper calyx lobes are joined to form a lip, and there are ten separate stamens. The fruits are small pods containing two seeds.

Called in Australia the large-leaf pea-bush, *P. daphnoides* is erect and about 6 feet in height. As its specific name indicates, it has somewhat the aspect of a daphne insofar as growth habit and foliage are concerned, but its flowers are very different. The leaves are slender-wedge-shaped with the narrow end at the base and the apex tipped with slender, sharp point. So tightly clustered are the yellow and red flowers that each head looks like a solitary bloom. The pods are about ¼ inch long. Although this is the kind best known in North America, other species, such as the good looking *P. stipularis,* are likely to be introduced.

Garden and Landscape Uses and Cultivation. These are attractive plants for borders and other places where flowering shrubs can be used advantageously. Only in California and areas of similar climates are pultenaeas hardy. They need sun and grow in well-drained ordinary soil. Propagation is by seed and by cuttings made of firm terminal shoots inserted under mist or in a greenhouse propagating bench.

PUMELO or PUMMELO is *Citrus maxima.*

PUMPKIN. Although there are no consistent botanical differences between pumpkins and squashes, the two are distinct in common usage. The characteristics that separate them are explained in the Encyclopedia entry Squash. Belonging in the gourd family CUCURBITACEAE, pumpkins are mostly varieties of *Cucurbita pepo,* but some are referable to *C. maxima, C. mixta,* and *C. moschata.* Characteristically, they have sprawling stems, often of great length, and fruits, frequently immense, orange when ripe, which are used for pies, jack o'lanterns, and stock feed. The seeds are sometimes roasted and eaten.

Harvesting pumpkins

Because of the amount of space they occupy, pumpkins are more often grown as a field crop than in gardens. However, gardeners sometimes plant them. Favorite varieties are 'Big Max', 'Cinderella', 'Connecticut Field', 'Jack o'Lantern', and 'Small Sugar'. In the south 'Cushaw' pumpkins are often preferred. Gross feeders, pumpkins are warm-weather annuals that for the best results need fertile ground enriched with generous amounts of manure or rich compost and an application of complete fertilizer.

Sow the seeds after the weather is warm and settled, about three together in hills, which need not be raised above the level of the surrounding ground, 4 to 8 feet apart, in rows 8 to 12 feet apart, and when the seedlings begin to crowd, pull out all except the strongest one. Where spring comes late, an early start can be had by sowing indoors three weeks or so before setting the resulting plants in the garden, which may be done about the time it is safe to plant tomatoes.

Because pumpkins tolerate light shade they are sometimes interplanted with corn, but the two crops then compete for moisture and nutrients and so it is better to plant them separately. To obtain huge pumpkins, limit each plant to one or at most two fruits, take care that at no time the plants lack for water, and fertilize lightly once a month or more frequently.

Harvesting is delayed until the fruits, which may be stored in the same way as winter squashes, are fully mature. Pests and diseases are those that affect squashes.

PUNA-WETA is *Carpodetus serratus.*

PUNICA (Pù-nica) — Pomegranate. The pomegranate, native from southern Europe to the Himalayas, and widely naturalized in warm countries elsewhere, together with a species not in cultivation that is endemic to the island of Socotra in the Indian Ocean, are the only members of *Punica,* which is the only genus of the pomegranate family PUNICACEAE. The common name comes from the Latin *pomum,* an apple, and *granatum,* having many seeds; the botanical one from the Latin *maium punicum,* apple of Carthage.

Punicas are deciduous small trees or shrubs, their branches often ending in spines, with undivided, opposite or sub-opposite, frequently clustered, toothless leaves that when young are coppery or have reddish veins. The flowers, solitary or in small clusters at the ends of the branches and short axillary shoots, have leathery, tubular calyxes with five to eight lobes (sepals), the same number of crumpled petals, many stamens, and one style. The fruits, thick-skinned, and containing numerous seeds surrounded by juicy pulp, are technically similar to berries. At the end opposite the stalk they are crowned with a conspicuous, persistent calyx. This served as an inspiration for the crown of Solomon, and thus for those of all succeeding monarchs. Cultivated since antiquity, and referred to in Holy Writ, the pomegranate was well known to the Israelites during their sojourn in Egypt. Its fruits have long been accepted as symbols of fertility, and since very early times used as decorative motifs. From the juice of the fruit cooling beverages and grenadine syrup are made. The explosive missiles called grenades were named because of the similarity in size and shape of sixteenth-century examples to the fruits. The pomegranate is the national emblem of Spain.

A deciduous shrub or tree up to 20 feet tall or sometimes taller, but often lower, the pomegranate (**P. granatum**) has blunt, short-stalked, lustrous, oblong to elliptic-lanceolate leaves 1 inch to 2 inches or more in length. Its bright orange-red flowers, 1 inch to 1½ inches in diameter, are decidedly showy. They are succeeded by brownish-yellow to reddish, orange-sized, compartmented, spherical fruits that contain numerous seeds encased in pink or red, acid-flavored pulp. In addition to *P. granatum,* a number of its variants are cul-

Punica granatum

Punica granatum (fruits, with one cut open)

tivated. These include several orchard varieties as well as *P. g. albescens,* with whitish flowers; *P. g. flore-pleno,* with double red blooms; *P. g. alba-plena,* with double white flowers, *P. g. legrellei,* which has double flowers striped with red and yellow; popular *P. g. nana,* a compact variety with smaller, narrower leaves and red flowers that does not exceed 5 or 6 feet in height; and a double-flowered variant, *P. g. plena.*

Garden and Landscape Uses. As an orchard fruit, the pomegranate is cultivated to only a limited extent in North America, but the species and some varieties are popular ornamentals in the south and southwest, where they are employed as hedges and for display in groups, interplanted with other shrubs and trees, and as single lawn specimens. They are also grown in pots and tubs, the dwarf variety especially, in greenhouses and as a window plant. The species and dwarf varieties are hardy about as far north as Washington, D.C. Other varieties are slightly more tender. All succeed in well-drained soil of ordinary garden quality and prefer sunny locations.

Cultivation. Pomegranates can be raised from seed, but are more commonly propagated by leafless hardwood cuttings taken in winter, by summer cuttings of leafy shoots planted in a greenhouse propagating bench or under mist, rooted shoots taken from the bases of established specimens, layering, and by grafting onto seedling understocks. In orchards, pomegranates are spaced 12 to 18 feet apart and trained to tree form by pruning out the many shoots that naturally develop from the bases of the plants. For ornamental purposes, and especially when used as hedges, the plants are spaced more closely. Annual pruning of established trees consists of cutting back the current season's shoots in winter after the leaves have fallen, and at that time any pruning deemed desirable to keep the plants shapely and of appropriate size is done. Hedges may be sheared in winter. No other special care is needed. In pots and tubs, they succeed in well-drained containers in porous, fertile soil and are watered freely from spring through fall, sparingly in winter. During their season of active growth, well-rooted specimens benefit from dilute liquid fertilizer applied at biweekly intervals. In the north, the protection of a greenhouse or other light place where the temperature can be maintained between 35 and 50°F through the winter is needed. Attention to pruning and repotting is given in late winter or spring before new growth begins. The plants are benefited by being stood outdoors in a sunny place for the summer.

PUNICACEAE — Pomegranate Family. The botanical description of this family of dicotyledons is that of its only genus, *Punica*.

PUNK TREE is *Melaleuca leucadendron*.

PURPLE. The word purple forms parts of the common names of these plants: purple bell vine (*Rhodochiton atrosanguineum*), purple coneflower (*Echinacea purpurea*), purple-leaf wintercreeper (*Euonymus fortunei coloratus*), purple-leaved plum (*Prunus cerasifera atropurpurea*), purple-loosestrife (*Lythrum salicaria*), purple mombin (*Spondias purpurea*), purple osier (*Salix purpurea*), purple passion vine (*Gynura aurantiaca* 'Purple Passion'), purple ragwort (*Senecio elegans*) purple viper's grass (*Scorzonera purpurea*), and purple wreath (*Petrea volubilis*).

PURSHIA (Púrsh-ia) — Antelope Brush. The rose family ROSACEAE includes among its many genera the only two species of *Purshia*. They are natives of western North America, named in honor of Frederick T. Pursh, botanist and author of an early flora of North America, who died in 1820.

Purshias are shrubs or small trees with crowded, rigid, clustered, alternate, deeply-three-cleft leaves with rolled-under margins. Solitary at the ends of short branches, their flowers have five sepals, five white to yellow petals, eighteen to twenty-five stamens, and usually one pistil with a short style that remains with the fruit (technically an achene).

Ranging from California to British Columbia, Montana, and New Mexico, **P. tridentata** is a grayish shrub up to 10 feet in height, but often lower, with young shoots more or less glandular-hairy. The leaves are wedge-shaped and three-toothed or three-lobed at the apex. They are ¼ inch up to 1 inch long or a little longer. Above they are pubescent and without sunken glands; their undersides are covered with white hairs. They are apparently deciduous. The flowers, with creamy-yellow petals, are about ⅓ inch long.

Differing from the last in being of greenish appearance and in having glandular, but not hairy twigs, and the upper sides of its leaves hairless and speckled with tiny sunken glands and their undersides only sparsely-hairy, **P. glandulosa** is a greenish shrub 3 to 6 feet tall or sometimes

taller, with leaves under ½ inch long and three- or rarely five-lobed. Native from California to Nevada and Arizona, its flowers are white.

Garden and Landscape Uses and Cultivation. Purshias make no appreciable display of bloom and are of minor horticultural importance. They are sometimes planted in and are well adapted to dry soils and arid climates. In humid regions, pruning may be needed to shorten long shoots and thin out crowded branches. This is done after blooming in spring. Propagation is by seed, by summer cuttings under mist or in a greenhouse or cold frame propagating bed, and by layering. They are hardy in climates not colder than those of their natural ranges.

PURSLANE is *Portulaca oleracea*; water-purslane, *Ludwigia palustris*; winter-purslane, *Montia perfoliata*.

PUSCHKINIA (Pusch-kínia) — Striped-Squill. The name *Puschkinia* commemorates the Russian chemist and botanist Count Apollos Apollosovich Mussin-Puschkin, who died in 1805. It belongs to a genus of two small, deciduous bulb plants, natives of western Asia, related to *Chionodoxa* and *Scilla* and belonging in the lily family LILIACEAE.

Puschkinias are spring-bloomers. They have a few all-basal leaves, those first to appear strap-shaped, the later ones linear. The leafless, erect flower stalks carry one or a raceme of several bell-shaped blooms with short perianth tubes, six somewhat spreading perianth lobes (tepals), six stamens, and one style. The fruits are capsules. These plants differ from *Scilla* and *Chionodoxa* in having the stalks of their stamens joined in a conelike arrangement that projects beyond the anthers.

The only species cultivated, the pretty striped-squill (**P. scilloides**), has channeled, dark green leaves 4 to 7 inches long. Its flowers, ½ to 1 inch across and milky-blue with a darker mid-vein to each petal, are in somewhat one-sided racemes 4 to 8 inches tall. Although less richly col-

Puschkinia scilloides

Puschkinia scilloides libanotica in a rock garden

ored than the flowers of scillas or chionodoxas, they are not drab. The flowers of *P. s. alba* are white, those of *P. s. libanotica* have rather longer petals than the blooms of the typical species.

Garden and Landscape Uses and Cultivation. The striped-squill, hardy as far north as Canada, is a delightful addition to such other harbingers of spring as chionodoxas, crocuses, grape-hyacinths, narcissuses, scillas, and tulips, with which it can be associated to produce charming effects. It succeeds under conditions that suit these other bulb plants.

PUSSY. The word pussy forms parts of the common names of these plants: pussy paws (*Calyptridium umbellatum*), pussy toes (*Antennaria*), and pussy willow (some sorts of *Salix*).

PUTA-PUTA-WETA is *Carpodetus serratus*.

PUTORIA (Putòr-ia). At least one of the three species of the Mediterranean region genus *Putoria*, of the madder family RUBIACEAE, is worthy of cultivation. The name, from the Latin *putor*, a disagreeable smell, alludes to the unpleasant odor of the foliage when crushed.

Putorias are low, spreading shrubs with opposite, undivided leaves. Their flowers, in terminal clusters, have a four-toothed calyx, a tubular corolla with four short, spreading lobes (petals), four stamens, and one style. The fruits are berry-like.

In appearance much resembling *Daphne cneorum*, but with glossier, more yellow-green foliage, **P. calabrica** (syn. *Asperula calabrica*) forms mats of prostrate, rooting branches. From 9 inches to 1 foot tall, and with slender, downy shoots, it has linear-lanceolate leaves up to 1 inch long by under ¼ inch wide, and with recurved margins. The flowers have corollas with slender tubes ½ to 1 inch long and faces about ¼ inch across. They are in crisscross-patterned clusters about 1 inch wide, of a dozen or so, and are borne freely over a long summer period. Unfortunately, they lack the delightful fragrance of those of *Daphne cneorum*; instead, have a faintly disagreeable odor. They are clear pink to purple-rose-pink and are succeeded by red berries that gradually deepen in color as they mature and provide some display.

Garden and Landscape Uses. This desirable shrub is not hardy in the north, but prospers near San Francisco, in other parts of California, and elsewhere where winters are mild, reveling in summer heat and withstanding several degrees of frost. It provides splendid furnishing for niches in rock garden cliffs, banks, and slopes and promises well as a groundcover where it is not subject to walking upon. For its greatest satisfaction, this plant needs a porous, reasonably fertile, well-drained soil.

Cultivation. New plants of *P. calabrica* are easily raised from seed and cuttings taken in summer root. Small-scale propagation can be accomplished by carefully removing rooted portions of established plants. As routine care, a spring application of a slow-acting fertilizer is helpful and, where long dry summers prevail, watering should receive attention. When setting plants as groundcover, a spacing of about 2 feet is satisfactory. Mulching with gravel or stone chips to retain moisture and minimize fluctuations in soil temperature is recommended.

PUTTY ROOT or ADAM-AND-EVE is *Aplectrum hyemale*.

PUYA (Pù-ya). The kinds of *Puya* grow with their roots in the ground. Unlike most of their bromeliad relatives, they do not perch on trees. There are 120 species, natives of the Andean region, which belong to the pineapple family BROMELIACEAE. They vary greatly, from comparatively small, trunkless plants to impressive giants with trunks up to 15 feet tall and flower spikes that sometimes attain heights of 40 feet. The name is one used by the Araucanian Indians of Chile.

Puyas are close relatives of *Dyckia*, differing in that their petals are not joined at their bases. They are evergreen herbaceous or woody plants with rosettes of spreading or erect, usually spine-toothed, sharp-pointed, tough leaves. Handsome and showy, their large panicles of flowers terminate erect stalks that usually tower high above the foliage. The flowers have three sepals, three petals, six stamens, and a slender style with three stigmas. The ovary is superior, which means that the sepals and petals come from below it. The fruits are capsules. Most puyas die after blooming, but some branch from the base or develop new rosettes at the ends of stolon-like shoots.

Botanically puyas are divided into two groups, one of kinds in which the main flowering stem and its branches, for at least one-half their lengths from their ends, have bracts without flowers in their axils, and the other group in which flowers are produced to the tips of the flower-

ing stem and its laterals. The projecting flowerless portions of the branches are used as perches by birds that extract nectar from the flowers and in doing so effect pollination. It is thought that puyas without such convenient perches are pollinated by hummingbirds that need no such rests.

One of the most remarkable plants in the world, rare *P. raimondii,* which grows in Peru at elevations of about 13,000 feet, has a branchless trunk that may exceed 12 feet in height, surmounted by a dense, globular crown of slender, 3-foot-long leaves. When, after many years of gathering strength for such a supreme effort, the plant blooms, it shoots to a height of 30 or 40 feet or more, an immense, uncompromisingly erect, columnar flower spike that points like a dagger to the sky. As the very numerous greenish-white flowers fade the leaves droop, the food resources of the plant are devoted to seed production, and when that objective is served the plant dies.

A massive species, Chilean *P. chilensis* develops a distinct, often candelabra-branched trunk up to 10 feet tall. Its leaves, of which there may be more than a hundred in each dome-shaped rosette,

Puya chilensis

are distinctly channeled and dark green and have few scales. From 3 to 4 feet long, at their bases 2 inches broad, they have slightly recurved tips and margins armed with rather distantly spaced vicious spines. The spikelets of greenish-yellow flowers are eighty to one hundred together in dense panicles 2 to 3 feet in length, lifted high above the foliage on long, stout, erect stalks. The outer portions of the panicle branches, and the end of its main axis, are without flowers. The green sepals are one-half as long as the 2½-inch-long petals. Variety *P. c. gigantea,* is described as having trunks up to 15 feet tall, shorter, erect leaves, more formidably armed with prickles, and smaller flowers.

Often confused with *P. chilensis,* but with laxer, markedly recurving, more flex-

Puya berteroniana (a young plant)

Puya berteroniana, in bloom

ible foliage, **P. berteroniana,** of Chile, has, in panicles of eighty to one hundred or more spikelets, beautiful metallic-blue flowers. Flowerless portions of the main stem and branches of the panicles extend well beyond the blooms. The leaves, 2 inches broad at their bases, are densely clothed with white scales on their undersides and sparsely, but distinctly above.

The hardiest puya, **P. alpestris** (syn. *P. whytei*), of Chile, belongs to the group in which the main axis and branches of the flower panicles extend well beyond the blooms. It has rosettes of recurved leaves up to 3 feet long and ½ to 1 inch wide at their bases. They are bright green above and thickly coated with white scales on their undersides. The blue-green flowers, in lax panicles carried on erect stalks to a height of 4 or 5 feet, are of up to twenty spikelets.

Two Chilean kinds that have flowers out to the tips of the panicle branches are *P. coerulea* and *P. venusta*. As young plants they are very alike. When mature, **P. coerulea** is larger. It has leaves up to 2 feet long, densely coated on their undersides with white scales. Its clearly separated, dark blue flowers are in panicles of ten to twenty spikelets that reach a height of 4 or 5 feet. The hemispherical rosettes of **P. venusta** are of leaves not over 1 foot long. Its flower panicles, often branchless or with few branches, have their reddish-violet blooms much crowded at the ends of the main axis and branches.

Puya coerulea

Puya coerulea (flowers)

Without trunks or stems, **P. spathacea,** a native of Argentina, has many-leaved rosettes and flowers with brownish-pink sepals, and dull greenish-blue petals about ¾ inch long, produced in panicles up to 2 feet in length. The leaves, up to 1½ feet long by ¾ inch broad or slightly broader at their middles, have edges furnished with incurved spines. Stemless or very short-stemmed **P. nana,** of Bolivia, forms a flattish, crowded rosette of many spreading, narrow-lanceolate leaves up to

Puya nana

2 feet long by 1 inch wide, their edges furnished with stiff brown spines, and their undersides densely covered with scales. The bluish-green flowers, accompanied by more evident brown bracts, are crowded in stalkless or almost stalkless heads that nestle in the centers of the rosettes.

Garden and Landscape Uses. In southern California and other areas of warm, dry climates, these noble bromeliads are magnificent landscape components. They associate with succulents, such as cactuses, and with other plants of desert and semidesert habitats, and show to great advantage both in and out of bloom. They should be located where their spiny leaves are unlikely to tear clothing or otherwise inconvenience or harm passers-by. As indoor plants, they are most frequently cultivated in succulent collections, especially in large greenhouses and conservatories. Stony, porous, reasonably fertile soil and locations in full sun are most favorable to these plants. Because of their spiny leaves it is well to wear leather gloves when working close to them.

Cultivation. In climates favorable to the growth of warm temperate and subtropical desert plants, no difficulty is ordinarily experienced with puyas. The hardiest, *P. berteroniana* stands considerable cold and even occasional light frosts. In greenhouses winter night temperatures of 50°F or thereabouts are favorable. By day five to fifteen degrees more is advantageous, and at other seasons much warmer conditions are in order. Water moderately from spring to fall, more sparing in winter, but extreme dryness of container-grown specimens is to be avoided. Puyas prosper either in dry or fairly humid atmospheres. Well-rooted specimens benefit from occasional applications in summer of dilute liquid fertilizer. Propagation is easy by seed, and those kinds that produce offsets or suckers can be multiplied by removing and potting or planting them.

PYCNANTHEMUM (Pycnánth-emum) — Mountain-Mint. Of minor horticultural interest, the genus *Pycnanthemum,* of the mint family LABIATAE, consists of perhaps twenty species. The exact number is open to question because natural hybridization occurs, and mongrel progeny may have been identified as species. The generic name, from the Greek *pyknos,* dense, and *anthemon,* a flower, refers to the crowded clusters of flowers with, immediately below them, small leafy, more or less hoary, bracts. These plants are confined as wildlings to North America, chiefly to the eastern part, but one species is a native of California. They are closely related to beebalms (*Monarda*), but have much smaller heads of bloom.

Mountain-mints are erect, perennial, aromatic herbaceous plants with rhizomes and branched or branchless, four-angled stems. Their short-stalked or stalkless leaves are undivided, opposite, linear to ovate, and toothed or toothless. The small, tubular flowers have a more or less two-lipped calyx and a white to purple corolla, with a lower, often purple-spotted, three-lobed lip and an upper lip sometimes slightly notched. Commonly, the four stamens protrude. The fruits are nutlets, usually called seeds.

One of the more common species, *P. virginianum* occurs in upland woods and meadows from Maine to North Dakota, Georgia, and Oklahoma. From 1½ to 3 feet tall, its stiffly erect stems are much branched above their middles and finely-hairy along their angles. Its many leaves, linear or linear-lanceolate, are sometimes hairy on the mid-veins beneath, but otherwise smooth. They are 1¼ to 2¼ inches long. The flower heads, about ½ inch in diameter, are nearly flat and have white, tightly crowded blooms. Generally similar, but with somewhat broader leaves is *P. flexuosum.* It grows in similar habitats, from Maine to Wisconsin, South Carolina, Tennessee, Louisiana, and Texas. It is suspected that hybrids between *P. flexuosum* and *P. virginianum* occur.

Pycnanthemum flexuosum

Garden and Landscape Uses and Cultivation. The species mentioned above and others have some appeal as furnishings for native plant gardens and semiwild areas. They are not showy enough to earn places for themselves in more formal beds and borders. Their culture is extremely simple. Any ordinary soil, neither excessively wet nor dry, satisfies. They are planted in spring or early fall and will grow in sun or light shade. Increase is by division and seed.

PYCNOSTACHYS (Pycno-stáchys). The East African and Madagascan genus *Pycnostachys,* of the mint family LABIATAE, is represented in cultivation by perhaps only two of its nearly forty species. These are ordinarily grown in greenhouses for late fall and winter bloom, but undoubtedly would prove satisfactory outdoors in climates not subject to frost. The group is closely related to *Coleus* and *Plectranthus,* but has flowers in much more compact clusters than those genera. Its name alludes to this characteristic; it comes from the Greek *pyknos,* dense, and *stachys,* a spike.

Both annual and herbaceous perennial species of *Pycnostachys* are known to botanists; those cultivated are tender perennials. The genus consists of erect plants with square stems, opposite, long-stalked, linear-lanceolate to broadly-ovate, coarsely-toothed leaves, and whorls (circles of several) of blue flowers in terminal spikes. The calyxes are evenly-fine-toothed. The asymmetrical, tubular, two-lipped corollas curve downward. The upper lip is notched into four teeth, the lower concave and not toothed. There are four stamens. The fruits are nutlets, commonly called seeds.

Gardeners are indebted to the African explorer David Livingstone for first collecting seeds of *P. urticifolia.* He sent them to England in 1859. This species attains a height of 4 to 6 feet. It has pointed-ovate, nettle-like leaves, downy on their undersides. Its flowers are in broad-based,

Pycnostachys urticifolia

pointed, conical spikes. Quite different is *P. dawei,* a stouter-stemmed plant of about the same height, that has narrow-lanceolate, somewhat drooping, pubescent leaves 6 inches to 1 foot long and ¾-inch-long, rich cobalt-blue flowers in shorter, squatter spikes than those of *P. urticifolia.* The bracts of the flower spikes are edged with long white hairs.

Garden Uses. As greenhouse and conservatory ornamentals, these are highly esteemed because their flowers are blue, a color not too common among winter-flowering plants. From a decorative point of view, *P. dawei* is superior, but the other is well worth having. They are easier to grow than their beautiful blue-flowered relative, *Coleus thyrsoideus,* and their blooms do not shatter as readily; in fact, provided most of the leaves are stripped

Pycnostachys dawei

from their stems, they last fairly well as cut flowers. These plants have the bad habit of growing excessively tall and leggy unless they are properly cared for. Compactness is encouraged by not propagating them too early, by correct pinching of the shoots, by allowing plenty of space between individual plants, and by avoiding excessively high temperatures.

Cultivation. Seed or cuttings started from April to July provide easy means of increase. Home-saved seeds are perfectly satisfactory; they ripen in spring. The young plants must be kept potted on (transferred successively to larger containers) until in August, early propagated specimens occupy pots or tubs 9 or 10 inches in diameter. They need fertile, loamy soil of a kind satisfactory for chrysanthemums. To encourage branching and to discourage excessive height, the shoots are pinched once, twice, or three times (depending upon the date the plants were propagated) during the growing season, the last pinch being given in September or October. At all times these plants need full sun. Their soil must never be permitted to dry to the extent that the foliage wilts. After their final pots are filled with roots, a program of regular applications of dilute liquid fertilizer should be instituted. A winter night temperature of 50 to 55°F and daytime temperatures only a few degrees higher are satisfactory.

PYRACANTHA (Pyr-acántha) — Firethorn. The genus *Pyracantha,* of the rose family ROSACEAE, comprises ten species of hardy and nonhardy shrubs or sometimes small trees native from southeastern Europe to the Himalayas, China, and Taiwan. Botanically they are closely allied to *Cotoneaster* and *Crataegus.* From the first they differ in mostly having thorns and toothed leaves, from *Cretaegus* in their leaves being evergreen, at least in mild climates, and not lobed. The name, alluding to the brightly colored fruits and to the thorns, comes from the Greek *pyr,* fire, and *akantha,* a thorn.

Pyracanthas are evergreens but a few sorts hardly enough to survive winters in

the north may be partly or wholly deciduous there. They have alternate, short-stalked, usually toothed leaves and rather crowded clusters of small, white, hawthorn-like flowers with five short sepals, five spreading, roundish petals, twenty stamens, and five pistils. The fruits are small, red, orange-red, or yellow berry-like pomes (fruits constructed like apples) containing five seedlike nutlets.

The hardiest sorts are *P. coccinea* and some of its varieties and *P. atalantioides.* Frequently planted, **P. coccinea** is a dense shrub, up to about 6 feet tall or taller when espaliered against a wall. Toward the northern limit of its hardiness, which in sheltered places is about New York City, it loses its foliage in winter. This has lustrous, narrow-obovate to elliptic, short-stalked leaves 1 inch to 2½ inches long, or smaller on the flowering shoots, with blunt teeth toward their bases. The stalks of the flower clusters are pubescent. The abundant fruits, ¼ inch or a little more in diameter, are bright red. Native from Italy to western Asia, *P. coccinea* is naturalized to some extent from Pennsylvania southward. In the north more common in cultivation than the species, more vigorous and hardier *P. c. lalandei* survives in southern New England. This has fruits slightly orange-red. About as hardy are *P. c.* 'Kasan', with orange-red fruits, and *P. c.* 'Thornless', the fruits of which are red. Less hardy *P. c. pauciflora* has orange-red fruits, those of *P. c. aurea* are yellow. Native to China and with scarlet to bright crimson fruits slightly smaller than those

Pyracantha coccinea lalandei (flowers)

Pyracantha coccinea lalandei (fruits)

of *P. coccinea*, beautiful, more desirable **P. atalantioides** (syn. *P. gibbsii*) is as hardy. A vigorous grower up to 20 feet high, this has flower clusters with hairless stalks and fruits that remain attractive for a month or longer than those of *P. coccinea* and its varieties. The leaves of *P. atalantioides*, elliptic to oblanceolate and usually pointed, have slightly glaucous undersides and are 1¼ to 1½ inches long. Toward the northern limit of this sort's hardiness, in sheltered places about New York City, they are shed in winter. Yellow fruits distinguish *P. a. aurea*.

Allied to *P. atalantioides* and like it with long-persisting fruits, very spiny **P. fortuneana** (syn. *P. crenato-serrata*), of China, is hardy in mild climates only. It has blunt, obovate to elliptic, toothed leaves, dark green above, lighter green on their undersides, and 1 inch to 2¼ inches long. The stalks of the flower clusters are hairless. The coral-red fruits are under ¼ inch in diameter. Those of *P. f.* 'Knap Hill Lemon' are yellow. Another not hardy in the north, **P. crenulata** is a variable native of China. A shrub or small tree, this has round-toothed, pointed and bristle-tipped to bluntish, oblong-lanceolate to oblanceolate leaves ¾ inch to 2 inches long, with wedge-shaped bases. The stalks of the rather loose flower clusters are without hair. The fruits, up to ⅓ inch in diameter, are orange-red. From the typical species, *P. c. kansuensis* differs in having flower clusters with pubescent branches, narrow-oblong to oblanceolate leaves up to 1 inch long, and fruits smaller than those of the species.

Akin to *P. crenulata* and sometimes considered a variety of it, Chinese **P. rogersiana** is more decorative and hardier, although not sufficiently so to survive in the north. Not over about 10 feet tall, it has lustrous, bright green, irregularly-toothed leaves approximately 1½ inches long and orange-red fruits as large as those of *P. crenulata*. Varieties are *P. r. aurantiaca*, with orange-colored fruits, and *P. r. flava*, with yellow fruits.

Most popular and satisfactory in the

Pyracantha rogersiana flava (flowers)

Pyracantha rogersiana flava (fruits)

southeastern United States, but not hardy in the north, excellent **P. koidzumii**, of Taiwan, is allied to *P. crenulata*. Its toothless leaves, mostly toward the branch ends, are oblongish to obovate; they have blunt, bristle-tipped apexes and are about 1 inch long. The flower clusters are nearly hairless, the orange-scarlet fruits are flattened and about ¼ inch in diameter. Horticultural varieties include 'San Jose', with wide-spreading branches, prostrate 'Santa Cruz', and 'Victory', with dark red fruits. Another species, somewhat hardier than the last, but suited for mild climates only, **P. angustifolia,** of southern China, is a tall to prostrate shrub with blunt, narrow-oblong to oblanceolate-oblong, few-toothed or toothless leaves ¾ inch to 2 inches long, grayish-hairy on their under surfaces. The long-persistent, bright orange to brick-red fruits are up to ⅓ inch in diameter.

Hybrid firethorns are plentiful, in fact it is thought that most of those in cultivation as species are probably of mixed parentage. In recent years, nusersymen have engaged in deliberate hybridization and given names to many offspring, some of which are too alike or so closely resemble earlier kinds to warrant this distinction. Hybrid sorts are described and offered in nursery catalogs.

Garden and Landscape Uses. Among the most decorative shrubs in fruit, attractive in bloom, and with handsome foliage, firethorns are magnificent as free-standing specimens, in foundation plantings, as hedges, and particularly for espaliering. Their greatest disadvantage is their susceptibility to fire blight and to a disease called scab, both of which cause the fruits to turn black. Scab can be controlled by spraying when the flower buds first open and twice later at ten-day intervals with fermate. There is no cure for fire blight. Pruning out affected branches early is important.

Firethorns adapt to a wide variety of well-drained soils not excessively dry. They need sun for at least part of the day, but when espaliered usually are best on walls facing directions other than south. On west-facing walls they are likely to do well.

Espaliered pyracanthas: (a) Fan-form

(b) Branches trained horizontally

A hedge of pyracantha

Cultivation. These shrubs make few demands on gardeners' skills. Do not prune more often than necessary, which with espaliered specimens means annually. Prune specimens trained in this way immediately after flowering so that as much bloom (the source of future berries) as possible is retained. Free-standing specimens that become too big may be pruned in early spring. Old, straggly specimens, if cut back really hard soon recover and if not crowded make shapely specimens. Propagation is frequently done in nurseries by grafting onto seedling pyracanthas, cotoneasters, or hawthorns, but good results can be had from cuttings planted under mist or in a cold frame or greenhouse propagating bed in late summer. Seeds, stratified for three or four months at 40°F and then sown germinate satisfactorily.

A garden pyrethrum

is fatal to many insects and harmless to warm-blooded animals including man. Because of this, it is an effective insecticide safe to use on vegetables and fruits. It is used as a fine powder made by grinding the dried flower heads and as a liquid extract diluted and applied as a spray.

PYRETHRUMS. Garden pyrethrums, or painted daisies as they are sometimes called, are charming hardy herbaceous perennials with finely-divided, ferny foliage and long-stalked, daisy-like flower heads 2 to 3 inches across, chiefly in shades of pink and red, but also white. There are single-, semidouble-, and double-flowered varieties. Botanically varieties of *Chrysanthemum coccineum* (syn. *Pyrethrum roseum*), which is a native of the Caucasus, belong in the daisy family COMPOSITAE.

Pyrethrums are choice in beds and borders for early summer bloom and as sources of excellent, long-lasting cut flowers. They prosper in sunny locations in very well-drained, preferably sandy soil that is not too rich. Plant in early spring or in regions of fairly mild winters early fall, spacing them 1¼ to 1½ feet apart. Where winters are severe, protect them with a light cover of salt hay, corn stalks, or branches of evergreens.

Propagation may be by division as soon as flowering is through, or in early fall, or if one is willing to forego much display of bloom the first year, early spring. Seeds sown in May in a cold frame or outdoor bed, shaded until they sprout, germinate readily, but the resulting plants are mostly inferior to choice horticultural varieties. Unfortunately, few of the latter are available from commercial sources in North America. Often the best plan is to work up stocks by sowing seeds and after the resulting plants bloom to discard the less desirable ones and multiply the better ones by division.

PYRACOMELES (Pyraco-mèles). An infrequently cultivated bigeneric hybrid between *Pyracantha crenato-serrata* and *Osteomeles subrotunda* bears this name, a combination of those of its parents. Raised in 1922, *Pyracomeles vilmorinii* is a low, half-evergreen shrub hardy perhaps as far north as Washington, D.C. From *Pyracantha* it differs in having spineless branches and pinnately-cut leaves, from *Osteomeles* in its leaves not being of all separate leaflets. The branches are slender and at first grayish-hairy. The leaves have five to nine lobes or divisions, the lower ones often separate leaflets, the upper ones divided by clefts that reach only partway to the midrib. The white flowers, ⅓ inch across, and many together in clusters, are followed by red, berry-like fruits about ⅙ inch across.

Garden Uses and Cultivation. Grown as a botanical and horticultural curiosity, this plant responds to treatment appropriate for *Pyracantha*. Propagation is by cuttings and by grafting onto one of its parent sorts.

PYRAMIDAL. The word pyramidal, used to describe the natural forms of plants, most commonly trees, has in many horticultural and botanical works, including this Encyclopedia, a different meaning from its common dictionary one. By definition a geometrical pyramid is a solid with a polygonal base and flat, triangular sides that meet at its apex. No plant, unless trained or sheared, has that form. Kinds described as pyramidal are geometrically conical; from more or less circular bases they taper gradually to a pointed apex.

PYRETHRUM. A product of *Chrysanthemum cinerariaefolium* and *C. roseum*, pyrethrum

PYROLA (Py-ròla)—Shinleaf, Wintergreen. The genus *Pyrola* belongs in the heath family ERICACEAE, or according to some interpretations to a segregate of that group called the shinleaf family PYROLACEAE. The name, from a diminutive of the Latin *pirus*, a pear, alludes to a fancied resemblance of the shapes of the leaves of some kinds to those of pears. The colloquial name wintergreen is also used for *Gaultheria*. Pyrolas are natives of North America, Europe, and Asia. There are about twelve species.

Pyrolas usually have rosettes of evergreen leaves, but sometimes are apparently leafless. In racemes, their small white, greenish, or purplish flowers have five-lobed calyxes, five separate petals, ten stamens, and one style. The fruits are capsules.

Chiefly natives of conifer forests, often favoring moist places, pyrolas are more or less saprophytes (plants that live on dead organic matter impregnated with microscopic organisms that aid them to obtain the nutrients they need). Singularly uncooperative in cultivation, they will not grow in ordinary soils. Failure commonly follows attempts to transplant them from the wild.

Pyrola, undetermined species

The species of *Pyrola* are mostly separated on slight differences not easily observable by other than trained botanists. Widely distributed as a native of bogs and moist woodlands in Europe and temperate Asia, *P. rotundifolia* is represented in North America from Newfoundland and Nova Scotia northward, and by its variety *P. r. americana*, which is slightly larger in its parts, from Quebec and Nova Scotia to Minnesota, Indiana, North Carolina, and Kentucky. This has thick, lustrous, broadly-elliptic to nearly round leaves 1 inch to 2½ inches long, and flower stalks from 6 inches to 1 foot tall that bear sweet-scented, white blooms in loose racemes.

Usually smaller than the last, *P. elliptica* favors dry upland woods. It is found from Newfoundland and Quebec to Minnesota, British Columbia, Virginia, Indiana, and Iowa and has broadly-elliptic to more or less obovate leaves 1½ to 2½ inches long. Its white flowers veined with green are in racemes similar to those of *P. rotundifolia*. Easy to identify because its greenish to white flowers are in one-sided racemes, *P. secunda* grows in moist woodlands and wet places from Greenland to Alaska, Maryland, Indiana, Minnesota, and New Mexico. Its elliptic to broadly-elliptic or nearly round, sometimes toothed leaves are about 1½ inches long.

Garden Uses and Cultivation. Challenging to grow, pyrolas are unlikely to be attempted by other than keen native plant gardeners. About the only advice about their cultivation that can be offered is to duplicate as closely as possible the conditions under which they grow in the wild, providing them with sandy, boggy soil which has been mixed with, if possible, a proportion of earth in which they grow naturally, the latter serving as an inoculum of required microorganisms.

PYROLIRION. See Zephyranthes.

PYROSTEGIA (Pyrostè-gia) — Orange-Trumpet-Vine. Five woody vines, natives of South America, of the bignonia family BIGNONIACEAE, constitute *Pyrostegia*. The name is from the Greek *pyr*, fire, and *stege*, a roof. It refers to the color and shape of the upper lip of the flower.

Pyrostegias have leaves of two or three leaflets and slender, three-branched tendrils. Their flowers, in terminal panicles, have a bell-shaped or tubular, toothed or toothless calyx and a tubular, funnel-shaped corolla with a curved tube. There are four slightly protruding stamens and a slender style tipped with a two-lobed stigma. The fruits are long, slender capsules containing seeds in two rows or zigzag.

The only species commonly cultivated is the orange-trumpet-vine (**P. venusta** syns. *P. ignea*, *Bignonia venusta*), of Brazil. A very vigorous grower, this has leaves of pubescent-stalked, pointed-ovate to pointed-ovate-oblong leaflets 2 to 3 inches long. The brilliant red-orange, slender-tubed flowers, in large pendulous clusters, are very showy. They are 2 to 3 inches long. Their petals are reflexed and fringed with white hairs. The fruits are 1 foot long or longer.

Pyrostegia venusta

Garden and Landscape Uses. Employed for covering arbors, balustrades, archways, fences, walls, trees, and even telegraph poles in the warmer parts of the United States and in other subtropical and tropical climates, the orange-trumpet-vine will, under favorable conditions, climb to a height of from 40 to 50 feet, but may be restrained by pruning. In California, it blooms from November to April, depending upon local climate. In Florida, it often blooms twice, once in midwinter and once in early summer. It is easily harmed by cold, but stands temperatures down to 28°F. This is a handsome adornment for large conservatories.

Cultivation. It thrives in any ordinary garden soil, but seems most responsive to a medium to heavy well-drained loam that is never very dry. For satisfactory blooming, full sun is required. In regions where frost occurs, it is advisable to protect the vines for the first two or three years after planting until their stems have developed a protective woody bark. Pruning, consisting of cutting back shoots that have bloomed to within a foot or two of their bases, should be done as soon in late winter or spring as the plant is through blooming.

In greenhouses, the main stems may be trained to pillars or to wires stretched beneath the roof, with the flowering shoots allowed to cascade. This vine succeeds in ground beds or large boxes in rich, well-drained soil. Winter temperatures of 45 to 50°F at night with a daytime rise of five or ten degrees are appropriate. From spring through fall the minimum temperature should be 65°F. Copious watering is desirable from spring through fall, less in winter. Weekly applications of a dilute liquid fertilizer during the active growing season are beneficial. At all times a humid atmosphere is needed. Propagation is very easy by cuttings of partly ripened shoots, each consisting of about three joints. Pests that may be troublesome are scales, mealybugs, and red spider mites.

PYRRHOCACTUS (Pyrrho-cáctus). As here accepted, *Pyrrhocactus*, of the cactus family CACTACEAE, consists of less than a dozen species, natives of Argentina. In the past other sorts, now referred to other genera, were included and in trade catalogs species of *Neochilenia*, *Neoporteria*, and *Horridocactus* are not uncommonly offered as *Pyrrhocactus*. Its name, from the Greek *pyr*, fire, and cactus, alludes to the colors of the blooms.

Pyrrhocactuses are small, spherical to short-cylindrical plants with conspicuous, notched ribs. They are formidably armed with clusters of strong, awl-shaped spines. The bell-shaped, reddish-yellow flowers open by day, come from the tops of the stems. Their perianth tubes and ovaries as well as the fruits are furnished with scales, woolly hairs, and slender bristles.

Its solitary, grayish-green stems or plant bodies spherical to ovoid, and up to 6 inches tall by 4 inches wide, *P. strausianus* is attractive. Its stems have twelve or thirteen notched and slightly spiraled ribs with areoles woolly at first and each sprouting nine to twenty reddish-brown spines scarcely distinguishable as radials and centrals, but the inner four slightly thicker and up to 1¼ inches in length. The flowers, ½ inch long or slightly longer, have brownish outer petals and salmon-pink inner ones. The stamens and style, the latter with twelve lobes, are white. In the wild inhabiting barren, sandy soils at high elevations in the Andes, *P. umadeave* has a long, thick taproot and a more or less spherical stem, solitary or branched from its base and up to 1¼ feet tall by 10 inches thick. The stems have eighteen to twenty-seven slightly notched ribs with woolly areoles and clusters of, in older specimens thirty to thirty-five, in younger specimens, fewer, awl-shaped, dark-tipped brownish-pink spines 1 inch to 1½ inches long, the radials and centrals similar. The tops of the stems are especially spiny and from that region are borne the yellow flowers, reddish on the outsides of the petals. They are nearly or quite 1½ inches long.

Garden and Landscape Uses and Cultivation. These are plants for collectors of cactuses and choice succulents They may be grown in rock gardens and similar places outdoors in mild, desert. and semi-desert regions and in greenhouses. The second species described above is reported to be difficult to grow on its own roots and grafting onto *Cereus*-type cactuses as understocks is recommended. Full sun and extremely well-drained sandy soil are needed. For more information see Cactuses.

PYRROSIA (Pyr-ròsia) — Felt Fern or Tongue Fern. About 100 species of small to moderate-sized ferns, ranging in the wild from southeast Asia, where the species are most numerous, to Siberia, Africa, Polynesia, Australia, and New Zealand, belong here; in addition, two species of South America, by some botanists thought to be distinct, are sometimes included in *Pyrrosia*. The genus, previously named *Cyclophorus*, belongs in the polypody family POLYPODIACEAE. Its species are often difficult to distinguish one from another. The name is from the Greek *pyrrhos*, reddish, in allusion to the coatings of reddish hairs.

Epiphytes, these ferns perch on trees, without extracting nourishment from them, and sometimes on rocks. They have creeping, scaly rhizomes and usually undivided, rarely lobed, toothless, leathery, more or less scaly fronds (leaves) clothed with stellate (star-shaped) hairs that soon fall from the upper sides, but are persistent beneath. In the polypody family only this genus, *Platycerium*, and *Pteropsis* have such hairs. The clusters of spore capsules are generally round, but sometimes elongated, and often merge.

The felt fern or tongue fern (*P. lingua* syn. *Cyclophorus lingua*) is a native of Japan, the Ryukyu Islands, Taiwan, China, and Indochina. It has wiry, long-creeping, reddish to yellowish-brown rhizomes and firm, generally lobeless, lanceolate to broad-lanceolate leaves with stalks a little shorter to a little longer than the blades. When young, the leaves are thickly clothed on both sides with a felt of brown hairs, but this soon disappears from the upper surface. The blades of the sterile fronds are 4 to 10 inches long by up to 2 inches wide; those of fertile fronds are usually a little smaller and narrower. Round clusters of spore capsules cover the undersides of the fertile fronds so thickly that they touch each other and often produce a quilted effect. Varieties include *P. l. cristata* (syn. *P.* 'Obake'), which has the apexes of its fronds conspicuously broadened and several times forked; *P. l. montrifera* (syns. *P. l. lacerata*, *P. l.* 'Hagoromo'), with the margins of its fronds irregularly fringed with deep lacerations; *P. l.* 'Nankin-shishi', which resembles *P. l. cristata* but has the broad apexes of its fronds more finely lacerated and the lacerations more congested and twisted rather than in one plane; *P.* 'Nokogiri-ba' (syn. *P. l. serrata*); and *P. l. variegata*, with fronds with yellowish streaks or bands running from the midrib to their round-toothed margins.

Much like *P. lingua* is *P. stigmosa* (syn. *Cyclophorus stigmosus*), a species common in teak forests in Java, and in Malaya favoring limestone rocks. Indigenous also to

Pyrrosia stigmosa

Pyrrosia heteractis

India, Ceylon, and the Celebes, this sort has bright green fronds with blades 10 inches to 1½ feet or slightly more in length and 1 inch to 2½ inches wide. The under surfaces of the leaves are thickly felted with persistent brown, stellate hairs. The small clusters of spore capsules do not touch each other. Of much the same aspect, *P. heteractis*, of Ceylon and the East Indies, has slender, shaggy, creeping rhizomes. Its fertile fronds have stalks somewhat shorter to rather longer than the ovate-lanceolate to lanceolate-elliptic blades, which are 4 to 7 inches long by up to 2½ inches wide. Their undersides are wholly or only in their upper halves evenly speckled with clusters of spore capsules that do not touch each other. The sterile fronds are smaller than the fertile ones.

Pyrrosia macrocarpa

Pyrrosia serpens in Scotland

Of tufted growth, *P. macrocarpa*, of southern Asia and some Pacific islands, has nearly linear to narrowly-lanceolate, wavy-edged leaves covered on their undersides with a thick, persistent felt of hairs and having very large clusters of spore capsules in two rows in their upper halves.

Native to New Zealand, Australia, and Polynesia, *P. serpens* (syn. *Cyclophorus serpens*) has long, slender, creeping rhizomes and numerous thick, occasionally shallowly-lobed, leathery leaves densely clad with matted, brownish hairs on their undersides. They are of two types, broadly-obovate to subcircular and ½ inch to 1½ inches long, and linear to oblongish or elliptic and 2 to 6 inches long. The first rarely bear spore capsules, the others may or may not do so in two rows near their margins, or densely covering most of their undersurfaces. This species prospers outdoors in favored places in Scotland.

Other sorts cultivated include these: *P. adnascens,* perhaps correctly identified as *P. lanceolata,* is native to southern China, Malaysia, India, and Polynesia. It is a variable species with slender, creeping rhizomes and glossy green fronds. The sterile fronds are elliptic to ovate-lanceolate and about 2½ inches long by one-fourth as wide. The fertile ones are up to 6 inches long and proportionately narrower. The clusters of spore capsules are in oblique rows. *P. angustata,* native from Malaysia to Polynesia, has long, creeping rhizomes and erect fronds that when young, like those of *P. samarensis,* have white, soon-deciduous hairs. Oblong-lanceolate, the sterile fronds are 5 inches to 1 foot long by up to 1¾ inches wide. The fertile fronds, strap-shaped and narrower than the sterile ones, are up to 1½ feet long and 1¼ inches wide. In single rows on both sides of the mid-vein on the narrower upper part of the blade, the rather large clusters of circular to more elongate spore capsules, partially sunken into the leaf tissue on the undersides of the fronds, show as little bumps on their upper sides. *P. beddomeana,* the largest species known to be in cultivation, is native to southern China, Malaysia, and southern India. From short rhizomes it produces close clusters of oblanceolate fronds 1 foot to 2½ feet long and, at their broadest, 2½ inches wide. The upper surfaces of the fronds are dark green, their undersides are brownish-tan. *P. hastata,* of Japan, Korea, and Manchuria, is hardy. It has short rhizomes and fronds under 1 foot long. Their blades are three-lobed with the center lobe long and narrowly-triangular and the basal lobes very much shorter and also triangular. Sometimes the basal lobes each develop a much smaller lobe. *P. longifolia,* native from Malaysia to Australia and Polynesia, in cultivation is sometimes misnamed *P. eberhardtii.* It has narrow, strap-shaped fronds 8 inches to 2 feet long by ½ inch to 1½ inches wide and normally of much thicker texture than those of any other cultivated kind. The midribs are conspicuously raised on the gray-hairy undersides of the fronds. The upper surfaces of the fronds are smooth and green. Fertile fronds may about equal the sterile fronds in length or may be longer. *P. obovata,* native from northern India to Java, has long slender rhizomes and thickish, longish-stalked, obovate, sterile fronds with blades about ¾ inch long and somewhat larger fertile fronds. *P. piloselloides,* native from India to New Guinea, has long rhizomes and glossy, fleshy fronds, the sterile ones stalkless or nearly stalkless, oblongish to nearly circular, and up to 2½ inches long. The fertile fronds are short-stalked, linear-oblong, and up to 4½ inches long by ⅖ inch wide. From sorts of similar aspect, *P. piloselloides* is distinguished by its clusters of spore capsules being in a continuous or interrupted band along the margins and around the tips of the fronds. *P. polydactylis,* endemic to Taiwan, is an attractive species with short rhizomes and long-stalked fronds that are distinct from those of all other pyrrosias in being up to 1 foot long by 8 inches wide and deeply-divided in palmate or pedate fashion into five to nine slender, finger-like lobes. *P. rupestris,* of Australia, has long rhizomes and short-stalked sterile fronds with broad-elliptic to roundish blades about ¾ inch long. Much narrower, the fertile fronds are mostly up to 3½ inches long, sometimes considerably longer. The clusters of spore capsules are in one to four rows on both sides of the midrib. *P. samarensis,* of the Philippine Islands, like closely related *P. angustata* has its young fronds conspicuously furnished with white hairs that soon shed. Its rhizomes are long. Its shortish-stalked, linear- to broad-lanceolate fronds, from 6 inches to 1½ feet long and up to 1½ inches wide, taper to both ends. The fertile fronds are frequently longer and narrower than the sterile ones. *P. varia,* native from Sumatra to New Guinea, resembles *P. adnascens* but has slightly bigger fronds, the sterile ones ovate-lanceolate and up to 9 inches long, the fertile fronds longer and narrower. This sort is said to respond better to cultivation than *P. adnascens.*

Garden and Landscape Uses and Cultivation. Except in frost-free and nearly frost-free climates, most pyrrhosias are not hardy outdoors, but where they succeed they may be attached to trunks of trees or grown on rocks in accumulations of loose organic debris that epiphytes find agreeable. They are grown in greenhouses in winter night temperatures of about 55°F. By day the temperatures may be increased by five to fifteen degrees before ventilation is needed. The atmosphere should be humid, and shade from strong sun afforded. Pans (shallow pots), extremely well drained and containing loose, very porous, highly organic soil, or a soil substitute such as a mixture of shredded fir bark, peat moss, and perlite, provide suitable growing conditions for pyrrosias, or they may be attached to slabs of bark or tree fern trunks in the manner that suits some orchids. Watering is done to keep the rooting medium moderately moist, not constantly saturated. Propagation is easy by division and by spores. For additional information see Ferns.

PYRUS (Pỳ-rus) — Pear. The genus *Pyrus,* as commonly defined, consists of about thirty species of spineless or more or less spiny trees or shrubs called pears. Some authorities include with it apples (*Malus*) as well as certain other genera. The more restricted view is accepted here. Belonging to the rose family ROSACEAE, pears are natives only of Europe, temperate Asia, and North Africa. Some kinds are naturalized in North America. The name is a modifications of *pirus,* the Latin name of the pear.

Pears are deciduous, rarely semievergreen or evergreen. They have alternate, undivided, mostly lobeless, toothed or toothless leaves. Occasionally pinkish, more commonly white, the flowers, which appear before or with the new leaves, are in more or less umbel-like clusters. They have a five-lobed calyx, five obovate to nearly round petals, twenty to thirty stamens with usually red anthers, and two to five separate styles closely constricted at their bases. The fruits, technically pomes, are typified by the familiar orchard pear. Absolute distinction between pears (*Pyrus*) and apples (*Malus*) is not simple. A combination of factors rather than any one must be considered. In general pears differ in usually having hairless or almost hairless, firm, lustrous leaves with toothed or toothless margins, and in the fruits, often, but not always pear-shaped, having abundant grit cells.

The common pear (*P. communis*) is cultivated in many pomological varieties, such as 'Bartlett', 'Clapp Favorite', and 'Winter Nelis', for their edible fruits. Characteristically, it is broad and pyramidal, and 40 to 60 feet tall. Its hard-textured, short-pointed, broad-elliptic to oblong-ovate, veiny leaves are finely-round-toothed or nearly toothless, and when mature, hairless. White or very rarely pinkish, the slender-stalked flowers, in clusters of up to a dozen, appear with the foliage. They have fifteen to twenty stamens, usually five styles, and are 1 inch or more in diameter. Most commonly the fruits, fleshy, sweet, and 2 to 6 inches long, are pear-shaped, less often nearly apple-shaped. The calyx lobes persist with the fruits. The common pear, cultivated for centuries, is of complex hybrid origin. For additional information see the Encyclopedia entry Pear.

The sand pear, Japanese pear, or Chinese pear (*P. pyrifolia*) is represented in cultivation by varieties grouped as *P. p. culta.* These differ from the wild species in having larger leaves and fruits. From 30 to 50 feet tall, they have lustrous, ovate-oblong leaves from 4 to 6 inches long and about one-half as broad. Like the shoots, they are hairless or soon become so. Their margins are prominently furnished with bristly teeth. White, and about 1½ inches across, the flowers, in clusters of up to nine, come just before or with the new foliage. They have five or less often four styles. The very gritty, hard, usually rough fruits are generally more apple- than pear-shaped and have a distinct depression at the stem end. The dried calyxes soon fall. Some orchard pears, including 'Kieffer' and 'LeConte', are hybrids between this and the common pear. They are given the group name of *P. lecontei*.

The Callery pear (*P. calleryana*), hardy through southern New England, is an excellent ornamental and is also used as an

Pyrus salicifolia

Pyrus kawakamii

Pyrus calleryana (foliage)

Pyrus salicifolia (foliage)

understock on which to graft orchard pears. Native to China, this tree is 15 to 30 feet tall. It normally has thorny branches. Its firm, ovate to broad-ovate, short-pointed, practically hairless, lustrous, finely-toothed leaves are 1½ to 3 inches long. In fall they assume striking tones of russet and red. Not exceeding 1 inch in diameter, the white flowers have two or three styles. The nearly spherical, brown fruits are about ½ inch in diameter. They have calyxes that fall before maturity. Variety *P. c.* 'Bradford' is exceptionally good. More erect and narrower than the species, and with upswept branches, this is spineless. It attains a height of 40 to 50 feet.

The snow pear (*P. nivalis*), sometimes cultivated for ornament, in Europe is used for making a cider-like beverage called perry. From other pears it is distinguished by its shoots and undersides of the leaves being clothed with persistent white hairs. Toothless or nearly so, the broad-elliptic leaves are 2 to 3½ inches long. The pure white, 1-inch-wide flowers are succeeded by nearly spherical fruits, 1 inch to 2 inches in diameter. This kind inhabits dry, open woodlands and sunny slopes in southern and southcentral Europe. An attractive intermediate hybrid between it and *P. salicifolia* is *P. canescens*.

Its foliage resembling that of a willow, *P. salicifolia* is a beautiful 25-foot-tall native of southeastern Europe and adjacent Asia. Its leaves are clothed in spring and early summer with silvery hairs. Later their upper sides become hairless and lustrous. Narrowly-lanceolate with pointed apexes, they are 1½ to 3½ inches long by ⅓ to ¾ inch broad. The downy-stalked, creamy-white flowers, ¾ inch wide, are succeeded by pear-shaped fruits up to 1¼ inches long. This is hardy through most of New England. Variety *P. s. pendula*, with pendulous branches, is most often cultivated.

Hardiest of pears, surviving throughout most of New England and into southern Canada, *P. ussuriensis*, of northeastern Asia, is up to 50 feet in height. Of dense habit and practically hairless, it has pointed, round-ovate to ovate leaves 2 to 4 inches long, with bristle-toothed edges. In fall they turn bronzy-crimson. The crowded flower clusters, appearing earlier in spring than those of other pears, are of white, or in bud pale pinkish flowers 1¼ to 1½ inches wide. The subspherical, yellow-green fruits are up to 1½ inches in diameter.

The evergreen pear (*P. kawakamii*) is an evergreen or semievergreen shrub or tree

12 to 30 feet tall, endemic to Taiwan, and the only pear native there. Hardy in southern California and places with similarly mild, practically frostless climates, it often has spiny branchlets. Its glossy, leathery, ovate to obovate leaves, 2½ to 4½ inches long, have round-toothed margins. Fragrant, the white blooms are in clusters of few. The nearly spherical fruits are under ½ inch in diameter.

Garden and Landscape Uses. Orchard pears, varieties of *P. communis*, *P. pyrifolia*, and hybrids between them, are widely cultivated for their edible fruits. Although of distinct ornamental merit, they rarely are planted for that, but are well worth preserving where old specimens exist as perhaps the remnants of an abandoned orchard. As a group, ornamental pears are much less important than ornamental crab apples, nevertheless, they are lovely in bloom, and some in foliage, and can be used effectively as individual specimens and in groups. The Callery pear and more especially its variety 'Bradford' are good street trees, especially esteemed for their fine fall foliage color. In mild climates, the evergreen pear is useful. Unless supported it becomes a wide, sprawling shrub, but staked and pruned during its early years it can be encouraged to assume tree form. It also lends itself to espaliering against walls and fences.

Cultivation. The cultivation of orchard pears for fruits is dealt with under Pear. Other kinds succeed in a variety of reasonably nourishing, well-drained soils. They are less responsive to sandy soils than those with a greater clay content. Sunny locations are best, but they stand part-day shade. No more pruning than is necessary to shape them or restrict them to size is needed. As mentioned above, training the evergreen pear to tree form involves regular pruning in its early years. This consists of shortening the side branches back to well-placed up-pointing buds or branchlets. The main shoot is allowed to develop without pruning. The diseases and pests of ornamental pears are the same as those of orchard pears, but since the ornamentals are not grown for their edible fruits, following a strict spray schedule is usually less important. For more information see Pear.

PYXIDANTHERA (Pyxid-anthèra)—Pyxie or Flowering-Moss. America has many native plants that challenge even the most expert gardeners' skills, among them the two species of *Pyxidanthera*. Yet dedicated, skillful rock gardeners will persist in their efforts to tame these pretty wildlings and, if success be theirs, it will abundantly repay their efforts. Belonging to the diapensia family DIAPENSIACEAE, and thus related to *Galax*, *Pyxidanthera* is completely different from that genus in appearance. The name, from the Greek *pyxis*, a box, and the Latin *anthera,* an anther, refers to the way in which the anthers are constructed.

Pyxidantheras are prostrate, evergreen shrubs with slender, branching stems crowded with alternate or clustered, heathlike leaves. The numerous, solitary, stalkless flowers terminate short branches. They have five separate sepals, a bell-shaped corolla deeply-cleft into five spreading, slightly reflexed lobes (petals), five stamens with flat, broad stalks, and a slender style. The fruits are tiny, spherical capsules.

The pyxie or flowering-moss (*P. barbulata*) occurs in sandy pine barrens from New Jersey to Virginia and North Carolina. It forms dense, low mosslike mats up to 3 feet in diameter and not much over 1 inch high. In spring it is thickly besprinkled with up-facing white, pale pink, or rose flowers, up to ⅓ inch wide. Its sharply pointed oblanceolate leaves are up to ⅓ inch long. The second species, *P. brevifolia* is confined in the wild to North Carolina. It is distinguished from the last by its very short leaves, mostly ⅟₂₅ to ⅟₁₂ inch long.

Garden Uses and Cultivation. Gems for choice locations in rock gardens, and for pans (shallow pots) in alpine cold frames or greenhouses, pyxidantheras have proved so difficult to tame that few gardeners have long succeeded with them. They need acid soil and perfect drainage. One that consists of largely gritty sand with a generous lacing of peat or leaf mold would seem to afford the best chance of success. It should not dry excessively, but stagnant moisture invites disaster. A cool location where the air is humid is appropriate. Exposure to scorching sun and drying winds is detrimental. It seems probable that in the wild the roots of these plants live in a mutually beneficial association with a fungus of the mycorrhiza group. If this be so, even though soil be brought from where the plants flourish naturally, the fungus may not be able to survive the inevitably different conditions of the garden, and when it perishes, death of the pyxie follows. Suggested methods of propagation are by seed, careful division, and cuttings.

PYXIE is *Pyxidanthera barbulata.*